BEYOND BABYLON

BEYOND BABYLON

Art, Trade, and Diplomacy in the Second Millennium B.C.

Edited by Joan Aruz, Kim Benzel, and Jean M. Evans

THE METROPOLITAN MUSEUM OF ART, NEW YORK

YALE UNIVERSITY PRESS, NEW HAVEN AND LONDON

This volume is published in conjunction with the exhibition "Beyond Babylon: Art, Trade, and Diplomacy in the Second Millennium B.C.," held at The Metropolitan Museum of Art, New York, November 18, 2008–March 15, 2009.

The catalogue is made possible by The Hagop Kevorkian Fund.

Additional support is provided by Mr. and Mrs. Malcolm H. Wiener.

The exhibition is made possible by Dorothy and Lewis B. Cullman and The Hagop Kevorkian Fund.

Corporate sponsors are

DEIK / TURKISH - AMERICAN BUSINESS COUNCIL

Additional support is provided by the Oceanic Heritage Foundation and the National Endowment for the Arts.

The exhibition is supported by an indemnity from the Federal Council on the Arts and the Humanities.

Published by The Metropolitan Museum of Art, New York

John P. O'Neill, Publisher and Editor in Chief
Gwen Roginsky, General Manager of Publications
Margaret Chace, Managing Editor
Emily Radin Walter and Harriet Whelchel, Editors
Bruce Campbell, Designer
Peter Antony and Sally Van Devanter, Production
Robert Weisberg, Assistant Managing Editor
Jean Wagner, Bibliographic Editor

Maps by Anandaroop Roy

Translations from the French by Jean-Marie Clarke and Jane Todd; from the German by Russell M. Stockman; from the Greek by Eleni Drakaki; from the Arabic by Eriksen Translations, Inc.

Typeset in Bell Std, Trajan Pro, and Warnock Pro
Color separations by Professional Graphics, Inc., Rockford, Illinois
Printed on Lumisilk 135 gsm
Printed and bound by CS Graphics PTE, LTD, Singapore

Jacket/cover front: Ivory pyxis lid with Mistress of Animals scene. Minet el-Beidha, Tomb III. Late Bronze Age, 13th century B.C. (cat. no. 261)

Jacket/cover back: Gold medallion pendant with four-rayed star and eight curved rays. Uluburun shipwreck. Late Bronze Age, 1300 B.C. (cat. no. 217b)

Endpapers: Wall painting with foreign emissaries bearing gifts. Thebes, Tomb of Rekhmire. Dynasty 18, reigns of Thutmose III–Amenhotep II (see fig. 85)

Frontispiece: Bronze and gold nude female figure. Uluburun shipwreck. Late Bronze Age, ca. 1300 B.C. (cat. no. 212)

Library of Congress Cataloging-in-Publication Data
  Beyond Babylon : art, trade, and diplomacy in the second millennium B.C. / edited by Joan Aruz, Kim Benzel, and Jean M. Evans.
    p. cm.
  Catalog of an exhibition at the Metropolitan Museum of Art, New York, Nov. 18, 2008–Mar. 15, 2009.
  Includes bibliographical references and index.
  ISBN 978-1-58839-295-4 (Metropolitan Museum of Art : hc)—ISBN 978-1-58839-296-1 (Metropolitan Museum of Art : pb)—ISBN 978-0-300-14143-6 (Yale University Press : hc)
  1. Art, Middle Eastern—Exhibitions. 2. Art, Ancient—Middle East—Exhibitions. 3. Middle East—Civilization—To 622—Exhibitions. I. Aruz, Joan. II. Benzel, Kim. III. Evans, Jean M. IV. Metropolitan Museum of Art (New York, N.Y.)
N5345.B38 2008
709.3'0747471—dc22
                                                                    2008037268

CONTENTS

DIRECTOR'S FOREWORD

Having ourselves just emerged from the second millennium A.D. and the dramatic effects of an age of intensive intercultural communication, we have the opportunity with this exhibition to reflect on the momentous developments that initiated these advances in the wake of the creation of the world's first cities. Three to four thousand years ago, with the formation of powerful kingdoms and large territorial states during the second millennium B.C., rising social elites fostered the impetus to acquire precious materials and to fashion objects in styles that reflected contacts with foreign lands. In this "open world," seemingly without borders, merchants from Mesopotamia established trading centers throughout central Anatolia while also exploiting its rich metal resources. Local Anatolian rulers embellished their palaces with luxurious furnishings that incorporated prestigious Egyptian imagery, and powerful kingdoms in Syria were linked through commerce and diplomacy with other Near Eastern and more distant centers. These contacts are reflected in the magnificent finds—some imported from Egypt—in royal tombs at Ebla and in the extraordinary sculptures and wall paintings from the renowned palace at the emporium of Mari, which stood at the crossroads between Mesopotamia and the Mediterranean. Much international exchange flowed through the port of Byblos on the Levantine coast, with its close ties to Egypt. The Nile Valley also actively participated in this exchange, as demonstrated by an exceptional hoard of foreign silver and seals in the Temple of Montu at Tôd.

Neither political nor physical barriers appear to have stemmed the flow of cross-cultural exchange, which took the form of booty and tribute, as well as trade and diplomatic gift giving, thus providing the means for the circulation of precious goods while stimulating the exchange of ideas and fostering artistic creativity. Craftsmen—most remarkably those responsible for fresco-painted palaces around the eastern Mediterranean littoral—traveled long distances, bearing imagery most familiar in the Aegean world. And the interaction of great and powerful rival states, from Babylonia to the Nile Valley, was expressed in the arts by the creation of new international styles. But perhaps the most dramatic evidence for such far-flung connections emerges out of tragedy—the wreckage of the oldest known seagoing ship with its wealthy cargo, found off the cape of Uluburun, on one of the treacherous stretches of the southern Turkish coastline.

In creating "Beyond Babylon: Art, Trade, and Diplomacy in the Second Millennium B.C.," Joan Aruz, Curator in Charge of the Department of Ancient Near Eastern Art, has been guided by her vision of the significance of representing the past as an integrated whole, not limited by modern boundaries. Following five years after the landmark exhibition, "Art of the First Cities: The Third Millennium B.C. from the Mediterranean to the Indus," this attempt to illuminate both a phase of human history over a wide geographic expanse and the impact of cultures on one another has presented enormous challenges. We are deeply grateful to participating institutions, to their directors and their curators, who have shared our commitment. Countries such as Turkey, Syria, Lebanon, Egypt, Greece, Georgia, and Armenia have generously lent treasures in their national collections, allowing us to represent their ancient cultures. The rich resources of the museums of western Europe, whose pioneering archaeological work in many of these lands has been rewarded with a division of the finds, have also ensured that we are able to present as full a picture as possible of the intricacies of the age, and to offer many of its most significant works. For this we are indebted to our colleagues in London, Paris, Berlin, Turin, and Brussels as well as in the United States. An exhibition of this scope could not be realized without the assistance of many people, listed by Joan Aruz in the acknowledgments.

We are also indebted to the contributors to the catalogue—archaeologists and art historians in thirteen countries—whose efforts were skillfully integrated in this comprehensive volume. Along with the lenders and our supporters, they have played a key role in realizing this ambitious project, elucidating a fundamental phase of human history. Looking back upon the legacy of the vibrant Bronze Age civilizations represented in "Beyond Babylon," an enduring message emerges: The impetus toward cross-cultural exchange is more powerful than the imposing barriers of geography and political conflict. Indeed, it has led to some of the greatest advances of our shared civilization.

Mention of this exhibition and catalogue cannot go without acknowledgment of the many important funders involved in the project. Our deepest thanks go to Dorothy and Lewis B. Cullman, whose generosity toward this project has been simply astounding. The Hagop Kevorkian Fund's extraordinary support has also allowed for many critical aspects of the project to be achieved. To our colleagues at the Turkish-American Business Council, we offer our appreciation for their newfound interest in the Museum's work. All of these contributors, together with Mr. and Mrs. Malcolm H. Wiener, the Oceanic Heritage Foundation, the National Endowment for the Arts, and the Federal Council on the Arts and the Humanities, have made possible the realization of this project.

Philippe de Montebello
Director
The Metropolitan Museum of Art

ACKNOWLEDGMENTS

"Beyond Babylon: Art, Trade, and Diplomacy in the Second Millennium B.C." focuses attention on the cultural interaction and artistic enrichment shared by civilizations over vast distances from western Asia to the Mediterranean islands, Egypt, and the Greek mainland, during nearly one thousand years of intense commercial, diplomatic and artistic exchange. The challenges involved in selecting the specific works that would best illustrate the extraordinary developments of the era, displaying them, and analyzing their significance in the exhibition catalogue has required an immense effort on the part of many individuals and institutions. Forty-four lending institutions in Europe, the Middle East, Egypt, and the United States have generously contributed to the project, and more than eighty authors in thirteen countries have shared their expertise to create a coherent narrative of the momentous developments of the period; their names and affiliations are cited in the List of Contributors. We are extremely grateful both to them and to the many other colleagues who provided curatorial and other scholarly and logistical assistance at different stages of the project.

Certain individuals deserve very special thanks for their belief in the importance of the concepts of this show and for their tireless efforts on our behalf to secure loans. First and foremost, profound gratitude goes to Philippe de Montebello, Director of The Metropolitan Museum of Art, who—despite the numerous difficulties involved during the preparation of this exhibition—has demonstrated his deep understanding of its value and significance and shown his support in so many fundamental ways. Mahrukh Tarapor, Associate Director for Exhibitions and Director for International Affairs, Geneva Office, also deserves much praise for her travels on our behalf and for her assistance and advice throughout the complex negotiations for loans. For the loans from Turkey, Mrs. Gülgün Şensoy, wife of the Ambassador of Turkey to the United States, along with Kıvılcım Kılıç, Political Counselor, translated their enthusiasm for this project into intense efforts to ensure that the loan negotiations went as smoothly as possible. Special thanks goes to Cemal Pulak, who demonstrated his dedication to this project with many trips to Bodrum to help with the selection, study, and photography of objects recovered from the Uluburun shipwreck and with his extensive contributions to the catalogue. For our efforts to secure loans from Syria, we owe a debt of gratitude to Madame Asma Assad, First Lady of Syria, to His Excellency Dr. Imad Moustapha, Ambassador Extraordinary and Plenipoteniary of the Syrian Arab Republic to the United States, and to Dr. Rafif al Sayed Moustapha. Their belief in cultural diplomacy energized the quest for some of the most significant works of Syrian cultural patrimony, discussed in this catalogue and illustrated by the wonderful photographs of Abdel Anwar Ghafour. We also thank Ambassador Dr. Bashar Ja'afari, Permanent Representative, Syrian Mission to the United States, and Mrs. Ja'afari, as well as Giorgio and Marilyn Buccellati, directors of the archaeological excavations at Tell Mozan/Urkesh, for their unflagging support. In Lebanon, Suzy Hakimian, Curator of the Beirut National Museum and a contributor to the catalogue, was instrumental in assisting us with the selection of spectacular loans, shepherding them through the administrative process. For the precious objects coming from Egypt, we are very grateful for the permissions granted by Dr. Zahi Hawass, Director General of the Supreme Council of Antiquities of Egypt, and the encouragement offered by Wafaa el Saddik, General Director of the Egyptian Museum, Cairo, whose assistance, along with that of the indefatigable May Trad, and Janice Kamrin, Director of the Egyptian Museum Database and Registrar Training Projects, American Research Center in Egypt, was invaluable during two trips to Egypt. Peter Lacovara provided introductions to many colleagues in Egypt, resulting in unprecedented research opportunities. In Greece, Lena Papazoglou-Manioudaki, Head of the Prehistoric Collection, National Archaeological Museum, Athens, deserves special gratitude for her conviction regarding the importance of this show and for her attempts to secure the loans needed for its realization; we extend similar thanks to Maria Andreadaki-Vlazaki, Director, 25th Ephorate of Prehistoric and Classical Antiquities, Khania, Crete, whose support and friendship over the years has been greatly appreciated. Nikos Stampolidis, Director of the Museum of Cycladic Art, Athens, was always available to offer valuable advice, and Professors Yannis Sakellaraki and Efi-Sapouna Sakellaraki, are to be especially thanked for their attempts on our behalf and for their encouragement.

In New York, special thanks goes to Bruce White, who demonstrated his photographic expertise and professionalism under many trying circumstances during trips to Turkey, Egypt, and Greece, to the admiration of all. He also beautifully photographed a select group of loans from the Musée du Louvre. I would like also to give special thanks to our colleagues in the Department of Egyptian Art at the Metropolitan Museum, Dorothea and Dieter Arnold, Susan J. Allen, Catharine H. Roehrig, Marsha Hill, Diana Craig Patch, and Isabel Stuenkel, in particular, for answering innumerable questions and extending generous assistance during every phase of this project. The efforts of Michael Batista, Exhibition

Design Manager, on behalf of the exhibition are deeply appreciated; his trips to Syria and Turkey inspired an evocative display. Thanks also go to Barbara Weiss, graphic designer for the exhibition.

The organization of an international loan show such as "Beyond Babylon" requires an enormous amount of cooperation from many other colleagues as well, all of whom have shared our vision and contributed generously to the exhibition. They include:

In BELGIUM: Eric De Gelaen, Exhibition Services of the Royal Library of Belgium, Brussels.

In EGYPT: Curator Waheed Edwar, Stephanie Boucher, and Gustavo Camps at the Cairo Museum; William Raymond Johnson, Director, Epigraphic Survey, Oriental Institute, University of Chicago; Mansour Bouriak, Chief Inspector for Luxor and Upper Egypt; and Sanaa Ali, Director, Luxor Museum.

In FRANCE: Henri Loyrette, Président-Directeur of the Musée du Louvre, Paris, which provided highly significant works of art; Béatrice André-Salvini, Conservateur général, chargée du Département des Antiquités Orientales, and Curators Agnès Benoit, Françoise Demange, Elisabeth Fontan, and Sophie Cluzan; Guillemette Andreu-Lanoë, Conservateur général, chargée du Département des Antiquités Égyptiennes, and Genevieve Pierrat-Bonnefois, Curator, whose assistance was invaluable during visits to Paris, as well as Caroline Biro, Registrar; Jean-Luc Martinez, Conservateur général, chargée du Département des Antiquités Grecques, Étruscques et Romaines, and members of his staff, particularly Christelle Brillault, Registrar. Sincere gratitude goes also to Annie Caubet, Conservateur général honoraire du Patrimoine, who was always available to assist.

In GEORGIA: David Lordkipanidze, General Director of the Georgian National Museum, and his assistant, Anna Chkonia.

In GERMANY, we thank Beate Salje, Director, Vorderasiatisches Museum, Staatliche Museen zu Berlin, and Ralf-Bernhardt Wartke, Deputy Director, and Curators Lutz Martin and Joachim Marzahn; Andreas Scholl, Director, Antikensammlung, Staatliche Museen zu Berlin, and Curator Ursula Kästner; Dietrich Wildung, Director, Aegyptisches Museum, Staatliche Museen zu Berlin, and Curator Bianca Hoffmann. Special gratitude also goes to Professor Peter Pfälzner, Institute for Ancient Near Eastern Studies, University of Tübingen, for publishing his spectacular finds from Qatna for the first time in this catalogue, and to Constance von Rüden, DAI scholarship holder, Deutsches Archäologisches Institut, Athens.

For the loans from GREECE, we are grateful to Alexandros P. Mallias, Ambassador of the Hellenic Republic, Embassy of Greece, Washington, D.C.; Michalis Liapis, Minister of Culture; Vivi Vassilopoulou, Director General of Antiquities and Cultural Heritage, Hellenic Ministry of Culture; Nikos Kaltsas, Director, National Archaeological Museum, Athens, as well as Curators Eleni Konstandini-Sivridi and Constantine Paschalidis, for their collegiality and assistance during visits to Athens; Nota Dimopoulou, Director, and Giorgios Rethymniotakis, Curator, Heraklion Museum; Vili Apostolaki, Director of the Hagios Nikolaos Museum; Marisa Marthari, Director, 21st Ephorate of Prehistoric and Classical Antiquities of Cyclades and Samos; Christos G. Doumas, Director of the Excavations at Akrotiri, Thera, and archaeologist Andreas G. Vlachopoulos; Vasilis Aravantinos, Director, Archaeological Museum of Thebes, whose generosity is demonstrated by the loans from Thebes, and archaeologist Ioannis Fappas; Toula Marketou and Fotini Zervaki, Curators of the 22nd Ephorate of Prehistoric and Classical Antiquities, for their hospitality and collegiality during two trips to Rhodes; and Evangelia Pappi, Curator in Charge, Nafplion Archaeological Museum, whose contribution is deeply appreciated.

In ITALY, we thank Eleni Vassilika, Director, Fondazione Museo delle Antichità Egizie di Torino, and Marco Rossani, Registrar.

For loans from LEBANON, we are indebted to Frederic Husseini, Director General of Antiquities, Directorate of Antiquities, Beirut, and Leila Badre, Museum Director, American University of Beirut.

In the REPUBLIC OF ARMENIA: Anelka Grigorian, Director of the History Museum of Armenia, Yerevan.

In SYRIA, where extraordinary efforts were made to realize this project, we thank Vice President Najah al-Attar; His Excellency Riyad Nassan Agha, Minister of Culture; Bassam Jamous, Director General, Directorate General of Antiquities and Museums, Ministry of Culture, Syria, and members of his staff, particularly Michel Al-Maqdissi, Director of Excavations and Archaeological Studies, Ahmad Ferzat Taraqji, Assistant to the Director of Excavations and Archaeological Studies, Myassar Yabroudi, Curator, National Museum, Damascus, as well as Samer Abdel Ghafour, Chief of Staff, all of whom did everything possible to enable us to borrow highly significant loans; Nadim Fakesh, Director of Aleppo Antiquities and Museums; and George and Miriam Antaki, who received us in Aleppo and offered much valued advice.

In TURKEY, we are indebted to Ertuğrul Günay, Minister of Culture and Tourism; Orhan Düzgün, General Director, and Abdullah Kocapinar, Deputy Director General for Cultural Heritage and Museums, assisted by Nilufer Ertan, Director of the Cultural Activities Bureau, as well as Melik Ayaz, Head of the Excavations and Surveys; Hikmet Denizci, Director of the Ankara Museum of Anatolian Civilizations, and Curators Nihal Turpan and Emel Yurttalgül; Ismail Karamut, Director of the Istanbul Archaeological Museums, and Curator Zeynep Kiziltan; Izmet Ediz of the Çorum Museum; Hasan Elmaağaç of the Kayseri Museum; Yaşar Yıldız, Director of the Bodrum Museum of Underwater Archaeology, deserves special thanks for his kind assistance with every facet of the preparation of loans from the Uluburun shipwreck, as does Erhan Özcan, for loans from Müskebi. At the Institute of Nautical Archaeology, Bodrum, Conservators Edith Trnka, Gülser Sinaci, and Tuba Ekmekci worked on the Uluburun shipwreck objects, and Don Frey provided the beautiful underwater photographs displayed in the catalogue and the galleries of the exhibition.

In the UNITED KINGDOM, at the British Museum, London, we thank John Curtis, Keeper, Department of the Middle East, and members of his staff, particularly Senior Administrator Dean Bayliss; J. Lesley Fitton, Keeper, Department of Greek and Roman Antiquities, who worked to secure important loans for the show, as well as Senior Administrator Trevor Coughlan, Senior Museum Assistant Kim Overend, and Museum Assistant Alex Truscott; Vivian Davies, Keeper of the Department of Ancient Egypt and Sudan, and members of his staff, including Claire Messenger, Senior Administrator; Steven Quirke, Curator, and Carolyn Perry, Manager of the Petrie Museum of Egyptian Archaeology.

In the UNITED STATES, special gratitude goes to the Institute of Nautical Archaeology for its support of our efforts to bring the precious artifacts from the Uluburun shipwreck to the United States for the first time. We make special mention of its founder, George Bass, Distinguished Professor Emeritus, Texas A&M University, as well as Executive Director James Delgado, and Jack Kelley. Special thanks also go to Gary Beckman, Chair, Department of Near Eastern Studies, Professor of Hittite and Mesopotamian Studies, University of Michigan, for sharing his expertise on Hittite history and language. In New York, we are grateful to William Griswold, Director, and Sidney Babcock, Associate Curator of Seals and Tablets, at The Pierpont Morgan Library, New York, as well as Patricia Courtney, Associate Registrar. Thanks also go to Rita Freed, Norma Jean Calderwood Curator, and Kim Pashko, Registrar, Museum of Fine Arts, Boston; Edna R. Russmann, Curator, Egyptian, Classical and Ancient Middle Eastern Art, and Elisa Flynn, Assistant Registrar, Brooklyn Museum, New York. We are also grateful to Richard M. Keresey, Head of Antiquities Department, Sotheby's New York, who aided in the preparation of the Federal Indemnity, and Jeanette and Jonathan P. Rosen, New York.

Many members of the staff of the Metropolitan Museum have been working hard for a number of years in the preparation of this complex exhibition. I would like to make special mention of my two co-editors, Kim Benzel, Associate Curator, and Jean M. Evans, Assistant Curator, Department of Ancient Near Eastern Art, who spent countless hours in the preparation of every aspect of the catalogue and provided their expertise and generous assistance as we developed and realized the concepts of the show. Sarah Graff, Curatorial Assistant, contributed to the catalogue and did an excellent job in coordinating the catalogue illustrations and layout with the Editorial Department. Aubrey Baadsgaard, Assistant Curator, displayed her dedication to the project with careful checking of the final manuscripts and other work on the exhibition, and Elisabetta Valtz-Fino, Curator, as well as Yelena Rakic, Hagop Kevorkian Research Scholar, prepared the various maps in the catalogue. Ira Spar advised on matters relating to the ancient texts. Tim Healing, Administrator, expertly coordinated the loan process and ensured that the many events surrounding the show would run smoothly. Susanna Lee, Assistant for Administration, demonstrated meticulous attention to the catalogue and exhibition preparation. We also thank Shawn W. Osborne for his skillful work as an art handler, Morena Stefanova and Eleni Drakaki, who assisted with research, Victoria Southwell, for her work on the exhibition database, as well as Nanette Kelekian, Monica Velez, Paul Collins, Eduardo Escobar, My Chau, and Ayşegül Vural.

This complex and beautiful catalogue was produced by the Editorial Department of the Metropolitan Museum. John P. O'Neill, Publisher and Editor in Chief, provided patience, understanding, and expert guidance throughout the writing and production. Special thanks go also to editors Emily Radin Walter, whose sensitivity to the project and elegant literary style are expressed throughout the volume, and to Harriet Whelchel, whose organizational skills and attention to detail were invaluable. Peter Antony adeptly oversaw production and printing of the catalogue along with Sally Van Devanter. Jean Wagner skillfully created the bibliography and ensured the accuracy of the footnotes. Bruce Campbell lent his expertise to creating an ideal design for the book. Anandaroop Roy produced the maps that illustrate the catalogue. Robert Weisberg, Assistant Managing Editor, deserves special mention for his heroic efforts. We also thank Margaret Chace, Pamela Barr, and Laura Perry.

Many other departments at the Museum were involved in the realization of this exhibition. For important loans and help with references, we thank Carlos Picón, Curator in Charge of the Department of Greek and Roman Art, and Curator Joan Mertens, as well as Mark Santangelo and Matthew Noiseux. Martha Deese, Office of the Director, and Linda Sylling, Manager, Special Exhibitions, deserve special gratitude for their support and advice throughout. We also thank Emily Kernan Rafferty, President; Doralynn Pines, Associate Director for Administration; Sharon H. Cott, Senior Vice President, Secretary, and General Counsel, Rebecca Murray, and Kirstie Howard in the Counsel's Office; Nina Diefenbach, Senior Vice President for Development, and members of her staff, including Andrea Kann, Christine Begley, Katie Holden, Kristin MacDonald, and Thea Hashagen; and Harold Holzer, Senior Vice President for External Affairs, as well as Elyse Topalian, Jennifer Oetting, Diana Pitt, and Egle Zygas in the Communications Department. In the Design Department, we are grateful to Norie Morimoto, Clint Coller, and Richard Lichte, as well as Joseph Smith, John Muldowney, and Andrey Kostiw, who worked on the production team. From Objects Conservation, we especially thank Jean-François de Laperouse, for advice on technology and conservation matters and for his lucid contributions to the catalogue, and preparators Alexandra Walcott, Fred Sager, Jenna Wainwright, and Matthew Cumbie. Kent Lydecker, Associate Director for Education, as well as Alice Schwarz, Michael Norris, Joseph Loh, Ines Powell, Terry Russo, William Crow, and Theresa Lai are to be thanked for their dedication to the educational aims of the exhibition. Vivian Gordon applied her skills to the writing of the audioguide. Chief Registrar Herbert M. Moskowitz deserves special praise for dealing with the complex job of coordinating the packing and transportation of loans, a task in which he was ably supported by Erin Mallay.

Finally, I would like to give my warmest thanks to Malcolm Wiener, member of the Visiting Committee of the Department of Ancient Near Eastern Art, for his contributions, as well as to Ralph Minasian, President of The Hagop Kevorkian Fund, New York, for his continuing support and encouragement, not only of this project but of the Department of Ancient Near Eastern Art.

Joan Aruz
Curator in Charge
Department of Ancient Near Eastern Art

LENDERS TO THE EXHIBITION

CONTRIBUTORS TO THE CATALOGUE

SA   Susan J. Allen
Associate Research Curator, Department of Egyptian Art,
The Metropolitan Museum of Art, New York

MM   Michel Al-Maqdissi,
Director of Excavations and Archaeological Studies,
Directorate General of Antiquities and Museums, Ministry
of Culture, Syria

MA-V Maria Andreadaki-Vlazaki
Director, 25th Ephorate of Prehistoric and Classical
Antiquities, Khania, Crete

BA-S Béatrice André-Salvini
Conservateur général, chargée du Département des Antiquités
Orientales, Musée du Louvre, Paris

VLA   Vasilis Aravantinos
Director, Archaeological Museum of Thebes, Greece

DA   Dorothea Arnold
Lila Acheson Wallace Chairman, Department of Egyptian Art,
The Metropolitan Museum of Art, New York

JA   Joan Aruz
Curator in Charge, Department of Ancient Near Eastern Art,
The Metropolitan Museum of Art, New York

SB   Sidney Babcock
Associate Curator of Seals and Tablets, The Pierpont Morgan
Library, New York

LB   Leila Badre
Museum Director, American University of Beirut

GB   Gary Beckman
Chair, Department of Near Eastern Studies, Professor of
Hittite and Mesopotamian Studies, University of Michigan,
Ann Arbor

AB   Agnès Benoit
Conservateur en chef, Département des Antiquités Orientales,
Musée du Louvre, Paris

KB   Kim Benzel
Associate Curator, Department of Ancient Near Eastern Art,
The Metropolitan Museum of Art, New York

LMB   Lawrence M. Berman
Norma Jean Calderwood Senior Curator of Ancient Egyptian,
Nubian, and Near Eastern Art, Museum of Fine Arts, Boston

MB   Manfred Bietak
Professor and Chairman of the Institute of Egyptology and
The Vienna Institute of Archaeological Science, Institut für
Ägyptologie der Universität, Vienna , and Chairman of the
Commission for Egypt and the Levant, The Austrian Academy
of Sciences

FDC   François de Callataÿ
Professor, Coin Cabinet, Royal Library of Belgium, Brussels

MC   Michèle Casanova
Maître de conférences, Archéologie du Proche-Orient Ancien,
Université de Paris

AC   Annie Caubet
Conservateur général honoraire du Patrimoine, Musée du
Louvre, Paris

PJC   P. J. Chatzidakis
Curator, Archaeological Museum, Delos

EHC   Eric H. Cline
Associate Professor and Chair, Department of Classical and
Semitic Languages and Literatures, The George Washington
University, Washington D.C.

SC   Sophie Cluzan
Conservateur, Département des Antiquités Orientales,
Musée du Louvre, Paris

DC   Dominique Collon
Assistant Keeper (retired), The British Museum, London

ED   Ella Dardaillon
Associate Researcher, Maison de l'Orient et de la Méditerranée,
Université de Lyon

FD   Françoise Demange
Conservateur en chef, Département des Antiquités Orientales,
Musée du Louvre, Paris

CGD   Christos G. Doumas
Emeritus Professor, University of Athens, and Director of the
Excavations at Akrotiri, Thera

ELD   Eleni Drakaki
Hagop Kevorkian Curatorial Fellow, Department of Ancient Near Eastern Art, The Metropolitan Museum of Art, New York

JME   Jean M. Evans
Assistant Curator, Department of Ancient Near Eastern Art, The Metropolitan Museum of Art, New York

IF   Ioannis Fappas
Archaeologist, Archaeological Museum of Thebes, Greece

MHF   Marian Feldman
Associate Professor, Departments of Arts and Near Eastern Studies, University of California, Berkeley

ILF   Irving Finkel
Assistant Keeper, Department of the Middle East, The British Museum, London

JLF   J. Lesley Fitton
Keeper, Department of Greek and Roman Antiquities, The British Museum, London

EF   Elisabeth Fontan
Conservateur en chef, Département des Antiquités Orientales, Musée du Louvre, Paris

SG   Sarah Graff
Curatorial Assistant, Department of Ancient Near Eastern Art, The Metropolitan Museum of Art, New York

SH   Suzy Hakimian
Curator, National Museum, Beirut

NH   Nicolle Hirschfeld
Assistant Professor, Department of Classical Studies, Trinity University, San Antonio

BJ   Bassam Jamous
Director General, Directorate General of Antiquities and Museums, Ministry of Culture, Syria

RBK   Robert B. Koehl
Associate Professor, Department of Classical and Oriental Studies, Hunter College, New York

EK-S   Eleni Konstandinidi-Sivridi
Curator, Prehistoric, Anatolian, and Egyptian Collections, National Archaeological Museum, Athens

PL   Peter Lacovara
Senior Curator of Ancient Egyptian, Nubian, and Near Eastern Art, Michael C. Carlos Museum of Emory University, Atlanta

J-FL   Jean-François de Lapérouse
Conservator, Department of Objects Conservation, The Metropolitan Museum of Art, New York

MTL   Mogens Trolle Larsen
Professor (retired), Carsten Niebuhr Institute for Near Eastern Studies, The University of Copenhagen

ML   Mario Liverani
Professor of Ancient Near East History, Sapienza Università di Roma

J-CM   Jean-Claude Margueron
Professeur honoraire, École Pratique des Hautes Études, Paris

TM   Toula Marketou
Curator of Antiquities, Ministry of Culture, 22nd Ephorate of Prehistoric and Classical Antiquities, Rhodes

LM   Lutz Martin
Curator, Vorderasiatisches Museum, Berlin

JM   Joachim Marzahn
Curator, Vorderasiatisches Museum, Berlin

PM   Paolo Matthiae
*Director, Italian Archaeological Mission at Ebla, Syria
Professor of Archaeology and History of Art of the Ancient Near East, University of Rome La Sapienza*

DMB   Danièle Morandi Bonacossi
Professore associato, Dipartimento di Storia e Tutela dei Beni Culturali, Università degli Studi di Udine

SM   Sarah P. Morris
Steinmetz Professor of Classical Archaeology and Material Culture, Department of Classics, University of California, Los Angeles

AM-K   Andreas Müller-Karpe
Professor, Vorgeschichtliches Seminar, Philipps-Universität, Marburg, Germany

DOC   David O'Connor
Lila Acheson Wallace Professor of Egyptian Art and Archaeology, Institute of Fine Arts, New York University

LP-M   Lena Papazoglou-Manioudaki
Curator in Charge, Prehistoric, Anatolian, and Egyptian Collections, National Archaeological Museum, Athens

EP   Evangelia Pappi
Curator in Charge, Nafplion Archaeological Museum, Greece

KP   Constantinos Paschalidis
Curator, Prehistoric, Anatolian, and Egyptian Collections, National Archaeological Museum, Athens

DCP   Diana Craig Patch
Associate Curator, Department of Egyptian Art, The Metropolitan Museum of Art, New York

PP   Peter Pfälzner
Professor, Institute for Ancient Near Eastern Studies,
University of Tübingen, Germany

GP-B Geneviève Pierrat-Bonnefois
Conservateur, Département des Antiquités Égyptiennes,
Musée du Louvre, Paris

CP   Cemal Pulak
Associate Professor, Department of Anthropology,
Texas A&M University

CHR   Catharine H. Roehrig
Curator, Department of Egyptian Art, The Metropolitan
Museum of Art, New York

KR   Karen Rubinson
Independent scholar

ERR   Edna R. Russmann
Curator, Egyptian, Classical and Ancient Middle Eastern Art,
Brooklyn Museum, New York

JR   Jeremy B. Rutter
Sherman Fairchild Professor of the Humanities, Professor of
Classics, Department of Classics, Dartmouth College, Hanover,
New Hampshire

JMS   Jack M. Sasson
Werthan Professor of Judaic and Biblical Studies, Vanderbilt
University, Nashville

ANS   Andreas Schachner
Director, Boğazköy-Hattusa Expedition, German
Archaeological Institute, Istanbul

THS   Thomas Schneider
Professor of Egyptology, School of Humanities, Swansea
University, Wales

GMS   Glenn M. Schwartz
Whiting Professor of Archaeology, Department of Near
Eastern Studies, Johns Hopkins University, Baltimore

TS   Tunç Sipahi
Professor, Faculty of Language, History and Geography,
Department of Archaeology, Ankara University

SAS   Anthony Spalinger
Professor, Department of Classics and Ancient History,
University of Auckland, New Zealand

IS   Ira Spar
Professor of History and Ancient Studies, Ramapo College
of New Jersey, Mahwah

IST   Isabel Stuenkel
Curatorial Assistant, Department of Egyptian Art,
The Metropolitan Museum of Art, New York

AS   Aygül Süel
Professor, Faculty of Language, History, and Geography,
Ankara University

MS   Mustafa Süel
Professor, Faculty of Art and Science, Uludağ University,
Bursa

AFT   Ahmad Ferzat Taraqji
Assistant to the Director of Excavations and Archaeological
Studies, Directorate General of Antiquities and Museums,
Ministry of Culture, Syria

JHT   John H. Taylor
Assistant Keeper, Department of Ancient Egypt and Sudan,
The British Museum, London

EV   Eleni Vassilika
Director, Fondazione Museo delle Antichità Egizie di Torino

AV   Andreas G. Vlachopoulos
Archaeologist, Akrotiri Excavation, Thera

CVR   Constance von Rüden
DAI scholarship holder, Deutsches Archäologisches Intitut,
Athens

R-BW Ralf-Bernhardt Wartke
Deputy Director, Vorderasiatisches Museum, Berlin

JW   James M. Weinstein
Editor, Bulletin of the American Schools of Oriental Research,
Department of Classics, Cornell University, Ithaca, New York

MY   Myassar Yabroudi
Curator, National Museum, Damascus

KAY   K. Aslihan Yener
Associate Professor of Anatolian Archaeology, The Oriental
Institute, and the Department of Near Eastern Languages and
Civilizations, The University of Chicago

TY   Tayfun Yıldırım
Professor, Faculty of Letters, Department of Archaeology,
Ankara University

FZ   Fotini Zervaki
Curator, 22nd Ephorate of Prehistoric and Classical
Antiquities, Rhodes

CHRONOLOGY

	Southern Mesopotamia/Elam	Northern Mesopotamia	Syria and the Levant
2000 B.C. **Middle Bronze**	Isin-Larsa period, 2004–1763 Old Babylonian period, 1894–1595 Hammurabi of Babylon (1792–1750) Dadusha of Eshnunna (ca. 1780) Samsu-iluna of Babylon (1749–1712)	Amorite dynasties Old Assyrian period, 1920–1740 Shamshi-Adad I (1808–1776?) Ishme-Dagan I (1775–?)	Middle Bronze Age, 2000–1600 Old Syrian period, 2000–1600 Yahdun-Lim of Mari (1810–1794) Alalakh VII Yarim-Lim of Alalakh (1780–1765?) Zimri-Lim of Mari (1775–1760) Destruction of Mari, ca. 1760 Immeya of Ebla (1750–1700)
1600 B.C. **Late Bronze**	Destruction of Babylon, 1595 Middle Babylonian/ Kassite period, 1595–1155 Kara-indash (ca. 1415) Kurigalzu I (ca. 1390) Kadashman-Enlil I (ca. 1370) Burnaburiash II (1359–1333) Untash-Napirisha of Elam (1340–1300) Kurigalzu II (1332–1308) Nazi-Maruttash (1307–1282) Shagarakti-Shuriash (1245–1233) Kashtiliashu IV (1232–1225)	 Mitanni, 1500–1330 Parattarna (ca. 1500) Saushtatar (?) Artatama I (?) Middle Assyrian period, 1400–1000 Eriba-Adad I (1390–1364) Tushratta (1365–1330?) Ashur-uballit I (1363–1328) Shattiwaza Adad-nirari I (1305–1274) Shalmaneser I (1273–1244) Tukulti-Ninurta I (1243–1207)	Late Bronze Age, 1600–1200/1150 Middle Syrian period, 1600–1200/1150 Alalakh IV Idrimi of Alalakh (ca. 1500) Niqmaddu of Ugarit (1353–1318) Destruction of Qatna, ca. 1340 Battle of Qadesh, ca. 1275 Treaty of Qadesh, ca. 1258 Ammistamru II of Ugarit (1250–1210)
ca. 1200/ **1150 B.C.** **Late Bronze/** **Early Iron**	Meli-Shipak (1186–1172) Shutruk-Nahunte of Elam (1185–1155) Marduk-apla-iddina I (1171–1159) End of Kassite dynasty, ca. 1155	Ashur-dan I (1178–1133) Ashur-resha-ishi (1132–1115) Tiglath-pileser I (1114–1076)	Beginning of Iron Age, ca. 1200/1150 Destruction of Ugarit, ca. 1180

This Chronology uses the Middle Chronology for the Near East, the Metropolitan Museum List of Rulers for Egypt, and a modified Traditional Chronology for the Aegean. All dates are approximate. See also Appendices on pages 250–54.

Anatolia	Egypt	Greek mainland	Crete/Cyclades
		Middle Helladic, 2090–1625	
Old Assyrian Trading/ Merchant Colony period *karum* Kanesh, 1950–1700	Middle Kingdom Dynasty 12, 1981–1802 *Amenemhat I (1981–1952)* *Senwosret I (1961–1917)*		Middle Minoan (MM) IB–IIA–B/ Protopalatial period, 1950–1750
Kültepe *karum* II (1950–1836)	*Amenemhat II (1919–1885)* Tôd Treasure *Senwosret II (1887–1878)* *Senwosret III (1878–1840)* *Amenemhat III (1859–1813)* *Amenemhat IV (1813–1805)*		
Kültepe *karum* Ib (1800–1700)	Dynasty 13, 1802–1640		
			MM IIIA–B/Neopalatial period, 1750–1625
Hittite Old Kingdom (1650–1500) *Hattusili I (1650–1620)*	*Neferhotep I (1722–1711)* Second Intermediate Period (Hyksos), 1640–1550		
		Late Helladic (LH) I/Early Mycenaean period, 1625–1525	MMIIB–Late Minoan (LM) IA/ Late Cycladic (LC) I, 1625–1525
Mursili I (1620–1590)			
	Kamose (1552–1550) New Kingdom Dynasty 18, 1550–1295 *Ahmose (1550–1525)*	Shaft Graves at Mycenae	Thera eruption, ca. 1525? LM IB, 1525–1450/LC II, 1525–1425
Telipinu (1525–1500) Hittite Middle Kingdom (1500–1344)	*Thutmose I (1504–1492)* *Thutmose III (1479–1425)* *Hatshepsut (1473–1458)*	LH IIA, 1525–1450	
		LH IIB, 1450–1425	LM II/Final Palatial period, 1450–1425
Tudhaliya I/II (1430–1390)	*Amenhotep II (1427–1400)*	LH IIIA:1, 1425–1375	LM IIIA:1/LC III (early), 1425–1375
	Thutmose IV (1400–1390) *Amenhotep III (1390–1352)*	LH IIIA:2 (early), 1375–1325	LM IIIA:2 (early), 1375–1325/ LC III (middle), 1375–1200
Tudhaliya III (1360–1344) Hittite New Kingdom/Hittite Empire (1344–1200) *Suppiluliuma I (1344–1322)*	*Amenhotep IV/Akhenaten (1353–1336)* *Tutankhamun (1336–1327)*		
		LH IIIA:2 (late)–IIIB/Late Mycenaean period, 1325–1200	LM IIIA:2 (late)–LM IIIB/ Postpalatial period, 1325–1200 Destruction of palace at Knossos
Mursili II (1321–1295) Uluburun shipwreck, ca. 1300 *Muwattalli II (1295–1272)*	*Haremhab (1323–1295)* Dynasty 19, 1295–1186 *Seti I (1294–1279)* *Ramesses II (1279–1213)*		
Hattusili III (1267–1237)		Theban Hoard	
Tudhaliya IV (1237–1209)	*Merneptah (1213–1203)*		
Destruction of Hattusa, ca. 1200	Dynasty 20, 1186–1070 *Ramesses III (1184–1153)*		LM IIIC/LC III (late), 1200–1125
Neo-Hittite and Aramean states	*Ramesses IV (1153–1147)*		

45°N

15°E   30°E

Rome

Sardinia   Black Sea

Sozopol

Istanbul

Troy   Ferzant
Ortaköy•   •Tokat
Aegean   Boğazköy• Alaca Höyük
Sea   Ankara•   Şarkışla• Dövlek
Ithaka   ANATOLIA   Kültepe
Thebes   Kayseri•
Mycenae• •Athens   Acemhöyük
Tiryns•   •Konya
Cyclades   Karahöyük   Bolkardağ
                  Bodrum•   Carchemish
Thera   Taurus Mountains •Tarsus   Tell al-Hamidi
                  Rhodes •Kaş   Aleppo•
Knossos   Uluburun   Alalakh•   •Ebla
Crete   Ugarit•   Deir ez-Zor•
                                    Nicosia•   Latakia•
                              Enkomi•   Qatna•
Mediterranean Sea   Homs•   •SYRIA   Euphrates M
                              Byblos•
                              Beirut•   Damascus•

Marsa Matruh   Megiddo•
                  Alexandria•   Jerusalem• •Amman
                        •Tell el-Dab'a   Dead
                                                Sea
                  Cairo•

Faiyum Oasis

Nile   Tell el-Amarna

EGYPT

Dakhleh Oasis   Abydos•   Karnak
                              Tôd• •Thebes
                                    •Luxor
                                    •El-Kab   Medin•

                              Aswan•
                        Wadi el-Hudi   Red
                                                Sea

                  Abu Simbel•   Mec•

Sesebi•   NUBIA
        •Kerma

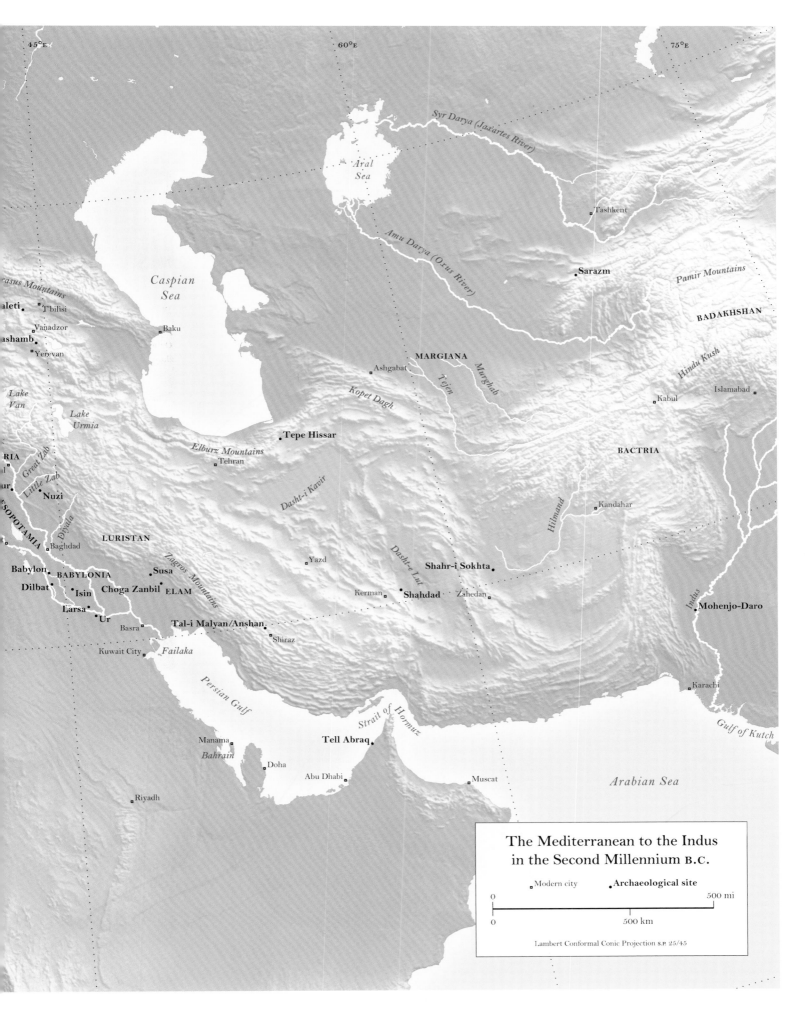

Syr Darya (Jaxartes River)

Tashkent

Aral
Sea

Amu Darya (Oxus River)

Sarazm

Pamir Mountains

*Caspian
Sea*

BADAKHSHAN

...asus Mountains

aleti · T'bilisi

· Vanadzor

...ashamb · Yerevan

Baku

Hindu Kush

MARGIANA

Ashgabat

Kopet Dagh

Tejen

Marghab

Islamabad

Kabul

*Lake
Van*

*Lake
Urmia*

Tepe Hissar

Elburz Mountains

Tehran

BACTRIA

...RIA

Great Zab

Little Zab

...ur

Nuzi

Dasht-i Kavir

Hilmand

Kandahar

Diyala

...SOPOTAMIA

LURISTAN

Baghdad

Zagros Mountains

Dasht-e Lut

Babylon · BABYLONIA

Dilbat

Susa

Yazd

Shahr-i Sokhta

Indus

Isin

Choga Zanbil ELAM

Kerman **Shahdad**

Zahedan

Mohenjo-Daro

Larsa · **Ur**

Basra

Tal-i Malyan/Anshan

Shiraz

Kuwait City · *Failaka*

Persian Gulf

Karachi

Manama

Bahrain

Tell Abraq

Strait of Hormuz

Gulf of Kutch

Doha

Abu Dhabi

Muscat

Arabian Sea

· Riyadh

The Mediterranean to the Indus
in the Second Millennium B.C.

· Modern city   **·** **Archaeological site**

0   500 mi

0   500 km

Lambert Conformal Conic Projection s.p. 25/45

THE AEGEAN AND WESTERN ANATOLIA

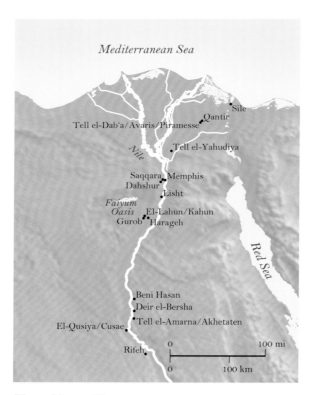

THE NILE VALLEY

THE LEVANT

THE AEGEAN AND THE NEAR EAST IN THE SECOND MILLENNIUM B.C.

CENTRAL ANATOLIA

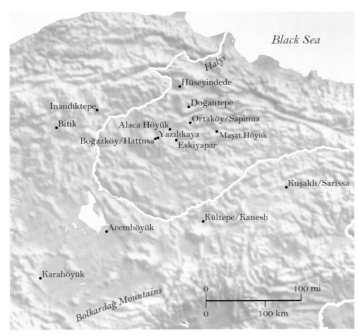

Black Sea

Halys

Hüseyindede

İnandıktepe

Doğantepe

Bitik

Ortaköy/Sapinua

Alaca Höyük

Yazılıkaya · Maşat Höyük

Boğazköy/Hattusa · Eskiyapar

Kuşaklı/Sarissa

Kültepe/Kanesh

Acemhöyük

Karahöyük

Bolkardağ Mountains

0   100 mi

0   100 km

MESOPOTAMIA

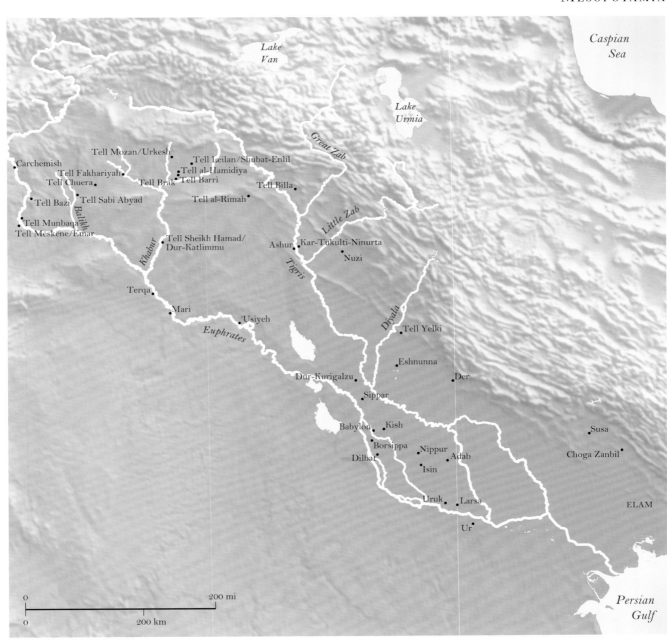

Lake Van

Caspian Sea

Lake Urmia

Great Zab

Tell Mozan/Urkesh

Carchemish

Tell Leilan/Shubat-Enlil

Tell Fakhariyah · Tell al-Hamidiya

Tell Chuera · Tell Brak · Tell Barri

Tell Billa

Little Zab

Tell Bazi · Tell Sabi Abyad

Tell al-Rimah

Tell Munbaqa

Tell Meskene/Emar

Balikh

Khabur

Tell Sheikh Hamad/Dur-Katlimmu

Ashur · Kar-Tukulti-Ninurta

Nuzi

Tigris

Terqa

Diyala

Mari

'Usiyeh

Tell Yelki

Euphrates

Eshnunna

Der

Dur-Kurigalzu

Sippar

Babylon · Kish

Susa

Borsippa · Nippur

Dilbat · Isin · Adab

Choga Zanbil

Uruk · Larsa

Ur

ELAM

Persian Gulf

0   200 mi

0   200 km

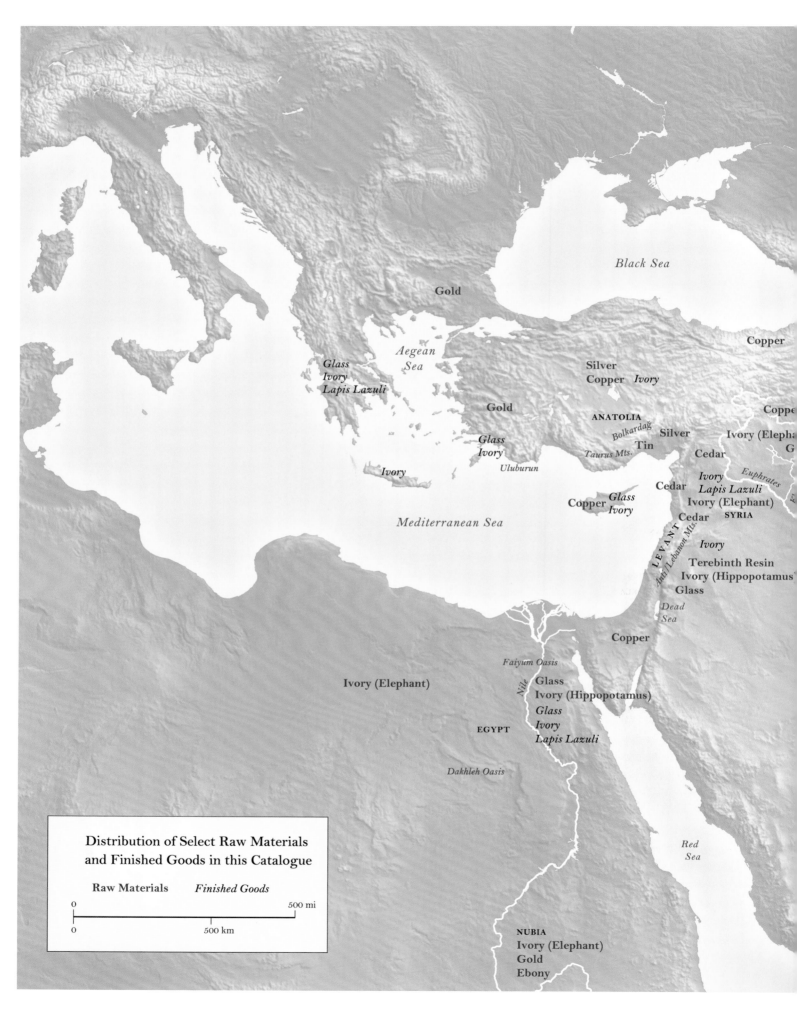

Black Sea

Gold

Copper

Aegean
Sea

Silver
Copper *Ivory*

Glass
Ivory
Lapis Lazuli

Copp

Gold

Ivory (Eleph

ANATOLIA   G

Bolkardağ Silver

Glass   Tin   Cedar
Ivory

Taurus Mts.
                    Uluburun   Cedar   *Ivory*
Ivory   *Lapis Lazuli*
                                                              Ivory (Elephant)

                    Copper *Glass*   SYRIA
                              Ivory   Cedar

Mediterranean Sea   *Ivory*

                                                    Terebinth Resin
                                                    Ivory (Hippopotamus

                                              Dead Glass
                                              Sea

                                        Copper

                              Faiyum Oasis

Ivory (Elephant)   Glass
                              Ivory (Hippopotamus)
                        Nile *Glass*
                                Ivory
                    EGYPT   *Lapis Lazuli*

Dakhleh Oasis

                                              Red
                                              Sea

Distribution of Select Raw Materials
and Finished Goods in this Catalogue

Raw Materials   *Finished Goods*

0 ————————————————— 500 mi

0 ————————————————— 500 km

                    NUBIA
                    Ivory (Elephant)
                    Gold
                    Ebony

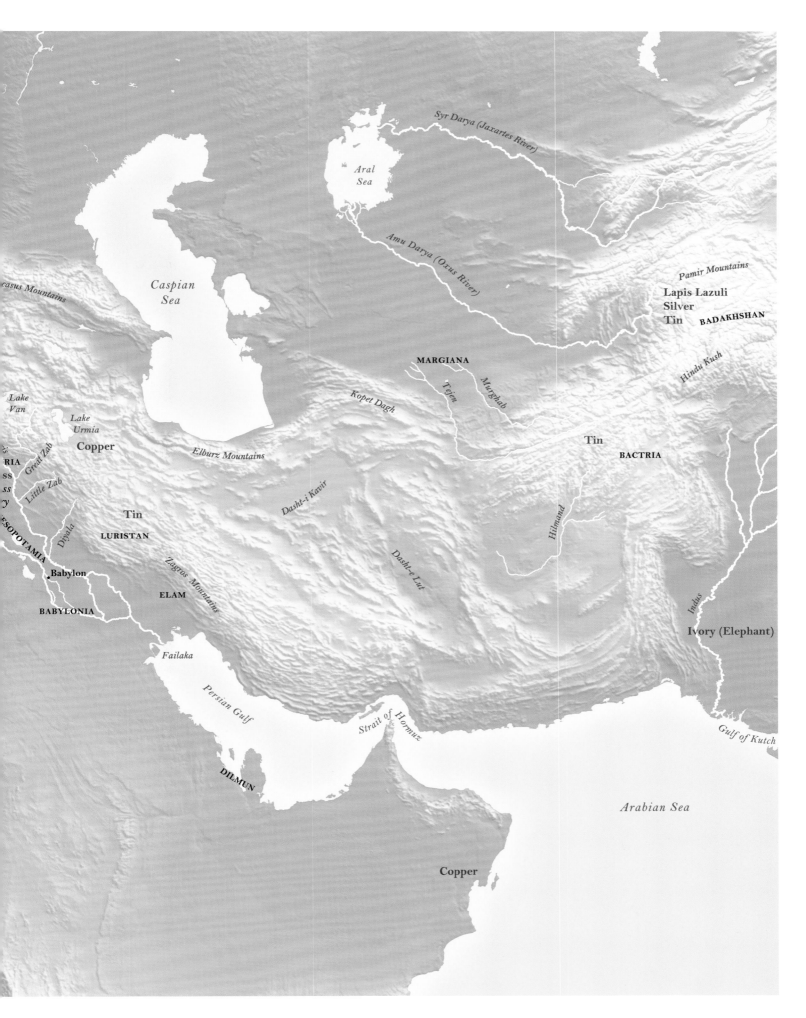

Syr Darya (Jaxartes River)

Aral
Sea

Amu Darya (Oxus River)

Pamir Mountains

Lapis Lazuli
Silver
Tin   **BADAKHSHAN**

*Caspian
Sea*

casus Mountains

Hindu Kush

MARGIANA

Kopet Dagh

Tejen

Murghab

*Lake
Van*

*Lake
Urmia*

Copper

Elburz Mountains

Tin

BACTRIA

RIA

Great Zab

Little Zab

Diyala

ESOPOTAMIA

Dasht-i Kavir

Hilmand

Tin

LURISTAN

Zagros Mountains

Dasht-e Lut

Indus

Babylon

ELAM

BABYLONIA

Ivory (Elephant)

Failaka

Persian Gulf

Strait of Hormuz

Gulf of Kutch

DILMUN

Arabian Sea

Copper

BEYOND BABYLON

INTRODUCTION

JOAN ARUZ

The Greek poet Hesiod, writing in the eighth century B.C., was the first to point out the significance of metals—gold, silver, bronze and iron—in defining the Ages of Mankind. In the Bronze Age,

Zeus the Father made a third generation of mortal men, a brazen race . . . no way equal to the silver age. . . . Great was their strength and unconquerable the arms which grew from their shoulders on their strong limbs. Their armour was of bronze, and their houses of bronze, and of bronze were their implements: there was no black iron. . . . But when earth had covered this generation also, Zeus the son of Cronos made yet another . . . a god-like race of hero-men . . . the race before our own, throughout the boundless earth. Grim war and dread battle destroyed a part of them, some in the land of Cadmus at seven-gated Thebe when they fought for the flocks of Oedipus, and some, when it had brought them in ships over the great sea gulf to Troy for rich-haired Helen's sake (Works and Days 109–201).[1]

THE BRONZE AGE

More than two thousand years after Hesiod, in the early nineteenth century, the first curator of the Nationalmuseet in Copenhagen, Christian Thomsen, again invoked the Bronze Age in his attempt at scientific classification of the development of civilization—part of a threefold system characterizing the advances in technology from the Stone to the Bronze and Iron Ages. With some modifications these terms have survived, and the Middle and Late phases of the Bronze Age—encompassing the early and late second millennium B.C.—are the subject of this volume and this exhibition. Indeed, the quest for metals—especially for copper and tin primarily to make bronze weapons and tools and precious gold and silver for display and exchange—was the driving force that led to the establishment of merchant colonies in central Anatolia at the inception of the second millennium and to the intensive trade and diplomatic exchange among the great powers of the later centuries of this era. The astounding discovery of an estimated one ton of tin along with ten tons of copper in the wreckage of the oldest surviving seagoing ship, sailing from the Levant toward the Aegean around 1300 B.C., provides perhaps the most tangible testimony to this major impetus for interaction. The cargo and other contents of the ship, which spilled onto the seabed off the southern Anatolian coast, have been the subject of intensive analysis since their discovery just a few decades ago (see pp. 289–305).

The pursuit of metals and the advances in metallurgy may be counted among the great developments that sparked the unprecedented intensity of interaction that characterized the second millennium B.C. A remarkable record of this exchange during the eighteenth century B.C., in the form of a cuneiform tablet, provides perspective on the peoples involved, their motives, and the routes they traveled. The tablet, discovered in the archives of the palace at Mari in the Middle Euphrates region, outlines the distribution of tin from east to west. In his interpretation of the document, Jack Sasson points to the presence in Ugarit, of Mari merchants who, with the service of translators, distributed tin in the Levant and Anatolia (fig. 1).[2] The places mentioned in this single disbursement list extend from the kingdom of Anshan in southwestern Iran (and, by extension, to tin sources probably located in Central Asia) to Kaphtor, identified with Minoan Crete.

In addition to the tin trade, there was also long-distance traffic in lapis lazuli—again from a Central Asian source in the mountainous Badakhshan region of Afghanistan—to centers in the Near East, Egypt, and the Aegean, as well as in other resources such as elephant ivory from Asia and Africa (see maps on pp. xxii–xxiii and fig. 97). Such exchange also testifies to the vast distances that goods were transported, across lands with a great diversity of peoples who spoke many languages. These included Elamites on the Iranian Plateau, Hurrians in northeastern Mesopotamia, Indo-Europeans (Hittites and Luwians in Anatolia and Mycenaean Greeks), Kassites (who came to rule Babylonia), Egyptians, and Semitic speakers. The last included descendants of Akkadians in southern Mesopotamia, Assyrians in the north, Amorites in Syro-Mesopotamia, and Canaanites and Aramaeans along the Levantine coast.[3] As Mario Liverani points out in his essay (pp. 161–68), the complexity of the human dimension—the array of languages, customs, and social practices to be mastered

Line no.	Text in translation	Places where tin was accounted	Comments
1	14 talents* 30 pounds tin, taken out of Mari		about 1230 pounds
3	1 talent tin that Hammurabi of Babylon conveyed	*in Aleppo*	
5	20 pounds tin: from the contribution of Sheplarpak		king of Anshan (Elam)
6	20 pounds tin: from the gifts of Ishhi-Dagan and Yatar-Addu	*in Ugarit*	two merchants of Elamite tin
9	Total: 16 talents, 10 pounds—available stock		
10	out of this (amount):		gifts to the royal circle of Yamhad
	11 pounds, 40 shekels tin: to Samsi-Addu [Shamshi-Adad]		Aleppo army general
11	9 talents, 27 pounds, 38 shekels tin: to Yarim-Lim		king of Yamhad
13	1 talent, 37 shekels tin: to Gashera		his wife, the queen
14	30 pounds tin: Hammurabi		their son, the crown prince
15	16 pounds, 40 shekels tin: to Tab-balat		the king's private secretary
16	8 pounds tin: to Sin-abushu	*in Aleppo*	the prince's private secretary
18	10 pounds tin: Sumu-barah	*in Muzunnum*	prince of Yamhad, ruling at Muzunnum
20	8 pounds, 20 shekels tin: Ewri-Talma	*in Layashum*	Layashum is not yet identified
22	30 pounds tin: Ibni-Addu, king of Hazor intermediary: Addi-Addu	*in Hazazar, the first time*	Hazazar is likely near Ugarit Addi-Addu: agent
25	20 pounds tin: Amud-pi-El		king of Qatna
26	20 pounds tin: Ibni-Addu	*in Hazazar, the second time*	Ibni-Addu of Hazor receives second shipment
	1+ (?) pounds and [40?] shekels tin: to a Kaphtorite		Kaphtor is Crete
28	20 shekels tin: the translator (*targamannum*) chief Kaphtor merchant	*in Ugarit*	*targamannum* is the precursor of "dragoman"
26	[x amount of tin: Ibni-Addu]	*the third time, in [....]*	Ibni-Addu of Hazor may have received a third shipment
	2 talents tin: [?] in Dūr-Sumu-epuh		Yamhadi town where final draft was likely drawn up
	*1 talent = 60 pounds		

Figure 1. Mari tablet. A. 1270 (ARM 23:556) Translated by Jack M. Sasson.

in the long-distance quest for resources and exotica—not only provided challenges but served as catalysts for contact, enlivening our picture of the world three to four thousand years ago.

THE LANDSCAPES OF INTERACTION

The defining features of the varied landscapes over considerable distances include the great river valleys—those of the Tigris and Euphrates (fig. 2), the Nile, and the Indus—with their relatively easy access to land and sea routes, fertile highlands, and arid lowlands and plateaus. Imposing barriers also exist, such as the Zagros Mountains on the border between Iran and southern Mesopotamia, as well as the vast Syrian and Arabian Deserts. Along the eastern coast of the Mediterranean extends the Levant (see p. 2), the region referred to by a term coined in the fifteenth century A.D. to designate the eastern lands in the direction of the rising sun. It runs south of the Amanus range, which along with the Taurus Mountains

naturally divides the region from Anatolia—signifying the area now encompassed by modern Turkey—restricting access to the central Anatolian plateau to a narrow winding track from the Cilician Gates close to Tarsus. One of the most dramatic features of this region is the great cross-continental rift caused by the meeting of two tectonic plates, the African and the Arabian. This created the 100-meter-long Beqa' Valley, which divides the Lebanon and Anti-Lebanon Mountain ranges that separate the Syrian Desert from the coast. Their primary resource—verdant cedar forests—is immortalized in the Babylonian Epic of Gilgamesh (fig. 3). Indeed, mountains ring the eastern Mediterranean, creating littoral zones limited in extent and access to the interior. One exception is the broad coastal plain that runs south of the Lebanon range and then west to the Nile Delta and beyond.

Neither land nor sea, however—or even such cataclysmic disasters as the eruption of the volcano on the island of Thera in mid-second millennium B.C.—impeded the movements of traders and other travelers over great distances and at great

Figure 2. Aerial view of the Euphrates River south of Deir ez-Zor, Syria.

Figure 3. Aerial view of the Cedars of Lebanon in the Chouf district, Lebanon.

risk. By the Middle Bronze Age (ca. 2000–1600 B.C.), the focus of the first section of this volume, certain cities—particularly Ashur on the Tigris, Mari in eastern Syria, Ugarit with its Mediterranean harbors, and the seaport of Byblos with its close ties to Egypt—developed special prominence as centers through which goods flowed to the west. As discussed by Mogens Trolle Larsen (pp. 15–17, 70–73), Assyrian merchants established a network of trading settlements around such cities as Kültepe on the Central Anatolian Plateau, traveling in donkey caravans laden with tin and textiles and assuming control of the internal trade in local copper. While their activities are documented in great detail, thanks to the discovery of their archives over the course of the last century, one must imagine the numerous other ventures that crisscrossed western Asia, carving paths out of mountain passes and deserts, as illustrated by a wall painting preserved in an Egyptian

Middle Kingdom tomb showing a donkey caravan with Asiatics wearing colorful textiles and carrying foreign products to Egypt (fig. 4). The figures have been variously interpreted as traders or tributaries, itinerant tinkers or mining specialists.[4]

Long-distance trade in the eastern Mediterranean is already implied in the third millennium B.C. by mention of "Byblos ships," a term used for seagoing vessels not only on the usual Byblos–Nile Delta route but for other destinations as well. "Byblos ships" voyaged to Punt during both Dynasty 6 and Dynasty 18, the time of Hatshepsut's famous expedition to this exotic land (fig. 5).[5] "Keftiu ships" (the term "Keftiu" alluding to the Minoan world) were possibly being repaired at the naval yards of Thutmose III, according to Manfred Bietak in his essay on Tell el-Dabʿa (p. 112).[6] Myriad other sailing vessels plied the seas (fig. 6). But it is the tragic consequences of those that met with disaster—like the Uluburun ship, discussed by Cemal Pulak—which provide a window into the sea trade that fed the intricate diplomatic and commercial enterprises flourishing among the great powers. In an age of large territorial states in the Near East, these included Kassite Babylonia in southern Mesopotamia, Mitanni and then Assyria in the north, and Hatti in central Anatolia. From time to time, some of these powers dominated smaller polities in the Syro-Levantine region. Forming a kind of international alliance along with Egypt and involving the Mycenaean world, their interactions forecast the explosion of Mediterranean commerce in later Phoenician times under very different sociopolitical circumstances.

TRADE, TRAVEL, AND TRANSFORMATION

The terms "global" and "multicultural" are often applied to our contemporary society, which has just stepped out of the second millennium A.D. Remarkably, such concepts are relevant as well to the second millennium B.C. when, building upon the momentous developments of prior millennia—the origin of cities and the invention of writing—an expanding social elite required bronze and demanded exotic luxury goods from distant lands. These needs fostered the creation of an era of intense foreign contacts, with new technological breakthroughs, such as the invention of glass, and a revolution in travel with the introduction of the horse into the Mediterranean region. The mechanisms and modes of interaction were complex. They included immigration and mixed marriages, and involved traveling merchants and diplomats, warriors, skilled specialists, kings, and princess-brides in a world seemingly without borders. The social consequences were also complex, some of their intricacies captured in surviving texts. Among the thousands of documents retrieved from the trading towns of central Anatolia are not only merchant accounts but also letters from home (Ashur), allowing us a glimpse into the lives of profit-driven businessmen living abroad, their day-to-day

Figure 4. Facsimile of wall painting with western Asiatic nomads. Tomb of Khnumhotep II, Beni Hasan. Dynasty 12, reign of Senwosret II.

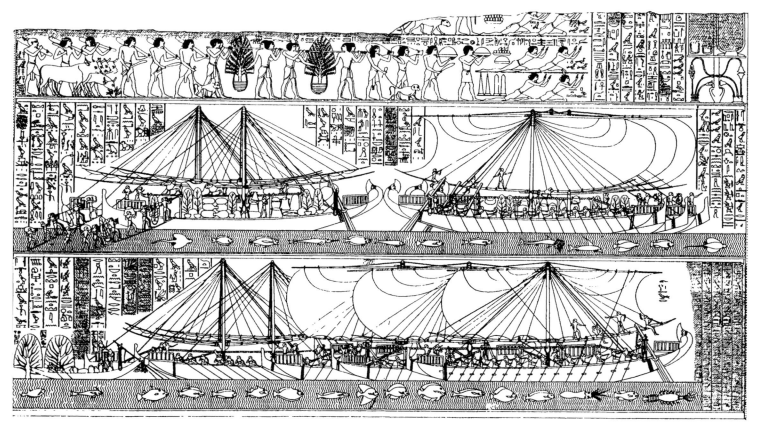

Figure 5. Drawing of stone relief with Hatshepsut's expedition to Punt. Mortuary temple of Hatshepsut, Deir el-Bahri.

dealings, and their personal problems. In one letter, a distraught wife and sister warn: "You love money! You hate your life! . . . Please . . . come, see Assur's eye and save your life! As to the proceeds from my textiles, why don't you send that to me?"[7] Rulers and other elite personages traveled abroad—Zimri-Lim, for example, who went from Mari to the Mediterranean, and an envoy of the king of Ugarit, who ventured eastward to see Zimri-Lim's own glorious palace (see pp. 96–100).

During the Late Bronze Age (ca. 1600–1200/1150 B.C.), with the formation of large political powers, historical accounts of Egyptian pharaohs and detailed depictions of conquests, booty, and tribute portray the riches of foreign lands brought to the Nile Valley as a result of war and in the context (and pretext) of domination. Precious goods described in letters circulated among the great rulers—Burnaburiash II in Babylonia, Tushratta in Mitanni, Ashur-uballit I in Assyria, Suppiluliuma I and later Muwattalli II in Hatti, and pharaohs from Amenhotep III to Ramesses II in Egypt (ca. 1390–1213 B.C.)— cast light on courtly diplomacy to secure not only necessities but also shared "symbols of excellence."[8] The Amarna Letters and Hittite diplomatic texts enumerate goods exchanged in the context of gift-giving, dowries for foreign princesses, and lavish wedding presents from one ruler to another. Made of the rarest and most precious materials, they must have been masterworks of elaboration—a metal horse-shaped bottle with gold eagles and lapis lazuli inlays; helmet-shaped containers of alabaster and malachite, gilded and inlaid

with lapis lazuli; saltcellars formed as bull-calves and lions; a gilded ebony plaque with winged discs and Deluge monsters; ceremonial weapons embellished with gold and precious stones; and gilded rhyta adorned with ivory, ebony, and lapis lazuli.[9]

The more intangible wealth—of ideas—that circulated in the interactive environment of the second millennium B.C. further stimulated the creativity that characterizes the Late Bronze Age. The transmission of literary traditions, enabled by "guest professors," is dramatically documented in fragments of the Epic of Gilgamesh, discovered in the Hittite capital at Boğazköy and at other sites such as Megiddo (see p. 192 and cat. no. 117). Scholarly texts found at Ugarit and Amarna attest to the spread of Mesopotamian intellectual traditions.[10] The impact in foreign lands of Mesopotamian concepts, practices of governance, views of the cosmos, and elements of language is also significant.[11]

Homer's *Odyssey* reveals attitudes to foreigners and the elevated status of experts from abroad:

Who would call in a foreigner?—unless an artisan with skill to serve the realm, a healer, or a prophet, or a builder, or one whose harp and song might give us joy. All these are sought for on the endless earth. (Odyssey 17.501–5).[12]

Indeed, in the Hittite texts we learn of physicians and conjurers sent by Ramesses II to Anatolia at the request of Hattusili III, who also expresses a desire for "some statues to put in my family house," pleading, "Do not refuse me a sculptor!"[13]

Figure 6. Miniature Frieze, detail. Thera, West House, Room 5. Late Cycladic I. Museum of Prehistoric Thera 5824

STYLES OF INTERACTION

Foreign "symbols of excellence" included not only exotic works but also, apparently, artisans. Such acquisitions would seem to imply that, alongside the development of individual expression characterizing distinct civilizations, there grew a shared appreciation of skills as well as aesthetic standards and qualities—in particular, the talent to transform raw materials into lifelike images infused with vitality.[14] The celebration of expertise is also conveyed in mythology, as in the story of the Ugaritic creator-god Kothar-wa-Hasis of the Baal epic. A divinity called "son of the sea" and "son of the confluence," with Kaphtor (Crete) as "the throne of his dwelling" and Memphis as "the land of his inheritance," Kothar appears elementally associated with these realms. Divinely inspired to prepare gifts for Lady Athirat of the Sea, the creator-god "poured silver, he cast gold . . . he cast a canopy and a reclining couch, a divine dais . . . a divine throne . . . a divine table filled with figures creatures from the foundation of the earth, a divine bowl."[15]

Texts mention master craftsmen sent by one Near Eastern ruler to another, and certainly imports and shared royal and ritual imagery are illuminating. However, the groundbreaking discoveries of Minoan-style fresco paintings at Tell el-Dabʻa in the Nile Delta, at Qatna in Syria, and at other sites in the Levant and Anatolia over the last few decades have truly transformed our picture of this form of exchange. There can be no doubt that prestige was attached to such exotic works, but perhaps more interesting is the uncommon receptivity to the artistic approaches and imagery of the Minoan world,

which were devoid of the symbolism of royal and divine power that otherwise permeated official decorative programs in these regions. The dynamic Aegean animal style invigorated the arts of the eastern Mediterranean (see figs. 7, 119) and was an essential factor in the development of international styles in the fourteenth and thirteenth centuries B.C., (see pp. 387–95). Scholars, building on the seminal work of Helene Kantor,[16] have wrestled with the interpretation of the magnificent objects in gold, ivory, and other materials that display elements absorbed from eastern and western traditions—the largest corpus among the dazzling works from the Tomb of Tutankhamun (see figs. 121, 122, 131). The creation of an "international koine" reflected and may also have served to foster diplomatic and other exchanges among the royal courts of the fourteenth and thirteenth centuries B.C.[17] With recent discoveries, such as the intact Royal Tomb at Qatna, new opportunities arise for further analysis of this artistic phenomenon and the differentiation of local versions of hybrid styles.

THE LEGACY OF THE BRONZE AGE

Art and texts alert us to crises that arose throughout the second millennium B.C. and eventually overwhelmed the eastern Mediterranean at the end of the Late Bronze Age (see fig. 141). Evocative of the world described in the Homeric epics, and hundreds of years before the traditional date of the Trojan War, names appear in Hittite documents that may allude to Ilion, Atreus, Alexander, and the Achaeans, and warriors in boar's tusk helmets and oxhide shields march to battle

Figure 7. Wall painting with hunting scene. Thebes, Tomb of Rekhmire (TT 100). Dynasty 18, reigns of Thutmose III–Amenhotep II.

on the Thera frescoes (see fig. 137). The impact of the Age of Heroes is the subject of Sarah Morris's essay (pp. 435–39), and the survival of its artistic traditions is explored by Marian Feldman in the concluding section of the catalogue (pp. 445–48).

The burst of creativity inspired by the intensity of exchange that marks the second millennium B.C. characterizes one of the first of many international ages in human history.[18] Walter Burkert, in his work on the Orientalizing Revolution of the seventh century B.C., concludes that "culture is not a plant sprouting from its seed in isolation; it is a continuous process of learning guided by curiosity along with practical needs and interests. It grows especially through a willingness to learn from what is 'other,' what is strange and foreign."[19] As he points out, the "miracle" represented by such an environment manifested itself repeatedly, notably during the Persian Empire. Here, in the sixth century B.C., within an imperial framework, we have perhaps the best-documented encounter in antiquity between local and foreign styles, with evidence for the presence of eastern Greek craftsmen among the foreigners at the Achaemenid court and even for the adoption of the Aegean animal style on the seal of a Persian royal courtier.[20] Whereas the creation of styles that crossed boundaries during the second millennium B.C. appears to have expressed the alliance of great kings, the use of borrowed forms in this later context may be a manifestation of the encompassing ideology of empire.[21]

Some scholars have recognized the relevance of these early beginnings to contact and exchange in later eras. In a plea for the application of global historical analysis to premodern as well as modern periods, Jerry Bentley notes that "networks of cross-cultural interaction, communication, and exchange are defining contexts of human historical experience just as surely as are the myriad ostensibly distinct societies....Thus attention to processes of cross-cultural interaction is . . . indispensable for . . . understanding the trajectories of individual societies and the development of the larger world as a whole"[22] It is this approach that has informed two exhibitions that we have had the privilege to mount at the Metropolitan Museum. The first, in 2003, "Art of the First Cities: The Third Millennium B.C. from the Mediterranean to the Indus," set the stage for our exploration of the art and culture that developed in the second millennium B.C. in the context of expansive trade and diplomacy both in the Mesopotamian heartland and "Beyond Babylon" (fig. 8).

1. Hesiod *Works and Days*, translation by Hugh Evelyn-White (1914).
2. Jack M. Sasson, personal communications. Mari tablet: A.1270 (ARM 23 556).
3. Åhlström 1993, pp. 58–59, with a discussion of the association of *kinahhu* with the famous crimson-purple dye working. Åhlström also discusses the terminology used in scholarly literature to describe the Syro-Levantine region.
4. See Newberry 1893, p. 69; Helck 1971, pp. 72ff.; Saretta 1997, pp. 130ff.; Kessler 1987; Staubli 1999, pp. 30–35; and Kamrin 1999, pp. 93ff., all of whom offer various levels of interpretation of this scene.
5. Wachsmann 1998, p. 19.
6. For a discussion of "Keftiu ships," see ibid., 1998, p. 51.
7. Larsen 1982, pp. 213, 219.
8. Clark 1986, p. 3, defined as "materials comparatively rare in nature, frequently . . . from distant sources and . . . useless for the purposes of daily life."
9. EA 22 and EA 25; Moran 1992, pp. 52, 54, 78.
10. For Akkadian rituals, see Izre'el 1997; Huehnergard 1989; and Pardee 2002.
11. See West 1997, pp. 14–18, for such fundamental concepts and loan words that spread to the Mycenaean world.
12. Homer *Odyssey*, translation by Robert Fitzgerald (1990).
13. Zaccagnini 1983, pp. 252–53; in the Amarna texts (EA 35, Moran 1992, p. 107) the king of plague-ridden Alashiya asks the pharaoh for an expert in vulture augury.
14. EA 10, Moran 1992, p. 19. For a discussion of the transformative powers of skilled artisans and their importance for long-distance acquisition, see Helms 1993, p. 63.
15. S. Morris 1992, pp. 80–81, 92–93, who associates the Canaanite god with Hephaistos and the Cretan Daidalos.
16. Kantor 1948; Kantor 1956.
17. The most recent comprehensive treatment of this subject can be found in Feldman 2006b; for archives in the Hittite capital, see Beckman 1996.
18. For the first international styles, see *Art of the First Cities* 2003, pp. 325–45. See also Van de Mieroop 2002.
19. Burkert 1992, p. 129.
20. For references, see Aruz 2008, p. 237.
21. Nylander 1979, p. 356.
22. Bentley 2006, p. 26.

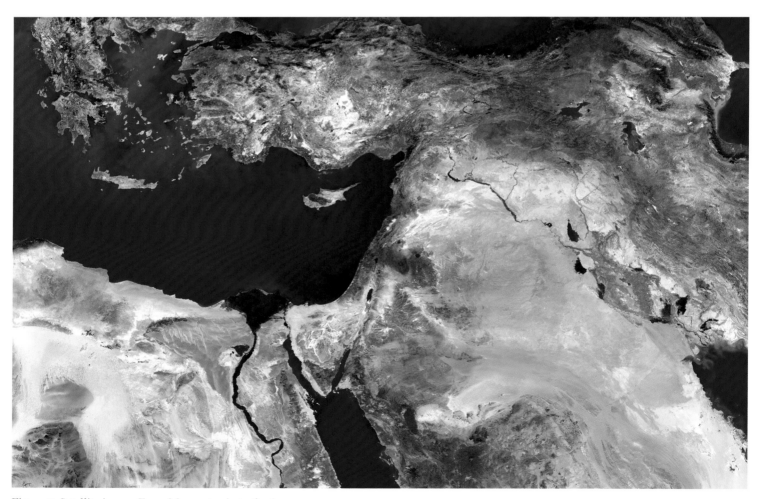

Figure 8. Satellite image: From Mesopotamia to the Aegean.

CATALOGUE

THE MIDDLE BRONZE AGE

MOGENS TROLLE LARSEN

The world of the Middle Bronze Age in the Near East, 2000–1600 B.C., was vast and open. We have direct textual evidence testifying to contacts and connections that linked areas from Khuzestan in present-day Iran and the Persian Gulf to the Mediterranean and the Black Sea coast; even the Aegean world and Egypt were involved in the exchanges of goods, people, and ideas. Indirect evidence shows that more distant areas were part of the network centered on the Near East: Iran and Central Asia produced important goods such as tin and lapis lazuli, which flowed into Mesopotamia from the east, and copper came from Oman via commercial centers in the Persian Gulf.[1]

All these connections are directly attested in an elaborate and varied textual documentation and supported by archaeological data from the many excavations that have been carried out in the Near East. However, although the texts are numerous they illuminate only certain regions and some sharply defined historical and political situations. From the city of Mari on the Middle Euphrates we have enormous palace archives, but the extensive information that they provide concerns only a few decades in the eighteenth century B.C. and throws light on only a limited geographic area in what is now northern Syria. Another major textual find stems from the site of Kültepe, the ancient city of Kanesh, in central Anatolia, where so far nearly twenty-three thousand documents from private merchant archives have been uncovered. From Ebla, some 50 kilometers south of modern Aleppo, we have a much smaller group of texts, mainly from a palace context. And from various places in Mesopotamia itself, notably the city of Sippar, we have thousands of documents, some from administrative areas, others from private archives. But these texts normally lack a primary context, and only rarely can they be restructured as parts of ancient archives.

Artifacts of all kinds have turned up in cities and towns throughout the region, and they can often be shown to have originated far from where they were found. In some cases this is apparent because the material of which an artifact is made does not exist locally, and in other instances clear stylistic differences show an artifact to have been brought from far away.

Despite the contacts linking the entire Near Eastern region together in a vast network, this world was not at all a uniform one. It included a variety of ecological zones—enormous floodplains in southern Mesopotamia, open steppes in the north, and highland plateaus in Anatolia and Iran. In the same way, we find many different cultures and ethnic and linguistic groups—Elamites in the Khuzestan Plain, Akkadians in Mesopotamia, Amorites in the Syrian region—and a variety of Indo-European languages, especially Luwian and Hittite, spoken in Anatolia. In terms of material culture there were great distinctions, seen in ceramics, architecture, and other artistic forms. Nevertheless, the Near East was also a world that shared many cultural and political traits and traditions. Towns and cities were ubiquitous; writing was used for everyday purposes, employing the cuneiform system on clay tablets; and there was even a certain sharing of religious concepts and divinities. As documented in this exhibition, there was also an intense exchange of ideas and luxury artifacts alongside the trade in such commodities as metals, stone, wine, wool, and textiles.

THE HISTORICAL DEVELOPMENT

The period began with the collapse of the so-called Third Dynasty of Ur (Ur III) in southern Mesopotamia about 2000 B.C. The Ur III kings brought large areas under military control, with the southern floodplain as the economic and political center. Northern Mesopotamia, with towns such as Ashur and Nineveh, was part of the Ur III state, as was the Diyala region, with its main city Eshnunna. Its power also reached into the Khuzestan Plain, where governors from Ur were installed at the old political center of Susa.

However, the Ur III kings never managed to establish real control over the regions along the Euphrates toward the northwest. In the Syrian and Mesopotamian areas, a major change in ethnic composition took place during the Middle Bronze Age with the influx of the Amorites. These Semitic-speaking tribes pushed down along the river toward the floodplain from the Levant and eventually helped bring the Ur III state to its knees. After its final collapse, a complex pattern of smaller states emerged. The most distant regions, such as northern Mesopotamia and Elam, were the first to escape from Ur's domination, and local dynasties seized power. The states in Mesopotamia proper were thereafter dominated by Amorite dynasties.

The Amorite chieftains became the rulers in the cities that came under their control, and they not only shared a common language but also had political and religious institutions and traditions that bound them together as a cultural unit. Perhaps the most striking example is the list of tribal ancestors invoked in funerary rituals, for it was an identical list that was used by the new rulers in Babylon and the one that reflects the traditions of the Amorite dynasty of Shamshi-Adad in the Syrian region. Curiously, not a single text is known to have been written using the Amorite language, which is identified exclusively from the thousands of personal names attested in the period.[2]

In political terms, the region was a patchwork of states. The period from about 2000 until 1600 B.C. was one of constant change, frequent warfare, shifting alliances, and the creation and subsequent dismantling of short-lived territorial states. At the same time, there is a clearly visible long-term trend throughout this period toward increasingly bigger political units, from a system of city-states in constant contact and competition to the final creation of large, stable territorial states. However, that final development happened only in the succeeding period, the Late Bronze Age.

At one moment in the eighteenth century B.C., a political agent attached to the court of the king of Mari wrote to his lord that "no king is great on his own," and he continued with a list of the major players on the Near Eastern scene, mentioning that some ten or fifteen lesser kings "followed" (that is, were subordinate to) each of the major political states—Hammurabi's Babylon, Rim-Sin's Larsa, Ibal-pi-El's Eshnunna, and Amud-pi-El's Qatna—whereas twenty kings followed Yarim-Lim's Yamhad, whose capital city was Aleppo.[3] A few decades later, all of the Mesopotamian floodplain had been brought under military control from Babylon by Hammurabi, who outmaneuvered his opponents through a bewildering progression of shifting alliances that allowed him to pick off his enemies one by one until only Babylon remained. Of the states mentioned in the letter, only Qatna and Yamhad in Syria were unaffected by Hammurabi's campaigns.

The letter from Mari gives us a snapshot of one particular situation that lasted a few decades. Yet it is characteristic of the dynamics of the period. Shortly before, a very large area in Syria and northern Mesopotamia had been united under Shamshi-Adad in a brief imperial venture, which collapsed with almost frightening rapidity upon his death.

Over this vast area, from the Persian Gulf to the Mediterranean, we find city-states or small territorial states centered on major cities. In some states, dynasties that rose to power were able to effect a certain expansion, conquering

rivals and sometimes conducting military campaigns hundreds of kilometers from their own political centers. Such successful powers could gather vassals around them and maintain their grip on large areas over one or two generations, but in most cases the life span of such states was quite short. The extensive palace archives from Mari show that the world in which these fragile structures were created was marked by almost constant warfare. The same picture seems valid also for Anatolia. Here we find a similar political development that led from a pattern of small states to the creation of the Hittite kingdom about 1650 B.C.

At a certain point in this process Anum-hirbi, who ruled a state called Mamma located in a valley system of the inner Taurus Mountains, wrote to Warshama, the king of Kanesh, and in this letter he described the character of the political system of kings and vassals, contemptuously characterized as "dogs":

> *You wrote me and said: "The man of Taishama is my slave; I shall deal with him. But will you then deal with the man of Sibuha, your slave?" Since the man of Taishama is your dog, why does he negotiate with other kinglets? Does my dog, the man of Sibuha, negotiate with other kinglets? Is a king of Taishama to become the third (real) king together with us? Earlier, when an enemy defeated me, the man of Taishama invaded my country and destroyed 12 of my towns and carried away their sheep and cattle. . . . Instead of protecting my country and encouraging me he not only burnt up my land but left evil-smelling smoke.[4]*

About a hundred years later, the great city of Kanesh itself was conquered and destroyed.

AN OPEN WORLD

The agent who told his master in Mari about the general political situation in the region from the Persian Gulf to the Mediterranean obviously had a clear idea of the extent and nature of this vast area. He knew which major players operated here, and he must have been perfectly aware of their location—in fact, he may have visited several of them. For it was a well-traveled world, where quite a large number of people felt at home and moved with relative ease.

The letters from the Mari archives give us countless examples of diplomats, agents, and spies who traveled extensively.[5] Diplomatic missions could go from Elam to Qatna, crossing frontiers between a number of smaller states along the way. Occasionally they would be stopped and questioned or even turned back in accordance with the political and diplomatic stance of the rulers, but the important thing here is that they had a mental map of the entire region, one that allowed the king at Susa to have a clear understanding of the military and political relevance of cities some 1,500 kilometers away.

One of the most illuminating instances of such diplomatic travels concerns the king of Mari, Zimri-Lim (ca. 1775–1760 B.C.), who journeyed to Aleppo and farther on to the Mediterranean port city of Ugarit, where he met traders from Crete (see pp. 94–100). Texts from the Mari palace inform us that he had a retinue of no fewer than 4,145 persons (including a large military contingent), for part of the reason for the journey was to offer assistance to the ally in Aleppo in a confrontation with a neighboring state.[6] It was presumably as a result of this trip that the ruler of Ugarit later expressed his desire to visit Mari in order to see the large palace in which Zimri-Lim had his royal residence, obviously a building that was admired far and wide.

The lack of political stability and the many wars that consumed this world also meant that armies of sometimes thousands of men walked hundreds of kilometers to reach their destination. Hammurabi of Babylon campaigned on the southern Mesopotamian floodplain, and he sent armies far to the north to fight the kings of Ashur. His final military adventure was the campaign against Mari, his earlier ally, some 500 kilometers from Babylon. Hammurabi's armies conquered the city in 1760 B.C., razing the walls and looting the palace. A considerable number of soldiers must have taken part in such a campaign; we hear in the diplomatic correspondence of armies of twenty, thirty, and even forty thousand men. Because these forces were made up of the ordinary population of cities and states, a large proportion of the male population would have traveled in regions far from their home.

The real travelers, however, were the merchants. Donkey caravans—sometimes with hundreds of pack animals—crossed the wide steppes and plains, even the formidable barrier of the Taurus Mountains, penetrating Anatolia's highlands all the way up to the coast of the Black Sea. A Bedouin sheikh wrote to his overlord, the king of Mari:

My lord knows that I command the bedouins and that just as a merchant travels through war and peace, the bedouins travel through war and peace . . . learning during their movement what the country talks about.[7]

This ability to carry on their business even in places ravaged by war is illustrated by the activities of the Assyrian merchants in Anatolia during the period from about 1950 to 1700 B.C. In their commercial letters, we find several references to military activities and political unrest. These events are mentioned simply because they created difficulties for commercial endeavors. When warfare erupted the merchants had to accept that, at least for a time, markets in certain towns were paralyzed and roads were closed, and that it was impossible to move into or out of the towns affected. However, the fragmented political pattern also allowed for great flexibility, and if one road was closed for a time, another one would nearly always be available.

THE IMPACT OF TRADE

The chronological term "Middle Bronze Age" tells us about some of the most important trade goods that passed through this vast area: copper and tin, which combine to produce the alloy bronze. Copper was available from several sources in the region, notably from Anatolia and Cyprus. But another major source that supplied the southern Mesopotamian floodplain was Oman. In the Persian Gulf the traffic of large boats took merchants from southern Mesopotamian cities such as Ur to the island of Bahrain, where there was an important market, and perhaps all the way to Oman itself. Copper from Oman is known to have reached even Mari, where it had to compete with imports from Cyprus.[8]

The strategic metal, however, was tin, for this had to be acquired from very far away. Small deposits of tin are known to have been worked during the Early Bronze Age in the Taurus Mountains, but it is clear from the textual documentation that large quantities of tin flowed into the Near Eastern region from the east. Where precisely the ancient tin mines were situated is still a matter for debate. A mine has recently been discovered in western Iran, but most scholars seem to support the view that the metal was brought to Susa and farther into Mesopotamia from mines in Central Asia. How such a commercial system, crossing vast distances, was organized is currently unknown, but we do know that considerable quantities of the popular semiprecious stone lapis lazuli came to the Near East from the same region (see p. 68).

When Zimri-Lim of Mari visited the Mediterranean coastal region on his diplomatic tour mentioned earlier, he brought with him sizable amounts of tin that he had acquired from his ally in Elam, and which were used as royal gifts.[9] This system of gift-exchange among rulers was, however, quite small compared with the commercial tin trade conducted by merchants.

We are particularly well informed about one element in this system of long-distance commerce because of a large find of texts in central Anatolia at Kanesh. These document the activities of Assyrian merchants who based their livelihood on a commercial penetration of Anatolia. During a period of more than two centuries, they were engaged in a flourishing trade in tin and textiles that were shipped in donkey caravans from Ashur on the Tigris to cities on the Anatolian plateau. It is assumed that most of the textiles were produced in workshops at Ashur, but many also came together with the tin from the cities on the southern Babylonian alluvium. Tens of thousands of textiles and hundreds of tons of tin were sent to Anatolia during the period of about forty years that is covered by the bulk of the textual documentation. Having built up a system of commercial colonies and stations, large numbers of traders lived permanently in these settlements far from their home cities.[10]

Once installed as the commercial experts in Anatolia, the merchants from Ashur also began to exploit the internal trade routes with such goods as copper and wool.[11] Copper was mined, it appears, primarily in the Black Sea region of Anatolia, and vast quantities were shipped from there to a major city called Burushaddum, which was situated strategically to connect with the roads leading down the river valleys toward the Aegean.

Ashur was one of many cities that seem to have specialized in long-distance foreign trade. Other such commercial centers included Ur, where activities were directed primarily toward the Persian Gulf; Der, in the region east of the Tigris, serving as a gateway to Elam, which distributed tin to the west; Sippar, on the Euphrates, where a lively trade along the river toward Syria and the Levant was organized; Eshnunna, in the Diyala region, close to one of the main passes through the Zagros Mountains to the Iranian highlands; Emar, on the Upper Euphrates; and probably Ebla, an old political center some 50 kilometers south of Aleppo.

Merchants all over the Near East traded in bulk goods such as metals, wool, and textiles. The donkey caravans made use of a well-developed system of roads with inns, where they could stop overnight, and guards, who secured a measure of safety. Large-scale river-borne transportation of wine from the Syrian region on the Euphrates to Babylonia is known from the customs office at Mari, where the boats from the direction of Carchemish had to stop to pay their dues to the palace officials. At Mari itself wine was consumed, sweetened with honey and cooled with ice from a special "ice house" built by Zimri-Lim. All such commodities have naturally disappeared, with only a very few carbonized fragments of textiles now known, in addition to the metal objects found in excavations. The trade in these bulk goods formed the basis for the constant exchange of objects, ideas, and people that marked the period. Cultural influences were transmitted as a consequence of these contacts. Along the routes that crisscrossed the entire region traveled not only diplomats, soldiers, and merchants, but also ideas and influences that had a profound impact.

CULTURAL EXCHANGE
An example of how these contacts sometimes had enduring reverberations is known from Mari. At one point, armies from Eshnunna forced Mari to accept a status as vassal on a campaign that took them toward Syria along the banks of the Euphrates. The army from Eshnunna brought a new and different scribal practice, one that was introduced at Mari during its brief period of control there. This scribal tradition became standard at Mari after the men from Eshnunna had left. Documents were set up in accordance with a new set of rules, the writing style itself changed, and from then on the chancery at Mari simply adopted the Babylonian scribal culture brought by the conquering army.[12] Bureaucrats are not generally known as great innovators, so there must have been political and probably other interests involved in this shift.

In the same way, we can follow how the merchants from Ashur brought a developed scribal tradition to Anatolia that was then adopted also by the local palaces and even private individuals. The Anatolians began to use the cuneiform system of writing, and they wrote all of their texts in Assyrian. Even more remarkable is the development of a special practice of sealing in which the cylinder seal almost completely replaced the traditional stamp seal and became the standard in the region until the end of the first phase of the Assyrian colonies, when the old practice was reintroduced. Not only did the Anatolians begin to use cylinder seals, but they produced seals in a distinct local style quite different from that used by the Assyrian merchants in their home city. The iconography of these often very beautiful Anatolian seals presents a mixture of imported, Mesopotamian elements and local scenes and topics (see cat. no. 37b). This hybrid style is an impressive achievement that shows the fusion of different cultural elements into a new and unique type of design.[13]

At the same time, Assyrians and Anatolians used seals that had been cut in a variety of other local styles, in the so-called Old Assyrian style, and in a special Syrian style characterized by the appearance of several specifically Syrian religious motifs; additionally, some seals were cut in the style in vogue in Babylonia. Some people even used old seals, presumably bought as antiques, and these would often be recut to include the name of the new owner. These seals were probably among the most private objects. Used as signatures on all kinds of documents, they must have had a special meaning for the individual owner. So it is highly interesting and significant that we can see in the same family of Assyrian traders that one man used an antique seal from the Syrian city of Ebla, whereas his brothers and children used seals cut in Anatolian and Syrian styles.[14] We are dealing with a cosmopolitan world where influences met and where people moved with confidence across cultural boundaries of all kinds.

When Zimri-Lim at Mari imported tin from Elam, some to be sent farther on toward the west, part of his payment was made in stone vases. We do not know where these luxury objects were produced, but they could have originated in a local craft tradition at Mari. Clearly they were assumed to be valued and appreciated in Elam. In central Anatolia, we have a set of ivory carvings that, as elaborate luxury items stemming from the Syrian region, could well have ended up there as the result of diplomatic contacts. Indeed, in the palace of Acemhöyük (perhaps ancient Ulama) were found several tags sealed and with brief texts that indicate that the ruler here received packages from kings in Syria and Mesopotamia.[15] Such gifts may well have accompanied other shipments of a strictly commercial nature, but the relevant fact is that they testify to a brisk exchange of luxury objects that were regarded as beautiful and interesting as well as unusual and perhaps exotic.

A large proportion of the goods traded in the ancient Near East was composed of textiles. Although the ancient textiles are no longer extant, we know a great deal about them. The texts speak of many different types, nearly always defined by reference to the name of a specific town, clearly the place where that particular combination of pattern and color was invented or developed. The parallel with Middle Eastern carpets and kilims is obvious, even though rugs were not normally in the repertoire of the ancient merchants. But it is striking that a textile produced perhaps at Ur could end up as a prized possession of an Anatolian living in a town on the coast of the Black Sea. Such objects were so costly that they must have carried with them a very special significance. The Anatolian weavers were themselves of course fully competent to produce beautiful textiles, and it may be argued that they had a weaving technology with an upright loom that was in some respects superior to what was used in Mesopotamia. Nonetheless, imports were more highly valued as they were not only luxurious but carriers of a significance beyond their commercial value.

Whether we are dealing with decorated stone vases, carved ivories, or textiles, it is certain that these objects, carried over long distances and across cultural boundaries, suggest an awareness and appreciation of cultural differences. It is therefore not surprising that we find in palaces from Mari to Qatna (cat. no. 69a, b) and to the Nile Delta (figs. 39, 40, 120) fresco paintings on the walls that exhibit many common traits and, moreover, indicate links with the Cretan tradition as known from Knossos (see fig. 42).

The so-called Investiture Scene, on a wall in Zimri-Lim's palace at Mari (fig. 13), gives us the same sense of hybridity of form, style, and iconography as the seals from Kanesh mentioned earlier.[16] The gods and human figures represented are fully Mesopotamian, and the central scene, which shows the handing over of the royal insignia to the king by his god, is known from, for instance, Hammurabi's stele of laws (fig. 10). But the style of the composition as a whole and several elements such as borders, trees, and birds seem to point to a craftsman from the the eastern Mediterranean. Nevertheless, the Mari wall painting is complete and coherent, embedded in royal ideology and palatial ritual. We should not regard it as a foreign or exotic import, but as a fully integrated work of art, one that could not have existed anywhere other than where it is, in front of the throne room in the palace of Zimri-Lim.

A WORLD OF INFLUENCES

The almost bewildering variety in the Middle Bronze Age Near East must be appreciated as a reflection of a lively, vibrant world of movement, ideas, and exchanges that linked societies otherwise very different in terms of political, social, linguistic, and commercial patterns. We find city-states that were almost entirely occupied with long-distance trade and ruled by an oligarchic elite, and we have centralized kingdoms governed by royally appointed officials. The region was crossed by countless routes, and it was linked also to a wider network reaching into the Mediterranean, over the Persian Gulf, and with tentacles deep into Central Asia.

Diplomatic contacts and military alliances united rulers and cities in a vast network from the Mediterranean to the Persian Gulf, and merchants moved with great ease throughout this system. These contacts—despite the many differences—illustrate the unity of the entire region, a unity in diversity that can be traced in the many texts left by the ancients as well as in their precious artifacts.

We cannot know precisely in which way the king of Elam would have appreciated the stone vases sent to him from Mari, or what motivated people in Anatolia to spend considerable amounts on textiles imported from Ashur. We know that they would have been happy to have deliveries of strategic commodities, such as the metals they needed for the production of tools and weapons; however, it is important to keep in mind that, for example, the Old Assyrian merchants made a greater profit on the trade in textiles than on that in tin. Luxury items certainly played a role in lavish display by the political elite everywhere, but that is hardly the entire story.

The situations where we find different cultural traditions fusing in new, hybrid forms tell us only a little about the way in which the interaction was managed and understood by the people who left us these magnificent treasures. We can also get a glimpse of the way in which such objects as seals, vases, and wall paintings became deeply meaningful in their concrete setting. And we can observe how the contacts that bound this world together resulted in a burst of innovative energy that led to the creation of new styles and imagery.

1. See the general discussion in Charpin, Edzard, and Stol 2004.
2. Such names were usually formed as brief phrases, such as "Yasmah-Addu," meaning "(the god) Addu has heard."
3. See Dossin 1938, pp. 117–18.
4. Text published by Balkan 1957.
5. See Durand 1997–2000 (LAPO 16–18).
6. See Villard 1986. See also Charpin 2004b, pp. 211–12.
7. See Charpin 2004a, pp. 58–59.
8. For a general discussion, see Larsen 1987. See also Stol 2004, chap. 15, "Der Handel."
9. Joannès 1991; see also Dossin 1970.
10. For a selection of letters, see Michel 2001.
11. Dercksen 1996.
12. See Durand 1992, pp. 121–23.
13. N. Özgüç 1965; Teissier 1994.
14. Larsen 2002, pp. xxix–xxxiii.
15. Veenhof 1993.
16. Parrot 1958, part 2.

BABYLON

BÉATRICE ANDRÉ-SALVINI

Although founded during the third millennium B.C., Babylon did not become an important city until after it was conquered by an Amorite tribal chief named Sumu-abum, in about 1894 B.C. The Old Babylonian period began with the founding of the first dynasty by his successor, Sumu-lael, who annexed older and more prestigious neighboring cities. Knowledge of these and other events during this period has come down to us through administrative and legal documents appended with elaborate year names, so called because the king named each year after the event he considered the most significant.

HAMMURABI, KING OF THE AMORITES[1]

Because of Babylon's central location in Mesopotamia, its history can be understood only within the historical and cultural context of the greater Near East. Babylonia was still a minor kingdom when Hammurabi, the great-great-grandson of Sumu-lael, took the throne in 1792 B.C., after the death of his father, Sin-muballit. At its northern frontier, 60 kilometers north of Babylon, lay the twin city of Sippar, famous for its oracle of Shamash, the sun god and divine judge. The southernmost point was Dilbat, situated about the same distance from Babylon as Sippar. Other major cities of the kingdom included Kish, several kilometers east of Babylon, and Kutha, east of Sippar on the Tigris.

Several powerful Amorite states surrounded Babylon. To the north lay the kingdom of Upper Mesopotamia, ruled by Shamshi-Adad, the most powerful monarch in the region. His influence extended west as far as Mari, in the central Euphrates region, and his realm shared a border to the south with Babylonia. Hammurabi also shared a border with Eshnunna (Tell Asmar), another important state that neighbored Babylonia to the northeast, in the Diyala region. To the south lay the great state of Larsa, corresponding more or less to the boundaries of ancient Sumer, which had been governed for more than thirty years by Rim-Sin. To the west of Mesopotamia lay the powerful kingdom of Yamhad, whose capital was Halab (Aleppo); the land to the east was ruled by Elam.

For many years, Hammurabi remained just another powerful monarch among others. The death of Shamshi-Adad in about 1776 B.C., however, opened the door to shifting military allegiances. In order to establish Babylon as the most influential kingdom of his time, Hammurabi played a complex game of alliances and counter-alliances. In the twenty-ninth year of his reign, supported by his allies Zimri-Lim of Mari and the king of Yamhad, Hammurabi successfully defended his kingdom against the forces of Siwapalarhuhpak, the king of Elam. In the process, he sacked the city of Eshnunna, which Siwapalarhuhpak had captured the year before; yet later he joined forces with Eshnunna's new monarch, who was his son-in-law. Thus the foe of one day became the ally of the next.

In the south, which had been relatively calm up to this point, raids on Babylonian territory by the king of Larsa gave Hammurabi a pretext for military intervention. In the thirtieth year of his reign, he acted on the advice of a divine oracle and, again with the help of Zimri-Lim, set out with his army to lay siege to Larsa. For months, the city walls withstood the onslaught of siege towers, ramps, and battering rams, but Larsa's fierce resistance was ultimately overcome and the city

Figure 9. Diorite head of a ruler, found at Susa. Old Babylonian period. Musée du Louvre, Paris sb 95

capitulated. The thirty-first year of Hammurabi's reign was named to commemorate this great victory:

The year: Hammurabi, the king, with the help of An and Enlil, went before the army [and], by the supreme power which the greatest gods had given to him, conquered (Isin), [and] the land of Emutbal and its king, Rim-Sin; he brought forth his life to its . . . [and] caused . . . Sumer and Akkad to dwell at his command.[2]

After the conquest and annexation of Larsa, Hammurabi took on the ancient and prestigious title of King of Sumer and Akkad. Babylon became a center of power, and Hammurabi the arbiter of conflicts in the region. He appointed high officials to govern the territories of Larsa under Babylonian domination, and from his correspondence with these officials, we know that the great local clans swore obedience to him in exchange for the maintenance of their privileges.

In the thirty-second year of his reign Hammurabi conquered Mari, returning eighteen months later to tear down its walls. He also took control of Eshnunna, then conquered the territories of Upper Mesopotamia, and, after routing the forces of Elam, dispatched his troops as far north as Tuttul, on the Balikh River. The fall of Mari was a major event in the history of Babylonia and the Near East, for it meant that the Babylonians no longer had any rivals in Mesopotamia. After sacking the city, Hammurabi took on the additional title of King of All the Lands of the Amorites. Indeed, he had defeated and united all of the Amorite kingdoms that had come to power in Mesopotamia after the fall of the Third Dynasty of Ur. From then on, the Near East was divided into two poles of influence: Aleppo in the west and Babylon in the east.

The name of the king's thirty-third regnal year commemorates these and other accomplishments:

The year: Hammurabi, the king, dug the canal "Hammurabi means abundance for the people, the beloved of (An) and Enlil"; provided perennial water of abundance for Nippur, Eridu, Ur, Larsa, Uruk and Isin; restored Sumer and Akkad which had been scattered; overthrew in battle the army of Mari and Malgium; subjugated Mari and its villages and the many cities (of the mountain land) of Subartu, (Ekallatum, (all of) Burunda and the land of Zalmaqum on the bank of the Tigris up to the Euphrates): and caused [them] to dwell at his command in friendship.[3]

The new canal served all of the cities located on or near the Euphrates and belonging to the ancient territory of Sumer. The king was concerned with restoring the canal system for the regions he had conquered the previous year, which must have suffered from lack of maintenance during the war. Hammurabi then adopted the imperial title King of the Four Regions, or "king who gives peace to the four regions." This title, which refers to the four cardinal directions, had been used for the first time around 2250 B.C. by Naram-Sin of Akkad after his victories

Figure 10. Diorite stele of Hammurabi, found at Susa, detail. Old Babylonian period. Musée du Louvre, Paris sb 8

over Ebla and Elam—that is, the lands to the west and east—and signified "king of the universe."

Except for occasional uprisings, Hammurabi's power was no longer overtly called into question, and he was able to devote himself to organizing the administration of his kingdom and applying a unified system of justice. During his last years, the king undertook major campaigns to repair the damage caused by floods or warfare, helping to relocate the inhabitants. Under his rule, and for more than one thousand years afterward, Babylon prospered as a center of literary, philosophical, and religious activity. Added to the city's oracle of Shamash was a priesthood devoted to Marduk, whom the king had promoted to chief divinity of the Babylonian pantheon.

THE STELE OF HAMMURABI

The prologue inscribed on the Stele of Hammurabi is one of our best sources for the history of his reign. In it, he lists the territories that formed the historical core of his kingdom as well as those that were added to the Babylonian empire by his triumphs. This information, supplemented by year names, dynastic lists, the Mari correspondence, and victory stele, provides an itinerary of Hammurabi's deeds and enables us to retrace the outlines of his empire.

The prologue of the stele reveals that at the end of his reign, Hammurabi no longer made a distinction between central Babylonia and the ancient cities of Mesopotamia that he had annexed. He listed them on his stele according to the topographical criteria of religious tradition and their regional distribution along the two major rivers and the main canals that ensured the unity and prosperity of Mesopotamia.

After Hammurabi

Toward the end of his reign, Hammurabi marched north as far as the foothills of the Zagros Mountains to consolidate some short-lived victories in the rebellious mountain regions. Soon after the king's death, his son Samsu-iluna (ca. 1749–1712 B.C.) was beset by enemies from several sides. The states of Larsa and Uruk in ancient Sumer revolted in 1741 B.C., and an economic crisis forced the inhabitants of the south to migrate to northern Babylonia. The invasion of the Hittite king Mursili I in about 1595 B.C. put an end to the reign of Samsu-ditana, Hammurabi's last descendant. After a period of obscurity, the Kassites, who had been infiltrating Babylonia over several generations, came to power in Babylon. The Kassite dynasty reigned for the next four hundred years, stimulating a spread of Babylonian culture.

1. Durand 1997–2000; Charpin 2003; Charpin 2004b; Charpin and Ziegler 2003; André-Salvini 2008.
2. After Horsnell 1999, p. 141.
3. Ibid., p. 147.

1, detail

The statue was attached to the hollow trapezoidal base in three places. A vase welded to the front of the base was likely intended for aromatics. Both long sides of the base are decorated in relief: on the right, a praying figure similar to the three-dimensional worshipper kneels before a seated god. The deity wears the horned headdress and traditional robe of divine figures and sits on a high-backed throne. The other side of the base depicts a recumbent ram, an animal associated with Amurru, originally considered the master shepherd of the nomadic herds. An inscription in Sumerian has been chased between the figure of the ram and the throne of the deity. It is read horizontally—which in this period is unusual in a medium other than clay—and records a dedication by a certain Lu-Nanna, who asks the god for the protection of Hammurabi:

For the god Martu, his god, for the life of Hammurabi, king of Babylon, Lu-Nanna, [. . .], son of Sin-le'i, fashioned for him, for his life, a suppliant statue of copper, [its] face [plat]ed with gold. He dedicated it to him as his servant.[2]

The description of Lu-Nanna's office has been mutilated, but Lu-Nanna was most likely a dignitary from the nobility or upper class of merchants who rallied around the king of Babylon after his victory over Larsa. Other depictions of dignitaries or members of the ruling family shown in the same pose as that of the figure here have been preserved, but none of them were gilded.[3] Lu-Nanna would have commissioned the statue to kneel in eternal prayer before the divinity. Raising issues of royal iconography, it is a representation of either the king or the donor, on behalf of his king, in royal guise.   BA-S

1. For further reference, see Dussaud 1933, pp. 1–10, pl. 1; Sollberger 1969, pp. 90–93; Sollberger in Sollberger and Kupper 1971, p. 219; Spycket 1981, pp. 246–47; André in *Naissance de l'écriture* 1982, no. 170; Frayne 1990, p. 361, no. 2002; and André-Salvini in *Babylone* 2008, p. 77, no. 31.
2. After Frayne 1990, p. 360.
3. See Sollberger 1969.

1

KNEELING WORSHIPPER

Bronze, gold, silver
Height 19.6 cm (7¾ in.)
Mesopotamia
Old Babylonian, ca. 1760 B.C.
Musée du Louvre, Paris, Département des
Antiquités Orientales AO15704

This votive statue is said to have been found among a series of objects from a metal workshop at Larsa that existed before Hammurabi's conquest of the kingdom and continued in the service of the new ruler of the land.[1] According to the inscription, it was dedicated to the Sumerian god Martu (Akkadian Amurru) and likely would have been intended for the temple of that deity.

Since the Early Dynastic period in Mesopotamia, it was common for dignitaries to dedicate votive objects to various deities, with inscriptions requesting intercession "for the life" of the king. These inscriptions carved on precious objects were commissioned not only to curry favor with the king but also to secure his protection and the prosperity of his kingdom.

The statue is of a male figure with right arm bent and hand raised to the mouth, a traditional gesture of deference, supplication, or prayer. The barefoot worshipper wears a headdress with a wide folded edge. His short, curly beard covers his cheeks. The eyes were originally inlaid with shell and lapis lazuli, and the hands and face are covered with gold leaf. The gilding ends at the wrist, around which a raised band could represent a bracelet. The figure wears a garment that opens at the front and is adorned with tassels along the lower edge.

pattern along the bottom of the relief suggests mountains.

Because her identity is uncertain, the goddess has been named the Queen of the Night. Some think she could be Lilitu (the biblical Lilith), but as Lilitu was a demoness, this is unlikely. Her horned headdress and rod-and-ring symbols indicate that she was a high-ranking deity, perhaps Ishtar, goddess of sexual love and war, who normally stands on a lion. The lowered wings, owls, and black background, however, would associate her with the Underworld, whose tutelary goddess was Ereshkigal, Ishtar's sister. Normally, deities have only one rod-and-ring symbol, but Ishtar's was taken from her when she visited Ereshkigal in the Underworld: the Queen could therefore represent Ereshkigal holding divine symbols for both herself and Ishtar. The plaque probably stood in a shrine, the location of which is unknown.

The Queen has been dated by thermoluminescence to between 1765 and 45 B.C.[1] This date and the geographic origins of the plaque can be more closely defined thanks to small, crude, mold-made plaques with figures of the same type that have been excavated in Babylonia in contexts dating from about 1850 to 1750 B.C. A vase of the same period was excavated from a grave at Larsa in 1933. On four miniature plaques on one side of the vase are depicted figures similar to the Queen.

2
PLAQUE WITH NUDE GODDESS

Ceramic
Height 49.5 cm (19½ in.); width 37 cm
(14⅝ in.); thickness 4.8 cm (1⅞ in.)
Mesopotamia
Old Babylonian, ca. 1850–1750 B.C.
The Trustees of the British Museum, London
2003–7–18, 1

This large, high-relief plaque was made of straw-tempered clay pressed into a mold from the back so that relief and slab form an integral whole. The clay relief was smoothed and further details were added before the plaque was fired. The body of the curvaceous nude female at center was then painted in red against a black background. She wears the horned headdress of a deity as well as a necklace and bracelets, and she holds two rod-and-ring symbols, representing justice. Her long wings, which hang downward, were painted red, black, and white, as were the two large barn owls that flank her. On her legs are projections that resemble dewclaws, and instead of feet she has talons similar to those of the owls. She stands on the backs of two small lions, painted white. Their black manes, the black bands of fur along their bellies, and the whorls on their shoulders indicate that they are Asiatic lions. A black scale

Figure 11. Reconstruction drawing of cat. no. 2, with color restored.

22

On the other side is a similar figure, painted and incised. An unsuccessful attempt to roll out a cylinder seal of a winged figure resulted in the presence of a hole near the base of the vase. The sun god on the Stele of Hammurabi in the Louvre (see fig. 10) wears the same headdress as the one seen here, and he extends a rod-and-ring symbol to Hammurabi. A fragmentary god of unbaked clay from the same period (cat. no. 3), excavated at Ur in southern Mesopotamia, also wears a similar headdress and necklace and is of the same high quality of manufacture as that of this plaque. Further, it is painted in the same range of colors, with yellow pigment for the headdress; yellow has therefore been inferred in the color reconstruction of this relief.[2]

The Queen of the Night relief may have come to England as early as 1924, and it was brought to the British Museum in 1933 for scientific testing. Following its publication in 1936, it was known as the Burney Relief, after its owner.[3] The plaque remained in private hands until 2003, when the British Museum acquired it to celebrate its 250th anniversary.[4]

One would expect a piece as unique as the Queen of the Night to have its detractors, and doubts were raised about its authenticity as early as 1936. These were withdrawn in 1971, and various scholars have shown arguments against its authenticity to be flawed.[5] One of the most convincing excavated objects for the study of the plaque is the upper part of the enthroned deity from Ur. The plaque is beyond doubt a masterpiece of ancient Mesopotamian art dating to the Old Babylonian period.

DC

1. British Museum, Department of Scientific Research, 1975.
2. See Collon 2005b, p. 8, fig. 2. In addition to the yellow on the headdress, yellow may have also occurred on parts of the necklace, the bracelets, and the rod-and-ring symbols, i.e., all the items that may have been made of gold.
3. F. Davis 1936.
4. See Collon 2005b, pp. 7–11, concerning the circumstances of the plaque's acquisition. The acquisition was supported by the Heritage Lottery Fund, the British Museum Friends, the National Art Collections Fund, the Friends of the Ancient Near East, The Sir Joseph Hotung Charitable Settlement, and The Seven Pillars of Wisdom Trust.
5. For a summary of the issues regarding the authenticity of the plaque, see Collon 2007.

3
DEITY

Ceramic
Height 7.3 cm (2⅞ in.); width 5.3 cm (2⅛ in.)
Ur, AH site
Old Babylonian, ca. 1850–1750 B.C.
The Trustees of the British Museum, London
122934

This fragment preserves the upper part of a figure that is identified as divine by a headdress consisting of four pairs of horns. The head, shoulders, and left arm down to the elbow are intact. The upper part of a chair back also remains, indicating that the deity would have been seated. The tip of what may have been a weapon rests against the left arm. Much of the paint that originally covered the figure has survived. The tufted garment, which appears to have been white with black lines between the tufts, leaves one shoulder bare. The hair, beard, and chair back are painted black, and the flesh of the face and arms is red. The headdress is yellow, and the necklace consists of alternating red and yellow beads. The paint on this deity has been used as a guide in reconstructing the Queen of the Night (cat. no. 2 and fig. 11).[1]

Clay was a popular medium for Mesopotamian images in the second millennium B.C. The skill evident in the modeling and painting of many of these figures would suggest that the medium was highly valued even though it would have been less expensive than metal or stone. The findspot of the deity—in the fill of a chapel belonging to a house in a residential neighborhood—indicates that it was used in a private, domestic cult.[2] The chapel also contained an altar of baked brick preserved to a height of some 50 centimeters; nearby was a mud-brick "table," and a large clay pot was sunk in the floor. In contrast to the finely made objects discussed above, various contemporary small-scale clay plaques were mass produced in molds. These plaques display consistent cultic themes and had a wide distribution. The adoption of clay as a medium for cultic images likely had an ideological significance.[3]

JME

1. Collon 2005b.
2. Woolley and Mallowan 1976, U.16993.
3. Assante 2002.

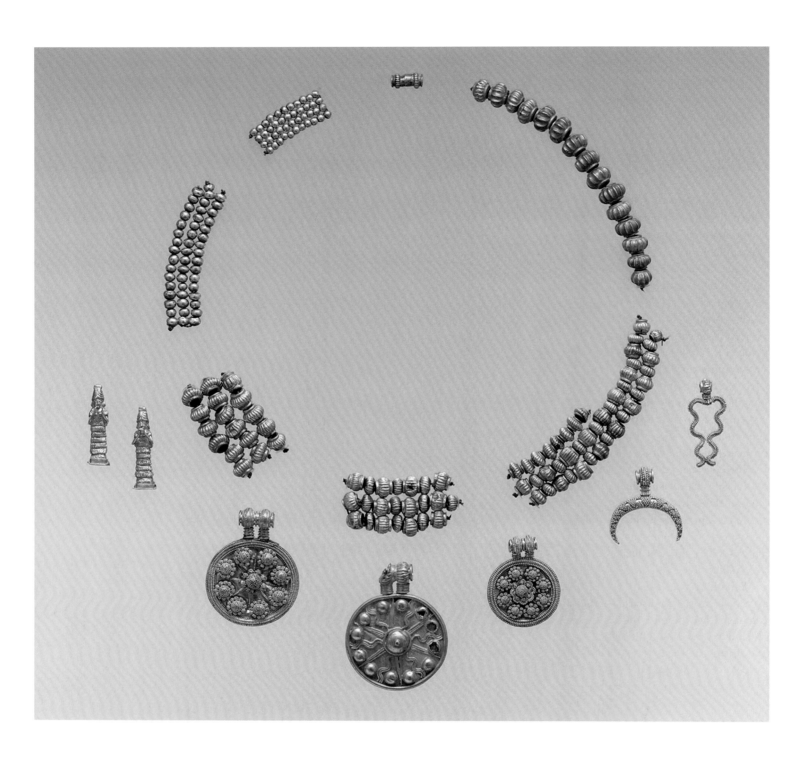

4

PENDANTS AND BEADS

Gold

Diameter of largest medallion 3.6 cm (1½ in.)

Mesopotamia

Old Babylonian, ca. 18th–17th century B.C.

The Metropolitan Museum of Art, New York,
Fletcher Fund, 1947 47.1a–h

The ornaments that make up the collection of objects better known as the "Dilbat necklace" or "Dilbat hoard" are among the most important extant examples of ancient goldsmithing from Mesopotamia. The seven pendants and various beads shown in the present arrangement came to the Metropolitan Museum in 1947 along with four cylinder seals, gold seal caps unrelated to those seals, a partially finished ear or nose ring, and some additional beads and fragments. According to notations made by the original owner and published in 1931, these disparate items (and others that did not make their way into the Museum's collection) were found in a pot in Dilbat (Deylam), a site south of Babylon.[1]

The pendants display a range of styles, gold alloys, and levels of craftsmanship that make it unlikely they were designed as part of a single necklace.[2] The small rosette medallion and the crescent are the most expertly crafted of the group and are decorated with finely executed granulation. The large rosette medallion appears similar in iconography and technique but was overheated in the process of manufacture so that the granulation is not as refined. And while all three pendants share the same design of suspension loop, they differ dramatically in color.

The other pendants in the group include a lightning fork, which is suspended from a different style of loop and therefore probably

24

designed for yet another piece of jewelry. The two small figures in flounced garments are the most exquisitely rendered pieces of all; their mechanisms of attachment, however, would make them difficult to combine with any of the other elements or with the large beads.[3] Finally, the large sun disc not only differs in iconography and style of manufacture but must also be considered a jeweler's mistake because of the melted domes on the medallion and the melted left loop of the suspension element.

It is also worth noting that images of necklaces depicted on reliefs, wall paintings, and terracotta figurines rarely show more than one pendant hanging from a string of beads until the first millennium B.C. (see cat. no. 5).[4] In addition, the beads in the group comprise a variety of shapes and sizes that would be difficult to incorporate into one or more coordinated strands to match the sizes and types of suspension loops on the pendants. It therefore seems reasonable to attribute the pendants and beads to a hoard rather than to a unified piece of jewelry.[5] The overall virtuosity of workmanship and the importance of the individual elements to our understanding of the goldsmith's craft in the second millennium B.C. are in no way diminished by this conclusion.

Visually each pendant signifies the emblematic form of a major Mesopotamian deity. The large sun disc represents Shamash (the sun god); the crescent, Sin (the moon god); the lightning fork, Adad (the storm god); the rosettes, Ishtar (the goddess of war and sexual love); and the females in flounced garments, Lama (the protective goddess). Symbols of divinity have a long tradition of representation in various media throughout the ancient Near East.[6] They were certainly meant to be apotropaic, but likely had far greater efficacy than the purely protective. An emblem was considered one mode of presencing a deity.[7] As such, the Dilbat ornaments did not simply allude to the divine beings they represented but testified to their virtual presence,[8] not unlike similar symbols on later *kudurru* (cat. no. 122). The power embodied in these ornaments thus would have been analogous to the power embedded in a cult statue—which is perhaps why in the later religions, along with idol worship, jewels were banned.[9]

KB

1. Unger 1931.
2. See Lilyquist 1994 for a complete history and reconsideration of the Metropolitan Museum's group of gold ornaments and cylinder seals said to come from Dilbat.
3. Their attachment mechanisms (as well as the fact that they are a pair) seem most suitable for suspension from hoop earrings. In addition, they are decorated on the reverse as fully as on the front, with even the minute detail of the necklace counterweights indicated. This suggests that they were designed to be seen in the round, as with hanging earrings. It is also noteworthy that a flat sheet of gold was left at the base of each figure, suggesting that they were either unfinished or intended to be placed on a pedestal, again as statues in the round would be shown (see cat. no. 7).
4. See Maxwell-Hyslop 1971, pp. 86–87, for examples.
5. Indeed, much of the extant jewelry from the Middle and Late Bronze Ages comes from hoards: Larsa, Byblos, Tell el-'Ajjul, and the Uluburun shipwreck, for example. See Lilyquist 1993.
6. Some, such as the rosette, can be traced back to the Uruk period while others, such as the sun disc, the crescent, the lightning fork, and the females in flounced dresses, to the Akkadian and Ur III periods. For more on the long tradition of using divine symbols in jewelry across the ancient Near East, see pp. 350–52, this volume.
7. Spaey 1993; Bahrani 2003, p. 127.
8. Bahrani 2007.
9. See Wildberger 2002.

5
FRAGMENT OF A VICTORY STELE

Diorite
Height 49 cm (19⅜ in.); width 55 cm (21¾ in.)
Mesopotamia
Old Assyrian, reign of Shamshi-Adad I (?), ca. 1808–1776 B.C.
Musée du Louvre, Paris, Département des Antiquités Orientales AO2776

This stele is carved on both sides, one of which still bears traces of an inscription in Akkadian.[1] The top probably would have been arched. This fragment represents the remains of what must have been several registers.[2] The inscription records the victory over the city of Qabra, on the Little Zab, a tributary of the Tigris River. Although the name of the victorious king was effaced, the stele came from the region controlled by Shamshi-Adad, who probably commissioned it. Another stele commemorating the same battle and commissioned by Dadusha in Eshnunna is preserved in the Iraq Museum, Baghdad.[3] The stele here therefore likely commemorates a successful

5

military campaign, commanded jointly by Shamshi-Adad of Ekallatum in Upper Mesopotamia and Dadusha of Eshnunna against Qabra and the kingdom of Urbilum (Arbeles), which corresponds to the present city of Erbil and the surrounding region.

The fighting figure on one side may personify the victorious king in the pose of the god Adad: he brandishes a battle-axe and tramples his victim underfoot, a motif that goes back to the third millennium B.C. The king's tunic leaves one shoulder bare and extends to the knees. Over the tunic is a fringed and embroidered shawl and a belt, typical attire for a king in battle. The king also wears jewelry on his wrist and around his neck, including a pendant hanging from a chain. A facing figure is dressed in a type of military garb—a short open garment with fringed edging or tassels falling below the knees—that identifies him as an officer of the victorious army. The crouching victim is probably the king of Erbil. He is clad in a long, belted V-neck tunic with short sleeves and embroidered along the edge.

On the other side of the stele, two men stand face to face flanking an inscription. One, whose hands are tied, probably represents a defeated king. Both figures wear royal garments with double tassels or fringes. On the figure that is the best preserved, a grid pattern is visible on the shoulder left uncovered by the tasseled garment. It is difficult to say whether the grid pattern depicts a piece of clothing or, more likely, a sort of net thrown over the figure's head; ensnaring enemies in a net

5, alternate view

was a Mesopotamian custom, both symbolically and in reality.

Since the figures face each other, they do not signify a procession of defeated adversaries (all of whom would normally face in the same direction). Nevertheless, the garments are similar and the protagonists are the same size, which suggests that the second figure (whose hands are missing) could also represent a royal captive.   BA–S

1. For further reference, see Genouillac 1910, pp. 151–56; Börker-Klähn 1982; Charpin and Durand 1985, pp. 293–343; Frayne in Grayson 1987; Ismail and Cavigneaux 2003; Charpin 2004b; and André-Salvini in *Babylone* 2008, pp. 68–69, no. 23.
2. Grayson 1987, A.O.39.1001.
3. The stele was discovered in the 1980s by Iraqi archaeologists in a field near Tell Asmar, the site of ancient Eshnunna (Iraq Museum, Baghdad, inv. no. IM 95200); see Ismail and Cavigneaux 2003.

MARI

JEAN-CLAUDE MARGUERON

By the time the *shakkanakku* ruler Hannun-Dagan started building his great palace at Mari, about 2000 B.C., the city had been the northern center of the Syro-Mesopotamian basin for nearly a millennium. Situated on the east bank of the Euphrates, halfway between Babylon and the Mediterranean coast, Mari controlled all the trade routes that crossed its territory to and from Babylon and the mountains in the north.

The palace of Mari is the best known in the period extending from the Third Dynasty of Ur to the Amorite kingdoms. With walls towering to a height of nearly 5 meters, it is one of the best-preserved palaces in the Near East. More than fifteen thousand complete or fragmentary tablets have been excavated there, as well as objects from daily life, wall paintings, and statues. When the Babylonian king Hammurabi took the city in 1760 B.C., he left behind everything he deemed useless and let the city burn. The wealth of material abandoned by Hammurabi was first brought to light in 1933. Excavations carried out under the direction of the French archaeologist André Parrot over the next several years would reveal the importance of Mari within the Syro-Mesopotamian world at the beginning of the second millennium B.C.

The palace was the most imposing of its time, covering an area of more than 25,000 square meters, with about three hundred units including rooms, courtyards, and corridors (fig. 12). This last number can in fact be doubled, as there was at least one upper story. The excavations have enabled us to understand the organization and operation of the palace and the role it played under the Amorite rulers. The organization is fairly simple: six sectors were grouped into two main areas. The first sector, which occupies the entire eastern half of the building, includes the entrance area (supervised by the official who orchestrated all the activities in the palace), a large court (131) that served as a central meeting place, a temple precinct to the southeast, and, to the south, storerooms for daily provisions and the distribution of wages. The location of the temple precinct is unusual for a Mesopotamian palace; it was perhaps built over the previous mid-third-millennium B.C. palace. A single door provides access to the second sector—the most important because it gave the building its palatial function. It includes the king's quarters, the administrative area, and to the northwest, the women's quarters. These are all grouped around the administrative sector,

consisting of a courtyard (106), a vestibule (64), and throne room (65). Communication between these different units, and between the ground and the upper levels, is laid out in such a way that all comings and goings could be closely controlled; no one was free to move about at will.

The king's and the women's quarters were characterized by luxury and refinement, as demonstrated especially from the fragmentary remains of the wall paintings. The reception rooms were on the upper story and have not survived, and we can only imagine their former splendor from the few vestiges that have come down to us. On the other hand, the official or royal sector on the ground level reveals the importance of the king's omnipotence because it literally pervades the living space. It was in the throne room that royal power was fully expressed and where the king appeared to his subjects in all his glory; his throne occupied one end of the room, a vantage point that permitted him to dominate the entire assembly. From there, he received tribute from his subjects or his visitors, in accordance with established rituals. Opposite the king, at the top of a majestic staircase, stood a platform with statues of ancient rulers from whom the dynasty claimed legitimacy. And finally, in a room at the southeast corner, another grand staircase led to the king's private chambers.

The throne room was not simply the place where the king's majesty was manifest. Although not a temple in a literal sense, it was imbued with an atmosphere of sanctity, for the king was presented as the intermediary between the realm of the gods and that of mankind, and was therefore related to the divine. The throne room aptly expressed that function as well, as the placement of the throne is identical to that of a divine throne in a temple. Other features of the palace complex also clearly expressed this aspect. The throne stood at the end of a route that first passed through the Court of Palms (fig. 14), which bore the tree symbolizing the king's beneficence to his subjects. From the Court of Palms, one passed through the southern facade, which was richly decorated with wall paintings that recounted the king's sacred deeds. Visitors would then enter the vestibule (64)—the *papahum*, a term that implies a further step along a sacred trajectory—where they would pass by the statue of a goddess holding a vessel that dispensed life-giving waters (cat. no. 7). From there one arrived in the throne room, which necessarily took on the appearance of a veritable royal sanctuary.

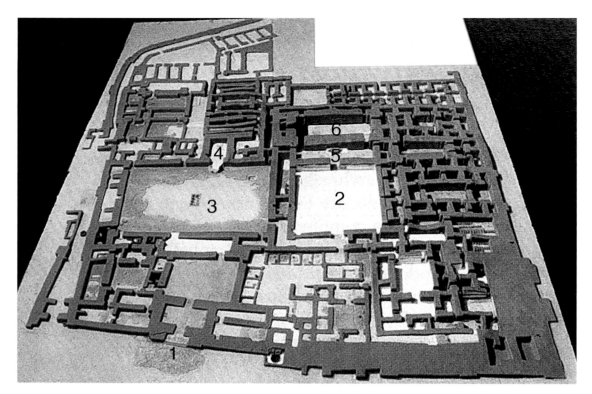

Figure 12. Model of the Palace of Zimri-Lim, Mari. Musée du Louvre, Paris

A. Entrance to Palace
B. Court 106, Court of Palms
C. Court 131
D. Room 132, Chapel of Ishtar
E. Vestibule 64, *papahum*
F. Throne room 65

Figure 13. Wall painting of Investiture Scene. Mari, Palace of Zimri-Lim. Musée du Louvre, Paris A019826

Figure 14. Reconstruction of the south façade of the Court of Palms. Mari, Palace of Zimri-Lim.

While the architecture of the palace expresses a strong Mesopotamian tradition, the material objects recovered from the ruins reflect the diverse influences that converged on this capital along the Euphrates. The extent of Mari's relations abroad is clearly attested in the textual documentation. As a result of these finds, we have an idea of the life of the kingdom, which extended northward almost to the foothills of the Taurus Mountains, southward to Hit at the far reaches of the plateau, and to the northwest as far as the stronghold of Halabiya. The king maintained a regular correspondence with the governors of the provinces and with his many agents. He was also in contact with the rulers of the kingdoms of western Syria, from Carchemish to Aleppo, Ugarit, and Qatna. His correspondence with the kings of the north and northeast, not to mention central Mesopotamia and the southern regions, was no less extensive. Despite the fact that only a fraction of these archives have come down to us, they tell us that diplomacy and trade relations were part of the active exchanges that Mari conducted with regions hundreds of miles away. Relations between the cities were much closer than we might imagine. It is not astonishing to discover that the king counted and recapitulated the tin holdings that he entrusted to private individuals in cities of western Syria, assets that permitted him to make purchases and to compensate for the transfer of funds; that the envoy of the king of Ugarit paid a visit to Mari; that Zimri-Lim went on a long voyage that took him to Aleppo and Ugarit (see pp. 95–100); and that princesses were summoned from distant foreign courts to secure alliances by marriage.

Strangely enough, although the Mari archives chiefly pertain to areas west of Mari—perhaps an accident of pillaging—the record left by works of art points to Mesopotamia, so much so that some specialists consider Mari to have been only an extension of Babylon. This view is incorrect. For one thing, we know nothing about the city of Babylon during the reign of Hammurabi, for the modern water table has made excavations of these strata impossible. And while it is true that some statuary exhibits a strong Mesopotamian influence, the specific characteristics of the statue of the goddess with the flowing vase (cat. no. 7), for example, can be attributed only to the craftsmen of Mari. To be sure, Mari's contacts with Babylonia as well as kingdoms such as Eshnunna introduced features that have often led scholars to overestimate their influence. For instance, the adoption of Babylonian cuneiform by the scribes of Mari certainly argues for the predominant influence of the capital of Hammurabi's kingdom. On the other hand, this view overlooks the fact that, until then and from the time of the accession of the *shakkanakku* to power in the twenty-second century B.C., Mari had remained faithful to the refined Neo-Sumerian style of writing, keeping its tradition very much alive.

It is also clear that diplomatic and military relations between Mari and the Taurus Mountain region played a part in religious practices. Traces of religious life left by both the male and the female workers in their quarters at the palace point to stimuli from the north. This would suggest that conquered populations found their way into royal service. Such influences were no doubt more extensive than might be extrapolated from the scant evidence that remains.

Among the major finds of the excavation were elaborate wall paintings that exemplify the originality and virtuosity of Mari's artistic production. With a few exceptions, the paintings occupied the upper portions of the walls and were found in fragments among the debris. Nevertheless, a meticulous excavation process made it possible to reconstruct certain scenes (for example, cat. no. 8), incomplete of course, but often comprehensible and significant, and even to propose general interpretations.

The connection between the king and religious practices at court are expressed not only by the Investiture Scene discovered in situ on the south wall of Court 106 (fig. 13), just west of the door leading to the *papahum* (64) but also in the Chapel of Ishtar (132), in which were found the remains of two compositions dominated by the goddess Ishtar and the god Sin. In addition, above Room 220, in the great reception hall of the king's apartments, a very large and remarkable painting glorified the king in his various roles as warrior, hunter, destroyer, and builder. Nevertheless, because it was found at eye level and was well preserved, the Investiture Scene is the most imposing, with an extraordinary presence, displaying a skillful blend of realism and symbolism. A remarkable work, it offers ample testimony to the creative power of the artists of Mari.

6

STANDING FIGURE
OF IDDI-ILUM

Steatite
Height 41.4 cm (16⅜ in.)
Mari, Palace of Zimri-Lim, Court 148
Shakkanakku period, late 3rd millennium B.C.
Musée du Louvre, Paris, Département des
Antiquités Orientales AO19486

This statue of Iddi-ilum was discovered in the palace of Zimri-Lim, the last king of Mari.[1] Iddi-ilum belonged to a line of monarchs who governed the kingdom at the end of the third millennium B.C. after its destruction by the Akkadians. These rulers of local origin were given the title *shakkanakku*, which means governor or general and alluded to the virtual dependence of their lineage on Akkad. This title survived the fall of the Akkadian empire, and the rulers of Mari continued to use it for a time. The *shakkanakku* rulers reconstructed the city when they came to power, but their archives have not yet been found. Some of the royal names that have come down to us are those whose memory was perpetuated in statues such as the one here.

Iddi-ilum is depicted standing with hands joined. His robe, which is unrealistically draped over the body, is made of a fine-weave fabric and richly adorned with fringes and tassels; unlike Mesopotamian garments of a similar type, it covers both shoulders. The outer garment, too, more closely resembles those characteristic of western regions of the Near East. The king's beard is divided into a symmetrical arrangement of braids that increase in length toward the middle and end in curls, a fashion that is well documented in Mari during the third and second millennia B.C.

The Akkadian cuneiform inscription on the robe tells us the names of both the ruler and the goddess to whom he dedicated his likeness:

Iddi-ilum, shakkanakku of Mari, for the goddess Ishtar dedicated a statue of himself. As for the one who removes this inscription, may the goddess Ishtar destroy his progeny.[2]

Ishtar is known to have played an important part in the royal institutions of Mari, as she did also in Mesopotamia, conferring power upon the ruler, as seen in the large wall painting in the royal palace that depicts the investiture of Zimri-Lim (fig. 13).

In addition to the lavish decoration with which he embellished his palace, this last king of Mari had statues set up to commemorate his predecessors, the present image of Iddi-ilum among them. Texts from Mari include records of rituals that were performed by rulers to honor their forefathers; the presence of these statues at the heart of the royal palace must therefore have involved these dynastic practices.

The sack of the city by the Babylonian king Hammurabi virtually emptied the city's institutions. Nevertheless, several statues of former kings, including Iddi-ilum, did not fall into the hands of the looters because they were buried in the rubble of the burned palace. Others were carted away to Babylon. One of these helped prove that royal ancestors in Mari were sometimes deified, a status symbolized by bovine horns on the headpiece.[3] The state of the present figure does not permit us to determine whether Iddi-ilum was also promoted to divinity, but the presence of the statue in the palace of one of his successors would suggest that his image helped legitimize the power of the dynasty that ruled the city two centuries later.

sc

1. See pages 27–29, this volume. For further reference, see Parrot 1938, pp. 17–18, pl. VII:1; Parrot 1958, pp. 18–20; Sollberger and Kupper 1971, p. 166, pl. IIIE:2a; Orthmann 1975, p. 179, pl. 67a, b; and Spycket 1981, pp. 242–43.
2. Frayne 1997, p. 441.
3. Moortgat 1967, fig. 181.

7

GODDESS WITH FLOWING VASE

White stone
Height 142 cm (56 in.); width 48 cm (19 in.)
Mari, Palace of Zimri-Lim, Room 64 and Court 106
Old Syrian, early 2nd millennium B.C.
National Museum, Aleppo, Syria 1659

This nearly life-size statue, found in the Palace of Zimri-Lim at Mari, had been broken into several pieces, with the body at the foot of the podium in Room 64 and the head in a basin in Court 106.[1] The headdress—featuring a pair of sinuous horns—indicates that the figure is divine. Beneath the headdress, the hair falls around the shoulders before being bound up at the back. The material of the long garment crisscrosses over the chest and back, with two wide bands incised at the waist; the skirt then falls in wavy incised lines over sculpted tiers, ending in volutes. The hem curves up at the front in order to reveal the feet. Short sleeves resembling those of figures in wall paintings from Mari end in incised scallops (see cat. no. 8). Carved in relief is elaborate jewelry befitting a goddess, including six rows of large beads that encircle the neck and are balanced by a counterweight at the back, as well as three bracelets on each wrist and multiple rings around the ears. The eyes would have been inlaid.

The goddess holds a vase tilted slightly away from her body. A vertical channel drilled inside the statue leads from its

7, front

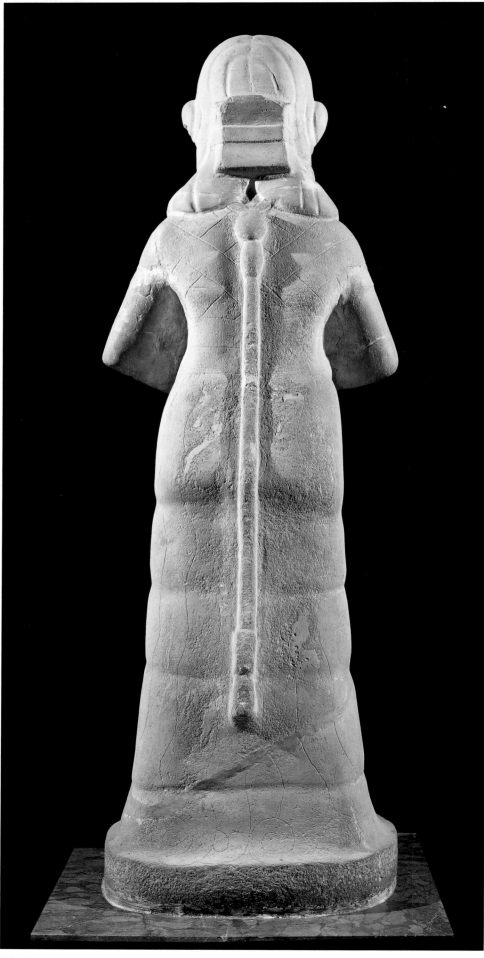

7, back

base to the vase. Water from a tank or container placed at a certain height would have risen through the channel to flow out of the vase, a mechanical feature unique among surviving Near Eastern sculpture. Streams and rows of fish were also incised along the front of the garment to evoke this same effect in the absence of real water.

The original location of the goddess is unknown, but she is the sculptural counterpart of two identical goddesses with flowing vases depicted in the lower register of the so-called Investiture Scene of Zimri-Lim (fig. 13), painted on the south wall of Court 106 (see fig. 12), which led to the vestibule (64) and beyond to the throne room (65) of the palace. Perhaps the statue originally stood in the vestibule, where its base was found. Alternatively, one could easily imagine the goddess as one of a pair set up in the courtyard not far from the painted counterparts.[2] Finally, it is also tempting to associate this hypothetical pair with the two mud-brick platforms, which could have been bases for statues, that flank the entrance into the east end of the throne room.[3]

JME

1. Parrot 1959, no. 2.
2. Parrot 1950, p. 39; Al-Khalesi 1978, p. 41.
3. Parrot 1959, no. 2; Al-Khalesi 1978, p. 41.

8

WALL PAINTING FRAGMENT

Plaster, painted
Height 52 cm (20½ in.); width 47 cm (18½ in.)
Mari, Palace of Zimri-Lim, Court 106
Old Syrian, early 2nd millennium B.C.
National Museum, Aleppo, Syria M10119

Figural wall paintings were recovered from five rooms of the Palace of Zimri-Lim. Only four compositions could be reconstructed, the most famous of which is the so-called Investiture Scene of Zimri-Lim on the south side of Court 106, the only figural wall painting to be discovered in situ (fig. 13). The thick plaster walls of Court 106 were decorated with various other wall paintings, however, some of which could be reconstructed from the numerous fragments found in the debris. One proposed reconstruction of a group of fragments depicts a multiregister composition in which male figures escort sacrificial animals in a procession, perhaps led by a figure portrayed at a much larger scale than that of the others. The fragment seen here, from that procession, shows a bearded male figure leading a bull by a rope fastened to a nose ring. The figure wears a garment with a scalloped border, and his soft, bulbous hat is held in position with two bands. The animal is rendered with the horns and forehead en face and the remainder of the head and neck in profile. Metal tips adorn the bull's horns, and a crescent decorates the forehead. The scene was painted on thick gypsum plaster with white, black, yellow, red, and brown pigments, outlined with thick black lines.[1] The Investiture Scene, in contrast, was painted on thin mud plaster applied directly onto the mud-brick wall.[2]

JME

1. Parrot 1937; Parrot 1958.
2. Gates 1984, p. 77.

EBLA

PAOLO MATTHIAE

During the third millennium B.C., the powerful kingdom of Ebla, south of Aleppo in northern Syria, twice flourished and twice collapsed. It was devastated first by Sargon of Akkad and the second time by unknown enemies, possibly related to the Amorites. The final renaissance of Ebla probably began soon after 2000 B.C. and marked the beginning of the early Old Syrian period. This third and last version of the city extended nearly 60 hectares (more than 148 acres), encompassing the area occupied by the older town, and the huge earthenwork rampart probably followed the traces of the earlier mud-brick fortification. It is quite likely that one of the first sovereigns responsible for the rebuilding of the town was Ibbit-Lim, who also established Ishtar, the goddess of fertility, love, and war, as the city's patron deity.[1] The new foundation followed an urban pattern different from that of the earlier ones: in the center of this new settlement was a small citadel surrounded by an inner wall; the lower town encircled the wall, forming a ring of public buildings, temples, and palaces stretching to the foot of the acropolis. This urban area was in turn surrounded by an oval outer fortification, including the enormous rampart, which measured 60 meters wide at its base and between 18 and 22 meters high.

During Ebla's early Old Syrian period, which corresponds to Middle Bronze I (ca. 2000–1800 B.C.), the city was among the leading political powers between the Euphrates and the Mediterranean. It flourished during the same long decades when, in Babylonia, the rival kings of Isin and Larsa battled for preeminence and lesser kingdoms such as Eshnunna began to expand. Large territorial states—the Upper Mesopotamian kingdom of Shamshi-Adad, Yarim-Lim's kingdom of Yamhad in northern Syria, whose capital was Aleppo, and Hammurabi's kingdom in southern Mesopotamia—were gaining in power. This shift probably ended Ebla's hegemony over northern Syria, to the advantage of Yamhad. During the classical Old Syrian period (corresponding to Middle Bronze II, ca. 1800–1600 B.C.), Ebla was compelled to enter Aleppo's sphere of influence and to share political and cultural authority with several centers, including Carchemish to the north and Qatna to the south.

The political balance of the Old Syrian period was maintained through a continuous succession of short-lived alliances and temporary shifts in power. A reconstruction of Ebla's foreign relations during the early Old Syrian period relies not on written evidence—in contrast to Mari, with its cache of letters[2]—but on archaeological findings. During the first two centuries of the second millennium B.C., the time of the dynasties of Isin and Larsa, Ebla is not mentioned in texts from southern Mesopotamia, which suggests a marked diminution of relations between northern Syria and southern Mesopotamia. Relations among central Syria, Anatolia, and Assyria are, however, suggested in the strong stylistic consistency among Old Assyrian Colony period glyptic of the so-called Syrian style, known from the impressions found on documents in Level II of *karum* Kanesh at Kültepe and reflected in the material culture of Ebla. Moreover, it is certain that one route taken by Old Assyrian merchants, from Ashur to Kültepe and other trading centers of Cappadocia, passed through the region surrounding Ebla en route to central Anatolia. Hints of this material connection can be seen in the bronze artifacts found in the Tomb of the Princess, dating to 1850 B.C. or shortly thereafter, which also seem to point to exchange between northern Syria and the Susa region in western Iran, possibly mediated by Assyria.

During this time, contact between Ebla and the coastal centers of the northern Levant, in particular with Byblos, was intense, as is demonstrated, for instance, by the precious gold situlae of Byblos, represented on the carved basins of Ebla; the bronze vases with round body, cylindrical neck, and flat expanded rim found at both Byblos and Ebla; and the globular jugs with short and narrow neck and one vertical handle, often with polished body, found in the royal tombs of Ebla and believed to have been imported from the coast and imitated in Syrian workshops. The artisans in these palace workshops, established first at Ebla, then at Aleppo, were well versed in the Old Syrian style (fig. 16). At the same time, frequent exchange with the Egyptian world brought pharaonic gifts, such as pectorals, maces, and jewels, enriching the artistic language of the royal production centers.

The relations established between the Egyptian court of the Middle Kingdom based at Thebes and important Syro-Levantine kingdoms were particularly strong. Egypt's interactions with Byblos were probably constant between Dynasties 11 and 13 (ca. 2124–1640 B.C.), and contact with Ugarit dates back as far as the twentieth century B.C., as evidenced by a bead inscribed with the name of Senwosret I found there. Communications between Thebes and the cities of Aleppo and Qatna were especially active under Amenemhat II, at the end of the twentieth century B.C., and again during the reigns of Amenemhat III and Amenemhat IV, in the last years of the nineteenth century B.C., when Egyptian statues of small size, especially sphinxes bearing names of princesses of the pharaonic court, were sent as gifts to those prestigious Asiatic courts.

Egyptian connections with coastal centers like Beruta (Beirut), Byblos, and Ugarit were still in place during Dynasty 13, a

Figure 15. View of the site of Ebla.

period of particularly meaningful, and documented, contact between Ebla and Egypt. For example, an obscure early Dynasty 13 pharaoh, Hetepibre Harnedjheriotef, who sometimes called himself "Son of the Asiatic," sent to Immeya, the king of Ebla, a ceremonial mace made in Egypt (cat. no. 12). This precious, and quite rare, pharaonic insignia was placed with other jewels of certain Egyptian manufacture in the so-called Tomb of the Lord of the Goats, tentatively identified as Immeya's grave, based on the presence of a silver bowl bearing his name found in the same tomb.

Relations between Ebla and Egypt reached their highest level during the Middle Bronze II period. Inspired by Egypt's cultural traditions and the concept of pharaonic rule, the kings of Ebla began to adopt classical Egyptian iconography for the representation of kingship, as seen in ivory inlays with motifs and style strongly inspired by Egypt (see cat. no. 9). Found in a room of the Northern Palace, they probably decorated a bed or a ceremonial throne. This appropriation of the Egyptian figurative language in order to represent the Old Syrian kings also appears in contemporary Old Syrian cylinder seals, which include characteristic figures from the Egyptian pantheon (see cat. no. 248).

The great cultural flourishing of the classical Old Syrian period ended during the last years of the seventeenth century B.C., perhaps partly as a consequence of a long climatic crisis. Two successive Old Hittite kings, Hattusili I and Mursili I, took advantage of this general and widespread economic and social crisis in Syria and, shortly before 1600 B.C., began a series of devastating military campaigns. Lesser towns such as Alalakh, Urshu, and Khashshu fell first, followed by the more powerful centers, Aleppo and Ebla. To celebrate the conquest of Ebla, the epic poem "Song of Liberation," was composed in Hurrian and soon translated into Hittite. The song's themes, which eerily prefigure some situations and expressions from the *Iliad*, include the siege of Ebla and its subsequent conquest by Pizikarra of Nineveh, an ally of Mursili I. As would happen several centuries later at Troy, Ebla was besieged after illegally imprisoning the lord of Igigallish. Hittite gods, such as the great Teshshup of Kumme, and heroes like Pizikarra fought together against the city. An assembly of allied princes of Ebla gathered and, against the wishes of the king, followed imprudent advice given by a clever orator. Divine banquets were held in heaven to ratify the fate of the town, which was perhaps defended by the goddess Ishkhara, as Aphrodite defended Troy.

The terrible final destruction of Ebla, which likely occurred about 1600 B.C., was probably the result of a large alliance among Hittites, Hurrians, and Kassites. Soon after, this powerful coalition, led by Mursili I, defeated even the mighty Babylon, although Mursili immediately abandoned the city to the control of a Kassite king. Within a very few years, the political balance of the region, previously anchored by the major powers of Babylon and Aleppo, was also destroyed, opening the way to new political alliances and new kingdoms.

1. It was also Ibbit-Lim who, with his inscription discovered in 1968, allowed the Italian Expedition to identify Tell Mardikh with ancient Ebla. See Gelb 1984.
2. A fascinating span of nearly thirty years, just before Hammurabi's conquest of Mari in about 1760 B.C., is illuminated by the so-called Mari Letters. Although these letters peculiarly do not mention Ebla—the main protagonists were Shubat-Enlil, Ashur, Aleppo, Carchemish, Larsa, Eshnunna, Babylon, Elam, Mari, Qatna, and Hazor—the quantity and quality of information about those very few years have no comparison in previous decades, or in the following ones.

Figure 16. Basalt stele, three views. Ebla. Old Syrian period.
Idlib Museum 3003

other slightly smaller ivory inlays representing Egyptian figures of divinity. These included the crocodile god Sobek, gods having the head of the falcon Horus, and a goddess bearing the horns and the sun disc of Hathor. Such figures appear frequently in the contemporary Syrian glyptic of the classical Old Syrian style, where they are shown with divine figures of the Syrian pantheon and kings and officials of the northern Syrian kingdoms.

It is difficult to ascertain the precise meaning of these images, but judging from the Egyptian figurative canon, they possibly represented Syrian deities. Knowledge of the iconography and style of the pharaonic masterpieces must have resulted from the fact that royal gifts were frequently sent to the courts of the Syrian kingdoms. These included pectorals, sphinx sculptures, maces, and jewels bearing the symbols of kingship over the Two Lands. It is likely that figures such as the one whose head is represented in this fragment were depictions in the Egyptian style of deified royal ancestors, the *rapi'uma* of the Ugaritic texts, who corresponded to the *rephaim* of biblical texts and who, in Syrian kingdoms during the Middle and Late Bronze Ages, were the object of a widespread cult.   PM

1. For further reference, see Matthiae 1989a, p. 46; Scandone Matthiae 1991a; Scandone Matthiae 1991b, p. 432, figs. 1, 2; Scandone Matthiae in *Ebla* 1995, p. 458, no. 372; and Scandone Matthiae 2002, pp. 16–24, 57, pls. I, VI.

10

BEADED BAND

Gold, amethyst, blue-gray stone
Height 0.5 cm (¼ in.); width 2.4 cm (1 in.);
length 3.4 cm (1⅜ in.)
Ebla, Tomb of the Princess
Old Syrian, early 2nd millennium B.C.
National Museum, Aleppo, Syria M10591

The oldest and only inviolate tomb of the three thus far excavated in the Old Syrian Royal Necropolis of Ebla, situated below the crown prince's Western Palace, is called the Tomb of the Princess because a young woman was buried there. Along with a large number of clay vases, all of her gold personal ornaments were found:

9

FURNITURE INLAY

Ivory (hippopotamus)
Height 13.4 cm (5⅜ in.); width 5.3 cm (2⅛ in.);
thickness 0.2 cm (⅛ in.)
Ebla, Northern Palace
Old Syrian, early 2nd millennium B.C.
Idlib Museum, Idlib, Syria 3495

This beautiful head in the Egyptian style belongs to an important group of ivory inlays found in a peripheral room—probably a workshop—of the Northern Palace at Ebla in western Syria. Probably made to embellish a bed or a ceremonial throne, they date from between 1725 and 1600 B.C. The head is shown wearing the *atef,* the typical Egyptian crown with feathers and horns, royal headgear related to the symbolism of the afterlife and to renewal in the Underworld.[1] From the time of the Old Kingdom, the *atef* crown was worn by the pharaohs of the Nile Valley. Later it became associated with Osiris, lord of the Underworld. Another head, probably a copy of this piece, was found with it and with several

10

this piece, a pin with a star-shaped head, six twisted-bar bracelets, and an earring with granulated decoration. The different elements of this jewel were found close to one another, trapped in the mud of the hypogeum after the threads holding them together had been lost. The central piece includes a gold rectangular setting with paste forming a cloisonné decoration, surrounding an oval setting, where a scaraboid of blue-gray stone is still preserved.[1] The beads included the usual melon-shaped elements with plain collars, as documented in the Levant, particularly at Tell el-'Ajjul, as well as in Mesopotamia. In the latter region they were parts of such famous jewelry collections as the Larsa Treasure, dating from shortly before 1738 B.C.; the beads belonging to the Dilbat hoard in the Metropolitan Museum (cat. no. 4); the jewels from Zimri-Lim's palace at Mari; and the ornaments found in the Old Assyrian tombs at Ashur. Other melon-shaped beads in the Tomb of the Lord of the Goats are cast in gold; these beads are of hammered gold foil. All the pieces of the princess's furnishings are without doubt products of the palace workshops at Ebla and probably date to the years between Middle Bronze I and Middle Bronze II, as this tomb is certainly older than the Lord of the Goats burial, where Immeya was likely interred.   PM

1. For further reference, see Matthiae 1981, pp. 212–13, fig. 47a–b, and Matthiae in *Ebla* 1995, pp. 470, 479, no. 393.

11
EARRING OR NOSE RING

Gold
Diameter 3.2 cm (1¼ in.);
thickness 0.6 cm (¼ in.)
Ebla, Tomb of the Princess
Old Syrian, early 2nd millennium B.C.
National Museum, Aleppo, Syria M10786

This large ornate jewel, weighing 6.85 grams, is a unique piece found in the intact Tomb of the Princess, and it may be interpreted as an earring or nose ring.[1] It is made of two gold sheets, curved and bossed in such a way that it is nearly round in section, and ends in two short stems. The sheets are covered with triangles and lozenges in granulation of highly refined workmanship. This type of jewel, quite rare in Syria, is well known in the Levant from examples of the same shape and technique and similar granulated decoration found at Tell el-'Ajjul. The pieces from Tell el-'Ajjul, however, do not end in bars but in two suspension loops; moreover, the granulated decoration is coarser and more irregular.

Technical analogies have been observed in jewels of contemporary Mesopotamia (see pp. 101–3), specifically in the pendants of the Dilbat hoard (cat. no. 4), but this evidence is not enough to assume a

11

Mesopotamian production for the jewels from Tell el-'Ajjul or for the Ebla earring. Indeed, this style of earring, with granulated decoration, is a product of the Syro-Levantine region, within which there were strong qualitative differences. The examples from Tell el-'Ajjul, and others of unknown provenance but certainly from the Levant, are more summary in execution, particularly in the curving and joining of the sheets and the granulated decoration.

The earring from Ebla is a wonderful object, made in a palace workshop and reflecting the excellent quality of the royal workshops, likely not only of the great political center of Ebla, but of the entire Yamhad milieu and of northern Syria in general.   PM

1. For further reference, see Maxwell-Hyslop 1971, pp. 116–18; Matthiae 1981, pp. 213–14; and F. Baffi Guardata in *Ebla* 1995, pp. 470, 480, no. 394.

12
EGYPTIAN MACE

Ivory, marble, silver, gold
Mace head: height 4.4 cm (1¾ in.);
diameter 5.6 cm (2¼ in.)
Handle: length 19 cm (7½ in.);
diameter 2.4 cm (1 in.)
Ebla, Tomb of the Lord of the Goats
Old Syrian, early 2nd millennium B.C.
Idlib Museum, Idlib, Syria 3184

This precious pharaonic gift was placed in the Tomb of the Lord of the Goats, the burial of Immeya, a king of Ebla, who probably lived in the second half of the eighteenth century B.C. In the same tomb was found a silver bowl bearing his name in cuneiform writing, and an Old Syrian letter addressed to him was found in the Lower Town of Ebla. The mace, an exquisite example of the most refined jewelry produced by Middle Kingdom palace workshops in Egypt, originally had an ivory handle likely covered by a netlike motif composed of small alternating silver and gold lozenges (now mostly lost). The handle included a silver cylinder, with applications of gold cynocephali in adoration of gold Egyptian hieroglyphs that form the name—but without the royal

12

 cartouche—of Hetepibre Harnedjheriotef, an early Dynasty 13 pharaoh. This king also used the unusual appellation "Son of the Asiatic," sometimes incorrectly read as "Son of the Farmer." Probably as a result of damage the object suffered at the Ebla court, the placement of the hieroglyphs is anomalous. In all likelihood, they were lost, and then replaced by someone who did not know hieroglyphic writing: the offering table *hotep* is upside down, the phonetic complement *p* is missing, and the other phonetic complement *t* was added in place of the *p*; the heart *ib* leans slightly to one side. It is also possible that during this unskilled repair the royal cartouche was lost.[1]

Little is known about Harnedjheriotef, but a carved block with one of his inscrip-

12, detail

tions was found near Asyut. A statue of a seated figure discovered at Tell el-Dab'a is similarly inscribed, and two scarabs associated with him were uncovered at Jericho. This evidence, combined with the fact that he sent his mace—a very important pharaonic insignia frequently represented on Middle Kingdom reliefs—to Ebla, suggests that Immeya descended from one of the most important ruling families of his time in Upper Syria.

The motif of the adoration of the pharaonic name by two cynocephali is related to a well-known theme of solar cults, the adoration of the sun god Ra-Harakhty. The motif was also reproduced by the Ebla craftsmen at the court of Immeya, who would surely have drawn inspiration from Harnedjheriotef's mace. An ivory amulet in the Old Syrian style, found nearly intact in the same burial, shows two identical cynocephali in adoration of a human-headed bull, certainly a representation of Immeya, ascended in heaven among the *rapi'uma*, the deified royal ancestors, following the funerary ceremonies.   PM

1. For further reference, see Archi and Matthiae 1979; Scandone Matthiae 1979; Scandone Matthiae 1988, pp. 71–73, pl. XV:1, 3, 4; and Scandone Matthiae in *Ebla* 1995, pp. 464–65, 478, nos. 383, 384.

13

CYLINDRICAL HANDLE COVER

Gold
Length 6.5 cm (2⅝ in.); diameter 2.4 cm (1 in.)
Ebla, Tomb of the Lord of the Goats
Old Syrian, early 2nd millennium B.C.
National Museum, Aleppo, Syria M10587

This refined gold cover for a cylindrical handle, most probably the work of Egyptian jewelers of early Dynasty 13, bears an elegant continuous decorative motif, a repetition of scales surrounded by a delicate filigree and enriched with individual elements of granulation; at both ends are series of thin rope-shaped elements, alternatively smooth and segmented.[1] It is possible, notwithstanding some slight difference in size, that this covered the handle of Harnedjheriotef's mace. The refined scale-and-filigree motif can be found on an Asiatic sickle sword inlaid in black metallic substance (cat. no. 30), nearly contemporary with or slightly older than this piece, belonging to Ip-shemu-abi of Byblos, probably a local work bearing Egyptian hieroglyphs; it is found also in Late Bronze II, in the top part of an ivory comb from Megiddo and in cylindrical ivory elements from the tomb of Minet el-Beidha, where the famous relief of the *potnia theron* (cat. no. 261) was discovered. The motif, probably elaborated in the most exquisite forms

13

by Egyptian jewelers of the Middle Kingdom, may not be of Egyptian origin but perhaps spread to other areas after its adoption in Old Syrian jewelers' workshops. It became common on ivory inlays and jewels in Syria and the Aegean as a consequence of frequent cultural and mercantile exchanges during Late Bronze II.

PM

1. For further reference, see Scandone Matthiae 1979, p. 119, and Scandone Matthiae in *Ebla* 1995, pp. 466, 479, no. 385.

14

JEWELRY ELEMENTS

Gold
Band: length 10.4 cm (4⅛ in.); height 4.4 cm (1¾ in.)
Discs: diameter 2.5 cm (1 in.)
Ebla, Tomb of the Lord of the Goats
Old Syrian, early 2nd millennium B.C.
National Museum, Aleppo, Syria M10783

For originality of concept and refinement of execution, this ornament is one of the finest accomplishments of classical Old Syrian jewelry crafting.[1] Quite likely a personal ornament of Immeya, it includes three elements in a row, each made of an upper horizontal rectangular section with a disc-shaped pendant at the bottom. The weight is impressive (left to right: 9.72 g, 8.63 g, 10.78 g). The outer edges of the two side pieces are curved;

the central plaque is rectangular. These upper elements are composed of front and back sheets—one smooth, one bossed. The bossed front sheets are decorated with four horizontally placed braided bands that join in an arch at the two curved ends of the side plaques. Corresponding to these four elements are the narrow long holes for the strands. The three discs have similar granulated decoration that forms a six-pointed star; between the points are small granulated spheres. The discs are circled by three rows of granulation.

This type of jewel is frequently represented on Old Syrian clay figurines of Middle Bronze II, but its combined structure, technique, and style find no comparison. The granulation technique used for the Dilbat pendants (cat. no. 4), as well as for a medallion from Larsa, is quite similar, including such details as the rows of granulation around the border. The feature that distinguishes the pendants from one another is the decoration of the discs: the Ebla pendants comprise a six-pointed star with spheres, while the Dilbat pendants are designed to show eight rosettes surrounding a larger central rosette.

It is quite likely that in the two cultural regions both the star and the rosette alluded to the goddess Ishtar. The star is an Old Syrian motif, although it spread to Anatolia and Elam, while the rosette is specifically Mesopotamian. It is also possible that at Ebla Immeya's jewelry was related to kingship, as the region was under that goddess's protection. In Middle Assyrian texts she is called Ishtar of Ebla, and in the

bilingual Hurrian-Hittite poem "Song of Liberation," discovered at Hattusa in 1986, the Star of Ebla refers to the king.

PM

1. For further reference, see Matthiae 1981, pp. 217–18, fig. 59, and F. Baffi Guardata in *Ebla* 1995, pp. 471, 480, no. 396.

15

CHAIN WITH TWO PENDANTS

Gold, rock crystal, gray-green translucent stone
Pendants: length 2 cm (⅞ in.)
Chain: length 22 cm (8¾ in.)
Ebla, Tomb of the Lord of the Goats
Old Syrian, early 2nd millennium B.C.
National Museum, Aleppo, Syria M10790

Judging by its form, this jewel may have been a necklace. It consists of a thin chain with two acorns with gold caps decorated in filigree hung by means of a gold ring and two small suspension rings. The acorns, made of rock crystal and a gray-green translucent stone, are very realistically represented. This is a unique piece, but its individual components may have parallels. The chain type is well known, though not common, particularly in the jewelry of the Levant, at Byblos and Megiddo, and at Beth-Shemesh and Tell el-'Ajjul, areas known for the production of earrings. Of note is the refined taste in the choice of the shining rock crystal joined to the elegant linear veins

16

15

this ring. The ring features a central oval space in which a much-damaged paste scarab is set, flanked by an openwork design of opposed lilies and blossoms that was originally inlaid with polychrome enamel.

The flower—symbol of Upper Egypt—the red color of the gold, typical of several Egyptian jewels from the tomb, and the fine quality of the typically Egyptian rendering of the flowers are evidence that this ring was made in Egypt. It likely was part of a gift sent by the pharaoh Hetepibre Harnedjheriotef to Immeya, the probable owner of the tomb, which also included the mace on which the pharaoh's name is adored by cynocephali (cat. no. 12).[1]

PM

1. For further reference, see Matthiae 1981, p. 224, fig. 66; Scandone Matthiae 1988, p. 71, pl. XIV:2–3; and Scandone Matthiae in *Ebla* 1995, pp. 467, 479, no. 387.

of the greenish stone. Rock crystal, which is difficult to work, was highly valued and frequently employed in the finest jewels of the ancient Near East, particularly in Mesopotamia, Anatolia, and Syria (see cat. no. 189a–c). Its sources were in Anatolia, Iran, and Cyprus, though Pliny observed that, in the classical age, the most precious examples came from India. The acorns, on the other hand, because of the rare combination of gold and stone, are an original creation and certainly from a palace jewelry workshop at Ebla.[1]

PM

1. For further reference, see Matthiae 1981, p. 219, and F. Baffi Guardata in *Ebla* 1995, pp. 472, 480, no. 398.

16

RING

Gold, blue paste
Height 2.2 cm (⅞ in.); width 1.4 cm (⅝ in.);
diameter 2.4 cm (1 in.)
Ebla, Tomb of the Lord of the Goats
Old Syrian, early 2nd millennium B.C.
National Museum, Aleppo, Syria M10791

In the partially sacked Tomb of the Lord of the Goats, several precious objects inexplicably escaped the notice of the looters. This oversight perhaps occurred because the looting was hastily done, and because mud probably covered much of the floor, thus concealing small objects such as

THE DEVELOPMENT OF TRADE ROUTES IN THE EARLY SECOND MILLENNIUM B.C.

MICHEL AL-MAQDISSI

The Levant played a major role in international relations throughout the ancient Near East as early as the third millennium B.C. Recent excavations at several sites have contributed valuable information about the communication routes between the ports along the Syro-Levantine coast and cities in Egypt, Mesopotamia, Cyprus, and the Aegean. The region consisted of a number of distinct geographic areas, described as follows:

- A long coastal corridor directly bordering on foothills and mountains, with occasional broad plains, including those of Latakia in the north, Jable in the middle, and Akkar in the south. These plains served as passages and communication axes between the coastal area and the Syrian hinterlands.
- A chain of mountains running parallel to the coast along a north-south axis, with summits reaching higher than 2,500 meters. This natural chain separates the coastal region from the interior, but the plains provided easy access and a direct passage between the harbors along the eastern Mediterranean coast and the settlements and urban centers of the Syrian interior.
- A fertile region with rich agricultural lands well irrigated by the Orontes River. Several major geographic features dominate this area, such as the plain of Aleppo in the north, the plain of Homs and the Qatna (Tell Mishrifeh) region in the middle, and the plain of Damascus in the south. This territory, of great significance, also bordered directly on the Syrian steppe to the east and partially desert regions to the north.
- Farther east, a geographic area characterized by a vast steppe watered by the Euphrates River and forming a broad valley marked by intensive human settlement.
- At the eastern end, close to northern Mesopotamia, a fertile region irrigated by several rivers.

The various western regions of the ancient Near East were subject to a series of occupations. Excavations at Tell Sianu, situated on the Jable Plain along the Syrian coast at Qatna, an urban center facing the broad valley of Homs, and at other key sites extending from the Syrian coast to northern Mesopotamia have provided clear evidence of the beginnings of urban organization during Early Bronze Age II (ca. 2700–2600 B.C.), which was linked to a second urban revolution in the ancient Near East. This process brought with it a variety of economic, social, and agricultural shifts in the organization of human settlements.

This phase of urbanization was also characterized by the development of roads to connect different parts of the coastal Near East with the Syrian hinterlands, the middle valley of the Euphrates, and northern Mesopotamia. The roads facilitated trade and the exchange of cultural traditions between the Mediterranean basin and the Iranian plateau. All of the great urban centers of the second half of the third millennium B.C., such as Byblos, Qatna, and Mari, played an important part in the development of these caravan routes.

Geological surveys conducted in areas through which the caravans passed have provided information about the placement of the way stations along these routes. On the plain of Akkar, halfway between the great Mediterranean port of Byblos and the major central Syrian urban center of Qatna, are vestiges of a communications system, dating to as early as the middle of the third millennium B.C., that connected three major centers separated by a distance of 20 kilometers, which was about a day's journey for a mule caravan. A similar system focused on the city of Qatna and the surrounding plain. This oriented the caravans in four different directions: either north to the kingdom of Yamhad, south to the kingdom of Apum, east to the kingdom of Mari, or west to the kingdom of Amurru. A detailed study of the satellite outposts around Qatna revealed the presence of several fortified towns, including Tell Safinat-Nouh and Tell Sour-Sinkari, which formed a defensive perimeter, with a radius of 35 kilometers, around the city. These outlying sites also acted as way stations for merchants.

The Mari texts provide further information about the trade routes that passed through the Syrian steppe, including descriptions of several types of trade caravans that connected the kingdoms of Mari and Qatna. Observations made in the field uncovered the existence of important way stations at sites like Nashala (Qariatayn) and the oasis of Palmyra. Roads subsequently developed around such watering spots, forcing the caravans to negotiate passage agreements with the nomadic groups that controlled the area. The importance of water to travel in the Levant can be illustrated by the latter-day example of Lawrence of Arabia, who, in order to pass safely through the region of Rubi' al-Khali and join the

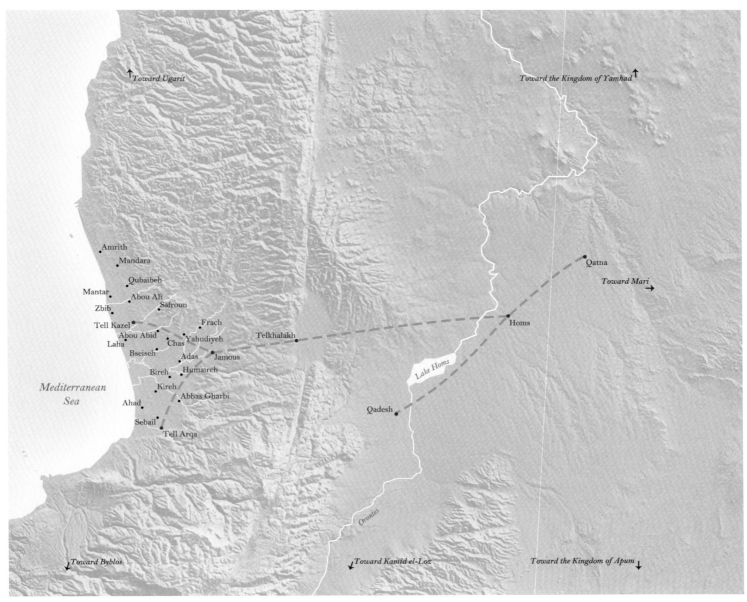

Figure 17. Map showing communication routes in the Plain of Akkar during the Bronze Age.

Christian forces in Jordan, had the watering places dried up and camouflaged.

Thus, the political balance of the Levantine region was important to the safe passage of trade caravans. The Akkadian period (ca. 2334–2154 B.C.) witnessed a flowering of trade throughout the Near East, with routes extending as far east as modern-day Iran and Afghanistan. During the Third Dynasty of Ur (ca. 2112–2004 B.C.), most of the major urban centers experienced crises that disrupted movement along the communication routes. With the subsequent rise of Amorite kingdoms in the western and eastern regions of the Near East, trade was soon restored on a large scale. After the fall of the Amorite kingdoms, about 1600 B.C., however, the geopolitical context changed again, primarily as a result of conflicts that pitted Egypt against the Hittite and Mitanni kingdoms. The need for access to routes affected by these conflicts fostered the forma-

tion of a constantly changing series of alliances between the various rulers of the kingdoms.

Despite the political difficulties that affected them, the routes provided an ideal stage for active commercial exchange and for the dissemination not only of artistic techniques and conventions but also of social ideas and traditions. This international phenomenon promoted the merging of artistic styles and, in general, broadened the cultural and religious spheres of these societies. Similarly, architectural knowledge and methods of urban planning, especially where palaces, temples, and large dwellings were concerned, also seem to have been shared during this fertile period in the history of the Levant, and the ancient Near East as a whole.[1]

1. For further reference, see Dossin 1954; Finet 1969; Dossin 1970, pp. 97–106; Durand 1987; Margueron 1989; Abdallah 1996; Joannès 1997; Durand 1997–2000, vol. 3, pp. 7–68; and Al-Maqdissi 2003b.

17

17
CUNEIFORM TABLET

Clay
Height 4.5 cm (1¾ in.); width 5.4 cm (2⅛ in.)
Tell Sianu, Chantier B
Middle Bronze Age, 18th century B.C.
National Museum, Damascus, Syria 8719

This is the oldest tablet found in the course of systematic excavations along the Syrian coast. It is an administrative text written in Akkadian, listing various types of objects—gold, fabric, oil jugs—of mixed provenance: Subartu (Jazira, Syria) and Alashiya (Cyprus). The discovery of this document at Tell Sianu provides evidence for the presence of a scribal tradition within the Mari and the Amorite kingdoms in the eastern Mediterranean region.[1]   MM

1. For further reference, see D. Charpin, "Document administratif," in *Le royaume d'Ougarit* 2004, p. 111, no. 85.

18a, b
TWO VESSELS

a. Chlorite
Height 11.5 cm (4½ in.)
b. Calcite
Height 14.1 cm (5½ in.)
Tell Iris, Chantier A
Middle Bronze Age, 17th century B.C.
Department of Antiquities, Jable, Syria
Iris 03/42, 43

Both of these intact vessels were found in a hypogeum carved out of rock. Also included in the find were rich furnishings, some dated toward the end of the Middle Bronze Age. This type of vessel is associated with an Egyptian tradition; comparable objects found in Syria have come principally from funerary contexts at Ugarit, Ebla, and Qatna.   MM

18a

18b

UGARIT

BASSAM JAMOUS

The Syrian coast has long attracted the attention of scholars, historians, and travelers. The people who lived there exhibited great creativity in the economic, artistic, and literary fields; most notably, they invented the Ugaritic alphabet. Interest in the Syrian coast has been triggered not only by accounts of historians and travelers but by modern archaeological discoveries, which have contributed to the reassessment of many early assumptions. The last sixty years have given prominence to the role played in history by Syria in general, and the Syrian coast in particular, which—because of its important geographic location and the influence of Mediterranean civilizations—has served as a stage for cultural convergence and contact between various peoples.

Political and commercial relations among the peoples along the Syrian coast with the kingdoms and cities of the eastern Mediterranean basin led to the spread of cultures and crafts, and to the boosting of international trade relations. Syrian exports included olive oil, pottery, timber, and other goods in exchange for gold, jewelry, precious stones, and stoneware. Thus the Syrian coast, along with Rhodes, Cyprus, and eventually Carthage, among other cultures, was an intermediate station for trade and communications, governed by internationally accepted trading principles.

Ugarit (Ras Shamra) is situated 10 kilometers north of Latakia. An important town with Mediterranean harbors, it was discovered accidentally by a farmer, Mahmud Menalla, who was plowing his fields. The initial discovery led to the unearthing of a tomb near the bay of Minet el-Beidha, which was still in use in the fourteenth and thirteenth centuries B.C. A French expedition, led by Claude Schaeffer, was soon formed to conduct excavations. The first dig on the *tell*, or mound, took place in 1929.

The city name Ugarit is known from several Ugaritic texts including *nqmd mlk'ugrt*, "Niqmaddu, king of Ugarit," in the colophon at the end of tablets in the Baal cycle. The place name is also attested in the Amarna Letters.

With Syrian participation, excavations have continued uninterrupted on the mound over the past fifty-one seasons. The central focus has been the palace at Ugarit, which has yielded important political, economic, social, and religious documents—hundreds, if not thousands, of studies have been published. On the basis of the discoveries made during the excavations, it has been established that humans settled in Ugarit during the middle of the seventh millennium B.C. There they hunted, cultivated the land, made tools, and excelled in the arts.

ARCHAEOLOGICAL LEVELS AT UGARIT

The mound is divided into five levels, each in turn subdivided into several layers. The levels are as follows:

Level V: Neolithic (8000–6000 B.C.)

Level IV: Chalcolithic (5000–4300 B.C.)

Level III: Ubaid to Early Bronze (3500–2100 B.C.)

Level II: Middle Bronze (2000–1600 B.C.)

Level I: Late Bronze (1600–1180 B.C.)

Three palaces have been unearthed in the mound area: the Royal Palace, the North Palace, and the Small Palace.

The city eventually grew into a kingdom extending from Jebel al-Aqra in the north to the Al-Sin River in the south. The Syrian coast became a great center of international relations and trade. Indeed, economic factors can be said to have played a fundamental role in its contact with the many civilizations of the eastern Mediterranean. The fourteenth and thirteenth centuries B.C. saw the cultural flowering of Ugarit and the rise of its economic and political influence—a virtual golden age.

statues probably represent a divine pair. Both are adorned with a spectacular torque of gold (or electrum), each made of a single thick, twisted wire. Laboratory analysis of the smaller figure established that it was made of silver, the surface of which is now oxidized.

The context and date of the find are unclear. Style and technique distinguish this pair from other divine statues made in the Late Bronze Age at Ugarit. Indeed, the excavator, Claude Schaeffer, has dated them to the early centuries of the second millennium B.C., positing an invasion of "torque people" to explain the major cultural changes that occurred in the course of the Middle Bronze Age. In addition to the torque, the figure wears a short kilt made of a hammered sheet of gold or electrum. He stands in a static position, his bent arms raised symmetrically to the level of his waist. The mace in the left hand is a reconstruction made by the excavator.

The body is schematically rendered in either flat or cylindrical shapes. Only the head is three-dimensional, with an emphasis on the eyes and nose, as if to identify the senses of sight and smell as important elements of the deity's personality. The empty eye sockets and brows were perhaps originally inlaid, as were many sculptures throughout Mesopotamian history. On the flat torso, two small pellets were applied for the nipples, and on the back two incisions were made to indicate the collarbones. Knobs delineate the knees and identify the gender. The parallel feet stand on the casting "mushroom," which served as a pedestal instead of having been sawed away as was generally the case. In the absence of analysis, one can only assume that the statue was cast in the lost-wax technique and that the deep incisions on the face, hair, and torso were made before the metal cooled. The arms also were probably bent before cooling.   AC/ED

1. Schaeffer 1949, pp. 71–80, pls. 17–19. The smaller figure is now in the Musée du Louvre, Paris, Département des Antiquités Orientales AO15733.

19
STANDING FIGURE

Silver, gold or electrum
Height 28 cm (11 in.); width 5.5 cm (2⅛ in.)
Ugarit, Acropolis
Middle Bronze Age manufacture,
early 2nd millennium B.C.
National Museum, Aleppo, Syria M8162

This statue is the largest metal figure found at Ugarit in western Syria and one of the largest from the Bronze Age Levant. It was discovered in the acropolis sector of the city, hidden in a vase together with a second, smaller figure.[1] The two

20
STANDING DEITY

Bronze
Height 25 cm (9⅞ in.)
Ugarit, Ville Sud
Middle Bronze Age manufacture (?),
early 2nd millennium B.C.
National Museum, Damascus, Syria S3574

This female figure is depicted in a static and frontal attitude. Her right arm is raised, palm outward, in a gesture of peace and benediction; the left arm is missing. Also missing is a headdress, as indicated by a cast tang on the back of the head. It had probably been used for the attachment of a tiara made in another material.[1] The mantle is crossed in the back and tied in front, emphasizing the breasts. A thick woolly edge borders the garment. Such a costume appears frequently on Syrian cylinder seals of the Middle Bronze Age.

The missing arm may have been bent horizontally, with a symbolic instrument in the hand. The unshod feet are resting on two tenons joined at the base, the remains of the cast jets. Deep grooves—set alongside the nape of the neck, the arms, and from the hip down to the lower part of the skirt—were meant to hold a thick gold leaf.[2] Applications of gold served the dual functions of protecting the piece from oxidation and emphasizing the eternal character of the goddess.

The fabrication technique and garment style point to a date early in the Middle Bronze Age. The figurine escaped being melted and recycled as so many other metal artifacts were. It was preserved into the last phase of the life of the city, though whether it remained a cultic image for the entire period remains a question.

AC/ED

1. See Dardaillon in *Le royaume d'Ougarit* 2004, no. 235, for a stone crown on a bronze figurine.
2. See ibid., no. 272, for another example of this groove from Ugarit.

21

SEATED FEMALE

Copper alloy
Height 24.8 cm (9¾ in.)
Ugarit, "Hurrian" Temple
Middle Bronze Age manufacture,
early 2nd millennium B.C.
Musée du Louvre, Paris, Département des
Antiquités Orientales AO19397

This statuette of a seated woman was found in Ugarit together with a figurine of a standing man. The dating of the deposit is confirmed by that of nearby strata that contained objects from the twentieth, nineteenth, and seventeenth centuries B.C. Unfortunately, this does not tell us when the objects were made, which may have been long before they were buried.

The two statuettes are both of copper alloy, but were given different treatments.

The man is represented in the round; the woman both flat and in the round. Her seated body resembles a twice-bent metal bar. The chair on which she sits is lost, but a small base with attached tenons under the feet indicates that the figure must have rested on a base.

The eyes (now missing) were inlaid, and slits in the back of the head and neck show that the head must have been gold- or silver-plated. The metal was welded in place with a lead wire hammered into the grooves. A slit in the shoulder blades that extends to the lower part of the arms suggests that the torso and arms were also plated. Two grooves on the side of the body indicate that it was covered with another metal. The back probably was not plated.

21

The figure's arms are outstretched. The right hand is open in a gesture of greeting or receiving, while the left hand is closed, with a space between fingers and palm for the insertion of a symbolic object. The robe, with a rounded, thick border, is typical of the costumes of Syrian kings and deities of the Middle Bronze Age. The texture, however, is unusual in that it appears to represent quilted fabric. The resulting lozenge pattern is interspersed with vertical lines that were probably meant to represent tufts of wool, according to a fashion then in vogue throughout the Near Eastern world. The headpiece—a turban that peaks in a kind of knot—is otherwise unknown in Bronze Age metal figurines from the Levant. Overall, the shape recalls horned headdresses worn by gods.

The gesture and the flattened appearance of the body present analogies to other Syrian figurines, but this woman, like her male counterpart, is unusual in the context of Ugarit, where figures were usually marked by Egyptian or regional influences. The large inlaid eyes and the treatment of costume and turban point away from the standard repertoire of Near Eastern fashions to the hinterlands of Syria, Mesopotamia, or Anatolia. Indeed, a male statuette with many stylistic similarities dating from the twentieth century B.C. was found at Boğazköy, in Anatolia.

When these statuettes were presumably made, Ugarit had many Hurrian inhabitants. The relative archaism in the treatment of the figures together with the influences visible in the costumes suggest an origin in northern Syria, where the Mesopotamian and Hurrian worlds converged.

No attribute indicates that these figures were associated with the divine realm. Perhaps they represent a royal couple or foreign dignitaries. The woman's turban and tufts of wool point to northern Syria and Mesopotamia, while the rounded, thick borders are attributes of royalty or divinity in Syria, a double legacy that raises the issue of the role played by these two spheres both in the culture of Ugarit and in the configuration of the dynasty itself.[1]

SC

1. For further reference, see Schaeffer 1939, pp. 128ff., and Negbi 1976, p. 90, no. 1648.

47

22

SEATED DEITY

Bronze
Height 17.1 cm (6¾ in.)
Syria
Middle Bronze Age, 17th century B.C.
Musée du Louvre, Paris, Département des
Antiquités Orientales A03992

This statue represents a bearded male figure wrapped in a tasseled and fringed garment that leaves the torso bare and the arms free. In keeping with Mesopotamian tradition, the ovoid headdress with four sets of horns identifies him as a high-ranking divinity.[1]

The deity is seated on a stool with four legs, one of which is missing; only fragments of the crosspieces remain. In his left hand, which rests on his lap, he seems to hold the cloak; the extended right hand once held an additional object, probably a scepter likely of another material. The bare feet have pegs that must have fit into a base, most likely made of wood, on which the seat could also rest.

The bronze was originally highlighted on the face and headdress with plating, gold or silver, as indicated by the two vertical grooves on the neck behind the ears. The eye sockets were inlaid with semiprecious stones or another colored material. This figure, entirely in the round, is one of the finest examples of seated divine figures among the type representing serene, older deities often depicted making a gesture of blessing.[2]

Found at the beginning of the twentieth century, the statue is said to have come from north of Homs, from the site of Tell Mishrifeh (ancient Qatna). It has been dated to either the Middle or the Late Bronze Age,[3] but a number of details point to the older date. The cloak, with its thick fur edging, and the ovoid headdress are typical of the Syrian iconography of the Middle Bronze Age. On glyptic from Level VII at Alalakh, which exemplifies the classic Syrian style, royal figures are depicted with the same slender proportions and drapery. A basalt head found out of context at Djabbul, east of Aleppo, which was once part of a life-size statue, wears a similar headdress with four pairs of incised horns;[4] here they are separated by a vertical band. The treatment of the beard as a smooth and compact chin piece may also be seen on a portrait head thought to represent that of Yarim-Lim, king of Alalakh (fig. 64).

Excavations at Qatna in 2002 brought to light two basalt statues flanking the entrance to a royal tomb (figs. 72, 74).[5] The figures, draped in the traditional Syrian cloak with thick edging, are depicted in exactly the same pose as the present statue but hold a vase in the right hand. Their hair is secured with a band, like that of Yarim-Lim. These clues may further confirm the identification of the bronze figure as the portrait of a deified king.[6]

EF

1. For further reference, see Dussaud 1926, pp. 336–46; Negbi 1976; Caubet in *Au pays de Baal et d'Astarté* 1983, p. 131, no. 165; and Moorey and Fleming 1984, pp. 67–90.
2. It was cast in the lost-wax method. The peg on the inside and the hole in the back were part of the arrangement that kept the core in place during the casting.
3. Negbi 1976, p. 53, dated between the eighteenth and twelfth century B.C.
4. Spycket 1981, fig. 181; Musée du Louvre, A010831.
5. Reproduced in *Le monde de la Bible*, no. 159 (2004), p. 11.
6. See Frankfort 1977, pp. 258, 396 n. 60, and Matthiae in Orthmann 1975, p. 478, no. 399.

BYBLOS

SUZY HAKIMIAN

Byblos is situated 45 kilometers north of Beirut. Its Akkadian name, Gubla, from a West Semitic root meaning "boundary" or "territory," survives in the modern place-name, Jbeil. The Egyptians gave it the name *kpn* or *kbn*. The Greeks called the city Byblos (from the Greek word for papyrus) because in the first millennium B.C. it was the center for trade in papyrus, used to make *byblia*, or books.[1] The role of Byblos in the papyrus trade resulted in its close association with alphabetic writing on papyrus scrolls. Because of its name, and because of many other legends that grew up around the origin of the alphabet, Byblos earned the reputation of being the place of origin of the alphabetic writing that the Phoenicians spread around the Mediterranean. Byblos is also famous for having been settled without interruption for nine thousand years, from the Neolithic period to the present day.

The site was surveyed for the first time in 1860 by Ernest Renan, but archaeological excavations did not begin until 1922, when a cliff collapse unveiled the royal necropolis. The first excavator was the Egyptologist Pierre Montet; he was succeeded by Maurice Dunand, who worked on site until the end of the 1970s, uncovering the ancient settlement down to bedrock.

The first human settlement at Byblos was a Neolithic village of single-room huts with a square plan and white plastered floors. Much later, in the third millennium B.C., the village developed all the features of an urban center, including a fortification wall, part of which is still preserved. The wall's two gates were strengthened with buttresses and retained by earthen works. During the same period, the city's streets were laid out, its sewers installed, and its houses built, all around a natural spring at the center of the mound. No royal palace was found in Byblos,[2] but temples from the third millennium B.C. were uncovered. One was dedicated to the cult of the main female goddess of Byblos, worshipped as Baalat-Gebal, the "Lady of Byblos." She was assimilated with the local goddess, Astarte, and represented as the Egyptian goddess Isis-Hathor.

Byblos became a major player in the trading network throughout the eastern Mediterranean, reaching the height of its wealth and power in the second millennium B.C., largely because of the city's privileged relations with Egypt. Indeed, the Nile Valley was the main trading partner of Byblos, and Egyptian influence was deeply felt in the religion, art, and culture of this ancient coastal settlement.[3] The famous Temple of the Obelisks and its offering deposits clearly illustrate this cultural symbiosis.

The temple was built in the second millennium B.C. on the ruins of an older L-shaped temple, which had been razed. It owes its name to the standing stones with pyramidal heads that were deposited in the temple courtyard as votives (fig. 19). Other offering deposits were put inside the cella and periodically collected by the priests and placed in jars, which were then buried under the floor of the sanctuary. The jars and their contents were found during the excavation and relocation of the temple, and today they form one of the most beautiful and valuable collections of the Beirut National Museum: gold daggers and axes, more than fifteen hundred copper-alloy figurines representing the god worshipped in the sanctuary, and finally, zoomorphic figures imported from Egypt (cat. nos. 23–25 and fig. 44).

Egyptian influence is also clearly detected in the funerary offerings and personal belongings found in the royal necropolis. Byblos has yielded eight royal rock-cut tombs, each consisting of a large square shaft 8 to 12 meters deep, with one or two rock-cut chambers at the bottom. The oldest tombs are dated to the beginning of the second millennium B.C., contemporary with Dynasties 12 and 13. The personal belongings of the rulers—gold pendants, a dagger and scepter bearing the name of the king, and Egyptian obsidian vessels—add further evidence for the close relationship between Byblos and the Nile Valley. The kings of Byblos also adopted the Egyptian tradition of using cartouches and Egyptian hieroglyphs to write their royal inscriptions, as seen in an inscribed pendant bearing the name of Ip-shemu-abi (cat. no. 29).

Evidence of continuity into the Phoenician era can be seen in the famous Ahiram sarcophagus, found in Tomb V of the Royal Necropolis (fig. 18).[4] Today it is displayed in the Beirut National Museum and counts as one of its masterpieces. Scenes carved on the stone coffin relate closely to the art of the Late Bronze Age and offer an insight into local funerary practices. On one long side of the sarcophagus is a funerary banquet scene representing the dead king Ahiram seated on a throne and flanked by winged sphinxes. He holds a faded lotus flower, symbolizing death, while the lotus-bud frieze that surrounds the scene symbolizes regeneration. Placed in front of him is a funerary meal, and a procession of officials carries additional offerings of food and drink. Women mourn the dead king, wailing and tearing their clothes and hair. The inscription, which was carved about 1000 B.C., begins on the short side of the coffin and continues on the lid.[5] It is the oldest known text written in the Phoenician alphabet.

As early as the nineteenth century B.C., the people of Byblos had developed a script of their own, consisting of signs very

Figure 18. Limestone sarcophagus of Ahiram. Byblos, Royal Necropolis, Tomb V. Direction Générale des Antiquités, Beirut 2086

similar though not identical to Egyptian hieroglyphs. Known as the pseudo-hieroglyphic script of Byblos, it remains undeciphered; scholars cannot agree even on the number of its signs. It fell into disuse around 1200 B.C. and was replaced by alphabetic script.[6]

Fortunately, the great upheaval of the twelfth century B.C., ascribed to the Sea Peoples (see fig. 141), did not destroy Byblos. The city is mentioned in the eleventh century B.C., in the annals of the Assyrian king Tiglath-pileser I, to whom it paid tribute, and in the account of the journeys of an Egyptian official (possibly apocryphal) named Wenamun, in which Zakar-Baal of Byblos appears as a powerful king exacting payment for the wood needed by the pharaoh Ramesses XI (ca. 1099–1070 B.C.).

The ancient site of Byblos, which is today dispersed around a Frankish Crusader castle, is a key site in the history of the Levant during the Bronze Age. Sixty years of excavations have yielded a huge number of finds, many of which still await publication. The city's important role in history was acknowledged by the international community when UNESCO declared it a World Heritage Site.

1. Huot, Thalmann, and Valbelle 1990, pp. 99–104.
2. Salles 1998, pp. 66–70.
3. Thalmann 1998, p. 51.
4. Montet 1998, pp. 228–38, pls. CXXVIII–CXLI.
5. Both the sarcophagus and the inscription were first dated to the thirteenth century B.C. Scholars subsequently revised the date of the inscription to the end of the eleventh century B.C.; however, because the sarcophagus showed clear signs of reuse, the original thirteenth-century B.C. date has been generally maintained for the sarcophagus.
6. Sader 1998, p. 61.

The Cedar Forest

In the standard Babylonian version of the epic of Gilgamesh, the hero and his companion, Enkidu, starting out from Uruk, traveled for fifteen days until they arrived at the mountain where the cedars of Lebanon grow, and there they gazed in wonder at the majestic trees:

> They saw a mountain of Cedar, seat of gods' and goddesses' throne. [On the] face of the mountain the cedar proffered its abundance; its shade was sweet and full of delight. [Thick] tangled was the thorn, the forest a shrouding canopy.[1]

Then they killed Humbaba, the monster guarding the forest, cut down cedars, and fashioned them into a raft upon which they floated down the Euphrates. When they arrived home, the tallest cedar was crafted into a great door for the temple of the god Enlil.[2]

Renowned in antiquity for their sweet fragrance, beauty, and durable strength, the cedars of Lebanon (Cedrus libani) grew in the high altitudes of the Lebanon and Anti-Lebanon Mountains as well as in western Syria and south-central Anatolia. Scarce and expensive because of the cost of transport over long distances, cedar was nevertheless an important item of trade in much of the ancient Near East. In Mesopotamia, Egypt, and the Levant, cedar beams were used primarily in the construction and paneling of palaces and temples. The wood was used also for gates and furniture and for images of the gods. And merchant ships, such as the Uluburun vessel that sailed the Mediterranean, were constructed of wood including cedar (see pp. 302–3). During the third millennium B.C., southern Mesopotamian city-states obtained cedar wood from sources in the Levant, as well as from the southern extension of the Zagros Mountains.[3] Records of commercial trade are limited, but literary and royal sources attest to continual import of cedar from the west. During the latter part of the twenty-third century B.C. both Sargon of Akkad (ca. 2334–2279 B.C.) and his grandson Naram-Sin (ca. 2254–2218 B.C.) claimed to have defeated enemy cities in Syria and established control of the valued forests of the Cedar Mountain, which can be identified as Mount Amanus (see map on pp. xxii–xxiii).[4] According to an inscription of Naram-Sin, timber from the mountain was used to rebuild a temple to the goddess Ishtar.[5] Approximately fifty years after Naram-Sin's reign, Gudea, the ruler of the city-state of Lagash, arranged for the importation of huge cedar logs from the Amanus, for the reconstruction of the Eninnu, the temple of his patron god Ningirsu.[6]

In the second millennium B.C. Yahdun-Lim of Mari (ca. 1810–1794 B.C.), a royal city situated on the Euphrates in Syria, marched his forces to the Mediterranean. Arriving at the Cedar and Boxwood Mountains, he set up a monument where he proclaimed himself the first king of Mari to reach this site; there he felled boxwood, cedar, and juniper trees.[7]

In the first millennium B.C., cedar was listed in Mesopotamian royal inscriptions as an item of booty or tribute.[8] Cedar was used in the preparation of medicines,[9] burned as incense, and employed in rituals. The resin was used for perfumes, and cedar oil served as an aromatic.[10]

In ancient Egypt cedar imports are first attested in Egyptian records beginning in Dynasty 4, although cedar was already used in earlier periods for construction.[11] The wood was used to construct royal barges and coffins and other items used in funerary rites. In the Levant cedar timber was used in the construction of Canaanite and Philistine temples. Archaeological evidence indicates that cedar was also used for tomb furniture in Middle Bronze Age Jericho.[12] The Bible makes reference to the cedars of Lebanon in connection with the building of the Temple in Jerusalem in the tenth century B.C., during the reign of Solomon (I Kings 5:5–6), as well as to a building referred to as the House of the Forest of Lebanon (I Kings 11:21). All that remains today of the great cedar forests are isolated groves, remnants of deforestation in the post-Roman period (see fig. 3).[13]

IS

1. George 1999, p. 39.
2. Ibid., pp. 22–47.
3. Ibid., p. 163; George 2004, p. 452.
4. Frayne 1993, pp. 28–29.
5. Ibid., p. 133.
6. Edzard 1997, pp. 33, 78.
7. See Kupper 1992, p. 165; Frayne 1990, p. 606.
8. See J. Postgate 1990.
9. See Chicago Assyrian Dictionary, vol. 8, s.v. "kisittu," p. 423, and vol. 4, s.v. "erēnu," pp. 276–79.
10. Ibid., vol. 4, s.v. "erēnu," pp. 276–79; Van de Mieroop 1992, p. 158. For an English translation of a prayer that included cedar as part of a ritual, see B. Foster 2005, pp. 209–11.
11. Egyptian records from the beginning of the Middle Kingdom continue to document journeys to Lebanon for the purpose of obtaining cedar. For a summary of Egyptian texts pertaining to the use of the cedars of Lebanon, see Briquel-Chatonnet 2004, pp. 465–68.
12. See Cartwright 2004, pp. 473–79, and Kenyon and Holland 1983.
13. Mikesell 1969.

23

STANDING FIGURES

Copper alloy, gold
Height 10.1–23 cm (4–9⅛ in.)
Byblos, Temple of the Obelisks,
Champ des Offrandes
Middle Bronze Age, early
2nd millennium B.C.
Direction Générale des Antiquités, Beirut,
Lebanon 11346, 16560, 22049, 22390, 22400,
22403

More than fifteen hundred male figurines made of bronze, silver, or copper alloy—some nude, with emphasized sexual organs, some wearing a short kilt, helmet, or conical cap—have been found at Byblos on the Levantine coast. Ranging in height from 3 to 38 centimeters, most are armed with a stick, dagger, mace, axe, or spear and are represented standing or walking, with one hand raised. Tangs projecting down from their feet indicate that they were meant to be stood upright on bases, perhaps of clay or wood, which no longer exist.

The figurines constitute one of the most famous finds at Byblos. Most date to the second millennium B.C. and may represent the god worshipped in the Temple of the Obelisks, probably Reshef, as suggested by a hieroglyphic inscription found on one of the obelisks. Written about 1800 B.C., the inscription mentions the name of a king of Byblos, Ip-shemu-abi, "the beloved of Herishef," the Egyptian name for Reshef.[1]

The nude and armed figurines symbolize both fertility and protective power and were offered by worshippers as a plea for the god's intervention. They were placed either inside small stone shrines that were sometimes cut into an obelisk or on benches inside the cella. To make room for new offerings, the priests would periodically remove the older ones and place them in jars that were then buried under the temple floor. The most famous of these jars was discovered by the Egyptologist Pierre Montet and now carries his name.[2]

Mass-produced in the temple workshop, most of the figurines were cast by the lost-wax method using a copper alloy, and many—as seen in this group—were fully or partially covered with gold foil. Surface finishing was probably done in a jeweler's workshop located in the temple precinct, where piles of ashes were found. The simplest and lightest, and probably the cheapest, were cut from a metal sheet. Although Egyptian influence can be traced in the frontal representation and short kilts of many of the figurines,[3] their overall schematic rendering, rigid posture, and oval-shaped heads have affinities to the so-called Syrian style represented by a group of earlier warrior figures said to have been found in the Lebanon Mountains.[4] It is likely, therefore, that these statues were locally produced. Closely related figures have been found at other sites on Cyprus and in the Levant.   SH/J-FL

1. Salles 1998, p. 70.
2. Seeden 1998, p. 95.
3. Parrot, Chéhab, and Moscati 1975, pp. 51–54.
4. D. Hansen 1969, pp. 283–84.

Figure 19. View from inside the Temple of the Obelisks, Byblos.

24

DAGGER AND SHEATH

Gold, ivory, silver
Dagger: length 39 cm (15⅜ in.);
width 6.5 cm (2⅝ in.)
Byblos, Temple of the Obelisks
Middle Bronze Age, early
2nd millennium B.C.
Direction Générale des Antiquités, Beirut,
Lebanon 16492

This dagger features a sharp blade with a hollowed central ridge, a gilded crescent-shaped ivory pommel, and a gold and silver sheath. The sheath is decorated with the same scene on both sides: a figure holding a sickle sword rides an equid and receives animal offerings—an antelope, a lion, a baboon, a dog, and a fish—brought by two kneeling men. On one side of the hilt is a figure wearing a short kilt and a conical cap. On the other side, two antelope stand face to face above the back of a third one. A fourth one grazes above the first three.[1]

Bronze Age daggers with decorated handles are well documented in the Levant.[2] This ceremonial weapon was offered to the warrior god Reshef of the Temple of the Obelisks, and the figure with conical cap represents in local tradition the god worshipped in the temple. While other offerings from the temple betray Egyptian influence, the motifs on the dagger, such as facing antelope or the standing lion in an attacking posture, were borrowed from Mesopotamia.[3]

The dagger blade's articulated central rib and beveled edges are like those found on weapons made for actual use. The sumptuous materials used here, however, indicate that this object was meant to serve a votive or ceremonial function similar to that of another dagger, with a sheet-metal blade, found in the same hoard. The hilt and the sheath are clad in gold sheet decorated with repoussé edged with silver. These precious metals could have originated in Egypt, Anatolia, or lands to the east of Mesopotamia and may have been acquired through trade or royal gifts.

SH/J–FL

1. Dunand 1958, p. 696, no. 14443, pl. CXVII.
2. Chavane 1987, p. 365.
3. Parrot, Chéhab, and Moscati 1975, pp. 62–64.

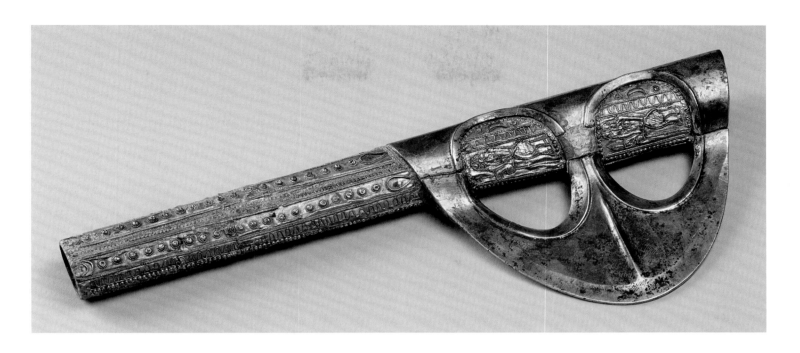

25

FENESTRATED AXE

Gold
Length 22.5 cm (8⅞ in.)
Byblos, Temple of the Obelisks
Middle Bronze Age, early
2nd millennium B.C.
Direction Générale des Antiquités, Beirut,
Lebanon 16132

The fenestrated axe is a semicircular weapon with a socket into which the handle is inserted.[1] On the socket, visible through the fenestration of the blade, are two standing figures surrounded by a semi-circular granulated line. The figures appear to represent Gilgamesh and Enkidu, the famous heroes of the Mesopotamian epic of Gilgamesh (see cat. no. 117). Other motifs, such as the moon crescents that complete the decoration, are typically Near Eastern and also have parallels in both Iran and Mesopotamia.[2]

This axe is part of a votive deposit found under the cella of the Temple of the Obelisks. Several fenestrated axes were recovered at Byblos, and molds for the casting of this weapon type have been found at this site and at Ugarit, attesting that they were locally produced. Ceremonial axes such as this one were offered to the warrior god Reshef. They demonstrate the wealth of their donors and the skills of the local craftsmen who had mastered the jewelry techniques represented here.

The bodies of the figures were raised by repoussé, chased on the front to provide linear details and outlined with fine granulation. Surrounding surfaces were then encrusted with individual elements, including twisted wire, domed hemispheres, and crescent-shaped cloisons made for semi-precious stone inlays that are now lost. These elements were most likely bonded to the surface using colloidal solder—a mixture of copper salts and an organic binder that when heated formed a localized alloy whose melting point was lower than that of the surrounding gold.[3]

The most conspicuous decorative feature of this axe is its extensive use of granulation. This technique, which involves the melting of tiny filings of gold to form small spheres that were then soldered onto the surface, required considerable practical knowledge and skill. Although granulation in simple linear designs is found on earlier jewelry from Troy and Poliochni, the type of fine granulation found here was a relatively recent innovation at the time this axe was produced, which undoubtedly added to its prestige as an elite object. It was during this period that the first examples of granulation appeared in Egypt, perhaps due to the importation of this technique through contacts with the Levant.[4]   SH/J-FL

1. Parrot, Chéhab, and Moscati 1975, pp. 64–68.
2. Caubet 1998b, p. 85.
3. Ogden 1982, pp. 64–66.
4. Ogden 2000, p. 165. See also Lilyquist 1993.

26

HATHOR PLAQUE

Ivory, silver
Height 9.5 cm (3¾ in.)
Byblos, Temple of the Obelisks
Middle Bronze Age, early 2nd millennium B.C.
Direction Générale des Antiquités, Beirut,
Lebanon 19287

The Egyptian goddess Hathor is represented on this ivory plaque with bovine ears and horns ending in a spiral, of which only her right ones are preserved. Above the horns, the figure wears the Hathor wig, which ends in two long braids resting on the chest. The face is entirely preserved, and the elongated eyes are underlined with silver. The plaque terminates in five horizontal bands.[1]

One of the oldest Egyptian deities, Hathor was believed to be the protector and nurturer of the pharaoh. Her cult appeared at Byblos in the third millennium B.C., and she was assimilated with the local goddess Astarte, also known as Baalat-Gebal, the "Lady of Byblos."[2] The latter borrowed some of the attributes of Hathor, including the sun disc worn between a pair of cow horns on her head. This plaque is most probably an Egyptian import, a testament to the trade connections between Byblos and Egypt during Middle Bronze Age.[3]

SH

1. Dunand 1958, no. 12166, pl. CLXIV.
2. Baurain and Bonnet 1992, pp. 44–46.
3. Caubet 1998a, p. 89.

27
VULTURE

Gold
Height 2.5 cm (1 in.); length 5.6 cm (2¼ in.)
Byblos, Temple of the Obelisks
Middle Bronze Age, early 2nd millennium B.C.
Direction Générale des Antiquités, Beirut, Lebanon 16554

This flying vulture is remarkable for the minutely carved details of the feathers on its wings. It was among the offerings found inside jars hidden under the floor of the Temple of the Obelisks.[1] In Byblos, zoomorphic objects representing animals such as hippopotami, apes, dogs, and bulls—made of metal and faience—were derived from Egypt. In Egypt, the vulture represented Nekhbet, goddess of El-Kab, a city south of Luxor, who was in charge of protecting the king. This royal symbol appears as a crown on Egyptian queens.

The object displays skilled craftsmanship in metalwork, but it is unclear whether it was locally made or imported. The artist's intimate relationship with nature is evident in the way the vulture is depicted, with outstretched wings, presumably circling high in the sky, ready to attack its prey.   SH

1. Dunand 1954, pp. 858–59, no. 16732, and p. 950, pl. CXXXIV.

27

28
FALCON PECTORAL

Gold
Height 12 cm (4¾ in.); width 20.5 cm (8⅛ in.)
Byblos, Royal Necropolis, Tomb III
Middle Bronze Age, early 2nd millennium B.C.
Musée du Louvre, Paris, Département des Antiquités Orientales AO9093

This gold pectoral was found in the Royal Necropolis of Byblos, whose extensive commercial and diplomatic relations with Egypt found dramatic expression in the art that it produced.[1] During the second millennium B.C., the city covered an area of about 16 hectares (39½ acres) and was fortified by strong walls. At the center were assembled the main shrines of the tutelary gods of the kingdom, while a Royal Necropolis was established at the northwest corner. Given the close association between the royal residences and the hypogea, the palace must have stood close to the funerary chambers, where the kings would perform commemorative ceremonies dedicated to their ancestors. Several funerary chambers have been discovered, each located at the bottom of a deep well carved out of bedrock. Two of them have yielded objects inscribed with the names of Ip-shemu-abi and his father, Abi-shemu, kings of Byblos (see cat. nos. 29, 30). These were found near objects bearing inscriptions with the names of Amenemhat III and Amenemhat IV, Egyptian pharaohs of Dynasty 12, who were likely contemporaries of the Byblos rulers.

The pectoral was found in a tomb without inscriptions, so it cannot be associated with any certainty to a specific ruler. Nevertheless, it is one of the most striking examples of Egyptian influence on local production. The overall form recalls Egyptian necklaces of the *ousekh* type, and the iconographic elements all refer directly to attributes of Egyptian pharaohs. It is the Levantine goldsmith's interpretation of the iconography, however, that reveals the very sophisticated nature of the art of Byblos. Deviating from Egyptian models, the craftsman created an original composition, setting a falcon with outspread wings between two falcon heads in profile. The central falcon holds in its talons a pair of *shen* signs attached to ropes that terminate in signs similar to the Egyptian *ankh*, symbol of

28

the region and generated symbolic expressions with mixed features in both the royal and religious spheres.

SC

1. For further reference, see Montet 1923, p. 337; *Monuments et mémoires* (Fondation Eugène Piot, Académie des Inscriptions et Belles Lettres, Paris) 27 (1924), p. 129, pl. 1; Montet 1928–29, p. 166, no. 619, pl. XCV; Dussaud 1930, fig. 6; Contenau 1949, p. 123, fig. 135; Dussaud 1949, p. 46, fig. 11; Parrot, Chéhab, and Moscati 1975, fig. 27; I. Winter 1976, p. 9, pl. 5:C; *I Fenici* 1988, p. 525; Baurain and Bonnet 1992, p. 43; Caubet and Pouysségur 1997, pp. 94–95; *Liban: L'autre rive* 1998, p. 87; Thalmann 1999, p. 119, fig. 5.

life. Versed in the symbolic language of Egyptian kingship, as well as in the ornamental motifs associated with its ideology, the maker of this pectoral adapted the motif of the divine falcon or vulture that spreads its wings protectively above the king, creating an original image for the royalty of Byblos.

The object is of a high technical and aesthetic quality, and it situates its maker within the current of cosmopolitan art that developed and was disseminated during the second millennium B.C. This current culminated in the artistic achievements of the next millennium, which were nourished by lively cultural interaction in

29

PENDANT OF IP-SHEMU-ABI

Gold, semiprecious stones
Height 7.5 cm (3 in.); width 7 cm (2¾ in.);
depth 1.5 cm (⅝ in.)
Byblos, Royal Necropolis, Tomb II
Middle Bronze Age, early 2nd millennium B.C.
Direction Générale des Antiquités, Beirut,
Lebanon 16235

This oval pendant is made of gold inlaid with semiprecious stones of red, green, and yellow color. At its center, a falcon with a gold head and wings outspread holds a ring in its talons, a possible allusion to the *shen* sign. On the bird's head is a white cartouche topped by a scarab, inside which the name "Ip-shemu-abi, Prince of *kpn* [Byblos]" is written with gold wire. On both sides of the scarab, *uraei* wear the white and red crowns of Upper and Lower Egypt, respectively. The edge of the pendant is decorated with four-petal flowers.

This pendant was excavated from Tomb II of the Byblos Royal Necropolis where Ip-shemu-abi, son of Abi-shemu, was buried. Egyptian influence on local artistic production, the result of trade between Byblos and Egypt, is evident as early as the fourth millennium B.C. and reached its height in the Middle Bronze Age, when the local kings borrowed the attributes of the pharaohs, such as rings, necklaces, pectorals, and crowns, and wrote their own names in hieroglyphs inside a cartouche.[1] Byblite craftsmen copied Egyptian motifs and adapted them to their taste and needs. The local manufacture of

29

the pendant is indicated by details such as the placement of the sun disc on the chest rather than on the head of the cobras, and in the poorly reproduced hieroglyphic signs.[2]

SH

1. Parrot, Chéhab, and Moscati 1975, p. 39.
2. Montet 1998, pp. 165–66, no. 618, pl. XCVII.

30

SICKLE SWORD

Bronze, gold, silver
Length 57 cm (22½ in.)
Byblos, Royal Necropolis, Tomb II
Middle Bronze Age, early 2nd millennium B.C.
Direction Générale des Antiquités, Beirut, Lebanon 16256

30

Ceremonial weapons like this one were presented to kings or high officials to symbolize victory. This sickle sword (*harpé*) belonged to Ip-shemu-abi, the king of Byblos during the early eighteenth century B.C., and was found inside his tomb in the Royal Necropolis at Byblos.

The curved blade is attached with a gold ring to a wood handle that terminates in a crescent-shaped gold pommel. The ring is decorated with an eight-petal flower. On each side of the blade is a bronze *uraeus* with scales and head made of gold. A hieroglyphic inscription, written in gold on the body of the cobra, reads, "Prince of Byblos, Ip-shemu-abi, born of Prince Abi-shemu, deceased."[1]

Egyptian influence can be seen in the representation of the *uraei* and in the use of hieroglyphic signs to name the kings, but anomalies in the Egyptian script point to local manufacture. This weapon differs from the Egyptian scimitars, or *khopesh*, held by gods and pharaohs and seems instead to copy Mesopotamian prototypes, which have a complete volute at the edge of the blade.[2]

The *uraei* are composed of gold wire set into a raised dark substrate. Although this dark material has been described as niello, it has not been analyzed. It may consist instead of a copper alloy to which small amounts of precious metal were added in order to provide a lustrous black-copper-oxide patina after treatment with acidic solutions. The technique of inlaying black

copper with gold wire appears to have been developed in Egypt during the Middle Kingdom and does not appear to have spread any farther east than the Levant.[3] In this case, the comparatively maladroit execution of the decoration further suggests that it was done by local craftsmen. The collar of a battle-axe (cat. no. 148) and a small falcon figure found at Ugarit and Minet el-Beidha, respectively, were embellished in a similar manner.

SH/J-FL

1. Montet 1998, pp. 174–77, no. 653, pl. XCIX; Parrot, Chéhab, and Moscati 2007, pp. 67–73.
2. Pottier 1922, pp. 301–3.
3. Issues regarding the still inconclusive identification of this black material are discussed in Thomas 2005, pp. 719–27.

Minoan Kamares Ware in the Levant

Kamares ware, the fine black-slip, polychrome-decorated pottery of the Protopalatial era on Crete (also called Middle Minoan IB–II, ca. 1950–1750 B.C.), was named after the cave on Mount Psiloritis in southern Crete where it was first discovered. It has also been found in the Levant, especially in the north.[1] Indeed, other than one sherd from Ashkelon and two from Hazor whose identities are debated, most examples come from Byblos (see cat. no. 32) and from Ugarit (Ras Shamra), followed by Beirut, Sidon, and Qatna.[2] The vessel from Byblos is a bridge-spouted jar, a vessel with a wide lipless mouth, two horizontal loop handles, a spout on the shoulder, and a globular body. While most of these vessels have a continuous convex profile and wide base (cat. no. 31), the Byblos vessel tapers to a narrow raised base, perhaps indicating that it was made at the end of the Protopalatial era.[3] Its shape and distinctive Wavy Line Style decoration may also indicate that it was made at Knossos.[4]

Texts from the palace of Mari attest to a wide range of products sent from Crete (if Kaptara refers to Crete), including leather footwear, inlaid bronze weapons, and silver and gold vessels; ceramics, however, are not among them.[5] Indeed, the Kamares pottery from the Levant appears to have been intended for the middle class rather than for a royal or elite clientele, suggesting that commercial interactions between Crete and the Levant operated on different levels, targeting different markets and, most likely, involving different reciprocal goods.[6] Crete lacked metals, and it seems reasonable that its trade with the Levant was aimed primarily at procuring copper and tin.[7]

Although historical texts may be silent on the importation of Minoan pottery, the archaeological record is informative. Of the minimum of twenty-two Kamares-ware vessels from the Levant, sixteen are cups, five are bridge-spouted jars, and one is a large coarse-ware jar.[8] The two predominant vessels, which have open shapes, presumably would have been imported to the Levant for use as tableware, not as containers. Obviously the cups were for drinking. While the bridge-spouted jar is surely a pouring vessel, its form may explain its broad use. Texts and organic residue analyses reveal that mixed fermented beverages, including wine, beer, and various flavoring ingredients, were popular in the eastern Mediterranean during the Bronze Age.[9] A vessel that closely resembles the Minoan bridge-spouted jar is the Egyptian beer strainer, which also has a wide, open mouth and a spout on the shoulder.[10] With both the Minoan and Egyptian vessels, particles in the liquid would float to the top; when the vessel was tipped, a clear liquid would pour from the spout, as the vessel's shoulder wall would retain the unwanted particles. With its wide mouth, the Minoan bridge-spouted jar would also have functioned ideally as a mixing bowl. If wine was added to the mix, the lees would settle to the bottom. Kamares-ware cups (see fig. 24) and bridge-spouted jars clearly appealed to a populace that enjoyed relatively inexpensive yet exotic goods from Crete which were compatible with indigenous drinking habits.   RBK

1. On Kamares ware, see Walberg 1976; Betancourt 1985, pp. 90–102; and MacGillivray 1998. For a recent survey of Kamares ware in the Levant, see Merrillees 2003.
2. Merrillees 2003; MacGillivray 2004.
3. MacGillivray 1998, pp. 80 (Type 6), 106.
4. Ibid., p. 106.
5. Guichard 1999. The archaeological evidence for Protopalatial artifacts in the Near East is summarized in Betancourt 1998.
6. Merrillees 2003, p. 139.
7. Wiener 1987.
8. Based on Merrillees 2003.
9. See articles in McGovern, Fleming, and Katz 1996; and Minoans and Mycenaeans 1999, pp. 140–209.
10. Hayes 1953, figs. 54, 68.

31

BRIDGE-SPOUTED JAR

Ceramic
Height 31.9 cm (12½ in.); diameter 36.6 cm
(14⅜ in.)
Crete, Phaistos, Palace, Room XXVII
Middle Minoan II, 18th century B.C.
Archaeological Museum, Heraklion, Greece HM5834

31

32
Bridge-Spouted Jar

Ceramic
Height 14.4 cm (5¾ in.);
diameter 15.5 cm (6⅛ in.)
Byblos
Middle Minoan II, 18th century B.C.
The Archaeological Museum of the American
University of Beirut, Lebanon 55.121

This Middle Minoan II Kamares-ware bridge-spouted vessel was discovered in 1955 by laborers digging for the foundations of a house at Byblos on the Levantine coast.[1] The Archaeological Museum of the American University of Beirut acquired the vessel along with twelve other locally made ceramics from an antiquities dealer. This example of Kamares ware is covered with an uneven dark-gray slip and painted with white dashes on the rim and handles. Wavy horizontal bands enclose three-leafed petals on the body, uneven bands circle the base, and rows of red blobs appear on the shoulder, lower body, and base. Byblos has yielded about ten other fragmentary Kamares-ware vessels, although none come from well-documented contexts.[2]   LB

1. Baramki 1967, p. 25. See also Baramki 1973.
2. Merrillees 2003.

EGYPT AND THE LEVANT

THOMAS SCHNEIDER

The intensity of Egypt's engagement in the Levant during the Middle Bronze Age is still difficult to assess.[1] By comparison with the establishment of a colonial empire in Nubia during Dynasty 12, when the region between the first and the second cataract of the Nile was controlled and exploited by a chain of forts and regular military campaigns, Egypt's foreign policy in the Syro-Levantine region seems more modest, though recent evidence suggests that this view may be based on incomplete evidence.

Egypt maintained the city of Byblos on the Lebanese coast as a political outpost that gave access to natural resources—among others, cedars of Lebanon—and facilitated economic control. A recently discovered text from the mastaba of Khnumhotep at Dahshur from the reign of Senwosret III (1878–1840 B.C.) mentions a conflict between Byblos and Ullaza and Egypt's involvement as a mediator in the politics of the region.[2] The rulers of Byblos bore the Egyptian title "prince of Byblos," and appear to have been Egyptianized; they adopted not only Egyptian hieroglyphs for their stelae and reliefs but also architectural and religious concepts; the local Astarte-type goddess, for example, was identified with the Egyptian goddess Hathor. Numerous Dynasty 12 kings are attested at the site: Amenemhat III (1859–1813 B.C.) with an obsidian jar from Tomb III of the Royal Cemetery and a gold pectoral from Tomb I, and Amenemhat IV (1813–1805 B.C.) with a box from Tomb II. The outpost was upheld in Dynasty 13; a relief depicting Antin, the king of Byblos, also bears the cartouche of Neferhotep I (1720–1711 B.C.).[3]

Intensive commercial contacts between Egypt and the eastern Mediterranean and the promulgation of Egyptian culture can be inferred both from texts and from the discovery of Egyptian objects throughout the region. A cuneiform tablet from Tell Sianu mentions trade relations between Egypt and Cyprus (cat. no. 17).[4] A sphinx of Amenemhat II's daughter Atar was found at Qatna. In Egypt, the Tôd Treasure from the foundation deposit of the Temple of Montu from Amenemhat II's reign contained silver and gold vessels identified by some scholars as Cretan, as well as a variety of stamp and cylinder seals. Amenemhat III is attested by sphinxes in Neirab, Ugarit, and Hazor, and Amenemhat IV by a sphinx found in Beirut. A ceremonial mace of the Dynasty 13 ruler Harnedjheriotef was uncovered in the Tomb of the Lord of the Goats at Ebla (cat. no. 12).

When these and other Egyptian objects reached the region is not confirmed. Nor is it known whether, beyond the exchange of trading goods and cultural knowledge, objects found in the Levant could imply a form of political supremacy by the Egyptian state.[5] Until recently the only explicit document about a military campaign was the Stele of Khu-Sobek,[6] with reference to a raid in the region of Shechem. A more energetic policy in the Levant is now fairly plausible as a result of the discovery of a fragment from the annals of Amenemhat II at Mitrahine[7] and the aforementioned Khnumhotep inscription. The tale of Sinuhe from the time of Senwosret I or later assigns the fictional protagonist Sinuhe the title Administrator of the Provinces of Majesty in the Countries of the Asiatics, and encourages the establishment of diplomatic contact with rulers of the Near East.[8] The Amenemhat text reports the Egyptian conquest of Cyprus and Ura in southeastern Anatolia, and states as one objective the capture of workers for the king's pyramid city; other Asiatics are given to Egypt as tribute. A fascinating detail here is the explicit information that the Egyptian soldiers ate the food of the Asiatic prisoners. As part of a ritual aimed at securing order, the Execration texts from Dynasty 12 list the names of Levantine princes and their cities and territories and so provide important information about the topography and population of the Middle Bronze Age Syro-Levantine region. Whether allusions to Asiatic incursions in Egypt during the First Intermediate period and early Middle Kingdom are trustworthy is uncertain.[9]

Figure 20. Facsimile of wall painting with western Asiatic nomads. Tomb of Khnumhotep II, Beni Hasan. Dynasty 12, reign of Senwosret II. The Metropolitan Museum of Art, New York, Rogers Fund, 1933 33.8.17

Beyond an ideological dismissal of the inhabitants of the Levant as the enemies of Egypt, there was also a desire to raise Egyptian awareness and understanding of Levantine culture. This is reflected in the tale of Sinuhe, who is transformed into an Asiatic chieftain and gains influence and prestige before returning to Egypt. The story suggests that a career abroad was viable for Egyptians in the Middle Bronze Age. Other texts can be quoted in this respect. A priest of Sekhmet appears to have presented his experiences abroad,[10] and the tale of Papyrus Lythgoe features as its protagonist an Egyptian merchant traveling to Byblos.[11] The presence of Egyptian scarabs highlights the regional popularity of the amulet, which also functioned as a means of promulgating Egyptian ideas.[12] Local workshops emulated Egyptian scarabs in the Levant and on Crete, where an active engagement with and remodeling of Egyptian concepts is apparent. It is notable that Levantine, Mesopotamian, and Aegean concepts and motifs were also transferred to the Egyptian province. The Tomb of Baqet at Beni Hasan displays a scene of the Mesopotamian tree of life and bull-leaping, together with fabulous creatures and griffins that reoccur in the Aegean.[13]

The Sinai Peninsula was the destination of mining expeditions throughout the Middle Kingdom, and sporadic resistance may have occurred (the stele of Nesmonth, dating to the reign of Amenemhat I, mentions confrontations with Bedouins). The employment of local personnel and workers from the Negev for quarrying is attested under Amenemhat III and Amenemhat IV. From the time of Senwosret II (ca. 1887–1878 B.C.) comes the depiction of a caravan of Asiatic nomads (from the Sinai or Negev) in the Tomb of Khnumhotep II at Beni Hasan, perhaps mining specialists searching for galena under the nomarch's protection (figs. 4, 20).[14]

The first half of the second millennium B.C. is marked by a great increase in evidence regarding foreigners in Egypt. This influx is attested throughout the socioeconomic and professional spectrum,[15] from prisoners of war and compulsory workers to cultic and priestly functions, high administrative offices, and royalty.

1. For a general overview, see Redford 1992.
2. J. Allen 2008.
3. Ryholt 1997, pp. 86–90.
4. Ahrens 2006, p. 26, n. 66.
5. Ibid., pp. 15–36; Schneider 2002.
6. Manchester Museum, acc. no. 3306.
7. Altenmüller and Moussa 1991; C. Eder 1995, pp. 176–95; Obsomer 1995, pp. 595–607.
8. Schneider 2002.
9. Gnirs 2006.
10. Parkinson 2002.
11. New York, MMA 09.180.535. See Parkinson 2002.
12. Bietak and Czerny 2004.
13. Morenz 2000.
14. Staubli 1991, pp. 30–35.
15. For a comprehensive analysis of this material, see Schneider 2003.

33

Vessel with Dolphins and Waterbirds

Ceramic
Height 14 cm (5½ in.); max. diameter 14.5 cm
(5¾ in.)
Lisht North, Pit 879
Middle Kingdom, Dynasty 13,
ca. 1802–1775 B.C.
The Metropolitan Museum of Art, New York,
Rogers Fund and Edward S. Harkness Gift,
1922 22.1.95

The so-called Dolphin Vase is a unique and important vessel that exhibits aspects of two eastern Mediterranean cultures of the first quarter of the second millennium B.C. Although the vase was found in Egypt, in form and clay it is a product of the Levant in the Middle Bronze Age. The entire body of the vessel is covered with carefully placed groups of plump, long-necked waterbirds similar to Egyptian Geese and leaping dolphins common in Minoan art. The decorative technique employed—combining dark, burnished surfaces and incised and filled lines—is similar to that of Tell el-Yahudiya pottery, which was produced in both Egypt and the Levant and was widely distributed. Since its discovery, many scholars have attempted to use this vessel to correlate the chronology of the later Middle Kingdom in Egypt with that of the Levant in the Middle Bronze Age and Crete during its Middle Minoan period.[1]

The jar was found in a shaft tomb, Pit 879, located beneath a later private house that had been built in the cemetery surrounding the pyramid of Amenemhat I (ca. 1981–1952 B.C.) at Lisht North in Middle Egypt. This tomb contained multiple burials and was probably reused. A study of the contents of the tomb by Janine Bourriau[2] has shown that the artifacts found there—pottery, stone vessels, objects of faience and Egyptian Blue, beads, and the remains of at least two coffins—can be dated to the first part of Dynasty 13. One of the coffins was decorated with bands of gold foil inscribed with the name of Debeheni, overseer of faience workers.[3] It appears that Pit 879 contained at least one rich and well-equipped burial, though we cannot with certainty associate it with the Dolphin Vase.

The vase is wheel-made of a very fine clay of non-Egyptian origin. Results of a neutron activation analysis indicated that the clay derived from a source in southern Canaan.[4] Its slightly piriform shape, tripartite loop handle, and ring base (now lost) are also similar to juglets found in the Levant during the Middle Bronze II period.[5] The surface of the vessel was first

33

Figure 21. Drawing of scene on cat. no. 33.

Figure 22. Ceramic vessel. Sidon. Middle Bronze Age. Direction Générale des Antiquités, Beirut 108501

burnished, and then the birds and dolphins were painted on with a purplish black slip containing manganese-iron pigment. The outlines, eyes, and body markings of the animals were incised over the painted shapes, and other parts of their bodies were filled with punctate patterns. After firing, the incisions were filled with a white paste of calcium carbonate.

While remarkable, the combination of Levantine, Minoan, and possibly Egyptian influences seen on this vase is not unparalleled. Tell el-Yahudiya juglets found at several sites in Egypt, the Levant, and Cyprus show long-necked water birds, leaping fish or dolphins, and running spirals.[6] An unpublished vessel from Tell Beit Mirsim, of shape and fabric similar to those of the Dolphin Vase, is decorated on its shoulder with black-painted and incised birds and lotuses.[7] More recently, a large vessel of local manufacture was found in a burial at Sidon in Lebanon and dated by the excavator to the final phase of the Middle Bronze Age (fig. 22).[8] On its shoulder is a sequence of leaping dolphins placed above a repeat pattern of waves rendered in Minoan fashion. The dolphins and waves are painted in black against a light-colored ground and outlined by incising. The size and sharply carinated form of the jar are very different from that of the Dolphin Vase and characteristic of the end of the Middle Bronze–early Late Bronze Age.[9]   SA

1. Kantor 1965, pp. 23–24, fig. 6A,B; Kemp and Merrillees 1980, pp. 220–25, pls. 29–31.
2. Bourriau 1997, pp. 115–16.
3. This coffin has been dated by James P. Allen, on the basis of texts and orthography to the reign of Awibre Hor (1774–1772 B.C.); forthcoming in *Funerary Texts from Lisht*, Publications of The Metropolitan Museum of Art Egyptian Expedition, New York.
4. McGovern et al. 1994, p. 38.
5. Amiran 1970, pp. 106–7, pl. 34:7, 8.
6. Bietak 1991b, p. 29, fig. 4, pp. 123–25, fig. 80; Arnold 1977, pp. 22–24, pl. 4.b; Kaplan 1980, pp. 326–28, figs. 127, 128.
7. Personal communication, Sarah Ben Arieh to Dorothea Arnold, August 1992.
8. Griffiths 2004, p. 117; Mommsen 2006, p. 49; Doumet-Serhal 2004a, p. 142, Doumet-Serhal 2004b, p. 106.
9. Amiran 1970, pp. 152–60, pl. 49.9.

34

VESSEL FRAGMENT WITH DOLPHINS

Steatite
Height 16.5 cm (6½ in.)
Crete, Palaikastro, Well 605
Late Minoan I, 1625–1450 B.C.
Archaeological Museum, Siteia, Greece

34

The tip of a serpentinite conical rhyton, carved with relief decoration, was discovered discarded in a well at Palaikastro, presumably after it had been broken (on conical rhyta, see pp. 426–30).[1] Like many other relief stone vases, it may originally have been covered with gold foil, as is suggested by another relief-carved rhyton from Palaikastro that has a depiction of a running boar to which fragments of gold foil still adhere.[2] Perhaps these relief-carved vessels were intentionally smashed at the time of the town's destruction in Late Minoan IB, to more easily strip them of their gilded surfaces.[3] From the scene on this rhyton, which must have been rather large and heavy, three dolphins are preserved. One facing right and two facing left, one above the other, swim toward each other above a pattern of coral work that covered the vessel's tip.

A fragmentary relief-carved rhyton from Zakros is also decorated with dolphins.[4] Indeed, dolphins are a common motif in Minoan Neopalatial art, from Middle Minoan III to Late Minoan IA–B, when they also occur on pottery, in intaglios, and possibly on wall or floor paintings.[5] Their earliest depictions seem to be on pithoi from Pachyammos, dated to Middle Minoan III (fig. 23). Painted with white interior markings on a dark ground, these dolphins resemble those incised on the Tell el-Yahudiya ware jug from Lisht (cat. no. 33), which may well be contemporary and whose appearance may be attributed to influence from the Aegean. The ubiquity of dolphins in Minoan art at the very least underscores the close ties between Cretan Bronze Age culture and the sea.   RBK

1. MacGillivray, Sackett, and Driessen 1998, p. 226; Koehl 2006, p. 181, no. 772; classified as Type III.
2. Koehl 2006, p. 181, no. 771.
3. Ibid., p. 53.
4. Ibid., p. 181, no. 773.
5. Vanschoonwinkel 1990, pp. 341–43.

Figure 23. Ceramic vessel. Pachyammos cemetery. Middle Minoan III. Archaeological Museum, Heraklion 7374

The Tôd Treasure

In 1936, the French archaeologist Fernand Bisson de la Roque discovered a treasure of lapis lazuli, gold, and silver objects in the foundations of the temple of Tôd, south of Luxor in Egypt, causing quite a stir within the scholarly world.[1] Because most of the objects had originated outside of Egypt, the treasure was a rich source of information, revealing the extent of international exchange in antiquity.

Four copper-alloy chests—two large and two small—containing the treasure bore inscriptions with the name of Amenemhat II (ca. 1919–1885 B.C.). The lid and the bottom half of the small chest in the Louvre (cat. no. 35b), recently reexamined for restoration, were each cast in one piece, surely through the lost-wax method. The craftsman who modeled the wax added the king's cartouche below the knob and on the lid. Traces of two round ventilation holes are visible on the sides. The many bubbles caused by the discharge of gases attest to the difficulty of the casting.[2]

The two small chests (one in the Egyptian Museum, Cairo) contained silver in the form of ingots, crude chains, and 153 vessels, most of them flattened and folded in four to reduce their volume. There were also a few objects in gold, all intact. Ever since these vessels were worked back into shape more than sixty years ago, scholars have been searching for comparable objects. Only a gold kantharos with decorated handles presented exact analogies with one of the pieces from the portion of the treasure in Cairo.[3] This object was discovered in a Mycenaean burial dating to the sixteenth century B.C., and the parallel would be plausible only if one accepts the late date for the treasure proposed by some scholars.[4] While this is not impossible, it is improbable.[5]

Among the lapis lazuli and other stone objects found in the two large chests, there is a collection of seals and amulets of diverse origins from Central Asia (fig. 26), the Levant, and the Aegean (see p. 388 and fig. 25). None can be dated beyond the Isin–Larsa period.[6] The context of the discovery—a ritual deposit—and the royal

inscription on the chests argue for a burial date under the reign of Amenemhat II, after which the treasure was left undisturbed.

We will never know the circumstances under which the Tôd Treasure was brought together, but they were most likely complicated. Like the lapis lazuli seals, the various objects in silver may not be contemporary. Different forms of treatment are visible: undecorated cups, fluted cups, and those adorned with maeandroid loops. The metal was probably hammered out of a rough silver mass, which would explain the irregular surfaces. In the fluted cups with thin walls, the inner surface is not as smooth and shiny as the outer surface. The restoration could not remove the many folds that distort our view of the objects, but did not change appreciably the original shapes.[7]

For the past sixty years, no specialized area of ancient archaeology has convincingly claimed "jurisdiction" over the cups from the Tôd Treasure. The Aegean, Anatolia, and northern Syria have all been advanced as possible places of manufacture. Laffineur raised the question of this very diversity.[8] An answer may be found on tablets from northern Syrian palaces of the second millennium B.C., such as at Mari. These document the important role played by silver vessels in

Figure 24. Kamares ware cup. Middle Minoan II. Knossos. Archaeological Museum, Heraklion π 14273ww

35a, bowls

exchanges between cities, noting that they were sometimes referred to toponymically, according to their style or place of origin.[9]

On the Egyptian side, the Annals of Memphis tell us that, during the first year of Amenemhat II's reign, two Egyptian ships returned from Lebanon with, among other materials, a cargo of 150 kilograms of silver.[10] Donations were made to the temples, especially to commemorate the memory of Amenemhat's father, Senwosret I, who had reestablished the temple of Tôd.[11] The context of the Tôd Treasure assumes its full significance when we consider that it was the property of Montu, the god who endowed the king with his martial strength and who was the lord of foreign dominions, lands that were symbolized for the Egyptians above all by the silver and lapis lazuli that they themselves lacked. In burying the objects beneath the temple, the king offered these lands to his god.　　　GP–B

1. Bisson de la Roque 1937. For further reference, see Bisson de la Roque 1937; Vandier 1937, pp. 174–82; Bisson de la Roque 1950; Bisson de la Roque, Contenau, and Chapouthier 1953; Seyrig 1954, pp. 218–24; E. Davis 1977; Kemp and Merrillees 1980, pp. 290–96; Matthäus 1980, pp. 249–50; Porada 1982; Cadogan 1983; Maran 1987; Laffineur 1988; Warren and Hankey 1989; Altenmüller and Moussa 1991; Thalmann 1991, pp. 21–38; Pierrat 1994; Maxwell-Hyslop 1995; Pierrat-Bonnefois 1999; Crete–Egypt 2000; Guichard 2005.
2. Observations of M.-E. Meyohas, restorer.
3. Laffineur 1988; Maran 1987.
4. Kemp and Merrillees 1980.
5. Pierrat 1994.
6. Pierrat-Bonnefois 1999.
7. Observations of A. Laurent, restorer.
8. Laffineur 1988.
9. Guichard 2005.
10. Lebanon is the traditional translation for henty-she; see Altenmüller and Moussa 1991, p. 14.
11. Altenmüller and Moussa 1991.

35a, b
BOWLS, CUPS, AND CHEST

a. Bowls and Cups: silver
Height 3.3–9.3 cm (1⅜–3¾ in.);
diameter 7.7–15 cm (3⅛–6 in.)

b. Chest: copper alloy
Height 14.3 cm (5⅝ in.); width 29.6 cm
(11¾ in.); depth 18.8 cm (7½ in.)

Tôd, Montu Temple
Middle Kingdom, Dynasty 12, reign of
Amenemhat II, ca. 1919–1885 B.C.
Musée du Louvre, Paris, Département des
Antiquités Égyptiennes, E15148, E15149,
E15166, E15167, E15169, E15129

The silver ware in the Tôd Treasure includes bowls (cat. no. 35a) decorated with flutes disposed either straight and vertically, in curves following a whirling pattern, merging with the rim or leaving either a smooth edge or a decorated edge with a row of beads. The most spectacular design is of continuous loops, with parallels in the Aegean world (fig. 24).[1] There are also various decorations for the bases: plain, with a rosette, with a rosette with whirling petals, or with concentric ribs. The latter design has analogies with ceramics of the Middle Minoan Age at Knossos.[2]

Most of the cups are so fragile that they could hardly have been intended for actual use. Their execution, however, is coarse, as if their weight in silver counted more than the quality of the craftsmanship. If we are to adopt the hypothesis that they were manufactured as a means of exchange—in a more elegant form than ingots or chains—thus permitting the tradition of gifts of precious metalwork to be perpetuated, then their folding for storage in the chests was probably intended from the outset.

The cup with a ribbon handle comes the closest to a utilitarian object because of its solidity and the thickness of its sides. This type of handle can also be seen on objects found in the royal tombs of Alaca Höyük in Anatolia dated about 2200–2000 B.C.[3] and on vases from the Middle Minoan period. The craftsmanship is mediocre (surface, rims, rivets). Scholars have suggested that the pedestrian quality of the silverwork at Tôd might indicate a region rich in minerals, but without a craft tradition of precious metalwork.[4]

One object is unique within the Tôd Treasure: an ovoid goblet with a cylindrical spool handle, a smooth, shiny surface, and a flat base. The handle especially has been given much attention: it consists of a hollow cylinder made of a sheet of metal rolled together and soldered to two small tongues riveted to the goblet. Precisely this type of handle has been found on wide-mouthed Mycenaean cups, but it was fashioned in ceramic versions as early as the beginning of the second millennium B.C. in Anatolia, at Kültepe.[5] Terracotta cups from Tell Arqa in the Levant (ca. 2400–2000 B.C.) display the same ovoid shape as this goblet.[6]　　　GP–B

1. Editor's note: For a parallel for this motif from Ebla, see Matthiae 1984, pl. 38d.
2. Warren and Hankey 1989.
3. Matthäus 1980, pp. 249–50.
4. E. Davis 1977, p. 75, and Cadogan 1983, pp. 515–16.
5. E. Davis 1977, pp. 71–72.
6. Thalmann 1991.

Figure 25. Steatite seal-amulet, carved on two faces, from the Tôd Treasure. Tôd, Montu Temple. Egyptian Museum, Cairo JE 66479

35a–c

Lapis Lazuli

Lapis lazuli is a fine stone of a blue hue with specks of pyrite. Its characteristic dark blue color is determined by the abundance of its main mineral constituent: lazurite. The best-known deposits are located in the Afghan province of Badakhshan, where its most famous site is Sar-i Sang. Deposits are also found at a high altitude in the Pamir Mountains, notably at Ladjevar-Dara.

After a first occurrence in a tomb in the Indus Valley in the seventh millennium B.C., lapis lazuli is found in archaeological contexts across Iran and Mesopotamia in the following millennia. Originating in northeast Afghanistan, it traveled through Iran before reaching Mesopotamia, the Levant, and Egypt. Its occurrence in Mesopotamia and Egypt in the fourth millennium B.C. clearly demonstrates that lapis lazuli was central to one of the oldest commercial networks. The number of objects made from the feldspathic mineral does not grow significantly until the Bronze Age, more specifically the second half of the third millennium B.C.

The earliest traces of lapis lazuli manufacturing are found in southern and Central Asia and Iran, at sites such as Mehrgarh, Mundigak, Sarazm, and Tepe Hissar, and date from the beginning of the fourth millennium to the beginning of the third millennium B.C. Lapis lazuli was still being worked at Shahdad, Tepe Hissar, Susa, and Shahr-i Sokhta during the third and the beginning of the second millennia B.C. Evidence of lapis jewelry manufacture in Syria and Mesopotamia is found at only a few sites: Ebla, Jebel Aruda, Larsa, and Ur.[1] Although workshops were not discovered at Mari, the texts confirm that craftsmen were working lapis lazuli in the city during the second millennium; fine objects found in the excavations date to the third millennium as well.

Thutmose III plundered gold, lapis, and precious stones from the city of Megiddo, but rulers obtained such materials by other means as well. Emissaries would be entrusted with negotiating purchases in the markets independent of the local palaces. The value of the prestige articles was measured in shekels of silver. At Sarazm, Mundigak, and Shahr-i Sokhta, lapis lazuli appears to have been both imported—the craftsmen adapting their work to meet local demand—and exported, to Elam. Goods made from lapis lazuli could be purchased in markets at Susa, Dilmun, Ur, Eshnunna, Ashur, Mari, and Emar.

Sites in Iran, the Persian Gulf, Ur, and along the Diyala and the Euphrates must have formed a series of posts that served as intermediary markets between the different centers. Goods would travel along these routes, and their arrival at their destinations was thus the culmination of a journey through a long-distance network rather than the result of direct contacts between emissaries.

Blue was the color of prestige in the Near East of the Bronze Age. It was associated with one material: lapis lazuli. The stone was

Figure 26. Lapis lazuli stamp seal, carved on two faces, from the Tôd Treasure. Tôd, Montu Temple. Egyptian Museum, Cairo JE 66485

offered to the gods by the princes of Mesopotamia and Egypt. It was used by the elite for personal adornment and seals, serving as a material representation of authority and entitlement. And it was the source of the power of the gods. The blue of lapis lazuli symbolized divinity, life, fertility, desire, sexuality, beauty, perfection.[2]

MC

1. Some 22 kilograms of unworked lapis lazuli were found in the destruction level of Palace G at Ebla; see Pinnock 1986.
2. For further reference, see Herrmann 1968; Pritchard 1969; J. Wilson 1969; Lichtheim 1973; Tosi 1974; Herrmann and Moorey 1980–83; Nibbi 1981; Wyart, Bariand, and Filippi 1981; Pettinato 1981; Porada 1982; Casanova 1992; Pierrat 1994; Casanova 1995; Michel 1996; Michel 1999; Pierrat-Bonnefois 1999; Casanova 2002; Warburton 2003a; Warburton 2003b; and Casanova 2006.

LAPIS LAZULI IN THE TÔD TREASURE

35c

BEADS AND RAW MATERIAL

Lapis lazuli
Raw material: height 4.8 cm (1⅞ in.);
width 7.7 cm (3⅛ in.)
Beads: max. length 5.8 cm (2⅜ in.)
Tôd, Montu Temple
Middle Kingdom, Dynasty 12, reign of
Amenemhat II, ca. 1919–1885 B.C.
Musée du Louvre, Paris, Département des
Antiquités Égyptiennes E15303–5, E15307,
E15313, E15316, E15318-1–4, 26-1, 40-2,
E15280 A-2/B1

The Tôd Treasure is remarkable not least for the quantity and variety of the lapis lazuli finds. The several thousand pieces excavated include the raw material and unfinished pieces, in addition to inlays, beads, pendants, amulets, and seals (fig. 26). Ranging from a pale gray blue to a deep ultramarine, the artifacts date from the mid-third millennium to the early second millennium B.C. and most of them were manufactured outside Egypt.

Some of the beads relate specifically to the assemblage discovered in the tombs of the Royal Cemetery of Ur: flattened date-shaped beads, faceted biconical beads, spherical and melon-shaped pinheads, squared spacer beads carved in the shape of a snail, and triangular spacers shaped as a panpipe with multiple perforations. Like the artifacts from Ur, they are often of poor quality and display a dull pale blue color with inclusions of brownish pyrite. This would indicate that some of the Tôd beads are indeed close in date to those from the Royal Cemetery.

The biconical and carved beads are the legacy of Susa, Mesopotamia, and Syria, with spacers characterized by multiple perforations common to all three regions. It is very likely that Ur was one of the most important centers for the manufacture of objects in lapis lazuli, specifically those found in the Royal Cemetery and in the Early Dynastic IIIA grave of Puabi (ca. 2500–2350 B.C.).   MC

35c, beads

THE OLD ASSYRIAN MERCHANT COLONIES

MOGENS TROLLE LARSEN

Kültepe, "Ash Hill" in Turkish, is a large mound in central Anatolia that covers the remains of the ancient city of Kanesh (fig. 27). It is approximately 500 meters in diameter and nearly 20 meters high, and it dominates the fertile valley northeast of the modern metropolis of Kayseri. To the east of the mound itself lies a lower city that covers a fairly large area, although the limits of this settlement are presently unknown. The site has been under excavation since 1948, but it seems clear that only a relatively small portion of the Lower City has been uncovered. It may extend nearly all the way round the central mound, in which case we are dealing with a very considerable urban site indeed. The ancient city that is being excavated here played a major role in Anatolia in the Middle Bronze Age.

On the mound itself excavators have uncovered palaces, temples, and official buildings. The main palace is vast and still an impressive sight; the walls stand 2 to 3 meters high. When it was destroyed by fire around 1700 B.C. the brick walls were exposed to such a violent heat—because of the timber used as a building material—that the mud brick melted and vitrified, now standing hard as glass.[1]

Unfortunately, very little has been found in the buildings on the mound, whereas the houses excavated in the Lower City have turned out to be veritable treasure chests. Here, too, we find that a fire destroyed the town and that the people who lived in the houses had only a short time in which to take their most valuable belongings and flee before the disaster struck. Therefore we find in the ruins not only the pots and pans used in daily activities, but also stocks of goods such as fine pottery in storerooms, and, not least, extensive collections of cuneiform texts, the remains of the commercial archives used by the inhabitants. To date, about twenty-three thousand texts have been discovered here. The ongoing publication and study of the archives left behind in the burnt-down houses have revealed the existence of a commercial society that flourished for more than two centuries and built up an impressive system of long-distance trade.[2]

Many of the excavated houses in the Lower City were those of merchants who came from Ashur, situated on the Tigris River in northern Mesopotamia more than 1,000 kilometers from Kültepe. The home city of these Assyrian merchants was excavated in annual campaigns by German archaeologists before World War I. The dig, directed by Walter Andrae, was an impressive undertaking and led to the discovery of palaces, temples, fortifications, and private houses plus some ten thousand texts. But the earliest period, corresponding to the settlement at Kültepe in Anatolia, was barely touched at Ashur. All we have from the Middle Bronze Age are scattered fragments of public buildings and practically no texts. There was nothing in the discoveries made here that even hinted at a special role for Ashur at this early time, when it appeared to have been simply another relatively small provincial town. It has thus been a revelation to learn from the finds from Anatolia that Ashur in fact played a central role in a vast network of international trade, a role that is not documented from the city itself.

Kültepe became known as the source of a considerable number of cuneiform texts, which were sold on the antiquities market already in the late nineteenth century, and a few incompetent "excavations" were started there on the mound. No texts were found. But the diggers could buy tablets from the local villagers, who not surprisingly declined to reveal where they came from. Only in 1925 did the Czech scholar Bedřich Hrozný succeed in getting that information from his local cook. As it turned out, he should have been digging outside the mound, in fact on the very spot where he had pitched his tent. It was in this way that the existence of an unsuspected Lower City was established.[3] Since 1948 annual campaigns have been conducted at Kültepe by a team of Turkish archaeologists, led for nearly sixty years by the late Tahsin Özgüç.

The town at the foot of the mound at Kültepe is a maze of narrow streets, many of them paved with very large stones under which are drains. Occasionally the streets, which in general run in a pattern away from the mound, broaden to become small plazas, and it seems likely that there would have been trees to provide some shade in such places. The houses were of half-timber construction and not very large, between 50 and 100 meters square; most or all of them had a second story. In the traditional manner of ancient Near Eastern towns, the houses turned their backs on the street, fronting a courtyard instead, so that a walk along the streets would be dominated by blank walls with only doorways to break the monotony; some of these, however, led to shops and occasionally into workshops. In fact, the part of the Lower City where the Assyrian merchants lived may well be understood to have been a kind of bazaar, the *karum*, where buyers of all kinds of goods could go from house to house to make deals and inspect the wares on offer. It was undoubtedly a busy place with a great deal of traffic.

It would also have been a world inhabited by many different peoples, speaking a variety of languages and presumably wearing many different types of dress. The names of the persons appearing as customers and assistants show that Indo-European

Figure 27. Aerial view of the site of Kültepe.

languages such as Hittite and Luwian were spoken by the local population, and some Anatolians would have spoken Hattian, a non-Indo-European tongue at home in the more northern areas. Many of the people in the Taurus Mountain regions spoke Hurrian, a language that is unrelated to any of the others. The merchants spoke and wrote their own Semitic language, and we also know that they were in contact with people from Syria, for instance from Ebla, who spoke different Semitic languages. Life in the Lower City at Kanesh was cosmopolitan and varied, a world that was created on the basis of the rich profits gained in long-distance trade.

Donkey caravans arrived regularly at Kanesh, having traveled for more than a month all the way from Ashur. They carried sealed packages with either tin or textiles, and before they could go to their destination at one of the merchant houses in the Lower City, they had to go up to one of the palaces on the mound, where they were checked and where taxes were paid. After that, the owners of the goods entered a busy period, during which they had to make sales as profitably as possible. This activity was in most cases organized by way of credit sales

whereby other traders took over smaller consignments that they would then sell within a stipulated time, mostly about three months, on business trips to the many other commercial settlements in Anatolia.

We know of about forty such Assyrian settlements in the region, a few very large with presumably no less than a hundred merchants stationed more or less permanently. Others were much smaller. And some would undoubtedly be manned irregularly by a few agents. The best-known sites are found at Hattusa (Boğazköy), the later capital of the Hittite Empire, where the Assyrian merchants had a small trading settlement, and Acemhöyük, a large mound south of the Salt Lake, which may have been called Ulama. Here excavations have been ongoing for decades, and impressive palaces have been uncovered.[4]

These colonies and stations were spread all over Anatolia from the Black Sea region, where copper was mined, to the Taurus Mountains in the east and southeast and to the west, beyond the Konya Plain and the Salt Lake. It would seem that the merchants from Ashur had managed—at least for a time—to establish a veritable trade monopoly in Anatolia, where they kept out merchants from other regions. We do hear occasionally of traders from Ebla as active in Anatolia, but with our present knowledge we must conclude that the Assyrian traders were completely dominant there.

It is likely that some of the tin and copper imported into and traded in Anatolia found its way to the Aegean region, but that section of the commercial system was not controlled by the merchants from Ashur, so it is never referred to in their correspondence. It is also noteworthy that the large and fertile Cilician Plain seems to have belonged to a different commercial circuit, perhaps one controlled from Ebla or Emar in Syria. For Ashur was just one of several commercial centers in the larger Near Eastern region, and its own trade was possible only in close contact with other networks.

The tin and large quantities of textiles, often referred to as "Akkadian" textiles, came to Ashur by caravan from what was known as the Lower Land—i.e., the northern part of the large Mesopotamian floodplain—and that part of the system was controlled by southerners. The market in Ashur could function only on the basis of a regular supply of these goods from the south, and we know that the king and city assembly in Ashur passed various regulations that were intended to attract this trade to Ashur, which functioned largely as a transit center. Some Assyrian traders certainly had relations with their southern colleagues; a few even spent years in the city of Sippar at the northern end of the floodplain, and we know of marriages between traders from the two cities.[5]

The Assyrians in Anatolia in the first generation known to us from the texts remained closely tied to their home city, Ashur. Some of them spent most of their adult life in Anatolia and eventually died and were buried there, although their wives and families remained in Ashur. The separation obviously placed a heavy emotional burden on them, and especially on their wives, who had to take over the responsibility for the running of the house and the family, bringing up the children alone. Since they were economically dependent on their husbands, some of whom neglected to send funds adequate to cover the costs of daily life, it is not surprising that we have a number of letters from such women in which they complained, often in very bitter, strong language. They were lonely, and at times they lacked money even to buy food for the household, so they had to sell their personal jewelry or borrow money against interest. One of these women wrote to her husband:

As you hear, mankind has become wicked. Brother stands ready to devour brother. Honour me by coming here and breaking the fetters that keep you. Place the girl in divine Ashur's lap.[6]

The last sentence probably refers to a religious ceremony in which their daughter was to be initiated as a priestess, as we know happened from several other texts. Clearly, the woman in Ashur was worried about having to go through such a significant ritual event alone, without the support of her husband.

The next generation of traders in Anatolia regularly married local women and established families in one of the colonies. We have several letters exchanged between such men and their Anatolian wives, and we can follow certain individuals through their life. A particularly poignant example is the lady called Kunnaniya, who married the son of Pushu-ken, one of the most influential Assyrian traders of the first generation. Some letters indicate that she led a peaceful life in charge of the household in Kanesh. However, her husband died young and she then became involved in acrimonious conflicts with her powerful in-laws. At some point, she went all the way to Ashur to plead her case. She appears to have been treated very badly also by her own Anatolian relatives, for while away she lost control of her house to her own sister. The last text we have that refers to her is a pathetic letter written by Kunnaniya to her grasping sister, and it begins as follows:

As you are my sister—truly, if you love me—I can no more. I am dying and the ground disappears under me![7]

Such texts provide the emotional, personal background for the meeting of different cultural traditions and the exchanges that we see exemplified in the material finds from the excavations. Marriages across cultural, religious, and linguistic boundaries represent the most intimate contact on the personal level, and apart from unhappy examples such as Kunnaniya, these interactions appear to have worked well in most instances. Such mixed households obviously involved close social contact between Anatolian and Assyrian families, where a great many compromises must have been made. This led to the occasional writing of marriage contracts, where the rights of both parties were spelled out. It seems clear that women had a different, freer status in Anatolian society than was the case among the Assyrians, but such problems were addressed and dealt with.

In fact, the Assyrian merchants moved with confidence in this complex world. Their houses in the colonies were constructed entirely according to local traditions, and the pottery found in them consists almost completely of local wares. In contrast to the seal cutters, who developed a unique hybrid style that mixed Anatolian and Mesopotamian elements, the potters excelled in a dramatic, purely Anatolian style that in many cases represents a playful adaptation of forms and patterns that must have originated in metal.

The basis for the Assyrian presence in Anatolia was the existence of treaties drawn up between the Assyrian community and the local kings. There were clear rules for taxation, of course, and the palaces retained the right to buy up to 10 percent of the imported textiles at a set price. These local authorities, on the other hand, were responsible for the safety of the roads and would have had to pay damages in cases of robbery or murder in their territory.[8] Also on this institutional level it seems that in most instances relations were positive and built on mutual trust. Yet there were drastic differences between the two interacting political systems: whereas in Anatolia we find politically centralized kingdoms with a long list of palace officials in charge of sectors of economic and social life, Ashur was in effect ruled by an oligarchy of leading businessmen with a king who may perhaps be described as "first among equals." The Anatolian king was the undisputed ruler who, for instance, dispensed justice by issuing royal verdicts, while in Ashur the highest judicial authority was constituted by the city assembly.[9]

Such differences are important to keep in mind as evidence of the great variety and flexibility in the world in which the Assyrian merchants moved, and they indicate how diversity and complexity were dealt with. Trade could go on for as long as it was seen as being of mutual benefit to the parties involved. It united a truly vast region, probably reaching from Central Asia to the Aegean; the evidence we have from Kanesh throws direct light on only a relatively small part of the much larger system that was in operation for at least two centuries.

About the year 1836 B.C., the colony in the Lower City at Kanesh was destroyed by fire, a disaster that sealed the immensely rich houses with their household goods and their archives. We must assume that the kingdom of Kanesh was involved in a war that went badly and which led to the capture and sack of the city. The merchants were obviously at the mercy of such events, but it is likely that their commercial activities in the other colonies and stations continued, and after about a generation the Lower City was reoccupied and there a new group of Assyrian traders began their life. This later settlement is not nearly as well known, since the merchants left us only a small archive. The political climate had changed as well, for a process of stabilization of much larger political units, true territorial states, was under way in Anatolia, a development that concluded with the establishment of the early Hittite kingdom around 1650 B.C. By that time the Assyrian traders had already left the region and a new world, one in which a small number of empires and great states ruled the entire Near East, was beginning to dawn.

1. See T. Özgüç 1999.
2. The period during which merchants from Ashur operated in Anatolia is divided into phases referred to with the archaeological terminology "Level II" and "Level Ib," based on the stratigraphy in the Lower City at Kanesh. This article presents primarily a picture of conditions during the older phase, that of Level II, ca. 1950–1836 B.C. See, for a general presentation, Veenhof n.d. (forthcoming). The excavator Tahsin Özgüç gave a general overview in 2003.
3. Hrozný 1927.
4. See preliminary reports by Nimet Özgüç in *Türk Arkeoloji Dergisi* 13 and 14 (1964 and 1965) and in *Anatolia* 10 (1966). The ancient name of the town hidden under Acemhöyük is assumed by many to have been Burushaddum; see most recently Forlanini 2008. However, a new interpretation of the political geography (see Barjamovic 2008) makes this identification unlikely, and Ulama seems to be a better choice.
5. Veenhof 1991.
6. MAH 16209 published in Garelli 1965, pp. 158–60. Translation from the Assyrian by the author.
7. See Michel 1997. See also Larsen 2001.
8. See Günbattı 2004.
9. Larsen 1976.

36a, b

CUNEIFORM TABLET AND CASE

Clay
a. Tablet: height 16.9 cm (6⅝ in.);
width 7.3 cm (2⅞ in.)
b. Case: height 18.5 cm (7⅜ in.);
width 9 cm (3½ in.)
Anatolia
karum Kanesh II, ca. 1950–1836 B.C.
The Metropolitan Museum of Art, New York,
Gift of Mr. and Mrs. J. J. Klejman, 1966
66.245.5a, b

Assyrian traders at *karum* Kanesh kept their business accounts in special strong rooms called *massartum*. Within these locked rooms cuneiform records and cylinder seals were placed in sealed containers. Many of the documents were negotiable contracts that were bought from and sold to other traders. Possession of a tablet such as a loan or quittance document, which was often encased in an envelope impressed with one or more cylinder seals, could be used to certify proof of a claim.

Assyrian merchants dealt with large amounts of capital and traded in vast quantities of goods, primarily tin and textiles. With profits from the sale of textiles estimated to be as high as 200 percent, it is not surprising to find tablets among the traders' archives that describe legal depositions regarding private disputes and decisions by the *karum* court.

In this legal deposition, sworn before witnesses upon the dagger of the god Ashur, two merchants accuse each other of theft. The first merchant, Suen-nada, claims that while he was in his home in Kanesh, another merchant, Ennum-Ashur, traveled to the nearby city of Durhumit, where he illegally entered Suen-nada's guesthouse and stole personal valuables, as well as two sealed containers that housed the business records of his firm. Stolen documents included records of debts, credits, quittances, purchases, memoranda, and court decisions, as well as tablets and seals deposited for safekeeping by "strangers" and company shareholders and their employees. In response to this accusation, Ennum-Ashur declares that the firm's accounts in fact belong to him and had been stolen from his agent's home three years earlier.

(Ever since then) I have been chasing you and repeatedly set witnesses for you, and they have bound you over! Three years have now passed, and the Kanesh harbor has learned of your robbery and your lies, and after they have had you yourself and your partners extradited to the Kanesh harbor, and I have stated formally

73

36a   36b

*under oath in the Kanesh harbor to you and to
your partners the (facts about the) robbery and
the lies, and after our tablets were written a
month ago and were entrusted to the bureau of
the harbor, stating that I have not entered your
house and have not taken anything belonging
to you— (after all this) you go on asking me
questions in court concerning many tablets![1]*

The court's verdict is unknown.

This tablet, attributed to Kültepe, was
found encased in its envelope, which was
impressed by two different cylinder seal
impressions, on the obverse, the reverse,
and on the sides.[2] The impressions illustrate the work of local seal carvers, who
adapted Mesopotamian subjects to local
taste. Scenes such as the procession to a
seated divinity were often embedded
within a larger corpus of Anatolian motifs.
The use of the foreign cylinder seal to roll
impressions on documents also represents
a departure, for the stamp seal was the
preferred form of sealing in Anatolia.

The seal impressions from Kültepe provide graphic evidence for the interaction of
peoples established in the *karum* from the
twentieth to the eighteenth century B.C.

Merchants from Ashur, representing the
dominant foreign presence, used seals in a
variety of styles, most prominently those
in a linear Old Assyrian style (cat. no. 37a).
More modeled seals, in Old Babylonian and
Old Syrian styles, also marked the envelopes of documents from the *karum*.

IS/JA

1. Larsen in Spar 1988, p. 119, no. 84a.
2. For further reference, see ibid., pp. 115–
   20, 178, nos. 84a, 84b, pls. 83–85, 129, 137,
   138, 147.

37a

37b

37a, b

CUNEIFORM TABLET CASES

Clay
a. Height 5.6 cm (1⅞ in.); width 4.6 cm
(1⅞ in.); thickness 2.5 cm (½ in.)

b. Height 5.2 cm (2 in.); width 5.4 cm (2⅛ in.);
thickness 2.5 cm (1 in.)

Anatolia
karum Kanesh II, ca. 1950–1836 B.C.
The Metropolitan Museum of Art, New York,
Gift of Mr. and Mrs. J. J. Klejman, 1966
66.245.15b, 66.245.16b

These two documents can be attributed to *karum* Kanesh. The quittance (receipt) for a loan of 9⅔ minas of silver is encased in an envelope (above left). It bears the cylinder seal impressions of four witnesses to the transaction.[1] Two are in Old Assyrian style, with depictions of worshippers being led by deities in horned crowns toward a seated god and a scene of kneeling nude belted heroes bearing a flowing vase (upper impression). A third seal impressed on the envelope (not visible in this photograph) is an heirloom of the Ur III period, the original seal perhaps originating in Ashur, where a lapis lazuli seal of this period from the grave of an Old Assyrian merchant was recut with Anatolian motifs.[2] One Anatolian-style cylinder seal is also impressed on the case (lower impression), on which the seated divinity is part of

a group that includes a figure holding the reins of a bull.

The quittance for a loan of 7 minas of silver was preserved in its envelope (above right). It bears three cylinder seal impressions.[3] One of them presents what is perhaps the most refined example of the Anatolian style (see detail below), with beautifully carved figures in procession moving toward a seated god wearing a conical cap. Led by a cupbearer, the Mesopotamian suppliant goddess is followed by a god whose tall cap, shoulders, flounced garment, and legs burst with flames, and by a warrior in a short kilt holding a shield in "oxhide" form. The two other seals, which have been termed Syro-Cappadocian, were executed in styles

that combine Syrian, Mesopotamian, and Anatolian features.[4] Characteristic of this manner are a fuller rendering of the figures and the introduction of distinctively Syrian motifs such as, on one impression, the nude goddess (see lower impression). Here the goddess is flanked by two bull-men, while a divinity in an ascending posture approaches a seated god.   JA

1. Larsen in Spar 1988, pp. 134–35, nos. 92a, 92b; Pittman in Spar 1988, pp. 186–88, nos. 53–56, pls. 132, 152, 153.
2. Aruz 1995c, p. 60, no. 41; Wartke 1995, pp. 44–47.
3. Larsen in Spar 1988, pp. 134–36, nos. 92a, 92b; Pittman in Spar 1988, pp. 188–89, nos. 57–59, pls. 132, 153, 154.
4. Teissier 1994, pp. 57–58.

37b, detail of upper impression

38
BOOT VESSELS

Ceramic
Height 12.3 cm (4⅞ in.); length 12.4 cm (4⅞ in.)
Kültepe
karum Kanesh II, ca. 1950–1836 B.C.
Kayseri Museum, Kayseri, Turkey
86/267, 268

During the Middle Bronze Age at Kanesh, a number of ceremonial libation vessels whimsically mimicked the shapes of human body parts. The salient characteristic of these anthropomorphic vessels was the significance given to the male and female face, torso,[1] and even shoes. Indeed, the shoe with upturned toe became the typical footware of deities and royalty in ritual scenes in Anatolia (see cat. no. 107). A variety of shoe-shaped vessels were found at the site, with surface treatment exemplified by red burnish or slip, polychrome painted geometric designs, or combinations of both. Also depicted on seal impressions from Kanesh, this shoe type becomes the preferred footwear of deities, especially the goddess.[2] By the Hittite period, such shoes appeared on the entire pantheon of Hittite deities, and also on Tudhaliya IV, in the Yazılıkaya outdoor sanctuary near Hattusa (fig. 55). In Turkey today, this footwear is still made and worn in the rural highland regions.

Apotropaic amulets of human parts such as hands, liver, heart, eyes, and feet have been found in the ancient Near East at Halaf-period sites dating all the way back to the fifth millennium B.C. It has always been difficult to ascribe symbolic meaning to amulets of disarticulated body parts, but often they have been interpreted as elements of sympathetic magic. In Central Asia shamans carried amulets shaped as human parts to give to the ailing to aid in the healing process. The upturned-toe shoe was perhaps initially related to gear for mountainous terrain. A first foreshadowing of its divine nature is seen on a late-fourth-millennium B.C. copper-alloy figurine of a bearded shaman or horned deity.[3] In Anatolia, however, the significance of boot-shaped ritual vessels dates back to the seventh millennium B.C., with a boot vessel from Höyücek.[4] Found in a context with grain bins and artifacts of cultic nature, the shoe-shaped vessel took on ritual significance from the Late Neolithic period onward.

KAY

1. A. Erkanal 1995.
2. N. Özgüç 1965, pl. 24: no. 71.
3. Porada 1985, pl. XII.
4. Duru and Umurtak 2005, pl. 101:6.

39
BULL-HEADED RHYTON

Ceramic
Width 7 cm (2¾ in.); length 14.5 cm (5¾ in.)
Kültepe
karum Kanesh II, ca. 1950–1836 B.C.
Ankara Museum of Anatolian Civilizations,
Turkey 15016

40
LION-HEADED VESSEL

Ceramic
Height 9.8 cm (3⅞ in.); width 7.3 cm (2⅞ in.)
Kültepe
karum Kanesh II, ca. 1950–1836 B.C.
Ankara Museum of Anatolian Civilizations,
Turkey 1-72-98

Animal-shaped drinking and libation vessels have been ubiquitous in Anatolia and neighboring regions as far back as the Neolithic era (7th millennium B.C.). While their origins are found in ambiguous religious iconography involving animals, zoomorphic vessels are said to be attributes associated with the pantheon of Anatolian gods and goddesses, especially those of the second millennium B.C. Animal-headed cups played an important

38

39

40

role in libation rituals and are depicted in seal impressions on tablets from Level II at Kanesh (Kültepe), dating from about 1950 B.C. to 1836 B.C. These presentation scenes verify their ceremonial context, in which acolytes carrying a lion-headed vessel move in processions toward seated or standing gods and goddesses, presumably chief tutelary deities of Kanesh.[1]

Animal-shaped silver and gold cups, called *bibru*, were highly esteemed as royal diplomatic gifts and, as documented in texts, were exchanged between Mari and other kingdoms in Syro-Mesopotamia during the early second millennium B.C.[2] Relief-decorated silver examples representing stags and bulls, as well as fist-shaped vessels, have been found in Anatolia (see cat. nos. 107–109). Through palace patronage, these exotic vessels became visual metaphors for crown, deity, and state, and they traveled extraordinary distances. Indeed, with the aid of lead-isotope analyses, a silver stag-shaped theriomorphic vessel discovered in Shaft Grave IV at Mycenae (fig. 54), was found to be made of Taurus Mountain silver from southern Turkey.[3]

At Kanesh a vast quantity and diversity of ceremonial libation vessels were given whimsical animal shapes, including those of donkeys, bulls, bears, snails, pigs, rabbits, lions, deer, and birds.[4] Often made of ceramic, these well-modeled menageries accentuate specific physical attributes— gaping jaws, voluminous manes, elegantly elongated necks. Surface treatment includes red burnish or slip and polychrome

painted geometric designs, or a combination of the two. And while these animals amuse—sometimes to the point of caricature—they also inspire awe.

The primary association of animal-shaped vessels was with deities. For the Hittites the bull was linked with the storm god Teshshup, while the lion was depicted with Hepat, the sun goddess of Arinna, and often also with her son Sharruma. As the vessels became more widely distributed, they were transformed and imbued with emblematic meanings relating to city, ruler, and religion. Thus a zoomorphic vessel used as a diplomatic gift might also serve as a three-dimensional emblem; that is, as a rebus in the round, which could be "read" as signifying the city, a tutelary deity, or the name of the gift giver. This type of modeled picture writing would have been very much at home in Anatolia, a region that, along with Egypt, developed hieroglyphic writing.

The bull-headed vessel from Kanesh (cat. no. 39) is properly termed a rhyton as there are two holes in the snout through which liquid may flow. Its ears and horns are modeled, while other features, such as the reins, are in relief. This combination of linear and three-dimensional treatment is also found in lion-headed cups from Kanesh (cat. no. 40) and from Ugarit, near the Syrian coast (see cat. no. 155). The Ugarit example, found in a Late Bronze Age context, shares such features as inlaid eyes and a handle that loops up toward the rim. Both the bull and the lion cups from

Kanesh reflect the popularity of red-burnished pottery characteristic of Hittite production.

KAY

1. N. Özgüç 1965, pl. 23, no. 70.
2. S. Dunham 1989.
3. Yener 2007.
4. T. Özgüç 2002b.

41

LION-SHAPED RHYTON

Ceramic
Height 20.5 cm (8⅛ in.)
Anatolia
karum Kanesh II, ca. 1950–1836 B.C.
Musée du Louvre, Paris, Département des Antiquités Orientales AM1517

Zoomorphic rhyta are surely among the most spectacular examples of the ceramic work produced during the age of the Assyrian trading colonies in central Anatolia. They display both the great technical mastery of the potters and their extraordinary creativity. This rhyton in the shape of a lion, acquired at Kültepe, is remarkably well preserved.[1] The animal is represented standing firmly on its legs; each paw has four curved claws. The jaws are open, as if the lion were roaring, revealing four fangs that show the animal's strength and fierceness and a protruding tongue. During the modeling process, a hollow space was left in the head and body. The spout on the back allowed the vessel to be filled with liquid that was then poured through the two holes pierced in the nostrils. The dark brown glaze, applied directly on top of the cream-colored slip, covers only the head and neck. Some details—tail, claws, jowls, and the roll of skin at the base of the mane, indicating that the animal is male—are accentuated by a uniform line. The fur on the muzzle and the shoulders is rendered by stippling, while the longer hair of the mane is represented by a series of spirals.

These motifs are characteristic of the decoration that adorns the group of rhyta in the form of standing lions that were recovered from Level II of the *karum* during the excavation of Kültepe. The similarities permit us to date the Louvre vase to the same period. Several of these zoomorphic vases were discovered in the rooms where the *karum* merchants kept their archives, usually accompanied by all manner of tableware: goblets, cups, and jugs. These vessels were probably used for ceremonies that took place inside the house itself, during the course of which the zoomorphic vases, which surely had a symbolic meaning, were used to pour libations.

FD

1. For further reference, see Genouillac 1926, pp. 52–53, no. 141, pl. 8; Bossert 1942,
no. 398, pl. 79; Bittel 1976b, p. 85, fig. 64; *Huit millénaires de civilisation anatolienne* 1981, no. 10; Dupré 1993, p. 69, no. 44; and B. Collins 2002, p. 312, fig. 112.

42

ANTELOPE-SHAPED VESSEL

Ceramic

Height 21 cm (8¼ in.); max. width 5.7 cm (2¼ in.); length 22.2 cm (8¾ in.); diameter 5.7 cm (2¼ in.)

Anatolia

karum Kanesh II, ca. 1950–1836 B.C.

Staatliche Museen zu Berlin,

Antikensammlung VI 5930

This antelope[1] with a pouring spout on its back is the earliest of a group of zoomorphic vessels and dates to Kanesh II. The polychrome geometric painting on the body—red and black on a cream ground—recalls third-millennium B.C. painted ceramics in Anatolia. The most common motifs in prehistoric Anatolia were wild animals shown with human figures, more often females. Over time, specific animals became associated with specific deities, thereby attaining the identification of an attribute. The antelope was associated with a goddess, perhaps Innara. Indeed,
the antelope often appears with a seated goddess surrounded by mountain goats, lions, sphinxes, birds, and supernatural creatures, a context typical of the Mistress of Animals theme found on seal impressions from Kanesh Level II. In Syria, on the other hand, the antelope was associated with Reshef, the god of death and war,[2] as seen in a lead figurine at Umm el-Marra. Stone molds and three-dimensional lead figurines of deities with their individual attributes were ubiquitous throughout Anatolia.[3]

Animal vessels with pouring spouts are in evidence as early as the sixth millennium B.C. at Hacılar, but they became the preferred type during the Hittite Empire. Kanesh provided an entire menagerie of animal-shaped pouring vessels; the antelope, however, is quite rare. The bridle painted across the muzzle and circling the head of this vessel suggests the antelope's strength. Such harnessed animals were often depicted in Old Hittite imagery as decoys during the royal hunt. The texts suggest that images of specific animals may carry metaphorical meaning signifying glory, power, fertility, fecundity of the land, and royalty. Indeed, images of the royal hunt often culminate in celebratory scenes of libations before the slain animals, emblematic of the ruler's vision of a

41

42

world suffused with sacred power. The motif of the harnessed animal decoy is also found on Hittite relief-decorated silver ceremonial vessels.

In the Hittite period, the preferred representation for ritual spouted zoomorphic vessels was a pair of bulls (see cat. no. 114). Found in public buildings and temple contexts during the early stages of the Hittite kingdom, twin-spouted bull figurines said to represent *hurri* and *sheri* (day and night) have been excavated at Hattusa (Boğazköy) and other Hittite sites.[4] The sacred animals are often depicted pulling the chariot of the storm god, Teshshup.

KAY

1. The stylized representation makes a definitive identification difficult to ascertain.
2. Matthiae 2007.
3. Tefnin 1990; Emre 1971.
4. Bittel 1976b; İnandıktepe, Kuşaklı/Sarissa and Maşat; T. Özgüç 2002b.

43

43

SPOUTED VESSEL

Ceramic
Height 16 cm (6⅜ in.); width 27.5 cm (10⅞ in.)
Kültepe
karum Kanesh II, 1950–1836 B.C.
Ankara Museum of Anatolian Civilizations,
Turkey 15012

This highly burnished vessel from Kültepe features an oval body set on a small ring base, a long, pointed spout, and an arched handle. Perched atop the handle is a miniature eagle with bulging eyes and sharply pointed beak; its heavy talons clutch the handle and its head faces in the same direction as the spout. The eagle's intent gaze, echoed in the exaggerated profile of the vessel's spout, lends a sense of vitality to the object. Eagles were sacred to the Hittites and appear frequently in both single- and double-headed forms on clay sealings from the site of Karahöyük.[1] Later Hittite texts describe a Protective Deity of the Countryside, who holds an eagle in his fist.[2]

This object is classified as a "teapot," which is defined as a round-bodied vessel with handle and spout set across from each other. Although teapots have been excavated at many Anatolian sites, this particular form is most commonly found at Kanesh, where the present example was discovered.[3] Its closest parallel, found at the same site in an archive of *karum* Level II, is a vessel comprising two spouted pitchers joined by a horizontal bar across the handles on which an eagle perches. This double vessel displays the same form and technique of manufacture seen in the single-bodied piece, and both were most likely produced in workshops within *karum* Kanesh.[4] Given their highly decorative, rather impractical form, vessels of this type likely served a ceremonial function. Although a number of Hittite pots incorporate animal forms into their spouts, handles, or decoration, vessels with perching eagles are unique to this site.[5]

SG

1. Alp 1968, pp. 177–82. Later Hittite texts describe statues of gods holding "eagles," perhaps drinking cups in the shape of eagles, crafted of gold, silver, iron, ivory, or lead plate; Rost 1961–63, pp. 179, 184, 193, cited in T. Özgüç 2003, p. 205.
2. Canby 2002, pp. 161, 168. I thank Gary Beckman for this reference.
3. T. Özgüç 1986b, p. 60, pl. 107:2.
4. Ibid., p. 60.
5. T. Özgüç 2003, p. 179; T. Özgüç 1986b, p. 58.

44

FEMALE FIGURE

Ivory
Height 9.4 cm (3¾ in.)
Kültepe
karum Kanesh Ib, ca. 1800–1700 B.C.
Ankara Museum of Anatolian Civilizations,
Turkey 11966

One of the earliest and most significant works of ivory sculpture from central Anatolia is the diminutive statuette of a nude female, discovered in a Level Ib pithos grave under the floor of a room with stelae in the merchant settlement (*karum*) at Kültepe.[1] The ivory material conveys the quality of a youthful body, nude except for a broad turban on the head, with arms drawn in and hands cupping the small breasts.[2] The figure's generous lower body has ample hips, with the navel indicated and an emphasized pubic triangle defined by deep incisions inlaid with silver, now blackened. Fingers and toes are well differentiated. In frontal view, the goddess appears to be standing with her stocky legs on a platform; actually, however, she is seated on a stool, which is evident in profile view. The full, rounded face exhibits large, exaggerated features. The almond-shaped eyes—below incised brows—were originally inlaid with stone pupils much like those of the sphinxes on the ivories attributed to Acemhöyük (cat. no. 46a, b). In typically Anatolian

style, the long nose, flattened at the bridge, curves downward, extending to a broad mouth with lips curved upward. The ears protrude from the distinctive circular head covering, flat at the back and in the front framing the face with two deeply incised lines. The hair is parted in the middle, and strands are lightly incised on the forehead.

Describing this sculpture, Tahsin and Nimet Özgüç have drawn attention not only to contemporary works, such as the ivories in the Metropolitan Museum, but to images of enthroned goddesses from such sites as Alaca Höyük, Çiftlik, and Eskiyapar.[3] These comparisons reinforce the view that the essential characteristics of Hittite artistic style were already formed during the latter phases of the Old Assyrian Trading Colony period. They also suggest that this divinity may be

44, front

44, back

associated with the principal fertility goddess Kubaba.[4]

The figure was fashioned at a time that frontal nude female divinities were depicted in both foreign and local styles in *karum* Kanesh at Kültepe, carved on Old Babylonian- and Old Syrian-style cylinder seals impressed on the envelopes of merchant documents.[5] Glazed faience figurines from burials at the site display Anatolian facial characteristics and similar headdresses, hairstyles, and body forms.[6] They derive from a long tradition in Anatolia of representing nude females with exaggerated hips and with hands cupping their breasts, as expressed on images dating from the late third to the early second millennium B.C. Notable within this tradition are statuettes from Alaca Höyük and Hasanoğlan, as well as lead figurines and stone molds from Titriş Höyük, Troy, and Kültepe itself.[7]   JA

1. T. Özgüç and N. Özgüç 1959, pp. 107–8, pl. XXXIV:2.
2. See Barnett 1982, p. 32, on the artistic intent in using ivory.
3. T. Özgüç 2003, p. 236; Bittel 1976b, p. 161, fig. 172, dated to the 14th–13th centuries B.C.
4. T. Özgüç 2003, p. 236.
5. N. Özgüç 1968, pp. 52, 54, pls. XII, XIII.
6. T. Özgüç 2003, p. 236, figs. 243, 244; T. Özgüç 1986c.
7. Muscarella in *Art of the First Cities* 2003, p. 279, no. 181; Aruz in ibid., p. 256, fig. 75, p. 257, fig. 163b, pp. 256–58, no. 163c; and also Demange in ibid., p. 258, no. 164, colorpl. on p. 259; Emre 1971, pls. I:1, 3; II:1–5; III:1–3, IV:1, V:1, 3; , VII:3.

45

WINGED GODDESS

Bronze
Height 6 cm (2⅜ in.); width 2.7 cm (1⅛ in.)
Karahöyük
Middle Bronze Age, 18th century B.C.
Konya Museum, Konya, Turkey 1971.26.374

This lead alloy figurine of a winged goddess provides insight into the influence of religious imagery imported into Anatolia during the early second millennium B.C. and the role that deities played in the domestic life of the region. Numerous one-sided lead figurines and the open-faced stone molds used to cast them have been found in ancient Anatolian houses or related debris pits. These diminutive

castings, which were made up to the end of the Old Assyrian Trading Colony period, may have served an apotropaic function for the individuals or households that acquired them.[1] It is likely that lead was used for these mass-produced objects due to its ease of casting at relatively low temperatures and to its softness, which facilitated subsequent working.

This figurine was found in a pit near the citadel of the ancient town at Karahöyük, in a level that also contained a lead figurine of an addorsed lion and sphinx, a stone mold, and numerous seals and sealings (for a relief vessel from the site, see cat. no. 81).[2] Karahöyük, near modern-day Konya, was located within the network of trade routes that passed through the Taurus Mountains, connecting central Anatolia with northern Syria. The associated glyptic finds suggest that this figurine was produced toward the end of the first quarter of the eighteenth century B.C., during the same period represented by Level Ib of *karum* Kanesh, the larger trading center located approximately 230 kilometers to the northeast.

Although the identity of this carefully modeled deity is not known, she is typologically related to the "winged Ishtar" form known from contemporary cylinder seal imagery; her close association with generative forces is indicated by the enlarged pubic triangle revealed by her raised arms. This figure also exhibits striking similarities to the ivory statuette excavated at Kanesh (cat. no. 44).[3] Other features, including her large, Hathor-style curls and the partially preserved projection at the top of her horned headdress—which may represent a celestial body—suggest a synthesis of Egyptian, Mesopotamian, and indigenous traits.[4]   J-FL

1. For the most comprehensive study of these figurines and their molds, see Emre 1971.
2. See Alp 1961–62, p. 220, n. 7, and Alp 1968, p. 15.
3. Site report in "Karahöyük kazısı," 1962, p. 621. For a discussion of winged goddess iconography, see Barrelet 1955.
4. A similar combination of iconographic traditions in the depiction of Levantine goddesses is fully discussed in Cornelius 2004.

45

Central Anatolian Ivories

With only indirect access to the sea, Central Anatolia can seem quite remote from the interaction among coastal areas of the eastern Mediterranean and the pervasive impact of Egypt throughout this region. Yet, it was the center of a vast trading network that brought rare materials to the west through the Mesopotamian city of Ashur (see pp. 70–73). By the nineteenth and eighteenth centuries B.C., central Anatolia also attracted traders from the Levant and, indirectly, from as far away as the Aegean, seeking access to these resources.[1] In such an environment, the discovery of a Middle Kingdom plaque at Alaca Höyük (cat. no. 87) and the imagery on the Pratt ivories in the Metropolitan Museum, attributed to Acemhöyük while featuring stylistic allusions to Egypt, do not come as a complete surprise.[2] Indeed, among the remains of luxurious furnishings discovered in the ruins of the Sarikaya Palace at the latter site were a piece of textile, possibly linen, with dark- and light-blue faience beads sewn with gold thread in a geometric pattern, and the remains of an Egyptian-type game board made of Egyptian Blue and pierced with holes lined in gold (see cat. no. 93).[3]

Most of the Museum's ivories collected here were carved in a local style, combining features that prefigure those of later Hittite art (see fig. 53) with a rich pictorial repertoire derived ultimately from the Nile Valley.[4] They comprise small inlay panels with low relief or incised decoration; figures in the round or in high relief, many of them with attachment holes; and furniture legs in the shape of sphinx and lion's legs, the latter a standard Egyptian form. Although an uncut elephant tusk and precut pieces were found at Acemhöyük,[5] the main corpus of ivories was fashioned out of hippopotamus incisors and lower canines (see cat. no. 198a, b).[6] Some were further embellished with gold leaf and inlays placed in the eye sockets.

Questions relating to the original appearance and function of these ivories have aroused intense interest. The red and light pink coloration visible on some examples call to mind ancient textual references to stained ivories.[7] Whether gold was applied all over the surface or only on specific details, such as the hair curls of sphinxes (cat. no. 46a) and the belt of a small kneeling figure (cat. no. 51), is unclear. The clean edges that define these details suggest partial rather than overall gilding, but other instances in which traces of gold appear randomly on the surface may contradict this view.[8] In addition, plaques that vary in size but not iconography may represent multiple pairs of elements that adorned more than one piece of furniture.

Perhaps the most vexing question concerns the identification of the school of ivory carvers responsible for this central Anatolian phenomenon. The most prominent images on these works are interpretations of Egyptian divine creatures with feline aspects, such as the sphinx, the griffin, and the human with a lion head. They were probably produced about the same time that Syrian-style seals with griffins and heraldically positioned female sphinxes were impressed on the envelopes of documents from the site of Kültepe.[9] Other depictions, such as an impressive relief carving of a falcon with wings outstretched (cat. no. 49), as well as small incised plaques representing geese in a marshy setting and a monkey holding a vessel (cat. no. 54), are also evocative of Egyptian art and suggest possible input from Syria, where Egyptian imports and imagery are more expected. This suggestion may be reinforced by the decoration on an extraordinary ivory box excavated at Acemhöyük. The box was made in one piece from an elephant tusk and encrusted with copper, iron, gold, and lapis lazuli studs.[10] Some of the images carved on this receptacle—sphinxes with Hathor curls, a crouching monkey, and the lion-legged throne for a ruler or deity—recall those on the ivory furniture elements (fig. 28). Their overall flat rendering against an obliquely striated ground and their arrangement in registers further suggest similarities with both Anatolian and Syrian glyptic. Whether they were produced in a center such as Carchemish or—as suggested by unfinished pieces—are perhaps the work of northern Syrian craftsmen or local apprentices at the Anatolian court, the ivories represent an early instance of the melding of traditions.[11] This synthesis not only laid the foundations for later Hittite art but also set the stage for an emphasis on ivory—used to fashion containers for precious materials and elegant furniture—as the premier medium in the creation of international styles of great variation during the Late Bronze and early Iron Ages, explored in subsequent essays in this volume.   JA

1. Kupper 1966, pp. 12–13; Dossin 1970, pp. 97, 101ff.; Malamat 1970, p. 168; Malamat 1971, esp. p. 38.
2. For the history of the Pratt ivories, given to the Metropolitan Museum in the 1930s, and their eventual attribution to Acemhöyük, which was subsequently excavated beginning in 1962, see Harper 1969, pp. 156–57, and N. Özgüç 1966, pp. 43–44.
3. N. Özgüç 1966, pp. 46–47; the textile recalls Egyptian beaded-linen garments with linen rather than gold thread: Rigault 1999, p. 306, no. 94.
4. Canby (1989, p. 112) points to the stylistic relationship between the ivories attributed to Acemhöyük and later Hittite sculptures.
5. Bourgeois 1992, p. 62 (identified as Elephas Maximus); precut pieces suggest ivory working at the site.
6. For the use of hippopotamus ivory, see Caubet and Poplin 1987, pp. 278ff.
7. EA 11 and EA 14, Moran 1992, pp. 21, 34; Güterbock 1971, pp. 2, 5: ivories are "white" and "red"; Bourgeois 1992, p. 64.
8. For Hittite texts referring to gilding, see Güterbock 1971, 3:5, 4:7.
9. N. Özgüç 1969: griffins: pls. VIIIA, XXII:1a, XXIIIB (with head curl), XXC (with horns); sphinxes: pl. XVD.
10. N. Özgüç 1976.
11. Ibid., p. 559; Mellink 1993, p. 426; Güterbock (1971, p. 3), writing about ivory in Hittite texts, lists images or figurines fashioned of the material, including a lion and an eagle.

46a, b

Furniture Support and Plaque

Anatolia
Middle Bronze Age, 18th century B.C.

a. Support: Ivory (hippopotamus), gold leaf
Height 12.5 cm (5 in.); width 9.9 cm (4 in.)
Middle Bronze Age, 18th century B.C.
The Metropolitan Museum of Art, New York,
Gift of George D. Pratt, 1932 32.161.47

b. Plaque: Ivory (hippopotamus)
Height 7.3 cm (2⅞ in.); width 5.7 cm (2¼ in.)
The Metropolitan Museum of Art, New York,
Gift of Mrs. George D. Pratt, in memory of
George D. Pratt, 1936 36.70.11

Among the most recognizable pieces in the collection of central Anatolian ivories attributed to Acemhöyük are four small furniture legs.[1] The legs were fashioned out of sections of hippopotamus incisors (see cat. no. 198a, b) into compact seated sphinxes without wings. They appear to have formed the (rather fragile) supports for a small piece of furniture that would not have held much weight.[2] Mortises were drilled into the tops of the heads and then squared out with chisels, after which holes were drilled across the mortises for the insertion of pins to secure tenons. All of the bases are solid and flat, with the exception of one leg in which the original pulp cavity has been preserved. Some idea of the original relative positioning of the legs can be inferred by aspects of their manufacture and condition: on one side of each head the curls are either omitted or simply blocked out, suggesting that this side may not have been visible. In addition, the legs can be paired based on the position of the tenon pins—either front to back or side to side—and on their surface coloration (fig. 30).

The compelling faces of these female sphinxes are the earliest known expressions of an artistic style that came to fruition during the Hittite Empire period, as exemplified by the monumental gateway sculptures at Alaca Höyük.[3] They feature large incised almond-shaped eyes and inlaid round pupils, long sharp noses, upturned mouths, and raised cheeks. Their foreheads display narrow fillets beneath full wigs, with central protrusions that suggest the *uraeus* of Egyptian royal headdresses. The wigs terminate in a number

46a

of curving locks with spiral curls, two of them behind the oversize ears, framing the faces as on images of Hathor.[4] Upper bands, which may indicate headdresses, as well as the hair, fillets, and eyes, retain traces of gold leaf, in some areas with a clean edge but in others extending beyond the hairline. An inlay for the pupil of the eye was preserved on only one sphinx. Another

survives in a pupil hole carved into a gray-colored ivory plaque that represents the upper body of a female sphinx in profile (cat. no. 46b). The sphinx plaque—one of two in the Metropolitan Museum—shows the same facial and body characteristics as the images in the round, but it has a more elaborate hairstyle, with three short curls added above the fillet binding the hair.[5]

46b

of kneeling heroes with similar curls and Mesopotamian-type divine horned crowns.[9]

Various opinions have been offered regarding the origin of (winged) sphinxes with Hathor curls in the arts of central Anatolia during the Middle Bronze Age.[10] Contemporary Syrian-style cylinder seals, replete with Egyptian imagery, may provide the immediate source for the introduction of Nilotic elements into depictions of fantastic creatures on the Anatolian plateau.[11] The rendering of an incised griffin (cat. no. 76) and images on an ivory box from Acemhöyük (fig. 28) further point to Syrian input.[12]

Male and female sphinxes in Anatolian-style glyptic appear to have specific links to local divinities.[13] It is possible, however, that the original association of sphinxes having Hathor attributes with the Egyptian royal female added a further dimension to their meaning.[14] If so, this choice of imagery for luxury furnishings in a central Anatolian palatial setting would be most appropriate.

JA/J–FL

Some scholars have noted resemblances with later depictions of Aegeans in Egyptian tomb paintings, although connecting links are hard to establish.[6]

The bodies of the sphinxes are leonine in form. Their limbs are clearly defined in an abstract style rendered in flat relief and incision to differentiate the massive seated haunches from the upright forelegs, with the large paws and dewclaws indicated. Their tails run vertically up the back, fanning into a lozenge shape at the tip (see fig. 30).

With their aprons, crowns, Hathor-like locks, and smooth faces, these creatures represent a variation on two of the earliest renderings of an Egyptian sphinx found in Anatolia, one with the head of a bearded man and a feline body and long tail, another beardless and wearing a skullcap. The bearded male sphinx continued to be prominent in the art of the trading towns on the central plateau (see cat. no. 81); by the Kültepe Ib period these sphinxes were adorned with curling locks evoking the Hathor wig and may display wings.[7] On one bulla in the Acemhöyük corpus, two addorsed striding male sphinxes serve as supports for the throne of a goddess.[8] Female sphinxes with curling locks emerging from skullcaps also appear in the local-style glyptic from the burned ruins of the Sarikaya Palace at Acemhöyük, where they are represented under the feet

1. For an ivory lion excavated at Acemhöyük, similar in form, see N. Özgüç 1966, pp. 43–44, pl. XIX.
2. Small objects, such as game boards (see cat. no. 92), also had animal legs.
3. Canby 1989, p. 112, who suggests an early date for the Sphinx Gate at Alaca Höyük; Mellink 1969, p. 285.
4. For a Middle Kingdom example of a woman wearing a Hathor wig, see Bourriau in *Pharaohs and Mortals* 1988, p. 49, no. 37; the multiple curls are not Egyptian.
5. For discussion of the other plaque, whose surface is extensively damaged, see Canby 1975, p. 237, fig. 10 (MMA 36.152.2).
6. Barnett 1982, p. 33.
7. N. Özgüç 1965, pls. XI: no. 31A, XXI: no. 63, XXIV: no. 71 (Kültepe II, *karum* phase); N. Özgüç 1991, pp. 296–301.
8. N. Özgüç 1991, p. 295, fig. 5; the sphinx is interpreted as the attribute of the goddess of mountain sheep.
9. N. Özgüç 1971, p. 25, fig. 4.
10. Canby 1975, pp. 234, 248, discusses the possibility of Anatolian sources for this imagery.
11. Teissier 1996, p. 148:203 and passim, for other Egyptianizing imagery.
12. N. Özgüç 1976.
13. N. Özgüç 1991, p. 298.
14. Teissier 1996, p. 194.

Figure 28. Ivory box, detail. Acemhöyük. Middle Bronze Age. Ankara Museum of Anatolian Civilizations, Turkey AC 0:24

Technical Notes on the Metropolitan Museum Ivories

The varied surface coloration of the Pratt ivories has elicited considerable interest since the objects' acquisition by the Metropolitan Museum.[1] The gray hue of the flat plaques (cat. nos. 46b, 48a, b) and one of the lion legs (cat. no. 47a) indicates exposure to considerable heat prior to burial. Both elephant- and hippopotamus-derived ivories contain oils and proteinaceous matter that assist in the maintenance and growth of the ivory in the living animal. Heating results in the combustion of these organic proteins until they are completely removed. During this process, the ivory becomes progressively darker, then lightens in color as the carbon becomes completely oxidized. In addition, the ivory shrinks slightly, with associated cracking and planar deformation. At the same time, the removal of organic matter may render the ivory less susceptible to subsequent biological attack.

Many of these ivories exhibit opaque black stains identified by X-ray fluorescence spectroscopy (XRF) as rich in manganese. Such deposits, which are often found on archaeological objects, result from microbial action on manganese in the surrounding soil and have been known to cause magenta-colored stains on other excavated ivories.[2] While deposits of manganese are scattered across the surfaces of the ivories, they are concentrated particularly in areas where gilding has been lost, perhaps due to the use of a comestible adhesive to attach the metal leaf. Those objects darkened by heating are relatively free of these deposits, perhaps due to a lower amount of protein surviving at or near the surface.

The red staining, which varies from the light pink on the kneeling human figure (cat. no. 51) to the rather intense color of one of the sphinx legs (cat. no. 46a), is a result of the presence of iron oxides.[3] Whether this staining was intentional or accidental, however, is difficult to determine conclusively. Close examination of the staining pattern on the surface of one of the sphinx legs in the area of the hair curls (below), which were originally gilded, indicates that the staining occurred after some of the leaf had been lost but was partially masked by the remaining gilding until parts of it too were removed. This pattern suggests that, if the staining was intentional, it was carried out after the gilding was applied and became solubilized during burial. Alternately, the staining may have been caused by conditions in the burial environment.

The two eye inlays (fig. 29) preserved in this group of ivories do not appear to have been added or repositioned since excavation. Both inlays consist of thin discs made of a slightly friable material with a darkened surface and light-colored core. Surface scans of these inlays using XRF indicate the presence of copper and silica. Although the identity of the material has yet to be confirmed, its appearance and composition suggest that it may be faience, colored green or blue by the copper. Objects made of faience, although rare, have been found in early second-millennium B.C. contexts in central Anatolia.[4]

J–FL

1. See Baer et al. 1971, pp. 1–8, and Baer, Jochsberger, and Indictor 1978, pp. 139–49.
2. For a thorough discussion of burial alterations and the associated staining of ivory, see Ecker 1989.
3. Unpublished analyses of fragments by R. J. Koestler, N. Indictor, and R. Harneman, using both environmental and conventional scanning electron microscopy, indicate that the red coloration is due to the presence of iron; there was no trace of the organic adhesive that may have been used to secure the gold leaf.
4. For an overview of contemporary faience finds in Anatolia, see Moorey 1994, pp. 176–77.

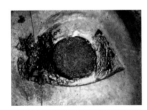

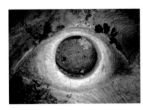

Figure 29: Details of eye inlays. Above: fig. 30, third from left. Below: cat. no. 46b.

46a. Detail showing red staining on surface.

Figure 30. Reconstructed positioning of ivory furniture supports as discussed in cat. no. 46a, b (far right).

47a, b

FURNITURE SUPPORTS

Ivory (hippopotamus)

a. Height:14.2 cm (5⅝ in.); width 5.9 cm (2⅜ in.)

b. Height 13.9 cm (5½ in.); width 7.6 cm (3 in.)

Anatolia

Middle Bronze Age, 18th century B.C.

The Metropolitan Museum of Art, New York,
Gift of Mrs. George D. Pratt, in memory of
George D. Pratt, 1936 36.70.7, 36.152.1

Perhaps the most visually compelling evidence for the Egyptian derivation of furniture elements in the corpus of ivories attributed to Acemhöyük are two furniture supports in the form of lion legs with broad flanks and curving outlines that taper downward to indicate the rear leg of the animal.[1] On one piece, now stained pink with some darker reddish areas, the animal's ankle is articulated, the upper part of the leg is well modeled, and the massive paw displays extended claws in the form of inverted triangles, with one hooked claw projecting to the side. The second completely preserved rear leg, gray-blue in color, is less detailed but retains the menacing hooked claw. The legs sit on bases with horizontal grooves, the gray one retaining

remnants of an original gold-leaf overlay.

The legs were most likely carved out of hippopotamus incisors; the ends of the pulp cavities are preserved in the upper part of both legs. Dowel holes on the flanks allowed for attachment to an upper element. The positioning of mortises and dowel holes on the paws suggests that struts connected the legs to one or more small pieces of furniture; the pink-colored leg would have supported the front left side, and the grayish one was the rear leg on the right side.[2] There are also mortises cut into the bases for further attachment.

There can be no doubt regarding the origin of furniture legs of this type. One early and impressive example, carved on a famous Dynasty 4 statue of Khafre, already displays the characteristically Egyptian differentiation between front and back legs to reflect the natural appearance of the animal's limbs, as well as lion heads attached above the forelegs to protrude from the seat. These features persisted in Egypt, on chairs depicted in private tombs, for example, and on royal thrones, such as found in the tomb of Tutankhamun.[3]

By contrast, the ivory lion legs were positioned without concern for the anatomy of an actual lion. Lion legs were atypical for Anatolian furniture, where

bovine legs were more often depicted, although they do support the throne of the seated figure on the Acemhöyük ivory box (fig. 28), a work with Syrian features.[4]

JA

1. The Metropolitan Museum collection also includes a fragment of a third lion leg, reddish in color.
2. See Kuhlmann 1977, pl. II:4a, for a later Egyptian throne with similar supports.
3. Ibid., pl. II; Hayes 1953, p. 298, fig. 195; see also Killen 1980, p. 28.
4. N. Özgüç 1976, pl. III.

48a, b

LION-DEMON PLAQUES

Ivory (hippopotamus), gold leaf

a. Height 11.1 cm (4⅜ in.); width 5.1 cm (2 in.)

b. Height 9.9 cm (4 in.); width 4.8 cm (1⅞ in.)

Anatolia

Middle Bronze Age, 18th century B.C.

The Metropolitan Museum of Art, New York,
Gift of Mrs. George D. Pratt, in memory of
George D. Pratt, 1936 36.70.14, 15

Two of the most fascinating ivories in the Metropolitan Museum are the pair of kneeling human figures with lion heads, holding flowering stems. Both plaques, which have attachment holes at top and bottom, have been discolored by burning to a gray-blue color. Gilding is preserved not only in well-defined areas, such as the borders of the long open kilts (see also cat. no. 51), on the mane area, and in the whites of the eyes; it also appears, on the creature on the left, in the arm crease, and, on the creature on the right, on the chest, overlapping part of the bent arm, and between the plant stem. This may indicate that the entire plant surface was originally covered in gold leaf.

The style of these pieces—with squared-off heads and blocky bodies executed in flat relief—is consistent with a number of other ivories in the group (see cat. no. 46a). Their leonine features include large eyes drilled for circular inlays and mane areas stylized to resemble wigs rather than tufts of animal fur. With their closed mouths, indicated by diagonal grooves, the creatures do not appear menacing. They are each shown in nearly three-quarter view, one arm drawn across the chest with the outer part of the hand visible; the other arm is bent upward, with the

47a

47b

48a   48b

palm and clenched fist holding a flowering stem (see fig. 53 for another example of this hand position).[1] The clearly human torso shows no indication of gender. The lower body is depicted in a kneeling posture, one leg exposed and the other covered by the long kilt, from which emerges a well-formed foot.

There is little doubt that—despite the appearance of a variety of lion-human hybrid creatures in the local Anatolian glyptic[2]—the ultimate derivation of the imagery on these plaques lies in the Nile Valley, where already during the Old and Middle Kingdoms, lioness goddesses were depicted with wigs, sometimes similarly striated.[3] Certain other details, such as the droop of the chin below a closed mouth—typical in Egyptian portrayals of lion's heads—were also rendered by the

carver who produced the ivory plaques.

It is likely that this imagery was transmitted through Syria, the most probable source of the kneeling posture. Syrian-style cylinder seals include depictions of kneeling figures wearing wigs and kilts; one holds papyrus stems and flanks an Egyptianizing bird of prey with outspread wings. The image of a kneeling lion-headed nude hero also appears on such seals.[4] The closest glyptic parallel for the kneeling kilted lion-demon, however, comes from central Anatolia itself, excavated at the site of Alishar Höyük. Here, the creature appears, with wings, on a Syrian-style import and includes other images familiar on the ivories, including a seated (albeit winged) sphinx and a crouching monkey.[5] A very closely related seal in the collection of the Pierpont Morgan

Library shows a kneeling lion-demon, nude, placed in a hunting scene above a griffin and next to a double-headed bird of prey with extended talons.[6]   JA

1. Harper (1969, p. 159) draws parallels with this Hittite sculpture.
2. N. Özgüç 1991, pp. 295–96.
3. Borchardt 1907, p. 41, fig. 23, p. 94, fig. 72; Metropolitan Museum excavations: Pyramid Temple of Senwosret III, Dahshur (unpublished); Yoshimura, Kawai, and Kashiwagi 2005, pp. 393–94, pl. 55d. Their breasts are prominent, and their lower bodies are covered with long garments. Some are associated with papyrus stalks.
4. Teissier 1996, p. 16:174, p. 18:245, 265.
5. See N. Özgüç (1991, pp. 295, 313, pl. 2:3), who points also to a second example from Kültepe; for a kneeling lion-demon dominating animals on a stamp seal from Boğazköy, see Boehmer and Güterbock 1987, pl. V:47.
6. Porada 1948, pl. CXLI:936.

FALCON WITH PREY

Ivory (hippopotamus)
Falcon: height 11.2 cm (4½ in.); width
5.8 cm (2⅜ in.)
Left plaque: height 3.8 cm (1½ in.); width
6.4 cm (2½ in.)
Right plaque: height 4.8 cm (1⅞ in.); width
7.4 cm (2⅞ in.)
Anatolia
Middle Bronze Age, 18th century B.C.
The Metropolitan Museum of Art, New York,
Gift of Mrs. George D. Pratt, in memory of
George D. Pratt, 1936 36.70.6, 36.152.4,
36.70.4

50

LID WITH FALCONS

Painted ceramic
Diameter 11 cm (4⅜ in.)
Crete, Mallia, Quartier Mu
Middle Minoan II, 19–18th century B.C.
Archaeological Museum, Heraklion, Greece
18712

More than five separate plaques originally formed the composition of a falcon with outstretched wings, grasping antelopes in its extended talons. The central plaque, which forms the head and body of the bird, captures its distinctive character with a well-formed beak, stylized peregrine falcon cheek markings ending in a spiral curl (see also cat. no. 76), and large eyes with holes for inlaid pupils.[1] The falcon is represented frontally, and areas of the plaque are executed in high relief to express the swelling of the breast and the shape of the head. Traces of gilding extend beyond the whites of the eyes to the beak. The surface is unevenly (dis)colored with red on parts of the head and tail feathers, which are demarcated by deep incisions. There is one hole in the top of the head for attachment to another furniture element and two on the bottom, probably for attachment to the missing legs. Mortises at the sides of the breast held the tenons that extended from the large wings, which feature a row of primary feathers below a plain covert area; only one of the original wings survives in the Metropolitan Museum collection.[2]

Two small plaques depicting antelopes held by powerful talons must have belonged to such a creature. While there are two

50

holes at the bottom of each plaque, there are no visible means by which to attach them to the bird's body. The antelopes respond to the attack by turning their heads toward their backs, with curving necks and mouths open and forelegs collapsing. The larger of the two is light pink in color, with much black discoloration on the surface. The smaller is red and the surface has bubbled from burning. As only one of the plaques is in proper proportion to this falcon, they probably belonged to two different falcon compositions.

There can be no doubt that the rendering of the bird, with stylized markings

49

and wings recalling Nilotic depictions of the Horus falcon, is of foreign inspiration. Similar birds of prey, with outspread wings and exaggerated talons and wearing Egyptian crowns, are found on Syrian Middle Bronze Age glyptic.[3] This imagery appears to have traveled to the west at this time, evidenced by two such birds applied in relief to a ceramic lid found in the Protopalatial town complex of the site of Mallia on Crete (cat. no. 50). In their position and in the treatment of their heads and wing feathers, they provide close parallels for the Anatolian ivory composition while recalling much earlier stone discs from Saqqara in Egypt.[4]

The transformation of this animal from divine symbol to hunter on the furniture plaque, clasping prey in its talons, may derive from a Near Eastern tradition in which the lion-headed eagle, or Imdugud bird, is sometimes depicted with stags in its talons.[5] A bird of prey with long hair curls and outspread wings clutches its prey on an Anatolian-style stone stamp seal in the Metropolitan Museum.[6] It is a motif also perpetuated in Hittite relief sculpture, with the depiction of a double-headed bird of prey holding hares in its talons.[7]

Scans of the falcon's surface using X-ray fluorescence revealed traces of silver in the more intensely red areas of surface staining. Although the origin of this silver— either from a metal overlay that is no longer preserved or from the proximity of a silver object during burial—cannot be confirmed, its presence reinforces the precious nature of the object.[8]   JA

1. See Harper 1969, p. 162.
2. A fragment of a similar but smaller wing comes from the Sarikaya Palace at Acemhöyük: N. Özgüç 1966, pl. XX:2.
3. Teissier 1996, p. 16:143, 145, 146.
4. Poursat 1980, pp. 119–20, fig. 169; Poursat in *Crete–Egypt* 2000, p. 58, no. 34.
5. Barnett 1982, p. 33; Collon 1987, p. 185:889.
6. Hogarth 1922, pl. XXV, no. 33 (MMA 99.22.3).
7. Bittel 1976b, p. 190, fig. 215, from the Sphinx Gate at Alaca Höyük.
8. Technical notes were provided by Jean-François de Lapérouse.

51
KNEELING FIGURE

Ivory (hippopotamus), gold leaf
Height 6 cm (2⅜ in.); width 2.6 cm (1⅛ in.);
depth 2.9 cm (1⅛ in.)
Anatolia
Middle Bronze Age, 18th century B.C.
The Metropolitan Museum of Art, New York,
Gift of Mrs. George D. Pratt, in memory of
George D. Pratt, 1937 37.143.2

52
KNEELING FIGURE

Ivory (hippopotamus)
Height 3.9 cm (1⅝ in.); width 1.7 cm (¾ in.)
Alaca Höyük
Middle Bronze Age, 18th century B.C.
Ankara Museum of Anatolian Civilizations,
Ankara, Turkey 9737

Two small sculptures of kneeling figures, fashioned from hippopotamus ivory,[1] expand our picture of ivory carving on the central Anatolian plateau. One (cat. no. 51), in the Metropolitan Museum, which is missing its head, has been attributed to the site of Acemhöyük. The other (cat. no. 52) was discovered at Alaca Höyük; the excavation report dates it to the Middle Hittite period but provides no further information.[2] In this case the head is preserved, showing a young male with short bobbed hair or a wig that lacks surface detail. He has almond-shaped eyes with holes for the inlaid pupils, a flat nose, small lips, and a heart-shaped face.[3] The figure is nude to the waist, with a well-defined collarbone and rounded chest. The torso is otherwise obscured by the left arm, which crosses the body to hold the right shoulder. The right arm extends down and touches the knee, a gesture in Egyptian art that conveys respect and submission.[4] This sculpture may thus represent a supplicant rather than a foreign captive.[5]

The figure from Alaca Höyük wears a long kilt with elaborate raised-loop edging at the hem and a similar pattern in the waist area. A prominent knot suggests that the garment was belted, with a striated sash adorning the front. This contrasts with the figure in the Metropolitan Museum, who wears, just below the navel,

51

52

a simple but clearly defined (gilded) belt and a sash indicated by vertical lines. The feet of the two sculptures, seen in profile emerging from the kilt, are treated in a similar fashion. In the back view, however, only the Alaca Höyük piece differentiates the bottom of each foot. Both figures probably adorned wood furniture, as indicated by attachment holes, either at the top of the head for the Alaca Höyük figure, or in the flat base of the ivory attributed to Acemhöyük.　　　　　JA

1. Caubet 1991, p. 224.
2. Koşay and Akok 1966, p. 183:Al m 84, pl. 31.
3. Harper 1969, p. 161, figs. 10, 11, draws comparisons with a small head attributed to Acemhöyük.
4. R. Wilkinson 1994, pp. 194, 198, 208.
5. Mellink (1969, pp. 285–86, fig. 5) compares him to a Dynasty 12 wood figure, possibly of a Nubian captive from Thebes, victimized by a rampant lion: Hayes 1953, p. 225, fig. 141.

53

BULL-MAN

Ivory (hippopotamus)
Height 5.5 cm (2¼ in.); width 2.5 cm (1 in.)
Anatolia
Middle Bronze Age, 18th century B.C.
The Metropolitan Museum of Art, New York,
Gift of Mrs. George D. Pratt, in memory of
George D. Pratt, 1936　36.70.3

Among the plethora of Egyptianizing creatures on the Metropolitan Museum ivories is one exceptional little figure of a Near Eastern bull-man. He is executed in the round, with arms cut away from the body and the front surface finely modeled. As is typical for this divinity, a human head and a frontal nude torso join at the waist with the lower quarters of a bull shown in three-quarter view (the ridge of his tail is visible at left). The lower limbs have not survived. The bull-man's distinctive face, framed by Hathor curls, is stylistically related to those of sphinxes and humans from the same collection. His braceleted arms are drawn toward the chest, with fists clenched above a belt with rolled edges and a lappet (or tassel) that covers one thigh. The ivory is deep red in color, including the portion of the interior surface that was exposed when the legs were lost. This seems to indicate non-intentional staining. There are no traces of gilding. A hole at the top of the head allowed for attachment to another element.

Both its hairstyle and adornment set this figure apart from the more traditional Mesopotamian-type bearded bull-man with bovine horns and ears. The latter

53

already appears on the earliest local-style cylinder seals at the site of Kültepe and was a popular image on contemporary Acemhöyük stamp seal impressions, where the creature retained his traditional characteristics but took on a variety of new poses and functions.[1]　　　　　JA

1. N. Özgüç 1965, pp. 70–71; N. Özgüç 1991, pp. 308–9.

54

MONKEY

Ivory (hippopotamus)
Height 2.2 cm (⅞ in.); width 0.9 cm (⅜ in.)
Anatolia
Middle Bronze Age, 18th century B.C.
The Metropolitan Museum of Art, New York,
Gift of Mrs. George D. Pratt, in memory of
George D. Pratt, 1936　36.152.9

This small incised hippopotamus-ivory plaque attributed to Acemhöyük, along with a tiny amulet made from a piece of elephant tusk in the Metropolitan Museum, captures the characteristic cheek ridges and body form of the African guenon monkey.[1] The monkey on the plaque, shown squatting and holding a jar, is depicted with a spotted coat, a striated ridge of fur down the back, and a beaded necklace, details that parallel two images of squatting apes found in Egypt. The first is on a

late Old Kingdom vessel from the site of Balat, in the Dakhleh Oasis, and takes the form of a guenon holding a baby and wearing an actual necklace of alabaster beads. The second, a Middle Kingdom baboon from Abydos (in the Metropolitan Museum), holds a jar and also wears a beaded necklace, this one incised on its body along with a shell-shaped pendant.[2] There can be no doubt that the representation is a remarkable quotation of unexpected details from Egyptian originals—such as the wearing of jewelry.[3] In the Nile Valley, the monkey was not only a beloved pet—accompanying sailors on ships, perched on the backs of chairs, and, beginning in the Old Kingdom, shown meddling with offerings in private tombs—but it also appeared on scarabs and amulets as a symbol of fecundity and of magical sexual powers in the afterlife.[4]

The image of a seated animal holding a vessel resonated in the ancient Near Eastern world, with its long tradition of representing animals acting like humans.[5] On cylinder seal impressions on documents from Kültepe, rows of crouching monkeys are shown holding ewers, in association with a water god.[6]　　　　　JA

1. Harper 1969, p. 161, fig. 10.
2. Vallogia 1986, pp. 116–17, pl. LXIV, no. 1045, pl. LXXXI, no. 1046: Balat; Hayes 1953, p. 245, fig. 157: MMA 10.176.54.
3. Arnold (1995, no. 81) also mentions the wearing of bracelets and armlets.
4. Andrews 1994, pp. 66–67.
5. See Pittman in *Art of the First Cities* 2003, pp. 43–45.
6. N. Özgüç 1965, pl. XX:60.

54

55

VESSEL

Silver
Height 13.2 cm (5¼ in.); diameter
10.5 cm (4⅛ in.)
Karashamb, Great Kurgan
Middle Bronze Age, early 2nd
millennium B.C.
History Museum of Armenia, Yerevan,
Republic of Armenia 2867–1

56

VESSEL

Silver
Height 11.3 cm (4½ in.); diameter 9.8 cm
(3⅞ in.)
Trialeti, Kurgan V
Middle Bronze Age, early 2nd
millennium B.C.
Georgian National Museum, Tbilisi, Georgia
s9–63:348

These two silver goblets were excavated about fifty years apart—in 1937 and 1987—from rich burials in Karashamb and Trialeti in the southern Caucasus.[1] Similar in size and shape and made of single sheets of silver, they are decorated with raised figural imagery with chased and punched details arranged in horizontal registers that share several elements: the pointed rosettelike ornament on the lower body, a procession of two alternating animals, and a central scene of an important personage holding a goblet and seated on a stool with crossed struts; in front of the figure is a table with hooved feet approached from the other direction by an individual also holding a goblet. All figures wear footgear with upturned toes, and walking figures wear garments that seem to be tunics and trousers. While the human figures on both vessels have large eyes, a prominent nose, and a receding chin, those on the Karashamb goblet are hairless, while those on the Trialeti goblet have both hair and beards. The relief on the Trialeti goblet is flatter, and there are fewer figure types; overall, it presents a relatively static and quiet scene in contrast to the greater variety, movement, and violence on the Karashamb vessel. The goblet from Trialeti Kurgan V bears two registers of figural ornament, while the goblet

55

55, alternate view

91

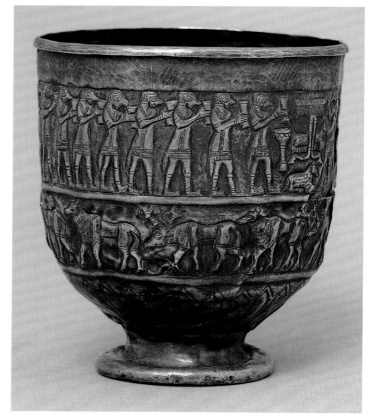

56

56, alternate view

from the Great Kurgan at Karashamb has five. Many of the images and compositions on these vessels are rare or completely absent in earlier periods in the southern Caucasus and uncommon during this period as well.[2]

From the time they were first published, connections between the imagery on the goblets and that seen on artistic production of the ancient Near East have been noted.[3] Among the parallels drawn by Kuftin was that to Cappadocian cylinder seals;[4] indeed, Anatolian local style seals of the Old Assyrian Trading Colony period found at Kültepe share many details with the imagery on the goblets, which may indicate that the origin of such Near Eastern motifs as the seated personage was Anatolia.[5]

There has been much discussion of the meaning of the scenes on these goblets.[6] Kuftin suggested a cult scene connected with a forest divinity on the Trialeti goblet,[7] while others have seen Indo-European

myth on both vessels.[8] The Karashamb goblet is interpreted as a reflection of political authority[9] or bearing images of earthly princes and mythical realms.[10] The variety of interpretations results from the appearance of new (and ancient Near Eastern) motifs in a cultural setting without written texts. Thus many approaches and points of view, including art-historical analysis, anthropological theory, archaeological typology, and national traditions, have been brought to bear.

The goblets are assigned to the Trialeti-Vanadzor (Kirovakan) culture, known almost exclusively from burial remains and thus dated primarily on the basis of internal typologies and external comparative materials to the early centuries of the second millennium B.C.[11] The location of most of the richest burials in areas of high pasture and the fact that settlements were few and mostly insubstantial suggest a primarily pastoral economy in the southern Caucasus and nearby

areas in this period.[12] Through the goblet imagery and other goods found in these burials, one can argue that the elites of this region were enriched by interaction with the Near East through exchange stimulated by or heightened through the Assyrian trade network.　　　KR

1. Kuftin 1941; Oganesian 1992a; Oganesian 1992b.
2. For a detailed discussion, see Rubinson 2006, pp. 254–61.
3. Kuftin 1941, pp. 86–88; Oganesian 1988; Oganesian 1992a; and see Rubinson 2003 for a review of previous research and literature.
4. Kuftin 1941, p. 88.
5. Rubinson 2003, pp. 140–41; Rubinson 2006, pp. 255–58.
6. Kushnareva 1997, pp. 111–12.
7. Kuftin 1941, p. 163.
8. Oganesian 1992a, pp. 93–98; Areshian 1988.
9. A. Smith 2001, p. 166.
10. Boehmer and Kossack 2000, pp. 18, 24.
11. Kuftin 1941; Gogadze 1972; Rubinson 1977; Kushnareva 1997, pp. 108–14; Avetisyan and Bobokhyan 2007, pp. 126–27.
12. Kushnareva 1997, pp. 208–9; Puturidze 2003.

57
NECKLACE BEADS

Gold, agate, carnelian
Length 36 cm (14¼ in.)
Trialeti, Kurgan VIII
Late 3rd–middle 2nd millennium B.C.
Georgian National Museum, Tbilisi, Georgia
s9–63:622–628

This spectacular group of gold and semiprecious stone beads exhibits an array of elements that were likely not produced together or originally strung together. They were found in Kurgan VIII at Trialeti in the southern Caucasus, a region that has yielded some extraordinary and sophisticated finds but has yet to be fully understood chronologically (see cat. nos. 55, 56).[1] Because the people of this area were primarily nomadic, few settlements with stratified finds have been discovered. Consequently, the chronology is based largely on stylistic comparisons of external material with the objects from the burial kurgans that are the hallmark of this culture. Furthermore, the kurgans are above-ground structures that have been entered repeatedly over time. The objects found within them thus may have been produced and deposited at different times, and dating them can be controversial. For example, this group of beads, and Kurgan VIII itself, has been assigned conflicting dates, spanning from the late third to the mid-second millennium B.C.[2]

In fact, on technical grounds it is most plausible that, considered individually, the beads indeed span the entire range of dates. In addition, they find parallels in several cultures (see pp. 101–3). They may have been manufactured locally with inspiration from various sources, collected from the sources themselves and deposited together at Trialeti, or a combination of both. Most interesting is the central element of agate, which is likely an heirloom from third-millennium B.C. southern Mesopotamia.[3] It was reused here in a setting with garnet and granulation that is similar in style and technique to a medallion from Byblos that dates from the first half of the second millennium B.C.[4] When the element was taken apart for conservation, it was discovered that the agate stone had been broken in half and covered by the design of the later setting. Amazingly, this one bead alone combines elements that date from the late third to the middle of the second millennium B.C. and demonstrates influences from Byblos to southern Mesopotamia.

The presence of such a diverse group of beads in the elite burial assemblages of the Trialeti kurgans is an indication not only that the people buried there used objects and employed styles from a range of times and places but also that they considered them highly prized possessions.   KB

1. There is a large body of literature on the chronology of the region, much of it published only in Russian or in Georgian. For a comprehensive review of the chronological issues in English, see Rubinson 1977.
2. Maxwell-Hyslop 1971, pp. 74–75; Lilyquist 1993, p. 41; Puturidze 2005, pp. 16–19.
3. Maxwell-Hyslop 1971, p. 26, fig. 19a, p. 65, pl. 45.
4. Ibid., pl. 69; Lilyquist 1993, p. 38, fig. 11.

TEXTS, TRADE, AND TRAVELERS

JACK M. SASSON

Zimri-Lim had been on the throne of Mari for less than ten years, weathering tribal insurrections and attacks from neighboring powers, when he made his famous trip to the Mediterranean (fig. 31). He could not refuse a summons from his embattled father-in-law, Yarim-Lim, who ruled from Aleppo in a large kingdom in Syria called Yamhad. Zimri-Lim (ca. 1775–1760 B.C.) assembled more than four thousand men and sealed in coffers a goodly portion of his movable wealth, including precious gifts and tin ingots. Together with an enormous retinue that included soldiers, officers, wives, concubines, administrators, artisans, and servants, the king set forth on a journey that covered hundreds of kilometers and lasted about six months. Zimri-Lim was not the only ruler of this era to embark on such an expedition; the legendary Gilgamesh had sought to make his name in the Cedar Forest and the troops of Zimri-Lim's predecessor, his father Yahdun-Lim, had waded in the Mediterranean. But the voyage of Zimri-Lim is exceptional, not least because its itinerary is charted by administrative documents, to which we shall return.

PEOPLE

By the end of the third millennium B.C., much of western Asia had fallen into increased political fragmentation, perhaps as a result of climatic changes and environmental degradation. A major shift in the power structure had occurred: from the flanks of the Zagros Mountains westward to the Mediterranean, the landscape was dotted with city-states, each with a relatively small area of influence. Dynasties rose and collapsed and territories swelled and eroded faster than the hopes and fears of their leaders. We recognize the existence of many ethnic groups in this area—Elamites in the Iranian plateau, Hurrians in northeastern Mesopotamia (which likely also included related peoples such as the Turukkus and the Lullus), Indo-Europeans (among them the Hittites and the Luwians of Anatolia), and Kassites, the future rulers of Babylon—but the major stock was Semitic, with remnants of Akkadians in the Babylonian south, and Assyrians, best known for their merchant colonies in central Anatolia. Arameans may have made an early appearance as Sutu nomads and later as Ahlamus.

Our sources, however, tell us most about the Amorites. We apply this ethnic term to several different tribal groups. Some regarded themselves as heirs to the third-millennium B.C. Sumerian and Akkadian dynasties. (One Amorite king of Mari, Yasmah-Addu, is scolded for speaking only Akkadian!) Others, such as the Numha and the Yamutbal, were pastoralists who gathered about the walls of fortified areas. The largest groups belonged to the Yaminite (southern) and Sim'alite (northern) coalitions, and these in turn embraced subtribes and clans, each with ambitions to overtake neighboring cities. What they did have in common, however, was a language: Amorite, the "Western" branch of Semitic. Amorites spoke their language in a variety of dialects, but strangely hardly used it when writing letters on cuneiform tablets. (We know the language mostly from names, nouns, and occasionally verbs.) They also had an extended kinship organization that they adapted to political life, with kings and vassals referring to each other as "fathers, sons, and brothers," exchanging gifts that included garments and beloved daughters, and orchestrating symbolic arrangements at ceremonial tables.

TRADE AND EXCHANGE

In this period of obligatory gift-giving, regulated by strict etiquette as well as by commercial value,[1] we have more details about what was exchanged than what was traded, the difference being that the former included objects and materials swapped between rulers. Merchants would supply materials from one region where there was a surplus to another where there was a shortage. Among the goods and products they bought and sold were people (slaves), livestock, grain, oils, wine, and honey. Raw materials—wool, leather, wood, reed, stones, metals—were purchased and processed locally or acquired as basic stock (mostly textiles and pottery). We learn from the Mari archives that merchants also played a crucial role in restoring harmony after wars, moving freely across frontiers to ransom prisoners and then returning them to their homes for profit.

Detail of cat. no. 65

Musicians came to Mari from Qatna, Aleppo, and Carchemish; but traffic in talent moved also in the opposite direction. We know, for example, that Mari sent singers to Aleppo. Women from the courts of defeated enemies were sent to Mari maestros who trained them to chant, sing, dance, and play instruments.[2] Male musicians often attempted to escape their employment for more favorable situations.[3] It may have been to prevent them from escaping that young men were sometimes blinded before being handed over for instruction.[4]

The traffic in professional artists and artisans was not limited to musicians; indeed, any specialist was a candidate—physicians, translators, incantation specialists, gymnasts, seamstresses, and all manner of kitchen workers. There is a whole category of individuals whose expertise was needed to sharpen the solemnity of religious ceremonies and perform at festivals. Not far from Mari, at Der, an annual ritual to honor Ishtar was held before the king, with priests and choristers chanting dirges and laments. The program included a precisely choreographed performance of fire and sword swallowers, jugglers, wrestlers, acrobats, and masqueraders. These performers may have been local, but we can also imagine that they made the circuit from one fixed festival to another. Their services were rewarded with gifts of jewelry, garments, and meat.[5]

In the Mari archives, we read also about the movement of smiths, weavers, masons, dressers of menhirs, jewelers, scribes (especially those with a knowledge of Sumerian), barbers, animal fatteners, and vintners. But most frequently recorded is the transfer of diviners and physicians, no doubt because the age was troubled by warfare and the epidemics that ensued. We know many such professionals by name and can even follow their careers as they shuttled from one trouble spot to another. Diviners would decipher the will of heaven by examining the innards of a sheep, and no army would set forth without a diviner in tow—and presumably also a flock of sheep. We read about diviners dispatched by allied rulers meeting far from home to collate auguries. Physicians attended the sick, and the best among them would travel long distances to collect a particularly efficacious herb. Not surprisingly, we occasionally find diviners and physicians working in tandem:

My lord should give strict orders to make Meranum, the physician, reach me by boat so that he can join me quickly. My lord should also send along with him (the diviner) Ishkhi-Addu. As Ishkhi-Addu takes the omens, Meranum will dress wounds. My lords must give strict orders so that these men will get here quickly by boat or by chariot.[6]

Elsewhere, we read of the same physician, Meranum, being fetched to attend to an elderly chief musician, who was suffering from debilitating anxiety.[7]

Some physicians earned prestige because they practiced abroad. A provincial governor requests that a physician from Mardaman (in Hurrian territory) clear an obstinate abscess

behind the ear,[8] and a letter from Zimri-Lim's personal valet indicates that such a reputation was well earned:

My lord had written me about the [herbal] drug for an inflamed blister by a Mardaman physician attached to the administrative bureau. I have placed under seal the drug that has come to me from the mountain regions, and I have sent to my lord with Lagamal-abum these physicians and their drugs. Now my lord has already tried the drug against an inflamed blister by the physician attached to the administrative bureau. I myself have tried the drug for an inflamed blister by the Mardaman physician, and it was effective. Together with Hammi-shagish, I have tried it several times, and it was effective. Abuma-nasi drank it, and it was effective.[9]

Exchanges among the elite included ceremonial weapons and finished products such as garments, shoes and belts, jewelry, and furniture. There was also traffic in the unusual (glass), the artistic (vessels shaped as animals, real or imagined), and the distinctive (models of Cretan ships). Much in demand were seasonals (desert truffles) and exotic animals (wild cats, bears, elephant hides, ostriches and their eggs). Anything that entered or left the palace as a gift was duly registered, for example: "3 oxen, 12 sheep, stored and sealed in 2 containers and 15 reed baskets; to remove from a depot at the Terqa palace, for taking to Mari. Assigned to Palusu-lirik; at the loft of the 'Meat-storeroom.'"[10]

Occasionally, a surplus of precious goods would lead a king to sell rather than hoard them for future disposal. To do so, diplomats were commissioned to secure the best price during their journeys, and they eagerly tried to gain favor with their lord, as this letter to Zimri-Lim makes clear:

About the rock-crystal that my lord conveyed to me and the price he set for it, writing "Regarding the price for this rock-crystal: it could be higher than what I am setting it for you, but not less." This is what my lord wrote me. However, on the price of the rock-crystal that my lord has set for me, what if people lower it by 10 or 20 shekels, what would my decision be? My lord has sent me this letter as if I had not been part of the palace! In fact, I had said, "I need to sell the rock-crystal that my lord sent me at a higher price than what he had set for me; I should fetch 10 to 20 shekels more!"

Now then, according to my lord's instruction, I will sell this rock-crystal and I shall use as much money as my lord had assigned me to purchase either tin or lapis-lazuli, depending on what I find available. It is possible that rock-crystal is abundant or scarce in this land; but who can tell? Regarding what my lord has instructed, I will not be negligent.[11]

Kings sent statues of themselves to distant gods and thrones to newly installed vassals, a gift symbolic of their authority. Earlier in the second millennium B.C., horses of specific regions (Qatna and Carchemish) or of specific colors (white) were highly sought. Their care received the highest attention, with

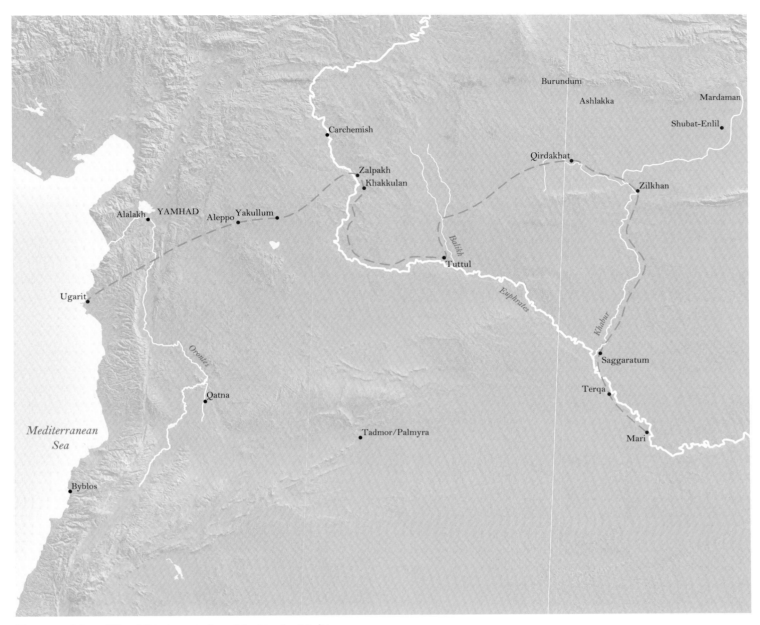

Figure 31. Map of Zimri-Lim's route from Mari to the Mediterranean.

one letter from Zimri-Lim urging that Qatna horses be kept in the largest space *within* the palace—one decorated with wall paintings, no less—where they could avoid direct sunlight.[12] In another letter the king of Qatna complains bitterly to his peer in Ekallatum about lack of reciprocity:

This matter is not for discussion; yet I must say it now and vent my feelings. You are the great king. When you placed a request with me for 2 horses, I indeed had them conveyed to you. But you, you sent me [only] 20 pounds of tin. Without doubt, when you sent this paltry amount of tin, you were not seeking to be honorable with me. Had you planned sending nothing at all—by the god of my father!—would I be angry?

Among us in Qatna, the value of such horses is 600 shekels [that is, 10 pounds] of silver. But you sent me just 20 pounds of tin! What would anyone hearing this say? He could not

deem us equal! This house is your house. What is lacking in your house that a brother cannot fulfill the need of his equal? If you do not plan to send me any tin, I should not have been in the least upset over it. Are you not the great king? Why have you done this? This house is your house![13]

Travel

Travel during this period was extensive, on rivers, by sea, and across the land. The great rivers, the Tigris and especially the Euphrates, their tributaries, and the many canals cut from them teemed with boats, barges, and rafts shuttling merchants, soldiers, and diplomats up and down the Syro-Mesopotamian heartland. Some cities, such as Mari, profited from hefty imposts on river traffic. The king of Aleppo, in a letter in the Mari archives, recalls sending five hundred boats to control

Diniktum, across the Tigris toward Elam, an expedition beyond our easy fathom.

To the west the Mediterranean connected western Asia, Egypt, Anatolia, Cyprus (the source of much copper), and the Aegean. Although we do not know the vocabulary for sea travel until the Late Bronze Age, the presence of merchants and dragomans in such places as Ugarit assures us that this sea trade was already active.

To reach some cities, however, such as Aleppo in Syria or Kanesh in central Anatolia, and when hostilities prevented riverine connections, feet and hooves were necessary. To enter Qatna from the Mari region, caravans traveled along the Euphrates, veering sharply westward into the Syrian Desert, reaching Palmyra before heading to Nashala and Qatna. The journey took about twelve days and was made on donkeys, since camels had not yet been widely domesticated. This is the route that the armies of Shamshi-Adad (Samsi-Addu) likely took on their mission to the Beqa' Valley or when his troops went to fetch a Qatna bride for his son.

Overland routes were heavily used, with caravan stops along the way; the itineraries are occasionally preserved in letters. There were many reasons for setting forth, but essentially they fall into four categories:

1. *Commercial.* To eager consumers, merchants distributed materials from distant locales—lapis lazuli was imported from Afghanistan and copper from Sinai and Cyprus. Mesopotamia, a breadbasket, imported practically everything else. While most distributions were done by relay, many merchants themselves traveled far beyond their hometowns. In doing so, they were inviting targets for brigands who, not infrequently, were supported by local rulers. To give themselves clout, merchants often formed associations, selecting an "overseer" to represent their interests. They also benefited from protective agreements between rulers. The shielding of merchants from abusive hosts is described in an epic that featured the great Sargon of Akkad (ca. 2334–2279 B.C.), who allegedly drove his armies deep into Anatolia to punish their oppressors. The Mari tablets include frequent reports of harm that came to merchants in transit, occasionally initiated by rulers themselves.[14] But there is also the statement by a high officer about the freedom merchants enjoyed in crossing borders, both in peace and in war, gathering gossip along the way.[15]

Merchants paid all sorts of tolls (and likely also bribes) when traversing territory or navigating past major cities, and officials kept a sharp eye on smuggling, occasionally using the gods or their emblems to uncover illicit traffic in slaves. We can reconstruct the affairs of many individual merchants from tablets said to come from Dilbat, Larsa, Kish, Sippar, Ur, and other Babylonian towns. But our best example of long-distance trading comes to us from the Old Assyrian period (see pp. 70–73).

2. *Diplomatic.* Many activities kept the powers of western Asia tightly knit. Though largely administrative, the palace archives of Mari include hundreds of letters that flesh out a world in which movement to and from capitals by ambassadors and messengers was recorded with exceptional detail. Light is shed even on the private undertakings of rulers investing in foreign lands. Kings would maintain large estates in friendly territories, run by trusted officials and overflowing with the necessities of the good life. Hammurabi of Babylon settled one of his sons in such a unit near Mari, thus providing him with a useful diplomatic apprenticeship. These units also functioned as banks, with payments made upon handing over receipts. Kings are even known to have purchased entire towns in areas far from their homeland, likely hedging against politically troubled times. Late in his career, Zimri-Lim purchased towns near Alalakh, close to the Mediterranean coast. The traffic required to maintain such long-distance purchases was undoubtedly impressive.

There is ample testimony also about the art of diplomacy. Ambassadors were charged with smoothing out relations with—no less than spying on—allies, overlords, and vassals. Rarely did they travel without gifts. And when they reached their destination, they would collect for their sovereign the same, a form of recycled wealth. Their appearances at court were highly choreographed, with seating arrangements reflecting the status of their lords.

A fine example of a grand send-off comes from Shamshi-Adad, writing to his son in Mari:

> *The day after sending this letter of mine, the messengers from Dilmun (Bahrain) will leave Shubat-Enlil (Tell Leilan). Wealthy men at their arrival should hire 10 poor folks who can accompany them, so that with their wages they could support their people, therefore traveling happily. If you send off the wealthy [by themselves], they will simply abandon the caravan. You must simply not send the wealthy off. [To be sent]*
> *-30 rams, 30 liters of fine oil, 60 liters of linseed oil—poured into leather bottles, (plus) 3 liters of juniper seed, and boxwood (essence);*
> *-For the 10 Dilmun (messengers) and their servants: leather bottles (outres), 1 per person; shoes, 2 each*
> *-For servants of mine: leather bottles, 1 each; shoes, 2 each;*
> *-For 7 craftsmen: leather bottles, 1 each; shoes, 2 each;*
> *-For the 10 men who accompany them from Shubat-Enlil: leather bottles, 1 each; shoes, 2 each;*
> *-For the 10 load-donkey: 10 ropes, each 1.5 cubits.*
> *Total: 52 leather bottles; 64 pairs of shoes, one large bag; 10 ropes, of 1.5 cubits. Let it be arranged as per this tablet.[16]*

3. *Dynastic marriages.* With western Asia fractured into many powers, each with satellite dependents, interdynastic marriage

became widespread. Princesses, sisters, and daughters of rulers normally married below their own status, thus retaining importance in the palace of vassal husbands.

Daughters and sisters of kings often functioned as pawns in diplomatic marriages, and Zimri-Lim had many to give away. Some were honored in their new homes, while others were humiliated and wrote back heartbreaking notes. They were all, however, expected to be the eyes and ears of their kin, and to aid in this purpose, scribes were often included in the dowries. Zimri-Lim gave his sister Liqtum in marriage to one of his early supporters, Adalshenni, king of Burundum, a town near Tur Abdin, a mountainous region in northern Syria, which was a major stop along the trade route between Assyria and Anatolia. Liqtum apparently used her scribe to argue her husband's cause, and we have a letter from Zimri-Lim responding to her efforts:

> *About what you wrote me on establishing peace and good-will between me and Adalshenni and on engaging in frank discussions between us; who would not want to have peace and good-will? I am herewith sending a long communiqué to Adalshenni about establishing peace and good-will. May peace and good-will be established between us.*[17]

But he also admonishes her:

> *In the land where you dwell, there are many ostriches; why have you not sent to me ostriches?*[18]

Marriage was achieved after much negotiation, requiring frequent diplomatic travel.[19] Marriage was also the occasion of broad disbursement of gifts: father to daughter (*nidittum*; "dowry"), groom to bride (*terhatum*; "bride-wealth"), and in-laws to each other (*biblum*; "marriage gifts"). Feasting promoted bonding and continued for days on end. The Mari archives contain records of many such transactions, with bride-wealth and dowry lists that included garments, jewelry, furniture, servants, and even scribes. We know of negotiations between the houses of Qatna and Mari that resulted in the princess Beltum being taken to a husband who did not fully appreciate her—especially as she had cost his father 4 talents (240 pounds) of silver.[20] In Mari, Beltum went dancing one midafternoon in an open courtyard, suffering a severe sunstroke.[21]

Our fullest documentation, however, concerns Zimri-Lim's own marriage to Shiptu, daughter of the king of Aleppo. The *terhatum*, sent through intermediaries, included necklaces of gold and lapis lazuli, with intricate clasps and precious stones, pectorals, leather objects, and hundreds of animals.[22] How she arrived at Mari is revealed in a series of letters the ambassadors wrote to Zimri-Lim during the mission.[23]

4. *Military.* The role of armies in promoting trade contacts is not always apparent, since their primary goal was to intimidate, in the process of which they would maim, capture, and ransack. Armies marched on their bellies, plundering food and equipment in enemy territory. But they also took along a vast array of auxiliaries, among them diviners, gods (as images), cooks, smiths, and, for all sorts of reasons, women. The hope was always to complete a mission in one season, around springtime; some operations, however, took armies far distances and assignments could stretch on for months. Troops could also be stuck in garrisons for years, keeping watch on unstable vassals.[24]

Nevertheless, in its wake, a successful military venture often led to the dispersal of people and goods. When Zimri-Lim conquered Ashlakka from his rebellious son-in-law, he sent to Mari his share of the spoils: more than one hundred women from the harem of the defeated king, among them the victims of previous conquests. Some of the women, bringing their talents to Mari, served as musicians, but most were assigned to weaving, making garments that were later sold by the palace or offered as gifts.

The Trip Westward

We return now to Zimri-Lim's trip to the Mediterranean with which we began this essay (fig. 31). During his reign the king was practically always on the road, inspecting strongholds, bringing peace to warring allies, visiting daughters given to vassals as "trophy" wives, and paying homage to diverse gods. This trip westward, however, was not exactly a social outing. The ruler who summoned him, his father-in-law Yarim-Lim, had conferred on him status and legitimacy by giving him Shiptu, his daughter from a concubine, and in return Yarim-Lim was now calling on him to help against a pesky opponent.

We know that the trip began at the turn of the twelfth month of the Mari calendar, not easily matched to ours but likely just as the rains were slackening and before the brutal summer was to set in. So let us imagine it was mid-April when the caravan lumbered out of Mari. The king stopped by a number of towns that were under his control, first along the Euphrates and then up the Khabur. As he moved up the river, he received gifts—mostly jewelry—from a number of his vassals. This phase took about a month. The next phase brought him farther upriver, and by mid-May, he was in territory under the control of Haya-Sumu, a vassal made loyal by marrying two of Zimri-Lim's daughters.

Three weeks later we find the king having crossed to the region of the Balikh River, though some of his emissaries must already have reached the Euphrates near present-day Tell Munbaqa. Nearby was a temple to the god Dagan, and Zimri-Lim paid him homage. He also offered his first gifts to Yarim-Lim and his primary wife, Gashera. There were also gifts to the great god Addu (Adad) of Aleppo.

Zimri-Lim stayed in Aleppo, his host's capital, for the next few weeks, but toward the end of June, he was again on the move, making his way toward the seacoast and sending gifts far and wide in Syria; tin was the most sought-after present, as it was a major component of bronze. We have the names of a number of local rulers who received his gifts, including Ibni-Addu, king of Hazor.

Nearly three months after he had left Mari, Zimri-Lim came to Ugarit. It was the first week of July, and the sea breezes must have helped sustain him and his court during the hot days. We do not know if Ugarit was yet the commercial metropolis it came to be in the Late Bronze Age, but undoubtedly it was under Aleppo's sphere of influence. From Ugarit, Zimri-Lim continued to dispatch gifts, some to people who had already benefited from his largesse, but also to new recipients, including a songstress, Niqmi-Lanasi, who was a member of Yarim-Lim's court. No doubt because his emissaries were returning from their missions, we begin to read about gifts, especially wine, from such cities as Qatna, Hazor, Ulme, and Byblos.[25] Egypt—unless it is concealed under an undeciphered name—is strikingly absent from the cuneiform records of the time, when it was still ruled by the glorious Dynasty 12.

During his stay in Ugarit, Zimri-Lim likely visited neighboring villages. It would appear that one of these locales, a town called Alahtum, took his fancy as a safe haven where he might end his days. A few years later we find his emissary negotiating its purchase, and in spite of the incompetence of his agent, Zimri-Lim eventually succeeded in obtaining his wish. His hold over Alahtum, however, could not have lasted long; for if that town proves to be Alalakh (Tell Atchana, near the Orontes in the Amuq Valley; see pp. 197–98), it reverted back to Aleppo's control fairly soon after the demise of Mari.

Zimri-Lim's stay in Ugarit lasted an entire month, after which he retraced his steps before heading home. Soon he was back in Aleppo. The administrative archives on this leg of the journey begin to diminish around the beginning of September. By this time, however, Zimri-Lim had received urgent news of insurrections abroad, likely fomented by his erstwhile allies the Elamites. A gruesome report reached him, too, about the murder and beheading of one of his faithful vassals, Qarni-Lim of Andariq. Zimri-Lim was at his capital by the end of the month.[26] The vacation was over.

1. See Lerouxel 2002.
2. Dossin 1978 (ARM 10 126); Durand 1997–2000 (LAPO 18 1166), pp. 349–51.
3. Durand 1997–2000 (LAPO 16 11–14).
4. Charpin et al. 1988 (ARM 26 297).
5. Sasson 1968.
6. Durand 1988 (ARM 26 125).
7. Dossin 1950 (ARM 1 115); Durand 1997–2000 (LAPO 16 168), p. 169.
8. Birot 1974 (ARM 14 3); Durand 1997–2000 (LAPO 16 172), p. 307.
9. A.2216; Durand 1997–2000 (LAPO 16 171), pp. 306–7.
10. Bardet et al. 1984 (ARM 23 224).
11. A.2993+; Durand 1997–2000 (LAPO 18 855), pp. 15–17.
12. Dossin 1978 (ARM 10 147); Durand 1997–2000 (LAPO 18 1110), pp. 290–92.
13. Dossin 1952 (ARM 5 20); Durand 1997–2000 (LAPO 16 256), pp. 403–5.
14. Charpin et al. 1988 (ARM 26 532).
15. A.350+; Durand 1997–2000 (LAPO 16 333), pp. 518–20.
16. Dossin 1950 (ARM 1 17); Durand 1997–2000 (LAPO 16 417), pp. 610–12.
17. Dossin 1978 (ARM 10 140); Durand 1997–2000 (LAPO 18 1184), pp. 372–73.
18. Ibid.
19. Two fine overviews of the archives on Mari marriages are Lafont 1987 and Lafont 2001, pp. 322–25.
20. Durand 1997–2000 (LAPO 18 1005–13), pp. 169–78.
21. Charpin et al. 1988 (ARM 26 298).
22. Ibid. Limet 1986 (ARM 25 616); improved edition in Durand 1988 (ARM 26/1), pp. 100–101.
23. The story is presented as one example of interdynastic marriages in Sasson 2006.
24. We have the complaint of a man kept five years in one such post; see Charpin et al. 1988 (ARM 26 345).
25. The exchange of tin for wine seems to have been an accepted barter, as documented from an earlier generation; see Charpin and Ziegler 1997.
26. See Villard 1986.

ORNAMENTS OF INTERACTION:
THE ART OF THE JEWELER

KIM BENZEL

Many of the most spectacular works of art from the ancient Near East and the eastern Mediterranean in the second millennium B.C. are not easily attributable to a specific culture or region or, by extension, to a place of manufacture. The jewelry finds from this era are prominent among the luxury items that elude attribution primarily because of the mix of styles and iconographies they present. Much has been written about the hybrid nature of these ornaments from both art historical and archaeological perspectives in an effort to sort out possible sources of inspiration and manufacture; relatively little, however, has been said about the methods used to produce them.[1] By examining the technical aspects of these finds, it is possible to discern nuances that may help shed light on the range of their cultural contexts.[2]

The Middle Bronze Age in the Near East and eastern Mediterranean boasts a series of extraordinary caches of jewelry. Among the sites from which they were excavated are Ebla in Syria, Larsa in southern Mesopotamia, Trialeti in the Caucasus, Byblos and Tell el-'Ajjul in the Levant, Mallia on Crete, and Tell el-Dab'a in Egypt. Because most of them were found in hoards or graves, they are difficult to date with precision despite having excavated contexts. Unexcavated items from this period include the hoard considered to be from Dilbat, in southern Mesopotamia; the pendant in the Petrie Museum of Archaeology in London, thought to come from Egypt; and the Aigina Treasure, allegedly discovered on the Aegean island of Aigina. While some of these pieces clearly exemplify jewelry traditions from which they derive, others appear stylistically and technically diverse.

The ornaments from Ebla (cat. nos. 10–11, 13–16) display designs and techniques with strong affiliations to those seen on objects from both mainland Mesopotamia and Egypt. Some may have been imports; others were made locally by craftsmen who drew inspiration from these outside sources. The jewelry related to Mesopotamian designs features simple, geometric background forms densely covered with motifs and patterns composed of finely executed granulation and wirework. The overall pieces were then neatly trimmed and finished. In both style and workmanship, several of the Ebla ornaments (cat. nos. 11, 14) may be compared to pieces in the Dilbat hoard (cat. no. 4), specifically the crescent and the granulated rosette medallions. Other related examples from Mesopotamia are two medallions from a hoard at Larsa[3] and an heirloom medallion from a grave at Lefkandi on Euboia;[4] like the Ebla jewels they display elaborate patterning beautifully executed on simple background forms.

Farther down the Levantine coast, at the site of Byblos, jewelry styles and techniques are more difficult to assign. Some objects show clear connections to Egypt (cat. no. 29). Others display distinctly Mesopotamian iconography, but in a style found in other media at such sites as Ebla[5] rather than in Mesopotamia proper. One example of this style can be seen on the fittings for a fenestrated axe from Byblos (cat. no. 25). Instead of richly ornamented and densely granulated surfaces, the fittings are adorned with figural scenes executed in linear granulation. One might note that linear granulation is technically much more difficult to produce than the triangle and rosette patterns seen on the previous examples. However, while the technique as practiced in Egypt approached perfection,[6] that seen on the axe fittings from Byblos is executed in a less careful manner.

At Tell el-'Ajjul a style of technology that is quintessentially Levantine can be clearly identified. While the iconography and designs relate to the broader context of Mesopotamia, Egypt, and Syria, the craftsmanship is marked by a summary execution of techniques used elsewhere with greater success. The falcon (cat. no. 221) is decorated with casually placed granules of varying sizes and has edges that are imprecisely finished, and the nude female pendant (cat. no. 216) comprises a roughly cut-out sheet incised in a schematic and inexact manner. This somewhat casual style remains typical for purely Levantine workmanship for much of the second millennium B.C.

Somewhere between the Mesopotamian and Egyptian-type ornaments, with their refined design and workmanship, and the locally produced Levantine pieces lies the disparate assortment of beads from Trialeti (cat. no. 57). This group was perhaps never actually strung together, as they are seen here. The stone of the central element is possibly an heirloom from third-millennium B.C. southern Mesopotamia.[7] It is reused in a setting with stone inlays that, along with one of the large beads, is related in style and workmanship to the medallion found in the Montet jar at Byblos,[8] a roundel from Ebla,[9] and third-millennium B.C. pinheads from Alaca Höyük in Anatolia.[10] A different style and level of execution are manifest on the Trialeti

Figure 32. Gold pendant. Mallia, Chrysolakkos cemetery. Middle Minoan II. Archaeological Museum, Heraklion 559

bead decorated with linear granulation, resembling that on the Byblos axe fittings. The workmanship here, as on the fittings, is of lesser quality. Yet another bead has been linked to the design and craftsmanship of a ring from Dahshur,[11] while the beads with punched dots appear the most indigenous in style. Dot decoration is seen on other objects produced in the vicinity of Trialeti.[12] It is difficult to say if the beads were manufactured locally with inspiration from various sources, collected from the sources themselves and deposited together at Trialeti, or a combination of the two.

The cultural connections between the pendant from Tell el-Dab'a (cat. no. 62), the Petrie pendant (cat. no. 63), and the Master of Animals pendant from the Aigina Treasure (cat. no. 58) have been a source of great controversy. From a technical standpoint, there is a strong link between the Dab'a and Petrie pendants. In both the emphasis is on the figural, cutout shape rather than on decorative details; the front sheet is rendered in low repoussé and attached to a flat back sheet, presumably by means of solder; and neither is carefully finished at the seams, most particularly at the seams inside the openwork portions. Surface details of the figures are chased but not with great precision. In

Figure 33. Gold jewelry of Khnemet. Dahshur, funerary complex of Amenemhat II, Tomb of Khnemet. Dynasty 12. Egyptian Museum, Cairo 52975-9

their lack of technical virtuosity they appear to be of Levantine production, an attribution supported by at least one scholar's analysis of the stylistic and iconographic features (see cat. no. 62).

While the Master of Animals pendant from the Aigina Treasure appears similar on a superficial level to the Dab'a and Petrie pieces, the method of its manufacture is distinctly different. The emphasis here is also on the openwork shape, but the front sheet in low repoussé is embedded into the flat back sheet whose edges are folded upward to form what can best be described as a shallow "pan." These edges are then smoothed out against the openwork designs on the front sheet. There is no flush join with a seam, as on the Dab'a and Petrie pendants, but overlapping front and back sheets that appear to hold together more or less on their own. The result is not much neater than the poorly trimmed edges on the Dab'a and Petrie pendants, but in approach and concept the technique is dramatically different. It is also used on what are perhaps earrings from the Aigina Treasure (cat. no. 59).[13]

Mention should be made as well of the famous Minoan bee ornament from Mallia on Crete (fig. 32). The Dab'a, Petrie, and Aigina pendants are frequently compared with it and, based on this relationship, attributed to Minoan manufacture. It must be said that, on purely technical grounds, none of the three bear any resemblance to the exquisitely made bee, whose masterly workmanship combines extraordinarily fine granulation and nearly perfectly trimmed edges and overall finishing. While the openwork technique is employed in the composition, the style is more sculptural than the flat, low relief of the other three pieces. This sculptural quality compares with objects from Minoan Crete[14] but contrasts with the three pendants. In its use of undecorated but beautifully polished open areas combined with areas of densely clustered granules and clean finish, the bee pendant is reminiscent of jewelry from Dahshur, Egypt (fig. 33). Only the pectoral from the Aigina Treasure (cat. no. 60) compares in its technical mastery with the bee, although its imagery derives from a different source.

1. See Lilyquist 1993 for the most comprehensive treatment of granulated jewelry dating from 2500 to 1400 B.C. The study, however, does not address jewelry without granulation such as the Tell el-Dab'a pendant (cat. no. 62), the Petrie pendant (cat. no. 63), and the Aigina group (cat. nos. 58–61).
2. The author was able to examine firsthand some of the pieces discussed; observations about other pieces are based on detailed photography or available published images.
3. Arnaud, Calvet, and Huot 1979, pl. II:8.
4. Popham, Touloupa, and Sackett 1982, p. 172, pl. XXIIIb; of further interest is that the suspension loop on the Lefkandi medallion is made and attached exactly like the ones on each of the the Dilbat medallions.
5. See Matthiae in *Ebla* 1995, p. 421, no. 290, and p. 422, no. 291.
6. See Lilyquist 1993, figs. 8c, d, 10b.
7. See Maxwell-Hyslop 1971, pp. 74–75, fig. 19a, pl. 45.
8. Ibid., pl. 69.
9. F. Baffi Guardata in *Ebla* 1995, p. 481, no. 400.
10. Maxwell-Hyslop 1971, pp. 42–43, fig. 25a.
11. Lilyquist 1993, p. 41, fig. 8f.
12. *Unterwegs zum goldenen Vlies* 1995, p. 72, pl. 51.
13. For other uses of a similar "pan" technique, see Effinger 1996, pls. 19a, 24a, 30a, 38b, 44d. Interestingly, these examples are all Minoan in origin.
14. Wolters 1983, p. 100, pls. 49, 50.

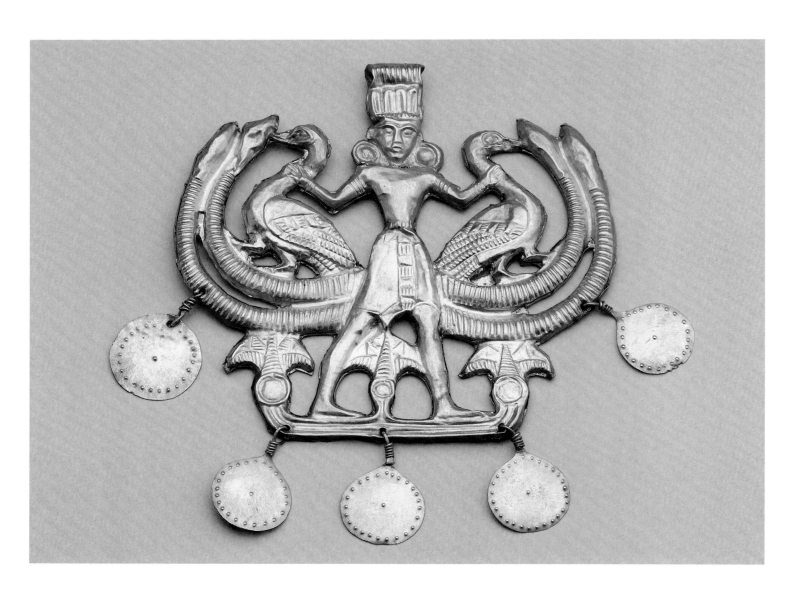

58

58
MASTER OF ANIMALS
PENDANT

Gold
Height 6 cm (2⅜ in.); width 6.3 cm (2½ in.)
Aigina Treasure
ca. 1750–1550 B.C.
The Trustees of the British Museum, London
1892.5–20.8

This pendant is perhaps the best-
known element in the so-called
Aigina Treasure, a remarkable group of
jewelry said to have come from the island
of Aigina in the late nineteenth century.[1]
Because the circumstances of the find are
not known,[2] the Treasure remains somewhat mysterious, and the dating and
primary stylistic affinities of the group
are open to debate.

The pendant is made of two sheets
of gold, one folded over the other (see
pp. 101–3). The front sheet is embossed

in the repoussé technique, and the imagery appears in relief. Central to the piece
is a male figure whose outstretched hands
touch the necks of two large birds, perhaps geese, which face away from him.
He stands among lotus flowers on what
may be a stylized boat. Pairs of ridged,
curving elements with budlike ends flank
the figure and enclose the birds. Five
hanging discs decorate the lower edge
of the pendant.

The figure stands with his upper body
facing front and his legs in profile to the
right. He wears a tall, apparently feathered
headdress, the top of which is formed into
a loop for suspension. His face is somewhat
triangular, with the features carefully
delineated. Two large discs may be earrings or curls. He wears a belted, kiltlike
garment with a long tassel down the front,
and possibly boots. His upper torso is
bare, and he wears armlets and bracelets.
The pose, in which a central figure sub-
dues pairs of animals, is known as the

Master (or Mistress) of Animals stance. It
signals that this figure is a divinity who
controls nature through his power over
wild animals.

In the first modern publication of the
Aigina Treasure,[3] Higgins identified
the figure as a Minoan nature god, pointing out affinities between his costume and
examples in Minoan iconography.[4] The
strange ridged elements with budlike ends
curving up from behind the god may be
vegetal, or they may be stylized bull's
horns, which would again reflect Minoan
artistic convention and underline the
divinity of the male figure.

In addition to Minoan iconography,
the pendant displays other influences, not
least that of Egypt. Lotus flowers, for
example, are common in Egyptian art, and
the figure stands on something resembling
the stylized papyrus boats known from
later Egyptian representations. Close
comparisons can be made between this
piece and two examples found in Egypt,

59

the Tell el-Dab'a and Petrie pendants (cat. nos. 62, 63).[5] Like Aigina, Tell el-Dab'a saw the importation of Minoan Kamares pottery—the fine ware used in early Minoan palaces (see p. 59).

Scholars have also noted both technical and stylistic affinities between this piece and the Bronze Age jewelry of Anatolia and Syria-Levant.[6] The inhabitants of Aigina were great sailors and were clearly far from isolated; it is not surprising that jewelry attributed to the island should partake of a broader international style.

JLF

1. A. Evans 1892–93.
2. The site of Kolonna, on Aigina, flourished in the Middle Bronze Age, and the tombs of the wealthy Middle Helladic inhabitants are a feasible, though unproven, findspot for the Treasure. See Kilian-Dirlmeier 1997.
3. Higgins 1957.
4. Higgins has not gone unchallenged: see Rehak 1996.
5. These interconnections are discussed in two forthcoming papers, Aruz 2008b and Collon 2008; see also Aruz 2008a, p. 109.
6. First published as Minoan in Walberg 1991a, pp. 111–12. See also Schiestl 2008.

59

EARRINGS (?)

Gold, carnelian
Diameter ca. 6.5 cm (2½ in.)
Aigina Treasure
ca. 1750–1550 B.C.
The Trustees of the British Museum, London
1892.5–20.11, 12

Within a hoop in the form of a double-headed snake is a symmetrical arrangement of two dogs face-to-face and, beneath their forepaws, a pair of back-to-back monkeys. Because of their slender bodies and elongated muzzles, the dogs have been described as greyhounds. Their tails are formed from wire, and wire also decorates their ears. One forepaw rests on

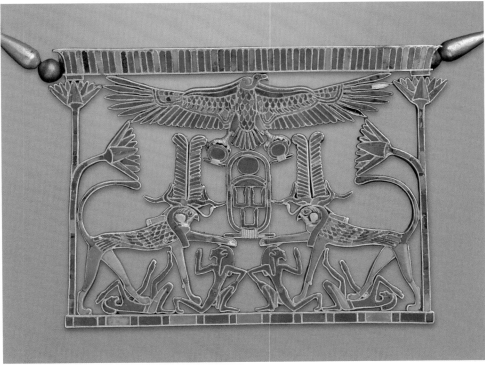

Figure 34. Pectoral of Mereret, gold and semiprecious stones. Dahshur, funerary complex of Senwosret III, Tomb of Mereret. Dynasty 12. Egyptian Museum, Cairo JE 30875

60

the monkeys' heads; the other forepaw is raised to rest on a carnelian bead. Fine wire around their necks represents their collars, with two chains decorated with carnelian beads attached to the inside of the hoop, serving as leashes. The seated monkeys, also with slender bodies, raise their hands to their faces. Their heads are rather shapeless, though a large eye is indicated on each. A curving element springs from their feet to support the dogs' hind paws.

Fourteen pendants were originally suspended from the hoop: seven in the form of plain discs on chains and seven in the form of birds on chains, each decorated with a carnelian bead. The birds, which are suspended from the tail and thus hang upside down, can probably be identified as owls. Their faces are frontal, and they each have two big eyes and outspread wings with beaded upper edges.

The ornaments are hollow and essentially identical on each side. This would fit with their identification as earrings, though it is not entirely clear how they were worn. They lack any obvious means of suspension from the ear, and if they were indeed worn as earrings, the dangling elements would have fallen together in a rather tangled way. They show almost no sign of

wear, so it remains possible that they were made specifically for the grave and were arranged with the elements radiating from the disc (as they are for museum display).

The earrings have no close parallels as complete objects. Large earrings are known in Aegean iconography and are shown, for example, on the Thera frescoes,[1] though they seem less elaborate than the Aigina Treasure examples. Higgins compared the general scheme of the confronted animals to a well-known Egyptian pectoral ornament of princess Mereret[2] that dates to about 1850 B.C. (fig. 34); the suspended birds (rather than owls) also find parallels in the jewelry of princess Khnemet from Dahshur (see fig. 33).[3] Monkeys as motifs in art have been discussed by Collon in her survey of Near Eastern connections with the Aigina Treasure.[4]   JLF

1. Doumas 1992.
2. Higgins 1979.
3. For Khnemet's jewelry, see Terrace and Fischer 1970, pp. 69–71.
4. Collon 2008.

60

PECTORAL WITH SPHINX HEAD TERMINALS

Gold
Length 10.6 cm (4⅛ in.)
Aigina Treasure
ca. 1750–1550 B.C.
The Trustees of the British Museum, London
1892.5–20.7

This sweeping curve of double-thickness gold terminates in two striking profile heads, with ten discs suspended from its lower edge. Suspension loops above the heads show that the ornament was originally attached to cords or chains and was presumably worn around the neck or on the chest.

The heads have straight profiles, large oval eyes, and two backward-sweeping locks of hair terminating in large curls. The curls indicate that these should probably be seen as the heads not of humans but of sphinxes. The eyes and eyebrows are now empty spaces, but early observers noted traces of blue, indicating that they were probably originally inlaid, perhaps with lapis lazuli.

The front and back sheets of the pectoral were carefully soldered all the way around the edge, and the back is flat. As

61

a result of the very solid, high-quality workmanship, this piece stands out from the other items in the Aigina Treasure. The low-relief design of the heads on the front sheet was worked initially by repoussé from behind. Details of the noses and mouths and the long hair curls were chased in from the front.

The sphinx heads can be compared to Minoan works, and they bear a fairly close resemblance to the sphinx of a ceramic appliqué for a vessel found at Mallia on Crete (see fig. 46b).[1] It has also been pointed out, however, that they resemble sphinxes both on bullae and on ivories attributed to Acemhöyük (see cat. no. 46b).[2] Thus, as with other items in the group, the purely Minoan interpretation perhaps does not tell the whole story.   JLF

1. Heraklion Archaeological Museum Π 19818, illustrated in *Krete–Aigyptos* 2000, no. 33.
2. Poursat 1973; Aruz 2008a, p. 100; Collon 2008.

61

ROUNDELS

Gold
Average diameter 0.4 cm (¼ in.)
Aigina Treasure
ca. 1750–1550 B.C.
The Trustees of the British Museum, London
1892.5–20.42/33/64/63/31/47/27/35/70/66

These ten gold plaques come from a group of fifty-four essentially identical plaques that are part of the Aigina Treasure. Each features a convex central boss surrounded by a border of eight running loops. Each boss is decorated with an eight-petal rosette, indicated by dotted lines, and has a raised edge with hatched lines. Each loop is decorated with grooved lines. It is probable that the basic dome and loop form was made by embossing the gold sheets into a single open mold. The plaque decoration was finished by chasing details from the front and by punching dots along scored guidelines seen on the surface of the domes.

Each disc is pierced in four places at the outer edge of the spirals. It seems probable that they were originally sewn to fabric as decoration for a garment or a shroud. Larger, flatter plaques with a variety of different motifs, found in considerable numbers in the Shaft Graves at Mycenae,[1] are probably the closest parallels to the Aigina plaques,[2] although, unlike the latter, they were not mass-produced.   JLF

1. Schliemann 1878.
2. For an alternative interpretation of the design, which has clear parallels in central Anatolia, the source of some elements in the Aigina Treasure, see cat. no. 62, and Aruz 2008a, p. 110.

EGYPT, THE LEVANT, AND THE AEGEAN FROM THE HYKSOS PERIOD TO THE RISE OF THE NEW KINGDOM

DAVID O'CONNOR

Between about 1640 and 1550 B.C., geopolitical and cultural interaction between Egypt and the Levant intensified to an unprecedented degree, motivated primarily by a dynasty of Levantine origin—the Hyksos—which dominated northern Egypt.[1] Their kings were described in Egyptian records as *heka khasut* ("rulers of foreign lands"), which was transformed by Greek sources into Hyksos.[2] This symbiotic relationship between the two regions not only was an important prelude to Egypt's deep involvement in the Levant during the subsequent New Kingdom, but it also generated tensions between the Hyksos in northern Egypt and the Theban-based rulers in the south. Eventually, open warfare led to the overthrow of the Hyksos in 1550 B.C. and to the rise of the New Kingdom, here defined as the period spanning the reigns of kings Ahmose I (1550–1525 B.C.) and Thutmose I (ca. 1504–1492 B.C.).[3] During the New Kingdom, Egypt, like much of the Near East, developed strong contacts with the Aegean world.

GEOPOLITICAL CONTEXTS

Even prior to the Hyksos period, the geopolitical situation in the Levant, and in the Near East in general, was extraordinarily volatile.[4] Throughout the Tigris–Euphrates Valley and in Syria, relatively small states, led by local dynasties, competed for power. Periodically, larger states were formed out of these disparate elements but sooner or later collapsed back into fragmentation. It was during a marked period of decline that new powers and larger entities came into being, generated in part by peoples long resident in the region but formerly peripheral to the mainstream of political development. These consisted of a Babylonian state, created by the Kassites, controlling the lower Tigris-Euphrates system, and the extensive Hurrian presence dominating the upper Euphrates and much of Syria, surmised by some to have generated population movements that coalesced to form the intrusive Hyksos dynasties in northern Egypt.[5] The reality, however, is more complex. The gradual settlement of Levantines in the eastern Nile Delta reflected a Dynasty 13 policy of Egyptian rulers co-opting alien peoples to provide desired services, and was paralleled in the province of Wawat, or Lower Nubia, also held by Egypt. The latter situation prepared the way for a takeover of Wawat by the independent kingdom of Kush, centered at Kerma,[6] and a similar process may have led to the development of the Hyksos state in the Delta. It is also possible that the relevant dynasties arose from the Levantine peoples already settled in Egypt, who were wealthy and prestigious enough to merit mortuary statues more than twice life-size, even when under Egyptian control.[7] Some scholars, however, argue for a closer connection, with Levantine invaders taking control by force at the outset of Dynasty 15, or even earlier.

As the Levant proper came out of its period of decline, its urban centers grew strong again, a process documented archaeologically and reflected (very randomly) in Egyptian Middle Kingdom execration texts. These texts consisted of the names of potentially (though not necessarily actual) rebellious peoples and towns, many located in the Levant,[8] written on figurines or vessels that were then ritually destroyed and buried to unleash a magic spell against the offenders. The city-states involved included Hazor,[9] with its rough equivalent to the south at Sharuhen (possibly Tell el-'Ajjul).[10] Farther north was Byblos, whose importance for Middle Kingdom Egypt declined in the Hyksos period,[11] when other northern Levantine ports may have competed for trade with the Egyptians. At this point, contacts with the Aegean, throughout the Levant and Egypt, existed but were slight.

EGYPT

Debate about Egyptian-Levantine relationships in the Hyksos period, and even during the rise of the New Kingdom, is lively but inconclusive.[12] Despite its ambiguities, the Hyksos occupation raises serious questions about the internal structure of the Egyptian political system and social order, which allowed a Levantine city-state to establish itself in the northeastern Delta and to build up a system of vassal towns, ruled by Egyptians on behalf of the Hyksos, that extended as far south as Cusae (El-Qusiya).[13] This incursion may have triggered the retreat of the Dynasty 13 rulers from the original capital, near the Faiyum, to Thebes in southern Egypt, although the remarkably short reigns of many rulers of this dynasty hint at instabilities within the Egyptian kingship itself.[14] Whether Thebes was actually conquered by the Hyksos during Dynasty 16 or 17 is uncertain.[15] Dynasty 17 rulers launched wars of liberation against the Hyksos and their Egyptian vassals, and the dynasty's last ruler, Kamose, reached the Hyksos capital at Avaris, but the final expulsion remained to be achieved by his brother Ahmose.[16] Kamose contented himself by taunting the Hyksos ruler:

As mighty Amun endures, I shall not leave you, I shall not allow you to tread the fields even when I am not (here) with you! Does your heart fail you, O vile Asiatic? Look! I drink of the wine of your vineyards which the Asiatics whom I captured pressed out for me. I have smashed up your rest house, I have cut down your trees, I have forced your women in ships' holds . . . I haven't left a thing to Avaris of her (own) destitution: the Asiatic has perished! Does your heart fail, O you vile Asiatic, you who used to say: I am lord without equal from Hermopolis to Pihathor upon the Rekhty water?[17]

The Hyksos period in Egypt left a distinctive material culture, combining both Egyptian and Levantine elements. This is especially evident at the site of Tell el-Dab'a (Avaris) in the northeastern Nile Delta, where substantial amounts of Canaanite material have been attributed to the Hyksos period.[18] At Tell el-Dab'a, Dynasty 15 rulers adopted Egyptian royal titles but also proudly displayed their status as "rulers of foreign lands" through temples in the Canaanite style, presumably built for Canaanite deities, which stood alongside others that were Egyptian in form, and through burials that often followed Levantine customs.[19] Despite this cultural integration, the wars of liberation were fierce, and later generations of Egyptians excoriated the Hyksos, who had—in their view—ruled "without Re," the sun god, and thus temporarily dragged much of Egypt, in symbolic terms, into the realm of chaos.[20]

The Levant

Ceramic and other materials found at Tell el-Dab'a reveal the existence of a highly developed trade network, linking the site to the Levant as a whole. Near the close of the Hyksos period, the Egyptians noted that "hundreds" of ships laden with Levantine products were to be found in the harbors of Tell el-Dab'a,[21] and it has been estimated that some two million Levantine storage jars may have reached the site.[22]

Within the Levant, Canaan was the region most influenced by the hybrid culture developed during the Hyksos period. In particular, scarabs with a variety of designs on their bases, typical for Egypt at that time, were found throughout Canaan.[23] Most seem to have been made locally, however, and there is little evidence to suggest the region was actually ruled by the Hyksos.[24]

Ahmose followed his expulsion of the Hyksos from Egypt with an attack on Canaan, specifically Sharuhen. Many of the heavily fortified Middle Bronze Age towns of the region were destroyed,[25] yet whether this was a result of Egyptian initiatives or due to other attackers, perhaps from the north, has not been determined. The Egyptians, in any event, soon realized that the wider geopolitical horizon held more opportunities for them than narrowly defined Canaan.

Both Ahmose and Amenhotep I were militarily active in the northern Levant, and they prepared the way for a spectacular initiative by Thutmose I, who not only brought the kingdom of Kush (which the Hyksos had tried to involve in their war with Thebes) to an end, but also successfully attacked Mitanni— an unprecedented geographic expansion for the Egyptians. Moreover, he declared Egypt's dominion up to the Mitanni border, upon which he erected a frontier stele.[26] Thutmose's gains were followed by a lull in Egyptian expansion; activity was ultimately resumed by his grandson Thutmose III, with more enduring results. The Egyptian empire had begun.

The Aegean

Farther afield, and more tenuously, most of the Hyksos period and the earliest reigns of the New Kingdom correspond to the Middle Minoan III and early phases of the Late Minoan and Mycenaean (Late Helladic) periods.[27] Aegean interaction with Egypt was especially intense by the reigns of Hatshepsut and Thutmose III (ca. 1479–1425 B.C.),[28] and images of Aegean tributaries under Hatshepsut and Thutmose III apparently depict both Minoans and Mycenaeans.[29] Prior to this time, materials of Aegean origin appear to have been quite rare in Egypt and the southern Levant,[30] although Cretan residents in Syrian coastal cities had contacts as far east as Mari on the upper Euphrates.[31] This theory of minimal contact was briefly overturned by the discovery of frescoes—Minoan in style, content, and technology—that had decorated what were believed to be Hyksos palaces in Egypt; the buildings were subsequently redated, however, to the later reigns of Hatshepsut and Thutmose III (see pp. 110–12).[32] This situation highlights the ambiguity of much of the textual and archaeological data for the period covered here, yet it also illustrates how exciting and stimulating continuing discoveries and debate are likely to be.

1. Redford 1992, chap. 5; Redford 1997; O'Connor 1997. According to a seemingly reliable Egyptian king list, now housed in Turin, Dynasty 15 (the Hyksos) lasted 108 years, plus some months and days, and thus began in about 1630 B.C. Yet other Levantine rulers were active in Egypt prior to this time (they are attested only on scarab-shaped seals but are identified as Dynasty 14). How far back they extend is uncertain, but they would have overlapped in part with the later rulers of Dynasty 13, whose authority was likely restricted to southern Egypt and centered at Thebes. Similarly based in Thebes were the successive Dynasties 16 and 17, both seemingly coeval with Dynasty 15 and hence part of the Hyksos period. See Ryholt 1997, but note the qualifications expressed in D. Ben-Tor, Allen, and Allen 1999.
2. On the term *heka khasut*, see Redford 1992, pp. 99–100; Redford 1997, p. 25; and Ryholt 1997, pp. 123–25, 303–4.
3. Redford 1997, pp. 12–16 (texts 61–71). The chronology of the New Kingdom is relatively well fixed, and its "rise" can be dated fairly precisely, in contrast to that of the preceding dynasties, which is less easily defined.
4. Van de Mieroop 2004, chaps. 5 and 6.
5. Ibid., p. 116.
6. Lacovara 1997; on Kerma, see Bonnet 1986 and Bonnet 2004.
7. Schiestl 2006.
8. Redford 1992, pp. 87–93.
9. Ibid., pp. 44, 121, 130.
10. Oren 1997b.
11. Redford 1992, pp. 96–97; Ryholt 1997, pp. 86–90.

12. See, for example, Ryholt 1997 and critiques in D. Ben-Tor, Allen, and Allen 1999.
13. O'Connor 1997, pp. 56–57 and p. 47, fig. 2.2.
14. Quirke 1991; Ryholt 1997, pp. 69–74, 209–51, 295–99.
15. Redford 1992, p. 125, and O'Connor 1997, p. 56 and n. 19.
16. Redford 1997, pp. 11–16.
17. Ibid., p. 14 (doc. 69, lines 10–18).
18. Tell el-Dab'a and other contemporary sites in the eastern Delta provide important synchronisms, via archaeological data, with contemporary Levant. Tell el-Dab'a's latter phases (D/2–E/2) correspond to the Middle Bronze IIB and, partially, IIC periods in the Levant; the other Hyksos period phases (E/3–G/1–3) correlate with the Middle Bronze IIA period. See the comparative table, Bietak 2002b, p. 41.
19. Bietak 1996.
20. See the text of Hatshepsut recalling the shame of Hyksos rule some fifty years later; Redford 1997, pp. 16–17 (doc. 73).
21. Ibid., p. 14 (doc. 69, lines 13–15).
22. Bietak 1996, p. 20.
23. Exhaustively covered in D. Ben-Tor 2007.
24. Ibid., pp. 190–93; see also Ryholt 1997, pp. 138–40, 301–4, 308–9.
25. Redford 1992, pp. 138–40.
26. For early Dynasty 18 campaigning in the Levant, see ibid., pp. 148–55.
27. Stager 2002, p. 359, fig. 22; Preziosi and Hitchcock 1999, p. 8. See also Phillips 1991 and Betancourt 1997.
28. For the dates utilized in this essay, see Baines and Malék 2000, p. 36; see also the relevant sections of Hornung, Krauss, and Warburton 2006.
29. For depictions of Aegean peoples in Dynasty 18 Egypt, see Panagiotopoulos 2006, pp. 392–94.
30. See, e.g., Merrillees 2003, and Crete–Egypt 2000, regarding evidence of Egyptian imports to Crete in the Early Bronze Age.
31. Redford 1992, p. 122 and n. 127; Fitton 2002, p. 99.
32. Jánosi 1995; Bietak et al. 1994, esp. pp. 44–45.

Tell el-Dab'a in the Nile Delta

One might have the impression that ancient Egypt, isolated by the Nile oasis, was a monolithic culture. This was not, however, the case. In fact, Egypt was a faceted cultural matrix, absorbing influences from the Near East, the Western Desert, and Nubia. The most prominent example of multiculturalism in Egypt during the second millennium B.C. was found at Tell el-Dab'a, site of the Hyksos capital Avaris, in the eastern Nile Delta, the subject of more than four decades of archaeological research by the Austrian Archaeological Institute in Cairo (fig. 35).

During Dynasty 12, the site was a planned Egyptian settlement. Later in the dynasty it expanded with the arrival of western Asiatics, most likely soldiers, sailors, and shipbuilders in the service of the pharaoh. The new members of the community appear to have come largely from the northern Levantine coast, and perhaps also from Sinai. Women may have been brought in from the Delta region.

By Dynasty 13, this now-settled population commanded the army and was in charge of ships and foreign relations. The new arrivals also wielded considerable political power, and eventually, with the dissolution of the Egyptian state, they established a kingdom in the eastern Delta. About 1640 B.C. they gained suzerainty over all of Egypt, establishing a vassal system that followed the Near Eastern model. The era that followed is called the Hyksos period (ca. 1640–1550 B.C.).

The settlers brought with them their own traditions, in architecture, religion, and funerary practices. The new temples were based on Near Eastern "broad room" and "bent axis" plans. The Syrian storm god and patron of seafarers Baal Zephon/Haddad was worshipped, as were other gods of the Canaanite pantheon, probably including Asherah, consort of the god El. For mortuary chapels, however, the Egyptian plan was used. The dead were buried within houses or in cemeteries and, contrary to Egyptian practice, were not mummified. Male burials had weapons such as daggers, axes,

javelins, and sickle swords. Beasts of burden (donkeys) and attendants were buried outside the tomb chamber so as to serve the deceased in the afterlife.

Of particular interest is the partially excavated Palace F/II, from the middle of the Hyksos period. Structured not on an Egyptian linear plan, the complex is arranged in a series of courtyards and buildings characteristic of the Near Eastern model. A ramp leads to an upper story where one would normally expect to find official presentation rooms. In one of the courtyards, funeral feasts were celebrated and the remains of the repasts interred in pits. Together with animal bones and charred wood, at least three thousand plates, goblets, ring stands, and ritual vessels were found; these had been intentionally broken. Among the pottery remains were also ceramics from the Nubian Kerma culture, the material culture of the African kingdom of Kush more than 2,000 kilometers to the south. Because most of these pots are beakers and cups, open forms that would not have served as containers of trade commodities, we can assume that their makers worked at Avaris. It is likely that the Nubians were initially employed as soldiers in the Hyksos military, which could explain their presence at the palace, perhaps as guards.

The palace was eventually abandoned. Another palace, dating from the Late Hyksos period, with vast gardens behind buttressed fortification walls, was built west of Avaris on the banks of the Pelusiac branch of the Nile. It is likely that these were originally the gardens of Apophis, the Hyksos ruler whose trees the rebellious vassal Kamose (according to the text of his stele) had threatened to uproot.

Avaris was ultimately overrun by the Upper Egyptian vassals under Ahmose I, founder of Dynasty 18 and the New Kingdom. The town was largely abandoned, although settlement activity continued within the temple precinct of the god Seth. While Seth of Avaris was an Egyptian adaptation of Baal Zephon—the principal god of the

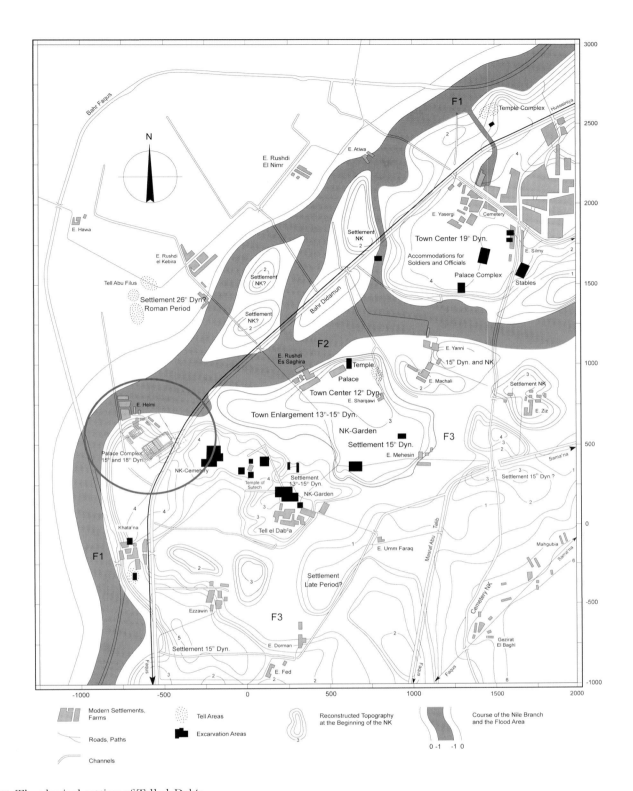

Figure 35. The physical setting of Tell el-Dab'a.

despised foreign rulers—the victorious Upper Egyptians appear to have respected his abode. Settlement life also continued south of the former palace. Notably, the ceramic industry continued to produce pottery in the hybrid style established during the Hyksos period, a clear indication that members of the community remained to serve the new overlords of Egypt, the Thebans.

During Dynasty 18, a huge military compound was set up at the site of the former Hyksos palace, with great fireplaces and enormous ovens. Silos were constructed to store grain. The dead were interred in a special complex, mainly for young men between the ages of eigh-

teen and twenty-five years. Few women and infant burials were found. In general, single burials without offerings were the norm, but there were also a series of tombs with double and triple burials, the bodies positioned on their stomachs tête-bêche. The impression is of a ritual execution, supported by the evidence of two male skeletons at the bottom of a deep pit found facedown beneath more than three hundred smashed pots and limestone fragments.

Later, in the Thutmosid period, a vast precinct that was constructed on the Nile covered more than 5 hectares (13 acres) and included three palaces (G, F, and J), each built on a raised podium of mud brick, accessible via a ramp with a landing, and an immense building for administration. The largest, Palace G, measured more than 160 meters in length and had a spacious courtyard, a portico, a broad vestibule, and a highly unusual square throne room with five aisles situated side by side with a typically Thutmosid temple. The placement of the temple—probably dedicated to the god Amun—parallel to the throne room made a clear ideological and symbolic juxtaposition of the king with the god. The private quarters were in the back, together with the cellars, where remains of military equipment such as Aegean arrow tips were found.

The most astonishing discovery at Tell el-Dab'a comprised thousands of fragments of Minoan wall paintings on lime plaster. Most of them came from Palace F, some from Palace G. They testify to a special relationship with Crete, which may be explained when we consider the function of the site. Tell el-Dab'a was an important harbor town from the Hyksos period (as stated in the Kamose stele) until the Ramesside period, when it was known as Piramesse. This Delta residence of the Ramesside kings is described as "the marshalling place of thy chariotry, the mustering place of thy army, the mooring place of thy ships' troops."[1] Furthermore, from inscriptions on naos doors in the Pushkin State Museum of Fine Arts, Moscow, one may conclude that Avaris was still the harbor of Piramesse during Dynasty 20.

We now also have firm proof of actual harbors at this site.[2] If the site is identified with the famous naval base Perunefer of Thutmose III and Amenhotep II, all evidence falls into place.[3] Not only do we have palaces from exactly this period at Tell el-Dab'a and nearby 'Ezbet Helmy, but Nile physiography makes it clear that Perunefer could never have been situated at Memphis, as nearly all Egyptologists still believe.[4]

Support for this idea may come from the British Museum papyrus 10056, a document from Perunefer mentioning Keftiu (i.e., Cretan) ships that were docked in its harbor. The usual interpretation is that these ships, which are mentioned only during the reign of Thutmose III, were of Cretan type or were sailing to Crete. However, it would be more logical to assume that Minoan ships actually moored and were repaired at Perunefer. If one can identify Tell el-Dab'a with its palatial Minoan wall paintings as Perunefer, then it is conceivable that Egypt fostered its special connections with the Minoan thalas-

socracy in order to build up its navy for military enterprises in the Near East.

We hear nothing of Perunefer in the texts after the reign of Amenhotep II, when the site was abandoned, until the Amarna period. Haremhab later constructed a huge fortress and rebuilt both the palace and the temple of the local god Seth. It is notable that the international character of the site is retained in the late period. The foreign variant of Seth, whose origins are found in Baal Zephon, was adopted by the kings of Dynasty 19 as the god from whom they claimed their lineage. The dynasty seems to have originated in Avaris. Several kings used the name Seti, meaning the One Belonging to Seth. Seti I rebuilt the temple and constructed a palace in nearby Qantir, laying the foundations of Piramesse (the city of Ramesses), which took the name of his successor Ramesses II. Traditions of the Hyksos period resurfaced. Not only do we have, besides Baal Zephon, evidence of Canaanite gods (Anat, Astarte, Qudshu, Reshef), but we find in glyptic art a revival of Hyksos motifs. The religious topography of Piramesse, for example, was designed according to a concept very different from that of Thebes, where Amun-Re and the Theban triad were central. In Piramesse, Canaanite cults were integrated into the religious landscape. A cosmopolitan cultural milieu was thus created where delegations were welcomed from throughout the eastern Mediterranean and indeed the entire Near East.[5]

MB

1. Papyrus Anastasi III: 7.5–6, translated in Caminos 1954, p. 101.
2. Geophysical surveys by the Austrian Archaeological Institute revealed a harbor basin about 450 meters square, with a canal connected to the Pelusiac branch of the Nile. A second harbor was identified beside Palace F/II, of the Middle Hyksos period, and a third north of Avaris at the Nile branch itself. The identification was secured according to sediment analysis conducted by the University of Lyon.
3. Daressy 1928–29, pp. 225, 322–26; Habachi 2001, pp. 9, 106–7, 121.
4. From January until June, navigation in the Delta would come nearly to a standstill as a result of water reduction to about one-fifth the usual level. Furthermore, from November until the middle of April, ships were moved to shelters in the wake of fog and stormy weather. Memphis as a harbor for seagoing ships was therefore active only from July through October.
5. For further reference, see Habachi 1972; Bietak 1975; Bietak 1981; Bietak 1996; Pusch, Becker, and Fassbinder 1999; Pusch and Herold 1999, pp. 647–49; Habachi 2001; Bietak, Marinatos, and Palyvou 2007; Bietak and Forstner-Müller 2008; and Forstner-Müller 2008.

62

PENDANT

Gold
Height 3.7 cm (1½ in.); width 3.8 cm (1½ in.);
thickness 0.2 cm (⅛ in.)
Tell el-Dabʿa
Middle Kingdom, Dynasty 13,
ca. 1780–1740 B.C.
Egyptian Museum, Cairo, Egypt JE 98553
(TD–7315 [72])

A fascinating gold pendant found in a Dynasty 13 tomb at Tell el-Dabʿa in the Nile Delta has provoked great interest and controversy for students of ancient jewelry technology and Bronze Age Mediterranean interconnections. Executed in an openwork technique, this small jewel depicts two confronted collared animals standing on a groundline, with lotus flowers emerging from circular elements. The rendering of the animals, with their foreground hind legs extending back to provide a sense of stability, are most closely paralleled on Syrian seals.[1] Their collars suggest that they are dogs rather than lions; canines are sometimes represented in Levantine art with open jaws.[2] Their postures, however, are more

common in the Levant on images of felines. The gold pendant from Egypt is thus likely to be Canaanite, either made locally at Tell el-Dabʿa or in the Levant by a craftsman versed in the Syrian animal style.

Further support for a Levantine attribution has been revealed by a startling discovery in the Petrie Museum of Archaeology, London, of a second Dabʿa-type pendant with symmetrically placed Egyptianizing griffins (cat. no. 63).[3] The characteristic elements of these creatures include the hawk's head, wings folded against the body, displayed tail feathers, and an upcurved tail, details familiar from Middle Kingdom Egyptian griffin depictions.[4] Sphinxes on Syrian glyptic share some of these features (see discussion in cat. no. 247).[5] The griffins' spiraling horns may evoke the headdress associated with Hathor, as rendered on an ivory plaque from Byblos (cat. no. 26).[6]

Walberg has expressed the view that, despite its typically eastern aspects, the Dabʿa jewel "does not show any Egyptian, Egyptianizing or Oriental features."[7] Rather, she attributes the pendant to Minoan workmanship, comparing it with the Middle Minoan bee ornament from the funerary complex at Chrysolakkos at Mallia

(fig. 32) and the Master of Animals pendant from the Aigina Treasure (cat. no. 58).[8] A similar view is expressed in this catalogue by Fitton (see cat. no. 63), who also attributes the Petrie pendant to Minoan manufacture, despite its many Near Eastern features. Such differences of opinion point to the difficulties of assessing works with features deriving from many traditions, symptomatic of an intense interchange of artistic ideas.

The Master of Animals pendant, along with other objects in the Aigina Treasure, is controversial in many respects, including associations with the island of Aigina.[9] Some pieces have clear parallels with the arts of Anatolia. The form of the small roundels in the hoard and their pattern of triple-line loop spirals (cat. no. 61, where they are interpreted differently) are best compared with seal impressions from Karahöyük and Acemhöyük.[10] The human- or sphinx-head terminals on a pectoral in the Treasure (cat. no. 60) may be compared with Anatolian ivory furniture elements shaped as sphinxes (cat. no. 46a, b).[11] The Master of Animals pendant, with its allusion to Egyptian scenes of fowling in a marshy setting, is a curious piece that presents an unexpected combination of iconographic features (see cat. no. 58). Certain aspects of the male figure seem atypical for the Aegean, including the possibly foreign details of his kilt;[12] the headdress and hair-style, reminiscent of those worn by nude goddesses with disc-shaped Hathor curls on Canaanite pendants; and the bow-shaped extensions emerging from the body that, rather than Aegean "snake frames," may be lotus tendrils with buds like those on a pendant from Minet el-Beidha (cat. no. 214).[13]

Several features that have been considered to relate the Tell el-Dabʻa pendant most closely to the Aigina Treasure Master of Animals ornament—the flat sheet backing, the openwork technique, and a groundline with lotus flowers emerging from circular elements—are referred to below.[14] The style and workmanship are hardly comparable.

On a purely technical level, the Dabʻa pendant appears closely related to the Petrie pendant, less so to the Master of Animals pendant, and not at all to the Mallia bee ornament. The emphasis in both the Dabʻa and Petrie pendants is on the figural, openwork shape, where the front sheets are rendered in low repoussé and attached to a flat back sheet, presumably by means of solder. They are not carefully finished at the seams, especially at the seams inside the openwork portions, where the edges are clearly somewhat ragged. Surface details of the figures are chased, but again, not with great precision. In contrast, the Aigina pendant is significantly more exact in its chased details; furthermore, it is manufactured in a distinctly different manner (see pp. 101–3). The Mallia bee ornament exhibits an altogether different style and a more sophisticated level of workmanship than the other three pieces. By its very lack of technical virtuosity, the Dabʻa pendant would appear to be of Levantine production, an attribution supported by the above analysis of its iconographic features.　　　JA/KB

1. See Aruz 2008a, fig. 223. Differences between Near Eastern and Aegean heraldic lion postures are discussed in Aruz 1993, p. 40, pl. 8:11: the foreleg posture for confronted lions and sphinxes in Syrian art is a variation of the Egyptian victory stance that first occurs in the Old Kingdom.
2. Compare the gold dagger sheath from Byblos (cat. no. 24 in this volume): the diagonal

hatched lines on the body may be part of a harness and not indicating animal fur, which is generally shown as a hatched band outlining the belly. For heraldic compositions of canine-bodied Seth animals in Egyptian art, see A. Wilkinson 1971, pl. xx (Middle Kingdom pectoral); Kaplony 1981, pl. 170:121 (Old Kingdom cylinder seal with linear Seth animals).
3. Schiestl 2000, pp. 127–28.
4. A. Wilkinson 1971, pl. xvii; C. Wilkinson and Hill 1983, p. 68: 33.8.14.
5. Teissier 1996, p. 146: 143 (sphinx with wing folded against body).
6. Salles 1998, p. 70. I thank Catharine Roehrig and Christine Lilyquist for their input.
7. Walberg 1991a, p. 111.
8. Ibid., pp. 111–12; Bietak and Marinatos 2000, p. 40; Hood 1978, pp. 195–97; Higgins 1979, pp. 21ff., who raises the possibility that the Treasure in fact derives from the Chrysolakkos cemetery; Higgins 1987; E. Davis (1977, pp. 321–22, no. 145) posits an Aiginitan origin for the gold cup in the Treasure, with its mixed Minoan-Mycenaean style. For a fuller discussion of this subject, see Aruz 2008a, pp. 109–10, and Aruz 2008b.
9. Higgins 1979.
10. Alp 1968, pl. 78:209; N. Özgüç 1983, p. 419, fig. 8; see Aruz 1993, p. 42, for a discussion of this Anatolian motif.
11. This parallel was first cited by Poursat 1973.
12. Rehak 1996, p. 43.
13. Schaeffer 1949, p. 36, fig. 10; Barrelet 1958, pp. 34ff., pl. xxv:c–e; Negbi 1970, pp. 30ff., pl. iv; Platt 1976, pp. 103ff.
14. For some of these features in Levantine jewelry, see Lilyquist 1993, p. 87, fig. 21d; Dunand 1937, pl. cxxxvi:1442, 3287; Dunand 1950, pl. cxxxviii:17754, 7727.

63

PENDANT WITH GRIFFINS

Silver
Height 3.5 cm (1⅜ in.); width 5.4 cm (2⅛ in.)
Egypt
Middle Kingdom, Dynasty 12–13,
ca. 1981–1640 B.C.
Petrie Museum of Egyptian Archaeology,
UCL, London UC34342

This delicate silver pendant is in the form of two Egyptian-style confronted griffins with lion bodies and hawk heads. Standing beak to beak, they are also linked by the overlap of their extended forepaws. Their heads are decorated with spirals or spiraling horns, and they wear long Egyptian headdresses that fall to the chest. Their wings are neatly folded against their bodies, and the curl of their rather doglike tails echoes the curling finials of the bases on which they stand. Although at the time they were obscured by heavy corrosion, they were accurately described by Petrie, who dated them to Dynasty 12.[1]

Formed from two sheets of silver, the pendant is a rare survival of silverwork from this time. The back is flat, and the front is worked in the repoussé technique, with details added by chasing. The back sheet was extended to form a loop for suspension from a chain. Three small wire loops soldered along the bottom edge must have been used to attach other elements, possibly discs, which have not survived.

63

114

64

Although the iconography of the pendant looks very Egyptian, the technique is closely paralleled by that of the Master of Animals pendant (cat. no. 58) and of a gold pendant from Tell el-Dab'a with confronted dogs (cat. no. 62). These three pendants are also linked by their symmetrical compositions and, especially, by the close similarity of the bases on which the figures stand. The three of them can therefore be considered to belong to the same craft tradition;[2] however, the question of where they were made cannot definitively be answered. The Aegean, the Levant, and Egypt are the three main possibilities.

A recent study has been made by Schiestl,[3] whose sharp eyes first spotted the potential significance of the Petrie pendant under the layers of corrosion. His cautious conclusion was to suggest an Aegean manufacture for the Petrie pendant, though under both strong Egyptian and Near Eastern influence. In his view, Egypt contributed the griffins, while their pose was adapted in the Near East. He argues that all other details—the technique, the shape of the griffins' bodies, the overlapping of the front legs, the spirals on the heads, the base, and the loops that are perhaps for pendant discs—point to the Aegean.

The jewelry workshops of Minoan Crete would certainly have been capable of producing such a piece. Indeed, possibly the most famous item of Minoan jewelry is the bee pendant from Mallia (see fig. 32), which also takes the form of confronted creatures, is similarly backed with a flat sheet of gold, and has three pendant discs. The bee pendant can be dated to the time of Crete's First Palaces period, when contact with Egypt, often mediated via the Levantine coast, certainly occurred.

JLF

1. Petrie 1927, p. 9, pl. VIII:110.
2. For alternate interpretations of the imagery and manufacturing techniques used in the works, see cat. no. 62 and pages 101–3 in this volume.
3. Schiestl 2008.

64

DIADEM

Gold
Length 49.1 cm (19⅜ in.)
Eastern Nile Delta
Hyksos Period, Dynasty 15,
ca. 1640–1550 B.C.
The Metropolitan Museum of Art, New York,
Purchase, Lila Acheson Wallace Gift, 1968
68.136.1

This striking diadem belonging to an elite lady[1] came to the Metropolitan Museum as part of a group of objects allegedly found in the neighborhood of Tell el-Dab'a, in the eastern Nile Delta.[2] It is not clear whether all the pieces in the group originated from one tomb or were a hoard brought together (in ancient or in more recent times) from a number of burials. Objects in the group either are of well-known late Middle Kingdom Egyptian types—scarabs and scarab rings, a cylinder amulet inscribed for Amenemhat III, gold shell pendants, various types of beads, a *shen* (protection) amulet, a small gold lion—or reflect Levantine jewelry styles, such as gold hoop earrings, a torque, and a toggle pin.[3] The diadem is usually considered to be contemporary with two Canaanite scarabs in the group that are part of the so-called Late Palestinian series (late Middle Bronze IIB).[4]

The head ornament consists of a band of hammered sheet gold whose ends have been tapered to a narrower width and rolled to form loops. A string threaded through the loops served to fasten the band around the head. Attached to the front of the band is the head of a deer with imposing antlers; it is flanked on either side by two gazelle heads. Four starlike elements are positioned between the animal heads.[5]

Parallels for headbands of this type are almost exclusively from either western Asia or Egypt's eastern Delta region.[6] In the rest of Egypt, especially during Dynasty 12, circlets with no opening at the back predominated.[7] The concept of decorating an object with animal heads is likewise more directly paralleled by Canaanite pieces[8] than by Egyptian ones,[9] and the eight-pointed star elements could well derive from the Mesopotamian "star of Ishtar."[10]

This said, it is striking how far the shapes and execution of the animal heads exhibit the typical realism of Egyptian animal representation.[11] The broad, triangular deer head, for instance, with its furrowed forehead and small pores on the muzzle, accurately depicts the Persian fallow deer (*Dama mesopotamica*), a native of western Asia but known to Egyptian hunters, presumably from individuals who had wandered into the country by way of the northern Sinai.[12] The gazelle heads, too, show the essential features of the species—the narrow, rounded snout and the fold at the forward corner of the eye.[13] The Egyptians' keen sense for specificity in the representation of natural phenomena may also have induced the designers of the diadem to reinterpret the eight-pointed Ishtar stars as representations of plants.[14] A plant that first appears in Dynasty 18 in Egypt and could well have been introduced during the Hyksos period is the mandrake.[15] Its pointed leaves are layered in a manner very similar to those seen in the stars of the diadem. In the center of the leaves small flowers grow, ripening into the bright yellow fruits that delighted New Kingdom Egyptians. Representations of flowers or fruit stems on this diadem could well have been inserted at the center of the stars.

The presence of multiple western Asiatic traits and a fundamentally Egyptian approach to animal and plant representation make the diadem a perfectly fitting product of the eastern Delta Hyksos culture.[16] DA

1. H. Fischer 1969; Aldred 1971, pp. 204–5, pl. 59; H.-W. Müller and Thiem 1999, p. 128, figs. 244–46; Lilyquist 1993, pp. 54–55; Lilyquist 2003, pp. 159–60.
2. Lilyquist 1993, pp. 54–55, 63 n. 99.
3. The pin has a tiny glass inlay at the top: ibid., pp. 55–56.
4. Their design is similar to D. Ben-Tor 2007, pl. 85, nos. 1, 10. The Late Palestinian series is dated by Ben-Tor to later Middle Bronze IIB, or, in Egyptian terms, Dynasty 15 and the very beginning of Dynasty 18 (ca. 1630–1500 B.C.): ibid., p. 155.
5. Each animal head consists of two halves of hammered sheet gold soldered together along the center. Separately cut and rolled ears and gazelle horns were inserted into holes in the heads. The antlers of the deer consist again of two halves, each with the edges folded over for joining; twisted wires cover the joins between the head and the antlers and ears of the deer. The star elements are each made of at least eleven pieces. In the center is a raised dome with a hole in the middle surrounded by a collar made of strips of gold. The leaves may have been inlaid, but the dome was certainly visible; the stem of some further element must have been inserted into the hole.
6. Philip 2006, pp. 86–88, 154–56, 220. The only somewhat similar head ornament from an entirely Egyptian context is the fillet of Senebtisi: Mace and Winlock 1916, pp. 58–59, fig. 28, pls. 15b, 21.
7. Andrews 1990, pp. 101–6; H.-W. Müller and Thiem 1999, pp. 102–4. Not to be confused (as also in Philip 2006, p. 156) with the simple headbands of the western Asiatic type should be the Egyptian "boatman's" fillet, whose manifestations as jewelry represented not only the headband but also the knot and falling ends of a tied piece of flexible material worn around the head: Andrews 1990, pp. 107–8. This is certainly an indigenous Egyptian type of head ornament with state, funerary, and religious meanings whose long history is amply documented in two- and three-dimensional art: Jéquier 1921, pp. 43–47; Kerrn-Lilleso 1986.
8. See, for instance, the stone and wood dishes: *At That Time the Canaanites Were in the Land* 1990, p. 30, figs. 27, 28. For floral or similar ornaments on Canaanite headbands see also the Tell el-'Ajjul jewelry; for instance: ibid., p. 68, fig. 73.
9. The use of heads alone for ornamentation is rare in Egypt. Among extant examples are the falcon heads on poles to which rudder oars are fastened (Winlock 1955, p. 61, pls. 48, 80), hedgehog heads on the stern and prow of boats (Hayes 1953, p. 99, fig 56), and the flattened falcon head on the ends of collars (H.-W. Müller and Thiem 1999, pp. 102–3, figs. 203, 205). Heads functioning as images of deities (such as the imposing cow head from the Tomb of Tutankhamun [Reeves 1995, p. 87]) are objects of a different nature.
10. Black and Green 1992, pp. 169–70. For stars as jewelry elements from Tell el-'Ajjul, see *At That Time the Canaanites Were in the Land* 1990, p. 70, fig. 76. On the eight-pointed stars with granulation from the late Dynasty 12 jewelry
of Khnemet (see fig. 33), see Lilyquist 1993, pp. 36–37 (suggested origin: Crete-Anatolia).
11. Compare, for contrast, the magnificent but highly abstracted gazelle head on the earrings from Tell el-'Ajjul: *At That Time the Canaanites Were in the Land* 1990, p. 66, fig. 69.
12. Boessneck 1988, pp. 36, 39. That Egyptian artists knew this animal is documented by a number of fine representations: ibid., fig. 21; Leclant 1978, p. 296, fig 330.
13. Compare cat. no. 158: Lilyquist 2003, p. 156, fig. 92b, pp. 159–60.
14. Egyptian stars have only five points: Gardiner 1988, p. 487 n. 14.
15. Germer 1985, pp. 169–71. A good example of how Egyptians observed the layering of the pointed leaves of this plant is on the box from the Tomb of Tutankhamun, below the representation of king and queen among flowers: Reeves 1995, pl. opposite p. 7.
16. A gold feline head in the Ahhotep Treasure is strikingly similar to the deer head on the diadem: Egyptian Museum, Cairo, CG 52.703, Vernier 1927, pp. 235–36, pl. 39. Was this a piece of booty taken by Theban rulers at Avaris?

65

DAGGER

Bronze and wood with gold overlay
Height 35.5 cm (14 in.)
Saqqara
Hyksos Period, Dynasty 15, reign of Apophis, ca. 1581–1541 B.C.
Luxor Museum, Egypt JE 32735

This dagger was found with a burial deposited inside the no longer functioning funerary temple of the Dynasty 6 queen Iput, at Saqqara.[1] Covered by sand, a painted wood coffin rested on the stone pavement of one of the chambers.[2] Between the head end of the coffin and a wall were placed a number of pottery vases,[3] animal bones (from food offerings?), and the remains of a wood stool. Inside the coffin, whose lid had caved in under the weight of the sand,[4] the excavators found at the side of the head a wood headrest and two more pots. By the right leg was a piece of wood (*taillée en pointe*,[5] perhaps a throw stick), and by the left leg, the dagger. The owner of the coffin was a man with the Semitic name *abd* (shortened from *abd*-NN, or Servant of the God NN).[6]

The dagger is of a type that not only was to become typical for New Kingdom Egypt[7] and the Late Bronze Age Levant[8] but also turned up, albeit more rarely, at

roughly the same time in the Aegean.[9] It is at present impossible to say where the type first originated.[10] The blade and handle of such weapons were cast in a single piece, with a comfortable grip ensured by a pair of hilt plates of wood or another organic material, and—in the case of luxury items—covered with hammered sheet gold as in the present case. Flanged rims on both sides of the handle served to fasten the hilt plates. One side of this dagger's handle is embellished with the inscription, "The perfect god, lord of the two lands Nebkhepeshre Apophis."[11] On the other side a man is depicted spearing a lion, while on top a horned animal flees in the opposite direction (see frontispiece, p. 94). A leafy plant fills the space in front of the horned animal, and a single leaflike object is squeezed between the hunter's right hand and an L-shaped bit of ground on which the hind legs of the lion rest.[12] Below the hunter are the words, "Follower of his lord Nehemen,"[13] the "lord" in question doubtless the Hyksos king named on the other side of the dagger.

After having been described in the past as a copy of an Aegean prototype, this dagger was more recently ascribed to Levantine workmanship based on comparisons with Syrian seals (see fig. 43).[14] Tightly packed groups of similarly lively animals appear as well on Canaanite-influenced Egyptian scarabs.[15] The curious climbing stance of the hunter, although known from Levantine seals,[16] occurs also in a Middle Kingdom Egyptian tomb.[17] Punched stipples and small parallel engraved lines not only are familiar from earlier Egyptian gold work[18] but also are found in a manner comparable to their nearly painterly use on the Nehemen dagger with a number of late Middle Kingdom metal objects excavated at Thebes and Abydos.[19] In short: neither the type of dagger nor the style of the decoration on its handle speaks against a manufacture of the object on Egyptian soil during a period when foreign contacts were omnipresent. Since daggers of the Nehemen type were not found up till now at Tell el-Dab'a,[20] it may even be possible that this particular weapon was made close to its findspot, at Hyksos-ruled Memphis, although a minor detail that forms a link between the Metropolitan Museum diadem (cat. no. 64), an earring from Tell el-'Ajjul, and the dagger indicates connections between the makers of the dagger with the eastern Delta/southern Canaan area.[21]

The lion hunt remains a remarkable subject for an object made in Egypt. Known since at least Early Dynastic times in Mesopotamia,[22] the theme of slaying a lion (the symbol of the pharaoh) is widely avoided in Old and Middle Kingdom Egyptian representations[23] and even during the New Kingdom remained largely a royal prerogative.[24] The dagger image must be understood in the context of the aims and self-perception of the Hyksos. Their Semitic personal names notwithstanding, these rulers strove to establish themselves as the legitimate successors of the pharaohs, and Nehemen parallels this strategy by assuming the *shendyt* kilt (with a central lappet) of Middle Kingdom Egyptian officials. By appearing in the role of a lion hunter, however, a status symbol derived from a foreign culture, this follower of a Hyksos king delivered an unprecedented blow to Egyptian decorum.

DA

1. Daressy 1906, pp. 115–16. Saqqara was the cemetery of the Old and New Kingdom Egyptian capital Memphis, and this dagger is a rare indication of actual Hyksos present at that place. No technical examination has yet been performed on the piece.
2. Firth and Gunn 1926, p. 11, fig. 3.
3. A search for these vessels in the Egyptian Museum, Cairo, is under way with the help of museum director Dr. Wafaa el-Saddik.
4. Cairo JE 28108: Lacau 1904, pp. 86–87, pl. 19:1, 2; Porter, Moss, and Málek 1978, p. 552.
5. Daressy 1906, p. 115.
6. Schneider 2003, pp. 140–41.
7. Early datable examples of this type of dagger from Egypt in addition to the one here under discussion are: Corble dagger (present location unknown) with the name of Aqenenre Apophis (Dawson 1925; Ryholt 1997, p. 386); dagger handle grips with the names of Thutmose I, MMA 22.3.75a, b (Roth 2005); dagger of Djehuty, Hessisches Landesmuseum, Darmstadt, inv. no. Ae:I, 6 (Petschel 2004, p. 87, no. 76; Lilyquist 1988, p. 15); sword of similar type, MMA 16.10.453 (Hayes 1959, p. 68, fig. 36 left; Merrillees 1982, pp. 234–36: ca. 1500 B.C.); dagger from Zawiet el-Amwat (Wainwright 1925).
8. H.-W. Müller 1987, pp. 61–67; Gonen 1992a, p. 246; Gonen 1992b, p. 44. The daggers mentioned by Ziffer in *At That Time the Canaanites Were in the Land* 1990, p. 72, do not have the cast-on handles.
9. Papadopoulos 1998, pp. 16–17, pls. 10, 11.
10. I thank Graham Philip for discussing the question with me via e-mail.
11. For this king, see Ryholt 1997, pp. 385–87, and Schneider 1998, pp. 36–39, 71–73.

12. The area around the right hand of the hunter was better preserved when the object was first photographed: Daressy 1906, pl. 7.

13. Written in large hieroglyphs the name ending with a plant determinative (Gardiner M2), possibly because the word *nḥmt* (lotus bud) was brought to the scribe's mind when he looked at the name; see Schneider 2003, pp. 148–49.

14. Helck 1979, pp. 58–59; Ziffer in *At That Time the Canaanites Were in the Land* 1990, pp. 72–73; Aruz 1995b, pp. 36–40, figs. 10, 13, 14 [a, b], 17, 19, 25, 26; Aruz 2008a, pp. 140–41 (attributed to the Levant or the Nile Delta).

15. Aruz 1995b, p. 40, with figs. 25–28. See also Hayes 1959, p. 36, fig. 17 (second row from bottom, third from left): MMA 30.8.903, identified by Daphna Ben-Tor (personal communication) as Egyptian under Canaanite influence. For similar scarabs from Tell el-Dab'a, see Mlinar 2004, pp. 131–32, fig. 13b [14].

16. Porada 1973b, p. 269, fig. 4.

17. See Blackman 1914, pls. 6, 7.

18. See, for example, Andrews 1990, p. 128, fig. 111; Aldred 1971, pl. 81; and Bourriau in *Pharaohs and Mortals* 1988, pp. 148–49, no. 159.

19. Petrie Museum of Egyptian Archaeology, University College London 16229, from Abydos: Bourriau in *Pharaohs and Mortals* 1988, p. 155, no. 174; and MMA 13.180.2, from Thebes: Hayes 1953, p. 239, fig. 153.

20. The only vaguely similar example is a stray find: Philip 2006, pp. 54–55, no. 3995. For the common dagger types found at Tell el-Dab'a see ibid., pp. 42–55, 141–46, 218–19. Irmgard Hein (personal communication) has confirmed the absence of the Nehemen dagger type from finds at Tell el-Dab'a.

21. On the inside of the animals' ears a peculiar branch pattern is incised, an abstracted rendering no doubt of the minute hairs these animals have inside their ears: for the Tell el-'Ajjul earring, see *At That Time the Canaanites Were in the Land* 1990, p. 66, fig. 69. Another eastern Delta link was pointed out by Christa Mlinar (2004, p. 114, with nn. 51, 52), who argued that the crossed bands indicated by dots over Nehemen's chest are not the badge familiar from depictions of Egyptians soldiers and hunters, but connected with similar bands represented in the Near East as a method to fasten a dagger to a man's side. According to Mlinar, among the scarab corpus such bands are depicted only on those made in the southern Levant or the eastern Delta.

22. Collon 2005a, pp. 193–97.

23. See, for instance, Blackman 1914, pl. 8.

24. Hayes 1959, pp. 232, 390, fig. 245; Rössler-Köhler 1980.

66

DAGGER OF KAMOSE

Bronze, silver, gold
Length 31.8 cm (12½ in.)
Dra Abu el-Naga
New Kingdom, Dynasty 17, reign of Kamose,
ca. 1552–1550 B.C.
Royal Library of Belgium,
Brussels

The legacy of Kamose, despite his short reign, is that of the leader who succeeded in defeating the Kushites in the south and, more important, the Hyksos to the north. The last ruler of Dynasty 17 and the brother of Ahmose, who completed the task of expelling the Hyksos and founded Dynasty 18, Kamose was arguably the most brilliant pharaoh of the period.

The dagger of Kamose was found with a gold bracelet bearing his cartouche on a mummy in a nonroyal sarcophagus.[1] The sarcophagus had been placed at the exit of the Valley of the Kings on the west bank of Thebes, at Dra Abu el-Naga. Discovered by Auguste Mariette and Heinrich Karl Brugsch in December 1857, it was given by Mariette to the Egyptian viceroy Said Pasha to be offered to Prince Napoleon. In 1884, the dagger figured in the Parisian sale of the properties of the famous dealer and jeweler Alessandro Castellani. It was then bought by the young Lucien de Hirsch de Gereuth, whose mother offered the entire collection of antiquities—primarily Greek coins—to the Belgian nation in 1898 after his premature death.

This dagger of precious metals was not suited for actual use, and even as a ceremonial artifact it had to be carried with great care, since the blade is poorly attached to the handle. A similar dagger, now in the Egyptian Museum in Cairo, was found in 1859, also by Mariette, among the burial equipment associated with Ahhotep, Kamose's mother, along with other artifacts with clearly foreign elements (see cat. nos. 67, 68). In comparison with the dagger in Cairo, the precious metals used for the handle and the pommel of Kamose's dagger have been reversed (a gold handle and a pommel covered with a silver leaf). It is likely that these two royal objects of identical shape were originally intended to form a pair,

although the different decorative stud pattern on Ahhotep's dagger weakens this hypothesis.

These prestigious daggers, with a round pommel pierced by two D-shaped ears, reproduce a type known since the Middle Kingdom and still in use at a later date, as attested by the Metropolitan Museum's dagger with an ivory pommel.[2]

FDC

1. For further reference, see von Bissing 1900, pl. VIII.20; Gaspar 1901, p. 7; Vernier 1927, p. 211; Naster 1975–76, pp. 419–26, pl. XVI; Hein 1994, p. 272, no. 382, and p. 77, colorpl.; Ryholt 1997; Laffineur 1998; and Franco 2002, p. 428, no. 103, and p. 137, fig. 8.
2. MMA 1911 11.150.16.

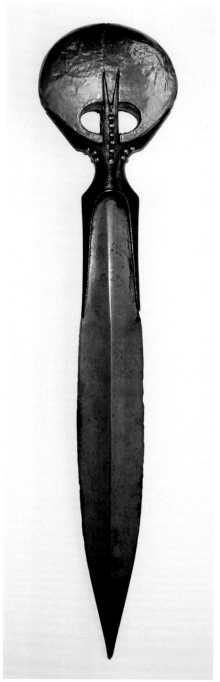

66

The Burial of Queen Ahhotep

One of the most important and intriguing finds linked to the beginning of the New Kingdom was made in 1859, when a gilded coffin and a trove of magnificent jewels and other objects belonging to a queen named Ahhotep were discovered, supposedly in a brick-lined vaulted tomb in the necropolis Dra Abu el-Naga in western Thebes.[1] Among the ornaments uncovered there were a number of precious metal fly pendants associated with military honor and derived from the Nubian Kerma culture.[2] The inclusion of this type of ornament reflects the queen's role, as recorded in an inscription from Karnak, as "the princess, the king's mother, the noblewoman who knows things and takes care of Egypt. She looked after its soldiers and protected them. She brought back its fugitives and gathered its dissidents together. She pacified Upper Egypt and expelled its rebels."[3]

Clearly Ahhotep had performed some part in ensuring the Theban triumph over the Hyksos. Most likely she was a princess of the Theban line, the wife of king Seqenenre, and perhaps the mother of both Kamose and Ahmose.[4] Inscribed materials for both of these rulers were found among her putative burial equipment. Another coffin inscribed for Ahhotep was discovered in the Deir el-Bahri cache[5] and has been taken as evidence that there were two early Dynasty 18 queens named Ahhotep.[6] The Deir el-Bahri coffin, however, was reused by Painedjem I of Dynasty 21, and its massive size suggests that it once formed the outer case to the Dra Abu el-Naga inner coffin. Such a pairing is evocative of the coffins of princess Meryetamun, indicating that the coffins of Ahhotep were originally made as a pair and separated at some point in the distant past.[7]

The Dra Abu el-Naga burial must have been a reinterment, as were the Kamose reburial[8] and possibly the Qurna rishi coffin group found by Petrie as well.[9] These reburials may have been necessitated by the tomb robberies of the late New Kingdom, but the quantity of precious items surviving in them suggests that they had been treated with more reverence than were the tombs of their successors.

PL

1. Reeves 2000, pp. 50–52; von Bissing 1900.
2. In addition to the well-known gold flies on a chain are smaller gold and silver flies from the tomb that are identical to the ones found at Kerma: cf. American Discovery of Ancient Egypt 1995, p. 167. The find was made during the early years of archaeological exploration in Egypt, and the lack of supervision at the time has made some scholars skeptical of the discovery, beginning with Winlock 1924, pp. 217–77, especially p. 254, and, more recently, Harvey 1998, pp. 20–21, and Arnold 2008, the latter two cautioning against any inferences made from the material. It could be at least as likely as not, however, that this material does form a singular group.
3. Jánosi 1992, p. 99.
4. Bryan 2000, pp. 228–29.
5. CG3872; Winlock 1932.
6. Roth 1999, p. 362.
7. Eaton-Krauss 2003, pp. 75–89.
8. Reeves 2000, p. 48.
9. The Ahhotep and Kamose reburials may be related to later reuse of the Dra Abu el-Naga tombs (Daniel Polz, personal communication). The circumstances of the rich rishi coffin burial from Qurna suggest that it could well have been part of the same project (Petrie 1909, pp. 6–11).

67

AXE

Gold, electrum, copper alloy, semiprecious stones, wood
Height 47.5 cm (18¾ in.); width 6.7 cm (2⅝ in.)
Thebes, Tomb of Ahhotep
New Kingdom, Dynasty 18, 16th century B.C.
Luxor Museum, Egypt JE 4673

68

DAGGER

Gold, electrum, copper alloy, semiprecious stones
Width 3.4 cm (1⅜ in.); length 28.5 cm (11¼ in.)
Thebes, Tomb of Ahhotep
New Kingdom, Dynasty 18, 16th century B.C.
Luxor Museum, Egypt JE 4666

The objects associated with the Ahhotep find reflect the cosmopolitan nature of Egypt at the outset of the New Kingdom, when contact with foreign cultures from both the north and south brought many new influences to the art and customs of the fledgling empire. The copper-alloy ceremonial battle-axe encrusted with semiprecious stones and gold cutouts inlaid into a black substance is an elaborate imitation (using precious metals) of a typical Egyptian weapon of the period, which would have had a copper-alloy blade, leather binding, and wood handle.[1] The now-missing bands on the handle would have evoked the contrasting bands of wood sometimes found in functional axes.[2] Running along the length of the handle is a gold band with inlaid hieroglyphs giving the titulary of Ahmose, and cartouches at the top side of the blade read, "The good god Nebphetyre, son of Re, Ahmose." Below this is a depiction of the king wearing a blue "battle" crown and smiting an enemy in the attenuated style of the late Second Intermediate Period. The pharaoh, depicted as an Egyptian sphinx on the reverse of the axe, is here rendered as a crested recumbent griffin, with a raised wing and eagle or vulture beak, in the lowest register, with the inscription "beloved of Montu," the god of war.[3] The tradition of depicting the pharaoh as a conquering falcon-headed winged feline extends back to the Old and Middle Kingdoms, as seen on the pectoral of Mereret (fig. 34), and similar imagery appears on a sword of Kamose.[4] The griffin on the axe blade of Kamose's brother, however, represents a departure from Egyptian convention with features that are distinctively Aegean.[5]

The developed Aegean griffin, which appeared at the beginning of the Late Bronze Age, has a large, elaborately feathered wing with bent profile and spirals;[6] two curls often fall over the animal's chest (see cat. no. 76 for a discussion of the spiral curl). An important detail of the wing patterning is the "notched plume" or "adder mark" design of dots and zigzags, which characterizes images of griffins on frescoes from Thera, Tell Kabri, Alalakh, Miletos, and possibly Tell el-Dab'a.[7] This Aegean "notched plume" design and spiral curls appear on the wings of the griffin on Ahmose's axe blade, and its head resembles a griffin on a dagger from the Shaft Graves at Mycenae.[8] The comb-like crest and the head in general find their best parallels in later Mycenaean art and on a gold vessel in the form of a griffin head depicted as part of the Aegean tribute in the Tomb of Useramun at Thebes.[9]

At the top of the reverse of the blade is a standard depiction of the god Heh, lord of eternity, holding palm fronds symbolizing the millions of years of rule offered to the pharaoh. Below this is the vulture goddess of Upper Egypt, Nekhbet, wearing the white crown and nesting above lilies, a heraldic plant of the south. Facing her is Wadjet, the cobra goddess of Lower Egypt,

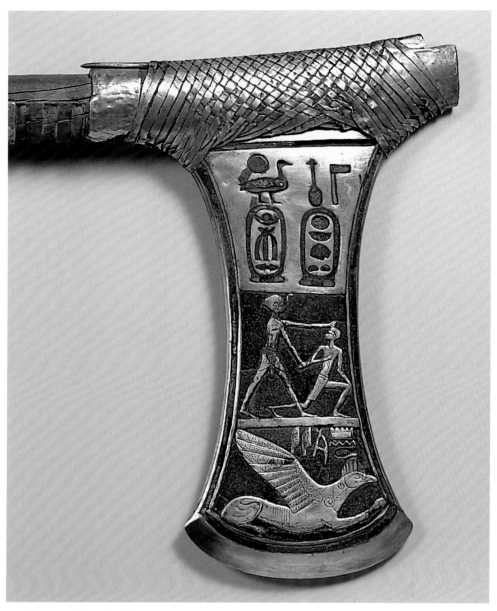

67, alternate view, detail

67

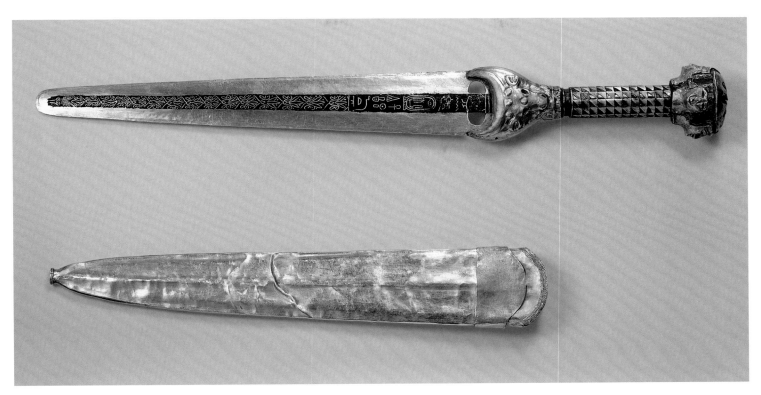

68

wearing the red crown and coiled above a
papyrus plant, symbolizing the north. The
hieroglyphic inscription "beloved" is positioned in the spaces around the plants.
At the edge of the blade is a depiction of
a sphinx offering a decapitated head, a
unique scene perhaps alluding to the function of the axe.

Also part of the Ahhotep assemblage
was an elaborate dagger, its pommel covered with gold leaf and embellished with
inlaid semiprecious stones.[10] The handle,
which was overlaid with silver and engraved,
has curving ends in the form of bucrania
covered in gold leaf. These hold the blade,
which is made of gold and tapers to a
rounded tip. Two holes on either side of
the midrib at the top of the blade are vestiges of the standard type of grip found on
Second Intermediate Period daggers.[11]

A dark strip of a black substance runs
down both sides of the blade, serving as a
background into which gold-wire figures
and hieroglyphic signs—possibly of foreign workmanship[12]—are inlaid. A lion
chases a bull down the length of one side,
both animals in flying gallop. A sedge plant
divides the chase from four locusts of comparable size. The flying-gallop and lion-
chase motifs, the curving landscape lines
above (indicating rock work), and the inlay
technique have all been linked to the decoration of daggers found in the Shaft Graves
at Mycenae (cat. no. 171), one of which has
a Nilotic theme, and at Rutsi (fig. 36).[13]

The juxtaposition of quadrupeds with
locusts is, however, unparalleled in the
Aegean world; rather, the insect is depicted
in Egyptian tomb paintings and on amulets, scarabs, jewelry, combs, and vessels

in the role of a destroyer. Its possible association with an army (multitude), as interpreted from art and texts, makes the
creature an appropriate image for an
Egyptian dagger blade.[14] The inlays on
the Ahhotep dagger also differentiate it
from weapons from the Aegean, where
daggers were set with gold- and silver-
leaf cutouts engraved with anatomical
details to provide body mass for each animal; here, gold wire is used for outlines
and inner markings, thus allowing the
background to show through and become
part of the body as well. Such a technique
was apparently already used in the nineteenth century B.C.—as evidenced by a
bronze sickle sword inlaid with electrum
wire into a black background, believed to be
from Middle Bronze Age Canaan.[15] The
significance of this piece is obvious when

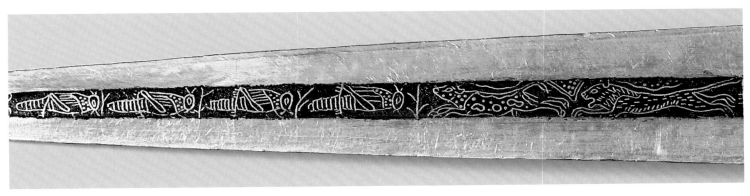

68, detail

121

Figure 36. Inlaid bronze and gold dagger. Rutsi, Tholos Tomb 2. Late Helladic IIA context. National Archaeological Museum, Athens 8340

compared with the sickle sword found in the tomb of the Syrian prince Ip-shemu-abi at Byblos (cat. no. 30).[16] On its blade is a narrow strip of black substance inlaid with gold; both wire and cutouts of gold leaf were used, the former to produce the dotted-scale pattern and the latter for the hieroglyphic inscription.

Metal inlay into a dark substance, often called niello (probably a blackened metallic alloy of copper), first appears in the Levant during the Middle Bronze Age and in Egypt during Dynasty 12.[17] It is significant that the first black-inlaid decoration in the Aegean, whether Near Eastern or Egyptian in origin, also appeared on a strip running the length of a weapon, although the Aegean cutout technique, which provides each figure with substance, imparts an artistic effect different from that of the wire that outlines the body. The griffin on the Ahmose axe blade is worked in the Aegean way and so looks more foreign in style than the design on the Ahhotep dagger and the design on the reverse of the axe blade, where semiprecious stones are set into forms cut into a gold background (cat. no. 67). Even though the iconography of both pieces exhibits foreign influences, alien motifs were not simply copied but were worked into an Egyptian

context. The unusual griffin of the axe takes the place of the Horus animal as the triumphant pharaoh, beloved of Montu, and the lion and bull, fashioned in outline on the dagger, gallop in a landscape of Egyptian locusts and plants.   JA/PL

1. Compare Hayes 1959, p. 68, fig. 36 (right).
2. The bands here may have been in ivory or some other delicate substance, which has not survived. Cairo Museum JE 17092.
3. We thank Dorothea Arnold for clarifying the meaning of the inscription.
4. A. Evans, PM IV, p. 914, fig. 888; Frankfort 1936–37, p. 110; Winlock 1924; von Bissing 1900, pl. XII.
5. Frankfort 1936–37, pp. 112–13; A. Evans, PM I, p. 551, fig. 402; Middle Kingdom Egyptian griffins: Newberry 1894, Tomb 15: pl. 4, and Tomb 17: pl. 13; Altenmüller 1986, p. 8, fig. 2, pl. 2:2.
6. This appears to be a very un-Egyptian characteristic. The only Egyptian bird represented with such a bent or pinioned wing is the lapwing, *rekhyt*, an image of subjugation, which, by the New Kingdom, had become associated with royal veneration: R. Wilkinson 1992, pp. 86–87.
7. See Doumas 1992, p. 65, no. 32; Bietak in *Pharaonen und Fremde* 1994, p. 204, no. 229: this element appears not to be preserved but is assumed in the restoration; Niemeier and Niemeier 1998, pp. 78, 84; Niemeier and Niemeier 1999, p. 548; for Minoan examples, see A. Evans, PM I, p. 549, fig. 400; Levi 1925–26, p. 178, no. 183, fig. 221, pl. XVIII; CMS I, no. 223, for example.

8. See Hood 1978, p. 178, fig. 176b.
9. Vercoutter 1956, pl. XXXVIII:259.
10. There is also a bronze spearhead related by Müller-Karpe (1977, pp. 44–45) to an example from Mycenae, but the correspondence is not exact.
11. For the typical Second Intermediate Period version, see *American Discovery of Ancient Egypt* 1995, p. 168. A simpler version of the Ahhotep dagger, with a gold-foil handle over copper alloy, comes from the Metropolitan Museum excavations in Thebes, now in the Egyptian Museum, Cairo JE 45699.
12. James P. Allen, personal communication regarding the hieroglyphs, January 2005.
13. Hood 1978, p. 180, fig. 179.
14. Keimer (1932, 1933, and 1937), who refers to the locust as symbolic both of multitude, especially in reference to armies, and of weakness, as swarms may be killed without a struggle. In an unusual passage in the Pyramid Texts (Dynasty 6), the soul of the dead pharaoh is referred to as a locust; a field of souls in the form of locusts is mentioned in the Book of the Dead: Keimer 1937; Brunner-Traut 1977, pp. 1179–80.
15. H.-W. Müller 1987, frontis., pp. 36ff. Purchased on the art market, it was believed to come from Balata-Shechem. For another object in this technique, see Wildung 1980, pp. 14–15 (crocodile).
16. Montet 1928–29, pl. XCIXc: 653, inlaid with silver and gold.
17. Ibid., pl. CII:655; Wildung 1982, p. 479; see *American Discovery of Ancient Egypt* 1995, and Giumlia-Mair and Craddock 1993, regarding the identification of niello.

PAINTED PALACES

JOAN ARUZ

Nothing, perhaps, would have impressed the ancient visitors to the courts of western Asia, the Nile Delta, and the Aegean more than the spectacular palace wall paintings, replete with divine, royal, and supernatural imagery. Indeed, they must have excited the enthusiasm of the king of Ugarit, who expressed his desire to see the palace of Zimri-Lim at Mari.[1] Here a strong figural tradition was established in the decorative program. At its core was the scene depicting the investiture of the ruler (fig. 13) using imagery derived directly from southern Mesopotamia. Flanking this impressive scene, however, are rows of supernatural creatures that create an overall composition familiar from local Syrian-style cylinder seals. The running spiral border, which appears to evoke the watery environment created by deities with flowing vases, is repeated in other parts of the palace, particularly in association with dadoes and platform slabs painted to resemble veined marble or gypsum.[2] This combination makes the suggested origin of such decoration in an Aegean stone rather than a mud-brick architectural tradition compelling—particularly at a site such as Mari, its treasury filled with precious items from as far away as Kaphtor (which has been identified with Crete). Similar painted stone imitations also occur at Qatna (where Aegean pottery has been found),[3] perhaps reflecting the wider desirability of stone in an area where it was scarce.[4] On Crete we have hardly a glimpse of the colors, patterns, and images that embellished the first palaces.[5] But even early on, foreign elements are visible—literally—in the use of imported Egyptian Blue.[6] At Knossos, two early dado fragments survive, possibly painted with veined rockwork.[7]

The stunning discoveries of unquestionably Aegean-looking frescoes around the Mediterranean littoral have dramatically enhanced our picture of cultural exchange during the second millennium B.C. Unlike Near Eastern and Egyptian wall paintings (see cat. no. 70 and figs. 13, 85), these were executed in the Minoan fresco technique.[8] Fragments of a swaying palm frond, a bucranium, a reclining griffin, and painted imitations of gypsum, all adorning the Level VII palace at Alalakh, are Aegean in motif and style.[9] The frescoes that apparently fell from the walls of the Late Bronze Age palace at Qatna, which appear to be Aegean in technique and imagery, feature details that recall designs on frescoes from Thera (see cat. no. 69 and fig. 38). The white lily fresco from Miletos[10] and flowers painted on the floors of a Canaanite palace at Tel Kabri (along with painted imitations of stone veining, and fragments of a miniature fresco with ships) are undoubtedly Aegean in inspiration.[11]

Scenes of griffins, bull hunts, and acrobatics were discovered at Tell el-Dabʿa (see p. 131), but uncertainty surrounds the ethnic identity of both patrons and painters. Model templates may have been used to produce bulls of identical proportions and unusual regularity on a bull-leaping frieze from Tell el-Dabʿa (see fig. 39).[12] Nonetheless, Aegean-trained craftsmen must have been responsible for the Aegean motifs and iconography painted in Minoan color conventions and technique. Their patrons certainly expressed an uncommon internationalism, not only commissioning work quite foreign to eastern artistic conventions but also choosing images that seem to lack the powerful political messages conveyed in the decorative programs of the Near Eastern world.[13]

1. Dossin 1937, p. 74.
2. Parrot 1958, part 1, pp. 67–69, fig. 54, p. 109, pl. XV, part 2, p. 165, pl. XXXIX:2; Niemeier and Niemeier 1998, p. 73, pl. V.
3. Du Mesnil du Buisson 1935, frontis.
4. I. Winter 2000, p. 751.
5. Militello 1999.
6. Immerwahr 1990, no. 1 (Middle Minoan IIA): for Egyptian Blue at Heraklion-Poros, see *Crete–Egypt* 2000, pp. 106–7.
7. A. Evans, PM I, p. 251, fig. 188a, pp. 252, 355–56; Immerwahr 1990, pp. 22–23, fig. 6f, pp. 178–79, no. 1 (Middle Minoan IIA): Kn no. 41; only by adopting the low Mesopotamian chronology would the Aegean and Syrian dadoes be roughly contemporary; for Egyptian Blue at Heraklion–Poros in Late Minoan IA, see *Crete–Egypt* 2000, pp. 106–7.
8. Regarding techniques of Minoan wall painting, see M. Shaw 1972, pp. 182ff.; Hood 1978, pp. 83ff.; Immerwahr 1990, pp. 11–20; and Doumas 1992, pp. 17–19. Tyrian purple has been identified as a pigment at Thera; see Sotiropoulou, Andrikopoulos, and Chryssikopoulou 2003.
9. Niemeier and Niemeier 1998, pp. 82ff.
10. Niemeier and Niemeier 1999, pp. 548ff., pl. CXIXb. The archaeological context suggests a Minoan colony, with Minoan kitchenware, ritual equipment, and a Linear A inscription. The Minoan settlement at Trianda on Rhodes also produced Aegean-style wall paintings.
11. Niemeier 1995; Cline and Yassur-Landau 2007.
12. Bietak, Marinatos, and Palyvou 2000, pp. 85, 89 (in the discussion, Kopcke observed a certain un-Minoan monotony in the rendering of the bulls); for bull-leaping scenes from Late Minoan IA Thera, see Televantou 2000, pp. 834–35, figs. 1, 2 (wall painting from Xeste 4); CMS V Suppl. 3, 2, no. 392 (sealing).
13. On decorative programs appropriate for public display, see I. Winter 2000.

The Wall Paintings of Thera and the Eastern Mediterranean

The catastrophic volcanic eruption that devastated the island of Thera in the early Late Bronze Age preserved—beneath layers of tephra at the site of Akrotiri—the evidence of a thriving town of multistoried mansions with luxurious furnishings and spectacular frescoes. A number of raw materials and artifacts demonstrate the island's foreign connections (see cat. no. 278). The world illustrated in the wall paintings is a further source of information about the island's relations with the eastern Mediterranean. Images of plants and animals revere the exotic world with which the Therans had contact. The depiction of the palm tree in Aegean art has been considered a Near Eastern influence, although the plant was not unknown in the Theran habitat. However, in the Miniature Frieze, which adorned the walls of a room in the West House (figs. 37, 137, 138), it defines, along with papyrus, the subtropical landscape populated by non-Aegean creatures. The lion, the deer, and the wild duck were certainly not indigenous Theran fauna, though their presence on the frieze does not necessarily imply that they were exotic, since they were known in other parts of the Aegean. However, monkeys, antelopes, and leopards are so realistically rendered in the Theran wall paintings that the artists must surely have traveled to the lands in which these animals thrived, that is, the lands of the east. The griffin, an imaginary creature introduced from the east, is quite common in Minoan and Mycenaean art; its early presence as a decorative motif on Middle Cycladic ewers may indicate that the Cyclades were

the gateway to its introduction to the Aegean. Whether it was accompanied by any specific religious meaning is not certain, but the flying gallop, in which the griffin is depicted in the Miniature Frieze (see fig. 138), may have been introduced to Aegean art along with it. As the archaeological evidence demonstrates, the borrowing of artistic motifs—abstract and geometric patterns—was reciprocal. For example, the stylized manner of rendering rocks, the imitation of veined stones, the interlace pattern, the checkerboard, and the spiral motif (fig. 38) are common in the art of Thera. Their discovery not only at coastal sites such as Tell el-Dab'a in the Nile Delta or Tel Kabri but also in places farther inland, such as Qatna (cat. no. 69b) and the palace of Mari in the Middle Euphrates (fig. 13), cannot be accidental. Rather, it confirms the close contacts between the eastern Mediterranean civilizations and the Aegean world.

The adoption of foreign artistic elements such as those described above could be understood simply as a means of promoting the status of their users by displaying their contacts overseas. However, iconographic conventions common to both Theran and Near Eastern art may reveal a much deeper interaction extending even into the ideological realm. The superimposition of different scenes, for example, or the use of lateral layering in the representation of moving figures and vertical layering of static figures to render depth may reflect contacts or influences (see fig. 137). In Egyptian art, human figures are shown with two left or two right hands or feet depending on the

direction in which they are moving. Although the Theran painters endeavored to deviate from this convention—and they were frequently successful—there are instances, such as the girl gathering saffron, in which such interventions were not possible.[1] Similarly, the standardized rendering of the piebald hide of cattle in Egyptian and Mesopotamian art, by three- or four-rayed stars with rounded spikes, is an artistic idiom found also in the art of Thera, as exemplified by the bulls in the Miniature Frieze or the structures made of bull hides, such as the so-called cabins on the ships of the flotilla scene (fig. 37) and the shields or palanquins that decorate the wall of Room 4 of the West House.

Personified animals, in particular monkeys, appear frequently in Near Eastern art (cat. no. 54); the monkey serving the Mistress of Animals in the wall painting of the saffron gatherers is a good Aegean example from Thera. Similarly, both Egyptian and Mesopotamian monuments with representations of monkeys playing musical instruments or dancing were surely the source of inspiration for the Theran artist who painted comparable scenes in Xeste 3, one of the spacious mansions of Akrotiri.[2]

The Egyptian pose for denoting pain or sorrow is recognized in the composition of the so-called Adorants in Xeste 3.[3] On the walls of funerary monuments in Thebes, Egypt, kneeling mourners are shown with one arm extended, the hand touching the ground, while the other hand supports the forehead. This pose was apparently borrowed by the Theran artist to express the pain of the young woman with the bleeding toe as, seated on a rock, she supports her forehead with her left hand, while with the right hand, extended downward, she holds her right foot. Another apparently Near Eastern convention is the rendering of inert bodies. Used from very early on in both Egyptian and Mesopotamian art, this style was applied by the painter of the Miniature Frieze to depict drowned warriors in the scene of a naval battle (see fig. 137).

Although later in date (12th century B.C.), the painting in the Tomb of Inherkhau at Deir el-Medina, Egypt, shows children with partly shaved heads, exactly as they are depicted in the Thera wall paintings. One cannot with certainty state that such hair treatment had the same meaning both in Egypt and in Thera (in the latter it was intended to designate stages of initiation). Nevertheless, the later date of the Egyptian example suggests an Aegean borrowing.[4]

All the examples cited suggest that interactions during the Late Bronze Age between the Aegean world and its contemporary civilizations in the eastern Mediterranean were neither temporary nor superficial.   CGD

1. Immerwahr 2005, pp. 176, 180. For lateral and vertical layering in Egyptian art, see Schäfer 1974, pp. 177–89, and Robins 1986, pp. 39, 41. For the representation of hands and feet of human figures in Egyptian art, see Robins 1986, pp. 12–16.
2. Vanschoonwinkel 1990, p. 332.
3. Immerwahr 2005, p. 177.
4. For representations of male and female children with partly shaved heads on Theran wall paintings, see Doumas 2000, pp. 972–73. For representations of children with partly shaved heads and locks of hair in the Tomb of Inherkhau at Deir el-Medina, see Weeks 2005, p. 507, and Meskell 2004, pp. 86–87, fig. 3.11.

Figure 37. Miniature Frieze, south wall, detail. Thera, Akrotiri, West House, Room 5. Late Cycladic I. Archaeological Museum of Thera 5824

69a, b
WALL PAINTING FRAGMENTS

Plaster, painted
a. Marine scene
Height 48 cm (18⅞ in.); length 51 cm (20⅛ in.)

b. Spiral frieze
Height 33 cm (13 in.); width 192 cm (75⅝ in.)

Qatna, Royal Palace, Room N
Late Bronze Age, 16th–15th century B.C.
Homs Museum, Homs, Syria MSH 00G–i
0092 et al.; MSH 01G–i 0052 et al.

More than three thousand fragments of wall paintings have been discovered in the Royal Palace of Qatna in western Syria (see pp. 219–21), most of them from Room N in the northwestern part of the building. When the palace was destroyed about 1340 B.C. during the wars with the Hittites, the fragments, together with the collapsed walls of the same room, fell into the ad-joining palace well, where they were discovered during the excavations of 2000 to 2004.[1] They are in part executed in fresco, the only examples of this technique to have survived from Bronze Age Syria.[2]

In both style and technique they closely resemble Aegean wall paintings from Minoan Crete and from the island of Thera. The most remarkable parallels can be found in frescoes from the Late Minoan I period, which seem to have had a strong influence.[3] The Qatna paintings can be dated to the sixteenth or early fifteenth century B.C.,[4] or, alternatively, to about 1400 B.C.[5] They were thus on the walls of Room N either for one hundred fifty to two hundred years, or—following the second proposal—for approximately fifty years.[6]

Many motifs on the Qatna paintings relate directly to Aegean archetypes, in terms of style, iconography, and color. Most prominent among these are palm trees with blue leaves that are integrated into a miniature landscape marked by rocks and grass which closely resemble Minoan landscapes at Knossos and on Thera.[7] The representations of papyrus and of a dolphin also clearly derive from Aegean models (see cat. no. 34).[8] The appearance of the dolphin is particularly striking as dolphins certainly were not seen in this inland Syrian city.

Two examples of the Qatna paintings from Room N, restored in 2008, are presented here.[9] One is a double frieze of running spirals with tripartite leaves[10] framed by a border of contour lines and dark red semicircles. The running spiral is a common motif in Aegean wall painting, abundantly present in the palace of Knossos[11] and in the houses of Akrotiri on Thera (fig. 38).[12]

The other fragment is a narrow, frieze-like composition originally nearly four meters long and only thirty centimeters high, of which the left half is presented here. It shows a water landscape populated by turtles and fish.[13] The two partially overlapping turtles are carefully rendered with naturalistic details, the heads cautiously poking out from under the expanse of the carapace. The landscape is divided into two zones, red and blue-gray.

The white area above the landscape seems to represent water. Red fish swim in the water, the fins clearly recognizable.

Red forms on the edge of the red landscape perhaps represent a stone and two grasslike plants along a riverbank.[14]

This scene is reminiscent of the Miniature Frieze at Thera, where in one scene a bending river is framed by a landscape populated with animals and covered with vegetation (fig. 138).[15] The only unfamiliar iconographic element in the Qatna wall painting is the turtle, which is not seen on Aegean wall paintings and is also rare in Near Eastern iconography.[16] Its representation on a wall painting might be regarded as an innovation of Qatna craftsmen.

It is highly likely that craftsmen trained in the Aegean fresco tradition were involved in the production of the wall paintings at Qatna. It may also be assumed, based on the non-Aegean technical and iconographic elements in the paintings, that local artists participated as well. Taken together, this suggests the existence of a workshop at Qatna with craftsmen trained in different regional art traditions.

Another possibility—based on the dating to 1400 B.C.—is that the wall paintings at Qatna are evidence not of direct cooperation between Aegean and Syrian craftsmen during the time the wall paintings were made but of a transfer over an extended period of time of style and techniques from the Aegean to Syria within the framework of interregional communication.[17]

In either case, the adoption of the Aegean style in a palace context may be understood as a means of increasing prestige and status among the ruling elite through the acquisition of exotica.[18]

PP/CVR

69a

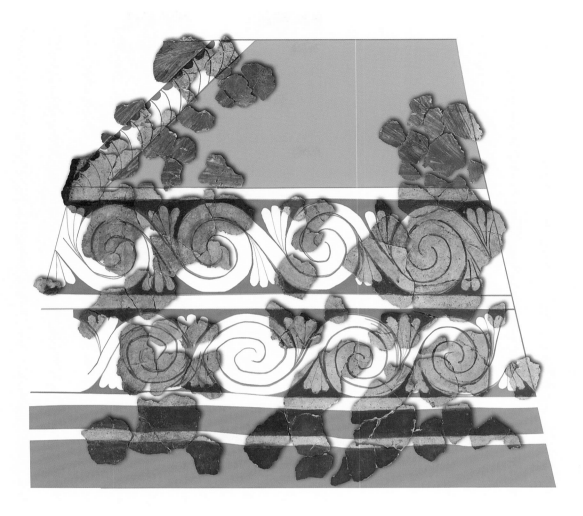

69b

Figure 38. Wall painting with spiral frieze, detail. Thera, Xeste 3, Room 2. Late Cycladic I–Late Minoan IA. Archaeological Museum of Thera

1. This catalogue entry is in large part based on von Rüden 2006.
2. Personal communication from Ann Brysbaert (in preparation for publication).
3. See Pfälzner 2008.
4. This date reflects the opinion of Peter Pfälzner; arguments are based primarily on direct stylistic comparisons.
5. This date reflects the opinion of Constance von Rüden; she argues (2006) that the wall paintings, for technical reasons, could not have been on the walls long before the destruction of the palace in 1340 B.C.; Bietak (2007) argues along the same line and proposes a date in the fourteenth century B.C.
6. Traces of the fire that raged when the palace was destroyed are visible on the paintings, clearly proving that they were at the time still on the walls.
7. Novák and Pfälzner 2001; Novák and Pfälzner 2002; von Rüden 2006; Pfälzner 2008.
8. Von Rüden 2006.
9. Restoration was overseen by Ilka Weisser and Andreas de Bortoli.
10. Von Rüden 2006.
11. A. Evans, PM III, pl. XXIII, figs. 221, 222, 228, 229, 252–54.
12. Doumas 1995, figs. 93, 94.
13. Reconstruction and description of the entire panel are described in von Rüden 2006.
14. A different interpretation is offered by von Rüden (2006), who interprets the entire representation as an underwater scene.
15. Doumas 1995, figs. 30–34. Von Rüden (2006) emphasizes parallels to painted ceramic motifs depicting underwater scenes from Late Minoan IB and Late Minoan II/Late Helladic IIA.
16. The turtle was known—though rarely depicted—as a symbol of the god Ea in the ancient Near East; see Black and Green 1992, p. 179.
17. Von Rüden 2006.
18. Feldman 2007.

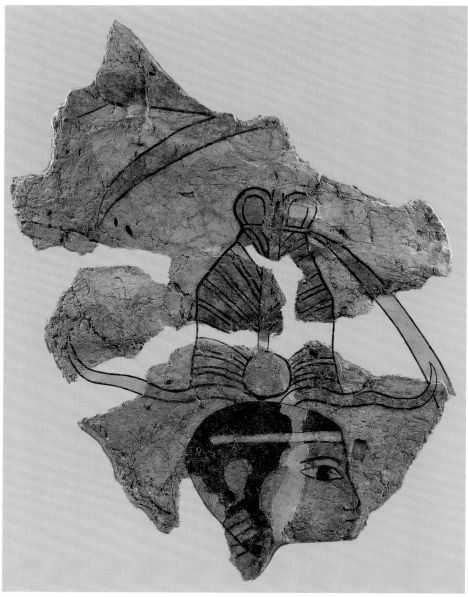

70a

70a, b
WALL PAINTING FRAGMENTS

Painted plaster
a. Height 50 cm (19¾ in.);
width 40 cm (15¾ in.)

b. Height 52 cm (20½ in.);
width 38.5 cm (15⅛ in.)

Tell Sakka, Palace
Middle Bronze Age II, early 2nd millennium B.C.
National Museum, Damascus, Syria
8911, 8290

The wall paintings in the Amorite palaces of Mari, Ebla, Alalakh, and Qatna attest not only to the opulent life-style that the rulers of those cities enjoyed but also to the aesthetic and artistic achievements of their artisans.

Fragments of the wall paintings at Tell Sakka began to appear during the fourth season of the excavations, in 1993, in the debris or on collapsed walls of the palace.[1] The wall paintings, which date to Middle Bronze II, were uncovered in four levels. The palace is a large architecturally sophisticated building with mud-brick walls between 140 and 180 centimeters thick, constructed with lime mortar and covered with a 1- to 2-centimeter layer of mud to which white lime plaster was applied. This surface was then painted with colorful compositions and decorative patterns.

The palace was destroyed during a military attack. The walls were intentionally damaged and the wall paintings forcibly removed and thrown to the ground before the palace was set aflame.

The Tell Sakka wall paintings depict both scenes from the daily life of the ruling class and scenes with religious or mythological significance. One fragment shows the profile view of a prince wearing a headdress reminiscent of an Egyptian type indicative of the divine authority embodied in the pharaoh. Other fragments depict women dressed in ornamented and colorful garments and a bearded male figure. Yet another fragment shows a goat climbing to eat from a tree, imagery that is Sumerian in origin but here executed in a different style. Many of the palace walls were fortunately unharmed by the fire. However, the wall paintings that survived in situ are not figural. In Room 9, for example, the designs follow the outlines of the stone and mud-brick architecture.

The Tell Sakka wall paintings clearly derive from Egyptian art, not only in

70b

the execution and arrangement of the decorative elements but in the prince's headdress, the face of the bearded man, and the colors of the women's garments. Near Eastern traditions, however, are evident in the ideas that underlie the thematic scheme.

AFT

1. The archaeological mound is situated some 20 kilometers southeast of the Damascus International Airport; a Syrian mission has been excavating there since 1989.

71

TRIPOD TABLE WITH ACROBATS

Plaster, painted
Height 7.6 cm (3 in.); width 12.1 cm (4¾ in.)
Rhodes, Trianda
Late Minoan IA, 1625–1525 B.C.
Archaeological Museum of Rhodes, Greece Δ 864

This fragment of an elaborate pictorial scene was part of a large round tripod offering table made of polished lime plaster. The plaster originally covered damp clay that formed the core of the table, a method known since Middle Minoan III on Crete and Late Minoan IA Akrotiri on Thera. The tripod was found in Late Bronze Age

IA deposits near a *polythyron* (a room with pier-and-door partitions) in the northeastern sector of the prehistoric town of Trianda on the island of Rhodes.[1]

The scene, which was from the side of the table just below the rim, shows two male acrobats performing on either side of a three-branched papyrus, their legs turned outward to parallel the bending papyri.[2] The acrobats wear flounced kilts fastened with belts over a short triangular element rendered in blue for the figure on the left and in yellow for the figure on the right. The dusky red stems of the plant emerge from what is likely a riverbed. Only the middle plant preserves the yellow fan-shaped head, which is overpainted with fine black veins terminating in an elegant scalloped top crowned by small red dots to mark the anthers. The calyx and head of the partially preserved external papyri are colored in reverse, with a yellow calyx and a blue head.[3]

The alternation of colors and the carefully drawn details render this composition a masterpiece of Aegean miniature painting, emphasizing the antithetical, tripartite syntax of the scene. Offering tables with pictorial compositions are known from Phylakopi on Melos,[4] Akrotiri on Thera,[5] Tiryns in the Peloponnese,[6] and Palaikastro on Crete.[7] All these examples share a triple, antithetical arrangement of animals and plants, with clearly Egyptian influence. This example, from Trianda, is the only known Aegean offering table with human representation.

TM

71

1. Marketou 1988, p. 30; Marketou 1990, pp. 107–9; Marketou 1998, p. 59.
2. Two acrobats are depicted on a cushion-shaped seal from Knossos and on a lentoid gem from Mycenae (A. Evans, PM IV, part 2, pp. 501–8, figs. 443, 444; Sakellariou 1966, p. 65, pl. 4e). A single tumbler is engraved on a sword pommel from Mallia (Chapouthier 1938, pp. 19–62).
3. Similar plants in Aegean iconography are identified either as papyri (*Cyperus papyrus*), by Warren (1976; 2000, pp. 375–78) and Morgan (1988, pp. 22–23), or as sea daffodils (*Pancratium maritimum*), by S. Marinatos (1972, p. 15, colorpls. E, F) and Baumann (1982, pp. 176–81, pls. 356–60), a confusion caused by the fact that anthers and calyx are features borrowed from lilies.
4. Morgan 2007, pp. 389–95.
5. Televantou 2007.
6. Ibid., p. 62 n. 19.
7. MacGillivray et al. 1991, p. 137, fig. 15, pl. 14c–d.

Figure 39. Reconstruction of Taureador Frieze. Tell el-Dab'a, Palace F. Dynasty 18, reigns of Hatshepsut–Thutmose III.

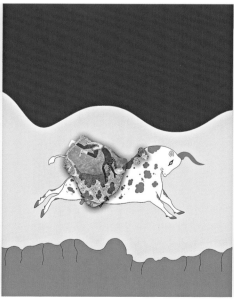

130

Minoan Artists at the Court of Avaris (Tell el-Dab'a)

The discovery of Minoan fresco painting at the site of Tell el-Dab'a, and therefore the presence of Minoan artists at foreign courts, has transformed our view of cultural interaction in the eastern Mediterranean world. These wall paintings on lime plaster have been partly reconstructed to reveal bull-leaping and bull-grappling scenes, some of them against a maze pattern (fig. 39) and felines (lions or leopards) chasing ungulates (fig. 120). Hunting scenes, life-size figures, men with staffs, and a white female wearing a flounced skirt, as well as heraldic griffins (fig. 40) have also emerged. As large as the griffins from Knossos, these griffins also probably flanked a throne. The hard lime plaster, which was used in the Aegean on walls with stone foundations built on rock, did not adhere well to the mud-brick walls at Avaris, which were built on alluvium. Furthermore, walls of this type tend to compress over an extended period of time. This is probably what happened in Palaces F and G,

causing the painted plaster to flake off the walls. The fragments must have been collected and dumped from the access ramp.

The fresco technique used to produce the wall paintings and the style and motifs employed leave no doubt that Minoan masters were at work. Also at this time, during the reign of Hatshepsut and the early years of Thutmose III, representations of Minoan delegations appear in tombs of Theban high officials (see fig. 85). The presence of Minoan art in Egypt cannot be explained simply as fashionable palace beautification. Rather, distinctive motifs such as the large griffins and the half-rosette frieze on the large Taureador fresco in Palace F (fig. 39) are emblematic of the palace at Knossos. The use of specifically Minoan royal motifs in a palace in the Nile Delta is a clear indication that an encounter on the highest level must have taken place between the courts of Knossos and Egypt. A proposed alliance between the Minoan thalassocracy and Egypt in the Thutmosid period would be reinforced by the identification of Tell el-Dab'a with Perunefer. The presence of Minoan royal emblems, the heraldic full-scale griffins, and the large-scale representation of the female in a flounced skirt may suggest that a political marriage took place. The palace was then perhaps equipped with wall painting imagery, indispensable for the spiritual life of Minoan royalty. It has been claimed that the throne room at Knossos was intended not for a king, but for a queen.[1] She would have taken her place between the two seated griffins depicted in the Knossos throne room, an allusion to the Minoan Great Goddess, Mistress of Animals. Such an iconographic scenario could also be claimed for Palace F at Tell el-Dab'a, with its heraldic Minoan style of griffins.

MB

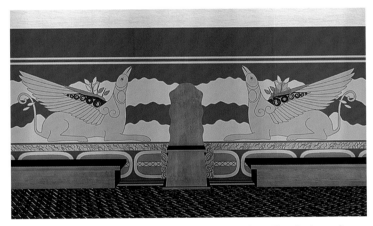

Figure 40. Reconstruction of throne room with wall painting of heraldic griffins. Tell el-Dab'a, Palace F. Dynasty 18, reigns of Hatshepsut–Thutmose III.

1. See Reusch 1958; Niemeier 1986; and N. Marinatos 1995. For an excellent overall reference, see Bietak, Marinatos, and Palyvou 2007.

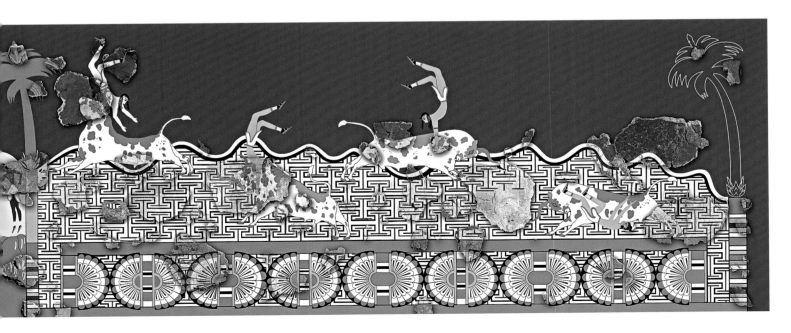

Bull Leaping

Depictions of figures grappling with bulls—sometimes shown in the context of the hunt—made their appearance during the late third to early second millennium B.C. Although this imagery ranged over a wide area, from the Indus Valley to Anatolia, Egypt (fig. 41), and the Aegean (fig. 42),[1] perhaps the most extensive narrative of bull vaulting and capture during the Middle Bronze Age is depicted on a tomb painting from Beni Hasan in Egypt.[2] Excerpts, possibly from this type of scene, showing leapers in various stages of vaulting over a bull, also appeared on old Syrian glyptic as small motifs embedded among a number of other figures.[3] Juxtaposed with kneeling archers, such representations seem to refer to the bull hunt rather than to an acrobatic ritual performance. By contrast, scenes of ceremonial performance on relief vases of central Anatolia,[4] such as the bull-vaulting scene on a large vessel discovered at Hüseyindede (cat. no. 73) may be interpreted in the latter way.

During the Level VII palace period at Alalakh (see pp. 197–98), scenes of animal combat and acrobatic bull leaping were juxtaposed on Syrian glyptic. This was a time during which two stylistic innovations occurred. First, spirited animals were shown breaking away from any groundline, without regard for traditional schemes of composition; second, images of gods and officials, while present, were no longer always clearly set apart, and they seem to have become less prominent. In one case (see fig. 124), an animal hunt takes up the entire seal surface, with a bull, ibexes, and lions charging across the field, albeit in a rather orderly fashion.   JA

1. *Aruz* in Art of the First Cities 2003, pp. 408–9.
2. *For the bull hunt in Egyptian art, see Galán 1994, pp. 81ff., 87, 93.*
3. *Collon 1994, p. 82, on seals that are stylistically earlier than those in the Aleppo Group; Seyrig 1955, pp. 34ff., pl. IV:2.*
4. *T. Özgüç 1988, pls. F, G; Akurgal 1962, pl. XIV.*

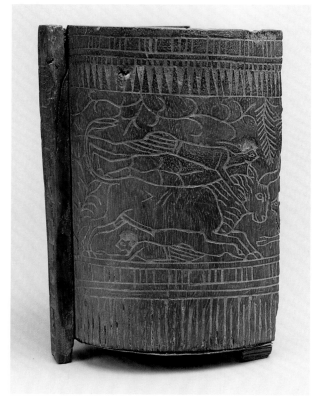

Figure 41. Wood box with bull-leaping scenes. Kahun. Dynasty 18. Egyptian Museum, Cairo JE 28754, CG 44707

Figure 42. Wall painting with bull-leaping scene. Knossos, Palace. Late Minoan II–IIIA:1. Archaeological Museum, Heraklion

became associated with the art of the Aegean throughout the Late Bronze Age: one was the act of subduing a wild bull, the other a theatrical/ritual exhibition.

JA

1. Aruz 1995b, pp. 36ff.; Aruz 1995a, p. 17, figs. 13, 14; Collon (2000, pp. 284ff.) denies any Aegean input; a seal impressed on a document of the time of the late seventeenth-century B.C. Babylonian king Samsu-ditana was published by Buchanan (1957, p. 49), who pointed to its Aegean-looking hunters attacking a large horned animal spread out over its prey; other hunting scenes also show similar figures and galloping animals.
2. See Zaccagnini 1983.

72

72

CYLINDER SEAL AND MODERN IMPRESSION: BULL LEAPERS

Hematite
Height 2.1 cm (⅞ in.); diameter 1.5 cm (⅝ in.)
Syria
Old Syrian, ca. 17th century B.C.
The Metropolitan Museum of Art, New York,
Anonymous Loan L.1992.43
Ex. coll.: Erlenmeyer

Two well-known works, one on loan to the Metropolitan Museum (seen here), the other impressed on the envelope of a clay document from Alalakh (fig. 43), depict bull leapers below animal hunt scenes. Both show nude belted acrobats with long hair, perhaps an allusion to foreign athletes (although leapers on Crete wore loincloths).[1] Acrobats, like musicians and fresco painters, were probably among the specialists who traveled to foreign lands.[2]

The bull vaulters are symmetrically posed, whereas the charging bulls below

them, with all limbs on the ground, impart a feeling of arrested movement. Yet, compared to the static imposing figures of deities and royalty that usually dominate Syrian compositions, the animal scenes here exhibit a new, distinctively loose and lively style. On the seal in the Metropolitan Museum, a figure in a royal robe with rolled borders approaches the Syrian weather god. A man attempts to control the charging bull with the leapers on its back; the horn of a bull galloping above is in the mouth of a seated lion with head reversed. On the Alalakh seal impression, a crouching lion with its head turned stretches its forelegs toward the neck of a large ibex whose body and limbs are extended so that they seem to thrust out of the conventional mold. While the composition appears confusing, the animal contest and bull-leaping themes probably belong together. They may allude to two types of bull-leaping scenes already introduced into the imagery of the Near East and Egypt during the early second millennium B.C. and which

Figure 43. Drawing of seal impression on tablet envelope with bull-leaping scene. Alalakh, Palace archive, Level VII. Antakya Archaeological Museum 7960-1

73

RELIEF VESSEL WITH BULL LEAPERS

Ceramic
Height 52 cm (20½ in.)
Hüseyindede
Hittite Old Kingdom, 17th century B.C.
Çorum Museum, Çorum, Turkey
1-1-99

Excavations at the Old Hittite settlement of Hüseyindede, in central Anatolia, uncovered two rare vessels with relief decoration.[1] This one, found in Room 1 of the temple complex, is a beautifully expressive example of the Hittite relief vase tradition. Hüseyindede is only the third site—along with İnandık and Bitik—to produce relatively complete examples of Hittite relief vases. The figurative art of the early Hittite period is known primarily through seal carving and such vases, which prefigure the style of the large-scale rock reliefs of the Hittite Empire (figs. 55, 56).

The larger of the two vessels from Hüseyindede with relief decoration resembles the İnandık and Bitik vases, with depictions of figures in horizontally stacked registers separated by bold geometric patterns. The smaller one, seen here, has only a single register of decoration. It lacks handles and the series of bull's heads around the top of the rim, as seen in other examples. The figurative panel on this vase, which is read from left to right, illustrates a Hittite ritual accompanied by dance and music. Thirteen figures form two main groups around a bull within the pictorial

73

frame. Two female figures dancing hand in hand on the left edge of the band seem to depict the type of dance known today as *halay*, which was also described in Hittite texts. The clothing of the dancing women is reflected in a type of garment still worn, and the stringed instruments depicted here are similar to modern versions that are played with a pick.

The figures shown around and on the bull portray the different acrobatic movements of a bull leaper. The scene probably depicts a ritual bull-leaping performance described in Luwian texts, which was accompanied by dancing and music. By the Old Hittite period, the bull as a focus of ritual action had a long history in Anatolia, dating back to the famous Neolithic period wall painting at Çatalhöyük, which depicts a giant bull surrounded by small human figures, and seal impressions from the Old Assyrian Trading Colony period showing bulls in religious scenes. This particular scene has no exact parallel among Aegean, Egyptian, or Syrian bull-leaping imagery, suggesting that a rich independent tradition existed in central Anatolia during the early second millennium B.C.[2]   TS/TY

1. The excavations were conducted between 1997 and 2004. The vase seen here was uncovered early.
2. See Sipahi 2001, pp. 109, 118.

73, detail

74

BULL AND ACROBAT

Bronze
Height 11.4 cm (4½ in.)
Crete
Minoan, ca. 1700–1450 B.C.
The Trustees of the British Museum, London
1966.3-28.1

74

Bull leaping, a frequent theme in Minoan art, probably formed a part of ritual activity. The strength and potency of bulls may have contributed to the religious importance of the animal to the Minoans.

In this bronze composition, the leaper is somersaulting over the bull's head in order to land with both feet on its back.[1] The sculptor has cleverly supported the acrobat by allowing his long hair to trail onto the bull's forehead. The work was cast in one piece using the lost-wax technique. The arms are not fully represented, but end in stumps; it is not clear whether this was by design or because the bronze did not flow into the extremities of the mold. The loss of the lower legs may also have been due to a casting fault. Minoan bronzes tended to be low in tin, which meant the alloy did not flow well. The low tin content also resulted in a characteristic bubbly surface.

Are such leaps possible? Because of the unpredictability of a bull's movements it seems highly unlikely that an acrobat could grasp a bull's horns and use the toss of its head to flip over onto its back. Judging from the large number of other representations now known, however, it appears that Minoan acrobats performed a variety of different types of leap.[2] Perhaps in some cases the bulls were restrained or even tamed. Certainly some Minoan imagery shows bulls being captured, tethered, and led, as well as apparently being held by the horns.[3] It is probable that the Minoans put considerable effort and long experience into the sport and were able to accomplish dramatic feats. Even so, the possibility of some artistic license having been taken in these representations should not be discounted.

Some scholars have suggested that Minoan iconography surrounding bulls was specifically associated with the palace of Knossos, and certainly the fresco decorations of the walls there included many images of bulls (see fig. 42).[4] One might thus expect that this fine bronze sculpture was produced in a palatial context, perhaps specifically at Knossos; however, it is said to have come from near Rethymnon. Although the provenance of this work is far from secure, along with other high-quality bronzes it may have traveled if intended as a dedication. Bronzes are often found in Minoan shrines and sanctuaries, particularly in sacred caves.

JLF

1. Arthur Evans (1921) considered this to be the "classic" bull leap, based largely on the evidence of this bronze sculpture.
2. Younger 1976.
3. Younger 1995.
4. Hallager and Hallager 1995.

75

RING WITH BULL LEAPER

Bronze, gold overlay
Height 1.8 cm (¾ in.); width 2.8 cm (1⅛ in.)
Asine
Late Helladic II–IIIA:1, 15th–early
14th century B.C.
National Archaeological Museum,
Athens, Greece 10275

The bronze bezel of this ring[1] is covered with gold plate, only the upper part of which is preserved. The hoop is also missing. It bears an engraved image depicting a scene of bull leaping. The massive body of the charging bull, worked in detail, dominates the composition. The long-haired bull leaper, wearing a Minoan loincloth and belt, jumps over the bull,

75

135

supporting himself on his hand and ready to land on the ground. The lower part of a second similar ring from the same tomb in Asine[2] completes the scene with the running bull's legs on the ground.

Bull leaping brings into the realm of ritual spectacle the struggle of man to subdue wild nature and to use it to his own advantage. The bull, symbol of fertility, was the strongest of the domesticated animals, and the hunting of bulls, some still in a feral state, was a dangerous enterprise. The bull as a symbol of power in Minoan Crete[3] and the scenes of bull leaping in Minoan art are well known, starting from the beginning of the early second millennium B.C.[4] Bull leaping is also depicted on the Minoan wall paintings at Tell el-Dab'a (Avaris) in Egypt (see fig. 39).[5] It is a known subject on seals and sealings, including a gold signet ring from Archanes,[6] now in the Ashmolean Museum, and the sealings from Akrotiri, Thera.[7]

On the Greek mainland, bull leaping is represented in art, but there it is uncertain whether the spectacle was part of Mycenaean cult. It is found in a variety of iconographic types on wall paintings from Mycenae, Tiryns, and Pylos, a Minoan stone vase from the Acropolis of Athens, and numerous seals and sealings. Bull-leaping scenes may be part of a broader symbolic imagery and used in initiation rites, as on the Boxer Rhyton from Ayia Triada. On a larnax from Tanagra, the scene includes competitions, perhaps funeral games, including goat hunting, chariot racing, and bull leaping, in honor of the dead.[8]

Outside the Aegean area, bull-hunting and bull-leaping scenes are also integrated into the artistic vocabulary. Cylinder seals and a sealed tablet from Syria dating to the seventeenth century B.C., and a Hittite relief vase (see cat. no. 73) provide additional evidence for the interaction of cultures in the eastern Mediterranean.[9]

LP-M

1. CMS I, no. 200.
2. Ibid., no. 201.
3. Hallager and Hallager 1995, pp. 547–56.
4. N. Marinatos 1993, pp. 218–20; Papazoglou-Manioudaki 2003, pp. 122–24.
5. Bietak, Marinatos, and Palyvou 2000, pp. 77–79.
6. *Archanes* 1997, p. 554, fig. 720.
7. CMS V Suppl. 3, part 2., nos. 392–95.
8. Immerwahr 1990, pp. 157, 195–96; Younger 1995, pp. 522–27; Morgan 1998, p. 31.
9. N. Marinatos 1994, pp. 89–90; Sipahi 2001, pp. 113–18, fig. 1; Aruz 2008a, pp. 139–41.

RITUAL AND ROYAL IMAGERY

JOAN ARUZ

The impact of Egyptian civilization on its neighbors can be measured to a large degree by the penetration of Nilotic imagery into the artistic expressions of the divine realm in the Near East and the Aegean. Paramount in these representations was the combination of humans and dangerous animals—or of animals alone—to create supernatural beasts that embraced their combined powers. Four creatures in particular enjoyed widespread popularity, with local adaptations both in physical appearance and presumably in function. The male bearded sphinx and the falcon-headed griffin, both with leonine bodies and associations with the sun god, first symbolized the elevated status and supremacy of the Egyptian pharaoh in the official art of the Old Kingdom.[1] With crowns worn by gods and kings, they were often shown in conquering postures, trampling enemies. Recumbent female sphinxes, at times associated with royal females, become more visible in subsequent centuries (see cat. no. 84).

During the Middle Kingdom, monstrous creatures with features of both the griffin and the sphinx appear on magical wands and in tombs of desert nobles.[2] Like the royal beasts they too combine feline, avian, and human aspects, but in an unnatural manner, creating ferocious apotropaic beasts.[3] Two other Egyptian creatures functioned largely on the popular level as protectors of households, women, and childbirth: Bes, the lion-headed god, and Taweret, the hippopotamus goddess with crocodilian attributes and the breasts and emphasized belly of pregnancy. Appearing with other monsters on magical wands, these protective deities seem to have derived their powers from the most

Figure 44. Faience figurines. Byblos, Temple of the Obelisks. Middle Bronze Age. Direction Générale des Antiquités, Beirut

Figure 45. Gold ring. Tiryns. Late Helladic II, 15th century B.C. National Archaeological Museum, Athens 6208

dangerous realms: Bes, like the griffin, from the remote deserts, and Taweret from the marshes of the Nile, which, with its annual inundation, also provided a metaphor for renewal and fertility.

By the Middle Bronze Age, griffins and sphinxes appear in the arts of Syria and Anatolia. Particularly striking are images on ivories and glyptic from cities in central Anatolia, where these hybrids retain traces of their pharaonic associations, evoked by their postures, which suggest conquest, by their crowns, and by specific features of their anatomy. The transmission of the sphinx and the griffin from the Near East to the Aegean occurred at this time, and such features as the spiral markings of the peregrine falcon head, feathered or curling crests, displayed wings with distinctive markings for the griffin, and elaborated Hathor curls for the sphinx were adapted to create distinctively Minoan creatures.[4]

The Minoan griffin—a hunter of lions and other creatures and a majestic attendant on frescoes, ivories, metalwork, and glyptic in the Aegean—had an enormous impact on the arts of the eastern Mediterranean. It became the symbol of the warrior Ahmose, "beloved of Montu," founder of the Egyptian New Kingdom, and was inlaid into the blade of the gilded axe among his mother's burial equipment (cat. no. 67). It also appears to have protected the throne, judging from the reconstructed wall paintings at Tell el-Dab'a (see fig. 40).

The goddess Taweret was well known in the Levant, as attested by faience figurines in the Temple of the Obelisks at Byblos (fig. 44) and by her depiction on cylinder seals at that site. We have no evidence that she acquired new attributes there, although a Byblos cylinder seal with two Taweret figures carrying sacrificial animals to a central human figure may indicate a new role for her in the Near East.[5] Taweret first appears in the Aegean during the Middle Bronze Age, on seal impressions from Phaistos and Knossos, where she retains the swollen belly of the protective female divinity. Carrying a libation ewer, she is transformed into the Minoan Genius and her hippopotamus head is replaced by that of a lion.[6] Later Minoan seal cutters

omit reference to her gender, and the creature receives the pinched-in waist characteristic of many human figures (fig. 45). This transformation of Taweret into a Minoan demon must have been dictated by Minoan religious needs. Taweret's two basic functions—as a libation bearer and as a lesser deity, probably attendant on a greater one—must also have originated in Egypt or the Near East.[7]

The Egyptian leonine demon Bes, Taweret's frequent companion, proliferates in the Levant and Cyprus—one image found in Anatolia—but is not adopted in the Aegean until the first millennium B.C.[8] A creature resembling this lion-faced demon (see cat. no. 87) appears on Middle Bronze Age Syrian seals with Egyptianizing imagery.[9] Elaborated New Kingdom versions, with ostrich-plumed crowns and spitting snakes (cat. no. 89), integrate exotic features such as kilts and wings. These elements are thought to derive from the Near East, where they are rendered on metalwork and ivory plaques from sites such as Ugarit (cat. no. 90), Megiddo, and Kition.[10]

1. Both creatures are represented in the funerary complex of Dynasty 5 ruler Sahure: Borchardt 1910, pl. 8.
2. Altenmüller 1965, figs. 1, 3, 6, 9, 12, 13, 16, 21; Meeks 2001, p. 506; the first griffin appears at the site of Susa in southwestern Iran, a proposed source of contacts with predynastic Egypt (see Teissier 1987, pp. 31, 32). Whether it may have been a distant prototype for the magical creatures on ivory wands is debatable, although predynastic-type serpopards also appear on these objects.
3. For a discussion of their Seth aspects and for hunting dogs disguised as monstrous griffins, see Meeks 2001, p. 505.
4. For discussion, see Aruz 2008a, pp. 106–8.
5. Dunand 1950, pl. CXCIII:11464. On another Syrian-style cylinder seal in the Metropolitan Museum (1999.325.151), two Taweret goddesses with knives confront each other, flanking a caprid and a waterbird.
6. Gill 1964, pp. 3ff. For discussion of the meaning of Taweret in Egypt, see Verner 1970, pp. 52ff.; see also Hornung and Staehelin 1976, pp. 127–29; Altenmüller 1965, pp. 148ff.; and Gundlach 1986. Phillips (1991, pp. 191ff.) emphasizes the Middle Kingdom deities that later coalesce into Taweret; see Phillips 2008, chap. 12; Weingarten 1991 charts the development of the appearance of the creature.
7. Weingarten 1991; Mellink 1987, pp. 67–71.
8. Aruz 2008a, p. 85 n. 70.
9. Teissier 1996, pp. 78–79, no. 132.
10. V. Wilson 1975; Loud 1939, pl. 8:24, 26; Barnett 1982, pl. 33b.

1. Houlihan 1986, pp. 46–48.
2. N. Özgüç 1991, pp. 301–2.
3. Teissier 1996, p. 146, figs. 145–47, p. 89, figs. 165, 166, p. 87, fig. 162; Porada 1948, pl. CXLIX, no. 981.
4. N. Özgüç 1968, pl. XX:C.
5. Ibid., pl. XXXII:2b.
6. N. Özgüç 1991, pp. 302–3.

76

FURNITURE PLAQUE WITH GRIFFIN

Ivory (hippopotamus)
Height 4.1 cm (1⅝ in.); width 2.6 cm (1 in.)
Anatolia
Middle Bronze Age, 18th century B.C.
The Metropolitan Museum of Art, New York,
Gift of Mrs. George D. Pratt, in memory of
George D. Pratt, 1936 36.152.7

One of the most interesting images in the corpus of ivories attributed to Acemhöyük is also one of the smallest: a sensitively drawn crouching griffin incised on a narrow plaque, now warped. Similarly incised images on other small plaques in the group include Egyptian-type waterfowl and a monkey holding a jar (cat. no. 54).

The lithe feline body and haunches of the griffin are rendered with a lively curving line, and its head is given the form of a bird of prey. A curving hatched line defines the edge of the massive falcon wing, feathered like those on Nilotic depictions of birds of prey. The leonine tail is raised and curled, and the claws of the visible hind leg are emphasized. Added to the bird and lion features are two long horns, with three tiny points between them, crowning the head. A pattern on the cheek, ending in a spiral curl, evokes the markings of the peregrine falcon, as rendered in Egyptian images of Horus in his animal aspect (see cat. no. 49).[1] This plaque may thus provide the source for one of the most characteristic features of griffins as portrayed later in the Aegean—the spiral curl on cheek or chest.

Although quadrupeds with feline and avian features first appeared on earlier Anatolian-style cylinder seals at Kültepe,[2]

the incised griffin, both in style and physical characteristics, finds its closest parallels in Syrian glyptic. There we find the source not only for the lithe rendering of the leonine body, but also for the allusion to Egypt, in both griffins and sphinxes, made by the addition of crowns composed of horizontally displayed ram's horns and upright feathers.[3] Furthermore, a Syrian-style cylinder seal impressed on a document from Kültepe Ib, a phase contemporary with this plaque, depicts a griffin that is similar in style, with long curving horns.[4] Other griffins, depicted on Anatolian-style seals in the *karum* settlements of the plateau, including Acemhöyük, lack horns but rather display a long head curl. They are portrayed as attackers mounted on the backs of their prey,[5] with one exception—a hunting griffin-demon with a rack of antlers, who stands on leonine legs and, beneath its spread wings, features human arms extended to grasp a hare and an antelope.[6]

JA

77

RING WITH GRIFFINS

Gold, silver
Height 1.7 cm (⅝ in.); width 3 cm (1⅛ in.)
Mycenae, Chamber Tomb 68
Late Helladic II, 15th century B.C.
National Archaeological Museum, Athens,
Greece 2970

This signet ring is made of hammered gold sheet. It has an oval bezel and a concave bedplate on the back side. A hammer-chisel was used for the engraving. The hoop has five ridges.[1] The ring was found in a chamber tomb rich in gold jewelry, which included the gold figurine of a reclining bull. Among the grave furnishings were five sealstones and a rare iron-and-silver ring.[2] Gold signet rings and sealstones were the *insignia dignitatis* of the ruling class—symbols of power, prestige, and wealth—and were associated as well with administration and trade.

The engraved scene on the ring depicts two griffins moving in opposite directions, their heads turned toward each other. Their impressive wings are widespread, and their chests are embellished with spirals.

77

A collar is visible on their necks. The griffins' raised tails form the axis of the symmetrical scene, and a schematic plant in front of each creature denotes the borders.

A mythical creature, the griffin has the body of a lion and the head and wings of an eagle, combining the powers of both. It is considered a guardian associated with deities and royal palaces. Adopted from the Near East, it was widely used in the artistic and symbolic vocabulary of the Aegean,[3] depicted on the wall paintings of Akrotiri at Thera, the throne rooms of Knossos and Pylos, and on seals and ivory pyxides.[4] A majestic reclining griffin is shown on a gold seal from Tholos Tomb IV at Pylos. The griffin rests on a zone of semirosettes, a motif symbolic of kingship known mostly from the stone frieze inlaid with glass of the palace of Tiryns[5] and the decoration of the Atreus tholos at Mycenae. On another seal from Mycenae two antithetically disposed griffins flank a column, an abbreviated form representing a building.[6] Their front paws and the column rest on a concave altar. This arrangement is the equivalent—only here, with griffins—of the Lion Gate at the entrance to the citadel (fig. 88).
                                                   LP-M

1. CMS I, no. 102; Xénaki-Sakellariou 1989, pp. 330, 335, fig. 8; Xénaki-Sakellariou 1995, p. 317; W. Müller 2003, pp. 476–77; W. Müller 2005, pp. 173–74.
2. Xénaki-Sakellariou 1985, p. 195, pl. 85.
3. N. Marinatos 1993, pp. 196–97.
4. Morgan 1988, pp. 49–54.
5. Panagiotaki et al. 2003, pp. 14–18.
6. CMS I, no. 98.

78
STAMP SEAL WITH MAN AND GRIFFIN

Red jasper
Diameter 2.2 cm (⅞ in.)
Vapheio, Tholos Tomb, Late Helladic IIA,
15th century B.C.
National Archaeological Museum, Athens,
Greece 1761

The tholos tomb at Vapheio,[1] known for the celebrated gold cups decorated with exquisite scenes of bull hunting found there,[2] is also rich in seals, approximately forty-four pieces, including two signet

78

rings, one in gold and the other in bronze. The tomb is dated to a time when the Greek mainland, especially Lakonia, had close relations with the Minoan civilization and adopted ideas from the Near East by way of Crete.

This seal[3] was found in the cist grave dug into the floor of the tholos. The imposing figure of a man, in profile, stands next to a majestic griffin. He holds a leash with a distinctive loop tied to the animal's neck. The griffin turns its head to look backward. The man is clean-shaven and wears a cap over his hair, which is cut short in front and longer in the back. There is a drill hole in the figure's wrist, suggesting that he wears a sealstone bracelet,[4] an adornment attested primarily in wall paintings.[5] The manufacture of the seal is attributed to the mainland artist called the Mycenae/Vapheio Lion Master.

The man wears a long robe with diagonal bands, recognized as a sacerdotal garment, probably of Syrian origin, though the exact significance is unknown. The robe certainly denotes an important and authoritative figure, who holds an insignia to indicate his rank. A number of Minoan seals present figures of priests or priestesses wearing similar attire and hairstyle and holding either a stone mace or a (possibly Syrian) lunate axe. An actual bronze axe of this type was found in the Vapheio tholos; a similar axe is also shown in the hand of a priest on another seal from the same tomb.[6]

The griffin, another Near Eastern import, was considered the ultimate predator and could be associated with a divine power, represented here by the priest.[7] The griffin

was widely adopted as a symbol of power and kingship in Aegean art.
                                                   LP-M

1. Kilian-Dirlmeier 1987, pp. 197–212.
2. E. Davis 1977, pp. 1–50, figs. 1–21.
3. CMS I, no. 223; for such scenes, see Aruz 2008a, p. 175.
4. Rehak 1994, pp. 76–77.
5. Younger 1992, pp. 272–73.
6. Regarding the axe, see Rehak 1994, pp. 79–80. The seal showing a man holding a similar axe is CMS I, no. 225.
7. On a Syrian cylinder seal discussed in N. Marinatos 1993, pp. 127–32, figs. 88, 95, 96, a frontal figure of a god or priest holds a griffin by the leash.

79
ROUNDEL WITH GRIFFINS

Gold
Diameter 6.5 cm (2½ in.)
Qatna, Royal Tomb
Late Bronze Age, 15th–14th century B.C.
National Museum, Damascus, Syria
MSH02G-i0765

This gold disc, a unique object, was found in the central chamber of the Royal Tomb of Qatna on a wood bier that had been placed on the chamber floor.[1] The relief is worked in repoussé from the back, with additional chasing of details on the front. The image is subdivided into three concentric circles. The inner circle is decorated with an eight-petal rosette. The middle circle, which dominates the composition, is embellished with four griffins in relief. Arranged in opposing pairs,

79

they comprise the elegant, slender body of a lion, the head of a bird of prey with a hooked beak and spread wings, and a long, curved tail ending in a thick tassel. The body and wings are impressed with circles.

The griffin does not conform to the so-called Aegean type[2] popular during the second millennium B.C. in Syria and the eastern Mediterranean, as the characteristic curl behind the head is absent;[3] rather, it is a local Syrian variant.[4] Stylistically, it derives from Egyptian art, evident from the standing position and the slender form of the body.[5] Iconographically, however, it is independent of the Egyptian model because it lacks the Egyptian crown. The closest parallel to the Qatna griffins is found on an ivory disc from Byblos dated to the Late Bronze Age (cat. no. 80).

Between each pair of griffins is another motif of Egyptian origin: an *ankh* framed on both sides by a stylized *was*-scepter. While the *ankh* has retained its Egyptian form, the scepter has degenerated to a nearly unidentifiable shape when compared to Egyptian examples, and its Syrian origin is undeniable.[6] The combined motif was introduced in the Levant

as early as the Middle Bronze Age, as indicated by the crown of Ip-shemu-abi from the Byblos royal tombs of the nineteenth century B.C.[7] On the much later Qatna gold disc, the *was*-symbol has evolved to a rounded, plantlike image.

The outer circle displays an alternating sequence of circular forms that can be identified as small sun symbols, and concave shapes that resemble sheaves of wheat. Around the edge of the disc are two parallel rows of perforations that served for sewing the object on to a textile or piece of leather. Traces of a dark organic material around most of the perforations are possibly the remains of leather, suggesting that the disc once decorated a leather band that was perhaps part of a sheath, a belt, or a jeweled ribbon.   PP

1. First published in Al-Maqdissi et al. 2003, p. 213, fig. 13.
2. See, for example, S. Marinatos and Hirmer 1973, fig. 33.
3. For the development of the griffin motif in the third and second millennium B.C., see Wild 2008.
4. For this Syrian griffin, compare seal impressions of the Old Syrian period: Otto 2000,

nos. 31, 122, 169, 173, 196, 201, 248, 306. Nearly all these griffins on Syrian seals are shown recumbent or seated. It is remarkable that a standing griffin, as on the Qatna disc, is so rare on Old Syrian seal impressions (ibid., no. 251). One example is depicted on a Middle Syrian seal from Ugarit (*Das Rollsiegel in Syrien* 1980, no. 58).
5. See the Egyptian griffin from the Middle Kingdom in Lange and Hirmer 1978, pl. XIV (center).
6. See T. James 2000, p. 303.
7. Parrot, Chéhab, and Moscati 1977, fig. 30.

80

PYXIS LID WITH GRIFFINS AND SPHINXES

Ivory
Diameter 10 cm (3⅞ in.)
Byblos
Late Bronze Age, 14th century B.C.
Direction Générale des Antiquités, Beirut, Lebanon 19295

One of the most intriguing ivory objects from Byblos is this irregularly shaped oval pyxis lid with incised designs of confronted griffins and sphinxes. There is little information about the exact findspot of the lid, which seems to have been discovered against the wall of a structure between Middle Bronze Age temple complexes and the Crusader Castle.[1] The lid appears to have been cut down for reuse on a smaller container than originally intended, without concern for the imagery, which is now partially obliterated. The central hole (now broken), surrounded by an eighteen-petal rosette inscribed in four circles, must have held a small knob, probably of a different material. Two confronted seated sphinxes are rendered with powerful haunches and large feathered wings, one emerging from behind the chest.[2] Another scene, repeated three times, shows a more dynamic confrontation, with falcon-headed griffins lunging toward one another, their forelegs crossing, foreground rear legs extended backward, and tails curling behind. The technique of overlapping is here employed to create a sense of space. This appears to be the impetus in the rendering of the wings, which are depicted one behind the other, the far one seeming to emerge from the neck. While two griffin pairs are almost fully preserved, the heads of the third set, as well as one extended hind leg, are now missing. Based on the pattern of loss and the spacing of the images, it is probable that the original lid was circular, about 16 centimeters in diameter, with an outer border of concentric bands.

The format of the design—incised concentric circles around a central rosette with a surrounding outer band, often undecorated—is paralleled on a number of ivory bowls and lids from the site of Megiddo.[3] In one instance, kneeling or collapsing horned animals are incised on the outer band of a pyxis lid with extensions for a swivel closure.[4] An ivory tabletop from Ugarit also has a central incised rosette surrounded by concentric bands of cutout designs, with confronted leonine creatures (probably griffins) on the outer frieze.[5]

The imagery on the Byblos lid depicts powerful supernatural forces in conflict, a common theme in the corpus of ivories produced in eastern Mediterranean centers toward the end of the Late Bronze Age. The use of incision instead of relief on this work of rather modest craftsmanship can be paralleled on ivories found over the wide span of western Asia from Ashur (fig. 69) to the Levantine coast, Cyprus, and the Cycladic island of Delos.[6] On Delos—in contrast to works created on the Greek mainland, which are in relief (see cat. nos. 268, 269)—the theme of clashing predators is rendered in a masterpiece of incised ivory carving, found deposited within the later Temple of Artemis (cat. no. 267).[7]   JA

1. Dunand 1939, p. 88: discussion of wall θ.
2. This scene was misinterpreted by Dunand (ibid., pp. 103–4, no. 1549, pl. CXXIII), who did not realize that the heads were missing.

3. Loud 1939, pls. 15, 26, 27; for rosette discs, see pl. 15.
4. Ibid., p. 13, fig. 54b.
5. Feldman 2006b, p. 52, fig. 34.
6. Barnett 1982, pls. 19, 33c, 35a, 36a.
7. Ibid., pl. 33d, possibly by the same hand as an ivory lid from Palaepaphos, Cyprus, which may be the source of the Delos ivory.

81
RELIEF VESSEL WITH SPHINXES

Ceramic
Height 10.2 cm (4 in.)
Karahöyük
Middle Bronze Age, 18th century B.C.
Konya Museum, Konya, Turkey 1975.25.41

The thin walls and burnished surface of this vessel, excavated at Karahöyük, near Konya, are characteristic of fine Anatolian ceramics, although its form, which incorporates images of a pair of bearded male sphinxes striding along the sides, is unique.[1] The body of each sphinx is depicted in profile and rendered in low relief, while the preserved head is turned 90 degrees outward and modeled fully in the round. A long tapered beard clings to the figure's neck, flanked by two locks of hair that end in symmetrical curls resting on the chest. Two additional locks fall to the back of the neck. The large forehead and bulging eyes are offset by a long,

81, detail of reverse

straight nose, small mouth, and receding chin, all framed by protruding ears. The other side of the vessel is damaged: only three paws and a curled lock remain of an identical sphinx that would have mirrored the existing figure. The superb workman-ship and unusual overall shape of this piece, which recalls the Hittite hieroglyph

for the sky, suggest that it was used to pour libations.[2]

Sphinxes, both male and female, appear frequently in Anatolian glyptic of the early second millennium B.C. A male sphinx with pointed beard and raised front paw, on an Acemhöyük clay bulla, closely resembles the Karahöyük figure.[3] A group of nine

Figure 46. Ceramic vessel appliqué in the form of a sphinx. Mallia, Quartier Mu, Building D. Middle Minoan II. Archaeological Museum, Heraklion Π 19818

bullae from Acemhöyük, all of which show impressions of the same seal, display pairs of addorsed, beardless sphinxes whose arrangement and long pendant curls also recall the Karahöyük sphinx.[4] Another comparison, surprisingly, is provided by a ceramic relief appliqué for a vessel excavated at Mallia on Crete, showing a wingless, bearded sphinx with dramatically full, curled locks (fig. 46).[5] The direct similarity in form between the two objects suggests that the Mallia sphinx vessel was also used in the performance of ritual. The relief combines an Egyptianizing beard and tail with facial features typical of Minoan wall painting, but its distinctive curls connect it with Anatolian sphinxes like the one seen here.[6] Finds such as these suggest some degree of interaction between central Anatolia and Crete during the early second millennium B.C., which remains as yet incompletely understood.[7]

SG

1. Alp 1978–80.
2. Ibid., p. 11; Alp 1950, p. 2.
3. N. Özgüç 1980, p. 76, fig. III-45.
4. N. Özgüç 1971, p. 25, fig. 4.
5. Poursat 1973.
6. Warren 1995, p. 3; Aruz 2008a, pp. 106–7.
7. Aruz 2008a, pp. 101–22.

82

SPHINX WITH PRISONER

Ivory
Length 5.8 cm (2¼ in.)
Abydos, Tomb 477
Middle Kingdom, Dynasty 12, ca. 1950 B.C.
The Trustees of the British Museum, London
54.678

This figurine from Abydos represents a sphinx seizing the body of a captive who lies prostrate, his head grasped between his captor's paws. The sphinx wears the striped *nemes* headcloth, the prerogative of Egyptian kings, with the royal protective *uraeus* at his brow. The carving is complete in itself, but the presence of two peg holes on the flat underside shows that it was intended to be attached to some larger object, such as a box or piece of furniture.[1]

In the years immediately after the discovery of the sphinx, some scholars deemed its large eyes and ears, long hooked nose, and high cheekbones un-Egyptian and suggested that it was a rare depiction of a Hyksos ruler of the Second Intermediate Period subduing an Egyptian prisoner. Other objects found in the group of tombs from which the sphinx comes were believed to support this dating. More recent studies, however, have shown that the archaeological context was too disturbed to exclude the possibility of an earlier or later dating, and a reassessment of the stylistic features of the sphinx has suggested that it fits more comfortably among Egyptian royal statuary of Dynasty 12. The shape of the *nemes* and the *uraeus* and even some of the facial peculiarities are paralleled on a statue from the reign of Senwosret I (ca. 1961–1917 B.C.). The figurine was therefore probably meant to represent an Egyptian king seizing one of Egypt's traditional foes, such as a Nubian; the captive's close-cropped hair and short kilt would be appropriate for an inhabitant of that southern region.

JHT

1. For further reference, see Garstang 1928, pp. 46–47, pl. VII; Schweitzer 1948, pp. 39–40, pl. IX:3B; Hornemann 1969, pl. 1526; Bourriau in *Pharaohs and Mortals* 1988, pp. 136–38, no. 138; M. Maree in *Pharaohs* 2002, p. 426, no. 97; and Strudwick 2006, pp. 100–101.

82

83

PYXIS WITH SPHINXES

Ivory

Height 4.8 cm (1⅞ in.)

Thebes, Chamber Tomb

Late Helladic IIIA–B, 14th–13th century B.C.

Archaeological Museum,

Thebes, Greece 42459

This cylindrical ivory pyxis is constructed of two separate pieces of ivory tusk, one for the main body and another for the base. A series of small holes indicates how the base and body were originally held together. The base was broken in antiquity; pairs of additional small holes pierced in each fragment provide evidence of attempts at repair. The vessel probably had a lid—made of the same or different material—which has not been preserved. Two small horizontal holes pierced through the pyxis's handles allowed attachment of the lid.

The ivory pyxis, a luxury object indicative of wealth and high social status, was found in a large chamber tomb cut into the side of a hill to the east of the citadel of Thebes and is dated from the fourteenth to the thirteenth century B.C. Such objects were used by the elites in their everyday life, specifically for the safekeeping of cosmetics or jewelry. This particular pyxis—

decorated in relief with two heraldic pairs of sphinxes and two shell-shaped handles placed at opposite sides—is a remarkable example of Mycenaean palatial art. It also provides evidence of influence from the Near East, where this type of walking sphinx in profile originated.

VLA/IF

84

PLAQUE WITH SPHINX

Sard

Height 3.4 cm (1⅜ in.); width 5 cm (2 in.); depth 0.8 cm (⅜ in.)

Egypt

New Kingdom, Dynasty 18,

ca. 1390–1352 B.C.

The Metropolitan Museum of Art, New York, Purchase, Edward S. Harkness Gift, 1926

26.7.1342

This sard plaque,[1] in the form of a winged female sphinx, was once part of a piece of jewelry similar to the *wedjat*-eye bracelet from the right arm of Tutankhamun's mummy.[2] The original setting, which would have been of gold, must have consisted of a curved backplate cut to match the outline of the plaque and possibly scored with a decoration. Gold strips were attached at right angles to the outer circumference of the backplate as well as along the edges of all the open spaces. Once the sard piece was set into place,[3] the gold strips covered the drill marks and uneven places along the edges. The inlay was at some time broken into two pieces along a vertical line that passes from the upper border along the front of the sphinx's wing to about the animal's chest and from there to the lower border. Losses occurred at the upper and lower borders of the inlay.[4] The break through the sphinx's body has been repaired.

A group of five similar bracelet plaques are thought to derive from the tomb of Amenhotep III,[5] although their decoration pertained more to ideas about kingship than to the afterlife. Because most of the plaques depict rituals performed at the king's thirty-year jubilee, the *Heb Sed*,[6] it has been suggested that the bracelets were in fact gifts to the king presented by high officials at the occasion of the feast,[7] and later deposited with the king's burial equipment.

In the past often identified as a representation of Amenhotep's wife, queen Tiye,[8] the sphinx of the sard inlay should more accurately be understood as a multifaceted mythical being that presents and protects the king whose cartouche she holds in her hands.[9] Female sphinxes were represented

83   83, alternate view

84

in Egypt at least since Dynasty 4, and then often during the Middle and early New Kingdoms.[10] Underlying such representations was the Egyptian belief that the female played a fundamental role in the creation of the universe and in maintaining the balance of the cosmos. In mythological terms this concept was expressed by the primeval pair Shu and Tefnut.[11] Tefnut, like her close associate Hathor, was also intimately linked with foreign countries. In the myth of the "faraway goddess," for example, Tefnut left Egypt to dwell as a fierce lioness in inner Africa, whence she could only reluctantly be coaxed to return to Egypt. Later transformed into the benevolent Hathor, she was joyously received in temples throughout the land.[12] The sphinx on the sard plaque is associated with this story through her Nubian accoutrements: the large circular earring and probably also the feathers on her head.[13]

To the southern exoticism the bracelet designers added the partly unfolded wings known in Egypt since the Middle Kingdom and Hyksos period first as part of griffin imagery (see cat. no. 67).[14] Egyptians from the time of Amenhotep III likely associated them with western Asia (see fig. 47).[15]

The sphinx's hairstyle has been likened to the headgear of the Shasu Bedouins living in Syria and the Levant during the New Kingdom.[16] But even more closely comparable are hairstyles seen on nude female figures on Egyptian ceremonial spoons[17] that have been convincingly

interpreted as representing the sky goddess Nut holding up the solar disc at sunrise.[18] This association would make the cartouche of the king an image of the sun disc.[19]

Thirty years later we encounter the winged female sphinx adorning the throne of a pair statue of Haremhab, the last ruler of Dynasty 18, and his queen Mutnodjmet.[20] Placed on the side of the throne closest to the figure of the queen, the sphinx is in this case coupled with the name of Mutnodjmet, and juxtaposed with the figures of foreign

male prisoners on the side of Haremhab—possibly in an attempt to differentiate the primarily symbolic role and mythical association of the queen from the more mundane function of the pharaoh. Mutnodjmet's sphinx wears a Nefertiti-type cap crowned by a Near Eastern–style plant motif; around her neck is a string with a large circular pendant such as was worn not only by the Shasu but by other Levantine peoples.[21] The sphinx thus acquired some more explicitly Levantine features on her journey from Amenhotep III to Haremhab. DA

1. Hayes 1959, pp. 242–43, fig. 147; Berman and Bryan 1992; Arnold in *Royal Women of Amarna* 1996, pp. xvi, 107, fig. 102.
2. Edwards 1976, pp. 21, 33, no. 11.
3. Presumably on some kind of bedding material. I thank Deborah Schorsch, Objects Conservation, The Metropolitan Museum of Art, for helping me understand the setting of the sard plaque.
4. The repaired break is today clearly visible on the back of the piece.
5. Hayes 1959, p. 242; Berman and Bryan 1992, p. 444 n. 2; Reeves and Taylor 1992, p. 118. For other finds from the king's tomb, see Hayes 1959, pp. 243–44.
6. For the scenes on the other bracelet plaques, see Hayes 1959, pp. 242–43, and Berman and Bryan 1992.
7. Hayes 1959, p. 242. For such gifts being presented to the king, see *Egypt's Dazzling Sun* 1992, p. 437, fig. xv.4.
8. Mainly on the basis of the appearance of the queen as a female sphinx at Sedeinga: Berman and Bryan 1992, pp. 443–44; of her throne in the Tomb of Kheruef: *Egypt's Dazzling Sun*

Figure 47. Ivory plaque with female sphinx. Megiddo, Palace Treasury. Late Bronze Age. Oriental Institute Museum, Chicago OIM A 22213

1992, p. 437, fig. XV.4; and of an ivory carving from Gurob: Borchardt 1911, pp. 21–22, fig. 30. For the same identification, see also: Arnold in *Royal Women of Amarna* 1996, p. 107. I thank George Johnson for making me consider the piece with renewed objectivity. Betsy Bryan (1996, pp. 69–70, fig. 15) had previously advocated a more general understanding of the figure.

9. The cartouche is, of course, an elongated version of the *shen* (protection) symbol so often appearing in the claws of mythical animals and lions. Otherwise, cartouches are held up in scenes of offering as in the various representations where the Aten's names are being offered by Akhenaten and Nefertiti: Davies 1906, pl. 31; Aldred in *Akhenaten and Nefertiti* 1973, pp. 104–6, no. 18. For the "offering of the name" as a ritual, see Osing 1982.

10. Fay 1996, pp. 62–69, nos. 1, 15, 16, 19, 24, 49–51, 60; Russmann 2005.

11. Assmann 1995, p. 80.

12. Verhoeven 1986. Cyril Aldred (1991, p. 225) saw Nefertiti very much in the role of the goddess Tefnut and described the queen's mortar-shaped crown as "the headgear of Tefnut in her leonine aspect of a sphinx," doubtless thinking of the sphinx on the throne of Haremhab in the Egyptian Museum, Turin (Aldred 1991, pl. 77 and below), and the plaque here under consideration.

13. Grumach-Shirun 1977, col. 144 n. 17; Valbelle 1981, p. 120. The identification of a curl of hair beside the sphinx's ear (Berman and Bryan 1992, p. 443; Bryan 1996, pp. 69–70) has to be corrected. *Royal Women of Amarna* 1996, p. 107, fig. 102, shows the circular ring in an ear that has been somewhat rubbed off during the varied history of the plaque.

14. Eggebrecht 1977.

15. See the box from Kum Medinet Gurob: Delange 1993.

16. Bryan 1996, p. 71. However, the Shasu headgear, besides being male attire, does not show the hair as tightly wound around the head as seen on the sard sphinx. See Giveon 1971, pp. 251–53, pl. 17, for Shasu headgear, and pls. 2–4 for the Dynasty 18 filleted hairdo of Shasu.

17. D. Dunham 1978, pl. 47, and Hayes 1959, pp. 268–69, fig. 163.

18. Kozloff 1992a, pp. 331–33; Kozloff 1992b, pp. 346–47, nos. 74, 75.

19. W. Johnson 1991.

20. Egyptian Museum, Turin, inv. no. 1379: Donadoni 1989, pp. 152–53, 159–60, figs. 236–38.

21. For the Shasu, see Giveon 1971, p. 253, pl. 19. For circular pendants worn by other foreigners from the Mediterranean area, see Bovot 1994. There is a possibility that the sard sphinx once wore such a necklace. It would have consisted of a gold strip that fit into the space on the front of the neck. The two incised lines on the neck could be Amarna-style "beauty lines" or could, alternatively, belong to the necklace.

85

QUEEN TIYE AS THE GODDESS TAWERET

Wood
Height 15 cm (5⅞ in.); width 5.5 cm (2⅛ in.)
Egypt
New Kingdom, Dynasty 18, reign of
Amenhotep III, 1390–1352 B.C.
Fondazione Museo delle Antichità Egizie di
Torino 566

Taweret was a folk goddess represented as a hybrid figure composed of a pregnant hippopotamus standing upright on leonine legs. She is generally depicted with pendulous breasts, human arms terminating in leonine paws, and the spine and tail of a crocodile. In this wood figurine the hippopotamus head is replaced with a beautiful head of a queen, who wears a long intricately striated wig bound by a wide circlet, which was originally gilded. A hole at the forehead marks the point where a *uraeus*, no doubt in another material, was inserted separately. Surmounting the head is a cylindrical element, which normally served as a base for a plumed headdress.

The face of the queen shows the unmistakable characteristics of Tiye, wife of Amenhotep III. The eyes slant down toward the root of the nose under naturally formed lids in a long shallow orbital. Black painted cosmetic stripes extend as far as the ears, whose lobes are scored to indicate piercing, a feature of the Amarna

85

period. The fleshy heart-shaped mouth is also suggestive of the Amarna style.

Taweret was a goddess of marriage, a protector of women, especially in childbirth, and children, and as such she shared traits with the goddess Hathor. By extension, Taweret also played a role in the rebirth of the dead. In one of the myths, Taweret was said to have held the crocodile Seth so that Horus could slay it. Children wore amulets of Taweret, perhaps to protect them from encounters with snakes and crocodiles. Remarkably, queen Tiye was worshipped as a living goddess and was variously associated with Taweret, Hathor, and Maat.

EV

86

MAGICAL WAND

Ivory (hippopotamus)
Width 5.3 cm (2⅛ in.); length 33.1 cm (13 in.)
Egypt
Middle Kingdom, Dynasty 12–13,
ca. 1981–1640 B.C.
The Metropolitan Museum of Art, New York,
Theodore M. Davis Collection, Bequest of
Theodore M. Davis, 1915 30.8.218

This magnificent magical wand, which retains the typical crescent shape of the hippopotamus tusk out of which it was carved, is one of the few completely preserved, extant examples.[1] To bring out its

decoration against the light-colored ivory, the incised lines were filled with a dark organic paste. At the narrow end is the usual relief depiction of the head of a fox; a feline head was incised onto the broader end. Between the two animal heads is a row of incised figures (from right to left): a seated baboon grasping a snake, a combination of a jackal's head with an animal's leg and a knife at the foot, a vulture on a basket with a flail over its back and a knife at its feet, a standing lion with a knife in each forepaw and right front leg raised, the goddess Taweret, a Bes image, and a sun disc on legs with a knife at the front foot.

Taweret stands upright on her hind legs, brandishing knives and devouring a snake. She is depicted as a composite of a lion and a hippopotamus and has a completely rendered crocodile attached to her back, rather than the usual crocodile tail fused with the back. Behind Taweret is an image of Bes but without snakes, a common attribute in contemporary depictions.[2] The frontal nude view and bowlegged stance with hands on his thighs are usual for Bes, however. His customary lion's tail hangs down between his legs, but his genitals are not represented. The tall headdress and leopard's skin appear only in later Bes imagery. This figure, without his usual lion's ears and with parted instead of the standard manelike hair, looks more human than others of the same period. Bes and Taweret were the most popular protective deities of children and mothers in ancient Egypt,

and their images also became very popular in the Levant (see cat. no. 90).[3]

Two short inscriptions on the wand read, "protection of the night" and "protection of the day." Several other wands bear similar inscriptions and give also the names of mothers and children, for whose protection they presumably served.[4] All the figures depicted on the magical wands were believed to help the sun god in the fight against his enemies, and their protective competence is demonstrated through the knives they hold. The child for whom such a wand was used could be magically identified with the sun god, who had been successfully defended by the figures depicted. Many wands, including this piece, show signs of wear, indicating that they were used over a period of time, possibly as part of a magical ritual. That the wands were found in tombs of adults can be explained by the Egyptian belief in rebirth: the protective wands thus not only protected newborns in life but also aided the deceased in rebirth. At a later stage, magical wands even seem to have been used for statuary. IST

1. For further reference, see Steindorff 1946, p. 43, fig. 4, pp. 46–47, no. 7; Altenmüller 1965, pp. 89–90, no. 106; Romano 1989, pp. 96–98, no. 30; and J. Allen 2005, pp. 28–30, no. 22.
2. For the Bes image, see Romano 1989 (especially pp. 33–57 for the Middle Kingdom and Second Intermediate Period).
3. See, for example, V. Wilson 1975 and Keel 1993.
4. For a detailed study and catalogue of magical wands, see Altenmüller 1965, 1983, 1986, and 1987.

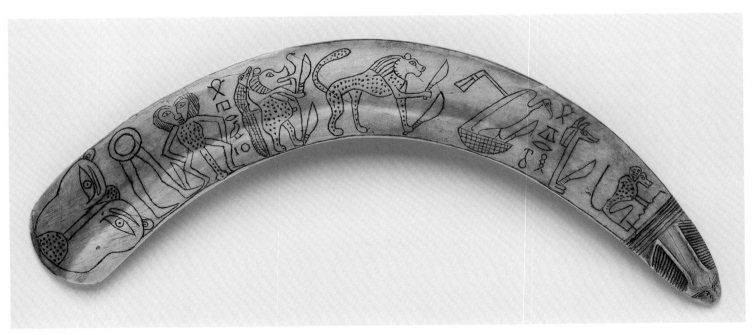

87

BES PLAQUE

Bone or Ivory
Height 4.9 cm (2 in.); width 3.5 cm (1⅜ in.)
Alaca Höyük
Middle Bronze Age, early 2nd millennium B.C.
Ankara Museum of Anatolian Civilizations,
Turkey 13186

87

A remarkable small relief sculpture, probably a furniture inlay, was found in the "deepest layer of the Hittite period" at Alaca Höyük during the 1936 excavations by Hamit Koşay.[1] It bears a sensitive rendering of the Egyptian lion-man Bes and is fashioned out of a gray-brown material that has been called bone or ivory. Some scholars originally assigned the piece to Anatolian or Syrian manufacture and sought the derivation of this leonine demon—with its unusual frontality and significance as a protective being—in the Near East.[2]

However, a thorough study of the creature by Romano convincingly placed the origin of the image of a nude male with the ears, mane, some facial features, tail, and bent-legged stance of a rampant lion in Egypt itself.[3] He also determined the particular rendering of Bes on the Alaca Höyük plaque to be fully consistent with the imagery and style of Egyptian renderings of Bes during the Middle Kingdom, despite the fact that no such inlays are extant in the Nile Valley as they are in Anatolia.[4] The closest comparisons, which suggest that the plaque was the work of an Egyptian craftsman and therefore a rare import to central Anatolia, are found on the numerous Egyptian magical wands made of the ivory of the formidable hippopotamus (possibly the same material used for the Alaca Höyük plaque) and incised with images of real and imaginary beasts (see cat. no. 86). Among these is the lean, naked bent-legged creature referred to as Aha, or fighter (protector), at times with prominently displayed genitalia, with the ears, mane, and tail of a lion, and with hands held toward the thighs and grasping snakes.

Only the upper portion of the Bes figure from Alaca Höyük is preserved, depicting his slender frontal human body with emphasized pectoral and arm muscles, a modeled ribcage, tapering waist, rounded belly with a drop-shaped navel, widely extended legs, and prominent genitalia. His fists are clenched on his thighs, which are preserved, as are his bent knees. The elliptical face, with horizontal almond-shaped eyes, a broad nose, and full lips, is framed by a slightly rounded trapezoidal mane that extends over the neck in strands of straight hair. Rounded leonine ears protrude from the mane.[5]

Another Bes image of this period, a statuette made of limestone, was found beyond the Nile Valley in the Temple of the Obelisks at Byblos along with many other offerings of Egyptian type in the form of animals and divine beings (some depicted in fig. 44). The piece probably dates to Dynasty 12–13 and is also considered to be an import.[6]

The presence of Bes in Anatolia and the Levant may, of course, signal more than simply the transfer of an exotic object or an exotic image. Rather, and more significantly, it may indicate the sharing of elemental ideas about the magical power of Bes and perhaps that of other Egyptian demons and symbols, which are found most profusely on Middle Bronze Age Syrian seals.[7] This possibility is supported by the discovery of a Middle Kingdom Egyptian magical wand in later context in a small tomb on the south acropolis at Ugarit. It was found not far from the House of the Priest-Magician, so named because of the divination texts and models of internal organs unearthed at the site.[8]

JA

1. Koşay 1944, p. 31, pl. XLIV (AL/A88).
2. Mesopotamian texts and iconography are replete with descriptions and images of apotropaic divinities with human and animal attributes, among them leonine demons, invoked as protectors against witchcraft and evil demons: Black and Green 1992, pp. 116, 119–21. Mesopotamian lion-demons, however, are generally depicted with the profile head of a lion and the body of a man, and they are often clothed in a kilt or robe and wield a weapon.
3. Romano (1980, pp. 39–43, 48; 1989, pp. 8–9, 14) cites Ballod in noting that the Bes image could have represented at least eight different divinities. See also Romano 1998, pp. 89–96, and Dasen 1993, pp. 55–56, 60, 63.
4. Romano 1989, pp. 150–51. This view is corroborated by Dorothea Arnold, Department of Egyptian Art, The Metropolitan Museum of Art (personal communication); V. Wilson (1975, p. 83) believes that "Egypt inspired the representation," which could have been imported from "Syria or Phoenicia." For Middle Bronze Age Anatolian ivory furniture inlays, see Harper 1969.
5. Romano (1998, p. 96) notes that by the reign of Senwosret I a rounded mane was introduced—perhaps dating this image to the mid–Middle Kingdom.
6. Dunand 1954, p. 767; Dunand 1950, pl. XCV; V. Wilson 1975, p. 84; Romano 1989, pp. 170–73, no. 53B. The Byblos image exhibits a different style, characterized by a grotesque large head with grimacing features.
7. See von der Osten 1934, pl. XXIII:329; Teissier 1996, pp. 78–79, no. 132, pl. 132. The impact

of Egyptian imagery is perhaps most apparent in the image of Taweret, the hippopotamus goddess frequently depicted alongside Bes, who was popular in the Levant and also in the Aegean, where she was transformed into the lion-headed "Minoan Genius": see Weingarten 1991.

8. Lagarce 1990.

88
FIGURE OF BES

Egyptian Blue
Height 8.5 cm (3⅜ in.); width 4 cm (1⅝ in.)
Egypt
New Kingdom, Dynasty 18, reign of
Akhenaten, ca. 1353–1336 B.C.
Staatliche Museen zu Berlin, Aegyptisches
Museum und Papyrussamlung 20484

This bright blue figure is an image of Bes, a being who was believed to watch over those in need of protection, such as mothers and children (see discussion in cat. no. 86).[1] A grotesque creature, with vaguely leonine facial features, he has a lion's ears, mane, and tail and a stocky, dwarfish body and limbs. His open-mouthed grimace seems both fierce and comic. Although Bes was most often

88

shown naked or wearing an animal pelt as a cloak, here he wears a kilt open at the front. He appears to be running or perhaps dancing.

Bes's physical peculiarities and his semidivine status have led some to suggest that he originated outside of Egypt, probably farther to the south in Africa. There seems to be no evidence to prove (or disprove) this theory, though it is certain that Bes—or Aha—was a force in Egypt as early as the Old Kingdom, when priests were represented wearing masks in the form of his head.

To judge from the many small figures of Bes that survive today, his protection was highly valued. Most such figures were made of Egyptian faience, a vitreous material consisting of sand or ground quartzite, which was usually pale greenish blue in color. This example, however, was made in a similar but rarer glasslike material known as Egyptian Blue (see pp. 419–20).[2] Its color, a deeper and more intense blue than that of faience, may have been intended to suggest the prized semiprecious stone lapis lazuli. The use of Egyptian Blue for this figure, together with the extremely fine and detailed modeling of its features, suggests that this Bes was intended for a person of high rank. It was probably placed in the owner's tomb, where, despite suffering the loss of both arms and legs, it survived.

ERR

1. For further reference, see Wildung in *Pharaohs of the Sun* 1999, p. 257, no. 181. For a brief description of Bes and his history, see Romano 1998.
2. For faience and Egyptian Blue, see Nicholson 2000, esp. p. 178.

89
HEADREST WITH BES IMAGERY

Wood
Height 15 cm (5⅞ in.); width 33 cm (13 in.);
depth 9 cm (3½ in.)
Egypt
New Kingdom, Dynasty 18, reign of
Akhenaten, 1353–1336 B.C.
Staatliche Museen zu Berlin, Aegyptisches
Museum und Papyrussamlung 11625

Ancient Egyptian headrests, like their modern counterparts, were intended to support the head of a sleeper while lying on his or her side. Like most Egyptian examples, this one consists of a curved support mounted on a column and fastened to a base large enough to provide stability.[1]

In addition to physically supporting and cradling the head, the headrest was believed to offer magical protection from evil animals and spirits that prowled in the dark. This magical power could be enhanced by the addition of images, often representations of the semidivine Bes, a guardian of sleepers. There are four such images on this headrest, two that show the upper body of Bes from the front and two of his entire figure in profile.

The frontal representations, which were carved on the undersides of the curved top, depict Bes's broad facial features and protruding tongue surrounded by his leonine mane and ears. He wears a short, flaring headdress, which appears to be a truncated version of the headdress worn by the full-length figures described below. His shoulders and arms are speckled with small incised dots, which may have been meant to indicate the leopard skin that he sometimes wears. In front of his torso, positioned as if he were holding it, is a lotus, an unusual accessory for Bes. Despite the similarity of the two half-length images, they vary in ways that suggest two different carvers: note, for example, the dissimilar shapes of the flowers and the presence of beard stripes on one figure but not on the other.

The full-length images of Bes in profile, placed on top of the base on either side of the central support, show him wearing a characteristic headdress that consists of a platform supporting tall, poorly delineated feathers. His stocky body, with bulging belly and stubby legs, sports a short lion's tail. In the hand nearest the viewer, which is raised above his head, he grasps the middle section of a large snake. In his other hand, Bes holds a large, leaf-shaped object, often shown with him, which appears to be a magic weapon. As with the pair of images discussed above, slight variations in the execution of these two figures, such as the texture of the manes, suggest that they were carved by different hands, or that perhaps they were differentiated in a way intended to reinforce their power.

Because of its magical properties, a headrest used in life often accompanied its

89

89, detail of base

owner to the tomb. That was probably the fate of this example, which, thus protected, survived in good condition.

ERR

1. For further reference, see Königliche Museen zu Berlin 1899, p. 196; Scharff 1923, pp. 32–33, pl. 26; and Schott 1958, p. 142.

unusual sexual practices. In the Levant, the image of this demon was supplanted by that of Bes, no doubt retaining its symbolic association with potency and fecundity.   AC/ED

1. Karageorghis and Demas 1985, pl. CXXIV, no. 4252; Loud 1939, pl. 8, nos. 24, 26.

90
FIGURE OF BES

Bronze
Height 10.4 cm (4⅛ in.);
width 2.2 cm (⅞ in.)
Ugarit
Late Bronze Age, 14th century B.C.
National Museum, Damascus, Syria 5722

Images of Bes appeared in the Levant during the second millennium B.C., notably at Ugarit, on various articles of personal adornment, jewelry, amulets, seals, terracotta figurines, and weights. He is usually represented as part human and part lion, with a beard or mane and feline ears, in addition to the lion skin worn as a mantle. On ivory plaques from Kition and Megiddo, Bes is depicted brandishing a large knife against nefarious demons.[1] The choice in this case of a protective demon for a razor—an instrument of toiletry and minor surgery—is therefore auspicious. This is the only sculpture of Bes known from Ugarit.

A similar apotropaic figure was popular during the Middle Bronze Age in Mesopotamia and inland Syria. He, too, is portrayed, in statuary and on terracotta plaques, full face, with bent legs and a paunch, and generously endowed. He is usually depicted playing a musical instrument. Dwarfs were said to be gifted with the power of music and to engage in

90

Board Games

Board games and their mechanisms of play are of surprising antiquity and are shared among ancient cultures. Archaeology establishes that abstract games of some form were already being played on flat stone boards with two or more rows of holes in the prepottery Neolithic period of the Near Eastern world. Such boards, dating to about 8000 B.C., occur at sites in the Levant and exemplify the principle that games find their natural function in settled communities, where shared labor and responsibility allow, crucially, for leisure.[1] For board games, whatever their literal origin and despite their occasional overlap with ritual or divination, have always been primarily for pleasure and the whiling away of unfilled hours. "Good" games, pared of inequalities down to a balanced medium for competition that can endure repetition, spread uninhibitedly from culture to culture, crossing political and language boundaries with freedom. Games—equipment and technique alike—traveled lightly, with merchant caravans along trade routes, in the aftermath of armies and mercenaries, and with itinerant preachers and runaway slaves. Really good games sometimes last for millennia.

Prior to the advent of Indian chess in the early centuries A.D., all ancient board games for which we have evidence today were "race" games. By this is meant a game—usually for two players—in which identical, matched pieces are maneuvered around a formalized track, their movements controlled by some form of random generator or dice. Often such a track will incorporate safe squares, hazards, penalties, or shortcuts. While local design and apparatus can vary drastically, the underlying aim, to be the first to get all the pieces off the end, is shared by all.

The board games of the second millennium B.C. illustrate this clearly. They are well known thanks to widespread archaeological discoveries. All three are classic examples of "race" games, with partly contrasting histories. One is the quintessentially Egyptian Senet (the Game of Thirty Squares), a game played at home for more than three thousand years, almost exclusively within ancient Egypt itself. By contrast, the Game of Twenty Squares (cat. no. 91, upper surface cat. no. 265) and the Game of Fifty-eight Holes (cat. nos. 92, 93) achieved widespread and similarly long-lived popularity across the Near East and Egypt, anticipating in some measure the later and enduring success of chess and backgammon.

SENET: THE GAME OF THIRTY SQUARES

A playing board of 3 × 10 squares characterizes the sedentary Egyptian game of Senet ("Passing"), a familiar aspect of daily life on the Nile from before 3000 B.C. to the second century A.D. Many boards with dice and pieces have come to light since the birth of Egyptology, and our knowledge of this game is much enhanced by wall paintings, tomb models, and even papyrus-and-ink narratives, so that we are in some ways better informed about Senet than almost any other of the world's ancient games.

This does not mean, however, that there is a consensus as to rules or direction of play. Certain squares at one end are usually marked, and each has a specific role in the final stages of the game.[2] Most scholars agree that the pieces begin lined up on alternate squares from the end with plain squares, and proceed boustrophedon-style around the track toward the other end according to the scores of knucklebones or, more commonly, two-sided "fingers," or throw sticks. Blocking strategy was evidently a crucial element. Many examples from tombs consist of well-finished boxes with a drawer for equipment and an elongated playing surface. In the New Kingdom it is evident that playing Senet could entail a deeper significance than mere amusement, since the passage of the soul of the dead through the Underworld involved playing a game to ensure a desirable outcome. The closest information we have about rules as such derives from a composition describing this process.

THE GAME OF TWENTY SQUARES

The first certain evidence for this game comes from mid-third-millennium B.C. cemeteries at Ur in southern Mesopotamia and Shahr-i Sokhta in Iran, although fragmentary boards from Habuba Kabira in Syria may prove to push the story back to the late fourth millennium B.C.[3] Two thousand years later the game was being freely played all over the Near East, as witnessed by boards known from Mesopotamia to Anatolia, and Cyprus. Fancy pieces, called "dogs," circulated as gifts, and known playing surfaces vary from the sketchiest of graffiti grids on brick or pavements to ivory-clad luxury items of furniture such as those made for Tutankhamun himself.[4]

Two players, usually with five pieces each, competed to enter their men via the left or right flank, then turned the corner to race up the central row of squares to the end. Five of the twenty component board squares are distinguished by a rosette, which probably conferred safety and/or a second throw. Dice at this time were most commonly sheep or goat astragals (knucklebones), each of which generated four possible scores. Rules that apply to this game from a Babylonian cuneiform tablet of the second century B.C. suggest that the game was called Pack of Dogs, and reveal that betting on the progress of the racing pieces had become an important pastime by that date.[5]

This race game would achieve remarkable longevity. While it was eventually supplanted in the Near East by a precursor of what later became backgammon, the original game survived against all odds under the name of Asha among the Jewish communities of Cochin in southwest India. It is evident that their remote ancestors, who likely made their way to India at an early period, must have brought with them from Babylon the traditional national board game and kept it alive into modern times.[6]

ILF

---

1. For a survey of these early game boards, see Simpson 2007 and the references given there.
2. The last five squares show typically, in order, nfr signs, X or "water," 3, 2, and a falcon; for a selection, see Kendall 1978, p. 25. For the Egyptian game of Senet, see, inter alia, Pusch 1979; Kendall 1982; and Piccione 2007. An innovative approach is that of Albertarelli 2002.
3. See Becker 2007.
4. For Tutankhamun's splendid collection of gaming equipment, including both the games discussed here and two-sided game boxes, see Tait 1982.
5. For details, see Finkel 2007b
6. For an equally remarkable case, with the Egyptian Game of the Snake (mehen) resurfacing in twentieth-century A.D. Sudan, see Kendall 1989, and Kendall 2007, pp. 43–44.

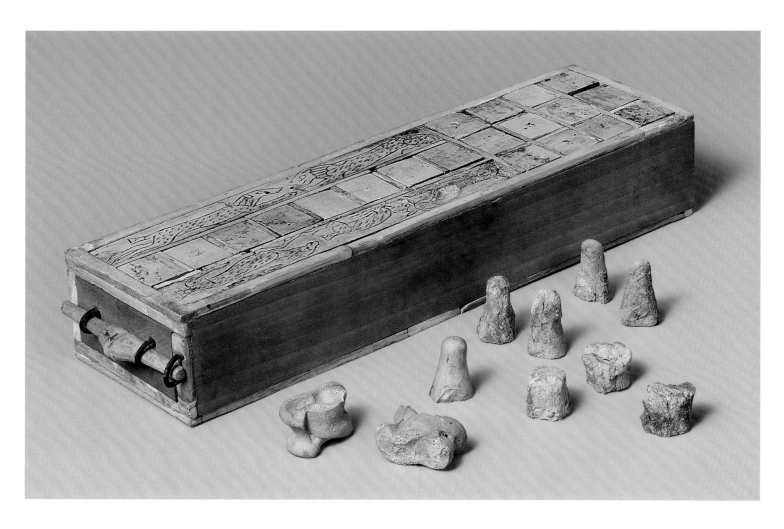

91

DOUBLE-SIDED GAME BOX:
GAMES OF THIRTY AND
TWENTY SQUARES

Ivory, wood
Height 5 cm (2 in.); width 6.7 cm (2⅝ in.);
length 25 cm (9⅞ in.)
Thebes, lower el-Asasif
Late Second Intermediate Period–
Early New Kingdom, Dynasty 17–18,
ca. 1600–1450 B.C.
The Metropolitan Museum of Art, New York,
Rogers Fund, 1916 16.10.475

With the advent of the Asiatic Hyksos during the course of the second millennium B.C., the Game of Twenty Squares was imported to Egypt, where it enjoyed fluctuating popularity between Dynasty 17 and 20. It was referred to as the Twenty-Square Game or Twenty Game, and Egyptian players even experimented with a double board when there were four players.[1] The double-sided potential of the traditional game boxes was soon exploited and used for both this game and Senet. Hieroglyphic inscriptions on the box sides often reveal that the import was uppermost, perhaps suggesting that the new game was a little more interesting. One-sided Egyptian boards for this game remain rare.

At the same time one- or double-sided game boxes in Egyptian style also occur outside of Egypt. This well-known example from the Metropolitan Museum is from Egyptian Thebes and has been dated to late Dynasty 17 or early Dynasty 18.[2] The box itself is carved from a block of wood and clad with strips, squares, and panels of ivory. It has a simple catch to secure the drawer, which contained two differentiated sets of six ivory pieces, six ivory casting sticks, and a pair of knucklebones. The upper surface is laid out for the Game of Twenty Squares, and the reverse is laid out for Senet. The appeal of the object was much enhanced by the elongated carved animals that appear at each side of the central path.

This Theban box has much in common with the ivory game box excavated some twenty-five years ago at the site of Kamid el-Loz, which dates approximately to the twelfth century B.C.[3] Here, too, opposite sides of the box are laid out for Senet and for the Game of Twenty Squares, with no squares marked. Although all second-millennium B.C. game boxes will naturally have points in common, the proportions, style of manufacture, bolt system, and, especially, the narrow animal decorations at each side of the playing track suggest that here is a style, if not a fashion, that led to local productions by Levantine workshops eager to imitate the Egyptian model. The point emerges even more clearly thanks to the recent discovery of yet another remarkably similar twelfth-century B.C. ivory box during the British Museum excavations at Tell es-Sa'idiyeh.[4]

ILF

1. A drawing occurs on a Dynasty 20 papyrus. See Pusch 1977. A similar earlier doubling experiment had taken place in Mesopotamia; see the lost board sketched in Banks 1912, p. 355.
2. See Hayes 1959, pp. 25–26 and fig. 10; Pusch 1979, pp. 199–201 no. 22; and Dreyfus 2005.
3. Full details of this important object and its context and construction are given in Meyer 1986.

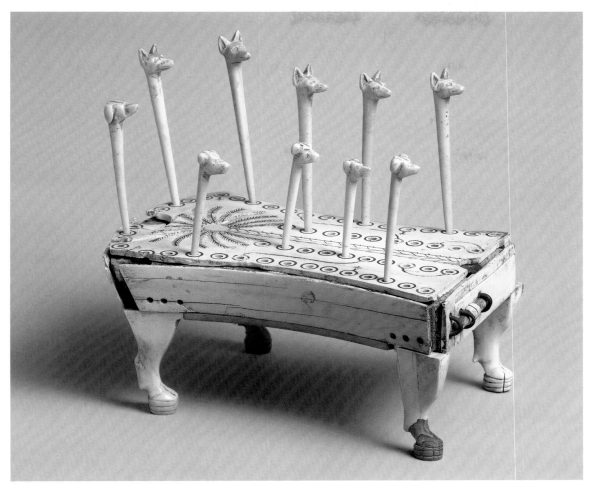

92

4. The Tell es-Sa'idiyeh box ZT204.7 (BM 1990-3-3, 102) is currently being assembled by the Department of Conservation and Science at the British Museum from hundreds of ivory fragments recovered from a disturbed double-pithos burial. The burial dates to the twelfth century B.C., contemporary with Egyptian Dynasty 20. The details of manufacture, carved animal decoration, and traces of the bolt device are directly comparable to the contemporary box from Kamid el-Loz. The writer is grateful to Jonathan Tubb, director of the British Museum Tell es-Sa'idiyeh Excavation, and Jack Green for the details quoted here in advance of the excavation report on the ivories.

92
GAME BOARD:
THE GAME OF FIFTY-EIGHT HOLES

Ivory, ebony
Height 6.3 cm (2½ in.); width 15.2 cm (6 in.)
Thebes
Middle Kingdom, Dynasty 12,
ca. 1981–1802 B.C.
The Metropolitan Museum of Art, New York,
Purchase, Edward S. Harkness Gift, 1926
26.7.1287

93
GAME BOARD:
THE GAME OF FIFTY-EIGHT HOLES

Egyptian Blue, gold
Width 3.8 cm (1½ in.); length 7.8 cm (3⅛ in.)
Acemhöyük, Level III
Middle Bronze Age, 18th century B.C.
Ankara Museum of Anatolian Civilizations,
Turkey 69–24–66

The first extant examples of the Game of Fifty-eight Holes come from Egypt, and it is possible that the game originated there. The wonderful table board with its unique set of original pieces, five per side, which was found by Howard Carter at Thebes, is now in the Metropolitan Museum (cat. no. 92).[1] The iconic designs for the pieces led him to call the game Hounds and Jackals; other writers have proposed the Palm Tree Game on the basis of the central design of this particular

example, while the more general Game of Fifty-eight Holes is often preferred, since this is the number of holes on the playing track.

The idea of a track of holes with peg-shaped men is surprisingly contemporary, and it brings the picture of the original players of the game that much closer to our own time, although any connection at all with devices such as the modern cribbage board must be firmly ruled out; it is even uncertain whether Drioton's claim is correct that the much later Coptic game which uses a similar device is truly descended from the more ancient game.[2]

The surviving corpus of boards of this type comprises more than forty to date. The earliest are Egyptian, from Dynasty 9 through 12, sharing with the Metropolitan's Theban board an "axe blade" shape, while later boards, in a variety of three further basic formats, are known from Mesopotamia and Iran to the Levant and Anatolia. Perhaps the majority are of stone; others occur in wood or ivory, with certain humbler Mesopotamian examples of worked clay. The Egyptian Blue fragment from Acemhöyük in central Anatolia (cat. no. 93) must once have been a much prized object. The holes were ringed with inlay. Every fifth hole is correspondingly larger, two retaining their original gold-leaf overlay.

Disregarding "starting holes" and the large final "goal" at the top, the track consists of fifty-eight holes divided into two sides, one for each player. The field of play shows every fifth hole marked. It seems beyond serious doubt that with most boards, each player was restricted to his own half of the field, and concentrated on steering his "hounds" (or "jackals") down the center of the board, round to the outer edge, and up to the top. The progress of the race would thus be affected both by the score thrown and by the presence of certain interhole links on each side (such as holes 6–20, or 8–10). These "shortcuts" must have been two-edged, in that—in contrast to Chutes and Ladders today—they would work in *both* directions, thus constituting benefit or hazard depending on the game. Two terracotta boards from Iran[3] show contrasting interhole links that cross over *from side to side*. This element changes the nature of the game, which becomes more complex, longer in duration, and involves greater interaction between the players. The Iranian version was thus likely a more enjoyable local innovation.

ILF

1. See Carnarvon and Carter 1912, pp. 56–59, pl. 50; Hayes 1953, p. 250, fig. 160; and Hoerth 2007, pp. 64–65.
2. See Drioton 1940.
3. One, from Tepe Sialk, is cited in Ghirshman 1938–39, vol. 2, p. 43. A roughly contemporary Iranian board of about 1000 B.C. that exhibits further and more complicated crossover lines is in the British Museum (ME 1991-7-20, 1). This seems to establish the correctness of Ghirshman's claim that the pegs could move from one side of the board to another. A further second-millennium B.C. example of black stone shaped like a neckless electric guitar that originated in Anatolia, also in the British Museum (ME 2003,12-1, 1), exhibits a different set of crossover lines. These variant and more complex versions of the Game of Fifty-eight Holes need investigation.

The Horse in the Ancient Near East

The wind of heaven is that which blows between a horse's ears.
—*Arabian Proverb*

Equids of varying sorts, both wild and domesticated, are clearly in evidence by the eighth millennium B.C. in parts of the Near East and the Eurasian steppe, although wild species likely existed during (and possibly before) the Ice Age.[1] It has been suggested that the horse (Equus caballus)—in contrast with other equids such as the onager, donkey, mule, and ass—was first domesticated as early as 4800 B.C. by nomadic peoples living in the Pontic-Caspian steppe, the area north of the Black and Caspian Seas.[2] While the horse would become the premier animal of transportation and warfare as well as a potent symbol of royalty throughout the ancient world, the initial incentive to tame it seems to have arisen from the need for inexpensive meat in the cold winter climate of the mountains and the steppes.

By the end of the third millennium B.C. the horse, described in Akkadian and Ur III sources as "the donkey of the mountain," had made its way to Mesopotamia.[3] The Sumerian and Akkadian words for the horse clearly reflect its geographic origins. It is also at this time that images of horses begin to appear, some of which show them mounted.[4] After 2000 B.C. horses enter the Near East in large numbers, a phenomenon that many scholars believe dovetailed with the ever-growing trade in metals, since the majority of ancient copper and tin mines have been found in the Eurasian steppe and in Central Asia, another area where horses thrived.[5]

A defining moment in the history of the horse came with the advent of the war chariot in the seventeenth century B.C. Both the Hittites in Anatolia and the Mitanni in northern Syria have been credited with this development.[6] Horses were highly valued and meticulously cared for, as demonstrated by a Hittite horse-training manual written by a Mitanni horse expert named Kikkuli (see cat. no. 96). It is widely thought that horses and war chariots were introduced to Egypt by the Hyksos in the first half of the sixteenth century B.C.[7] By the fifteenth century B.C., Asiatics are depicted bringing horses and a chariot to the Egyptian court (fig. 48). Eventually, the Egyptians themselves improved the chariot so that it could be more easily maneuvered than those used by the Hittites and the Mitanni.

Although there is little evidence that the Kassites used horses and chariots in the same manner as the Egyptians, the Hittites, and the Mitanni, it would appear that they served as major brokers in the trade and movement of horses around the Near East and the eastern Mediterranean.[8] It is clear from the Amarna Letters (cat. no. 97) that horses and chariots were among the most prized commodities in the elaborate system of royal gift exchange that dominated the Late Bronze Age. The ever-increasing importance of the horse in the second millennium B.C. is perhaps best expressed by its symbolic association with the goddess Astarte, a popular Near Eastern deity who was also adopted in Egypt. In earlier times Astarte was most often pictured with a lion; by Dynasty 19, however, she is shown, bejeweled, riding nude on horseback (cat. no. 95).[9] The raw power of this image speaks for itself—and volumes for the majesty of the horse.

KB

1. *Anthony 2007, pp. 197–99.*
2. *Ibid., pp. 200–201.*
3. *Weszeli 2003–5, pp. 469–71.*
4. *Buchanan 1966, p. 56, no. 290, pl. 23, no. 290b(E).*
5. *Anthony 2007, pp. 417–18 and fig. 16.1.*
6. *Littauer and Crouwel 1979, pp. 62–65, 68–71.*
7. *Rommelaere 1991, pp. 19–31.*
8. *Vermaak 2007, p. 521.*
9. *A stele recently excavated at the site of Tell el-Borg in North Sinai shows the unusual arrangement of Astarte sitting on a chair on the back of a horse. See Hoffmeier and Kitchen 2007 for a full description of the stele and for a discussion of the breed of horse depicted.*

Figure 48. Wall painting of Asiatics with horses and chariot. Thebes, Tomb of Rekhmire (TT 100). Dynasty 18, reigns of Thutmose III–Amenhotep II.

94
HANDLE IN THE SHAPE OF A HORSE

Ivory, stain, glass
Length 15 cm (5⅞ in.)
Egypt
New Kingdom, Dynasty 18, 1400–1350 B.C.
The Metropolitan Museum of Art, New York,
Purchase, Edward S. Harkness Gift, 1926
26.7.1293

Most scholars agree that the horse was imported into Egypt toward the end of the Second Intermediate Period (before 1550 B.C.) by the Hyksos kings who ruled northern Egypt as Dynasty 15.[1] The Egyptians used horses primarily for pulling chariots, either in battle or in the hunt. In such scenes, they are shown with their hind legs on the ground and their forelegs raised in a rearing stance, so that the enemy, or hunted animals, would fall beneath their hooves. Like domestic dogs (cat. no. 271), horses were seldom depicted in three dimensions.

This elegant handle for a whip, or fly whisk, provides a rare representation of the horse in a flying gallop, a posture often seen in Aegean animal imagery. The extended form allowed the horse's body to fit comfortably in a closed hand. It also evokes the animal's power, speed, and spirit, all of which were highly valued by the Egyptians.[2]

CHR

1. Rommelaere 1991, pp. 19–31.
2. For further reference, see Hayes 1959, pp. 314, 315, fig. 197; Rommelaere 1991, pp. 49, 224–25 (with bibliography); and Arnold 1995, p. 55, no. 71.

95

OSTRACON WITH NUDE GODDESS ON HORSEBACK

Limestone, painted
Height 10 cm (4 in.); width 16 cm (6¼ in.)
Thebes
New Kingdom, Dynasty 19,
ca. 1295–1186 B.C.
Staatliche Museen zu Berlin, Aegyptisches
Museum und Papyrussamlung 21826

This ostracon is painted with a representation of a youthful-looking female riding bareback on a horse whose reins she holds in one hand.[1] The feet of both horse and rider have been broken off, and damage to the top of the piece obscures what the female once held in her upraised right hand, almost certainly a bow and arrow. Although a curving line at the base of the figure's neck suggests that the artist may have originally intended to portray her clothed, she wears only a large beaded necklace with a heart-shaped pendant and hoop earrings. The top and back of her head are damaged, but it is clear that her hair was short; it seems to have been adorned with a lotus flower.

The figure's nudity, her weapon, and the fact that she is on horseback all suggest that she is not an Egyptian woman. She must be a goddess, but not a goddess of Egypt, as no Egyptian goddesses were associated with horses. Most likely she represents Astarte, a northwest Semitic deity brought to Egypt by immigrant soldiers and merchants, and associated with weapons and horses.

Astarte was imported into the Egyptian pantheon early in the New Kingdom. At Memphis, where she had her own temple, she was associated with Ptah, the chief Egyptian god of that city. The surviving representations of Astarte from Egyptian temple reliefs and stelae, however, show characteristics rather different from those of this drawing: in them, the goddess wears a tall crown and usually a robe, and she carries either a spear and shield or a bow and arrow. Occasionally she is shown on horseback, and on one such example she is nude, except for ornaments, and she shoots her bow. Even there, however, she wears her crown, and though she rides bareback, she is sitting sidesaddle.

Thus the figure on this ostracon, although almost certainly inspired by Astarte, remains somewhat shrouded in mystery. Together with a few similar images on other ostraca, she may be the only surviving evidence of a localized cult somewhere in Egypt; or she may bear witness to a story, now lost, in which the goddess was for some reason disguised. At the very least, she is evidence for the fact that, in crossing borders, the gods often underwent significant change.

ERR

1. For further reference, see Leclant 1960, pp. 40–41, pl. 3a (with earlier bibliography); Ägyptisches Museum Berlin 1967, p. 64, no. 728, illus.; and Stadelmann 1967, pp. 103–4.

The presence of this exotic vocabulary is undoubtedly related to the fact that, although the administrative language of the realm of Mitanni was the non-Indo-European Hurrian, the Mitanni rulers were of Indic origin, as revealed by their personal names.

The methods employed in the training program include carefully calibrated workouts and diet, as well as close attention to grooming the animals. An instruction from day 184, the last preserved, provides an indication of its character:[1]

In the morning (the horses) are hitched up and (the trainer) drives them for one-half mile and twenty "field lengths." Then he gallops them for one-half mile and seven "field lengths" (equivalent to three laps)—triwartanna. In addition, they return to the city at a gallop. When they are unhitched, then they are covered and brought into the stable.

After a while the stable becomes very warm. When the horses become restless and begin to sweat, (the trainer) removes their halters and blankets. Then he puts on their reins and they are led out of the stable. They are bathed in warm water. Furthermore, they are led down to the river and splashed four(?) times with water. Each time they are given one handful of hay and one handful of barley. When they come up from the water, they are led into the stable and now given one quart of groats. Afterward their barley ration is set out.[2]

GB

1. Unfortunately, we can give only very approximate modern equivalents of the measures of distance and capacity involved.
2. Translation by the author, previously unpublished.

96
HORSE TRAINING MANUAL

Clay
Height 28.5 cm (11¼ in.); width 16 cm (6¼ in.)
Boğazköy
Hittite Middle Kingdom, 14th century B.C.
Staatliche Museen zu Berlin,
Vorderasiatisches Museum VAT6693

An important factor in Hittite military success was the high quality of their chariotry, and this in turn was dependent on the stamina and agility of the horses that drew the chariots. This tablet is the fourth in a series of at least five that records the training regimen for chariot horses attributed by the Hittites to the Mitanni expert Kikkuli.

The text is composed in Hittite, but it borrows from an ancient Indic dialect a number of technical terms, including *triwartanna*, *panzawartanna*, *shattawartanna*, and *nawartanna*, which specify that the horses should be run in sequences of three, five, seven, and nine laps, respectively.

97
WEDDING GIFTS FROM TUSHRATTA

Clay
Height 31 cm (12¼ in.); width 17 cm (6¾ in.)
ca. 1365–1330(?) B.C., Tell el-Amarna
New Kingdom, Dynasty 18
Staatliche Museen zu Berlin,
Vorderasiatisches Museum VAT395 (EA22)

The inscription on the reverse of this
tablet from Tell el-Amarna reads:

*It is all of these wedding-gifts, of every sort,
that Tushratta, the king of Mitanni, gave to
Nimmureya, the king of Egypt, his brother
and his son-in-law. He gave them at the same
time that he gave Tadu-hepa, his daughter, to
Egypt and to Nimmureya to be his wife.*[1]

The rest of the tablet presents a minutely
detailed inventory of a shipment of gifts
sent to Egypt by the Mitanni king to celebrate the upcoming marriage of one of
his daughters to the Egyptian pharaoh, a
dynastic union intended to solidify relations between the two empires. Presumably
this document accompanied the princess
on her journey to Egypt so that with it she
could ensure the safe arrival of the various
goods and objects recorded there.

The gifts were apparently not an actual
dowry, but rather wedding presents
intended to promote good relations with
the king. Many of the numerous items
listed—the "beautiful horses that run
(swiftly)"; a "chariot . . . its covering all of
gold"; a "whip . . . overlaid with gold";
"necklaces for horses"; a "set of bridles . . .
of ivory"; and "reins . . . overlaid with
silver"[2]—as well as various weapons and
other military equipment that were surely
intended for display at the pharaoh's court,
would not have been among the accoutrements of a princess.

Almost completely preserved, the clay
tablet was produced in the Babylonian
style, with the front side flat and the back
convex. On both sides objects are listed,
separately or in groups, divided into four
columns and by double lines.

JM

1. EA 22: IV, 43–49; translated in Moran 1992,
   p. 57.
2. EA 22: I, 2, 4, 12, 15, 24; translated in Moran
   1992, p. 51.

THE LATE BRONZE AGE: MATERIALS AND MECHANISMS OF TRADE AND CULTURAL EXCHANGE

MARIO LIVERANI

THE REGIONAL SYSTEM

During the second millennium B.C., and especially during the Late Bronze Age, the entire area of the Near East, from the eastern Mediterranean to the Iranian plateau, was interlinked by a complex network of cultural, political, and economic relations. In previous periods the development of the region had been mostly centered on the great alluvial valleys of the Nile in Egypt and of the Tigris and Euphrates in Mesopotamia. The surrounding areas—hilly or arid—were less suitable to intensive settlement and urbanization, although important as reservoirs of raw materials such as timber, semiprecious stones, and especially metals, unavailable in the alluvial valleys. Trade networks for the dissemination of such materials had existed since prehistoric times; with the Late Bronze Age not only was there increased commerce but the entire system acquired a new configuration.

This system of heightened interaction can be defined as a "regional system," a description that avoids the exaggeration—and resulting misunderstandings—of that coined by Immanuel Wallerstein for the modern world, namely, "world-system."[1] The Bronze Age system was based on a formalized, and generally accepted, hierarchy that differentiates the Great Kings (*sharru rabu*) from the "small kings" (*sharru sehru*). The former were independent, the "lords" of the latter, who were their "servants." Because a small king could be the servant of no more than one Great King, the system was subdivided into half-a-dozen major political units.

Egypt had long been a unitary kingdom along the Nile from Aswan to the Delta. A densely populated land rich in agriculture resulting from the seasonal flooding of the river, it was a major power of the entire Near Eastern area, governed by a god-king, the pharaoh. After a period of inner division and domination by the Asiatic dynasty of the Hyksos people (ca. 1640–1550 B.C.), the beginning of the Late Bronze Age is marked by the expulsion of foreign rulers followed by the expansion southward (in Nubia) and northward (in the Levant) by Thutmose III (ca. 1479–1425 B.C.) and the other pharaohs of Dynasty 18. The Amarna period, during which the heretical pharaoh Amenhotep IV/Akhenaten (ca. 1353–1336 B.C.) took his residence at Tell el-Amarna, is the principal locus of study for interregional affairs, thanks to the discovery in 1887 of a stash of cuneiform tablets (the Amarna Letters) exchanged between Egypt and the Asiatic kingdoms.

Equally important in its concentration of people and power was Babylonia. In that region—Lower Mesopotamia, from modern Baghdad to the Gulf coast during the hegemony of Akkad (ca. 2334–2154 B.C.), Ur (ca. 2112–2004 B.C.), and Babylon under Hammurabi (ca. 1792–1750 B.C.)—periods of fragmentation alternated with periods of unity. But the end of Hammurabi's dynasty was marked by foreign domination by the Kassites, who descended from the Zagros Mountains, and by an economic and demographic decline resulting from the progressive disruption of the irrigation system. This decline is documented in the archaeological record as a reduction in the number and size of inhabited sites. Yet even in the wake of economic and demographic crisis, Babylonian prestige in culture and religion was strong enough to survive and to maintain supremacy (see fig. 49).

In Upper Mesopotamia the small polities of the Hurrian peoples were eventually unified, about 1500 B.C., in the kingdom of Mitanni, whose rise is possibly to be associated with the development of horse training and chariot warfare. The power of Mitanni, extending from the Mediterranean coast in northern Syria to the piedmont of the Zagros, had the effect of forestalling the growth of Ashur, the center of a lively trade network, from city-state to regional power. But when Mitanni was defeated by the Hittite king Suppiluliuma (ca. 1344–1322 B.C.), the kings of Ashur seized the opportunity to extend their domain during what is known as the Middle Assyrian period. Eventually they conquered all of Upper Mesopotamia, setting the stage for the growth to empire.

The Hittites were a relatively new power in the Near East, but already before 1600 B.C. they had unified most of central and eastern Anatolia and temporarily conquered Syria. The victories of Suppiluliuma led to the rise of Hatti as a powerful and respected kingdom facing Egypt in the Levant and Assyria along the Euphrates, and extending its boundaries to encompass all of western Anatolia to the shores of the Aegean Sea.

Although less well known in the extant textual records, the kingdom of Elam was equally powerful, dominating wide areas

Figure 49. The Kassite ziggurat at Dur-Kurigalzu (Aqar Quf) in Babylonia.

of southwestern Iran, with an unusual political organization that centered power both in Anshan (Tal-i Malyan) and in the southwestern outpost of Susa, and with connections extending into Iran and the Gulf area.

These were the members of the "club of the great powers," to use an expression coined by Hayim Tadmor.[2] The sociological (and mostly ideological) model for membership was "brotherhood" (*ahhutu*): the Great Kings considered themselves "brothers," and indeed they sometimes became brothers-in-law by marriage. Compared with previous periods, the military and political entrance of Thutmosid Egypt in the Levant, the waning of Babylonian hegemony, and the increased participation of the hilly regions instigated a broader and more variegated activity and challenged the preeminence of the river valleys. The hub of the Near East experienced a westward displacement to include the eastern Mediterranean. In addition to the officially recognized "members of the club," other polities connected with the Near Eastern regional system must be introduced.

In the west the role of Ahhiyawa (the Mycenaean world) as a great kingdom is doubtful,[3] possibly because it lacked a

central unifying power. During the Amarna period, the king of Alashiya (Cyprus) was considered a "brother" of the Great Kings because the state was independent (thanks to its insular location) and economically advantageous (with a monopoly in copper production and export). The regional system in general provided equilibrium and stability. A major change occurred with the earlier mentioned devolution of Mitanni following its defeat by the Hittites and the consequent rise of Assyria, although Hatti's resistance in accepting Assyria as a peer-ranking state is indicative of the club's exclusive and habitual nature. During shorter periods Kizzuwatna, in southeastern Anatolia, and later Carchemish, in northern Syria, would also assume the rank of a great kingdom.

The legal implications of the system were relevant. Each small, or vassal, king was responsible for what happened in his own territory, and each Great King was responsible for his entire domain. And while a Great King exercised authority over many vassal kings, a small king could address only his one master. Legal cases between states (these most frequently concerned the murder of merchants and the hiding of runaway slaves) were negotiated by the Great Kings acting on behalf of their vassals. Penalties and compensations, initially based on local models, became increasingly standardized over the centuries. There are also treaties (in the Hattusa, Alalakh, and Ugarit archives) that regulate specific problems and describe the procedures to be followed.[4]

This activity generated an overarching system of shared legal conventions and trade procedures.[5] Following the tradition of the Middle Bronze Age, Akkadian was adopted as the international language of diplomacy. Disseminated through the court schools, it was modified by the local languages of the scribes.[6] Misinterpretations were common, but for the most part they were intentional, serving to support or to undermine political interests. In some marginal centers—newcomers to the system—the use of Akkadian was difficult to implement. The king of Arzawa, for example, preferred to be addressed in Hittite;[7] scribal competence in the central hills of the Levant and Trans-Jordan was quite poor; and we have no evidence for the use of Akkadian by the Mycenaean merchants in the Levant.

THE GEOGRAPHY OF RESOURCES

The intensive interaction between the states was the result, in part, of a differentiated distribution of resources. The main fibers used in the production of clothing were wool in western Asia and flax in Egypt. Oil was made primarily from olives in Anatolia and the Levant, sesame seed in Mesopotamia, and flaxseed in Egypt. Dates were used as sweeteners in Mesopotamia, figs and honey in the Mediterranean. Beer was the most common fermented beverage in Mesopotamia and Egypt, while in Anatolia and the Levant wine was preferred. Such a distribution of food and fibers did not generate a significant flow of trade; that of minerals and metals, on the other hand, led to major commercial intercourse. Of the two metals used in the production of bronze, copper was abundant in Cyprus, while tin came from distant Afghanistan. Both were exchanged in their characteristic ingot form—usually oxhide ingots for copper (fig. 50), bun ingots for tin. Silver, the standard metal for comparative prices, was more abundant in Anatolia. There were no gold deposits in the Near East, and Egypt monopolized its export from Nubia. Generally speaking, Egypt had privileged access both to the "African" products (from Nubia) and to the "Asiatic" ones (from the Levant; fig. 51). Thus Egypt could negotiate from an advantageous position with the Asiatic kings, whose desire for the precious metal could best be described as an obsession. Semiprecious stones were also imported from afar—lapis lazuli from Afghanistan, carnelian and agate from Iran and India—though during the Late Bronze Age they became less common and were replaced, to a great extent, by artificial stones made of colored vitreous materials.

Trade was generated not only by the constraints of the geological distribution of metals, but also by local traditions in technology and fashion. Such trade would have applied especially to recently introduced technologies, while those long in use had already been widely disseminated. The manufacture

Figure 50. Wall painting with Syrians carrying copper ingot and Canaanite jar. Thebes, Tomb of Rekhmire (TT 100). Dynasty 18, reigns of Thutmose III– Amenhotep II.

of the light chariot, used in war and for hunting, and the concomitant training of horses were the major technological innovations of the Late Bronze Age, their use spreading southward. In the Amarna period, Egypt imported both chariots and horses from Mitanni and Syria. Also during these years glassmaking became more sophisticated, with Egypt, in addition to producing its own glass, importing raw glass from the Levantine coast (see cat. no. 187).[8]

In the case of technologies that did not materialize into products which could be easily transported, those who created the products were themselves transported: doctors, exorcists, and also artists were lent between kings. It was not unusual that a king attempted to retain a specialist as long as possible—even unto death.[9] Such specialists, unlike itinerant craftsmen, were part of the palace organization.

GIFTS, WOMEN, AND MESSAGES

According to the anthropologist Claude Lévi-Strauss, interaction among human communities is based on a threefold exchange—of gifts, women, and messages.[10] This analysis may appear rather crude, but it is certainly reflected in history. It also holds true, at least in part, in the modern world, though its use in the various historical civilizations is often mitigated or concealed by an ideology that tends to endow the exchange with a value inherent in itself, one that is different from and higher than that of purely material gain.

In a logical sequence the first exchange is that of matrimony, at least in small communities where survival and reproduction were based on exogamous alliances that proved more effective—both as a genetic imperative and as a risk-sharing strategy—than a strict endogamy. On a wider scale, as in international relations, exchange was pursued for social prestige and political aims:

> The Babylonian and Amorite girls whom I took [as daughters-in-law], were they not a source of praise for me before the people of Hatti? I did it: I took as a daughter-in-law the foreign daughter of a great king. Had I no girl from the Hatti Land? Did I not do this for the sake of renown?[11]

The increase of prestige was evident both to the inner audience (in the same kingdom as the issuer king) and the external, or international, audience. As for political reverberations, marriages between peers must be distinguished from marriages between social unequals. A marriage between family members of peer kings served either to reinforce a positive, already existing relationship or to subvert a relationship that was strained. Marrying off daughters to vassals, practiced most commonly by the Hittite kings, had the additional attraction of situating a member of the Great King's family as queen in the vassal court, a strategy that eventually landed a direct descendant of the sovereign's line on the throne of the small kingdom.

Figure 51. Wall painting with Nubian and Syrian bearing tribute. Thebes, Tomb of Rekhmire (TT 100). Dynasty 18, reigns of Thutmose III–Amenhotep II.

In the case of interdynastic marriages, the distance between the ideal—the model of reciprocity and generosity—and the reality was quite significant, especially in relations between the Egyptian pharaoh and his Asiatic colleagues. It was current practice among the Asiatic kings that when one of their daughters was wed to a peer-ranking king, she would become his first wife, that is, his queen. The Egyptian pharaohs, on the other hand, were willing to receive foreign princesses into their harems as a mark of prestige, but the queen had to be Egyptian; local public opinion would not have accepted a foreigner on the throne. Moreover, the Egyptian kings were not willing to reciprocate on equal terms, as peremptorily declared in the famous statement, "Since olden times, the daughter of a king of Egypt has never been given to anybody."[12] Such a lack of reciprocity could have resulted in the collapse of the entire system. But the Asiatic kings were content to receive gold in exchange—a solution the Egyptians considered demeaning to their colleagues, as the sarcastic tone of one pharaoh demonstrates: "Is it nice," he asks, "that you give your daughters away in order to obtain the gift of your neighbors?"[13]

Women and gifts were connected as well in the traditional model.[14] The bridegroom had to send "marriage gifts" to his future father-in-law; the bride had to bring with her a substantial dowry. The dowry, notably, would remain the wife's property, as a guarantee against divorce. Several lists of marriage gifts and dowries have survived, many that include huge quantities of metal vessels, wood furniture with ivory and gold inlays, clothing, servants—in short, necessities for the establishment of a new household (see cat. nos. 97, 118).

Of course, gifts unrelated to marriage were also exchanged. Two conditions were paramount. First, that a gift be given on a specific occasion—the enthronement of a new king, for example, or the building of a palace or temple—the least significant (and most common) occasion being the posting of a letter (always accompanied by a gift). The second condition was that a gift be "personalized," with reference to the sender and/or the recipient. Consequently, gifts tended to be gender specific: horses and weapons were given to males, clothes and perfumes to women.

The third item of exchange, namely, the message, functioned primarily in the service of the other two, since oral and written messages were employed to negotiate the terms of both gift exchange and marriage.[15] In some cases, however, one wonders whether it was the message that accompanied the gift or the gift that accompanied the message, as each was a necessary complement of the other and only together could they fulfill their social purpose. Sometimes the text of a letter lacks any apparent content and seems to have been sent simply to maintain contact. In Late Bronze Age diplomacy, the manner in which a formal letter is framed carries as much import as the information that it imparts. Titles of sender and addressee, forms of greeting, conventional inquiries, and reports regarding health are often nuanced in such a way as to underscore the different social status of both parties. In the greeting, the health of the sender and his family is always described as good, even when, a few lines below, serious problems are related. This first part of the letter, called the *shulma sha'alu*, "to ask about the health," is most important in formal relationships, and to omit or interrupt it implies hostility or political crisis.

The basic form of the letter derives from the Babylonian tradition, although local customs, if not properly understood, could lead to misunderstandings. In Babylonian epistolary courtesy, for example, the name of the addressee precedes that of the sender, while in the standard Egyptian address the order is reversed. In international usage, the position of the two names was dictated by rank. Reversals in order—intentional or by oversight—could result in protests. More serious problems were generated by the adaptation of Akkadian terminology to very different political views, in Egypt and Asia. The standard Egyptian exhortation "[to] keep the place in order," for example, usually addressed to petty officials, was translated as the Akkadian verb *nasaru*, "to protect," giving rise to protests by the Levantine vassal kings, who claimed (according to Asiatic usage) that it was the sovereign's duty to protect his loyal servants.[16]

TRADE AND DIPLOMACY

In the absence of substantial archives belonging to the merchants' firms (like those of the Old Assyrian period), we have to rely on the diplomatic correspondence (so well attested in the Late Bronze Age), though in so doing we risk overestimating the extent of sociopolitical gift exchange as compared with commercial exchange—even if we assume that all trade was carried out in the form of gift exchange, with the royal palaces acting as the sole agents in long-distance traffic. A quantitative evaluation of gift exchange versus commercial dealings can be attempted in the trade of copper. In the Amarna Letters, the maximum number of copper ingots given by the king of Alashiya to the Egyptian pharaoh was one hundred, or about 3 tons. But this is an exceptional case;[17] the usual number was only about ten. By comparison, the cargo of the Uluburun ship contained approximately 10 tons of copper ingots (see cat. no. 185). Can we assume that the copper traded in the form of gift exchange was in the order of 30 percent of the total? It is notable that the "gift" is called *shulmanu*, a term that has also the technical meaning (in Middle Assyrian usage) of "audience gift" and that, once paid, allowed an individual to carry out his commercial affairs. The similar *nishatum* tax, paid by the Old Assyrian merchants to the local Anatolian kings, was 5 percent on textiles, 3 percent on tin, and 4 percent on silver.[18] The amount of such percentages is not dissimilar, and suggests that the ceremonial gifts were the tip of the iceberg of a much larger commercial activity.

Obviously trade and diplomacy were functionally interlocked, since good relations between the royal palaces were a prerequisite for the favorable reception of merchants and a mutually profitable trade could generate a political alliance: "Between kings there is brotherhood, alliance, peace, and good words if there is an abundance of [precious] stones, silver, and gold."[19] The Babylonian kings would give merchants traveling to Egypt letters for the pharaoh, though in their role as goodwill ambassadors they were often faulted. The more economically savvy among the Great Kings, namely, those of Assyria and Cyprus, were vexed by the slow pace of diplomatic relations—the practice of waylaying messengers and the political strategy of prolonging negotiations. Still enigmatic is the behavior of Mycenaean merchants, who left no trace of diplomatic endeavors in the Ugarit archives, although their presence is archaeologically quite evident in that kingdom.

INNER AND EXTERNAL AUDIENCES

What we know about the nature and functioning of the regional system is found in written documents that follow genres and codes directed toward an intended audience. Celebratory texts and monuments address a more general public, roughly coincident with the populace of a kingdom. Letters have a more restricted audience—a foreign king or his court. The tone of any message, but also the selection of the information that could or could not be provided to an internal or an external public, to a general or an individual audience, differed in accordance with the addressee. Diplomatic negotiations required the presumption of peer reciprocity, while celebratory texts were based on the preeminence above all others of the country of origin. Celebratory texts thus present as "tribute" the same goods that diplomatic letters present as "gifts." The problem is apparently one of translation; the reality is more complex and more interesting. At the level of denotative meaning, ancient terminology is rather neutral. Terms such as the Egyptian *inw* or the Babylonian *biltu* and *mandattu* are designations for "supply," indicating anything that is brought in, regardless of the status of the participants in the exchange, whether the gift is given freely or is imposed, or of the implications of gain or loss of prestige in the exchange. A more precise translation, one that would better fit the categories of "gift" and "tribute," would have to take into account connotation and the context in which the terms were used. If the *inw* was supplied by a vanquished people asking to be spared, a translation of "tribute" is appropriate. If, in a diplomatic letter, the *mandattu* was provided by one king to another in exchange for *mandattu* previously received, a translation of "gift" is preferable.[20]

It was also essential that addressees be kept separate. If a message addressed to a peer king and using the conventions of reciprocity and brotherhood became known to the inner populace, it would create bewilderment. And if a celebrative presentation, intended for an inner audience, was revealed to a foreign king, the repercussions could be worse still. In one of the Amarna Letters a Babylonian king, informed by his messengers that the chariots filled with his gifts had been paraded alongside those of the vassals, which were loaded with tribute, vociferously expressed his displeasure: "You place my chariots together with those of the vassals! You did not display them separately! You denigrated them in the sight of your country as something yours. You did not show them separately!"[21] The response of the pharaoh is equally revealing (here paraphrased): Do you really think, he writes, that the Egyptian populace is interested in looking at them separately? Once I receive them, all the chariots belong to me and I can do with them whatever I choose.

A similar situation, described in the same letter, concerns the different perceptions of the same dynastic marriage—as seen through the eyes, respectively, of the Egyptian and the Babylonian courts. In a marriage between equals, a spouse was part of the gift exchange. A princess destined to enrich a harem, on the

Figure 52. Botanical reliefs. Karnak, Temple of Amun, Room X. Dynasty 18, reign of Thutmose III.

other hand, was considered tribute. The reaction of the Babylonian messengers to a woman in the harem, unidentified but assumed to be a Babylonian princess, was similar to that of the king mentioned above when informed that his chariots had been shown with those of the vassals: "While your wives were standing together in your presence you told my messengers: 'Look, you are in the presence of your lady.' But my messengers did not recognize her. . . . She did not open her mouth and did not say anything to them."[22] But the Babylonian king had no call to complain too loudly, as he himself had suggested to the pharaoh, when the latter was unwilling to provide him with a princess: "[Just] send me a nice girl—as if she were your daughter. Who could then say, She is not the pharaoh's daughter?"[23]

SELF-SUFFICIENCY AND INTERACTION

The desire for interaction, to the point of building up an international "club" of all the royal courts, sharing common values and behaviors and tastes, different from local ones, finds its limits in the pretension for self-sufficiency:

> I am told that in my brother's country there is everything and that my brother is in want of nothing. In my country as well there is everything and I am in want for nothing. Nevertheless, the custom of exchanging gifts, passed on from ancient times and early rulers, is a good thing. [Therefore] let this tradition remain firm between us![24]

But how, one might ask, could a king ask for a gift or for raw materials or for a person without implying that he was lacking such? The standard solution was to produce a reason—or an excuse—for the request by conjoining it to some ongoing project. The Mitanni king asks for gold because he is building a mausoleum for his father. The Babylonian king makes the same request because he is building a new palace:

> If you will not send me the gold in time to allow me to finish the work that I undertook, why should you send it to me at all? If the work I undertook will be finished, what could I then do with it? Even if you were to send me 3000 talents, I would not accept them. I would send them back. Nor would I give you my daughter.[25]

On the other hand, it was considered a courtesy to send a gift for a special occasion—palace furnishings to a newly enthroned king, for example. A gift not associated with a specific occasion would imply that the receiver was permanently in need, like a poor relative. For the same reason, silver (the equivalent of our money) could not be offered as a gift, as it would have been a source of humiliation for both the sender and the recipient. The rules of etiquette were in fact quite similar to those followed in modern societies today.

Another way to circumvent the need to demonstrate self-sufficiency was to show appreciation for foreign technologies and fashions in terms of their exotic appeal: materials were in demand because they were made "according to the style of country X" or "the workmanship of country Y," or because their raw material came only from a specific mountain or a specific territory. The ability to appropriate such goods was also a demonstration that the authority of the ruler receiving them extended to the most remote areas. The most famous example is the royal garden of Thutmose III (ca. 1479–1425 B.C.), who attempted to acclimate to his own botanical garden the many exotic trees and flowers that he had collected in Nubia and in Syria, images of which are represented in the paintings and carved reliefs in the Temple of Amun at Karnak (fig. 52).[26] Exotic plants were also common in the private gardens of high officials of that time. Hatshepsut (ca. 1473–1458 B.C.) had already tried to acclimate imported myrrh from Punt in the courtyard of the Temple of Amun. Her experiment failed, although the texts and carved reliefs lead one to believe that the imported trees in fact grew taller and flourished more exuberantly than in their original homeland. This connection between imperial ideology and exotic gardens is seen as well in the royal parks of later Assyria and, in our own times, in nineteenth- and twentieth-century Europe, where botanical and zoological gardens were presented to the public as evidence of colonial conquest in distant, exotic lands.

The Rules of Etiquette

Since the publication of Marcel Mauss's essay on the subject,[27] we know that to be effective the exchange of gifts had to conform to carefully prescribed rules of etiquette. It was expected that a gift would be offered without having to be requested; that it would be accepted unconditionally; and that it would be reciprocated, the value of the reciprocal gift exceeding that of the original offering. Were such rules known in the Late Bronze Age? Were they observed? Apparently they were known but rarely observed—and not infrequently subverted. The desire for profit superseded the desire for prestige; there was a pretense of caring for the recipient's prestige more than one's own; and the ideal of disinterested generosity was projected onto the recipient's behavior rather than one's own.

The Amarna Letters suggest that kings were more active in asking for gifts than in giving them:

> Since my fathers and your fathers established good relations between them, they have sent each other fine gifts and never refused requests for fine things. Now my brother sends me as a gift only two minas of gold! If gold is abundant, send me as much as your father did. If it is scarce, send me at least one half what your father did![28]

Preoccupied with tallying the monetary value of their gifts, the partners in this exchange appear quick to criticize rather than to appreciate: "[What you sent me] is not enough to cover even the round trips of my messengers!"; "The 30 minas of gold that you sent me hardly compensate for my gifts of the last year!"; "The 40 minas of gold they brought, once put in the oven [melted down] hardly added up to 10!"[29] The rule of increased return is acknowledged in general terms: "Every gift you sent me I reciprocated at double the value"; "I will give ten times what my brother desires!"[30] But in practice the focus is strictly on balancing the value of incoming and outgoing goods. The connection between gift exchange and trade is obvious: in spite of the ritualized procedures and the shows of generosity, the codes of practice are those of barter, carried out to please oneself rather than one's partner, and with a view to increasing one's wealth rather than one's prestige.

"Provocative Gifts" and "Diplomatic Excuses"

Other procedures well known from comparative anthropological evidence also make their appearance in gift exchange.[31]

One such procedure is the "provocative gift," which served to elicit incremental return on one's investment. A small amount of a desired product would be sent as a gift to a partner already well stocked in such goods in the expectation that, in accordance with the rule of increased return, the partner would send back a huge amount of the same product. A passage in a letter by the king of Alashiya to the Egyptian pharaoh is a clear example of such an exchange: "You sent me 200 shekels of copper, and now I am sending to you 10 talents of copper."[32] A letter from the governor of Alashiya to his Egyptian counterpart, in which he offers two elephant tusks, also exemplifies the seemingly irrational practice. The explanation is rational, although exaggerated, in terms of differentiated value: If I am generous enough to renounce a product that is scarce in my own country, my partner should reciprocate with a tenfold return to compensate for the lower value with an increased amount.

Another typical procedure was that of the "diplomatic excuse." When some commodity was requested without mention of a counter gift, the standard reply was that the merchandise was not available because of some occurrence beyond one's control. At the same time, a token amount of the requested product was dispatched to make clear that the product's "unavailability" was simply an excuse, and that the real problem was economic in nature. Thus the king of Alashiya:

> As to the fact that I am sending you only 500 [shekels of] copper, I send it as a greeting-gift to my brother. My brother, do not be concerned because the amount is so small. In my country all the men have been slain by the hand of Nergal [the god of pestilence] and there is nobody left to produce copper. . . . Send me silver in quantity and I will send you whatever you request.[33]

Similarly, the king of Hatti:

> As to the good iron about which you wrote me, I have no good iron in the Kizzuwatna warehouses, I wrote (there), but it is a bad time to produce good iron. . . . [Nevertheless,] I am sending herewith an iron blade.[34]

In the tale of the Egyptian priest Wenamun, the refusal of Zakar-Baal, king of Byblos, to send cedar trunks as tribute to the god Amun is accompanied by a gift of seven cedar trunks. The motive behind this tactic is perfectly clear to the Egyptian partner, who sends in advance adequate payment in the form of counter gifts, at which point Zakar-Baal fells hundreds of cedars to be sent to Egypt.[35]

The Endless Negotiations

When economic interests prevailed and the conventional etiquette of gift exchange was followed, deals were generally carried out with positive results within a reasonable time, although following the conventions of gift exchange with all its obligations. In some cases, however, when social or political interests were paramount, negotiations stymied to a pace too slow even for people accustomed to the endless bargaining of the bazaars. Actors in the drama of Late Bronze Age international relations appear to have lived by the motto "Better the chase than the capture," as they entered into protracted negotiations seemingly for their own sake, with no regard for the passing of time, and with no apparent intention of reaching a solution. The main purpose of such an exercise was to stay in touch, and for such a purpose, lengthy, complex negotiations were more advantageous than an impersonal and efficient conduct of business. Negotiations could be so protracted that they were passed down from one ruler to the next. Negotiations for marriage contracts could extend over years, so that a bride who had aged had to be replaced by a suitably nubile young woman. Messengers dispatched to distant territories were retained until they died, in an effort to exert political pressure on their master. Decades could be spent bargaining over the value or the number of reciprocal gifts, each move in the game lasting as long as a year, since the journey from Egypt to Babylonia or to Hatti and back again could take an entire season. Such conduct was counterproductive to the strictly commercial aims of the trade agents, who were interested not in the chase but in the capture—that is, in sealing the deal. But it was an excellent tool for improving political and cross-cultural contacts. Mutual accusations were in fact a highly efficacious way of discharging the aggression that inevitably came with international contacts without, however, reaching the frenzied level that could have led to war.

Because we deal for the most part with archaeological evidence, we are accustomed to evaluating a regional system on purely quantitative criteria: the value of ten pots is ten times that of one pot. But we should add—if such were possible—a qualitative appreciation as well, one that is based on the time it took to conclude a deal, how many people were involved, how many words were expended in reaching an agreement, how many languages were spoken (and with how many misunderstandings). Of course, this is not possible. But if it were, the Near Eastern regional system of the Late Bronze Age would appear even more lively, more rich in human values and in future prospects than it does in a purely material appreciation.

1. Wallerstein 1974–89.
2. Tadmor 1979, p. 3.
3. Beckman 1996, p. 101 and n. 23.
4. On the international relations in the regional system of the Late Bronze Age, see Liverani 1990 and 2001.
5. For a general introduction to the international laws, see Beckman 2003. On trade procedures, see Faist 2001, with previous literature.
6. H.-P. Adler 1976; Izre'el 1991; Rainey 1996; Cochavi-Rainey 2003. For a general introduction to the royal correspondence, see Bryce 2003.
7. EA 32: 24–25. A complete translation of the Amarna Letters can be found in Moran 1992. All translations in this essay are by the author.
8. Oppenheim 1973; McGovern, Fleming, and Swann 1993.
9. Edel 1976; Zaccagnini 1983.
10. Lévi-Strauss 1953, p. 536.
11. Beckman 1996, p. 128.
12. EA 4: 6–7.
13. EA 1: 61–62.
14. For a general introduction, see Zaccagnini 1987.
15. On Late Bronze Age diplomacy, see the essays collected by Cohen and Westbrook 2000.
16. Liverani 1983.
17. EA 34: 16–18; the Alashiya king adds a list of the reciprocal gifts he is asking for.
18. On Old Assyrian taxation on traded goods, see Larsen 1967 and Veenhof 1972.
19. EA 11: Rev. 22–23.
20. Liverani 1990, pp. 255–66; Liverani 2001, pp. 176–82.
21. EA 1: 89–92.
22. EA 1: 26–30, 41–42.
23. EA 4: 12–13.
24. EA 7: 33–39.
25. EA 4: 44–50.
26. On botanical gardens in Dynasty 18, see Manniche 1989, pp. 7–21.
27. Mauss 1923–24; English translation, 1967.
28. EA 9: 7–14.
29. EA 16: 27–31; EA 3: 21–22; EA 7: 71–72.
30. EA 35: 50–53; EA 19: 69.
31. Liverani 1979.
32. EA 33: 16–18.
33. Ibid., EA 35: 10–15, 19–22.
34. Beckman 1996, p. 140.
35. Liverani 1990, pp. 247–54; Liverani 2001, pp. 170–75.

The Amarna Letters

In autumn 1887, a Bedouin woman working in a field 160 kilometers (180 miles) south of modern-day Cairo discovered a cache of cuneiform tablets. The site, called in ancient times Akhetaten, "Horizon of the Sun," is commonly referred to as Tell el-Amarna, after the name of the woman's Bedouin tribe. It was the seat of government under the reign of the Dynasty 18 Egyptian king Amenhotep IV (ca. 1353–1336 B.C.), who took the name of Akhenaten. Over the next several decades excavators discovered additional tablets at Amarna; to date 382 tablets and fragments have been recovered and published.

The cuneiform texts, most of which are records of foreign correspondence with Near Eastern monarchs and local Syro-Levantine rulers, had been placed in the archives of the pharaoh's foreign ministry. The corpus of letters reflects the struggles for power and domination, as well as the trade and tribute, that characterized international relations in the mid-fourteenth century B.C. Three hundred and fifty letters date to the approximately thirty-year period from the thirtieth year of the reign of Amenhotep III (ca. 1390–1352 B.C.) to the third year of the reign of Tutankhamun. The tablets that date to the reign of Amenhotep III, the father of Akhenaten, were originally kept in the state archives at Thebes. These documents were transported to Akhetaten when Akhenaten, his son and successor, moved the capital to this new location in the desert between Thebes and Memphis.

Forty-four of the letters reflect the diplomatic correspondence between Egypt and the great powers of the day: Assyria, Hatti, Mitanni, Arzawa, and Alashiya. By far the largest portion of the correspondence deals with exchanges between the Egyptian pharaohs and the local rulers of vassal cities and states in Canaan and northern Syria.

The vast majority of the letters are written on clay in Babylonian Akkadian, an East Semitic language, which by the fourteenth century B.C. had acquired the status of an international language of correspondence.[1] One letter is written in Hurrian and two letters in Hittite, attesting to the fact that the scribes of the Egyptian foreign ministry were highly educated in the study of foreign languages and scripts. Thirty-two tablets contain texts that might have been used in the study of Akkadian language and literature. They include literary compositions, scholarly lists of words, signs, and gods, and an Egyptian-Akkadian dictionary.[2]

Most of the international correspondence found in the archive represents letters from foreign rulers; only a few include the pharaoh's replies or drafts of replies that were never sent. The Great Kings rhetorically addressed each other as "brothers," a designation that recognized their fellow monarchs as having equal political status. Contrary to what we might expect, the Great Kings did not address pressing political issues but restricted their correspondence to bickering and bargaining about exchanges of gifts, political marriages of the daughters of foreign rulers to the Egyptian king, and matters of trade, law, and the rules of diplomacy.

Gift exchange, especially regarding precious metals such as gold, was considered a sign of good relations. Diplomatic marriages between the Egyptian king and foreign princesses were used to symbolically cement political alliances and add to royal prestige. Although the pharaoh demanded marriage to a woman of royal blood, the Egyptian king did not send his daughters abroad to be married to foreign princes or kings. In a letter presumably sent by the Kassite king Kadashman-Enlil I to Amenhotep III, the Babylonian monarch quotes a letter from the pharaoh in which the Egyptian king states, "Since olden times, the daughter of a king of Egypt has never been given to anybody."[3] Kadashman-Enlil mocks his Egyptian brother in his reply by asserting that if the pharaoh does indeed command authority he should be able to send any beautiful woman as a gift. After all, he appears to reason, true prestige and friendship comes from reciprocal gift-giving.

Why is [she not given]? You are king—you do as you please. If you were to give (her), who would [say] anything? . . . (Surely) beautiful women, adult(?) daughters [of. . .] are available. Send me one beautiful woman as if she [were your daughter]! Who would say, "She is not the king's daughter?" (But) you, in accord with your refusal, did not send me

(anyone). Did you not seek brotherhood and friendship when you wrote to me about marriage so that we might become close relations to each other? . . . Why has my brother not sent me one woman? Perhaps, (since) you have not sent me a woman, just like you I should withhold a woman from you and not send her? (But) my daughters are available; I shall not withhold (one) from you.

The letter concludes with a demand that the pharaoh send him gold as a gift in exchange for a royal daughter, the gold to be used as part of a building project:

If you send me the gold I wrote you about this summer . . . I shall give you my daughter. So you do me a favor and send me [as much(?)] gold as you [can(?)].[4]

In contrast to this bickering between kings, imperial correspondence sent to the pharaoh's court from petty rulers in Egypt's western Asiatic empire dealt with political issues of domestic security and rivalry between vassals and matters of trade and tribute.

In other letters Rib-Hadda, the mayor of the city of Gubla (Byblos) desperately pleads with his lord, Amenhotep III, to send him provisions and garrison troops, as his impoverished town is in mortal danger of being overrun by a coalition led by their enemy Abdi-Ashirta, king of the state of Amurru, and the lawless Habiru militia.[5] Together they have conquered neighboring towns, and Abdi-Ashirta has urged other townfolk to revolt, assassinate their rulers, and join the growing traitorous insurgency:

May the lord king (Amenhotep III) know that Gubla, faithful maidservant of the king since the days of his ancestors, is safe. But now, the king has let go his faithful city from his hand. May the king look up the tablets of his father's house, (to check) whether the ruler who is in Gubla (Rib-Hadda) has not (always) been a faithful servant! Do not neglect your servant! For the war of the Habiru against me is severe. And, by the gods of your land, our sons and daughters are finished, (as well as) the wood of our house(s), through being sold for our sustenance in the land of Yarimuta. My field, for lack of a ploughman, is like a woman without a husband. All my towns that are in the mountains or on the seacoast have joined the Habiru. (Only) Gubla, together with two towns, is left to me. (Rib-Hadda admits that he fears for his life.) I am very, very afraid! Like a bird that is placed inside a cage, just so am I in Gubla.[6]

IS

1. For the most recent treatment of the diplomatic corpus of letters, see Moran 1992.
2. See Izre'el 1997.
3. EA 4, Moran 1992, pp. 8–10.
4. Translation, von Dassow 2006a, pp. 193–94.
5. See, for example, EA 74, Moran 1992, pp. 142–45.
6. Translation, von Dassow 2006b, p. 203.

THE HITTITE EMPIRE

ANDREAS MÜLLER-KARPE

As part of western Asia with its early advanced civilizations and also as a geographic bridge to Europe, Anatolia played a major role in the ancient world. One of the most splendid periods in Anatolian history was the time of the Hittite kingdom, from about 1650 to 1200 B.C. The Hittite-speaking population probably inhabited central Anatolia as early as the third millennium B.C., but the earliest clear evidence of Hittite presence dates to the nineteenth century B.C., when the cuneiform tablets of Assyrian merchants began to include typical Hittite names and terms. These tablets represent the earliest extant written documents from Anatolia.

The Hittite language belongs to the wide group of Indo-European languages. The Hittite people called their language *nasili*, derived from early spellings of the city of Kanesh/Nesha, indicating that this town and its surroundings were of great importance to Hittite identity. Archaeological research shows that the heartland of early Hittite culture was the fertile valley of the Halys River (Kızılırmak), with Kanesh (Kültepe) at its center. Furthermore, Hittite historiography begins with a story concerning the town. A king called Pithana, from Kushshara (which has not yet been located), "took Nesha in the night by storm . . . , but he inflicted no harm on the inhabitants of Nesha. Instead he made them mothers and fathers."[1] The town became Pithana's residence, and from there he and his son Anitta conquered other small city-states nearby.

Some generations later, the Hittite capital was moved to Hattusa, 160 kilometers to the northwest of Nesha (figs. 53, 59, 60). From Hattusa the kingdom quickly expanded in all directions, encompassing large parts of Anatolia, from the Black Sea in the north down to the Mediterranean coast. Yet the region of most interest to the Hittites lay to the southeast. Hurrian expansion in Upper Mesopotamia had cut off established trading routes, obstructing Anatolia's access to tin, which was essential to the production of bronze. In response, Hattusili I captured Alalakh (Tell Atchana), and his successor, Mursili I, took Aleppo and then Babylon. Large amounts of precious metal, as well as sheep, cattle, and prisoners of war, were brought back to Hattusa.

This booty helped to build the economy and consolidate the empire, but subsequent rulers, undermined by palace rivalries, lost large territories. Most Hittite kings of the sixteenth century B.C. were murdered by their successors. At the very end of the Hittite Old Kingdom, Telipinu (ca. 1525–1500 B.C.) tried to stop the bloodshed by proclamations in which he established a rule of royal succession: in the case of a murder committed within the royal family, the culprit—even the king himself—could be sentenced to death by the *pankus*, which translates roughly as "the whole body of citizens." The role of the *pankus* is quite remarkable in a period when kings in other lands were regarded as gods. During his lifetime, a Hittite king was a man—a servant (albeit a privileged one) of the gods—who did not become deified before his death.

Telipinu's proclamation also included regulations to improve the structure and efficiency of the state, serving as a kind of early "constitution," in an attempt to establish the empire on legal foundations. Telipinu not only tried to organize the internal affairs of the Hittite state, but he also pursued foreign relations. The first international treaty—made with Ishputashu, king of Kizzuwatna (Cilicia in southern Anatolia)—dates to his reign. More than seventy treaties (mostly fragments) from different periods were found in the archives at Hattusa. The introduction of this new written instrument for regulating intergovernmental relations marks a turning point in history and ranks as one of the most important Hittite achievements. Problems between competing states could be solved not only by military action but also through diplomatic negotiations and written agreements.

The oldest tablets outlining the Hittite laws most likely date to the reign of Telipinu as well. They differ from older Mesopotamian laws, such as the laws inscribed on the Stele of Hammurabi (fig. 10), in that they are more humane and considerate. The emphasis in Anatolia is placed on compensation rather than vengeance or retributive justice for its own sake. Corporal punishment and mutilation were rare, as was capital punishment.

The Hittite Old Kingdom came to an end with Telipinu, and the following Middle Kingdom is still an obscure period, about which little has been uncovered. We do know that during this time, the Hittites faced pressure from the powerful Hurrian kingdom of Mitanni. Egypt also expanded to the north under the reign of Thutmose III, who conquered Aleppo in about 1440 B.C., marking the Hittites' first direct contact with Egypt as a political rival. Twenty years later, Tudhaliya I succeeded in both regaining Aleppo and defeating Mitanni. He also directed a series of campaigns to expand Hittite supremacy in western Anatolia. One of his destinations was Assuwa, a confederation of small states.[2]

An inscription on a bronze sword found just outside Hattusa, part of the booty from one of the Assuwa campaigns, invokes the Storm God (cat. no. 292). The sword is doubtless of north-western Anatolian origin but displays Mycenaean affinities. The

Figure 53. Hattusa (Boğazköy), King's Gate relief. Hittite Empire period. Ankara Museum of Anatolian Civilizations

ground in about 1360 B.C. Over the next twenty years, however, the Hittite king Suppiluliuma I regained the lost territories and inaugurated a new and splendid period in Hittite history: the New Kingdom or Hittite Empire. Suppiluliuma expanded primarily to the southeast, destroying Mitanni; he also conquered Aleppo and Carchemish, where he established vassal states under the rule of two of his sons. Qatna was also captured, and life immediately before the siege of the city is well documented in recent archaeological excavations (see pp. 214–16, 219–21, 233).

Suppiluliuma used not only military force but also diplomacy, especially through marriage, to achieve his aims. He wed a Babylonian princess, and then married off one of his daughters to the Hurrian heir to the throne. He even had the chance to marry one of his sons to an Egyptian queen and thus to become the father of an Egyptian pharaoh: after the early death of Tutankhamun, his widow wrote to Suppiluliuma, saying, "My husband is dead. . . . If you would give me one of your sons, he would become my husband. I will never take a servant of mine and make him my husband."[3] Yet Suppiluliuma hesitated, and his decision to send one of his sons to Egypt came too late. The political situation in Egypt had changed, and the Hittite prince was murdered before reaching the Nile. Furious, Suppiluliuma attacked Egyptian territories in revenge. Egyptian prisoners of war were transported to the Hittite homeland, bringing with them a plague that decimated the population. Suppiluliuma himself was probably a victim of this plague. His son Mursili II later interpreted the catastrophe as a divine punishment for offenses committed by his father, most notably his attack on Egypt in violation of a treaty between the two countries. Mursili considered the attack not only a mistake, but also as a sin, which he called *wastul.*

The Hittites were no more peaceful than other contemporary states, yet they developed their own legal practices in handling conflicts with their neighbors. Hittite kings tried to avoid initiating wars, preferring to present themselves as defenders against external aggression or the breaking of a treaty. In Hittite ideology, aiding an ally or vassal state also justified attacking another country. The annals of Mursili II provide detailed information about military and civil activities during his reign and are masterpieces of Hittite historiography.

After Muwattalli II succeeded Mursili II to the throne, tensions with Egypt increased, eventually culminating in the Battle of Qadesh (ca. 1275 B.C.; see cat. no. 166 and fig. 84). In this clash of the two "superpowers" of their time, the Hittites successfully defended their southern border. Ramesses II, called the Great, fought at the head of the Egyptian army but failed to expand his empire any farther to the north.

After long negotiations Muwattalli's successor, Hattusili III, completed the now-famous Qadesh peace treaty with Ramesses II nearly twenty years later. The Treaty of Qadesh is the earliest fully preserved international treaty between two of the most important empires of the Late Bronze Age. A cuneiform tablet with the text of this treaty, recorded in the Akkadian language, was found in 1906 during excavations at Hattusa. A version

Hittites referred to the Mycenaean region (or at least part of it) as Ahhiyawa, which first appears in Hittite Middle Kingdom records as a hostile power that attacked Hittite vassals in western Anatolia. Nevertheless, the Aegean world seems not to have been of great interest to the Hittites, and cultural exchange was limited. A stag-shaped silver rhyton from the Shaft Graves at Mycenae might be of Hittite origin (fig. 54), and a few seals with Anatolian hieroglyphs found their way to Greece. Yet imports of Mycenaean pottery, ubiquitous at most of the coastal sites of this period (see cat. nos. 243, 244) and throughout the eastern Mediterranean, are noticeably few in the Hittite heartland.

Toward the end of the Hittite Middle Kingdom, enemies invaded the land of Hatti from all sides, burning Hattusa to the

Figure 54. Silver stag rhyton. Mycenae, Shaft Grave IV. Late Helladic I context. National Archaeological Museum, Athens 388

written in Egyptian hieroglyphs is carved on the outer wall of the Temple of Amun at Karnak; the text follows the Hittite formula for legal diplomacy as the Egyptians had no such tradition.

Friendly relations between the two kings were further strengthened by the marriage of a daughter of Hattusili III with Ramesses II. Surviving letters record the exchange of precious gifts on this occasion and during the following years. Such diplomatic gifts are known from earlier times as well. A fragment of an obsidian vase with the name of the pharaoh Khayan (late 17th century B.C.) in hieroglyphs was found within the royal residence in Hattusa, and an Egyptian gold jewel in the shape of a lotus flower came to light in the Hittite Middle Kingdom Palace of Shapinuwa (Ortaköy) (cat. no. 111). Judging from numerous texts excavated from the palace, the town served as a temporary residence for the Hittite king and his queen, who may have been the recipient of the foreign jewelry. Although everyday goods from Egypt have not yet been identified among the archaeological finds of central Anatolia, according to written sources, at least once in the late thirteenth century B.C. the pharaoh Merneptah sent a large amount of grain to Anatolia, which was suffering under a severe famine. This aid of food had been made possible by the Treaty of Qadesh, which brought both peace and political advantages for both sides.

Problems with Assyria, however, remained. Shalmaneser I conquered one of the richest copper-mining regions in the southeastern Hittite Empire, eventually reaching the Euphrates near Malatya. The ultimate goal of the Assyrians was the Mediterranean with access to international naval trading routes. But the key position on the Syrian coast was held by Amurru, an important Hittite vassal state, and the Hittite king Tudhaliya IV, son and successor of Hattusili III, took strong measures against the rising rival, writing to the Amurrite ruler: "As the king of Assyria is the enemy . . . , you must allow no merchant of Assyria to enter your land or pass through your land."[4] In attempting to counter military and political pressure from an opponent by economic means, Tudhaliya enacted what must have been one of the first trade embargoes in history.

Tudhaliya IV offset the loss of access to copper mines in the east by conquering Cyprus, which was equally rich in copper and also a nexus of international trade. Relations with western Anatolia and the Aegean states were intensified as well. Hatti was at the zenith of its power.

Toward the end of the thirteenth century B.C., however, internal and external troubles came to a head. Conflicts within the royal family concerning the legitimacy of the king, and pressure from the Kashka people in northern Anatolia as well as the Sea Peoples in the southern coastal regions, were exacerbated by increasing climatic change. Crop failure and famine weakened both the economy and the military strength of the Hittite Empire. The ever-expanding state bureaucracy was not flexible enough to react quickly to these changes, and the palace economy collapsed. Contemporary Anatolian, Aegean, and Levantine cultures shared similar fates, yet the exact circumstances of the fall of the Hittite Empire are still unknown.

1. Neu 1974, 10.11.
2. It is believed that the geographic term "Asia" may derive from the name Assuwa.
3. Bryce 1998, p. 193.
4. Ibid., p. 350.

98
EDICT OF SUPPILULIUMA I

Clay
Height 14.2 cm (5⅝ in.); width 8.8 cm (3½ in.)
Ugarit
Late Bronze Age, ca. 1344–1322 B.C.
National Museum, Damascus, Syria 17.227

Through a series of campaigns in the middle of the fourteenth century B.C., the greatest military commander among Hittite kings, Suppiluliuma I, broke the power of the Hurrian kingdom of Mitanni, thus adding much of northwestern Syria to the Hittite Empire. The usual practice for the Hittites was to expand their domain not through formal annexation of distant regions, but rather through the imposition of vassal status upon local princes. This subordination of conquered peoples to the Hittite Great King was sealed by a formal written treaty.

This tablet is composed in Akkadian, the diplomatic lingua franca of the time. It is a codicil to the treaty between Suppiluliuma and Niqmaddu II of the coastal city of Ugarit and concerns the tribute that Niqmaddu had to deliver yearly to the Hittite monarch and his court.

Following a brief historical introduction in which Suppiluliuma relates just how Ugarit had come to be a Hittite dependency, he writes:

Your tribute for His Majesty, Great King, your lord, is as follows: 12 mina and 20 shekels of gold and one golden cup one mina in weight as the primary portion of the tribute; four linen garments, one large linen garment, 500 shekels of blue-purple wool, and 500 shekels of red-purple wool for His Majesty, Great King, your lord.[1]

A major element of this payment consists of products of the dyeing industry for which the Syro-Levantine coastal region was famed throughout antiquity.

The remainder of the text lists smaller quantities of the same materials destined for the queen, the crown prince, the chief scribe, the vizier, and the royal officials known as *huburtanuri* (possibly a chamberlain) and *andubsalli* (perhaps a treasurer).

To prevent other Hittite bureaucrats from attempting to extort payments for themselves, Suppiluliuma decrees:

There is no one else to pay among the noblemen in the entourage of His Majesty, Great King, his lord. On the day when Niqmaddu brings his tribute, Niqmaddu shall not be obligated for any other gift.

The document concludes with the invocation of the chief Hittite gods—the Sun God, the Sun Goddess of the city of Arinna, and the Storm God—as witnesses to the edict's provisions and to the integrity of the tablet upon which it has been inscribed.   GB

1. Translations by the author, in Beckman 1999.

Figure 55. Rock-cut relief, detail showing the god Sharruma embracing Tudhaliya IV. Yazılıkaya, Room B, Relief 81. Hittite Empire period.

99

99

DECREE OF TUDHALIYA IV

Clay
Height 14.2 cm (5⅝ in.); width 8.9 cm (3½ in.)
Ugarit
Late Bronze Age, ca. 1237–1209 B.C.
National Museum, Damascus, Syria 3566

The Hittite Great King buttressed his relationships with his vassals through a number of diplomatic marriages—either between members of the Great King's immediate family and children of subordinate kings or among members of the various vassal courts. As these arranged unions involved men and women with individual personalities and desires, they did not always turn out happily. This Akkadian-language tablet formally dissolves the failed marriage of Ammistamru II of Ugarit and the unnamed daughter of Benteshina, who governed Ugarit's southern neighbor, Amurru. As its introduction relates:

Ammistamru, King of the land of Ugarit, took as his wife the daughter of Benteshina, King of the land of Amurru, but she sought trouble for Ammistamru. Ammistamru, King of the land of Ugarit, has irrevocably divorced the daughter of Benteshina.[1]

Unfortunately, we do not know the exact nature of the "trouble" caused by the princess. If, as some scholars believe, she can be identified as the "Daughter of the Great Lady" mentioned in other records from Ugarit, the offense might have been that of adultery.

Because the couple had children, the question of succession to the throne of Ugarit added an additional and extremely sensitive political dimension to the divorce. Thus, in order to mitigate tensions between two of his most important clients in Syria, the Hittite Great King Tudhaliya IV (see fig. 55) was forced to intervene in what might otherwise have been a purely domestic matter. He decreed that the princess leave Ugarit, taking only the property that she had brought into the marriage. In case of any dispute, the people of Amurru would be awarded anything whose ownership they were willing to claim under oath. Tudhaliya further dictated:

Utri-Sharrumma is the Crown Prince of the land of Ugarit. If Utri-Sharrumma says, "I want to follow my mother," he shall place his garment on the stool (a symbolic act of renunciation of his inheritance) and depart. Ammistamru, king of the land of Ugarit, will install another of his sons in the office of Crown Prince in the land of Ugarit. If Ammistamru goes to his fate (that is, dies), and Utri-Sharruma takes his mother and returns her to the office of Queen in the land of Ugarit, he shall place his garment on the stool and go where he pleases. His Majesty (Tudhaliya) will install another son of Ammistamru in kingship in the land of Ugarit.

The record closes with a clause forbidding the princess to initiate any future legal action concerning her sons, daughters, or sons-in-law. The document is authenticated by an impression of the official royal stamp seal of Tudhaliya.   GB

1. Translations by the author; see Beckman 1999.

100

SMITING DEITY

Bronze
Height 11.4 cm (4½ in.)
Anatolia
Hittite Old Kingdom, 17th–16th century B.C.
Ankara Museum of Anatolian Civilizations,
Turkey 8825

This bronze male figure, said to come from Dövlek in eastern central Anatolia, was cast in one piece, with tenons below the feet for insertion into a base.[1] The high conical headdress and horns identify him as a god. Details such as facial features are difficult to make out because of surface corrosion, but easily visible are earrings, a short necklace with a roughly cylindrical pendant, and a long, loose mass of hair extending down his back nearly to the waist. The objects originally held in the fists are lost, and the right leg is bent unnaturally from its original position. In spite of this damage, the figure's taut musculature and active stance present a compelling image.

Metal figures depicting "smiting gods" originated in the Syro-Levantine region during the early second millennium B.C., and they are later found throughout the eastern Mediterranean.[2] Comparison with well-preserved examples suggests that this figure originally held a weapon in his upraised right hand and a shield on the left arm (see also fig. 102). Such figures were sometimes embellished with gold or silver overlay (cat. no. 150).[3] Particularly fine examples such as this one are thought to have been set up in shrines within temples, where they served as votive offerings to ensure strength and fertility.[4] Based on stylistic criteria,[5] this figure has been widely dated from the seventeenth to the thirteenth century B.C.[6] Its slender, muscular form and dynamic posture argue for a date in the early part of this range, based on a comparison with an important stamp-cylinder seal dated to the Hittite Old Kingdom (cat. no. 101).   SG

1. N. Özgüç 1949.
2. See Muscarella 1988, pp. 360–62; Seeden 1980; Negbi 1976; and Collon 1972.
3. A comparable figure from a fourteenth-century B.C. context at Ugarit wears a steatite headdress with gold horns; see illustrations in von Reden 1992, p. 205, Abb. 23, 24.
4. Seeden 1980, pp. 153–54.
5. Cf. N. Özgüç (1949), who dates it ca. 1400–1200 B.C. by comparison with Yazılıkaya; Canby (1969, pp. 145–46) dates the figure significantly earlier by comparison with a cylinder seal in the Museum of Fine Arts, Boston (cat. no. 101, this volume).
6. Seeden 1980, p. 130; Orthmann 1975, p. 422; Akurgal 1962, p. 77.

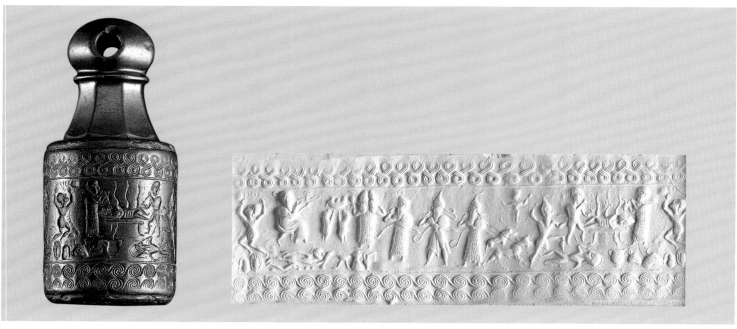

101

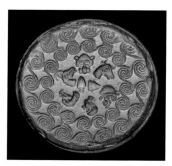

101, detail of end

101

STAMP-CYLINDER SEAL AND MODERN IMPRESSION

Hematite
Height 5.8 cm (2¼ in.); diameter 2.2 cm (⅞ in.)
Anatolia
Hittite Old Kingdom, 17th–16th century B.C.
Museum of Fine Arts, Boston
98.706

One of the most famous works of ancient glyptic is this hematite stamp-cylinder seal, purchased from the collection of Count Michel Tyszkiewicz in 1898 and eventually acquired by the Museum of Fine Arts, Boston. Originally published as from Cyprus, there can be no doubt—based on its form and imagery—of its central Anatolian origins.[1] The seal has a looped and faceted handle. It is designed to be both stamped and rolled, with decoration on its base and body. The

stamp-cylinder seal originated in northern Syria, but did not survive the influx of the Mesopotamian cylinder seal to the region. However, it came to be a standard form during the Hittite Empire, thus preserving the native predilection for stamping.[2]

Two ornamental bands, a guilloche pattern at the top and spiral quatrefoils below, frame the figural compositions. In a variation on the standard Near Eastern presentation scene, figures ascend steps toward a divinity on a platform. The deity, in a flounced garment and holding three curving stems and a cup, is seated on a throne with leonine legs (see cat. no. 47) before an offering stand with supports in the form of rampant lions. The first to approach is a double-headed god bearing a ewer, wearing conical caps and a long flounced robe. He is followed by another figure similarly dressed but with a broad cap. Next are a bearded god in more typically Hittite garb—a calf-length kilt and a spiked conical helmet (compare cat. no. 100)—and a deity in a flounced garment, with a crescent-shaped symbol on his headgear. All four figures carry the curved *lituus* (Hittite *kalmus*), associated with divine kingship during the Hittite Empire.[3] Adjacent to this scene a brutal confrontation ensues—interpreted by one scholar as a battle of the gods, as found on earlier Akkadian seals.[4] In a variation of the Syrian smiting posture for weather gods, a warrior in a conical spiked helmet and typically Anatolian dress plunges a

spear into the body of a fallen man wearing only a tight cap. Above him is a scene interpreted as either a sacrifice or a funerary ritual of a double-faced man in a cap and short kilt, flames rising from his body. A similarly dressed figure appears to fan the fire, while another holds a water pitcher. Most enigmatic are two "swimmers"[5]— one with a fish in his hand who seems to support the platform, and another who holds up the skeleton of a fish. There are also figures of a lion attacking a bull beneath a Syrian-type goddess with arms outstretched to reveal her nudity.[6] On the base of the seal, a band of spiral quatrefoils forms a border enclosing the heads of two lions, a bull, a caprid, an eagle, and a human circling two vessels.

The complex narratives on this seal—perhaps derived from local myths—are difficult to decipher. They have been compared with scenes on a stamp-cylinder seal, apparently purchased in Aydın, in southwestern Anatolia, where the bands and procession are repeated and the upright swimmer is depicted in a watery zone.[7] Both seals have been attributed to a group of Old Hittite glyptic of the seventeenth century B.C., with associations to elaborate ornamental stamp seal patterns from Karahöyük and figural imagery on sealings from Acemhöyük.[8] This group—with distinctive stamp-cylinder seals, designs combining ornamental bands and signlike elements, and specific figural imagery with later parallels—appears to bridge the gap between the glyptic of the Old Assyrian Trading Colony period and that of the succeeding Hittite Empire.[9]

JA

1. Tyszkiewicz sale 1898, pp. 80–81, no. 241, pl. XXVII, said to have been found on Cyprus; Frankfort 1939, pp. 285–88; Alexander 1985; Canby 1969, pp. 145–46.
2. This preference is visible throughout the history of Anatolian glyptic, even with the establishment of *karum*s and the use of local-style Anatolian cylinder seals. See Aruz 2008a, pp. 35–36, 61–62, for a discussion of the type, its transfer to the Aegean, and its use on pottery.
3. Collon 1980–83, p. 252 (Krummstab).
4. Canby (1989, p. 115) cites Hittite textual references to divine battles, which did not survive in imperial Hittite art.
5. Ibid.; interpreted as deceased on the Web site of the Museum of Fine Arts, Boston (www.mfa.org, search under collections).
6. For the nude Syrian goddess, see U. Winter 1983, figs. 279–89.
7. Boehmer and Güterbock 1987, p. 38, fig. 24b; Frankfort 1939, pp. 285–87; Alexander 1985.
8. N. Özgüç 1971, pp. 23–24; Alp (1968, pp. 271ff.) dates it to the last phase of the Colony period.
9. Boehmer and Güterbock 1987, pp. 33–39.

102

SMITING DEITY

Bronze
Height 9 cm (3½ in.)
Tiryns, Acropolis
Late Helladic IIIC context,
12th century B.C.
National Archaelogical Museum, Athens,
Greece 1582

This bronze figure of a smiting god was found intact during the late nineteenth-century excavations of the German archaeologist Heinrich Schliemann on the Mycenaean acropolis of Tiryns.[1] With a squarish face and stocky, muscular body, his right arm upraised and left arm held against his body, he wears a short loincloth and a high conical cap with vertical ridges and a knob at the peak, similar to the *hedjet*, or white crown, of Upper Egypt. On the left hip is a short dagger with a wide pommel. A small hole in the right fist indicates that the figure originally held a spear.

The Tiryns figure belongs to a general type known as the smiting god, which appears during the Late Bronze and the early Iron Ages as Sharruma in the Hittite Empire, as the Ingot God on Cyprus

102

(fig. 102), as Reshef in the Levant, as the Master of the Horse in the Mycenaean pictorial repertoire (on a krater from Ugarit),[2] and as Melqart in the Phoenician world.[3] With this figure type, the god is depicted poised to hurl a spear or smite the enemy with a mace. He bears a dagger secured at the waist and wears a high conical hat that, in some cases, is horned.

The smiting god figure from Tiryns probably represents an eastern Mediterranean god generally believed to be Reshef.[4] Such bronze figures, which were usually produced in Syro-Canaanite workshops, are distributed across a vast geographic area around the Mediterranean,[5] including the Mycenaean world; they have been found at Mycenae, Phylakopi on Melos, on the island of Delos, and at Lindos on Rhodes. The Aegean examples come from contexts of the late thirteenth and twelfth centuries B.C. but are thought to have been manufactured in earlier times.[6]

Although these figures have been interpreted as exotic gifts to the Mycenaean elite,[7] it is tempting to see them as personal belongings of Syrian merchants established at the Aegean emporia[8] or as their votive offerings at local shrines, such as at Phylakopi and on Delos. The smiting gods of the Aegean would thus represent a form of the religious syncretism that emerged toward the end of the Late Bronze Age and the beginning of the early Iron Age.[9]

CPA

1. Schliemann 1886, p. 187.
2. Paschalidis 2002–3, pp. 103–4; Niemeier 2003, pp. 106–7, figs. 7, 8.
3. For the morphological koine of these gods, see Gallet de Santerre 1987, pp. 15–17, where the origin of the smiting god is discussed in the context of early depictions of the pharaohs.
4. Ibid., pp. 8–9, 17, 23.
5. Ibid., p. 9. See also the examples listed together in *Sea Routes* 2003, pp. 455–57, nos. 799–806, from Syria, the Aegean, Italy, and Spain.
6. Gallet de Santerre 1987, pp. 9–14; Cline 1994, pp. 133–34.
7. N. Marinatos 1990b, p. 370, no. 356.
8. Cline 1994, pp. 54–55.
9. A phenomenon that is also apparent in the twelfth-century B.C. cemetery at Perati in Attica and at the Late Bronze and Early Iron Age site at Lefkandi in Euboia.

103

STRIDING MALE

Bronze
Height 15.5 cm (6⅛ in.)
Levant or Anatolia
Hittite Empire, 14th–13th century B.C.
Musée du Louvre, Paris, Département des
Antiquités Orientales AO11187

Acquired in the late nineteenth century in Latakia, near the ancient royal city of Ugarit, this figure in the Musée du Louvre belongs to the Syrian tradition of small cast-bronze statuary representing kilted warrior gods with elongated proportions and energetic poses dating to the second millennium B.C.[1] However, the figure also presents features that point to a strong Anatolian influence, if not place of origin. The statuette wears low boots and is clad in a short kilt decorated with parallel bands and held high on the waist by a belt, features that are typical of Anatolian costume. The hair, gathered into a thick plait, falls to the small of the back. The arms, which probably brandished weapons, were cast separately and later attached, as was

103

104

the headgear, which was likely of a different material. The headcovering was probably either a high conical cap, like that of a figure found at Doğantepe,[2] or rounded, like that on a large figure found near Afyon.[3] Horns symbolizing the divinity of these figures also may have adorned the headpieces.

Like all the other extant examples from a similar series produced either in northern Syria or in Anatolia,[4] this little bronze figure was covered with gold leaf, particles of which have been found in a slit on the left side that served to hold the plating. Grooves on the back of each leg and on the shoulders were used for the same purpose. There is a striking similarity between the Louvre figure and one in the Vorderasiatisches Museum, Berlin, that was long thought to have come from Boğazköy (cat. no. 104). But the provenance of the

latter, which lent credence to the idea that the Louvre figure could be associated with Anatolia, has been called into question as it now seems assured that the Berlin bronze was acquired in Sidon.[5] However, comparison with yet another Anatolian work speaks for this connection: the Louvre bronze can be seen as a miniature version of a warrior god carved in high relief on one of the doorjambs of the King's Gate from the Hittite capital of Hattusa (fig. 53). The two figures wear the same kind of kilt, woven with parallel horizontal bands, as well as the same type of high belt. The accentuated musculature enhances their martial aspect, and both the large-scale relief and the fragmentary figurine express the same dynamic energy.

Wherever the small bronze figure was produced, it bears witness to the fusion of Syrian and Anatolian influences during

a period in which the authority of the Hittite Great King extended as far as northern Syria. Soon thereafter, in the mid-thirteenth century B.C., it was superseded by the authority of a viceroy installed in Carchemish.   FD

1. For further reference, see Longpérier [1882], pl. 21:2; Ledrain 1888, no. 49; Bossert 1942, nos. 581, 582, pl. 140; Contenau 1949, p. 172; Bittel 1976c, p. 227, fig. 263; Seeden 1980, no. 1739; *Huit millénaires de civilisation anatolienne* 1981, no. 17; and Spycket 1981, p. 322 and p. 211, no. 134.
2. Seeden 1980, pl. 105, no. 1738.
3. Ilasli 1993.
4. Seeden 1980, p. 113, pl. 105.
5. Ibid., p. 113, no. 9.

104

STRIDING MALE FIGURE

Bronze
Height 14.7 cm (5¾ in.)
Levant
Late Bronze Age, 14th–13th century B.C.
Staatliche Museen zu Berlin,
Vorderasiatisches Museum VA4853

This cast-bronze statue, which, according to early publications is said to have come from Boğazköy, depicts a male figure wearing a short kilt and calf-length boots.[1] His broad face, large ears, and long slender nose are striking and well modeled. Incised details lend definition to the fringe of the tightly wrapped kilt and the thick belt around the waist. The figure is adorned with a short, V-shaped necklace. A drilled hole in the center of the flattened head could have been used to secure a horned crown, a wig, or a cap made of some other material, and the eye sockets may have been filled with glass paste or stone inlay. The arms—the left one is missing—were affixed to the shoulders with tangs and secured with rivets. Two tangs on the feet indicate that the figure could have been mounted on a separate base. Grooves on the body hold traces of gold leaf and lead, suggesting that the entire figure was gilded. This supposition is also supported by contemporary texts from Boğazköy that describe statues of gods overlaid with gold and silver.[2]

A bronze figure acquired in Latakia (cat. no. 103) with Anatolian features is closely related to this example, especially in the technique of its separately attached arms and headpiece (now missing). Numerous similar bronze statuettes discovered in excavations at Byblos and Ugarit were identified as Egyptian-influenced representations of weather gods. Veneration of the weather god, whose seat on the mountain Jebel al-Aqra was visible over an area of many miles, took on great importance during the second half of the second millennium B.C. It is therefore quite possible that this statuette represents the weather deity worshipped during the last third of the millennium.[3]   LM

1. For further reference, see Starke in *Die Hethiter und ihr Reich* 2002, p. 338, and Martin 2007, pp. 475–78.
2. V. Haas 1994, pp. 494–96.
3. Martin 2007, pp. 475–78.

105

AXE HEAD WITH MOUNTAIN DEITY

Bronze
Height 19.5 cm (7⅝ in.); width 9.2 cm (3⅝ in.)
Anatolia
Hittite Empire, 14th–13th century B.C.
Staatliche Museen zu Berlin,
Vorderasiatisches Museum VA15652

This shaft-hole axe head is the finest piece unearthed from a hoard in the vicinity of Şarkışla, in eastern Cappadocia

105

105, detail

between Kayseri and Sivas, which also includes bronze lugged axes, bowls, and pieces of snaffle bits.[1] The axe is elaborately ornamented both in high relief and fully in the round. On either side is a composition including a bearded mountain deity with a tall, pointed cap who supports a lion protome in his upraised arms. Atop the protome is another deity wearing a cap and a long robe, and above him are two kneeling creatures holding a winged sun disc. Three lion-griffin protomes with sharp wings crouch in front of spikes rising from the top of the axe, as pictured here. The narrow sides are decorated with additional lion protomes above and below the hole for the shaft. The blunt, rounded end of the axe blade terminates on either side in raptor heads.

The axe was made by the lost-wax process, with details added by chasing after casting. The elaborate religious and mythological content of the imagery and the detailed overall design of the axe rendered it unsuitable as a weapon, suggesting that it served some ritual purpose. The composition of the axe's decorative elements recalls a Hittite stele from Fasillar, which was perhaps originally intended to decorate a sanctuary at a freshwater spring.[2] An ornate shaft-hole axe (fig. 53) held prominently at chest height by the warrior god from the King's Gate at Hattusa suggests that such weapons served as symbols of

power, although more specific nuances of meaning remain unknown. No specific parallel to the Şarkışla axe has been recovered.

R–BW

1. Bittel 1976a, pp. 19ff., figs. 9–12; Bittel 1976b, p. 299, with figs. 341, 399; H. Erkanal 1977, suppl. and fig. 20; Wartke in *Das Schiff von Uluburun* 2005, p. 649, no. 224.
2. V. Haas 1994, p. 204, fig. 89; see also Mellaart 1962.

106
Relief with Deity on Stag

Steatite
Height 6.4 cm. (2½ in.); width 4.9 cm (1⅞ in.)
Alaca Höyük
Hittite Empire, 14th–13th century B.C.
Ankara Museum of Anatolian Civilizations,
Turkey 12467

Despite its small size, this stone relief of a deity acquired at Yeniköy, near Alaca Höyük in north-central Anatolia, evokes the monumental reliefs that were cut into living rock during the Hittite Empire period (fig. 56).[1] The dynamic pose of this deity, who strides forward with one arm bent against his body and the other extended, as well as his placement on a symbolically important base—in this case a sacred stag—became conventions in the depiction of Hittite gods and rulers as seen in the relief band encircling the rim of a stag vessel (fig. 57).[2] The god's conical headdress, short belted kilt, and shoes with upturned toes also reflect distinctive forms of Hittite ceremonial dress. The curved staff resting against his shoulder—referred to in Hittite texts as a *kalmus*—may derive from a beating staff used to flush out prey during the hunt and, by extension, the empire's enemies in battle. Under the Hittites, this staff became a symbol of authority.[3]

The rounded forms and naturalistic proportions of both the god and the stag in this relief contrast with the flatter and more abstract figural style of earlier art from central Anatolia. During the reign of the Hittites, contact with Egypt and eastern lands culturally tied to Mesopotamia introduced foreign stylistic idioms that became fused with indigenous traditions. The readily identifiable official style that resulted from this interaction may have helped to unite the previously disparate groups of the region under central rule.

J–FL

1. This unexcavated find was presented to members of the 1935 excavations at Alaca Höyük. See Arik 1937, p. 26.
2. For a general discussion of Hittite figural style, see Akurgal 1962, pp. 110–13.
3. Canby 2002, pp. 169–70.

106

Figure 56. Rock-cut shrine at Yazılıkaya. Hittite Empire period.

107
STAG VESSEL

Silver, gold inlay
Height 18 cm (7⅛ in.)
Anatolia
Hittite Empire, 14th–13th century B.C.
The Metropolitan Museum of Art, New York,
Gift of Norbert Schimmel Trust, 1989
1989.281.10

This silver alloy cup is among the few surviving objects that can attest to the highly accomplished metalwork produced during the period of Hittite hegemony in central Anatolia. Inventories of Hittite cultic objects include lists of ritual zoomorphic vessels, such as this stag, described as leaning forward or kneeling.[1] Essentially a sculpture in the round, the protome of this vessel captures the majesty of a fully antlered stag in repose with a naturalism that is characteristic of Hittite art.

The narrative relief encircling the upper section of the cup illustrates the type of libation ritual in which the cup may have been used. After a successful hunt, indicated by a butchered stag under a tree festooned with hunting paraphernalia, worshippers approach two deities who are identified by hieroglyphs chased on inlaid roundels of gold. Wearing a horned conical headdress and long robe, one deity sits to the left of an altar and holds a bird and a cup. The other deity stands on a stag in front of the altar. Dressed in a short kilt, with a long plait of braided hair running down his back, he holds a bird with his left hand and the curved rod known as the *kalmus*, a Hittite symbol of authority, in his right hand. Although the interpretation of the hieroglyphs remains unresolved, it is likely that the latter deity represents the Protector God of the Countryside, who is described in Hittite texts as standing on a stag.[2]

The approaching worshippers wear fillets in their hair and short robes that hang down at the back. The first figure—possibly a ruler—offers a libation from a beaker jug similar in shape to those excavated in central Anatolia. The second worshipper holds up what appears to be a round loaf of bread; the same object is depicted on an offering table in the relief on a fist-shaped cup in Boston (cat. no. 108). The third, kneeling worshipper holds a spouted jar.

Radiographs indicate that the vessel was produced from at least a dozen separate pieces of worked silver sheet that were sleeved together and soldered in place. The ring soldered around the neck serves both to hide and to reinforce the join between the head and the body. The lip of the cup was also strengthened with a separately fashioned section. The antlers, ears, and handle were made of tubes of metal with overlapping seams that were curved as needed, inserted into holes, and soldered in place. Although some restoration has occurred to these projecting elements, enough of the original silver remains to show that this reconstruction is accurate.

Both the checkerboard pattern on the neck ring and sections of the lip retain

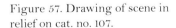
Figure 57. Drawing of scene in relief on cat. no. 107.

remnants of a black inlay material, which instrumental analysis indicates is neither niello nor bitumen.[3] Its composition suggests instead that it may have been a complex copper alloy intentionally formulated to turn dark when patinated. Used in Egypt already during the Middle Kingdom, this black copper also appears as an inlay material on mid-second-millennium B.C. Mycenaean daggers (see cat. no. 171 and fig. 36).[4]

J-FL

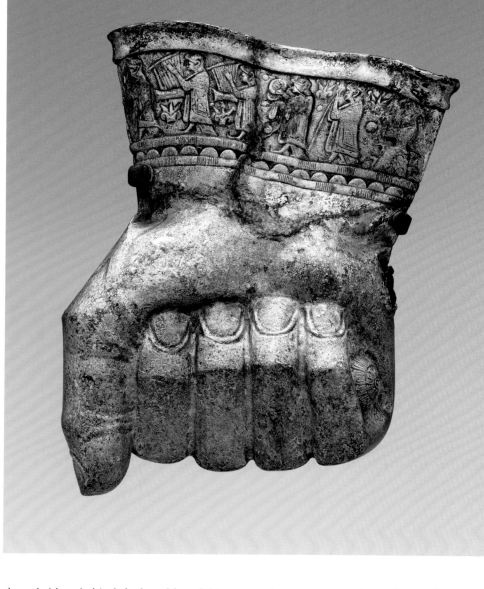

1. Koehl 1995, p. 63.
2. For a discussion and further references of the god on a stag, see Hellenkemper and Wagner 1977, pp. 70–71. For a discussion of the narrative relief, see Muscarella 1992 and Güterbock 1981–83.
3. Preliminary X-ray fluorescence and diffraction analysis performed by James H. Frantz at the Metropolitan Museum. Further analysis of this material will be required to confirm its identity.
4. See Ogden 1982, pp. 41–42, and Photos, Jones, and Papadopoulos 1994, pp. 267–75.

108

FIST-SHAPED VESSEL

Silver
Height 15.5 cm (6⅛ in.); width 10 cm (4 in.)
Anatolia
Hittite Empire, 14th–13th century B.C.
Museum of Fine Arts, Boston 2004.2230

The unusual shape of this cup may reflect the Hittite practice of venerating specific parts of their anthropomorphic divinities, as described in ancient texts. These body parts, fashioned of wood or metal, served as metaphors for divine attributes and became objects of worship. In this context, the forearm and hand were of particular importance as symbolic executors of divine will.[1]

Given the naturalistic quality of Hittite art, it is probable that the prominent V-shaped ridges behind the knuckles of this hand, as well as the bands and numerous wrinkles associated with the thumb, represent more than a mere stylization of physical features. It has been proposed that these details, along with the markedly flared profile of the wrist area, indicate that the hand wears a fingerless gauntlet of the type used in falconry.[2] Although falconry is not explicitly mentioned in Hittite texts, raptors are depicted in earlier and contemporary Anatolian art (see cat. no. 43). The important role of birds in Hittite cultic practices is also suggested by their prominent placement in Hittite reliefs, including the one on this cup.[3]

The relief scene in the wrist area appears to illustrate extant textual descriptions of Hittite libation rituals that were performed with musical accompaniment. On the left, the Storm God, wearing a short kilt and a horned conical headdress,

Figure 58. Drawing of relief encircling rim of cat. no. 108.

109

stands before an offering table while brandishing a mace in his right hand and holding on to the reins of a bull—now largely
lost—with his left. He is approached from
the right by a ruler dressed in a long robe
who pours a libation as he holds the crook-
shaped staff associated with Hittite authority. This ruler is followed by a large bird
with upswept wings standing on a slightly
raised mount. Although the next figure
is largely lost, the rest are similar to the
ruler in dress and coiffure. The first holds
aloft what appears to be a round loaf of
bread, similar to the one already placed on
the offering table. The next two figures
play stringed lyres, and the third holds
what appear to be cymbals. The last attendant grasps a long staff articulated with
horizontal banding.

Flowering plants and blossoms with
radiating petals appear between the figures.

These stylized foliate forms suggest that
the ritual shown here was connected
with the Spring Festival. The bearded and
horned god on the right, who seems to
rise out of a leafy mound, may represent
the rebirth of a vegetation or tree god
during the vernal season.   J-FL

1. Güterbock and Kendall 1995.
2. Canby 2002, pp. 169–70.
3. Ibid., pp. 170–72.

109

BULL-SHAPED VESSEL

Silver
Height 18 cm (7⅛ in.)
Anatolia
Hittite Empire, 14th–13th century B.C.
The Metropolitan Museum of Art, New York,
Gift of Norbert Schimmel Trust, 1989
1989.281.11

Hittite texts refer to a type of sculpted
vessel known as a *bibru* from which
the gods received libations.[1] This cup was
most likely dedicated to the Storm God,
chief deity of the Hittite pantheon, who was
closely associated with bulls. Its rounded,
naturalistically modeled body conveys a
sense of robust corporeal power characteristic of Hittite art and contrasts with the
earlier, more stylized depiction of bulls

found at central Anatolian sites such as Alaca Höyük. Although the original upper section was almost entirely lost and has been restored, it may have featured a narrative scene such as those found on similar Hittite vessels.

Benefiting from the extensive mineral resources in the mountainous areas to the north and south of their capital at Hattusa, the Hittites produced a broad array of metal artifacts, of which relatively few have survived. Hittite inventories of the thirteenth century B.C. identify two areas in north-central Anatolia where silver was obtained, but whether these were actual source locations or distribution points remains unclear.[2] Later texts of the Neo-Assyrian period mention a "silver mountain," most likely located in the Taurus Mountain range, which was within the southern reaches of Hittite control during the Empire period.[3]

Constructed of at least eleven individual sections of worked silver, this vessel reflects a considerable mastery of metal-forming techniques. The head and body were made separately of worked silver sheet, sleeved together at the neck, and secured in place by a raised band fixed with solder. The horns and ears were inserted into holes cut into the head. The fully modeled legs were each made in two pieces sleeved together at the knee and soldered on to stumps that project slightly from the body. The handle consists of a curved tube of silver, with a seam running down the inner face, which was soldered on to the cup at both ends. The recesses in eyes and eyebrows may have held stone inlays that are now lost.   J–FL

1. Tuchelt 1962, pp. 49–54.
2. Košak 1982, p. 197.
3. Luckenbill 1926–27, p. 246.

Shapinuwa: A Capital of the Hittite State

Shapinuwa (Ortaköy), one of the capital cities of the Hittite Empire, is situated 53 kilometers southeast of Çorum on the plateau between the Amasya and Alaca Plains, a strategic location in terms of governance, politics, and geography. The east–west trade route that ran along the Kelkit-Yeşilırmak Valley passed in front of the city and led to central Anatolia. Shapinuwa was also an important and special religious center. People journeyed to the city to be ritually cleansed, or they would read the texts that were prepared there so as to be absolved of their sins. Other rituals were established in Shapinuwa relating to sacrifices to the Underworld and invocations to the "Sky Gods." Documents also indicate that many other cities, both large and small, were under the authority of Shapinuwa and that the Hittite Great King lived there.

The more than four thousand tablets and tablet fragments found at Shapinuwa, written in Hattian, Hurrian, and Akkadian, include letters and historical and religious texts. The varied subjects and vast number of these cuneiform tablets tell us that they came from a royal archive. The archaeological and philological data show that most of the tablets date to the Hittite Middle Kingdom period, in the early fourteenth century B.C. At this time, the rulers of Shapinuwa were Tudhaliya III and his queen, Taduhepa. The city was later used by Mursili II in the thirteenth century B.C. and populated long after.

AS / MS

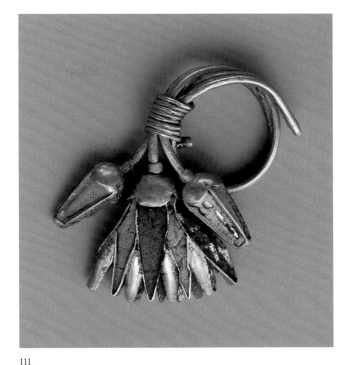

110

111

110

HEAD IN PROFILE

Bronze
Height 4.5 cm (1¾ in.); width 6.4 cm (2½ in.)
Shapinuwa (Ortaköy)
Hittite Middle Kingdom,
early 14th century B.C.
Çorum Museum, Çorum, Turkey 2–73–98

This unique bronze head in profile was found among the ruins of Ortaköy (ancient Shapinuwa) in Building B, which was destroyed in a devastating fire. Engraving, carving, and relief techniques were used together in making this piece. The face has a small chin, bold lips, and a wide nose. The almond-shaped eye and curved eyebrow were originally either inlaid or left as empty spaces to reveal a background material. The thick hair is combed toward the back of the head and falls to the shoulder. The ear is in relief, and the forehead is practically nonexistent. There is no visible beard. A now-missing metal piece was likely used for attachment.

The hair, at first glance, appears to be Egyptian. Generally, the figures on Egyptian papyri and wall paintings were represented without hair, with curly hair, or in a number of hairstyles. The face shares similarities with Egyptian renderings of the mouth and a small chin that does not protrude. However, unlike Egyptian images, the nose is wide and the outer wall of the nostril is expressive. Whether the figure resembles a Hittite or an Egyptian, it is a unique work.

AS/MS

111

LOTUS FLOWER ORNAMENT

Gold with inlays
Height 2.7 cm (1 in.); width 2 cm (¾ in.)
Shapinuwa (Ortaköy)
Hittite Middle Kingdom,
early 14th century B.C.
Çorum Museum, Çorum, Turkey
28–1874–90

This ornament was found at Shapinuwa in the ruins of Building A. Made of gold, it comprises a lotus flower with a bud on either side, each constructed separately and then joined with a gold wire to form a cluster. Each of the buds is made with four trapezoidal pieces of gold attached edge to edge. The petals were once filled with lilac- and blue-colored inlay. A calyx appears under the lotus buds. The stem is wound into a ring shape and held with a gold wire just beneath the sepals.

The flower depicted here is widely known as the Egyptian lotus, although it is actually a water lily. The closing and opening of the flower symbolizes rebirth. The lotus is believed to be connected to the cycle of the sun and to be sacred, divine, and related to the other world in Egyptian, Anatolian, and other Near Eastern cultures. In the archaic era, the roots of the lotus symbolized immortality and eternity; the stem, attachment to life; and the petals, purity and innocence. In Egypt, the blue and white lotus signifies peace and purity. Head ornaments in the form of a lotus were worn in life and death, both as festive attire and as funerary jewelry.

Shapinuwa was an important religious center in the Hittite world. It was quite natural to find there an object such as the lotus, which symbolizes purity and innocence. This precious ornament, which displays a high level of craftsmanship, was probably a gift sent from an important individual in Egypt to an important individual in Shapinuwa.

AS/MS

Figure 59. Hattusa (Boğazköy), Lower Town, Great Temple. Hittite Empire period.

Hattusa: Capital of the Hittite Empire

A landscape shaped by cutting and leveling rocks and mountains is one of the distinctive features of the Hittite capital Hattusa (Boğazköy) in the late thirteenth century B.C. With a more than 6.8-kilometer-long defense system (fig. 60), its imperial silhouette is crowned by a monumental artificial structure resembling a truncated pyramid punctuated by temples and palaces on different elevations in a rough, rocky landscape .

This unique setting was the outcome of a dynamic development over a period of more than 350 years, originating with the destruction and condemnation of the city in the late third and early second millennia B.C. by Anitta, king of Kanesh. Despite this negative omen, Hattusili I, the first Hittite king, chose this site for his new capital because of its strategic position. Partly founded on virgin soil in a rough terrain, it marks a fundamental change in the plan and structure of settlements in ancient Anatolia. Its largest extension, over more than 185 hectares, makes it one of the most extensive urban centers of its time.

Ongoing excavations by the German Archaeological Institute have revealed aspects of both royal and everyday life that are illuminated by archaeological evidence as well as by the contents of more

than thirty thousand cuneiform texts found in the royal archives. The palace compound, stretching out atop a large rocky outcrop, is one of the most distinctive features of the city. While its organization evolved over time, in its final configuration, myriad buildings were interconnected by large courtyards. A monumental fortification system guards the citadel. Access is gained by means of two gates, one of which is accessible over a bridgelike viaduct. This architectural structure distinguishes the Hittite royal citadel from all other palace compounds in the ancient Near East at this time.

The Great Temple, the largest temple of the Hittite world, was unearthed in the Lower Town, which is surrounded by complexes of storerooms and administrative buildings (fig. 59). An additional twenty-eight temples have been excavated in the specially designated area of the Upper Town, separated from the rest of the city by topography. Although it is impossible to associate a given temple with a specific god, the architectural development of Hittite temples can be traced over a period of at least 250 years. During the turbulent late days of the Hittite Empire, the temples fell out of use and pottery kilns and dwellings were built over them.

Communal installations for the storage of water and grain have been found over the past two decades of research, both within and in the close vicinity of Hattusa. Excavations in the southern part of the Upper Town indicate that such installations were in use beginning in the early sixteenth century B.C., and their location suggests that they were closely related to the early imperial extension of the city. Facilitating control over vital resources, the installations were important for the survival of the city in the dry climate of central Anatolia, enabling the Hittites to overcome the disadvantages of their natural setting. Indeed, they were crucial to the success of the Hittite economy and social system.

It is still not known where, specifically, the general population lived, although a relatively small area of dwellings was unearthed in the Lower Town west of the Great Temple. Excavated houses show that older Anatolian traditions of domestic architecture continued in Hittite times. New features and architectural forms indicate, however, that at least some houses were updated to conform to new urban functions. Recent research has located single buildings—some of which may be farmsteads—in the vicinity of the city.

A small necropolis was identified close to a rocky outcrop north of the urban settlement. The human remains indicate that cremation was the main practice there, but instances of inhumation were also present.

ANS

Figure 60. Hattusa (Boğazköy), Lion Gate. Hittite Empire period.

113

112

DEITY

Ivory
Height 5.8 cm (2¼ in.)
Boğazköy
Hittite Empire, 14th–13th century B.C.
Çorum Museum, Çorum, Turkey 1–166–82

This deeply carved ivory from Temple VII at Boğazköy presents an unusual image of a warlike divinity.[1] The figure wears the horned crown, a characteristic attribute of Mesopotamian deities, above an elaborate hairstyle that frames the face with two long curls ending in spiral locks that rest on the chest. A triple-strand necklace is visible between the curls. A kilt is wrapped tightly about the body, and a dagger is tucked sideways in an elaborate belt. Although the limbs are damaged, enough of the vigorously twisting legs remains to suggest the figure is dancing.[2] The left elbow is bent, either as part of the dance or perhaps in the act of raising a weapon. Holes in the irises suggest that the eyes were originally inlaid, giving a more powerful aspect to the stern expression.

The short kilt indicates an Anatolian milieu, but the horned crown differs from the headdresses generally worn by Hittite gods and points instead to this deity's origin in Mesopotamia. Furthermore, the figure displays attributes that could belong to either gender in Hittite art, including the long spiral curls worn by male and female creatures (see cat. nos. 46, 53, 81) and necklaces worn by gods and goddesses. Slight swellings at the chest could indicate either breasts or pronounced musculature. It is likely that this finely carved piece depicts Shaushga, the Hittite version of Ishtar, goddess of sexual love and war, whose dual aspects allowed her to occupy both female and male roles. On the rock reliefs at the Hittite shrine of Yazılıkaya (fig. 56), she is depicted twice: among the gods and among the goddesses.[3] Her cult, crucial in ensuring success in battle, in inducing fertility, and in guaranteeing oaths, seems to have flourished under royal patronage during the Hittite Empire.[4]   SG

1. For further reference, see Neve 1983, p. 447, fig. 22; Darga 1992, p. 110; Neve 1992, p. 33, fig. 82; and Starke in *Die Hethiter und ihr Reich* 2002, p. 344, no. 114.
2. Neve 1983, p. 447, fig. 22.
3. V. Haas 1994, pp. 350–51; Güterbock 1975, p. 173, no. 38 (male), p. 181, nos. 55a–56 (female).
4. V. Haas 1994, pp. 349–50.

113

PLAQUE WITH OFFERING BEARER

Bronze
Height 4.5 cm (1¾ in.); width 3.9 cm (1½ in.)
Boğazköy
Hittite Old Kingdom, 17th–16th century B.C.
Boğazköy Archaeological Museum, Turkey
1–30–66

This bronze fragment from the Hittite capital of Boğazköy, perhaps originally part of a vessel,[1] shows a striding figure dressed in a belted kilt. He holds aloft in both hands the head of an animal, perhaps a goat.[2] The composition is bordered on three sides by a raised line; beneath the groundline are running spirals. Similar compositions appear in wall paintings from private tombs in Egyptian Thebes dating to early Dynasty 18, in which Aegeans and Syrians offer animal-headed vessels as tribute to the pharaoh (see fig. 87).[3] The object held by this figure may also be a vessel. Despite the fragment's small size, embossed details lend definition to the extended arms and exposed leg. Its light color suggests that the piece may originally have been silver-plated.[4]

The fragment was excavated at Boğazköy in Level 3 of the Lower Town, dated by excavators to about 1700–1500 B.C.[5] Later inventories of cult objects from Boğazköy, dating to the time of Tudhaliya IV, list many vessels in the shape of animal heads, or protomes.[6] These vessels were often made of precious metals and used in cultic ceremonies by the king or royal couple, who would drink from the cup and then pour an offering to the deity.[7] Although this piece dates from an earlier period, it could depict a moment during a similar ritual. Alternatively, the figure could simply be offering a sacrificial goat's head to a deity.[8]   SG

1. Bittel 1976b, pp. 164, 332.
2. Bittel 1957b, pp. 16–17.
3. Wachsmann 1987, pp. 55–60.
4. Boehmer 1972, p. 68, no. 169.
5. Ibid., p. 68; dated "Zeit von Büyükkale IVc" in Neve 1982, pp. 2–6, 34–46.
6. Güterbock 1983, pp. 211–14.
7. Ibid., p. 212; see this reference for a discussion of the terms used in the inventory texts to refer to these vessels, Sumerian gú (neck or throat), and Akkadian *bibru*. In spite of its contemporary usage to refer to an animal-headed cup, the term *bibru* seems to designate an animal figure, while gú is more commonly used to identify animal-headed cups. However, these terms remain incompletely understood.
8. Bittel 1957b, p. 17.

the spout, which would then have been poured out of the nostrils; some bulls also had an additional opening, below the tail.

The bull was sacred to Teshshup, the Hittite weather god, and the use of paired clay bulls or bull vessels in rituals for this god—perhaps reflecting the sacred bulls Sheri and Hurri referred to in cuneiform ritual texts from Boğazköy—is well documented in Anatolia.[5] Furthermore, the İnandıktepe bulls were found in a pit together with a terracotta model of a shrine, suggesting that they had previously been kept in the city's temple.[6] The fragment seen here most closely resembles the pair from Boğazköy, which have been dated to the sixteenth century B.C.[7]   SG

1. See N. Özgüç 1956. For further reference, see also *Art Treasures of Turkey* 1966, p. 79, no. 71, and Bittel 1976b, pp. 151–52.
2. Neve 1965, pp. 35–68.
3. T. Özgüç 1988, pp. 111–12, pls. 60–62, pl. E, 1.
4. T. Özgüç 1978, p. 58, pl. 46:1–5.
5. V. Haas 1994, pp. 315–16, 320, 533–34.
6. T. Özgüç 1988, p. 112.
7. Bittel 1976b, pp. 151–52.

114

FRAGMENT OF BULL RHYTON

Ceramic
Width 21.4 cm (8⅜ in.); length 17 cm (6¾ in.)
Anatolia
Hittite Old Kingdom, 16th century B.C.
Ankara Museum of Anatolian Civilizations,
Turkey 8405

Even in its fragmentary condition, this terracotta bull's head, said to have come from Tokat,[1] displays a remarkable liveliness and high-quality workmanship. The alert posture of the head is underscored by the small extended ears and the bulging eyes, now missing their inlaid pupils. The cream-colored slip that indicates the base of the horns, triangular forehead patch, eyeballs, and reins stands in strong contrast to the deep reddish color of the bull's head and neck. Delicate incised lines trace the eyebrows and nostrils. Prominent reins connect with the bull's nostrils, which are pierced to allow for the flow of liquid.

In its original state, this piece would have closely resembled a group of large bull-shaped vessels found in pairs at Boğazköy[2] (fig. 61) and İnandıktepe,[3] and in fragmentary condition at Maşat Höyük.[4]

Complete examples allow us to reconstruct this bull as part of a rhyton that originally had a tall spout on the back, set just behind the neck. The hollow body could have been filled with liquid through

Figure 61. Pair of Hittite Old Kingdom ceramic vessels in the shape of bulls, in situ. Boğazköy, Royal Citadel of Büyükkale, Building M, Room 6. Hittite Empire period context.

189

115

SPOUTED VESSEL

Ceramic
Height 50 cm (19¾ in.); diameter 22.5 cm
(8⅞ in.)
Tokat-Sanusa
Hittite Old Kingdom, 17th–16th century B.C.
Ankara Museum of Anatolian Civilizations,
Turkey 4–10–68

The elongated forms of this pitcher's neck, handle, and spout are offset by its widely flaring body. The convex profile of the shoulders is further counterbalanced by the sharply tapered lower body, which terminates in a disc-shaped base. The surface has been burnished to a high shine, and two small triangular lugs have been applied to the shoulder on either side of the spout. The vessel belongs to a characteristic group of Hittite pitchers whose hooked spouts bring to mind the beak of a bird of prey, and whose crisply modeled forms and glossy surfaces evoke the shape and finish of metalwork.

Similar beak-spouted vessels have been excavated at the Hittite capital of Boğazköy,[1] at Alaca Höyük[2] and Eskiyapar,[3] and in Old Assyrian Trading Colony levels at Kültepe (the ancient *karum* of Kanesh).[4] This vessel, said to have come from a cemetery at Ferzant near Çorum,[5] closely resembles Old Hittite beak-spouted pitchers in its slender proportions and the sharp curvature of the spout. Vessels of this type have not, however, been otherwise attested in burial contexts. A stone relief from Alaca Höyük,[6] a jar decorated in relief from İnandıktepe,[7] and a small relief band running around the mouth of a stag-shaped silver drinking vessel (cat. no. 107) show similar beak-spouted pitchers being used to pour libations before Hittite deities.

The evidence of the pictorial reliefs and the magnificent craftsmanship of this vessel suggest that it, too, was used for ritual offerings.   SG

1. F. Fischer 1963, pp. 36–41.
2. Koşay and Akok 1947, pp. 155–57.
3. Temizer 1979, p. 87, fig. 123.
4. T. Özgüç 1986b, pp. 54–55, pl. B:8–13;
   T. Özgüç 2003, cf. figs. 109–15, pp. 152–53.
5. T. Özgüç 1986a, p. 398.
6. Bossert 1942, p. 112, fig. 505.
7. T. Özgüç 1988, pl. I:3.

116

Spouted Vessel

Ceramic
Height 30 cm (11⅞ in.); width at shoulder
11 cm (4⅜ in.)
Tokat-Sanusa
Hittite Old Kingdom, 17th–16th century B.C.
Eski Şark Museum, Istanbul, Turkey 12890

The spout of this vessel rises from a narrow, elongated neck in a dramatic curve that evokes the sharp beak of a bird of prey. Below the neck, the vessel's body is laterally flattened and tapers into a dagger-like shape that makes it impossible to stand the object upright. Its surface is highly burnished, with a pattern of uniformly sized circles impressed on to the body and a ring of small hatch marks encircling the juncture of neck and body. The suggestion of animal forms—a beak, pronounced shoulders, and spotted surface—gives this piece a vivid sense of animation.

Beak-spouted pouring vessels form a characteristic type of Anatolian pottery that recalls metalwork in its toreutic modeling and burnished surface[1] and that remained in use over a long period of time.[2] Early examples of pitchers with dramatically curved spouts were excavated in Old Assyrian Trading Colony levels at Kültepe and from a level contemporary with Kültepe Level Ib at the Hittite capital of Boğazköy.[3] Later beak-spouted vessels become more elongated in form, and many variations in the basic shape appear over time. Although its surface treatment is unique, this piece can be dated by comparison with a number of Hittite Old Kingdom spouted vessels with slender profiles.[4]

A relief-decorated sherd from the Hittite sanctuary at Yazılıkaya depicts a beak-spouted vessel with a pointed base carried in what appears to be a procession of figures with votive offerings.[5] Thus, it seems most likely that this vessel was used for pouring ceremonial offerings during religious rituals.   SG

1. Bittel 1955, p. 36.
2. F. Fischer 1963, pp. 38–41.
3. T. Özgüç 2003, pp. 152–53, figs. 109–15;
   F. Fischer 1963, pp. 36–41.
4. Akurgal 1962, fig. 38.
5. Bittel 1955, p. 31.

Literary and Cultural Connections

During the second millennium B.C., western Asia and northeastern Africa were divided into two cultural spheres. Egypt was centered around the glorification of its pharaoh and dominated not only the Nile Valley but also the adjacent areas of Nubia, Libya, and the Sinai Peninsula. This influence is attested by statements in texts from Egypt itself and the numerous objects of Egyptian manufacture found in these regions, as well as by the occasional use of the hieroglyphic script by those residing there.

By contrast, civilizations in Babylonia, Assyria, western Iran, northern Syria, and Anatolia were structured around the conceptions, lifeways, and cuneiform writing system originally developed by the Sumerians in southern Mesopotamia beginning in the late fourth millennium B.C., if not earlier. The southern region of the Levant, situated on the border between these two cultural zones, was subject to the influence of both hieroglyphic and cuneiform civilizations. Similarly, if to a lesser degree, traders in Minoan Crete and, later, Mycenaean Greece as well as the Aegean islands interacted with their counterparts in both Egypt and Mesopotamia.

The spread of Mesopotamian culture entailed not only the passive reception of objects and texts produced in the heartland, but also the active study of the cuneiform script. This task was accomplished by following the educational practices that had been employed for centuries in Sumer, Babylonia, and Assyria. Just as Babylonian apprentice scribes, preparing for a career writing in their own Akkadian tongue, continued to copy Sumerian-language texts as part of their advanced training, those learning to inscribe their native idioms of Hittite, Hurrian, or Canaanite, for example, also occupied themselves with the reproduction of classic texts in Sumerian and Akkadian.

Furthermore, in the Late Bronze Age—even in Egypt and Cyprus (ancient Alashiya)—Akkadian was in use as a lingua franca for diplomatic correspondence and for the composition of international documents. At every major royal court, a certain active knowledge of this language was necessary for the bureaucrats who were concerned with diplomacy. For example, the Hittite Great King and his high officials provided those vassals of Hatti situated in Syria with documents composed not in Hittite, the official administrative language of the Hittite state, but in Akkadian.

In this way, important Mesopotamian scholarly and literary texts were transmitted to various sites on what scholars have come to call the "periphery" of cuneiform civilization. For example, a copy of the historical epic The King of Battle, which tells of the campaigns of the Akkadian king Sargon the Great (ca. 2334–2279 B.C.) in Anatolia, was found in the ruins of the pharaoh Akhenaten's short-lived capital of Akhetaten (Tell el-Amarna) in Egypt, and fragments of the Epic of Gilgamesh have been recovered at Megiddo in the Levant, at the Hittite capital of Hattusa (Boğazköy) in central Anatolia, and at the commercial centers of Ugarit (Ras Shamra) on the Mediterranean coast and Emar (Tell Meskene) on the middle course of the Euphrates in Syria. Texts such as these from the periphery normally represent the often rather poor efforts of local students, but in some instances they have clearly been imported from Babylonia or Assyria, presumably by Mesopotamian "guest professors" for use in instructing their pupils.

During the second millennium B.C., the Mesopotamians showed relatively little interest in borrowing foreign cultural goods or technology, but people living in peripheral regions were happy to receive useful knowledge from their neighbors as well as from Assyria and Babylonia. We can see this process of transmission at work in the Hittite borrowing of certain Mesopotamian literary materials, not directly from Babylonia but from scribal centers in Syria. The Hittites also adopted a regimen for training warhorses seemingly developed for the chariotry of their one-time rival Mitanni.

Indeed, material from the periphery has played an important part in the efforts of modern researchers to reconstruct the development of the ancient Mesopotamian "canon," or core body of written cultural knowledge. Owing to the vagaries of discovery, few significant "libraries" of cuneiform scholarly and literary works from the second half of the second millennium B.C. have actually been excavated in Babylonia or Assyria. Consequently, contemporary tablets from peripheral sites, in particular those from Hattusa, constitute the primary testament to a crucial period in the evolution of the Mesopotamian intellectual tradition.

GB

117
Epic of Gilgamesh

Clay
Height 9.6 cm (3¾ in.); width 15.6 cm (6⅛ in.)
Boğazköy
Hittite Empire, 14th–13th century B.C.
Staatliche Museen zu Berlin,
Vorderasiatisches Museum VAT12890

The tale of Gilgamesh is one of the best-known literary works of cuneiform culture, not only to modern readers but also to the ancients themselves. Excerpts from this saga have been found as far from Mesopotamia as Megiddo. Two different versions of the epic in the Akkadian language, as well as translations into Hurrian and Hittite, were also discovered in Anatolia at the Hittite capital. It seems that local adapters of the tale made certain changes in the narrative to reflect local interests. In particular, Hurrian and Hittite versions slighted the hero's early activities in Mesopotamian Uruk in order to give greater prominence to his adventure in the fabled Cedar Forest, which contemporaries identified with the (relatively) nearby Mount Amanus.

This partially preserved tablet contains an Akkadian text describing one of a series of disturbing dreams experienced by Gilgamesh on his way to confront the fearsome guardian of the Cedar Forest, the monstrous Humbaba, and to cut the valuable timber Humbaba protected. Gilgamesh's companion Enkidu endeavors to bolster the hero's spirits by providing a positive interpretation of his nightmare. In this connection, he promises that the sun god will aid them in their perilous quest:

They traveled hand in hand, pitched camp, and lay down. Sleep, which pours out by night, overcame Gilgamesh. In the middle of the night his sleep was interrupted. He got up and related his dream to his friend Enkidu: "I have seen a dream. How can it be that you did not wake me? Why am I awake? Enkidu, my friend, I have seen a dream. How can it be that you did not wake me? Why am I awake?

"My second dream was more frightful than my first dream: My friend, in my dream a great mountain was cast down upon me, trapping my feet. An awesome glare intensified (the strength of) my arms. A certain young man appeared, dressed in power. He was the most handsome in the land. His beauty was surpassing(?). He pulled me out from beneath the mountain, gave me water to drink so that my feelings were settled, and set my feet back upon the ground."

Enkidu replied to Gilgamesh: "My friend, we are going to him—is he not the mountain? He is something strange. Humbaba, to whom we go—is he not the mountain? He is something strange. Come, cast off your fear!

"And the young man whom you saw in your dream, who found favor in your eyes, and who succored your body—he is the sun god. Without hesitation he will fight(?) by your side. Your dream is favorable." (Gilgamesh) rejoiced, his heart was gladdened, and his expression lightened.[1] GB

1. Translation by the author, previously unpublished.

THE MITANNI STATE

JEAN M. EVANS

Of the four great powers of the mid-second millennium B.C.—Egypt, Hittite Anatolia, Kassite Babylonia, and Mitanni—the last mentioned is the least well known. The land of Mitanni is also variously referred to as the land of the Hurrians by the Hittites; Hanigalbat by the Assyrians, Hittites, and Babylonians; and Nahrina by the Egyptians. The history of the Mitanni state is obscure, and the precise reign dates of Mitanni rulers—because of the absence of king lists—are unknown. The Mitanni heartland was in the upper Khabur region of northeastern Syria. By the eighteenth century B.C., small states with Hurrian inhabitants were established in the region, and these later joined to form the territorial state of Mitanni. During the reign of Parattarna, about 1500 B.C., the Mitanni state was at the height of its power and stretched from the foothills of the Zagros Mountains to the Mediterranean.

Mitanni was inhabited principally by the Hurrian people; the Hurrian language is already attested in the third millennium B.C. and is related to the later Urartian language. Some scholars have posited that this largely Hurrian population was subject to an Indo-European military class presiding over the Mitanni state. Mitanni rulers seem to bear Indo-European names, and gods of the later Indian Vedas, such as Mitra and Varuna, were worshipped as minor deities; Hurrian technical terms related to

horses are also Indo-European. Conversely, it has been suggested that these cultural elements associated with Indo-Europeans were brought by the Hurrians; the character of the military class with which these elements have been associated is difficult to determine.[1]

Mitanni power derived in no small part from equestrian skills and expertise in the use of the light two-wheeled chariot and the composite bow; Hurrian handbooks on horse training and racing have survived (cat. no. 96). In the fifteenth century B.C., the Mitanni successfully fought off the advance of Egyptian forces into northern Syria, most notably under Thutmose III (ca. 1479–1425 B.C.). Later in the fourteenth century B.C., peace negotiations were sealed with a succession of diplomatic marriages between Mitanni princesses and Egyptian pharaohs. Letters sent by the Mitanni rulers profess eternal friendship with the Egyptian rulers, list the contents of the dowries, and request quantities of gold in return (see cat. no. 118).

Until recently, Mitanni material culture was known primarily through early twentieth-century excavations at the sites of Nuzi (Yorgan Tepe) in northeastern Mesopotamia (see fig. 62) and Alalakh (Tell Atchana) in southeastern Anatolia (see pp. 197–98), two sites at either extreme of the Mitanni state. In recent years, an increase in archaeological activity in Syria has

Figure 62. Reconstruction of wall painting. Nuzi, Level II Palace. Mitanni period.

194

revealed Mitanni remains at several sites in the upper Khabur River valley, among them Tell Brak, Tell Barri, and Tell al-Hamidiya.[2] The principal Mitanni royal city, Washshukanni, still has not been identified, but Tell al-Hamidiya has been identified as Taide, a Mitanni royal city.[3] Excavations there have revealed a stepped platform upon which were the remains of a massive Mitanni palace that had been twice the size of the palace of Zimri-Lim at Mari (see pp. 27–29). Among the possible upper Khabur sites that may one day prove to be Washshukanni, Tell Fakhariyah is a plausible candidate.[4] The site was briefly excavated in 1940 and again in 1955–56. New excavations were begun in 2006.[5]

The recent excavations at Tell Brak (ancient Nagar) have supplemented our knowledge of Mitanni culture.[6] During the fourth and third millennia B.C., Tell Brak had been one of the largest cities in northern Mesopotamia; the southern part of the site seems to have been abandoned in the early second millennium B.C. Later in the second millennium B.C., a Mitanni temple and palace were built at the summit of the mound. The palace comprised large rooms surrounding a central court, and two stairways provided access to an upper story, possibly the residential part of the palace.[7] The Mitanni settlement at Tell Brak was destroyed in the early thirteenth century B.C. during the expansion of Assyria. Many objects, broken and scattered when the palace was looted and burned, were recovered: fragments of gold and glass; components of wood, ivory, and bronze furniture; and painted Nuzi ware (compare cat. nos. 119, 120). Evidence for international contacts at Tell Brak includes vessels of Egyptian travertine, Egyptianizing scarabs, and highly burnished plum-red vessels resembling Hittite pottery. A fragment of a stirrup jar from the Mitanni palace is the easternmost example of this Mycenaean type (compare cat. nos. 242b, 244); it was probably manufactured in the Levant to satisfy local demand.[8] A fragmentary duck vessel of hippopotamus ivory was also retrieved (compare cat. no. 199).

Developments in glassmaking in the mid-second millennium B.C. include elaborate techniques and the production of a wide range of colors. The glass excavated at Tell Brak includes vessel fragments decorated with motifs of wide geographic distribution, such as multicolored scallops and chevron inlay (compare cat. no. 274). Other small glass fragments bear a unique type of decoration consisting of flowers and patterned bands of triangles composed of tiny globules of yellow and white glass for an effect resembling that of gold granulation. It is thought that this type of glass may have been manufactured at Tell Brak; pieces of cullet and ingots of raw glass found in the palace provide evidence for glassmaking activities (see cat. no. 187).

Two complete Mitanni tablets from Tell Brak record royal legal transactions sworn in the presence of Tushratta and his older brother Artashumara, who is otherwise only known from an Amarna Letter in which Tushratta informs the Egyptian king that his brother has been assassinated.[9] Both tablets were sealed with a Mitanni dynastic seal carved for their forebear Saushtatar (see fig. 63). Mitanni cylinder seals bear

Figure 63. Impression of cylinder seal of Saushtatar.

designs combining international motifs with elements that may be distinctly Mitanni. The most substantial corpora of Mitanni glyptic—from Alalakh and Nuzi—show strong local characteristics.

Most of Syria and northern Mesopotamia was under Mitanni control when the Hittite ruler Suppiluliuma I (ca. 1344–1322 B.C.) ascended the throne. Suppiluliuma's first attempt to conquer northern Syria does not seem to have been a success. His second attempt, presumably many years later, was a decisive victory as he marched into the Mitanni heartland and sacked Washshukanni. These conquests possibly precipitated the internal strife in Mitanni that led to the assassination of Tushratta and the flight of the crown prince, Shattiwaza, to the Hittite court. Suppiluliuma eventually installed Shattiwaza as a puppet king in the western reaches of the state. What remained of Mitanni now served the Hittites as a buffer region until the expansion of Assyria dealt the final blow to the Mitanni state.[10]

1. Kuhrt 1995, pp. 297–98; Van de Mieroop 2003, p. 116.
2. For the identification of Tell Barri as ancient Kahat, see Pecorella 1998.
3. Kühne 1984; Eichler and Wäfler 1990, p. 219.
4. New petrographic analyses (Goren, Finkelstein, and Na'aman 2004, p. 44) of the Amarna Letters sent from Washshukanni contradicts prior studies (Dobel, Asaro, and Michel 1977) by indicating that the clay used for the tablets was taken from a geological milieu that is characteristic for the region around Tell Fakhariyah; see also Harrak 1987, p. 106.
5. A single campaign was also undertaken in 2001 by a joint Syrian–German mission; see Pruss and Bagdo 2002.
6. Oates, Oates, and McDonald 1997.
7. Ibid., pp. 9–11.
8. Ibid., p. 79.
9. EA 17, Moran 1992, pp. 41–42.
10. Kuhrt 1995, pp. 289–96.

118
Amarna Letter: List of Gifts from Tushratta

Clay
Height 36 cm (14⅛ in.); width 22 cm (8⅝ in.)
Tell el-Amarna
New Kingdom, Dynasty 18, ca. 1365–1330(?) B.C.
Staatliche Museen zu Berlin,
Vorderasiatisches Museum VAT340

This clay tablet, preserved only in fragments, includes a detailed list of gifts, apparently comprising the dowry of the Mitanni princess Tadu-hepa sent to the Egyptian court to be married to Amenhotep III (see cat. no. 97). The incomplete signature mentions "all these [ob]jects (and) dowry-personnel t[hat Tu]shratta, the king of Mitanni, [. . .] *her* [. . .] ga[ve]."[1] The addressee was doubtless either the bridegroom or one of his administrators.

In contrast to the inventory given in cat. no. 97, listed here are goods and objects intended only for the personal use and adornment of the princess and her staff. Foremost among them are full sets of jewelry and textiles, possibly scarves, for the princess, as well as necklaces, bracelets, pendants, earrings, rings, and ankle bracelets made expressly for one hundred dowry servants, as well as so-called eye agates and garment pins. All the objects were made of precious materials and richly ornamented, and frequently there is mention of the quantity of precious metal or fabric required to make them.

Also listed are toilet articles such as mirrors, bowls, and sets of "flagons," as well as salves and silver combs, of which—in the surviving text—nine different styles are named. The bride was given many articles of clothing—including chemises, skirts, and boots, not to mention additional necessities such as washbasins, rhyta, fly whisks, spoons, and bed linen. Judging from references to a sideboard and objects made of boxwood, we can assume that furniture, or portions of furniture, were also included.[2]

Despite the tablet's relatively poor state of preservation, it is apparent that its text was written with particular care because wherever possible, groups of words that belonged together were carefully placed one above another, a format typical in cuneiform writing. This must have made the work of the Egyptian translator-copyist considerably easier. JM

1. EA 25, IV: 65–67, translated in Moran 1992, p. 81.
2. See EA 25, IV: 17ff., Moran 1992, p. 80.

Alalakh (Tell Atchana)

A flurry of international archaeological research began in Hatay in today's Republic of Turkey in the early 1930s, when the Syro-Hittite Expedition team assembled by James Henry Breasted, director of the Oriental Institute at the University of Chicago, arrived in the Amuq Valley (Plain of Antioch). The 22-hectare mound of Tell Atchana (ancient Alalakh, site number 136) was first surveyed by Robert Braidwood,[1] although it was subsequently excavated from 1936 to 1939 and, after World War II, from 1946 to 1949 by the British archaeologist Sir Leonard Woolley.[2] The resumption of excavations and surveys at Alalakh began in 2000 under the direction of the author on behalf of the Turkish Ministry of Culture and Tourism and the Mustafa Kemal University in Antakya.[3]

The earlier Woolley campaigns conducted extensive horizontal and vertical excavations, especially on the northern end of the mound, called the royal precinct. The expedition uncovered archives, temples, palaces, administrative buildings, and other extraordinary architectural monuments ranging in date from the Middle to the Late Bronze Age. Sophisticated metallurgy, glass, faience, ivory carving, and especially bronzes characterize the prestige commodities produced in the workshops of Alalakh, while interregional trading networks facilitated the transport of materials across great distances. The ongoing work at Alalakh has concentrated on further fine-tuning the problematic chronologies of the second millennium B.C. At the same time, broad horizontal exposures have uncovered evidence of a city and its material culture functioning as the capital of a smaller regional state called Mukish.

Perhaps the greatest contribution of the work at Alalakh has been the historical information provided by the discovery of extensive royal cuneiform-tablet archives—written in Akkadian, Sumerian, and Hurrian—as well as inscribed materials in Hittite. The texts revealed a Near East that, during the early second millennium B.C., was the locus of a remarkable economic and political tableau. A kaleidoscope of changing political affiliations—Amorite, Egyptian, Hurro-Mitanni, and Hittite—nurtured a fusion of influences on the indigenous traditions of architecture and material culture. An exquisitely sculpted diorite head with inlaid eyes (fig. 64) exemplifies the local sculptural style during the time Alalakh was culturally and politically affiliated to the Amorite kingdom of Aleppo. It was found

Figure 64. Diorite head of a ruler. Alalakh, Level VII. Antakya Archaeological Museum 10022

197

discarded in the Level VII Temple and is thought to represent the king Yarim-Lim, who ruled sometime during the nineteenth and eighteenth centuries B.C.

After the period of Level VII, a second period of prosperity occurred in Alalakh Level IV. An archive of cuneiform tablets excavated from the palace indicates that, during the fifteenth century B.C., Alalakh was part of the Mitanni state. A seated royal figure attributed to Level IV bears a long autobiogaphical inscription of Idrimi and recounts his rise to power at Alalakh (fig. 65). A member of the royal house of Aleppo, Idrimi fled for unspecified reasons to the city of Emar along with other family members and then ventured south to Canaan, where he rose to prominence. Leading a diverse semi-nomadic contingency, including the Habiru, Idrimi captured Alalakh and then sought the endorsement of the Mitanni king, Parattarna, who made him his vassal. As the inscription of Idrimi makes explicit, Mitanni power was maintained in the region through the control of local rulers. The dominance of the Hurro-Mitanni kingdoms and Alalakh's subsequent incorporation into the Hittite Empire during the fifteenth and fourteenth centuries B.C. led to significant changes in the areas of religion, royal ideology, and governance.   KAY

1. Braidwood 1937.
2. Woolley 1953 and 1955.
3. Yener 2005.

Figure 65. Stone statue of Idrimi. Alalakh, Level IV. The Trustees of the British Museum, London
ME 130738A

119

NUZI WARE VESSEL

Ceramic
Height 21.5 cm (8½ in.); diameter 10 cm (4 in.)
Alalakh
Syro-Mitanni, 15th–14th century B.C.
The Trustees of the British Museum, London
125994

Nuzi ware—so named after the Late Bronze Age city where it was first excavated—is a type of painted luxury ware that was widely distributed during the Mitanni period. It has been found at sites from the Amuq Plain and Orontes Valley in the west to the Zab River valley in the east, as well as farther to the south in Babylonia.[1] Nuzi ware features design elements painted in white on monochromatic backgrounds that range from dark red-brown to black.

The form of the vessel illustrated here— a tall, thin-walled beaker with a small foot or button base—is most characteristic of Nuzi ware, although other vessel forms are

known. It is from a Level II house distinguished by monumental half-columns of mud brick flanking its entrance, an elite context befitting a luxury ware.[2] On the beaker, bands divide a compositional space painted with palmettes and blossoms linked by dotted, wavy bands; a band of blossoms and a row of triangles encircle the rim. Painted floral and vegetal motifs derived from the eastern Mediterranean were considered so particular to Nuzi ware from Tell Atchana (ancient Alalakh) that it was dubbed "Atchana ware" when first excavated.[3] Subsequent excavations have demonstrated, however, that the distinct floral and vegetal motifs on Nuzi ware are not restricted to Tell Atchana, although geometric motifs are more common on Nuzi ware from eastern sites, such as Tell Brak, Tell al-Rimah, and Nuzi.[4]

JME

1. Stein 1984, p. 24.
2. Woolley 1955, p. 186.
3. Ibid., p. 347.
4. Postgate, Oates, and Oates 1997, p. 55; Oates, Oates, and McDonald 1997, p. 68, and also figs. 99, 172.

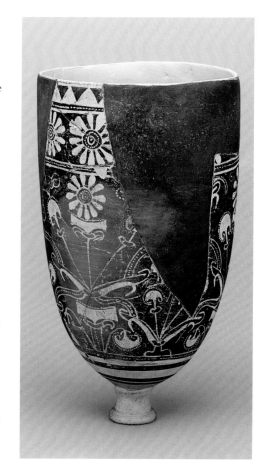

120a, b
Nuzi Ware Vessels

Ceramic

a. Height 13.3 cm (5¼ in.)

b. Height 12.4 cm (4⅞ in.)

Qatna, Royal Tomb

Late Bronze Age, Middle Syrian IA

ca. 1550–1400 B.C.

Homs Museum, Homs, Syria

MSHO2G–i1843G, MSHO26–io977

These two Nuzi ware beakers were found close to each other on the floor of the main chamber in the Royal Tomb of Qatna (see pp. 219–21).[1] They are typical examples of a pottery tradition seen throughout the region of the Mitanni Empire (see cat. no. 119). Their presence at Qatna is notable because the site is outside the area where the ware was commonly produced, suggesting that the two vessels were imports from a site in northwestern or northeastern Syria.[2]

The vessels have a small disc base, a globular body, and a short neck. The painted decoration, comprising three horizontal bands, is white on a dark background, a distinctive feature of Nuzi ware. The style of Nuzi ware suggests connections to Kamares ware from Minoan Crete (see pp. 59–60). This is evident not only in

the white-on-black scheme but also in single motifs such as the double spirals, the dotted leaves, and the dotted geometric forms.[3] The rosette with small inner circle and long petals, seen on the vessel at right, is very similar to the typical daisy-shaped rosettes of the Kamares style,[4] while the composition of the painted decoration in bands and the overlapping semicircles—representing a mountain—are characteristic features of Near Eastern art. Nuzi ware thus demonstrates the hybridity of Near Eastern art in the Late Bronze Age.

Interestingly, Kamares ware dates to the Middle Minoan II period (ca. 1850–1750 B.C.) and is thus Middle Bronze in date, while Nuzi ware first appears at the beginning of the Late Bronze Age. Both examples from Qatna can be attributed to the Early Mitanni type of Nuzi ware, datable to the Middle Syrian IA period (ca. 1550–1400 B.C.).[5] The apparent discrepancy can best be explained by the fact that Kamares ware vessels were imported during the Middle Bronze Age to the Levant (see cat. no. 32),[6] where they were likely treasured—and thus preserved—for their exotic appearance.[7]   PP

1. Dohmann-Pfälzner and Pfälzner 2006, pp. 104–5, fig. 33.
2. The same interpretation can apply to the rare appearance of Nuzi ware at Hama,

situated 30 kilometers to the northwest of Qatna (see Mazzoni 2002, pp. 132–33).
3. Compare: Schiering 1998, pls. 6:1 (dotted background), 6:5, 52:2 (dotted concave shapes), 27:3 (dotted leaves), 14:2+3, 15:1, 42:2, 52:2, 55:1–2 (spirals); all cited parallels date to the Middle Minoan IIB period.
4. S. Marinatos and Hirmer 1973, pls. 20a, 21; Schiering 1998, pl. 6:5; C. Hattler in *Im Labyrinth des Minos* 2000, p. 279, no. 181, p. 280, no. 186.
5. See Pfälzner 2007d; Dohmann-Pfälzner and Pfälzner 2006, pp. 104–5.
6. Kamares ware imports to the Levant are attested at Byblos (*Liban: L'autre rive* 1998, p. 96) and Ugarit (Caubet in *Im Labyrinth des Minos* 2000, p. 319, no. 305).
7. This idea is supported by the discovery of a Kamares ware vessel in a tomb at Ugarit, whose last phase of use dates from the fifteenth and fourteenth centuries B.C. (*Im Labyrinth des Minos* 2000, p. 319).

120a

120b

KASSITE BABYLONIA

JEAN M. EVANS

The Kassites ruled over southern Mesopotamia for nearly 450 years (ca. 1595–1155 B.C.), longer than any other dynasty in history. During the Kassite period, the concept of Babylonia—the land of Babylon—was established, and the Kassites made Babylonia into a major power. The diplomatic language of the time was Babylonian Akkadian, and the Kassites corresponded with the Egyptian, Hittite, and Assyrian courts. Diplomatic marriages were negotiated, and lavish gifts were exchanged. The Kassites undertook extensive building programs in important Babylonian cities and founded the royal city of Dur-Kurigalzu.

The Kassite language is not related to any known language and is largely preserved through names: no complete Kassite texts have survived, although some Kassite words appear in other texts and two Akkadian-Kassite word lists exist.[1] It is believed that the Kassites entered Babylonia from the Zagros Mountains of western Iran, but their homeland has not been identified. They are first documented during the eighteenth century B.C. in northern Babylonia—particularly around Sippar—as well as in the Middle Euphrates region. When Babylon fell to the Hittites in 1595 B.C., the Kassites took advantage of the power vacuum. The details of their rise to power are little understood, however, because the sixteenth and fifteenth centuries B.C. are poorly known in the Near East. Archaeological and textual evidence for the Kassites is particularly rich for the fourteenth and thirteenth centuries B.C. By then, the Kassites controlled all of Babylonia and regions beyond, including ancient Dilmun (Bahrain) in the Persian Gulf.[2]

Figure 66. Molded brick facade of the Temple of Inanna, Uruk, E-anna Precinct. Kassite period, reign of Kara-indash. Staatliche Museen zu Berlin, Vorderasiatisches Museum VA 10 983

Distinctly Kassite religious traditions are largely unknown, although at least one Kassite king received coronation rites at Babylon in the shrine of the Kassite mountain gods Shuqamuna and Shumaliya. Instead, the Kassite rulers strongly assimilated Babylonian culture.[3] The city of Babylon remained the most important political, religious, and commercial center of Babylonia, and the claim of an early Kassite king—possibly a scribal forgery—to have recovered the cult statue of Marduk and reinstalled it at Babylon suggests how closely the Kassite rulers observed and respected Babylonian traditions.[4] The ideology of Kassite rule over a unified Babylonian territory was bolstered by the rebuilding of earlier temples, and older architectural forms thus persisted. The Kassites rebuilt the Temple of Inanna and other temples in the great holy city of Nippur. Because the city had been abandoned for a period of time, these temples may have been "excavated" by the Kassites in order to locate and identify them for rebuilding.[5]

At Uruk, the new Temple of Inanna built by Kara-indash (ca. 1415 B.C.)—comprising a long cella with the entrance in the short wall opposite the altar—is one important exception to this practice, although it is nevertheless situated within the long-standing E-anna precinct at Uruk.[6] The remarkably well-preserved facade of the temple (fig. 66) is built of baked mud brick molded to form life-size deities set in niches; some fragments still show traces of paint. Identified as mountain and water gods by the patterns on their garments, the male and female deities hold vases from which water flows, recalling both earlier imagery (cat. no. 7) and Kassite cylinder seals (cat. no. 177a, b). The streams of water flow horizontally over to the buttresses, then well up and fall to the groundline, along which stelae are perhaps meant to be represented. The composition is framed by a pattern of raised circles. This type of exterior architectural embellishment appears earlier in unbaked mud-brick examples and continues a few centuries later at the site of Susa, perhaps transmitted there after the Elamite sack of Babylonia in 1155 B.C.[7] These second-millennium B.C. examples are the forerunners of the glazed bricks of the Ishtar Gate and Processional Way of Nebuchadnezzar II (ca. 604–562 B.C.) at Babylon, and of the Achaemenid palace of Darius (522–486 B.C.) at Susa.

Situated some 30 kilometers northwest of Baghdad, Dur-Kurigalzu ("Fortress of Kurigalzu") was probably founded by Kurigalzu I (ca. 1390 B.C.), although there was a later ruler of the same name (Kurigalzu II; ca. 1332–1308 B.C.). In addition to being a royal residence, Dur-Kurigalzu likely had a defensive purpose, safeguarding access to routes through the Diyala region that linked Babylonia with the Iranian Plateau and beyond. It was via this Kassite-dominated network that, for example, horses from the Iranian mountains and lapis lazuli from Afghanistan were obtained and distributed across the Near East (see map on pp. xxii–xxiii).[8] Excavations at Dur-Kurigalzu uncovered a vast palatial and administrative complex as well as a religious quarter dominated by a ziggurat.[9] Subsequent kings rebuilt and used the site until it was destroyed

Figure 67. Terracotta figure of a lioness. Dur-Kurigalzu, Palace. Kassite period. Iraq Museum, Baghdad IM 50920

sometime in the first half of the twelfth century B.C., possibly coinciding with the end of Kassite rule.

Four building levels of the palace, which consists of rooms grouped around a series of courtyards, were excavated; several elaborately vaulted rooms were perhaps meant for storage. In one wing of the latest level of the Dur-Kurigalzu palace, wall paintings at the doorways depict processions of male figures.[10] The procession motif was a traditional subject—preserved in a rare example of wall painting dating to about 3000 B.C.—that continued into the Neo-Assyrian period.[11] Other painting fragments rendered in shades of red, cobalt blue, dark blue, yellow, white, and black depict fruit clusters, rosettes, and other floral motifs, as well as guilloche, chevron, and geometric patterns.[12]

Located about 1 kilometer southeast of the palace, the ziggurat today rises some 57 meters above the plain (fig. 49). It is reinforced with a baked-brick facing; reed matting is also embedded in sand and gravel at every eighth or ninth course of mud brick, and plaited reed ropes some 10 centimeters in diameter are periodically laid side to side through the structure.[13] The ziggurat is located within a complex of courts surrounded by long, narrow rooms. Although the construction method of the ziggurat is unique, the overall plan of the complex resembles the sacred precinct at Ur, which Kurigalzu I likely restored.

The finds from the Dur-Kurigalzu palace represent the extent of our knowledge of Kassite palatial arts. Among the items recovered are fragments of monumental sculpture and mosaic glass vessels; animal figures of frit, bone, and terracotta; a relief-carved stone mace head; a gold bracelet with granulation and triangular inlays of blue paste; and other gold jewelry and ornaments. A small lioness or hyena (fig. 67) and a male head from Dur-Kurigalzu, both with traces of paint preserved, reflect the continued popularity of terracotta representations in Babylonia, and their subtle modeling shows a familiarity with the medium. Whether such a style originated in Babylonia proper or reflects international contact remains an open question. Egyptian influence has been suggested, however, for a finely rendered vulture of white paste inlay belonging to a fragmentary mosaic-glass vessel inlaid also with stars and circles.[14] Exchange with the west is exemplified by an oxhide ingot (see cat. no. 185).

By the reign of Kara-indash (ca. 1415 B.C.), envoys and gifts were being exchanged with the Egyptian court. When Kurigalzu I succeeded Kara-indash, Babylonia was receiving large amounts of gold from Egypt, and a Kassite princess was married to Amenhotep III (1390–1352 B.C.). Kassite diplomatic relations are best documented through the exchange of royal gifts chronicled in fourteen Amarna Letters dating to the reigns of Kadashman-Enlil I (ca. 1370 B.C.) and Burnaburiash II (ca. 1359–1333 B.C.; cat. no. 121). Protocol required elaborate salutations in which inquiries were made after the royal household, including family members, courtiers, troops, and even the king's horses and chariots. Diplomatic marriages accompanied by extensive bridal gifts and dowries were primary concerns. During the reign of Burnaburiash II, the Kassites were also linked by marriage to the Hittite and Assyrian courts.

Finished items such as ivory boxes, animal sculpture, ebony furniture embellished with ivory and gold, and jewelry were exchanged—many as greeting gifts—between the Egyptian and Kassite courts. Egyptian pharaohs repeatedly requested precious materials, including great quantities of lapis lazuli. Across the entire Near East, Babylonian horses, textiles, and chariots were in great demand. The skills of Babylonian physicians were held in high esteem, and Babylonian doctors as well as conjurers and sculptors were requested by the Hittite court.[15] A Kassite origin has been suggested for fragmentary glass beakers excavated in a later context at Hasanlu, Iran, apparently preserved there as heirlooms (fig. 116).[16]

The Kassite seals of lapis lazuli in the Theban Treasure (cat. no. 177a–c) might represent a standard type of diplomatic gift.[17] Two of these seals are the best examples of a distinct Kassite glyptic style with compositions that depict water or mountain deities with flowing vases; stylized trees sometimes complete the composition. Featuring elements related to Mitanni and Middle Assyrian seals, the Kassite seals also bear elements derived from Egyptian and possibly Aegean art.[18] By contrast, a direct descendant of Old Babylonian cylinder seals is represented by a second Kassite style of cylinder-seal carving in which elongated figures occupy a narrow compositional space dominated by extensive prayers inscribed in vertical columns (see discussion in cat. no. 231a, b).

Despite the international milieu in which Kassite royalty circulated, a distinctly Babylonian culture thrived under Kassite rule. Hard, polished stones inscribed and carved in relief with divine symbols are a Babylonian type of monument that began in the Kassite period and continued into the first millennium B.C. (cat. no. 122).[19] They have long been referred to as boundary or *kudurru* ("border," "boundary") stones because many of their inscriptions describe the boundaries of a royal land grant. In the inscriptions, however, these stone monuments are actually called *naru* ("stele," "monument").[20] The use of relief carving on stone for administrative documents concerning the sale or transfer of land is first attested about 3000 B.C.[21] The symbolic representational system depicted on these Babylonian stelae, however, is new and may have been developed for the system of royal land grants formulated under Kassite rule and commemorated in the majority of the inscriptions on the stelae.[22] Likely set up in temples, their irregular, boulder-like form was perhaps intended to evoke the actual fieldstones that would have marked boundaries.[23]

Babylonian scribal activity flourished under the Kassite dynasty and had a great impact on the Near East. Traditional learning was preserved from earlier periods, and distinct Babylonian genres of omen, magical, medical, and other texts were compiled into reference works. In courts across the Near East, Babylonian literary texts were preserved, studied, and imitated. The importance of second-millennium B.C. Babylonian scribes was acknowledged in the first millennium B.C., and many of the literary works found in the great libraries of the Neo-Assyrian rulers are copies of the texts that were compiled during the Kassite period.[24]

Clashes with Assyria and then Elam led to the downfall of the Kassites. The expansion of Assyria in the thirteenth century B.C. culminated in a successful attack by Tukulti-Ninurta I, who installed Assyrian governors in Babylonia for a brief time. After the death of Marduk-apla-iddina (ca. 1171–1159 B.C.), the Assyrians, under Ashur-dan I (ca. 1178–1133 B.C.), again raided Babylonia. The Elamites seized this opportunity to claim Babylonia for themselves. The Elamite king Shutruk-Nahunte (ca. 1185–1155 B.C.), who had married a Kassite princess, declared himself the legitimate ruler of Babylonia. The Elamite armies ransacked Babylonia, but fierce opposition continued for another three years. In 1155 B.C., the last Kassite king was taken to Elam and the Kassite dynasty came to an end.

1. Van de Mieroop 2003, p. 163.
2. Potts 1990, pp. 298–314.
3. Brinkman 1976; Brinkman 1976–80.
4. Kuhrt 1995, p. 338; J. Oates 2005, p. 112; P. Collins 2008.
5. Gibson 1992, pp. 44–45; Gibson 1993, pp. 8–9.
6. Heinrich 1982, pp. 221–22.
7. Harper in *Royal City of Susa* 1992, no. 88.
8. Kuhrt 1995, p. 341.
9. Baqir 1944; Baqir 1945; Baqir 1946.
10. Tomabechi 1983. Baqir (1946, p. 81) describes evidence for similar paintings in an earlier level.
11. Lloyd and Safar 1943, p. 143.
12. Baqir 1945, pp. 7, 14; Baqir 1946, p. 80.
13. Baqir 1944, p. 6.
14. Porada 1952, p. 185.
15. Zaccagnini 1983, p. 251.
16. Marcus 1991.
17. Porada 1981–82, pp. 68–70.
18. Porada 1948, pp. 63–65; Porada 1952, p. 186; Matthews 1990, p. 55.
19. Bahrani 2007, pp. 162–68.
20. Slanski 2000, p. 96.
21. D. Hansen 1975, no. 74.
22. Sommerfeld 1995, p. 920; Slanski 2000, p. 98; Bahrani 2007, pp. 162–68.
23. Buccellati 1994; Slanski 2000, pp. 96–97; Bahrani 2007, pp. 162–68.
24. Van de Mieroop 2003, p. 167.

back to Egypt was not imposing enough:

With Haya [the Egyptian ambassador] there are 5 chariots. Are they going to take her to you in 5 chariots? Should I in these circumstances allow her to be brought to you [from m]y [house], my neighboring kings [would say], "They have transported the daughter of a Great King [t]o Egypt in 5 char[iots]."[1]

JM

1. EA 11: 18–22, translated in Moran 1992, p. 21.

122
KUDURRU OF NAZI-MARUTTASH

Black limestone
Height 50 cm (19¾ in.); width 22 cm (8⅝ in.)
Susa
Kassite, reign of Marduk-apla-iddina I,
ca. 1171–1159 B.C.
Musée du Louvre, Paris, Département des
Antiquités Orientales sb21

Although discovered in Susa, in southwestern Iran, this stele, in the form of a large stone, belongs to the category of typically Babylonian monuments produced between the fourteenth and the seventh century B.C. and designated by the Akkadian term *kudurru*, which means "boundary," "limit," and by extension "boundary stone."[1] These stelae bear relief-carved decoration that represents deities in symbolic form and inscriptions that record gifts of lands or tax exemptions granted by the ruler to members of his family or to high dignitaries. Long believed to have been erected in the fields to mark property boundaries, studies now show that they were placed in temples.

The inscription on the *kudurru* of Nazi-Maruttash, which covers both sides of the stone, records a donation of lands to the god Marduk, granted by the Kassite king Nazi-Maruttash (ca. 1307–1282 B.C.). A certain Kashakti-shugab, whose function is not specified, also receives land. As is typical, the detailed description of the estates is followed by a series of ritual curses against anyone who would dare contest the legitimacy of the title deeds. The text clearly makes reference to the

121

121
AMARNA LETTER: THE BETROTHAL OF BURNABURIASH'S DAUGHTER

Clay
Height 14 cm (5½ in.); width 9.3 cm (3⅝ in.)
Tell el-Amarna
New Kingdom, Dynasty 18,
ca. 1359–1333 B.C.
Staatliche Museen zu Berlin,
Vorderasiatisches Museum VAT151 + 1878

Of the correspondence between Babylonia and Egypt, only fourteen texts have survived from the archives at Tell el-Amarna. The return messages have not been uncovered. In this letter, the Babylonian king Burnaburiash II (ca. 1359–1333 B.C.) sought to make his royal "brother" in Egypt, Amenhotep IV (Akhenaten) indebted to him through a policy of dynastic marriage. He offered his daughter as a bride, and the exchange of gifts ensued.

Amenhotep III, father of Amenhotep IV, had already married a princess from Babylonia. Accordingly, in this tablet Burnaburiash speaks of generous presents of gold previously received by his father, Kurigalzu, which had occasioned reciprocal gifts of lapis lazuli. Burnaburiash is concerned both for the welfare of his daughter and for his international reputation, and he complains that the entourage sent to Babylon to accompany the bride

one side of the stone, while Marduk's spade appears only on the third register, preceding the emblems of the war gods Ninurta, Nergal, and Zababa. The three celestial deities—Sin, the moon god; Shamash, the sun god; and Ishtar, the planet Venus—hover over the decoration on the other side, which is dominated by Gula, the goddess of medicine, depicted seated on a throne that rests on a dog. Although Gula dispenses cures, she can also spread terrible diseases. It is in this capacity that she is invoked in ritual curses and appears on the *kudurru* stones, where she is one of the few deities depicted in anthropomorphic form.

Two texts carved at the base of each side indicate that this *kudurru* is in fact a copy, fashioned during the reign of Marduk-apla-iddina I (ca. 1171–1159 B.C.), after a stele of clay that was made at the time of Nazi-Maruttash's gift and placed before the god. The clay stele was destroyed when a wall collapsed, and several generations later the heir of the first beneficiary made a stone replica, in turn erecting it before the gods and thus consolidating his title to the property. The inscription is evidence that, before the appearance of *kudurru* stones, there were clay monuments that fulfilled the same function.[3]

The *kudurru* of Nazi-Maruttash was unearthed at Susa in 1898 during the excavations of the French archaeological mission. It was one of the first monuments of this type to be discovered at this site, which unexpectedly yielded nearly fifty *kudurru* stones—approximately half the extant corpus. Part of the spoils of Shutruk-Nahunte, king of Elam (ca. 1190–1155 B.C.), they were carted back from the cities of northern Mesopotamia, which he had plundered many times. Apparently, these stelae were considered no less important as war trophies than monuments as prestigious as the Stele of Naram-Sin or the Stele of Hammurabi, also taken to Susa.   FD

122, alternate view

complementary role of the imprecations and the carved decoration, both of which contribute toward placing the legal instrument of donation under the protection of the gods, and thus guaranteeing its perpetuity. Seventeen deities are invoked, some with descriptions of their emblems, and seventeen gods and goddesses are represented, all but one in symbolic form.

While the correspondence between text and image is not exact, the elements provided by the inscription have allowed the symbols to be identified.[2] Their arrangement probably reflects both the hierarchy of the pantheon and the order of the cosmos. Thus the major deities—Anu, god of the heavens, and Enlil, god of air, wind, and storms, are represented at the top of

1. For further reference, see de Morgan 1900, vol. 1, pp. 170–72, pls. 14, 15; Scheil 1900, pp. 86–92, pls. XVI–XIX; Brinkman 1976, p. 265, U.2.19; Seidl 1989, no. 48, pl. 19; and Slanski 2003, pp. 22–23, 41, 128–30, 188–89.
2. Seidl 1989, pp. 33–35; Slanski 2003, pp. 129–30.
3. Brinkman 1980–83, p. 268.

THE MIDDLE ASSYRIAN PERIOD

JEAN M. EVANS

The tripartite division of Assyrian history into Old, Middle, and Neo-Assyrian is a modern construction (for the Old Assyrian period, see pp. 70–73). The Assyrians chronicled their own history as a succession of rulers lasting until the defeat of the Assyrian empire by the Babylonians in 612 B.C. The Middle Assyrian period covers the fourteenth to the eleventh century B.C., beginning with Assyria's rise after the collapse of the Mitanni state and ending with the decline of Assyria and the second dark age of the second millennium B.C. During the Middle Assyrian period, Assyria became a substantial territorial state and maintained international contacts with Egypt, Hittite Anatolia, and Kassite Babylonia.

Assyria corresponds roughly to the northern half of modern-day Iraq—Babylonia encompasses the southern half—and its name reflects that of its capital city, Ashur. Situated on a rocky plateau overlooking the Tigris River to the east, the city was enclosed by extensive fortifications, which allowed approach from the west via several gates. Although Ashur served only rarely during its long history as the sole residence of the Assyrian rulers, the city was of great religious importance as the home of the state god, Ashur.[1] Throughout Assyrian history, the temples and palaces of the capital were constantly rebuilt and maintained, and new ones were added.

The centuries in Assyria between the reigns of Ishme-Dagan I (ca. 1775 B.C.) and Ashur-uballit I (ca. 1363–1328 B.C.) are poorly documented. When Mitanni power was at its height, Assyria seems to have been restricted to the area immediately surrounding Ashur. As recorded in the treaty between the Mitanni king Shattiwaza and the Hittite king Suppiluliuma, an earlier Mitanni king, Saushtatar, had sacked Ashur and taken booty—including a silver and gold door for his palace—to his capital, Washshukanni.[2] When Hittite campaigns debilitated the Mitanni state in the second half of the fourteenth century B.C., Ashur-uballit I established Assyria as an independent regional power. Rich agricultural land north and east of Ashur came under Assyrian control: this was the Assyrian heartland, bordered by the Taurus Mountains to the north and the Upper Zab River to the east.

Two letters from Ashur-uballit I—the first Assyrian ruler to call himself "king of Assyria"—have survived among the Amarna Letters.[3] In one of them, he addresses the king of Egypt as "brother." This seems to have been controversial, however, as the Kassite king Burnaburiash II (ca. 1359–1333 B.C.) claimed that Assyria was his vassal state. Although there is some debate over their stature on the international stage, the Assyrian rulers certainly were among the so-called Great Kings. Moreover, the Assyrian princess Muballitat-sherua married Burnaburiash II during the reign of Ashur-uballit I, and their son Kara-hardash succeeded his father to the Kassite throne. When Kara-hardash was murdered by a usurper, Ashur-uballit I crushed the revolt and installed Kurigalzu II (1332–1308 B.C.).

After the death of Ashur-uballit I, subsequent rulers struggled to maintain an international presence. Under the rule of three successive kings spanning the thirteenth century B.C., Assyria once again rose to prominence: Adad-nirari I (ca. 1305–1274 B.C.), Shalmaneser I (ca. 1273–1244 B.C.), and Tukulti-Ninurta I (ca. 1243–1207 B.C.). In the first half of that century, the declining Mitanni state was ultimately destroyed by Assyrian aggression. Adad-nirari I marched west and conquered a succession of Mitanni cities, including the capitals of Washshukanni and Taide, creating an empire that stretched to the Euphrates River.[4] Shalmaneser I put down a rebellion by the last known Mitanni king, Shattuara II, who had been supported by the Hittites, and the eastern half of Hanigalbat—as the Assyrians called Mitanni—was annexed.[5]

In the upper Khabur River valley, Middle Assyrian remains have been excavated at several sites that had been Mitanni centers, including Tell Barri, Tell Brak, Tell Chuera, and Tell Fakhariya, as well as Tell al-Hamidiya, which has been identified as the Mitanni royal city of Taide.[6] Adad-nirari I boasted that during the conquest of Taide, he sent the contents of its palace to Ashur and subsequently built his own palace in the former Mitanni capital,[7] and excavations at the site have uncovered the remains of a Middle Assyrian palace built directly over a destroyed Mitanni palace.[8] Traces of paintings in black, red, yellow, and blue applied to whitewashed walls were discovered among the Middle Assyrian debris.[9]

Recent excavations have furnished an abundance of new data on the transformation of Hanigalbat under Middle Assyrian rule, when Assyrian governors were installed in centers from which they administered the surrounding province.[10] One such governor was installed on the lower Khabur River at Dur-Katlimmu (Tell Sheikh Hamad), where a large Middle Assyrian building with workshop areas and storerooms for grain was excavated.[11] An administrative archive of more than 550 tablets recovered in the debris covers a wide geographic horizon and dates to the reigns of Shalmaneser I and Tukulti-Ninurta I.[12] Although Dur-Katlimmu had been occupied by the Mitanni, it was located away from the traditional Mitanni centers on the upper Khabur River and was thus relatively close to Ashur; regular road stations along the route to Ashur have been identified.[13] Dur-Katlimmu also had an importance that extended beyond its own province, for the archive indicates that Ashur-iddin, the grand vizier and king of Hanigalbat, resided there for at least a short period of time.

Ashur-iddin was also the owner of a fortified agricultural estate (*dunnu*) recently excavated at Tell Sabi Abyad, one of a series of Middle Assyrian settlements in the Balikh River valley that provided a buffer against the Hittites.[14] It was inherited by his son, Ili-pada, who succeeded his father as the grand vizier and king of Hanigalbat in the late thirteenth century B.C.[15] Located at the summit of the mound, the *dunnu* centers on a well-preserved building, some 60 meters square, that incorporates an earlier Mitanni tower. An outer fortification wall, originally some 5 to 6 meters high, protected the building; a dry moat some 4 meters wide ran roughly parallel to the wall and provided an additional line of defense.[16] The owners seem to have visited only periodically. The *dunnu* was managed instead by chief stewards, including Tammitte, whose name is preserved on cuneiform tablets and on surviving impressions of his cylinder seal.[17] Some 400 Middle Assyrian tablets were recovered and indicate that the settlement also functioned variously as a military outpost, administrative center, customs office, and even a jail.[18]

Assyrian campaigns extended into Hittite Anatolia during the reign of Tukulti-Ninurta I (ca. 1243–1207 B.C.), and clashes with Babylonia culminated in the sack of Babylon. Tukulti-Ninurta I boasted that he captured Kashtiliashu, the Kassite king, and "trod with my feet upon his lordly neck as though it were a footstool. Bound I brought him as a captive into the presence of Ashur my lord."[19] A letter from the Dur-Katlimmu archive tempers the severity of this account: it suggests that the Kassite king and his entourage even visited Hanigalbat, where an elaborate reception was planned for them.[20] Nevertheless, in his conquest of Babylon, Tukulti-Ninurta I destroyed the city walls and seized numerous cuneiform tablets, which likely formed the foundations for an Assyrian royal library. Tukulti-Ninurta I's victory was commemorated as a major triumph in an Assyrian epic that survives in at least three separate editions, the latest of which was found in the Neo-Assyrian library of Ashurbanipal at Nineveh.[21]

Figure 68. Reconstruction drawing of wall painting. Kar-Tukulti-Ninurta, Palace. Middle Assyrian period.

Figure 69. Incised ivory pyxis. Ashur, Tomb 45. Middle Assyrian period. Staatliche Museen zu Berlin, Vorderasiatisches Museum VA ASS 1099 (ASS 14630 ao)

After his defeat of Babylonia, Tukulti-Ninurta I embarked on ambitious building programs. According to the epic, part of the booty from his Babylonian campaign was used for the decoration of Assyrian temples.[22] At Ashur, Tukulti-Ninurta I dug a moat around the city, rebuilt the Temple of Ishtar, and began construction of a palace. This last project was abandoned, however, and Tukulti-Ninurta I instead founded a new short-lived capital and cult residence of the god Ashur at Kar-Tukulti-Ninurta ("the harbor of Tukulti-Ninurta"), some 3 kilometers north of Ashur on the opposite bank of the Tigris River. Kar-Tukulti-Ninurta was first excavated for only a few months from 1913 to 1914.[23] Subsequent excavations and an archaeological survey conducted from 1986 to 1989 indicated that the city was much larger than had been suggested by the earlier research.[24] A substantial wall with at least four gates protected an official district with a massive palace, situated directly on the Tigris River, and a ziggurat complex dedicated to Ashur.

Glazed tiles in brilliant colors and fragmentary wall paintings were recovered at Kar-Tukulti-Ninurta. One reconstructed drawing of painting fragments from the palace depicts rosettes, palmettes, and other floral motifs forming bands that frame large rectangular compositional spaces in which recumbent caprids and stylized trees are represented (fig. 68).[25] According to a later chronicle, Tukulti-Ninurta I was assassinated by his own son, with the backing of Assyrian nobility. Kar-Tukulti-Ninurta ceased to be the Assyrian capital, and the kings once again ruled from Ashur (cat. no. 230). Parts of Kar-Tukulti-Ninurta nevertheless continued to be inhabited.

The arts of Assyria are still best known by the examples from Ashur (cat. nos. 123, 124, 126), although recent excavations in the Khabur and the Balikh River valleys have produced fine examples of Middle Assyrian glyptic and luxury grave goods, as well as evidence of wall paintings. Although royal Assyrian seals of the fourteenth century B.C. reflect Mitanni iconography, they also established a precision of line and clarity of form that would become characteristically Middle

Assyrian (cat. no. 125a, b). Dynamically posed animals and sparse spatial compositions also define the distinctly Middle Assyrian glyptic style.[26] The popularity of animal-combat themes during the thirteenth and twelfth centuries B.C. has been linked to contemporary political unrest and a growing militancy.[27]

Middle Assyrian artistic production balances the internationalism of its time with the emergence of a distinctly Assyrian idiom.[28] The best evidence for Middle Assyrian luxury goods at Ashur comes from Tomb 45, a private burial containing several individuals and grave goods, including ceramic and alabaster vessels, ivory objects, and jewelry of gold and semiprecious stones (cat. nos. 126, 206). A cylindrical ivory pyxis (fig. 69) from Tomb 45, carved from a section of tusk, is incised with a frieze of gazelles striding amid fruiting date palms alternating with conifers laden with cones as well as cocks and possibly hens perched on the branches. The sensitive treatment of animals and the interest in depicting natural settings are characteristic of Middle Assyrian art.[29] Date palms and conifers also alternate in garden scenes on later Neo-Assyrian reliefs, with the conifer signifying the Assyrian landscape and the fruiting date palm foreign lands where such trees thrived, such as Babylonia and Elam.[30] Tomb 45 may have belonged to the high-ranking family of an official named Babu-aha-iddina, who was active in the international affairs of Assyria during the reign of Shalmaneser I.

The assassination of Tukulti-Ninurta I was followed by a temporary decline in the power of Assyria, coinciding with the fall of the Kassites in Babylonia and lasting until the reign of Ashur-resha-ishi (ca. 1132–1115 B.C.). Remembered as one of the greatest kings in Assyrian history, Tiglath-pileser I (ca. 1114–1076 B.C.) aggressively campaigned north to Lake Van, west to the Mediterranean, and south into Babylonia. In his time, royal inscriptions were written in the standard form known as the annals, which would be maintained until the end of the Assyrian empire. The annals record military campaigns year by year, with lengthy royal epithets and accounts of building activities inserted between them. The annals of Tiglath-pileser I became famous again in modern times when they were used in 1857 as the test case by which the Royal Asiatic Society proved that Babylonian cuneiform had been deciphered.[31]

The hunting expeditions of Tiglath-pileser I are also chronicled in the annals. In one expedition in Upper Mesopotamia, the ruler boasts that he killed ten elephants and captured four more. Elephants are well documented in the region at that time. Egyptian sources state that Thutmose III hunted elephants in the Euphrates River valley, and the left femur of an elephant was discovered in the Middle Assyrian *dunnu* at Tell Sabi Abyad.[33] Basalt statues flanking the entrance to the palace of Tiglath-pileser I also included a replica of a *nahiru* sea creature, which the ruler slaughtered with his own harpoon.[32]

Under Ashur-bel-kala (ca. 1073–1056 B.C.), Assyria continued to play a role in international politics, and the Egyptian king sent gifts, including a crocodile, a monkey, and possibly a hippopotamus.[34] By the middle of the eleventh century B.C., however, Aramean tribal groups had settled in northern Syria and the Levant, and Assyria was reduced to its heartland. With the rise of the Neo-Assyrian empire in the first millennium B.C., Assyria once again encompassed a vast territory, and the many aspects of Assyrian identity and culture that had emerged in the Middle Assyrian period continued to thrive.

1. Lambert 1983.
2. Kuhrt 1995, pp. 292–93.
3. EA 15, EA 16, translated in Moran 1992.
4. Grayson 1987, A.O.76.1, A.O.76.3.

5. Harrak 1987.
6. For Tell Brak, Oates, Oates, and McDonald 1997; for Tell Barri, Pecorella 1998; for Tell Chuera, Orthmann 1995; for Tell Fakhariya, Pruss and Bagdo 2002; for Tell al-Hamidiya, Kühne 1984. For the identification of Tell al-Hamidiya as Taide, see also Röllig 1983; V. Haas and Wäfler 1985, pp. 53–76.
7. Grayson 1987, A.O.76.3, A.O.76.4, A.O.76.22; Reade 2004, p. 257.
8. Eichler and Wäfler 1990, pp. 241–54.
9. Ibid., p. 252.
10. Akkermans and Rossmeisl 1990, pp. 35–36; Kühne 2000; Akkermans and Schwartz 2003, pp. 348–50.
11. Kühne 1983–84, p. 168.
12. Cancik-Kirschbaum 1996, pp. 9–18; Kühne 2000, p. 271.
13. Kühne 2000, pp. 273–74.
14. Akkermans and Rossmeisl 1990; Akkermans, Limpens, and Spoor 1993; Wiggermann 2000; Akkermans 2006.
15. Jakob 2003, pp. 59–63, just as Ashur-iddin had succeeded his own father to this high royal office.
16. Akkermans 2006, p. 203.
17. Akkermans and Wiggermann 1999.
18. Wiggermann 2000, pp. 174–75; Akkermans 2006, p. 201.
19. Grayson 1987, A.O.78.5.
20. Cancik-Kirschbaum 1996, pp. 147–53, but see also Luppert-Barnard 2001, p. 58 n. 6.
21. Machinist 1978, p. 17.
22. Lambert 1957–58; Machinist 1978.
23. Andrae 1925; Eickhoff 1985.
24. Dittman 1992, pp. 310–11.
25. Wartke in *Assyrian Origins* 1995, no. 74a–c.
26. Venit 1986.
27. Ibid.; Matthews 1990.
28. Aruz in *Assyrian Origins* 1995, no. 45; Feldman 2006a; Feldman 2006b.
29. Aruz in *Assyrian Origins* 1995, no. 45.
30. P. Collins 2006, p. 102, who also suggests a relationship on the pyxis between the conifer and masculinity and date palms and femininity.
31. Grayson 1991, p. 7.
32. Ibid., A.O.87.4.
33. Akkermans and Rossmeisl 1990, p. 20.
34. Kuhrt 1995, p. 361.

123
CULT PEDESTAL OF THE GOD NUSKA

Alabaster
Height 60 cm (23⅝ in.); width 57 cm (22½ in.)
Ashur, Temple of Ishtar
Middle Assyrian, reign of Tukulti-Ninurta I,
ca. 1243–1207 B.C.
Staatliche Museen zu Berlin,
Vorderasiatisches Museum VA8146

One of the canonical monuments of the ancient Near East, this cult pedestal originally would have held an image or symbol of a deity. The stepped base supports the pedestal proper, which takes the form of a rectangle terminating in rounded, protruding corners on which rosettes are carved. Two representations of Tukulti-Ninurta I, holding the royal scepter, approach a pedestal resembling the one on which the scene is carved. Both figures wear a tunic and mantle comparable to that worn by later Neo-Assyrian kings. Both extend their right forefinger toward the object of veneration, divine symbols plausibly interpreted as a tablet and stylus.[1] Through the double representation of the royal figure, approaching and kneeling before the pedestal, the ritual of worship is performed continuously.[2]

Although the ending of the inscription has worn away, enough remains to identify the pedestal as that of Nuska, "chief vizier of Ekur, bearer of the just scepter, courtier of the gods Ashur and Enlil, who daily repeats the prayers of Tukulti-Ninurta, the king, his beloved, in the presence of the gods Ashur and Enlil and a destiny of power [for him] within Ekur [. . .]."[3] Primarily known as the god of light, Nuska was also the god of dreams. Bahrani argues that the divine symbols refer to Nuska in the latter role and perhaps signify the tablet on which the omen of destiny is inscribed.[4]

The pedestal was found along with two others—identical but lacking relief carving—in Room 6 of the Temple of Ishtar, which was built by Tukulti-Ninurta I. The temple's excavator, Walter Andrae, believed

123

that the three pedestals were originally placed in the main cult room, or cella, and had been moved for safekeeping.[5] Room 6 had been sealed, which was interpreted as a ritual burial intended to protect these sacred objects. Wherever the pedestals were originally placed, they were not meant for public display. Access to part or all of the temple—certainly the cella—was restricted. Although the cult pedestal of Nuska portrays a royal figure, its carving does not depict a public act, and this par-

ticular relationship with the divine was a prerogative that the majority of worshippers would never know.   JME

1. Muscarella in *Assyrian Origins* 1995, no. 75.
2. See Bahrani 2003, pp. 185ff.
3. After Grayson 1987, pp. 279–80; for the reading of Nuska, see Lambert 2002.
4. Bahrani 2003, p. 198.
5. Andrae 1935, pp. 57ff.

124
CONTRACT IMPRESSED WITH CYLINDER SEAL OF ERIBA-ADAD I

Clay
Height 4.4 cm (1¾ in.); width 4.3 cm (1¾ in.)
Ashur
Middle Assyrian, reign of Eriba-Adad I, ca. 1390–1364 B.C.
Staatliche Museen zu Berlin, Vorderasiatisches Museum VAT9009

124

The subject of this cuneiform tablet is a contract, and the presence of an impression from a seal of the Middle Assyrian king Eriba-Adad I indicates that it is a royal document.[1] The imagery of the seal derives from Mitanni glyptic, which favored fabulous beasts and compositions that fill the entire field (see cat. nos. 250, 251). On this seal, however, such images are translated into a Middle Assyrian idiom that drew on various sources and produced distinct glyptic styles during the fourteenth and thirteenth centuries B.C.[2]

The balanced composition on the seal of Eriba-Adad I consists of two distinct groupings of self-contained, antithetical motifs. In the first a pair of griffin-demons flank a small tree and support above their crossed wings a large winged sun disc. In the second a double-headed griffin-demon holds two griffin-demons by the hind legs. Beneath the head and forepaw of each victim is a cross. Particularly characteristic of the period are the feathers composed of tiny dots on the lower edge of the winged sun disc and on the wings of the double-headed griffin-demon.[3]

Winged griffin-demons holding up their prey by the hind legs were a feature of many glyptic compositions during the reign of Eriba-Adad I and his successor, Ashur-uballit I.[4] Examples dating to the second half of the fourteenth century B.C. display an even greater emphasis on heraldic compositions; small filler elements such as crosses are eliminated. The winged griffin-demon, added to a recut Old Babylonian seal from the Uluburun shipwreck, can be securely dated also to the fourteenth century B.C. (cat. no. 230).

The seal of Eriba-Adad I is an important chronological marker in the development of Middle Assyrian glyptic. A second major phase subsequently emerged during the reign of Adad-nirari I in the early thirteenth century B.C. (cat. no. 125a, b).[5]   JME

1. Klengel-Brandt in *Assyrian Origins* 1995, no. 66. The seal is not inscribed, but its royal owner is identified by the text of another clay tablet impressed with the same seal.
2. Matthews 1990, p. 89.
3. Klengel-Brandt in *Assyrian Origins* 1995, no. 66.
4. Collon 1987, p. 65.
5. Matthews 1990, p. 89.

125a, b

CYLINDER SEALS AND MODERN IMPRESSIONS

a. Milky chalcedony
Height 3 cm (1⅛ in.); diameter 1 cm (⅜ in.)

b. Banded agate
Height 2.8 cm (1⅛ in.); diameter 1.2 cm (½ in.)

Mesopotamia
Middle Assyrian, 13th century B.C.
The Pierpont Morgan Library, New York
Morgan seals 601, 602

One of the finest cylinder-seal styles developed in Mesopotamia in the fourteenth and thirteenth centuries B.C. in northern Assyria, where there were outstanding seal cutters at court. These artists created naturalism in the landscape elements and vitality in the modeling of figures that imparted a new sense of realism to their compositions, which perhaps reflects the general trend that characterized Egyptian and Aegean art during this period.[1] These two seals are among the most accomplished examples of Middle Assyrian glyptic of the thirteenth century B.C.[2]

One seal shows a stag leaping in a landscape.[3] A gnarled tree, perhaps an olive tree, stands on a hill; a bird perches in the flowers growing beside it. The stag, suspended in motion, descends from the hill, one hind leg held horizontal after an initial downward spring. The stylized pattern incised on the body not only depicts the animal's hide but adds a sense of corporeality. The muscles of the neck are clearly indicated and parallel the great arc that forms its outer edge. The artist who carved this stag must have been familiar with the grace and dignity of the animal. The significance of the scene is unknown. However, the word for stag in Assyrian, *lulimu*, was also an epithet for a king or a god.[4] An echo of the scene's meaning is surely to be found in a biblical text from the Song of Solomon (2:8–9), in which the bride describes her beloved:

Behold, he cometh leaping upon the mountains, skipping upon the hills. My beloved is like a roe or a young hart.

The other seal is no less remarkable, not only for the striking image of a lion attacking a mouflon but also for the beauty and complexity of the white-banded agate upon which the scene is carved.[5] Two tall straight trees and a six-pointed star set the scene. The carver has expressed the ferocity of the roaring lion through a series of arcs and curves beginning with the arc of the tail moving into the curves of the belly and back and culminating in the curve of the head in profile, the mouth open to expose sharp teeth. The mane and underbelly are delineated by a series of linear striations. The bulging muscles of the haunch provide power for the attack.

The mouflon's fear is expressed in its face as it turns its head sharply back toward its attacker and raises a foreleg in a vain attempt to escape; the haunch muscles are lean and taut.

Such extraordinary attention to detail in scenes of great artistic achievement in spite of their minute scale had not been seen in the art of Mesopotamia since the cylinder seals of the Akkadian period, nearly one thousand years earlier.[6]   SB

1. Matthews 1990, pp. 89–101, 115–17.
2. Ibid., p. 89. Only about 140 Middle Assyrian seals survive.
3. Porada 1948, pp. 68–69, pl. LXXXIV: 601.
4. *Chicago Assyrian Dictionary*, vol. 9, s.v. "lulimu," p. 241.
5. Porada 1948, pp. 68–69, pl. LXXXV: 602.
6. *Art of the First Cities* 2003, pp. 214–21, nos. 141–51, esp. no. 146.

125a

125b

126
Beads

Gold, semiprecious stones
Diameter 16.5 cm (6½ in.)
Ashur
Middle Assyrian, 14th–13th century B.C.
Staatliche Museen zu Berlin,
Vorderasiatisches Museum
VA ASS 1026–1034

During the excavation of Tomb 45 at Ashur, which contained impressive ivories (see fig. 69), stone vessels, and jewelry, more than a hundred beads came to light.[1] The majority were found loosely distributed in the silt at the bottom of the tomb, thus precluding associations with specific skeletal remains. It is likely that many beads originally formed necklaces or other items of jewelry. A selection of beads was arbitrarily combined to create this necklace, which centers on three spacer elements made of cat's-eye onyx in plain and granulated gold settings.[2] The spacers were found separately and can be assigned with certainty to one skeleton.[3] Such devices served both to organize necklaces into distinct strands and to enhance the overall design, in this case three strands graduating into two. The beads chosen to be combined with the spacers—lapis lazuli, agate, carnelian, smoky quartz, and onyx— are of different sizes and shapes. They have been arranged to augment the interplay of colors and forms, a design concept valued in the Near East and Egypt from earliest times.[4]

Evidence for assortments of beads of similar shapes and stones is found, for example, in Mitanni levels at Nuzi and Tell Chuera in northern Mesopotamia,[5] in Kassite graves at Babylon in the south and at Tell Yelki in the Hamrin,[6] and in other contexts at Ashur.[7] The great variety of forms and colors together with their symbolic associations—flies, frogs, birds, ducks[8]—strongly suggest that such beads in combination served a meaningful purpose when worn, by either the living or the dead. The use of cat's-eye onyx, a stone

that naturally resembles an eye, is linked to protective powers[9] and may be a conceptual forerunner of the "evil eye" popular today in the Middle East and eastern Mediterranean. Eye agates are specifically mentioned in the Amarna Letters in inventories of dowry jewelry and gifts from Tushratta (cat. no. 118). They were also prominently featured among the jewelry found with the Neo-Assyrian queens at Nimrud.[10]   KB

1. Haller 1954, pp. 125ff., pls. 34, 35, 36:f; Wartke 1992, pp. 111–12, figs. 7, 8, 10.
2. Nagel 1972, figs. 9, 20.
3. Wartke 1992, pp. 111–12.
4. Dubin 1987, pls. 10, 11, 21, 23.
5. Starr 1937–39, vol. 2, pls. 119, 120; Moortgat and Moortgat-Correns 1976, fig. 15.
6. Reuther 1926, pls. 47–49; Invernizzi 1980, fig. 73.
7. Haller 1954, pl. 14a.
8. Ebeling 1971, pp. 87 (s.v. "Fliege") and 118 (s.v. "Frosch"); Hilzheimer 1938, pp. 399–400 (s.v. "Ente").
9. Ebeling 1932, pp. 121 (s.v. "Apotropaeen") and 313 (s.v. "Auge"). See also Dubin 1987, pp. 307–12, for magical eye beads.
10. See Elmer-De Witt 1989, pp. 80–81.

SYRIAN ARCHAEOLOGICAL EXCAVATIONS AT QATNA

MICHEL AL-MAQDISSI

The site of Qatna (Tell Mishrifeh) stands on the eastern edge of the Syrian steppe, about 20 kilometers north of the city of Homs. It was systematically excavated at the time of the French Mandate over the course of four campaigns (1924, 1927, 1928, and 1929) by a French expedition under the direction of Du Mesnil du Buisson. Sixty-five years later, in 1994, a Syrian mission headed by the author undertook a series of surveys and surface excavations in various areas of the site. In 1996, a joint Syrian, Italian, and German mission led by Danièle Morandi Bonacossi, Peter Pfälzner, and myself undertook a new project that concentrated on the Royal Palace and a number of test pits. Since 2004, the diversity and development of these excavations led the Directorate of Antiquities and Museums to create two missions in addition to the Syrian mission: a Syrian-Italian mission codirected by Morandi Bonacossi and a Syrian-German mission codirected by Pfälzner.

The Syrian mission, under my direction, concentrated on fifteen different excavations located mainly on the western slope of the acropolis: in the Lower City, on the western and northern slopes of Lot's Cupola; at the north and west gates; and, recently, in the middle of the highest point of the acropolis, as well as to the east of the Royal Palace. Our objective was to uncover the Aramaic stratum of occupation and to establish a chronology of the development of the site. We also wished to examine work begun by Du Mesnil du Buisson in order to check the stratigraphy and dating of certain monuments.

Phases	Dating	Phases	Dating
Mishrifeh IB	Modern 19th century (village structures)	Mishrifeh VIC	Early Bronze IVB (beneath the palace) (in the foundation trenches)
Mishrifeh IA	Modern 19th century (ditches)	Mishrifeh VIB	Early Bronze IV B (soil)
Mishrifeh II	Iron III (domestic structures)	Mishrifeh VIA	Early Bronze IV B (ditches and silos)
Mishrifeh III	Iron II (domestic structures)		
Hiatus	Iron I	Mishrifeh VIIE1–A	Early Bronze IV A (domestic structures)
Mishrifeh IVB	Late Bronze II (Royal Palace)	Mishrifeh VIII	Early Bronze III–IVA (silos)
Mishrifeh IVA	Late Bronze I (palace foundations)		
Mishrifeh V	Middle Bronze I–II (sherds)	Mishrifeh IX	Early Bronze III (sherds) Virgin soil

Figure 70. Table summarizing the stratigraphic phases presented in this essay and associated with the sequence obtained in the drilling at Excavation R, courtyard of the throne room of the Royal Palace.

PHASES OF STRATIGRAPHIC OCCUPATION

Modern Period

At the surface of the excavations on the acropolis, we proceeded to clear the foundations of the modern village. The excavation occasionally turned up soundings by Du Mesnil du Buisson as well as large trenches running from the southern edge of the palace to the present-day Orthodox church.

Iron Age III

This phase of occupation, during the Iron Age, is indicated by only a few walls forming part of a domestic construction and associated with a pebble floor in Excavation C on the western slope of the site. There, we discovered some potsherds of local production and fragments of Attic ceramics imported from the Aegean.

Iron Age II

Structures from the Aramaean period were brought to light in the excavations on the Acropolis and in the Lower City, which revealed a variety of architectural vestiges. Examinations of the surface of Excavation C have uncovered a palace complex composed of a main building and sizable constructions to the north separated by a vacant area that may have connected the two. The palace has a rectangular ground plan laid around a long courtyard, with an entrance to the west and several storage areas. Its location on the western slope, facing the north gate, gives it prominence. This architectural ensemble is comparable to the palace complex at Hama, which consists of several juxtaposed buildings.

In Excavation O, at the foot of the eastern slope of the site, we found a block of structures dominated by an industrial building (which has been partially excavated), bordered to the south by a street that leads to the acropolis. The building was probably a commercial winepress, with areas for the preparation and pressing of grapes, as well as specialized structures and rooms for the storage of large jars of wine. The presence of this type of industry suggests that the Aramaean city supported a number of agricultural activities, resulting in products intended for both the local market and exportation. Other excavations around the Lower City have yielded traces of domestic architecture. The excavations of the Syrian-Italian team have brought to light other constructions that point to an intensive occupation throughout the site during this period.

In several places, levels of architectural collapse indicate a violent destruction, in some cases associated with fire. These remains are evidence of the triumphant passage of the Neo-Assyrian king Sargon II, who annexed the entire region after the fall of the kingdom of Hama in 720 B.C.

Late Bronze Age

This period involved a phase of intense urbanization. The Syrian efforts in Excavation C revealed a small palace to the south of the Royal Palace. Unfortunately, this building, one of several structures built around the palace, was in a poor state of preservation. Only part of it has been unearthed, and many elements of the public area and main entrance have disappeared as a result of erosion and the establishment of the modern village. Furthermore, this building was emptied and cleared before being abandoned during the fourteenth century B.C.

Figure 71. Aerial view of the site of Qatna.

215

Archaeological analysis has given us a clear idea of the organization of the most important part of the city, which focused around a Royal Palace (fig. 71) that was in turn surrounded by several smaller palaces having different functions: the residential South Palace, the residential East Palace (under excavation by the Syrian-Italian team), and the North Palace, which housed the high official who controlled the North Gate. The Lower City was occupied by domestic housing. This system reflects the same Late Bronze Age architectural model for palace complexes seen at Ugarit, Alalakh, and probably also at Ras Ibn Hani. The stratigraphic sequence in the palace area and at other locations documents the destruction that befell the city about 1350 B.C. at the hands of the Hittite ruler Suppiluliuma.

A subsequent phase of occupation is evident in the palace area, especially in certain parts of the Royal Palace and on the western slope of Lot's Cupola, where Excavation Q unearthed several juxtaposed houses containing local and imported ceramics as well as some pieces imitating late Mycenaean productions. The nature of the occupation at the end of this period remains unknown, but a study of the ceramics shows that it ended about 1200 B.C.

Middle Bronze Age

Excavations have not yielded much archaeological evidence from the first half of the second millennium B.C. Surveys of the surface and excavations around the north and west gates show that the site underwent a period of redefinition upon the arrival of Amorite tribes at the beginning of the second millennium B.C. This phase of urbanization gave the city its present form: a square ground plan of about 100 hectares (247 acres), a high city center, and four main gates facing the four cardinal directions.

In Excavation C, directly below the Aramaean palace, we came upon a relatively large edifice with stone walls and floors made of pounded earth and pebbles, reminiscent of the architecture of Ebla. The ceramics found there permit the elaboration of a stratigraphic sequence extending from the Middle Bronze Age I to the Late Bronze Age I. Soundings made in the courtyard where the royal throne stood confirm this evidence, despite the poor state of preservation of the remains. The Mari texts tell us that the city was also the capital of the Amorite kingdom of Qatna, which is why we think that a great deal remains to be uncovered from this period.

Early Bronze Age III–IV

Soundings made in the northern section of the courtyard of the throne room (Excavation R) have uncovered a level of occupation marked by the presence of several silos hewn out of the rock and associated with ceramics from the middle of the third millennium, about 2600 B.C. (Early Bronze Age III–Early Bronze Age IVA). This period was followed by two phases of architectural development: the first dates to the Early Bronze Age IVA (Mishrifeh VII) and presents a succession of domestic structures and material typical to this period; the second is dated to the Early Bronze Age IVB (Mishrifeh VI). The evidence from this sounding, the results of the more extensive tests made by the Italian team in Excavation J, and those of the surface survey all indicate that the initial occupation and first phase of urbanization took place at the site of the present-day Upper City and that the town was organized around a circular plan identical to those of other settlements on the edge of the Syrian steppe.

Thus, the results of the Syrian excavations have helped to determine four phases of urban development at Qatna. The first, during the second half of the third millennium B.C., corresponds to the initial foundation of the site according to a circular ground plan. The second phase saw the resettlement of the site on a square ground plan. This system of organization was maintained during the first two phases, and the subsequent slight alterations did not affect the overall plan. The circular core of the first settlement then became the upper city of the later phases, which was surrounded by a lower city fortified with a system of embankments and ditches typical of western Syria in the second millennium B.C. The destruction of the city by Sargon II marked the end of Qatna's fourth major period of urbanization, after which the site was virtually abandoned, although certain structures suggest the existence of a village dating from Iron Age III.[1]

1. For further information on the Syrian excavations, see Al-Maqdissi 1996; Al-Maqdissi 2001; Al-Maqdissi 2002a; Al-Maqdissi 2002b; Al-Maqdissi and Badawi 2002; Al-Maqdissi et al. 2002; Al-Maqdissi 2003a; Al-Maqdissi 2003b; Al-Maqdissi and Morandi Bonacossi 2005; Al-Maqdissi 2007a, pp. 75–82; and Al-Maqdissi 2007b.

127

Seated Figure

Basalt
Height 11.3 cm (4½ in.); width 6.6 cm (2⅝ in.)
Qatna, South Palace
Late Bronze Age, 14th century B.C.
Homs Museum, Homs, Syria Mish. 2004/34

This roughly carved dark gray basalt statuette represents a seated figure leaning back, with forearms on the lap. The bearing of the head and the voluminous torso suggest that the subject is not young. Rather, the figure expresses a solemnity that is proper to depictions of adults and the elderly.

The oblong head is shaved, and the high cheekbones are accentuated by projecting ears. The facial features are coarsely indicated, with only the eyebrows and upper lip clearly worked. The vacant gaze and ample costume, of which only the lower part remains, accentuate the disproportion between the volumes of the upper and lower halves of the figure. The seat is stylized and lacks armrests; similarly, details on the back and sides have been omitted.   MM

128a, b

Cylinder Seals and Modern Impressions

Frit
a. Height 1.5 cm (⅝ in.); diameter 0.7 cm (¼ in.)
b. Height 1.5 cm (⅝ in.); diameter 0.7 cm (¼ in.)
Qatna
Late Bronze Age, 14th century B.C.
Homs Museum, Homs, Syria Mish. 1995/12, 1996/18

These two intact cylinder seals are made of frit and display a Syro-Mitanni style typical of the second half of the second millennium B.C.[1] One depicts a row of fish above a lattice pattern representing a net, while the other shows a row of dancers holding one another by the shoulders in what is a presumably a ritual dance. These are common subjects, typical of seals found at Ugarit.[2] Similar seals were distributed around the eastern Mediterranean and imported to the Greek mainland.   MM

1. For further reference, see Al-Maqdissi 2002b, p. 112, fig. 3-a.
2. See Schaeffer-Forrer 1983, pp. 100–101.

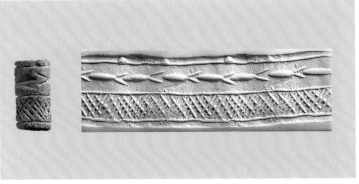

128a

128b

Figure 72. Basalt male figures. Qatna, Royal Tomb, Antechamber. Late Bronze Age context; Middle Bronze Age manufacture. National Museum, Damascus MSH02G–i0738, MSH02G–i0744; MSH02G–i0729, MSH02G–i0736

THE ROYAL PALACE AT QATNA: POWER AND PRESTIGE IN THE LATE BRONZE AGE

PETER PFÄLZNER

The seat of political power in Qatna was the Royal Palace, situated close to the center of the city (figs. 73, 77). Initially excavated by the French archaeologist Du Mesnil du Buisson in the 1920s, the site has been revisited by three missions since 1999—Syrian, Syrian-Italian, and Syrian-German.[1] The Syrian-German mission[2] was able to determine by stratigraphic and ceramic analyses that the palace was built in the Middle Bronze IIA period,[3] the time of the great Qatna kings Ishkhi-Addu and Amud-pi-El, contemporaries of Shamshi-Adad I of Ashur and of Hammurabi of Babylon.[4]

The building and its main halls are unique in their construction. The foundation walls rest on solid bedrock, in places 4 to 5 meters below the ground, and a system of wide stone-filled trenches along the foundation walls serves as a safeguard against humidity, thus protecting the mud-brick construction.[5] The assembly hall (Hall C), measuring 36 meters square, was equipped with four huge wood columns that rested on basalt bases and supported the wood roof.[6] Another extraordinary feature was the well, a shaft 9 by 9 meters square. Dug vertically about 20 meters below the palace, it was accessible by a basalt staircase leading all the way down to the bottom.[7]

The architectural construction of the palace projected a vision of monumentality and durability, symbolic of its power and enhanced by other features. For example, the palace was situated on top of a natural cliff, nearly 15 meters above the Lower City, creating an impressive, soaring view. The cliff itself was artificially cut into a straight, nearly vertical bloc encased in a terrace wall of mud brick.

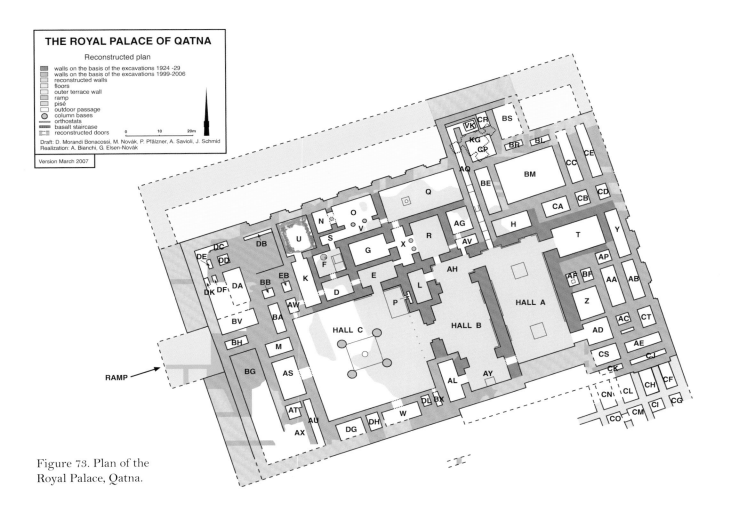

Figure 73. Plan of the Royal Palace, Qatna.

Palace Life and the Appropriation of Exotica

In the final destruction of the palace, probably about 1340 B.C., during the Hittite invasion of Syria, debris from the surrounding rooms collected in the well, with the fortuitous result that thousands of wall painting fragments survived (see cat. no. 69).[8] Reconstructed, they exhibit a conspicuously Aegean style, a reflection of the desire, on the part of the ruling elite, to create prestige through the appropriation of foreign techniques and styles.[9] This synthetic approach was in vogue from the turn of the Middle Bronze to the Late Bronze Age, when we see the apogee of the international style. The style emerged as a result of the intensive exchange of goods and ideas between the cultures of the Syro-Mesopotamia region, the Levant, Egypt, and the eastern Mediterranean.[10] The Qatna wall paintings exemplify the spirit of this age.

The wood finds in the shaft of the palace well are also revealing.[11] When the palace was demolished the beams of the wood ceiling collapsed into the shaft. Because of the wet soil in which the remains were embedded, the organic debris is exceptionally well preserved. The abundance of cedar used in the construction of the palace can be explained by Qatna's direct control over the Anti-Lebanon Mountains and the Syrian coastal mountains, the natural habitat of cedar forests. It may also be assumed, on the basis of Qatna's geographic location and regional authority, that the kingdom exported cedar in large quantities and that wood was an important international currency. The ostentatious presence in the palace of huge cedar beams was another means of creating an image of power.

Life within the palace is described in some of the seventy-three cuneiform tablets that fell from a scribal office into the corridor of the Royal Tomb.[12] We learn, for example, that members of the royal household owned many pieces of luxury furniture and precious objects of gold and lapis lazuli,[13] a surprising fact given that the tablets date to the final phase of Qatna's history, the fourteenth century B.C., when the heyday of the kingdom was long past. The language of the texts, a mixture of Akkadian and Hurrian,[14] is a clear indication that during the Late Bronze Age a heterogeneous population with multicultural practices lived in the city.

The Passage to the Ancestors

The most sensational discovery, in 2002, of the Syrian-German excavations at Qatna was that of the Royal Tomb, or hypogeum, below the palace.[15] Because it had not been looted during the destruction of the palace or thereafter, it offers a wealth of evidence of material culture, beliefs, and rituals. When the palace was destroyed, access to the burial chambers was covered in masses of debris that prevented entrance to the tomb and protected the objects within.

A 40-meter-long subterranean corridor led from the ceremonial hall (Room A) to the tomb. Several doors along the corridor established divisions between the palace—the upper world—and the tomb—part of the Underworld. The corridor led 7.5 meters below the palace floors to a room-sized shaft 4.5 meters deep, which functioned as the antechamber to the tomb.

In the antechamber were two exceptionally well preserved statues of basalt, slightly less than life-size (fig. 72).[16] Virtually identical, they represent two figures seated on low stools. Their garment, a long Syrian bordered robe, and headdress, a broad ring holding the hair, identify the figures as royal. The headdress is strikingly reminiscent of that on the so-called head of Yarim-Lim from Alalakh (fig. 64), which shows in more detail what is only schematically depicted on the Qatna statues.[17] The stylistic rendering of the face, in particular the short slightly protruding beard, also closely relates the Qatna statues to the

Figure 74. Basalt male figures in situ before the Royal Tomb, Qatna.

Figure 75. Inside the central chamber of the Royal Tomb, Qatna.

head from Alalakh. All three date to Middle Bronze Age II and exemplify the finest of Old Syrian statuary.

The two statues, positioned at either side of the entrance to the inner chambers (fig. 74), served as guardians to the Underworld. They also received offerings, indicated by the open vessel that each figure holds in the right hand. Deposited before them were several bowls and animal bones, remains of the last offerings. As royal figures in a royal tomb were surely ancestor statues, the antechamber was likely an important site of ancestor worship.[18]

RITUALS AND THE DISPLAY OF PRESTIGE

Cut into the natural bedrock 12 meters below the palace were the four inner chambers in the Royal Tomb, a large central chamber surrounded by three side chambers. While the central chamber served a variety of functions, from primary and secondary burial to the display of prestigious objects and collective meals, the side chambers were reserved for specific activities. The western chamber was used for burial rites. The eastern chamber was the ossuary of the hypogeum, where the bones were eventually deposited after a series of ritual ceremonies. The southern chamber has been interpreted as a symbolic throne or banquet room for deceased rulers and their spirits.[19] This chamber was particularly well furnished with luxury items such as calcite vessels, the carnelian vessel (cat. no. 132), and the gold duck heads (cat. no. 129).

The central chamber (fig. 75) held a basalt sarcophagus, in which the bones of several individuals were found together with pottery, gold pendants, and an ivory scepter, indicating that the tomb was a burial site for the royal family. The tomb held a minimum of nineteen to twenty-three individuals of various ages, both male and female.[20] (Other burials may have disintegrated, as the bones were poorly preserved in the chambers not filled with earth.)

Four wood biers—reconstructed from decayed remains—were placed on the floor of the main chamber, with scattered bones and an abundance of grave goods deposited on top, among them hundreds of beads, decorative plaques (cat. nos. 134, 135), quiver fittings (cat. no. 133), a lion-headed vessel (fig. 83), and

a modeled hand of gold (cat. no. 131). The objects show stylistic and iconographic influences from many neighboring cultures, ranging geographically from Egypt to Mesopotamia.

In the Syro-Levantine region during the second millennium B.C., these foreign influences were combined in a hybrid international style (see pp. 387–94).[21] Within this broad category several features can be distinguished as distinctly Syrian in character. Indeed, a specifically Late Bronze Age Qatna style can be identified. Had more objects survived from other Syrian centers, it would, in principle, be possible to identify other local styles. The material value of the objects recovered from the Qatna palace and Royal Tomb, their distant provenances, and their foreign iconography were for the ruling elite expressions of prestige, for through these objects it was possible to demonstrate the kingdom's far-reaching contacts and its participation in interregional exchange networks.[22] Prestige was also acquired from artifacts from foreign regions (exemplified here by Egyptian stone vessels, cat. no. 141), imported to Qatna either as objects of exchange or as diplomatic gifts.[23]

Many of the objects and materials in the grave chambers undoubtedly served ritual purposes. A large number of pottery vessels were used for the storage of food, and beneath benches in the main chamber were found animal bones that had been tossed as leftovers from meals. What this suggests is that communal consumption of food—in which the living and the dead participated, at least symbolically—took place within the central chamber.[24] The kispu ritual, the continuous supply of the deceased with food, is known from ancient Near Eastern texts as a major concern of the cult of the dead.[25] At Qatna, we have for the first time been given the opportunity to acknowledge this practice archaeologically, to observe its significance both for the living and as a guarantee for the political stability of the kingdom.

1. Al-Maqdissi et al. 2002.
2. Co-directed by Michel al-Maqdissi and the author.
3. According to the Babylonian Middle Chronology, ca. 1850–1750 B.C.; according to the Babylonian Low Chronology, 1800–1700 B.C.
4. Dohmann-Pfälzner and Pfälzner 2006, pp. 131–80; Pfälzner 2007a; Dohmann-Pfälzner and Pfälzner 2008.
5. Novák 2006.
6. Pfälzner 2007a.
7. Dohmann-Pfälzner and Pfälzner 2006 and 2008.
8. The wall paintings were studied by Constance von Rüden (2006).
9. On this, see Feldman 2007.
10. Caubet 1998c.
11. Dohmann-Pfälzner and Pfälzner 2008.
12. Richter 2003; Richter 2005.
13. Thomas Richter, personal communication.
14. Richter 2003, pp. 171–77.
15. Al-Maqdissi et al. 2003; Pfälzner 2006.
16. Novák and Pfälzner 2003, pp. 156ff., figs. 17–20.
17. Woolley 1955, pp. 235ff.
18. Pfälzner 2005.
19. See Al-Maqdissi et al. 2003, pp. 204–10.
20. Personal communication, Carsten Witzel, Syrian-German Mission, October 2007.
21. Caubet 1998c.
22. The author wishes to thank Elisa Roßberger for sharing her insights on the prestige function of Qatna jewelry. See Roßberger 2006.
23. See Pfälzner 2007b.
24. Pfälzner 2007c.
25. Tsukimoto 1985.

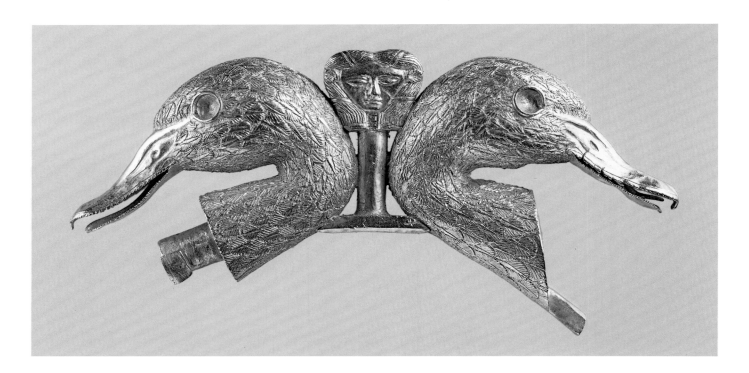

129
DUCK HEADS

Gold
Height 3.4 cm (1⅜ in.); width 7.2 cm (2⅞ in.);
diameter 1.3 cm (½ in.)
Qatna, Royal Tomb
Late Bronze Age, 15th–14th century B.C.
National Museum, Damascus, Syria
MSH02G–i2038

This object with two golden duck heads, discovered in the Royal Tomb of Qatna, is a masterpiece of Late Bronze Age art in Syria. It is made entirely of gold, including the fastening pegs. The two heads, with their elegantly curved necks, are mounted on a gold baton and face in opposite directions. They are rendered in a perfectly naturalistic style. The fine overlapping feathers are indicated by miniature incisions, and the beaks are subtly curved and characterized by anatomical details such as jagged edges along the upper and lower edges, with openings for the nostrils at the base of the upper beak. The tongues, which were fashioned separately, are visible through the half-open bills; the eyes were once inlaid. A pole down the middle bears a golden head of the Egyptian goddess Hathor, with a typically triangular face, a long headdress with bands, and cow's ears that are purely Egyptian in iconography.

The sophisticated production technique demonstrates the advanced level of crafts-manship of second-millennium B.C. gold-smiths.[1] The artifact is composed of fifteen individual pieces, all of which are soldered to one another. The two heads were produced using the lost-wax method, with the lower beak, tongue, eye rings, base, and fastening pegs attached by soldering; the incised decoration was added with a punch as the last step of manufacture. The work-shop where this masterpiece was produced must therefore have been organized by a division of labor involving various special-ists. Although the Hathor head suggests Egyptian influence, we can assume, based on the style of the heads, that the work-shop was in Syria. The object must have been made in the early phase of the Late Bronze Age, around the fifteenth or four-teenth century B.C.

It is difficult to ascertain how this object was used. The two fastening devices at the lower end of the necks clearly demonstrate that the heads were once attached to another object, probably of organic mate-rial, of which nothing survived in the tomb chambers. We can only speculate that these were two pieces of wood, into which the fastening pegs could have been inserted by screwing (on one side) and by plugging (on the other). In the Syro-Levantine region, sculpted duck heads, mainly of ivory, were generally connected to small shallow bowls, also of ivory (see cat. nos. 199–202).

Such vessels have been found at many sites, from Lachish in the south to Alalakh in the north (fig. 106) and Tell Brak in the east.[2] They are commonly thought to have served as containers for oils, perfumes, and cosmetics. They are also known from Egypt, mainly in wood, but in smaller quantities (cat. no. 200).[3] Duck-headed ves-sels were prestigious and cultic objects,[4] widespread and internationally distributed over the Levant and Egypt, including the eastern Mediterranean and the Aegean area.[5] Two also traveled on the Uluburun ship (see cat. no. 199). Their main center of production must have been in western Syria and the Levantine coast.

If the Qatna duck heads were, most plausibly, part of a cosmetic container, it could be reconstructed as a double vessel with one wood bowl attached to each of the two heads. The heads would in this way have functioned as a handle. This inter-pretation is supported by the observation, made by Edilberto Formigli, that there are traces of abrasion concentrated beside the eyes and on the Hathor head. The object is the only known example of this type.[6] The innovative character of the Qatna vessel together with the fact that it is made of pure gold signifies its unique and extraor-dinary importance.   PP

1. This technique was studied by Edilberto Formigli, Murlo, Italy, and Marta Abbado, Florence.
2. Findspots are Lachish, Megiddo, Tell Dan, Sidon, Kamid el-Loz, Tell Qasile, Ugarit, Alalakh, Tell Meskene, Tell Brak (summa-rized by Echt 1983 and *Das Schiff von Uluburun* 2005, p. 605).

3. *Schönheit im Alten Ägypten* 2006, p. 227,
   no. 196; Schoske in *Schönheit, Abglanz der
   Göttlichkeit* 1990, p. 94, no. 52; W. Peck and
   R. Freed in *Egypt's Golden Age* 1982,
   pp. 213–14, nos. 258, 260; Hermann 1932.

4. A cultic function, at least in New Kingdom
   Egypt, is evident from the depictions of two
   duck-headed vessels on a mural painting in
   the grave of Kenamun at Thebes (Dynasty
   18) where they function as offerings to the
   king in the New Year's ritual: see Davies
   1930, vol. 1, pls. 18, 20; vol. 2, pl. 22A (see
   fig. 107, this volume).

5. For a duck-headed vessel from Mycenae, see
   Sakellarakis 1971; see also S. Marinatos and
   Hirmer 1973, fig. 235.

6. A slightly different type is represented by an
   Egyptian object of wood composed of a bowl
   on one side and a duck's entire body on the
   other, with both sides functioning as interconnected containers. However, it features
   only a single duck head, which could be used
   as a handle (Hermann 1932, p. 93, pl. VIIIc).
   A pottery vessel with two duck heads, arranged not in opposition but parallel to each
   other, was found at Hattusa and dates to the
   fourteenth century B.C. (see Bittel 1976b,
   p. 157, fig. 165).

130

130

INLAID ROSETTE

Gold, lapis lazuli, carnelian
Diameter 6.9 cm (2¾ in.)
Qatna, Royal Tomb
Late Bronze Age, 15th–14th century B.C.
National Museum, Damascus, Syria
MSH02G–i1150

This extraordinary gold rosette is the most complex piece of jewelry found in the central chamber of the Royal Tomb.[1] The center of the solid gold disc is covered by a carnelian roundel bordered by a broad ring of carnelian set in gold. Twenty-six petals, each subdivided into nine compart-ments inlaid with lapis lazuli and carnelian, are arranged around the central roundel by a flaring ring of gold wire. The inlay at the end of each petal is alternately lapis or carnelian, so that two neighboring petals always show a different sequence of blue and red stones, creating a vivid and color-ful effect. The stone inlays are glued to the gold compartments with an adhesive of which a red crumbly substance remains partly visible.

The technique of gold jewelry inlaid with lapis lazuli, carnelian, and other semi-precious stones in contrasting arrange-ment of colors was developed to perfection in Egypt.[2] It was imported already to the Levant during the Middle Bronze Age, as is seen in the locally produced gold-inlay jewelry from Byblos that incorporates car-nelian combined with blue and green semi-precious stones (see cat. no. 29).[3] It must therefore be assumed that the inlay tech-nique was common in Late Bronze Age Syria. The absence of Egyptian symbols in the Qatna rosette is another clear indication of non-Egyptian manufacture. Most likely, it is a product of Syrian craftsmanship.

On the reverse are thirteen small gold loops soldered on to each second petal of the rosette and perhaps used for sewing the heavy ornament on to a textile or piece of leather. The rosette probably served to adorn a fine garment as a kind of brooch. Or perhaps it was attached to a leather ribbon to circle the arm. The latter recon-struction is supported by the slight convex curve along the middle axis, which could have enabled adjustment to the shape of the arm. If the latter interpretation is cor-rect, the rosette would be a typological predecessor of the rosette wrist straps worn by the Assyrian kings and winged Genii in Neo-Assyrian art.[4] Given the numerous smaller gold rosettes found in the Royal Tomb, most of which were prob-ably sewn onto garments, it can be argued that already in Late Bronze Age Syria the rosette served as a royal symbol.   PP

1. First published in Al-Maqdissi et al. 2003,
   p. 215, fig. 15.
2. See Lange and Hirmer 1967, pl. XIV, and
   T. James 2000, pp. 200–241.
3. Parrot, Chéhab, and Moscati 1977, p. 42,
   figs. 28, 29.
4. Hrouda 1991, figs. on pp. 124, 125, 126, 127,
   131, 326, 347, 355, 356; for Genii see figs. on
   pp. 126, 127, 232, 233.

131

HAND FRAGMENT

Gold
Width 4.2 cm (1⅝ in.); length 6.4 cm (2½ in.)
Qatna, Royal Tomb
Late Bronze Age, 15th–14th century B.C.
National Museum, Damascus, Syria
MSH02G–i0758

This fragment of a right hand was found in connection with a bier and a multitude of other grave goods in the cen-tral chamber of the Royal Tomb. The hand is about 6.4 centimeters long and about half natural size. Hollow inside, it consists of gold sheet in the shape of four fingers. The fingers are separated from each other by shallow flutes, and the details of the

131

fingers were traced on the surface during the final stage of production. The fingernails, cuticles, and skin folds at the knuckles are rendered in an astonishingly naturalistic fashion, and the lengths of the fingers are anatomically correct. There is a sharp edge on the gold sheet where the thumb may have broken off. It must originally have been set apart from the other fingers, probably below the palm. Thus the hand could possibly have held other objects.

The hand was probably part of a libation arm. Mounted on a wood stick inserted into the hollow end of the hand, the arm would have been held, allowing the offerings within to be presented without being directly touched by humans. Similar arms functioned as incense holders in Egypt.[1] Stone, faience, and clay examples known in Syro-Mesopotamia and Anatolia have also been interpreted as libation arms. While those that have survived are mainly dated to the Iron Age,[2] they are also known in the Middle and Late Bronze Ages,[3] with examples at Alalakh, Ugarit, and Boğazköy.[4]

The hand from Qatna is unique in being the only excavated example of its kind to be made of gold and must have had special prestige in the royal burial. Whether it was actually used as a libation arm within the grave chambers is difficult to say. Water libations (*naq ma*) in connection with food offerings (*kispu*) are well recorded in ancient Near Eastern texts as part of the rituals[5] performed to care for the spirits of the dead (*etemmu*). Ample evidence of food offerings in the Royal Tomb would tend to support the offering of liquid libations as well. PP

1. See, for example, Schoske in *Schönheit, Abglanz der Göttlichkeit* 1990, p. 66, no. 16, and *Schönheit im Alten Ägypten* 2006, p. 258, no. 282. For images on Egyptian wall paintings and reliefs, see Lange and Hirmer 1967, fig. 226, or *Schönheit im Alten Ägypten* 2006, p. 258, no. 284.
2. Kepinski 1987–90, pp. 12–14.
3. Kepinski 1977.
4. Alalakh: Woolley 1955, p. 297 (Yarim-Lim Palace, Level VII, Room 18). Ugarit: Calvet in *Le royaume d'Ougarit* 2004, p. 41, no. 22. Nimrud: Moortgat 1967, p. 115, fig. 237. Boğazköy: Bittel 1957a, pp. 33–42, tables I–III; Fischer 1963, pp. 149–51, pls. 122, 124.
5. Bayliss 1973, pp. 116ff.; Tsukimoto 1985, p. 239.

132

BOTTLE

Carnelian
Height 12.4 cm (4⅞ in.)
Qatna, Royal Tomb
Late Bronze Age, 15th–14th century B.C.
National Museum, Damascus, Syria
MSH02G–i0812

This miniature bottle is made from a single piece of carnelian of orange-red color with cloudy whitish patches. It was carefully carved to form a perfectly teardrop-shaped body with a narrow neck, and the surface was then polished to a shiny, eye-catching gloss.

The vessel is one of the largest extant pieces of carnelian worked into an object ever found in the ancient Near East. Natural occurrences of the stone are found

mainly in the region of the Persian Gulf and in India, and also, but to a much lesser extent, in the deserts of Egypt.[1] An eastern provenance is more likely. The difficulty of procuring the stone from such a long distance surely added to the object's prestige.

There are no parallels for this kind of carnelian bottle in Egypt, in the Levant, or in Syro-Mesopotamia. Nevertheless, it can be argued that the vessel was likely produced in Syria, adapting to stone a shape that closely resembles clay vessels made in the region from the Early to the Late Bronze Ages.[2] While it is difficult to date this object, theoretically it could have been made long before it was placed in the Royal Tomb.

The function of the bottle within the tomb can be seen in connection with the many other small stone vessels found nearby, in the southern chamber. These most likely contained precious oils, perfumes, and ointments. Undoubtedly, the contents of the little carnelian bottle, whatever it may have been, were enhanced by the rare and beautiful material in which it was contained. PP

132

133

1. Mineralogical determination and geological information kindly provided by Judit Zöld-földi, University of Tübingen.
2. For Early Bronze Age examples, see, for example, Fugmann 1958, fig. 98 (no. 3A647 [Niveau J2]); Mazzoni 2002, pl. XLV:135 (Zalaquiyate, Early Bronze IVB). For Late Bronze Age examples, see ibid., pl. LVIII:17 (Tell Afis, Level E 13).

133
QUIVER PLAQUE WITH HUNTING SCENE

Gold, silver
Height 9 cm (3½ in.); width 17.9 cm (7 in.)
Qatna, Royal Tomb
Late Bronze Age, 15th–14th century B.C.
National Museum, Damascus, Syria
MSH02G–i1588

This plaque was found in the central chamber of the Royal Tomb in close proximity to a larger decorative plaque fashioned for a quiver (fig. 76). As both are similar in style and made in the same, unusual technique of gold foil-on-silver sheet appliqué, it is highly probable that the two pieces were produced in the same workshop. Whether the present, smaller plaque was also decoration for a quiver—even the same one—or was decoration for a sheath accompanying the quiver remains unknown. The perforations along the border of the plaque indicate that it was sewn onto a textile or a piece of leather.

The figurative scene fills one register without subdivisions. Around the field is a decorative border, with the same hatched pattern as on the edge of the larger quiver

Figure 76. Gold and silver relief plaque for a quiver, detail. Qatna, Royal Tomb, central chamber. Late Bronze Age. National Museum, Damascus MSH02G-i1091

plaque, further attesting to a common place of production. The scene is depicted twice in exact symmetrical arrangement. The middle axis is formed by a stylized palm tree with leaves and dates. The figural representation shows two men, identical in appearance, both wearing a kilt with decorative bands and a fitted upper garment, killing a stag. The modeled rendering of the stag's head, the fine parallel incisions indicating the hide, and the irregularly branching antler are characteristic of the art of Qatna. The closed composition is created by the stag, which turns its head, the two figures who look toward each other, and the flying bird, apparently inserted to fill the void above the stag.

Scenes of animals in combat and the domination by men over wild beasts are deeply rooted in Mesopotamian iconography, dating back to the Early Dynastic and Akkadian periods of the third millennium B.C. The same motifs are still widespread in Late Bronze Age Syro-Mesopotamia, particularly in Mitanni-style glyptic. The compositional style is, however, specific to Qatna. It is characterized by a symmetrical, closed composition, the absence of overlapping, and static figural postures. Facial features typically include a large nose and ears, staring eyes, and a small mouth. The straight hair is marked by deeply incised parallel grooves. Fine parallel lines are used to indicate the hide of wild animals, conferring a note of elegance.

The stag hunt depicted on this plaque is a rare subject in Late Bronze Age art. On Syrian objects the stag is usually protected by man against the attack of wild animals such as lions, as on the gold bowl from Ugarit (cat. no. 146). By contrast, on contemporary Hittite figurative reliefs stags are hunted by men, as on a bowl from Kastamonu,[1] on the orthostats from Alaca Höyük,[2] and on relief vessels.[3] While a preference for stag hunts seems to be a common feature of Hittite art and of works from Qatna, the stylistic renderings follow very different principles. The Hittite scenes, though vivid and freely arranged, are executed in a rather flat style; the Qatna scenes are characterized by a static arrangement but are rendered in a plastic, more detailed manner. Furthermore, the stags in the Hittite representations are hunted with bow and arrow, while on the Qatna plaques the stags are captured by hand weapons. In Hittite Anatolia, the stag hunt belongs to a religious context (see cat. no. 107).[4] At Qatna, by contrast, the subject seems to symbolize man's domination over the wild and thus was used as an emblem of prestige by the Late Bronze Age political elite.

PP

1. Emre 2002, pp. 232–33, fig. 18.
2. Bittel 1976b, figs. 224, 225.
3. Ibid., p. 146, no. 146.
4. Emre 2002, pp. 220, 233; V. Haas 1994, p. 432.

134

PLAQUE WITH THE GOD HORUS

Gold
Height 5.6 cm (2¼ in.); width 4.4 cm (1¾ in.)
Qatna, Royal Tomb
Late Bronze Age, 15th–14th century B.C.
National Museum, Damascus, Syria
MSH02G–i1087

Among the finds in the Royal Tomb were a number of thin gold plaques with elaborate figurative representations in relief that reflect iconographic connections to different cultural regions. The plant and two gods on this U-shaped plaque are unambiguously Egyptian in influence, for they represent *sema tawi*, symbol of the Unification of the Two Lands, Upper and Lower Egypt. The god Horus, depicted twice, is shown binding

a lotus plant around a pole, signifying the act of unification. Horus is distinguished by his falcon head and wears the Egyptian double crown of Upper and Lower Egypt. Atop the pole is a bird with spread wings above a basket-shaped support. The bird's head is crowned by the winding head of a cobra. In a separate, lower register is another bird, also with spread wings.

While the Egyptian iconography appears authentic, closer examination reveals noticeable aberrations. An archetypal Egyptian representation would depict, opposite the falcon-headed Horus, the god Seth with his long curved muzzle.[1] Here, for the sake of symmetry, one of the main stylistic norms of Late Bronze Age art in Syria, Seth is omitted and replaced by a second Horus. Another modification is the replacement, on the central pole, of a cartouche with an inscription with the winged bird, since an Egyptian text would probably not have been understood in Syria. The basket-shaped object on the pole below the bird may be understood as a remnant of the lower half of the cartouche border.

The plaque thus demonstrates the adaptation by Syrian artisans of foreign iconographic models to local cultural principles. The meaning of motifs necessarily changed with modifications. In the case of the Horus plaque, while the symbolism of the Unification of the Two Lands would have been meaningless to Syrian elites, the exotic motif likely served as an emblem of prestige.

PP

1. For a standard Egyptian model, see Lange and Hirmer 1967, fig. 88.

135

PLAQUE WITH FIGURES FLANKING HATHOR STANDARD

Gold
Height 3.9 cm (1½ in.); width 4.6 cm (1¾ in.)
Qatna, Royal Tomb
Late Bronze Age, 15th–14th century B.C.
National Museum, Damascus, Syria
MSH02G–i1930

This gold plaque from the central chamber of the Royal Tomb is rectangular in shape, with a line of perforations along the upper and the lower edge. The plaque is broken on the left and right sides, but undoubtedly perforations were provided there as well, as the holes surely served as a means of sewing the plaque on to a textile or piece of leather. Because it was found on a burial bier, the plaque may have been attached to a shroud or a garment of the deceased. Or perhaps it was used as a piece of jewelry, affixed to a strip of hard leather that was worn as a belt, a pectoral, a necklace, or a headband. Its small size and singularity make the latter options more plausible.

The repoussé decoration on thin gold sheet of two figures at either side of a standard is rendered to create the effect of deep relief. The standard is surmounted by the head of the Egyptian goddess Hathor, depicted with typical Egyptian iconography: a rhomboid face, protruding cow ears, and long strands of hair held together by bands.[1] The two figures, wearing the Egyptian short kilt with a triangular projection in front of the body are

135

also represented in Egyptian imagery.[2] Attached to the kilt at the back is the artificial tail of a bull, derived from an Egyptian royal emblem. Even the figures' headdresses resemble the Egyptian *afnet*.[3] The two figures, nude above the waist, are nearly identical except for their jewelry. The figure on the left is adorned with a pectoral; the figure on the right wears a simple torque around the neck. Each holds a long scepter in one hand, similar to the Egyptian *heqa*-scepter or the longer *awt*-staff. The scepters held by these figures were probably incorporated into Syrian iconography as a fusion of the two.

The subject as it is depicted here does not appear in Egyptian art. Conforming as it does to the principle of symmetry characteristic for Syrian art in the Late Bronze Age, the plaque would seem to be the work of a Syrian goldsmith. The somewhat clumsy rendering of the faces, typical of Syrian craftsmanship, especially at Qatna, would further support such a provenance.   PP

1. The head of Hathor mounted on a pole is also seen in connection with Egyptian objects such as spoons (e.g.: *Schönheit, Abglanz der Göttlichkeit* 1990, p. 79, no. 33), mirrors (ibid., p. 120, no. 102), sistra (ibid., p. 142, no. 127), or capitals of columns (see Lange and Hirmer 1967, fig. 268).
2. This feature is strongly reminiscent of the two guardian statues at the entrance of the Tomb of Tutankhamun; see T. James 2000, pp. 60–61.
3. Seen, for example, on the left guardian statue of the Tomb of Tutankhamun (ibid.).

136
LOTUS PENDANT

Gold, lapis lazuli (?)
Height 2 cm (¾ in.); width 2.6 cm (1 in.)
Qatna, Royal Palace
Middle to Late Bronze Age, 17th–
14th century B.C.
Homs Museum, Homs, Syria MSH02G–i0391

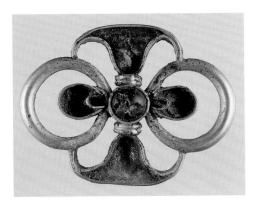

This small gold pendant, found in Room AL of the Royal Palace to the west of the throne room (Hall B), is composed of a number of single elements soldered together. Two gold rings and two papyrus-shaped parts are attached to a round central element. Both papyri and the central element are inlaid with a dark stone, probably weathered lapis lazuli. Within the two gold rings and attached to each side of the central element are two oval double compartments, in which stone inlays must once have been inserted.

The form of the pendant is symmetrical, closed, and flowerlike. It was possibly part of a necklace or a single pendant. There is no loop attached to the reverse, but one or both of the rings could have been used to suspend the object from a string or an earring, or for sewing it to a textile. The papyrus may be regarded as an Egyptianizing element in jewelry made in Syria, where the technique of stone inlay—originally imported from Egypt—had been common since the Middle Bronze Age.[1]   PP

1. This is demonstrated, for example, by the Egyptianizing but locally produced jewelry from the Middle Bronze royal tombs at Byblos (see Parrot, Chéhab, and Moscati 1977, p. 42, figs. 28, 29). See catalogue no. 29 in this volume.

137
SCARAB WITH ROBED FIGURE

Amethyst, gold
Length 2.4 cm (1 in.)
Qatna, Royal Tomb
Late Bronze Age context, 15th–
14th century B.C.
Old Syrian manufacture, 18th–
17th century B.C.
National Museum, Damascus, Syria
MSH02G–i0764

The beautiful amethyst scarab was found in the central chamber of the Royal Tomb.[1] On the back of the scarab the details of the beetle are only faintly indicated. The line between the *pronotum*, the shieldlike middle part of the body, and the *elytra*, the rear wings, is subtly indicated by two short engraved lines on either side of the body. The dividing line between the two wings of the *elytra* is missing, probably as a result of abrasion from use. In front of the head the long mandibles are rendered with deep grooves indicating teeth.

The base of the scarab bears the carefully modeled and deeply engraved image of a standing figure dressed in a long robe. The veil-like covering of the head and the absence of a beard identify the figure as female. The robe is fashioned from a single cloth wrapped around the body and draped over the head. Only the face—accentuated by full lips, a broad nose, and an enormous eye—is left uncovered. A drill was used extensively in the modeling of the face.

This type of dress, a robe pulled over the head, well known from Hittite art, however, is not specifically Anatolian and is frequently represented elsewhere in ancient Near Eastern art.[2] Representations of women with similarly covered heads occur also on Classic Syrian-style seals from the Middle Bronze Age.[3] A garment strikingly similar to the one on the Qatna scarab appears on a bronze plaque in a Late Bronze Age context at Hazor; that robe, however, is worn by a male.[4] This robe type and its specifically female rendering can thus be identified as typically Syrian. These observations leave no doubt that the scarab is of Syro-Levantine manufacture. Close stylistic parallels to the representation of a woman on a Classic Syrian-style seal allow us to date the scarab to the Middle Bronze Age.[5]

The scarab is held by a thick gold bezel, and two gold rings are attached to the openings of the central drill hole, an indication

that the scarab was originally part of a ring, most likely of gold.[6]　　　PP

1. Scarabs made of violet amethyst are frequent in the Levant and in Egypt during most of the second millennium B.C. as is demonstrated by finds from Byblos (*Liban: L'autre rive* 1998, p. 73; two pieces), from the Uluburun ship (cat. no. 226), and from the Tomb of Tutankhamun (T. James 2000, pp. 246–47).
2. Compare, e.g., the Hittite vases from Bitik and Inandik (Bittle 1976b, fig. 140) or Late Hittite representations of women at Carchemish or Maraş (Bittel 1976b, figs. 287, 289, 313, 315, 316).
3. Otto 2000, p. 214, figs. 104, 110, 116, 135, 147, 313, 317, 348, 355.
4. The parallel was cited by Argiro Mavromatis (University of Tübingen) during a seminar on the Qatna objects; for an illustration, see Weippert 1988, p. 215, fig. 3.25/5.
5. Otto 2000, fig. 355.
6. A similar Middle Bronze gold seal ring with an amethyst scarab was found in the royal tombs of Byblos (*Liban: L'autre rive* 1998, p. 73).

138

CYLINDER SEAL AND MODERN IMPRESSION: COLUMNS OF ANIMALS AND SYMBOLS

Gray hematite
Height 2.3 cm (⅞ in.); diameter 1.5 cm (⅝ in.)
Qatna, Royal Tomb
Late Bronze Age context, 15th–14th century B.C.
Old Syrian manufacture, 18th–
17th century B.C.
National Museum, Damascus, Syria
MSH02G–i1976

This perfectly preserved cylinder seal found in the eastern side chamber of the Royal Tomb of Qatna is made of dark gray hematite. The deeply engraved symbols are arranged in twelve vertical columns, the symbols differing from column to column but generally repeating within each column. A column of five bucrania is the most distinctive. The bull's heads depicted in frontal view have a rounded

mouth, large round eyes, long ears, and short horns. The bucranium at the bottom is, notably, turned on its side to accommodate the small amount of remaining space. To the left is a column of four figures in seated position though without chairs. In the next column are four crouching animals that in their posture resemble lions but with unusually long ears. This column is adjoined by a column of six birds, each with a raised wing and long tail feathers. To the left again is a row of six human heads in profile. The following column contains ten S-shaped symbols arranged in the form of a vertical guilloche band. To the left of it is a column of five large hands. The next column includes four crouching sphinxes with a raised wing; a small animal is inserted into the remaining space at the lower end of the column. In the next column are three masklike human faces in frontal view, with protruding ears and a long curl of hair on either side. At first glance, they resemble the Egyptian goddess Hathor, but the presence of a long beard makes them recognizable as Mesopotamian heroes.[1] Here again, to fit the space, one of the heads is depicted on its side. Below the three masks is a tripartite guilloche pattern composed of three parallel strands. The next column shows mixed symbols: (from top) a standing caprid, a seated monkey, and a series of crescents, symbols of the moon god. The following column again contains mixed symbols: (from top) a double lion-headed eagle,[2] probably the symbol of the god Ninurta; a kneeling man; and a bird with spread wings on top of a standard placed on the back of a lion. The last column shows a standing caprid, a standing lion, and seven crescents.

Altogether we find eighteen different symbols united on this seal, seventy-three images in total, an extraordinarily large number to be assembled on such a small surface. The symbols do not seem to carry a common message; it is doubtful even

whether each motif has a specific meaning. Rather, the images would appear to be mainly decorative. Such an assemblage of images arranged in columns is a familiar compositional type in Syrian glyptic of the Middle Bronze Age, known from Ugarit, Alalakh, and other sites in the Levant.[3] The vertical columns most frequently contain rows of seated animals, human and animal heads, birds, hands, and crescents.

Many of the individual motifs can be attributed to the Old Syrian style of the Middle Bronze Age,[4] and thus the Qatna seal can be dated from the eighteenth to the seventeenth century B.C.　　　PP

1. Compare: Boehmer 1965, nos. 9, 10a, 23, 31, 158, 176, 238, 279, etc.; for a similar Old Syrian head type, here connected to a full figure, see Kühne in *Das Rollsiegel in Syrien* 1980, p. 76, no. 32.
2. The same double lion-headed eagle is depicted on an Old Syrian seal in the National Museum, Damascus (Kühne in *Das Rollsiegel in Syrien* 1980, no. 31), where it is, however, described as a "double-headed eagle" (ibid., p. 74) because the leonine character of the heads is not as clearly visible as on the Qatna piece. The iconographic type of the double lion-headed eagle on Syrian seals can be defined more precisely on the basis of the Qatna seal.
3. Otto 2000, pp. 113–15, 143–44, nos. 35–65, 360–68; Kühne in *Das Rollsiegel in Syrien* 1980, no. 33.
4. Otto 2000, nos. 5, 24, 31, 49, 63, 115, 153, 155, 156, 158, 159; Elsen-Novák 2002, pp. 258–59, fig. 2; Kühne in *Das Rollsiegel in Syrien* 1980, nos. 31, 33.

139

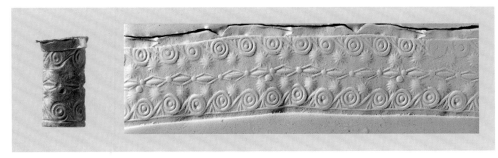

140

139

CYLINDER SEAL AND MODERN IMPRESSION: LOTUS CHAIN

Frit, gold
Height 2.2 cm (⅞ in.); diameter 1 cm (⅜ in.)
Qatna, Royal Tomb
Late Bronze Age, 15th–14th century B.C.
National Museum, Damascus, Syria
MSH02G–i0757

This cylinder seal was discovered in the central chamber of the Royal Tomb of Qatna. Both ends are covered by gold caps, lending prestige to the seal, which is made of inexpensive white frit. The seal image consists of purely geometric and floral designs. In the upper and lower registers is a wide, one-strand running spiral; the center of each spiral is accentuated by a drill hole. The spirals are separated from the middle register by horizontal incised lines. Between the lines is a pattern composed of two rows of stylized lotus flowers connected by a row of lozenges along the middle axis.

Both the material and the schematic composition indicate a Late Bronze date of manufacture. The running spiral with central drill holes appears on seals of the Mitanni Common Style,[1] and the lotus-flower pattern was a favorite motif on Syrian seals of the Late Bronze Age.[2]

This type of seal, made from a common, easily workable material, bearing a simple decoration, and embellished with gold caps, was surely appreciated as a grave gift in the Royal Tomb in much the same way as the older, more elaborate seals made of hard stones.   PP

1. Salje 1990, nos. 93, 94, 100, 124, 131, 141, 155, 163, 196, 221, etc.
2. For an example on a seal, also with gold caps, from Ugarit, see Kohlmeyer in *Land des Baal* 1982, p. 128, no. 108. An example of a Middle Syrian cylinder seal in the Badisches Landesmuseum Karlsruhe, with a comparable three-register division and double-lotus-flower tendril in the middle register, forms a close parallel: Rehm 1997, p. 162, S92, fig. 361.

140

CYLINDER SEAL AND MODERN IMPRESSION: RUNNING SPIRALS

Frit, gold
Height 1.7 cm (¾ in.); diameter 0.8 cm (⅜ in.)
Qatna, Royal Tomb
Late Bronze Age, 15th–14th century B.C.
National Museum, Damascus, Syria
MSH02G–i2209

The seal is very similar to catalogue no. 139 and was found close by in the central chamber of the Royal Tomb. It, too, is made of white frit and had two gold caps at both ends, one of which is now missing. The remaining cap partly overlaps the edge of the seal image, which indicates that it was a later addition. The caps were probably added when the seal was transformed into a grave good. They are not carefully made or well soldered, further supporting the notion that the seal was not used for sealing after they were attached.

Although frit is a very soft material, the seal image is deeply and sharply engraved. There is little abrasion to the surface, a sign that the seal had not been long in use before it was deposited in the grave. Based on material and style, the seal was—like catalogue no. 139—made in the Late Bronze Age. The image is divided into three horizontal registers. The middle register is filled with a continuous row of lozenges with an interior ridge and connected by drill holes. Above and below are pairs of stars roughly corresponding in alignment to each of the lozenges.

The upper and lower registers are symmetrically decorated with running spirals, between which are inserted paired leaves. The motif of the running spiral was perhaps borrowed from Aegean art, where it was widely used as a decorative element on wall paintings (see fig. 38) and pottery, among other artifacts.[1] At Qatna this type of spiral is most prominent on the wall paintings from Room N of the Royal Palace (cat. no. 69b), which are dated to the middle of the second millennium B.C. It is also seen, with less careful workmanship, on painted Qatna pottery. Its appearance on cylinder seals points to the popularity of this imported motif during the Late Bronze Age in Syria.   PP

1. Compare S. Marinatos and Hirmer 1973, figs. 22, IX, 39, 76, 78, 80, 81, 109, XXX, 154, 169, 171, etc.

141

141

EGYPTIAN VESSEL

Gabbro
Height 15 cm (5⅞ in.); diameter 29.1 cm
(11½ in.)
Qatna, Royal Tomb
Late Bronze Age context, 15th–
14th century B.C.
Egypt, Dynasty 1–2 manufacture,
ca. 3000–2700 B.C.
Homs Museum, Homs, Syria MSH02G–i2369

142

AMPHORA

White calcite
Height 43.2 cm (17 in.)
Qatna, Royal Tomb
Late Bronze Age, 15th–14th century B.C.
Homs Museum, Homs, Syria MSH02G–i1993

Fifty-six stone vessels were discovered
in the Royal Tomb of Qatna and in the
corridor leading down to it from Hall A of
the Royal Palace, most of them made of
white calcite, others of serpentine, granite,
and other hardstones.[1] Stone vessels found
at Qatna occur in various shapes, many of
which resemble Egyptian types. Some of
the vessels were imported directly from
Egypt, while others, derived from Egyptian
archetypes, were produced in local workshops in the Syro-Levantine region, a supposition supported by the quantity of such
vessels found at sites such as Qatna, Ugarit,
and Kamid el-Loz. However, in most cases,
it is difficult to distinguish between imported Egyptian vessels and locally produced, "Egyptianizing" types.

The vessel above, a large, heavy jar, was
found standing in the main chamber of the
tomb. It has a squat form without a neck
and two tubular lug handles on the shoulders. The type is usually termed an Archaic
jar, since it was produced in Egypt during
Dynasties 1 and 2 (ca. 3000–2700 B.C.;
see cat. no. 143). Such jars were often traded
or brought as gifts to Syria during the
second millennium B.C. When this vessel
was in the inventory of the tomb before
the destruction of 1340 B.C., it was already
one and a half millennia old. Although its
antiquity was probably not recognized, the
vessel must nevertheless have been highly
valued as an exotic item because of its

archaic shape and rare material; it is made of gabbro, a very distinctive gray-black stone with large white inclusions.[2]

The vessel at left, an amphora, was found in the sarcophagus of the western side chamber.[3] Made of white calcite, it is 43 centimeters high and thus one of the tallest stone vessels recovered at Qatna. A high base, worked from the same piece of stone as the vessel itself, supports a slender body with a high neck and equally high handles. The latter are angled at the top and directly connected to the rim. While this type of slender calcite amphora is principally found in Egypt, the Qatna vessel was probably manufactured during the Late Bronze Age in a Levantine workshop.[4]

The large number of stone vessels dating from the Early, Middle, and Late Bronze Ages that were assembled in the Royal Tomb of Qatna clearly demonstrates the high esteem in which these objects were held as grave goods. Within the burial chambers, their grouping is significant, with a high concentration in the prestigious southern chamber, which is identified as the "throne or banquet room of the deceased king."[5] Clearly separated from the pottery vessels that served as containers for food, they were likely containers for oils, ointments, or perfumes and functioned also as exotic prestige goods.   PP

1. The typological classifications and chronological determinations of stone vessels presented in this entry are based on Alexander Ahrens's master's thesis at the University of Tübingen (Ahrens 2005).
2. All mineralogical identifications in this section were made by Judit Zöldföldi, Tübingen.
3. For the location, see Al-Maqdissi et al. 2003, fig. 9.
4. Ahrens 2005.
5. Al-Maqdissi et al. 2003, pp. 206–8.

143
CONVERTED EGYPTIAN VESSEL

Porphyritic basalt
Height 16.5 cm (6½ in.)
Crete, Zakros
Late Minoan IB context, 15th century B.C.
Egypt, Dynasty 1–3 manufacture,
ca. 3000–2575 B.C.
Archaeological Museum, Heraklion, Greece
Λ 2695

This Egyptian globular vase of brown porphyritic basalt with white crystals was transformed by a Minoan artist into a bridge-spouted jar with the opening of a pouring hole just below the rim and the addition of a spout made of a probably local, soft gray-brown stone. The square depressions on the spout's outer surface may originally have been inlaid with some kind of white material in imitation of the white crystals of the vase's stone. Further alterations of the Egyptian vase included the removal of its original pair of cylindrical handles and their replacement by horizontal handles, which were attached to the body by four vertical paired openings, still visible today on both sides of the vessel at its maximum diameter.[1]

Egyptian vases of this type are dated to the Early Dynastic and Old Kingdom periods; this particular vessel, however, was altered on Crete much later, in Late Minoan IB.[2] Certainly valued as a prestige item, this vessel also acquired what was probably a ritual function connected with the offering of liquids: it was found safely kept in one of the clay cists inside the treasury room of the palace at Zakros, where excavations produced numerous objects (clay, stone, and faience rhyta, stone mace heads and lamps, bronze double-axes) believed to have formed the liturgical equipment of the palace's central shrine. Also found was a second altered Egyptian vessel of similar material and date.[3] The imitation of Egyptian prototypes and the adaptation of Egyptian originals according to Minoan aesthetics seem to have been common practice in Minoan lapidary art throughout its history of development.[4]

ELD

1. L. Platon in *Crete–Egypt* 2000, pp. 209–10, no. 208.
2. Warren 1969, p. 109, no. 8; *Crete–Egypt* 2000, p. 210.
3. Platon 1966, pp. 181–82; Platon 1971, pp. 133–48.
4. Warren 1995, excerpted in *Crete–Egypt* 2000, p. 200.

Figure 77. Royal Palace, Qatna, as restored, view from the east.

ITALIAN ARCHAEOLOGICAL RESEARCH AT QATNA

DANIÈLE MORANDI BONACOSSI

From the time of the Middle Bronze Age, Qatna was the capital of a territorial state of primary importance on the geopolitical chessboard of Syria, Mesopotamia, and the Levant.[1] The end of Middle Bronze Age II and the transition to the Late Bronze Age marked another important phase of reorganization at the site. In this period, the great Royal Palace (fig. 77) was constructed on top of the Middle Bronze Age cemetery. The Syrian-Italian team excavated the eastern portion, dominated by a grand ceremonial hall (A), which had access to an underground corridor leading to the Royal Tomb and, farther east, a series of probable warehouses for the storage of agricultural surplus. The city's new building program also included a series of buildings surrounding the palace in which the ceremonial, residential, administrative, and craft activities associated with court members and dignitaries were organized.

Two of these buildings, the Lower City Palace and the Eastern Palace, are currently being excavated. Sixty-five rooms belonging to the Lower City Palace, situated midway between the acropolis and the city's north gate, have been investigated, including a throne room with a large vestibule, warehouses, kitchens, a cellar, and bathrooms. In Rooms R and Y, hundreds of elephant ivory, antler, and bone inlays were discovered. These two rooms, probably used for finishing and storing precious goods destined for decorating luxury furniture, also contained about 50 cuneiform tablets belonging to an administrative archive. Most of these are records of animals owned by and cereal and beer rations destined for the residents of this large palace institution. Found in other rooms of the Lower City Palace were fine imported Cypriot and Mycenaean pottery,

evidence of the extensive commercial relations maintained by the building's inhabitants.

Excavation of the Eastern Palace, a vast building immediately to the east of the Royal Palace, was begun in 2006 by the Syrian-Italian mission. Although the plan is still far from complete, it includes at least one large courtyard and about fifteen rooms whose floors are covered with thick mortar, like those found in the other palace buildings.

Both of these structures, together with Residence C, situated south of the Royal Palace, were abandoned in the fourteenth century B.C., probably at the same time as (or shortly after) the destruction of the main palace. After a period of partial abandonment—or at least a reduction in size—during the final part of Late Bronze Age II and for most of Iron Age I (from the end of the 10th century B.C. onward), the site of Tell Mishrifeh underwent a new phase of economic and urban growth, this time not as the capital of an independent kingdom but probably as an administrative center of the Luwian-Aramaic principality of Hama. The archaeological evidence suggests that during Iron Ages II and III (ca. 900–550 B.C.) and until its abandonment, Qatna was an important agricultural center specializing in the working of wool and the production of colored textiles.[2]

1. Paleoenvironmental studies have shown that this urban center grew up on the eastern shore of a small lake, which probably originated from the water of karstic springs immediately southwest of the site. The name Qatna, probably documented in Egyptian Middle Kingdom sources of the early second millennium B.C., derives from a Semitic root meaning "narrow" and may refer to the artificial narrowing of an area of the springs to create the lake.
2. For further reference, see the papers in Morandi Bonacossi 2007.

144
FACE PLAQUE

Ivory (elephant), limestone, gypsum
Height 5.6 cm (2¼ in.); width 6.8 cm (2⅝ in.)
Qatna, Lower City Palace
Late Bronze Age, ca. 1500–1350 B.C.
Homs Museum, Homs, Syria
MSH02–3266.707

The Late Bronze Age Lower City Palace yielded partly worked bone, horn, and antler pieces, as well as bitumen lumps, glass beads and inlays, stone inlays and bronze slag, and more than 500 ivory, antler, and bone inlays in Rooms R and Y in the central and northwestern sectors. At least 340 of the inlays are of ivory, and most were probably destined to be fitted on to wood furniture. The majority of these are of elephant ivory, a type found much less frequently in Late Bronze Age Syria than hippopotamus ivory. It was used for the most precious royal furniture, as is demonstrated by ivory finds from the Royal Palace and other non-palatial contexts at Ugarit. That the Qatna ivory ornaments were found in a palace and are of the rarest and most costly variety, together with the evidence of secondary

workshop activities in Rooms R and Y of the Lower City Palace (as evidenced by large quantities of finished and partly worked inlay pieces), indicates that these ivory inlays were intended for a royal elite and that they were finished, stored, and assembled within palatial premises.[1]

The most striking among these objects in elephant ivory, which are cut into various shapes, primarily geometric, is an appliqué ornament in the form of a human face carved in low relief and highly polished. The eyes were inlaid in limestone and gypsum, representing the eye white and the pupil, respectively (only the inlay of the right eye is present). This face, which most likely embellished a furniture appliqué set or was part of a composite statuette (as the flat back and wedge-shaped mortise groove for tenon jointing would suggest), shows clear iconographic and stylistic similarities with the Hathor masks that were widespread throughout the Near East and eastern Mediterranean during the Late Bronze Age. This resemblance is evident in the strong frontality and the clearly Egyptianizing style (seen in the distinctly triangular composition of the face and the proportion and shape of the inlaid eye contour, with emphasized lower lachrymal

ducts); however, the characteristic Hathor wig framing the face and the cow's ears of the goddess are absent. Unfortunately, the context in which the face would have been placed remains unknown, which prevents a fuller comprehension of its iconography.

Carved in a manner that was highly modeled and at the same time extraordinarily delicate, this splendid appliqué ornament was probably intended to celebrate a Qatna royal or court personage by evoking, through familiar Nilotic imagery and composition, the epoch's most powerful political entity, Egypt. This assimilation of Egyptian (along with Aegean) cultural styles can be seen in all types of artistic endeavor—ivory, metalwork, jewelry, seals, wall paintings—found in Late Bronze Age Syrian palace culture. The local kings used luxury artifacts like this one to emulate the elite symbols of foreign states in order to legitimize their own authority. The final result is an appliqué ornament, most likely locally produced in a Syrian court environment, that skillfully blends Egyptian symbolism with local features.

DMB

1. For further reference, see Luciani 2006 and Gachet-Bizollon 2007.

UGARIT IN THE LATE BRONZE AGE

BASSAM JAMOUS

The Late Bronze Age (ca. 1600–1200/1150 B.C.) is one of the most important periods in the study of international and trade relations in the Near East. As a result of the wealth of documents passing from Egypt to the Syro-Levantine region, Anatolia, and northern Mesopotamia that have survived, we now know how international relations were formed and have a clear idea of the nature of political life at that time.

Toward the end of the thirteenth and the turn of the twelfth century B.C., the cities of the Syrian coast were invaded by the Sea Peoples. Nevertheless, relations and contacts continued between kingdoms of the region, as they did between east and west, as revealed by finds made in coastal sites along the Mediterranean. Relations with the Greek isles at the close of the Late Bronze Age and the beginning of the Iron Age are not clear, although there have been related discoveries at Tell Soukas, Hamam Tepe, Ras Ibn Hani, and Tell Kazel, as well as at Tell Arqa.

Our knowledge of relations between the Mediterranean kingdoms is based on archaeological finds and texts relating to activities of merchants, craftsmen, travelers, diplomats, and immigrants; political visits, gift exchange, and the conclusion of economic, political, and social treaties; and intellectual life represented by the visual arts and literature.

In his excavations of Ugarit extending over many decades beginning in 1929, the French archaeologist Claude Schaeffer was able to establish the fact that the city served as a link between the Near East and the Aegean world. Indeed, Ugarit became a center of interaction between Egypt, Crete, Cyprus, and Anatolia.

Excavation work at the site of Ugarit continues today. The Syrian-French mission recently unearthed a collection of cuneiform tablets at the home of a merchant named Urtenu that deal with the economic and commercial activity of Ugarit during the Late Bronze Age. They are currently being studied.

Figure 78. The site of Ugarit.

UGARIT: GATEWAY TO THE MEDITERRANEAN

JEAN-CLAUDE MARGUERON

Excavations begun nearly eighty years ago have given us a very precise picture of the city of Ugarit—its residential districts and its temples, its culture, activities, economic foundations, and daily life. The discovery of the palace just before World War II and its excavation from 1948 to 1954 provided important information in all these areas. Furthermore, evidence of the interplay between various influences permits us to measure the extent of Ugarit's relations with the rest of the world. The architecture of the palace and the archaeological discoveries made there were particularly significant because, unlike the written documents, which cover only a relatively short period at the end of the city's history, they preserve the traces of influences over a much longer period of time.

The royal fortress appears to have been a complex edifice (fig. 79). Before going into the stages of its evolution and what they can tell us about the interplay of external relations, let us look at how it appeared at the time of its discovery, that is, in its state before the destruction of Ugarit, about 1180 B.C. At that time the fortress was a vast complex composed of older buildings—generally called the Royal Palace—and more recent constructions: the guardhouse, a great banquet hall, and a small temple. The connecting element between these different parts was a royal square, on to which the doors of these buildings opened, and where the two major routes (eastern and southern) that connected the palace to the city converged. The whole formed a closed and very well protected ensemble, especially on the side facing the western plain, where the road to the port of Minet el-Beidha provided access to the sea. The imposing fortified gate attached to the ramparts gave the palace not only the appearance but also the function of a fortress.

The Royal Palace was only one part of the fortress and is so called today because it was long believed to represent the entirety of the buildings devoted to the ruler—which it did, but only during one particular period. Architecturally, it was composed of very different elements. The entrance porch opened on to a royal square supervised by an official and led to a ceremonial courtyard, at the far end of which was the throne room. Along the east side of this official compound a group of four units could be reached. The first, atypical because it was very densely built, continued to the east through a large courtyard (the second unit) bordered by a porch with a colonnade and

connected to the area of the royal tombs. The third unit was a large banquet hall with a sort of dais at the south end on which the king would take his place, and to the east was another unit (the fourth) organized around a courtyard closed off by a columned porch. From the banquet hall leading south, one came to a room furnished with a large, well-proportioned basin. Beyond the eastern limits of these four units stretched a garden bordered by elegant rooms and a kiosk.

The whole was in fact merely a juxtaposition of disparate elements; the principle of a central space surrounded by rooms, in keeping with the Mesopotamian model, had been applied, but new spatial arrangements—successions of rooms and courtyards, for example—were also created. Moreover, certain modules, such as the columned porches so frequently seen, were also characteristic. This demonstrates that the architects of Ugarit took their inspiration from sources quite different from those typical of Mesopotamia.

But the palace of Ugarit was not only a juxtaposition of more or less disparate units connected at the ground-floor level. It also had one or several upper levels. The life of the palace took place on the upper level; the storerooms and the common areas—with the exception of the official rooms—were located on the ground-floor level. The royal apartments were situated above the throne room and the adjacent units, the banquet hall, and the room with the basin. The arrangement of the staircases and the way the doors functioned indicate that access to the entire sector was controlled from the royal apartments; guests and courtiers were invited to assemble in one of the three ceremonial halls—a fine example of the precision with which the operation of the palace was planned.

We have at present no means to establish with certainty the date of the first building's construction; it may have been toward the end of the sixteenth or the beginning of the fifteenth century B.C. The construction was cumulative and included demolitions (sometimes deliberate) as well as renovations, such that the building as a whole perhaps displays a certain incoherence in terms of organization. The most telling evidence is the final phase, which allows us to see a precise moment in its operation, while it incorporates the traces of earlier modifications.

It thus appears that the oldest section was part of the unit with the very dense structural network that adjoined the official

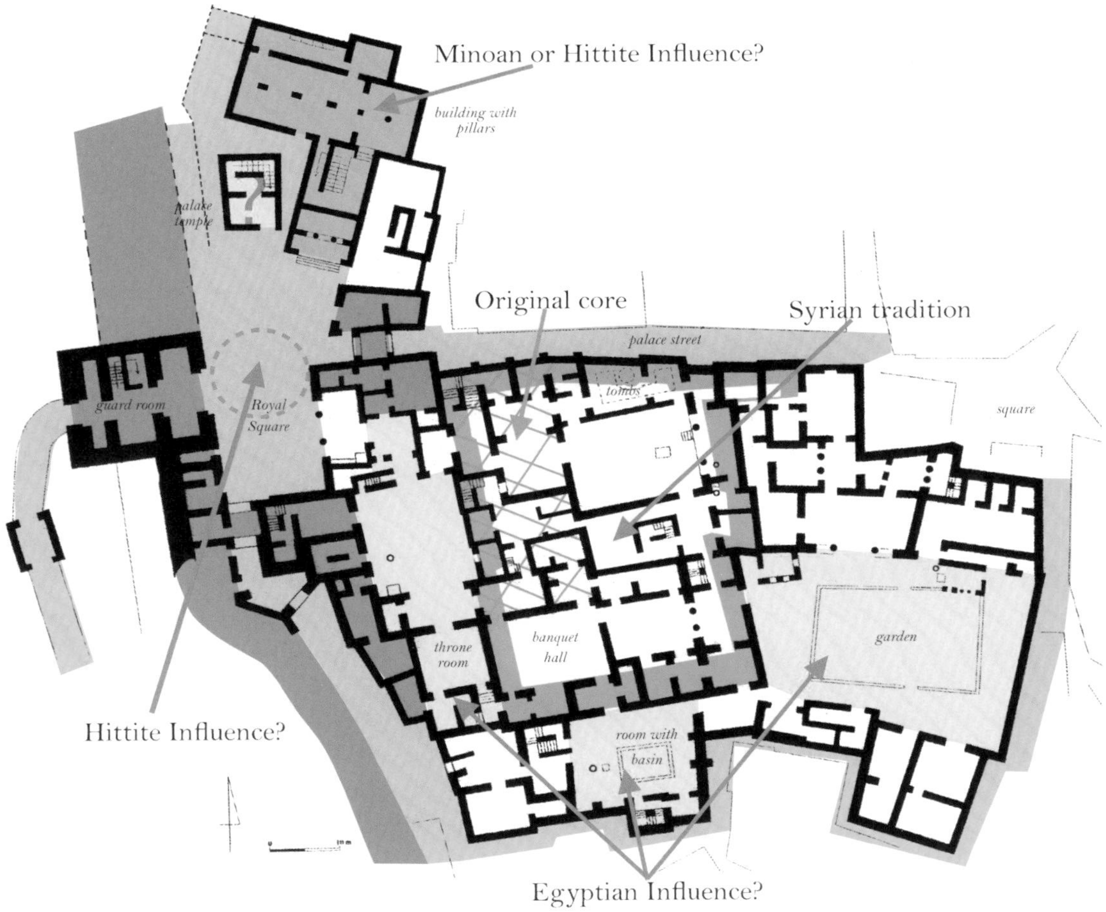

Figure 79. Plan of the Royal Fortress, Ugarit, showing stages of development.

Minoan or Hittite Influence?

building with pillars

palace temple

Original core

palace street

Syrian tradition

tombs

guard room

Royal Square

square

throne room

banquet hall

garden

Hittite Influence?

room with basin

Egyptian Influence?

courtyard on the east side, undoubtedly the one surviving element of an earlier, more complex building. This part is clearly marked by Syrian influences. Successive extensions to the east and south resulted in a coherent grouping of units that formed the sectors at the heart of the palace. But the most important addition was the official courtyard and the throne room adjoining the banquet hall, because it made use of an absolutely new architectural plan: an axial organization characteristic of Egyptian architecture. It would seem therefore that this part was built at the apogee of Egypt's influence on the kingdom of Ugarit, in the late fifteenth century B.C. Shortly thereafter, the palace was embellished with a room with a basin and a garden, elements that also point directly to Egypt. This is not surprising: Ugarit was a window from the east on the Mediterranean and, while it did not come under the hegemony of Egypt on land, the extensive trade channels by sea could certainly account for architectural influences. In any case, features such as axiality, basins, and gardens had Egyptian rather than Near Eastern characteristics.

With the rise of Hittite supremacy and Ugarit's quasi-protectorate status, new influences began to make themselves felt in the transformations that the palace underwent beginning in the fourteenth century B.C.; the monumental gate, the postern, and the ramparts that protected the entrance of the palace complex all bear a decidedly Hittite stamp. This new influence

also involved the very concept of the palace itself: instead of a palace comprising a single large building that included its various functions, the fortress plan was adopted so that the groups of different buildings within it formed a network of structured relationships. The old palace—bereft of its entranceway—was integrated in its entirety into the new zone. Architectural inspiration may also have come from Crete, since the new banquet hall replicates a plan well known from the Minoan palaces at Knossos and Mallia.

It is unusual for a palace to display such clear traces of the various and successive influences to which it was exposed. Architecture is not alone in attesting to the close relations between the kingdom of Ugarit and the thriving world of the eastern Mediterranean in the Late Bronze Age, or to its capacity to adapt foreign forms to its own genius. The material objects that have been recovered tell the same story. The cuneiform tablets, in particular, from archival deposits disseminated throughout the palace, have turned up documents written in eight different languages: Ugaritic, Hurrian, Akkadian, Hittite, Luwian, Sumerian, Egyptian, and Cypro-Minoan (see cat. nos. 98, 99). Ugaritic may have been a local language, but Akkadian was the language of diplomacy and culture, and it constituted half the texts recovered—proof enough of the dominant role that Mesopotamia still played at the time. Other influences also speak for the wide network of relations that the

237

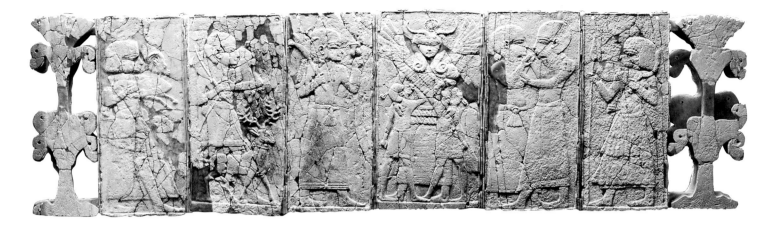

Figure 80. Carved ivory bed panels. Ugarit, Royal Palace, Room 44. Late Bronze Age. National Museum, Damascus RS 16.056+28.031, 3599

palace maintained with the Mediterranean world. The artifacts of daily life—ceramics, stone and bronze tools, figurines, seals, ornaments, weapons, weights, and molds—are not always revealing. More refined objects, however—gifts, perhaps, or objects left behind after extended sojourns—point to Ugarit's Hittite neighbors or Egypt (alabaster vases with hieroglyphic inscriptions and the wedding scarab of Amenhotep III and Tiye).

Ivory, a prized raw material sometimes of local origin but more often imported from Egypt, was used to make several remarkable pieces recovered from the palace. Among them are a horn carved from an elephant's tusk (see fig. 127) and a finely modeled head (cat. no. 145), no doubt part of a piece of furniture, and variously interpreted as male or female, both objects

demonstrating the mastery achieved by the ivory carvers of Ugarit. This same expertise is also evident in a round pedestal table, more than one meter in diameter, sculpted with animal figures drawn from the collective repertoire of the Levant during the Late Bronze Age. But it is the ivory bed with sculpted panels (fig. 80), with particularly marked Egyptian influence, that may best display the cosmopolitan milieu of the palace, where all the traditions of the eastern Mediterranean and Mesopotamia met face to face.

The palace of Ugarit, both by its architecture and by its furnishings and works of art, stands as the most eloquent expression of these forces, which created the flowering of civilization on the shores of the Near Eastern world.

145

HEAD OF A DEITY

Ivory, copper alloy, silver with gold inlay
Height 15.2 cm (6 in.)
Ugarit, Royal Palace
Late Bronze Age, 15th–13th century B.C.
National Museum, Damascus, Syria 3601

This exceptional ivory head was excavated in Courtyard III of the Royal Palace, generally believed to be a garden with a pleasure pavilion. Next to the head was an ivory bed (fig. 80) and table and an ivory frame that may have served for its presentation.[1]

The head was carved from elephant tusk, with metallic elements added, some now missing. The eye sockets, cast separately in copper alloy, retain an adhesive for the insertion of the eyes. Deep grooves in the ivory mark the brows, which were also encrusted with another material. Along the forehead are elements in the shape of semicircular silver plaques with gold concentric lines. X-radiographs show bronze pegs above the ears; these would have been used to secure horns, now missing, which were probably made of gilded bronze. Deep grooves alongside each cheek were likely inserted with metal to represent hair locks or a beard. Traces

of gold foil remain on the crown, the top of which is unfinished; it is not clear if the crown was broken or originally had a finial attached or inserted.

The specific identity of the figure is unknown, although it is certain that a deity was intended, as indicated by the now missing horns. There is no exact parallel for the shape of the headdress. While it is not clear whether the figure is male or female, the appearance is youthful, which could suggest the weather god Baal or his consort, Anat. The plaques on the forehead and the locks of hair originally affixed to the cheeks would seem to be significant traits, inviting comparison with images of

145

fertility goddesses displaying "love locks," such as the ivory lid with female feeding goats (cat. no. 261) or faience face vessels (see discussion in cat. no. 211). The proximity of the head to the ivory bed and table points to its possible use in rituals of the perambulation and clothing of divine statues. Such rituals are recorded in cuneiform archives at Ugarit.   AC

1. Gachet-Bizollon 2007, no. 408.

146

BOWL WITH HUNTING SCENES

Gold
Height 4.7 cm (1⅞ in.); diameter
17.5 cm (6⅞ in.)
Ugarit
Late Bronze Age, 14th century B.C.
National Museum, Aleppo, Syria M10129
(4572)

Two extraordinary gold vessels were discovered on the acropolis of Ugarit, calling to mind the luxury wares listed among the greeting gifts and dowries sent by Near Eastern rulers to the Egyptian pharaoh. Displaced from their original context, the vessels were found just 48 centimeters below the surface of the soil in the area of a structure southwest of the Temple of Baal.[1] While they differ in shape, format, and aspects of style, both render the royal theme of the hunt, one as a band of continuous narrative (cat. no. 147) and the other as a series of abstracted scenes arranged in registers.[2]

Hemispherical in shape and formed over a bitumen core, the bowl pictured here is more intricate in its design, which is executed in repoussé from the interior and chased on the outer face. Seven discrete compositions are disposed around a band bordered by a running spiral pattern beneath the rim. A second spiral border separates this register from a band that shows pendant pomegranates, striding lions, and collapsing bulls within zones created by voluted palmette plants.[3] A third band of fleeing and collapsing ibexes surrounds a rosette pattern at the base. Two hunters, wearing short-sleeved fringed tunics with cross-straps and tasseled belts,[4] spear and stab a rampant roaring lion that had apparently already felled a stag. Despite the danger of the encounter, the violence of the moment is barely conveyed by the posture of the figures.

Three other scenes echo the abstract quality of these savage encounters. A rampant lion paws a seated griffin with an exaggerated vulture beak, powerful wings, and a collar with a loop or medallion. With the crossing ibexes, they frame a heraldic confrontation of an Egyptianizing female winged sphinx and a horned lion flanking a voluted palmette.[5] Their movement toward one another is suggested only by their forelegs. More dynamic are three scenes of lions leaping onto their prey from behind; two of the lions appear in fully extended posture and the third mounts his victim, biting its back and pawing at its ribs. The reaction to the assault is expressed by the turn of one bull's head and the extension of its rear legs, and the collapsing forelegs of the remaining bull and ibex. Similar devices are used in the lower registers.

The postures of the lions and the semi-folded wings of the griffin and sphinx suggest reflections of Aegean art that may have infused Syrian styles centuries earlier. These contrast with the arrested movement and flat modeling of the human and animal figures, which, along with the general composition and such details as the shoulder star on the lions and the elaborate patterning on the sphinx, are unmistakably Near Eastern in origin.

146

Perhaps the closest parallels for both the combat groups and the vegetation on the Ugarit bowl can be found among the treasures of Tutankhamun. A gold dagger sheath (fig. 121), chariot attachments (fig. 122), and an alabaster vessel (fig. 131) are embellished with an array of scenes showing felines and canines attacking ibexes and bulls in a similar but perhaps more lively manner, without the restraint

of registers and symmetrically placed figures. Shared landscape elements include Egyptian pondweed shoots,[6] while the hybrid plants on the Ugarit bowl—combining "South flowers," volutes, leaves, tendrils, and papyrus tips—are derivative and demonstrate "ignorance of the naturalistic prototypes . . . borrowed from the Nile" (contrast fig. 121).[7] This further indicates that the international style bowl was

locally manufactured by a Canaanite craftsman. JA

1. Schaeffer 1949, pp. 4–5; Kantor 1945 (1999 ed.), p. 521, assigned to Stratum I (15th–14th century B.C.).
2. Schaeffer (1949, p. 23) notes the artistic differences between two contemporary vessels; Kantor (1945 [1999 ed.], pp. 522–28) considers the patera an "indigenous style" and the bowl Egyptianizing; see also Feldman 2002, p. 26 n. 25, and Feldman 2006b, pp. 51–53, 65.

146, alternate view

146, alternate view

3. See Ward 2003 for pomegranate imagery and trade in the commodity.

4. For Asiatics wearing cross-straps in Egyptian art, see W. S. Smith 1965, fig. 211.

5. For the winged lion with bull's horns on works from Ugarit, see Feldman 2006b, p. 81.

6. Kantor 1945 (1999 ed.), p. 524.

7. Ibid., pp. 527–28.

147

147

PATERA WITH CHARIOT HUNT

Gold
Diameter 18.8 cm (7⅜ in.)
Ugarit, Acropolis
Late Bronze Age, 15th–14th century B.C.
Musée du Louvre, Paris, Département des
Antiquités Orientales AO17208

This gold patera was found at a shallow depth near the Temple of Baal on the acropolis of Ugarit, buried with the gold bowl (cat. no. 146).[1] With straight sides and a rim molding, it was decorated in relief by embossing, probably with a wood relief template. Concentric circles define two separate relief friezes and an unadorned center.

The inner frieze depicts four ibexes, framing the central circle. The outer concentric frieze depicts a hunt. A man in a chariot chases animals, the last of which seems to be chasing the chariot. The whole forms a dynamic, endless composition.

The hunter's hairstyle and beard identify him as Near Eastern in the cosmopolitan world of the eastern Mediterranean during the Late Bronze Age. His bow is Mesopotamian in design. The light chariot is of a type invented in the Syro-Anatolian region during the second millennium B.C. Drawn by two horses, it is followed by a hound. Horses, introduced in the Near East during the second millennium B.C., were a privilege of the elite, especially at Ugarit, where the horse trade flourished.

The fleeing animals are not depicted naturalistically. Their legs are extended in the flying gallop, a convention developed in the eastern Mediterranean during the Late Bronze Age under the influence of Cretan and Mycenaean art. The hunter's first target is an ibex, in front of which four other animals—a mighty bull, a cow and her calf, and a smaller bull—flee for their lives.

This iconography introduces us to the symbolic language of the Near East, executed in the specific idiom of Ugarit. The hunt was a widespread expression of royal power. It represented not only the pleasures and privileges of royalty, but also its function with regard to external threats. Dangerous forces were usually symbolized by wild animals, such as lions, but, here, it is a family of bovines. In this author's opinion, this unusual scene may

be explained by Ugaritic mythology and religion, in which the major gods assumed the form of bovines—the god El as an adult bull, Baal as a wild young bull, and the goddesses, especially Anat, as cows.

The patera thus displays a traditional representation of power, but set in relation to the local deities. In this unusual confrontation between royal and divine power, the king is shown killing animals associated with deities, which could be interpreted as the divine endangered by the secular. It also may be understood through the role played by the king (as hunter) relative to that of the gods (as game) in religious ceremonies at Ugarit. A major part of the royal cult was animal sacrifice, and bovines were reserved for the highest gods, especially Baal and El.

Not surprisingly the patera was buried close to the abode of Baal, lord of the city, its decoration expressing the royal power of Ugarit while at the same time serving as an offering by the king to his gods. The patera perfectly illustrates the close relationships among the different civilizations in the region, combining aspects of the Aegean style with original forms to express beliefs that were essential to the cultural identity of the region.   SC

1. For further reference, see Schaeffer 1934, pp. 128–31, fig. 10, pl. XVI; Schaeffer 1949, pp. 1–48, pls. I, VII, figs. 3, 4; Amiet 1977, p. 392, fig. 509; Caubet and Stucky in *Au pays de Baal et d'Astarté* 1983, pp. 159–60, no. 177; and Matoïan in *Le royaume d'Ougarit* 2004, no. 1.

148

CEREMONIAL AXE

Iron, copper alloy, gold inlay
Length 19.5 cm (7⅝ in.); width 6.4 cm (2½ in.)
Ugarit
Late Bronze Age, 14th–13th century B.C.
National Museum, Aleppo, Syria M10127

This ceremonial axe—found in a small shrine in the northwest corner of the palace complex at Ugarit—is composed of an iron blade and a copper head. The blade is held between the heads of two lions with open mouths so that it is, in effect, the manifestation of their roar. The foreparts of a boar emerge from the back of the axe head, and gold inlay articulates the animals

as well as the floral elements of the background. The motif of an axe blade emerging from the mouth of an animal first appears at the end of the third millennium B.C. and ultimately may be Central Asian in origin (fig. 81). By the second millennium B.C., however, several examples of the motif are known. For instance, the blade of the Hittite sword god carved in relief at Yazılıkaya emerges from the open mouths of two flanking lions, and the blade of a Middle Elamite axe from Choga Zanbil (cat. no. 149) emerges from a roaring lion head. With the latter, a recumbent boar embellished with electrum appears on the back of the axe head.

Although the widespread use of iron did not occur until the early first millennium B.C., both meteoric and smelted iron played an increasing role as a valuable commodity in the ancient Near East in the preceding centuries. By the latter half of the second millennium B.C., textual inventories and archaeological finds indicate that iron objects were produced in Anatolia, northern Syria, and Egypt. This axe head is among the most metallurgically sophisticated objects recovered from this period.[1]

With a melting point beyond the capability of existing pyrotechnology, iron could not be completely separated from its slag or cast. Instead, partially reduced iron was wrought or hammered into shape while hot. The hammering resulted in a lamellar structure seen in the corroded surface of this blade. Wrought iron was relatively soft unless carburized by heating. As this axe has not been analyzed, it is not known if it was hardened after forming.

The copper alloy socket appears to have been cast directly onto the blade, providing a strong join. After casting, its surface was decorated with gold inlay imitating a decorative technique that probably developed in Egypt during the Middle Kingdom. It has been suggested that the copper alloy used in Egyptian inlay objects contained minor amounts of gold and little or no lead, which provided a thick, dark patina when treated with acidic compounds.[2] Although a similar alloy may not have been used here, the oxidized surface of the socket undoubtedly provided a dramatic visual contrast with both the gold inlay and the silvery appearance of the blade when it was new.[3] A falcon from Ugarit is inlaid in a similar manner.[4]   J-FL

148

1. An overview of iron finds prior to the Iron
   Age is provided by Waldbaum 1980.
2. Ogden 2000, p. 160.
3. Analysis done many years ago on this axe
   head revealed the presence of tin but no precious metals. See Thomas 2005, p. 725 n. 88.
4. *Ebla to Damascus* 1985, no. 137.

149

CEREMONIAL AXE

Silver, electrum, copper alloy
Length 12.4 cm (4⅞ in.)
Choga Zanbil
Late Bronze Age, reign of Untash-Napirisha,
ca. 1340–1300 B.C.
Musée du Louvre, Paris, Département des
Antiquités Orientales sb3973

This axe is one of the most remarkable
weapons to bear the name of Untash-
Napirisha, the Middle Elamite king. Ruling
Elam in southwestern Iran during the
second half of the fourteenth century B.C.,
Untash-Napirisha founded a new city,
Dur-Untash-Napirisha (Fortress of Untash-
Napirisha, modern Choga Zanbil), 45

kilometers southeast of Susa, and was
destined to unite the various cults of the
empire. At Dur-Untash-Napirisha, all
the deities of the kingdom of Anshan[1]
and Susa were placed under the aegis of
Inshushinak, god of the lowlands, and
Napirisha, god of the highlands. Both are
mentioned together in the inscriptions of
the temple built at the top of the ziggurat
that dominated the center of the city.

The axe was discovered northwest of
the stepped tower, in the eastern temple of
Kiririsha, the consort of Napirisha.[2] More
than a hundred maces inscribed with the
king's name were found in the temple,
as well as a group of bronze objects decorated with animal figures, a number of
bronze and faience animal figurines (especially boars), and three axes bearing the
name of Untash-Napirisha, the present one
included. They were presented by the king
as votive offerings in the temples of the
city. At the time of the Assyrian raids in
the seventh century B.C., they were taken
to the temple of the goddess Kiririsha
to be sorted out by the looters. The less
valuable objects were left behind, but the
present axe had been carefully buried

under the wall at the northern corner of
the cella.

The inscription on the axe head reads
simply: "I, Untash-Napirisha." This weapon
was not meant to be used in combat but to
symbolize royal authority. Starting in the
third millennium B.C., the king was represented leading his soldiers, weapon in hand,
to signify the duty of kings to defend their
subjects. Thus, on the Sumerian Stele of
the Vultures, Eannatum, king of Lagash,
brandishes a sickle sword in his right hand;
on the victory stele of the Akkadian king
Naram-Sin, the ruler presses his weapons
to his chest; in later periods, Assyrian
kings carried maces.

In the Elamite world, weapons were so
richly decorated that they became veritable
works of art. This was especially true of
axes and hammers, whose shapes lent
themselves particularly well to elaborate
ornamentation. They were often given by
the king to high functionaries as tokens
of appreciation. This custom—attested on
several seal impressions, the best known
of which is that of Kuk-Simut, an official
at the court of Idadu II, who ruled the
Shimashki before 2000 B.C.[3]—served to

244

149

Figure 81. Silver and gold-foil shaft-hole axe head. Central Asia, Bactria-Margiana. Late 3rd–early 2nd millennium B.C. The Metropolitan Museum of Art, New York, Purchase, Harris Brisbane Dick Fund and James N. Spear and Schimmel Foundation Inc. Gifts, 1982 1982.5

stimulate a creative production that found its highest expression in Margiana and Bactria. Beginning around 2300 B.C., axes were decorated with ibexes[4] and, even more often, with lions.[5] At the end of the third millennium B.C., lion heads were depicted as if they were "spitting out" the blade.

This motif can be seen here, where a crouching wild boar is attached with rivets to the external edge of the socket, while a trapezoidal silver blade emerges from the open mouth of a lion. The same tradition inspired the preservation of such ancient objects for centuries[6] and continued into the Iron Age, as seen in the Luristan culture.[7]

The polychromy of Untash-Napirisha's axe has faded: the electrum plating that covers the body of the boar—made of a material resistant to X-ray[8]—retains its sheen, but the transition between the shaft and the blade, made of an alloy of silver and copper mixed in varying proportions,[9] as well as the red of the inscription are now hardly visible.[10] This object is not unique to the second half of the second millennium B.C.: a silver ceremonial axe found in the palace temple at Ugarit presents a decoration with the same animals—a lion and a boar—and displays a similar play of colors and materials (cat. no. 148).

AB

1. Tal-i Malyan/Anshan was in the Fars region, not far from present-day Shiraz.
2. For further reference, see Ghirshman 1953, p. 227, fig. 9; Amiet 1966, p. 358, no. 265; Ghirshman 1966, p. 101, pls. LIII:1, 2, LXXXIII: GTZ 163; Orthmann 1975, fig. 301-c; Amiet 1977, p. 394, fig. 530; and Amiet 1988, p. 94, fig. 52.
3. Amiet 1966, p. 258, no. 1879. A similar gesture can be seen on the impression of the seal of Imazu, king of Anshan; ibid., pp. 256–57, no. 186.
4. Amiet 1976, no. 19.
5. Ibid., no. 18; at the Musée du Louvre, AO 24793 and 26757; at Shahdad, Hakemi 1997, Gp 9, pp. 542, 638.
6. An axe from the beginning of the second millennium B.C., with a wing and the head of a raptor on the neck, and a unicorn dragon spitting out the blade (sb 2888) was found in a Middle Elamite context.
7. For example, Amiet 1976, nos. 51, 52, 56–58.
8. Without further details, from the report of the Laboratoire des Musées de France, Analyse LRMF no. 6970, dated October 24, 1979.
9. According to the same source, there is up to 41 percent copper in the blade but only 20 percent in the lion head.
10. The paste encrusted in the inscription shows traces of calcium colored with iron and impurities.

El, father of the gods (cat. no. 151); another in the shape of a bull, symbolic animal of Baal; and the last showing a smiting god similar to this one. They all retained traces of cloth, possibly used to wrap them before they were stored. The hoard was discovered among dwellings in a southern area of Ugarit[5] and may have belonged to a residential shrine or to a cultic place enclosed within the urban network.

This figure wears the same short kilt and conical crown ending in a globular tip seen on a number of similar objects. In contrast to one standing figure (cat. no. 20), where a thicker sheet of gold was originally set into grooves, all statues from this hoard display gold leaf thin enough to be applied by pressure, a technique that leaves no indentations on the surface of the figurine. Here, the gold leaf was not restricted to the divine crown, as is often the case with sculptures from Ugarit, but also applied over the face, as with the kneeling figure inscribed with the name of Hammurabi (cat. no. 1). Because the bronze used for these figurines originally appeared golden, the gold leaf was not meant for contrast. Instead, it offered some protection against oxidation and expressed the eternal character of the deity. Thus, it is unknown whether the figure was originally meant to be gilded or if the gold leaf was applied by a worshipper at some later stage in the life of the image; cuneiform tablets record such offerings of gold to the gods.

AC/ED

1. Seeden 1980.
2. Yon 1991.
3. Yon (1997) 2006, no. 40.
4. Amiet 1992.
5. Callot 1994.

150
SMITING DEITY

Bronze, gold
Height 12.5 cm (4⅞ in.)
Ugarit, Ville Sud
Late Bronze Age, 14th century B.C.
National Museum, Damascus, Syria s3572

The youthful god depicted in a dynamic stride, with his right arm raised above the shoulder, is by far the most popular of the divine figures in Levantine art.[1] The stance is borrowed from Egyptian images of triumphant kings striding over fallen enemies. Statues of this type found at Ugarit are believed to represent the young weather god Baal, hero of several myths recorded on cuneiform tablets. Baal was also a popular figure on stone stelae (see fig. 82),[2] ceramic incense burners,[3] and cylinder seals.[4] The statue was found together with three others: one depicting a god seated on a throne, interpreted as

151
SEATED DEITY

Bronze, gold
Height 13.5 cm (5⅜ in.)
Ugarit, Ville Sud
Late Bronze Age, 14th century B.C.
National Museum, Damascus, Syria s3573

This statue of a seated god was discovered wrapped in a linen cloth and buried below a house in the Ville Sud of

151

of divinity in the Near East, were once attached separately to the headdress. The eyes are missing their original inlay. The figure wears the Syrian mantle with rolled border (see also cat. nos. 20–22) and raises his right hand in a gesture of benevolence; the fingers on his left hand are curved to hold a cylindrical object, perhaps a cup or scepter (now missing). The tall crown flanked by plumes derives from Egyptian art, where it is often worn by Osiris. It also appears on a similarly posed bronze deity in Egyptianizing dress from Ugarit.[4]

MY

1. Kohlmeyer in *Ebla to Damascus* 1985, no. 133.
2. Schaeffer 1961–62, p. 191; Schaeffer 1963, p. 206.
3. Kohlmeyer in *Ebla to Damascus* 1985, no. 151.
4. Eaton-Krauss in *Ebla to Damascus* 1985, no. 132.

Figure 82. Limestone stele of Baal. Ugarit, Acropolis. Late Bronze Age. Musée du Louvre, Paris AO 15775

Ugarit. A bull and two standing gods in the smiting position characteristic of the weather god were buried in the same cache (cat. no. 150).[1] The three images were overlaid with gold foil, well preserved on the seated god, an indication of their importance. A hoard of unfinished electrum and silver jewelry as well as gold and silver ingots buried in a jar nearby suggest that the house may have belonged to a goldsmith.[2]

This seated figure closely resembles a deity—probably El, principal god of Ugarit—shown receiving offerings from a king on a stele from Ugarit.[3] Drill holes above the ears indicate that horns, emblems

with the same pose and similar characteristics are well known from Ugarit. One example (cat. no. 151) was part of a group discovered in the Ville Sud along with two statuettes of a young smiting god and a bull. Ugaritic poetry identifies these statuettes as the gods El and Baal.

This statuette was found in 1981 during the excavation of the Temple of the Rhytons at Ugarit.[1] Although the building had been plundered, remains attested to its ritual use: a stone stele, a large terracotta incense burner with relief decoration of a king praying beneath a sun disc, and a number of fragmentary rhyta locally made or imported from the Aegean (see pp. 426–32). The temple, surrounded by streets and houses, follows a plan familiar from other Levantine Late Bronze Age sanctuaries, such as those at Enkomi and Lachish: a side entrance led to a main room lined with stone benches. On the wall facing the entrance was a three-tiered bench or altar. A smaller room stood to one side. The large number of rhyta suggests that the building may have been a *marzihu*, a place for meetings and ritual banquets.   AC

1. For further reference, see Yon and Gachet 1989, p. 349; Yon 1990, pp. 1–9; Connan, Deschesne, and Dessort 1991; Yon 1991, pp. 347–48; and Yon (1997) 2006, no. 13.

153

Seated Deity

Bronze
Height 16.7 cm (6⅝ in.)
Byblos
Late Bronze Age, 15th–13th century B.C.
Direction Générale des Antiquités, Beirut, Lebanon 16588

This figure was found in the surface rubble rather than among the offering deposits of the Temple of the Obelisks at Byblos.[1] It was identified by Maurice Dunand, who excavated at Byblos, as the god El, not Reshef, as most scholars have done. El was a cosmic deity, creator of heavens and earth, who, according to myth, built the walls of Byblos. He is also well known at Ugarit, but there he is represented as an old bearded man (cat. no. 152), whereas the Byblos figure shows a young clean-shaven god.[2]

152

Seated Deity

Limestone
Height 25 cm (9⅞ in.)
Ugarit, Temple of the Rhytons
Late Bronze Age, 14th century B.C.
Archaeological Museum, Latakia, Syria
RS88.70

This statuette depicts a male figure clad in a garment that covers his shoulders and upper arms and reaches nearly to his ankles. A ceremonial robe with a rolled border, it resembles those worn by deities and kings represented in ritual scenes of Bronze Age Syria. The figure, with slightly sagging shoulders, has a long flat beard and wears an ovoid headdress, but without the bull's horns that would have indicated divinity. He gazes with large eyes that, like the brows, were originally inlaid. The forearms (now missing) may also have been inlaid. Analysis has shown that the adhesive used for the inlays was bitumen, which was often used in the Near East following a Mesopotamian tradition. Here, however, the bitumen has been traced to deposits in the area of Latakia, near Ugarit.

The figure is seated on a chair with a subtly curved high back, his feet resting on a low stool. Thus enthroned, he conveys an impression of both majesty and weariness. Most likely, the hands were originally extended in a peaceful gesture, with one palm facing the viewer. Bronze statues

153

below the torso and feet were affixed to thrones made of materials that no longer survive. The eye sockets most likely held inlays that are now lost.　　　SH/J-FL

1. Seeden 1982, p. 115, fig. 20.
2. Parrot, Chéhab, Moscati 1975, p. 10, fig. 7.
3. Dunand 1954, no. 7190, p. 76, pl. CLXI.
4. This statue has not been technically examined.

154

STANDING DEITY

Bronze
Height 17.5 cm (6⅞ in.)
Levant
Late 2nd–early 1st millennium B.C. (?)
Musée du Louvre, Paris, Département des
Antiquités Orientales AO4049

This statuette from the Musée du Louvre belongs to the martial "smiting god" type popular in the Syro-Levantine world in the second millennium B.C., which depicts a youthful deity in a dynamic pose, striding with the left leg forward and brandishing a weapon in the raised right hand.[1]

Draped in a long, tight-fitting robe adorned with an undulating pattern and held by a low-slung belt with striped panels ending in two *uraei*, the goddess wears a short bouffant Egyptian wig that leaves the ears uncovered, with curls stylized as chevrons carved into vertical bands. The large almond-shaped eyes were originally inlaid, while the ears are perforated for earrings that would have been made of precious metal.

The composite crown displays several elements of Egyptian origin: the *atef*-crown is framed by two *uraei*, and the whole rests on two large ram's horns. A third, smaller *uraeus* connects the wig to the headdress.

Barnett compares the goddess to a representation engraved on two sides of a bronze axe in the Beirut National Museum, permitting some of the lost (removable) attributes to be reconstituted.[2] On the axe the goddess is depicted wearing a long pleated robe and an Egyptian-style composite crown similar to the one on the Louvre goddess. In the right hand she holds a sickle sword and in the left an oval object that has been interpreted as a shield.

The Louvre statuette is said to have come from Qalat Faqra in the northern

154

Levant.[3] Given the absence of a well-defined archaeological context, it has been variously dated. Negbi and Seeden argue for a date around the second half of the second millennium B.C., and indeed smiting god iconography enjoyed its greatest popularity during the Late Bronze Age.[4] It is seen primarily on male representations. Female versions are quite rare. Only two, both found in the Beqa' region, can be attributed with any certainty to this period.[5] The Louvre goddess may, however, be a Phoenician work dating to the Iron Age, marked by strong Egyptian influence. The crown and the *uraei* that decorate the belt— also found on the garment on a torso from Sarepta[5]—are examples of the adaptation of Egyptian themes and motifs that characterized Phoenician art. The elongated body, its slender forms showing through the tight-fitting tunic, is, however, reminiscent of small Egyptian bronze statuary

Seated on a throne with his right hand raised for blessing, the god may have held in his left hand a scepter, which has not been preserved. He wears a long garment, and his feet rest on a footstool decorated with vertical ridges. The throne, with legs in the shape of animal feet, is placed on a double podium. The god wears an Egyptian conical *atef*-crown decorated with a *uraeus*, feathers, and a ram's horn on either side. Only one of the horns has been preserved. The headdress ends with a ball-shaped top surrounded by bands.[3]

Both the figure and the throne appear to have been cast together by the lost-wax method.[4] The five metal projections below the throne and footstool may be the remains of runners that provided access into the mold during casting, presumably retained to secure the statue in place when on view. The complete image suggests that other seated deities with substantial tangs

of the Third Intermediate Period (ca. 1070–713 B.C.). Thus, Barnett's suggested dating to the ninth century B.C. is very plausible in the case of this statuette, which may represent the war goddess Anat.   EF

1. For further reference, see Falsone 1986, pp. 53–76; Falsone 1988, pp. 79–109; Moorey and Fleming 1984, pp. 67–90; Seeden 1980; and Spycket 1981.
2. Barnett 1969, pp. 407–11, p. VIII; Beirut National Museum, inv. no. 4046, reproduced as a drawing by Seeden 1980, p. 131.
3. Archives, Musée du Louvre, Paris, Département des Antiquités Orientales. Information provided by Father Sébastien Ronzevalle, who made the acquisition.
4. Negbi 1976, p. 86; Seeden 1980, p. 106, group XI and p. 109, no. 1722.
5. Seeden 1980, nos. 1723 and 1728.
6. Spycket 1981, fig. 276; Musée du Louvre, AO 4805.

155

155
VESSEL

Ceramic
Height 15.8 cm (6¼ in.); width 11.6 cm (4⅜ in.)
Ugarit
Late Bronze Age, 15th–14th century B.C.
National Museum, Damascus, Syria 4217

This vessel, found at Ugarit, takes the form of a lion with an open mouth. The incised lines that define the muzzle suggest muscular tension and add to the intensity of the threatening expression. The deeply carved eyes were originally inlaid in a different material. The ears are flattened back against the skull and highlighted by an incised line, as are the cheeks and the bridge of the nose. A looped handle extends from the side of the neck toward the rim. A similar lion-headed cup, with an Ugaritic inscription dedicating the vessel to the god *rshp-gn*, or Reshef the Protector, was found in a house on the south acropolis at Ugarit.[1]

In the looped handle and the forward-facing orientation of the head, the Ugarit cups recall two Middle Bronze Age vessels from Kültepe (Levels Ib–a) in the shape of lion heads (see cat. no. 40).[2] The surface treatment of the Anatolian lion's head is comparable, with incised lines delineating the features and the tensely furrowed brow modeled in high relief. Lion-headed cups were also found in the Aegean as early as the late seventeenth and sixteenth centuries B.C. (see cat. no. 170), and Mycenaean animal-headed cups have been found at Ugarit.[3] A small yet naturalistically detailed amber lion head from Qatna demonstrates a very different style, although it too may have been used as a vessel (fig. 83).   SG

1. Schaeffer 1978, p. 149; Yon 2006, pp. 148–49.
2. T. Özgüç 2003, pp. 220–22.
3. Koehl 2006, pp. 36–37; Schaeffer 1978, pp. 220–23.

Figure 83. Amber lion head. Qatna. Late Bronze Age. National Museum, Damascus MSH02G-i0759

NEW KINGDOM EGYPT

THOMAS SCHNEIDER

With the exception of the pyramids, the image of ancient Egypt is impressed most vividly in the collective consciousness by the monuments of the New Kingdom (ca. 1550–1070 B.C.)—the temple precincts of Luxor, Karnak, and Abu Simbel, and the tombs of the Valley of the Kings.[1] Named initially to indicate its chronological placement in the sequence of Egyptian history, the New Kingdom has increasingly been considered "new" in the sense also of being innovative. Tomb corridors hewn into bedrock replaced the pyramids that rose to the sky, and temples to the gods succeeded installations to house dead pharaohs.

The emergence of the New Kingdom can be regarded as the final stage of a process that began in the Hyksos period (ca. 1640–1550 B.C.).[2] Its most visible external feature, paralleling the emergence of territorial states in Anatolia and Mesopotamia, was an empire that embraced Nubia and parts of the southern Levant.[3] The most conspicuous internal feature was the expansion of the sacred precincts in the larger cities, where temples appropriated parcels of state property and allocated land to their dependants. The military and the priesthood emerged as decisive forces, the full-fledged army offering new avenues of professional advancement outside state administration.[4]

New Kingdom politics also demonstrated ruptures with past traditions. In the fifteenth century B.C., the throne was ascended by a woman, Hatshepsut (ca. 1473–1458 B.C.), in what was portrayed as a divine election. Her co-ruler and successor, Thutmose III (ca. 1479–1425 B.C.), would later erase Hatshepsut from the monuments; her name was later omitted from the Egyptian Kinglists. Other major departures from the past were the implementation of a new religion by Amenhotep IV, later known as Akhenaten (ca. 1352–1336 B.C.), the appropriation of royal prerogatives by private individuals, and the elevation of a nonroyal woman to the status of principal queen by Amenhotep III (ca. 1390–1352 B.C.).

The ultimate military triumph of Ahmose I (ca. 1550–1525 B.C.)—a king of transition still aligned to the Second Intermediate Period—over the Hyksos was traditionally perceived by the Egyptians as the foundation of a new era (for this period, see cat. nos. 67, 68). Measures to strengthen the pharaoh's base of power included the creation of the position of God's Wife of Amun, whereby a woman became the function of consort to the god, and the reshaping of the administration and the army. Indispensable to Egypt's economy, Nubia was reconquered and placed under a provincial governor. Cult and building practices emulated those of the Middle Kingdom; Ahmose I and Amenhotep I, for example, still had tombs on the slopes of Dra Abu el-Naga at Thebes, and chapels continued to be erected to the cult of the royal family at Abydos.

This first phase of state consolidation is quite distinct from the imperial policy of the Thutmosid kings that followed Thutmose I (ca. 1504–1492 B.C.), and Thutmose III[5] built a colonial empire that incorporated Nubia as far as the Fourth Cataract of the Nile and the southern Levant. The Levantine territory was governed by a colonial administration in Egypt, by Egyptian administrators in the provinces, and by a network of loyal local kings. This expansion was motivated by the desire to create a buffer zone beyond Egypt's traditional border on the Delta periphery; to establish control over economically profitable cities, territories, and trade routes of the Levant; and to disseminate Egyptian culture abroad as a means of strengthening regional loyalty.

The twenty years of military expansion under Thutmose III established Egypt's hegemony in the eastern Mediterranean and formed the basis of its cultural flowering. During these decades, the professionalization of the army not only guaranteed military success but was furthered by the allocation of substantial resources toward the formation of the infantry, the navy, and, in the Ramesside years, chariotry. The reign of Amenhotep III represents the cultural zenith of Dynasty 18,[6] its prosperity reflected in its art and architecture, both official and private, and in the royal building programs that extended from the Levant to Nubia. Among these were the Temple of Amun at Karnak and the king's great (later dismantled) funerary temple in western Thebes. Already in their lifetime, the king and his queen, Tiye, were worshipped as deities in Nubia.

The religious revolution initiated by their son Amenhotep IV, as well as the historical era of his and his immediate successors' reigns, the Amarna Age, is a topic that continues to fuel debate.[7] Radicalizing the earlier Dynasty 18 worship of the sun, the pharaoh implemented a far-reaching monotheism, eventually to the exclusion of all other gods. At its center was the god Aten, visible in the sun disc. His founding of a sacred residence at Tell el-Amarna, in Middle Egypt, represented an unprecedented departure from Egyptian tradition as well as from his own earlier commitment to Thebes. The city was given the name Akhetaten, "Horizon of Aten"; the king, too, adopted a new name, Akhenaten, "Efficient for Aten." The new doctrine was based on the empirical observation that nature is sustained by the sun. Replacing traditional belief, it denied the existence of an Underworld and suppressed established cultic practices. The second focus of the new religion was Akhenaten himself and his queen, Nefertiti (see cat. no. 224), mediators between mankind and the divine. The great artistic flowering of the Amarna Age also nurtured new styles and innovative means of expression (see pp. 387–94).

Why Akhenaten was given such unprecedented political support to abolish long-standing traditions is unclear; it was perhaps an attempt to vanquish the plague that devastated the Near East in the late fourteenth century B.C.[8] Following the reign of Akhenaten, Tutankhamun (ca. 1336–1327 B.C.) abandoned the city of Amarna and transferred his administration back to Memphis. The last ruler of Dynasty 18, Haremhab (ca. 1323–1295 B.C.), dismantled the temples to Aten; in the early years of Dynasty 19, Akhenaten's memory was obliterated.

The first of a number of emperors to have risen from the military, Haremhab, who stands on the cusp of the Ramesside period, consolidated Egypt's position in the Levant. The extensive building activity of the thirteenth century B.C.—above all, that of Ramesses II (ca. 1279–1213 B.C.)—not only mirrored the economic wealth of the empire, but served as an instrument of political and religious consolidation. The strong architectural and cult presence in the old religious centers of Thebes and Abydos compensated for the establishment, by Seti I (ca. 1294–1279 B.C.), of Piramesse as the new capital of Egypt, immediately adjacent to the ancient Hyksos capital of Avaris in the eastern Nile Delta (see pp. 110–12).[9] This has been seen as a decision required by strategic needs, but it also pays tribute to the fourth state god of Ramesside Egypt, the Syrian weather god Seth-Baal. Piramesse would be the stage of important ideological and political events—jubilee festivals of Ramesses II, Merneptah, and Ramesses III, and the signing of the peace treaty between the Egyptians and the Hittites in 1258 B.C. It also served as headquarters for the Ramesside army and navy as well as for chariotry.

The cultural changes brought about by the Ramesside period are particularly evident in the areas of religion and literature. The authority of the gods, channeled increasingly through oracles, gained in significance both public and private life ("personal piety").[10] In literature, while the classical texts of the Middle Kingdom were preserved, new genres were also created—love songs, burlesque, satire, and long tales composed in the new literary language of Late Egyptian.

The political and military activities of Ramesses II and his successor, Merneptah (ca. 1213–1203 B.C.), foreshadowed the crisis that paralyzed the Near East in the twelfth and the early eleventh century B.C., when the Hittite Empire collapsed and major states of the eastern Mediterranean were destroyed. The later history of Dynasty 19 was characterized by civil war and rival claims to the throne of Egypt. Only Ramesses III (ca. 1184–1153 B.C.), in Dynasty 20, was able to establish political stability, economic wealth, and extensive building activity.[11]

The demise of the New Kingdom shortly after 1100 B.C. cannot be separated from the wider crisis that affected the eastern

Figure 84. Battle of Qadesh relief. Abu Simbel, Temple of Ramesses II. Dynasty 19.

Mediterranean, coinciding with the end of the Bronze Age and the inception of the Iron Age.[12] Rather than ascribing the decline to incompetent rulers within Egypt, it can perhaps be attributed both to internal problems and to the disintegration of structures beyond Egypt's control. Central features of the ensuing Libyan era (ca. 945–712 B.C.) are already manifest under the last Ramesside kings of Dynasty 20, announcing a new period in the history of Egypt well before the end of the New Kingdom.

FOREIGN RELATIONS IN THE NEW KINGDOM

The emergence of the New Kingdom in Egypt coincided with the establishment of Kassite rule in Babylonia and the rise of the empire of Mitanni. With the reshaping of the Hittite Empire in the later fifteenth century B.C., the so-called concert of powers—so decisive for Egyptian politics in later Dynasty 18 and Dynasty 19—was in place.[13] During the first century of the New Kingdom, Egypt benefited from the relative vacuum of power in Syria, whereas in the last century it was responding to far-reaching crises in the eastern Mediterranean. More than in earlier periods, cultural innovation and a flourishing economy reflect engagement with Near Eastern cultures.

The building of the colonial empire was initiated under Thutmose I, with incursions into Nubia and the Levant. Taking advantage of the collapse of the empire of Kerma, Egypt extended her southern border to the area between the Fourth and Fifth Cataracts.[14] A region of critical importance for trade with Africa and access to Nubia's gold mines was thus brought once again within the reach of Egyptian rule and placed under the administration of local princes. One of Thutmose I's most significant military achievements was his campaign to the

Euphrates River in his fourth or fifth regnal year, legitimized as retaliation for the "evil," possibly an allusion to Hyksos rule. This meant a claim for the possession of Syria, which was confirmed by the consecration of tusks of Syrian elephants he had hunted to the god Amun. Hatshepsut undertook military forays in the south; her famous trading expeditions to the land of Punt on the Red Sea coast are meticulously depicted in her great funerary temple at Deir el-Bahri (see fig. 5).[15]

Egyptian control of the Levant was secured by Thutmose III in a series of seventeen campaigns conducted between his twenty-second year following the death of Hatshepsut and the forty-third year of his reign.[16] What we know of them comes almost exclusively from the royal annals in the Temple of Karnak, making their credibility difficult to verify. Egypt's long-term political and economic interests, supported by the dissemination of Egyptian culture in the Levant, are achieved in the fifth, sixth, and seventh campaigns with the establishment of a permanent military presence north of Byblos. In the eighth expedition, Thutmose III reached the Euphrates and pursued the army of Mitanni as far as Emar. Six campaigns followed in the Levant. The southern provinces were henceforth governed through a system of garrisons and administered by provincial governors at Gaza, Kumidi (Kamid el-Loz), Simyra, and the northern (Syrian) provinces through a system of political alliances. There are no campaigns recounted for the last twelve years of Thutmose III's reign, perhaps the result of a more settled situation in the north or a strategy of deterrence by a strengthened state of Mitanni. Minoan frescoes unearthed at Avaris (Tell el-Dab'a), now dated to the time of Thutmose III, could point to an alliance with the Minoan naval empire (see p. 31).[17] A tomb built by Thutmose III for three secondary wives

of Levantine descent suggests a network of diplomatic marriages (see cat. nos. 156–159).[18]

With the empire of Mitanni in its heyday and an increasingly powerful Hittite kingdom, the contest for Syria became a central focus of the fourteenth and thirteenth centuries B.C. A political agreement is referred to in the Amarna Letters when Artatama, king of Mitanni, married one of his daughters to Thutmose IV (ca. 1400–1390 B.C.). Indeed, diplomatic marriages now come to constitute an important political tool. In the Egyptian sphere of influence in the Levant, a *pax Aegyptica* holds firm. It is expressed in a festival building in the king's residence at Malqata, which the king ascended by means of more than thirty stairs, with depictions of prostrate captives.

Eventually, Mitanni succumbed to the expansionist policies of Assyria and the Hittite Empire, ceasing its existence as a viable power and surviving only as a truncated state under Hittite rule. The Hittites, while acknowledging Egypt's border on the upper Orontes River, assumed control over northern Syria. The plan devised after the death of Tutankhamun by his widow—to marry one of Suppiluliuma's sons, who would ascend the throne of Egypt—failed, a result of the prince's death. Had it been realized, it would have established a Hittite-Egyptian empire of unprecedented size.

The complex struggle for Syria at the end of Dynasty 18 and the early Ramesside period[19] came to a preliminary end at Qadesh in 1275 B.C. (see fig. 84); as a consequence the Egyptians had to abandon their aspirations in northern Syria. The definitive conclusion was reached with the Egyptian–Hittite treaty of 1258 B.C., binding the two parties to end hostilities and territorial conquests, and to extradite of political refugees.[20] With the Assyrians threatening Hittite territories, the treaty was of political and economic benefit to both states.

During the reign of Ramesses II, the Sea Peoples, a confederation of seafaring tribes, appeared as a new threat to the empires of the eastern Mediterranean. The first to repulse them, Ramesses II built a defense system along the coastal border with Libya. The Libyans and the Sea Peoples were repeatedly defeated by Merneptah and, in Dynasty 20, by Ramesses III. The latter's detailed account of Medinet Habu describes the destruction of the Hittite Empire, the Anatolian kingdoms, Cyprus, and Amurru, annihilated "as if they had never existed," and the progression of the "scorching flames" of the Sea Peoples. The early eleventh century B.C. saw the end of the territorial empires of the second millenium—those of Egypt and Middle Assyria—and Kassite rule in Babylonia.

Cultural exchange with the Near East and the Aegean was unprecedented during the New Kingdom,[21] embracing weaponry and warfare, glass and metal industries, textiles and dyeing, woodworking, shipbuilding, and lifestyles. It was also manifest in religion and literature. With the blessings of the Egyptian court, deities and beliefs from the Near East were integrated into the Egyptian religion, most notably the Syrian weather god Baal (named Seth in Egypt), who was raised to the patronage of Egyptian kingship, and including the gods Reshef,

Astarte, Anat, and Qudshu. The emergence of Late Egyptian narrative literature appears to have been inspired by Near Eastern tales. Moreover, the exchange of knowledge in mythology, magic, medicine, and crafts evokes the picture of an international koine of ideas that transcended political conflict.

1. Assmann 1993.
2. See Polz 2007.
3. See E. Morris 2005.
4. See Gnirs 1996.
5. Cline and O'Connor 2006; for the wars, see Redford 2003.
6. See *Egypt's Dazzling Sun* 1992; O'Connor and Cline 1998; Cabrol 2000; and Leospo and Tosi 2005.
7. Most recently, see Gabolde 1998; Hornung 1999; Montserrat 2000; Reeves 2001; and Silverman, Wegner, and Houser Wegner 2006.
8. Gnirs 2004. The arguments put forth by Kozloff 2006 are unwarranted.
9. Herold 1998.
10. Luiselli 2007.
11. Grandet 1993.
12. Lehmann 1985; Leahy 1990; Lehmann 1996; Oren 2000; Jansen-Winkeln 2002.
13. Klengel 1999; Liverani 2001; Van de Mieroop 2007.
14. Kendall 1997.
15. See, for example, the contributions in O'Connor and Quirke 2003.
16. Redford 2003; Cline and O'Connor 2006.
17. Caubet 1999a; Bietak 2000b.
18. Lilyquist 2003.
19. Murnane 1990; Van de Mieroop 2007.
20. Edel 1997.
21. See, among others, Cornelius 1994, Herold 1998, Wilde 2003, Cornelius 2004, and Feldman 2006b.

TOMB OF THE THREE FOREIGN WIVES OF THUTMOSE III

156
HORUS COLLAR AND VULTURE PECTORAL

Collar: Gold
Length 32 cm (12⅝ in.)

Pectoral: Gold
Length 37.3 cm (14¾ in.)

New Kingdom, Dynasty 18, reign of Thutmose III, ca. 1479–1425 B.C.
The Metropolitan Museum of Art, New York, Fletcher Fund, 1926 26.8.102, 105

157
HEADDRESS

Gold, carnelian, turquoise, glass, and clear glass
Height 35 cm (13¾ in.); diameter 40.2 cm (15⅞ in.)
New Kingdom, Dynasty 18, reign of Thutmose III, ca. 1479–1425 B.C.
The Metropolitan Museum of Art, New York, Purchase, Henry Walters and Edward S. Harkness Gifts, 1920 26.8.117A

158
DIADEM

Gold, carnelian, opaque turquoise glass, decayed crizzled glass
Length of forehead band 47.9 cm (18⅞ in.)
New Kingdom, Dynasty 18, reign of Thutmose III, ca. 1479–1425 B.C.
The Metropolitan Museum of Art, New York, Purchase, George F. Baker and Mr. and Mrs. V. Everit Macy Gifts, 1920 26.8.99

159
CUP

Glossy faience, gold
Height 10.2 cm (4 in.); diameter 7 cm (2¾ in.)
New Kingdom, Dynasty 18, reign of Thutmose III, ca. 1479–1425 B.C.
The Metropolitan Museum of Art, New York, Purchase, Edward S. Harkness Gift, 1926 26.7.1175

South of the Valley of the Kings are several wadis that house tombs belonging to family members of early Dynasty 18 rulers. Late in the summer of 1916, high in the cliffs of one of these valleys, Wadi Gabbanet el-Qurud, local villagers found the undisturbed tomb of three wives of Thutmose III.[1] The tomb was effectively cleared. Little remained except fragments of jewelry, gold leaf, and smashed pottery vessels; the rest of the burial goods had already been removed. Within a few months of the tomb's discovery, several archaeologists

156

had combed through the remaining debris and interviewed the local residents, who knew about the robbery. According to one villager's account, the coffins and mummies had already disintegrated as a result of age and ancient water damage.

The tomb itself was undecorated, but inscriptions on jars identified each of the tomb's burials as *hmt nswt*, a title that identifies a royal wife. The women's names are best read as Manuwai, Manhata, and Maruta, and because these names are West Semitic in origin, the original homes of all

three were most likely towns in Canaan or somewhere along the Levantine coast.[2]

THE FUNERARY ORNAMENTS
The surviving objects fall principally into two broad groups: jewelry and vessels. Jewelry found in a New Kingdom burial can be sorted into two basic categories: pieces worn during the individual's lifetime and those created solely for eternal use.[3] The fragility of the two gold-foil pieces (cat. no. 156), combined with their iconography, indicates that at one time

they adorned mummies. In this instance, foil was fashioned into a beaded collar with falcon terminals (a Horus collar) and a vulture with outspread wings, elements of funerary jewelry known at least since the Middle Kingdom.

THE WIG COVERING
The rosette wig covering (cat. no. 157) lacks clear parallels in representation or in the archaeological record in Egypt or the Near East.[4] The piece is composed of an ornamented plate and strings of graded

rosettes. Lilyquist identifies the decoration on the plate as fronds. Feathers are also possible, as in Egypt royal women occasionally wore feathers with their crowns.

Winlock was the first to reconstruct the large numbers of rosettes and the heavy flat gold plate as a headdress.[5] His version, however, was cumbersome and could not realistically have been worn. Lilyquist, after studying metallurgical manufacturing techniques, removed a number of rosettes from Winlock's reconstruction when they were determined to be of more recent manufacture. Her version of the wig covering depicted ribbons of rosettes hung from the plate in unattached and shorter strands, in a form that would allow the wearer to move her head;[6] if the piece was attached to the wig, rather than just sitting on the head, it might also have been easier to wear.[7]

The plate is decorated with a central element from which forty-one narrower versions extend outward, twenty of which were once probably inlaid with Egyptian Blue.[8] The plate has no parallel as headgear. Only a few illustrations of platelike

head decorations for women are extant; the closest parallel is a large flat lotuslike ornament on the statue of a queen from mid-Dynasty 12.[9]

Rosettes were long used as motifs on women's head ornaments. Many fillets and diadems from the Old and Middle Kingdoms make use of rosettes. Wig ornaments, however, which are consistently made from sheet gold, tend to be distributed throughout a wig as individual elements. Solid wig coverings seem not to be an Egyptian tradition.

By early Dynasty 18, the most common head ornament depicted on tomb walls was a fillet fashioned from flowers. By the Ramesside period, some 150 years after the burial of the foreign wives, these fillets could be ornate, widening into an elaborate head ornament framing the wearer's face, suggestive of the wig covering.[10] But unlike the wig covering, these fillets leave the crown of the head exposed.

The coffin of Meryetamun (ca. 1540 B.C.) has been suggested as a source of a parallel for the head plate and rosettes of the wig covering.[11] However, neither the inlaid

pattern nor the decorative motif at the crest of the wig matches what was found in this tomb. In all, the components of the wig covering suggest something worn in life, not funerary jewelry.

Because the plate and its pendants of rosettes do not have direct parallels in surviving Egyptian jewelry or in representations of jewelry, we cannot know what the piece looked like and thus why it was made. The rosettes are fragile and not well fashioned, unlike other ornaments in the tomb meant for use during their owners' lifetimes, such as the collars, bracelets, and earrings. If the wig covering was worn only rarely, perhaps during a yearly ritual, the ornament would not have needed to be made strong enough for daily use. The survival of additional strings of rosettes does not make interpretation any easier. Possibly the wig covering had its origins outside Egypt, given the lack of parallels.

THE GAZELLE DIADEM

Diadems ornamented with gazelle protomes are new to the jewelry repertoire of the New Kingdom, although diadems and fillets had long been worn by both sexes in ancient Egypt. The gazelle has a history of iconographic use in Egypt, although the inspiration to affix this animal head to a diadem seems to have come from the Near East (see cat. no. 64). A number of well-documented tomb paintings of the time depict women wearing diadems adorned with heads of gazelles.[12] Women who have been identified, adorned with such diadems and associated with the king's household, held titles indicating they carried out rituals on behalf of the cult of the goddess Hathor.[13]

The T-shaped diadem (cat. no. 158) is also a new form. Like the wig covering, it has no known parallels in either the Near East or Egypt. Tutankhamun owned an elegant example, so it is clear that the style rapidly became part of the repertoire.

Regrettably, the rosette decorations hamper a more thorough understanding of the appearance of the original diadem. All seem to be ancient, but the diadem may not have appeared in antiquity in the format seen here.[14] Lilyquist's analysis of the manufacturing techniques revealed that the soldering was poorly done, suggesting that the large rosettes may have been added to the older T-shaped diadem. Perhaps they were part of another hair ornament, like the one seen on a statue of queen Tiye.

158

The Drinking Vessel

Like the wig covering, the gazelle diadem, though composed of iconographic elements and utilizing metalworking techniques that seem to have originated in the Near East, was an ornament easily recognizable as Egyptian. Dynasty 17 to early Dynasty 18 was a period when new iconography and decorative styles were appearing on all types of traditional Egyptian objects.[15]

The Drinking Vessel

The vessels in the tombs were of many sizes, forms, and materials. One of the most unusual was a vessel with wide neck and everted rim (cat. no. 159) made from a glassy faience whose colors of brick red, camel, dark turquoise, and white are swirled together. This material is quite rare; the closest parallels, based on elemental analysis, are three fragments from Nuzi, a Mitanni site in northern Mesopotamia.[16] The rare material and the gold foil that trims the rim and base mark the vessel as a luxury item. The shape, which closely parallels drinking vessels from early second-millennium B.C. Mesopotamia, also testifies to its non-Egyptian origin.[17]

The Foreign Wives and International Exchange

Little about the objects identified as from the tomb of the foreign wives of Thutmose III may unequivocally be attributed to a Near Eastern origin. The drinking vessel may be the exception in that it seems most certainly to be foreign.[18] Although a number of granulated gold beads and the wig covering show metallurgical techniques identified with Near Eastern craftsmen, these pieces could have been made by Canaanite craftsmen working in Egypt or by Egyptians who learned the techniques from them.[19] The use of gazelle protomes originated in the Near East, but all the women represented wearing such a diadem are Egyptian.

The wives of Thutmose III were entombed together, but there is no evidence that they were related. No ancient records discussing the wives exist, and the assemblage of equipment provided each woman is now incomplete. The artifacts in the tomb suggest that Thutmose treated all three equally—but not necessarily identically. At the time of burial, each woman was accompanied by her own set of jewelry and cosmetic items and was given funerary equipment similar in date and manufacture to that of the others.[20] Many pieces were clearly personal gifts bearing the name of Thutmose III. In addition, the women had been in Egypt for some time, judging from the many pieces of Egyptian jewelry used during their lifetime and the general absence of items of foreign manufacture. This would suggest that they probably came to Egypt as a result of political marriage instead of capture during a military campaign.

The material evidence from the tomb demonstrates that the women were buried around the time of Hatshepsut's death, about 1458 B.C.[21] Their burial near the site of Hatshepsut's first tomb and that of her daughter Neferure would also suggest a date in the first half of Thutmose III's reign. Chronological considerations would then prevent their often-cited origin as women from Mitanni (for later references to Mitanni brides, see cat. no. 118). The first Egyptian campaign during the reign of Thutmose III that involved the Mitanni took place in the year after Hatshepsut's death. In fact, there is nothing in the burial of the three foreign wives, except the Nuzi-type cup, to connect these women to the Mitanni state. Their West Semitic names suggest that we could look to south Canaan for their origin; perhaps they went to Egypt as a result of marriages arranged by local rulers when the pharaoh was active in Gaza and south Canaan during the years of joint reign.[22] Another possibility is that they were sent from cities along the Levantine coast, perhaps even Byblos. Trade between Egypt and Levantine cities had a long tradition, and Hatshepsut's extensive building program required materials such as cedar from the Near East.[23] Perhaps local rulers in the Levant presented the women as political gifts to encourage their own profitable trade with Egypt. Although sent to Egypt in the wake of Hatshepsut's activities, such women logically would have been

159

married to Thutmose III. The presence of the Nuzi-type vessel could easily have been a result of trade between that city and regions farther north and east that were controlled by the Mitanni.

The three foreign wives seem to have been allowed to remain together after their arrival in Egypt.[24] Regardless of whether they were related or died within a short space of time—information that cannot be gleaned from the tomb—they were accorded burials which demonstrate that their identity had become Egyptian as a result of their time at court.   DCP

1. The author is indebted to Christine Lily-quist's 2003 study of the tomb and its contents. The author also thanks Christine Lilyquist, Dorothea Arnold, Catharine Roehrig, and Marsha Hill for their comments. For more details on the tomb's discovery, see Lilyquist 2003.
2. See Hoch in Lilyquist 2003, pp. 329–37.
3. For a discussion of the function of jewelry in early Dynasty 18, see Patch 2005.
4. Lilyquist 2003, pp. 164–66.
5. Winlock 1937.
6. Lilyquist 2003, pp. 164–69.
7. Ibid., p. 165.
8. Ibid., p. 166.
9. Ziegler 2001, fig. 18.
10. For example, see Quibell 1912, pl. 67, no. 2, pl. 68, no. 5, and pl. 69, no. 1; C. Wilkinson and Hill 1983, p. 143, MMA 30.4.29; see also A. Wilkinson 1971, p. 115.
11. Cairo Museum, JE53410. See Saleh and Sourouzian 1987, no. 127.
12. Lilyquist 2003, pp. 347–48.
13. Ibid., pp. 159–62; A. Wilkinson 1971, pp. 115–18.
14. See Lilyquist 2003, pp. 154–58.
15. See *Hatshepsut* 2005.
16. This cup is referred to here as a Nuzi type because of the parallel to glass found at that site. It is likely, however, that the cup could have been made at any glass-producing site within the Mitanni sphere of influence.
17. Lilyquist 2003, pp. 150–51, 220.
18. Ibid., p. 337.
19. Ibid.
20. Although the three sets of burial goods were possibly made in the same royal workshops, the same craftsmen do not seem to have made them.
21. Ibid., pp. 333–36.
22. Redford 1967, p. 62.
23. Bryan 2000, pp. 233, 239, 242–43.
24. For example, this consideration was extended to foreign women at Tell el-Amarna, where they are depicted together; see Manniche 1991, pp. 85–86.

160

160

FRAGMENTARY PATERA WITH INSCRIPTION OF GENERAL DJEHUTI

Silver
Diameter 18 cm (7⅛ in.)
Egypt
New Kingdom, Dynasty 18, reign of
Thutmose III, ca. 1479–1425 B.C.
Musée du Louvre, Paris, Département des
Antiquités Égyptiennes E4886

This fragment consists of the bottom of a patera in its original diameter. The sides can be reconstituted on the basis of another dish, of gold, that belonged to the same individual and that is also preserved in the Musée du Louvre.

Both objects bear the name "Djehuti" and have similar forms and decoration. The distinction between them is found in the details: the orientation of the fish, the papyrus, and the disposition of the decoration at the bottom. The craftsmanship of the silver patera is finer.

The outlines of the design were drawn with a stylus, then chased with a burin. The flowers and fish were worked in repoussé, the linear details added with a tracer. A recent restoration rendered the last character of the inscription legible (right to left): "He who amply fills the heart of the Lord of the Two Lands, esteemed of the good god, the royal scribe, Overseer of Northern Foreign Lands, Djehuti."

In her study of the furnishings belonging to this royal official, Lilyquist expressed doubts as to the authenticity of the gold dish and the inscription on the silver one.[1] Indeed, the quality of the inscription is inferior to that of the decoration in the center and the sign for "scribe" is reversed. However, the placing of the inscription in the largest space of the fragment suggests another scenario. The patera of silver, an unstable metal, may have been damaged in antiquity, possibly during Djehuti's life-time, and the finely decorated center kept for later use. The object was then hastily inscribed with Djehuti's name—in the largest available space—before being buried and forgotten.

The decoration of blue faience vessels with aquatic subjects painted in black during the reigns of Thutmose III and Hatshepsut present the closest analogies to that of Djehuti's paterae: a central rosette, the tilapia fish pattern, and Nile vegetation, occasionally stylized in the

161

same fashion. The faience vessels were presented as offerings in the shrines of the goddess Hathor, their decoration evoking her realm: the marshlands of the primordial world.

However, the bottoms of the faience vessels are never flat. This flat patera shape may be found at Ugarit (cat. no. 147).[2] The form of the present piece suggests that it may have been manufactured in Syria. Writing about the statuette of Djehuti made for the Temple of Hathor in Byblos, Yoyotte mentions Djehuti's career in the colonies as tribute collector for the king of Egypt. This suggests that Djehuti would have been in a good position to acquire precious metalwork of non-Egyptian origin, as well as to have it engraved by Egyptian craftsmen with motifs illustrating the religious beliefs of his homeland.[3] The gold dish, which bears an inscription identifying it as a royal "gift," may have been ordered locally by his administrator for himself and never found its way into the king's treasury.

GP-B

1. Lilyquist 1988.
2. Louvre AO 17208.
3. Yoyotte 1981.

161
DISH WITH SCENE OF THE RIVER NILE

Faience
Height 4.7 cm (1⅞ in.); diameter 9 cm (3½ in.)
Enkomi
Late Bronze Age, 14th–13th century B.C.
The Trustees of the British Museum, London
1897.4–1.1042

This attractive shallow bowl of pale blue faience is painted with the figure of a man wearing an Egyptian kilt and punting with a long pole a papyrus boat along a river. A cow or bull sits under a canopy, and in the water is a large fish. The shape of this thin-walled vessel was first modeled or cold-formed in a mold and then allowed to dry. After it was dipped in glaze, the outline drawing was added in black paint. The distinctive color of the glaze would have had specific cultural associations for the Egyptians: it was perhaps linked with ideas of prosperity and fertility. It may have had the same associations for its Cypriot users as well.[1]

Papyrus skiffs, made of bundles of reeds lashed together, were the simplest form of boat in ancient Egypt. They were used for

hunting and fishing, and for short journeys along the Nile. The animal in the boat is perhaps simply being transported from one place to another, but possibly it is to be sacrificed as part of a funerary feast. If this is the case, its use for a similar purpose on Cyprus may reflect the deliberate adoption of foreign traditions by local elites.

Faience, especially when made into elaborate vessels with figural decoration, was one of the luxury materials of the Late Bronze Age, forming part of the International Style that developed particularly during the fourteenth and thirteenth centuries B.C. (see pp. 419–20). The main workshops for high-quality faience were in Egypt and northern Syria, both areas from which other faience products can be found in the tombs of Enkomi and elsewhere on Cyprus in this period. By the thirteenth century B.C., fine faience vessels were also being made on Cyprus itself, perhaps with the help of itinerant craftsmen. This dish may well have been imported from Egypt, though it is the only example of this type to have a separately added ring base; this could indicate a different, perhaps local, manufacturing tradition influenced by contemporary Base Ring pottery vessels.

Objects such as this one appear to have been not so much traded on the open market as sent as diplomatic gifts. The correspondence of the period, especially the Amarna Letters between the Egyptian pharaohs and their allies, record constant reciprocal gift giving. The exchange of items such as this bowl was a nonverbal extension of this correspondence.

The Enkomi tombs housed a rich mix of local and imported products, illustrating the wealth of the site and the key position occupied by Cyprus in cultural exchange during the Late Bronze Age. Tomb 66 was the only stone-built tomb on the site to be found intact. The contents—more than 140 objects in total—included goldwork, bronze vessels and weapons, amber beads, glass vessels, a silver vessel, and pottery of Mycenaean, Cypriot, Levantine, and Egyptian origin.

JLF

1. For further reference, see Murray, Smith, and Walters 1900, p. 35 and fig. 63:1042; Courtois, Lagarce, and Lagarce 1986, pp. 42, 143, pl. XXVI:2; Peltenburg 1991; and Jacobsson 1994, p. 32, no. 164, pl. 19:164.

Depictions of Foreign Emissaries in the Theban Tombs

The international character of New Kingdom Egypt during early Dynasty 18 is vividly reflected in a group of painted tombs cut into the hilly landscape in Thebes west of the Nile River.[1] Built for Egyptian high court officials during the fifteenth and fourteenth centuries B.C., the tombs were entered through a forecourt that led into a chapel; the burial chamber itself was cut below this level.[2] For a time after the tomb owner's death, family members and priests would observe funerary rituals in the chapel; many other visitors also came to the tombs, where they admired the paintings prominently positioned on the walls of the chapel and sometimes added graffiti recording their appreciation.[3]

The varied subjects depicted in these paintings include craftsmen at work; scenes of the hunt (figs. 7, 119); and the tomb's owner receiving rich items of booty, trade, or tribute from processions of foreigners on behalf of the pharaoh. The last, in particular, has attracted attention for what these scenes can tell us about the nature of the interaction between Egypt and other eastern Mediterranean powers. The depiction of foreigners also raises the question of how to categorize those identified as men of "Keftiu," a term that may refer to Cretans or Aegeans in general.[4]

Paintings in the Tomb of Rekhmire, who was vizier under Thutmose III and Amenhotep II, show him receiving tribute from four delegations of foreigners (fig. 85). The offering bearers, differentiated by physical appearance, dress, and the goods they bring, are introduced in an inscription giving their places of origin: Nubia, Punt, Syria, and Keftiu. Others are identified as captives from several regions.[5] The impressive lineup of foreigners and their magnificent goods represented in the tombs of officials like Rekhmire reflected the power and influence of the pharaoh whom these officials served.

Actual vessels comparable to the bull- and lion-headed rhyta carried by men of Keftiu in several tombs are known from the Aegean (cat. nos. 169, 170).[6] In addition, certain jugs and vases painted in the tombs of Senenmut, Useramun, and Menkheperreseneb closely resemble contemporary Aegean metalwork.[7]

Not all the foreigners are shown bearing offerings characteristic of their homelands. Some bring objects that could have been acquired by way of the eastern Mediterranean trade route or originally received as gifts from their own royal treasuries. These include ivory tusks, tin and copper ingots, and what are perhaps colored glass ingots,[8] all of which were found among the cargo of the Uluburun ship (see pp. 289–305). Notably, some paintings depict people with hybrid regional attributes, such as the figure with the red skin and kilt of an Aegean and the coiffure and beard of a Syrian, and wares that are likewise composed of novel combinations of individually recognizable elements. The creation of these hybrids, perhaps driven by a desire to produce a varied and abundant visual repertoire in the tombs,[9] is a phenomenon deserving of further study.   SG

Figure 85. Wall painting with foreign emissaries bearing gifts. Thebes, Tomb of Rekhmire (TT 100). Dynasty 18, reigns of Thutmose III–Amenhotep II.

1. See map in Kozloff 1992c, p. 266, fig. IX.6. I thank Marsha Hill for sharing her insights on Theban tomb paintings.
2. Hartwig 2004, pp. 15–16; Kozloff 1992c, p. 263.

3. Hartwig 2004, pp. 8–18, 43–49.
4. Discussion in Vercoutter 1956, esp. pp. 33–38; Wachsmann 1987, pp. 93–102; see also Matthäus 1995, pp. 177–94.
5. Vercoutter 1956, p. 56; Wachsmann 1987, p. 36.
6. Wachsmann 1987, pp. 56–60; however, he notes that the bull-headed rhyta are portrayed with horns in profile, rather than en face as is typical in Egyptian painting, indicating that the rhyta shown in the Theban tombs are copied from Aegean depictions, not directly from the objects themselves.
7. Matthäus 1995, pp. 182–86.
8. Wachsmann 1987, p. 54.
9. Ibid., pp. 4–11; for a recent critical response, see Feldman 2006b, pp. 60–61.

162

RELIEF FRAGMENT

Sandstone, painted plaster
Height 18 cm (7⅛ in.)
Egypt
New Kingdom, probably Dynasty 18,
ca. 1550–1295 B.C.
Staatliche Museen zu Berlin, Aegyptisches
Museum und Papyrussammlung 21140

This fragmentary scene shows men identified as Syrians by their pointed beards, hair fillets, and long garments prostrating themselves before a fortress. Similar compositions, dating to the New Kingdom, are known from temples and from painted tombs of the Egyptian elite in Thebes. This fragment may originally derive from the wall decoration of one such temple or tomb. Carved in relief that has been plastered and painted, the figures, ramparts, and row of rosettes beneath the

Figure 86. Wall painting with Syrians bearing gifts. Thebes, Tomb of Sebekhotep (TT 63). Dynasty 18, reign of Thutmose IV. The Trustees of the British Museum, London EA 37991

163

groundline display a yellow coloration with red outlines likely meant to represent gold.

The scene has been interpreted in two ways: as a depiction of an elaborate metal vessel, such as those shown in wall paintings in Theban tombs, and alternatively, as representing a wall above the deck of a ship.[1] Although metal vases from tomb paintings do display fanciful handles and rim attachments, and would offer an explanation for the gold color of the figures, none are close parallels for this composition. Nor do they account for the sloping groundline of the scene, which is difficult to reconcile with the rim of a bowl or krater.

Indeed, the angle of the groundline lends support to the idea that the scene takes place on board a ship. Comparison with boats from the New Kingdom period—preserved in reliefs, wall paintings, and ship models—suggests that the rosette frieze could be taken as the painted decoration of the ship's hull.[2] A lavishly decorated divine boat carved in relief in the Temple of Seti I in Abydos shows figures flanking a central shrine.[3] The gold suppliant figures and the fortress-like structure on this fragment could thus represent features of a ship such as those carried in festivals or funeral processions.[4] However, the presence of foreigners whose appearance recalls Syrian envoys in Theban tributary scenes (see fig. 86) varies from typical representations of divine boats. A closer comparison may

be a relief from Tell el-Amarna showing Nefertiti smiting a prostrate foreigner aboard a royal ship.[5] However, any interpretation of this unusual composition without further evidence about the overall context of this scene must remain tentative.   SG

1. S. Martinssen-von Falck in *Pharao siegt immer* 2004, p. 160, no. 156; Priese 1991, p. 128, no. 79.
2. D. Jones 1995, pp. 66–68. I thank Dieter Arnold for sharing his thoughts on this piece with me and for bringing this and the following source to my attention.
3. Landström 1970, p. 199, fig. 369.
4. See, for example, ibid., p. 117, fig. 362.
5. Y. Markowitz in *Pharao siegt immer* 2004, p. 58, no. 52.

163

RELIEF FRAGMENT WITH VANQUISHED ENEMIES

Painted limestone
Height 61 cm (24 in.); width 115 cm (45¼ in.)
Thebes
New Kingdom, Dynasty 18, probably reign of Amenhotep II, ca. 1427–1400 B.C.
The Metropolitan Museum of Art, New York, Rogers Fund and Edward S. Harkness Gift, 1913 13.180.21

The reuse of this relief block in the foundations of the unfinished mortuary Temple of Ramesses IV (Dynasty 20, ca. 1153–1147 B.C.) kept the colors of its painted surface vibrant until the time of its excavation by the Metropolitan Museum's Theban Expedition in 1912–13.[1] The block is part of a larger scene that shows the Egyptian king vanquishing his Syrian enemies. At the upper right margin of the block, the Syrians fall beneath the pharaoh's chariot horses. Three of the fallen enemies have been struck by his arrows, one of which is painted over by the beard and hair of the two figures at right. The Egyptians depicted their neighbors in the Near East with characteristic pointed beards and with distinctive hairstyles and clothing, recognizing that the area was inhabited by a variety of peoples.

Scenes such as this one, some of battles against enemies to the east, some against the Nubians to the south, decorated the walls of Egyptian temples throughout the New Kingdom. Although they sometimes commemorate specific battles, their primary purpose was to portray the pharaoh in his role as the victorious defender of Egypt.

CHR

1. For further reference, see Winlock 1914, pp. 22–23, fig. 12; Hayes 1990, p. 340, fig. 214; P. Brand in *American Discovery of Ancient Egypt* 1995, pp. 170–71, no. 74 (with bibliography); I. Franco in *Pharaohs* 2002, p. 424, no. 92; and J. Allen 2005, p. 33, no. 33.

164

OPENWORK PANEL WITH PHARAOH SMITING ENEMY

Ivory
Length 11.2 cm (4⅜ in.)
Tell el-Amarna
New Kingdom, Dynasty 18,
reign of Thutmose IV,
ca. 1400–1390 B.C., or later
Staatliche Museen zu Berlin, Aegyptisches
Museum und Papyrussamlung 21685

This ivory plaque was apparently part of a bracelet, or perhaps a wrist guard intended to protect an archer's arm from the vibrating cord of his bow.[1] The elaborate openwork design shows Thutmose IV smiting an Asiatic enemy. This scene, symbolic of the king's fundamental duty to protect and enlarge his realm, was represented in Egyptian art throughout pharaonic history. Here, as on most other examples, the king grasps the groveling foe by a hank of his hair, a task apparently so easy for Thutmose that he is able to hold a tall bow and arrows in the same hand. The king's other arm is raised, wielding the weapon he is about to bring down on the head of his victim. In contrast to the mace held by kings in earlier depictions of the scene, Thutmose holds a sickle sword, a battle knife or short sword of Asiatic origin, which the Egyptians had recently adopted (see cat. no. 30).

The king wears a wig of short curls, with a *uraeus* at the front, two streamers hanging down behind, and a sun disc on top. His elaborate costume features a pleated knee-length kilt with a belt. Suspended from the front of the belt are a beaded sporran (pouch) and two cords with flowerlike tassels; a bull's tail hangs in back. On his upper body Thutmose wears a sort of vest in the shape of two falcons whose wings extend over his chest and back. He is also embellished with a necklace, armlets, and bracelets.

Behind the pharaoh is a stand of papyrus, crowned with a sun disc, in which a cobra is entwined. A disc, topped by two plumes, also appears on the falcon head of a god standing at left, probably Montu-Re, who proffers another sickle sword to the king so that he may, according to the inscription in front of him, "smite the chiefs of all foreign countries."[2] In his other hand, the god holds an *ankh*, symbol of life, and a tall sign representing millions of years. The final elements in the composition are two oval cartouches at the top of the frame, within which two of the king's names, Menkheprure Thutmose, are written.

The grandfather of Akhenaten, Thutmose IV initiated the increased attention to the cult of the sun that would culminate in his grandson's worship of the Aten. It is not surprising, therefore, that this object wound up at Akhenaten's capital city, Tell el-Amarna. It was not found in a royal building, however, but in the house of a courtier who, like the king himself, may have descended from a line of sun worshippers.

ERR

1. For further reference, see Porter and Moss 1934, p. 204; Ägyptisches Museum Berlin 1967, pp. 56–57, no. 590, illus.; and Bryan 1991, pp. 162–63.
2. Bryan 1991, p 163.

165

STELE OF AN ASIATIC SOLDIER

Limestone, painted
Height 29.5 cm (11⅝ in.); width 24 cm (9½ in.)
Tell el-Amarna (?)
New Kingdom, Dynasty 18, reign of
Akhenaten, ca. 1353–1336 B.C.
Staatliche Museen zu Berlin, Aegyptisches
Museum und Papyrussamlung 14122

This small stele was made for a Syrian immigrant to Egypt, whose name is given as Tarura in the painted inscription above his figure.[1] His bulging forehead, small nose, and full beard are not consistent with the features of an Egyptian native. His hairstyle and white headband are also foreign to Egypt, as is his colorful tasseled kilt. He is shown using a straw to drink from a two-handled jar, which was probably filled with beer. This type of

165

long metal straw, designed to help the drinker avoid sediment and other impurities, was a Near Eastern innovation that made its way to Egypt with travelers like Tarura.

Tarura's reason for being in Egypt is explained by the spear that stands behind him as if propped against a wall. He was a soldier and, to judge from the stool on which he sits, one of high rank. Like all the furniture represented on this stele, the stool is Egyptian, a portable type designed for military use, with legs that folded together for travel. The seat would have been of animal hide, with the tail hanging down on one side. The low stool of Tarura's wife appears well made, with braced, turned legs; a typical Egyptian jar stand

holds the pointed base of the jug from which Tarura drinks. With his long fine-linen kilt, his necklace, and his shaven head, the couple's companion also appears to be Egyptian. Because he is not identified as a family member, or even given a name, he was presumably a servant, or even a slave.

The most enigmatic figure on the stele is Tarura's wife. In most respects, she appears to be a prosperous Egyptian woman. She wears a long black wig, from which escapes a strand of her own hair, and a gauzy linen garment that partly conceals an imposing necklace. Her slumped posture suggests the relaxed pose in which Nefertiti was sometimes portrayed at this time. But her prominent nose and full

lips may be intended to convey a foreign appearance, and her name, written in the three right-hand columns above, is certainly not Egyptian. After the Egyptian title *nbt pr*, the equivalent of "Mrs.," she is called Arbura, a name as foreign as that of her husband. The many foreign soldiers who came to Egypt during this period apparently often married Egyptian women. Perhaps Tarura brought his wife with him, or perhaps he gave his Egyptian wife a name from his homeland.   ERR

1. For further reference, see Porter and Moss 1934, p. 232; Janssen 1951, pp. 52–53, fig. 10; Priese 1991, pp. 79–80, no. 80; and Kendall in *Pharaohs of the Sun* 1999, p. 239, no. 114.

166
STELE FRAGMENT RECOUNTING BATTLE OF QADESH

Stone
Height 33.5 cm (13¼ in.)
Thebes
New Kingdom, Dynasty 19, reign of
Ramesses II, ca. 1279–1213 B.C.
Staatliche Museen zu Berlin, Aegyptisches
Museum und Papyrussamlung 31604

This carved relief fragment from the mortuary temple of Ramesses II, called the Ramesseum, at Thebes represents a tiny portion of the extensive annals recounting the now-famous Battle of Qadesh (ca. 1275 B.C.) between the armies of the Egyptian pharaoh and the Hittite king Muwattalli II (see fig. 84). As part of his campaign to expand northward and recapture the province of Amurru, then under Hittite control, Ramesses amassed an army of nearly twenty thousand foot soldiers and charioteers and set out for Amurru's capital city of Qadesh, on the Orontes River in Syria. False intelligence led him to believe that he could take Qadesh and the surrounding region without opposition. Instead, he met with stiff resistance, and the battle was ended only with the signing of a peace treaty.[1] By mutual agreement, fighting ceased and the army of Ramesses was allowed to collect its dead and depart. Although the official Egyptian account interprets the outcome as an Egyptian triumph,[2] in reality, Ramesses suffered a strategic defeat by failing to regain control of Amurru and its capital city.

The Egyptian record of the Battle of Qadesh is preserved in two hieratic documents. The lengthy "official" version is referred to as the *Poem*; the accompanying pictorial records included captions as well as a detailed though relatively short account called the *Bulletin*.[3] Varying versions of these texts have been found carved on to the walls of five temples: Luxor, Karnak, and the Ramesseum at Thebes, one at Abydos, and Abu Simbel in Lower Nubia. The earliest reliefs, from Abydos, remain the most beautifully executed of all the variants, despite their fragmentary nature.

Correlating the five sets of carvings is a complex task, although an existing tentative chronology manages to integrate the texts and captions in all five locations.[4] Even more complex are the connections among the various records *within* each temple.[5] The Ramesseum fragments join to one another, as do the Luxor ones. The truncated text of the *Poem* at Abu Simbel, a grotto temple, can be attributed to a lack of available wall space there. At Karnak, where the situation is extremely complicated, the recent discovery of yet another palimpsest, this time of the *Bulletin*, has recently been added to the repertoire of Egyptian accounts of the battle.[6]

In many cases, the walls have disintegrated and what remains is difficult to decipher. Fortunately, this fragment from the Ramesseum is easy to identify. It belongs to version R2 of the relief captions[7] inside the temple on the north wall of the second court, close to the join of the interior north and east walls.[8] In the lower portion of the fragment, the Hittite king is seen in left profile (facing westward). Above him are brief captions written vertically. The more complete one, to the left (R42), reads, "the chief of every [foreign country] who came with him."[9] The fragment relates to Muwattalli's decision to avoid direct combat, preferring to manage his troops from a distance. Despite the Hittite king's subsequent success, Egyptian accounts focus on the "cowardly" nature of his actions.   SAS

1. The most recent analysis and translation of the campaign can be found in Kitchen 1996, pp. 2–26, and Kitchen 1999, pp. 3–54. See also Spalinger 2005, pp. 209–27.
2. For a translation of the text, see Kitchen 1979, pp. 2–147. The later hieratic account, a copy of an archive text, is edited and discussed in Spalinger 2002.
3. In a different approach to the Qadesh accounts, Sir Alan Gardiner (1960, pp. 1–4) argued for a bipartite division between text and pictures.
4. See Spalinger 1985 and Spalinger 2006.
5. The traditionally accepted scheme is that of Charles Kuentz (1928–32). The best diagrams of the carvings are those in Kitchen 1979, 125–28; see p. 179 for the Luxor version L2 of the *Poem* and the adjoining *Bulletin*, although the blank exterior east wall of the Colonnade of Dynasty 18 is where one would have expected the pictorial version of the campaign to appear. Gaballa 1976, pp. 113–19, also covers these details.
6. For more about this discovery by William J. Murnane, see Spalinger 2002, pp. 173–75 n. 31. The author is in possession of Murnane's notes of this text.
7. See Ägyptisches Museum Berlin 1967, no. 812; and *Pharao: Kunst und Herrschaft* 1997, no. 16.
8. See Porter and Moss 1972, p. 434 (10).
9. Kitchen 1979, p. 139; for translation, see Kitchen 1996, p. 22.

167

167

ASIATIC CAPTIVE

Ivory
Height 12 cm (4¾ in.)
Egypt
New Kingdom, Dynasties 19–20,
ca. 1295–1070 B.C.
The Metropolitan Museum of Art, New York,
Purchase, Fletcher Fund and The
Guide Foundation Inc. Gift, 1966   66.99.50

This ivory depicts a fettered captive. His pointed beard, facial creases, and elaborately patterned garment clearly mark him as an Asiatic. He stands with bent legs, the lower body shown in profile facing to his left, the upper body and face presented in frontal view. Egyptian representations of captives often show the upper body in profile with arms bound together in back. Because the upper body of this captive is presented frontally, the arms are pulled into a curious position over the head so that they remain visible. Fetters are usually wound about the elbows, but in this case they tie wrists to shoulders.[1]

In ancient Egypt, foreigners were a symbol of chaotic and evil forces threatening *maat*, world order and justice. It was the duty of the king to maintain *maat*. To portray a foreigner as a bound prisoner not only served to demonstrate the victory over such forces by the king; it was also a symbolic reassurance that these threatening forces were defeated and controlled. In the New Kingdom, bound Asiatics were often depicted on the king's throne together with bound Nubians. The extension at the top and the bar at the bottom of this figure demonstrate that it was originally part of another object, perhaps one in a row of fettered captives that embellished a piece of furniture—a wood chair or footstool.   IST

1. Compare a glazed tile from the palace of Ramesses III at Medinet Habu, MMA 26.7.969, for another Asiatic captive with the same position of the arms but bound at the elbows.

168a–d

GLAZED TILES WITH ASIATIC LEADERS

Polychrome faience
a. Syrian Leader
Height 25 cm (9⅞ in.); width 6 cm (2⅜ in.)

b. Amorite Leader
Height 29.5 cm (11⅝ in.); width 5.5 cm (2⅛ in.)

c. Philistine Leader
Height 30 cm (11⅞ in.); width 5.5 cm (2⅛ in.)

d. Hittite Leader
Height 16.8 cm (6⅝ in.); width 5.5 cm (2⅛ in.)

Egypt, Thebes, Medinet Habu, Mortuary
Temple of Ramesses III
New Kingdom, Dynasty 20, reign of
Ramesses III, ca. 1184–1153 B.C.
Museum of Fine Arts, Boston   Emily Esther
Sears Fund   03.1569, 03.1571–1573

These glazed tiles come from the site of Ramesses III's mortuary temple at Medinet Habu, on the west bank of Thebes. A ceremonial palace of mud brick provided a residence for the king's spirit and also for the king himself when he stayed at the temple for ritual ceremonies. The entrances to the palace were luxuriously decorated with inlay tiles picturing the king as a sphinx trampling his enemies above rows of bound foreign prisoners—Asiatics, Nubians, Libyans, and Sea Peoples—from the farthest reaches of the Egyptian empire.[1] Their gaily embroidered garments are brilliantly captured in polychrome faience, a technique that reached its apogee in the Ramesside period.[2]

Shown here in their finery, bound and helpless, are four Asiatic leaders: a Syrian, an Amorite, a Philistine, and a Hittite.[3] We should, however, be wary of these designations, for the Egyptian artist depicted their outlandish costumes and un-Egyptian facial features according to convention. So while it is a simple matter to distinguish an Asiatic from a Nubian or a Libyan, it can be difficult to distinguish one Asiatic from another: there is a certain interchangeability about their fringes and tassels, their wraparound shawls and tunics, leading one scholar, for example, to identify a "Hittite in Libyan costume."[4] As Hayes remarked apropos a related group of tiles from a palace of Ramesses II at Qantir:

The general standard of accuracy and consistency in such ancient "racial portraits" is seldom so high as to make the identifications of the types matters of certainty, even when labels accompany the figures. . . . In many instances the Egyptian sculptor or painter had only a vague idea of the exact physical characteristics of the foreigner he was portraying [or] the details of his clothes and accessories. . . . By the Nineteenth Dynasty, the names of certain peoples, once used in connection with closely defined tribes or nations, had been extended to include whole groups of neighboring outlanders.[5]

These figures, however, are not records of conquered peoples. Their main purpose was ritual, not historical. From ancient times the enemies of Egypt were known collectively as the "Nine Bows." Just as the figure nine, or three times three, signified a plural of plurals, so the number of enemies could increase to include the entire gamut of foreign peoples. New enemies made their appearance as the geographic knowledge of the Egyptians expanded. These representations of bound foreigners do more than record, advertise, or commemorate their defeat; they magically perpetuate it for all eternity. Like wild animals, foreigners living outside Egypt's borders represented the forces of chaos. It was the pharaoh's duty to subdue them and thus to preserve the harmony of the universe.

LMB

1. R. Anthes in Hölscher 1951, pp. 40–42, pl. 5.
2. See Crowell in *Gifts of the Nile* 1998, pp. 196–97, nos. 52–54.
3. L. Rowe 1908, pp. 47–50.
4. Anthes in Hölscher 1951, p. 42, pl. 30a.
5. Hayes 1937, p. 33.

168a

168b

168c

168d

AEGEAN INTERACTIONS WITH THE NEAR EAST AND EGYPT DURING THE LATE BRONZE AGE

ROBERT B. KOEHL

Contacts during the Late Bronze Age between the inhabitants of the Aegean and the cultures of the eastern Mediterranean are attested archaeologically by the discovery of Aegean-made artifacts in foreign contexts and of eastern-made artifacts in the Aegean.[1] To this evidence may be added a handful of visual and textual references to Aegean peoples preserved in eastern sources, primarily Dynasty 18 Egyptian tombs and several letters from Hattusa and Ugarit.[2] Since the Mycenaean Linear B texts (and most likely the undeciphered Minoan Linear A tablets) from Crete and the Greek mainland are mute on questions of foreign relations—with no records of diplomatic exchanges or trade agreements preserved—reconstructions of international relations in the Aegean, whether political or socioeconomic, are subject to a range of interpretations. Nevertheless, by observing changes in the distribution patterns of imports, noting their source and date of manufacture, their place of discovery, and the date of their find contexts, it may be possible to outline the role played by Late Bronze Age Aegean peoples in the thriving network of international exchanges that characterizes this era.

During the Middle Bronze Age, the Minoans of Crete pursued relations with eastern Mediterranean cultures more aggressively than did their Greek mainland and Cycladic island counterparts. We can deduce this activity from the widespread distribution of finely decorated Middle Minoan Kamares ware and references to Kaptara, widely believed to be Crete, in texts at Mari (see p. 59). These overseas ventures, surely efforts to obtain copper and tin, resources lacking on Crete, were provisioned by a string of colonies on Aegean islands reaching to the west coast of Anatolia.[3]

Crete continued to dominate Aegean interests with the eastern Mediterranean at the beginning of the Late Bronze Age, although Late Minoan IA ceramics are scarce in eastern contexts.[4] Rather, it would appear that Minoan interests began to focus on Cyprus, because of its copper resources. Indeed, the largest assemblage of Late Minoan IA pottery in the east comes from the site of Toumba tou Skourou, overlooking Morphou Bay on the north coast of Cyprus, where Minoan ships could conveniently load copper and then, for shipments of tin, sail one day north to the south coast of Anatolia.[5]

While many scholars believe that these Minoan trading ventures to the east were organized and financed by palatial institutions, the widespread distribution on Crete of bronze workshops and finished objects indistinguishable in type and quality from those found in the palaces suggests that independent entrepreneurs or cooperative ventures between communities or merchant families played a significant role in these exchanges.[6] Although Minoan pottery seems to have been regarded as a valuable commodity, to judge from the fine decorated cups and jugs found at Toumba tou Skourou, those items that would leave no trace in the archaeological record, such as wool textiles, herbs, and aromatics, may have been part of Late Minoan I trade.[7]

Despite the dominance of Crete during the early years of Egypt's Dynasty 18, finds of Near Eastern artifacts on Thera, albeit in small numbers, and in the Shaft Graves at Mycenae suggest more complex networks of exchange. Indeed, Thera may have played an active and independent role in eastern overseas ventures.[8] Although the gold source for the objects in the Shaft Graves has never been confidently identified, a stag-shaped vessel, or bibru, from Shaft Grave IV (fig. 54), was made from Taurus Mountain silver and was perhaps a royal gift from an Anatolian prince.[9]

It is difficult to gauge how the eruption of the Theran volcano at the end of Late Minoan IA affected Aegean contacts with the east. If the Minoan fleet was harbored on the island's south coast, it may have escaped such aftereffects as a tsunami. Indeed, based on the wealth of artifacts discovered in the destruction levels of the next era, Late Minoan IB, it would appear that Crete survived the event relatively unharmed. Thus gift-bearing embassies from Crete and the so-called Isles in the Midst of the Sea, probably a reference to the Cycladic islands, figure among the international delegations depicted on the walls of Egyptian noble tombs dated to the reigns of Hatshepsut and Thutmose III (see figs. 85, 87). Late Minoan IB ceramics have also been found in Egypt and the Levant.[10] Despite the small quantities of Late Minoan I pottery in the Nile Valley, the fact that the Minoan conical rhyton was adopted by Egyptian culture during early Dynasty 18 (see cat. no. 283) and used there as it was on Crete implies a degree of cultural influence that could only have come through sustained contacts.

Many scholars believe that the destructions on Crete which brought the Late Minoan IB era to a close, about 1450 B.C., were caused by a military invasion of Mycenaeans from the Greek mainland. It is therefore not surprising that Late Helladic or Mycenaean IIA and IIB ceramics suddenly appear in Egypt and the Levant in significantly greater numbers than Minoan pottery.[11] Most are cups, which again suggests that the ceramics themselves were valued commodities. Whatever else the Mycenaeans were marketing at this time has left no trace in the archaeological record.

Relations between the Aegean and Egypt continued, as witnessed by the large numbers of Egyptian stone vessels interred in tombs on Crete that may have belonged to the occupying Mycenaean forces.[12] Indeed, the shift from Minoan to Mycenaean seems to have been acknowledged by Egypt, as may be surmised from the repainting inside the Tomb of Rekhmire. After attending the coronation of Amenhotep II, following the death of Thutmose III, Rekhmire recorded his journey to Thebes on a new wall and, to make them appear more "Mycenaean," made changes to the costumes of the Keftiu and to their vessels.[13]

Mycenaean power during the fifteenth century B.C. appears to have expanded to include former Minoan settlements in the Aegean islands, as on Karpathos, Kos, and Rhodes, including the west coast of Anatolia.[14] Texts from Hattusa indicate that from this era until the end of the thirteenth century B.C., Mycenaeans were sporadically involved in Anatolian internal affairs, sometimes as allies of the Hittites, at other times acting independently and out of self-interest rather than loyalty.[15] Although the amounts of Mycenaean pottery in Anatolia are relatively small, compared with their distribution at this time in Cyprus and the Levant, Hittite influence on Mycenaean architecture, specifically corbeling and fortification walls and gates, implies a different level of contact.[16] Texts record that on occasion, the Hittite king regarded the king of Ahhiyawa, a reference to either one or all Mycenaean kingdoms, as his "brother," the term of mutual address used by Great Kings of equal status (see pp. 161–68). Perhaps Hittite kings sent architects to advise Mycenaean dynasts on the construction of their citadels.[17] It may be recalled that Pelops, the mythological founder of Mycenae, came from Anatolia.

Although Mycenaean texts do not provide information on the structure of trade with the east, the centralization of power in the hands of the *wanax*, the Mycenaean king, is undeniable. Based on the concentration of luxury items from the Near East in Mycenaean palaces and high-status burials, notably ivories and semiprecious stones in both raw and finished states, it is likely that a restricted class of society controlled access to elite eastern commodities more tightly during the Mycenaean era than during the Minoan. Yet the archaeological evidence of Mycenaean exports to the east suggests that commercial interactions were not based exclusively on high-status goods.

Whereas previously the quantities of Minoan and Mycenaean ceramic imports to the Egypt, Cyprus, and the Levant numbered in the dozens, Late Helladic IIIA:2–IIIB:1 ceramics, representing roughly a century, from 1350 to 1250 B.C., number in the thousands, a figure that was never again exceeded during the Bronze Age. Sites such as Marsa Matruh on Bate's Island provided conduits for the distribution of Aegean and Cypriot goods to Egypt.[18] Neutron activation studies of Mycenaean imports to the east confirm that the majority were made in the Argolid, home of the most powerful Mycenaean kingdom.[19] However, differences in the distribution of shapes may imply that Mycenaean merchants accommodated different tastes. Earlier, the most significant quantities came from Cyprus, Tell el-Amarna, and Alalakh.[20] At Alalakh the most common shapes are the amphoroid krater, probably used for mixing fermented, wine-based beverages, and the small globular vertical flask, which may have contained a concentrate that was diluted in the krater, such as *de-re-u-ko*, a sweet wine or must, and possibly the highest grade of Mycenaean wine, according to Linear B texts.[21] This flask is also the most common Mycenaean shape at Tell el-Amarna, although kraters are rare. While kraters are common in Cypriot tombs, stirrup jars and small piriform jars are the most common Mycenaean vessels. Stirrup jars (see cat. nos. 242b, 244) may have contained other grades of wine and oils, including perfumed oil.[22]

By about 1300 B.C., Mycenaean commercial contacts with the east may have reached their peak in frequency, to judge from the vast number of sites in the Levant, Cyprus, and Egypt with Mycenaean imports.[23] A trio of containers dominates the repertoire: the small- and medium-size stirrup jar, for transporting wine and oil; the small piriform jar; and the small, angular alabastron.[24] The wide mouths of the latter two vessels suggest they may have contained viscous substances, such as honey, or even dried herbs and spices, although only residue analysis will confirm these hypotheses. In addition, some vessels are known almost exclusively from the east, although they are made in standard Mycenaean fabric and hence called Levantine-Helladic or Cypro-Mycenaean ware.[25] These include angular, tall-stemmed chalices; painted shallow, rounded, and pedestaled bowls; and two kinds of rhyta, figural in the form of hedgehogs and head shaped in the form of rams. Their restricted distribution suggests they were made specifically for the eastern market. Finally, the maintenance of royal contacts between Egypt and the Aegean is suggested by the paintings in the Tomb of queen Nofretari, chief wife of Ramesses II, which appear to depict silver earrings very likely of Aegean manufacture.[26]

During the last quarter of the thirteenth century B.C., Mycenaean ceramic imports to the east dramatically decreased, surely related to the violence that plagued the Mycenaean world at this time and culminated about 1200 B.C. with the destruction of the Mycenaean palaces, essentially spelling the end of Aegean Bronze Age palatial culture. However, a market for Aegean products had been created over the preceding several centuries. To fulfill consumer needs, workshops on Cyprus and in the Levant began to produce imitation or "Derivative" Mycenaean wares, a practice that continued into the Iron Age.[27] While these certainly would not have included commodities from the Aegean, their distinct shapes and decorations may have become so closely associated with Aegean luxury items that, even if filled with the local version, their Mycenaean shapes may have enhanced their appeal, at a time when the imports were no longer available.

1. Studies include Leonard 1994; Cline 1991; papers in W. Davies and Schofield 1995; and papers in Karetsou 2000.
2. Cline 1991, pp. 108–31.
3. For views on Minoan settlement abroad, see papers in Hägg and Marinatos 1984; Niemeier 2005a; and Niemeier 2005b.
4. Warren and Hankey 1989, pp. 138–39.
5. Vermeule and Wolsky 1990.
6. On the role of the palaces in Minoan trade, see Wiener 1987 and Kopcke 1987.
7. Knapp 1991.
8. On the possibility that ostrich eggshell rhyta were fashioned on Thera, and not Crete, whence they were exported to Mycenae, see Koehl 2006, p. 357.
9. Koehl 1995.
10. Warren and Hankey 1989, pp. 138–44.
11. To the specimens listed in Leonard 1994 may be added more recently published fragments from Ugarit in Yon, Karageorghis, and Hirschfeld 2000.
12. Discussed in Warren 1995, p. 8.
13. Koehl 2006, p. 344.
14. Niemeier 2005a, Niemeier 2005b.
15. Cline 1994, pp. 121–25.
16. Özgünel 1996.
17. Zaccagnini 1983.
18. White 2002; Russell 2002.
19. French 2004.
20. L. Åström 1972, pp. 289–384; Hankey 1973; Koehl 2005.
21. Stanley 1982.
22. Leonard et al. 1993.
23. For the Levant, see Leonard 1994; also Yon, Karageorghis, and Hirschfeld 2000; for Cyprus, see L. Åström 1972, pp. 289–384; for Egypt, see Warren and Hankey 1989, pp. 154–55; Hankey and Aston 1995; Mountjoy and Mommsen 2001.
24. Cadogan 1973.
25. Karageorghis 1965.
26. Koehl 1999.
27. Leonard 1994; Koehl and Yellin 2007.

169

RHYTON

Chlorite
Height 15 cm (5⅞ in.); height with horns
21.5 cm (8½ in.)
Crete, Zakros, Palace
Late Minoan I, ca. 1625–1450 B.C.
Archaeological Museum, Heraklion, Greece
HM 2713

170

RHYTON

Ceramic, painted
Height 13.2 cm (5¼ in.); length 17.8 cm (7 in.)
Thera, Akrotiri
Late Cycladic I ca. 1625–1525 B.C.
Archaeological Museum of Thera, Greece
AKR 1855

At the start of the Neopalatial era, in Middle Minoan III, about 1700 B.C., Minoan artisans created a new type of animal-headed rhyton, classified as such from its two openings behind the head and in the muzzle.[1] Its immediate inspiration was undoubtedly the Protopalatial animal-headed rhyton, which may in turn have been inspired by Middle Bronze Age Anatolian animal-headed cups (see cat. nos. 39, 40).[2] On the Middle Bronze Age vessels the back of the head is open, ending with a short neck or rim. Similar vessels continue into the Late Bronze Age, as attested by the ceramic lion-headed cup from Ugarit (cat. no. 155).

169

170

By contrast, Neopalatial animal head–shaped rhyta sit majestically at a perpendicular angle to the neck, which is now closed. With a small opening behind the head, nearly all are lions or bulls, although two ceramic boar heads were discovered at Thera.[3] This type of rhyton is also depicted on the tombs of Dynasty 18 Egyptian nobles carried by the Keftiu, probably from Crete, and Islanders from the Great Green, probably from the Cycladic archipelago (fig. 87). In addition to bulls and lions or lionesses, dog- and griffin-headed rhyta appear. The white and yellow colors used for all may indicate that the vessels were originally silver and gold, following the standard Egyptian color conventions, while red and blue linear details may attest to inlays.[4] The only extant metal head-shaped rhyta are the silver and gold bull head and gold lion head from Shaft Grave IV at Mycenae, which were probably also made in the Neopalatial era.[5]

While the burnished reddish yellow surface on the ceramic lion-headed rhyton from Akrotiri, above, may have been meant to imitate the animal's coat, its facial planes separated by sharp transitions recall the gold lion head from Mycenae, perhaps its immediate source of inspiration. The rhyton was handmade, the flat back plate and pointed ears attached separately. The facial features are generally naturalistic, with a strong jawline, rounded muzzle with whisker roots in relief, squared nose, grooved mouth, pointed *barbiche*, amygdaloid eyes with thickened edges, and raised bosses at the base of the nose bridge for the brow nodules.

Naturalism reaches its apogee in Minoan art with the chlorite bull-headed rhyton from Zakros, opposite page, reassembled from fragments and with the horns, eye inlays, one ear, part of the muzzle, and lower left side of the face now reconstructed. The face is asymmetrical, with a higher left eye and ear. Flame-shaped locks of hair carved in relief flow freely over the head around a swirling tuft on the forehead, down the muzzle, and up to the brow ridges and smooth, fleshy sides of the face, neck, and dewlap. Gold foil, which adheres to a more fragmentary rhyton from Zakros, suggests that parts or all of the present example may also have been similarly sheathed.[6]   RBK

1. Koehl 2006, pp. 32–37.
2. Ibid., p. 41.
3. Ibid., pp. 21–38, classified as Type II.
4. Ibid., pp. 246–50.
5. Ibid., pp. 115, 121–22.
6. Ibid., p. 116.

Figure 87. Facsimile of wall painting, showing Syrian with his son and man of Keftiu with rhyton. Thebes, Tomb of Menkheperreseneb (TT 86). Dynasty 18, reigns of Thutmose III– Amenhotep II. The Metropolitan Museum of Art, New York, Rogers Fund, 1930 30.4.55

Mycenae

The Mycenaean civilization (ca. 1625–1125 B.C.), named after its greatest center, is marked by the rise in power of Mycenae in the Argolid.[1] The royal Shaft Graves (Grave Circles A and B) of the sixteenth century B.C. provide an impressive image of the accumulated wealth of the ruling warrior aristocracy and confirm the legend of Homer's "Mycenae rich in gold" (Iliad 11.51–52). The Mycenaeans developed relations with the Minoan civilization on Crete, then at the peak of its power. Luxury items that arrived at Mycenae by way of Crete included ostrich eggs,[2] alabaster vases from Egypt (later made into rhyta), objects of ivory, and semiprecious stones (carnelian and lapis lazuli). Itinerant artists also arrived via Crete, bringing with them new technical skills and new ideas of social organization. The exquisite Mycenaean inlaid daggers that depict lion hunts and Nilotic scenes, while locally made, betray a knowledge of the imagery and the techniques of the east. Among the grave offerings that have been excavated is a silver vessel (bibru) in the form of a stag that came from the land of the Hittites, possibly sent as a gift (fig. 54).[3]

During the fourteenth and thirteenth centuries B.C., the citadels of Mycenae and Tiryns were fortified with mighty walls fashioned from huge boulders, erected, according to legend, by the Cyclops, builders from Lycia. At Mycenae, the main entrance to the citadel, the monumental Lion Gate (fig. 88), has a massive lintel and imposing relief decoration: two heraldic lions, international emblems of kingship, face each other in profile on either side of a column. Originally, the citadel included a palace and a shrine—both decorated with wall paintings—artist's workshops, and storerooms. The administrative, economic, military, artistic, and religious center of the region, this central authority was organized hierarchically under the wanax, or king. Archives were kept on clay tablets in Linear B, the first Greek script. Agriculture and animal husbandry, the production of oil, wine, and perfumed oils, and the manufacture of textiles were centrally controlled. Magnificent tholos tombs, now plundered, were built for the ruling class, and around the citadel were clusters of ordinary chamber tomb cemeteries. Archaeological finds indicate a socially stratified and prosperous society.

The Egyptians took notice of the Tanaja (Homer's Danaoi) and their rise to power early in the fourteenth century B.C. Faience plaques, vessels, and figurines bearing the cartouches of the pharaohs Amenhotep II and Amenhotep III were imported to Mycenae, though there is no clear evidence of an official Egyptian delegation.[4] In the archives of the Hittite capital, letters mentioning the great power of "Ahhiyawa," possibly situated on the Greek mainland, give a vivid picture—long before the Trojan War and Homer's Achaeans—of the Mycenaean presence and the rivalry of the two powers around Millawanda (Miletos) on the eastern coast of the Aegean.[5]

The palace maintained trade relations with centers in the Syro-Levantine region, and ships crossed the Aegean laden with copper and tin ingots to be used in foundries, glass ingots for the glass workshops such as the one in Tiryns,[6] and elephant tusk and hippopotamus canines for the ivory workshops later excavated outside the citadel at Mycenae,[7] where faience objects exhibiting Near Eastern influence have also been found.[8] Canaanite jars were used to transport a number of goods, including glass beads and terebinth resin, used in medicine and for the production of wine.[9] The Uluburun ship (see pp. 289–305), the Cape Gelidonya, and the presumed Kyme wreck (off the coast of Euboia), carrying copper ingots, provide important evidence for Mediterranean interconnections. The extensive excavations at Mycenae, on the citadel and in the tombs, confirm the existence of both raw materials, such as copper ingots and hippopotamus canines, and finished goods,[10] such as Canaanite jars, Egyptian stone vases and scarabs, a bronze figure of the god Reshef, lapis lazuli cylinder seals with representations of heroes, glass pendants, and Cypriot wall brackets (compare cat. no. 193e).[11]

It is more difficult to trace the Mycenaean end of the exchange, which was perhaps in perishable goods. Elaborate metal artifacts and even textiles,[12] like those carried by the men of Keftiu on wall paintings in the tombs of fifteenth-century B.C. Egyptian dignitaries, may have been in demand. More substantial evidence is provided by the high-quality Mycenaean pottery that was distributed throughout the Mediterranean from Syria and Egypt to the Iberian peninsula. The pictorial pottery, produced at Berbati close to Mycenae, comprised mainly kraters with figural, chariot, and bull representations and was exported primarily to Cyprus and Syria,[13] where conical and zoomorphic rhyta were found in a temple complex (see pp. 426–32).[14] Coarse-ware transport stirrup jars of Cretan manufacture were stored in great numbers at Mycenae—some inscribed in Linear B and probably carried wine, olive oil, and perfumed oil both within Greece and to the eastern ports.[15]

The collapse of the palatial system at the end of the thirteenth century B.C. caused a decline in trade, but it did not altogether halt the network of exchanges. At the time of its sinking near the Argolid coast,[16] the Point Iria ship was transporting Cypriot, Cretan, and Mycenaean pottery, mainly storage jars and transport stirrup jars. Mycenae and Tiryns continued to thrive in the twelfth century B.C.; relations were strengthened especially with Cyprus, where there was a substantial Mycenaean Greek presence and metal artifacts such as the bronze tripod of the Tiryns Treasure were produced and exported.[17] It was also a time of renewed relations with the central Mediterranean region, attested in bronze weapons and other artifacts.[18]

Figure 88. The Lion Gate. Mycenae, Citadel. Late Bronze Age.

In the centuries that followed the demise of the Mycenaean civilization, new cultural and political centers emerged and the foundations of the Greek city-state were laid. The Homeric epics, the Iliad and the Odyssey, immortalized the heroic worlds of the Mycenaean era and the centuries that followed. These narratives were passed down to the poets who created Greek drama in the fifth century B.C. The city of Mycenae took part in the Persian Wars at a time when it had already entered the realm of legend and was part of the common Greek heritage.

LP–M

1. French 2002.
2. Sakellarakis 1990.
3. Koehl 1995.
4. Phillips and Cline 2005.
5. Niemeier 2005a.
6. Panagiotaki et al. 2003.
7. Tournavitou 1995.
8. Peltenburg 1991.
9. Minoans and Mycenaeans 1999, pp. 148–58.
10. Cline 1994.
11. Maran 2004.
12. B. Jones 2005.
13. Van Wijngaarden 2002.
14. Jung 2007.
15. Haskell 1984.
16. Phelps, Lolos, and Vichos 1999.
17. Maran 2006.
18. Papazoglou-Manioudaki 1994; Eder and Jung 2005.

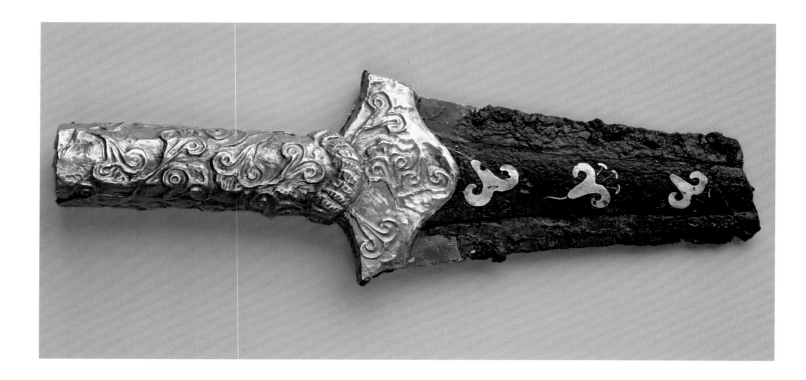

171

INLAID DAGGER

Bronze, gold, and silver
Length 32 cm (12⅝ in.)
Mycenae, Shaft Grave V
Late Helladic I, 16th century B.C.
National Archaeological Museum, Athens,
Greece 8340

The upper part of the blade and the gold sheathing of the hilt and the shoulder of this dagger are preserved. The sheathing is richly decorated with repoussé lilies, a motif that also embellishes both sides of the blade.[1] Cutouts in the shape of lily blossoms—in silver, with stamens in gold—are held in place with a black alloy consisting of low-tin bronze, with small quantities of gold and silver.[2]

Daggers with inlaid decoration, among the most exquisite works of early Mycenaean art, were buried with male warriors; such daggers were ceremonial rather than used in actual warfare. Twelve such daggers were found in Shaft Graves IV and V at Mycenae. Others were found in the rich tholos tombs of Messenia, Lakonia, and Achaia, and in the chamber tombs of Prosymna in the Argolid. Depictions on the blades include a lion hunt, Nilotic scenes, felines hunting prey (fig. 36), rows of spirals, birds and dolphins, and human bodies floating in water.[3]

The decorative technique is variously described as painting in metal, inlay, and niello. It is seen also on gold and silver vases from Mycenae, Dendra, Pylos, and Enkomi on Cyprus, and may have originated in the Levant (see cat. no. 30). The Minoan connection is here missing, as no such examples have been found on Crete. Wall paintings at Akrotiri, specifically the miniature fresco (see figs. 137, 138), may offer intriguing parallels with the scenes that appear on the daggers.[4] Inlaid daggers and vases developed to their most advanced form in early Mycenaean Greece. They were made locally in closed workshops by artisans who were not only trained in the difficult technique but knowledgeable in the iconography of kingship and elite status.[5]

LP-M

1. Xénaki-Sakellariou and Chatziliou 1989, p. 26, pl. v:3, Papadopoulos 1998, p. 11.45, pls. B, 7.
2. Demakopoulou et al. 1995, pp. 146–47, fig. 2; see also cat. no. 30, this volume.
3. Televantou 1994, pp. 204–5.
4. Ibid., pp. 303–8.
5. For further reference, see Xénaki-Sakellariou and Chatziliou 1989; Televantou 1994; Demakopoulou et al. 1995; Boss and Laffineur 1997; Papadopoulos 1998; and Thomas 2005.

172

OPENWORK RELIEF WITH LIONS ATTACKING BULL

Gold
Max. height 5.8 cm (2¼ in.);
max. length 14.5 cm (5¾ in.)
Mycenae, Shaft Grave IV
Late Helladic I, 16th century B.C.
National Archaeological Museum,
Athens, Greece 119

This openwork relief takes the form of lions attacking a bull. The relief, of fine reddish gold, originally formed part of a larger composition that probably covered the sides of a wood pyxis.[1] The three lions are smaller in scale than the bull. Two of the lions—shown in flying gallop—pounce while the third attacks from the front, biting into the neck and clawing the shoulders. The landscape is represented by the tops of two palms.

The lion is the animal most frequently represented in Aegean art, usually in a rocky landscape or amid reeds and palms, and commonly attacking bulls or cattle. Such scenes appear primarily on sealstones; representations also occur on the Theran frescoes (fig. 37),[2] on a gold pommel,[3] and on two niello daggers from Shaft Grave IV,[4] all datable to the sixteenth century B.C. The discovery of lion bones and teeth at Bronze Age sites

172

(Tiryns in the Argolid, Kalapodi in Lokris and Kastana in Macedonia),[5] and the large number of representations of lions in the wild, is evidence that the animal existed on the Greek mainland during this period. Lions were still being hunted in Thrace and Thessaly at the time of Herodotus (*Histories* 7.125–26).

In Assyrian and Persian contexts, the king is often represented hunting lions for sport.[6] In Egypt lions guarded the gates to the Underworld.[7] In Mycenae, because they were a threat to livestock, lions were killed.[8] While the lion hunt is rendered in different styles in the art of Egypt, the Near East, Crete, and Mycenae, the victory of the lion over its prey may be understood as the victory of the powerful over the weak or the victory of the ruler over his enemies.

The palm was associated with flourishing life. Imported from the Near East, it was also valued for the variety of its by-products. Virtually every part of the plant was used—in the production of wine, vinegar, perfume, and medicine.[9] There are relatively few representations of the palm in Aegean art; these mainly occur on pottery and seals.

EK-S

1. A wood pyxis with appliqué gold foil in the National Archaeological Museum, Athens (NAM 808, 811), representing lions chasing deer, was discovered in Shaft Grave V, Grave Circle A, Mycenae.

2. Morgan 1988, p. 45.
3. NAM 295.
4. NAM 394 and 395.
5. Bloedow 1999, p. 53, n. 1, for relevant bibliography of the sites.
6. Bloedow 1992, p. 302.
7. Ibid.
8. Bloedow 1999, p. 54.
9. L. Morgan 1988, p. 28.

173

RING WITH MASTER OF ANIMALS

Red jasper
Max. diameter 2.8 cm (1⅛ in.)
Mycenae, Chamber Tomb 58
Late Helladic II, 15th century B.C.
National Archaeological Museum, Athens, Greece 2852

173

This ring, with the bezel and loop carved from a single piece of jasper, is one of a small group of Mycenaean seal rings made of semiprecious stones. It was found in a chamber tomb along with two other signet rings—one in gold and the other with gold sheathing—six sealstones, and a Canaanite transport jar.[1]

At the center of the scene is the Master of Animals grasping two lions, one by the neck and the other by its hind paws. The massive bodies of the powerful lions are depicted in detail. The figure's broad chest is frontal, while the head and the legs are shown in profile. With short, curly hair and a beard, he wears a Minoan codpiece and a belt and what appear to be greaves on his legs.

The imagery of the Master of Animals has a long history in the Near East in the third millennium B.C.[2] It was widely adopted in Crete during the Neopalatial period and then brought to the mainland. In the Aegean the figure is often depicted as a beardless youth, taming wild nature as he brings animals—usually lions but also bulls, dogs, and others—to submission.[3] Here, he is shown bearded like the Mesopotamian hero. While the Master of Animals subjugates wild beasts, the Mistress of Animals is venerated by them, as is seen on a seal from Mycenae.[4] In the Aegean both figures are known almost exclusively in glyptic. A notable exception is the depiction of the Master of Animals with felines on a conical rhyton from Pylona, Rhodes (cat. no. 288), which also has a modeled bull's head affixed to the side to underscore its ritual character.[5]

LP-M

1. CMS I, no. 89, Xénaki-Sakellariou 1985, p. 182, pl. 77.
2. Barclay 2001, pp. 374–79, pl. CIVg.
3. N. Marinatos 1993, pp. 167–69, figs. 154–61.
4. CMS I, no. 144.
5. Karantzali 2001, pp. 34–35, fig. 28, pl. 33, colorpl. 1.

174

174
PLAQUE WITH HERALDIC LIONS

Ivory
Height 7.4 cm (2⅞ in.); width 4.7 cm (1⅞ in.)
Rhodes, Ialysos
Late Helladic IIIA2–IIIB,
14th–13th century B.C.
Archaeological Museum, Rhodes, Greece 7939

This ivory plaque was found in the votive deposit of the Sanctuary of Athena on the Acropolis of Ialysos.[1] Carved in fairly high relief is a pair of heraldic rampant lions with their heads turned backward. They stand on their hind legs, with raised forepaws resting on a typical Aegean concave altar.[2] Both the lions and the altar are placed on an elaborate epistyle that crowns a tripartite structure[3] or a gate. Three rivet holes arranged in a triangle correspond to the rivets for fastening the plaque to a bronze mirror or to the shaft of an elaborate scepter.[4]

One lion, with its slender proportions and the casual incisions on the upper body, is probably a female. The other, more robust lion is certainly a male, as indicated by the mane. The elaborate altar, represented with parallel incisions and granulation, shows details that commonly appear on jewelry and less frequently on ivories. Also unusual for ivories are the dotted outlines on the lions.[5]

The iconography is reminiscent of the monumental relief on the Lion Gate at Mycenae (fig. 88).[6] Similar arrangements of animals resting on concave altars appear on Minoan and Mycenaean sealstones,[7] as well as on a cylinder seal from Cyprus.[8] Altars in association with entrances and tripartite structures are shown on a seal impression from Zakros,[9] and in the gold-foil shrine from Mycenae.[10] Concave altars are depicted in Late Bronze Age I wall paintings. A monumental concave altar stands above the gateway of the Arrival Town in the Miniature Frieze of the ship fresco at Akrotiri in Thera.[11] And four concave altars are represented in association with a tripartite opening in another Theran fresco.[12] In the thirteenth century B.C., pairs of lions are shown above gateways in the frescoes of Pylos.[13]

The Rhodian ivory has affinities with the carved griffins on the ivories from the Megiddo hoard (fig. 128), the sphinxes on the Mycenaean plaques from Menidi, and other products of the Mycenaean workshops associated with the Near East.[14] According to Helene Kantor,[15] the Megiddo griffins represent the same school of carving that produced the monumental relief at Mycenae. Moreover, an Aegean concave altar is carved on a pyxis lid from Minet el-Beidha (cat. no. 261).[16] This ivory plaque is thus significant not only for its symbolic meaning but also for the evidence it provides for the circulation of similar luxury items along the Mediterranean trade networks. TM

1. The Italian excavation, conducted in the years 1923, 1925, and 1926, yielded approximately five thousand votive offerings dated mainly to the Geometric and Archaic periods. Among them were some Middle Minoan IB/Middle Minoan II stone vessels, a few Late Minoan I objects, fragmentary Mycenaean pottery, and other small objects along with a bronze tanged mirror; see Benzi 1984 and Martelli 1988.
2. See Barnett 1939, p. 13, n. 4; Kantor 1947, pp. 88–89; Poursat 1977a, p. 69, n. 29; Barnett 1982, p. 37, pl. 33a; Benzi 1992, pp. 193–94; Martelli 2000, p. 105, fig. 1; and Marketou n.d. (forthcoming), n. 19.

3. J. Shaw 1978; Gessel 1985, pp. 29–30.
4. Of all the known tanged Mycenaean mirrors from Rhodes, only one mirror is without tangs and bears three rivet holes: Ialysos, Tomb LXIX: 4, Late Helladic IIIA:1–IIIB; see Catling 1964, pp. 226–27; and Benzi 1992, p. 182, pl. 180:g, h.
5. The granulation-type borders on the lion legs and bodies are reminiscent of the pyxis from Mycenae; see Xénaki-Sakellariou 1985, pp. 129–30, E2477, pl. 36. Also similar are the frames on ivory combs, ibid., pp. 85–86, E2474, pl. 16, and on a comb from Megiddo; see Kantor 1947, p. 98, pl. XXIVE.
6. Wace 1949, pp. 22, 50, 52–53, figs. 73a,b, 74a, pp. 89, 132; Mylonas 1966, pp. 173–76.
7. Such as those from Zakros and Ayia Triada: A. Evans, PM IV, part 2, p. 611, fig. 599b, c, PM II, part 2, p. 607, figs. 380, 381; for other examples see CMS I, nos. 46, 73, 98, and Sakellariou 1966, pp. 37–40, 75, 92–97, pl. 2, no. 46, pl. 3, no. 98. A similar altar is depicted on the plaster tablet from Mycenae (Mylonas 1966, p. 162, fig. 131) and on the relief rhyton from Zakros (J. Shaw 1978, pp. 432–37).
8. Frankfort 1939, p. 303, pl. XLVI:5.
9. A. Evans, PM IV, part 2, p. 611, fig. 599a.
10. Mylonas 1966, p. 93, fig. 122e.
11. Morgan 1988, fig. 108.
12. The fresco depicts a goddess seated on the tripartite structure receiving an offering of saffron given by a monkey, see Doumas 1992, fig. 122.
13. Lang 1969, pp. 137–38, no. 2A2, pls. 76, 136, and no. 3A20, pl. 77.
14. Kantor 1960, pp. 18–22, figs. 9–11; Mylonas 1966, pp. 196–97.
15. Kantor 1960, p. 19.
16. Rehak and Younger 1998, pp. 249–50.

Mycenaean Thebes

The city of Thebes, like Mycenae, was advantageously situated at the crossroads of land and sea routes. Secure within its walled citadel, Thebes gradually developed into a dominant political and military power on the Greek mainland, reaching its height during the last centuries of the Bronze Age, usually referred to as the "Mycenaean palatial period" (1400–1200 B.C.). It is therefore possible that some of the traditional Greek myths about the city could reflect its fame during the Late Bronze Age.

The residential settlement and funerary remains of prehistoric and historic Thebes, whose name (te-qa) appears numerous times in its archival texts, were discovered within the modern city first by travelers and later through excavations, which began before the end of the nineteenth century and continue until the present day. These excavations have shed light on the everyday life of Thebes during the Mycenaean palatial period. Among the many finds, prestige items and texts, especially, have provided a record of the bustling settlement, which occupied the Kadmeion hill throughout the Bronze Age. With a network of primary and secondary dependent settlements, Thebes dominated nearly the whole of historic Boiotia in central Greece. With other powers of the Greek mainland, Theban rulers fostered cultural exchange and trade throughout the Aegean and the eastern Mediterranean.

The first excavations on the citadel of Thebes, which is also the nucleus of the modern city, took place from 1906 to 1929 and brought to light the architectural remains of an important building complex. The so-called House of Kadmos remains until today the only extant Mycenaean palatial building in central Greece. Grouped on the ground floor of this complex, which extended over the citadel hill, were archival, storage, and workshop areas; residential rooms occupied the first floor. The sudden conflagration that caused the building's destruction helped to preserve several prestige items, including precious jewelry, while within the storage rooms were found large stirrup jars, most of them with painted Linear B inscriptions. Clay analysis confirmed that they contained olive oil from western Crete.

Excavations, begun in 1963, have continued to the present day. They have uncovered several sections of the immense wall surrounding the citadel, and about 325 archival documents, inscribed on clay tablets and nodules, have come to light in storage rooms and workshop areas associated with the palace. Distribution centers contained weapons, tools, weights, bits of raw materials, and both finished and unfinished jewelry and furniture appliqués made of imported materials. The 1963–64 expedition uncovered an unexpected cache of jewelry made of precious materials, mainly gold, ivory, lapis lazuli, and agate, in the palatial building. Comprising the Theban Treasure, these objects, which came mainly from the eastern Mediterranean, were stored not only for safekeeping but also to be worked further. A variety of artifacts also came to light in the chamber tombs around the citadel.

The appearance of the Sea Peoples in about 1200 B.C., among other factors, contributed to the collapse of the centralized governments in the Aegean and the Near East, with the exception of Egypt. In the beginning of the twelfth century B.C., Thebes, like many other civil and palatial centers of the eastern Mediterranean, was violently destroyed, to rise again only in the historical period.

VLA

175

175
PLAQUE WITH RAMPANT GOATS

Ivory
Height 9 cm (3⅜ in.); width 7.7 cm (3 in.)
Thebes
Late Bronze Age, 13th century B.C.
Archaeological Museum, Thebes, Greece
383α

This ivory plaque with relief decoration shows a group of heraldically placed wild goats framed by a thin relief strip. It has been reconstructed from five pieces, although some fragments are missing from its body and frame. The plaque is dated to the thirteenth century B.C. and comes from a workshop within the Mycenaean citadel of Thebes, which operated under the auspices of the Royal Palace. It was found in a deposit with other ivory items and was probably attached to a larger object, perhaps a wood container (chest) or furniture item. VLA/IF

176a, b
BEADS

a. Lapis lazuli, max. height 4.5 cm (1¾ in.); max. width 4.9 cm (2 in.)

b. Agate, max. length 4.5 cm (1¾ in.)

Thebes, Palace Workshop
Late Helladic IIIB, 13th century B.C.
Archaeological Museum, Thebes, Greece

176a

176b

A rich and varied treasure of jewelry and cylinder seals of mainly eastern origin was discovered in the winter of 1963–64 in a building near the center of the Theban citadel.[1] The structure of the building, its location next to the palace (the so-called Kadmeion), and its contents identify it as associated with palace activity. The excavation uncovered two rooms, one housing the treasure and the other filled with pithoi. The treasure included beads and other jewelry made of gold, agate, lapis lazuli, and ivory, as well as eastern cylinder seals and Mycenaean seals of different materials. The beads, of various shapes and materials, mainly belonged to necklaces and have parallels in the wider Aegean area and the Near East. Of particular interest are those made of lapis lazuli, a material from Afghanistan, and of agate, also thought to be imported; objects made of these materials are not well known from other Mycenaean sites. The cylinder seals, the plain cylindrical beads of lapis lazuli and agate, and the majority of the gold jewelry arrived in Thebes in the thirteenth century B.C. from the eastern Mediterranean, perhaps the Syro-Levantine coast or Cyprus.

Some of these pieces were reworked at Thebes, where they were combined with locally produced objects. When much of the palace was destroyed at the end of the thirteenth century B.C., they were buried—and thus preserved—under a thick layer of debris. Recently, clay sealings and Linear B tablets were also found in excavation.

VLA

1. Displayed are lapis lazuli beads inv. nos. 221α, 221β, 221χ, 221δ, 221ε, 225α, 225β, 225χ, 227α, 227χ, 227σ, 163. and agate beads inv. nos. 160α, 160δ, 160ιε, 217α, 217β, 217χ, 218, 219, 220α, 220β, 220χ.

177a–c

KASSITE STYLE CYLINDER SEALS AND MODERN IMPRESSIONS

Lapis lazuli
a. Height 4.2 cm (1⅝ in.);
diameter 1.5 cm (⅝ in.)
Kassite, reign of Burnaburiash II, inscription
of Kidin-Marduk ca. 1359–1333 B.C.

b. Height 4.9 cm (1⅞ in.);
diameter 1.6 cm (⅝ in.)
Kassite, 14th century B.C.

c. Height 4.4 cm (1¾ in.);
diameter 1.5 cm (⅝ in.)
Kassite, possibly Cypriot re-carving,
14th–13th century B.C.

Thebes, Palace Workshop
Late Helladic IIIB context, 13th century B.C.
Archaeological Museum, Thebes, Greece
198, 191, 199

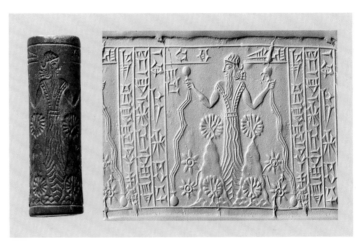

177a

177b

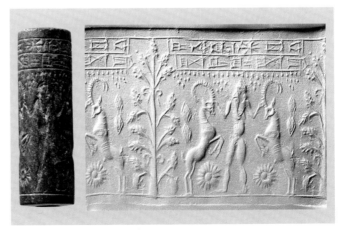

177c

The Kassite lapis lazuli cylinder seals from Mycenaean Thebes must be considered among the most impressive glyptic to reach foreign shores. They attest to a connection between Babylonia and the Greek mainland that extends beyond our expectations based on the rare importation of Mesopotamian cylinder seals to the Aegean.[1] When considered in a more global context, however, such an exchange becomes more understandable.

The only major ruler's name inscribed in the hoard of thirty-eight carved cylinder seals in the Theban Treasure is Burnaburiash II, whose greeting gifts to the Egyptian pharaoh, as documented in the Amarna Letters, invariably included large quantities of lapis lazuli, sometimes in the form of jewelry.[2] However, unlike the gifts of Ashur-uballit I of Assyria and Tushratta of Mitanni (who also sent large quantities of lapis jewelry), seals made of this precious and auspicious material do not count among his offerings.[3]

The Kassite cylinder seals imported to Thebes are eleven in number and varied in style, imagery, and quality. The most outstanding (cat. no. 177a) is a large piece with a nature divinity towering over a mountainous landscape with gnarled trees, perhaps olive trees, that bear circular crowns and star-shaped flowers (see cat. no. 125a). The god is bearded, and his hair is drawn back in a chignon with distinctive spiral curls. With muscled arms extended, he grasps streams that flow out of and into aryballos-shaped vessels. The belted garment that he wears transforms below the waist into undulating lines to suggest that he emerges from the mountain waters which flow from the two flanking peaks. Columns of inscription, carved to be read in the engraving rather than (as is more common) when impressed, identify the seal as that of "Kidin-Marduk . . . *sha reshi* official of Burnaburiash, king of the world."[4] When it is compared with an agate cylinder seal similarly inscribed, also finely carved but somewhat more traditional in its iconography, we can appreciate that the term "artistic revolution" may be appropriate to express the innovations that characterize the imagery on this object.[5]

A second Kassite seal from the Treasure (cat. no. 177b), even larger but not so finely detailed, presents another (perhaps later) version of the motif.[6] Here the bearded god wears the multiple-horned crown and

his strong arms are drawn in to the body; the streaming and branching waters appear to emanate from his shoulders. The source may be the rain clouds, perhaps symbolized by the double lion-headed eagle above. Streams cascade into the cupped hands of fish-men. They also grasp the waters that emanate, along with flowers, from the god's body, which is transformed into a mountainous peak with a cross-hatched pattern and rootlike extensions that join with those of an upright voluted tree. Leaping ibexes add vitality to the symmetrical composition, and typically Kassite cross-and-lozenge motifs fill the field. The inscription across the top of the seal is a prayer to Marduk, leading Porada to identify the nature deity with the chief god of Babylon and son of Ea, the god of sweet waters that flow beneath the earth.[7]

The imagery of divinities merging with the natural world recalls the alternating water and mountain deities as depicted on the molded brick facade of the Temple of Inanna built by Kara-indash (fig. 66). Produced in the Second Kassite style of the late fourteenth century B.C., the seals represent a significant departure from traditional Babylonian scenes of worship that characterize the First Kassite glyptic style.[8] Somewhat rigid compositional schemes are infused with a new vitality at a time when we find a similar spirit in the glyptic arts of Assyria (cat. no. 125). One of the most elaborately carved seals of this type shows a double-headed god whose mountainous body encloses a kneeling figure with flowing streams. This divinity is also a master of beasts, dominating two rampant griffins with displayed wings, while a flock of birds fills the sky. A closely related scene was impressed on a tablet bearing the seal of a governor of Nippur under Shagarakti-Shuriash (ca. 1245–1233 B.C.).[9]

Another superb Kassite seal in the Theban Treasure (cat. no. 177c) inscribed,

"By the command of Marduk, may its wearer stay in good health," bears the depiction of a nude Master of Animals grasping the massive horns of two rampant ibexes.[10] Edith Porada, contrasting the figures on this seal with a more finely modeled example, suggests that the hero's body, separated into segments, and the ibexes with protruding chests may be the work of a Mycenaean craftsman who re-engraved the original.[11] However, the segmenting of the human body with individual drillings is a feature alien to Aegean works, where a sense of organic form remains intact even during later phases of seal carving on the Greek mainland. This is evident in the depiction of an Aegean Master of Animals on the only cylinder seal in the Theban hoard that was made locally (cat. no. 183). In attempting to understand the unusual image of the hero, it might be instructive to compare the depiction on a seal from the Iraq Museum (fig. 89),[12] where a nature divinity very similar in form to one from Thebes (cat. no. 177a) grasps the horns of two rampant ibexes in a scene with birds perched on a palm tree. Could a foreign craftsman have replaced an image such as this one with the more familiar Master of Animals, transforming the outline of the undulating and spreading waters into the figure's bulging belly and widely spaced legs? If this is the case, then it would be more likely for such extensive re-carving to have taken place on Cyprus, where other seals were modified, and it is thus possible that the entire hoard of lapis lazuli came to mainland Greece in a single shipment.

JA

1. Only one Mesopotamian seal, of the Old Babylonian period, CMS I, no. 306, was found in archaeological context, on Crete in Platanos Tholos B; others, CMS II, nos. 206, 287, and CMS XI, no. 287, also come from Crete, but without clear provenance. For Syro-Mitanni

Figure 89. Modern impression of cylinder seal. Kassite period. Iraq Museum, Baghdad IM 22450

seals in the Aegean, see catalogue nos. 250, 251 in this volume.

2. Moran 1992, pp. 13 (EA 7: four minas), 18 (EA 9: 3 minas), 19 (EA 10: 2 minas and a necklace with 1048 "cricket-shaped" beads), 22 (EA 11: 10 lumps and 20 "cricket-shaped" beads).

3. Ibid., pp. 39 (EA 16), 52, mounted in gold (EA 22); also seal-shaped stones mounted in gold: pp. 73, 75 (EA 25); for the significance of lapis lazuli, see Moorey 1999.

4. For this seal, see Porada 1981–82, pp. 49–50, no. 26; Brinkman 1981–82, p. 74.

5. Matthews 1990, p. 60; see also Collon 1987, pp. 58–61.

6. Porada 1981–82, pp. 51–53, no. 27, who considers its looser style to indicate a later work.

7. Brinkman 1981–82, p. 74; Porada 1981–82, p. 50. This view is questioned by Matthews (1990, pp. 60–61), who notes that Klengel-Brandt interprets the mountain god on a relief from Ashur as a personification of Mount Ebikh.

8. For a review of the First Kassite Style, see Matthews 1992, pp. 4–32.

9. Ibid., pp. 34–36; see also Matthews 1990, figs. 132, 133 (Tell Subeidi), for the mountain god as Master of Animals.

10. Brinkman 1981–82, p. 75, no. 31.

11. Porada 1981–82, pp. 58–59, no. 31.

12. Beran 1958, p. 269, fig. 14.

178

SYRO-MITANNI CYLINDER SEAL AND MODERN IMPRESSION

Lapis lazuli
Height 2.2 cm (⅞ in.); diameter 0.9 cm (⅜ in.)
Thebes, Palace Workshop
Late Helladic IIIB context, 13th century B.C.
Syro-Mitanni re-carving,
15th–14th century B.C.
Old Syrian manufacture, 18th–
17th century B.C.
Archaeological Museum, Thebes, Greece 202

The dominant composition carved on this seal is Syro-Mitanni; however, an older inscription related to an unknown king and land of the eighteenth or seventeenth century B.C. and traces of an earlier, poorly preserved design indicate that the seal has been re-carved. In the later composition, two symmetrical griffin-demons stand beneath a winged disc and raise an object, which can be identified by its legs and crossbars as a seat or stool.[1] A human head or mask appearing below it assumes a demonic appearance, with an open mouth and vertical lines suggesting a long beard ending in two points. A vertical motif of seven intertwined loops occupies the full height of the compositional space.

Similar imagery on seal impressions from Ashur dated to the time of Eriba-Adad I (1390–1364 B.C.) and Ashur-uballit I (1363–1328 B.C.) point to a range of dates for the seal here. The Ashur sealings also show certain variations, such as a seat being supported by either bull-men or nude

heroes instead of griffins, and crescent and sun discs instead of the winged disc. The most important element in all these compositions is the raising of the seat, perhaps as a thronelike support for the symbol above it.[2]

The small drillings bordering the wings of the sun disc suggest a Syro-Mitanni style. In contrast, the Middle Assyrian depictions of wings usually have a more feathery appearance, created by vertically incised lines (see cat. no. 124). The winged sun disc on the seal here is closely related to that of a Mitanni cylinder seal found at Tiryns (cat. no. 250). The circumstances regarding the transition to the Syro-Mitanni style are poorly known, but the glyptic evidence at Alalakh shows that there, as elsewhere in Syria, the Syro-Mitanni style prevailed from the sixteenth to the fourteenth century B.C., and perhaps even longer.[3]   JME

1. Porada 1975, pp. 164–72.
2. Porada 1981–82, p. 38.
3. Porada 1980, p. 18.

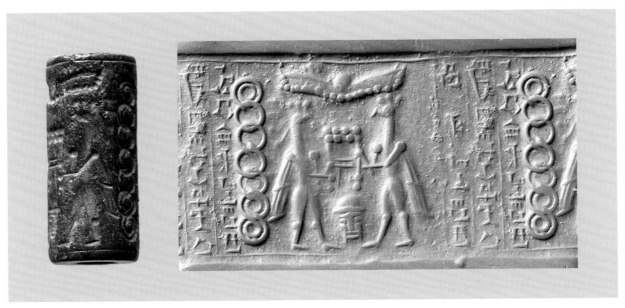

179

HITTITE CYLINDER SEAL AND MODERN IMPRESSION

Lapis lazuli
Height 3.2 cm (1¼ in.); diameter 1.9 cm (¾ in.)
Thebes, Palace Workshop
Late Helladic IIIB context, 13th century B.C.
Hittite Empire manufacture, 14th–
13th century B.C.
Archaeological Museum, Thebes, Greece 200

Among the large corpus of Mesopota-mian and Cypriot cylinder seals in the Theban Treasure is one that is distinc-tively Hittite in style. Like the large major-ity of seals in the group, it appears to have been carved more than once. The original design consists of a procession of four divinities wearing horned headgear. The female figure in a long robe revealing a bared leg may represent Ishtar/Shaushga. Behind her, the Protective Deity of the Countryside grasps a hare. He is followed by the Storm God, who is identified both by the W (thunderbolt) sign before him and by his associated animal, the bull (here possibly a calf). The sun disc over his head is atypical, as it usually denotes the sun god who wears a skullcap and long robe and carries an upside-down crook. The final standing god must remain unidenti-fied. The *ankh*-like shape, which appears four times, usually in conjunction with the small triangle, is the symbol for "life," while the triangle denotes "good fortune."[1] Above the goddess at right is the personal name of the seal owner: Ti-la-zi. On the left is the ideogram for his office: a spear (read HASTARIUS), indicating that he was a member of the royal bodyguard. A small seated figure suspended between two of

the striding gods and the animals, inter-rupting the original composition, appears to have been added later.[2]

The figures, while somewhat attenu-ated in form, exhibit the long nose and full cheeks, clothing, and wide stance typical of the arts of central Anatolia. The carv-ing of such imagery on a conventionally shaped cylinder seal, however, signals the absorption of foreign traditions. Anatolia can be considered a stamp-seal culture, although during specific periods such as the Old Assyrian Trading Colony era—under stimuli from Mesopotamia and Syria—the cylinder seal made its appear-ance (see cat. nos. 36, 37). This type of sealing device was eventually transformed in Hittite central Anatolia into an instru-ment for stamping as well as rolling (cat. no. 101). Exceptionally, conventionally shaped cylinders, such as the Theban seal, bear designs in Hittite style. They demon-strate the coming together of Syrian and Anatolian traditions once again during dif-ferent sociopolitical circumstances within a period of Hittite hegemony extending to the south (see pp. 170–72). The largest body of material consists of cylinder-seal impressions, on tablets from sites such as Ugarit and Emar, depicting complex scenes including those of divine processions.[3]

GB/JA

1. Laroche 1960, no. 369; triangle: BONUS2 : ibid., no. 370.
2. See Porada 1981–82, p. 46; the "stars" above the figures, part of the original composition, are not used analogously to the cuneiform DINGIR sign, as Porada suggests; see also Güterbock 1981–82.
3. See Porada 1981–82 p. 47; for similar scenes on more conventionally Anatolian glyptic meant to be stamped, see Schaeffer 1956, p. 41.

180

OLD BABYLONIAN CYPRIOT CYLINDER SEAL AND MODERN IMPRESSION

Lapis lazuli
Height 2.8 cm (1⅛ in.); diameter 1.6 cm (⅝ in.)
Thebes, Palace Workshop
Late Helladic IIIB context, 13th century B.C.
Cypriot re-carving, 13th century B.C.
Old Babylonian manufacture,
19th–17th century B.C.
Archaeological Museum, Thebes, Greece 196

181

CYPRIOT CYLINDER SEAL AND MODERN IMPRESSION

Lapis lazuli
Height 3.5 cm (1⅜ in.); diameter 1.2 cm (½ in.)
Thebes, Palace Workshop
Late Helladic IIIB context, 13th century B.C.
Archaeological Museum, Thebes, Greece 192

Before the discovery of the Theban Treasure, there was little to associate Cyprus with supplies of lapis lazuli, aside from a mention of tribute from Alashiya in the annals of Thutmose III. Indeed, cylin-der seals of this material have only rarely been found on the island, as pointed out by Edith Porada in her brilliant analysis of the Theban seal corpus.[1] The discovery of six imported lapis seals carved in local Cypriot style and at least four more col-lected and re-carved by a Cypriot engraver[2] thus transforms our view of the island's role in the dissemination of this exotic and prestigious material.

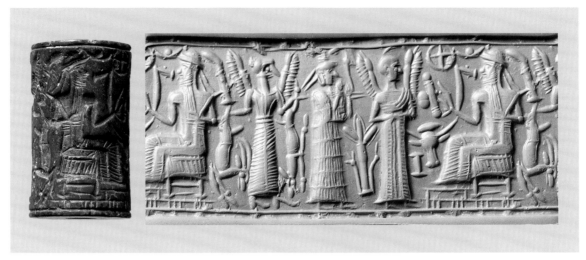

180

Three of the reused seals appear to
derive from Mesopotamian glyptic of the
Old Babylonian period.[3] In one case
(cat. no. 180), the beautifully carved original design is still visible, with a bald worshipper and a suppliant goddess approaching
an enthroned (divine) king. The Cypriot
engraver not only redefined the facial features, emphasizing the nose and eyes, but
added vertical wings on the worshipper and
streamers to the headdresses of the goddess and seated ruler. The ruler's fingers
were also extended and an axelike element
appears to rise from his wrist; he holds a
refashioned "ball staff." The original sun
disc was simplified with a cross inserted.

Of the purely Cypriot additions, most
prominent is the winged divinity grasping
the hind legs of a wild goat and a dog,
added in the space normally reserved for
an inscription. The originally bare field is
now cluttered with a plant, a bucranium,
and a local-type sun in a moon crescent.
The additions are not well executed and
contrast with the highest-quality cylinder
seals produced on Cyprus a century
earlier—one example also in the Theban
hoard.[4] The derivative style it represents
has been paralleled on mid-thirteenth-
century B.C. impressions of seals on tablets
from Ugarit.[5]

Among the original Cypriot cylinder
seals in the Theban hoard, one has been
attributed by Porada to a specific hand,
"the artist of broad-shouldered figures,
who worked during the 13th century B.C."
One of his works was found at Ugarit,
and he may have re-carved another older
Cypriot seal in the Theban collection.[6]
A related example, with imagery one
would associate with Syro-Mitanni glyptic,

181

is impressed on a tablet from Tell
Fakhariyah, a site in northeastern Syria
near the source of the Khabur River. It
shares, however, the emphasis on the
shoulders and full cheeks, pointing to for-
mative elements of this Cypriot style.[7]

Depicted on the Theban seal (cat. no. 181)
is an enthroned divinity, identified by
Porada as a goddess, wearing a long
(flounced?) robe and a horned knobbed
helmet of Syro-Mitanni type. Beneath
a winged sun disc, the deity attempts to
control a rampant winged sphinx, while
nearby a standing winged figure holds the
rear legs of two caprids. Below this scene
of domination are two confronted griffins
with bent Aegean-type wings, their heads
reversed. Cross-shaped elements further
fill the field.

Judging from the state of preservation
and the variety of the Cypriot seals in
the Theban hoard, there can be no doubt
that they were valued primarily for their
material. Porada posits that they were not

shipped together but rather were collected
at Thebes from the fifteenth through the
thirteenth century B.C.[8] While this is
possible, it may be unlikely. Lapis lazuli
glyptic is rarely found on the Greek mainland, which makes the Theban Treasure
so significant. The evidence from Crete
is somewhat more extensive. Two lapis
lazuli cylinder seals imported to Knossos
and Archanes were reworked, one of
them embellished further with gold caps.
Another seal in the Royal Cemetery at
Isopata may have been cut down to form
an amulet. There is also a Minoan-style
cylinder seal from Knossos and a stamp
seal from Palaikastro. One text from Mari
refers to a Kaphtorite dagger of lapis lazuli
and gold in the treasury of Zimri-Lim.[9]

JA

1. Porada 1981–82, p. 8, who refers to Helck and
   reports two lapis lazuli seals, one of them
   Syrian in origin.
2. Ibid., pp. 9–29.
3. Ibid., nos. 3, 7, 8; no. 11 is Syro-Mitanni.

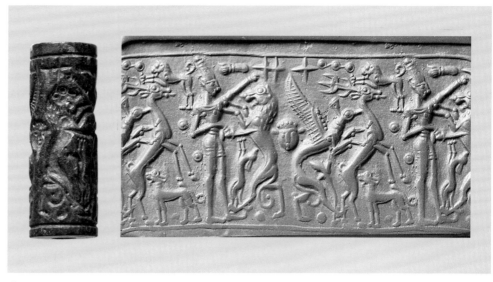

182

4. Ibid., pp. 10 (no. 1), 28, cites the western input essential for the creation of the Cypriot Elaborate Style. See also catalogue no. 252 in this volume.
5. Ibid., p. 16.
6. Ibid., p. 19; see also Porada 1973b, pl. XXXIII:2,3.
7. Porada 1981–82, pp. 17–19; Kantor 1958, p. 79; Porada (1973b, pp. 264, 265, fig. 2) notes an Aegean component in the treatment of the lion heads on the Ugarit seal.
8. Porada 1981–82, p. 29.
9. For a discussion of this material, see Aruz 2008a, pp. 95–96.

182
CYPRO-AEGEAN CYLINDER SEAL AND MODERN IMPRESSION

Lapis lazuli
Height 2.7 cm (1⅛ in.); diameter 1 cm (⅜ in.)
Thebes, Palace Workshop
Late Helladic IIIB context, 13th century B.C.
Cypro-Aegean manufacture, 14th century B.C.
Archaeological Museum, Thebes, Greece 203

One lapis lazuli seal in the Theban Treasure has been attributed to the hand of the master seal carver who created the intercultural style seal in the Yale Babylonian Collection (cat. no. 254).[1] Two scenes fill the height of the cylinder: a belted and kilted hero wearing a tall conical cap stabs a lion, and a griffin attacks a stag at the neck from behind. A human face, a horned animal, and signs fill the field. It may be significant that the only Aegean cylinder seal in the Theban hoard (cat. no. 183) also has the two separate motifs of a hero dominating lions and a griffin attacking a stag from behind.

The animal attack scenes on the lapis lazuli seal encapsulate the differences between the purely Aegean style, posture, and composition and those of the intercultural style. On the Aegean seal both figures leap into the air, the stag's front hooves indicating the struggle; its chest is full and curved. On the mixed-style seal, while the hind leg of one griffin kicks forward, its other leg and the hind legs of the stag are grounded. This static posture is emphasized by the stag's forelegs and lifeless upper body. The griffin, however, with its sinuously curving body, is similar in treatment to the lions of the Yale seal (cat. no. 254), deriving from a Minoan tradition.

Porada notes that the male attacking the lion on the lapis lazuli seal has one

foot placed slightly higher than the other, a concession to Aegean posture that destroys "the immutable solidity of the Western Asiatic figures."[2] Otherwise, his entire body exhibits a static quality that contrasts with an Aegean style. Absent in particular is the three-quarter twist of the torso extending toward the right shoulder that occurs even on standing male figures in the Aegean. The lion, too, mixes stylistic elements; compared with Near Eastern renderings of upright lions, it is very light on its feet, with one foot slightly off the ground, but the vertical posture again introduces a static quality.

The Theban seal is another fine example of the creation of a new style that goes beyond the juxtaposition of individual features from east and west. The use of lapis lazuli, and the fact that the piece comes from a hoard that includes many Cypriot-style lapis lazuli seals, may indicate a Cypro–Levantine home for the seal carver of this work and the seal at Yale. A date in the fourteenth century B.C. is indicated by its style, the period to which we also ascribe the only Aegean cylinder seal found in the same hoard (cat. no. 183). Both pieces must have been deposited in their final context sometime after they were made.   JA

1. Porada (1981–82, pp. 21–23, no. 6) comments on "the exquisite delicacy of the engraving and the use of minute drillings [that] evoke images of a goldsmith's work." Aruz 1997, pp. 277, 288, fig. 19.
2. Porada (1981–82, p. 22) assigns only the man's costume and signs in the field to Cypriot origin.

183
AEGEAN CYLINDER SEAL AND MODERN IMPRESSION

Agate
Height 1.8 cm (¾ in.); diameter 1 cm (⅜ in.)
Thebes, Palace Workshop
Late Helladic IIIB context, 13th century B.C.
Late Helladic II–IIIA manufacture,
15th–14th century B.C.
Archaeological Museum, Thebes, Greece 175

Among the riches of the Theban Treasure is a single Aegean cylinder seal.[1] Unlike the foreign cylinders in the hoard, many fashioned of lapis lazuli, it is made of agate. This material not only was among those preferred for Aegean cylinder and stamp seals but also was found in large quantities and in various states of manufacture both in the Old Kadmeion, dated to the fourteenth century B.C., and the New Kadmeion complex, dated a century later, where the agate cylinder was discovered (see cat. no. 176b).[2]

Two scenes are engraved on the cylinder seal: a nude male Master of Animals flanked by two reversed lions, and an upright griffin attacking an upright stag. The Master of Animals is a Near Eastern theme, introduced into the Aegean glyptic repertoire by the Middle Bronze Age and more evident during succeeding periods (see cat. no. 173).[3] In Mesopotamia and Syria, during the Middle Assyrian and Mitanni periods contemporary with the stylistic date of the Theban seal, the Master of Animals commonly holds lions or ruminants upside-down in mirror image, both

286

183

facing inward or outward. Only rarely on Cypriot and Aegean seals of the time is this careful symmetry observed.[4] The lions on the Theban cylinder seal, with their positions exactly replicated, can be paralleled on Aegean stamp seals.[5] Similarly, the hero extending his arms over the beasts rather than actually holding them can be found on Aegean stamp seals from Prosymna, and Knossos, as well as on some cylinder seals with mixed Aegean and Near Eastern features (see cat. no. 253), one excavated on Cyprus.[6] On other Cypriot and Near Eastern cylinder seals, however, the Master grasps the dominated animals.[7]

The head of the Theban Master of Animals also displays Aegean features, with drillings for the eye and hair and strokes for the head and jawlines. The thin neck emerges from an inverted triangular torso with an inside triangle that serves to outline the chest. The figure has a long, narrow waist and wears no belt; his legs are in profile, both relatively long and slender. The thigh also receives an inner triangle, and the buttock drilling is visible.

The lions on the Theban seal have drillings for the eye, in one case creating a double ring, and for the tip of the nose and the ends of the open jaw.[8] The mane consists of long vertical striations, with obvious drillings marking the chest and rump. Most of the lower body contour is outlined, with a rather exaggerated curve from the belly to the hind legs. Such features are Aegean, as are the prominent tool marks. Perhaps the closest stylistic parallels can be found on the Aegean stamp seals from Thebes itself.

The second scene consists of a griffin attacking a stag, both animals with feet well off the ground. Tool marks are again prominent in the small drillings for the head, joint, and paw details, the outlining of animal bodies, and the wing feathers. The griffin crest and stag antlers are close in form, again paralleled on an Aegean agate stamp seal from the same hoard.[9] The front limbs of both Theban animals are splayed, providing some variation and dynamism, and both scenes seem to have been conceived from the same point of view.

The contrast with a more eastern format, however, is apparent if one compares the image with a griffin attack scene on a companion piece from Thebes, the lapis lazuli seal with Near Eastern as well as Aegean features (cat. no. 182). Both seals may have been produced about the same time, and the sequence of events that might explain their relationship is intriguing but elusive.

In sum, one can relate the Theban agate cylinder seal to Aegean glyptic of the Late Helladic II–IIIA period and date the stamp seals in the hoard to the same time of manufacture, probably prior to the fourteenth-century B.C. destruction of the earlier Kadmeion—the site of an extensive jewelry workshop with many agate pieces.[10] Like the early Near Eastern seals at Thebes, the Aegean seals had been "collected" and were already heirlooms when they were placed in the Theban hoard.   JA

1. Salje 1990, p. 134, pl. XXV:453, for uncertain reasons, places it together with a variety of "Cypro-Aegean" seals.

2. Dakouri-Hild 2005, pp. 181–85.
3. CMS II 1, no. 469, suggests that the Near Eastern theme had already been transmitted, if in a rudimentary state, to the Aegean by the beginning of the Middle Bronze Age. Early versions: Demargne 1939, p. 122, fig. 1; for its appearance and meaning in Greece, see Spartz 1962.
4. See CMS VII, no. 173, CMS V Suppl. 2, no. 113 (with arms extended). For Cypriot asymmetrical compositions, see Boardman 1970, pl. 206; Porada 1981–82, p. 9, no. 1.
5. CMS I, no. 141, when turned 90 degrees.
6. Prosymna Tomb 33 (found in Late Helladic IIIA:2 context): CMS II 8, no. 250; a Minoan sealing dated stylistically to Late Minoan II–IIIA:1, Knossos destruction deposit.
7. There is one exceptional and unusual cylinder seal, published by Vollenweider (1967, p. 58, no. 141), which parallels the Theban agate seal in aspects of composition and style.
8. Younger (1986, p. 134) puts them in his Spectacle Eye Group C (Knossian IIIA:1/2).
9. See CMS II, no. 675.
10. Keramopoullos 1930, pp. 41–58; for later workshops in the new palace: Demakopoulou 1974.

THE ULUBURUN SHIPWRECK AND LATE BRONZE AGE TRADE

CEMAL PULAK

A shipwreck dating to the Late Bronze Age was excavated off Uluburun—or Grand Cape[1]—approximately 9 kilometers southeast of Kaş, in southern Turkey, between 1984 and 1994.[2] It was discovered by a sponge diver during the summer of 1982 and brought to the attention of archaeologists at the Institute of Nautical Archaeology (INA) conducting annual shipwreck surveys along the coast.[3] The original allure of the site was its cargo of copper ingots. Similar ingots had been discovered during the 1960 excavation of a seafaring merchant ship of around the twelfth-century B.C. off Cape Gelidonya, just 65.5 kilometers east of Uluburun. Analyses of finds from the Cape Gelidonya shipwreck had allowed George Bass to hypothesize about the central role of Near Eastern seafarers in Late Bronze Age trade in the Mediterranean.[4]

Excavations at Uluburun quickly revealed the true wealth of the ship. The vast cargo included ingots of copper and tin, other raw materials, several types of manufactured products, and a collection of premium exotic goods. The assemblage recovered from Uluburun has offered great insight into Late Bronze Age trade, both on land and at sea. The raw materials have yielded information on contemporary metallurgy and technology, and the exotic goods illustrate value-laden commodities. With its coherent artifact assemblage and extant hull remains, the wreck is considered the world's oldest seagoing ship and has pushed back the timeline of shipbuilding technology. Examination of the hull and cargo of the Uluburun ship has challenged many previously held assumptions about Late Bronze Age society, and ramifications of the excavation are still being interpreted. Conservation and analyses of the nearly 17 tons of artifacts recovered from the site continue today, demonstrating the multiplicity and complexity of the find.

THE SITE

Archaeologists first visited the site, situated 60 meters off Uluburun's east face and about 350 meters from the terminus of the cape, in the autumn of 1982. Immediately visible were several dozen ingots, still arranged in four discernible rows. Their shape was reminiscent of copper ingots recovered from the Cape Gelidonya shipwreck two decades earlier and termed "oxhide" for their rectangular, four-handled appearance. It had been assumed that each ingot represented the shape of an oxhide, possibly as a means of assigning value for trade, although this hypothesis has since been disproved. The form of the oxhide ingots and other artifacts from the wreck allowed us to propose a rough date of about 1300 B.C.[5] With this estimated date in mind, excavations began in the hope of uncovering items that would illuminate aspects of Late Bronze Age trade.

Because of the depth of the site—42 to 61 meters[6]—the cargo had been spared from salvage or pillage. Nevertheless, recovery of the artifacts was not easy. The depth created difficulties for archaeologists, who could dive only twice a day, each dive limited to twenty minutes of bottom time. Over the subsequent eleven seasons of excavation, more than 22,400 dives were conducted, logging a total of 6,613 hours underwater at the wreck site. The majority of the artifacts were scattered over about 250 square meters of the rocky bottom, which is characterized by a jagged, steep slope, averaging 30 degrees, and occasional pockets of sand (figs. 91–93). The ancient ship had come to rest listing 15 degrees to starboard, in an approximately east-west orientation (fig. 92). From the appearance of the cargo, particularly the copper ingots, and the discovery of several stone anchors, it was determined that the stern of the ship lay higher on the slope, on the western end, with the bow at the deeper end of the site. As the ship settled under the weight of the cargo, the wood hull gradually collapsed and eroded in stages. Some artifacts settled into level spots, while others tumbled down the slope. This led to problems, as many artifacts were found out of their original context. Because each sherd was numbered on the seabed and plotted on a site plan, ongoing reassembly of the pottery and other cargo revealed the trail of spillage, permitting, through detailed documentation and computer graphics, the reconstruction of the cargo's original placement within the ship's hold (fig. 94).

Figure 90. Archaeologist excavating copper ingots at site of Uluburun shipwreck.

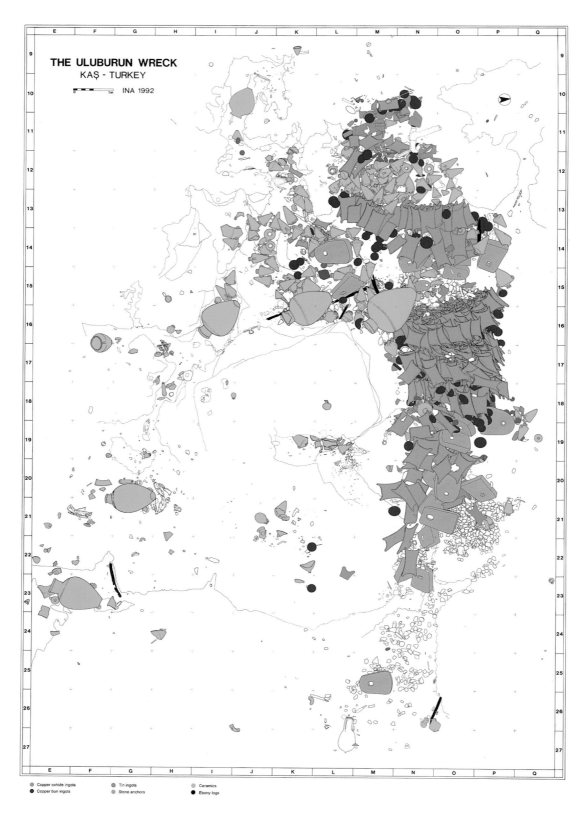

THE ULUBURUN WRECK
KAŞ - TURKEY
INA 1992

Copper oxhide ingots   Tin ingots   Ceramics
Copper bun ingots   Stone anchors   Ebony logs

Figure 91. Plan of seabed at the site of the Uluburun shipwreck.

CARGO

The Uluburun ship had a carrying capacity of at least 20 tons' burden.[7] This minimum capacity was calculated by tallying the recovered objects, which included more than 10 tons of copper and one ton of tin ingots, glass ingots, Canaanite jars, large ceramic storage jars (pithoi), stone anchors, and approximately one ton of cobblestone ballast. This estimate assumes that all transport and storage containers were filled with materials approximating the density of water (1 g/cm^3), although some large storage jars were originally packed with Cypriot pottery for export (see cat. no. 193). It is impossible to estimate exactly how much of the ship's original cargo perished, but some fragments of the more delicate items, such as ebony logs, riddled with teredo, or shipworms, hint at the harsh environment.[8]

Of the twenty-four stone anchors carried on the ship, eight remained in the hold in the midship area as reserve anchors

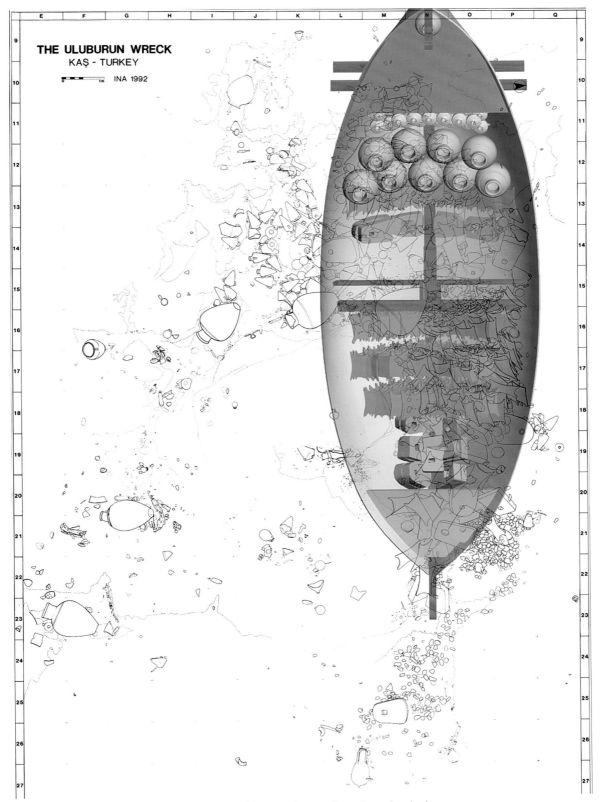

Figure 92. Reconstruction of the Uluburun ship superimposed on plan of seabed.

carried as ballast, while the remainder were stowed at the bow, with several ready for use. An analysis of the cargo provides our clearest glimpse thus far into Late Bronze Age trade in the Mediterranean.[9] The wreck itself is another indicator of a sea route for the east-west transport of materials. Many of the artifacts are Syro-Canaanite and Cypriot in origin, and it seems likely that the vessel was heading for a destination in the Aegean, probably on the Greek mainland (see fig. 97).

Copper and Tin Ingots[10]

The primary freight excavated from the wreck consists of about 10 tons of Cypriot copper in the form of 354 rectangular slab ingots, each with an average weight of about 24 kilograms.[11] Of these, 317 are of the typical oxhide shape, with a protrusion on each of the four corners (see cat. no. 185a); 31 ingots, while of similar form, have only two protrusions, both on the same long side (see cat. no. 185b). The latter are unique

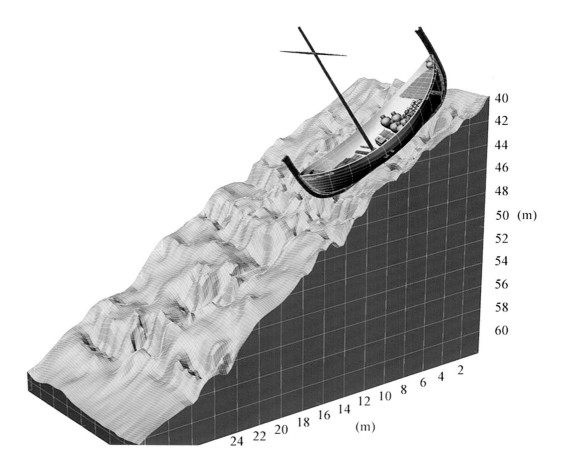

40
42
44
46
48
50 (m)
52
54
56
58
60

2
4
6
8
10
12
14
16
18
20
22
24
(m)

Figure 93. Three-dimensional reconstruction of the Uluburun ship with slope of seabed indicated.

to the Uluburun ship. There are also six smaller oxhide ingots (see cat. no. 185c, e), four of which have shapes of a seemingly earlier type,[12] and 121 plano-convex discoid, or bun-shaped, ingots (see cat. no. 185d), plus fragments of ten more.[13]

Metallurgical analyses of the oxhide and plano-convex discoid copper ingots have shown them to be raw or "blister" ingots of pure copper.[14] Lead-isotope analysis confirms that the Uluburun copper ingots, and most contemporary copper ingots found in the Mediterranean, originally came from Cyprus. Whether they were loaded on the island or at an entrepôt on the Levantine coast cannot be proved, but the latter is more likely.[15] In either case, the evidence provides significant information about how the ship was laden.

Although many ingots slipped down the slope after the ship sank or were displaced as the hull settled and broke apart under the tremendous weight of the cargo, their basic arrangement survived. Four distinct rows of copper ingots stretched transversely across the hull, overlapping like roof shingles. The direction of overlap alternated from layer to layer, apparently to prevent slippage during transit. In each row were as many as 12 ingots, stacked eight to eleven layers deep at the middle of the ship, with the number of ingots decreasing toward either side of the hull. The bottom layers were placed on beds of brushwood and branches, also known as "dunnage," to protect the hull timbers.[16] All ingots appear to have been stowed with their mold sides down, both to facilitate handling when loading and unloading and to increase friction between

ingots, thereby minimizing shifting during the voyage.[17] The weight of the ingots, in addition to that of the stone anchors, helped preserve some portions of the hull remains. Several more perishable artifacts were recovered here because they had become trapped between or beneath the copper ingots and thus saved from the ravages of marine organisms by the copper corrosion products.

In addition to the carefully stowed copper ingots, tin was also carried on board. The tin was cast in several ingot shapes: oxhide, discoid, slab, and a unique ingot shaped like a stone weight anchor, with a circular hole at one end. Many of these had been cut into quarters or halves before they were taken on board (see cat. no. 185f, g).[18] Some of the tin on the wreck had, through a complex change in its crystalline structure, converted to another, nonmetallic phase of tin with the consistency of toothpaste, which disintegrated during excavation.[19] For this reason, it is impossible to determine the exact amount of tin on the ship. Although nearly one ton was recovered during excavations, the original quantity carried must have been much greater. Alloying all the metal ingots on board would have produced 11 tons of bronze in the optimal 10 to 1 ratio of copper to tin.[20]

Lacking in the Mediterranean, tin was likely obtained through trade. Sources of Bronze Age tin remain unknown, although ancient texts indicate that it may have been obtained from regions east of Mesopotamia,[21] probably Central Asia,[22] and shipped via the Levantine coast.

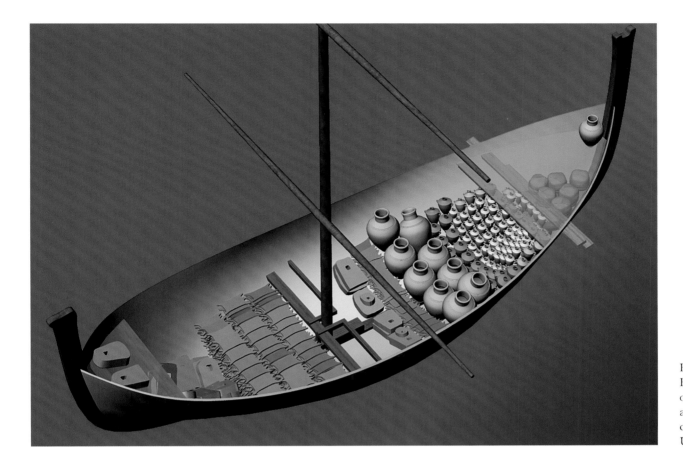

Figure 94. Reconstruction of original arrangement of cargo on the Uluburun ship.

Glass Ingots

Glass ingots, each in the shape of a roughly truncated cone, were also part of the cargo.[23] Some were in an excellent state of preservation, and others suffered partial or complete deterioration, but it is estimated that 175 pieces, totaling some 350 kilograms, were on board. The majority of the glass ingots were cobalt blue or turquoise in color, but at least two ingots of purple and one of amber are also represented (cat. no. 187).[24] These are among the earliest well-preserved examples of their type, as complete glass ingots in any quantity are rarely found in land excavations.

Chemical analyses of the alkalis and the coloring agents suggest that the glass was obtained from both Egypt and the Near East.[25] The transparent cobalt blue ingots, however, are chemically similar to core-formed vessels of cobalt blue glass from Amarna in Egypt and to typical cobalt blue Mycenaean relief beads (cat. nos. 239, 246).[26] This similarity is sufficient to suggest that the glass for all the cobalt blue ingots was probably made in the same general region at about the same time from similar raw materials and following the same batching and glassmaking processes.[27]

Wood

African blackwood (*Dalbergia melanoxylon*) was an important component of Bronze Age trade. This is the ancient *hbny* of the Egyptians, from which the English word "ebony" derives.[28] Ebony has become a generic name for many different dense,

black woods from around the world, whereas the *hbny* of the ancient Egyptians originated in tropical Africa.[29] It was the favorite material for furniture among the Egyptian elite, as attested by the bed frames, thrones, chairs, footstools, boxes, and walking sticks made from ebony and found in the Tomb of Tutankhamun.[30] Evidence of the ebony trade exists in both ancient texts and the archaeological record. About 18 intact and fragmentary small ebony logs were found on the Uluburun ship.[31] All are composed only of dark heartwood, the commercially valuable part; the bark and thin layer of yellowish sapwood were useless and therefore stripped from the log. The logs were cut to standard lengths of about one meter,[32] perhaps approximating two Egyptian royal cubits of 52.4 centimeters.

Several centuries before the Uluburun shipwreck, Hatshepsut's expedition to Punt (see fig. 5), probably somewhere in modern-day Somalia, brought back ebony wood, among many other exotic items.[33] Ebony continued to be exported from East Africa through Nubia, down the Nile, and into Egypt during the reigns of Thutmose III and Amenhotep II.[34] Several New Kingdom reliefs depict Nubians bearing ebony as tribute, including those in the mid-fifteenth-century B.C. Tomb of Rekhmire in Thebes (fig. 95),[35] the late fifteenth-century B.C. tomb chapel of Sebekhotep near Thebes,[36] and the thirteenth-century B.C. rock temple built by Ramesses II at Beit el-Wali in Nubia.[37]

The Egyptians exported ebony in the form of both logs and furniture, and the ebony furniture referred to in the Linear B

Figure 95. Wall painting with Nubians carrying ebony logs and ivory tusks. Thebes, Tomb of Rekhmire (TT 100). Dynasty 18, reigns of Thutmose III–Amenhotep II.

tablets from Pylos, on the Greek mainland, may have come from Egypt.[38] While ebony fits well with the valuable and rare goods that make up some of the cargo, it is remarkable that it was exported in unfinished state, for this suggests that it was destined for a palace or other centralized entity capable of mobilizing the resources necessary to operate a workshop for the final production of such luxuries.[39]

Ivory

The Uluburun ship carried a short section of a large elephant tusk (cat. no. 197) and 14 hippopotamus teeth (see cat. no. 198).[40] Combs, plaques, and furniture inlays made of ivory were common products of the Aegean during the Bronze Age, but ivory was also carved into figurines, containers, and pins.[41] Elephant tusk was the material of choice because it offered large quantities of solid ivory, although hippopotamus teeth were also commonly used.[42] It is not always easy to distinguish between the two types of ivory, and the full extent of the trade in hippopotamus ivory cannot yet be fully assessed. Based on existing finds, including the discoveries on the Uluburun ship, it would seem that hippopotamus teeth were a more common source of ivory than hitherto believed (see pp. 406–7).

Ostrich Eggshells

The Uluburun ship carried three ostrich eggshells, one of which was found intact (cat. no. 194a).[43] These were undoubtedly exotica destined to be transformed into ornate jugs or vases by the addition of spouts, handles, and bases of faience or precious metals.[44] Ostrich eggshell vases and eggshell fragments have been found at several sites on the Greek mainland and the major Aegean islands.[45] A blue glass disc found

separately, and in a poor state of preservation, may have been a base for one of the Uluburun eggshells (cat. no. 194b). If this is the case, it is evidence that the eggshells had already been made into luxury vases for use as prestige gifts or items of elite consumption before they were placed in the ship. The Uluburun ostrich eggshells could have been obtained in either Africa or the Near East, as ostriches inhabited both regions at the time.[46]

Orpiment

Orpiment, or yellow trisulphide of arsenic, was also carried on the Uluburun ship,[47] in a quantity that suggests that it was probably cargo, although some of it may have been intended for shipboard use as well. Orpiment was primarily used in Egypt, as a pigment,[48] and perhaps also as an ingredient for lapis lazuli–colored glass later on, in the seventh century B.C.[49] It was also mixed with beeswax, presumably to impart a more pleasing color, and used to create surfaces for wood writing boards,[50] two sets of which were found on the Uluburun ship, although their waxed surfaces did not survive (cat. no. 234). In classical times, orpiment served as a pigment in the encaustic paint used for the hulls of ships,[51] and, when mixed with lime, as a depilatory.[52] Pliny notes that it was mined in Syria,[53] which may have been the source of the Uluburun supply; it is also found elsewhere in the Near East.[54]

Murex opercula

Thousands of opercula from murex (*Murex* sp.) shells were lodged between the copper ingots and elsewhere on the Uluburun ship.[55] An operculum is the chitinous (hornlike material) or calcareous (shell-like material) plate attached to the foot of a gastropod that closes to form a protective barrier when the snail retracts into its shell. In *Murex* species, the operculum is of the chitinous type and, unlike the calcareous types of some species, normally would not have survived the ravages of the sea for extended periods. Most of the opercula have disappeared, but those that became trapped in the crevices between the copper ingots were preserved as a result of their impregnation with copper and probably also because the toxic environment created by the corroding ingots would have kept away predatory marine organisms. The number recovered suggests that a significant amount of opercula was originally carried on the Uluburun ship.

This is the first discovery of *Murex opercula* in any quantity from a Bronze Age archaeological context. Certain gastropod opercula may have been used in antiquity as an ingredient for incense. Under the Greek name *onycha*, opercula seems to have constituted one ingredient of the Holy Incense mentioned in Exodus (30:34).[56] The *shlt* listed in an Ugaritic inventory of foodstuffs, spices, and medicinal substances may also refer to opercula,[57] whose medicinal uses were noted by Pliny.[58] Opercula may have been procured as a by-product of the more lucrative dye-extraction process.[59] Whatever their purpose, their presence on the Uluburun ship has shown for the first time that they were an item of interregional trade along with spices and resins.

Terebinth Resin

Well over half of the approximately 150 Canaanite jars (see cat. no. 190) aboard the Uluburun ship contained an estimated half a ton of a yellowish substance chemically identified as terebinth resin,[60] making it the second-largest consignment on the ship, after the copper and tin ingots.[61] Terebinth resin has been identified with the Egyptian *sntr* and also possibly as the Linear B *ki-ta-no*.[62] Probably from the *Pistacia atlantica*, a tree common throughout the eastern Mediterranean region, the resin was noted in antiquity for its use in incense and scented oils, and it may have been added to wine to inhibit the growth of bacteria.[63] It is likely that the resin aboard the Uluburun ship was intended for use in the scented-oil industry in the Aegean.[64] If the interpretation of Egyptian *sntr* as terebinth resin[65] is correct, which seems likely, then Thutmose III imported it annually from the Near East, probably in quantities averaging 9,250 liters, to be burned as incense in religious rites.[66] Moreover, it was likely imported in Canaanite jars similar to those found on the Uluburun ship. A Canaanite jar depicted in a storeroom scene in the Tomb of Rekhmire in Thebes is labeled *sntr* (fig. 96).[67]

The terebinth resin on the Uluburun ship, the largest ancient deposit of the material ever found, provided the first opportunity for its identification by modern analytical methods. Analysis of pollen extracted from the terebinth resin cautiously suggests an origin in the general area of the northern Jordan River valley and the Sea of Galilee.[68] The malacological study of endemic terrestrial snails found in some jars similarly points to a nearby region west and northwest of the Dead Sea.[69] The discovery of such a large quantity of terebinth resin in a commercial context leaves no doubt that it was traded in the eastern Mediterranean during the Late Bronze Age.

Spices, Condiments, and Foodstuffs

Coriander, black cumin or nigella, and safflower were all carried on the Uluburun ship,[70] together with sumac, which was still being exported westward from the Levantine coast in medieval times.[71] Coriander and cyperus may have been imported from Cyprus, as they were described in texts from Minoan Crete as Cypriot.[72] Black cumin was traded at Ugarit.[73] Specialty oils mentioned in Linear B tablets from Pylos, Mycenae, and Knossos were pretreated with astringents such as coriander and cyperus and then scented with rose and sage.[74] The oil base for these specialty products was usually made from olives, almonds, and sesame,[75] some of which were recovered from the Uluburun ship; it is not known whether they were for export or shipboard use.

Organic remains of almonds, pine nuts, fig seed (from dried figs), grape pips (from either raisins or wine), and pomegranate seeds and fruit fragments; several Canaanite jars containing olives; and charred barley and wheat probably represent the ship's stores, although some of it could have been cargo.[76] The contents of one Canaanite jar, for example, consisted of at least 2,500 pits from olives that may have been a specialty product, since olive stones from this jar are generally larger than typical olive stones from most Near Eastern Bronze Age sites.[77] Pomegranate seeds and remains of anther, stamen, and skin were recovered from more than 25 percent of all sampled

Figure 96. Wall painting showing storeroom with goods of foreign manufacture. Thebes, Tomb of Rekhmire (TT 100). Dynasty 18, reigns of Thutmose III–Amenhotep II.

contexts on the Uluburun ship. Large, open ceramic storage vessels, such as a pithos and a pithoid krater, produced more than a thousand seeds and epidermal fragments, suggesting that the fruits stored inside it were likely among the products being exported to the Aegean.[78]

MANUFACTURED GOODS

Alongside raw materials, the Uluburun cargo included manufactured goods such as Cypriot pottery, copper-alloy vessels, glass and faience beads, and perhaps textiles. Ten large pithoi of varying sizes found on the ship served as containers during transit and likely as export pottery as well. These storage jars are typically Cypriot, known from a number of sites on the island.[79] Careful excavation and sieving of sediments from the more complete vessels have shown that they were used for carrying liquids (perhaps oil), fruit (pomegranates), Cypriot pottery, and probably other commodities.[80] In addition to high-end raw materials like ebony and ivory, some of the manufactured goods aboard the ship, including cosmetics containers of ivory, vessels of tin, and perhaps even dyed textiles or garments, appear to constitute value-laden gifts exchanged between royals or other high-ranking elites. Other manufactured articles offer insight into the number and ethnic identity of the crew and the passengers aboard the vessel, including evidence of their garments, adornments, and personal possessions.

Cypriot Pottery

The Cypriot pottery contained in the pithoi includes oil lamps, wall brackets, Bucchero jugs, White Shaved juglets, Base Ring II and White Slip II bowls and other vessels, making a total corpus of about 155 vessels, including possibly as many as 137 fine wares (see cat. no. 193).[81] The most common vessels are White Shaved juglets and White Slip II milk bowls.[82] If the intended destination of the Cypriot pottery cargo was the Aegean, the sheer quantities of these wares aboard the Uluburun ship contrasts with what has been found to date in the region. If one excludes the shipwreck evidence from Cape Gelidonya and Uluburun from an inventory of Cypriot pottery in the Late Bronze Aegean, one is left with only 68 ceramic vessels. Had the Uluburun ship reached its destination, the number would have been altered significantly. This great disparity clearly demonstrates that the archaeological record, even with respect to nonperishable goods, does not necessarily reflect the true nature and magnitude of the trade in question.[83]

Metal Vessels

In addition to pottery, copper-alloy vessels were carried aboard the Uluburun ship. They were primarily thin-walled and had for the most part disintegrated through corrosion, although their sturdier components, such as rims and handles, survived to reveal their approximate shapes and sizes. Among these are sets of bowls once composed of at least three graduated sizes

nested together, suggesting that other scattered bowl fragments may have been grouped in this manner. At least one of these bowl sets appears to have been stored in a large cauldron, identified by its handle and reinforcement straps. Elements of other vessels, such as a riveted spout, hint at the variety of metal forms that existed but which may never be fully reconstructed because of the lack of sufficiently preserved parts.[84]

In addition, several tin vessels, including a pilgrim flask, a plate, and a double-handled cup, have been found. Each is unique, suggesting that such vessels were among the prestige goods carried aboard to be presented as gifts to high-ranking individuals or elites.[85]

Wood Vessels

An oblong lid and a circular base for two containers of boxwood were among the perishable objects recovered from a squat, large-mouthed Cypriot pithoid krater. It is likely that these wood containers fell into the jar after the ship sank and were preserved by being quickly covered with sediments. These and several other poorly preserved fragments indicate that wood vessels of high-quality craftsmanship were carried on the Uluburun ship. Since nearly all of this cargo has perished, it cannot be determined whether these exquisite containers were primary cargo or additional prestige gifts.[86]

Beads

Several types of glass and faience beads were among the manufactured goods. Spherical glass beads were found among the copper oxhide ingots, suggesting that they were carried in perishable containers, such as cloth or leather bags, which have since disintegrated. An irregular, concreted cluster of seemingly white tiny faience beads, which undoubtedly have lost their original colors, was probably also carried in such a bag. Thousands of smaller glass beads were found inside a Canaanite jar (cat. no. 188) indicating that they were intended for export. Faience beads of red, yellow, green, black, and blue, found mostly in a shallow depression in the central part of the wreck site that served as a catchment basin for many objects rolling down the steep slope (see fig. 93), probably constituted a part of a cargo of bulk jewelry, and perhaps also were appliqués on garments or decorative attachments on the surfaces of boxes or other specialty items.[87] Many other types of faience and glass beads, as well as beads of agate, other stones, amber, and ostrich eggshell, may have been for the personal adornment of those aboard the ship.

Textiles

Bolts of dyed cloth may have been carried on the ship, although there is no conclusive evidence to suggest that textiles made up a significant portion of the original cargo.[88] The sediment contents of Canaanite jars contained a number of individual fibers dyed blue, purple, and red, but whether they were from lengths of cloth, luxury garments sent as gifts, or clothing of the merchants aboard cannot be determined. That some highly valued textiles were carried on the ship, however, is certain.[89]

The blue and purple color of some of the fibers almost certainly came from murex shellfish dye.[90] Who first developed purple dyeing is still unclear, although some of the earlier murex shell middens come from Middle Minoan Crete.[91] Near the dyers' workshops at Minet el-Beidha, the port of Ugarit, slightly later Late Bronze Age heaps of crushed murex shells were identified.[92] Other mounds and pits filled with murex shells abound along the Syro-Levantine coast.[93] Contemporary texts from Ugarit give evidence of a considerable trade in purple cloth.[94] Although murex can yield colors ranging across various shades of red, purple, and blue, it is not known whether the red fibers from the Uluburun ship were colored with shellfish dye or with red dye from another source.

Also in question is whether some of the faience beads from the ship were originally sewn on to cloth or garments. Some of these beads were found concreted, indicating that they were stored together, probably as cargo. The rest, however, may once have been decorative elements of fine cloth, either woven into the weft or embroidered on after the weaving was completed. Examples of cloth with sewn-on beads have been found in both the Aegean and the Near East in Late Bronze Age contexts.[95]

Gold and Silver

Gold and silver were also found on the Uluburun ship, mostly in the form of intact and scrap jewelry but also as a gold ring ingot, silver bar ingots, and amorphous lumps. Along with a large gold chalice (cat. no. 219) weighing about 236 grams, which may have been for personal or ritualistic use, or perhaps represented a prestige gift, approximately 530 grams of gold in total were found on the ship. Much of the gold and silver, whether intact or scrap, was excavated in the same small area of the site, indicating that it was kept together and probably used as bullion when required. Interestingly, two of the scrap silver pieces are debased, containing copper; one of them has a copper core. Two other pieces that appear to be silver bars also yielded high copper content. If these scrap silver pieces were intended as bullion in trade, one must wonder how ancient traders ensured the purity of the metal they received in payment. Even the most pristine jewelry may have been used as bullion when required, for a number of silver bangles and various gold pieces had sections removed with a chisel, apparently for use in previous transactions.[96]

Most of the gold and silver jewelry pieces are Canaanite, but Egyptian items and a few others of unknown origin were also present. One remarkable piece is a small gold scarab (cat. no. 223), inscribed with the name of Nefertiti, wife of the Egyptian pharaoh Akhenaten.[97] It would seem that gold from the Near East reached the Aegean largely as intact and scrap jewelry, not only supplying Aegean craftsmen with raw materials but introducing Near Eastern styles and examples of goldworking techniques.[98]

Based on lead-isotope analysis, the majority of the silver appears to have originated in southern Anatolia, as expected, since this region was well known for its silver. It was therefore traveling westward from eastern sources.[99] The gold and silver, both jewelry and scrap, were probably kept in a pouch or chest along with pieces of ingots, an Egyptian stone plaque, scarabs, and cylinder seals. The pouch was likely the possession of the chief merchant aboard the ship and kept at the stern in a secure compartment. Its precious-metal contents may have been used to provision the ship and crew during the voyage.

TRADE ROUTES

The westward flow of eastern materials indicates the proposed counterclockwise trade routes of the Late Bronze Age Mediterranean (fig. 97). The Uluburun ship epitomizes the various means by which Near Eastern and African raw materials and finished goods reached the Aegean and ports beyond. In addition, its cargo represents the commodities being shipped—utilitarian raw materials, products for elite consumption, and prestige goods for gift exchange.[100]

Using various chronological methods, both relative and absolute, it has been possible to date the Uluburun ship to the end of the fourteenth century B.C.,[101] one of the most active and colorful periods of the ancient world. During this century, seafaring Syrians and Canaanites, a general term used to denote the Semitic peoples along the Levantine coast during the second millennium B.C., traded extensively with Egypt, Cyprus, and the Aegean world. Syro-Canaanite cities served as hubs for overland trade connecting Egypt, Mesopotamia, and the Hittite Empire.[102] The exact nature of interregional trade is not fully understood. Textual evidence suggests, however, that much of the trade that took place at the palace level was conducted in the guise of gift exchange. Transactions, primarily commercial, also occurred at a lower level.

Gift exchange in the Late Bronze Age was, in a sense, a type of prenegotiated directed trade, inasmuch as a vessel was loaded in one port and had a specific destination. In other patterns of so-called tramping or cabotage,[103] the ship was loaded with goods, which it then traded when it made landfall, often without a distinct destination. Tramping was usually a low-commerce trade, whereas gift exchange was a high-commerce, prestigious trade, occurring over long distances and involving items of great economic value. The term is commonly invoked to describe interregional trade between entities of equal (or lesser) power who may also have been competitors. This is the type of trade illustrated by the Amarna Letters (see pp. 168–69), the correspondence between the Egyptian pharaoh and other royalty.[104]

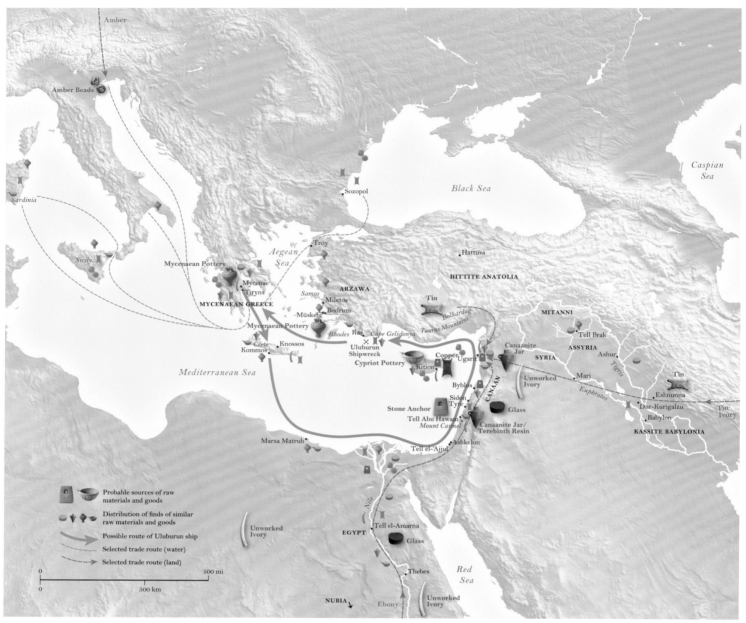

Figure 97. Possible route of the Uluburun ship.

The traditional view of gift exchange sees such transactions as reciprocal; trade relations were conducted between seemingly equal entities and were based on the creation of obligatory, continuing reciprocity. This vision of trade in the Late Bronze Age may seem somewhat altruistic. A closer reading of the Amarna Letters reveals that while luxury gifts were exchanged, they often served specific purposes such as dowries or tribute. Most tribute, on the other hand, may have been only perceived, and was the concept under which most trade was transacted (see pp. 161–68). The exchange of raw and finished goods may have operated through the use of "letters of credit."[105]

As a high-risk endeavor, long-distance trade necessitated extensive preparations, provisions for security during the voyage, and substantial capital investment for the procurement of goods. All these services were best provided by the state, which came to dominate nearly all aspects of social, economic, political, and military life.[106] While private merchants engaged in retail trade in domestic markets, most interregional exchange in the Near East during this time was probably controlled or influenced by the palaces or elite centers. Undoubtedly, some interregional trade must have occurred, but even seemingly private mercantile trade enterprises appear to have been mostly conducted through merchants who were in some manner connected to or operating around the palace. Thus the Uluburun ship probably represents a royal or elite shipment of the type exchanged between Egypt, the Levantine coast, Alashiya (Cyprus), and Anatolia, as is vividly revealed by the Amarna Letters, albeit one whose ultimate destination was in the Aegean. Unlike the Cape Gelidonya ship, which was engaged in opportunistic trade or tramping along the southern coast of Anatolia and Cyprus, probably between minor ports, and whose cargo included only a modest quantity and variety of raw materials and large amounts of scrap metal, the Uluburun cargo may be seen as evidence for directional trade where intra-Mediterranean voyages involved specific destinations.[107] The study of the ship, its immensely rich and diverse cargo, and the personal effects of those on board corresponds with the commercial activities conducted under the guise of royal or elite gift exchange and partly described in contemporary documents. This notion of distribution appears to be a working example of the concept of gateway communities, in which imported goods are directed to a few major centers characterized by long-distance trade connections.[108]

The Uluburun ship demonstrates the simultaneous flow of raw materials and manufactured goods from the Levantine coast and Cyprus into the Aegean. Some of the cargo was in transshipment, as it came over great distances; the ebony logs originated in equatorial Africa and some of the tin probably came from Central Asia, while other materials were obtained from closer sources—copper and pottery from Cyprus, for example, and glass ingots principally from Egypt. The assemblage reveals the way in which various goods reached the Aegean and, almost certainly, points farther north and west. While evidence for Bronze Age shipwrecks ceases west of the Aegean, goods similar to those found on shipwreck sites are known from mainland Greece, Crete and other islands, southern Italy, Sicily, Sardinia, and elsewhere, indicating that these goods certainly reached the Aegean and central Mediterranean in some quantity by sea.

THE ROUTE OF THE ULUBURUN SHIP

Assigning a specific home port for the Uluburun ship and its crew is difficult, but based on certain artifacts of a personal nature and those intended for shipboard use, it would appear that it was somewhere along the Levantine coast rather than on Cyprus.[109] The stone anchors of the type carried on the vessel are good indicators as these items were not cargo and most were probably not transported very far from their production centers before being loaded onto the ship.[110] Preliminary petrographic examination of the anchors indicates that most of them were hewn from beachrock, or coastal sandstone, found specifically in the vicinity of the Carmel coast in the Levant.[111]

Stylistic features of the ship's galley wares, such as bowls, jugs, and oil lamps, also support this hypothesis.[112] The source of the clay for nearly all the galley wares, including the oil lamps in use aboard the ship (see cat. no. 192), has also shown to have been in the same general area, but just north of the Carmel coast.[113] A site in this region, such as Tell Abu Hawam, may have been the home port of the ship, or at least the origin of its final voyage. Indeed, this site's well-placed location, its prominence in the region, and the period during which it flourished, along with the presence of many objects similar to

those found on the ship, make it a likely candidate. Although Tell Abu Hawam is a comparatively small site, excavations have uncovered an international assemblage of artifacts, leading to its identification as the port city associated with the major inland site of Megiddo.[114] Significant quantities of Cypriot pottery found at Tell Abu Hawam suggest that the pottery was imported from Cyprus and then stockpiled to await export aboard such ships as the one that sank at Uluburun.[115]

That the Uluburun ship took its cargo of Cypriot pottery—and probably also the copper ingots—from an entrepôt or way station like Tell Abu Hawam rather than directly from a Cypriot port is also suggested by the nature of the pottery assemblage and the manner in which the pots were stacked. While the pottery comprises nearly all major export types made on the island, there is considerable variation in the style, size, and quality of craftsmanship among individual pieces within a given type. This suggests that the assemblage consisted of leftover pieces obtained at different times from different shipments and, perhaps, from different workshops. Had they been procured directly from Cypriot purveyors as a single group, they would have been significantly more homogeneous within the type groups. On board the ship, Cypriot fine wares were stored along with mainland wares from just north of the Carmel coast, another indication that they were not taken directly from Cyprus.

From its presumed point of origin just north of the Carmel coast, the Uluburun vessel headed north along the Levantine coast and then sailed west along the coast of southern Anatolia, keeping the northern coast of Cyprus on its port side until it eventually foundered at Uluburun. The discoveries of contemporary shipwrecks along the southern coast of Anatolia at Antalya and Cape Gelidonya suggest that ships navigating this route hugged the coast during their journeys from east to west.[116] After negotiating Cape Gelidonya and the treacherous cape at Uluburun, westbound ships apparently continued toward the southwestern tip of Anatolia, as revealed by a copper ingot caught in a sponge trawler's net at Knidos, in water more than 100 meters deep.[117] From there, the ships appear to have sailed either west, in the direction of Greece, or north into the Aegean, as suggested by a shipwreck laden with oxhide ingots reported, but not yet verified, between Samos and the western Anatolian mainland.[118] A single oxhide ingot found on land near Sozopol, on the western coast of the Black Sea, and a corner fragment of an oxhide ingot found just inland of the northern coast of the Sea of Marmara may have originated from such northbound ships or, more likely, arrived there by overland routes after having been unloaded at a port on mainland Greece.[119] On the other hand, copper oxhide ingots, as well as tin and lead ingots of other forms, found south of Haifa represent lost cargoes from the maritime trade in metals along the Levantine coast.[120]

Why the wreck occurred at Uluburun will probably never be known with certainty; it is possible that the ship, sailing in a northwesterly direction, drew dangerously close to the point before tacking and then failed to clear it. It is also conceivable that the ship was dashed against the rocky promontory by an unexpected southerly gale, or that it experienced some difficulty in steering while trying to round the cape.[121]

The importation to the Aegean of foreign goods from the Levantine coast, Cyprus, and Egypt shows a shift away from Crete and toward mainland Greece at the end of the Late Helladic/Late Minoan IIIA period. This may be an indication that by the end of the fourteenth century B.C., the Mycenaeans had taken away from the Cretans control of the trade routes to the eastern Mediterranean.[122] This is noteworthy, since it coincides with the date of the Uluburun wreck. The importation of foreign goods to the mainland then peaks in the subsequent Late Helladic IIIB period. Based on the nature of the ship's cargo and the likelihood that the Mycenaeans aboard the ship were mainlanders, it would seem that the vessel's final destination was most likely on the Greek mainland. And while its ultimate port of call cannot be determined with certainty, there were in fact few palatial centers on the mainland that could have absorbed the quantity of goods carried on board. Such a center would have disseminated portions of the cargo to lesser centers through a system of redistribution. The most likely palatial center that could have adequately fulfilled these criteria is Mycenae itself, to which imported goods were funneled from the port city Tiryns to its south.

During this period of Levantine imports into Tiryns and Mycenae, Tiryns appears to have retained most of the Cypriot goods (except for copper ingots), which are exceedingly rare at Mycenae. Of the Syro-Canaanite goods, however, some were retained at Tiryns while most were forwarded on to Mycenae.[123] To that end, it may be of some interest to note that both Cypriot goods—mostly in the form of pottery, which seems to have been favored at Tiryns—and Syro-Canaanite goods and raw materials are represented in abundance on the Uluburun ship, perhaps to satisfy the needs of both centers.

The People Aboard the Ship

It is impossible to know the fate of the crew and passengers on the Uluburun ship; surviving artifacts, however, offer insight into their identities. Some of the manufactured goods have been identified as personal possessions of those on board, and give an indication of how many people were on the ship and where they might have come from. Careful study of these artifacts indicates that the ship was crewed by Syro-Canaanite merchants and sailors accompanied by two Mycenaeans of elite status and probably also a third individual who may have been from the area north of Greece.[124] The identifying personal effects are weapons, items of personal adornment, seals, pottery for shipboard use, and ship's tools. Sets of weights and balances, a merchant's most important tools, were also present, as these were essential for conducting trade.[125]

Analysis of the balance weights shows that three or four merchants were aboard, each of whom must have carried a pair of personal sets of weights. In all, 149 objects were catalogued as balance weights, the largest and most complete contemporary weight assemblage from the Bronze Age Mediterranean. As the weights were from a closed context and in use at the time of sinking, the assemblage must exhibit all standards and sets necessary for an effective maritime merchant venture, with the possible exception of smaller denominations in metal that may have been missed in excavation or corroded over the millennia. These weights are divided into three main groups based on shape: domed, sphendonoid, and zoomorphic (cat. no. 235). Many of the sphendonoid weights (oblong, with pointed or rounded ends) correspond to fractions and multiples of a unit mass, or shekel, in the vicinity of 9.3–9.4 grams.[126] It seems that there were at least seven weight sets (four sphendonoid, three domed) that were structured to that standard.

A small portion of the sphendonoid weights, however, do not conform to this mass standard. Most of these correspond to a few precision sets based on a unit mass, or shekel, of about 8.3 grams, a Mesopotamian standard, and a standard close to the Syro-Canaanite *peyem* that ranged from 7.4 to 8.0 grams.[127] Metal corrosion made it impossible to determine the standard(s) represented by the zoomorphic weights.

Each merchant was probably equipped with at least one sphendonoid-weight set (the precision set) for the accurate weighing of valuable commodities, such as gold and silver bullion, and one domed-weight set for weighing heavier or everyday goods.[128] Both sets, regardless of the shapes of their weights, conform to the same mass standard of 9.3–9.4 grams, but with different weighing ranges. This suggests the presence of four merchants, one of whom also carried the zoomorphic weights. This unique set probably belonged to the chief merchant. That these balance weights were for everyday use and not simply a part of the ship's cargo is indicated by their used state and the presence of odd and perhaps homemade pieces to replace those that were lost over time. The four Canaanite or Cypriot merchants proposed for the Uluburun ship compare favorably with the maritime scene depicted in the Tomb of Kenamun at Thebes, which shows a Syrian merchant fleet arriving in Egypt (fig. 98).[129] The four merchants shown on one of the ships are dressed in typical Syro-Canaanite robes with tasseled belts, and are engaged in various activities, including conducting rituals associated with a safe arrival. Three crewmen are also shown climbing around the ship's sail and rigging, while a fourth sits in the crow's nest atop the mast. To sail a ship of that size would have required no less than four crewmen. Even so, it has to be remembered that Egyptian tomb paintings do not necessarily depict reality but rather perception, and care must be used in their literal interpretation.[130]

The numbers of excavated weapons also appear to support the view that there were four merchants aboard. The chief

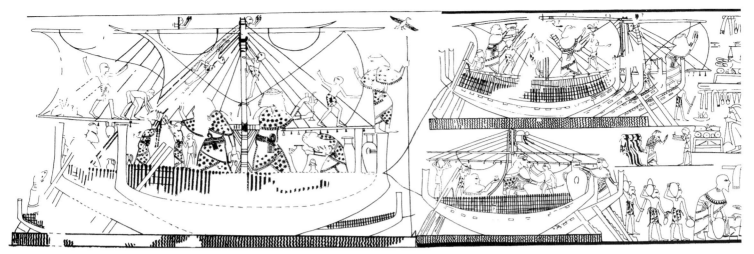

Figure 98. Drawing of wall painting with Syrian ships. Thebes, Tomb of Kenamun (TT 162). Dynasty 18, reign of Amenhotep III.

merchant was in charge of the ship and its cargo. He was also probably the ship's captain, and must have carried the only Canaanite sword found on the ship.[131] Almost fully preserved, it is a single-piece cast-bronze weapon with inlaid hilt plates of ebony and ivory, indicative of the owner's elite status. Among the daggers excavated—visible symbols of status roughly equivalent to the sword—two were nearly identical in make and design to the Canaanite sword; one of the daggers still retains its hilt plates and inlays of ebony and ivory (cat. no. 233).[132] A tanged dagger may have belonged to the fourth merchant.

To these merchants also probably belonged some, if not all, of a group of nine cylinder seals found mostly near the stern of the vessel in association with much of the silver and gold (cat. nos. 230–232).[133] It is uncertain if these items were in use as cylinder seals at the time the ship sank or if they served merely as elaborate beads. They are of different sizes and crafted from various materials: hematite, quartz, other stone, and faience, of which two were gold capped (see cat. no. 231a).

Little can be determined about the Uluburun crew, since their personal effects would not have included distinctive and valuable items. Among the objects recovered are several relatively plain daggers, knives, and simple pendants. Food was prepared by grinding in one of three stone mortars and eaten in simple bowls, and at night Canaanite oil lamps (cat. no. 192) were used for illumination.[134] Assorted fishhooks, lead line sinkers, troll line sinkers, a barbed trident, and a harpoon, along with more than a thousand lead net sinkers of two types, probably denoting seine and casting nets, indicate that the crew fished during the voyage to supplement their otherwise dull diets. What little free time was available may have been passed by playing the game of knucklebones, as suggested by their presence on the ship.

Mycenaean objects, such as fine tablewares, swords, spears, razors, chisels, axes, glass relief beads, faience and amber beads, quartz beads, and lentoid seals, were also discovered.[135]

That these artifacts speak to a Mycenaean as opposed to a Minoan presence is evident from three different artifact types: lentoid seals, deep-bar chisels, and double-axes.[136] The closest parallels to the lentoid steatite sealstones from Uluburun (cat. no. 241) belong to Younger's "Mainland Popular Group" from the Greek mainland.[137] Six deep-bar chisels are of the shorter, more robust types associated with the Greek mainland, rather than with the delicate-looking elongated versions found on Crete.[138] Two double-axes have ovoid shaft holes generally found on examples from the Greek mainland, rather than the circular ones seen on those from Crete.[139] The categorically Minoan artifacts aboard the ship were coarse-ware transport stirrup jars, a vessel type made primarily as a container for exporting oil. More telling of the Mycenaeans' identity are the utilitarian fine-ware pouring-and-drinking sets comprising a beaked jug, a narrow-necked jug, a cup, a dipper, and a kylix (see cat. no. 242a).[140] With the exception of the kylix, none in the assemblage is among the Mycenaean types commonly exported to the Levant.[141]

Two knives and a tang portion of a third are also among the Mycenaean artifacts.[142] A knife for everyday needs would have been an essential tool for a Mycenaean Greek, especially one enduring a long journey to and from the Levantine coast. Also on the ship were five typically Mycenaean razors.[143] These offer a glimpse into the grooming practices of these well-equipped individuals, and of the care they afforded to their appearance. Two of the razors are nearly identical in size and shape, and display a fine decorative ridge, just below the back edge, which extends the full length of the blade and tang.

The presence of at least two pouring-and-drinking sets, two swords, two relief-bead necklaces, two quartz beads, and two lentoid seals, along with the occurrence of other Mycenaean objects in multiples, strongly suggests that there were two Mycenaeans aboard the Uluburun ship.[144] These individuals do not appear to have been simple merchants, as they apparently lacked the single most important tool used to conduct commercial transactions in a precoinage society: balances and weight sets. Without weights, it would have been impossible to measure metals for payment of goods received.[145]

The wealth of their personal adornments and other items considered with the quality of their weaponry suggest that the Mycenaeans aboard the ship were elites. Two bronze swords, typical of Aegean products of the fourteenth century B.C., were also among the Mycenaean finds (see cat. no. 238a). In the Late Bronze Age Aegean, a sword probably served as an object of prestige signifying military rank, or was a weapon used in warfare by a select few.[146] That being the case, it is likely that the two Mycenaeans were of the warrior class or palace staff, perhaps acting as emissaries or ambassadors—the "messengers" mentioned in ancient texts—accompanying to the Aegean a cargo of reciprocated "gift exchange."[147] As representatives of palatial or elite interests, their purpose may have been to oversee the safe delivery of the ship and its precious cargo to its final destination at or near their homeland. Likely empowered to handle letters of credit or other methods of reciprocity by which interregional trade was conducted, they may also have served as pilots and negotiators for the ship in Aegean territorial waters, with which they would have been familiar.

A troubling aspect of the Mycenaean assemblage is the absence of sealstones appropriate to such elites or emissaries. The two steatite lentoid sealstones (cat. no. 241) are of a type predominantly found in simple burials, settlements, and even sanctuaries. Perhaps these items did not function as seals, but instead were strung as beads and served as amulets, talismans, or jewelry.[148] Conversely, they may have been intended as votive offerings to be placed in a sanctuary upon the safe conclusion of the voyage or certain portions of it.[149]

The identity of a third foreign individual on the Uluburun ship is more speculative than that of the Mycenaean emissaries. His presence is attested by an assemblage of loosely linked foreign (northern) artifacts, including a central Mediterranean–type sword, spearheads, a bronze pin, and a scepter-mace with its closest parallels in the northern Balkans (cat. no. 237).[150]

This shadowy figure, possibly hailing from a region north of the Greek mainland, may have served as an elite mercenary in the service of the Mycenaeans, or as another messenger.[151] Piracy on the high seas would undoubtedly have posed a threat for a high-profile mission like the one represented by the Uluburun ship. The shipment of valuable goods was a risky undertaking, and certain Amarna Letters refer to a messenger merchant killed by bandits.[152] These well-armed individuals, along with the armed Canaanite merchants and crew, would have served as a deterrent for looters and rogue seafarers.

THE HULL

Because most of the ship's hull as well as some of the cargo perished when the ship sank, and the position of the artifacts that had spilled down the slope no longer reflected their original locations, estimates of the ship's size and shape are, for the most part, necessarily speculative. Nevertheless, the distribution of the recovered remains and the surviving portions of the hull suggest that the ship had a length of about 15 meters and a beam of about 5 meters, with a cargo carrying capacity of at least 20 tons.

In some areas of the site, preservation was aided by conditions unfavorable to shipworms and other detrimental organisms. A portion of the hull remains was located underneath some of the copper ingots. The copper created a toxic environment that discouraged marine life, preserving the hull timbers and layers of dunnage placed over them. These surviving timbers allowed for the identification of the wood as Cedar of Lebanon (*Cedrus libani*), which Bronze Age sources often mention as the preferred timber for building ships.[153]

The ship was constructed in a "shell-based" method, in which the planking is joined edge-to-edge on either side of the ship's keel. In this type of construction, mortises or recesses are cut into the edges of adjacent planks, and a tenon is placed within the mortise. The mortises are then secured with a peg on either side of the plank seam, thereby locking all the planks together to form the hull. The planking of the Uluburun ship was made of cedar, with tenons and pegs cut and shaped from evergreen, or kermes, oak (*Quercus coccifera*).[154] In addition to the hull itself, remains of a bulwark fencing of branches have also been identified (fig. 99).[155]

Reconstructing any hull on paper is analogous to assembling a puzzle or solving a riddle. In the case of the Uluburun ship, this process was complicated by varying levels of preservation and disarticulation of some of the remains. Results of reconstruction studies, in spite of difficulties, have provided an invaluable glimpse into the construction of Bronze Age seagoing ships.

Perhaps the most unusual feature of the Uluburun hull is its keel, the primary longitudinal member forming the ship's spine. Unlike modern keels, it is wider than it is high and extends upward into the hull. Although the keel did not protrude more than a few centimeters beyond the outboard surfaces of the hull planking, it served as an effective spine for the ship. Designated as a proto-keel, it also protected the planking from damage if the ship ran aground, and supported the vessel when beached for repairs or for wintering. Unlike true keels in later sailing ships, however, it did not offer much lateral resistance, which is needed for the ship to hold course when sailing. This rudimentary feature therefore limited the headway a ship could make against counterwinds, which probably resulted in favoring certain maritime routes during certain sailing periods.[156]

The Uluburun ship is significant to any study of shipbuilding techniques, as it is the earliest seagoing ship to be found and excavated. Analysis of the hull, and the manner in which it was constructed, has provided new information regarding seagoing ships and the use of mortise-and-tenon joinery. Early

Egyptian examples of mortise-and-tenon joints, as seen in Khufu's funerary boat at Giza and Senwosret III's boat at Dahshur,[157] were freestanding and not pegged to lock adjacent planks to one another. Egyptian woodwork shows that, at least as early as Dynasty 3, the Egyptians, while fully aware of this type of fastening,[158] did not use it in shipbuilding, unless pegged tenons were restricted to ships for which we have no surviving examples.[159]

Exactly when and where pegged mortise-and-tenon joints were first used to build seagoing ships is not known. The earliest documented use of this type of joint in the Near East is much later than in Egypt and is seen in woodwork dating to the Middle Bronze IIB period.[160] Based on present evidence, it appears that the use of pegged mortise-and-tenon joints in shipbuilding developed on the Levantine littoral and spread westward. Their earliest archaeologically documented use in shipbuilding occurs on the Uluburun ship, which almost certainly was built somewhere along the Levantine coast.[161]

Because there is no evidence of frames or other internal lateral strengthening timbers, the strength of the Uluburun vessel must have come almost solely from the hull planking itself, with additional reinforcement provided by bulkheads and through-beams. The mortise-and-tenon joints must have been remarkably strong. The tenons were strikingly large, and frequently spaced.[162] Rather than evenly staggering the mortise-and-tenon joints in one edge of a plank from those in the opposite edge, each mortise cut was positioned immediately adjacent to the nearest joint in the opposite edge of the same plank, such that one mortise often intruded into the space of another. Placing tenons adjacent to one another would appear to have compromised the structural integrity of the planking

and thus of the hull. Studies of replicated sections of the hull have shown, however, that the arrangement probably made for a stronger plank than would have been the case had they been placed farther apart.[163] The tenons were obviously more than simple fasteners, serving as small internal frames and providing considerable stiffness and integrity to the shell of planking. The Uluburun ship relied heavily on these long oak tenons, which were clearly intended to supplement the hull's lateral rigidity and to compensate for the paucity or absence of proper frames. This method of construction partially explains how heavy cargoes could be carried directly on the hull planking without resorting to visible lateral support in the form of frames or bulkheads.[164]

Conclusions

Excavation of the Uluburun shipwreck recovered more than 15,000 catalogued artifacts, one of the largest and richest assemblages of Bronze Age goods ever found. The ship's cargo, perhaps of a royal nature, consisted mostly of raw materials, although finished goods were also present. Galley wares, tools, fishing implements, and some foodstuffs were for shipboard use, while cylinder seals, jewelry, weapons, and balance weights represent some of the personal effects of those on board. These items indicate that the likely site for the home port of the ship was just north of the Carmel coast. The finds further suggest the presence on board of three, possibly four, Canaanite merchants, two Mycenaeans of rank, acting as official messengers or envoys escorting a shipment of important cargo bound for their homeland, and another individual, who also may have been an escort in his own right or an elite mercenary for the two Mycenaean officials. The assemblage has provided evidence for a counterclockwise Late Bronze Age maritime trade network that circled the eastern Mediterranean; it appears the ship was a merchantman from the Levantine coast headed in a northwesterly direction for the Aegean (see fig. 97).

The Uluburun ship epitomizes the various means by which Near Eastern and other foreign goods entered the Aegean during the Late Bronze Age. New implications for the dynamic and far-reaching trade activities in this period are just beginning to emerge. The stunning diversity and wealth of artifacts found on the Uluburun wreck are products of numerous cultures: Canaanite, Mycenaean, Cypriot, Egyptian, Nubian, Baltic, northern Balkan, Old Babylonian, Kassite, Assyrian, Central Asian, and possibly south Italian or Sicilian. The ship and its cargo appear to represent an elite dispatch of an enormously wealthy and diverse cargo of raw materials and manufactured goods intended for a specific destination. In addition to utilitarian objects and raw materials, the presence of value-laden or prestige goods would appear to indicate that the Late Bronze Age Aegean was not far removed from the long-distance interregional trade that was based on royal or elite exchange in the Near East and reflected vividly in the nearly contemporary Amarna Letters. As was the practice in such ventures, the ship's cargo was probably placed in the care of an official who represented elite or royal interests, but who may have engaged in some private trade of his own on the side. This merchant emissary or messenger also was entrusted with a contingent of prestige goods that he would present personally to the royalty or elite receiving the cargo. The Uluburun ship captures, in transit, tangible evidence for the flow of goods and raw materials from the Levantine coast to the Aegean, while at the same time providing a rare glimpse of the individuals involved in long-distance trade and the ships with which it was conducted.

1. As is customary in nautical archaeology, when a shipwreck cannot be identified with a specific name, it and the artifacts found with it are often given the name of the site at which it was found, in this case, Uluburun. Each object was given a find number beginning with KW; originally the ship was referred to as the Kaş wreck.
2. The site was excavated with the permission of the Turkish Department of Antiquities and Monuments. The work was carried out under the auspices of the Institute of Nautical Archaeology (INA) at Texas A&M University, with funding from the INA Board of Directors and grants from the National Endowment for the Humanities, the National Science Foundation, the National Geographic Society, Texas A&M University, the Institute for Aegean Prehistory, and others. The post-excavation, conservation phase continues in the Bodrum Museum of Underwater Archaeology with support from the museum administration, and at the conservation laboratory of the INA Research Center in Bodrum, with grants from the Institute for Aegean Prehistory, funding by the INA Board of Directors and Texas A&M University, and contributions by many individuals and companies. For further reference, see Bass 1986; Pulak 1988; Bass et al. 1989; Pulak 1997; Pulak 1998; Pulak 2001; Pulak 2005c.
3. Bass, Frey, and Pulak 1984; Pulak and Frey 1985.
4. Bass 1967, pp. 163–67; Bass 1973.
5. Pulak 1998, pp. 213–14.
6. Ibid., p. 188.
7. Ibid., pp. 210–13.
8. Pulak 2002, p. 615.
9. Pulak 2001, p. 13.
10. Pulak 1998, pp. 193–201; Pulak 2000b.
11. Originally, the ingots would have been heavier, since the corrosive seawater environment dissolved some of the copper and reduced parts of the ingots to a spongy consistency. The original weight of an ingot is therefore impossible to determine with accuracy.
12. Pulak 2000b, p. 141; Pulak 2001, p. 18.
13. Pulak 2000b, p. 143; Pulak 1998, pp. 196–97.
14. Hauptmann, Maddin, and Prange 2002.
15. Pulak 2001, p. 21.
16. Pulak 2000b, pp. 140–41.
17. Ibid., p. 141; Pulak 1997, pp. 235–36.
18. Pulak 2000b, pp. 150–52, figs. 16–22; Pulak 1998, pp. 202–3, fig. 16; Bass 1986, pp. 281–82, ills. 15, 16.
19. For metallurgical aspects of the Uluburun tin ingots, see Hauptmann, Maddin, and Prange 2002, pp. 15–17.
20. Pulak 2001, p. 22.
21. L. Weeks 1999, p. 61.
22. Dossin 1970, pp. 101–6; Muhly 1985, pp. 282–83; Pulak 2000b, p. 153.

23. Pulak 2001, pp. 25–30; Bass 1986, pp. 281–82.
24. Pulak 2001, p. 25.
25. Lilyquist and Brill 1993, p. 41; Brill and Shirahata 1997, pp. 89–91; Henderson 1997, pp. 94, 97–98; Rehren, Pusch, and Herold 1998, p. 243; Brill 1999, vol. 1, pp. 47–48, 280, vol. 2, pp. 53–54; Shortland and Tite 2000, pp. 16–17, 50, 98, 147–49, 183, fig. 3.1, table 3.2; Pulak 2001, pp. 27–30.
26. Bass 1986, p. 282; Brill 1999, pp. 53–54; Pulak 2000b, p. 28.
27. Brill, personal communication, 1997.
28. Gardiner 1950, pp. 517, 579, 611.
29. Lucas and Harris 1962, pp. 224–28; Hepper 1977, p. 129.
30. Pulak 2001, p. 31.
31. Bass et al. 1989, pp. 9–10.
32. None of the ebony logs is complete, with worm damage on surfaces and ends rendering them somewhat shorter than their original lengths.
33. Naville 1896, pp. 1–3.
34. Davies 1973, p. 14, pl. 17.
35. Ibid., pp. 19, 26, 46, pls. 17–20, 40.
36. Taylor 1991, title page.
37. Ibid., p. 33, fig. 37.
38. Meiggs 1982, p. 284; Ventris and Chadwick 1973, pp. 342–43; EA 1, 31, 34 (Moran 1992, pp. 1–3, 101–2, 105–6).
39. Pulak 2001, pp. 31–32. One ebony piece from Uluburun was worked.
40. Bass 1986, pp. 282–85, figs. 18, 19; Bass et al. 1989, p. 11, fig. 20; Pulak 1995, p. 16, fig. 14.
41. Poursat 1977a.
42. Reese 1985b, pp. 393–94.
43. Pulak 2001, pp. 39–40; Pulak 1997, p. 242.
44. This appears to be their only use in the Bronze Age Aegean (Renfrew and Cherry 1985, p. 324, pl. 64a–b).
45. Cline 1994, pp. 237–38, nos. 945, 946.
46. Conwell 1987, p. 29; Reese 1985a, p. 378.
47. Bass 1997, p. 159; Bass 1986, p. 278.
48. Bass 2004, p. 280, and n. 61; Bass 1986, p. 278, n. 37.
49. Bass 1997, p. 159, citing Oppenheim et al. 1970, pp. 40–43, and nn. 52, 91.
50. Mallowan 1954, p. 99; Wiseman 1955, p. 5.
51. Pliny Natural History 35.31.
52. Ibid., 34.56; Bass 1997, p. 159; Bass 2004, pp. 280–81.
53. Pliny Natural History 32.22.
54. Schafer 1955, pp. 73–74.
55. Pulak 1988, p. 5; Pulak 2001, pp. 32–33.
56. Hart 1888, p. 200.
57. UT 12, Robert Stieglitz, personal communication, 1994.
58. Pliny Natural History 32.41.

59. Pulak 2001, p. 33.
60. Mills and White 1989; Hairfield and Hairfield 1990.
61. Pulak 2001, p. 36; Pulak 1998, pp. 201–2.
62. Bass 1997, p. 164; Melena 1976, pp. 177–90.
63. McGovern 1997, pp. 84–85.
64. Pulak 2001, pp. 35–36.
65. Serpico and White 2000, p. 894.
66. Loret 1949, pp. 20–23.
67. Davies 1973, pl. 48.
68. Jacobsen, Bryant, and Jones 1998, p. 80.
69. Welter-Schultes 2008, pp. 84–85.
70. Haldane 1993, p. 352; Pulak 2001, p. 37.
71. Haldane 1993, p. 352; Bass 1997, p. 167, n. 209.
72. Bass 1997, p. 167; Ventris and Chadwick 1973, pp. 221–22.
73. Heltzer 1978, p. 20.
74. E. Foster 1977, pp. 32–35.
75. Shelmerdine 1985, pp. 17–18.
76. Pulak 2001, p. 37; Haldane 1990, pp. 57–59; Haldane 1993, pp. 352–56.
77. Haldane 1993, pp. 353–55.
78. Ward 2003, pp. 530, 537.
79. P. Åström 1999; Schaeffer 1949, pp. 208–9, fig. 86, pl. 31.2; Watrous 1992, pp. 157–58, fig. 70, pl. 52; Karageorghis 1993, p. 584, fig. 3; Vagnetti and Lo Schiavo 1989, pp. 220–21, fig. 28.1a–b; Vagnetti 1999, pp. 189–90, 206, fig. 4.
80. Pulak 2001, p. 40.
81. Ibid., pp. 41–42. Although the numbers of Cypriot vessels in the cited article are lower, based on ongoing conservation and mending of these vessels, Nicolle Hirschfeld, who is studying the Cypriot fine wares for publication, reports the higher numbers indicated here.
82. Pulak 2001, pp. 41–42; Bass 1986, pp. 279–82, ills. 10–14.
83. Pulak 1997, pp. 242–43.
84. Pulak 2001, pp. 42–43; Pulak 1997, p. 243, fig. 11.
85. Pulak 1997, p. 243.
86. Pulak 2001, p. 43.
87. Ibid., pp. 43–44.
88. Ibid., pp. 44–45.
89. For similar, purple-dyed wool fibers on an eighth-century B.C. Phoenician ship discovered off the coast of Ashkelon, see Stager 2003, pp. 242–43. These fibers suggest the presence on board the ship of prized purple textiles or garments for export, as may have been the case on the Uluburun ship.
90. Pulak 2001, p. 44.
91. Reese 1980, pp. 81–82; Reese 1987, pp. 203–6.
92. Schaeffer 1951, pp. 188–89.
93. Pulak 1988, p. 5, n. 5, with references; Reese 1987, pp. 205–6.
94. Schaeffer 1951, pp. 190–92.
95. Barber 1991, pp. 171–74; Persson 1931, pp. 29–30, 39–41, 60, 106, no. 51, pls. VIII, XV, XXXIV, XXXV; Carter and Mace 1923–33, pp. 167–71, pls. 34, 37, 38; N. Özgüç 1966, p. 47, pl. 22.
96. Pulak 2001, pp. 24–25.
97. Weinstein 1989.
98. Pulak 2001, p. 25.
99. Ibid., pp. 24–25; Zofia Stos-Gale, personal communication, 2000.
100. Pulak 2001, pp. 13–14.
101. Ongoing dendrochronological wiggle-matching and 14-C dating of short-lived specimens from the wreck such as leaves, young branches, olive pits, nuts, and resin suggest a date at the end of the fourteenth century B.C. for the sinking of the ship.
102. Knapp 1993, pp. 334–36.
103. Horden and Purcell 2000, pp. 365–66.
104. Zaccagnini 1987, pp. 47–56; Moran 1992.
105. Manning and Hulin 2005, pp. 286–88.
106. Liverani 1987; B. Foster 1987; Peltenburg 1991, pp. 161–70.
107. Pulak 1998, pp. 215–16.
108. Cline 1994, pp. 87–88; Cline 2007, p. 199.
109. Pulak 1997; Pulak 1998.
110. Pulak 1997, p. 252; J. Shaw 1995, pp. 281–82.

111. Based on petrographic analysis with Yuval Goren.
112. Pulak 1997, pp. 252–53.
113. See note 111 above.
114. Loud 1948.
115. Schaeffer 1939a, p. 19. For similar stockpiling of Cypriot export wares at Minet el-Beidha and in a house at Ugarit, see Schaeffer 1937, p. 128, pl. 20:3; Schaeffer 1962, p. 100, figs. 83, 84, p. 119.
116. Pulak 1997, p. 2.
117. Ibid., pp. 234–35; Bass 1986, p. 272; Buchholz 1959, pp. 27, 29, pl. 3:5–6; Buchholz 1966, pp. 63, 65, fig. 2b.
118. A hoard of 19 copper ingots from a shipwreck near Kyme on Euboia is probably not of Bronze Age date, as the size and shapes of these ingots are very different from the typical Bronze Age oxhide ingot.
119. Pulak 1997, pp. 255–56.
120. Pulak 2001, pp. 16–17.
121. Pulak 1998, pp. 188–89, 218–20.
122. Cline 2007, pp. 194–95.
123. Ibid., p. 195.
124. Pulak 1998, pp. 216–18.
125. Pulak 2001, pp. 13–14.
126. Pulak 2000a, p. 261.
127. Ibid., pp. 256, 261.
128. Ibid., pp. 262–64.
129. Davies 1963, p. 14, pl. 15; Davies and Faulker 1947, pp. 40–46.
130. Wachsmann 1987, p. 4.
131. Pulak 1988, p. 20, fig. 20, p. 21.
132. Pulak 1997, p. 246.
133. See Collon, this volume; Bass et al. 1989, pp. 12–16.
134. Pulak 2005a, p. 296. Ongoing petrographic analysis has shown that the used lamps, revealed by charring around their wick nozzles, were all made with clay from the vicinity of Tell Abu Hawam and slightly farther north.
135. See Pulak 2005a for the Mycenaean objects on the Uluburun ship.
136. Ibid., p. 296; Cline 2007, p. 129; Bachhuber 2006, pp. 351–55.
137. Pulak 2005a, p. 305; Younger 1987, p. 65.
138. Pulak 2005a, p. 302.
139. Ibid., p. 302, n. 58.
140. Ibid., pp. 296–98.
141. Ibid., pp. 297–98.
142. Ibid., pp. 300–301.
143. ibid., pp. 301–2.
144. Ibid., pp. 296ff.
145. Ibid., p. 306.
146. Driessen and MacDonald 1984, p. 56; Pulak 2005a, p. 298.
147. Pulak 2005a, pp. 306–9.
148. Ibid., p. 305; Betts 1997, pp. 63, 65.
149. Pulak 2005a, pp. 307–8.
150. Vagnetti and Lo Schiavo 1989, pp. 223–24; Buchholz 1999; Bodinaku 1995, p. 268; Pulak 1997, pp. 253–54, fig. 22; pp. 254–55; Pulak 2005a, p. 209.
151. Pulak 2001, pp. 48–49.
152. EA 8 (Moran 1992, pp. 16–17); Pulak 2005a, p. 308.
153. Pulak 1999, p. 212. This wood was used for Egyptian funerary ships and for the Cape Gelidonya ship; see Pulak 2001, pp. 27–29, 33.
154. Pulak 2001, p. 13.
155. Pulak 1999, p. 212.
156. Pulak 2002, pp. 618–21, figs. 1–4.
157. Lipke 1984, p. 64; Steffy 1994, pp. 25–27, 32–36; Patch and Haldane 1990, pp. 34–35, fig. 19.
158. Lucas and Harris 1962, p. 451.
159. Pulak 1999, p. 213.
160. Ricketts 1960, p. 530, fig. 229.1.
161. Pulak 1999, p. 215.
162. Pulak 2002, p. 629, fig. 2.
163. Ibid., pp. 626–27, fig. 1.
164. Ibid., p. 626.

Figure 100. Archaeologist preparing to raise anchors from seabed. Uluburun shipwreck.

184

WEIGHT ANCHOR

Beachrock
Height 75.4 cm (29¾ in.); max. width 61 cm
(24 in.); max. thickness 22 cm (8¾ in.);
weight 148.3 kg
Uluburun shipwreck
Late Bronze Age, ca. 1300 B.C.
Bodrum Museum of Underwater
Archaeology, Turkey 37.1.94
(KW 3330)

The Uluburun assemblage of 22 large coastal sandstone, or beachrock, anchors[1] and two smaller ones of limestone, the latter possibly for the ship's boat, collectively weighs 3.3 tons and is the largest group of anchors found associated with any shipwreck (fig. 100).[2] This example is of beachrock, trapezoidal in shape, with rounded corners and a square apical hole for an anchor cable or hawser at its narrower end. It is one of four with incised marks on the surface, in this case an inverted V.

Because the Uluburun anchors were preserved in their original context, they offer insight into specific onboard uses of stone anchors during this period. The anchors were found in two groups: 16 were strewn in a line at the eastern end of the site, corresponding to the ship's bow, and another line of eight lay two deep across the keel, extending from one side of the hull to the other, near the center of the ship, just aft of the mast step. The anchors found near the center of the wreck were spares stored in the hold and were also used as temporary ballast, while those at the bow were for immediate use.

At least two of the bow anchors were originally stored on the ship's foredeck, ready for deployment, with others stowed in the area under the foredeck and immediately aft of it. These spare bow anchors were meant to be used in addition to those on the foredeck, or as equivalent substitutes in their absence. Although the anchors were intended to be retrieved after use, the large number aboard the ship suggests that they were frequently lost or had to be cut loose in an emergency.[3]

Weight anchors moored ships by sheer mass, in contrast to stone composite anchors, which gripped the seabed with wood stakes.[4] Anchors excavated on land usually represent votive and funerary offerings deposited in wells, temples, and tombs at sites such as Ugarit and its port at Minet el-Beidha,[5] Byblos,[6] and Kition on Cyprus.[7] In marine contexts, however, they often mark offshore moorings, inshore anchorages, and proto-harbors.[8] Other

Bronze Age shipwreck anchors include 15 found off Newe-Yam on the Carmel coast,[9] and a single anchor associated with the Cape Gelidonya ship,[10] although the Uluburun assemblage is the only complete set found to date.

The weight anchor is virtually unknown in the Aegean,[11] although some examples have been found at Mallia and Kommos on Crete as well as off Cape Iria in the Gulf of Argos.[12] Ongoing petrographic analysis of the Uluburun anchors suggests an origin in coastal regions in the vicinity of Tell Abu Hawam or slightly farther north, the same area where the ship's galley ware (see cat. no. 192), much of its pottery cargo, and probably the very ship itself appear to have originated.[13]   CP

1. Beachrock is formed by sedimentation of beach sand and sediments in intertidal zones: Beachrock formations occur only a few meters from shore and generally run parallel to the coastline.
2. Pulak 1997, p. 252, fig. 20; Pulak 1998, p. 216. The twenty-two large anchors are loosely grouped into three basic weight categories: the heaviest at about 201 kg, the midrange at 164–82 kg, and the lightest at about 97 kg, averaging 147.7 kg. The two small anchors have an average weight of 23.9. Pulak 1999, pp. 210–11, fig. 1.
3. Pulak 1999, pp. 210–11.
4. Kapitän 1984, pp. 33–36; for Bronze Age anchors in general, see also Wachsmann 1998, pp. 255–93.
5. Schaeffer 1978, pp. 371–81; Frost 1969b; Frost 1991.
6. Wachsmann 1998, pp. 271–73; Frost 1969a.
7. Karageorghis 1976b, pp. 60, 69, 72, 78, 169; Frost 1985; Wachsmann 1998, pp. 273–74.
8. Galili, Sharvit, and Artzy 1994, pp. 93–95, 106–7.
9. Galili 1985, pp. 144–49.
10. Pulak and Rogers 1994, pp. 20–21, fig. 7; Wachsmann 1998, pp. 283, 285.
11. The few stone anchors found in the Aegean and in the western Mediterranean are usually much smaller than those from Uluburun or are of the composite type with three holes, rather than the single-holed weight type recovered from the Uluburun ship. They are catalogued in Wachsmann 1998, pp. 279–83; for Italy and Sardinia, see Lo Schiavo 1995, pp. 406–21.
12. J. Shaw 1995, pp. 280–82, 290, n. 8.
13. Based on preliminary results from Yuval Goren.

CARGO

185a–g

SELECTION OF INGOTS

a. Large oxhide ingot incised with image of ship
Copper
Height 43.7 cm (17¼ in.); length 77.1 cm (30⅜ in.); thickness 4.2 cm (1⅝ in.); weight 20.4 kg
35.4.88 (KW 1526)

b. Large oxhide ingot with two protrusions
Copper
Height 37.8 cm (14⅞ in.); length 62.2 (24½ in.); thickness 4.5 cm (1¾ in.); weight 22.7 kg
38.4.88 (KW 1549)

c. Small oxhide ingot
Copper
Height 25.6 cm (10⅛ in.); length 32.7 cm (12⅞ in.); thickness 3.7 cm (1½ in.); weight 10.7 kg
104.24.86 (KW 389)

d. Plano-convex discoid (bun-shaped) ingot
Copper
Diameter 22 cm (8⅝ in.); thickness 4.6 cm (1¾ in.); weight 6.6 kg
2006/4/10A (KW 3108)

e. Small oxhide ingot
Copper
Height 24.7 cm (9¾ in.); length 26.7 cm (10½ in.); thickness 6.6 cm (2⅝ in.); weight 10.1 kg
39.5.90 (KW 1983)

f. Quarter-oxhide ingot
Tin
Width 17.4 cm (6⅞ in.); length 29 cm (11⅜ in.); thickness 4 cm (1⅝ in.); weight 6.3 kg
5.1.2000 (KW 3061)

g. Half-oxhide ingot
Tin
Width 29.1 cm (11½ in.); length 29.1 cm (11½ in.); thickness 7.5 cm (3 in.); weight 11.7 kg
60.4.88 (KW 1371)

Uluburun shipwreck
Late Bronze Age, ca. 1300 B.C.
Bodrum Museum of Underwater Archaeology, Turkey

Of the 354 copper oxhide ingots found in the Uluburun wreck,[1] 317 feature protrusions, or "handles," at the four corners,[2] and an average weight of just under 24 kilograms.[3] While of similar form, 31 have only two protrusions or handles on the same long side.[4] There are also 6 smaller ingots, 4 of which are nearly identical,[5] consisting of two pairs of mold siblings, cast in the same mold;[6] a small ingot that has the same general shape as the others but lacks corner protrusions; and an ingot that is much thicker than the other small ingots, with exaggerated corner protrusions.[7] These 6, as well as the two-handled and the small ingots, are unique to the Uluburun shipwreck. There are also 121 intact ingots of a plano-convex discoid, or "bun," shape.[8] As with the oxhide shape, these ingots vary in weight but average about 6.2 kilograms apiece. The recurrence of differing weights for the Uluburun oxhide ingots indicates that they constituted a quantity of "blister," or raw, copper probably subject to weighing and evaluation during each commercial transaction. Although they were not of a standardized quantity of metal, their broadly common weight groupings would have simplified accounting procedures.[9]

The Uluburun shipwreck yielded some of the earliest known tin ingots,[10] most apparently in the same oxhide shape as the majority of the copper ingots. Except for three intact specimens, however, nearly all of the tin oxhide ingots had been cut into quarters or halves before they were taken on board. Other tin ingot shapes from Uluburun include bun ingots, two complete rectangular slab ingots, sections of slab ingots, thick wedge-shaped sections cut from large ingots of indeterminate shapes, halves of elongated ovoid loaves, and a unique ingot shaped like a stone weight anchor with a large hole near one end.[11] The intact tin ingots are of approximately the same weight range as the copper oxhide ingots.[12]

Tin and raw copper were probably transported as whole oxhide ingots, overland from mines, primary smelting works, or central ore-processing installations to distribution or manufacturing centers, where they were cut into fractions of their

185a

185b

185c

185d

185e

308

185f, g

original form. The Uluburun assemblage contains many partial tin ingots, which were probably gathered by barter, levies, taxes, gifts, or some other mechanism for constituting the appropriate counterpart to the amount of copper loaded on board the ship. This suggests that the ship owners had direct access to sources of copper, whereas most of the tin was procured through indirect sources.[13]

Preliminary examination of the Uluburun copper oxhide ingots has shown that no fewer than 162 ingots are incised with at least one, and possibly as many as three, marks on their upper surfaces (a).[14] Of the bun ingots, 62 are marked on their lower or mold surfaces.[15] That similar marks were found on both the copper and tin ingots,[16] and that the marks were all incised after casting or cooling, rather than stamped during the casting process, suggest that they were probably made at a point of export or receipt rather than at primary production centers.[17]

The earliest evidence for full-size oxhide ingots comes from sixteenth-century B.C. sites on Crete[18] and depictions in Egyptian tomb paintings, where they are frequently associated with Syrian merchants and tribute-bearers (fig. 101).[19] Later copper-oxhide ingots of the fourteenth, thirteenth, and early twelfth centuries B.C. have been found as far west as Sardinia and Sicily, and as far east as central and eastern Anatolia, Syria, and Mesopotamia.[20] They also occur in southern Germany,[21] Bulgaria, mainland Greece, western and southern Anatolia, Cyprus, the southern Levant, and the Nile Delta.[22]

Thirty-four oxhide ingots were also recovered from the Cape Gelidonya shipwreck.[23] Lead-isotope analysis has shown that oxhide ingots postdating the mid-fourteenth century B.C. differed in the source of their metal from those of earlier Cretan finds. The analysis further indicates that ingots dating from the mid-thirteenth century B.C. to the early twelfth century B.C. were produced from Cypriot copper ores mostly originating in the

Apliki mines in the northwestern foothills of the Troodos Mountains.[24] Lead-isotope analysis of the Uluburun oxhide ingots[25] shows that they form a relatively homogeneous Cypriot group and were probably derived from a hitherto undiscovered deposit, almost certainly among the Solea axis ores of northwestern Cyprus, which includes the Apliki deposits.[26]

Sources of Bronze Age tin remain unknown, although ancient texts indicate that

Figure 101. Wall painting with Syrian carrying copper oxhide ingot. Thebes, Tomb of Rekhmire (TT 100). Dynasty 18, reigns of Thutmose III–Amenhotep II.

it may have been obtained from regions to the east of Mesopotamia.[27] Although lead-isotope analysis of tin is in its infancy,[28] preliminary results suggest two sources, one in the Bolkardağ Valley in the central Taurus Mountains in south-central Anatolia,[29] the other probably located in Central Asia, possibly Afghanistan.[30] CP

1. Pulak 2000b, pp. 140–41, fig. 3, pp. 141–53; Pulak 2001, pp. 18–22; Pulak 2005c, pp. 59–65, figs. 5–13.
2. Such rectangular ingots with a projection at each corner were originally termed "oxhide" when it was believed, erroneously, that they were cast to resemble dried oxhides (Bass 1967, p. 69). The shape itself probably evolved to facilitate loading of the ingots onto specially designed saddles or harnesses for transport over long distances by pack animals (Pulak 1998, p. 193; Pulak 2000b, pp. 137–38).
3. The original weights would have been heavier prior to the corrosion and metal leaching that occurred during three millennia in the undersea environment.
4. Pulak 2000b, p. 141, fig. 4.
5. The four small ingots are roughly pillow shaped, seemingly a type more common in the sixteenth and fifteenth centuries B.C. Rather than representing the earlier ingot type, the Uluburun examples are seen as fractional copper ingots, which would have been handled differently and not have required the large corner projections (Pulak 2000b, p. 138).
6. Mold siblings are revealed by identical impressions on the surfaces in contact with the mold. At least six ovoid bun ingots, which also bear identical incised marks, are also mold siblings. It is likely, therefore, that these ingots may have been cast in reusable stone or clay molds, rather than in temporary sand molds. Although not yet studied, a single pair

7. of "two-handled" oxhide mold siblings has also been identified (Pulak 2005c, pp. 59–60, fig. 8, p. 567, figs. 30, 31; Pulak 2000b, pp. 141–42, fig. 5).
7. Pulak 2005c, p. 568, fig. 32; Pulak 1998, pp. 193–94, fig. 9.
8. Pulak 2005c, pp. 59–60, figs. 9, 10, pp. 569–71, figs. 33–46; Pulak 2000b, pp. 143–46, figs. 8–12.
9. Pulak 2001, p. 18; Parise 1968, p. 128; Zaccagnini 1986, pp. 414–15. For a discussion of the chemical composition of the copper and tin ingots, see Hauptmann and Maddin 2005, pp. 133–40; Hauptmann, Maddin, and Prange 2002.
10. Pulak 2005c, pp. 63–65, figs. 12, 13; Pulak 2001, pp. 22–23; Pulak 2000b, pp. 150–55; Pulak 1998, pp. 199–201, figs. 13, 14. Although poorly preserved, a single tin ingot resembling one from the Uluburun shipwreck was found in a foundation deposit in the House of the Metal Merchant on Mochlos, Crete, in a Late Minoan IB context. It is more than a century older than the Uluburun tin ingots (Soles 2008). Tin ingots were also found on wrecks off Cape Gelidonya (Bass 1967, pp. 52–83) and Haifa (Stos-Gale et al. 1998, pp. 119, 123, fig. 6; Galili, Shmueli, and Artzy 1986).
11. Pulak 1998, p. 199, fig. 14. For other tin ingot shapes from Uluburun, see Pulak 2005c, pp. 572–75, figs. 47–61; Pulak 2000b, pp. 150–53, figs. 16–22.
12. Pulak 2000b, p. 152.
13. Pulak 2001, p. 22; Pulak 2000b, pp. 152–53.
14. The marks vary in shape from a simple cross to more complicated forms, some associated with the sea and ships (cat. no. 185a), such as fishhooks, a trident, a fish, and possible quarter rudders. Pulak 1998, pp. 194–96; Pulak 2000b, p. 146, fig. 13.
15. There are thirty-two different types of marks on the ingots. Of these, only thirteen appear more than once, and one is repeated as many as seventeen times. Only seven different

marks are found on the bun ingots, five of which are also occur on the copper oxhide ingots (Pulak 2000b, p. 146, fig. 13).
16. Ibid., pp. 146, 153, figs. 13, 21.
17. Pulak 1998, pp. 194–96.
18. Buchholz 1959, p. 33, pl. 4; Platon 1971, pp. 116–18; Hazzidakis 1921, pp. 56–57, fig. 31; Gale 1991b, pp. 202–3, pls. 1–2d. The Cretan ingot finds are listed in Evely 1993–2000, vol. 2, pp. 343–46; and in Hakulin 2004, pp. 19–20, 54–55.
19. Pulak 2000b, p. 138; Pulak 1998, p. 193; Bass 1967, pp. 62–67.
20. Muhly, Maddin, and Stech 1988, pp. 281–85, fig. 1; Gale 1991b, pp. 200–201.
21. Primas and Pernicka 1998, pp. 27–50.
22. Gale 1991b, pp. 200–203, fig. 2; See also Stos-Gale et al. 1997, pp. 109–15, for lead-isotope data for most of these oxhide ingots.
23. Bass 1967, pp. 52–60; for lead-isotope results of the Cape Gelidonya ingots, see Gale 1991b, pp. 227–28.
24. Gale and Stos-Gale 2005, pp. 117–31; Gale, Stos-Gale, and Maliotis 2000, p. 339; Stos-Gale et al. 1997, pp. 109–12; Stos-Gale et al. 1998, pp. 115–26.
25. Gale and Stos-Gale 2005, pp. 117–31.
26. This is supported by recent analysis of copper ores from the nearby Phoenix mine and fourteenth century B.C. copper-smelting slag from Enkomi and Kalavassos. See Pulak 2001, pp. 20–21; Stos-Gale, personal communication, 2000.
27. Descriptions of the tin trade in ancient texts from western Asia hint at a tin source located somewhere to the east, perhaps Iran or Central Asia. Pulak 1998, p. 199; Dossin 1970, pp. 101–6 (see fig. 1, this volume); Muhly 1985, pp. 283–85; L. Weeks 1999, p. 51.
28. Gale and Stos-Gale 2002, pp. 279–302.
29. Pulak 2000b, pp. 153–55, fig. 23; Stos-Gale et al. 1998, pp. 119, 123, fig. 5.
30. L. Weeks 1999, pp. 60–61.

Cyprus: An International Nexus of Art and Trade

During the Late Bronze Age, a period marked by increasing international contacts within the eastern Mediterranean world, the geographic position of Cyprus, together with its historical role as a crossroads of the Near Eastern, Egyptian, and Aegean worlds, stimulated artistic creations that benefited from many influences. Its natural wealth and resources, especially its many copper mines, encouraged the development of a thriving trade. Metalwork in particular prospered on the island. While the objects manufactured in its many workshops drew upon techniques known throughout the eastern Mediterranean, Cypriot craftsmen achieved an even greater mastery and became the foremost producers of cast-bronze objects.

Enkomi, a prosperous center on Cyprus, seems to have held a leading position in this industry. Various metallurgic installations dating from different phases of the Bronze Age have been identified there as using copper extracted from the nearby ore deposits of Troulli, Mthiati, and Sha. Much of the copper produced was apparently intended for export and shaped into oxhide ingots (see cat. no. 185). Copper was also alloyed with tin to manufacture objects of bronze. Iron, too, was mined on Cyprus, its production mastered as early as the twelfth century B.C. It is unknown whether iron technology was developed locally or imported from Iran, the Caucasus, Anatolia, the Aegean—or even central Europe.

Oxhide ingots constitute a category of object that sheds light on the trade between Cyprus and other regions of the Mediterranean ranging from Sardinia to Crete, mainland Greece, and the Levantine coast. Large quantities dating from the Late Bronze Age have been found in the cargoes of sunken merchant vessels discovered near land, especially off the coast of southern Anatolia (see cat. no. 185). Egyptian paintings of the fifteenth and fourteenth centuries B.C. depict Asiatics and Aegeans bearing gifts of ingots to pharaohs (figs. 50, 85, 101). Although these ingots traditionally signify Cyprus, their production was not restricted to the island, as evidenced by the discovery of a mold in a royal palace at Ras Ibn Hani, near Ugarit.

The significance of oxhide ingots on Cyprus can be seen by the fact that they were used as motifs in religious contexts. They were associated with the deities whose figures they came to represent, and miniature ingots—some with inscriptions in Cypro-Minoan writing or Egyptian hieroglyphs—have been found in shrines, where they may

Figure 102. Bronze statue of armed god standing on base in the form of an oxhide ingot. Enkomi, Sanctuary of the Ingot God. Late Bronze Age. Cyprus Museum, Nicosia Field no. 1142

have been deposited as votives. The association of the realm of the gods and copper ingots is further confirmed by another category of objects typical of Cyprus during the Late Bronze Age: bronze stands with openwork decoration. They appear to have been offered as symbolic representations of shrines, made to hold vases or basins that were probably used in religious ceremonies; their surfaces were decorated with scenes that represented the rituals or mythologies involved.

One of the stands depicts the bearer of an ingot moving toward a pillar that is topped by a series of volutes, an ornamental motif associated with a female deity (cat. no. 186). The combination of this motif with the oxhide ingot created a general association of copper and metallurgy with the realm of gods and wealth.

Other objects demonstrate the religious syncretism that stemmed from repeated foreign contact. Metal statuettes of standing male deities were widely distributed throughout the Near East beginning in the Middle Bronze Age, illustrating these shared tendencies. With their combative stance and specific attributes, Cypriot divine figures from the Late Bronze Age are related to Canaanite representations of Baal, god of storms, thunder, and lightning. On Cyprus such a god was represented on an oxhide ingot (fig. 102), thus linking his image directly to the art of metallurgy. This would have involved not only a knowledge of deposits and techniques, but also his control of thunder and lightning, which are evoked in turn by the fire and the din of the forges. This association recalls similar connections made between technology and deities, between artisan gods and guardians of knowledge—Ptah in Egypt, for example, Kothar at Ugarit, and Hephaistos in Greece. Cyprus thus participated in the religious world that was shared by the regions of the eastern Mediterranean and that entailed the creation of closely related forms of artistic expression. In the midst of this iconographic mainstream, however, the island also developed its own characteristics, which added a further dimension to the international repertoire. As in the preceding millennia, the craftsmen of Cyprus, immersed in a sea of different cultures, drew inspiration from their great neighbors—Egypt, Crete, Mycenae, the Aegean islands, and Canaan—and developed their own forms of expression in masterful syntheses of artistic and iconographic currents.

SC

186

OPENWORK STAND

Bronze
Height 12.5 cm (4⅞ in.); width 11 cm (4⅜ in.);
diameter 8.5 cm (3⅜ in.)
Episkopi (?)
Late Bronze Age, ca. 1250–1050 B.C.
The Trustees of the British Museum, London
1920.12–20.1

The Amarna Letters between the Egyptian pharaoh and the king of Alashiya record a shipment of 500 talents of copper from Cyprus.[1] While a major source of the metal in the Late Bronze Age, the island produced metal wares that remained conservative in form and technique until the thirteenth century B.C., when contact with surrounding regions, particularly the Mycenaean world, dramatically transformed Cypriot bronze making.[2]

This well-executed four-sided stand, decorated on each face with a man and a stylized tree, would have supported a large vessel such as a cauldron.[3] It represents the flowering of Late Cypriot craftsmanship and imagery, with iconography reflecting Aegean and Near Eastern symbolism. This is particularly significant in view of the probable religious, funerary, or ceremonial context in which the stand would have been used.

The rods of the frame and the supporting ring for the vessel were cast or hammered, while the figures, with shallow, subtle detailing, were made in open molds; the various parts of the stand were hard-soldered (brazed). Both techniques require high levels of skill. Each of the trees is shown with volutes of twisted bronze rods representing leaves. The male figures are similar and may represent the same individual. They wear only a long kiltlike garment. The face is fleshy, the nose prominent, and the hair (or wig) falls to the nape of the neck. One figure carries what looks like a fish; the other bears over the left shoulder a long, sinuous object that trails on the ground. The copper oxhide ingot carried by the third figure recalls scenes of Minoans and Mycenaeans in Dynasty 18 Egyptian tombs (see figs. 85, 134). It was also featured widely in Cypriot religious imagery of the thirteenth and twelfth centuries B.C., where it was sometimes associated with a divinity. The Late Cypriot IIC–IIIA temple complex at Kition

in southeastern Cyprus included metal workshops within the sacred enclosure, indicating a further link between the alchemic nature of metallurgy and religious (or ideological) forces.[4]

The final scene shows a man playing a multistringed instrument and possibly singing. He is perhaps an archetype of Kinyras, the legendary musician-king of Cyprus and also perhaps of Levantine

186, alternate view

bardic figures such as King David, or even of the Greek Homer. The relationship of music to ritual or to religious activity is strong in all the cultures that came together in areas like Cyprus in the thirteenth to the eleventh century B.C. Music was commonly used to evoke a divinity, prophesy the future, or accompany recitations to honor distinguished ancestors. While the tree may simply indicate a landscape, it may be a sacred image, perhaps a goddess of fertility. Stylized trees, sometimes in association with ingots, appear on locally produced cylinder seals throughout the Late Bronze Age.[5]

The exact find context of the stand is not known, apart from its association with the village of Episkopi, near ancient Kourion. No examples of its type were found in the many tombs of the thirteenth and twelfth centuries B.C. at Kourion.[6] Excavations at the Early Iron Age necropolis of Kaloriziki revealed several rich tombs of the late eleventh and tenth centuries B.C. containing bronze stands of a simpler rod type without figures.[7]

Stands became common in burials of the aristocracy of Kourion and of its neighbors on Cyprus.[8] The present stand is a precocious early example originating in the metallurgical revolution of the thirteenth and twelfth centuries B.C. that gave rise to the adoption of iron technology in which Cypriot artisans played a leading role.

JLF

1. EA 35, Moran 1992, pp. 107–9.
2. Catling 1964, pp. 299–302; Catling 1986, p. 99.
3. Catling 1964, pp. 205–7, pl. 34; Matthäus 1985, pp. 314–15; Papasavvas 2001, pp. 239–50, no. 23, pls. 42–47; Macnamara and Meeks 1987, p. 58, pl. XVIII.
4. Webb 1999, passim; Knapp 1986.
5. Zevit 2001, pp. 321–22, 325, with further references.
6. Murray, Smith, and Walters 1900, pp. 56–86; Benson 1972.
7. Benson 1973; McFadden 1954.
8. See Matthäus 1985 and Karageorghis 1983 for examples from Palaepaphos, and, more generally, for Cyprus in this period see Karageorghis 2002, pp. 115–49.

187

GLASS INGOTS

Cobalt, turquoise, purple, and amber-colored glass
Max. diameter 11–16.2 cm (4⅜–6⅜ in.);
max. thickness 3.7–7.2 cm (1½–2⅞ in.);
max. weight 0.8–2.8 kg
Uluburun shipwreck
Late Bronze Age, ca. 1300 B.C.
Bodrum Museum of Underwater Archaeology, Turkey
7.7.95 (KW 3950), 55.7.95 (KW 3576), 9.1.2000 (KW 4532), 70.7.92 (KW 2923), 10.1.2000 (KW 3779), 2003.1.23A (KW 3163)

The Uluburun ship's cargo included approximately 175 glass ingots of cobalt blue, turquoise or light blue, amber, and purple color, each roughly in the shape of a truncated cone. Of these, 112 essentially retained their original shape and color, while 32 were fragmentary and ranged in size from one-quarter to three-quarters of an ingot. The remaining ingots, however, had partially or completely weathered and transformed into amorphous lumps that for the most part crumbled or disintegrated.[1] Although the sizes of the ingots vary, using an average weight of 2 kilograms, it is estimated that some 350 kilograms of glass must have been on the ship.[2]

While most of the glass ingots were found scattered among the rows of copper ingots stacked forward of midships, a group of 20 found at the stern suggests they were stored there, just aft of the Canaanite jars, with several copper and tin ingots. Only half of the ingots were sufficiently pre-

served to reveal their cobalt blue color. These formed a relatively tight cluster on the seabed, suggesting that they were originally kept in a perishable container, perhaps a bag. Evidence for the stacking of the ingots is tenuous, as they were displaced during the wrecking of the ship, but in situ positions of six in the group kept at the stern suggest that they were placed with the larger surface of one ingot adjacent to the smaller surface of the next ingot.

The Uluburun glass ingots are among the earliest known examples of their shape.[3] Other excavated glass ingots include three fragments of a mid-fifteenth to early fourteenth-century B.C. dark blue ingot from Nuzi,[4] 13 light and dark blue ingots and fragments from the fourteenth-century B.C. Mitanni palace at Tell Brak,[5] a number of small ingot chunks from fourteenth-century B.C. Tell el-Amarna,[6] a thirteenth-century B.C. dark red ingot from Qantir in the Nile Delta,[7] and chunks from blue glass ingots from Ugarit.[8] Two pieces of cobalt blue glass and two fragments of light blue ingots from the island of Failaka (ancient Dilmun) in the Persian Gulf[9] suggest that glass was also exported to areas outside the greater Mediterranean basin.[10]

It is not known where the Uluburun glass ingots were made, whether all the ingots of different colors were obtained from a single location, or if they came from different sources specializing in the production of specific colors. A series of fragmentary cylindrical terracotta vessels excavated at Tell el-Amarna may be similar to the crucibles used in producing glass ingots of the type found at Uluburun. Although no complete ingots themselves

187

survive,[11] traces of cobalt blue glass in these crucibles suggest that the dark blue glass commonly found at Amarna was made there. If so, Amarna would rank among the earliest glass-producing centers in the ancient world.[12] In fact, a replica of a cobalt blue glass ingot from Uluburun fits snugly into several of the Amarna crucibles.[13]

Glass is formed by melting silica, lime, and soda. The silica is commonly obtained from sand or crushed quartz pebbles; lime, which is required as a stabilizer for the silica, is also often naturally found in sand. The soda, which serves as a flux for lowering the melting temperature for the silica, may be obtained either from natron, a mineral that occurs naturally in Egypt, or from the ash of saline plants, usually used in glass manufactured outside Egypt. Different colors are produced by the addition of various metal oxides.[14] The chemical composition of the Uluburun cobalt blue glass ingots matches that of contemporary Egyptian core-formed vessels, fragments of cobalt blue ingots from Amarna, and Mycenaean relief beads (see cat. nos. 239, 246), which suggests a common source for all.[15] Based on the chemical composition and the use of natron in production, the cobalt blue ingots from Amarna were probably manufactured locally, using local materials.[16] It would appear that the Egyptians manufactured cobalt blue glass as imitation lapis lazuli during the Late Bronze Age.

One Amarna Letter, however, lists both "genuine lapis lazuli" and simple "lapis lazuli" as coming to Egypt from Mitanni.[17] Cakes of "lapis lazuli" and "turquoise" (as opposed to "genuine lapis lazuli" and "genuine turquoise") are shown as tribute from Syrians in a relief at Karnak (fig. 96).[18] Glass ingots such as these are quite likely the *mekku* and *ehli-pakku* listed on Amarna and Ugaritic tablets as trade items.[19] They were apparently exported to Egypt from Tyre, Akko, Ashkelon, Lachish, and Yura on the Levantine coast.[20] A Ugaritic text reveals that Ugarit also exported raw glass.[21]

Light blue glasses are regarded as typically Mesopotamian products. The basic composition, which almost certainly involved the use of quartz pebbles and plant ashes, appears in Mesopotamia at the very beginning of glassmaking.[22] Chemical analysis of the two light blue ingots from Uluburun, however, reveals a composition somewhat different from that of blue glass from Mesopotamia and Egypt,[23] although excessive weathering of the Uluburun sample in seawater may have altered its chemical composition. Furthermore, as most of the variations in their compositions may be explained by the difference in colorants,[24] there is nothing to suggest that the Uluburun light blue glasses were made in a workshop other than the one that produced the glasses of cobalt blue.

One of the purple glass ingots from the Uluburun ship was found to be consistent with a plant-based alkali and is chemically similar to a rare purple ingot fragment from Amarna.[25] If the use of plant ash is considered indicative of glass manufactured outside Egypt, it would appear that the Uluburun ship was carrying a cargo of glass obtained from both Egypt and the Near East.[26]

Chemical analysis of a limited number of cobalt blue ingots from Uluburun suggests that they were made in Egypt,[27] but there may be additional evidence for determining their origin. A fragment of the crucible used in making glass had adhered to one of the Uluburun ingots and became separated from it after the ship sank. If the source of the clay from which the crucible was made can be identified, this would provide conclusive evidence not only for the provenance of some of the Uluburun glass ingots, but also the first definitive indication of the location of a Bronze Age glass-production site.[28]   CP

1. Pulak 2005c, pp. 68–71; Pulak 2001, pp. 25–30; Pulak 1998, pp. 202–3; Bass 1986, pp. 281–82. The better preserved cobalt blue ingots vary from 1.3 to 3 kg, the turquoise ingots from 1.1 to 1.4 kg: Pulak 2005c, pp. 68–69, figs. 21, 22; Pulak 2001, pp. 25, 27; Nicholson, Jackson, and Trott 1997, pp. 147–50; Rehren, Pusch, and Herold 1998, pp. 244–45.
2. Pulak 2001, p. 25.
3. Nicholson 2007, pp. 23–24.
4. Barag 1988, pp. 140–41, fig. 16.
5. Oates, Oates, and McDonald 1997, pp. 85–86, fig. 124.
6. Petrie 1974, p. 26, pl. 13.40.
7. Rehren 2005, p. 538; Rehren and Pusch 1997, pp. 134–35, pl. 18.3.
8. Matoïan, personal communication, 1998.
9. Pollard 1987, pp. 186–87.
10. Pulak 2001, p. 26.
11. Nicholson 2007, pp. 13–82.
12. Nicholson 1995c, p. 127; Nicholson, Jackson, and Trott 1997, pp. 147–50; Rehren, Pusch, and Herold 1998, pp. 244–45.
13. Nicholson 1993, pp. 49–51; Nicholson 1995a, pp. 14–16; Nicholson 1995b, pp. 17–18; Nicholson 1995c, pp. 127–28.
14. Nicholson 2007, pp. 118–21.
15. Bass 1986, p. 282.
16. Shortland and Tite 2000, pp. 147–49; Nicholson 2007, pp. 102–7; Brill 1999, p. 280.
17. EA 25 (Moran 1992, pp. 72–81).
18. Sherratt and Sherratt 1991, p. 386.
19. Oppenheim 1973, pp. 259–63.
20. Pulak 2001, p. 26; Bass 1997, pp. 161–62; Heltzer 1978, p. 80; EA 148, EA 235, EA 327, EA 323, EA 331, EA 314, Moran 1992, pp. 235, 293, 351, 355, 347.
21. Heltzer 1978, p. 80; Nougayrol, PRU, VI, 6 (RS. 17.144, 40).
22. Brill and Shirahata 1997, pp. 89–94.
23. Pulak 2001, p. 29.
24. Brill, personal communication, 2001.
25. Shortland 2000, p. 17, table 3.2, pp. 50, 98, fig. 3.1, p. 183.
26. Pulak 2001, p. 29.
27. Bass 1986, p. 282; Brill 1999, pp. 53–54.
28. Pulak 2001, pp. 29–30.

188

CANAANITE JAR WITH GLASS BEADS

Ceramic, glass
Jar: height 32 cm (12⅝ in.); width at base
4.5 cm (1¾ in.)
Beads: average length 0.6 cm (¼ in.);
diameter 0.8 cm (⅜ in.)
Uluburun shipwreck
Late Bronze Age, ca. 1300 B.C.
Bodrum Museum of Underwater
Archaeology, Turkey 62.1.2000 (KW 8)

Tens of thousands of beads found in the Uluburun shipwreck represent a wide range of materials, including glass, faience, amber, rock crystal, agate, carnelian, bone, and ostrich eggshell (see cat. nos. 189, 195).[1] Some probably represent personal belongings; others, however, were items of cargo, as evidenced by a concreted cluster of some 70,000 tiny faience beads,[2] which, based on the shape of the cluster and lack of pottery sherds associated with it, represent the contents of a bag, now lost, and by the glass beads transported inside this Canaanite jar (for Canaanite jars, see cat. no. 190). Contained within the preserved section of the jar was a mass of heavy encrustation consisting of approximately 8,000 small glass beads.[3] When filled to capacity, the jar would have held approximately 26,000 beads.[4] The preservation of these glass beads and others found elsewhere at the site is quite poor, and their original color is now lost.

188

and Tell Abu Hawam,[13] as well as blue-colored beads from Egypt at Gurob[14] and el-Lahun.[15] Although none survived the excavation, several hundred glass beads, including small spherical ones, were also carried, in a pottery vessel, on the Cape Gelidonya ship.[16]

The missing portion of this dark reddish brown Canaanite jar was not found during excavation, suggesting that the jar may have been broken prior to loading and was being reused as a transport container for the beads. Moreover, the clay used to make the jar is believed to come from a northern Syrian source, indicating that the jar and its contents could have been imports whose origin differed from that of the two other groups of Canaanite jars aboard the ship, traced to clay sources farther south.

Because beads found in archaeological sites are notoriously difficult to date as a result of their extended use over time, the discovery of beads clearly representing items of cargo is significant in that their production dates are more secure. The abundance of beads aboard the Uluburun ship also supports their likely function as an imported trade commodity during the Bronze Age.   CP

1. Pulak 1998, p. 206.
2. Pulak 2005c, p. 590, fig. 98; Pulak 2001, p. 44.
3. Pulak 2005c, pp. 74, 590, fig. 97; Pulak 2001, pp. 41–42; Bass 1986, pp. 278, 289.
4. Ingram 2005, pp. 207–9. The Canaanite jar is of the smallest standard size of about 6.7 liters represented on the Uluburun ship; for other Uluburun jar capacities, see Pulak 1998, p. 201.
5. For this type of glass bead and four other types used in the Bronze Age, see Beck 1981, pp. 60–62.
6. Ingram 2005, pp. 61–66; the author also discusses a variant of the decorated glass bead termed "crumb" bead where colored glass crumbs are worked into the matrix of the bead, also found on the Uluburun wreck.
7. Tomb XIX at Prosymna yielded 97 glass beads (Blegen and Blegen 1937, pl. 1:298) and chamber tomb 524 at Mycenae revealed more than 110 beads (Wace 1932, p. 43, no. 31).
8. Persson, Hammarstrand, and Hamilton 1942, p. 86, no. 32c.
9. Rudolph 1973, p. 118.
10. A. Evans 1906, pp. 71–72, no. 66f.
11. L. Åström 1967, p. 55, no. 1.
12. Tufnell, Inge, and Harding 1940, pl. XXXIV, nos. 19, 20.
13. Hamilton 1935, pp. 61–62.
14. Brunton and Engelbach 1927, pl. XLV, no. 80B.
15. Petrie 1974, pl. LXII, no. 80N.
16. Bass 1967, p. 132, Type 2 shown in figs. 139.B and 142.

Although all are devitrified, a single bead retains a bright blue glassy area. The poor condition of the beads found on the ship makes it impossible to determine their original numbers, but surviving artifacts and observations of bead impressions suggest that, in addition to the glass beads found in this jar, another 1,500 were on board, and the actual number carried was significantly higher.

All of the glass beads, with the exception of mold-cast Mycenaean relief beads (cat. no. 239), are of the type known as "wire wound," formed by trailing molten glass around a wire, mandrel, or some other core material.[5] The wound-glass beads from Uluburun are grouped according to two sizes: either large glass beads, which may be plain or possess decorative "eyes" of a different color of glass applied to the bead,[6] or small globular beads. About 9,000 of the glass beads on the Uluburun ship, including those in this jar,

are generally considered small glass beads. The average bead is either spherical or slightly oblate in shape. Some have tapering holes that are either impractically narrow on one end or fail to penetrate the full diameter of the bead completely. Since these were found intermixed with completely perforated beads, it is likely that they represent manufacturing flaws. The presence of these flawed beads also indicates that the jar's contents were not strung into necklaces but carried as raw cargo.

Similar glass beads have been found at sites throughout the Levant. Nearly identical examples were found on the Greek mainland at Prosymna and Mycenae,[7] with similar ones also coming from Dendra[8] and Tiryns,[9] as well as on Crete[10] and Cyprus,[11] perhaps representing Near Eastern glass beads imported to the Aegean like those on the Uluburun ship. Additional close parallels have been found along the Levantine coast at Lachish[12]

189a–c

Beads

Rock crystal

a. Beads
Average height 2 cm (¾ in.)
79.5.87 (ᴋᴡ 716, ᴋᴡ 728, ᴋᴡ 758, ᴋᴡ 765,
ᴋᴡ 815, ᴋᴡ 882, ᴋᴡ 911, ᴋᴡ 922

b. Cylindrical bead
Height 2.3 cm (⅞ in.); diameter 1.2 cm (½ in.)
40.24.86 (ᴋᴡ 379)

c. Mycenaean bead
Height 1.35 cm (½ in.); diameter 1.55 cm (⅝ in.)
79.5.87 (ᴋᴡ 767)

Uluburun shipwreck
Late Bronze Age, ca. 1300 ʙ.ᴄ.
Bodrum Museum of Underwater
Archaeology, Turkey

Fourteen beads fashioned from white, transparent quartz or rock crystal were found on the Uluburun ship (ten are on exhibition). They were imported either as finished products or as raw material and manufactured locally or elsewhere in the Near East. Most are amygdaloid, or almond-shaped, and their sides taper toward truncated ends. The beads are of different sizes, some flatter on one side than the other and at least one exhibiting a pronounced triangular cross section.[1] Unique in the group is a single well-formed and polished barrel-shaped bead. The cylindrical bead, lower left, is similar in size and shape to two quartz cylinder seals found on the wreck (cat. no. 231), although it is not engraved.[2] Ten of the beads were found in close proximity to one another, which suggests that they were originally strung together. Another three amygdaloid beads found slightly farther down the slope, in a trail leading away from the main cluster, delineated the path of spillage. The two quartz cylinder seals were also found among the bead cluster, but whether they were strung into a necklace (compare cat. no. 258) or simply stored in a bag with the beads is not known. Located at the stern of the ship, the beads were most likely personal possessions for adornment rather than items for exchange.

Although a study of the drilling technique used in perforating the beads for stringing has yet to be completed, preliminary observations reveal that nearly all of the quartz beads, including the cylinder

seals, were bored from both ends, in the common manner of drilling ancient beads. Most of the drilled holes meet slightly askew, approximately at the center, although some meet much closer to one end of the bead than the other. Four of the beads, however, were either drilled through in a single pass or, equally likely, were drilled from opposite ends in perfect alignment. The profiles of the perforations indicate use of a bevel-tipped copper drill used together with an abrasive powder.[3] Also found on the wreck were nearly 1,200 agate beads, which were probably items for trade. Most are irregularly shaped discoids, although some retain much of their roughly chipped shape, with only minimal smoothing or surface treatment; because of the thinness of these beads, drilling was performed from one side only.[4] They contrast with the quartz beads, which are more uniformly shaped and polished smooth on all surfaces.

Amygdaloid and cylindrical quartz beads are rare in the Aegean, but the former shape is reminiscent of some Cretan and Mycenaean engraved seals made of a variety of hard stones, including carnelian,

sard, agate, and jasper.[5] Although these bead forms occur in the Levant, they do not appear to have been very common there. Similar examples, including the barrel form, are found among a group of beads from Middle Bronze II period Megiddo.[6] A number of truncated amygdaloid and cylindrical beads were also recovered at Megiddo from the Early Iron I (ca. 1150–1100 ʙ.ᴄ.) level,[7] some of which may well have been heirlooms from earlier periods.

At least one of the quartz beads (c, bottom row, center) is of a typical Aegean shape.[8] It is decorated with five plain flutes and five gently undulating ribs, consisting of three spines each, oriented along the bead's longitudinal axis. Like the other quartz beads, this one was found at the stern of the ship near most of the gold artifacts and other items of personal value, suggesting that it belonged to one of the Mycenaeans aboard the ship (see cat. nos. 238–242) and therefore was not a gift item or part of the cargo. A smaller plain spherical quartz bead (bottom row, right),[9] also almost certainly of Aegean origin, was found farther downslope, near the mast-step, and must have rolled from an area near the stern.

A fluted quartz bead from a tomb near Knossos is similar in size and overall shape but carved with seven ribs.[10] Fluted beads of similar shape but with differing styles of ribbing were found on the Greek mainland at Prosymna.[11] Similar beads from tombs at Mycenae, made of sard, a reddish variety of agate, have only four flutes.[12] One of the beads from Tomb 91 at Mycenae, perhaps the closest visual parallel for the Uluburun bead, is of similar gadrooned form but of discoid shape; it is believed to be carved of fluorite, a softer material than quartz.[13] This tomb also yielded a plain spherical bead of approximately the same size as the one from Uluburun (KW 5144).[14]   CP

1. Pulak 2005c, p. 82, fig. 34, p. 592, fig. 100:a–o.
2. Pulak 1988, p. 25, fig. 28.
3. Kenoyer 1997, p. 270, fig. 3a; see Gorelick and Gwinnett 1987, pp. 37–38.
4. Pulak 1988, pp. 24–25, fig. 27.
5. See, for example, Kenna 1964, p. 9, pls. 1:29, 31–33, 36, 37, 3:23, 24, 26, 30, 32–35, 37. Boardman (1970, pp. 36, 47, 57, 59, and ills., p. 39, figs. 7–10, p. 49, fig. 2, for some examples) notes that on Minoan Crete, from the Middle Minoan III period on, the most common shapes for sealstones were lentoids and amygdaloids, and in Late Minoan II–IIIA:1 the lentoid became the preferred form, but amygdaloids were also still quite common. There is a similar pattern in Late Helladic I–IIIA Mycenaean Greece, with lentoids of banded agate and onyx as the preferred sealstones; only a few amygdaloid examples are still present.
6. Loud 1948, pls. 209:24, 209:35, 36 (more of ovoid form than amygdaloid), 211:52.
7. Ibid., pl. 216:122.
8. Bass et al. 1989, pp. 8–9, and fig. 16; Pulak 2005a, pp. 304–5; Pulak 2005c, p. 592, fig. 100:f.
9. KW 5144: height 1.01 cm, width 1.11 cm.
10. Hood, Huxley, and Sandars 1958–59, p. 250, no. X.11, fig. 35:X.11; also in Effinger 1996, p. 25, no. KNG 10f, pl. 5:c.
11. Blegen and Blegen 1937, fig. 599:10.
12. Xénaki-Sakellariou 1985, p. 73, no. 2387(15), p. 293, type 6, p. 196, no. 2927(2), p. 293, type 7, pl. 85:2927(2).
13. Ibid., p. 261, no. 3192(6), pl. 127:3192(6).
14. Ibid., p. 261, no. 3192(2), pl. 127:3192(2). Another similar spherical bead was found at Prosymna. Blegen and Blegen 1937, p. 293, fig. 169:6.

190a, b

CANAANITE JARS

Ceramic
a. Canaanite jar
Height 53.5 cm (21 in.); max. diameter
26.4 cm (10⅜ in.); capacity 9.7 liters
50.31.84 (KW 102)

b. Canaanite jar with shoulder markings
Height 48.8 cm (19¼ in.); max. diameter
23.7 cm (9⅜ in.); capacity 6.5 liters
44.31.84 (KW 93)

Uluburun shipwreck
Late Bronze Age, ca. 1300 B.C.
Bodrum Museum of Underwater
Archaeology, Turkey

More than 150 Canaanite jars were found on the Uluburun shipwreck, two of which are included here, one marked with three incised parallel lines on its shoulder.[1] The decanted contents of both jars revealed a quantity of yellowish matter identified as terebinth resin. Body sherds found inside some of the intact Canaanite jars suggest that they had been stoppered with organic material, over which was placed a potsherd, after which the jar was sealed with mud or clay. All of the Uluburun Canaanite jars were stored aft of the large storage jars at the stern of the ship, regardless of their size and type, with the smaller jars stacked two deep.

The Uluburun jars fall into three general size groups, with the smallest (representing about 75 percent) having an average capacity of 6.7 liters, the medium (about 11 percent) about twice that volume, and the largest examples some 26.7 liters.[2] This last value may correspond to a *kd*, meaning "jar," mentioned in Ugaritic texts of the thirteenth century B.C., which corresponds to the eighth to seventh century B.C. Judean *bat*, a unit of liquid measure usually calculated during the Iron Age as about 22 liters, or a derivative thereof.[3]

Despite the size differences, nearly all Uluburun Canaanite jars conform to a single morphological type.[4] Further analysis, however, reveals two fabric groups corresponding to two different manufacturing methods for their inner bases. The two groups seem to correspond to two different cargoes: terebinth resin and a vegetable oil, possibly olive. Petrographic analysis of the two clay matrices of the fabrics has shown that the majority of the jars were of clay found immediately north of the tip of the Carmel coast, while those

Figure 103. Facsimile of wall painting showing Syrians with Canaanite jar and gold vessel. Thebes, Tomb of Rekhmire (TT 100). Dynasty 18, reigns of Thutmose III–Amenhotep II. The Metropolitan Museum of Art, New York, Rogers Fund, 1930 30.4.83

190a

of the second group seem to have come from the general region of Sidon.[5]

Canaanite jars, widely found in the eastern Mediterranean, were the most popular type of vessel imported into the Aegean. In Egyptian tombs such as those of Kenamun and of Rekhmire at Thebes (fig. 103),[6] the jars are depicted as cargo or tribute brought by Syrian merchants to Egypt. The best morphological parallels for the Uluburun Canaanite jars are from Tell Abu Hawam, Tell el-Amarna, Mycenae, and Menidi.[7] A storeroom at Minet el-Beidha, one of the two ports servicing

Ugarit, contained some 80 Canaanite jars, possibly awaiting export by sea.[8]

Unlike the fine wares aboard the Uluburun ship, the Canaanite jars themselves were valued primarily for their contents, although empty containers were sometimes recycled and pressed into everyday use. These contents could have included wine, oil, olives, and honey.[9] One jar from Uluburun was filled with glass beads (cat. no. 188), several others with olives.[10] The chemical analysis of preserved organic residues, however, revealed that more than two-thirds of the jars were probably car-

rying *Pistacia* species resin, most likely terebinth resin from the *Pistacia atlantica* tree,[11] which produces more abundant resin than the other *Pistacia* species found in the eastern Mediterranean. The Uluburun resin cargo—originally at more than half a ton—represents the largest ancient deposit of the material ever found.

Before this discovery at Uluburun, in an unmistakably commercial context, the best evidence for the trade of terebinth resin was in textual references and iconographic depictions, with nearly all the ancient authors agreeing on its superiority

190b

over other resins.[12] Its medicinal qualities as an antiseptic and its use in the preparation of incense and scented cosmetics have long been recognized.[13] A few Linear B tablets from Knossos contain the word *ki-ta-no*, which has been translated as "terebinth fruits,"[14] but, more recently, possibly as "terebinth resin."[15] Terebinth resin may also be the Egyptian *sntr*, the aromatic most often mentioned in Egyptian texts, brought from the Near East to the pharaoh primarily in Canaanite jars. Large quantities of *sntr* were recorded over a period of five years in the annals of Thutmose III, and

sntr is found among the hieratic inscriptions on the Canaanite jars from Tell el-Amarna and Memphis.[16] A depiction of a storeroom in the Tomb of Rekhmire shows a representative group of Canaanite jars, with the contents of one jar labeled *sntr* (fig. 96).[17] The jars were most likely inscribed to indicate the commodity they contained upon first reaching Egypt. Chemical analysis of residues from two Canaanite jars from Tell el-Amarna, inscribed *sntr*, as well as from many other uninscribed jars confirmed the identification as terebinth resin.[18] These jars are made of the same clay fabric

as the resin-bearing jars from Uluburun, indicating a common source for both the jars and, perhaps, also their contents in the vicinity of Tell Abu Hawam.[19] CP

1. Bass 1986, pp. 277–79, ills. 7, 8; Pulak 1988, pp. 10–11; Pulak 1997, pp. 240–41, fig. 9; Pulak 1998, pp. 201–2, fig. 15; Pulak 2005c, p. 581, figs. 80, 81.
2. Pulak 1998, p. 201; Pulak 1997, p. 240. These values were obtained early in our study and, therefore, represent only the intact jars that were devoid of encrustation. As jars are cleaned and mended and capacity measurements taken, the average values and their percentages within the cargo assemblage will vary accordingly.

3. Heltzer 1989, pp. 197, 201.
4. They have conical bodies, pointed bases with slightly convex toes, carinated body-shoulder junction, and slightly convex shoulders leading to a narrow, cylindrical neck and a tall lip defined by an incised line. Vertical ovoid loop handles are attached opposite each other at the junction of the shoulders and bodies of the jars.
5. Yuval Goren, personal communication. Clay, from near the sites of Tell Abu Hawam and Tel Nami, was identified from the Amarna project's petrographic analysis of the Canaanite jars from Memphis and Tell el-Amarna. See Bourriau, Smith, and Serpico 2001, p. 140.
6. Davies 1963, pl. 15; Davies and Faulkner 1947, pl. 8.
7. Bass 1986, p. 277.
8. Schaeffer 1949, p. 209, pl. 31:1; Schaeffer 1932, p. 3, pl. III:3.
9. Leonard 1996, p. 251.
10. Pulak 1997, p. 240.
11. Mills and White 1989; Hairfield and Hairfield 1990; Haldane 1991, p. 219; Haldane 1993, pp. 352–54.
12. Stol 1979, p. 15.
13. Ibid., pp. 3, 16; Pulak 2001, pp. 33–36.
14. Pulak 2001, p. 36; Bass 1997, p. 164; Melena 1976, pp. 177–90.
15. Pulak 2001, p. 36
16. Loret 1949, pp. 20–25.
17. Davies 1973, pl. 48.
18. Serpico and White 2000, p. 894.
19. Stern et al. 2000, p. 412.

191

PILGRIM FLASK

Ceramic
Height 29.5 cm (11⅝ in.); width 24.2 cm
(9½ in.); capacity 3.2 liters
Uluburun shipwreck
Late Bronze Age, ca. 1300 B.C.
Bodrum Museum of Underwater
Archaeology, Turkey 63.1.2000 (KW 3686)

192

LAMP FOR SHIPBOARD USE

Ceramic
Height 5.7 cm (2¼ in.); width 13.8 cm (5⅜ in.);
length 14.3 cm (5⅝ in.)
Uluburun shipwreck
Late Bronze Age, ca. 1300 B.C.
Bodrum Museum of Underwater
Archaeology, Turkey 10.5.90 (KW 1742)

191

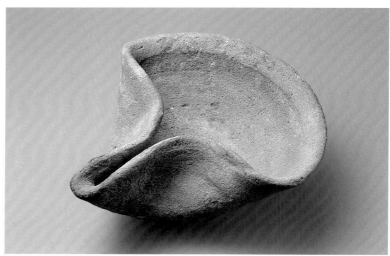

192

This Canaanite pilgrim flask from the Uluburun ship has a round, lentoid body with a sharply carinated edge and a narrow neck widening to a small mouth with a thick, triangular-sectioned rim.[1] Two round vertical handles project from the top of the body and rejoin the vessel about halfway up the funnel-like neck, which appears to sprout from between the handles with the rim resting on them. The body of the flask was thrown on its side on a potter's wheel as a single piece, and the resulting hole at the middle of the top half of the body was sealed and smoothed over.[2] The flask is in good condition, with a rich, light brown color, buff to greenish gray surface slip, and a somewhat coarse fabric with finely scattered dark inclusions and a gritty, sandy surface. At least sixty such pilgrim flasks, forming a homogeneous group but of varying sizes, were found on the Uluburun ship. They represent the second largest group of vessels carried on board.

The flasks appear to be undecorated, though a few may show remnants of the usual red concentric circles seen embellishing better preserved examples of this type known from excavations elsewhere. Had decorative painting been present, it would have disappeared, along with much of the original surface slip, as a result of the underwater environment. Pilgrim flasks of this type are common in fourteenth-century B.C. assemblages, with good parallels found at Tel Dan,[3] Hazor,[4] Tell Abu Hawam,[5] Beth-Shan,[6] Gibeon,[7] Akko,[8] and Lachish,[9] among others. Ongoing petrographic analysis of the flasks indicates that they are all of the same fabric and probably originated in the same workshop located somewhere along the southern Levantine coast.

The 60 pilgrim flasks on the Uluburun ship vary greatly in size. Only 46 were recovered intact or could be later restored into complete vessels for taking capacity measurements. They range in capacity from 0.16 to 8.84 liters.[10] As with the Canaanite jars, the pilgrim flasks almost certainly served simply as containers and were in demand for their contents, and not for the vessels themselves.

Sieving the sediments decanted from the flasks during excavation yielded many varieties of seeds, but most frequently encountered were those of figs. Because fig seeds were recovered in great quantities throughout the shipwreck site, indicating that they were carried aboard the ship either for consumption or as cargo, they may have been intrusive elements deposited in the flasks after the ship sank. The narrow necks of the flasks indicate that they probably carried a liquid such as oil. A pilgrim flask, along with Canaanite jars and several other items of the type represented on the Uluburun ship, can be seen being unloaded from a ship in the scene of a Syrian merchant venture to Egypt in the fourteenth-century B.C. Tomb of Kenamun at Thebes (see fig. 98).[11]

Sixteen Canaanite oil lamps were found on the vessel. They are made of medium coarse red-orange gritty fabric with a reddish brown surface.[12] One corner of the saucer-shaped lamp bowl is pinched to form a nozzle for the placement of the wick. On one side of the nozzle is a semicircular impression in the clay resulting from pinching between a thumb and index finger, and around the interior circumference is a slightly raised ridge. The nozzle exhibits soot stains from burning, suggesting use aboard the ship. Similar charring is seen on

several other lamps, all of the same type, although two types of lamps were found on board. The lamps that exhibit charring are larger, and more coarsely made than the more numerous second type,[13] which is of Cypriot manufacture (cat. no. 193d); some were found still nested one inside another along with Cypriot export pottery within one of the large storage jars or pithoi. These Cypriot lamps are in pristine condition, thus representing cargo. Unlike the Cypriot examples, the Canaanite lamps may provisionally be taken as an indicator of the ship's point of origin.[14]

Similar lamps have been found at Tel Michal,[15] Tell Abu Hawam,[16] Megiddo,[17] Tel Dan,[18] Hazor,[19] and Lachish,[20] among many others. Ongoing petrographic analysis reveals that all of the heavier lamps were made of the same type of clay as that used in producing most of the ship's cargo of coarse wares such as the pilgrim flasks (cat. no. 191), most of the Canaanite jars (cat. no. 190), and several types of bowls, suggesting that all were taken on board in the same general region. Unlike the cargo, which cannot be used to indicate a ship's home port, a ship's galley wares, among which oil lamps are to be included, are excellent indicators of a ship's port of origin. The evidence of these oil lamps, along with several bowls for shipboard use thus represents one of the strongest indications that the ship's home port was in the vicinity of Tell Abu Hawam or slightly farther north along with Levantine coast.   CP

1. Pulak 1988, p. 12, fig. 7, p. 13; Bass 1986, pp. 284–85, 286, ill. 21.
2. For a similar fabrication method of pilgrim flasks from Beth-Shan, see James and McGovern 1993, pp. 100–101.
3. Biran and Ben-Dov 2002, pp. 77–78, 88–91.
4. Yadin et al. 1960, pl. CXXX:8–13.
5. Hamilton 1935, p. 42, no. 255.
6. Oren 1973, figs. 41:4, 44b:27, 30, 31.
7. Pritchard 1963, fig. 8:25.
8. Ben-Arieh and Edelstein 1977, p. 23, fig. 11.1–4, pls. III:4, IX:3–4, XII:3.
9. Tufnell 1958, p. 217, pl. 84, no. 955.
10. Nearly half the flasks have capacities of under 2 liters, and seven are more than 6 liters, approximately the average capacity of the small Canaanite jars on the ship (see cat. no. 190).
11. Davies and Faulkner 1947, pl. 8; Davies 1963, p. 14, pl. 15.
12. Pulak 1988, p. 12, fig. 6, p. 13; Bass 1986, pp. 285, 287, ill. 22.
13. Bass 1986, pp. 285–87, ill. 22; Pulak 1988, pp. 12–13, fig. 6. A total of 27 Cypriot lamps were among the assemblage of Cypriot pottery on the Uluburun ship.
14. Pulak 1997, p. 252.
15. Negbi 1989, fig. 5.7: 9.
16. Hamilton 1935, p. 23, no. 93, p. 49, no. 300.
17. Loud 1948, pls. 9–12.
18. Biran and Ben-Dov 2002, pp. 78, 92–93.
19. Yadin et al. 1960, pp. 149–50.
20. Tufnell 1958, pl. 73, especially classes F and G.

193a–e

CYPRIOT POTTERY

Ceramic
a. Bucchero jug
Height 16.2 cm (6⅜ in.); diameter 11.4 cm
(4½ in.)
8.31.84 (KW 15)

b. White Slip II milk bowl
Height 8.2 cm (3¼ in.); diameter 15.1 cm (6 in.)
27.6.98 (KW 5734)

c. Base-Ring bowl
Height 7.5 cm (3 in.); width 18 cm (7⅛ in.)
11.31.84 (KW 18)

d. Lamp
Height 4.3 cm (1¾ in.); length 13.3 cm (5¼ in.)
15.31.84 (KW 23)
(Three lamps are shown on p. 322)

e. Wall bracket
Length 39 cm (15⅜ in.)
14.4.88 (KW 1539)

Uluburun shipwreck
Late Bronze Age, ca. 1300 B.C.
Bodrum Museum of Underwater
Archaeology, Turkey

At least 3 of the 10 pithoi (large ceramic transport containers) stowed on the ship that sank at Uluburun contained Cypriot pottery: Bucchero jugs, lug-handled bowls, milk bowls, Base Ring bowls and a single juglet, White Shaved juglets, lamps, and wall brackets—about 140 pieces in total, excluding the pithoi. The Uluburun shipment and the ceramic cargo jettisoned off Point Iria on the Greek mainland a century later are the only extant excavated direct archaeological evidence for the transport of pottery in the eastern Mediterranean during the Late Bronze Age.[1] These examples of ceramics-in-transport are highly significant for what they tell us about how pottery was procured and organized for shipment. This, in turn, is important because archaeologists often view imported ceramics as significant indicators of exchange and chronological synchronization.

193a

193b

193c

193d

The Cypriot ceramic cargo at Uluburun was not the primary cargo of the ship, nor even of the containers in which it was packed. Bowls found on the seabed in tightly packed stacking arrangements would have only partially filled the pithoi. Each pithos carried a different assortment of pottery. The Bucchero jug (a), for example, was one of three found on the wreck, all packed into a single pithos. Similarly, another pithos held the only examples of a unique variety of White Slip bowls. None of the pithoi contained a homogeneous shipment, and there was diversity even among vases of a particular type shipped in one container. For instance, the Base Ring bowl (c) is one of two varieties of this shape found on the wreck. Both types were found nested together in a spill of pottery that fell from the third pithos (fig. 104), still in a coherent stack in spite of having been shaken out of their container as it lurched down the sloping surface.

The wall bracket (e) fell from the same pithos. Whatever the function of these enigmatic objects—most likely they served as lamps or lamp holders—it is somewhat surprising to find these clunky, coarse-ware

193e

Figure 104. Author excavating Cypriot ceramics spilled on seabed. Uluburun shipwreck.

pieces packed alongside fine tablewares. Also surprising is the discovery of non-Cypriot ceramics packed together with Cypriot vases. Inside the krater was a White Slip bowl (b) stacked with another milk bowl in a carinated bowl that was probably made in the Levant. Herein lies the key to understanding the diversity of this mixed lot: it was a secondary cargo, relative not only to the shipment of ingots and luxury items carried on board this ship, but also in the sense that it was picked up not at any single primary production center, but rather at a trading entrepôt, likely located on the Levantine coast. These Cypriot artifacts thus provide a view into the complexity of exchange within the eastern Mediterranean during the latter half of the second millennium B.C.

NH

1. Most of the ceramics found on the Cape Gelidonya ship, the one other excavated wreck from this area and era, were probably in use on board the ship rather than transported as cargo.

Exotic Materials and Prestige Goods

194a, b
Ostrich Eggshell and Glass Base

a. Ostrich eggshell
Height 13.6 cm (5⅜ in.); diameter 12.4 cm
(4⅞ in.)
7.4.88 (KW 1391)

b. Base
Blue glass
Diameter 6.4 cm (2½ in.)
Lot 3783 (2006/4/28A)

Uluburun shipwreck
Late Bronze Age, ca. 1300 B.C.
Bodrum Museum of Underwater
Archaeology, Turkey

In addition to many ostrich eggshell beads (cat. no. 195), the Uluburun ship carried three ostrich eggshells, one of which was found intact.[1] All three eggs had been decanted of their contents in antiquity by means of a 2.5 centimeter hole chipped through at one end. The thickness of the eggshell at the hole is about 0.2 centimeters, roughly the same as that of the ostrich eggshell beads. The eggshells were undoubtedly exotica destined to be transformed by local artisans into ornate jugs or vases by the addition of bases, spouts, and perhaps other components of faience, precious metals, and additional materials. That the hollow eggshells did not float away in the course of the ship's sinking, and that one of them survived intact, suggests they were

packed snugly in a strong container, perhaps a box made of wood, kept in a compartment at the stern of the ship. Nearly all the eggshell fragments recovered from the site during excavation joined one of the two broken eggshells, indicating that only three eggshells were carried on the ship.

The eggshells could have been obtained in Africa or the Near East, since ostriches inhabited both continents in the Late Bronze Age.[2] Cups made by slicing off the top quarter of an ostrich eggshell—found in burials dating to the mid- to late third millennium B.C., in Syria and Mesopotamia—probably came from the Asiatic variety of the ostrich.[3]

On the Levantine coast, excavations at Byblos have also revealed a complete

eggshell found in an Early Bronze I tomb,[4] and eggshell fragments have been found at Tel Arad.[5] Two intact eggshells were recovered at Sahab from a Late Bronze II–Early Iron I tomb.[6] Eggshells have been unearthed in three tombs at Enkomi on Cyprus.[7]

Ostrich eggshells, along with ebony, ivory, and other exotic goods, were transported to the Aegean in unfinished form. They are conspicuous indicators of long-distance trade between the Levant and the Aegean (especially Crete), from the Early Minoan II period at Palaikastro[8] until the Late Cycladic period at Phylakopi on Melos. This trade cannot have involved many recipients. It is highly likely that only palace residents or the affluent could mobilize the resources necessary to operate a workshop for the final production of such luxury goods.

One popular use of ostrich eggshell was in the manufacture of rhyta, or ritual libation vessels, two examples of which were found at Akrotiri on Thera.[9] Rhyta were fashioned by making a large hole in one end of the eggshell for the attachment of a neck piece, while a second hole was made at the opposite end for the positioning of a foot. These attachments were made of gold, silver, bronze, faience, or wood.[10] Rhyta were important pieces of cultic equipment, often imitated in both stone and clay (see pp. 426–30).[11] An ostrich eggshell rhyton with mountings of gold, silver, bronze, and faience was discovered in a royal tholos tomb at Dendra,[12] reflecting the prestigious value of such items. Ostrich eggshell vases have been found on Crete, Rhodes, the Greek mainland at Mycenae, and Ayios Stephanos;[13] they are often embellished with incised decoration. On Crete they are found at Zakros,[14] and an eggshell—originally identified by Evans as fragments of a marble vase[15]—was excavated in the palace at Knossos in the Middle Minoan IA level of the Vat Room deposit.[16] On the Greek mainland they are found at Mycenae and Gla.[17] Painted fragments have been recovered from the Temple of Athena on Chios.[18]

Elsewhere in the Aegean, eggshell fragments are found at Troy.[19] Unworked ostrich eggshell fragments excavated at the fourteenth-century B.C. outpost at Marsa Matruh on Bate's Island off Libya were found with Minoan, Mycenaean, and Near Eastern ceramics.[20] Presumably, ostrich eggshells could have been transported directly to the Aegean from the Libyan coast. More likely, they were shipped eastward to Egypt and the Levantine coast, perhaps by ships returning from the Aegean in a counterclockwise circuit or by overland routes. Eggshells from both Africa and Asia would have been exported by ships sailing from Late Bronze Age Levantine ports to the Aegean,[21] perhaps by way of Cyprus, where contemporary finds of such shells are abundant.[22]

The purpose of the blue glass disc, found at the stern of the ship, was undetermined until recent examination suggested that it served as a base for an ostrich eggshell vase. If so, this would provide unique evidence for the exportation of ostrich eggs to the Aegean as finished products.[23] The glass base appears to be mold formed with a raised rim and a concave center, which would have supported the egg, though the thinnest portion is worn through. Originally opaque blue in color, these devitrified areas are now covered with a whitish crust.

At present, it is not known whether two of the eggshells were being shipped as raw exotica or if all three were intended to be worked into ornate vases displayed atop bases of glass or another material. In either case, these eggshells were most likely destined to serve as gifts for elite recipients.

CP

1. Pulak 2005c, p. 79; Pulak 1997, p. 242. For a discussion of ostrich eggshells in antiquity, see Caubet 1983; Reese 1985a; Conwell 1987; and Moorey 1994, pp. 127–28.
2. Conwell 1987, p. 29; Reese 1985a, p. 378.
3. Mackay 1925, p. 136; Moorey 1970, pp. 105, 116, 118, 120, 122. See also Hansen in *Art of the First Cities* 2003, no. 70b (Ur), and Porter and McClellan in ibid., p. 184 (Tell Banat).
4. Dunand 1945, pl. I:b, d.
5. Amiran 1978, p. 58, pl. 120:8.
6. Dajani 1970, p. 34, pl. II:SA151, 52.
7. Dikaios 1969, p. 367, pl. 211:42; Åström 1972, pp. 557, 616; Reese 1985a, p. 371. One example, from a Late Cypriot II tomb, had a hole and is believed to be associated with an ivory piece from the same tomb, which may have been a spout: Åström 1972, pp. 557, 616.
8. Dawkins 1904, pp. 201–2.
9. S. Marinatos 1972, p. 35, pls. 36:b, 81:a,b.
10. Sakellarakis 1990, p. 285. For a broad discussion of ostrich eggshells in Aegean contexts, see Sakellarakis 1990. Sometimes the underside was only painted and, rarely, handles were added.
11. Ibid., p. 295. Sakellarakis (p. 285) notes twelve examples of such rhyta from the Aegean.
12. Persson 1931, pp. 37, 54, pl. III.
13. Cline 1994, pp. 237–39, nos. 940–43, 947–49, 951–54.
14. Platon 1971, p. 159.
15. Panagiotaki 1998, p. 180, pls. 33:a, 34:b.
16. Cadogan 1980, p. 28.
17. Cline 1994, pp. 237–38, nos. 945, 946.
18. Boardman 1967, p. 243, pl. 97:604.
19. Blegen, Caskey, and Rawson 1953, p. 264.
20. White 1986, pp. 79, 82; Conwell 1987; White 2002, pp. 60–64.
21. Caubet 1983, p. 195.
22. Reese 1985a, pp. 371–72. See Reese 1985a for a summary of ostrich eggshells in Cypriot, Aegean, Near Eastern, and western Mediterranean archaeological contexts.
23. Unlike Aegean examples, this base would have allowed the egg to stand upright on its own.

195
DISC-SHAPED BEADS

Ostrich eggshell
Length 19 cm (7½ in.)
Uluburun shipwreck
Late Bronze Age, ca. 1300 B.C.
Bodrum Museum of Underwater
Archaeology, Turkey 2006/4/30A

Seventy-six individual disc-shaped ostrich eggshell beads were gathered from the Uluburun shipwreck.[1] All are cylindrical in shape, with smooth edges. Most have an hourglass-shaped cross section at the perforation, which likely resulted from the method of drilling the central stringing hole.

The Uluburun ship carried many exotic items, both as raw materials and in finished form. Among the more delicate were ostrich eggshells (cat. no. 194a) and these beads. It is difficult if not impossible to determine whether the beads were personal possessions of those on board or if they were intended as gifts along with the eggshell vases and other items on the ship.

Most ostrich eggshell beads are initially shaped roughly by chipping, after which a hole is bored at the center to produce a bead with jagged edges. These crude forms are then ground smooth on their circumference by rubbing the edges against an abrasive stone, which usually produces an asymmetrical bead with irregular edges. The Uluburun examples, however, were manufactured in a different manner. Their central holes and outer edges exhibit great regularity and were

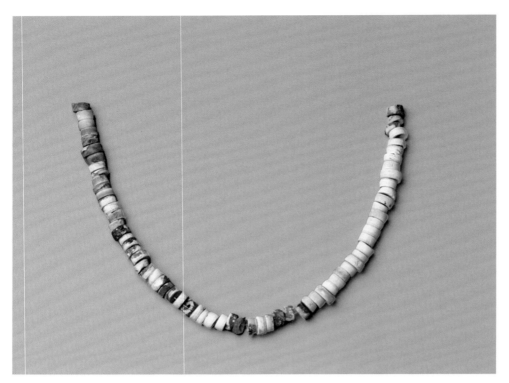

195

INLAID RINGS

Shell, bitumen
Diameter 2.1–2.5 cm (⅞–1 in.); thickness
0.3–0.5 cm (⅛–¼ in.)
Uluburun shipwreck
Late Bronze Age, ca. 1300 B.C.
Bodrum Museum of Underwater
Archaeology, Turkey
14.6.98 (KW 5106), 16.19.90 (KW 2201),
22.8.96 (KW 4182), 26.19.90 (KW 2335), 9.6.98
(KW 4877), 8.13.93 (KW 3259), 32.7.95
(KW 3525), 10.4.88 (KW 1501), 35.5.90
(KW 1952), 7.13.93 (KW 3219)

Included in the finds from the Uluburun ship were 28 shell rings.[1] The groove cut around the exterior circumference of each ring contains bitumen, a petroleum-based natural asphalt, for affixing decorative inlays, now lost. This characteristic is unique to the Uluburun rings. Most of the rings were found scattered just aft of amidships, indicating that they were originally stored at the stern along with most of the other precious items on board. The large number of rings suggests that they were likely prestige gifts or valuable cargo items rather than personal effects of those on the vessel.

The ring assemblage exhibits three different patterns of inlays, as revealed by the impressions visible on the bitumen layer. Of these, 19 rings are embellished with the same pattern, while one pattern is either unique or also represented on a second ring but on which the bitumen is too poorly preserved to be certain. The sharp, irregular edges of the impressions suggest that the inlays were fashioned from bits of colored glass, which have since disintegrated.[2] This conclusion finds some corroboration in traces of a white powdery material in the recesses of some inlay depressions.[3] The black bitumen used as the adhesive backing for the inlays also forms a part of the decorative scheme, visible around many of the inlay pieces.

The most common pattern of embellishment used on the rings is that of a varied number of alternating circles and rectangles (seven rings depicted).[4] The bitumen on some of the rings is poorly or only partially preserved, making it impossible to determine with certainty the number of inlays used in each ring, although it would appear to range from eleven to thirteen.

likely formed with a tubular drill, allowing the outer surface to be shaped simultaneously with the central perforation by means of an added central projection on the drill bit. Although tubular drills existed as early as the late third millennium B.C.,[2] this particular method of bead manufacture has yet to be verified by technical examination.

Discoid ostrich eggshell beads are among the earliest known manufactured ornaments and are quite common at Late Paleolithic and later prehistoric sites along the Nile in Egypt.[3] Since Neolithic times, ostrich eggshells have been fashioned into beads and other shapes to make pendants, necklaces, belts, and anklets.[4] Outside of Africa ostrich eggshell beads are rare. They have been found in Early Bronze IV–Middle Bronze I transition (ca. 2300–1900 B.C.) contexts in the Negev Highlands, where Rekhes Nafha and the Camel Site have revealed implements, debris, and sandstone grinding stones associated with the manufacture of beads.[5]

In the Early Bronze Age cemetery of Bab edh-Dhra, on the southeastern Dead Sea plain, ostrich-eggshell beads were placed with the skeletal remains.[6] The so-called Copper Age Site H at Beth-Pelet produced not only ostrich eggshell beads, but also sandstone bead grinders.[7] Ostrich eggshell beads—blackened from either fire or cremation[8]—have also been found

in the central Mediterranean in the Bronze Age Tarxien Cemetery of Malta (ca. 2500–1500 B.C.);[9] the presence of these imported items in Tarxien may reflect possible connections with the eastern Mediterranean. The frequent occurrence of ostrich eggshells or their fragments at many Late Bronze Age sites in the eastern Mediterranean demonstrates their popularity as objects, yet the near total absence of ostrich eggshell beads at the same sites is difficult to reconcile.   CP

1. Owing to their minute size and indistinct creamy white color, some beads could undoubtedly have been missed during excavation.
2. Kenoyer 1997, p. 271; Moorey 1994, p. 56.
3. Manlius 2001, p. 947.
4. Such objects are still made today by the Bushmen of the Kalahari Desert in southern Africa. Conwell 1987, p. 30.
5. Saidel 2002, pp. 40, 58–59, 60.
6. Chesson 2007, pp. 117–19.
7. MacDonald 1932, p. 12, pls. XXIV:45, XXVI:54.
8. M. Murray 1934, p. 3.
9. J. Evans 1959, p. 175.

196

At least seven rings are of a design in which standing triangles alternate with inverted triangles, resulting in a close-fitting arrangement. Again, the number of inlay pieces varies, in this case from 26 to 36.[5] The most intricate and possibly unique inlay design in the assemblage consists of rectangles alternating with larger rectangles composed of four triangles, sometimes quadrilaterals, placed so that their peaks meet at the center.[6]

The effort expended in acquiring, shaping, and polishing the Uluburun rings would have followed the practice in crafting shell rings found elsewhere, but the exterior grooves were a further complication. The inlay work would have required much additional patience and skill. The Uluburun shell rings must therefore have been highly prized prestige items, products of an accomplished artisan operating in a controlled workshop environment.

The rings are shaped from the apical ends of marine gastropod shells, most likely those of cone (*Conus*) or conch (*Strombus*) species.[7] Although the exact species cannot be determined because of the extensive modification of the shells by cutting and grinding, the large size of the rings indicates that they were not crafted from the Mediterranean cone shell (*Conus ventricosus*); rather, they were imported, almost certainly as finished products, along with five "buttons" or ornaments found on the wreck, also of cut and ground-down cone or strombus whorls. These finely crafted imported objects contrast sharply with the simplicity of the few objects found on the ship that were made of local shells, such as beach-polished apertural lips of Mediterranean bonnet shells (*Phalium undulatum*), two cockleshells (*Glycemeris*) used as spoons or scrapers, and water-polished fossil and semi-fossil shells and shell fragments.

Chemical analysis conducted on the bitumen from three of the Uluburun shell rings has revealed that it originated from a single Mesopotamian source, probably one of the natural seepages in the region of Hit,[8] where bitumen was also extracted for use at Mari.[9]

Seashell rings have been found in Late Bronze Age contexts in the Aegean, Cyprus, and Syria,[10] but these examples are carved from native Mediterranean top shells (*Mondonta* sp.). Two shell rings, contemporary with and probably made of a species similar to those at Uluburun, were found at Megiddo.[11] While such shell rings are rare in the Mediterranean, they are not uncommon in Mesopotamia, with more than 1,431 examples coming from 'Usiyeh alone, dating to the early second millennium B.C.[12] Other Mesopotamian examples have been found in burials, one including 19 ring-shaped shell ornaments laid across the midsection of a body, which were likely strung together for interment.[13] This suggests that they may have been linked together to form a belt as was probably the case earlier at Kish[14] and also at Ur.[15] Contemporary parallels are also found in Dilmun (Bahrain).[16] Although some of these rings were intricately decorated with incised figured and geometric designs, none display the expert craftsmanship of the Uluburun rings, nor do they retain traces of bitumen. Nevertheless, the Uluburun rings provide evidence for trade between the Persian Gulf and the Levantine coast during the fourteenth century B.C. Shells of Indo-Pacific origin were either imported into Mesopotamia as finished rings, as may have been the case at 'Usiyeh, or they were made into rings there and probably also embellished with inlays affixed with Mesopotamian bitumen before being exported to the Levant.

CP

1. Pulak 1988, pp. 26–27, fig. 31; Bass et al. 1989, pp. 11–12, fig. 20; Pulak 1998; Pulak 2005c, pp. 85, 593.
2. In the event that inlay pieces had fallen off the rings but had survived, the sand around and under each ring was recovered and raised to the surface for sifting through fine-mesh sieves. No inlays were recovered during this procedure.
3. The white powder could be remnants of de-vitrified or weathered glass. The inlays could presumably have been of colored bits of faience as well, but it would seem that the impressions of the inlay edges preserved in the bitumen would have been more regular and smooth, since such faience inlays would have been shaped by casting and firing. Even in the event that they were cut and ground to shape, they still would have produced smoother edge impressions on the bitumen.
4. Catalogue nos. KW 1501, 3219, 3259, 3525, 4182, 4877, and 5106.
5. Catalogue nos. KW 1952 and 2335.
6. Catalogue no. KW 2201. Catalogue no. KW 3525 may have been embellished with the same inlay design, but its bitumen layer is too poorly preserved to make a positive attribution.
7. Moorey 1994, p. 133.
8. The bitumen from the Uluburun rings was analyzed by J. Connan of Elf Exploration Production (personal communication, May 25, 1993) using gas chromatography, for which I am most grateful; also briefly mentioned in Connan et al. 1999, p. 36.
9. Moorey 1994, pp. 332–35; Connan et al. 1999, pp. 33–38.
10. Reese 1984, pp. 237–38; personal communication.
11. Loud 1948, pl. 224:14–15.
12. Oguchi 1992, p. 69, fig. 4:1–10, pl. 4:a, b. Because partially worked shells or shell waste were not found at the site, it is likely that the rings were imported as finished items (ibid., pp. 69–70).
13. Boehmer and Dämmer 1985, pp. 8–9, 58–60, pls. 21, 22, 145, 17:2.
14. Moorey 1978, p. 77.
15. Woolley 1934, p. 243.
16. Ibraham 1982, p. 88, no. 54:9, p. 216, pl. 54:9.

197
ELEPHANT TUSK

Ivory
Height 20.1 cm (7⅞ in.); max. diameter
14.6 cm (5¾ in.)
Uluburun shipwreck
Late Bronze Age, ca. 1300 B.C.
Bodrum Museum of Underwater
Archaeology, Turkey 73.31.84
(KW 162)

197

A length of elephant tusk, cleanly sawn off at both ends, was recovered in good condition from the shipwreck.[1] Oval in cross section, the tusk is slightly curved and narrows toward the distal end. In addition to the saw marks evident on both ends, several cut marks are visible on the sides. The lack of any trace of the pulp cavity indicates that it was cut from the distal two-thirds of a sizable tusk. Its color is a mottled light brown stained gray green from the copper ingots on the wreck, and it exhibits slight surface pitting and deep longitudinal grain cracks. The tusk was located at the stern of the ship along with 14 hippopotamus teeth (see cat. no. 198) and other delicate and valuable objects.[2] Its placement with other trade items and the raw nature of the tusk are clear indicators that the ivories aboard were intended for trade. Small pieces of roughly worked raw and scrap ivory were also found on the ship.

Elephant and hippopotamus ivories were traded as a luxury commodity as early as the Chalcolithic period and onward.[3] An elephant tusk and worked

elephant and hippopotamus ivories have been excavated in a late fourth-millennium B.C. Levantine workshop at Bir es-Safadi.[4] The Middle Bronze Age palace at

Figure 105. Facsimile of wall painting showing Syrians with elephant and ivory tusks. Thebes, Tomb of Rekhmire (TT 100). Dynasty 18, reigns of Thutmose III– Amenhotep II. The Metropolitan Museum of Art, New York, Rogers Fund, 1931 31.6.43

Alalakh (see pp. 197–98) produced five tusks belonging to the Asian elephant; tusks have also been found at Megiddo.[5] The Amarna Letters reveal that ivory objects and tusks were a part of the gift-exchange system in the eastern Mediterranean.[6] Lacking local supplies of its own, Egypt acquired elephant ivory from Syria and Nubia. The fifteenth-century B.C. Tomb of Rekhmire at Thebes vividly depicts ivory brought to Egypt in the form of raw elephant tusks as well as a live elephant (fig. 105).[7] Extant texts from the same period in Qusr Ibrim, Nubia, mention 250 "man-loads," or up to 500 tusks, imported from "southern countries," as well as 700 tusks obtained by Hatshepsut from eastern Tjehenu (eastern Libya/ western Egypt).[8] Hatshepsut also sent a fleet to the fabled land of Punt (see fig. 5) to acquire African elephant tusks,[9] and in northern Syria Thutmose III hunted Asian elephants for ivory.[10]

The probable Near Eastern origin of

the Linear B word for ivory, *e-re-pa*,[11] hints at a Near Eastern source for the early ivory that reached the Aegean, but it was also imported from Nubia and, probably, from North Africa.[12] The only unworked elephant tusks from the Aegean are four complete ones excavated in fifteenth-century B.C. Crete in a Late Minoan IB context at Zakros,[13] and partly worked tusk sections recovered in fourteenth-century B.C. (Late Helladic IIIA) levels at Kommos.[14] Sections of elephant tusk[15] and hippopotamus canine[16] were also found in thirteenth-century B.C. (Late Helladic IIIB) contexts at Mycenae.

From the sixteenth to the thirteenth century B.C., both elephant and hippopotamus ivory were used in the Levant and the Aegean (see pp. 406–7). Elephant tusk was the material of choice for large objects because it offered large quantities of solid ivory for carving. These objects included combs, relief plaques, figurines, and cosmetic containers or pyxides.[17] The large central pulp cavity of an elephant tusk would have facilitated the carving of a pyxis; its base and lid would have been fashioned from separate, transversally cut slabs of ivory, with the base pegged to the bottom of the pyxis body.[18]

While physical and chemical analyses can distinguish between hippopotamus and elephant ivories, there are no known scientific methods at present for differentiating between Asian and African elephants.[19] Whatever the original source, it appears that elephant and hippopotamus ivory, in the form of complete tusks and teeth as well as partly modified pieces, reached the Late Bronze Age Aegean and the central Mediterranean on ships like the one that sank off Uluburun.   CP

1. Pulak 2005c, p. 583; Bass 1986, pp. 282–83, 284, ill. 18; Pulak 1995, p. 51, fig. 14.
2. Bass et al. 1989, p. 11; Pulak 2001, pp. 37–39.
3. Tusks, teeth, and bones of elephants and hippopotamus found in the Near East and the Aegean, as well as possible sources of elephant and hippopotamus ivory, are discussed in Reese 1985b.
4. Ibid., pp. 394, 399; Mellaart 1966, pp. 28–31; Perrot 1955, p. 172, n. 24.
5. Barnett 1975, pp. 164–65, n. 3; Scullard 1974, p. 30.
6. Peltenburg 1991, p. 170.
7. Davies 1973, pls. XIX, XX, XXIII.
8. Hayward 1990, pp. 104, 107.
9. Breasted 1962, p. 109, no. 265.
10. Crowfoot and Crowfoot 1938, p. 54; Collon 1977, pp. 219–20.

11. Ventris and Chadwick 1973, pp. 343–46.
12. Hayward 1990, pp. 103–4.
13. Platon (1971, pp. 116, 120, 245, 61 with figure) mentions only three, but Reese (1985b, p. 400) notes that four tusks were found; Krzyszkowska 1988, p. 230.
14. Reese and Krzyszkowska 1996, p. 324.
15. K. Wardle 1973, pp. 339–40, fig. 23, pl. 61; Reese 1985b, p. 400; Cline 1994, p. 234, no. 908.
16. Cline 1994, p. 235, no. 917; Reese 1985b, p. 393; Krzyszkowska 1984, p. 124.
17. For the variety of Mycenaean objects made of ivory, see Poursat 1977a; Krzyszkowska 1988, pp. 209, 230–31.
18. Krzyszkowska 1988, p. 212.
19. Stable isotope analysis has been used to source ivory from modern African elephants, but the methodology for its application to archaeological specimens has yet to be developed. See Vogel, Eglington, and Auret 1990.

198a, b

HIPPOPOTAMUS TEETH

Ivory

a. Incisor
Length 31.2 cm (12¼ in.); diameter 5 cm (2 in.)
2006/4/12A (KW 2893)

b. Canine
Length 25.5 cm (10 in.); diameter 4.5 cm (1¾ in.)
2006/4/11A (KW 5187)

Uluburun shipwreck
Late Bronze Age, ca. 1300 B.C.
Bodrum Museum of Underwater Archaeology, Turkey

198a, b

The Uluburun ship carried 14 complete and unmodified hippopotamus teeth consisting of eight incisors and six canines.[1] The lower left canine (p. 329, right), which is the largest tooth of a hippopotamus, is naturally curved, is of subtriangular cross section, and has a pulp cavity occupying its proximal end. A hard, ridged enamel covers the two outward faces, with the third covered only with cementum. A marked wear facet at the distal end was caused by grinding against the upper canine. Other than a crack along the natural fracture of the tooth, it is well preserved.

The lower incisor (left) is straight, with a subcircular cross section. As with the canine, a tapering pulp cavity occupies its proximal end, which is chipped and cracked. The distal end, which shows some surface loss, is partly flattened by grinding, with the outer surface covered only with cementum.

Hippopotamus ivory is generally denser, harder, finer grained, and whiter than elephant ivory, and retains its whiteness over time instead of turning yellow.[2] Its limited size, however, precludes the carving of large pieces. Moreover, both the enamel and cementum have to be removed to facilitate carving, which is one of the drawbacks of using lower canines.[3]

Hippopotamus ivory was commonly exploited in the Levant at least from the Chalcolithic period into the Iron Age (see pp. 406–7).[4] Archaeological evidence shows that hippopotamus teeth were fashioned into a variety of small objects, including seals, inlays, and plaques.[5] It was traded over long distances, reaching Cyprus[6] and the Aegean by sea, where ivory objects on Crete first appeared during the third millennium B.C.[7] A fragment of a hippopotamus lower canine was found at Knossos in an Early Minoan context, suggesting that ivory in the form of hippopotamus teeth reached in the Aegean from the earliest days of ivory working in the region.[8]

The concentric growth rings, or lamellae, of hippopotamus ivory are wavy and discontinuous, unlike elephant ivory, which has smooth, even layers, making distinction possible between the two types.[9] It would now appear that certain small carvings, previously assumed to be of elephant ivory, may instead be of hippopotamus ivory. Reexamination of some earlier Bronze Age Minoan ivory objects has shown this to be the case[10] and indi-

cates that the use of elephant ivory became more the norm in the Aegean later, during the Mycenaean period.[11] A similar reexamination of Late Bronze Age ivory objects from Ugarit in Syria has shown the majority to be of hippopotamus rather than elephant ivory.[12]

Quantities of hippopotamus and elephant ivory reached Aegean artisans in the form of raw teeth and tusks on ships like the one that sank at Uluburun. While the full implications of the trade in hippopotamus ivory cannot be assessed based on the existing finds, it would seem that hippopotamus teeth were more commonly used as a source of ivory than hitherto believed.

CP

1. Bass 1986, pp. 283, 285, ill. 19; Bass et al. 1989, p. 11, fig. 20; for color illustration, see Pulak 1995, p. 51, fig. 14; Pulak 2001, p. 39; Pulak 2005c, pp. 78, 583.
2. Krzyszkowska 1990, p. 38; Horwitz and Tchernov 1990, p. 67.
3. Krzyszkowska 1990, p. 42.
4. Horwitz and Tchernov 1990, pp. 67–68.
5. Krzyszkowska 1988, pp. 215–26.
6. Various Bronze Age ivory objects from Cyprus have recently been shown to be made of hippopotamus incisors and canines. See Reese 1998, p. 140.
7. Krzyszkowska 1984, p. 123.
8. Ibid., pp. 124–25, pl. XIIIa (right); Reese 1985b, p. 393; Reese 1998, p. 142. A large fragmentary hippopotamus lower canine was discovered in a much later context at Mycenae. See Krzyszkowska 1984, p. 124, pl. XIIIa (left); Krzyszkowska 1988, p. 210; Reese 1985b, p. 393.
9. Krzyszkowska 1988, pp. 211–15, pls. 24:b–d, 25:b; Krzyszkowska 1990, pp. 42–47, figs. 17–19.
10. Krzyszkowska 1988, pp. 228–29.
11. Ibid., pp. 230–32.
12. Caubet and Poplin 1992, pp. 92–93, 100.

199a, b
DUCK-SHAPED VESSELS

Ivory

a. Height 9.2 cm (3⅝ in.); width 8.8 cm (3½ in.); length 20.4 cm (8⅛ in.)
62.7.92 (KW 2818), 53.8.96 (KW 2818), 58.7.95 (KW 2818), 26.8.96 (L10019)

b. Height 8.8 cm (3½ in.); width 5.7 cm (2¼ in.); length 17.8 cm (7 in.)
60.7.95 (KW 2534), 51.19.90 (KW 2534), 63.7.92 (L6582), 59.7.95 (L9014)

Uluburun shipwreck
Late Bronze Age, ca. 1300 B.C.
Bodrum Museum of Underwater Archaeology, Turkey

Among the most impressive finished-ivory objects recovered from the Uluburun ship are two duck-shaped vessels, presumably containers for holding cosmetics, unguents, or other similar materials. Although different in shape and style, both vessels have a pair of pivoting wings that serve as lids for the body cavities.[1] They were found disarticulated, with various components spilled into deeper parts of the site; most of them, however, were recovered among the three rows of copper oxhide ingots stowed forward of amidships. Because this is an unlikely area for such delicate objects, we can assume that the vessels floated down from the stern of the ship where most of the other fragile and valuable objects were kept.

The duck vessel shown opposite, above, is the larger and more complete of the two vessels. It is composed of an ivory head, hollow body, neck, two wings, two wing

Figure 106. Fragmentary ivory duck-shaped vessel. Alalakh, Level II. Late Bronze Age. Antakya Archaeological Museum 6082

199a

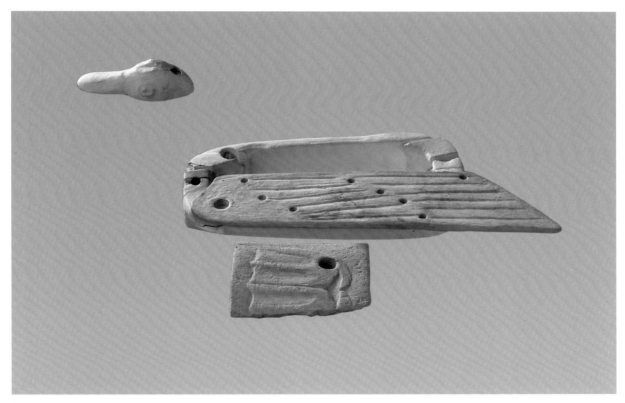

199b

pins, and a base plaque.[2] These pieces, as well as the missing legs, were held together with pins. The shape of the back of the head and the upper neck clearly indicates that the head faced forward. The hollow body was covered by the wings, which pivoted on small mushroom-headed pins to reveal the contents inside. The double lids are flat pieces of ivory carved into the shape of wings, and include a portion of tail feathers, or retrices. Two S-shaped bands, one wide and one narrow, divide the wings into three zones, and a third band separates the wing from the integrated partial tail. The wings are embellished with shallow carved and incised designs that represent long flight feathers, or remiges, and greater and primary covert feathers. Compass-incised overlapping circles on the anterior third of the wings represent lesser and median covert feathers. The wide S-shaped band frames a guilloche pattern. The center of each guilloche circle is pierced by a small hole, which was probably accentuated by inlays, perhaps of colored glass or semiprecious stones. The narrower central band is decorated with a series of semicircles. The wing lids were designed to create a complete tail when the two pieces were brought together to close the vessel. The shape of the tail is echoed in the carving of the body, with the wings overhanging slightly on all sides. The entire assembly is supported by a base plaque, which features a pair of duck feet carved in low, rounded relief and incised with web detailing. There are two rectangular mortises on the underside of the body for attaching the legs to secure the vessel to the base.

The vessel on page 331, below, is the smaller and less well preserved of the two. It comprises a head, a body, one wing, and a feet plaque. Like the larger example, it too is a double-winged container, although only one wing was recovered during the excavation. This wing is also a flat piece of ivory with two S-shaped bands of equal width, creating three zones. The stylized design on the wing consists of shallow carved and incised lines that represent greater and primary covert feathers. The wing's anterior zone is embellished with overlapping compass-incised circles to indicate the lesser and median covert feathers. The small holes piercing the bands likely held decorative inlays. A single larger hinge-peg hole pierces the anterior of the wing; a smaller hole on the inner posterior edge probably held a knob to manipulate the lid and to secure the two wing lids together when they were closed.

The shape of this wing differs from those of the larger vessel. The posterior end is cut at an angle, giving it a swept-back appearance. Unlike the larger vessel, the duck's body does not have an integrated tail projection. Rather, it was fitted with a separate tail component, now lost, that was attached with a pair of pins driven into two holes in the rump. The underside of the body also has sockets for the attachment of the missing legs, which would have been inserted into the webbed feet carved in low relief on the base plaque. The neck would have been affixed by a single peg inserted into a hole on the forward edge of the body. Judging from the shape of the head, it must also have faced forward. Both duck vessels were probably produced in the same workshop, perhaps even by the same hand.

The elite nature of ivory and the high level of craftsmanship suggest that the vessels represent prestige gifts or valuable trade items. Likely they served as toilet accessories of a ritual nature for cosmetics.[3]

Many duck vessels and their components have been found in the eastern Mediterranean. Although sometimes believed to represent geese rather than ducks,[4] the birds are mostly modeled after the Egyptian Goose, of the Shelduck subfamily. The vessels may be grouped into two general types: those with single oval lids and those with double-wing lids. The former appear to be of Canaanite inspiration and the latter, to which the Uluburun examples belong, are of Egyptian derivation.[5] The more naturalistically rendered double-lidded duck vessels have two wings that pivot outward in opposite directions from a point on the forward edge of the body, while the stylized single-lidded variety pivots in either direction from a similar point (see cat. nos. 201, 202). Both vessel types appear to have been equally valued, with the single-lidded version encountered slightly more frequently in the archaeological record.[6]

Duck vessels from the Levantine coast are approximately contemporary with those found in Egypt. The Uluburun examples seem to incorporate features of both types. The compass-drawn circles and straight lines representing feathers appear to be Canaanite in style. The integration of the tail into the body is probably an Egyptian trait.[7] The transformation of the Egyptian-style tailed body into an ovoid shape and its embellishment, including the entire underside, with chevrons or circles and semicircles representing body feathers, seem to be of Cypriot design.[8]

The closest parallels for the Uluburun ducks are seen among vessels from Egypt that represent a double-winged duck held by a nude swimming girl with outstretched arms (see cat. no. 200).[9] They are often referred to as "spoons"[10] and are almost exclusively made of wood.[11] Although there are differences in material and the Uluburun vessels do not feature a nude swimming girl, the waterfowl portions of the spoons are remarkably similar to the larger of the duck vessels.[12]

No complete double-winged duck vessels are known from outside of Egypt. Many incomplete vessels or fragments have been found on the Levantine coast and Cyprus.

Examples are found at Megiddo,[13] Tel Dan,[14] Kamid el-Loz,[15] Meskene-Emar,[16] Ugarit,[17] Alalakh (fig. 106),[18] and Tell Qasile.[19] On Cyprus, parallels are found at Enkomi[20] and Kition.[21] The earliest duck vessels with both single and double lids are found in Late Bronze Age II contexts, but the great majority of them are from the Late Bronze Age III period, with the exception of a single-lid type body fragment found at Ugarit and a pair of wings from Kamid el-Loz, which date to Late Bronze Age I.[22] They continue in use until the early Iron Age.

The Uluburun duck vessels represent the only relatively intact examples of the two-winged type found in this region. They provide the only evidence for the manner in which these vessels were fitted with base plaques having carved duck feet, and they help us to interpret similar plaques found elsewhere.[23] The wings of the Uluburun examples are also distinctive, with the addition of a central zone representing primary and greater covert feathers. In Egypt, the cosmetic spoons with ducks and nude swimming girls also feature a middle zone of feathers. Outside Egypt, the closest parallels in style and execution for the Uluburun wings are from Megiddo, although these do not denote the central feather zone. The Uluburun duck vessels thus represent Canaanite versions of Egyptian spoons in which the female form has been eliminated and the swimming duck is instead supported with legs and feet for a base. As such, they provide strong stylistic evidence of an Egyptian origin for the two-winged duck vessels produced in the Levant.

Ivory held an important place among value-laden objects used as prestige gifts, whether in raw form, such as tusks, or as finished products. It was also the material of choice for Near Eastern duck containers. Only four duck vessels, all of the single-lidded type, have thus far been found in the Aegean.[24] If the Uluburun duck vessels were part of the cargo, as is likely, evidence is provided for the exportation of the first double-winged vessels from the Levant.

CP

1. Pulak 2005c, pp. 83, 605, fig. 128; Pulak 1997, pp. 244–45, fig. 13; Pulak 1995, pp. 54–55, fig. 28.
2. The components of the duck containers have not yet been examined to determine if they are of elephant or hippopotamus ivory. The body of cat. no. 199a is quite wide and likely to

have been fashioned from elephant ivory, while the other components are smaller and may have been crafted from hippopotamus ivory.

3. Reports of a Dynasty 18 vessel in the form of a swimming nude female pushing a duck, which contained ointment (Kozloff 1992, p. 331), have been disputed; see cat. no. 200.

4. Ibid., p. 332.

5. Gachet-Bizollon 2007, p. 66.

6. Ibid.; see also the convenient inventory of both types compiled on pp. 67–70.

7. Ibid., pp. 60–61, 65.

8. Ibid., pp. 61, 66.

9. The only example of this type of vessel outside of Egypt was found on Cyprus. Perhaps in keeping with the tradition of Near Eastern duck vessels, it is made of ivory. Murray, Smith, and Walters 1900, pp. 14–15, with fig. 21; Gachet-Bizollon 2007, p. 64, fig. 20, p. 66.

10. Although there are many more examples of spoons with nude swimming girls supporting various spoon bowls, only about a dozen complete or nearly complete duck versions are known with perhaps another dozen or more fragmentary examples throughout the museums of the world; Egypt's Dazzling Sun 1992, pp. 331, 347–48.

11. Drioton 1949, pl. 105; Petrie 1891, pl. 18; Vandier d'Abbadie 1972, pp. 44–45 от 117–19. For examples of these vessels, see Egypt's Dazzling Sun 1992, p. 331, fig XI.1, p. 347, fig. XI.75, with color photograph on p. 365, pl. 39; Vandier d'Abbadie 1972, pp. 10–11, 13 от 1–3; Saleh and Sourouzian 1987, pl. 157.

12. An example from the Musée du Louvre (cat. no. 200) is particularly close; Vandier d'Abbadie 1972, pp. 10–11, 13 от 3. See also Egypt's Dazzling Sun 1992, pp. 347–48, fig. 75, p. 365, pl. 38.

13. At Megiddo, there are at least five heads, three bodies, and six different wings of which three are paired. This indicates that there must have been at least six double-winged duck vessels among the ivories found (Loud 1939, pl. 12:45–53, pl. 24:129, pl. 30:157, pl. 31:158, with various duck heads in pl. 45).

14. Biran and Ben-Dov 2002, pp. 141–44, with figs. 2.101 and 2.102, pl. IIIa; Biran 1971, pl. a; Biran 1970, p. 119.

15. W. Adler 1996, p. 105, fig. 2; Metzger 1993, pl. 46:3, nos. 9976, 1143, 1149, and also no. 1034; Hachmann in Frühe Phöniker im Libanon 1983, p. 163; Hachmann and Kuschke 1966, pl. 20:9.

16. Beyer 1982, p. 123, fig. 1.

17. Gachet-Bizollon 2007, pp. 46–47, 357, pl. 7, p. 415, pls. 65, 66.

18. Woolley 1955, pl. 75.

19. Although of a later, Iron Age date, the rectangular body with integrated tail is of interest in showing the continuation of this style; Mazar 1975, p. 81, pl. 7:C.

20. Murray, Smith, and Walters 1900, pp. 32, 41; Gallis 1973, figs. 4, 5; Courtois 1984, p. 576, fig. 18:12, pl. 6:11; Gachet-Bizollon 2007, pp. 69–70, and p. 63, figs. 16a and 18a, for drawings of one of the unpublished examples.

21. Karageorghis and Demas 1985, pls. CXXI no. 5332, CXXXV, and CCIV no. 2526.

22. Gachet-Bizollon 2007, pp. 50, 66.

23. Three base plates with crudely incised duck feet are found at Megiddo (Loud 1939, pl. 25:143–45) and one from Tel Dan (Biran and Ben-Dov 2002, pp. 142–43, fig. 2.101:204).

24. They are from Rhodes (Ialysos), Crete (Zafer Papoura), and the Greek mainland (Mycenae and Asine), all listed in Gachet-Bizollon 2007, p. 51, table 4.

200

DUCK-SHAPED CONTAINER WITH FEMALE SWIMMER

Wood, ivory
Width 5.5 cm (2⅛ in.); length 29.3 cm (11½ in.)
Egypt
New Kingdom, Dynasty 18, reign of Amenhotep III, ca. 1390–1352 B.C.
Musée du Louvre, Paris, Département des Antiquités Égyptiennes E218

Although often referred to as cosmetic spoons because they were found among personal belongings in Egyptian tombs, the meaning of these fascinating Egyptian offering containers remain to be fully explained. No clear traces of the original contents have been detected on their wood or ivory surfaces, unlike Egyptian cylindrical compartmented boxes (see cat. no. 270). Moreover, the often fragile handles, made of thin layers of carved wood, hardly lend themselves to frequent use.

Lacking evidence of a practical purpose, the form and decoration of these objects may help with their interpretation. The absence of any explicit correspondence with deities, in the form of attributes or inscriptions, encourages us to seek a symbolic system common to the entirety of the imagery they bear. Scenes presented include ritual offerings, the royal cartouche, the bucolic world of the Nile as an emblem of rebirth (marshes, boats on the river, harvesting, tilapia fish, ducks), and female eroticism (nude young women, swimmers). The rare inscriptions, with wishes for the new year or good fortune, may provide a key to their meaning; such vessels could have been objects for private use exchanged on the occasion of the great renewal feast of the Egyptian calendar, a time when Egyptian royalty also renewed itself.

This object, in the shape of a duck and a female swimmer, presents a surprising combination of Egyptian and Levantine elements. The woman's form and facial features unquestionably speak for the Egyptian style under the reign of Amenhotep III. On the other hand, the wings of the duck have the same contours as those (in ivory) found in the Uluburun shipwreck (see cat. no. 199a, b). As for the duck's head, which is of ivory and disproportionately large in relation to the swimmer, the

details around the base of the beak are similar to those on lidded boxes discovered at Ugarit (see cat. no. 201),[1] on the basis of which one may suppose a common place of manufacture. This type of object, made during the fourteenth century B.C., hints at an artistic community that shared forms and exchanged detachable parts, with itinerant craftsmen active in an area that stretched from the Levant (especially Ugarit) to the palaces of Egypt.

Here, the duck's body is carved from the same piece of wood as that of the swimmer, which certainly marks it as Egyptian. Nevertheless, the origin of the lidded boxes of wood in the form of ducks and gazelles found in Egypt has yet to be elucidated. Conceptually similar to ivory boxes of the "duck and duckling" type of Levantine manufacture (cat. no. 202 and fig. 107), they were often inlaid with ivory in zigzag patterns, like the pyxides with handles found in Egypt (made of wood) and at Ugarit (made of ivory). The place of discovery of the former could simply correspond to the context most favorable to the conservation of wood: Egyptian tombs.   GP-B

1. See also Louvre AO 14778; Gachet-Bizollon 2007.

201
DUCK-SHAPED VESSEL

Ivory (hippopotamus)
Height 7.6 cm (3 in.); length 14.5 cm (5¾ in.)
Minet el-Beidha
Late Bronze Age, 14th–13th century B.C.
Musée du Louvre, Paris, Département des Antiquités Orientales AO14779

Nearly thirty duck vessels and fragments were discovered at Late Bronze Age Ugarit. This example was found in its port at Minet el-Beidha, in Deposit 213, which possibly represented the remains of a rich tomb. Many such containers have been unearthed in the eastern Mediterranean, from Mycenae and Rhodes to inland Syria.

This vessel is made of hippopotamus ivory, specifically the lower canine.[1] One defect of the hippopotamus canine, the commissure or crack that occurs with age, is cleverly concealed along the ridge. Such sophistication in using this material suggests that the container was made by a Levantine craftsman, possibly working at Ugarit.

Duck vessels from the Levant derive from Egyptian prototypes. The model would have been a spoon in the shape of a duck or goose, made in boxwood, ivory, or alabaster, often propelled by a nude swimming girl (see cat. no. 200). Such spoons are typically thought to have been used for cosmetics, but no doubt had a symbolic meaning as well, associated in Egyptian imagery with annual gifts deposited by the river god of the Nile. In the Levant, the motif was adopted and transformed, the lower part of the vessel carved in the shape of a boat. There are several variants.[2] Ducklings may sit on the back of the mother duck (cat. no. 202), the swivel lid may be oval, as here, or in the shape of wings (fig. 106 and cat. no. 199); a fan tail may or may not be included. The lid on this vessel is bordered with holes that originally contained blue pigment, another allusion to water.   AC

1. Gachet-Bizollon 2007, no. 22.
2. See W. Adler 1996 and Gachet-Bizollon 2007.

202
DUCK-SHAPED VESSEL

Ivory (hippopotamus)
Length 25.1 cm (9⅞ in.)
Kamid el-Loz
Late Bronze Age, 14th–12th century B.C.
Direction Générale des Antiquités, Beirut, Lebanon 24410

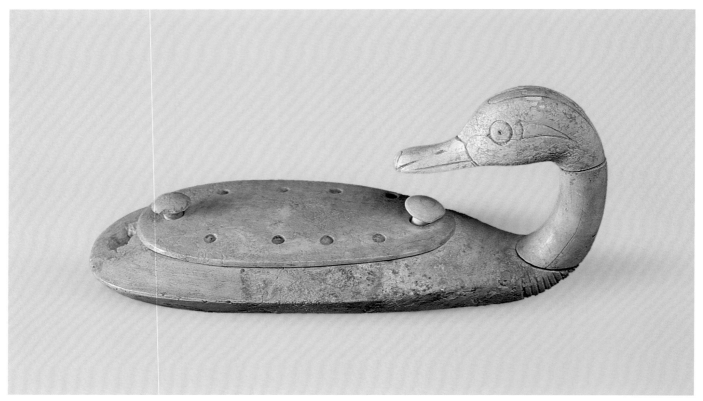

201

202

Figure 107. Facsimile of wall painting with duck-shaped vessel. Thebes, Tomb of Kenamun (TT 93). Dynasty 18, reign of Amenhotep II. The Metropolitan Museum of Art, New York, Rogers Fund, 1930 30.4.177

The dramatically curved head and neck of a duck serve as a handle for this cosmetic box. The duck is turned to face two ducklings placed on the lid, one made of ivory, the other identified as jade. The receptacle rests on a folded rectangular base carved with two rows of five dot-circles. Its lid was fixed with three mushroom-headed nails, two of which are missing. At one time a fourth nail was also fixed on the body. The duck is incised with three concentric circles at the base and upper part of the neck. The bird's eye is represented as three concentric circles with a hole in the middle.[1]

Carved from a hippopotamus tusk,[2] this remarkable box imitates Egyptian prototypes. Together with other alabaster and ivory artifacts, it was found in the "funerary deposit" inside the palace at Kamid el-Loz and shows the high quality of workmanship that Levantine ivory carvers attained in the Late Bronze Age, especially between the fourteenth and the twelfth century B.C. Such artifacts—illustrated in Egyptian wall paintings (fig. 107)—were widely distributed throughout the eastern Mediterranean, and examples have been found at Byblos, Sidon, and Ugarit and as far north as Alalakh; farther south they were found at Lachish, Megiddo, and Akko, as well as at sites on Cyprus and in the Aegean.

Ivory-working, with elephant instead of hippopotamus tusks, continued to flourish in the Iron Age. Phoenician ivory workshops were famous for the quality of their products, which were disseminated far from their land of origin through the wide trade network established during that era. SH

1. Hachmann in *Frühe Phöniker im Libanon* 1983, p. 119, no. 8; Miron 1990, no. 502, fig. 58, pl. 38:2.
2. Caubet and Poplin 1987, p. 281; Caubet 1998a, p. 89.

CULT, RITUAL, AND PERSONAL ADORNMENT

203

HANDLE IN THE FORM OF AN ACROBAT

Ivory
Height 4.1 cm (1⅝ in.); width 5 cm (2 in.)
Kamid el-Loz
Late Bronze Age, 14th–13th century B.C.
Direction Générale des Antiquités, Beirut,
Lebanon 24394

This exquisite ivory handle in the shape of an acrobat was carved from a hippopotamus tusk. Its body is curved and its legs rest on the figure's head, with the arms extending on either side of a hollow socket. The object to which the handle would have been attached was not preserved. The figure wears a short kilt, and the details of the body—hair, facial features, fingers, toes, and navel—are carved with great precision.

The handle was discovered in the "funerary deposit" of the Levantine palace at Kamid el-Loz together with other ivory objects, including figurines, deity masks, cosmetic containers, and game boxes with their gaming pieces. These finds not only provide insight into the daily life of the royal family,[1] but they also illustrate the mastery of Kamid el-Loz ivory carvers during this period.

Dance and acrobatics were popular in antiquity. In Egypt and Crete there is evidence of both ritual and secular dancing and acrobatic scenes (fig. 108, cat. no. 71). It is difficult, however, to interpret the significance of the Kamid el-Loz acrobat. Similar handles were also found at Byblos, Megiddo,[2] and on the Uluburun shipwreck (cat. no. 204).   SH

1. Hachmann in *Frühe Phöniker im Libanon* 1983, pp. 82–84, 114, no. 2.
2. Loud 1939, nos. 182–84, pls. 41, 42.

204

HANDLE IN THE FORM OF AN ACROBAT

Ivory
Height 3.7 cm (1½ in.); width 7.4 cm (2⅞ in.)
Uluburun shipwreck
Late Bronze Age, ca. 1300 B.C.
Bodrum Museum of Underwater
Archaeology, Turkey 34.6.98 (KW 5754)

This ivory object is in the form of a contorted human, with legs that bend backward at the knee so that the soles of the feet rest against the head. A solid cylindrical extension protrudes from the chest in place of outstretched arms.[1] The legs, buttocks, shoulders, and facial features are clearly defined, although the figure appears unfinished and coarse around the head and upper legs, perhaps in part from weathering caused by millennia underwater. The gender is difficult to ascertain, but the shorter hair and lack of breasts suggest a male or, less likely, an adolescent female. The protruding cylinder has a slightly narrower and rounder end to allow for insertion into another component, which does not survive. This may explain why the arms were not rendered along its sides, as they would have been concealed. The missing second piece may have been of a perishable material such as wood.[2] The figure was found just aft of amidships, suggesting that it was stored at the stern, where valuable personal and ritual objects were kept.

The carved ivory handle from Kamid el-Loz, also in the form of an acrobat (cat. no. 203), provides the only clear parallel

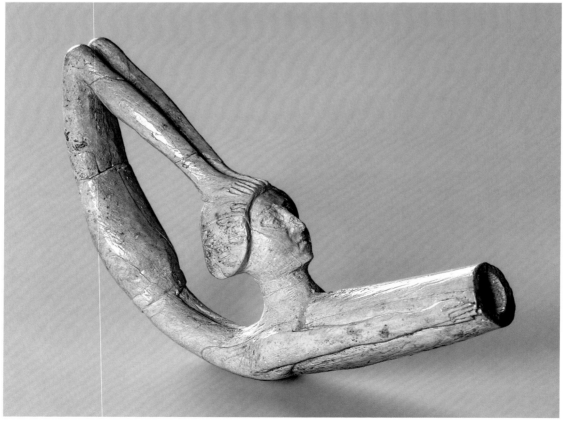

203

for the Uluburun piece.[3] Although remarkably similar in posture, the Kamid el-Loz acrobat, shown clothed in an Egyptian-style kilt, is more slender, more detailed, with elaborately rendered eyes, fingers, and toes, and more finely carved than the Uluburun piece. The cylindrical protrusion of the Kamid el-Loz example is hollowed out to form a shallow tube in order to receive the complementary component. Unlike the example from Uluburun, however, the figure's arms are carved in relief alongside the cylindrical tube, almost in a gesture of offering. The Uluburun handle's lack of similar details, such as the garment, arm positioning, and hollowed-out protrusion, as well as its bulkier and shorter body proportions and less graceful modeling, point to cruder craftsmanship.

Egyptian artists made little distinction between dancers and acrobats. Depicted in a relief in the Dynasty 18 Red Chapel at Karnak are two pairs of acrobatic dancers performing backbends, accompanied by a man playing a harp.[4] Dancers in similar backbend poses are shown on two later ostraca from Deir el-Medina (fig. 108).[5] In these representations, the acrobatic dancers wear small kilts or loincloths, probably for decoration and ease of movement rather than for modesty.[6] None of the acrobatic

Figure 108. Painted limestone ostracon with dancer, detail. Deir el-Medina. Dynasty 19. Fondazione Museo delle Antichità Egizie di Torino c. 7052

dancers display the exact pose of the Uluburun and Kamid el-Loz handles.

Several ivory handles in the shape of human figures from Byblos and Megiddo display the same general spirit in form and function, even though their outstretched bodies do not match the backbend of either the Uluburun or Kamid el-Loz acrobats. The Byblos handle, modeled as a female stretched out on her chest and grasping a

cylindrical projection,[7] represents a transition between the acrobatically posed figures of the Uluburun and Kamid el-Loz handles and four others from Megiddo. Nearly identical to one another, the Megiddo handles are carved in the form of human figures lying flat on their stomachs, heads upright, with their bodies supported by arms bent at the elbows. The surviving pair of hands on one example, shown as clenched fists, are vertically perforated, likely for the mounting of a spoon bowl, thus associating the Megiddo handles with the offering gesture of the Byblos, Kamid el-Loz, and Uluburun examples.[8]

While the latter two handles appear to be male figures, numerous iconographic representations associate such gestures of offering with females.[9] These spoons may be related to well-known Egyptian examples of nude females swimming and holding spoons of various forms, each outstretched in a gesture of offering (cat. no. 200).[10] If the female figures, such as that of the Byblos handle, whose gender is clearly indicated by her breasts, are represented nude, then figures wearing kilts, such as the Kamid el-Loz and Megiddo handles, perhaps represent males. The style and other rendered features of the Uluburun acrobat nevertheless suggest a male figure whose kilt simply was not indicated, a theory reinforced by the object's crudely worked, unfinished quality.   CP

1. Pulak 2005c, p. 606, fig. 131.
2. Boxwood was the wood of choice for nearly all of the finely carved objects recovered from

the Uluburun shipwreck, including an ovoid box lid, a circular base for a cylindrical container, writing boards, and many other fragments whose function cannot be determined. Had the component been of metal, it would have corroded and stained the ivory.

3. Miron 1990, p. 113, fig. 67, pl. 37.1; Hachmann in *Frühe Phöniker im Libanon* 1983, pp. 82–84, 114, fig. 2.
4. Peck 1978, p. 138, fig. 67; Vandersleyen 1975, no. 282a, b. The Red Chapel dates from the time of Hatshepsut.
5. One of these (fig. 108) is more naturally rendered than the second one (Vandersleyen 1975, pl. 333b; see also Goelet 1993, p. 23, fig. 1). A third is from the Ramesside period (Peck 1978, p. 138, fig. 68).
6. Goelet 1993, p. 28.
7. Dunand 1950, pl. 151:17241.
8. Loud 1939, p. 18, nos. 182–85, pls. 41:182, 42:183–85. The hands reach forward, and the legs stretch backward, terminating in flattened handles perforated vertically at the ends, perhaps for suspension from a cord. They have short hair, wear short kilts, and lack cylindrical protrusions from the upper chest. Although they have no breasts, they have been identified as females.
9. See, for example, much larger ivory spoons depicting outstretched females from Megiddo (Loud 1939, p. 18, nos. 177–79, pls. 40:177, 41:178, 42:179).
10. For the importance and symbolism of Egyptian spoons, see Kozloff 1992, pp. 331–39.

205a, b

205a, b
COSMETIC SPOON AND TUBE

a. Spoon
Ivory
Length 9.9 cm (3⅞ in.)
23.8.96 (KW 4246)

b. Tube
Bone
Length 8.8 cm (3½ in.); max. diameter
1.5 cm (⅝ in.)
24.8.96 (KW 4251)

Uluburun shipwreck
Late Bronze Age, ca. 1300 B.C.
Bodrum Museum of Underwater
Archaeology, Turkey

This ivory Egyptian-style spoon in the form of an extended arm was probably used for applying salve, unguents, or cosmetics.[1] The handle is carved in the shape of a clenched right fist—except for the straight thumb—perforated laterally

by a narrow hole. Two bands encircling the wrist represent bracelets. The forearm terminates just below the elbow, and the spoon continues as a straight, narrow cylindrical shaft, gently tapering to form the tiny, shallow spoon bowl. Two small wear marks at the junction of the arm and the spoon shaft suggest that a sleeve or case originally enclosed the spoon and part of the handle, fitting tightly over the widest point. A cord running through the hole of the clenched fist may have secured the spoon to its case or served as a lanyard to be worn around the neck.

Found in an area corresponding to the after half of the ship, the spoon probably belonged to one of the merchants aboard. An undecorated, thin-walled, bone tube found next to the spoon, and of the appropriate length and diameter, may have served as its case.[2] It was cut flat at either end, one of which was probably capped with a wood plug, now lost, while the other

accommodated the spoon. It may have been a homemade replacement for the original tube, possibly also of ivory or finely carved wood.

Bronze Age cosmetic vessels, mostly in the form of kohl tubes and commonly found in Egypt,[3] were probably introduced there from the Near East during the time of Thutmose III.[4] Kohl applicators generally took the form of long rods tapering to a blunt tip to facilitate application,[5] making it unlikely that the Uluburun spoon was used for kohl. Nor was it likely to have been used as an ear spoon, which required a smooth, uniformly tapering shaft. Two bronze handles found at Tell Abu Hawam[6] are of slightly larger proportions, but they closely approximate the Uluburun spoon's handle in both design and construction,[7] although the bowl ends do not survive. Several pins from Mesopotamian sites, with heads in the form of clenched fists, are similar to the fist of the Uluburun spoon, although none are pierced (see cat. no. 206).

The use of armlike handles as spoons was quite ancient in Egypt. Two small ivory spoons from Dynasty 3 were modeled as outstretched right arms,[8] each grasping a spoon by its handle; one is shown with a pair of bracelets. On two spoons from the end of Dynasty 6, the hand is positioned in reverse, at the end of the handle intended to be grasped by the user.[9]

Early versions are seen in Dynasty 3 and four depictions of offering tables with votive gifts placed on them. Above the table is a list of offerings, foremost among which is "washing," represented by an outstretched arm presenting water from a jar. A mid–Dynasty 5 offering table labeled with the hieroglyph for "offering" features an outstretched arm hieroglyph, shown with a pair of bracelets and holding a pot of water, providing the closest known link to Egyptian censers that incorporate a hand holding a plain incense bowl.[10] Perhaps the feature of the clenched fist grasping a bowl, common to Uluburun and Tell Abu Hawam handles, echoes the offering concept. If so, the spoons could have been used in personal rituals.   CP

1. Pulak 1997, p. 224; Pulak 1998, p. 205.
2. Additional color photographs of the spoon and bone tube are in Pulak 2005c, p. 606, figs. 129, 130, and Pulak 1995, p. 56, fig. 29.
3. Petrie 1974, pp. 27–28, pl. XXII for bone, wood, and reed tubes from Egypt.

4. Ibid., p. 28.
5. See ibid., p. 28, pl. XXII for kohl applicators found in Egypt.
6. Hamilton 1935, p. 59, nos. 367, 368.
7. The longer of the two handles has a swelling two-thirds of the way down, probably serving as the articulation between the arm and shaft sections; the second appears to have a distinct carination between the arm and shaft, although it is much closer to the clenched fist than in either the first handle or the Uluburun spoon. The fists of both Tell Abu Hawam handles are pierced through, and both are shown with a single bracelet.
8. H. Fischer 1963, p. 32, fig. 8:a, b.
9. Ibid., p. 32, fig. 8:d, e, p. 33.
10. Ibid., pp. 30–31.

206

FIST-SHAPED PIN

Ivory
Length 7.6 cm (3 in.)
Ashur, Tomb 45
Middle Assyrian, 14th–13th century B.C.
Staatliche Museen zu Berlin,
Vorderasiatisches Museum VA Ass1102

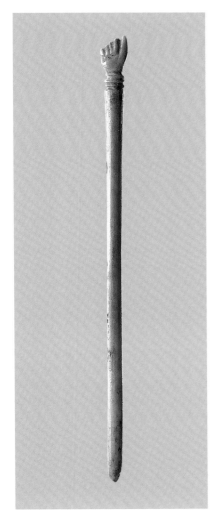

206

This delicately carved pin in the form of a fist exemplifies the Middle Assyrian affinity for naturally rendered forms. The fist was carved with great precision and attention to anatomical detail, each knuckle clearly defined both front and back. Even the impression of the fingertips in the fleshy palm of the hand is marked.

The pin was discovered above the head of a skeleton in Tomb 45 at Ashur, prompting the excavator, Walter Andrae, to consider it a hairpin or headdress pin, possibly for a headband found in the same tomb.[1] Alternatively, it may have been used as a pin for clothing. Judging from the grave goods found alongside the skeleton, recent studies have concluded that it was female.[2]

A silver pin in the shape of a clenched fist from an Early Dynastic grave in the Royal Cemetery at Ur is very close in appearance if not in date of manufacture to the Ashur pin,[3] indicating that the use of fist imagery on objects of personal adornment had a long tradition. A fist pin made of bone, less carefully rendered, was excavated in a Mitanni level at Nuzi in northern Mesopotamia and provides a chronologically more appropriate parallel.[4] However, it is the cosmetic spoon of ivory recovered from the Uluburun shipwreck (cat. no. 205) that offers the closest parallel in all respects, save for the fact that it was not found in a burial context.

The meaning of the fist itself is unclear. Andrae suggested that it might be related to the modern Near Eastern gesture of the clenched fist, which is associated with procreation.[5] The fist has also been associated with the manifestation of physical strength,[6] and with the Egyptian hieroglyph for "offering" (see cat. no. 205).

KB

1. Haller 1954, pp. 132–33, pl. 30:h; see also Klein 1992, pl. 169:4.
2. Wartke in *Assyrian Origins* 1995, p. 82.
3. Woolley 1934, pls. 189, 231.
4. Starr 1937–39, vol. 2, pl. 127:z.
5. Haller 1954, p. 132; see also Musche 1988, pl. LVII, for same in the Parthian period.
6. Ebeling 1932, p. 121 (s.v. "Apotropaeen").

207

HORN

Ivory (hippopotamus)
Length 24.3 cm (9⅝ in.); max. diameter
4.2 cm (1⅝ in.)
Uluburun shipwreck
Late Bronze Age, ca. 1300 B.C.
Bodrum Museum of Underwater
Archaeology, Turkey 66.7.95
(KW 3526)

This horn was fashioned from a single hippopotamus lower incisor. The exterior of the incisor is carved to represent the natural spiraling of an animal's horn—probably that of a ram[1]—with its pulp cavity forming the horn's hollow bell. A hole, approximately 0.8 centimeters in diameter, was drilled from the tip of the pulp cavity along the full length of the incisor. The spiraling tapers toward the distal end, terminating in a short, narrow, cylindrical shank with a protruding ring or band. A second, similar ring carved on the distal tip of the incisor, about 5 centimeters below the first ring, forms a mouthpiece. The incisor's full length was used to shape the horn, with only minimal trimming at the extremities in order to provide a smooth edge for the bell and flat mouthpiece. A guilloche pattern encircles the edge of the bell. The horn, discovered wedged between bedrock and copper ingots stowed just forward of amidships, was stained light blue from the corroding copper.

Even though the Uluburun ivory horn is carved in the likeness of a natural horn, it does not appear to be long or hollow enough to have produced even the limited range of harmonics one would expect of a sounding horn (like those traditionally used by shepherds). Its presence on board might suggest that it was part of the ship's permanent equipment and was used for signaling purposes, yet a real animal horn would have been more durable and practical for shipboard use and would have performed better than one emulated in ivory.

Because ivory is an exotic material, the Uluburun horn was likely a valued ritual object. It may represent a Canaanite precursor to the shofar, a ceremonial instrument usually made of a ram's horn,[2] and may have had a similar function. Although the modern use of the shofar is much more celebratory,[3] an important early use

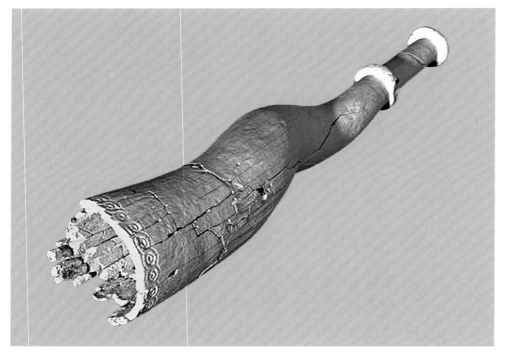

207

9. Caubet 1996, p. 14.
10. Hamilton 1935, p. 61, no. 376, pl. 32:376.
11. Bass 1986, pp. 288–90, ill. 28.
12. Caubet 1996, p. 10; Koitabashi 1992; this particular type of cymbals occur only as pairs (Wulstan 1973, p. 44).

208a, b
Vessels

Faience
a. Ram-headed vessels
Length 20.1 cm (8 in.); diameter 7.9 cm
(3⅛ in.)
16.5.87 (KW 707)

b. Female-headed vessel
Height 10.1 cm (4 in.); diameter 7.6 cm (3 in.)
2006/4/31A (KW 5919)

Uluburun shipwreck
Late Bronze Age, ca. 1300 B.C.
Bodrum Museum of Underwater
Archaeology, Turkey

Four ram-headed faience cups and one female-headed example were excavated from the Uluburun ship. (see p. 342)[1] Found in the after half of the ship, they were stored at the stern, along with the other fragile and valuable objects aboard, both of commercial and personal nature.

This nearly complete ram-headed cup is the only one to survive intact. The other, fragmentary ram-headed cups appear to have been of the same general size and shape and may have been formed in a common mold (fig. 109). They are rendered in a detailed and naturalistic manner, the only stylized feature being the slightly bulging, circular eyes. For practical reasons, certain features, such as incised growth rings on the horns and details of the eyes, mouth, and nostrils, were probably worked in afterward. The protruding tips of the relief-modeled, close-adhering horns and the small ears also must have been added after the cup was formed. The original glazing has long disappeared, but a vestigial patch in the folds of one eye and the overall hue of the intact cup suggest that it was yellow in color.[2] A crack that extends from the rim of the cup approximately halfway down to the arc of the left horn probably occurred during drying or firing. It was repaired in antiquity with a white pastelike filling, and then refired without glazing.

appears to have been as a signaling instrument during wartime;[4] it was also sounded to evoke divine compassion and protect believers, including sailors, from various misfortunes or perils—blown during times of crisis, such as a storm.[5]

A fragmentary object carved from a hippopotamus incisor in a spiraling shape, but missing both ends, was found at Ugarit and previously published as the twisted leg of a statue.[6] Based on the discovery of the Uluburun ivory horn, however, the object has now been correctly reidentified.[7] The bell of the Ugarit horn is also embellished with a guilloche design, but there applied as three separate vertical bands rather than a single one like that encircling the bell of the Uluburun horn.[8] That the horn was discovered in a pit in the Temple of Dagan[9] also hints at its ceremonial use.

Another incomplete object similar to the Uluburun example, presumably also carved from a hippopotamus incisor in the likeness of a twisted animal horn, comes from Tell Abu Hawam, where it was originally identified as an ivory handle.[10] Like the Uluburun horn, the Tell Abu Hawam piece is also decorated around its bell, this time with a band consisting of three closely spaced parallel, incised lines. Because the distal extremity is missing, it is not known whether it carried a mouthpiece similar to that of the Uluburun horn.

It seems likely that the Uluburun horn was not a simple signaling device but an instrument employed in rituals that may have taken place before, during, and after the completion of a journey. Moreover, a pair of small bronze cymbals, or crotals,[11] found at the stern of the Uluburun ship may have also been used during shipboard rituals. Similar bronze cymbals have been found at a number of Levantine sites and on Cyprus. Several pairs from Ugarit were identified as musical instruments that played an important part in the local religion, especially in rites celebrating Baal.[12]

CP

1. Pulak 1998, p. 205, fig. 18; Pulak 1997, p. 245, fig. 14.
2. The word "shofar," generally meaning "ram's horn" but specifically "as an instrument," originated from the Akkadian word *sapparu*, meaning "wild sheep" or "goat." A shofar was not provided with holes, which would have rendered it "invalid" (Wulstan 1973, pp. 21, 29, 41).
3. Werblowsky and Wigoder 1966, p. 358.
4. It is not clear if the shofar was originally used for ritual or for warfare (Wulstan 1973, pp. 31, 41).
5. This use was recorded in the Tosephta, a collection of statements and traditions closely related to the Mishna and compiled about A.D. 200 (Patai 1998, pp. 69, 93).
6. Caubet and Poplin 1987, p. 302, no. AO 14797; Gachet 1992, p. 72.
7. Caubet 1996, pp. 14–15, 30, fig. 10; Gachet-Bizollon 2007, pp. 186–87, fig. 66, p. 395, pl. 45:388.
8. Gachet-Bizollon 2007, p. 187. The guilloche design is also found on bone inlays from Uluburun and on ivories at Samaria (Crowfoot and Crowfoot 1938, p. 41, fig. 12).

The female-headed cup originally had a flat-footed base attached to the neck and, unlike the ram-headed cups, was free-standing. The lower half and base are missing. The head made up the body of the cup, and a tall, inverted conical crown positioned on heavy plaits of hair formed the upper portion and rim. Fine details were incised after the cup was formed. A faint yellowish hue on some of the crown fragments is the only surviving indication of that portion of the cup's color. The overall artistic style of production and similarities in the rendering of the rams' horns and female's hair strongly suggest the same production center or workshop for the Uluburun cups.

Zoomorphic and anthropomorphic cups were common in the Near East during the second and first millennia B.C. (see cat. nos. 209–11).[3] Because of their stylistic similarities, it has been suggested that they could have been made in a single center,[4] either in Cyprus,[5] Syria,[6] or northern Mesopotamia.[7] It is more likely, however, that they came from several local production centers in the Levant.[8] Made of metal, faience, and ceramic, animal-headed and female-headed cups constitute an important aspect of Syro-Canaanite art and cultic practice.

The Uluburun cups are paralleled in examples at Enkomi (cat. nos. 209, 210)[9] and Tell Abu Hawam.[10] Additional parallels for the female-headed cup are found at Ugarit (cat. no. 211),[11] Ashur,[12] and possibly Rhodes,[13] and, for the ram-headed cup, at Kition.[14] An approximately contemporaneous counterpart of the ram-headed cups, albeit in bronze, displaying similar V-shaped nostrils, was found at Qatna.[15] The closest matches to the Uluburun cups, in overall shape and style, are from Tell Abu Hawam.[16]

Animal-headed cups, or *bibru*, were used as gifts in diplomatic exchanges among Late Bronze Age courts.[17] Thus, the cups on board could indicate that the ship's cargo was not merely commercial but also, at least partially, intended for "gift exchange." Such gifts, however, were generally of silver or gold,[18] and animal-headed cups were found for the most part in temple and tomb contexts. Their ritual function appears to be demonstrated by a clay cup from Ugarit carrying a dedicatory inscription to the Canaanite god Reshef.[19]

Further, many ram-headed cups dating to the fourteenth and thirteenth centuries B.C. have been found together with female-headed cups,[20] suggesting that the two cup types were used together for ritual purposes.[21] In the temple at Tell Abu Hawam, they were found with a gilded-bronze figure of an enthroned male deity with the left hand clenched and the right hand open, palm downward.[22] This gesture is similar to that of the partially gilded female deity (cat. no. 212) found, like the Uluburun cups, near the stern of the ship.[23] That the Uluburun finds appear to replicate the temple context at Tell Abu Hawam in form and proximity suggests a similar ritualistic function for them. Consequently, the presence of four ram-headed cups, concurrent with the presumed number of merchants on board, supports the possibility that the cups and statuette were used in shipboard rituals intended to ensure a safe and productive voyage.   CP

1. Bass 1986, pp. 290–91, pl. 17:5, 6; Pulak 1988, p. 32, fig. 40; Bass et al. 1989, p. 8, fig. 12; Pulak 1997, p. 244.
2. Whether the cups were originally polychrome, with certain features highlighted by additional glaze or underglaze colors, cannot be determined.
3. Tuchelt 1962, pp. 40–60.
4. Frankfort 1970, pp. 274–76.
5. L. Åström 1972, p. 595.
6. Culican 1971, pp. 86–89, nn. 19–22.
7. Tuchelt 1962, pp. 55ff.
8. Zevulun 1987, p. 104.
9. Murray, Smith, and Walters 1970, p. 33, fig. 61.1212, pl. III.
10. Hamilton 1935, p. 65, nos. 425–29, pls. XXVII:427, 429, XXX. Of the distinct three-color glazing scheme used on the Tell Abu Hawam cup—golden yellow for details, pale pinkish white for the face, and yellowish white for the crown and hair—the last color is in keeping with that suggested for the Uluburun cup's crown.
11. Schaeffer 1933, p. 105, pl. XI, p. 106, pl. XII; Caubet and Pierrat-Bonnefois 2005, pp. 49–50, and figs. 98, 99.
12. Hall 1928, pp. 64–74; Andrae 1935, pp. 78–80 ("Funde aus dem Tukulti-Ninurta-Bau"), fig. 62; Bossert 1951, pp. 24, 102, no. 343.
13. Frankfort 1955, p. 161, cites an unverified reference to a female-headed faience goblet from Rhodes.
14. Peltenburg 1985, pp. 258–59, pls. X:1131, XXXIX:1131.
15. Du Mesnil du Buisson 1928, p. 19, pl. XVI:1. Although this cup's head is perpendicular to its neck, unlike the straight-necked cups under consideration, it is nevertheless a representative of this category of vessels, and is the only published example in metal.
16. The preserved ram's eye of fragment 429 from Tell Abu Hawam closely approximates

those of the Uluburun ram-headed cups; the Uluburun female-headed cup and cup 425 are so similar, and skillfully modeled, that both may be products of the same craftsman or workshop. See Hamilton 1935, p. 65, no. 425, pls. XXVIII:427, 429, XXVII:429, XXX.
17. An Amarna Letter refers to silver stag and ram vessels sent by the Hittite king Suppiluliuma I to the Egyptian pharaoh (EA 41:39–43; Moran 1992, p. 114); and earlier texts from Mari mention vessels in the form of animals, of which at least seven are animal-headed cups, but none of them rams (Limet 1986, p. 275, n. 82); Zevulun 1987, p. 100; Peltenburg 1991, pp. 168, 170.
18. See Moran 1992, p. 114; for a bronze example from Qatna, see note 15 above. See also Zevulun 1987, pp. 100–101.
19. Zevulun 1987, p. 100.
20. Pulak 1997, p. 244.
21. Zevulun 1987, pp. 92–93, 100, 102.
22. Hamilton 1935, p. 60, no. 370, pl. XV:2. The gold foil has largely fallen off, but the face, neck, back of left upper arm, and feet are still covered.
23. The clenched and open hands of the Uluburun statuette appear in reverse.

209

Ram-Headed Vessel

Faience
Height 11.3 cm (4½ in.)
Enkomi, Tomb 86
Late Bronze Age, 14th–13th century B.C.
The Trustees of the British Museum, London
1897.4-1.1212

210

Female-Headed Vessel

Faience
Height 15.7 cm (6¼ in.)
Enkomi, Tomb 19
Late Bronze Age, 14th–13th century B.C.
The Trustees of the British Museum, London
1897.4-1.875

The vessel in the form of a ram's head from Enkomi, on Cyprus, is endowed with magnificent curling horns. The face is naturalistically rendered, with folds above the eyes and indications of curly fleece. Yellow and white color is preserved on the face and on a thick yellow band near the rim. Like the head of the goddess, the vessel was made in a mold, with incised details added.[1]

208a

Figure 109.
Fragmentary
ceramic ram-
headed vessels.
Uluburun ship-
wreck. Bodrum
Museum of
Underwater
Archaeology
2006/4/4A,
(KW 565),
2006/4/5A
(KW 42)

208b

209

210

211

343

Presumably used as a drinking cup, the vessel has similarities with the animal-headed rhyton, or ritual sprinkler, that was common in the Aegean world (see cat. no. 170). The mouth of the rhyton, however, was always pierced to allow liquid to pass through; here, the mouth is not pierced, which suggests that it was used for drinking.

Tomb 86 at Enkomi was a chamber tomb, disturbed when found but nonetheless rich in content. Other finds included gold and silver jewelry, faience and carnelian beads, a stamp seal, and pottery, including imports from the Aegean and Egypt.

The goblet in the form of a female head is probably the representation of a goddess. She wears a tall cylindrical headdress with a spray-shaped ornament in front; her hair is visible beneath, swept back and caught up in a net. Elaborate ornaments adorn the top of her ears, and a necklace fits closely around her neck. While the eyes are prominent, the facial features were likely even stronger when the original color was fresh.

The goblet was made in a mold, with the details then incised in the surface. The white glaze of the face, ears, and neck is well preserved but other colors have largely disappeared. The vessel may originally have been yellow or brown, with the facial features painted in brown glaze. Traces of blue survive on the necklace. The semicircular fittings with drilled holes on the inside of the rim were perhaps designed for the attachment of another element or a lid, which has not survived.[2]

Tomb 19 at Enkomi was seemingly disturbed. It was nonetheless a rich chamber tomb that had been used for successive burials throughout the Late Cypriot period. Finds included goldwork and silver jewelry, local and imported pottery, ivories, and a lapis lazuli cushion-shaped seal. A set of hematite weights is also associated with this tomb, perhaps the property of a wealthy artisan or trader, providing a possible context for the arrival of this object at Enkomi.

Polychrome glazed objects may owe something to the Minoan Cretan elaboration of a craft tradition originally invented in Egypt. By the Late Bronze Age, head vessels in the form of females and animals seem to have been a specialty of Syrian workshops, where complex shapes rather than colorful effects were most highly desired. It is not certain whether such pieces were always imported, or whether some were made on Cyprus itself.   JLF

1. For further reference, see Murray, Smith, and Walters 1900, pp. 22–23, 33, fig. 61:1212, pl. III; Courtois, Lagarce, and Lagarce 1986, pp. 155–56, pl. XXVII:7, 10; and Peltenburg 1991, esp. p. 165.
2. For further reference, see Murray, Smith, and Walters 1900, pp. 22–23, 33, pl. III; Peltenburg 1972; Courtois, Lagarce, and Lagarce 1986, pp. 152–55, pl. XXVII:7; and Peltenburg 1991, esp. p. 165.

211
FEMALE-HEADED VESSEL

Faience
Height 12.9 cm (5⅛ in.)
Minet el-Beidha, Tomb VI
Late Bronze Age, 14th–13th century B.C.
Musée du Louvre, Paris, Département des Antiquités Orientales AO15732

Faience face vessels count among the most charming artistic creations of the Late Bronze Age. These high-footed conical cups present a female head molded in relief. More rarely, as in this example, two heads are joined back to back.[1] One example from Ugarit preserves their main characteristics: thick black contours of the eyes and brows under an elaborate braided coiffure and a hooked lock falling in the middle of the forehead, its black color contrasting with the pale skin. Two more locks are painted on the cheeks.[2]

The chemical composition of the glazes points to production by a Levantine workshop. The decorative style, using broad bands of yellow and light green, with a transparent glaze over the light color or the underlying siliceous paste, is also typically Levantine.

Other such vessels have been found over a wide geographic area, from Cyprus (Enkomi) to Ashur and the southern Levant (Tell Abu Hawam). The vessel from the Uluburun shipwreck (cat. no. 208b) is evidence for the overseas trade in these artifacts. Several come from Ugarit, such as this one from a rich tomb at the harbor of Minet el-Beidha. Double-headed vases from southwestern Iran, though related to this group, are technically different.

The female face motif was frequently used to represent the divine powers of love and fecundity. It appears on a number of artifacts used by women, such as gold and faience pendants. The emphasis on black hair and locks—the equivalent of the up-turned locks on females depicted on ivory reliefs from Ugarit (see cat. no. 261) and Mycenae—was an expression of seduction and may be compared with images on a number of Minoan wall paintings from Crete and Thera.[3] A similar concept is represented in Egypt by the thick, curly wig worn by the goddess Hathor. In the Levant, artifacts decorated with Hathor masks combine the mask motif with luxuriant hair.

The purpose of these face vessels is still a matter of speculation. They were frequently found in conjunction with other faience vessels in the shape of heads of animals—horse (Enkomi), ram (Enkomi, Uluburun), or lion (Hazor)—animals more often associated with males. They were part of the same assemblage as the flower bowls (see cat. nos. 276–277). Those from Ugarit are similar in style and chemical composition. Unlike the face vessels and flower bowls, the animal-headed cups, like rhyta, were not made to stand and were probably used in libation rituals. It is possible that different categories of faience vessels were intended for different genders, to be used in complex symbolic ceremonies.   AC

1. See Matoïan in Caubet 2007, no. 206.
2. Caubet and Pierrat-Bonnefois 2005, p. 149, fig. 98.
3. Immerwahr 1990, pl. 21 (West House, Akrotiri); pl. 43 ("dancing lady," Queen's Megaron, Knossos).

212

NUDE FEMALE FIGURE

Bronze, gold
Height 16.4 cm (6½ in.); max. width 6.1 cm
(2⅜ in.)
Uluburun shipwreck
Late Bronze Age, ca. 1300 B.C.
Bodrum Museum of Underwater
Archaeology, Turkey 52.7.95
(KW 3680)

This bronze figure of a youthful nude female in frontal pose may have been one of the most precious objects on board the Uluburun ship.[1] The slender figure, with outstretched arms bent at the elbow, a clenched right fist and an open left hand with the palm facing down, small breasts, and a distinctive pubic triangle, was cast by the lost-wax method. The head, face, hair, hands, ankles, feet, parts of the arms, and a collar around the neck are all covered in sheet gold.[2] An irregular pattern formed by the gold surviving on the left upper arm suggests that the statuette was originally clad mostly or entirely in gold. On the other hand, the uniform edges of the gold foil covering the bare feet and collar may indicate that the rest of the body was clad in some other material, such as silver,[3] or even dressed up as part of a ritual activity.[4] The figure's hair is arranged in shoulder-length twisted plaits on either side of the face, with a central braided lock that terminates in a loop halfway down the back and is perforated with a hole at the center. The head is adorned with a simple, narrow headband. The tenon protruding from under the feet would have affixed the figure to a base, now lost, probably of wood.

Although the type is unique, the style, craftsmanship, and theme are typically Canaanite and can be compared with other goddess figures from the Levant.[5] Several parallel figures (see fig. 110) and a gold plaque from Lachish display similar hairstyles.[6]

While the Uluburun figure wears only a simple headband and no crown, she is adorned with a broad multi-strand collar worked on the gold foil covering her upper shoulders. Such multi-strand collars of beads and amulets in precious materials are depicted in Egyptian art, usually worn with cuff bracelets and armlets on deities as well as on rulers and nobles.[7] Solid and plated gold figures in the likenesses of royal wives and daughters are mentioned

212

212, back

Figure 110. Ivory figure. Megiddo, Palace Treasury. Late Bronze Age. The Oriental Institute Museum, University of Chicago
OIM A 22257

in the Amarna Letters as Egyptian gifts to Kassite and Mitanni rulers,[8] but it would be unlikely for a noblewoman to have been represented in the nude.[9]

The archaeological contexts in which most such anthropomorphic figures have been found suggest that they were votive offerings placed in temples and sanctuaries.[10] That the Uluburun figure also represents a deity is suggested by the peaceful gesture of the hands.[11] In the seated and standing male and female deity figures, the extended or raised open hand is associated with the act of blessing, an attitude recognized as a gesture of peace through all ages and across cultures.[12] In these figures the clenched right hands are often pierced, suggesting that they originally held a shafted device such as a scepter, symbolizing divine power.[13] Although the clenched fist of the Uluburun figure is bare, it is not known whether it is perforated to hold a shaft because of the crumpled gold covering.

Although divine images are abundant, it may not be possible to ascertain their specific identities because of the near absence of named representations.[14] While the identity of the Uluburun figure and the message it carried must have been known to the ancients, it continues to elude us today.[15]

A gold-clad bronze figure of an enthroned male deity with the same hand gesture, but in reverse form to that of the Uluburun female, was found in a temple at Tell Abu Hawam, along with faience ram-headed and female-headed cups, both types also represented on the Uluburun ship (cat. no. 208a, b). Therefore, it is likely that the female figure, the faience cups, and other objects, such as an ivory horn (cat. no. 207), were brought on board to ensure a safe and productive passage. The presence of images of deities on seafaring vessels is vividly described in the early eleventh-century B.C. story of the priest Wenamun, who sails to Byblos to procure lumber for the bark of Amun-Re. Wenamun's remarkable tale involves diplomacy, sailing, shipbuilding, hazards of navigation, theft, and attempted murder. During the ordeal, Wenamun carries a small figure of Amun-Re, of great personal value to him, which he hides while aboard ship.[16]

Although the Uluburun figure was located on the seabed in an area outside the limits of the ship's hull, near the forward half of the ship, its trajectory indicates that before rolling down the slope, when the ship broke apart, it had been placed at the stern.[17] Most likely, it was brought on board to guard against the very fate that befell the ship, its crew, and its passengers.

.   CP

1. Pulak 1997, p. 246, fig. 15; Pulak 1998, p. 207, fig. 20; Pulak 2001, pp. 22–28.
2. Judging from a New Kingdom text in which Re is described as having "bones being of silver, his flesh gold, his hair true lapis lazuli," the use of specific ritually charged materials may have been deliberate (Lichtheim 1976, p. 198).
3. Many such figures are partly or fully covered in gold but some in silver; see, for example, Seeden 1980, p. 34, nos. 56, 56A, 59, 105, 108. An unpublished bronze figure from Ugarit, also modeled nude, is completely sheathed in silver (Ella Dardaillon, personal communication).
4. Linen-swathed painted wood images, some also with gilded faces and feet, were found in the Tomb of Tutankhamun (Allen and Allen 2006, p. 49, fig. 37, p. 61, fig. 49, pp. 72–73, figs. 61, 62). For a discussion of garments and cults in later Mesopotamia, see Zawadzki 2006, pp. 153–207 (chap. 7).
5. See Negbi 1976, pp. 86–95, and Seeden 1982, pp. 117–19. All of these figures have the same general hand gestures of the Uluburun figure: an extended arm with an open hand, and a clenched fist usually, but not always, extended outward.
6. Clamer 1980, p. 153, fig. 1, pp. 155, 157. For a close parallel to the coiffure of the Uluburun figure, see Negbi 1976, no. 1563 on pp. 70, 73, 181, pl. 42.
7. Patch in *Hatshepsut* 2005, pp. 198–99. A collar-type necklace is seen on a nude Syrian figure (Negbi 1976, pp. 86–87, no. 1632, fig. 99).
8. Figures of royal family members are mentioned in EA 14 (Moran 1992, pp. 28, 29); EA 24 (Moran 1992, p. 68); EA 27 (Moran 1992, p. 87), but other figures were also given as gifts, some of silver and stone (see, for example, EA 14, Moran 1992, pp. 28, 33).
9. Goelet 1993, p. 21.
10. Seeden 1982, pp. 119–20; Seeden 1980, pp. 95–96; Negbi 1976, pp. 2, 141–42.
11. The gesture of the clenched left hand and the open right hand, usually shown angled, with the palm facing out but also facing down, as in the Uluburun example, is relatively common in Levantine figures; see examples in Seeden 1982, p. 116, figs. 20, 23–25, and Schaeffer 1966b, pp. 6, 7, figs. 2, 3, pls. II, III. However, the positions of the hands on the Uluburun figure are in reverse, like those of a seated male deity from Qatna (see cat. no. 22).
12. Seeden 1982, p. 119. A large late thirteenth-century B.C. bronze male cult statue wearing a horned helmet was found in the Sanctuary of the Horned God at Enkomi. The statue is shown with the right hand open, palm facing down, in a gesture of blessing, and the left hand clenched into a fist and bent toward the chest (Karageorghis 2002, p. 97, fig. 196,

p. 98). For a general discussion of the identification of this god, see Hadjioannou 1971, pp. 33–42, and Karageorghis 1998, pp. 30–33.
13. A standard of embossed sheet gold with a four-pointed star is preserved in the clenched left hand of a gold-covered seated male figure from Megiddo (Negbi 1976, p. 50, no. 1453, p. 51, fig. 59.1453, p. 172, no. 1453, pl. 33.1453).
14. Cornelius 2004, p. 5.
15. Brody (1998, p. 68) suggests that the figure represents Asherah, since she is the only Late Bronze Age goddess who protected Canaanite sailors. Cornelius (2004, p. 100), however, argues that the image of Asherah is that of a more senior female, which the Uluburun female does not appear to represent.
16. Wenamun refers to the figure several times, and twice calls it "Amun-of-the-road" (Goedicke 1975, pp. 45, 110).
17. The tradition of housing representations of guardian deities on board ships in Roman times is demonstrated by a reference to an image of Libyan Amun placed at the stern of a Punic war galley (Silius Italicus *Punica*, 16.436–40, 458–61; also cited in Brody 1998, p. 68), and a stele from Carthage that depicts a small shrine housing a figure placed at the stern of a vessel, aft of the quarter rudders (Brody 1998, pp. 71, 135, fig. 19, p. 164, fig. 69).

213

PENDANT WITH NUDE FEMALE

Gold
Height 9.1 cm (3⅝ in.); width 4.7 cm (1⅞ in.);
max. thickness 0.9 cm (⅜ in.)
Uluburun shipwreck
Late Bronze Age, ca. 1300 B.C.
Bodrum Museum of Underwater
Archaeology, Turkey 1.5.87
(KW 703)

Found on the Uluburun ship were pendants of well-known Syro-Canaanite types and styles. One of the most impressive, made of a single sheet of gold, depicts a nude female.[1] Its wide, ribbed bail or suspension loop, typical of Syro-Canaanite jewelry, was formed from an extension of the pendant that was folded over the edges twice for reinforcement and then rolled forward and backward on itself. The pendant is roughly triangular, or piriform, tapering toward the bottom, with rounded corners and edges folded over from the front to the back and crimped. The central nude female is worked in repoussé, with certain details incised on the obverse. The figure appears as a mature female with a rounded belly, full breasts, and a pubic triangle, depicted by dots. Her well-defined feet are oriented toward her right, unusual for pendants of this design, which usually show the feet facing left or forward.[2] Her arms are bent at the elbow, and in either hand she clutches an upright horned gazelle, forming an addorsed symmetrical composition. She wears a cylindrical crown delineated by a pair of parallel horizontal lines at the base and a single one at the top, with paired vertical striations between rectangular spaces (see also fig. 110).[3] The hair or wig under the crown hangs down as five twisted locks on either side of her face, partly covering her shoulders; her ears protrude from between the locks. Three horizontal bands below the chin represent strands of a beaded collar or choker.[4] She wears four bracelets on each wrist and a pair of anklets. The pendant was found at the stern of the ship with most of the other valuable objects. Its weight corresponds to one shekel (9.46 g).

The Uluburun figure recalls the nude goddess depicted on a group of Egyptian votive stelae, shown frontally standing on the back of a lion, and wearing a Hathor wig with spiraling curls and usually a Hathor headdress. Her outstretched arms clutch lotus flowers in one hand and snakes in the other. The figure is identified by the accompanying hieroglyphs as "*kdsh/kdsht*, the lady of heaven."[5] She resembles images on pendants of sheet gold, bronze, faience, and glass, as well as on terracotta plaques found from Syro-Cilicia to the southern Levant.[6] Unlike their Egyptian counterparts, however, these figures are usually shown clutching only lotuses or long-stemmed flowers (or papyrus), and only a few of them stand on lions.[7] They undoubtedly represent one or more goddesses, but none are found with identifying texts. The overlapping attributes and functions of three major goddesses—Asherah, Anat, and Astarte—among others, appear to have caused frequent confusion even in antiquity, making their identification on plaques and other objects uncertain.

The image of a female holding a horned animal in each hand—limited to the Uluburun pendant and three others from Ugarit[8]—is usually connected with the Mistress of Animals motif. Generally associated with Astarte,[9] she is sometimes also identified with Asherah, who is often shown with lions. Even among this group, the Uluburun goddess is unique in that she wears a crown instead of a Hathor headdress. Of the five known gold pendants depicting a full-length standing female deity, the one closest to the Uluburun figure in shape and overall design is from Minet el-Beidha (cat. no. 214).[10] Based on Ugaritic texts, she may represent Astarte and Shapash.[11] It has also been suggested that such imagery may have originated to the north, where the Hurrian goddess Shaushga represents another variant of Ishtar as a fertility deity.[12] Perhaps the piriform shape of the pendants evokes a stylized pubic triangle and, therefore, symbolizes fertility and fecundity.

Although the Uluburun pendant is highly wearable, it may have been kept with the rest of the gold at the ship's stern also to be used as bullion if required during the voyage.[13] Its ritual significance may be suggested by a hoard of gold pendants found at Ugarit, one with a stylized female figure and others in forms symbolizing the major Canaanite pantheon. Such an assemblage was also found on the Uluburun ship (see cat. no. 217 and fig. 111).   CP

1. Bass et al. 1989, pp. 2, 4–5, and fig. 3; Pulak 1997, pp. 243–44; Pulak 1998, p. 206, fig. 19; Pulak 2005c, p. 595, fig. 104.

2. In a comprehensive list of sixty-six items representing a "naked woman holding objects [Qedeshet, see note 5 below]," assembled by Cornelius (2004, pp. 45–48), which also includes the Uluburun pendant, twenty-three are incomplete or damaged so that the direction of the feet can not be ascertained. Of the remaining figures, only five show the feet facing right, and none are found on pendants.

3. Although the name of this distinctive head-dress is not known, Barnett (1975, pp. 104–5) likens it to a Greek *polos*, which he notes was derived from this eastern prototype. A fragmentary glass plaque from Megiddo shows a female head with a headdress marked by parallel vertical flutings, again probably representing the same kind of crown, McGovern 1985, p. 30, pl. 5; Loud 1948, pl. 241:1 (misidentified as faience), also a clay example on pl. 241:6. Crowns of this type are commonly shown on female figurines carved in ivory, from ninth- to eighth-century B.C. Nimrud (see Barnett 1975, pls. LXXII:S192–96, S198, S200, S201, LXXXIII:S197, S202, S203, S206, LXXIV:S207, S208); the coiffure of these ivory figures is also remarkably similar to that of the Uluburun figure. See also Maxwell-Hyslop 1971, pl. 233.

4. Barnett (1975, p. 105) notes that in Syria the necklace was a feature of an Ishtar-like cult figure and, perhaps, of her devotees. Multi-strand necklaces are shown on the necks of nearly every ivory female from Nimrud; see, for example, ibid., pls. LXX–LXXVI.

5. Cornelius 2004, pp. 45, 83–84. Of these stelae, seven are clearly inscribed *kdsh* or *kdsht* (vocalized for convenience as Qedeshet), along with other attributes including "lady of heaven"; one inscription reads "Qedeshet, Astarte, Anat" (ibid., p. 84, no. 5.16). From these inscriptions, it is clear that *kdsh(t)* is a proper divine name in Egypt, unlike in the Levant, where it was used as an epithet or a title.

6. These pendants have been considered by Maxwell-Hyslop under her "pictorial" group (1971, p. 139), and by Negbi in her "pictorial '*qudshu*' group (Negbi 1976, pp. 99–100). McGovern, who treats pendants of various materials from the Levant, lists few examples found under his "type II.B.1" pendants in human form (1985, pp. 30–31). He further notes that these pendants (his type II) are clearly related to terracotta figurine plaques found throughout Mesopotamia and the Levant. The most recent and extensive study of the iconography of the Levantine goddesses represented on these pendants is Cornelius 2004.

7. A gold appliqué shows the figure standing on a horse (Clamer 1980, p. 153, fig. 1; Cornelius 2004, pl. 5.22).

8. These are collected in Cornelius 2004, pls. for nos. 5.20, 5.20a, and 5.27. A standing nude female figure on a Late Bronze Age cylinder seal (pl. 5.11) from Cyprus holds two horned animals, one by the legs and the other by the horns. For the gold pendants, see also Schaeffer 1932, pl. IX:1 (fourth from left); Maxwell-Hyslop 1971, pls. 106, 107.

9. Cornelius (2004, p. 91) notes that representations of Astarte bearing weapons may be compared with the Mesopotamian Ishtar. Several pendants carry rosettes, perhaps also representing the star disc of Ishtar. See ibid., pls. 5.23, 5.28, and 38. This is contra Cornelius (ibid., p. 91) who proposes that the Qedeshet figure represented on many of these Syro-Canaanite pendants is a separate entity.

10. Also in Maxwell-Hyslop 1971, pl. 106.

11. Schaeffer 1939a, p. 62, pl. XXXII.

12. Maxwell-Hyslop 1971, p. 140.

13. Pulak 2001, p. 24.

214

214

PENDANT WITH NUDE FEMALE

Gold

Height 6.5 cm (2⅝ in.); width 2.8 cm (1⅛ in.)

Minet el-Beidha

Late Bronze Age, 14th century B.C.

Musée du Louvre, Paris, Département des Antiquités Orientales AO14714

215

PENDANT WITH NUDE GODDESS

Gold

Height 7 cm (2¾ in.); width 4 cm (1⅝ in.)

Minet el-Beidha, "Depot d'enceinte" (dépot 11)

Late Bronze Age, 15th–14th century B.C.

National Museum, Aleppo, Syria M10450

Several gold pendants representing a nude goddess were found at Ugarit and its port of Minet el-Beidha. Most of them are composed of a fairly thin gold sheet with one end rolled into a ring for hanging. The decoration is in repoussé, with details chased or punched. The pendants are different in form, more or less oval or round, and display an iconography that was traditional in the Levant and variously represented in a schematic, symbolic, or realistic manner.[1]

Many pendants represent a star, symbol of the planet Venus and goddess of love and life. Others depict the goddess in human form. Her distinguishing features are nudity, frontality, a dominant stance, and an emphasis on her hairstyle. Whether she is shown in part—reduced to a few anatomical details as face, breasts, or pubic triangle—or in full, this deity is nearly

215

always surrounded by patterns of globules that indicate her heavenly origin.

The nudity and frontality in images of female deities is characteristic of divine representations in the Levant during the second millennium B.C. At the same time, the hairstyle of the images from Ugarit attests to the close relations with Egypt, which led to religious syncretism. Accordingly, the Levantine goddess was given certain attributes that relate her to Egyptian deities, in particular the symmetrically disposed locks of hair that frame the face and end in prominent curls, an attribute of Hathor, goddess of the Nile.

The forms of the pendants that show the goddess in full length are fairly homogeneous, with the authoritative bearing being a constant feature. The imagery through which this trait is expressed—domination over the wilderness (represented by animals) and over plant life—however, varies considerably. These variations complicate our interpretation of the nude goddess with Hathor locks. Indeed, while the domination of plant life can be explained by Ugaritic mythology, the deity's power over serpents and her association with lions connect her more with the Egyptian goddess Qadesh and recall deities from the Aegean world, especially Knossos, where the taming of snakes was the prerogative of certain female deities.   SC

1. For further reference, see Schaeffer 1932; Schaeffer 1949, p. 36, fig. 10; Barrelet 1958; Caubet 1990, p. 33, no. 67; Caubet 1999c, pp. 32–38; and *Le royaume d'Ougarit* 2004.

216
PENDANT WITH SCHEMATIC NUDE FEMALE

Gold
Height 3.5 cm (1⅜ in.); width 2.1 cm (⅞ in.)
Tell el-ʿAjjul, Hoard 277
Middle/Late Bronze Age, 17th–
15th century B.C.
The Trustees of the British Museum, London
130761

This pendant depicts a highly stylized frontal nude female with Egyptianizing features. It is of a general Syro-Canaanite type that is related to pendants found on the Uluburun ship (cat. no. 213) and at Minet el-Beidha (cat. nos. 214, 215). Like those examples, it is constructed from a single sheet of gold with the top rolled up and forward into a suspension loop. The figural details are executed in repoussé with some chasing and punching, while the border is decorated with incised cross-hatching.[1] The craftsmanship, while casual, is in keeping with works of Levantine manufacture (see pp. 101–3).

The form of the pendant comprises the entire female figure, schematically rendered to emphasize face, breasts, navel, and pubic triangle to the exclusion of other anatomical details. The overall shape of this and similar pendants is most often described as piriform when, in fact, the reference to the pubic area that is so dramatically featured on the plaque itself seems obvious. As such, it reflects a remarkably sophisticated use of conceptual self-reference, a representational scheme not uncommon in the ancient Near East.[2] For this reason, among others, it has been suggested that such ornaments may not have been necklace pendants at all but plaques suspended from pelvic girdles.[3]

Because these ornaments so clearly accentuate the life-giving aspects of the female anatomy, they are often labeled "Astarte" plaques to suggest a link to the Canaanite goddess of fertility.[4] Other divine associations are also possible (see cat. nos. 213–215). There is, however, no obvious marker of divinity on this particular example. Ambiguous representations, often schematic, of nude females in various media have a long history in the ancient Near East and have yet to be fully understood. Whatever the ultimate identification of the females depicted, this pendant

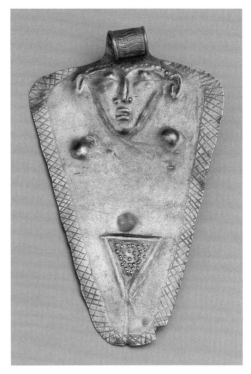

216

and others like it should not be considered simply decorative; rather, they must have been charged with sexual and procreative power and possessed of potent agency.

The present example comes from an important hoard of jewelry found at Tell el-ʿAjjul, a site in the Levant possibly associated with ancient Sharuhen, the last stronghold of the Hyksos (see pp. 108–10). The hoard was one of several at the site, all of which included sizable assemblages of gold ornaments. Why these items were hidden away, and whether they were made at the site or brought there by itinerant craftsmen or merchants, remains open to debate.[5] On purely technical grounds, however, the jewelry seems typical of a local Canaanite style of manufacture.   KB

1. Petrie, Mackay, and Murray 1952, pls. VI:13, VIII:1, B:17; Negbi 1970, p. 42, no. 130; McGovern 1985, pp. 32, 114, no. 74, pl. 6, II.B.2.b 74.
2. Bahrani 2002.
3. Platt 1976.
4. For examples, see Maxwell-Hyslop 1971, pp. 138–40; Lilyquist 1993, p. 49; Pulak 1998, p. 206; and Cornelius 2004.
5. See cat no. 220 and Politis 2001 for a discussion of various interpretations.

217a, b

PENDANTS WITH RAYED STARS

Gold

a. Medallion with four-rayed star and four curved rays

Height 10.3 cm (4 in.); width 11 cm (4⅜ in.); thickness 0.1 cm (¹⁄₁₆ in.)

2.5.90 (KW 1672)

b. Medallion with four-rayed star and eight curved rays

Diameter 7.5 cm (3 in.); thickness 0.2 cm (¹⁄₁₆ in.)

68.31.84 (KW 138)

Uluburun shipwreck

Late Bronze Age, ca. 1300 B.C.

Bodrum Museum of Underwater Archaeology, Turkey

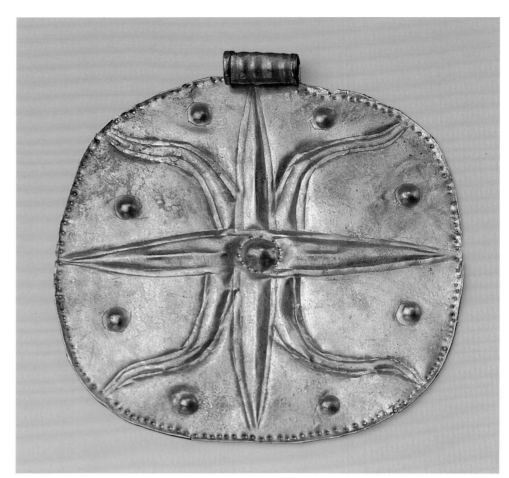

217a

Four gold Canaanite medallions in the form of thin roundels were found on the Uluburun ship.[1] They were each fashioned from a single sheet of gold, with a cylindrical bail or loop at the top for suspension formed by rolling forward an extension of the roundel that had been reinforced by folding over the edges. Two of the roundels show edges folded back and crimped irregularly on the reverse, and those of the other two appear to have been left unaltered. Their decoration consists of a four-rayed star with opposed, curved rays in between, all worked in repoussé and defined on the obverse by incision.

There are two variations of this design. The largest (this page), which is also the largest example of its type known in gold,[2] and the smallest medallion in the group (KW 756; not on exhibition) have a single curved ray between each pair of straight rays, for a total of eight rays. The other two (opposite page, above, and KW 1512, not on exhibition) are similar to one another in both size and design, each bearing a pair of opposed, curved rays between the pair of straight rays, for a total of twelve rays. At the center of each medallion, and also centered in the fields between each of the rays, are single bosses in the first type, and repoussé dotted rosettes in the second type in imitation of gold granulation. In the latter design there are also four repoussé-dotted "triangles" pendant from the rim between the pairs of opposed rays. The peripheral edges of the roundels are milled in repoussé dots.[3]

Although one of the medallions was found farther down the slope than the others, it is likely that all four were originally kept at the stern of the ship together[4] with most of the other gold pendants and objects. These and other symbolically charged pendants are impressive pieces of jewelry and were probably intended for personal adornment. Some, however, were associated with scrap gold and silver jewelry (fig. 114), all of which was probably kept in one or several pouches at the stern, suggesting that, if required, they could also have been used as bullion during the voyage.

Pendants with star motifs, found in many varying forms with or without curved rays throughout western Asia, probably originated in Mesopotamia, where they were known since the Akkadian period. The star disc as a symbol of Ishtar, the sun disc in the form of a four-rayed star with undulating rays between them as Shamash, and the lunar crescent as Sin are found in Mesopotamia throughout the Bronze Age. Ishtar, the goddess of love and war, was manifest as Venus, the morning and evening star, and was often

represented as a disc inscribed with an eight-rayed star, but sometimes also with fewer rays.[5]

The hoard of jewelry presumably found at Dilbat (cat. no. 4) also includes several medallions. One of these is somewhat similar in its design and execution to catalogue number 217a, apart from the extra pairs of rays and the presence of undulating instead of curved rays in a reversed orientation.

In Anatolia, the eight-pointed star is associated with the goddess Shaushga, the Hurrian form of Ishtar.[6] The Hittites were strongly influenced by Hurrian cults and adopted Hurrian gods and goddesses; the sun disc, known as the *sittar*, reflects this influence.[7] One of the two variants of the so-called Cappadocian symbol occurs in the form of a four-rayed star with curved rays between them, and bosses centered in the field between all the rays.[8]

Pendants with star motifs were also used throughout the Bronze Age Levant.[9] The motif with the single curved ray (cat. no. 217a and KW 756), however, is found mostly along the Levantine coast. Although gold pendants with only the star motif

217b

(generally with eight rays) have been found at Ugarit,[10] Tell el-ʿAjjul,[11] and elsewhere, the sun-disc motif of straight and opposed curved rays was also used at Ugarit from the first half of the fourteenth century B.C. It appears on the famous ivory bed panel, carved with an image of a goddess displaying Hathor locks and with a sun disc between the bovine horns on her head (see fig. 80),[12] and also on a silver-plated bronze disc, which may have been part of a divine headdress.[13] Several partly gilded ivory discs of this design, perhaps used as furniture inlays, are known from approximately the same period at nearby Alalakh.[14]

Although of a much smaller size, two gold disc pendants with the star-and-curved-ray motif, found discarded along with a group of other gold pendants and jewelry pieces at Shechem,[15] have a design similar to that of catalogue number 217a. The same motif is found on the three considerably smaller disc pendants from Kamid el-Loz and one from Qatna (cat. no. 218).[16] A parallel in both dimension and design is seen in a silver medallion from Shiloh.[17] A stone jewelry mold

for a disc pendant with a similar motif was found at Megiddo,[18] which also yielded a gold pendant of the same design from an Early Iron Age context;[19] a mold for the same type of disc pendant is known from Tell el-Amarna in Egypt.[20]

Disc pendants bearing the opposed, double curved rays framed by straight rays also occur as representations. Sun- and star-disc pendants are shown around the necks of bearded Asiatics with short kilts on wall paintings depicting foreign tribute bearers and prisoners in the tombs of Puimre and Kenamun.[21] Disc pendants, one of which bears a pair of opposed rays, are seen on the necks of vanquished and captured Syro-Canaanites, worked in relief on the side of a chariot body from the Tomb of Thutmose IV, of Dynasty 18.[22] Carved on a wood ceremonial footstool from the Tomb of Tutankhamun are four of Egypt's enemies, including a Syrian captive wearing a clearly depicted sun-disc pendant with a pair of opposed, curved rays between each pair of straight rays of the type on cat. no. 217b from Uluburun.[23] Although their motifs are not indicated, disc pendants are also shown in the Tomb

of Kenamun around the necks of the bare-chested crew aboard the Syrian ships arriving at an Egyptian port (fig. 98).[24] The merchants on the ships do not appear to wear any medallions, though it is likely that they were hidden from view beneath the merchants' robes.

A hoard of gold pendants found at Ugarit, including six-rayed and four-rayed star-disc pendants, as well as two crescent pendants and one of a stylized female, suggests a group of goddess, solar, and lunar divine symbols. Ugaritic texts refer to these types of pendants as Astartes, suns (Shapash), and moons (i.e., crescents).[25] Perhaps the most complete textual reference to pendants can be found in the Old Testament. The term "little sun," interpreted as a star disc, appears with "crescents" and "drop pendants" (triangular goddess pendants?) as part of the catalogue of finery that the Lord will take from the "haughty daughters of Zion."[26] It is therefore noteworthy that a pendant depicting a nude goddess (cat. no. 213), a pendant shaped like a crescent (fig. 111), and also sun-disc pendants (but none with only the eight-rayed star motif) found together on the Uluburun ship perhaps replicate the symbols of the Canaanite pantheon.

The Syro-Canaanite disc pendants with the four-rayed star and opposed single or double curved rays between them, as represented on the Uluburun medallions, are difficult to attribute to a specific deity. Although they appear to be related to the symbol of the sun god Shamash, the opposed curved rays shown between the

Figure 111. Gold pendant in the form of a crescent. Uluburun shipwreck. Bodrum Museum of Underwater Archaeology 7.5.87 (KW892)

four-rayed star are unlike the undulating rays typical of this motif, and might represent the double lightning bolts of the Mesopotamian god Adad. Perhaps in the Syro-Canaanite region, the double lightning, which is also the symbol of the Hurrian god Teshshup, replaced the undulating rays of the original Shamash symbol and was joined with the four-rayed Shamash star to represent both deities, thereby combining their apotropaic aspects.[27] Alternatively, rather than representing lightning bolts, the curved rays may resemble bovine horns, in which case they are to be associated with the goddess Hathor, who is often shown wearing a headdress formed of a wig, horns, and sun disc. Either way, because the medallions with the curved-ray motifs appear to have a more widespread distribution in the Levant, they may represent the Canaanite version of a symbol for syncretic deities.

In view of the importance of both sun and star symbols in the Semitic, Hurrian, and Hittite religions, disc pendants may be regarded as amulets bearing divine symbols. They were transportable versions of the large cult symbols and were charged with their apotropaic powers. As such, the pendants were an essential part of personal equipment, representing both the gods and goddesses in the temple, and probably also the king.[28]   CP

1. Bass 1986, pp. 289–90, pl. 17:4; Bass et al. 1989, p. 4, fig. 4; Pulak 1997, p. 244, fig. 12; for color photographs, see Pulak 2005c, p. 596, figs. 105–8.
2. Pulak 1997, p. 244; Pulak 2001, p. 24.
3. Catalogue no. 217a weighs 46.2 grams and catalogue no. 217b weighs 10.11 grams; these weights probably correspond to 5 and 1 shekels, respectively, although the latter weight is on the high side, based on a unit of 9.3–9.4 grams.
4. Pulak 2001, p. 24.
5. Maxwell-Hyslop 1971, pp. 141–42. This star symbol was at times juxtaposed with the image of an armed goddess, probably representing Ishtar standing on a lion; see Barrelet 1955, pl. XXI:4.
6. Maxwell-Hyslop 1971, p. 143.
7. Texts from Boğazköy mention *sittar* of metal, at least one of which was worn as a pendant on a necklace. Maxwell-Hyslop 1971, p. 146.
8. Wainwright 1956, pp. 137–38; Maxwell-Hyslop 1971, pp. 146–47, pl. 115. Assyrian connections may be seen in the eight-pointed gold star pendants of fourteenth-century B.C. Tell al-Rimah and on a limestone relief carving of Ashurnasirpal (Maxwell-Hyslop 1971, pp. 177–78, 241, pls. 130, 220).
9. See McGovern 1985, pp. 75–77.
10. Schaeffer 1932, pl. XVI:2; Maxwell-Hyslop 1971, p. 141, pl. 109; Negbi 1970, p. 32.
11. The star on the Tell el-'Ajjul disc pendant has eight straight rays with bosses between the rays (Maxwell-Hyslop 1971, pp. 140–41, pl. 108). A type of star pendant in which the stars are cut out from a piece of sheet gold also occurs. In Tell el-'Ajjul these cutout star pendants are found in earlier deposits than the disc-star pendants (Negbi 1970, p. 31).
12. Schaeffer 1954, pp. 54–55, 58–59, pl. VIII; Gachet-Bizollon 2007, pp. 137–38, with pls. 26:269 no. 2/H, 80:269, 82:269 no. 1/K. Gachet-Bizollon proposes a date in the first half of the thirteenth century B.C. for the panels (p. 146).
13. Schaeffer 1931, pl. XIII:4.
14. Woolley 1955, p. 290, AT/38/79, pl. LXXVII:A; Woolley 1939, p. 12, pl. XIV:4B (AT/8/79).
15. Maxwell-Hyslop 1971, p. 144, pl. 115:d, e; an eight-rayed star pendant is also represented in this group; see pl. 115:c.
16. W. Adler 1994, pp. 84–85, figs. 21–23.
17. Finkelstein, Bunimovitz, and Lederman 1993, pp. 243–44, fig. 9.12:1–2.
18. Lamon and Shipton 1939, pl. 105:6.
19. Guy and Engberg 1938, p. 162, fig. 169, p. 163, pl. 166:8.
20. Petrie 1894, pl. XVIII:440.
21. Davies 1922–23, pp. 90–91, pl. I.
22. Yadin 1963, pp. 192–93. The disc pendant shown around the neck of the figure indicated as no. 1 has the double opposed rays of catalogue. no. 217b but lacks the straight star rays between them, undoubtedly stemming from the Egyptian craftsman's poor understanding of the symbolism. Another disc pendant around the neck of the figure indicated as number 2 has the single curved ray between the pairs of straight rays, as in catalogue no. 217a.
23. Desroches-Noblecourt 1963, p. 51, fig. XI:a, p. 296:XI.
24. Davies 1963, pp. 14–15, pl. XV; Davies and Faulkner 1947, pp. 40ff., pl. VII.
25. Dussaud 1931, p. 375; Jack 1935, p. 45.
26. Isaiah 3:18–23; Platt 1979, pp. 72, 80–81.
27. Maxwell-Hyslop 1971, p. 147.
28. Ibid., p. 142.

218

PENDANT WITH RAYED STAR

Gold
Diameter 3.9 cm (1½ in.)
Qatna, Royal Tomb
Late Bronze Age, 15th–14th century B.C.
National Museum, Damascus, Syria
MSH02G-i0829

This round pendant displays an astral motif consisting of a four-pointed star with four curved rays inserted between the points.[1] The motif, symbol of the solar disc, is associated with the sun god Shamash.[2] Gold solar discs were widespread in the ancient Near East and were particularly popular in Late Bronze Age Syria and neighboring regions, with examples known from Kamid el-Loz,[3] Ugarit,[4] and the Uluburun shipwreck (cat. no. 217). A suspension loop is always attached to the edge so that the disc could be worn as a pendant on a necklace. Most likely, they

218

had both decorative and apotropaic functions. This example, from the Royal Tomb at Qatna, was obviously long in use before it was deposited as a grave good. The original loop was broken off and replaced by a gold melon bead soldered on to the edge of the pendant. Additionally, a small strip of gold was soldered onto this weakened spot to stabilize the connection with the new loop.

The pendant is carefully decorated both in repoussé and with granulation. The star and the rays are worked in repoussé from the reverse, as are the eight rounded projections between the rays and the points of the star. On the front, fine granulation follows the center lines of the points of the star, encircles each of the projections, and highlights the perimeter of the disc. With these lavish embellishments, the Qatna solar-disc pendant is one of the finest examples of its type.   PP

1. See Dohmann-Pfälzner and Pfälzner 2006, p. 97, fig. 29.
2. This sun symbol should not be confused with the star symbol of the goddess Ishtar, which consists of eight straight rays; compare Black and Green 1992, p. 16, fig. 7, p. 168, fig. 140, p. 169, fig. 143.
3. *Frühe Phöniker im Libanon* 1983, pp. 154–55, no. 90, fig. on p. 176.
4. *Le royaume d'Ougarit* 2004, p. 242, no. 269, p. 266, no. 312.

219
CHALICE

Gold
Height 13.1 cm (5⅛ in.); diameter of mouth
11.2 cm (4½ in.); diameter of base 6 cm
(2⅜ in.); max thickness 0.1 cm (¹⁄₁₆ in.)
Uluburun shipwreck
Late Bronze Age, ca. 1300 B.C.
Bodrum Museum of Underwater
Archaeology, Turkey 47.31.84
(KW 99)

This biconical chalice is the largest gold object from the wreck (fig. 112),[1] yet one of the few Uluburun artifacts to have defied convincing attribution. It is crafted from three components: a nearly conical bowl with a slightly flaring rim, a conical pedestal base, and a small collar covering the junction where the bowl and base are joined by three gold rivets clenched in the base. The bowl lacks handles and is full bodied, with two repoussé bands; the upper is pronounced and rounded in section, and the lower, directly below it, is carinated. The bowl section is thicker than its pedestal base and was shaped from a single sheet of gold hammered from the inside out. The chalice was discovered at the stern of the vessel near the gold falcon pendant (cat. no. 220) and one of two small bronze cymbals, or crotals, which probably were for ritual use.

Although the Uluburun chalice has no exact parallels in the Aegean,[2] the resemblance of its cup section, with its general profile and pronounced rounded band, to well-known gold cups from that region[3] has led to suggestions of an Aegean origin.[4] The orientation and appearance of the second carinated band, as well as the plain conical pedestal base, however, set the Uluburun chalice apart.[5] The Uluburun chalice has neither a ring handle nor a full handle, both types of which are found on Aegean cups. Such handles are fastened with multiple rivets, yet there are no rivet holes on the Uluburun chalice to indicate that it ever carried a handle. Nor is there any evidence to suggest that it was formed by modifying another cup type.

Handleless, pedestal-footed chalices or goblets of pottery and stone, usually alabaster, occur commonly in the Levantine region. Although the bowls of these chalices are embellished with two or three bands or ribs located on the rim, midbowl,

and bowl skirt, the bands are thin and the bowl is cylindrical in shape, having a diameter wider than the bowl's height, which makes their proportions unlike that of the Uluburun chalice.[6]

A type of biconical chalice or goblet of pottery and faience, with a bell-shaped bowl often painted to represent a stylized lotus bud and a conical stem and ring foot, is known from Egypt.[7] Such vessels, along with two faience examples from Minet el-Beidha,[8] probably of Egyptian origin or Egyptian-inspired local production,[9] are similar in their general profile to the Uluburun chalice but lack its banding.

As with several other objects on the ship, the unique Uluburun chalice may be seen as a hybrid vessel or a version of the typical banded Levantine cylindrical-footed stone vessel, which incorporates the form of Egyptian lotus-shaped vessels. Biconical chalices or goblets, usually of pottery but sometimes of other materials, also occur on the Levantine coast.[10] All these vessels, however, have a single band of rounded or angular section located slightly above the bowl-base juncture and lack the second carinated band of the Uluburun chalice. It may then be suggested that the Uluburun chalice was made in the Levant or at least modified there. This attribution is also supported by its weight of 236.8 grams, which rather closely corresponds to 25 units of a shekel, or half a mina, based on a unit of approximately 9.3–9.4 grams, the mass standard predominantly represented by the weights aboard the Uluburun ship (see cat. no. 235).[11]

The chalice may have been a valued personal possession of the ship's captain and/or head merchant or it may have been a prestige gift to be presented at the ship's destination. Conversely, it may have been an item of ritual or cultic use for ceremonies conducted on the ship when setting out on a journey and also upon reaching shore safely. Pictorial and artifactual evidence have shown that chalices were used as incense burners in the Levant. A wall painting in the Tomb of Kenamun in Thebes (see fig. 98) depicts a fleet of Canaanite ships arriving and docking in Egypt, where the captain of one ship holds a raised tall cup (or chalice) in one hand and incense burners in the form of a chalice in the other.[12] The captain of a second ship also raises an incense burner, while a second man on the same ship holds in

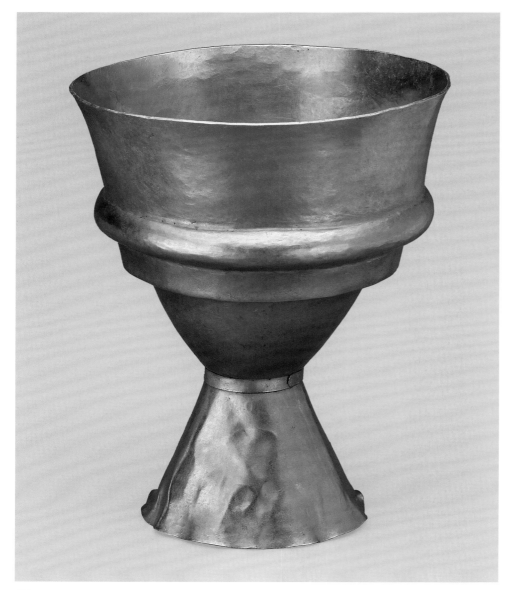

219

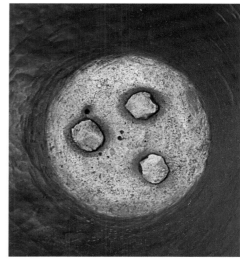

219, detail of interior

raised hands a tall offering cup and a carinated bowl. Several bronze chalices of Late
Bronze IIIB, used for burning incense, have
been found at the coastal site of Tel Nami,
and more than 50 chalice-shaped pottery
incense burners have been excavated from
the Late Bronze Age anchorage of Tell Abu
Hawam.[13] A chalice-shaped pottery incense
burner has also been found on an eighth-
century B.C. shipwreck off Ashkelon.[14]
While the Uluburun cup could have been
used as an incense burner aboard the ship,
biconical incense chalices generally have
flatter bowls.

If not an incense burner, perhaps the
Uluburun chalice served as an offering
cup onboard, as seen with the two men
clutching such cups aboard their ships in
the Kenamun wall painting. Although
much later in time, Thucydides writes of
shipboard libations offered in silver and
gold cups before departing on a voyage.[15]
Polemon, too, tells of such offerings,
though after the offering was made, the
cup was tossed into the sea.[16]   CP

1. The weight of the cup, 236.8 grams, may be
   approximately 1 gram heavier owing to a
   small patch of encrustation preserved inside
   the base. A total of approximately 530 grams
   of gold in the form of various objects, an
   ingot, and scrap were found on the Uluburun
   ship; this chalice accounts for half the total
   weight. See Bass 1986, pp. 286, 289, ill. 24;
   Pulak 2005c, pp. 67, 594.
2. For Middle Minoan III–Late Minoan I chalices of a variant form found in ritualistic contexts, see Wright 1996, pp. 289–93; Warren
   1969, pp. 36–37, pls. 392, 393.

Figure 112. Author excavating gold chalice on seabed. Uluburun shipwreck.

3. See, for example, gold cups nos. 102, 108–12, 185, 196, 197, and especially the plain-bodied cup no. 136 in E. Davis 1977.

4. Lolos 1989, pp. 8–9.

5. Pulak 1997, p. 244.

6. A few examples of this type include an alabaster group of differing sizes and banding arrangements found together with other stone and pottery vessels in a storeroom at Minet el-Beidha (Schaeffer 1932, p. 6, pl. VIII:1), and a small, two-banded version with separately made bowl and pedestal from Gezer (Seger 1988, p. 196, no. 10, pls. 13:10, 73:B).

7. For faience examples, see Caubet and Pierrat-Bonnefois 2005, p. 74, fig. 200, p. 62, fig. 142; for those of pottery, see Rose 2007, p. 214, no. 263, p. 218, no. 293, p. 266, no. 557.

8. Schaeffer 1929, p. 288, pl. LII:6; Schaeffer 1932, pp. 6, 12, fig. 8; Caubet 2007, pp. 226–27; for a color photograph of one of the cups, see Caubet and Pierrat-Bonnefois 2005, p. 62, fig. 142.

9. Schaeffer (1932, p. 6) surmised a Cypriot origin for a similar footed cup found at Minet el-Beidha, although he did not discount the possibility of Syrian manufacture.

10. Among others, pottery examples of biconical bowls with banding have been found at Lachish (Tufnell, Inge, and Harding 1940, pl. XLVIIA, B:222, 232); Hazor (Yadin et al. 1960, p. 57, pl. CXIII:21); Gezer (Macalister 1912, pp. 163–64, fig. 325); an earlier chalice of Middle Bronze IIC period at Tel Dan (Biran 1994, p. 101, fig. 68:9); Samaria (Crowfoot and Crowfoot 1957, pp. 175–76, fig. 25:1, 2, 4, 7, for some examples), and in alabaster at Shiloh (Finkelstein, Bunimovitz, and Lederman 1993, p. 249, fig. 19.15:4, p. 252, fig. 9.18:2, p. 255, no. 19). Early copper examples of this general type have been found in the royal tombs of Dynasty 1 in Egypt. See Petrie 1901, pl. IXa:3.

11. A text from Ugarit (RS 11.732) mentions a gold cup to be sent as a gift to the Hittites as weighing a Ugaritic mina of 50 shekels, which is twice the weight of the Uluburun chalice, suggesting that vessels of precious metals were made according to specific weights; see Parise 1984, p. 128.

12. Davies 1963, pp. 14–15, pl. XV; Davies and Faulkner 1947, pp. 40ff., pl. VII; see also Brody 1998, p. 79.

13. Yoselevich 2006, pp. 27–28.

14. Ballard et al. 2002, p. 158, fig. 8, p. 159, fig. 9:2, p. 163.

15. Thucydides 6.32.1–2.

16. Athenaeus 11.426.

220

FALCON PENDANT

Gold
Height 3.5 cm (1⅜ in.); width 6.3 cm (2½ in.)
Uluburun shipwreck
Late Bronze Age, ca. 1300 B.C.
Bodrum Museum of Underwater
Archaeology, Turkey 45.31.84
(KW 94)

A gold pendant in the form of a falcon is one of the most elaborate pieces of jewelry discovered on the Uluburun shipwreck.[1] The falcon is depicted with its head facing front, outstretched wings, and legs spread on either side of the tail feathers, with the talons of each foot clutching a hooded cobra. The pendant, with two small hoops attached to the upper edge for suspension, is made of two sheets of gold, with the back sheet folded over the front sheet and crimped around the edges. The body is worked in repoussé. The falcon is distinctive both in form and in the use of fine granulation, which covers the entire body and wing coverts of the bird, as well as the addorsed cobras. Lines of larger granulation define the outline of the pendant, the body of the bird, and the flight feathers of the wings and tail.[2] The granulation appears to be sweated in place, but further analysis is needed to confirm the metalworking method used to affix the granules to the gold sheet.

The somewhat crude craftsmanship of the pendant suggests that it was probably of Syro-Canaanite make and design, as the pendant does not display the level of skill commonly associated with Egyptian and earlier Mesopotamian goldwork.[3] Its granulation, however, exploits the reflective qualities of gold and was an elite metalworking technique that displayed power and prestige.[4] The Uluburun pendant was found in the part of the site corresponding to the stern of the vessel, the same area where much of the gold jewelry and gold scrap were found, suggesting that these pieces, no matter the quality, were kept together and used as ready bullion when necessary.

Because some of the granulation has been lost, the original weight of the falcon can only be estimated at approximately 12.5 grams, which may correspond to 1.5 units of the Mesopotamian shekel of about 8.4 grams or possibly one unit corresponding to the lighter end of a mass standard based on the Egyptian gold *dbn*.[5]

The pendant is evocative in subject of the well-known falcon earrings from the hoards at Tell el-'Ajjul (cat. no. 221),[6] but a closer stylistic parallel can be found in a pair of matching earrings in Leiden,[7] which are also thought to come from Tell el-'Ajjul.[8] A falcon earring in the Musée du Louvre is virtually identical to the Leiden pair, and may have come from the same original source.[9] The Leiden earrings are closest to the Uluburun pendant: the falcon's head faces front and the talons are shown clasping cobras. The Leiden earrings are also made from two sheets of gold, with the features raised by repoussé and outlined with gold granules, and are more elaborately decorated than the Uluburun pendant. While the falcon is a common symbol in Syro-Canaanite iconography, the presence of the hooded cobra in both the Leiden earrings and the Uluburun pendant may reflect contemporary Egyptianizing tastes.

Goldwork found in tombs at Byblos may represent an earlier stage in the use of granulation and other techniques (see cat. no. 25).[10] Gold funerary collars from these burials introduce falcon imagery into the Levantine jewelry repertoire (see cat. no. 28). Middle Kingdom collars and pectorals are the most likely sources of inspiration.[11] It is believed that by the early fifteenth century B.C., the goldworking tradition may have moved from Tell el-'Ajjul to another center, such as Ugarit, where it lasted until the late fourteenth century B.C.[12] Recently, other areas of influence suggested for the Tell el-'Ajjul goldworking tradition have included Ebla and Megiddo.[13]

The earrings from Tell el-'Ajjul were also found in association with other pieces of gold in hoards, which have been identified as the possessions of itinerant craftsmen or peddlers.[14] It is probably through such individuals that the styles and techniques of goldworking were spread throughout the ancient Near East. Goldworking techniques from the Near East may have reached the Aegean through intact jewelry, like this pendant, and scrap jewelry, represented on the Uluburun shipwreck by cut-and-folded granulated pendants and other pieces (see fig. 114). These imports supplied Aegean craftsmen with raw materials and exposed them to Near Eastern artistic styles.[15]   CP

220

1. Bass 1986, pp. 287–88, pl. 17, fig. 3; Pulak 1998, p. 206; Pulak 2005c, p. 597, fig. 110.
2. Bass 1986, p. 287.
3. Politis 2001, pp. 174–77, 180.
4. Ibid., pp. 161, 180–81.
5. The pendant presently weighs 12.08 grams; granulation has been lost, especially from the body of the cobra clutched in the falcon's left foot.
6. The four falcon-shaped earrings from Tell el-'Ajjul, along with other gold objects from the hoards, have been dated to between about the mid-sixteenth and the early fifteenth century B.C. by Negbi (1970, pp. 29, 36–37). For the Tell el-'Ajjul falcon earrings, see ibid., pp. 26, 38–39, nos. 14–17, pl. I:1; Maxwell-Hyslop 1971, pp. 117–18, pl. E; Tufnell 1983, pp. 61–63, pl. XXI.
7. Tufnell 1983, pp. 63–64, pl. XXII.
8. Maxwell-Hyslop 1971, p. 117, Tufnell 1983, p. 64.
9. Lilyquist 1994, p. 27, figs. 46, 47. Lilyquist (ibid., p. 28) suggests that both the Leiden earrings and the example at the Louvre were found in Egypt.
10. Maxwell-Hyslop 1971, pp. 103–4, 107–9; Lilyquist 1993, p. 41, fig. 13.
11. Negbi 1970, p. 26.
12. Ibid., p. 37.
13. Politis 2001, pp. 171–75; Lilyquist 1993, pp. 44–47.
14. Politis 2001, p. 176; Petrie, Mackay, and Murray 1952, pp. 8–10; others understand them as being hidden by their owners in times of stress (Tufnell 1983, p. 60; Negbi 1970).
15. Pulak 2001, p. 24; Politis 2001, pp. 177–80.

221

FALCON EARRING

Gold
Height 1.4 cm (⅝ in.); width 1.3 cm (½ in.)
Tell el-'Ajjul, Hoard 277
Middle/Late Bronze Age, 17th–15th century B.C.
The Trustees of the British Museum, London
130764

This ornament has been interpreted as both a pendant and an earring. The latter identification, however, would seem more appropriate, as a nearly identical

piece, now in the Fitzwilliam Museum, Cambridge, was discovered in the same hoard at Tell el-'Ajjul.[1] The shape is that of a bird of prey, the body and tail feathers depicted frontally, the head in profile. Constructed from sheet gold worked in repoussé, the ornament was then decorated with granulation and wires to demarcate

Figure 113. Drawing of gold earring inlaid with stones, glass, and faience from the Tomb of Tutankhamun. Dynasty 18. Egyptian Museum, Cairo JE 61969

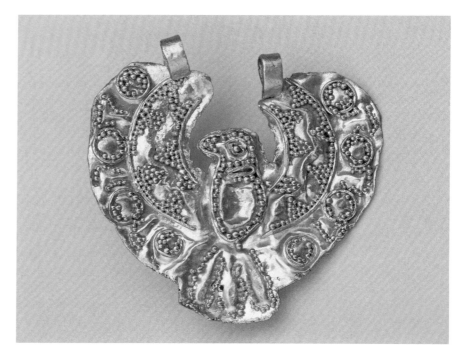

221

356

the head, eye, neck, body, and tail feathers. While the body is rendered in a more or less realistic manner, the wings are embellished with granulation in purely decorative triangular and circular patterns.

The bird is generally described as a falcon, which has both royal and divine associations in Egypt and is frequently portrayed on pectorals going back to the Middle Kingdom, as well as on objects produced at contemporaneous Levantine sites with strong Egyptian connections (see cat. no. 28). It has also been suggested that the bird is a wryneck, primarily because its beak is straight rather than hooked.[2] In its anatomical details, the Tell el-'Ajjul bird can be linked to those depicted on the well-known examples belonging to Tutankhamun (fig. 113).[3] While the connection between the two sets of earrings is apparent, the falcon as a symbol for a royal personage such as Tutankhamun is better documented and more appropriate, supporting the identification of both sets as falcons.

It would, however, be impossible to attribute to the two sets of earrings the same level of craftsmanship. As is typical for Levantine manufacture (see pp. 101–3), the Tell el-'Ajjul earring is worked in a rather crude and casual manner, with granules of uneven size and imprecise placement, edges inexact and poorly finished, and evidence of overheating. While the iconography may ultimately derive from Egypt, the workmanship is not on the level of that found on pieces of Egyptian origin, or on material produced at Ebla or in Mesopotamia.[4] Quintessentially Canaanite or Levantine, the ornament, despite its less than expert execution, is pivotal to our understanding of both the goldsmith's art and the use of shared imagery throughout the Near East and eastern Mediterranean in the second millennium B.C.   KB

1. For both earrings, see Petrie, Mackay, and Murray 1952, pl. VI:1, 3; Negbi 1970, p. 38, nos. 15, 16; McGovern 1985, p. 36, no. 78.
2. Tufnell 1983, esp. p. 64 for a discussion of beak types.
3. Ibid., p. 58, fig. 1.
4. See also Lilyquist 1993, p. 50; Ziffer in *At That Time the Canaanites Were in the Land* 1990, pp. 54–55; Politis 2001, pp. 170–74.

222

BRACELET

Silver
Diameter 8.7 cm (3⅜ in.); thickness 0.8 cm (⅜ in.)
Uluburun shipwreck
Late Bronze Age, ca. 1300 B.C.
Bodrum Museum of Underwater Archaeology, Turkey 14.1.2000
(KW 92)

A total of four intact, wearable silver bracelets, and seven others, consisting of crumpled specimens and cut fragments of scrap metal ready for the melting pot, were excavated from the wreck.[1] This bracelet, weighing 69.5 grams,[2] consists simply of a solid bar of silver,[3] circular in section and bent round in a circle, leaving a gap of 1.6 centimeters between the two flat ends. The ends are ornamented with five to six incised parallel lines or threading, followed by a wide band of double chevrons, a motif seen on some of the other bracelets.[4] One other bracelet is identical in shape, size, and decoration, and the two were probably a matching pair. Another, with plain ends, is much smaller, and was likely intended for a child. A unique bracelet fragment is made of a copper alloy sheathed in silver.

This silver bracelet was found at the stern end of the wreck, along with most of

Figure 114. Gold and silver scrap. Uluburun shipwreck. Bodrum Museum of Underwater Archaeology

the other silver and gold jewelry, scrap pieces of silver and gold, and pieces of silver and gold ingots (fig. 114). It would thus seem likely that the precious metals aboard the ship, along with other valuables, were stored in a bag of cloth or leather, or

perhaps in a small wood chest, now lost, in a compartment at the ship's stern. That readily usable intact jewelry was kept alongside scrap jewelry and other bits of silver and gold suggests that the intact examples, in addition to their use as a means of personal adornment, could have served as a supply of ready bullion for use when needed. One of the complete bracelets was crumpled, rather than cut into manageable smaller pieces, as was the case with two gold medallions (whose matching halves were recovered) and fragments of other silver bracelets, indicating that the intended value of much of the hoard was monetary rather than one of adornment.[5]

Originally, such bracelets were mostly worn after the fashion of the multiple bracelets represented on some of the "Astarte" pendants (cat. no. 213) and plaques. Bracelets with thread-ornamented ends, with or without chevrons, are paralleled in gold and silver in Late Bronze Age contexts at Tell el-'Ajjul[6] and on Cyprus,[7] gold at Megiddo,[8] silver at Ugarit,[9] Gezer,[10] and Amarna,[11] and bronze at Byblos.[12] A bronze bracelet of a different form but with threaded ends and double chevrons similar to the examples from Uluburun was found at Beşik-Tepe in the Troad.[13]

CP

1. Bass 1986, p. 288, ill. 27; Pulak 1988, pp. 25–26, figs. 29, 30.
2. Another, nearly identical, silver bracelet is lighter, at 60.6 grams. A third bracelet, complete but crumpled, weighs 68.7 grams.
3. Analyses by Zofia Stos-Gale using ED XRF indicates the silver is 96.3% pure, and lead-isotope compositions using TIMS are consistent with lead-silver ores from south-central Turkey's Bolkardağ in the southern Taurus Mountains (personal communication).
4. This decoration is one of four different varieties seen in the Uluburun shipwreck assemblage; two other bracelets have cross-hatching at their ends with a band of double chevrons above it. One bracelet fragment has an end with a wide band of cross-hatching bordered by a row of dotted circles, framed with a pair of parallel lines on either side above which are triple chevrons embellished with the same circles both inside and outside the chevron field. A good parallel for this type of decoration is seen on a silver bracelet from Cyprus (Marshall 1969, p. 39, no. 607, pl. V:607).
5. Pulak 1988, p. 26, n. 153; Pulak 2001, pp. 24–25.
6. Petrie 1932a, p. 6, pl. II; Petrie 1932b, pp. 44–45, fig. 5; Petrie 1934, pp. 5, 7–8, pls. XII, XV, XVI:68, XIX, XX:155–58; Negbi 1970, pp. 48–49; Maxwell-Hyslop 1971, pp. 123–24, fig. 88, pl. 90.
7. Lassen 2000, pp. 242–43 fig. 16.3; Marshall 1969, p. 39, no. 607, pl. V:607.

8. Loud 1948, pl. 226:3.
9. Schaeffer 1939a, pp. 42–44, fig. 31.
10. Macalister 1912, pp. 98–100, fig. 286.
11. Pendlebury 1931, p. 236, pl. LXXIII:3.
12. Dunand 1939, p. 174, pl. LXXII:2540, 2542.
13. Lassen 1994, pp. 132–35, ill. 3.

223

NEFERTITI SCARAB

Gold
Height 0.5 cm (¼ in.); width 1 cm (⅜ in.);
length 1.4 cm (⅝ in.)
Uluburun shipwreck
Late Bronze Age, ca. 1300 B.C. context
New Kingdom, Dynasty 18, reign of
Amenhotep IV–Akhenaten,
ca. 1353–1336 B.C. manufacture
Bodrum Museum of Underwater
Archaeology, Turkey 6.5.87 (KW 772)

The decline in the production of royal-name scarabs during the Amarna Age was a result of Akhenaten's proscription of all deities except for the Aten; this ban included the god associated with the scarab-headed solar deity, Khepri. This scarab recovered from the Uluburun shipwreck is the only extant gold specimen attested with the name of Akhenaten's wife, Nefernefruaten Nefertiti.[1] Because of the scarab's small size, the signs forming the name were packed close together onto three lines rather than the usual four. The scarab shows evidence of considerable wear, especially on the back, though the wing cases retain a series of thin ribbed lines like those on the back of an equally fine gold scarab of Akhenaten in The Metropolitan Museum of Art (fig. 115).[2]

The original owner of the scarab is likely to have been an official (or spouse) of the Amarna era who disposed of it after the royal couple's death, when an object naming a member of the widely despised royal family could no longer be displayed safely in public. The owner may have sold it to a merchant who kept it for himself or planned to peddle it at one of the ship's Mediterranean stops for its metallic value or for reuse in jewelry. The scarab provides a terminus post quem for the date of the Uluburun wreck as the post-Amarna phase of late Dynasty 18, that is, the end of the fourteenth century B.C.

JMW

223

223, back

Figure 115. Gold scarab with inscription of Akhenaten. Dynasty 18. The Metropolitan Museum of Art, New York, Purchase, Edward S. Harkness Gift, 1926 26.7.201

1. Weinstein 1989, pp. 17–29. The normal practice in the Amarna period was to show the god's name, Aten, in the top line facing the seated-queen determinative at the bottom. On this scarab, the reed leaf (the Egyptian letter *i*) in the god's name is reversed and faces away from the queen.
2. Ibid., p. 19, fig. 31, with previous bibliography.

224
PLAQUE WITH HEADS OF AKHENATEN AND NEFERTITI

Limestone
Height 15.7 cm (6⅛ in.); width 22.1 cm (8¾ in.)
Egypt
New Kingdom, Dynasty 18, reign of
Akhenaten, ca. 1349–1336 B.C.
Brooklyn Museum, New York 16.48

This plaque is carved in sunk relief with representations of the heads of Akhenaten and his queen, Nefertiti.[1] The couple are portrayed in the style developed toward the end of their reigns, with features far less exaggerated than in earlier years. That is particularly true of the king, whose earlier representations depicted him with heavy-lidded eyes, drooping lips, elongated chin, and two fleshy creases on the front of his neck. Although those peculiarities are only hinted at here, he is also recognizable by his headdress, the baglike royal *khat* that he often wore.

Nefertiti's headdress, which was worn by no other queen, is a bulbous cap. In painted examples, it is shown as blue. Her earlobe is pierced for earrings, as is the king's, and the front of her neck is marked by a single fleshy crease. Her facial features are more regular than those of her husband, and they subtly suggest a woman who, though still beautiful, is no longer young. Note, for example, her rather gaunt cheek and the hint of a double chin.

This small relief is clearly the work of a master sculptor. The hole at the top indicates that it was meant to be hung on a wall, probably to serve as a guide to lesser artists. Other comparable three-dimensional sculptors' models have been excavated at Tell el-Amarna, including the famous head of Nefertiti in Berlin, which represents her wearing a cylindrical blue crown.

This relief is often referred to as the Wilbour Plaque, named after the early American Egyptologist Charles Edwin Wilbour, who purchased it in 1881 near the site of Tell el-Amarna, the city founded by

Akhenaten. There, temples decorated with reliefs showed the king, Nefertiti, and their daughters worshipping his sun god, the Aten. It was at Tell el-Amarna that this relief was doubtless made and used.   ERR

1. This plaque has been frequently discussed and illustrated; see, most recently, Arnold in *Royal Women of Amarna* 1996, pp. 79, 90, fig. 81; Fazzini, Romano, and Cody 1999, p. 101, no. 54; and Fazzini in *Pharaohs of the Sun* 1999, p. 245, no. 135.

225

225
RING FRAGMENT

Electrum
Height 1.6 cm (⅝ in.); width 1.4 cm (½ in.);
length 1.6 cm (⅝ in.)
Uluburun shipwreck
Late Bronze Age, ca. 1300 B.C. context
New Kingdom, Dynasty 18, 14th century B.C.
manufacture
Bodrum Museum of Underwater
Archaeology, Turkey 83.24.86 (KW 603)

This Dynasty 18 signet ring fragment, made of a gold and silver alloy, has suffered significant wear and chipping, and chisel marks along the break at the bottom edge show that it was deliberately cut in half. The lower half of the bezel and most of the hoop are gone, leaving the remaining segment as little more than a piece of scrap metal eventually to be melted down for reuse.

Of the three surviving signs on the upper part of the bezel, only the neatly cut ostrich feather on the left, symbol of Maat, the Egyptian goddess of truth and justice, is completely legible. The figure in the center is a vulture with carefully detailed plumage and a head which may be that of a vulture or of a human. If the former identification is correct, the bird could possibly represent Nekhbet, the vulture goddess of Upper Egypt; if the latter, then a better connection might be to a royal statue of probable Middle Kingdom date in Cairo that has a female human head on the body of a vulture.[1] The partially preserved, more roughly cut figure on the right is difficult to identify. It appears to be the upper part

of a seated woman possibly wearing a crown, but an inverted triangular chip, perhaps deliberately cut out of the face of the bezel above the head, has obliterated nearly all of what was once there. Overall, the signs on the bezel seem to relate to a woman, specifically a queen, but the exact significance of the composition remains elusive.   JMW

1. Keimer 1935. See also Weinstein 1989, pp. 22–23.

226
SCARAB

Amethyst
Height 0.8 cm (⅜ in.); width 1.5 cm (⅝ in.);
length 1.9 cm (¾ in.)
Uluburun shipwreck
Late Bronze Age, ca. 1300 B.C. context
Middle Kingdom, Dynasty 12–13, 19th–18th
century B.C. manufacture
Bodrum Museum of Underwater
Archaeology, Turkey 4.6.98 (KW 4851)

The scarabs found in the Uluburun shipwreck come from a variety of periods and places. The earliest is this one, made of amethyst. Like most amethyst scarabs of the early second millennium B.C., it has a plain base, with the side and back features of the beetle defined only perfunctorily.[1] The legs are rendered as several short lines down the sides between two horizontal lines; on the back are three lines carved in the form of the Roman numeral I, with the top line delineating the back of the head area and a line near the base perhaps for

226

the back of the wing cases. The head area is blank, and no prothorax is indicated.

Amethyst is a translucent variety of quartz whose purplish color comes from ferric-oxide impurities. The amethyst used by Egyptians during the Middle Kingdom comes from deposits at Wadi el-Hudi, about 35 kilometers southeast of Aswan, in Egypt's Eastern Desert.[2] Inscriptions left by pharaonic expeditions in this mining region attest to the widespread exploitation of the amethyst deposits from late Dynasty 11 through the late Middle Kingdom, during which the use of this gemstone in Egyptian jewelry and seals—for both royal name and private name and title scarabs—reached its peak. The hardness of amethyst made it much more difficult to work than softer materials, yet this very quality also explains why many amethyst scarabs created in the early second millennium B.C. have been found in archaeological deposits dating hundreds of years later.   JMW

1. E.g., A. Rowe 1936, pls. 10, 11, and passim; Tufnell 1984, p. 39, fig. 15, nos. 1–18.
2. Sadek 1980–85; Shaw and Jameson 1993.

227
SCARAB

Gold, faience
Height 1.9 cm (¾ in.); width 1.8 cm (¾ in.);
length 2.5 cm (1 in.)
Uluburun shipwreck
Late Bronze Age, ca. 1300 B.C. context
Second Intermediate Period, 17th century B.C.
manufacture
Bodrum Museum of Underwater
Archaeology, Turkey 28.24.86 (KW 338)

This scarab is an heirloom of Levantine rather than Egyptian manufacture. The design on the base is of a type that initially appeared in the seventeenth century B.C. on scarabs in the southern Levant. It still occurs occasionally in the early sixteenth century B.C. but is rarely seen on contemporary Second Intermediate Period scarabs in Egypt or Nubia.[1] The hieroglyphs are arranged in three vertical columns, with the central column of signs set within a "shrine," above which is a winged sun disc. The four signs in the two flanking columns are identical. The signs on the base

227

227, back

228

228, back

are purely decorative and amuletic in nature; their arrangement does not form a comprehensible text.

The beetle's back is executed in a highly schematic fashion typical of the period. The trapezoidal head has double side lines and a simple open clypeus (the shieldlike plate at the front of the head). A single horn protrudes from the center of the head, and small squared eyes flank the base.[2] The rest of the back is blank except for a single small notch along each side to indicate the division between the prothorax and the wing cases. The thin gold mount and attached tubular endings were made separately, after which the endings were soldered to the band. The scarab was probably threaded with gold wire to create a finger ring.   JMW

1. D. Ben-Tor 2007, pp. 87, 135, 168, pls. 58, 86; cf. Tufnell 1984, pp. 123–24, pl. 20.
2. Tufnell 1984, p. 34, fig. 12 (head type D6). A good illustration of the head appears in *Das Schiff von Uluburun* 2005, p. 599, no. 113.

228

SCARAB

Maroon jasper with inclusions
of quartz
Height 0.7 cm (¼ in.); width 1.3 cm (½ in.);
length 1.8 cm (¾ in.)
Uluburun shipwreck
Late Bronze Age, ca. 1300 B.C. context
New Kingdom, Dynasty 18, 15th–14th
century B.C. manufacture
Bodrum Museum of Underwater
Archaeology, Turkey 45.7.95 (KW 3699)

The baboon was an exotic creature that the Egyptians obtained from the land of Punt, in the area of northern Ethiopia, or Eritrea.[1] Together with the ibis, it was a sacred attribute of Thoth, whose numerous identities in Egyptian mythology included god of writing, god of justice, and god of the moon. In his capacity as the moon god, Thoth is depicted as a baboon wearing a crescent moon and a full lunar disc on his head.

Steatite scarabs inscribed with designs that incorporate representations of baboons

were quite numerous in both Egypt and the Levant during the New Kingdom.[2] This is a rare example made of maroon jasper, a semiprecious stone that occurs geologically in a variety of colors at several places in Egypt's Eastern Desert.[3]

Many New Kingdom scarabs show a baboon placed variously on a stool or a standard, or in the hieroglyph *neb*, and facing—sometimes in a pose of adoration—the name of a king.[4] The baboon on this very fine scarab sits on a stool, with the crescent moon and lunar disc on his head; he holds between his paws what appears to be a *wedjat*, in Egyptian mythology the eye of Horus stolen by Seth and retrieved by Thoth. The animal is cut in simple outline form with no delineation of the interior details of the body.   JMW

1. Houlihan 1996, index s.v. "baboon."
2. E.g., Petrie 1925, pp. 16, 19, 23, pl. 13, nos. 840–46; Hornung and Staehelin 1976, p. 107, nos. 244, 265, 266, 401, 664, 697, 744, 747, B30, D3, MV6. On some of these pieces, the baboon hieroglyph actually substitutes for the Egyptian *Djehuti* (Thoth).
3. Aston, Harrell, and Shaw 2000, pp. 29–30. Scarabs made of jasper are rare prior to Dynasty 18.
4. The two kings most often named on these objects are Thutmose III and Ramesses II; see, e.g., Jaeger 1982, pp. 79, 151, ills. 158, 159, 430, 537, 591, 594, figs. 85, 96.

229

SCARAB

Green stone
Height 0.9 cm (⅜ in.); width 1.4 cm (½ in.);
length 1.5 cm (⅝ in.)
Uluburun shipwreck
Late Bronze Age, ca. 1300 B.C. context
Cypriot or Levantine manufacture
Bodrum Museum of Underwater
Archaeology, Turkey 46.5.90 (KW 2012)

This enigmatic scarab, originally located toward the stern area of the ship along with other glyptic and jewelry, has certain features typical of New Kingdom and later scarabs. These include V-shaped nicks (the humeral callosities) marking the shoulders on the back, and the incised lines radiating out across the beetle's clypeus (the latter trait common only starting in Dynasty 19). Nevertheless, the piece is clearly of non-Egyptian manufacture.

229

229, back

It is nearly circular in shape with somewhat flattened ends, quite unlike the typical Egyptian scarab which is more elongated and has rounder ends. In addition, the oversized V-shaped nicks and the schematically rendered beetle legs on the sides suggest an origin outside the Nile Valley, as does the very non-Egyptian design engraved on the stamping surface.

A roaring lion with raised tail strides to the left. Its head is well defined, with the eye formed as a dot within an almond-shaped depression creating an angled profile from the ear and forehead to the nose, with a raised area for the cheek and a gaping jaw. The animal's heavily muscled but lithe body is captured in this rendering both by its posture and by the use of strong curves and high modeling for the belly, rump, and thigh areas. The lower limbs are, by contrast, formed of thin double lines, perhaps to indicate leg tendons; the lines thicken and bend to evoke such features as dewclaws and paws.

Various aspects of this image can be paralleled in glyptic representations of felines from Cyprus and Ugarit. The posture of the animal—with all four legs placed firmly on a groundline, the (partially missing) rear leg nearest the viewer extending backward, and the tail raised and curled over the back—as well as such details as the placement of one foreleg in

line with the chest curve, can be compared with images on seals and seal impressions found at Ugarit (some of them attributed to Cypriot manufacture).[1] While individual features such as the linear depiction of the legs occur on seals from Syria,[2] others such as the form of the head and eye are found on Cyprus.[3] The treatment of the body as a sum of parts rather than as an organic whole places this representation outside the Aegean world. However, both the rendering of individual elements and the overall sense of movement suggest that it was made by a seal carver working on Cyprus or at Ugarit, where Aegean traditions were embedded into local styles.

JMW/JA

1. See two ring impressions on tablets from Ugarit: RS 17.141, showing a griffin with the far foreleg emerging from the chest and front hind leg extended back, and RS 16.400, depicting a lion in a similar posture, which Beyer (1997, p. 175, fig. 24) attributes to possible Cypriot manufacture; a steatite rectangular prism seal from Ugarit: AO 28277: RS 10.001, depicts a similar though fuller, treatment of the head, chest, and forelegs, but with the foreground rear leg kicked forward in the Aegean manner, perhaps indicating Cypriot manufacture; for a steatite scarab from Kition with a striding griffin, its foreground rear leg extended back and far foreleg also emerging from the chest, see Karageorghis 1980, pp. 784–85, fig. 66; by contrast, note the more characteristically Aegean posture of the lion on a gold ring from Enkomi (Karageorghis 1968, pl. XXXVII:5, 6) with a natural transition from chest to far foreleg and rear leg nearest the viewer kicked forward; see also felines incised on ivories from Megiddo: Loud 1939, pl. 52:266, 228.
2. Hammade 1987, fig. 159.
3. Karageorghis 1968, pl. XXXVII:3.

230

CYLINDER SEAL

Hematite
Height 2.9 cm (1⅛ in.); diameter 1.2 cm (½ in.)
Uluburun shipwreck
Late Bronze Age, ca. 1300 B.C. context
Old Babylonian manufacture,
18th century B.C.
Middle Assyrian recarving, 14th century B.C.
Bodrum Museum of Underwater
Archaeology, Turkey 11.5.87 (KW 881)

This seal was probably first carved in Babylonia during the second half of the eighteenth century B.C., when the cutting wheel was used for the deep grooves that form the basis of the figures, and recut on several occasions.[1] The initial design was one of the most popular in the Old Babylonian period. The so-called king with a mace faces the suppliant goddess who raises both hands in intercession for the owner of the seal. The bearded and kilted king wears the round-brimmed Babylonian royal headdress and holds a mace at his waist. The goddess wears the horned headdress of a deity (see cat. no. 7), has looped hair, numerous necklaces (now barely visible), a necklace counterweight down her back, and a tiered, flounced robe. Between the figures are a star disc and a crescent above the small figure of a kilted priest holding a cup and, originally, a small bucket for libations.

The seal must have been extremely worn when, at some later date, the king's beard was partially recut, his kilt altered, his cup recut, and his bucket erased; the priest was given a headband. The original owner's three-line cuneiform inscription

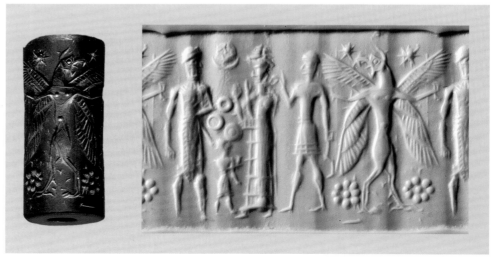

230

was also erased so that only illegible traces remain, and over it a four-winged lion-demon was cut with considerable expertise. Two stars and two rosettes further mask some of the cuneiform signs (perhaps the rosettes and the circular drillings between the original two figures at left were added at the same time, as both appear to have been cut with a worn tubular drill). The lion-demon stands upright, its beaklike jaws open to reveal fangs and a pointed tongue, its staring eye set below a sharply angled brow. A mule's ear rises from its head, and small drill holes indicate nipples. Its arms and legs end in talons, two wings rise from its shoulders, and two hang down. The recutting of earlier seals was frequent in the Late Bronze Age, and the lion-demon addition can be securely dated to the second half of the fourteenth century B.C. by comparing similar creatures on seal impressions used on clay tablets from the reigns of the Middle Assyrian kings Eriba-Adad I (cat. no. 124) and Ashur-uballit I. There follows a hiatus in the archival evidence until the reign of Adad-nirari I (ca. 1305–1274 B.C.); by then the lion-demon had disappeared from the repertoire.

The final change to the seal was the insertion of a thin, kilted figure behind the interceding goddess. He faces left, raises his right hand, and holds a sickle sword in his lowered left hand. His dress, particularly the two tabs at the back of his cap, identify him as the so-called Assyrian hero, who appears in this posture after Ashur-uballit's reign but not later than 1290 B.C. His presence supports a date for the final recutting of this seal between about 1320 and 1290 B.C., which fits perfectly with a date of about 1300 B.C. for the wreck of the Uluburun ship.[2]   DC

1. The material of the seal is probably hematite, but it has not been analyzed and could be magnetite or goethite, as all three iron oxides were used.
2. For further reference, see Collon 1987, no. 570; Collon 1989, pp. 14–16, figs. 26–28; Matthews 1990, no. 285; Collon 2005a, no. 570; Collon in *Das Schiff von Uluburun* 2005, pp. 110–11, no. 125, and p. 603.

231a

231b

231a, b
CYLINDER SEALS

a. Rock crystal, gold
Height 2.8 cm (1⅛ in.); diameter 1.1 cm (½ in.)
2.5.87 (KW 714)

b. Rock crystal
Height 2.2 cm (⅞ in.); diameter 1 cm (⅜ in.)
10.19.90 (KW 2159)

Uluburun shipwreck
Late Bronze Age, ca. 1300 B.C. context
Kassite manufacture, 14th century B.C.
Bodrum Museum of Underwater
Archaeology, Turkey

The two seals seen here were probably cut shortly before 1300 B.C., as they were newly made at the time of the shipwreck. They were worked with cutting wheels and drills of different sizes on very clear rock crystal, and both have slightly convex ends.[1] Over the ends of the first seal (cat. no. 231a), strips of gold were roughly shaped and braised together to form rudimentary caps about 7 millimeters high; they hide the upper and lower parts of the design.[2] Depicted are three bearded male figures, probably gods, approaching a fourth, probably a royal worshipper, in postures and garments characteristic of Kassite procession scenes (see fig. 116, here possibly as dignitaries). Each of the first three figures stands with one foot forward and left arm bent; the first approaching figure holds a short bow in his lowered hand, but the other two are empty-handed. All three wear globular headdresses and robes with double diagonal hems. The fourth figure is smaller and wears a flatter headdress. The hem of his long robe is indicated by two heavy lines meeting at a slight angle; his right arm is bent, and his left hand is raised in greeting. Various symbols are inserted between the figures, and linear borders encircle the top and bottom of the seal. The symbols may identify the gods: the cross could be an abbreviated star indicating an astral deity; a diagonal

Figure 116. Suggested reconstruction of designs on glass beakers from Hasanlu. Kassite period. Extant fragments: University of Philadelphia Museum of Archaeology and Anthropology 65-31-403, 65-31-404, 65-31-405

V might be a fish, signifying the water god; the crescent could stand for the moon god; and the sideways V, which may represent a fly, symbolizing courage and victory, is appropriately placed next to the deity with a bow—presumably a warrior god. The lozenge and eye shapes are probably the same symbol (known as the *rhomb*) placed on either side of the worshipper for good luck; this symbol is found on royal and other seals from Babylonia during this period but seems to have been absent in northern Mesopotamia.

The second seal (cat. no. 231b) is slightly flattened on one side, although there is no indication of earlier cutting and erasure. A small chip at the lower end, probably caused during manufacture, was filed down and polished. The design shows a standing bearded worshipper facing right, with one hand raised before a seated, bearded king (or god?) who holds a cup beneath a star; behind the king is a suppliant goddess of Old Babylonian type. All three figures are robed, and they wear their hair in buns beneath their domed headdresses. At the end of the scene stands a frontal nude figure with her head turned toward the right. Linear borders circle the top and bottom of the seal.

Although both seals incorporate Babylonian motifs belonging to earlier periods, there are several indications that these seals were not cut in Babylonia. The figures on catalogue number 231a are paralleled on seals of what is known as the First Kassite Style of fourteenth-century B.C. Babylonia, but those seals are rigidly conventional. They generally depict only one or two figures, and are inscribed, often with long prayers. This seal is unusual, therefore, in that it is uninscribed and depicts four figures. The posture adopted by the first three figures is that of the "king (or god) with a mace" of Old Babylonian seals (see cat. no. 230), a figure that seems to derive from the victorious warrior king and that probably represented a beneficent being. The posture of the fourth figure is that of the king in ceremonial robes, found on Mesopotamian seals from the late third millennium B.C. into Kassite times. Deities normally face left when a seal is impressed; as a king, therefore, he should face right. On the present seal, however, the scene is reversed: the more imposing size, headdress, and stance of the three advancing figures, and the attitude of worship of the fourth, suggest three gods approaching a worshipper,

perhaps a king. The reversed design may, therefore, indicate that the seal cutter was copying seal impressions rather than an actual seal.

Seated deities appear frequently on seals of the First Kassite Style, but the composition on catalogue number 231b derives from much earlier seals of the Third Dynasty of Ur and early Old Babylonian period (2100–1850 B.C.); on those seals, the suppliant goddess is sometimes replaced by a goddess who leads the worshipper. The nude female appears on Old Babylonian seals made predominantly between about 1820 and 1740 B.C., but it is only on Late Bronze Age examples that she turns her head to one side. Such figures are often referred to as "nude goddesses," but they may be priestesses or apotropaic figures, as they never wear the horned headdress of deities. On First Kassite seals, the nude female would be shown smaller than the other figures; the suppliant goddess would be in front of, and not behind, the god; and a star would be most unusual. The theme of a figure standing before a seated figure with a globular cup is found on pseudo-Kassite seals from southwestern Iran about 1300 B.C.

There is yet another reason for suggesting that the seals probably originated outside Babylonia. Although rock crystal is an extremely hard form of quartz, few Kassite cylinder seals were made from it, possibly because it fractures easily when drills and cutting wheels are used. Therefore, to avoid overheating the drill bit, rock-crystal seals were always perforated from each end, and this can clearly be seen here through the translucent material. In addition to cylinder seals, the Uluburun ship carried a number of pre-drilled rock-crystal beads and amygdaloid seal blanks suitable for the Mycenaean market (cat. no. 189), suggesting that the rock crystal came from or via the Levant. The Uluburun rock-crystal seals may, therefore, have been imitations of Babylonian seals made in the Levant to satisfy a demand for Kassite seals. Indeed, genuine Kassite seals excavated at Thebes in Boiotia testify to this demand (see cat. no. 177).

Although the two seals may have been products of the same workshop, we know they were not produced by the same seal carver because of differences in the way various features were cut; for example, the

bodies on catalogue number 231a are outlined, but on catalogue number 231b they
are recessed on the seal. The designs of
both seals were based on Old Babylonian
prototypes, but the techniques used were
later, and thus the designs are archaizing.
Furthermore, had the seals been produced
in Babylonia in the fourteenth century B.C.,
they would have been cut in one of the
Kassite styles then in vogue, but this was
not the case. These two seals are more
closely related to each other than to any
other Kassite seals.   DC

1. For further reference, see Collon 1987,
   no. 571; Collon 1989, pp. 12–15, figs. 24, 25;
   Matthews 1990, no. 124; Collon 2005a,
   no. 571; Collon in *Das Schiff von Uluburun*
   2005, pp. 110–12, nos. 123, 124, and
   pp. 602–3.
2. The caps are easily removed, allowing the
   whole design to be studied.

232

232

CYLINDER SEAL

Orange, yellow, and brown faience
Height 2.6 cm (1 in.); diameter 1.1 cm (½ in.)
Uluburun shipwreck
Late Bronze Age, ca. 1300 B.C. context
Syro-Mitanni manufacture,
ca. 1500–1320 B.C.
Bodrum Museum of Underwater
Archaeology, Turkey 56.7.95 (KW 3405)

This is one of two seals from the
Uluburun wreck that belong to a
distinctive workshop of faience seals in
the Mitanni Common Style[1] and are a
counterpart to the rock-crystal pair
(cat. no. 231a, b).[2] This seal depicts a figure who faces right in the impression and
grasps a horn and the beard of a rampant
goat that stands in front of a stylized tree
and looks back over its shoulder at its
assailant. On the other side of the tree is a
seated deity facing left, wearing a horned
headdress, with one hand extended toward
the tree and holding one of its branches.
Standing behind the seat, an attendant
holds a staff or mace in his right hand and
a curved sword by his side. The two standing figures wear globular brimmed headdresses, and all three wear fringed robes.
Linear borders ring the top and bottom of
the seal.

Once glazed in bright colors, faience
seals were mass-produced in several centers between about 1500 and 1320 B.C. and
were traded in large numbers. Because
they were so common, they were seldom
kept as heirlooms and are therefore useful
for dating the houses and burials in which
they have been excavated. Seals from this
particular workshop are unusual in that
they show heroes fighting animals—a
subject rarely depicted on Mitanni seals.
Products of this workshop have been excavated at sites that span a vast area of the
Levant, from Tell Kazel and Tell al-
Hamidiya to Kamid el-Loz, Hazor, Beth-
Shan, and were also found at Dhekelia on
Cyprus. Three have been excavated in
northern Mesopotamia, at Tell Mohammad
ʿArab, Tell Billa, and Ashur. There are
also many unprovenanced examples. All
these seals show heroic figures with similar round double-brimmed hats and huge
noses, either nude or wearing fringed,
open robes.

With the exception of an unprovenanced example in a private collection that
provides a very close parallel, this is the
only seal to show a seated figure. The tree
on this seal is also closely paralleled on
many other seals from this workshop and
on related seals from Beth-Shan, Tell Abu
Hawam, and Lachish, on the Kamid el-Loz
seal, and even on a seal from Marlik, near
the Caspian Sea in Iran. The provenanced
examples from this workshop have been
found over such a wide area that it is

unfortunately impossible to establish their
place of manufacture. The form of the tree
indicates close links with sites in the
southern Levant, and a workshop in that
area is possible.   DC

1. The other Mitanni Common Style seal from
   Uluburun, KW 4266, is not included here.
2. For further reference, see Collon in *Das Schiff
   von Uluburun* 2005, pp. 112–13, no. 127, and
   p. 604.

365

233

CANAANITE DAGGER

Bronze with ebony and ivory inlays
Max. height 4.1 cm (1⅝ in.); length 34.6 cm
(13⅝ in.); max. thickness of blade 0.6 cm
(¼ in.)
Uluburun shipwreck
Late Bronze Age, ca. 1300 B.C.
Bodrum Museum of Underwater
Archaeology, Turkey 30.1.2000 (KW 1393)

Among the bronze weapons found on
the Uluburun wreck were a flanged-
hilt short sword and two daggers, the
shorter of which is pictured here.[1] The
pointed, slender blade is leaf-shaped, widening along the middle of its length and
tapering slightly toward the hilt.[2] A band
of decorative punched dots at the base of
the blade forms three transverse parallel
lines. Between the hilt and the three
punched lines is an incised zigzag motif
filled with punched dots. At its juncture
with the blade, the hilt forms protuber-
ances, or "horns," on either side, which
serve as a handguard or quillon. At the
opposite end of the hilt is an integrated
pommel of an inverted crescent shape. The
hilt edges are raised to form flanges for
the insertion of ivory and ebony inlays,
probably originally affixed with an adhesive and fully preserved on one side. The
grip is inlaid with ebony, the pommel and
quillon with ivory, and each end is separated from the grip plate by four bands of
alternating strips of ivory and ebony.

A second flanged-hilt dagger is similar
to the first, except that it is longer (39.3 cm),
and poorly preserved, and its hilt plates
are completely missing. Still longer is a
unique short sword, one of four found on
the Uluburun ship but the only one of
Canaanite origin. Both the daggers and
the sword were cast in one piece, a manufacturing technique that strengthens the
integrity of the weapon while allowing
it to remain narrow.[3] With a length of
45.7 centimeters, the sword is similar in
size to the shorter of the two Mycenaean
swords found on the ship (cat. no. 238a).
This is the only known example of a

flanged-hilt Canaanite sword of its type.[4]
Its leaf-shaped blade is decorated with two
transverse bands across the base, each
composed of three finely incised longitudinal grooves; the flanged hilt is inlaid with
ivory and ebony.[5]

There were either three or four
Canaanite merchants on board the
Uluburun ship (see pp. 301–2).[6] The larger
size and the high quality of craftsmanship
of the only Canaanite sword found on the
vessel suggest that it probably belonged
to the chief merchant,[7] who may also have
been the ship's captain. Although the
present dagger may have been a companion piece also belonging to the captain, the
discovery of additional bronze daggers of
various types indicates that each merchant
carried a weapon. All four Uluburun
swords were found at the stern of the ship,
while one flanged-hilt dagger was located
just aft of the mast and the second was
found among the copper ingots near the
ship's bow. Clearly, at least one and perhaps both of the daggers were originally
located in the stern half of the ship but
possibly somewhere forward of the
swords. If so, the placement of personal
possessions in different areas of the ship
may reflect a social hierarchy observed
among those on board, with the higher-
ranking individuals bearing swords using
the stern of the vessel and the subordinate
merchants perhaps using the area around
the mast or just aft of midships.

While these weapons would have provided a measure of personal protection for
the merchants and the truncated size of
the swords would have been more practical for shipboard activities, their primary
function was probably as an indicator of
status. Daggers were common weapons on
the Levantine coast in the Bronze Age, but
flanged-hilt daggers were considered a
luxury item.[8] The Uluburun examples,
with their inverted crescent-shaped pommel, leaf-shaped narrow blade, and rivetless construction, are typical products.[9]

Flanged-hilt daggers of various types
are found on Cyprus,[10] along the Levantine
coast,[11] and at sites farther inland,[12] but
the closest parallels to the Uluburun

flanged-hilt daggers and sword come from sites such as Tel Dan, where two daggers with pointed, leaf-shaped blades decorated at the base and crescentic handguards and pommels were found in a fourteenth-century B.C. tomb.[13] Two flanged-hilt daggers, with partly preserved less exotic wood hilt inlays, were found in fourteenth-century B.C. tombs, near the Persian Garden at Akko, thought to belong to wealthy merchants.[14] Similar examples are seen at Ugarit,[15] Shechem,[16] Beth-Shan,[17] Fara (Beth-Pelet),[18] and Tel Aphek.[19] Some of these daggers retain remnants of their hilt plates, all of which are reported to be of wood, but without mention of any ivory inlays. This points to the unique nature of the Uluburun pieces.[20]   CP

1. Pulak 1988, pp. 20–23, figs. 20–24; Pulak 1997, pp. 246–47, fig. 16.
2. The hilt is the handle of the dagger and consists of three parts: the handguard, the grip, and the pommel. The handguard is a widening of the hilt at the juncture with the blade, the grip is the middle section of the hilt where the dagger is held, and the pommel is a widening at the end of the hilt, usually for balance and ease of grip.
3. Maxwell-Hyslop 1946, p. 33.
4. Using an arbitrary length of about 45 centimeters to distinguish between daggers and short swords, among the Bronze Age flanged-hilt bladed bronze weapons cast in one piece found on the Levantine coast, only the Uluburun specimen would qualify as a short sword. Only three daggers exceed 40 centimeters in length: Shechem (43.8 cm), Megiddo (40.0 cm), and Beth-Shan (43.9 cm); Shalev 2004, p. 43, no. 143, p. 46, nos. 147, 148, pls. 14:143, 15:147, 148.
5. Pulak 1988, p. 20, fig. 20; Pulak 1995, p. 50, fig. 11, pp. 54–55; Pulak 1997, pp. 246, 248, fig. 16.
6. Pulak 2000a, pp. 247–66; Pulak 1998, pp. 209–10.
7. Pulak 2001, p. 45.
8. Biran and Ben-Dov 2002, p. 121. Chavane 1987, p. 366, figs. 27–29. This type also approximately corresponds to Shalev's Type 7 daggers; Shalev 2004, pp. 41–54, pls. 14–18. The Uluburun daggers and sword fall into Maxwell-Hyslop's Type 31 category of Asiatic weapons: "flanged-hilt" swords and daggers. These bronze weapons are cast in one piece and the edges of the hilt are flanged to receive hilt inlays, either of wood, ivory, or bone, held in place by adhesives or rivets; see Maxwell-Hyslop 1946, pp. 33–36, pl. IV:31A.
9. Maxwell-Hyslop's suggestion that flanged-hilt swords are Aegean in origin has since been refuted: Maxwell-Hyslop 1946, p. 34; Sandars 1961, p. 22; Catling 1964, p. 129.
10. Flanged-hilt daggers found in Nicosia on Cyprus are attributed to Syro-Canaanite origins. (Catling 1964, pp. 128–29, pl. 15:i–l).
11. Petrie 1934, pl. XXVIII:295; Guy and Engberg 1938, fig. 171:8, pl. 149:8; Yadin 1963, pp. 187, 209; Schaeffer 1936a, figs. 13, 22A; Schaeffer 1939a, pp. 67–68, fig. 63u.
12. Medvedskaya 1982, pp. 68–70, figs. 9.8–9.13.
13. Biran and Ben-Dov 2002, pp. 120–21, figs. 2.88–2.90:117–18.
14. Ben-Arieh and Edelstein 1977, pp. 33, 36, 40, figs. 18:1, 18:3. Two tanged-dagger types from the tombs are also similar to one found on the Uluburun ship (ibid., pp. 33–41, fig. 19:1, 2).
15. Chavane 1987, pp. 364–67, figs. 19, 20, 27–29.
16. M. Tadmor 1970, p. 63.
17. James and McGovern 1993, pp. 212–13, fig. 159:5, pl. 51:h; Rowe 1940, p. 9, pls. XXXII:3, XLIXA:6. A second flanged-hilt dagger with a more slender form was found at Beth-Shan; Shalev 2004, p. 53, no. 163, pl. 18:163.
18. MacDonald 1932, pls. XLVII, XLVIII:2; Shalev 2004, p. 52, no. 162, pl. 18:162. In this example, the arch of the pommel is a full semi-circle, and the entire weapon is of a more slender form, but the decoration at the base of the blade is somewhat similar to that of the Uluburun dagger.
19. Kochavi 1977, p. 9.
20. While other flanged-hilt daggers have been found with preserved hilt inlays of wood, those of the Uluburun weapons are the only ones identified as ebony. Variants of some flanged-hilt daggers from Gezer, Fara (Beth-Pelet), and possibly Megiddo retain ivory or bone hilt plates, but the use of ornate alternating ebony and ivory hilt inlays are peculiar to the Uluburun weapons.

234
WRITING BOARD

Boxwood, ivory
Height 9.5 cm (3¾ in.); width 13.5 cm (5⅝ in.); thickness 0.9 cm (⅜ in.)
Uluburun shipwreck
Late Bronze Age, ca. 1300 B.C.
Bodrum Museum of Underwater Archaeology, Turkey 61.1.2000 (KW 737)

Reassembled from more than twenty-five fragments, this boxwood writing board[1] consists of two rectangular leaves of similar dimensions, originally joined on their longer sides with a cylindrical ivory hinge.[2] The hinge's missing central segment was longer than the preserved hinge segments on either side. The three hinge segments rotated around small wood dowels, and each was affixed with two small wood pegs to the grooved edges of the leaves forming the board's spine. This method of hinging allowed the writing board to lie flat when open. Two small holes on one leaf and a small depressed area and a hole on the inner-margin edge of the opposite leaf originally accommodated a fastening device for folding the two leaves tightly together when not in use.[3] The innermost margin corner of one leaf was incised with geometric marks, which may have been repeated on the opposite corner. The recessed areas, incised with irregular cross-hatched lozenge patterns, would have been filled with wax held securely in place by the incisions. The writer would press the tip of a stylus into the wax surface. After the writing was registered, the wax surface could easily be modified or smoothed out, probably with a flattened, spatula-shaped back end of the stylus, for repeated use.[4] The wax surfaces and any texts have disappeared over time.[5]

The writing board was found in a large pithos that had contained whole pomegranates, a fortuitous situation that prevented complete destruction by marine organisms. Although the outer surfaces are heavily eroded, the interior is fairly well preserved, possibly because the board was closed when it was buried. Another boxwood leaf from a second writing board was found nearby.[6] Surviving holes on the edge of the leaf indicate that there were three hinge segments, each affixed with small wood pegs. Found elsewhere on the site were two disarticulated ivory hinge segments, one incomplete, probably belonging to this writing board, although damage to the hinge edge and the absence of the second leaf make this difficult to verify.

While no trace of the wax survived on this writing board either, the surfaces of both would have been prepared probably with beeswax mixed with a bulking and coloring material such as orpiment (trisulphide of arsenic).[7] Quantities of arsenic were found on the Uluburun ship,[8] although it is unlikely that the preparation of the boards actually would have occurred on the ship.

The written surfaces once may have recorded the ship's manifest, perhaps a list of the intended destination and designation of the cargo, or even a message from one court to another.[9] After the text had been inscribed, the writing board would have been closed, tied with string attached to the clasp, and sealed in order to prevent any unauthorized alteration to the original message. Removing the string to open the writing board would have required breaking the sealing.[10]

234

The Uluburun writing boards are the only known examples of their type from the Bronze Age. Archaeological examples of similar boards are not found until the end of the eighth century B.C.[11] That they were used elsewhere in the Late Bronze Age, however, is revealed by surviving texts[12] as well as the discovery of perforated cylindrical hinge segments, most of ivory, similar to those used on the Uluburun writing boards, at Megiddo, Byblos, and Ugarit. This suggests that these writing boards with wax surfaces were of Near Eastern origin and were used in the Levant during the Late Bronze Age.[13] They are mentioned by Homer in his only reference to writing, when Bellerophon, who had been sent from Greece to Lycia, carried a folded tablet bearing baneful signs (*Iliad* 6:178–80).[14]

A Neo-Assyrian letter from the eighth century B.C. seems to fit the context of the Uluburun writing board remarkably well: "The goods of *Umbakidini* which *Rashisi-ilu*, the third messenger brought down by boat, they checked in the city of Sudanina according to the writing-board and accepted them. Everything was intact. There was nothing missing."[15]   CP

1. The term writing board rather than writing tablet is used here in keeping with recent epigraphical terminology; see Symington 1991.
2. Pulak 1998, p. 216; Pulak 1997, pp. 252–53, fig. 21; Bass 1990, pp. 168–69; Bass et al. 1989, pp. 10–11. For the identification of the wood, see Warnock and Pendelton 1991, pp. 107–10. Detailed physical study of the writing board is in Payton 1991, pp. 99–106.
3. Each central section has a carved recess 2 millimeters deep, with borders 0.8 to 1.0 centimeters wide on all sides.
4. Symington 1991, pp. 114–15.
5. Bass et al. 1989, p. 10.
6. This one is more slender (5.7 cm), slightly longer (12.4 cm), and of about the same thickness (max. 1.0 cm) as the first board.
7. An eighth-century B.C. writing board discovered in a well at Nimrud still retained traces of beeswax bearing cuneiform inscriptions. Analysis of the beeswax showed it to be mixed with about 25 percent orpiment (Mallowan 1954, p. 99; Wiseman 1955, pp. 5–6). For the likely use of orpiment, see also Symington 1991, p. 114.
8. Bass 1986, p. 278; Pulak 1988, p. 11.
9. Pulak 1998, p. 216; Symington 1991, pp. 111–23.
10. Symington 1991, pp. 120–21.
11. For multileaved writing boards of wood and ivory from Nimrud, see Mallowan 1954, pp. 98–99; Wiseman 1955, pp. 3–6.
12. Symington 1991, pp. 111–12.
13. Two of the four Megiddo hinges still retain their attachment pins or pegs (Loud 1939, p. 20, nos. 305–8, pl. 58:305–8). There are fifteen cylinders from Ugarit (Gachet-Bizollon 2007, p. 401, pl. 51:434–44), most of which are hinge components but a few are of unknown purpose. Two hinges from Byblos are said to be of bone, and a third of ivory (Dunand 1954, p. 16, no. 6853, fig. 12,

pp. 103, 135, no. 7469, and fig. 127:7469, p. 425, fig. 451:11466, p. 450, no. 11466). Although found near a box, an ivory hinge segment from Hala Sultan Tekke on Cyprus is more likely from a writing board than an element from a box hinge or a furniture component (Niklasson 1983, p. 16; Gachet-Bizollon 2007, p. 213). This type of hinge is not found in the Mycenaean realm.
14. For the possible use of similar wood writing boards in the Aegean, as suggested by the discovery of small bronze hinges associated with burned wood found amid clay tablets at the palaces of Pylos, Knossos, and Zakros, see Shear 1998, pp. 187–89.
15. Refer to Symington 1991, p. 123.

235 a–f

SELECTION OF ZOOMORPHIC WEIGHTS

Bronze

Clockwise from left:

a. Sphinx-shaped weight
Height 2.7 cm (1⅛ in.); width 1.7 cm (⅝ in.);
length 5.6 cm (2¼ in.); weight 80.7 g
55.24.86 (KW 468)

b. Lioness-shaped weight
Height 2.3 cm (⅞ in.); width 2.3 cm (⅞ in.);
length 4.2 cm (1⅝ in.); weight 26.8 g
3.1.94 (KW 3081)

c. Duck-shaped weight
Height 1.7 (⅝ in.); width 1.6 cm (⅝ in.); length
2.2 cm (⅞ in.); weight 8.3 g
29.24.86 (KW 350)

d. Bull-shaped weight
Height 1.3 cm (½ in.); width 1.1 cm (½ in.);
length 2.3 cm (⅞ in.); weight 5.2 g
41.1.2000 (KW 4504)

e. Frog-shaped weight
Height 1.5 cm (⅝ in.); width 1.3 cm (½ in.);
length 2.2 cm (⅞ in.); weight 6.6 g
39.1.2000 (KW 237A)

f. Fly-shaped weight
Height 0.5 cm (¼ in.); width 1.4 cm (⅝ in.);
length 1.8 cm (¾ in.); weight 1.2 g
40.1.2000 (KW 2128)

Uluburun shipwreck
Late Bronze Age, ca. 1300 B.C.
Bodrum Museum of Underwater
Archaeology, Turkey

The balance weights excavated from the Uluburun wreck were well-used, personal weights belonging to the merchants aboard the ship.[1] Evidence suggests that, in addition to the weights, at least three sets of balances were also on the ship. Surviving are two pairs of nested pans or scales from handheld beam balances, one of which is still partly preserved in its walnut sleeve-type case, and fragments of a third pair.[2]

Of the 149 weights found on the ship, 78 were fashioned from hematite or similar iron-bearing minerals, 38 are of bronze, 25 of diorite, steatite, or limestone, and the remaining eight of lead. The hematite and other stone weights were for the most part carefully shaped and polished, but a few are minimally worked chunks.[3] The corpus of the Uluburun balance weights can be divided into morphological groupings. The great majority represent the two most common balance-weight shapes found during the Bronze Age: sphendonoid (oblong, with rounded or pointed ends) and domed. Zoomorphic weights and a few disc-shaped weights make up the rest. The zoomorphic

group consists of 19 bronze balance weights, some hollow cast, with lead cores.

Bronze weights recovered from marine environments are usually severely altered or deformed because of corrosion and are always considered underweight.[4] While many of the zoomorphic pieces are seemingly well preserved, it is apparent that they have lost an indeterminate amount of mass as a result of metal leaching. A few weights are seriously damaged, and the animal shapes they represent are uncertain. Because the hollow-cast weights were significantly damaged by the expanding lead core, which shattered the weight's bronze shell, their unit attributions are extremely difficult, if not impossible, to determine with any degree of accuracy.

Owing to their corrosion resistance in salt water, hence their relatively stable mass, only the non-metallic Uluburun weights were analyzed to determine the mass standards represented. The results revealed that several different weight sets in different mass standards were carried aboard the ship, but the great majority conform to a single mass standard based on a unit of 9.3 to 9.4 grams.[5] This unit of mass undoubtedly represents a shekel of the Syrian standard, commonly used along the Levantine coast, on Cyprus, and in Cilicia,[6] and based on the Egyptian *qedet*. There appear to have been four sphendonoid (for precision weighing) and three domed (for bulk weighing) weight sets aboard the ship conforming to this mass standard, with each merchant probably carrying one set of each weight type. Precision sphendonoid weights with unit masses of about 7.4 grams (most likely the Syro-Canaanite *peyem* standard), 8.3 grams (based on a shekel of the Mesopotamian standard), and 10.5 grams (another norm used in the Syro-Canaanite region) were also carried on the ship, most likely for assaying precious metals or performing conversions to other mass standards.[7] Although the mass standard of the corroded zoomorphic weights cannot be determined with accuracy, these weights, based on the presence of large denominations in the group, probably incorporate at least one additional set based on the 9.3–9.4 gram standard for bulk weighing.

The Uluburun zoomorphic weights take the forms of a fly, two frogs, two ducks, a waterfowl, a recumbent calf and five recumbent bulls, a probable canine head, a couchant lion and lioness, a sphinx, a unique cylindrical weight surmounted by a bucolic scene of a herdsman kneeling before three calves, one of which is lost, and two weights that are too corroded for identification.[8] The Uluburun assemblage constitutes the largest group of such weights from the Bronze Age.[9] The next largest set, a late fourteenth-century B.C. hoard of fourteen balance weights from Kalavassos–Ayios Dhimitrios, includes only eight zoomorphic or anthropomorphic forms.[10]

Of the six zoomorphic weight forms represented here, the recumbent bull (d) is of a type commonly seen in the Levant, Cyprus, and Egypt.[11] The couchant lioness (b) represents another animal shape seen in some numbers, with a similar distribution.[12] Duck-shaped weights, mostly of stone, commonly occur among weights of Mesopotamian origin (see cat. no. 236). Those of bronze are much rarer; the Uluburun ship carried two, the larger of which is shown here (c). At least two bronze examples are known from Cyprus, with other bronze pieces found in Mesopotamia, along the Levantine coast, and in Egypt.[13] The Uluburun sphinx weight (a) is one of the best-preserved zoomorphic weights in the group. Sphinx-shaped weights are otherwise unknown outside of Egypt, except for one from Byblos, covered in gold foil and of uncertain function.[14] A zoomorphic weight unique to the Uluburun group is in the form of a fly (f), also an Egyptian motif. It is the lightest in the assemblage. The smaller of the two frog weights (e) is well preserved, while the larger is badly damaged owing to the expansion of its lead core. Balance weights in the shape of frogs and toads, especially those of bronze, are extremely rare in the Near East and Cyprus, but they do occur in Egypt.[15]

Zoomorphic weights were quite widespread in the ancient Near East during the Late Bronze Age. Their use is depicted in New Kingdom Egyptian tomb paintings, where gold ring ingots are shown in one pan of a balance and animal weights in the other pan.[16] Bronze zoomorphic weights (with and without lead cores) have been found in numbers along the Levantine coast and on Cyprus,[17] as well as in Egypt.[18] To what special purpose these weights may have been put, if any, is now lost to us. The high level of craftsmanship and expense of their materials may hint at their use by the affluent and by elites. On the Uluburun ship, therefore, these weights could have been among the personal possessions of the head or senior merchant, with the simpler weight sets of geometric shapes being used by the lesser or junior merchants. The mass standards of the weight sets on the Uluburun ship provide near-conclusive evidence that Syro-Canaanite merchants were aboard. CP

1. Pulak 2000a, p. 248.
2. Ibid., p. 248, fig. 17.1. The sleeve-type case is the only Bronze Age wood case of this type found outside Egypt, where it is commonly known. For Egyptian balance cases of this type, see Petrie 1974, p. 47, pl. 40, pp. 73–74; Randall-MacIver and Mace 1902, p. 91, pl. 51, D77; Schiaparelli 1927, p. 83, fig. 51; Brunton and Engelbach 1927, p. 18, pl. 13:7; and Bruyère 1937, pp. 199ff., fig. 68.
3. Geometric weights in various shapes from Uluburun are in Pulak 2000a, p. 255, fig. 17.2.
4. Ibid., pp. 253–54.
5. Ibid., pp. 257–60.
6. Petruso 1984, pp. 302–4.
7. Pulak 2000a, pp. 260–63.
8. Ibid., p. 256, fig. 17.3; Pulak 1988, pp. 30–31, figs. 37, 38; Bass et al. 1989, pp. 8–9, fig. 14.
9. Pulak 2000a, p. 262, table 17.1.
10. Courtois 1983, p. 117; Lassen 2000, pp. 235–41.
11. Cypriot examples include one from Maroni (Catling 1964, pl. 44.e; Johnson 1980, p. 25, pl. XXIX), two from Enkomi (Karageorghis 1964, p. 310, fig. 31; Courtois 1984, p. 43, no. 407, fig. 15.36, pl. III), and an example of unknown provenance (Catling 1964, p. 251, pl. 44:d; Karageorghis 1976b, pp. 206–7, fig. 174; Karageorghis and Demas 1985, pp. 130–31, fig. 112). A much corroded, lead-filled bull-calf weight was found at Kition on Cyprus (Karageorghis and Demas 1985, pp. 179, 290, pl. CLII:1267; Buchholz and Karageorghis 1973, pp. 162, 746, no. 1737). Ugarit in Syria has produced more than half a dozen bull weights (Schaeffer 1929, p. 287, fig. 2d; Schaeffer 1937, pp. 148–50, pl. XXIII:4; Schaeffer 1963, p. 209, fig. 25). Others are from Sarepta (Pritchard 1975, p. 69, fig. 62.6), near Akko (Eran and Edelstein 1977, p. 57, with fig. 25:24, p. 62, no. 58), and Tel Nami (Artzy 1993, p. 12).
12. Ugarit has yielded at least three examples of such felines (Schaeffer 1963, p. 209, fig. 25, no. 23-475; Gray 1964, fig. 53). Many more are found farther south: at Akko (Eran and Edelstein 1977, pp. 57, 62, fig. 25.23, pl. XX:37), a lead-filled lioness from Tell Abu Hawam (Hamilton 1935, p. 18, no. 39), a lion cub from Megiddo (Loud 1948, pl. 240:3), one from Hazor (Yadin et al. 1960, p. 159, pl. CXCVI:14), and two others from 'En Shemer (Eran and Edelstein 1977, p. 57). Only a single example is known from Cyprus at Kalavassos (Courtois 1983, pp. 126–27, pl. 17:10; Lassen 2000, p. 236, fig. 16.1, no. 7, p. 241). In Egypt, lion

236

weights in both stone and bronze are known: see Petrie 1926, pl. IX; and Roeder 1956, pp. 365–66, figs. 510–13. For two from Tell el-Amarna, see Pendlebury 1951, pp. 109, 125, pl. LXXVII, nos. 32.250, 33.280.

13. Cypriot examples are from Kalavassos and Enkomi (Courtois 1983, pp. 120, 123, pl. XVII:5), several later Mesopotamian ones from Khorsabad (Braun-Holzinger 1984, pl. 74, nos. 387–90), and two from Alalakh (Arnaud 1967, pp. 152, 154, 167). For Egyptian examples, see Petrie 1926, pl. IX:4815; Skinner 1954, p. 783, fig. 569; Skinner 1967, pl. 5; Weigall 1901, p. 386, no. 7056, pl. 5.

14. Dunand 1954, pl. CXVI, no. 14499; Jidejian 1968, p. 24.

15. Petrie (1926) lists two bronze toads (nos. 4986 and 5245) and five frogs (nos. 4775, 4913, 4986, 5083, 5146).

16. For depictions and lists of Egyptian weighing scenes, see, for example, Regling 1926, pl. 98; Petrie 1926, p. 6; Davies 1933, pl. 11; Skinner 1954, p. 784; Eran and Edelstein 1977, p. 57 n. 33; and Cour-Marty 1985, p. 192 n. 22.

17. Courtois 1983, pp. 117–30.

18. Cour-Marty 1990, p. 27.

236

DUCK-SHAPED WEIGHT WITH CUNEIFORM INSCRIPTION

Diorite

Length 41 cm (16⅛ in.); weight 26.7 kg

Babylon

Late Bronze Age, 13th century B.C.

Eski Şark Museum, Istanbul, Turkey 7878

This weight is in the form of a duck with the head and neck turned back and carved in relief against the body. On the highly polished surface, a cuneiform inscription gives its weight as one "true" talent.[1] A talent was approximately 30 kilograms, and the duck weighs 26.7 kilograms. However, Mesopotamian systems for recording weights and measures often varied. Weights were based on the arbitrary concept of the load, or talent, that could be carried by a man or animal.[2] According to the Sumerian sexagesimal system for counting, the load was then divided into 60 minas, and a mina was divided into 60 shekels.[3]

Zoomorphic weights were widespread in the Near East during the Late Bronze Age, and duck-shaped weights are commonly of Mesopotamian origin. This duck weight, found at Babylon in one of the storerooms on the eastern side of the ziggurat precinct, is dated to the mid-second millennium B.C. on the basis of its inscription.[4] It is one of the rare second-millennium B.C. objects excavated at Babylon because the majority of those levels at the site fall below the modern water table and are largely inaccessible. Stone was preferred for weights of different standards during this period.[5] Although a gradual shift to metal weights occurred in the first millennium B.C., both metal and stone weights were found on the Uluburun shipwreck (see cat. no. 235).   JME

1. Koldewey 1908, p. 16.

2. J. Oates 2005, p. 251.

3. Powell 1987–90, p. 508.

4. Koldewey 1913, pp. 185, 187. The inscription reads: "1 true talent belonging to Mushallim-Marduk son/descendant of the (family) of the shangu-priest of Kish. May Shamash take away whoever removes (this weight)."

5. Zeyrek and Kızıltan 2005.

237

Scepter-Mace

Stone (andesite?)

Max. height 7.8 cm (3⅛ in.); length 19.2 cm

(7½ in.); thickness 5.2 cm (2⅛ in.)

Uluburun shipwreck

Late Bronze Age, ca. 1300 B.C.

Bodrum Museum of Underwater

Archaeology, Turkey 12.7.92 (KW 2742)

This scepter-mace is carved from a gray-green volcanic stone, probably andesite.[1] The mushroom-shaped butt end is incised with spiraling grooves, most of which radiate from its center and end near the knob's edge. The recessed neck is plain and polished smooth. Beginning at the shoulder, the body is embellished with longitudinal fluting consisting of a pair of raised ridges encircling a central ridge. These run the entire length of the body and terminate at the tip of the blade, which curls back on itself to form a loop with a small hole. At its widest part is a transverse shaft hole parallel to the direction of the curl of the blade. The fine modeling of the curled blade suggests that the form was based on metal types. The shaft itself is missing, an indication that it may have been made of wood that disintegrated over time, although a hole of approximately 1 centimeter in diameter seems somewhat narrow for a wood shaft. This may hint at a symbolic or ceremonial rather than functional use for the weapon. The scepter-mace was discovered far down the steep slope of the wreck site; the direction of spillage indicates that it had originated from an area somewhere aft of amidships, probably near the stern.

The Uluburun scepter-mace discovery is unique for the Aegean and the Mediterranean. Judging from a few similar examples from the Balkans and regions farther north, its presence aboard the Uluburun ship provides an indisputable link for an Aegean connection that extends into these regions.[2] It has long been argued that such a connection existed, which resulted in a flow of materials and influences, especially weaponry but also other goods, between the Aegean and the Mediterranean, and eastern Europe and the Black Sea.[3] This scepter-mace now

demonstrates conclusively that such a connection existed from at least the middle of the second millennium B.C.

The Uluburun scepter-mace is a rare variant in stone of a Late Bronze Age bronze axe type found in southeastern European cultures of the Carpathian-Pontic region.[4] In these variants, the blade is drawn out to form a long pick-like spike, which is then rolled into a spiral. As the Uluburun example is fashioned from stone, its blade configuration is simplified to form a single loop rather than an intricate free spiral. Unlike typologically similar counterparts, which are functional axes,[5] these rare scepter-maces were probably of symbolic or ceremonial use—as the Uluburun example must have been—possibly symbols of royal power held by tribal chiefs who may also have been head priests.[6]

A close parallel for the Uluburun scepter-mace, albeit of bronze and with long tubular flanges around the shaft hole, was found in a hoard discovered at Drajna de Jos, north of Bucharest in Romania.[7] A pair of two-part (bivalve) stone molds for casting similar weapons in bronze was found at Pobit Kamuk, near Razgrad in Bulgaria.[8] Another bronze weapon with a partly spiraling blade, but cast with a long cylindrical shaft socket, was found in the Lozovo II hoard in Moldava.[9] These bronze examples, however, probably date to the thirteenth century B.C. or later, slightly postdating the Uluburun example. Stone weapons, however, may have been

more common than similar bronze versions in earlier periods.[10] A similar stone example from Bulgaria, near Ljulin, has a fluted blade and a plain mushroom-shaped butt end. Its blade tip, however, is only bent downward, and not coiled into a full spiral (fig. 117).[11] Another stone scepter-mace, similar to the one from Ljulin, but with spiral grooving on the knobbed butt end, was found in southeastern Bulgaria, near Glavan.[12]

Undoubtedly, the Uluburun scepter-mace was not a trade item or an object left on the ship from a previous voyage. It is a carefully worked symbolic or ceremonial weapon for personal use, representing power and prestige for its owner. As such, its presence may help explain several other items aboard the ship: a seemingly anachronistic globe-headed bronze dress pin with southern Greek parallels of sub-Mycanaean dates;[13] solid-socketed spearheads that occur in Macedonia during the Late Helladic IIIA–B period and subsequently farther south[14]; and a bronze sword with central Mediterranean parallels.[15] It is hypothesized that such "northern" dress pins and spearheads were introduced into the Aegean region by emerging contacts with the cultures of the Balkans to the north. While the peculiar Uluburun sword is attributed to southern Italy and Sicily, somewhat similar examples, albeit of smaller, dagger-sized weapons, are also found in Albania.[16] These objects, along with the scepter-mace, may therefore have

Figure 117. Stone mace head. Thrace, Ljulin. Late Bronze Age. National Archaeological Institute with Museum, Bulgarian Academy of Sciences, Sofia 3500

237

belonged to an individual from the northern Aegean or the Balkans.[17] This person, of some rank, could have represented northern interests in part of the ship's cargo, especially its metal component. Alternatively, he may have functioned in the role of an elite mercenary for the two Mycenaean messengers or envoys, in whose interest it was to negotiate the Uluburun ship through the dangerous waters of the Aegean and to ward off any potential attack by rogue seafarers.[18]

CP

1. The scepter-mace weighs 690 grams. Pulak 2005c, pp. 94, 608; Pulak 1997, pp. 253–54, fig. 22; see also Buchholz and Weisgerber 2005, pp. 149–53.
2. Pulak 1997, pp. 253–54; Buchholz 1999, p. 77.
3. See discussion in Sandars 1983, pp. 43ff., where the emphasis is on weaponry and warfare, although the period discussed is a little later than that of the Uluburun ship. Sandars (1983, pp. 53–55) also notes a close similarity between a spearhead excavated in a grave on the island of Kos and one from the hoard at Drajna de Jos.
4. For this axe type and its variant, see Vulpe 1970, pp. 13–25.
5. The Uluburun scepter-mace and other similar weapons have also been interpreted as deriving from pickaxes rather than bladed axes (Buchholz 1999, p. 74).
6. Tončeva 1982, p. 180; Buchholz 1999, p. 74.
7. Buchholz 1999, pp. 72, fig. 4:b, 75; Vulpe 1970, p. 59, pl. 41:565. This hoard is dated to the Romanian Late Bronze Age (ca. 1300–1200 B.C.), making it a little later than the Uluburun example (Vulpe 1970, p. 59).
8. This hoard is attributed to the Lesura-Verbica group and is dated to the twelfth century B.C. (Hänsel 1976, p. 39, pl. 13). For illustrations and color photographs of the mold, see Buchholz 1999, p. 75, fig. 6:c; Buchholz and Weisgerber 2005, p. 150, figs. 3, 4, where the same mold is illustrated twice. For photographs of both molds, see Venedikov 1988, pp. 70–71, figs. 54, 55.
9. S. Hansen 2005, p. 93; Chernykh 1976, p. 246, fig. XLII:9; Lichardus et al. 2002, p. 159, fig. 6:6, p. 160.
10. Vulpe (1970, p. 24) notes that stone knob-headed axes are found at the very beginning of the Bronze Age in Romania and were more abundant than those in bronze.
11. Lichardus et al. 2002, pp. 158–59, fig. 16:3; Buchholz 1999, p. 76, fig. 6:a; Chernykh in *Gold der Thraker* 1979, p. 62, nos. 81, 82; Tončeva (1982, p. 180) dates the site to the local Late Bronze Age (ca. 13th–11th century B.C.).
12. Unpublished, found in a fill, out of context, but without doubt contemporary with the Ljulin example.
13. Pulak 1997, pp. 254–55; Pulak 1988, pp. 29–30, fig. 36.
14. Pulak 1997, pp. 255–56, fig. 23; Pulak 2005a, pp. 299–300, pl. LXX:d.
15. Pulak 2001, pp. 45–46, fig. 5; Vagnetti and Lo Schiavo 1989, pp. 222–23, fig. 28:2.
16. Bodinaku 1995, p. 268.
17. Another connection through the Balkans is indicated by the presence on the Uluburun ship of beads of Baltic amber, some of which are of shapes seen in the Balkans. These may, however, have been in the possession of the Mycenaeans aboard the ship, who are also known to have commonly used amber beads for adornment; Pulak 2005a, p. 304, pl. LXXI:d; Bass 1986, pp. 286, 289, ill. 25.
18. Pulak 2001, pp. 45–48; Pulak 1997, pp. 254–56.

MYCENAEAN ENVOYS

238a, b
SWORD AND SPEARHEAD

Bronze
a. Sword
Length 45.5 cm (17⅞ in.); max. width 7.2 cm
(2⅞ in.); thickness of blade 0.7 cm (¼ in.)
16.24.86 (KW 301)

b. Spearhead
Length 25 cm (9⅞ in.); width of blade 4.7 cm
(1⅞ in.); diameter of socket 3.4 cm (1⅜ in.)
21.24.86 (KW 309)

Uluburun shipwreck
Late Bronze Age, ca. 1300 B.C.
Bodrum Museum of Underwater
Archaeology, Turkey

238a

238b

Mycenaean bronze weapons recovered from the Uluburun shipwreck
include ten spearheads and two swords.[1]
The swords range in length from 45.5 to
51.3 centimeters, shorter than most conventional examples, and are, therefore,
referred to as short swords. Both the
swords and spears were found in the after
half of the ship.

The two swords have similar single-
cast construction, finely grooved blades,
flanged hilts, and cruciform handguards
with rounded lobes, all features of a type
existing during the fifteenth and fourteenth centuries B.C. (conforming to
Sandars' Class Di and Kilian-Dirlmeier's
Type 1f).[2] Their pommels and the tangs
for attaching them are lost,[3] as are their
hilt plates, which were probably of wood.
Two holes just below the shoulder, and
higher up on the hilt of this one, indicate
where rivets would have secured the plates.
The blades have seemingly convex sections, without true midribs, and with three
fine-grooved lines down the center of this
one and four in the other. While this blade
section differs considerably from the typical high midribbed blade of Di swords,
other swords of this class have only a broad
flat midrib or convex section without
any midrib.[4]

During the fourteenth century B.C., the
ornate version of the Di sword type[5] was
replaced by more efficient and utilitarian
ones, such as those from Uluburun. Although the variants of Di swords without the pronounced midrib are confined

mainly to weapons shorter than 50 centimeters, the loss of the midrib is recognized
as leading to moderately thickened double-
convex blades. Typologically, therefore, the
Di variants, including the Uluburun swords,
mark the end of the ornamental sword-
making tradition of the fifteenth and early
fourteenth centuries B.C. and a transition
to later sword forms.[6]

Of the 22 spearheads found on the
Uluburun ship, ten display characteristics
of later Mycenaean or Aegean spearheads, which are shorter than the earlier
Mycenaean spears.[7] Although the Uluburun
spearheads vary in their dimensions, all
were cast with distinct, leaf-shaped blades

and, with one exception, had solid-cast, seamless sockets to fit the wood shaft of the spear. The spearheads were secured to the shaft with bronze nails or rivets driven through holes at the base of the blade. Spearheads with solid-cast sockets were probably influenced by spears made in the northern Balkans and eastern Europe, but most examples found in the Aegean are thought to be local products.[8] Nearly all of the spearheads on the Uluburun ship appear to be short, stocky weapons with leaf-shaped blades (Avila's Type VI, which usually have split sockets cast flat and rounded in the forge).[9] The Uluburun spearheads are among the earliest securely dated examples of their type found in an Aegean context.

Solid-cast, seamless-socketed spearheads are rare on the southern Greek mainland and appear rather late, with all securely dated examples coming from the late thirteenth and early twelfth centuries B.C.[10] A similar solid-socket spearhead from a chamber tomb at Antheia near Patras, dated to Late Helladic IIIB or Late Helladic IIIC, is classified as a variant of Type VI, with a "short broad blade."[11] Farther north, solid-socketed spearheads from western Macedonian graves at Áno Kómi and Åani date to the Late Helladic IIIA– Late Helladic IIIB:1 period, as does a stone mold for a spearhead of this type found in Macedonia.[12] A spearhead of similar construction was found at Enkomi, and probably dates to the first half of the twelfth century B.C. Owing to the lack of any close Aegean parallels for the spear, its provenance has been debated.[13] Some of the Uluburun spears, along with the scepter-mace (cat. no. 237), a Thapsos-type sword, and perhaps also a globed cloak pin, may have belonged to the third foreigner aboard the ship, thought to have been an elite mercenary from the central or northern Balkans but associated with the Mycenaeans.[14]

Analysis of wood-shaft fragments preserved within several spearhead sockets reveals the wood to be *Pinus sylvestris*,[15] a pine species whose southernmost distribution in Greece is in the northern Pindos Mountains.

In the Late Bronze Age Aegean, a sword was an object of status symbolizing military standing; in warfare, swords were used by a select few.[16] Spears, commonly used in battle and perhaps the warrior's

most effective implement, were also prestige objects, with a similar distribution in Mycenaean burials.[17] Thus, it is likely that the swords aboard the Uluburun ship belonged to two warrior-class or elite Mycenaeans.[18] The swords and the wealth of their other personal adornments suggest that they represented elite or palatial interests and may have been the "messengers" of ancient literary sources, returning from a diplomatic mission to the Near East.[19]

CP

1. Pulak 1988, pp. 20–24, fig. 21; Pulak 1997, pp. 247–48, figs. 16, 17, pp. 255–56, fig. 23; Pulak 1998, pp. 207–8, fig. 21; Pulak 2005a, pp. 298–300, pl. LXX:c, d.
2. Specifically, variant 1f. Sandars 1963, pp. 123–25, 146–48; Kilian-Dirlmeier 1993, pp. 61–62, pl. 25.
3. Pommels are knoblike pieces attached to the end of the hilt in order to ensure a firm grip; they also serve as counterweights for balancing the sword, and are often made of or embellished with precious and semiprecious materials.
4. Kilian-Dirlmeier 1993, pp. 61–62, pls. 25:134, 136–38, 26:140–44; probably also one found at Panaztepe but missing its hilt, see Ersoy 1988, pp. 58–59, 61–64, fig. 3:1, pl. 5. Swords with grooved blades similar to that of sword KW 4193 are found in Mycenae Tomb 91 (Xénaki-Sakellariou 1985, p. 127, nos. 3196, 3197, pl. VIII:3196, 3197) and at Ialysos, Rhodes (Kilian-Dirlmeier 1993, p. 62, no. 139, pl. 25:139). A sword from Khania, Crete, with a slightly different hilt profile but nearly identical blade grooving is similar to catalogue no. 238a (ibid., no. 137, pl. 25:137).
5. The finest specimens of Di swords may have come from Knossos in the Late Minoan II period, but the possibility of other mainland production centers has also been proposed. See Driessen and MacDonald 1984, pp. 64–65, and Sandars 1963, p. 126.
6. Pulak 2005c, p. 298.
7. Ibid., pp. 299–300, pl. LXX:d.
8. Corresponding to Bouzek's Type B3 and Höckmann's Group KII. Bouzek 1985, pp. 138, 141; Sandars 1983, p. 53; Höckmann 1980, p. 69, fig. 15:K18,19, p. 70.
9. Avila 1983, pp. 38–46.
10. Hochstetter 1987, pp. 20–21; Bouzek 1985, p. 139; Höckmann 1980, pp. 20–21, 68, 149, pls. 5:3, 28:7.
11. Avila 1983, pp. 43–44, pl. 15:98.
12. Hochstetter 1987, pp. 20–21.
13. Catling 1964, p. 122, nos. 1, 2, fig. 14:6, 7, pl. 14:e, f.
14. Pulak 2001, pp. 45–48.
15. Nili Lipschitz, personal communication, 2007.
16. Driessen and MacDonald 1984, p. 56.
17. Ibid., p. 58; Sandars 1963, p. 128.
18. Mycenaean swords are rarely found outside the Aegean or in non-Mycenaean contexts.
19. Pulak 2005a, pp. 308–9.

239

MYCENAEAN RELIEF BEADS

Glass
Max. width 1.2 cm (½ in.); max. length 2.9 cm (1⅛ in.); max. thickness 0.4 cm (⅛ in.)
Uluburun shipwreck
Late Bronze Age, ca. 1300 B.C.
Bodrum Museum of Underwater Archaeology, Turkey 2006/4/26A (KW 3498), 2006/4/25A (KW 5753), 2006/4/27A (KW 3344)

Beads of amber, faience, quartz, and glass were among the personal adornments belonging to the two Mycenaeans aboard the Uluburun ship.[1] A total of 17 rectangular, flat-backed, glass relief beads, or plaques, were recovered. These beads are severely weathered and mostly fragmentary, and their original translucent dark blue color, resembling lapis lazuli, has faded. Many more relief beads must have been aboard, but most disintegrated over time in the corrosive seawater.

Of the 17 beads, 12 are of a type adorned with spirals, possibly representing highly stylized hair curls,[2] positioned one above another and separated by a line of dots. They have yet to be studied fully, but the better preserved examples also reveal a ribbed band at the upper end, perforated transversally for stringing, with another perforation on the opposite end through the lowest spiral.[3] Similar relief beads are found in Late Helladic III Aegean contexts, with many examples of the three-spiral variety coming from Rhodes,[4] Crete,[5] and Mycenae.[6]

The remaining five relief beads, three of which are shown here, are of a less common type, adorned with paired horizontal figure-of-eight shield motifs arranged one above the other, separated by a line of dots.[7] Transversally perforated ribbed bands at either end allowed for stringing. Beads with shield designs similar to those from the Uluburun wreck have been found on the Greek mainland at Prosymna[8] and on Rhodes.[9] Both Uluburun glass relief bead types share the common decorative line of dots placed between or on either side of the central motifs, perhaps indicating a common workshop for both.

Iconographic evidence suggests that beads were worn primarily by women, less often by children and men.[10] Found in tombs all over the Mycenaean world,

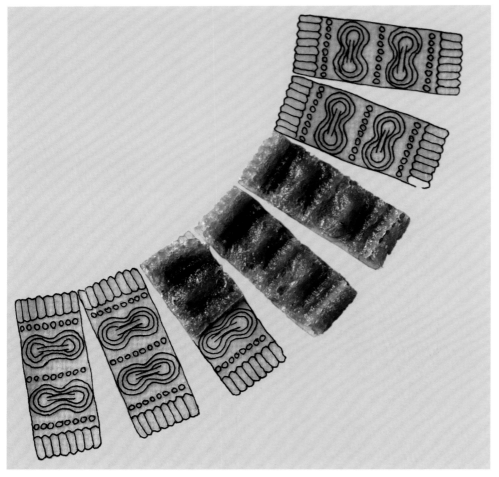

239

glass relief beads are believed to have been used in necklaces, as adornments sewn singly or in groups on garments, or for diadems.[11] These uniquely Mycenaean objects disappeared from the archaeological record with the end of Mycenaean society.[12]

Glass was mass-produced and apparently imported in great quantities to the Aegean as disc-shaped cakes like those found on the Uluburun ship (see cat. no. 187).[13] Along with faience, it probably represented an economical alternative to semiprecious stones such as lapis lazuli and turquoise.[14]

Relief beads are formed by pressing molten glass into open or closed stone molds. Approximately two dozen molds for producing glass ornaments and jewelry have been found in the Aegean.[15] Of these, only one was recovered from a tomb; the majority have been found in two major centers of the Mycenaean world: Mycenae and Knossos.[16] This suggests that the primary, or perhaps the sole, centers of production were in major palatial workshops and that relief beads bearing symbolic motifs may have served as insignias of a

certain religious standing, social status, or perhaps official rank. Relief beads do not appear to have been exported as trade items. The few found in graves outside the Mycenaean realm have been associated with Mycenaean individuals.[17] In contrast to the numerous finds of plain globular glass beads in simple pit or cist grave burials for those of humble means—most probably imported from the Levant (see cat. no. 188) or produced locally from imported raw-glass ingots—the glass relief beads occur almost exclusively in elite burials of affluent families.[18]

Thus, the two types of relief beads found on the Uluburun ship were almost certainly used for personal adornment and, hence, are a virtual indicator of the ethnicity and high standing of the two Mycenaeans on board the ship. They also demonstrate that men wore such beads. Moreover, the Uluburun relief beads represent items of everyday life, rather than commercial goods or specific funerary furnishings.[19]   CP

1. See Pulak 2005a, pp. 303–6.
2. Yalouris 1968, p. 12; see also Harden 1981, pp. 39, 45.
3. For discussion of relief beads with spiral designs and examples in the British Museum, see Harden 1981, pp. 45–46, nos. 56–59, pl. IV:56, 59; fig. 3.56, 57, 59. Another example is found in Grose 1989, pp. 64–65, 397, fig. 24.
4. Harden 1981, p. 46, nos. 56–60, pl. IV.57, 59, fig. 3:56, 57, 59, with other examples given on p. 45; Benzi 1992, pp. 200, 294, pl. 119:I; Dietz 1984, pp. 49–50, fig. 51.
5. Effinger 1996, p. 36, variant E: nos. Ar 2a, Kal la, Mi 6c, pls. 3:n, 25:d.
6. Xénaki-Sakellariou 1985, pp. 100–101, pl. 26, no. 2373.
7. For a discussion of relief beads with figure-of-eight shield motifs and examples in the British Museum, see Harden 1981, p. 47, pl. V, fig. 3. A photograph of figure-of-eight shield relief bead KW 829 is in Bass et al. 1989, pp. 8–9, and fig. 5.
8. Blegen and Blegen 1937, pp. 62, 305, fig. 121:2.
9. Harden 1981, p. 47, pl. 5:62, fig. 3:62, with other unprovenanced examples on p. 47.
10. Younger 1992, pp. 261–69.
11. Harden 1981, p. 39.
12. Hughes-Brock 1999, p. 291; Grose 1989, p. 57.
13. Bass 1986, pp. 281–82, ills. 15, 16; Pulak 2001, pp. 25–30.
14. Hughes-Brock 1999, p. 285; Harden 1981, p. 39. Analysis by Robert Brill of the Corning Museum of Glass indicated that the chemical composition of the Uluburun cobalt blue glass ingots matches those of contemporary Egyptian core-formed vessels and the Mycenaean glass relief beads, which suggests a common source for the glass from which both objects were made (Bass 1986, p. 282).
15. Tournavitou 1997, pp. 212–29.
16. Hughes-Brock 1999, p. 289.
17. They include a tomb at Kolophon in western Anatolia (Greenwell 1902, p. 6, fig. 6) and two others on Cyprus (P. Åström 1989, p. 47, Tomb 80, no. 321). The second Cypriot tomb, at Kalavassos-Ayios Dhimitrios, containing a group of women and children, yielded relief beads and a single amber bead, which is suggested as marking the identity of those interred as Mycenaean (Hughes-Brock 1993, p. 223).
18. Lewartowski 2000, p. 35; Hughes-Brock 1999, pp. 287–89.
19. This theory has been suggested because the beads have been discovered predominantly in burial contexts. See Panagiotaki 2000a, p. 169.

240
LENTOID BEADS

Agate
Max diameter: 2.5 cm (1 in.);
thickness: 0.9 cm (⅜ in.)
Uluburun shipwreck
Late Bronze Age, ca. 1300 B.C.
Bodrum Museum of Underwater
Archaeology, Turkey 78.5.87 (KW 793)

The Uluburun excavation has revealed one dozen lentoid beads. Several were found in the stern half of the ship, while the others were found farther down the slope toward the ship's bow, indicating that they were probably all stored at the stern but spilled into deeper areas of the site after the ship sank. The beads are of varying shapes and sizes, ranging in diameter from 1.5 to 2.5 centimeters and in thickness from 0.6 to 0.9 centimeters. With the exception of a single discoid bead, all are of the same general lentoid shape, with convex faces that curve uniformly to thin flattened or band edges of varying widths, which swell to blunt ends where the stone thickens to accommodate a string hole.[1]

The bead surfaces exhibit swirls and wavy bands of muted colors, alternating among white, yellow, and bluish gray, with various intermediate tones in between. All are smooth and well polished, without any indication of carved or incised surface decoration. It is likely that these beads were originally stored together either in a bag or strung with other stone beads. Three flattened ovoid or amygdaloid beads found in the same general area are of a similar marbled agate, and they all may have belonged to the same necklace.

Aegean lentoid hardstone seals are of similar shape but generally larger.[2] The two Mycenaean soft-stone seals recovered from the Uluburun shipwreck are

also lentoid but of much cruder craftsmanship (cat. no. 241). The preferred material for Aegean sealstones was banded agate,[3] and the principal source was Egypt, although it has been suggested that some were imported from the Indus Valley to the Aegean as finished beads and then recut.[4] Whether the Uluburun lentoid beads were personal possessions of the ship's crew or represented gifts or cargo is not known. Regardless of their source, they demonstrate conclusively that at least some lentoid agate beads reached the Aegean on ships like the one that sank at Uluburun.[5]

CP

1. Bass et al. 1989, pp. 7–8, and p. 6, fig. 11, where KW 793 is shown with a smaller lentoid bead, KW 840.
2. Of the twelve agate lentoid beads from Uluburun only six are 2 cm or greater in diameter, whereas of the thirty-seven agate/chalcedony beads listed in Boardman (1970, pp. 95–96, 101–5) for Mycenaean Knossos and the Greek mainland, only six have diameters less than 2 cm, but there are many more lentoid seals of different stone types that have diameters less than 2 cm.
3. Boardman 1970, pp. 47, 57; see also ibid., p. 49, nos. 3 and 12, for agate banding and varying colors similar to those on the Uluburun lentoid beads.
4. Hughes-Brock 1999, p. 284; Younger 1979, p. 42.
5. While lentoid agate beads are uncommon in the Levant, good parallels, albeit of a later date, occur at Hama in Syria; see Riis 1948, p. 161, fig. 203.F.

241a, b
MYCENAEAN LENTOID SEALS

a. Green steatite
Diameter 2.2 cm (⅞ in.); thickness
0.8 cm (⅜ in.)
7.6.98 (KW 4855)

b. Dark brown-black steatite
Diameter 1.8 cm (¾ in.); thickness
0.6 cm (¼ in.)
63.31.84 (KW 134)

Uluburun shipwreck
Late Bronze Age, ca. 1300 B.C.
Bodrum Museum of Underwater
Archaeology, Turkey

Two fairly worn Mycenaean steatite sealstones of lentoid shape were found in the excavation of the Uluburun ship,[1] at opposite ends of the site. The sealstone (cat. no. 241a) found farther down the slope, just forward of the area corresponding to the bow of the ship, was with a glass relief bead and several other small objects in loose sand, indicating that they were not in situ when found and were inadvertently missed by excavators pushing down sand from areas higher up on the steep slope of the site. In all likelihood, this sealstone was originally located at the stern of the ship, along with most of the objects of Mycenaean origin, including swords, chisels,

241a, b

240

knives, various beads (see cat. no. 240), and pottery.

The smaller of the two sealstones (cat. no. 241b) is of a brown-black steatite with light brown mottling and a slightly asymmetrical cross section. The flatter face is adorned with a double "triskeles"—three-legged designs with each terminating in drilled points—and incised curved double lines.[2] The seal is slightly ovoid in shape and perforated on its longer axis for a suspension string. Both faces of the seal are worn smooth, with parts of the worked design on the flatter face obliterated as a result. The seal has also been worn down around the perforation, resulting in indentations.

The larger sealstone (cat. no. 241a) is of a green steatite with some brown streaks, polished smooth. One face is significantly more raised, becoming quasi-conical; the engraved flat face, sloping gently toward the sides, bears what appears to be a highly stylized ungulate.[3] The design seems to be bordered by a circle, with a series of short parallel strokes above and below the animal's forefeet. Like the other sealstone, this one is perforated laterally for stringing, and the stone has been ground or worn down around the string-hole.

Aegean lentoid seals were worn on the wrist or around the neck, imparting status to the owner.[4] Their primary use may have been to make the owner's mark if necessary, but they could have also served as amulets, talismans, or simply as jewelry.[5] Although there is no evidence that they were impressed on clay tablets, as in the Near East,[6] they were used to seal bindings around boxes or possibly documents, and to seal clay stoppers in stirrup jars.[7]

Like most Aegean sealstones carved of steatite and bearing schematically rendered designs with little or no modeling, the Uluburun seals belong to Younger's Mainland Popular Group.[8] The type first appears on the Greek mainland in Late Helladic IIIA:2 contexts, and its popularity peaks during the Late Helladic IIIB period, with a great many examples coming from the mainland and, to a lesser extent, from the Cyclades, Crete, other Aegean islands, the Troad, Cyprus, and even fewer examples from outside the Aegean.[9] It may be significant that the smaller Mycenaean sealstone from the Uluburun ship finds its closest parallels at Tiryns and Mycenae, and to a lesser extent

at two sites a little farther north in Boiotia and Thessaly.[10]

Because Mycenaean sealstones of the Mainland Popular Group are found predominantly in simple burials,[11] often bear simple carvings, and are fashioned from a common, easily carved stone such as steatite, it is generally agreed that their owners were of humble means.[12] These two seals are therefore at odds with the other personal effects of the two Mycenaeans aboard the Uluburun ship (cat. nos. 238, 239). Had these other Mycenaean objects been recovered from a grave, their owners would have been considered well-to-do elites.[13]

Furthermore, two Late Minoan IIIA burials at Sellopoulo on Crete contain grave goods similar to the Uluburun Mycenaean assemblage, including lentoid sealstones[14] meticulously crafted of hardstone and appropriate to the elite status of their owners. Why, then, were seals of such quality not found on the ship? Perhaps they were lost when the Mycenaeans perished in the shipwreck.

The two steatite sealstones must, therefore, have served a different purpose. Hardstone seals are known from temples and shrines,[15] but soft sealstones of the Mainland Popular Group, well worn rather than pristine, were also deposited as votive offerings at sanctuaries and shrines. Perhaps the Uluburun sealstones were intended as offerings to be made upon completion of a successful crossing or journey.[16] Alternatively, worn soft-stone sealstones have been found in burials strung on necklaces adorning the deceased,[17] and the two steatite sealstones from Uluburun, also fairly worn, could have been part of necklaces belonging to either or both of the Mycenaeans aboard the ship.   CP

1. See Pulak 2005a, pp. 305–6, pl. LXXI:f; Bass 1986, pp. 283–85; Dickers 2001, p. 49, pl. 24:6, no. 399; CMS V Suppl. 1B, pp. 453–54, no. 473.

2. CMS V Supp. 1B, pp. 453–54, no. 473, with figure. Dickers 2001, p. 229, pl. 24. The design of catalogue no. 241b is assigned by Dickers to the "triskel" motif, consisting of two subtypes. The Uluburun sealstone conforms to the subtype with finely incised legs terminating in dots, for which there are two examples from Tiryns and one from Mycenae. The two subtypes date to the Late Helladic IIIA–B (Dickers 2001, p. 49, pl. 24.3–6). Paired and antithetical triskeles motifs are seen only on the Uluburun sealstone and one other from Medeon in Boiotia (ibid., p. 49, pl. 25:2, no. 296).

Younger (1988, pp. 190–91) places the design in his "5B-animal faces: bucrania" motif.

3. About one-sixth of the seal's edge has broken away, obliterating the hind legs of the ungulate. See Pulak 2004, pp. 651–52, no. 454, with figure.

4. Boardman 1970, pp. 62–63.

5. Betts 1997, pp. 63, 65.

6. Boardman 1970, p. 62; Aravantinos 1984, pp. 41–48.

7. Boardman 1970, p. 62.

8. Younger 1987, p. 65; Younger 1989, p. 106; Younger 1985, p. 290. Within this group, the renderings are so varied that no internal development or workshop attribution can be detected. It may be that this group was produced in many workshops over a relatively short period of time during the Late Helladic IIIA:2–IIIB:1, and that most sealstones from Late Helladic IIIB–IIIC contexts, usually worn from use, were made earlier. See Younger 1985, p. 290.

9. Dickers 2001, pp. 6–9, with map 1.

10. For Tiryns, see ibid., p. 49, pls. 3, 5; for Mycenae, see ibid., p. 49, pl. 4; and for other sites to the north in Boiotia and Thessaly, see ibid., p. 49, pls. 24:7, 9 and 25:1, 2.

11. Ibid., pp. 7, 72–73.

12. Younger 1987, p. 58; Younger 1985, p. 290.

13. Pulak 2005a, p. 307.

14. Burial I of Tomb 4 yielded a gold-capped lentoid seal and Burial II two lentoid seals, one of rock crystal and the other of carnelian. Other grave goods include a jug and a kylix, a Type Di sword, two spears, a razor, and faience and gold-relief beads, and those from Burial II include a conical cup and two kylixes, a Type Di sword, a bronze knife, and relief beads of glass and gold (Popham, Catling, and Catling 1974, pp. 199, 201–2, 224–25, 229, pl. 35d).

15. Dickers 2001, pp. 71–73; Younger 1985, pp. 294–95.

16. Pulak 2005a, p. 306, citing Bachhuber 2003, pp. 126–30.

17. Dickers 2001, p. 76.

242a, b

MYCENAEAN POTTERY

Ceramic

a. Kylix
Height 11.7 cm (4⅗ in.); diameter 11.9 cm
(4¾ in.)
28.31.84 (KW 57)

b. Stirrup jar
Height 16.8 cm (6⅝ in.); max. diameter 14 cm
(5½ in.); diameter of rim 2.1 cm (⅞ in.)
104.31.84 (KW 137)

Uluburun shipwreck
Late Bronze Age, ca. 1300 B.C.
Bodrum Museum of Underwater
Archaeology, Turkey

Among the hundreds of ceramic containers that constitute a major portion of the Uluburun ship's cargo are 25 complete or largely restorable vessels that originated in locales around the shores of the southern Aegean. Unlike the scores of Canaanite amphoras designed to transport liquids in bulk (see cat. no. 190), or the dozens of Cypriot bowls and juglets in mint condition that had been packed in a pithos (cat. no. 193) and were evidently being delivered as new tablewares, these Aegean objects served a multiplicity of functions and had seen a fair amount of earlier use before they came to rest on the seabed off Uluburun about 1300 B.C.

Three jugs and three cups were used for drinking.[1] No two cups or jugs closely resemble each other, nor are any jug-cup pairs decorated so similarly as to suggest that they constituted a set. Indeed, each of these six vessels is unique within the ship's cargo in terms of its combination of shape and decoration. Of the three jugs, one unmistakably Mycenaean example is attractively decorated with a painted floral pattern; neutron activation analysis of its fabric identifies it as an Argive product from the northeastern Peloponnese. The two other jugs, both considerably more fragmentary, are likely to have come from coastal regions of southwestern Anatolia. One has a burnished reddish brown surface, a narrow neck, and an angular body profile,[2] the other a brown-slipped but unburnished surface and a shorter and substantially wider neck.[3]

All three of the drinking cups are Mycenaean painted pots, but they differ in shape, volume, and decorative elaboration.

Figure 118. Cemal Pulak holding Mycenaean kylix and Canaanite pilgrim flask (cat. no. 191) during excavation; chalice (cat. no. 219) and Canaanite amphora in foreground. Uluburun shipwreck.

The simplest, a banded semiglobular cup, would have held only about a sixth of a liter when filled to the brim. Another is a ladle, or dipper, decorated with the abstract motif known as the N-pattern and would have held about a quarter of a liter; its handle, now missing, would have been sizable and might have been broken off even before the ship sank. The third and most elaborately painted of the cups is the two-handled stemmed cup, or kylix (cat. no. 242a), decorated with two large birds on each side. Unfortunately, after more than three millennia underwater (fig. 118), its painted pattern is not very well preserved. The closest parallels for this distinctively ornamented piece come from cemeteries on the island of Rhodes,[4] and this may well be where this particular cup was produced. It is tempting to link it with the most elaborate of the decorated jugs, leaving the linear cup and the simply patterned ladle to be paired with the two much plainer jugs, and to see in these three jug-cup pairs the personal drinking

equipment of a trio of passengers on board the ship: the Mycenaean emissaries and the bearer of the scepter-mace (cat. no. 237). Sadly, there is nothing about the find-spots of these six pots or the details of their decoration to support this interpretation. Mainland Mycenaean drinkers often made use of a large mixing bowl, or krater, to mix wine with water when they drank socially, but nothing remotely resembling an Aegean krater has been recovered from the Uluburun wreck. Perhaps there were not enough Aegean drinkers on board to make one necessary.[5]

A second major group of Aegean vessels from Uluburun consists of nine small- to medium-size containers notable for the slow-pouring design of their spouts and the density of their painted decoration. Eight of the nine are examples of the quintessentially Aegean ceramic form known, by the distinctive design of the handles and solid neck, as the "stirrup" or, alternatively, "false-necked" jar (the ninth is a neck-handled flask). These diminutive vessels,

242a

242b

specially shaped for careful pouring of liquids such as perfumed oils, have capacities ranging from as little as one tenth of a liter to slightly more than 3 liters; the example here (cat. no. 242b) holds approximately one liter. Produced in the thousands by Mycenaean palatial administrations, they dispensed a comparatively high-priced commodity that was widely distributed throughout the eastern Mediterranean.[6] So popular were these gaily decorated stirrup jars among Egyptian and Levantine consumers that they were imitated in more exotic materials, such as, in Egypt, faience and even translucent stones. The decoration of stirrup-jar shoulders with schematic flowers, as on this one, may be an allusion to the fragrance of the perfumed oil within. The number of these small jars from Uluburun, even with a few miscellaneous spout and base fragments added, is far too few to identify Mycenaean perfumed oil as a significant component of the ship's overall cargo. Moreover, the impressive range of different shapes, sizes, and fabrics represented by this small group of jars identifies them as a motley collection, many of them possibly in secondary use, rather than a shipment of freshly made and stoppered perfume vessels. It may be that they, like the Aegean drinking equipment described above, were personal possessions.

Of the ten giant stirrup jars from the wreck, each with a capacity of between 12 and 18 liters, at least half were wheel-made Cretan products decorated very simply with two or three groups of broad bands. Two handmade examples, however, one burnished dark but otherwise plain and the other banded in an atypical fashion, were clearly manufactured elsewhere, possibly along the western coast of Anatolia or on one of the eastern Aegean islands. Four of these large jars bear incised marks on their handles showing that at some point they had passed through the hands of Cypriot middlemen as reusable transport vessels for the shipping of oil and wine in bulk.[7]   JR

1. Pulak 1998; Rutter 2005.
2. Compare Günel 1999, pp. 179, 365, figs. 104:1, 2, 158:1, 2.
3. Compare ibid., p. 181, figs. 113:6, 115:6.
4. Benzi 1992, pl. 8a (Ialysos Tomb 7:6).
5. Pulak 2005a.
6. Haskell 1984; Shelmerdine 1985; Shelmerdine 1998.
7. Hirschfeld 1993; Hirschfeld 1999.

MÜSKEBI TOMBS

243

MYCENAEAN KYLIX

Ceramic
Height 17.8 cm (7 in.); diameter of mouth
15.2 cm (6 in.)
Müskebi, Chamber Tomb 12
Late Bronze Age, 14th century B.C.
Bodrum Museum of Underwater
Archaeology, Turkey
Müskebi 688 (#23)

244

MYCENAEAN FOOTED STIRRUP JAR

Ceramic
Height 19.5 cm (7⅝ in.); diameter 15.3 cm
(6 in.)
Müskebi, Chamber Tomb 15
Late Bronze Age, 14th century B.C.
Bodrum Museum of Underwater
Archaeology, Turkey
Müskebi 698 (#43)

The Late Bronze Age cemetery at Müskebi is on the Halikarnassos (Bodrum) peninsula in southwestern Anatolia, part of the ancient region of Caria. Excavated by the Turkish archaeologist Yusuf Boysal from 1963 to 1966,[1] it was the first cemetery with standard Mycenaean-type chamber tombs— intended to hold multiple burials of what were probably individual families—to be explored on the Anatolian mainland. The tombs are similar to those of contemporaneous burials on the nearby islands of Rhodes, Kos, and Kalymnos, where, by the end of the fifteenth century B.C., Mycenaean culture from the Greek mainland had largely supplanted the earlier Minoan culture of Crete. The same is true of their contents: more than 250 vases and substantial numbers of bronze weapons, jewelry, and miscellaneous other finds. Even though the burials at Müskebi were an unusual mixture of both inhumations and cremations (the latter were not common in Mycenaean cemeteries of this date), most authorities have identified the

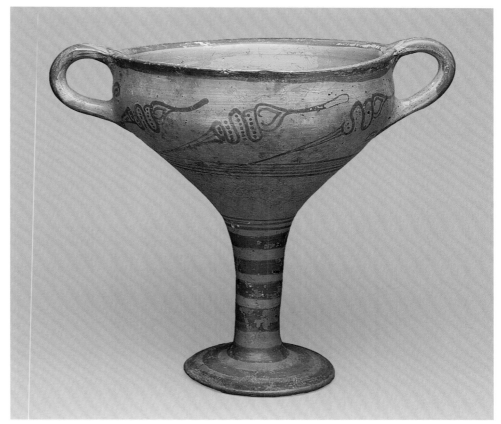

243

244

tombs as those of a group of Mycenaean colonists who had migrated from the islands of the southeastern Aegean to the mainland early in the fourteenth century B.C.[2] This migration was thus believed to have taken place about a generation before the massive destruction of the hybrid Minoan-Mycenaean palatial center at Knossos. As a result, Knossian cultural dominance throughout the southern Aegean was replaced by a more decentralized Mycenaean hegemony focused on palatial sites on the central and southern Greek mainland, including Mycenae, Tiryns, Thebes, and Pylos.

The high point of the Müskebi cemetery's history occurred in the second half of the fourteenth century B.C.; it was during this time that the Uluburun ship sank with its fabulously rich cargo of metals, incense, glass, and other raw materials. It is therefore not surprising to find examples of southern Aegean ceramic types like those represented on the Uluburun ship also deposited in the tombs at Müskebi. A two-handled drinking cup, or kylix, from Tomb 12 (cat. no. 243) is very similar in shape to the lone kylix found on the wreck (cat. no. 242a), and both were probably produced on Rhodes. The diagonal whorl shells that decorate the Müskebi kylix are much more common on this shape than are the large birds decorating the Uluburun vase, but both motifs are good examples of the simplification and conversion to pure pattern of the far more naturalistic depictions of living creatures that were characteristic of Minoan ceramic ornament during the preceding fifteenth century B.C. It is interesting that the Müskebi kylix was accompanied in its tomb by a plain western Anatolian jug,[3] in much the same way that two of the three Mycenaean drinking cups from the Uluburun wreck appear to have been paired with plain Anatolian rather than pattern-decorated Mycenaean jugs.

The piriform stirrup jar from Müskebi Tomb 15 (cat. no. 244), decorated with intersecting hatched semicircles on the shoulder and with lentoid shapes hatched in a zigzag arrangement on the body below, is closely comparable in shape and date to the single piriform stirrup jar from the Uluburun wreck (cat. no. 242b) and likely to be another Rhodian product. The neck-handled flask and more common small- and middle-size globular stirrup

jars from Uluburun, all designed to hold expensive perfumed oils, similarly have close parallels in the Müskebi tombs. Even the giant stirrup jars used for bulk liquid transport—the most common form of Aegean ceramic container found on the Uluburun ship—can also be found at Müskebi.[4] Thus, the entire southern Aegean ceramic repertoire documented on the wreck could easily have been acquired in the eastern Aegean, whether at an inland settlement on the Anatolian mainland, whose inhabitants were buried at Müskebi, or at one of the numerous Mycenaean coastal sites ringing the islands of Rhodes and Kos.   JR

1. Boysal 1969a.
2. But see Mountjoy 1998, esp. pp. 36–37, for the possibility of acculturation playing a greater role than simple migration.
3. Özgünel 1996, p. 104, pl. 15:3 (Bodrum Museum 668).
4. Ibid., p. 53, pl. 5:6 (Bodrum Museum 987).

245

Dagger

Bronze
Length 32.3 cm (12¾ in.)
Müskebi, Chamber Tomb 11
Late Bronze Age, 14th century B.C.
Bodrum Museum of Underwater
Archaeology, Turkey
Müskebi 675 (#18)

This dagger, or dirk, was found in Chamber Tomb 11 of the Late Bronze Age cemetery at Müskebi.[1] It is unique among the limited number of bronze weapons, mostly spears and knives, excavated from the forty-eight Mycenaean tombs at the site.[2] Two Mycenaean vases found in the same tomb date it and its contents to the Late Helladic IIIA:2 period.[3]

The dagger originally would have been longer, probably 34 centimeters or more, but the pommel tang did not survive intact and the tip of the blade was damaged by corrosion. Its unusual hand guard, or "quillon," with horn-shaped projections curving slightly downward at the tips, and the rivetless flanged grip configuration narrowing to an elongated extension for attaching the pommel, now lost, are typical of Sandars's Class H short swords or daggers.[4] The hilt flanges would have

retained hilt plates, and the pommel would have been attached to the hilt by the rod-like extension, of which only the base survives.[5] A seam is visible on the horn-shaped pointed ends of the quillon, suggesting that they were shaped on an anvil after the dagger was cast in a mold. The surface of the pointed blade is heavily pitted from corrosion, but four grooves down its center can readily be discerned.

The small group of Class H bronze daggers, according to Sandars, borders the Minoan-Mycenaean worlds in both time and space. These weapons are an amalgamation of Aegean and Near Eastern characteristics: the flat-blade type, although not originally Aegean, had been developing in that direction in Mycenaean swords; the quillon horns were undoubtedly of Aegean origin; and the rod-shaped pommel extension parallels Near Eastern and Cypriot weapons.[6] A dagger, reputed to have been found in a Mycenaean tomb at Siana, Rhodes, together with a knife and spearhead, forms the basis of this class. A second dagger, said to be from Pergamon in northwestern Anatolia, is nearly identical in shape and size to the Siana dagger except for the lines down the blade center, which are worked as grooves on the Siana dagger and as ridges on the Pergamon example. Another example, with the ridges down the blade's center, was found at Pyli on the island of Kos.[7] The grooved blade of the Müskebi dagger, which represents a fourth example of this class, is similar to the one from Siana.

The knife found with the Siana dagger, with its rod-shaped pommel extension, is of similar construction to one found at Troy and to two others, from Ialysos on Rhodes and at Kolophon in western Anatolia. Based on the only datable example from Ialysos, both the knife type and the Class H daggers had been attributed to the Late Helladic IIIB–early IIIC period (late thirteenth–early twelfth century B.C.), characterized by Sandars as a time of confused frontiers and even more confused politics preceding the collapse of nearly all eastern Mediterranean Bronze Age cultures except Egypt.[8] The Ialysos tomb, however, has since been redated to Late Helladic IIIA:2–IIIB.[9] Two unpublished knives found in Tombs 7 and 14 at Müskebi are dated by the Mycenaean pottery found with them to the Late Helladic IIIA:2–IIIB period,[10] as are two

other examples from tombs T 48 and T 59 on Rhodes.[11] Two incomplete knives from the Uluburun shipwreck are dated to the late fourteenth century B.C.[12] Based on the datable examples, we can infer that the use of these knives spanned the Late Helladic IIIA:2 and most likely the earlier part of the Late Helladic IIIB periods rather than being confined to the end of the Late Bronze Age as previously suggested. Whether the Class H swords have the same date range as that of the knife with rod-pommel extension is not certain, but the similar construction features of both weapons, and the dates of the Müskebi dagger and the knives, suggest that they were both in use during the same approximate period.   CP

1. Boysal 1969a, p. 33. The Müskebi tombs and a group of Mycenaean pottery found by locals, as well as initial observations at the site, were first were noted by Bass (1963, pp. 353–56). The tombs were subsequently excavated by Yusuf Boysal, yielding more than 250 terracotta vessels, along with bronzes and jewelry; the last two categories of artifacts have not been published. General discussion of the tombs and their finds are in Boysal 1964 and 1969a.
2. Boysal 1964, p. 83. Mee (1978, p. 137) notes that the bronzes on display in the Bodrum Museum of Underwater Archaeology consisted of seven spears, three knives, a razor, and a dagger, all of which have since been placed in storage.
3. For the two Mycenaean piriform jars found in Tomb 11, see Boysal 1969b, pp. xi, 3, Taf. I:1, 6, V:2, and pls. I:1, V:2; see also Mee 1978, p. 137, no. 1:1–11, p. 139, no. 5:2–11.
4. Sandars 1963, pp. 140–42, pl. 27:52, 53.
5. Mee (1978, p. 137), while correctly attributing the dagger to Sandars's Class H, notes that the dagger is outfitted with a short pommel tang rather than the typical rodlike extension with a square cross section that characterizes this type. The rough edge of the pommel tang indicates, however, that the rodlike extension broke off and was lost.
6. Sandars 1963, pp. 140–41.
7. Kilian-Dirlmeier 1993, p. 49, pl. 18:99, designated as Type 2b.
8. Sandars 1963, pp. 140, 142.
9. Mee 1982, p. 60 n. 5. Discoveries since the original publication have increased the number of known examples of knives of this type to sixteen; even so, only a few are from contexts with useful dates. References are compiled in Pulak 2005a, p. 300 and n. 34, where the number of known knives of this type is given incorrectly as seventeen, and is corrected herewith; Benzi 1992, pp. 177–78; and Ersoy 1988, p. 67 n. 56.
10. One knife (Bodrum inv. no. 676-B), 29.5 cm long, was found in Tomb 7 with a Mycenaean mug and pyxis: Boysal 1969b, pp. xi, 17, pl. XX:6, p. 22, pl. XXV:3, and pls. XX:6,

xxv:3; and Mee 1978, p. 142, no. 20:6, 7,
p. 140 no. 25:3–7, where the two vessels are
dated to the Late Helladic IIIA:2–IIIB
period. The second knife (Bodrum Museum
inv. no. 677-B), 27.4 cm long, was found in
Tomb 14 with a Mycenaean pyxis and bowl:
Boysal 1969b, pp. xi, 22, pl. XXV:8, p. 27,
pl. XXXI:5; and Mee 1978, p. 141, no. 31:5–14,
p. 140, no. 25:8–14, where the vessels are
dated to the Late Helladic IIIA:2–IIIB
period. I am grateful to the former director
of the Bodrum Museum of Underwater
Archaeology, Oğuz Alpözen, for giving me
information on and access to these knives.

11. Benzi 1992, pp. 177–78, 334, pl. 179:f (for
T 48/15), and p. 360, pl. 179:n (for T 59/C).

12. Pulak 2005a, p. 300, pl. LXXI:a. One of the
knives (KW 4452) is missing the rodlike
extension at the terminus of the hilt, and
the second (lot no. 3242) is missing the
entire blade.

246

MYCENAEAN RELIEF BEADS

Glass
Average bead dimensions: length 2.1 cm (⅞ in.);
width 1 cm (⅜ in.); height 0.9 cm (⅜ in.)
Müskebi, Chamber Tomb 22
Late Bronze Age, 14th century B.C.
Bodrum Museum of Underwater
Archaeology, Turkey Müskebi 711 (#101)

Among the objects excavated from
Chamber Tomb 22 in the Late Bronze
Age cemetery at Müskebi were glass relief
plaques, or beads, a uniquely Mycenaean
product that disappeared from the archaeological record with the end of the Mycenaean culture.[1] Of the forty-eight tombs
excavated at Müskebi, Tomb 22 is the only
one to have contained glass relief beads.
The burial is dated to the Late Helladic
IIIA:2 period, based on the Mycenaean
pottery evidence,[2] and was thought to
belong to a woman.[3] Since relief beads do
not appear to have been exported as trade
items outside Mycenaean society, and
occur almost exclusively in monumental
and other elaborate burials for affluent
families,[4] the individual buried in Tomb
22 must have been an influential member
of the Müskebi society.

Inside the tomb were 33 flat-backed
relief beads, all made of a translucent, deep
blue glass—presumably in imitation of
lapis lazuli. Their cream-colored, non-
glasslike crust is the result of weathering;

they are otherwise in good condition.[5]
Cast in open, one-piece molds, probably
from imported raw glass, each bead is
modeled as a single ornament, likely representing a stylized curl of hair.[6] The curl
emanates from a ribbed band or headpiece
with a semicircular convex profile, pierced
transversally for stringing; a second
transverse perforation runs through the
center of the curl. The curl itself is highlighted with four curved parallel lines or
ridges, the outermost of which ends in a
multiwhorled, conical spiral, forming the
highest point of the bead.

Objects of glass, such as star-disc
pendants and certain beads, were imported
to the Aegean during the late sixteenth
and early fifteenth century B.C. The deep
blue color and unusual material of these
fine objects must have delighted the
Mycenaeans, who soon began using *kyanos*,
as they called the glass, to manufacture
objects of their own. The physical and
chemical similarity between imported glass
objects and those produced locally indicates that the latter were made from imported glass ingots like the deep and light
blue examples carried on the Uluburun
ship (cat. no. 187).[7] The great majority of
Mycenaean relief beads are made of deep
blue glass, though light blue or turquoise
beads are occasionally found, often with
the former, indicating that these two colors
were preferred by the Mycenaeans. It is
noteworthy, therefore, that all but three
glass ingots found on the Uluburun shipwreck represent these two colors.

Relief beads in the form of spiral hair
curls are well represented in Late Helladic
III contexts in the Aegean. Two classes of
relief beads, one with triple spirals positioned one above the other and separated
by a row of dots between them, the other
bearing a figure-of-eight shield motif, were
found on the Uluburun ship (cat. no. 239).[8]
The hair-curl motif probably began as a
simple, volutelike circular curl emanating
from a pierced suspension band.[9] The motif
was later modified to include an elongated lock attached to the curl that could
be used singly or paired with another one
suspended below the first, facing in the
opposite direction. At about this time, the
single elongated-curl motif was also featured on flat, rectangular, cast plaques.
Somewhat later, the end of the hair curl
appeared as stylized, multiwhorled, spiral-
and plaque-shaped bead forms. The former

was ultimately dropped altogether in favor
of the plaque-shaped relief bead with two
or three superimposed spirals and a lock
represented by curved parallel lines or ribs.
Eventually, these lines were replaced by
simple spirals. In this hypothetical progression, the Müskebi relief beads would
thus appear to be early variants of the
hair-curl motif, with the Uluburun beads
belonging to the later plaque versions
having just three spirals to represent the
hair lock.

The contents of the Müskebi tombs
are typical of contemporary Mycenaean
burials on the nearby islands of Kos,
Kalymnos, and, especially, Rhodes in the
fourteenth century B.C.[10] It is not surprising, therefore, that many relief beads similar to those from Müskebi, including the
single- and multiple-curl and the spiral
varieties, were found on Rhodes, both in
glass[11] and gold,[12] although the suspension
band or headpiece for these beads is usually ornamented with designs other than
ribbing; furthermore, the borders, and
sometimes also the fields between the
lines representing the lock of hair, are
trimmed with rows of raised dots, perhaps
in imitation of gold granulation. Glass
examples also occur on the Greek mainland, at Prosymna[13] and Ayios Ilias,[14] with
gold versions found at Mycenae[15] and at
Thisbe in Boiotia.[16] The Müskebi relief
beads are, however, unique. Although no
known examples embody all four of their
defining features—ribbed suspension
band, cutout form, plain line ornamentation without raised dots, and locks with
spiral ends—an example from Ialysos,
Rhodes, exhibits the cutout form and
spiral,[17] and another from an unknown
provenance features the cutout form and
ribbed suspension band.[18]

Glass relief beads have been found
throughout the Mycenaean world, but
those recovered in any quantity have come
almost exclusively from Mycenaean burials. Although iconographic evidence suggests that beads were worn primarily by
women, they were also worn by children
and men.[19] The peculiarly Mycenaean
glass plaques, with their perforations for
stringing, have been interpreted as beads
for necklaces, adornments sewn on garments, or for use as diadems.[20] With
regard to diadems, two or three chamber
tombs near Olympia, one of which may be
that of a female, contained relief beads

246

with rosettes and ivy-leaf motifs scattered around the skulls; those found in the third burial, of a male, were recovered as an intact diadem on the forehead of the skeleton.[21] The diadem beads display the triple-spiral hair curl, a motif surmised to be particularly appropriate for placement on the forehead. However, no single use can be ascribed to any relief-bead motif. The discovery on the Uluburun ship of relief beads with two different motifs—one with a triple-spiral design—suggests not only that there were two pieces of Mycenaean jewelry on board but also that they were worn by men as necklaces. They represent the only discovery of their kind in a personal, everyday context, suggesting that those from Olympia and Müskebi were not intended exclusively for use as grave offerings. Rather, they would have been used during the owner's lifetime and, in some instances, placed near the skull or on the forehead as a diadem when the deceased was interred.   CP

1. Hughes-Brock 1999, p. 291; Grose 1989, p. 57.
2. The eleven Mycenaean vases found in the tomb are in Boysal 1969b, p. xii: five piriform jars (pp. 3–4, 6, pls. I:3, II:2; V:1, 3, 4), four mugs and cups (pp. 17–19, pls. XXI:3, 4, 6, XXIII:6), brazier (p. 27, pl. XXXI:2), and a flask (p. 27, pl. XXXII:1, 3). See also Mee 1978, pp. 137–42, for a listing and discussion of the Mycenaean pottery.
3. A comprehensive list of grave goods and analysis of the tomb itself have not been published. It seems likely, however, that the female attribution is based on the presence of relief beads and the lack of weapons. The spatial relationship of the relief beads to the skeletal remains is not indicated.
4. Lewartowski 2000, p. 35; Hughes-Brock 1999, pp. 287–89.
5. Due to the thick weathering crust on the beads, they were initially reported to be of a stonelike material (Boysal 1964, p. 83).
6. Yalouris 1968, pp. 12–14; see also Harden 1981, pp. 39, 45.
7. Robert Brill of the Corning Museum of Glass, who is analyzing all of the Uluburun ingots for publication, reported that the chemical composition of the Uluburun cobalt blue glass ingots matched those of contemporary Egyptian core-formed vessels and Mycenaean glass relief beads, which suggests both were manufactured from glass obtained from a common source (Bass 1986, p. 282).
8. For discussion of relief beads with spiral designs and examples in the British Museum, see Harden 1981, pp. 45–46, nos. 56–59, pl. IV:56, 59, fig. 3:56, 57, 59. Another example is found in Grose 1989, pp. 64–65, 397, fig. 24.
9. Yalouris 1968, pp. 13–14.
10. Mee 1978, pp. 149–50.
11. Harden 1981, p. 46, nos. a, b, pl. IV:52, 53, fig. 3:52, 53.
12. Benzi 1992, pls. 116:I, 182:1.
13. Blegen and Blegen 1937, p. 305, fig. 300:8.
14. Mastrokostas 1966, pp. 205–7, pl. 17a.
15. Yalouris 1968, p. 13, fig. 13.
16. A. Evans 1925, p. 2, fig. 1:j; Yalouris 1968, p. 13, no. 16, figs. 13–15, for other examples in gold and glass.
17. Harden 1981, p. 46, no. 52, pl. 4:52, fig. 3:52.
18. Goldstein 1979, p. 94, fig. 177, indicated to be from Crete or the Peloponnese.
19. Younger 1992, pp. 261–69. There is no extant pictorial evidence for relief beads.
20. Harden 1981, p. 39.
21. Yalouris 1968, pp. 10–13, and figs. 1–11; the assignation of the burial to a male is made primarily on the presence of weapons, and that to a female, from the lack of such and also on the presence of other grave goods. A burial at Dendra, also containing weapons and relief beads, is that of a male (Wace 1932, p. 193).
22. Yalouris 1968, p. 15.

THE ART OF EXCHANGE

JOAN ARUZ

The inception of the Late Bronze Age heralds a new era, one in which developing centers in the Near East, Egypt, and the Aegean express their growing power and prestige through the creation of monumental and brilliantly decorated palaces and lavishly furnished tombs. The age is characterized in contemporary texts as one of intense interaction during which rulers, engaging in war and diplomacy, sought to acquire valuable resources and exquisite works of art. The year-by-year records of pharaonic campaigns carved on the walls of the Temple of Karnak recount the enormous wealth accumulated during Thutmose III's Asiatic wars. The Amarna Letters highlight more peaceful aspects of interaction, in the form of greeting gifts, dowries, and wedding presents circulated among the great royal houses of the late fourteenth century B.C. Through these texts, a picture emerges of a world in which Egypt was admired not only for its gold resources, which were as abundant as "dirt," but also for its artistry in capturing lifelike images. Addressing the Egyptian pharaoh, the Kassite king Burnaburiash writes:

> *There are skilled carpenters where you are. . . . Let them represent a wild animal, land or aquatic, lifelike, so that the hide is exactly like that of a live animal.*[1]

Elements such as the stained ivory plants and a cedar ship towing six smaller ships mentioned in one of the Amarna Letters must have been part of the many tableaux crafted as gifts for the Babylonian ruler. Tushratta of Mitanni asks for the solid-cast gold statues of himself and his daughter Tadu-hepa, sent as a bride to the Egyptian court.[2]

While Egypt was amassing large quantities of precious materials from the Near East—lapis lazuli, horses, chariots—special mention is made in the Egyptian annals and diplomatic correspondence of the peculiarities of foreign workmanship. Animal-headed vases are listed among the tribute from Retenu ("heads of goats, head of a lion," and "a vessel with the head of an ox"). There is a "silver vessel of the workmanship of Keftiu,"[3] gilt horn-shaped (?) vessels sent by Tushratta and silver vessels in the form of a stag and a ram, a gift from Suppiluliuma, the Great King of Hatti.[4]

The material record reinforces this notion of the prestige attached to exotic objects. These were not only admired but imitated and adapted, certainly by the early sixteenth century B.C. As Mary Helms has stated, for the ruler, "the act of acquisition in itself becomes a mark of exceptionality, exclusivity, ability to control, and allows the cultivation of a kingly image."[5] Large-scale works of art, such as Minoan-style frescoes, become the preferred form of decoration in royal palaces around the Mediterranean littoral, introducing a new emphasis on a natural world devoid of direct messages of divinely imbued royal power so prevalent in Near Eastern and Egyptian iconography (compare fig. 13). Reference to royal prowess is now oblique, the human element in scenes of the hunt and animal combat often alluded to by the presence of attacking hounds. The focus shifts to animal predators and prey, a subject represented in Egyptian tombs from the Old Kingdom onward, but now infused with a new sense of dynamic movement evocative of animal styles one associates with Minoan Crete and Mycenaean Greece. Such scenes appear in the private tombs of officials in Egyptian Thebes during the fifteenth century B.C. in the local technique of low relief painted in tempera (fig. 119).[6] These may have been directly inspired by such works as the hunting fresco with predatory leopards, lions, and griffins from Tell el-Dab'a, which we can only glimpse from the fragments that remain (fig. 120).[7]

Precious works of foreign type in small scale are represented in the Theban tombs by vessels held by Aegean and Asiatic envoys and illustrate the written accounts of booty and tribute. Such objects must have been highly prized, and their appearance in Egyptian workshop scenes perhaps suggests that they were being copied locally, providing one avenue for the coming together of traditions that characterize some of the finest display pieces of succeeding centuries.[8] The creation of new styles combining elements from different cultures becomes especially apparent in the depiction of such themes as the Mistress of Animals (cat. no. 261) and animal combats. The latter proliferate on works of gold and silver, ivory, and vitreous materials and are carved on cylinder seals, where the artistic manifestation of cultural interaction can be traced back to its incipient phases.

Figure 119. Drawing of wall-painting scene with animal hunt. Thebes, Tomb of Puimre (TT 39). Dynasty 18, reign of Hatshepsut–Thutmose III.

SEALS, TRADE, AND CULTURAL EXCHANGE

Seals, small and easily portable, were integral to the trade process, worn and used for reasons of security, identity, status, and adornment. Imported seals reflect the movement of peoples—merchants, craftsmen, officials, immigrants—and in many instances, the transfer of ideas. Seals and seal-shaped stones of precious materials such as lapis lazuli—mentioned in texts as gifts from Assyria and Mitanni to the Egyptian court[9]—were intentionally collected, as witnessed by two spectacular discoveries, one near Egyptian Thebes and the other in Mycenaean Thebes. These rich hoards of lapis lazuli glyptic were found in very different circumstances, one in bronze caskets of the twentieth–nineteenth century B.C., found under the Temple of Montu at Tôd, and the other in a thirteenth-century B.C. Mycenaean palace workshop. An inscription from the temple, "representing what foreigners and explorers, who travel across the lands, had delivered," may reflect the circumstances under which silver vessels, gold and silver ingots, and lapis lazuli beads, pendants, and seals in the Tôd Treasure came to Egypt from sources extending from Afghanistan possibly to Crete (cat. no. 35).[10] While the origin of the silver vessels remains in dispute—attributed to either Crete or Anatolia[11]—a wedge-shaped steatite seal-amulet with bees and spiders engraved on its two main faces looks like a Minoan-style piece and could have been made close to the time of deposition (fig. 25).[12] Two lapis lazuli stamp seals in the hoard were produced in eastern Iran and Bactria-Margiana (fig. 26), areas close to the source of this material.[13] The cylinder seals appear to have been made over a long span of time in areas along the lapis lazuli trade route—eastern Iran, Mesopotamia, and the Syro-Levantine region, with one piece that could have come from central Anatolia.[14] How these objects came together, along with lapis lazuli amulets and inlay pieces in the form of frogs, bulls, hair curls, and a beard, has remained a matter of speculation. As many similar assemblages were retained in Near Eastern temples, particularly at

the site of Mari,[15] Edith Porada conjectured that part of the Tôd Treasure entered the commercial sphere after being forcibly removed by conquest. The random selection of lapis lazuli Mesopotamian glyptic in the hoard was, she believed, separately procured.[16]

The desire for this valuable and ritually charged material was apparently not confined to Egypt and the Near East, but also appears to have extended as far as the Aegean, where, although it may not have retained all its original associations, it was highly prized as jewelry. One imported cylinder seal of fine-quality lapis lazuli was discovered in the Palace of Minos at Knossos. Originally carved in the Early Dynastic period, it has features that indicate later recutting in central Anatolia and further reworking on Crete, where it was embellished with Minoan gold caps.[17] Some centuries later, the Palace of Kadmos in Mycenaean Thebes yielded a spectacular collection of thirty-six lapis lazuli cylinder seals carved in various regions from Mesopotamia to the Levant and Cyprus (cat. nos. 177–82). There were also floral elements of lapis lazuli, appropriately sized perhaps to form an ensemble with the exotic stones (cat. no. 176a). Other jewelry elements may have included nine unworked lapis lazuli cylinders, and others cut down into various shapes.[18] There were also Cypriot and Mitanni faience cylinder seals, agate cylinders, one in Aegean style, and Aegean agate stamp seals.[19] As with the Tôd Treasure, the Theban hoard is difficult to interpret and may not represent a single group of exports. It contains official Kassite seals, Mesopotamian heirlooms, and Syro-Mitanni and Hittite cylinder seals, some in pristine condition, others abraded, damaged, repaired, or recut. There is also a large group of finely carved Cypriot pieces, as well as Cypriot recyclings of Mesopotamian works. Porada hypothesized that this last group reached the Aegean from its established trading partner over a long period of time, and that the Kassite seals, originally dedications in the Temple of Marduk at Babylon, were taken by Tukulti-Ninurta I of Assyria, who conquered the city around 1225 B.C. Because the seals represented one mina, the weight of Kassite diplomatic gifts recorded in the Amarna Letters, she also suggested that they may have been sent to the king of Thebes, with the promise of access to sources of gold beyond Egypt.[20] While these scenarios are possible, it may be more probable that the lapis lazuli cylinder seals, made in a variety of styles, were part of a single shipment. The evidence may lie in the interpretation of a single Kassite seal, which was re-carved to create a very unusual image (cat. no. 177c).

Other definable groups of traveling seals have also invited historical interpretations, such as the scarabs of Amenhotep III and his queen, Tiye. Together with other objects bearing their names, those found in burial, palatial, and ritual contexts in the fourteenth- and thirteenth-century B.C. Aegean have been considered evidence for an Egyptian embassy to Crete and the Greek mainland.[21] However, we cannot be certain either that all these objects were shipped together to the Aegean or that they came directly from Egypt. One notable example from a warrior grave on Crete was part of a necklace of variegated glass spherical beads (possibly Egyptian imports) and faience beads. Based on the peculiarities of its cartouche, it has been suggested that the scarab may have been made by a foreigner not familiar with the hieroglyphic script, possibly in a Canaanite workshop.[22]

Perhaps the largest category of imported cylinder seals found in Aegean burials is that of the Mitanni Common Style. These colorful objects, made of glazed faience and other vitreous

Figure 120. Wall painting details with leopards. Tell el-Dab'a, Palace F. Dynasty 18, reigns of Hatshepsut–Thutmose III.

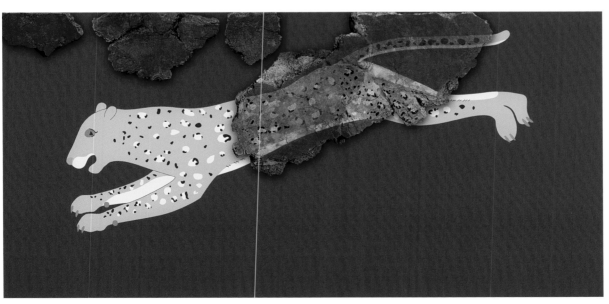

materials, were mass-produced (see pp. 419–20). Although used to impress documents in the Syro-Mitanni heartland at Nuzi and Alalakh in the fifteenth century B.C., the largest concentration of actual seals comes from the southern Levant, particularly from Beth-Shan and Megiddo, as well as from Cyprus, in contexts down to the thirteenth century B.C.[23] While there is no evidence for their administrative use in the Aegean, these seals were valued enough to be buried with their owners and may have been worn as jewelry in life as well as in death. They appear to reflect a new Near Eastern fashion at a time when seals were still made of colorful hardstones in the Aegean and in southern Mesopotamia. Perhaps they were acquired or received as gifts; possibly they were talismans and symbols of social status, displayed by traders as proof of voyages in the eastern Mediterranean.[24]

One such voyage with its complement of seals has been preserved thanks to the meticulous excavation of the Uluburun shipwreck off the southern coast of Anatolia (see pp. 289–305). Found on the seabed near intact gold pendants, other jewelry elements, ingots, and scrap gold and silver, the seals originated in various areas of the Near East, Cyprus, Egypt, and Mycenaean Greece. Some are made of precious materials, for example the unique gold scarab of Nefertiti (cat. no. 223), or

Figure 121. Gold sheath and dagger with glass inlay. Tomb of Tutankhamun. Dynasty 18. Egyptian Museum, Cairo JE 61584A, 61584B

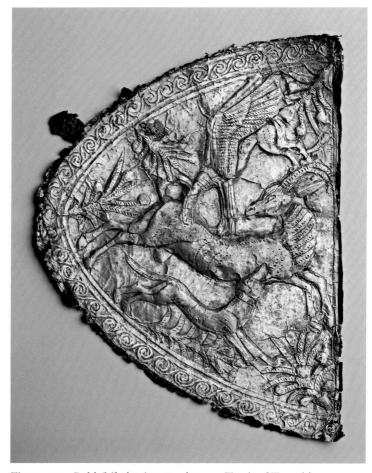

Figure 122. Gold-foil chariot attachment. Tomb of Tutankhamun. Dynasty 18. Egyptian Museum, Cairo TEMP. NO. 30.3.34.52

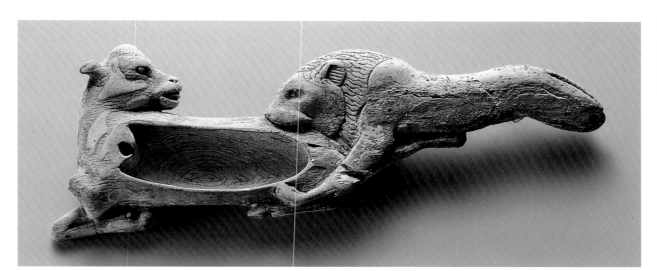

Figure 123. Ivory cosmetic spoon. Egypt. Dynasty 18. Egyptian Museum, Cairo JE 47009

have gold mounts. Others are in provincial styles, such as the Kassite rock-crystal cylinder seals (cat. nos. 231a, b), or recut, such as an Old Babylonian piece later carved in the Middle Assyrian style (cat. no. 230). There are also scarabs of Egyptian and Levantine type and Mycenaean Popular Style lentoids (cat. no. 241a, b). Some of these items may have been personal belongings and may suggest the identification of travelers on board the ship. Others, however, may have been destined for foreign palace treasuries or workshops, to be incorporated into jewelry.

The environment of intense interaction in which seals traveled abroad also led to the creation of international glyptic that crossed stylistic boundaries. This phenomenon is manifested in various ways under differing social and historical circumstances—including trade, movements of populations and craftsmen, and political and cultural domination. In one well-documented era spanning the first centuries of the second millennium B.C., the need to enact business in the Assyrian trading colonies, or *karum* settlements, on the central Anatolian plateau (see pp. 70–73) affected the choice of seal shape and imagery. At that time, during which thousands of cuneiform document envelopes were marked with the impressions of Mesopotamian and Syrian cylinder seals, the Anatolian stamp seal itself was largely supplanted by a native version of the cylinder seal, embedding the Mesopotamian presentation motif into a plethora of locally inspired scenes (cat. no. 37b). Not much later, cylinder seals clearly made by Syrian craftsmen appear to demonstrate a growing affinity for artistic styles with dynamically rendered animals in free space, reflecting a sensibility generally associated with Minoan Crete (see fig. 124).[25] These were produced close to the time that Minoan-style frescoes came into fashion at foreign courts (see cat. no. 69a, b and figs. 39, 40, 120), which included Alalakh, the source of many innovative seal designs.[26] The vehicle for such exchanges and for the initiation of a "litorally based internationalism" was probably the movement of artisans across the Mediterranean during a period of transition from the Old to New Palace period on Crete.[27]

A few hundred years later, during the fourteenth century B.C., craftsmen may have dispersed to foreign lands in the wake of the Minoan palatial collapse (see pp. 270–72). Seals exhibiting a subtle integration of Aegean and Near Eastern styles, syntax, and iconography were produced, most likely for an international clientele, by carvers intimately familiar with both traditions. Perhaps the finest surviving example is a cylinder seal in the Yale Babylonian Collection (cat. no. 254), reported to have come from the Levantine coast. It is one of two works attributed to a master engraver, the other a lapis lazuli cylinder that was part of the treasure of Cypriot and Near Eastern seals at Mycenaean Thebes (cat. no. 182).

The iconography of intercultural style seals appears to convey notions of conquest and control, with some notable themes being the Master of Animals, often combined with scenes of animal combat, a hero stabbing a lion, or a chariot hunt. Similar depictions in various media (see fig. 123) and in later times, particularly in the Near East, continue to be metaphors for virile royal supremacy.[28] Such an image choice is perhaps not unconnected to international trade, a subtle allusion to the ruler's power to acquire wealth and ensure prosperity.

LUXURY METALWORK

Ceremonial Weapons

Among the inventory of elaborately worked gifts of precious materials sent by the Mitanni ruler Tushratta to the Egyptian ruler are ceremonial weapons of precious materials such as gold, ebony, and iron.[29] These were sent to Egypt not long before daggers with iron and gold blades and gold sheaths, and with animal-hunt imagery of foreign inspiration, were buried in the Tomb of Tutankhamun—a repository of an impressive collection of international style hunting scenes depicted on weapons, chariots, and wood chests.[30] However, as we have seen reflected in the glyptic, the impetus to create such styles can be traced back to the transitional phase represented by the Hyksos in Egypt and their overthrow. A lively

Figure 124. Modern impression of hematite cylinder seal. Old Syrian. Ashmolean Museum, University of Oxford 1914.161

hunting scene and inscriptions, including the cartouche of the Dynasty 15 Hyksos king Apophis (ca. 1581–1541 B.C.), were carved on a gilt wood inlay set into the hilt of the famous dagger from Saqqara, Egypt (cat. no. 65). Daggers of roughly this form are later held by Syrians depicted in wall paintings in the tombs of Rekhmire, Menkheperreseneb, and Amenmose in Thebes.[31] Animal-combat scenes on Syrian seals (fig. 43 and cat. no. 72) look somewhat similar to images on the Apophis dagger and suggest a strong Levantine element. If actually produced in Egypt, as most recently suggested, this piece should be considered an early mixed-style work of the Hyksos period produced not far from the Nile Delta.

Ahhotep, the mother of Ahmose, who defeated the Hyksos and established Dynasty 18, may be associated with jewelry, weapons, and other items made of precious materials originally reported to come from a tomb at Thebes (see pp. 119–22). One outstanding piece is an openwork gold collar with terminals in the form of Egyptian falcon heads—a type of jewelry that can be traced back to Dynasty 12. Here, however, the elements of the collar are unusual and include the lion and the goat—animals typically depicted in Aegean hunting scenes—as well as the gazelle, all in dynamic galloping postures, along with spiral coils and other decorative elements.[32] An axe blade bearing the name of Ahmose from Ahhotep's burial equipment incorporates Aegean features into a purely Egyptian setting (cat. no. 67).

Also found was an elaborate dagger with a blade of gold (cat. no. 68). Although the weapon form is in the tradition of Middle Kingdom/Second Intermediate Period types,[33] aspects of its decoration may point to foreign influences. A dark strip serves as a background into which gold wire figures and hieroglyphic signs, possibly of foreign workmanship,[34] are inlaid. A lion chases a bull down the length of one side, both animals in flying gallop, with curving lines above to indicate rockwork. These features have been linked to the decoration of Aegean inlaid daggers (see fig. 36), one of which itself has a Nilotic theme.[35] Within a century, during the reigns of Hatshepsut and Thutmose III, there can be no doubt that the Aegean spirit was infused into traditional scenes of the hunt, particularly evident in the Tomb of Puimre, high priest of Amun (fig. 119).[36] Egyptian craftsmanship is obvious in the adherence to the

undulating groundline, as well as in the rather stiff forequarters of some of the wild goats. Yet the movement of their lifted hindquarters and the innovative contorted postures of the predatory lions, combined with the immediacy of their attack, brings a new dynamism and expressiveness to these scenes.[37] Such depictions reflected aspects of the life of the deceased. These scenes are depicted in the burial chamber or the entrance corridor, preceded by images of foreign envoys bearing riches for the pharaoh (fig. 85). There are also workshop scenes, some showing foreign craftsmen alongside Egyptians.[38]

About a hundred years later—during the era of intense trade and diplomacy framed by the Amarna Letters and the cargo aboard the Uluburun ship—Tutankhamun's magnificent burial accoutrements include a gold dagger and gold-foil chariot attachments, with imagery that emphasizes the traditional association of the pharaoh with the power of feline predators in a similarly dynamic manner (figs. 121, 122). While the superb workmanship on the handle and sheath, with cloisonné featherwork, together with the execution of the hieroglyphs on the dagger, may suggest its fabrication in an Egyptian workshop, the triangular patterns of granulation on the hilt and the violent animal combat scenes on the sheath—in a style that captures both the violence of the moment in the Aegean manner and the somewhat arrested movement of Levantine interpretations—present a truly intercultural amalgam.

Gold and Silverware

If the depictions of envoys in Theban tombs are any guide, Aegeans and Syrians were associated with elaborate metal vessels in the minds of Egyptians, as they are depicted bearing luxury wares that the Egyptians considered worthy of diplomatic gifts or tribute. Nevertheless, the objects depicted in the Theban tombs cannot be definitively cited to determine specific trade goods. The accuracy of representations and the identification of envoys must be questioned, not least because Egyptian artistic convention permitted hybridization, the mixing of features of both objects and persons.[39] Furthermore, the ostensible purpose of these visits was to bring tribute or to exchange diplomatic gifts between one ruler and another. Royal gift exchange had its own rules, the aim of which was to create links between the parties concerned:

Between kings there is brotherhood, alliance, peace, and good words if there is an abundance of (precious) stones, silver, and gold.[40]

Rulers could exchange anything in the royal treasury, whether local products or acquired as diplomatic gifts (see pp. 161–68). It is thus not surprising to find Aegean envoys carrying metal ingots and tusks to Egypt (see fig. 85), as they are raw materials that have been found together in the palace treasury at Zakros on Crete.[41]

The annals of Thutmose III reveal that metal vessels from foreign regions were also considered worthy as tribute or booty. Such objects—which appear in the Theban tomb paintings and on the walls of the Temple of Karnak—must have been highly prized in Egypt, and their appearance in Egyptian workshop scenes could mean that they were copied locally.[42] Diplomatic correspondence between the Great Kings, who emerged during the fourteenth and thirteenth centuries B.C., displays a similar admiration for metalwares of precious materials.[43] While few of these survive, two exceptional gold vessels from Ugarit escaped destruction, a patera and a small hemispherical bowl (cat. nos. 146, 147). Although both pieces depict hunting scenes disposed concentrically, they are conceptually quite different. The patera shows an archer in a chariot, the reins tied around his waist in Egyptian fashion, chasing a fleeing wild goat, its body fully extended as it leaps with rump lifted, as well as galloping and charging bulls. In posture and exuberance, the escaping prey are reminiscent of the innovative design on a Mediterranean-style seal probably produced in Syria many centuries earlier (fig. 124). The overall composition is a simplified version of hunting scenes depicted on weapons and chests from the tomb of Tutankhamun and foreshadows the chariot hunt on the ivory game box from Enkomi (cat. no. 265).

The scene on the bowl is quite different, with the hunt abstracted into static confrontations and heraldic compositions, more in keeping with traditional Near Eastern renderings that persist into the Phoenician era (see pp. 445–48). Certain artistic elements, however—the lions leaping onto their prey, the bent-wing profiles of fantastic beasts, and the vegetation emerging from above and below—reflect the impact of Aegean imagery as interpreted in a style that removes the viewer from the immediacy of the attack. Predators have rear limbs firmly planted on the ground, and their vicious chase evokes at most the turn of a head and an open mouth. A bronze plaque said to come from Tyre on the Levantine coast (cat. no. 259) offers yet another interpretation of the feline hunt, with two- and three-figured combat scenes infused with the energy of a life-and-death struggle that ultimately derives from Aegean sources and is preserved in late Cypriot metalwork (fig. 125).

The violent confrontation between two formidable predators—the lion and the griffin seen interlocked over a dead

Figure 125. Detail of animal-hunt scene on rim of bronze tripod. Cyprus. Late Bronze Age. The Metropolitan Museum of Art, New York, The Cesnola Collection, Purchased by subscription, 1874–76 74.51.5684

victim on the Tyre plaque—is also evident on Mycenaean seals and ivories. This theme is most sensitively rendered on a plaque preserved for centuries on the island of Delos (cat. no. 267). The creatures on this ivory are "powerfully immobile, drawing strength from . . . old (Aegean) conventions for speed and locked struggle."[44] Yet the carver did not model the bodies in relief but rather used an eastern idiom for the expression of musculature and other anatomical details, which are reduced to linear patterns.

Such works reveal the internationalism of the age, and analyses of their underlying structure and the manner in which specific elements were interpreted illuminate questions regarding the social climate that occasioned this coming together of traditions.[45] Innovations in the rendering of animal combat—a theme popular both east and west—appear to derive from a growing affinity in the Levant and Egypt for Minoan artistry. This is most clearly demonstrated in the material remains of two periods: the transition to the New Palace phase on Crete and the years around and following the destruction of Knossos as a center of Minoan culture. These were times during which historical events may have caused Aegean craftsmen to travel abroad, eventually participating in the creation of a great intercultural koine. Innovative styles of art that crossed boundaries—as in earlier periods of long-distance trade and later periods of empire—reflect, and were probably occasioned by, the historical realities we glimpse by reading the letters of the Great Kings, discovered by chance at Tell el-Amarna.[46]

1. EA 19, EA 10, Moran 1992, pp. 44, 19.
2. Moran 1992, pp. 68, 85, 87.
3. See Breasted 1906, pp. 210, 211, 217; Liverani 1990, p. 258, with further references; Van de Mieroop 2007, p. 92.
4. Moran 1992, pp. 78, 114.
5. Helms 1993, p. 165.
6. See Kantor 1947, pp. 66–69, pl. XIII.
7. Morgan 2004.
8. Vercoutter 1956, pp. 332–33, 321, nos. 283, 284, p. 333, no. 345; e.g., in the workshop depicted in the Tomb of Puimre; see also Wachsmann 1987, pls. XV, XI.
9. Amarna Letters: "seal of genuine lapis lazuli," EA 22: 48–54, Moran 1992, p. 52; there are also mentions of "seal-shaped stones" embedded in jewelry in EA 25, Moran 1992, pp. 73, 75; see also Oppenheim et al. 1970, pp. 11–12.
10. Posener 1971, p. 543. Warren and Hankey 1989, pp. 131–34; E. Davis 1977, pp. 69–78; Wiener (1991, p. 332) sees the vessels (or their raw material?) as part of a palatial gift exchange; A. Sherratt and S. Sherratt (1991, p. 361) mention the treasure in connection with the movement of precious metals; Kantor (1965, p. 20) refers to the small objects in the hoard as a "motley stock of jeweler's materials"; Porada (1982, p. 292) says they were originally collected as usable materials rather than a foundation deposit.
11. E. Davis (1977, pp. 69ff., 75) points to the cups' central Anatolian characteristics. Warren and Hankey (1989) relate these features to Middle Minoan IB–II Cretan pottery, itself seemingly inspired by metalwork.
12. Posener (1971, p. 544) identifies it, along with the cups, as Cretan or Asiatic imitations of Cretan objects; see also Yule 1985, pp. 43–44; Aruz 1995b, pp. 34–35; and Aruz 2008a, p. 87.
13. See Porada 1982, p. 290, figs. 8, 9, p. 288: these include fragmentary, recut, crude, and fine pieces, one attributed to a royal personage but with the inscription abraded.
14. Porada (1982) makes it clear that the Near Eastern amulets and seals come from various original sources and date from the Early Dynastic to the Isin-Larsa period.

15. Parrot 1956, pp. 159ff.; Parrot 1967, pp. 265–67, pl. LXXVII.
16. Porada 1982, pp. 290–91.
17. Aruz 2008a, pp. 96–98; Aruz 1995a, pp. 6–11.
18. Porada 1981–82, pp. 4–6.
19. A second treasure in a nearby room yielded lapis lazuli and gold beads and figure-of-eight shields of blue vitreous material; the site of an extensive jewelry workshop with many agate pieces was destroyed in the fourteenth century B.C.: Keramopoullos 1930, pp. 41–58; for later workshops in the new palace, see Demakopoulou 1974.
20. Porada 1981–82, p. 70.
21. See Cline 1987 and 1995. Lilyquist (1999a) questions the origin and interpretation of the faience fragments from Mycenae inscribed with the name of Amenhotep III.
22. Discussed in Aruz 2008a, p. 184, from Sellopoulo, Crete. Further examples are from Enkomi, from a tomb north of Acre, and from Panaztepe, cited in Aruz 2008a; Jaeger and Krauss 1990; and A. Erkanal 1986, p. 258.
23. See discussion in Aruz 2008a, pp. 192–95, and Aruz 2005.
24. Salje (1997, pp. 251ff.) notes that one import was found along with an Egyptian cowroid and suggests that some found in the Aegean were imitations.
25. Discussed in Aruz 2008a, pp. 139–43.
26. Collon 1981; Niemeier 1991.
27. S. Sherratt (1994, pp. 237–38) applies this description to the frescoes, some of which also resist simple ethnic identification.
28. In an extraordinary expression of empire, a stamp seal used by the Persian courtier Gobryas, an intimate of Darius the Great, bears an image of two lions attacking a stag, and displays the dynamic modeled animal style of the Greek world; see Aruz 2008a, p. 237.
29. EA 22, Moran 1992, pp. 51, 53; for iron weapons in later correspondence from Ramesses II to the Hittite king, see Beckman 1996, p. 140.
30. Lilyquist (1999b, pp. 214–16) notes that a mixture of Egyptian and foreign goods may have been present in the tomb. She observes that the "objects from Egypt are rich but comparatively simple in form, pattern, or material, those from the Near East more colorful and varied."
31. Ziffer (in *At That Time the Canaanites Were in the Land* 1990, p. 73) identifies the dagger as Syro-Canaanite in manufacture; Vercoutter (1956, p. 360, pl. LXII:467), however, identifies this as a misattributed Aegean weapon with a pommel; Helck (1995, p. 48) considers the design to indicate an Egyptian copy of an Aegean work.
32. Andrews 1990, p. 178, fig. 163; A. Evans, PM II, p. 361 and PM I, pp. 714–15; von Bissing 1900, pls. I–III, VIII–VIIIA; for the identification of Ahhotep, see Eaton-Krauss 1990 and Jánosi 1992; on possible relations with the Aegean world, see Bietak 1997, p. 124, and Hughes-Brock 2000, p. 123.
33. Von Bissing 1900, pl. II; Wolf 1926, pls. 4, 5; Vercoutter 1956, pp. 359–60, nos. 462–67, pl. LXII; Eggebrecht 1975; Müller-Karpe 1977, pp. 41ff.; W. Smith 1981, p. 222.
34. James P. Allen, personal communication, January 2005.
35. Hood 1978, p. 180, fig. 179.
36. Wachsmann (1987, p. 29) believes that his association with foreigners stems from his role in dealing with temple revenues.
37. Kantor 1947 (reprinted 1997), pp. 66–67, pl. XIII; for Aegean and Egyptian hunt scenes, see Morgan 2004, pp. 288–93; for an exceptional Dynasty 11 precedent, see Hayes 1953, p. 164, fig. 100.
38. See Wachsmann 1987, p. 29, pl. XXIV, where the third foreigner could be an Aegean.
39. Ibid., pp. 4–9.
40. Liverani 1990, p. 213: Amarna Letter EA 11; see also Papadopoulos 2001 on distinctions between trade and royal gifts.
41. On such "irrational" trade, see Liverani 1979, pp. 22–26; Wachsmann (1987, pp. 50–55) considers that scenes appropriate for Syrians in some cases may have been transferred to Aegeans, and cannot be used as evidence for objects of Minoan gift exchange; for the Zakros Treasury (and Ayia Triada ingots): Platon 1971, p. 116.
42. Vercoutter 1956, pp. 332–33, 321, nos. 283–84, p. 333, no. 345; e.g., in the workshop depicted in the Tomb of Puimre; see also Wachsmann 1987, pls. XV, XI.
43. EA 22, 25, Moran 1992, pp. 52, 54, 78.
44. Vermeule 1964, p. 221. For similar features on ivories from Cyprus, see Feldman 2006b, pp. 44–45.
45. For a lucid discussion of this issue during the Achaemenid Empire, see Nylander 1970, pp. 17–20.
46. See Feldman 2006b for the most recent comprehensive treatment of this subject; for similar archives in the Hittite capital, see Beckman 1996.

247

CYLINDER SEAL AND MODERN IMPRESSION: ANIMAL COMBAT AND SPHINX

Hematite
Height 1.2 cm (½ in.)
Syria–Levant
Old Syrian, early 2nd millennium B.C.
The Metropolitan Museum of Art, New York,
Gift of Mr. and Mrs. John J. Klejman, 1966
66.76.2

247

248

CYLINDER SEAL AND MODERN IMPRESSION: PHARAONIC SCENE

Hematite
Height 1.9 cm (¾ in.)
Syria–Levant
Old Syrian, early 2nd millennium B.C.
The Metropolitan Museum of Art, New York,
Gift of The Right Reverend Paul Moore Jr., 1985
1985.357.16
Ex coll.: Mrs. William H. Moore

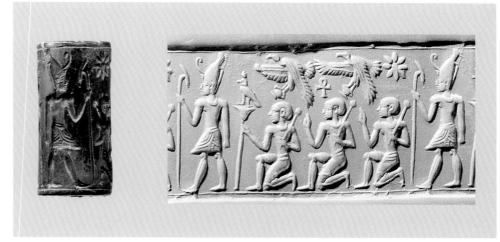

248

Two hematite cylinder seals in the Metropolitan Museum offer a glimpse into the various ways in which Egyptian and possibly other foreign imagery were absorbed into the Syrian glyptic repertoire. The seal above has been attributed to a workshop that may have been located at Ugarit.[1] The seals ascribed to this workshop share some stylistic characteristics, especially the rendering of animals with sweeping strokes that create a sense of movement.[2] They vary significantly, however, in composition. While some of the seals have imagery that covers the entire field, others are less densely carved, arranged in one or two registers. This seal shows a hunting scene with an antelope galloping above a lion that appears to be pawing at its mate, whose head is turned back. A second image introduces what may be an Egyptianizing motif of a female winged sphinx standing on a cobra, its head lifted as if to strike, below a typically Syrian guilloche chain.[3] The sphinx—sometimes depicted in this group in the Egyptian manner, with wing folded against body[4]— is one of the most prominent images on these seals, along with Horus falcons, vultures, and monkeys.

Of particular interest is the rendering of movement by the use of a dynamic stance that becomes a hallmark of Aegean art—the flying gallop. This posture, which makes isolated appearances in the art of western Central Asia and Egypt during the late third and early second millennia B.C.,[5] first appears on Crete in the corpus of stamp seal impressions found in the Palace of Phaistos.[6] Dated to some time in the eighteenth century B.C., they are contemporary with the earliest use of this posture on Syrian glyptic.

The seal below is part of a large corpus of Syro-Levantine cylinder seals with Egyptian royal and divine imagery. A pharaonic figure, wearing the double crown and royal kilt, strides forward holding a backward *was*-scepter. He is attended by three kneeling nude belted figures with maces, the first also bearing a standard crowned by a Horus falcon. Vultures fly above holding *shen* signs, with an *ankh* beneath their wings. It has been suggested that the scene may derive from Egyptian depictions of protective spirits, possibly ancestral kings, attending the pharaoh.[7]

JA

1. Collon (1985b, p. 58), points to three seals from Ugarit in the group; Amiet 1992, pp. 26–30, nos. 28, 29, 36.
2. Teissier 1996, pp. 16–17, Workshop A.
3. Ibid., pp. 80–83, 146, IIA, p. 149, points out that sphinxes trampling snakes are not found in Middle Kingdom imagery; for a double-headed sphinx with a cobra below, see Altenmüller 1965, fig. 10.
4. For an Egyptian griffin from Beni Hasan, with wings similarly folded against the body, see Wilkinson and Hill 1983, p. 68: 33.8.14.
5. Pittman in *Glories of the Past* 1990, pp. 43–44, no. 30 (Bactrian vessel); Hayes 1953, p. 164, fig. 100 (Dynasty XI).
6. CMS II 5, nos. 276, 277.
7. Teissier 1996, pp. 55, 56, no. 31.

249

CYLINDER SEAL AND MODERN IMPRESSION: DEITY AND OFFERING BEARER

Hematite
Height 2.4 cm (⅞ in.); diameter 1.1 cm (½ in.)
Crete, Mochlos, Tomb Λ
Early Minoan II–Middle Minoan IB/IIA context
Old Syrian manufacture, early 2nd millennium B.C.
Archaeological Museum, Siteia, Greece
8540

249

The site of Mochlos on Crete—a gateway from the east—produced a remarkable collection of foreign imports. Discovered here, in addition to a fragment of Old Hittite pottery, an Egyptian bronze sistrum, and copper and tin ingots found with a ceremonial trident,[1] were two Syrian cylinder seals. One, made of silver, comes from an Early Bronze Age tomb.[2] The second, represented here, belongs to a small body of Near Eastern cylinder seals that arrived on Crete during the Middle Bronze Age and were deposited in elite burials.[3] Datable from the late nineteenth to the early eighteenth century B.C., it was found in a disturbed tomb with Early Minoan II–Middle Minoan IB/IIA pottery, suggesting that it arrived at a time close to its manufacture.[4] It is unflawed and exhibits little wear.

A male offering bearer is depicted wearing a long fringed garment and holding a hare before an enthroned deity in a flounced robe. Framing this scene (when the seal is impressed) is a guilloche chain dividing two rows of figures, males striding to the right above females striding left between linear borders. Seals with similar imagery and figural style are widely distributed in northern Syria at Alalakh, Chagar Bazar, and Ugarit; in central Anatolia at Boğazköy; and in Canaan at Gaza and Balata. Some of these belong to a group that has been attributed to an origin in Ugarit.[5]   JA

1. Soles 2004, pp. 2–5.
2. See Aruz 2008a, pp. 40–41.
3. Ibid., pp. 90–93, 96 (Platanos, Archanes, Knossos, and Tylissos).
4. Soles and Davaras 1992, pp. 423–24; CMS V Suppl. IB, no. 332. The date of the tomb extends into Middle Minoan IIA, based on some carinated cup fragments: Thomas

Brogan, personal communication to Colin Macdonald, 2006.
5. A. Rowe 1936, pp. 234–35, pl. XXVI:S4; Nougayrol 1939, pp. 49–50, pl. 8:S.B.1; Petrie, Mackay, and Murray 1952, pl. IX:33; el-Safadi 1974, pl. XII:86, 89; Collon 1982, pp. 56–57, no. 22; Schaeffer-Forrer 1983, p. 34 (RS 9.888), (RS 9.300).

250

CYLINDER SEAL AND MODERN IMPRESSION: BULL-MEN

Hematite
Height 2.8 cm (1⅛ in.); diameter 1.3 cm (½ in.)
Tiryns Treasure
Mitanni manufacture, 15th century B.C.
National Archaeological Museum, Athens, Greece 6214

251

CYLINDER SEAL AND MODERN IMPRESSION: WINGED DEMONS

Hematite
Height 3.2 cm (1¼ in.); diameter 1.5 cm (⅝ in.)
Perati, Chamber Tomb 1
Late Helladic IIIB–IIIC: 1 context
Mitanni manufacture, 14th century B.C.
National Archaeological Museum, Athens, Greece 8088

These two Mitanni cylinder seals found on the Greek mainland date to the period of Mycenaean domination of Aegean trade with the east.[1] The largest class of imported Mitanni cylinder seals is that of

the mass-produced Common Style (see pp. 388–91). The imported seals illustrated here are carved in the Elaborate Style, distinguished by the use of a fine drill, small size, and relatively hard stone, usually hematite, the mineral form of iron oxide.

The seal at right, above, is from the Tiryns Treasure, a hoard found in 1915 inside a bronze cauldron buried in a house belonging to the Lower Town of Tiryns.[2] The objects in the treasure are of various dates and range from gold rings (see fig. 45) to scrap bronze. On the seal two symmetrical bull-men stand beneath a winged disc holding a standard and occupying the full height of the composition. The winged disc with small drillings bordering the wings is typically Mitanni (see cat. no. 178). A horizontal row of concentric circles divides the remaining space into two registers, in which caprids, griffins, and a stylized tree are depicted.

The seal at right, below, is from a much later tomb context at Perati and was found along with a Cypriot cylinder seal and ten Egyptian scarabs.[3] Two principal figural groups are depicted. The first consists of a winged demon with feline legs and tail holding two griffin-demons by the hind legs in a typically Near Eastern Master of Animals pose. In the second group, two figures—identified as divinities by their horned conical headdresses—have bull legs and tails. Each raises one arm in a smiting pose and with the other hand grasps the hind leg of the ibex suspended between them. Rosettes, stars, birds, and a frontal head fill the compositional field, while a band of running spirals and a lion stalking its prey appear along the bottom. In addition to the

250

251

Syro-Levantine aspects of the composition, the first figural group has Middle Assyrian parallels (see cat. no. 124), while the second group has Anatolian parallels (cat. no. 100), attesting to the eclectic character of the Mitanni style.

JME

1. Aruz 2008a, pp. 181ff.
2. Maran 2006, pp. 129ff.
3. CMS I Suppl., no. 54.

252
CYLINDER SEAL AND MODERN IMPRESSION: DEMONS AND ANIMALS

Hematite
Height 2.8 cm (1⅛ in.)
Cypriot with Aegean elements
14th century B.C.
The Metropolitan Museum of Art, New York,
Purchase, Friends of
Inanna Gifts, 2008 2008.27

This beautifully carved hematite cylinder seal, published by Boardman in 1970, bears an elaborate multifigured design. Two demonic figures known as Minoan Genii—lion-headed creatures derived from the Egyptian hippopotamus goddess Taweret—face one another. Holding vessels by the handle, they appear to stand on the backs of seated confronted lions, with heads of horned animals in the field. Above them, between a small leaping ibex and crossing lions, signs of the Cypro-

252

253

Minoan script flank a central rosette over a winged sun disc. A second group is composed of two figures grasping a lion suspended between them, one by the tail and the other by the hind leg. It is a depiction of domination rendered in a manner that becomes typical for Cypriot seals. Both are probably divinities. One, in human form, wears a knobbed cap and a belted flounced garment that covers the entire body. The other is a bull-headed demon with a narrow waist and undulating lower body suggestive of the human female form, revealed through a kilt that exposes one leg. Approaching the scene is an upright human-headed lion. A typically Near Eastern hero head with a horned cap, curls, and a beard appears above the defeated lion, with the head of another lion below.

This is one of the most important cylinder seals for understanding the development of the finest glyptic styles on the island of Cyprus. While the format of aligned figures certainly derives from Near Eastern seal compositions, many features appear to be local stylistic elements adapted from Aegean glyptic. These include the shapes of the lion heads, the movement expressed by the bull-demon, and the exaggerated curves of the Minoan Genii with the dotted outline of their dorsal appendages.[1] Other stylizations, such as the depiction of human faces with a long line for the nose, human feet with high heels, and lion claws as a crescent with raised dot, come to be diagnostic features of Cypriot work.

JA

1. Boardman 1970, pp. 64–65, 106:206, pl. 206; Porada 1973b, pp. 260–64; Pini 1979, p. 127.

253

CYLINDER SEAL AND MODERN IMPRESSION: MASTER OF ANIMALS

Hematite
Height 2.3 cm (⅞ in.); diameter .8 cm (¼ in.)
"Cypro-Aegean," 14th century B.C.
The Metropolitan Museum of Art, New York,
Gift of Nanette B. Kelekian, in memory of
Charles, Dikran, and Beatrice Kelekian, 1999
1999.325.223
Ex coll.: Dikran Kelekian

An extraordinary seal with a famous twin—discovered near the House of the Bronzes at Enkomi on Cyprus[1] and now in the Cyprus Museum, Nicosia—came to light as part of the important collection of seals formed during the early years of the twentieth century by Dikran Kelekian. Sometime around 1910, before the start of excavations at Enkomi, the collection was placed in the care of the British Museum, where it remained until 1952. It was given to the Metropolitan Museum in 1999.

Both cylinder seals are made of hematite and are close in size. Each depicts a hero in a short kilt, arms outstretched, and flanked by lions with their heads reversed and forelegs on altars. A Minoan Genius stands behind the left lion; it has a ring eye and a carapace indicated by drillings, which narrows at the waist, and holds a vessel, schematically rendered by three drillings. In an upper register, two facing birds flank the hero's head and above the Genius a griffin is shown in flying gallop. The seals vary in certain details, however. On the Metropolitan seal, the hero appears

to wear a crested (horned?) Mycenaean boar's tusk helmet. There is also variation in the small motifs in the field: a human head, a rayed sun disc, and a figure-of-eight shield on the Enkomi example, and a sun disc in crescent and dot rosettes on the Metropolitan Museum seal.

In style and composition the two seals are identical, mixing Aegean and Near Eastern elements. The animal bodies are finely modeled with supple curves, thrusting foreground hind legs forward in the Aegean manner. Cuts and small drillings indicate outlines and details.[2] The lions are in the Aegean heraldic posture, their forelegs resting on an altar. Nevertheless, they have a wooden appearance, created by a nearly horizontal chest and belly, and no torsion or thrust. The griffins, too, lack dynamism; though in flying gallop, the downward motion of head, chest, and forelegs stops their movement.[3] The hero's head looks Aegean, having a line for the nose, chin, and jaw, and drillings for the long curl of the hair and the eye. The torso is modeled, slightly twisting toward a three-quarter view, the back arched with a wasp waist. The legs are straight, with feet on the groundline in the Near Eastern manner; the extended arm position, however, is characteristic for the Aegean Master of Animals.

The discovery of this pair of seals points to the rare production of look-alikes made by the same hand. This phenomenon is identified otherwise by seal impressions that are often mistaken for imprints of one rather than separate seals.

JA

1. Built in Late Cypriot II (ca. 1450–1350 B.C.), damaged by earthquake, and used through the

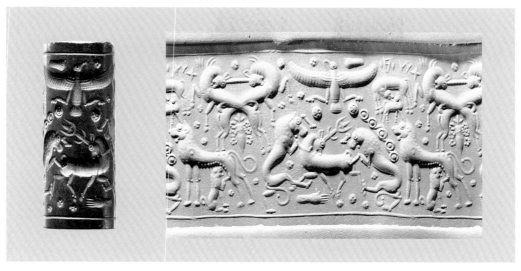

254

end of the Bronze Age: Schaeffer 1936b, pp. 89, 112–113, figs. 48, 49; Schaeffer-Forrer 1983, p. 56 (Enkomi 1.002).

2. Boardman 1970, pp. 48, 393 (Common Palatial Group: Late Minoan II–IIIA), pl. 114 for a lion parallel; Pini 1980, p. 80, no. A7, places the Enkomi seal in the "Cypro-Aegean" group closest to Minoan.

3. The griffin on a Late Cypriot I–II seal from Maroni is similarly restrained, in contrast to the more dynamic horned animal beneath it; see Kenna 1971, pl. VII:31.

254
CYLINDER SEAL AND MODERN IMPRESSION: ANIMAL COMBAT

Hematite
Height 2.5 cm (1 in.); diameter .6 cm (¼ in.)
"Cypro-Aegean," 14th century B.C.
Yale Babylonian Collection, New Haven 358

On this masterpiece of seal engraving from the Yale Babylonian Collection, reported to come from Latakia, near Ugarit, the carver has integrated eastern and western elements to a degree that they are inseparable.[1] The central theme is animal combat: two lions, each upright on a single hind leg, attack a stag, with an eagle above. The pyramidal composition is framed on a higher level with two motifs: crossing goats and a horned animal nursing its young. A lioness, suckling her cub, stands on the groundline adjacent to the combat scene. The field is filled with signs, a hand device, an octopus, a spiral chain, and tiny rosettes.

The pyramidal scheme is a traditional feature of Near Eastern glyptic, with two predators attacking a fallen victim beneath an eagle or a lion-headed (Imdugud) bird. However, the style and postures of the animals are quite different. On Old Syrian and Syro-Mitanni seals, attacking felines are rooted to the ground despite their raised forepaws, whereas the bodies of the lions are oblique and maintain balance on one thin hind leg only, the other leg kicking forward in a characteristically Aegean manner. On the Yale seal, the stag, too, while horizontal like those on sealings from the northern Mesopotamian site of Nuzi, is in motion, with its head dramatically turned back and downward, exposing the chest, its limbs moving to express its struggle. The prototypes for the style and postures of lions and stag in three-animal combat are Minoan-Mycenaean.[2] The Aegean figures are generally more massive and powerful looking. By comparison, the animals on this seal are static. The lions' feet are on the same ground level, the stag's leg movements are less well defined, and the turn of its head lacks the tension of purely Aegean representations. Thus, in style and posture the Yale seal stands between Aegean and Near Eastern traditions, providing a subtle blend of elements, further emphasized by the scene of the lioness suckling her cub.[3]

The group of crossing goats, like the central triad, blends the sensitive modeling and dramatic curves of animals in Aegean gem engraving with postures that are rather static for Crete but animated in contrast to standard Syrian work. Like the wild goats on ivory plaques from the Mycenaean palace at Thebes (cat. no. 175), they are symmetrically positioned. The detail of the horizontal line connecting the animals' heads, however, suggests that the motif of crossing addorsed animals ultimately derives from Syro-Mitanni glyptic, where addorsed stags are bound by a similar connecting line.[4]

Finally, the filling motifs, such as the hand, rosettes, and Cypriot signs, are common on cylinder seals with mixed imagery and designated as "Cypro-Aegean." The hand can be traced to a Mitanni Common Style origin, where rows of this device occur.[5] The octopus must derive from the Aegean, but the tiny drillings of the tentacles are similar to the granulation effect on the carapaces of Minoan Genii on Cypriot seals.[6]

The overall syntax of the Yale seal, with individual self-contained scenes juxtaposed at different levels to fill the entire field, is eastern in derivation. It contrasts with the Minoan approach of producing a unified picture: drawing in all parts of the field by the use of thrusts in different directions, varied perspective, and changes in orientation. The carver of the Yale seal remained sensitive to the Minoan treatment of organic form—but developed a new style, fully and successfully integrating Aegean and Near Eastern aspects of style, posture, individual schemes of composition, iconography, and overall syntax.

JA

1. For further reference, see Buchanan 1968, pp. 410–11; Pini 1980, p. 81, no. C1, p. 96, fig. 11; Symeonoglou 1973, p. 48, fig. 225a; Porada 1981–82, p. 22, fig. c; Aruz 1997, pp. 275–77, 287, fig. 15; Aruz 1998, p. 306, pl. XXXIII.

2. See Aruz 2008a, fig. 428, with other striking parallels on a seal in Munich (fig. 429), as on a ring impression from Knossos (fig. 397).

3. Unlike Aegean suckling scenes, the lioness is aloof from the cub and faces the combat scene. Legs are aligned on the groundline; the only movement is created by extension of the hind legs. The forelegs are straight. The body is smooth and supple, marked by a full chest and rump curves. In execution, posture, and details such as the shoulder drilling, the lioness is close to that on cat. no. 253.
4. See Aruz, 2008a, fig. 427.
5. See ibid., fig. 431.
6. Compare the Aegean octopodes on CMS I, no. 312; Pini 1997, pl. 19:40, 40A, pl. 20:40B–G: sealings from Pylos with ring impressions of an octopus motif, dated stylistically to Late Bronze II–Early IIIA.

255
CYLINDER SEAL AND MODERN IMPRESSION: ANIMAL COMBAT

Hematite
Height 3 cm (1⅛ in.); diameter 1.2 cm (½ in.)
"Cypro-Aegean," 14th century B.C.
Jeanette and Jonathan Rosen, New York
Ex coll.: Colville Collection

The field on this hematite cylinder seal is divided into informal registers without dividers or border lines. The central animal combat triad consists of two lions attacking a bull collapsed on its haunches with forelegs enfolded. Above the bull is an eagle with wings outspread, beneath which two quadrupeds emerge. A second eagle hovers beside the combatant lion on the right, forming a symmetrical pattern with the addorsed lions when the cylinder is rolled more than once. Above the eagle is an adoration scene of a frontal bull-headed demon in a long garment flanked by Minoan Genii holding ewers above stands. The Genii have pinched-in waists marked by belts and plain carapaces; they are posed in the Aegean manner with vessels extended.[1]

Stylistically, the curvaceous bodies of the animals, with the foreground rear legs of the lions kicked forward and the belly–hindquarter transition scooped out, relate to the animals on the masterpiece of intercultural style seal carving in the Yale Babylonian Collection (cat. no. 254). The Aegean treatment of hind leg kicked forward—here also combined with horizontal rather than diagonal bodies and

with a straight foreleg on the ground—makes for a more static, eastern posture. The overall composition, divided into registers with little relationship between scenes and multiple "filler" devices, also creates more of a Near Eastern than an Aegean effect; although constructed on similar principles, it is somewhat less integrated than the design on the Yale seal.

This seal could have been made by an apprentice of the carver of the Yale seal—hence its derivative features. Compositional schemes such as the pyramidal syntax of combatant animals with an eagle above also occur on the Yale seal, pointing to ultimate origins in Mitanni glyptic. The eagle, placed to create a symmetrical composition between two quadrupeds (lions below, horned animals above), is Near Eastern in origin. Heraldic scenes with Genii occur on Aegean stamp seals, where they flank a nude male.[2]

While the animal combat triad and the eagle with prey in its talons find their closest parallels in Near Eastern glyptic, Genii libating at altars are Minoan in derivation.[3] The frontal horned figure in a long garment, however, seems to combine the imagery of Near Eastern horned deities and Cypriot long-robed demons usually with profile animal heads rather than frontal human heads. The motifs in the field—Cypro-Minoan script, rayed sun disc, and hand device—are also part of the "Cypro-Aegean" repertoire, the latter two probably of Syro-Mitanni origin.   JA

1. For further reference, see Kenna 1967b, pp. 251–53, fig. 1; Pini 1980, p. 81, no. B3, p. 95, fig. 10; Weingarten 1996, p. 82(c), pl. 25A.
2. Gill 1964, pl. 7:3.
3. A Genius attends a goddess with upraised arms and "snake frames" on a sealing from Pylos: CMS I, no. 379.

256
CYLINDER SEAL AND MODERN IMPRESSION: HERO DOMINATING LIONS

Hematite
Height 2.3 cm (⅞ in.); diameter .9 cm (⅜ in.)
"Cypro-Aegean," 14th century B.C.
The Metropolitan Museum of Art, New York, Rogers Fund and funds from various donors, 1992 1992.288
Ex coll.: Erlenmeyer Collection

This hematite cylinder seal, with many motifs juxtaposed at different levels in the field, displays both Aegean and Near Eastern features. The dominant figure is a hero, nude except for a tasseled belt of Near Eastern type and a conical plumed cap. His head is in profile, his torso in three-quarter view, legs striding to his right with the front one slightly raised. His right arm, bent at the elbow, holds the leg of a reversed lion with the head turned toward him. Behind him is an upright lion in adorant posture, with forelegs on an altar and hind legs on the

255

256

CYLINDER SEAL AND MODERN IMPRESSION: DEMON AND ANIMAL COMBAT

Brownish hematite
Height 2.5 cm (1 in.); diameter 1 cm (⅜ in.)
"Cypro-Aegean," 14th century B.C.
The Pierpont Morgan Library, New York,
Morgan seal 1077

A number of cylinder seals manufactured during the Late Bronze Age reflect the mixed artistic styles that are also found in other media. This hematite example in the Pierpont Morgan Library is of particular interest because of the manner in which the field of a Near Eastern cylinder seal is adapted to render a scene with clear Aegean associations.[1] Depicted are combatant animals, a goat-headed demon, an "impaled triangle," and a tree with a dotted stalk topped by a flower and drooping leaves. Similar motifs occur on Aegean lentoid stamp seals of the fifteenth century B.C.[2] The goat-man in three-quarter pose, with his lively posture, head turned in one direction, and bent limbs in the other, appears Minoan in style. If the cylinder is read horizontally, he stands on a baseline. The animal combat, however, is to be seen from a different vantage point, at a 90-degree angle to the goat-man. A griffin, formally similar to those on mixed-style seals associated with Cyprus, attacks a bull from above; other animals leap below.

The composition, with its varied vantage point and dynamic action, which take

---

ground. To the right is a smaller scene of a griffin confronting a running stag. A double-headed eagle hovers between the two scenes and, at the same level, another nude belted hero is flanked by heraldically addorsed dogs.

The style, like that on the Yale seal (cat. no. 254), is one of supple, well-curved bodies, spindly limbs marked with small drillings, and movement mixed with restraint.[1] Aegean inspiration is evident in the torsion of the human bodies. The torso of the large hero is turned, a swayed back narrowing to a wasp waist, and he steps with his feet off the ground. There is a similar twist to the body of the small male figure above. Aegean parallels exist for all the animal postures, such as the reversed lion.[2] The second lion's body is vertical, recalling postures of many upright animals on Cypriot seals. The stag is in the Aegean wounded-animal posture. The griffin may relate in stance to the vertical leaping griffin on the Thebes agate cylinder seal (cat. no. 183).[3] The posture of the Master of Animals in the upper field and the confinement of the composition of the three figures make it clear that the scene was excerpted from the circular field of an Aegean lentoid seal.[4] With this exception, the overall composition of the field is Near Eastern. Major and minor actors are in distinct scenes at different heights in the field and with no specific registers. Such syntax is found on works by the master carver of the Yale seal and his followers. The composition, with an eagle above an animal combat, may allude to Mitanni pyramidal schemes, also popular in this group.

Certainly the carver of this seal achieved an integration of Minoan, Cypriot, and some Mitanni elements.[5] His production is closely related to, or derived from, the art of the "Yale Master," who must have worked in the fourteenth century B.C.

JA

1. These stylistic features may ultimately derive from the Rhodian Hunt Group (see cat. no. 257).
2. See Aruz 2008a, figs. 388, 389.
3. See also an Aegean lentoid seal: ibid., fig. 402.
4. A close parallel can be found on the Knossos sealings: ibid., fig. 435.
5. Pini (1980, p. 80, no. A9, p. 90, fig. 7) considers this seal to have Aegean style and iconography and Near Eastern syntax; M. Erlenmeyer and H. Erlenmeyer (1964, pp. 201ff.) and Schachermeyr (1967, p. 55, pl. 54:194) call it Mitanni in Aegean style.

257

the eye all over the field, is also Minoan. Birds fly in empty spaces as they do on Late Minoan style cylinder seals.[3] The smooth modeling of the attenuated animal bodies, with exaggerated curving outlines, connects this seal with one found on the island of Rhodes, possibly another place where eastern and western traditions came together.[4] The use of hematite, a favorite material for Near Eastern cylinder seals, suggests a desire to create a Near Eastern–looking product. The lines defining the upper and lower limits of the field, often an indication of the addition of gold caps, is the main concession to Near Eastern syntax on this otherwise Aegean creation.   JA

1. Pini 1980, p. 79, no. A5, p. 86, fig. 4; Porada 1948, no. 1077.
2. CMS I, nos. 52, 57, 73, 74, 88, 105.
3. Hood 1959–60, pp. 23, 24; CMS II 3, no. 65.
4. Younger 1987.

258

NECKLACE WITH SEALS AND BEADS

Carnelian, amethyst, glass, and gold
Max. length 2.9 cm (1⅛ in.); max. diameter
2 cm (¾ in.)
Kazarma, Tholos Tomb
Late Helladic IIA, ca. 1525–1450 B.C.
Nafplion Archaeological Museum, Greece
15024–15038, 15120

258

These stamp and cylinder seals were found loose around the neck of a body in Burial Pit II of a tholos tomb situated on the southern slope of Kazarma hill (fig. 126), which lies inland and east of the Argive Plain on the Greek mainland.[1] The strategic position of the tomb along a roadway and its rich, cosmopolitan offerings imply that it was built by a local elite who controlled land routes between the Argive Plain and the area of Epidauros. The monumental tomb was likely an expression of autonomy and local dominance during a period of instability and social competition that preceded the formation of the hierarchical and centralized Mycenaean political system of the nearby citadels and palaces.

The three intact pits dug into the floor of the chamber contained one female and two male burials, respectively. Apart

from the seals and amulets, Burial Pit II contained five squat alabastra, a silver cup with gilded rim and handle, lead balance weights, bronze knives and daggers with silver rivets, flint arrowheads, and boars' tusks.

The necklace consists of eight spherical glass beads of various sizes; a glass bead in the shape of a bull's head; two amygdaloid seals of amethyst and carnelian, one in talismanic style with a Minoan dragon,[2] the other with three birds; a glass cylinder seal with a winged griffin, embellished with gold caps;[3] an amethyst cylinder seal with a unique lion-drawn chariot;[4] and an amethyst cylinder seal with a griffin and a lion bearing a female figure on its back.[5] It was not possible to accurately reconstruct the original

arrangement of the beads as the thread that once held them together had disintegrated. Although the amethyst cylinder seals must have been made on the Greek mainland, they present evidence that Near Eastern seal forms and imagery were imitated and adapted to Mycenaean art and craftsmanship.[6]   EP

1. On the tomb, see Protonotariou-Deilaki 1968; Protonotariou-Deilaki 1969; *Archaiologikon Deltion* 24 (1969), B1, pp. 104–5, pls. 83, 84; see also *Bulletin de correspondance hellénique* 94 (1970), p. 961, and 95 (1971), p. 867.
2. CMS V 2, nos. 581, 582.
3. Ibid., no. 583.
4. Ibid., no. 585.
5. Ibid., no. 584.
6. For the most recent discussion of the cylinder seals, see Aruz 2008a, pp. 167–69.

258, detail

258, detail

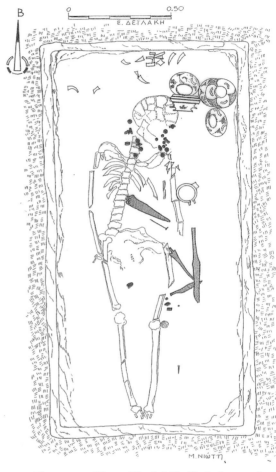

Figure 126. Plan of Burial Pit II, tholos tomb, Kazarma, showing placement of necklace. Late Helladic IIA.

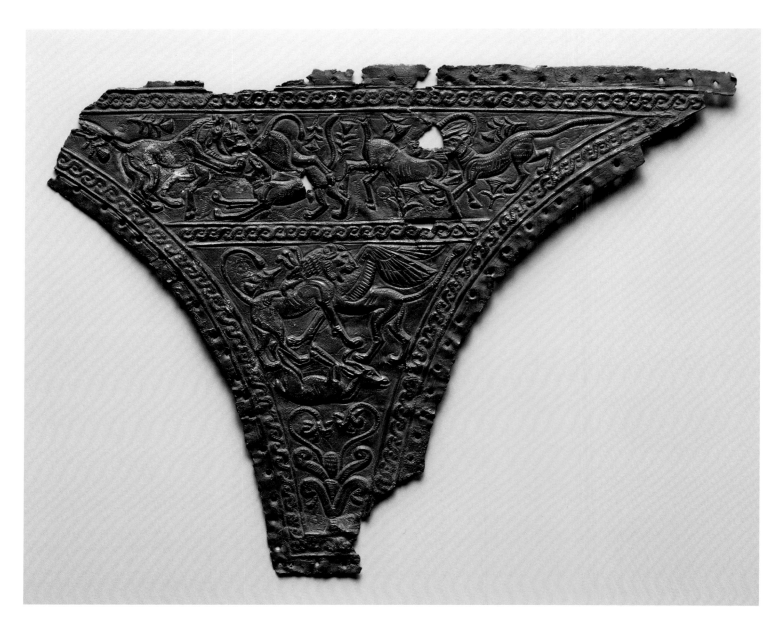

259

PLAQUE WITH ANIMAL
COMBATS

Bronze
Height 12.1 cm (4¾ in.)
Levant
Late Bronze Age, 14th century B.C.
Musée du Louvre, Paris, Département des
Antiquités Orientales AO 15557

This small bronze plaque, which came
to be attributed to the site of Tyre on
the Levantine coast, is triangular in form,
with holes for attachment to another material.[1] Hunting scenes are depicted above a
scene of powerful beasts from the natural
and supernatural realms—a lion and a
griffin—clashing over their prey. The vegetation and the overall arrangement of two-
and three-figure combats in registers—

here bordered by a simplified Syrian
guilloche pattern—relate this plaque to
a suite of international style metalwork
that includes the gold bowl from Ugarit
(cat. no. 146) and the dagger sheath of
Tutankhamun (fig. 121). Of great interest
is the differentiation within this community of styles, in the details of rendering
of the predatory beasts, the vegetation,
and the ornamental motifs, as well as the
degree to which the dynamic, modeled
images associated with the Aegean world
are absorbed and integrated.

Two distinct combats—one with a lion
and a hound attacking a bull and the other
with a leopard or cheetah biting the throat
of an ibex—fill the upper horizontal band.
In contrast to the scenes on the Ugarit
bowl and the dagger sheath from Egypt,
the violence of the moment is captured in
these compositions of frontal attack and

permeates the bodies of the victims, their
heads contorted, their limbs lifted off the
ground. The lions leap onto their prey
with the rear leg nearest the viewer kicked
forward in the Aegean manner, while a
hound with open jaws bites into the belly,
his body overlapped by the raised limbs of
the bull. Egyptian pondweed stalks with
papyrus flowers provide the landscape.[2]

A voluted palmette with curving tendrils—closer to Egyptian models than
those on the Ugarit bowl—occupies the
lower register,[3] over which a lion and a
griffin are locked in fierce combat over a
prostrate, probably dead, calf. This scene
may perhaps recall an Aegean composition
surviving on a jasper stamp seal from
Mycenae, where two crossing lions bite
each other.[4] Here, however, the griffin,
while grasping the back of its adversary in
its beak, is itself shielded by its enormous

wings, which serve as a backdrop for the head of the lion. This powerful animal is rendered with ripples rather than patterning at the neck, to indicate perhaps the lack of a mane. The griffin, too, is distinctive, with its great wings shown in profile, one behind the other, displaying the characteristic Aegean bent-wing form and a narrow head with exaggerated vulture beak and three crest curls. It shares features with the seated creature on the Ugarit bowl and, more closely, with the griffin on a gold-foil chariot attachment from the Tomb of Tutankhamun (fig. 122). There, the beast pounces on its prey while a hound bites its belly, in a scene that captures the dynamic spirit and composition of Aegean animal confrontations. As already mentioned, the fashion for such imagery appears to have originated earlier in the New Kingdom, perhaps introduced to Egypt by the craftsmen responsible for the Tell el-Dab'a feline hunt frescoes (see fig. 120).[5]   JA

1. Perrot and Chipiez 1885, p. 813, fig. 565; Longperier 1882, pl. XXI:4. According to Annie Caubet (personal communication), the bronze plaque came to the Musée du Louvre with the Salt collection, which was built in Egypt at a time that artifacts from Lebanon came into the hands of dealers in Alexandria and Cairo. The origin of the attribution to Tyre, however, is unknown.
2. See Kantor (1945) 1999, pp. 524, 533, for the identification of pondweed, or *Potamogeton*.
3. Kantor (ibid., pp. 33–34) considers this a possible indication of a southern Levantine artistic tradition, with close ties to Egypt.
4. CMS I, no. 117, with two clashing lions; for the prostrate victim, see CMS II 6, no. 103.
5. Morgan 2004.

260
PLAQUE WITH ANIMAL COMBATS

Gold
Width 5.6 cm (2¼ in.); length 14.6 cm (5¾ in.)
Levant (?)
Late Bronze Age, 14th–13th century B.C.
Musée du Louvre, Paris, Département des Antiquités Égyptiennes E17383

This concave elliptical gold plaque came to the Musée du Louvre in 1950. A complex design, chased rather crudely on the surface, is surrounded by a hatched border with holes at the ends for attachment. The animal combat imagery seems to relate the plaque to a corpus of metalwork—executed in a much more refined manner—found in both the Levant and Egypt. Closest in composition is the upper band of a bronze plaque, also in the Louvre, reportedly from Tyre (cat. no. 259), on which are depicted two contiguous scenes of feline predators, a lion and a cheetah, violently attacking ruminants among Egyptian pondweed with papyrus tips. On the gold plaque, in a setting marked by papyrus clumps on curving stems, are two combat scenes of a more unusual nature. In one, a lion with protruding tongue, bared teeth, a shoulder star, and extended forelegs—having perhaps thrown a bull in the air—is shown below his victim; the bull is in a galloping posture, its forelegs touching the lion's tail and rear legs extended above its gaping mouth. In the other, a griffin is executed in a particularly crude manner, with no line

differentiating the rear thighs. It looks like a provincial version of the beautifully rendered crested griffin with elongated vulture head, collar, and powerful wing with bent profile and detailed feathers depicted on another elliptical gold plaque, one that embellished chariotry in the Tomb of Tutankhamun (fig. 122). In both instances, the griffin pounces on the back of its prey. On the chariot appliqué, the beast descends from above the head of a fleeing ibex, biting its rump while a dog, with protruding tongue, bites its belly. On the Louvre plaque, surprisingly, the victim is a cheetah—generally depicted in the international style corpus as a predator—and there is little connection between the two felines. On the gold dagger sheath (fig. 121), as well as on a gold appliqué from the Tomb of Tutankhamun,[1] cheetahs join with lions to bring down ibexes, biting their neck or rump.

The craftsman who made this provincial work, which appears to quote many details from the so-called Tyre plaque, may have misunderstood the narrative, which on the plaque is excerpted into vignettes of animal contest. While the lion may attack from below, as on the dagger sheath, it seems unconnected with the bull over its body; the cheetah, with its extended body and reversed head, seems to take the place of the expected ibex or cow, the usual victims of feline attack.

The slightly reddish surface coloration suggests that the gold alloy used contains traces of copper and silver. Although some elements are raised from the back by repoussé, the design was produced primarily by chasing from the front, using pointed punches and linear tracers of at least three different widths. No sign of modern tool marks are evident other than surface abrasions resulting from intensive cleaning.[2]   JA

1. Feldman 2006b, p. 34, fig. 6.
2. Technical notes were provided by Geneviève Pierrat.

260

IVORY, SHELL, AND BONE

ANNIE CAUBET

Many artifacts from the Near East seemingly made of ivory or bone turn out, on examination, to derive from a larger variety of materials, the common denominator being their animal origin and their glossy, cream-colored appearance. These materials range from the bones of domestic and wild animals to seashells, ostrich eggs, and, of course, ivory. Ivory came from various species indigenous to the Near East, including elephants, hippopotami, wild boars, and sea cows. Each of these materials possesses specific qualities that the ancient craftsmen used to their best advantage.

Crafts using hard animal materials underwent a major transformation at the beginning of the second millennium B.C. Real ivory, which had been practically nonexistent in Mesopotamia during the Early Dynastic period, made a first appearance in the form of a few elephant-ivory figurines depicting what are believed to be nude goddesses, their hair tied in tight buns, with examples from Mari, Tell Brak, and Ashur. During the first half of the second millennium B.C., the use of ivory, almost all of it from the hippopotamus, was limited to specific regions. Some fine examples from about 2000 to 1800 B.C. come from Egypt and Cappadocia (cat. nos. 46–54). Crete was known for its production of stamp seals and amulets, and, about 1700 B.C., craftsmen in the ateliers at Ebla near Aleppo fashioned silhouette figures in Egyptianizing styles (cat. no. 9). At Pella, in the Jordan Valley, a box decorated with lion motifs and prophylactic eyes of Egyptian inspiration was found in a tomb dated to about 1600 B.C. (fig. 139).[1]

Throughout the early second millennium B.C., in inland Syria and Mesopotamia, large seashells were imported from the Indian Ocean and Persian Gulf. They were no longer used for inlay plaques, but rather for the creation of new forms, in particular statuettes carved from the central axis of gastropods. This was the case of a figurine found in Susa that depicts a standing woman clad in a tight-fitting robe and wearing a necklace with a counterweight in the back.[2]

In the second half of the second millennium B.C., which corresponds to the Late Bronze Age, the use of ivory spread over a vast geographic area, stretching between Mesopotamia, the Levant, Cyprus, Egypt, and the Aegean. A favorite material of the elite, it was used to make luxury objects, furniture, game boards, cosmetic boxes, musical instruments, and chariot elements, all of which were exchanged internationally. Most of the ivory used was hippopotamus tusk. Elephant ivory remained quite rare and was reserved for pieces of larger size and significance. In fact, only one section of an elephant tusk was found in the wreckage of the Uluburun ship, while there were many hippopotamus tusks (cat. nos. 197, 198a, b).

Trade in ivory tusks was related to the habitat of these animals. The hippopotamus was indigenous to the Nile and to smaller river deltas along the Levantine coast, especially in the region around what is now Haifa. Hippopotamus ivory supplied to Near Eastern craftsmen was thus of local origin. The incisors and lower canines could be carved into objects of up to 10 centimeters in diameter, such as small musical instruments, cases, toilet articles, and spindles. The pronounced curvature of the canines was skillfully worked into clappers in the form of hands or graceful boxes in the shape of aquatic birds (see cat. nos. 199–202), a specialty of Levantine artisans.

Elephant tusks, having greater volume, could be used for larger pieces. The shaft could be carved into freestanding figures or sawed along the vertical axis to make large panels, boxes for precious objects, and bedsteads such as the one found in the palace at Ugarit (fig. 80). The natural hollow at the base of the tusk often formed the bottom half of cylindrical containers, flasks, and horns.

Yet where did these elephants come from? Thutmose III boasted of having slaughtered 120 elephants in the "land of Niyi," which has been located in the region of Qatna, near Homs in western Syria, and Assyrian annals from the twelfth century B.C. mention tribute in the form of elephants being exacted from Levantine kings. Later texts mention only hides and tusks, which perhaps suggests that elephants were extinct in that region. Elephant bones dated to the second millennium B.C. (but not earlier) have also been found among animal remains unearthed at a number of sites between eastern Anatolia and the Euphrates.

Although there is little doubt that elephants existed in inland Syria, the region was densely urbanized at the time, and it is difficult to imagine the presence of herds of wild animals. Some scholars believe that an isolated colony of Asian elephants inhabited the Syrian hinterlands during the second millennium B.C. According to another hypothesis, the elephant herds slaughtered by Thutmose III were kept in a royal preserve near the present-day Lake of Homs. Archives from Mari and Assyrian texts tell us that Near Eastern rulers were fond of maintaining hunting preserves, in which rare wild animals were kept. Did the elephants of the land of Niyi belong to the king of Qatna? Recent excavations at the site have uncovered workshops in which deer antlers and elephant ivory plaques were carved (see cat. no. 144). There is also evidence of hippopotamus ivory found at Qatna.

Late Bronze Age objects of ivory and shell provide the clearest expression of the ideology of the international elite as described in the Amarna Letters (see pp. 168–69). Objects and motifs often glorified the ruler or exemplified a heroic warrior ethic; they also reflected beliefs in the powers of fertility. Other aspects of palace life are represented in games and musical instruments—small horns (cat. no. 207) and castanets. Larger pieces made of elephant tusk found at Megiddo, Mycenae, and Ugarit may also have been used as oliphants, unless they were vessels (fig. 127). The natural hollow of the tusk was widened and worked, possibly to accommodate a mouthpiece or a rim. A female head of Egyptian inspiration that probably decorated a lyre found at Tell Miqne, ancient Ekron, is an example of the association of a musical instrument with a local divinity.[3]

Among the ivory game boards that have been found, the most interesting are those fitted on rectangular boxes with side openings for storing the game-pieces (see pp. 151–54). Some boxes, such as those from Enkomi on Cyprus or from Ugarit, were carved from large ivory plaques and feature relief carvings of the hunt with chariots (cat. no. 265). The panels from Megiddo depict prisoners being presented to a seated ruler.[4]

A cuneiform tablet listing the trousseau of Ahat-milku, wife of the twelfth-century B.C. king of Ugarit, included "three beds inlaid with ivory, with a footboard, beds made of boxwood and armchairs with gold and lapis-lazuli inlays and a footboard."[5] Among the furniture found in the Royal Palace at Ugarit was a two-sided bedstead of rectangular panels topped by two friezes with scenes of lion and deer hunts. Each of the panels depicts a separate scene—the king killing an adversary or returning from the hunt, the wedding feast of a princess, the symbolic nursing of princes by a winged goddess (fig. 80). The refined style combines Egyptian elements, such as dress and coiffure, with more Levantine aspects, the bearded figures, for example, or the ubiquitous lion and deer.

The objects found at Ugarit relate most often to the world of women—their beliefs, their finery, and the utensils they used for domestic tasks. One of their main occupations was the weaving of textiles. Luxury versions of wood spindles and spindle whorls were usually carved of hippopotamus ivory, which was not valued as highly as elephant ivory. The inventory of the queen's trousseau also lists twenty ivory cosmetic boxes and four ivory saltcellars.

Figure 127. Carved ivory tusk. Ugarit, Royal Palace, Pavilion 86. Late Bronze Age. National Museum, Damascus RS 16.404, 7360

Large cylindrical pyxides, a specialty of Cyprus, were made of elephant ivory and closed with a lid often engraved or carved in relief. A box discovered in a tomb at Ashur features an engraved landscape with fruit-laden trees, a symbol of fertility (fig. 69). The cock crowing in the branches is one of the earliest representations in the Near East of this bird imported from east Asia.[6]

More common objects included simple containers carved of hippopotamus teeth. Some are lenticular in shape, with discoid lids pivoting on lateral tenons; others are fashioned in the shape of waterfowl. The latter form was probably of Egyptian inspiration and associated with the symbolism of animal life along the Nile (cat. no. 200). The examples produced in the Levantine workshops may be recognized by the oblong shape of the lower part, which exploits the natural shape of the canine (cat. no. 198b). Such items were widely distributed to the Aegean and inner Syria.

Late Bronze figures of ivory sculpted in the round seem to have been made for religious purposes. The head of a divinity from the palace at Ugarit probably belonged to a cult statue (cat. no. 145). The fittings for the horns (now lost) and the locks of hair with gold inlays on the forehead suggest that it is probably the same goddess depicted on the faience goblets and between two caprids on the lid of a box from a rich tomb at Minet el-Beidha (cat. no. 261). Smaller statuettes depicting votaries and musicians were usually carved from hippopotamus teeth, like the lady seated on a throne from Kamid el-Loz.[7] A cymbalist from Ugarit and a lyre player from Kamid el-Loz are offerings perpetuating the memory of musical ceremonies.[8]

1. Gachet-Bizollon 2007, nos. 275, 276, pl. 21.
2. Caubet in *Royal City of Susa* 1992, p. 95, no. 59.
3. S. Gitin, personal communication.
4. Loud 1939, pl. 4, no. 2.
5. Nougayrol 1955, pp. 182–86.
6. See Aruz in *Assyrian Origins* 1995, pp. 83–85, no. 45.
7. Metzger 1993, pl. 49:1.
8. Gachet-Bizollon 2007, no. 409; Miron 1990, no. 501.

261

PYXIS LID WITH MISTRESS OF ANIMALS

Ivory
Height 13.7 cm (5⅜ in.); width 11.5 cm (4½ in.)
Minet el-Beidha, Tomb III
Late Bronze Age, 13th century B.C.
Musée du Louvre, Paris, Département des
Antiquités Orientales AO11601

The second half of the second millennium B.C. was a time of rapid progress in the art of ivory making, especially along the Syrian seacoast and on Cyprus.

Many pieces found at Ugarit display a remarkable mastery of this craft and a perfect adaptation to the artistic currents that marked the eastern Mediterranean. The internationalization of art trends, however, makes it difficult to identify the provenance of such objects, especially for unusual pieces in which artists gave expression to the widest possible range of stimuli. This pyxis lid is such a piece, reflecting the complexity of a world in which a single image could serve different cultural principles and religious beliefs.

The lid, which did not survive intact, originally fit on a round box. Carved and engraved with great skill, the motif was adapted to a circular space (which usually calls for a concentric or radiating composition). A female on an incurving seat flanked by two caprids, offers them palm fronds. Her torso is bare except for a necklace with pendants, and she wears a long flounced skirt rendered by parallel bands with central chevrons below a scale pattern.

The face in profile exhibits fine features, with a sharp nose and lips that seem to smile. The dome-shaped coiffure is held by a band with a spiral on the forehead; wavy locks hang down the back. The figure sits on a mountainous rise textured with drill holes that may have been inlaid. Her seat is placed on an inverted, patterned cone on which the goat at right rests his left leg. A second conical element appears at the left, and it too is used as a footrest for the other caprid. The scene is encircled by a band of scale patterns that formed the edge of the lid.

The scene represents the popular Near Eastern motif of the Master—or, in this case, Mistress—of Animals, the earliest examples of which have been found on seals from the site of Susa and the region of Luristan. While the motif occurs in many variations, with natural and divine protagonists throughout its long history, there are certain constants, such as the symmetrical composition in which the center is occupied by a figure dominating a pair of animals of the same species. The scene represents the balance of forces and their mastery, but not their destruction. The female figure seen here expresses less the mastery over these forces than the idea of balance through nurturing that fosters life.

The scene is set in a mountainous landscape, from which the female seems to emerge. Indeed, if the feet are set on a hill, the lower part of the body is framed by two mountains, and the garment itself evokes, on the sides, the mountainous element, in accordance with an ancient near Eastern convention associating scales and mountains. The image thus understood could recount the appearance of a mythical being, who is manifest at the top of the mountain and who dispenses life-giving nourishment. The pattern along the border also evokes the mountains and reaffirms the nature of the space in which the scene unfolds.

The association of mountains and divinities permeates Near Eastern religions and was characteristic of the mythological literature of Ugarit during the Late Bronze Age. The god Baal inhabited the mountains, and there he was manifested in the form of clouds and lightning, the prelude to the coming of life-giving waters. As the storm god he is linked to the world of vegetation and thus subject to a life cycle. He dies and returns to the Underworld (the mountain itself) while the world is laid waste. The goddess, known also as the Source, intervenes, gathers up the fragments of the god's body in the mountain, reconstitutes it, and so ensures life and regeneration.[1]

This is perhaps the meaning of this Near Eastern scene in which, like a spring, the goddess appears out of the mountain holding palm fronds, new vegetation symbolizing the god's seed and the restoration of the balance of life. Style, pose, features, and costume, however, recall figures from the Aegean world. The question thus arises: Was this luxury Aegean object adopted by Ugarit because it fit the symbolic and religious imagery of the Syrian kingdom? Or was it made by local craftsmen who produced an image to express their own beliefs—albeit in Aegean fashion? While the female's costume resembles those of similar figures found at Mycenae and most recently in ancient Kydonia (cat. no. 263), it differs in one detail that may provide a clue. The torso is entirely bare. This is not the case with most depictions of Aegean women, who wear a tight-fitting, short-sleeved blouse with a breast exposed. The nudity of the goddess displayed here is more specific to the Syro-Levantine world.[2]   SC

1. Caqot, Sznycer, and Herdner 1974, pp. 223–74.
2. For further reference, see Schaeffer 1929, p. 292, pl. VI; Kantor (1947) 1997, pp. 99–103; Poursat 1977b; *Au pays de Baal et d'Astarté* 1983; Gates 1992; Caubet and Matoïan 1995; Caubet 1999c, pp. 32–38; Poursat 1999; *Ivoires* 2004, pp. 63, 68, no. 67; Gachet-Bizollon in *Le royaume d'Ougarit* 2004, no. 164; and Gachet-Bizollon 2007, pp. 87–92.

262
PLAQUE WITH SEATED FEMALE

Ivory
Height 8.5 cm (3⅜ in.)
Mycenae
Late Helladic III, 14th–13th century B.C.
National Archaeological Museum, Athens, Greece 5897

Represented on this relief plaque is a female figure, probably a goddess seated on a rock.[1] Turned toward her

262

right, the torso is shown in frontal view and the legs are in profile. The head, forearms, and hands are missing. The proper right arm bears the mark of an ancient repair, indicated by two round incisions. The back of the plaque is flat and bears no signs of attachment.

With a beaded necklace, the goddess is dressed in the typical Aegean costume, a flounced skirt and a sleeved bodice perhaps fastened by means of a loose belt or double girdle.[2]

With a thick torso, narrow waist, and full breasts, the deity belongs to the Aegean tradition. Earlier precedents that may have served as an inspiration are the life-size clay statues found in the shrine of Ayia Irini on the island of Kea, dated to Late Minoan IA–IB.[3]

Both standing and seated ivory figures in similar postures and dress were found at Mycenae and Prosymna.[4] A seated goddess on a gold ring from the Acropolis Treasure at Mycenae receives offerings of poppies and lilies. Only one such representation has been found outside the Aegean, the pyxis lid from Minet el-Beidha with a female figure seated on a Minoan incurved altar extending handfuls of palm fronds to flanking goats (cat. no. 261).[5]

Figures making this gesture, which must have had symbolic meaning, are seen in various guises—painted frescoes, gold rings, and ivory plaques, among other media. It is also possible that such figures all represent the same divinity.

Ivory is included among the prestige gifts exchanged in the eastern Mediterranean during the Late Bronze Age. While there is no evidence for the exact findspot of this goddess from Mycenae, it may be placed in the fourteenth–early thirteenth century B.C., a period during which some of the most impressive ivories were produced.[6]

EK-S

1. Poursat 1977a, p. 19, no. 48.
2. Wardle 1988, esp. p. 471.
3. Caskey 1986, passim. For plaques of a standing goddess (from Mycenae), see Poursat 1977a, p. 93, no. 299, pl. XXIX, and Rehak 1992, p. 53; (from Prosymna), see Poursat 1977a, pp. 121–22, no. 375, pl. XXXIX.
4. Poursat 1977a, p. 80, no. 270, pl. XXIX, and p. 91, no. 295, pl. XXIX. For the same gesture with grain, see Rehak 1992, p. 52.
5. Gates 1992, passim.
6. The plaque comes from the excavations conducted by Christos Tsountas at Mycenae prior to 1900. Unfortunately, there is no other information available.

263
PLAQUE WITH SEATED FEMALE

Ivory (hippopotamus)
Height 8.6 cm (3⅜ in.); width 3.8 cm (1½ in.)
Crete, Kydonia, Rovithaki Plot
Late Minoan IIIA:2–IIIB:1, ca. 1375–1250 B.C.
Khania Archaeological Museum, Greece K 115

This rectangular, nearly complete ivory plaque represents a female figure seated on what is probably a rock; in her right hand she holds a lily. The face is rendered in profile to the right, the torso is shown frontally, and the legs are also turned toward the right. A gentle smile forms on her lips beneath a well-defined brow, large, almond-shaped eye, accentuated cheek, and markedly protruding nose. The long hair, delineated by parallel incisions, is partially swept up in a ponytail. A double ribbon wreathes her narrow forehead, and a necklace adorns her throat. The breasts are not pronounced, and there is no clear evidence of a bodice. Barefoot, she wears a long elaborate flounced garment that covers her lower body. The plaque is carved in relief and incised. The reverse has three dowel holes for bone rivets.

The interpretation of the figure as a deity (the "goddess with the lily") is sup-ported by the seated posture, which is identical to that of a Minoan goddess on frescoes and seals.[1] The posture is seen frequently in Aegean ivory work, as on objects found on Crete itself, at Mycenae (cat. no. 262), on Cyprus,[2] or even at Ugarit (cat. no. 261).

Excavated at Kydonia, the plaque (like those from Knossos, Archanes, Phylaki, Mycenae, and Spata) was part of the applied decoration of a wood object, probably a chest deposited as a grave offering in an important burial. Several other plaques adorned the chest, including representations of another flower-bearing female figure, helmeted warrior heads, heraldic lions, figure-of-eight shields, columns, and rosettes. Many were made of hippopotamus tusk (more widely used in Kydonia than elephant tusk).[3]

Kydonia was the most important Minoan center in western Crete and a thriving harbor during the Final Palatial period. The plaque was found in a monumental Late Minoan III chamber tomb that had been plundered. The remaining grave offerings—jewelry of faience, rock crystal, and gold leaf, and stone and clay vessels, including a Canaanite jar fragment—were, however, sufficient to indicate the wealth of the deceased and to provide evidence of Kydonia's contacts with the Levant during the fourteenth and thirteenth centuries B.C. MA-V

1. CMS V Suppl. 1A, no. 177; KH 2097: clay sealing from the Neopalatial archives of Khania.
2. See the Lady with the Mirror, from Kition: KEF-141. Poursat 1999, pl. CXLV:d, a
3. For further reference, see Poursat 1977a, pl. II (48/5897); Poursat 1977b, pp. 231–32, 242–43; Sakellarakis 1979; Krzyszkowska 1990; Fitton 1992; and Gates 1992.

264
Plaque with Animal Combat

Ivory
Height 3.8 cm (1½ in.); width 6.5 cm (2½ in.); thickness 1.1 cm (½ in.)
Byblos, Royal Necropolis, shaft of Tomb of Ahiram
Late Bronze Age, 13th century B.C.
Direction Générale des Antiquités, Beirut, Lebanon 2461

This ivory plaque from Byblos, which once adorned a rectangular wood box or piece of furniture, was discovered along with two tusks in the shaft leading to the royal tomb that contained the renowned sarcophagus of Ahiram (fig. 18).[1] The elaborately carved sarcophagus has been dated to the thirteenth century B.C. by scholars who recognize its Bronze Age associations. Others consider it to be a transitional early Phoenician work and date it to the late eleventh century B.C., when its funerary inscription was added.[2] The contents of the tomb and its shaft contained Bronze Age remains, including fragments of alabaster vessels with inscriptions of Ramesses II,[3] as well as Mycenaean and Cypriot pottery.[4]

The plaque is carved in relief with a scene of a bull being attacked by two predators: a griffin, whose body is abraded, and a lion, which is only partially preserved. Although the general scheme finds precedence on Aegean lentoid seals,[5] significant differences characterize the ivory as a work produced outside Greece itself.[6] While the bull's body remains horizontal, the bent foreleg and extended (missing) rear leg, the lowered head with furrowed brow, and the forward position of the horns all signal the reaction of the massive animal to the ferocious attack. The rampant griffin bends

264

Figure 128. Ivory plaque with griffin. Megiddo. Late Bronze Age. The Oriental Institute Museum, University of Chicago OIM A 22212

Figure 129. Roll-out drawing of scene on ivory pyxis from Athenian Agora. Late Helladic IIIA. Agora Museum, Athens BI 511

over its victim, biting and mauling him with its avian claw, while the powerful lion, also rampant, bites the bull's back.

Many stylistic features of the Byblos ivory plaque are paralleled on works excavated both in the Levant and on Cyprus,

possibly pointing to manufacture on the island. The massive bull, with thick dewlap folds and a distinctive flame pattern for leg musculature and with one foreleg bent and head lowered to gore its attacker, resembles those on an ivory cosmetic box found in a hoard in the Fosse Temple at Lachish, as well as on a game box from Enkomi (cat. no. 265).[7] These formidable creatures exude raw power but lack the dynamic movement and sense of engagement displayed in purely Mycenaean scenes (see fig. 129).[8] Ivory mirror handles from Enkomi (cat. no. 266), also feature abbreviated scenes of violent combat with awkwardly placed predators, although the bovine victims appear to move somewhat more responsively than does the Byblos bull.[9] Individual details—the spiral curls and overlapping wing feathers of the griffin and the abstract patterns of animal musculature—are also found on ivory plaques from Megiddo and Delos (fig. 128 and cat. no. 267); the latter, however, are more refined in execution.[10]

Many scholars have recognized that Aegean and Near Eastern features were intentionally melded into an international style, or koine, which is particularly evident on portable luxury objects made for a royal elite. Vermeule, in assessing the array of expressions of bloody combat in ivory (fig. 129), noted that "the source of artistic power seems to come from the (Greek) mainland."[11] Kantor distinguished stylistic groups according to their mixture of Mycenaean and Levantine elements.[12] More recently, Feldman has focused attention on the intent of international styles in the eastern Mediterranean, addressing this issue in the context of diplomatic gift exchange as documented in the Amarna Letters and the Hittite archives.[13]   JA

1. Montet 1928–29, p. 220.
2. Doumet-Serhal et al. (1998) believe that the thirteenth-century B.C. sarcophagus was reused; Porada (1973a) interprets the style as transitional between the Late Bronze and early Iron Ages, dating the work to 1000 B.C. with the tomb reused; Markoe (1990, pp. 19–21) concurs, considering the sarcophagus to be the earliest major work of Phoenician art.
3. One was found in the shaft; a second was found in the tomb chamber itself: Montet 1928–29, pp. 225, 227, nos. 883, 890; Stubbings 1951, p. 75, reports Late Helladic III sherds.
4. Dussaud 1924, p. 142; Porada (1973a, p. 356) reports Cypriot White Slip II milk bowl fragments of fourteenth-century B.C. date and later White Painted ware with circular patterns on the shaft.
5. See CMS I, no. 186.
6. Kantor 1956, p. 167, classifies this work as "Hybrid Canaanite-Mycenaean."
7. Feldman 2006b, pp. 56, 57, figs. 38, 39.
8. The scenes on the ends of the Enkomi box relate closely to ivories from the Greek mainland; see cat. no. 265, this volume.
9. Two examples depicting animal combats were discovered in different tombs, each with Mycenaean pottery; see Murray, Smith, and Walters 1900, pp. 31–32, nos. 872, 402, pl. II.
10. Kantor 1956, p. 163, fig. 3:b, c, d; for similar muscle patterns on the Enkomi box, see Murray, Smith, and Walters 1900, pl. I.
11. Vermeule 1964, p. 218.
12. Kantor 1956.
13. Feldman 2006b, pp. 57–58.

265

GAME BOX WITH CHARIOT HUNT

Ivory (elephant)
Length 29.1 cm (11½ in.)
Enkomi, Tomb 58
Late Bronze Age, ca. late 13th–12th century B.C.
The Trustees of the British Museum, London
1897.4–1.996

Ivory carving flourished on Cyprus in the thirteenth and twelfth centuries B.C., with a rich mixture of stylistic influences from Mycenaean Greece and western Asia. The ivory itself must have been imported from Egypt or Syria. A letter from the king of Alashiya mentions ivory among the items sent to the pharaoh in the late fourteenth century B.C.[1]

The top of this game box is laid out for the Game of Twenty Squares. The playing pieces were probably kept inside the box. Similar game boxes were used at Ur in the third millennium B.C. and in New Kingdom Egypt. We do not know exactly how the game was played, but such games may have formed part of court rituals and elite entertainments (see pp. 151–54).

The box is beautifully carved from elephant ivory and must have been a rare and valuable object. The sides are decorated with animal scenes and scenes of the hunt. On the better preserved of the two long sides a figure, perhaps a king, stands in a chariot drawing his bow. A charioteer controls the pair of horses pulling the light, two-wheeled chariot, while behind a man

on foot, in what appears to be a feathered headdress, carries an axe, presumably to dispatch wounded prey. A third hunter, on the left, spears a lion. Five animals flee the hunters: probably a deer, a wild goat, and a bull below, and perhaps two bulls above them. Another, larger bull, pierced by an arrow, puts its head down to charge the oncoming chariot. A large bird flies above the horses, and a dog runs alongside.[2]

This scene and the similar, though less well preserved, depiction on the other side show strong traditions from western Asia. A ninth-century B.C. lion-hunt pyxis from Nimrud displays both hunters and horses in similar dress.[3] The hairstyles of the two hunters on foot are found in representations of the Sea Peoples on the Medinet Habu reliefs in Egypt (fig. 141), which date to the early twelfth century B.C., contemporaneous with the box. The ends of the box are Mycenaean in style, one with two seated bulls before a tree, the other with two goats flanking a tree.

Mycenaean objects, especially pottery and metalwork, were imported to Cyprus in the centuries before this box was made, resulting in imitation by local artists. While the combination of styles has been interpreted as reflecting the migration of new peoples to Cyprus, it perhaps owes more to the mobility of craft workers and to new iconographic ideas. A comparable box was discovered in fragmentary state in a tomb at Tell es-Sa'idiyeh.[4]

Tomb 58 at Enkomi, where the box was found, was situated in the central part of a Late Cypriot settlement. It was a rich burial; other finds included gold jewelry, bronze and iron knives with ivory handles, an elaborate bronze vessel stand, and Bucchero pottery vessels. The surviving finds suggest a date in the late thirteenth or twelfth century B.C., the so-called Crisis Years. The box sits comfortably in either century, a period of considerable cultural continuity despite the political and economic turbulence.   JLF

1. EA 40, Moran 1992, p. 113.
2. For further reference, see Murray, Smith, and Walters 1900, pp. 12–14, 31, fig. 19, pl. 1; L. Åström 1972, pp. 554–55, fig. 78; Poursat 1977b, esp. pp. 74–77, 159–62, pl. XVII:3; Courtois, Lagarce, and Lagarce 1986, pp. 137–38, pl. XXIV:9; Krzyszkowska 1990, fig. 9; and Caubet 2008.
3. Barnett 1975, p. 190, pl. 18.
4. British Museum, London ME BM 1990–3–3, 102.

266
MIRROR HANDLE WITH COMBAT SCENES

Ivory
Height 20.3 cm (8 in.)
Enkomi, Tomb 17
Late Bronze Age, ca. late 13th–12th century B.C.
The Trustees of the British Museum, London
1897.4–1.872

This beautifully carved handle must originally have been attached to a circular bronze hand mirror of common Late Cypriot type. Most likely it belonged to a wealthy individual and accompanied the person to the grave. The groove and holes for the attachment of the mirror can be seen on the upper edge. The roughly square plaques are carved in relief with scenes on each side of combat, one between a warrior and a griffin, the other between a lion and a bull. The shaft is decorated with foliate patterns.

As is the case with most Cypriot ivories of the Late Bronze Age, the decoration shows a mix of influences from both east and west. The lion attacking the bull is a familiar motif in Mycenaean art, while the theme of a warrior slaying a griffin perhaps owes its inspiration to western Asia. The vivid representation of the griffin combat may, however, have been a Cypriot innovation. In this violent confrontation the

266

266, alternate view

413

warrior, elaborately dressed and armed, lunges toward the griffin, which throws back its head in an attitude of despair.

The warrior is dressed in the banded body armor associated with the Sea Peoples, as depicted on the Medinet Habu reliefs in Egypt (fig. 141). He wears an elaborately decorated helmet and carries a round shield. Using a short sword to attack the griffin, he holds his arm in an anatomically impossible position that enhances the sense of forward thrust. The griffin falls backward, with closed wings and gaping beak. The epic nature of the conflict may be hinted at by an indication of rocky or mountainous ground.

The warrior could be either a god or a hero. The theme may derive from a now-unknown tale of heroism, its underlying symbolism perhaps connected to the idea of man's defeat over the forces of chaos. There is an obvious link with the scene on the other side, where the lion pounces ferociously onto the back of the apparently unsuspecting bull. Both lion and hero are filled with energy and both are victorious.

Tomb 17 at Enkomi was a chamber tomb with three burial chambers situated in the northern part of the ancient town. It had been extensively looted when excavated. Only this mirror handle and two Mycenaean vases dating to the later fourteenth or thirteenth century B.C. and now in the British Museum survive, along with several Late Helladic vases preserved in the Cyprus Museum, Nicosia. The original excavation notebook also records gold diadems, bronze knives, Mycenaean sherds, and "stone figurines of the Cypriote type," the latter possibly intrusive Cypro-Archaic votives.[1]   JLF

1. For further reference, see Murray, Smith, and Walters 1900, pp. 10–11, 32–33, pl. II; L. Åström 1972, p. 555 (Handle, 1a); Poursat 1977b, esp. pp. 52–54, 65–68, 159–62, pl. XVI:3; Courtois, Lagarce, and Lagarce 1986, pp. 130–34, pl. XXIV:2; and D'Albiac 1992, pp. 105–12, fig. 1a.

267
PLAQUE WITH ANIMAL COMBAT

Ivory
Height 5.1 cm (2 in.); length 22.5 cm (8⅞ in.)
Delos, Artemision
7th century B.C. context
Late Bronze Age manufacture,
14th–13th century B.C.
Archaeological Museum, Delos, Greece
B 07075

The powerful image on this incised ivory plaque, the confrontation of two predators, a lion and a griffin, is an heirloom discovered in a much later context. It was found in a small rectangular structure on Delos dating to the early seventh century B.C., which was itself within a Hellenistic temple dedicated to Artemis, the twin sister of Apollo. There were many structures inside the later temple, one a Mycenaean cult building associated with the worship of Potnia Theron, the Mistress of Animals, a deity later identified with Artemis.

In the northeastern corner of the seventh-century B.C. structure were found charred bones, sherds, and Mycenaean artifacts of bronze, gold, and ivory. Among the 2,533 fragments of ivory is a plaque with a Mycenaean warrior, possibly the product of a Cypriot workshop (see frontispiece, p. 434); parts of a frieze representing, in relief, lions mauling deer and a bull and a griffin attacking a deer; columns and capitals; and ivory cutouts with incised decoration, most likely remains of richly decorated furniture.[1] Judging from this evidence, it is probable that there were ivory workshops on Delos or on neighboring Mykonos, where a Mycenaean royal tholos tomb was excavated in 1994.

It was thought that these objects came from the Mycenaean cult building, but this seems unlikely. The finds comprise a variety of items—gold diadems for use in funerals, steatite buttons, beads, sealstones, arrowheads, sword fragments—objects usually found not in sanctuaries but in graves. These may have originated from a neighboring Mycenaean tomb later identified as that of the Hyperborean Maidens, considered sacred in the Archaic period.   PJC

1. For these ivories, see Tournavitou 1995.

268
PYXIS LID WITH ANIMAL COMBAT

Ivory
Diameter 6 cm (2⅜ in.)
Thebes, Mikro Kastelli, Chamber Tomb 23
Late Helladic IIIA–IIIB, ca. 14th–13th century B.C.
Archaeological Museum, Thebes, Greece
42458

This ivory pyxis lid was discovered in a chamber tomb cut into a hillside east of the citadel of Thebes. It bears a scene in

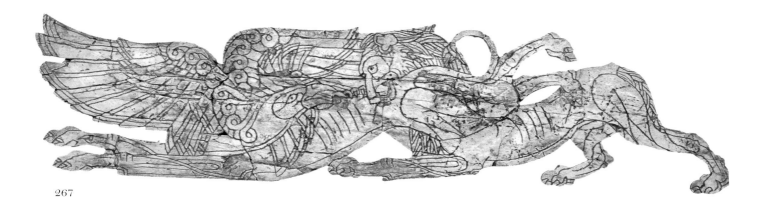

267

268

became widespread in the eastern Mediterranean world. Scenes with both a lion and a bull may be understood not only as realistic representations but as having symbolic content. In Aegean iconography, the bull is generally shown being hunted by predatory beasts such as the lion. It has been argued that the victory of the lion, king of beasts, over the bull signifies the victory of the ruler over his enemies.[2] Scenes of gods or heroes as the Master of Animals dominating lions (see cat. nos. 173, 253) may further allude to such a divine hierarchy.

The plaque was discovered in one of the two chamber tombs at Spata in Attika, which, although robbed, revealed hundreds of ivories.[3] Among them were finely carved combs and mirror handles, and dozens of comparable plaques. The majority of the finds date to the fourteenth century B.C. Rectangular plaques such as this one were commonly affixed to furniture; some of them imitate metalwork. The present example is reassembled from several pieces; the surface is well preserved.[4]

EK–S

relief of a lion attacking a bull, framed by a narrow border, also in relief. The lid constitutes a fine example of Mycenaean ivory carving of the fourteenth and thirteenth centuries B.C. The scene has been executed to conform to the circular surface. A favorite theme in the iconographic corpus of Mycenaean art, it is often found engraved on seals.

VLA/IF

anatomy, especially that of the lion, is clumsily executed; the lion's eyes, for example, are too large for the head. The plaque is nearly identical to another one, also in the National Archaeological Museum, Athens; only the rendering of the lion differs slightly.[1]

Both the subject of animal combat and the motif of the Aegean flying gallop

1. NAM, inv. no. 2045.
2. Morgan 1988, p. 49.
3. Haussoullier 1878, passim.
4. Poursat 1977a, pp. 155–56, no. 453.

269

PLAQUE WITH ANIMAL COMBAT

Ivory
Height 6.5 cm (2½ in.); width 9.2 cm (3⅝ in.)
Spata, Chamber Tomb
Late Helladic IIIA, ca. 14th century B.C.
National Archaeological Museum, Athens,
Greece 2046

This dynamic, beautifully integrated composition shows a lion attacking a bull, the lion's body stretched horizontally along the bull's back as he violently claws and bites into the neck. The bull turns its head backward, the long, curved horns harmoniously echoing the form of the lion. The carving is finely worked, although the

269

270

CYLINDRICAL BOX

Carob wood, ivory
Height 13.5 cm (5⅜ in.); diameter 7 cm (2¾ in.)
Egypt
New Kingdom, Dynasty 18–19, 14th–13th
century B.C.
Musée du Louvre, Paris, Département des
Antiquités Égyptiennes N1698

This type of compartmented box carved from a hardwood branch—here, that of a carob tree—belongs to a well-known production in New Kingdom Egypt. More often than not, such boxes have a semi-cylindrical shape and close with a flat lid. This object is of a much rarer type, in which two halves of the same piece of wood have been fitted together, one half sliding over the other. Once closed, the cylinder can stand vertically, which is the position in which the decoration is meant to be seen. The "palace facade" motif at the bottom, the scenes on both halves, and the rows of petals and pendants all belong to the repertoire of Egyptian necklace decoration.

On one side (below left) a calf is attacked by two dogs—one wearing a collar—rendered with great freedom of movement; the landscape is limited to a cluster of water lilies below the hooves of the calf. On the opposite side a lion carries off a calf, while the cow behind it raises its head expressively. The reeds and plants typical of this period appear mostly under the lion's paws. These scenes are carved in relief with incised details. The cavities were originally filled with a blue pigment—probably Egyptian Blue—except for the cow, which was colored in red. The body of the calf in the lion's jaws was filled with a black material and partially inlaid with bits of ivory (a fragment remains). The same black and white treatment of an animal can be seen on a lid also in the Musée du Louvre, as well as on a vase held by a kneeling servant figure that was found in Gurna and dated to late in Dynasty 18.[1]

Animal life, wild and domestic, was the usual subject depicted on this kind of box (see fig. 130). The style sometimes belongs to the pure flying-gallop tradition, but the animal's feet on this box are positioned on the register. Both style and scenes belong to a repertoire that we are tempted to call "international" and is seen on objects made outside Egypt, such as a faience rhyton from Kition (fig. 132). Although the

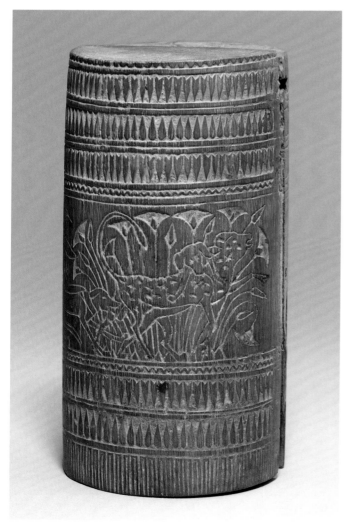

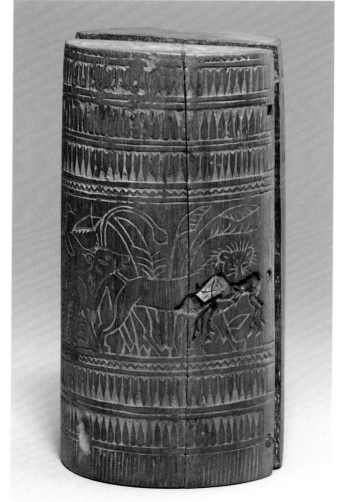

Figure 130. Carved, inlaid wood box. Egypt.
Dynasty 18. Egyptian Museum, Cairo
CG 44717

Figure 131. Calcite pyxis with recumbent lion on lid. Tomb of
Tutankhamun. Dynasty 18. Egyptian Museum, Cairo JE 62119

objects were discovered in Egyptian cemeteries, their unusual shape and occasional hieroglyphic inscriptions—restricted to terse formulas such as "all beauty" and "all abundance"—raise doubts about their Egyptian origin.

The inside of this box has nine compartments, four on one side and five on the other. Because the compartments are on both halves, they could only have held materials that adhered to the sides. Traces of a light brown substance have been found, hinting at cosmetics.[2] A spectacular alabaster balsam jar found in the Tomb of Tutankhamun is decorated with a similar scene of dogs and a lion attacking an ibex and a bull (fig. 131), as well as color inlays and prophylactic Egyptian motifs. For the Egyptians such scenes apparently carried apotropaic meaning.   GP-B

1. Musée du Louvre N1711a; Egyptian Museum, Cairo, CG 44745–JE 31382. Saleh and Sourouzian 1987, no. 158; *Parfums et cosmétiqués* 2002, pp. 39, 152.
2. Freed in *Egypt's Golden Age* 1982, pp. 202–3, no. 236, n. 7.

271
MECHANICAL DOG

Ivory, garnet inlay
Length 18.6 cm (7⅜ in.)
Egypt
New Kingdom, Dynasty 18,
ca. 1390–1352 B.C.
The Metropolitan Museum of Art, New York,
Rogers Fund, 1940   40.2.1

This small sculpture of a dog fits comfortably in a closed hand. A lever jutting out of the chest allows the mouth to open and shut. The lower jaw has two teeth and a red-stained tongue. The collar inscribed around the dog's neck indicates that he is a domestic animal.[1] During the New Kingdom dogs are often depicted in the hunt (see cat. 272); they also occasionally appear in scenes of battle, attacking

fallen enemies. It is, however, unusual to find a domestic dog depicted in a three-dimensional representation, so the purpose of this object is difficult to determine. It may have been a toy for a child of an elite family, or perhaps it was a ceremonial object.

The dog is posed in a flying gallop, its legs fully extended as though leaping through the air. This convention for depicting speed is thought to have originated in the Aegean. Its earliest known occurrence in Egypt dates to the beginning of the Middle Kingdom in the Tomb of Khety at Thebes (ca. 2030 B.C.). A fragmentary hunting scene from this tomb, now in the Metropolitan Museum, shows dogs leaping through the air after fleeing antelopes.[2]   CHR

1. For further reference, see Lansing 1941, pp. 10–12, fig. 1; Hayes 1990, p. 315, fig. 197; Kozloff in *Egypt's Dazzling Sun* 1992, p. 427, no. 114; and Arnold 1995, p. 57, no. 75.
2. Hayes 1990, p. 164, fig. 100.

272

272

OSTRACON

Painted limestone
Height 12.5 cm (4⅞ in.); width 14 cm (5½ in.)
Western Thebes, Valley of the Kings
New Kingdom, Dynasty 20,
ca. 1186–1070 B.C.
The Metropolitan Museum of Art, New York,
Purchase, Edward S. Harkness Gift,
1926 26.7.1453

This ostracon was uncovered in the Valley of the Kings during Howard Carter's search for the Tomb of Tutankhamun early in the twentieth century. As the principal cemetery of the New Kingdom pharaohs, the valley was a sacred place, and thousands of painted ostraca have been found there, most of them dating to the Ramesside period. These ostraca are thought to be votive offerings; usually they depict a king worshipping one of the gods. Occasionally, the scenes are more symbolic, like this one, in which the king, acting as the protector of Egypt, is shown spearing a lion, representing Egypt's enemies.[1]

The pharaoh is accompanied by a hunting dog similar to the Dynasty 18 mechanical dog (cat. no. 271). Here, however, though depicted in an extended leap identical to that of the ivory dog, he does not fly through the air. Rather, his hind legs are firmly planted on a groundline, as is more typical of Egyptian art.   CHR

1. For further reference, see Carter and Mace 1923–33, vol. 2, p. 16, pl. IIA; Hayes 1990, p. 390, fig. 245; Reeves and Taylor 1993, p. 135; and Arnold 1995, pp. 16–17, no. 12.

VITREOUS MATERIALS

ANNIE CAUBET

Egypt and the Near East played a major part in the invention of vitreous materials. Production techniques, types of objects, and their size and color (long limited to blue from a copper colorant), which were diversified and expanded during the third millennium B.C., underwent major trans-formations at the turn of the next millennium.

Faience in the archaeological sense consists of a body made of silica and lime coated with glaze, a thin, transparent siliceous slip or cover. Frit is distinguished from faience by the absence of glaze. The most famous frit is Egyptian Blue, a copper silicate pigment that can be used as paint or refired and molded into small beads, figurines, and vases. Glass is made by fusing the silicate completely; it is shaped while hot, using molds or rods, and can be recycled.

The bright colors and brilliance that give faience and other vitreous materials their appeal are obtained from metallic oxides. Light blue was the earliest and most frequently used glaze color. Made from copper oxides, it would turn a light green when the ore used in the composition contained lead impurities, as was frequently the case in the Near East. Copper is responsible for the color of Egyptian Blue frit. Brown and black colors were obtained by mixing iron and manganese. Dark blue was made from cobalt; yellow and orange from lead antimony; and red and pink from iron oxide. Antimony was used as an opacifier for white.

THE MIDDLE BRONZE AGE

The technical skills of the faience makers, initially limited to the manufacture of small pieces cast in simple molds, became increasingly inventive during the Middle Bronze Age. The material was used to replicate beads made of metal and precious stones, and the first faience figurines made their appearance. In Egypt, figures of hippopotami and graceful female statuettes called Concubines of the Dead offered a poetic analogy, with their bright blue color, to the life-giving waters of the Nile. During the same period in Mesopotamia and the Levant there began the production of blue and black faience figurines identified as nude goddesses—of the same type as on terracotta plaques—and of symbolic animals such as the lion and the bull. These new productions bear witness to the exchange of technical information, as well as to the wide dissemination of beliefs in the powers of storm gods and of fertility goddesses: Hathor in Egypt, and Astarte and Ishtar in the Near East.

Figure 132. Faience rhyton. Kition. Late Bronze Age, Cyprus Museum, Nicosia

THE LATE BRONZE AGE

The Late Bronze Age in Mesopotamia, Egypt, and the Levant experienced a technical revolution in the manufacture of vitreous materials resulting from a mastery of their mechanical properties and the use of new oxide pigments. Glass was invented, and the secrets of its fabrication, set down in technical treatises written in cuneiform script, would be used for millennia (see cat. no. 273). At the same time, the oxides used to color the glass also helped to expand the palette for faience wares. Although the primary components remained the same— copper for blue and green, for instance, lead antimonate for yellow, ferrous manganese for black and brown—physiochemical analysis of the pigments has revealed groups of compounds and recipes specific to certain regions. Traces of specific compounds indicate the presence of impurities in the minerals and permit their place of extraction to be identified. Thus, we can distinguish two separate sources for the cobalt oxides, namely, Egypt and western Asia. Recipes and stylistic characteristics were developed. A palette of yellow, black, and light green applied in broad stripes was more popular in the Levant and Mesopotamia than in Egypt. The so-called Egyptian manner, which involved black line drawings on a blue ground, was a specialty in Egyptian and Levantine workshops. Hemispherical bowls decorated with stylized tendrils and trees were found only along the Euphrates.

Egyptian Blue was widely used in the manufacture of beads, amulets, and larger objects such as goblets. During the last phase of the Late Bronze Age, faience workers succeeded for the first time in applying glaze to clay, a procedure that required solving problems arising from the different retraction of clay bodies and vitreous glazes during cooling. This also permitted the use of a potter's wheel, which helped speed production.

The Late Bronze Age also witnessed the development of architectural decoration in faience, a technique that would be much used in Babylon and Persia during the first millennium B.C. Faience tiles and knobs were applied to walls to cover the ends of beams and often bore inscriptions with the name of the king who commissioned the construction. For special monuments, faience bricks were sometimes used as substitutes for clay bricks.

Faience, frit, and glass were subsequently used for a variety of applications, in particular the fabrication of cylinder seals (see pp. 388–91) and ceremonial weapons. Glass and faience mace heads sometimes bore inscriptions with royal names. The same regal status was conferred on certain spool-shaped objects—the end fittings of yokes and bridles—widely distributed from the Mediterranean to Elam. Fabricated of vitreous materials or ivory, they were made for a new type of light war chariot used by the armies of the Late Bronze Age.

If vitreous materials were put into the service of the male world and royal ideology, they were also used extensively in the women's world. Jewelry, musical instruments, and cosmetic boxes were given shapes and decorations that alluded to fertility beliefs—a goddess represented in the form of a mask of a bejeweled female, a crown of petals, or a star. Most characteristic are the rectangular pendants in the shape of a woman's face, with ears pierced, eyes inlaid, and necks painted with bead necklaces. These symbolic ornaments have been discovered at sites extending from Cyprus to Iran and passing through Mesopotamia.

Face goblets were widely distributed and have been found at sites on Cyprus (cat. no. 210) and at Ugarit (cat. no. 211), Tell Abu Hawam, Ashur, and Susa. They have often been associated with vessels in the form of horses, and of rams, with examples from Uluburun (cat. no. 208a). Unlike the goblets—which stand on a stem—rhyta had to be held in the hand when full and could not be set down until empty; most likely, they were meant for ritual libations. Also made of vitreous materials were cylindrical vases, drinking cups with fluted rims, rimmed bowls, bowls with spouts, and thin-necked oval bottles.

ease. Furthermore, cuneiform writing can sometimes entail true cryptography, which is quite another matter.

The text provides practical instruction for making glass, colored like *samtu*, a red stone,[2] and is among the best preserved and fullest of all the surviving glass recipes. The first two sections give the materials and quantities needed for two such types of glass, (1) perhaps "Assyrian" and (2) "Akkadian":

1. For each mina of zuku-glass (you take) 10 shekels of lead, 15 shekels of copper, a zuz of anzahhu-glass and a half of antimony. This is the mixture for Assyrian (?) red-stone glass.

2. For each mina of zuku-glass (you take) 1 sixth of lead, 10 shekels of copper, 1 shekel of antimony and 1 shekel of anzahhu-glass. This is the mixture for Akkadian red-stone glass.

The following, longer section (3) describes a procedure whereby the two types are combined, while a sort of codicil (4) describes what to do if this fails:

4. If (with) this red-stone glass inside the clay cover you get "copper dust" and "copper exudation" you mix into it 10 shekels of zuku-glass, one twelfth of copper, one twelfth of lead, one twelfth of anzahhu-glass. But do not bring in any antimony—per mina, and inspect it. During the mixing-in you must . . . and (then) remove it.

The text of the tablet bears some relation to that of the Neo-Assyrian library copies of glassmaking recipes from Ashurbanipal's Nineveh. Interestingly, the Middle Babylonian document can be said to operate on a less elementary level than its later counterparts, since it is obviously assumed that the craftsman knows how to produce the primary *zuku* and *anzahhu* glasses and is competent to do so. There was obviously a seasoned tradition of workshop expertise, but seldom would details of the operations ever come to be written down. Little is known of the artisans who practiced this craft, although the production of colored glass covered by the document likely concerns the beads and baubles that would eventually find a secure market where equivalents in stone were inevitably more costly.   ILF

273
CUNEIFORM TABLET WITH MANUAL FOR GLASS MANUFACTURE

Clay
Height 8.3 cm (3¼ in.); width 5.2 cm (2 in.)
Mesopotamia
Kassite, 14th–12th century B.C.
The Trustees of the British Museum, London
120960

Cuneiform tablets with technical or procedural instructions have always been rare, and few have attracted as much attention as this celebrated second-millennium B.C. tablet. Quite aside from the rarity of technical glass-making texts generally, two features make this document particularly unusual.

The colophon names one Le'e-kali-Marduk, son of Ussur-ana-Marduk, scribe of (the god) Marduk and a native of Babylon, and gives the date "month *tebitu*, 24th day of the year after (that in which) Gulkishar became king." This dating, to a little-known sixth king of the Sealand Dynasty in the early sixteenth century B.C., has seemed improbable for a number of reasons. Oppenheim, in his standard discussion of this genre of texts, wonders whether the date formula might not be an intentional device to make the tablet look older than it was, in that the scribes, father and son, on the basis of their names, belong in the Kassite period, between the fourteenth and twelfth century B.C.[1] In addition, the style of writing employs a conspicuous number of strange usages and sign values, leading previous editors to suggest an attempt to safeguard professional secrets by deliberate cryptography. Again it was Oppenheim who brought clarity, dismissing the "cryptographic" school on the grounds that any literate Babylonian could have read the text with

1. Oppenheim 1970, esp. pp. 59–65.
2. Often it is clear that the word literally means "carnelian."

patterns such as the arcades, intersecting loops, bold dots, and stripes preserved here. Originally a bright yellow, the base color of the flask is now a yellowish white.

Core-formed glass vessels were first produced in Egypt and Mesopotamia. Major advances in the technology of glassmaking were introduced in the middle of the second millennium B.C., and the vitreous materials recovered from Ashur represent one of the largest and best-preserved corpora so far recovered.[2] The example here is from part of a grave inventory.[3] In the sixteenth century B.C., glass imports and evidence of glassmaking began to appear in the Aegean. Two core-formed flasks of lentoid form—variously considered Cretan, Egyptian, or Syrian in origin—contribute to the evidence of a foreign stimulus to the Aegean glassmaking industry.[4]

JME

1. Wartke in *Assyrian Origins* 1995, no. 69.
2. Barag 1970, p. 141.
3. Haller 1954, p. 18.
4. Aruz 2008a, p. 171.

275

VESSEL WITH LID

Glazed vitreous material
Height 5.3 cm (2⅛ in.); diameter
10.7 cm (4¼ in.)
Ashur
Middle Assyrian, 14th–13th century B.C.
Staatliche Museen zu Berlin,
Vorderasiatisches Museum VA5930

Both the vessel and its flat lid are of a white vitreous material to which a secondary glaze has been applied.[1] The yellow lid has a brown circle at the center, and the fluting on the body of the vessel alternates white, brown, and greenish yellow. The fluting and the alternating colors give the effect of a flower, resembling in this manner the so-called petal or blossom bowls (see cat. nos. 276–78). Now faded, the glaze was likely a much brighter color, and areas have flaked off or weathered. Small holes would have allowed the lid to be fastened to the jar.

Glazed vitreous material is commonly called faience in Near Eastern literature, but this is a misnomer for a composite material consisting of a sintered quartz body and glaze (see pp. 419–20).[2] The

274

274

FLASK

Glass
Height 23.3 cm (9⅛ in.); max. diameter 8.2 cm
(3¼ in.)
Ashur, Sherd Grave
Middle Assyrian, 14th–13th century B.C.
Staatliche Museen zu Berlin,
Vorderasiatisches Museum VA5699

This flask, with a piriform body, knob base, and high neck, was manufactured by the core-formed technique. The walls of the flask were formed by the application of a layer of hot viscous glass over a core composed of a mixture of clay and sand that was modeled into the precise shape desired.[1] While the glass was still malleable, glass threads and drops of blue, red-brown, and white were fused onto the body of the flask and worked into

richness of the finds at Ashur in northern Mesopotamia suggest that the city was a prominent center for the production of vitreous materials. Yet the striking similarities between this vessel and others found as far from Ashur as Enkomi on Cyprus suggest an international commerce in vessels of standard shapes and forms.   JME

1. Wartke in *Assyrian Origins* 1995, no. 72.
2. Moorey 1994, p. 167.

275

276

277

276

PETAL BOWL

Faience
Height 6 cm (2⅜ in.); diameter 12.2 cm (4¾ in.)
Ugarit
Late Bronze Age, 14th–13th century B.C.
Musée du Louvre, Paris, Département des
Antiquités Orientales   AO17370

277

PETAL BOWL

Faience
Diameter 14.4 cm (5⅛ in.)
Mari, Tomb 123
Late Bronze Age, 13th century B.C.
Musée du Louvre, Paris, Département des
Antiquités Orientales   AO18929

A number of Late Bronze Age hemispherical bowls are molded in the shape of an open flower with petals ending in triangular tips, raised in low relief or incised on the body of the vessel. Each petal has a different glaze—yellow, pale blue, or green; the background is plain; and the inside of the bowl is often a different color. Petal relief decoration was applied on a number of pyxides with a depressed globular body and a swivel lid pegged into large horizontal lug handles (see cat. no. 275); several examples come from Mari.

The distribution of the flower bowls is similar to that of face vessels (see cat. nos. 208b, 210, 211)—from Cyprus (Enkomi) to Babylonia—with many examples from Ugarit. The chemical composition, particularly of the black glaze, colored with iron manganese oxides, is compatible with an origin in Levantine workshops. Pyxides from Mari are made with cobalt oxides to produce a blue color, using a technique observed mostly in Babylonia.

The range of colors, the chemical composition, and the similarity of distribution relate the flower bowls to the face vessels, with which they are not infrequently associated in the context of several rich tombs at Ugarit. Their function is unclear. While the pyxides may be cosmetic boxes, the open shape and porous material of the bowls would have made them inappropriate for the conservation of precious liquids or for drinking. It is possible that, like the face vessels and the animal-headed goblets, they were used in ritual libations. The flower motif, like the ubiquitous rosette on cylinder seals, jewelry, and painted vases, may be related to beliefs associated with fertility. AC

278a

278a, b

PETALED LIDS OR PLAQUES

Faience

Max height 3 cm (1⅛ in.); max. diameter 17.6 cm (7 in.)

Thera, Akrotiri

Late Cycladic I, ca. 1625–1525 B.C.

Archaeological Museum of Thera, Greece 417, 418 (3763, 6481)

Both these faience rosettes were probably lids for luxury pyxides.[1] Although found on the paved rectangular square south of Xeste 3, a three-story mansion on the seafront of Akrotiri on the island of Thera, they probably came from the building's interior, which had collapsed after the earthquake that preceded the massive Thera eruption. Xeste 3 was an important public building. It contained many precious objects and was embellished with extensive wall paintings, sophisticated compositions associated with rites of passage in Theran society.

278b

The motif of the colorful, multipetaled rosette is a major theme in the geometric imagery of the wall paintings on the third floor of the building. The rosette is also seen in Akrotiri on other wall paintings, incised on a bronze talent (weight), and in relief on an alabaster lid.

In the Near East, faience rosettes are seen on furniture and jewelry. The pointed petals of the rosette were possibly inspired by the art of Mesopotamia and the Levant, where petal bowls were found.

Faience technology is attested in Mesopotamia beginning in the fifth millennium B.C. and in Egypt in the fourth millennium B.C. The first faience objects found on Crete date to the mid-third millennium B.C. The manufacture of faience was further developed in the mid-second millennium B.C. at Knossos, the major palatial center of Minoan culture, with evidence for a local workshop.

Widespread in the minor arts of both the Minoan and the Mycenaean civilizations, faience was used primarily for decorative objects and jewelry and less commonly for vessels. The Late Cycladic I settlement of Akrotiri, on the island periphery of the Minoan and early Mycenaean worlds, has yielded a considerable number of miniature faience artifacts in the Aegean style—rosettes, shields, dolphins—and beads, sherds from relief goblets, and fittings for ostrich-egg rhyta. Copper from Lavrion, richest on the Greek mainland, was used to produce the glaze for these objects.[2]

AV

1. Akrotiri excavation nos. 3763, 6481.
2. For further reference, see S. Marinatos 1976, pp. 31–32, pl. 55b; K. Foster 1979, pp. 149–50, pl. 52; Doumas 1992, p. 131, figs. 136, 137; Doumas 1993, p. 234, pl. 146β; *Gifts of the Nile* 1998; *Crete–Egypt* 2000; Karetsou 2000; Panagiotaki 2000a, pp. 154–57; Panagiotaki 2000b, pp. 93–96, 103, no. 103; Bichta 2003, pp. 545–47, fig. 2; K. Foster and Laffineur 2003; Pantazis et al. 2003; and Vlachopoulos and Birtacha 2003.

279

279

VESSEL

Glass
Height 8.5 cm (3⅜ in.); diameter 6.5 cm
(2½ in.)
Enkomi, Tomb 66
Late Bronze Age, ca. 1340–1200 B.C.
The Trustees of the British Museum, London
1897.4–1.1052

This vessel, shaped like a pomegranate, is made of clear brown glass with opaque white, light blue, and orange trails in two antithetical festoon patterns. It was made by the core-formed technique, in which the glass was wound around a shape made of friable material that was later scraped out of the interior.

Glass pomegranate vessels are common in Egypt in the Late Bronze Age, and a number have been found also on Cyprus, particularly at Enkomi. The examples from Cyprus have a shorter neck than the contemporary Egyptian versions and have six upward-pointing calyx tips. They are actually closer in form to the real pomegranate fruit than their Egyptian counterparts. Because most examples of this form have been found on Cyprus, it seems likely that they were made there. Core-formed glass vessels were not produced in the Aegean at this time.

The pomegranate shape was clearly attractive to the glassmakers and could be easily adapted to create a small flask. Pomegranates, with their many seeds, were frequently associated with fruitfulness and fertility in the ancient world (see cat. no. 146).

The Enkomi tombs contained a rich mixture of local and imported products. They illustrate the wealth of the site and the key position occupied by Cyprus in cultural exchange during the Late Bronze Age. Tomb 66 was the only stone-built tomb on the site that was found intact. The contents—more than 140 objects—were very rich and included goldwork, bronze vessels and weapons, amber beads, glass vessels, a silver vessel, and pottery of Mycenaean, Cypriot, Levantine, and Egyptian origin.[1]

JLF

1. For further reference, see Murray, Smith, and Walters 1900, pp. 23–24, fig. 63:1052, and Harden 1981, p. 37, no. 14.

CONICAL RHYTA

280
Approx. 40 cm (15¾ in.)
Marble
Crete, Zakros, Treasury of the Shrine
Late Minoan I, ca. 1625–1450 B.C.
Archaeological Museum, Heraklion, Greece
2747

281
Ceramic
Max. height 33.2 cm (13⅛ in.); diameter
12.2 cm (4¾ in.)
Thera, Akrotiri, Complex Δ
Late Cycladic I, 1625–1525 B.C.
National Archaeological Museum, Athens,
Greece AKR 1493

282
Ceramic
Height 37.5 cm (14¾ in.); diameter 11 cm
(4⅜ in.)
Rhodes, Kameiros
Late Helladic IIIA:2, 14th century B.C.
Musée du Louvre, Paris, Département des
Antiquités Grecques, Étrusques et Romaines
A 276

283
Faience
Height 17.5 cm (6⅞ in.); diameter 7.5 cm
(3 in.)
Abydos
New Kingdom, Dynasty 18, reign of
Thutmose III, ca. 1479–1425 B.C.
Museum of Fine Arts, Boston 00.702A-D

284
Ceramic
Height 36.5 cm (14⅜ in.); diameter 14.3 cm
(5⅝ in.)
Ugarit
Late Helladic IIIB, ca. 1300–1200 B.C.
National Museum, Damascus, Syria
6891 RS 24.521

280

The conical rhyton had a greater impact on the cultures of Egypt, Cyprus, and the Levant than did any other single Aegean vessel. No other type was imitated as frequently or as widely and in so broad a range of materials. Invented on Crete near the end of the Protopalatial period (Middle Minoan IIB) or early in the Neo-palatial (Middle Minoan III) period, about 1750 to 1600 B.C., this type of rhyton has a wide opening at the mouth and tapers evenly or in a convex curve to a narrow tip perforated with a tiny opening that rarely exceeds .05 centimeter in diameter.[1] Because its Minoan or Mycenaean name is unknown, archaeologists have borrowed the Greek word *rhyton* (from ῥέω, "to flow"), which identifies a Classical-era vessel that also has openings at either end.

Neither a container nor a drinking cup, the conical rhyton was rather a vessel through which liquids passed from one source to another, such as from a jug to a cup. As with other Aegean vessels, such as

281

282

animal-headed rhyta, the general shape
may derive from Anatolia, where convex-
conical cups of stone and clay have been
found at several Old Assyrian Trading
Colony sites.[2] The underlying explanation for these intercultural borrowings
may be traced to contacts between Crete
and Anatolia, initiated by the Minoans
to obtain much-needed metals, such as
copper, tin, and silver, which were available in Anatolia, but rare or absent in
the Aegean.

By the developed Neopalatial era of
Late Minoan I, the conical or convex-
conical was the most popular shape of
rhyta in the Aegean. Ubiquitous on Crete
and the Cyclades, they were quickly
adopted into the Mycenaean world. Some
of the finest Neopalatial stone vases are
conical rhyta, including the so-called
Boxer Rhyton, featuring carved figural
reliefs of Minoan athletes,[3] and a group
of marble examples from the palace at
Zakros (cat. no. 280). Ceramic conical

rhyta are among the most beautifully
painted vases of their era (cat. no. 281).
During the Mycenaean period, ceramic
conical rhyta generally increased in size
and were often decorated with a wide zone
on the upper body and narrow linear
zones below (see cat. nos. 282, 284, 288).
Frequently, the upper zone included an
octopus, a motif that had its origins in Late
Minoan IB Marine Style vase painting but
was adopted into the Mycenaean ceramic
decorative repertoire (cat. no. 282). This

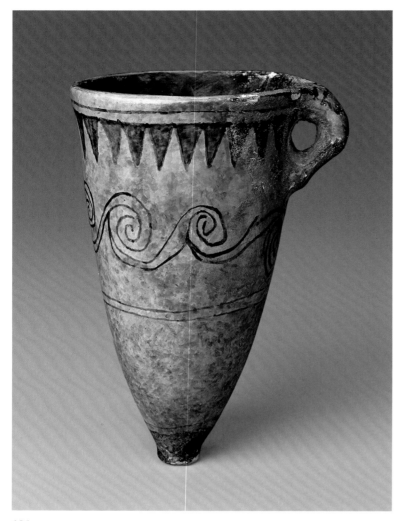

283

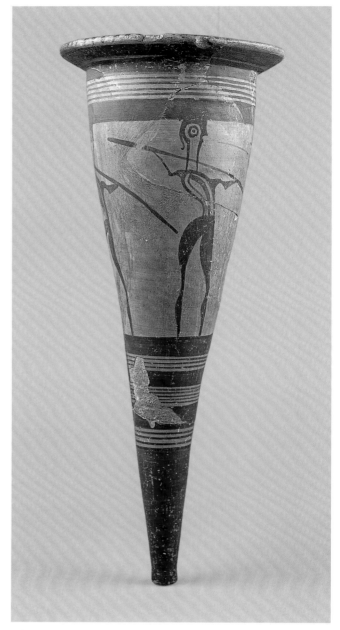

284

motif remained popular on Crete into the fourteenth and thirteenth centuries B.C., where it also appears on conical rhyta, including one example exported to Ugarit. Other Mycenaean ceramic conical rhyta were painted in the so-called Pictorial Style, including one from Rhodes (cat no. 288) and one from Ugarit (cat. no. 284).

Without descriptions in the texts, it is difficult to know how the conical rhyton was used. A wall painting from Knossos shows a conical rhyton carried by a male youth in a procession (fig. 133). Large groups of vessels composed predominantly of conical rhyta have been discovered in Minoan palaces and in one or two houses in every Minoan town. The internal

arrangement of the rooms and their locations near roads or open spaces suggest that conical rhyta were distributed to be carried in processions that may have culminated in public ceremonies, perhaps involving libations and drinking.

The association of conical rhyta with beverages, specifically those that were fermented and flavored, may be surmised from several sources, including two imitations of Aegean rhyta fitted with strainers. The first is an early Dynasty 18 convex-conical rhyton from Tell el-Dab'a in Egypt, which has a clay strainer that fits precisely on the mouth,[4] suggesting they were made as a set. A variant of a conical rhyton from Ugarit made in Cypriot Base Ring ware

had a strainer attached to the mouth.[5] The discovery of rhyta with grinding tools in several contexts on Crete and on Thera at Akrotiri complements this evidence and suggests that rhyta were used with beverages whose flavor was enhanced with freshly ground additives. Strainers would have prevented unwanted particles from clogging the tip of the rhyton while still improving the taste of the beverage when poured into the mouth.

No strainers have as yet been found with rhyta in the Aegean. A Linear B tablet from Pylos,[6] which may list the ingredients for manufacturing perfume, concludes with the word for "wool," and it has been suggested that the wool was

Figure 133. "Cupbearer" fresco. Knossos, Palace. Late Minoan II. Archaeological Museum, Heraklion

used as a filtering device. Using a scale reproduction of a conical rhyton, the present author placed a tuft of wool inside and sprinkled ground herbs and spices onto the wool. When wine or beer was poured into the rhyton, the wool became saturated with the beverage but also trapped the aromatics, preventing them from clogging the small secondary opening at the tip. A clear stream of richly aromatic and flavor-enhanced liquid, naturally intensified by aeration, emerged. The use of the conical rhyton as both an aerating, flavor-enhancing filter and a filler may explain its popularity in the second-millennium B.C. southeastern Mediterranean, where fermented beverages were imbibed as part of daily life. The impact of the conical rhyton on these societies may be gauged from its importation, depictions in art, and local imitations made in a range of materials that include electrum, ivory, faience, and clay.

Beginning in early Dynasty 18, Egyptian artists manufactured convex-conical rhyta based on Late Minoan IA or Late Cycladic I prototypes. Indeed, the running spiral on a rhyton from Abydos (cat. no. 283), a motif otherwise rare at this time in Egypt, is probably in imitation of a typically

Minoan motif especially common on Late Minoan IA conical rhyta (cat. no. 281). Paintings on the walls of Dynasty 18 Theban tombs from the era of Thutmose III depict rhyta being carried by the men of Keftiu, which suggests that they were presented to the pharaoh at these international gatherings (fig. 134). According to Egyptian color conventions, they were probably made of gold or silver and embellished with color inlays.

Current evidence indicates that conical rhyta were first exported from the Aegean to Cyprus and western Asia in the late fourteenth century B.C., probably from the Argolid on the Greek mainland and from Crete. The largest number of imported conical rhyta and local imitations in the Levant come from Ugarit, where more than forty were excavated in houses, graves, and temple contexts (cat. nos. 284, 285). The discovery of clusters of conical rhyta in Levantine contexts recalls the Neopalatial and Final Palatial Cretan and the Late Mycenaean mainland contexts with clusters of conical rhyta, from which they were distributed to be carried in processions. It thus appears that their adoption for use in Canaanite processions may be attributed directly to influence from the Aegean.

By the thirteenth century B.C., conical rhyta were imitated in various media on Cyprus and in the Levant. Few artifacts better articulate the international spirit of the second-millennium B.C. eastern Mediterranean than a faience rhyton from Kition, Cyprus (fig. 132). Its handle, now missing its strap, perhaps formed an S-curve, as is typical of Late Minoan IA conical rhyta (cat. no. 281). This type of handle occurs also on the electrum rhyton from Ugarit (cat. no. 285). It contrasts with the loop handle seen on Mycenaean conical rhyta. Also typical of Neopalatial Aegean rhyta (e.g., cat. no. 281) is the composition of the Kition rhyton, which is divided into narrow zones, the lowest decorated with vertical rows of spirals. The imagery on the upper two zones, however, seems Levantine, especially the male figures on the second zone who wear tall conical headdresses.

A group of Base Ring ware rhyta, found thus far only at Ugarit, may also have been made on Cyprus (cat. no. 287). The piriform bodies appear to have been based on Aegean prototypes known from

Figure 134. Facsimile of wall painting showing men of Keftiu with conical rhyton, ingot, and gold vessel. Thebes, Tomb of Rekhmire (TT 100). Dynasty 18, reign of Thutmose III–Amenhotep II. The Metropolitan Museum of Art, New York, Rogers Fund, 1931 31.6.42

Mycenaean imports to Cyprus and the
Levant. Several feature a clay bull's head
attached to the shoulder opposite the handle.
The practice of adding zoomorphic attachments to rhyta may have begun in the Late
Minoan IA and continued into the Mycenaean era (see cat. no. 288).

Only a few conical rhyta from the
Aegean dating to the early twelfth century B.C. have been found. As a result
of the collapse of palatial Mycenaean civilization at the end of the thirteenth
century B.C. and the concomitant abandonment of international trade networks
established with the east, conical rhyta
also disappeared from the cultures of
Cyprus and the Levant. Perhaps the wines,
herbs, and spices that had been traded
from the Aegean and that required the
use of a conical rhyton were no longer
exported; hence the need for the vessel
died out. The unique qualities of the rhyton, simultaneously enhancing and transforming the liquid that flowed through
it, may account for its adoption into cultic
or ritual practices from the Aegean to
the Levant.   RBK

1. For a thorough examination of the types,
   mechanical functions, contexts, and uses of
   Aegean rhyta, see Koehl 2006.
2. Ibid., pp. 44, 47.
3. Ibid., frontis., pp. 164–66, no. 651.
4. Ibid., p. 239, no. E6, p. 271, ill. 12.
5. Ibid., p. 244, no. C5.
6. Ibid., p. 271.

285

286

285

R H Y T O N

Electrum
Height 34.6 cm (13⅝ in.); diameter 10.6 cm
(4⅛ in.)
Ugarit, South Acropolis
Late Bronze Age context,
14th–12th century B.C.
Late Helladic IIIB manufacture,
1300–1200 B.C.
National Museum, Damascus, Syria
3590 RS 25.407

286

D A G G E R

Gold
Height 3 cm (1⅛ in.); length 27 cm (10⅝ in.)
Ugarit, South Acropolis
Late Bronze Age, 14th–12th century B.C.
National Museum, Damascus, Syria
3587 RS 25.410

This unique electrum conical rhyton from Ugarit (see p. 45) was excavated in 1962 along with a gold dagger. The blade and handle of the dagger were cast in a single piece, starting with a plate of hammered triangular section. The handle is decorated with scrolls that terminate in two palmettes. Several daggers of this type but in bronze, used both as utensils for cutting meat and as weapons, were also found at Ugarit. Both the electrum rhyton and the gold dagger were part of a treasure discovered in an overturned jug that had been buried in a building in the middle of a residential district.[1] The plan of the building and the presence of stone benches are unusual for a dwelling in Ugarit, suggesting that it may have served a special purpose, possibly as a place of assembly. The treasure also included six electrum bowls, electrum and silver pins and earrings, and miscellaneous cut or folded pieces made of gold and electrum (wire, rings, a plate, a rod). There was also a Cypriot ceramic pitcher of the so-called White Shaved type. While the jewelry and precious-metal fragments suggest a goldsmith's cache, the bowls and rhyton point instead to objects used in ritual banquets. Such banquets, attested in Ugaritic documents as *marzihu*, were held in buildings specially constructed for the purpose. The use of precious metals indicates the high social rank of the participants, probably members of the royal court.   AC

1. For further reference, see Schaeffer 1966, p. 131, figs. 8–11, and Courtois 1979, pp. 1165–66 ("TJ"), 1268.

287

R H Y T O N

Ceramic
Height 30.5 cm (12 in.); diameter 7.9 cm
(3⅛ in.)
Minet el-Beidha
Late Bronze Age context,
14th–12th century B.C.
Late Cypriot II manufacture,
14th–13th century B.C.
Musée du Louvre, Paris, Département des
Antiquités Orientales   AO14913

288

R H Y T O N

Ceramic
Height max. 40.5 cm (16 in.); diameter 11 cm
(4⅜ in.)
Rhodes, Pylona Cemetery, Tomb 2
Late Helladic IIIA:2, 14th century B.C.
Archaeological Museum of Rhodes, Greece
17964

The rhyton is found both in settlements and in funerary contexts on Crete, mainland Greece, and in the Levant.[1] Its presence in tombs is evidence for the practice of funeral rites.

The Pylona rhyton is the most common shape of Mycenaean rhyta, with a thick, rounded lip, conical body, and a loop handle at the rim. The lower part of the vase is missing. The scene depicted, the Master of Animals standing between felines, underscores the ritual character of the vase. Details on the costume of the male divinity—a loincloth and a headband or diadem—as well as the felines' skin are highlighted with white paint. The space between the figures is filled with decorative motifs, papyrus, chevrons, and stroke marks. The main register is framed by groups of fine and broader bands.[2]

The theme of the Master of Animals, the domination over animals—and, by extension, over the natural world—by a male divinity, is common in the east, especially on cylinder seals. The Pylona rhyton is the only known example of the scene's representation on pottery, and one of the few depictions in Mycenaean art.

A bull's head, modeled in the round, with one of the horns restored, is attached to the rim opposite the handle. This feature is unique in the Aegean. Its closest parallels are the Cypriot Base Ring II conical rhyta from Ugarit (cat. no. 287), which were found in a sanctuary.[3] Bull protomes on ritual vessels, as well as Minoan and Mycenaean bull-headed rhyta, reflect the worship of a bull-god and the performance of bull sacrifices throughout the Aegean and the Near East.

Clay analysis has indicated that the Pylona rhyton was imported from an unidentified source, probably in the southeastern Aegean—the Dodecanese, western Anatolia, or eastern Crete.   FZ

1. Koehl 2006.
2. See Karantzali 2001, pp. 34–35, 175; see also Karantzali 1998 and Karantzali in *Sea Routes* 2003, p. 286, no. 238.
3. Yon 1980, pp. 79–83; Yon 1986, pp. 275–78.

287

288

288, alternate view

BRIDGES TO BABYLON: HOMER, ANATOLIA, AND THE LEVANT

SARAH P. MORRIS

Bronze Age rulers and merchants of the Near East, their clients, and their armies circulated not only material wealth but also cultural capital—poetry and ritual. Their adventures survive in narratives of the first millennium B.C., particularly in the epic poetry of Homer. The earliest epic poems of Greece, Homer's *Iliad* and the *Odyssey*, embrace much older traditions from the Near East, beginning with Anatolia, its nearest neighbor. A Luwian poem found at the Hittite capital at Hattusa (Boğazköy) refers to "steep Wilusa" (Homer's Ilion?), and a bilingual Hurrian-Hittite poem offers poetic patterns and themes close to those found in Homer.[1] A treaty between the Hittite king Muwattalli II (1295–1272 B.C.) and Alaksandu of Wilusa suggests an ancestor for Alexandros (Paris) of Troy, and perhaps a motive for an Anatolian (rather than Greek) destruction of the city.[2] The Ahhiyawa, who appear twenty-eight times in Hittite texts with the same name Homer gave the Greeks (Achaeans) at Troy, must have been early speakers of Greek who encountered the Hittites in western Anatolia. What light do the objects in this exhibition shed on early military and diplomatic relations between these peoples—and on how those relations were transformed into literature?

Greek epic poetry is largely a story of war, and weapons and images of warriors made war glamorous and its heroes glorious. In Homer, a helmet plated with the tusks of boars worn in battle (cat. nos. 289, 290 and fig. 135) signifies both a hunting trophy—a souvenir of a young hero's early exploits (*Odyssey* 19.392–466)—and an heirloom handed down through generations (*Iliad* 10.261–71). Such equipment also distinguishes Aegean warriors in Near Eastern art and narrative. The warrior on a Hittite bowl (cat. no. 291), with his plumed helmet, cuirass adorned with tangent circles that suggest spirals, and an Aegean sword like those found at Boğazköy (cat. no. 292), Müskebi (cat. no. 245), and on the Uluburun ship (cat. no. 238a), could be an early "Carian" mercenary, from Miletos in western Anatolia, who fought with the Trojans against the Greeks (*Iliad* 2.867), or an Ahhiyawa soldier captured in battle with his alien weapons. Memories and impressions of the Achaeans and the Hatti (Hittites) fertilized the great sagas of the first millennium B.C.

The distances such Aegean soldiers and their outfits traveled in the Bronze Age Mediterranean emerge in Odysseus's "false" adventures related after his return to Ithaka, many of which take place in Egypt (*Odyssey* 3.300–303, 14.240–97, 17.424–44). Additional clues are provided by an illustration in a remarkable painted papyrus from Akhenaten's short-lived capital (1349–1336 B.C.) at Amarna (fig. 136).[3] A battle scene takes place at sea or near shore. The prows of ships frame nonnative warriors who prefigure those in monumental battle reliefs of the Sea Peoples (Libyans, Asiatics, and other foreigners) who would attack Egypt toward the end of the Bronze Age (see fig. 141). Some of the warriors fighting against them wear oxhide tunics and helmets that resemble Aegean ones made of boars' tusks. When Odysseus tells Penelope of fighting for and against Egyptian pharaohs, his fictive adventures draw on real experiences of Bronze Age warriors, ancestors of those "men of bronze" who sold their fighting skills to the pharaohs of Egypt (Herodotus *Histories* 2.152).

Aegean art made hundreds of years before the *Iliad* and the *Odyssey* were composed depicts stories of war and travel abroad to places such as Anatolia. A panorama of Aegean adventures is displayed on wall paintings in a house excavated at Akrotiri, a town on the Cycladic island of Thera that was destroyed by the eruption of the island's volcano in the late sixteenth century B.C. (see pp. 124–25). The east wall of an upper room is decorated with a lush river landscape reminiscent of the Nile in Egypt or the Orontes in Syria (fig. 138). Such landscapes, whether seen firsthand or imagined in travelers' tales, but always evoked by the exchange of exotic objects, inspired Homeric stories of sojourn in Egypt. This scene joins two others: a seascape on the south wall, where warriors on ships sail from a small city to a grander one (fig. 37), and a landing scene with a sea battle on the north wall, where heroes in Homeric gear march uphill to attack a walled city reminiscent of Troy, the site of the greatest of all the Greek epics (fig. 137).

A different relationship between the Hittites and the Mycenaeans is reflected in silver vessels from royal workshops in Anatolia (cat. nos. 107–109). A vessel in the shape of a stag (see fig. 54) reached a grave at Mycenae about the time Thera was buried by volcanic ash. Nearly pure in its silver content

Figure 135. Ivory plaque with Mycenaean warrior. Delos, Artemision. Late Bronze Age. Archaeological Museum, Delos B7069

Figure 136. Painted papyrus fragments. Tell el-Amarna, House R 43.2. Amarna period. The Trustees of the British Museum, London ᴇᴀ 74100

(99 percent), its shape and material point to Anatolia and a type of zoomorphic vessel exchanged by elites, referred to as a *bibru* in their correspondence. In letters written on clay tablets and found at Amarna, a Hittite ruler received gold and silver *bibru* from the pharaoh and recycled them as gifts to the king of Ahhiyawa,[4] from whom he received bronze objects.[5] If a *bibru* traveled from a ruler of Hatti to his "brother," king of the Achaeans, it was put to local use. For example, the zoomorphic vessel from Mycenae, originally with a single opening in its back, at some point had the holes that represented nostrils pierced and was reborn as an Aegean ritual rhyton, for pouring rather than drinking.[6]

Ivory work in Homer is imagined as a product of Anatolia—made by either Maionian or Carian artists (*Iliad* 4.141–45)—and indeed the ship wrecked at Uluburun off the southern coast of Anatolia (see pp. 289–305) carried a raw elephant tusk and many hippopotamus teeth to Aegean workshops like those that produced fine boxes for the Palace of Kadmos at Thebes (cat. no. 83). The ivory-paneled box from Pella (fig. 139)— possibly a Late Bronze Age Canaanite work in Egyptian style—inspired distant designs such as the Lion Gate at Mycenae (see fig. 88; see also cat. no. 174). Even more powerful in Homeric poetry is lion imagery, especially in similes where heroes are compared to lions (e.g., *Iliad* 20.164–73),[7] in part inspired by the presence of mountain lions in northern Greece but more dramatically by the models of the royal lion hunt, the lion emblem, and lion tamers of the Near East.

In Homer, the exchange of exotic and valuable objects plays a role in cult and in royal relations, even in wartime. Achilles uses a gold chalice (*depas amphikypellon*) for special libations (*Iliad* 16.221–30; 23.196, 219) that brings to mind the gold cup from the Uluburun ship (cat. no. 219).[8] Agamemnon receives a magnificent cuirass, inlaid with tin and lapis lazuli from Kinyras, king of Cyprus (*Iliad* 11.19–28), and carries a scepter (*Iliad* 2.100–108, 9.38) like one found at Kourion, also on Cyprus. In the *Iliad* (6.150–211) two warriors, Diomedes and Glaukos, one Greek and the other Anatolian (Lycian), meet in battle, as on the bowl from Hattusa. Recognizing that their families once regaled each other with gifts (including a gold *depas*; *Iliad* 6.220), they too exchange offerings and refrain from combat. Other treasures described in Homer—the Phoenician silver krater gifted to the island of Limnos, ransomed for a Trojan hostage, and ultimately offered as a prize for athletic prowess (*Iliad* 21.134–35, 23.740–49), or the krater Menelaos and Helen receive as a gift in Phoenicia and later present to their visitor Telemachus, son of Odysseus (*Odyssey* 4.612–19, 15.103–4)—reflect earlier practices of gift-giving.

The export of Aegean artistry is also reflected in painted palaces of the Near East, including Tell el-Dab'a in the Nile Delta (figs. 39, 40, 120) and Alalakh, Qatna (cat. no. 69a, b), and Tel Kabri.[9] In style and subject, they suggest the work of local artists trained in the Aegean style or artists who traveled

from Greece to work for Near Eastern rulers. Many years later, in palaces visited by Homeric heroes (*Odyssey* 7.81–132), Greek poets were inspired to write elaborate descriptions of other Near Eastern settings (Neo-Assyrian palaces), returning in poetry a compliment to their Levantine ancestors.[10] Finally, in epics of the Late Bronze Age—Ugaritic poems such as the epic of Baal, whose gods and heroes resurface in later Greek and Semitic literature—the craftsman god Kothar-wa-Hasis holds twin seats of power: "His throne is at Kaphtor [Crete, or the Aegean], his seat at Memphis [Egypt]."[11] In such tributes, poets expressed international connections that bridged the Aegean, Egypt, and the Levant.

How did luxury objects travel from port to port and palace to palace? The rich cargo of the Uluburun ship offers an answer in the form of a wood tablet (cat. no. 234) found in a large storage pithos, one of two double-leaved "pages" of lost history from the ship. By coincidence, the ship sank off Lycia in southwest Anatolia, home of the Trojan warrior Glaukos and destination of Bellerophon, the Homeric hero who carried from Corinth a "folding tablet with baleful signs"—orders for his own death (*Iliad* 6.178–80).[12] This reference to writing, the earliest in Greek literature, implies that the Mycenaean Linear B script had been long forgotten by Homer's time, and that the alphabet was not yet in wide use. Phoenician letters from

Figure 137. Wall painting with warriors. Thera, West House, Room 5. Late Cycladic I. Museum of Prehistoric Thera

Figure 138. Wall painting with river landscape. Thera, West House, Room 5. Late Cycladic I. Museum of Prehistoric Thera

Figure 139. Wood box
(modern reconstruction)
with carved ivory inlays.
Pella. Late Bronze Age.
Jordan Archaeological
Museum, Amman 70402,
70415

the east, perhaps inscribed on tablets like this one, eventually brought oral composition and performances of Greek poetry into written form as the earliest Greek literature. Originally coated with wax in which to incise letters or signs that could be "erased" for reuse, this tablet once bore writing, but in what script or language we are not certain. Ancient cargo, both Aegean and Near Eastern, often carried commercial notations from Cyprus,[13] and surely the island was in a pivotal position, given that it straddled the routes of the eastern Mediterranean. Like the poetry of Homer, this witness to writing, now silent, may link Aegean, Cypriot, and Near Eastern traditions.

More articulate connections between east and west repose in the hoard of lapis lazuli cylinder seals from the palace at Thebes in Boiotia (cat. nos. 177–183), the largest concentration of inscribed Near Eastern objects found in Bronze Age Greece.[14] Perhaps a royal gift, they recall to some the myth of Kadmos, the Phoenician who founded Thebes (Herodotus *Histories* 5.58) and brought "letters" to Greece, just as the Phoenicians introduced the alphabet to the western Mediterranean. Finds such as these give Mount Helikon in Boiotia, home of the Greek Muses, an "east face" that attracted Greek poets to Near Eastern ideas.[15]

Long after the great battles and voyages of the Bronze Age, and their commemoration in art and text, echoes of these adventures survived in Greek epic poetry. In the Homeric world, relations between royalty are not just temporary or convenient friendships but lasting alliances, inherited by later generations. How long did memories of past exchanges sur-

Figure 140. Stone relief with Amenhotep II shooting an arrow through an ingot. Dynasty 18. Luxor Museum J. 44

vive, and how did they inform Homeric epic poetry? Glaukos's gift to Diomedes of a gold shield in exchange for a lesser bronze one was appropriate in light of their individual ranks. Homer's misinterpretation of this earlier custom leads him to deride Glaukos for giving so much in return for so little (*Iliad* 6.234–36).[16] Thus did some Greek heroes suffer for their distance from Bronze Age realities.

Others, however, benefited, most notably Odysseus, who, returning home disguised as a beggar, recounts tales of slavery and combat in Egypt, Cyprus, and Phoenicia. In relating Odysseus's campaign to reclaim his throne and his wife, the poet borrowed from Anatolian legends of kings. Like Gurparanzah of Ailanuwa, who wins an archery contest at a feast,[17] Odysseus achieves his great homecoming victory when he bests Penelope's suitors in the contest of the bow, stringing it and shooting arrows "through twelve axes" (*Odyssey* 21.393–421). No ordinary man could have accomplished this feat, only a hero and a king: the privilege of performing it once belonged to Egyptian pharaohs alone. If the Greek poet ever saw such an image (fig. 140), he did not recognize the pha-

raoh's actual target, copper ingots, common currency in the Bronze Age and the chief cargo of the Uluburun ship (cat. no. 185). To him they resembled the bronze double axes familiar in his time.[18] Here Greek epic poetry evokes the art and power of royalty in the distant Near East, and images long lost to history take on a vibrant new life.

1. S. Morris 1997; Watkins 1986; West 1997; Bachvarova 2005.
2. Basedow 2007, pp. 55–56.
3. Schofield and Parkinson 1994.
4. *Keilschrifttexte aus Boghazköi* 2.11.
5. Listed in an inventory, *Keilschrifttexte aus Boghazköi* 18.181.
6. Koehl 1995.
7. Laffineur 2007, pp. 79–85.
8. Bloedow 2007, esp. pp. 91–92, 94.
9. See Feldman 2007, pp. 39–65.
10. Cook 2004; see also Feldman 2007.
11. S. Morris 1992, chap. 4, pp. 73–100.
12. Bellamy 1989.
13. Hirschfeld 1999.
14. Porada 1981–82.
15. West 1997.
16. See *Keilschrifttexte aus Boghazköi* 2.11, 18.181.
17. Laroche 1971, no. 362.
18. S. Morris 1992, p. 116; S. Morris 1997, pp. 621–22.

289
Helmet

Boar's tusk
Height 29 cm (11⅜ in.); diameter at rim 21 cm
(8¼ in.)
Mycenae, Chamber Tomb 518
Late Helladic II–IIIA, 15th–14th century B.C.
National Archaeological Museum, Athens,
Greece 6568

This reconstruction of a helmet is fashioned of sixty boar's tusks pierced at the ends and attached to a modern conical leather cap.[1] The larger tusks are set in four horizontal rows around the helmet, curved alternately to the right or left as indicated by Homeric description and several surviving pictorial representations.[2] The rectangular pieces, falling into a graduated series, cover the cheekpieces. An exceptional bow-shaped element with curls or horns crowns the top as a kind of crest, seen also in contemporary illustrations.[3]

This type of helmet must have first been in use on mainland Greece in the late seventeenth century B.C. The earliest examples come from both settlements and warrior tombs of the Middle Helladic III period, such as Eutresis and Malthi, and the first royal shaft graves at Mycenae, Thebes, and Aigina-Kolonna.[4] Over the following five centuries, the boar's tusk helmet became very popular. Because each helmet required the tusks of thirty-three boars, to possess one was considered the ultimate *insignium* of prowess and high social—even divine— status. A symbol of power on early Mycenaean and contemporary Minoan vases, the boar's tusk helmet appears also on a fresco frieze at Thera (cat. no. 290). It was carved on numerous miniature ivory plaques depicting the heads of Mycenaean warriors and included in Linear B script as an ideogram and as the word *ko-ru* (κόρυς).

Boar's tusk helmets are depicted on several wall paintings. They are worn by soldiers on a fresco from the Palace of Nestor at Pylos, which likely represents a Mycenaean army in combat.[5] They are also worn by warriors in procession on the Miniature Fresco at Thera (fig. 137),[6] on a ceramic bowl fragment from Hattusa (cat. no. 291,[7] and on a papyrus from Tell el-Amarna in Egypt (fig. 136),[8] in all cases to signify the figures' ethnicity. Finally, the image of a helmeted female figure holding

a griffin on a fresco fragment from the Cult Center at Mycenae has been interpreted as the depiction of Athena Potnia, the Mycenaean goddess of war.[9]

The legend of the Mycenaean helmeted warriors long outlived the warriors themselves and the era in which they lived. Their presence, however, is felt in the Homeric epics in a surprisingly accurate description of a helmet very similar to this one, lent by Meriones to Odysseus.[10]

CPA

1. Published in Wace 1932, p. 85, pl. 38, no. 65.
2. See, for example, the helmet depicted on a fresco from Thera; Akrivaki 2003, p. 528.
3. Akrivaki 2003.
4. Kilian-Dirlmeier 1997, pp. 35–50, esp. pp. 40–45, where a list of sites with helmet tusks is cited.
5. Lang 1969, pp. 43–49, pls. M, N.
6. Negbi 1978.
7. Niemeier 2003, pp. 104–5, fig. 4.
8. Schofield and Parkinson 1994.
9. Boulotis 1988, pp. 181, 182, no. 149, p. 189, no. 163.
10. Wace 1932, p. 213; Homer *Iliad* 10.260–65.

290
Wall Painting Fragment

Plaster, painted
Height 48 cm (18⅞ in.); width 38 cm (15 in.)
Thera, Akrotiri
Late Cycladic I, ca. 1625–1525 B.C.
Archaeological Museum of Thera, Greece
11548

This fragment shows one boar's tusk helmet and the partial crest of another helmet. It belonged originally to a frieze that decorated the upper part of the wall of a room in Xeste 4 at Akrotiri, on the island of Thera. Dated to the final phase of the city's history, the building is one of the most important at the site. It was imposing in its dimensions—probably four-storied in the eastern wing. Its construction consisted entirely of ashlar masonry, and the grand staircase was decorated on either side with an impressive wall painting of men who appear to be climbing steps, suggesting that it served a public function.

Although the fragment was found in the debris of Room 2, at ground-floor level, the absence of other fragments of the same composition indicates that it fell from an upper story. It is quite well preserved, and the impression of timber on the top edge indicates that the frieze touched a beam near the ceiling. The plaster was applied in two layers. The first layer, containing sand, ceramic grits, and bits of straw, was spread directly on the clay-coated wall surface, while the second was very fine, its surface polished before being painted.

The representation of the helmet is incised and painted in the *al secco* fresco technique. Unique in being nearly life-size, it includes a crest and cheekpiece; structural details, such as the holes through which the tusks were sewn to the lining, are also depicted. The projection of the helmet over painted horizontal bands creates a trompe l'oeil effect and the impression that it was hanging on the wall. Because it is not isolated but part of a frieze, the image recalls Homeric descriptions of shields hanging in similar manner inside a warriors' hall. Indeed, the artist's intention may well have been to reproduce such a hall. As symbols of power, the helmets may also allude to the function of the building as a seat of authority.

This early depiction of a boar's tusk helmet far from the Greek mainland, where it is believed to have originated—specifically on an island that enjoyed close connections with Crete long before the Mycenaean expansion into the Aegean—raises new

290

questions about relations not only between Thera and continental Greece just prior to the volcanic eruption at Thera, but between the Aegean peoples in general at the very beginning of the Late Bronze Age.   CD

291

INCISED BOWL FRAGMENT

Ceramic
Height 14.7 cm (5¾ in.); width 5.1 cm (2 in.)
Boğazköy, Lower Town
Hittite Middle Kingdom, late 15th–14th century B.C.
Çorum Museum, Çorum, Turkey
1–329–75

The unusual image of an armed warrior is finely incised on the interior of this Hittite redware bowl from Boğazköy.[1] It has been interpreted as visual evidence for the conflicts between Anatolia and the Aegean, as possibly recounted in contemporary Hittite documents and glorified in the Homeric epics.[2] The warrior is shown in a dynamic stance, with his body thrust forward, the calf of his extended back leg perhaps preserved in a few curving lines, and his right arm in a downward position to thrust a sword into the (now missing) body of his opponent. The feet of what appears to be a defeated combatant are visible horizontally below him.

The warrior's very distinctive armor may identify him as a foreign fighter. Unlike the more typical Near Eastern headgear worn, for instance, by the imposing warrior god on one of the city gates at Boğazköy (fig. 53), this one is detailed with horizontal zones, suggestive of the Mycenaean boar's tusk helmet (cat. no. 289). Such helmets, which were worn by Homer's Achaeans, are more realistically depicted on Aegean objects—wall paintings, silverware, weapons, ivories, and seals—showing rows of curving teeth instead of zigzags.[3] Emerging from a crowning knob or point on these images is an impressive crest, textured in the more modeled renderings with ridges that may suggest the horns of a wild goat. Sometimes streamers are also depicted. Both a crest and streamers are carefully detailed on the Boğazköy bowl.[4]

As for the curved bovine horn shown emerging from the front of the warrior's helmet, this is a traditional Near Eastern feature that appears in the Aegean only at the end of the Late Bronze Age—presumably centuries after this image was made. Mycenaean warriors first wear horned helmets in the twelfth century B.C., when the Sea Peoples are similarly depicted on the walls of the Temple of Ramesses III at Medinet Habu (fig. 141).[5]

The warrior on the Hittite bowl appears to wear an open garment ornamented with zigzags on the fringed sleeves and tangent triple concentric circles on the chest, perhaps intended to suggest an Aegean spiral-form pattern.[6] Such garb, however, is unparalleled in Aegean combat scenes, where plain tunics are worn or, more commonly, warriors are shown heroically nude to the waist as they are in the Near East.[7] The triangular sword with rounded pommel may further allude to the west, where this type of weapon appears in war and hunt scenes.[8] Some Mycenaean-type bronze swords (lacking their pommels) were in fact discovered in Anatolia (cat. no. 245). One possible spoil of war from Boğazköy (cat. no. 292) was later inscribed in Akkadian with a dedication to the Storm God by the late fifteenth-century B.C. Hittite ruler Tudhaliya I/II.[9]

The image on the bowl gives rise to many questions. Although well executed, it represents a secondary sketch, like the much later Greek graffito on a foot fragment of a statue from Persepolis.[10] Most intriguing is the fact that while the iconography is somewhat unconventional in Mycenaean terms—suggesting a foreigner's perspective[11]—the dynamic style is unusual in Hittite art.[12] Attenuated figures with dramatically extended legs can be found on seals from the Greek mainland, as well as on combat scenes in the frescoes from Pylos, where defeated enemies have similarly dangling limbs.[13] The original composition remains a mystery, but it is likely that there were a number of warriors. Some scholars have suggested that the image is a record of an actual encounter, like that described in the Indictment of Madduwatta.[14] This important Hittite text recounts the attack by Attarisiyas, "a man of Ahhiya" (the Achaean hero Atreus?), on Madduwatta, perhaps a local western Anatolian ruler, whose changing allegiances caused him

to be both rescued and confronted by the Hittites.[15]   JA

1. Bittel 1976d.
2. Güterbock 1984, pp. 115–19; S. Morris 1989, p. 532.
3. Borchhardt 1972, pls. 2–4; Niemeier 1998a, p. 42, fig. 13b. For a schematic Minoan zoned helmet with zigzags, floating like a sea creature on a pithoid jar from Katsamba near Knossos, see Borchhardt 1972, pl. 8:1; Schofield and Parkinson (1994, pp. 164–65) discuss variations in rendering the zoned helmet.
4. For divine headgear with curving horned crests on Anatolian seal impressions, one from Crete, see Pini 1977–78, pl. 3, nos. 1–4; Kültepe: T. Özgüç 1953, pl. LXII, fig. 692; for streamers: Borchhardt 1972, pls. 7:7, 8:1; on the silver siege rhyton from Mycenae, warriors with crests and streamers stand behind tower shields: Hiller 1999, pl. LXIX:1b; see also Lang 1969, pl. 124:29H64.
5. Borchhardt 1972, pp. 113–14; often in Near Eastern depictions, both horns are shown. On the Ugarit Baal stele (fig. 82, this volume), they are depicted in profile.
6. For concentric circle decoration on an ivory helmet from Knossos, see Borchhardt 1972, pl. 8:3.
7. We must assume that elite Aegean warriors were in fact well protected, based on the discovery at Dendra in the Argolid of a full set of bronze-plated body armor, along with a boar's tusk helmet: ibid., pl. 6.
8. Hiller 1999, pl. LXIX:2–5.
9. Niemeier 1998a, p. 42; Cline (1996) suggests that the sword may have not been imported and discusses it in the context of the Assuwa rebellion and the possible role of Mycenaean combatants.
10. Roaf and Boardman 1980, pp. 204–6; the style indicates a Greek hand.
11. See Niemeier 1998a, p. 42, for this view; see also figure 136 in this volume for the Egyptian rendering of possibly Mycenaean armor on a painted papyrus from Tell el-Amarna.
12. Also unusual is the treatment of the eye, which appears to be in profile; the two-horned helmet is also modified for profile view.
13. Hiller 1999, pl. LXIX:1, 2; J. Davis and Bennet 1999, pl. XIV:a–c: this means of depicting a defeated enemy is visible centuries earlier on the Thera Miniature Fresco; see fig. 137, this volume.
14. Güterbock 1984, pp. 115–19; S. Morris 1989, pp. 532–33; Niemeier 1998a, pp. 41–43.
15. Güterbock 1984, pp. 116–19; see also Cline 1996, pp. 140ff.

291

Figure 141. Stone relief with battle between Egyptians and Sea Peoples. Medinet Habu, Temple of Ramesses III. Dynasty 20.

292
SWORD

Bronze
Length 79 cm (31⅛ in.)
Boğazköy
Hittite Middle Kingdom, ca. 1430–1390 B.C.
Çorum Museum, Çorum, Turkey
10–1–92

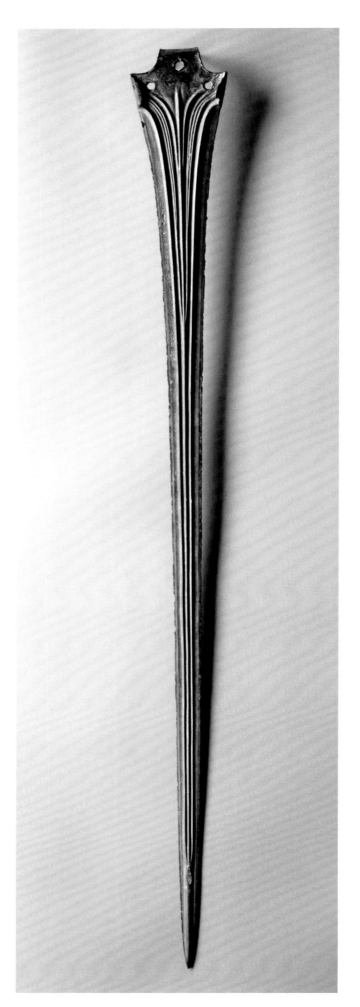

This bronze sword was discovered in 1991 at Hattusa, capital city of the Hittites, by the operator of a bulldozer doing repair work. It has a raised midrib and several secondary side ribs on the blade, square flanged shoulders, and four rivet holes (two in the hilt and two in the tang) for the attachment of a now-missing handle. The blade tapers sharply from hilt to point, and the rectangular tang is now bent back.

On the blade is an Akkadian inscription stating that the sword was among those dedicated at Hattusa by Tudhaliya I/II following his successful quelling of the Assuwa rebellion in northwestern Anatolia about 1430 B.C.:

As Tudhaliya the Great King shattered the Assuwa-Country, he dedicated these swords to the Storm-God, his Lord.[1]

The sword has no parallels in Anatolia or, indeed, anywhere in the eastern Mediterranean. It was the subject of much discussion in the years immediately following its discovery. Current scholarship holds that it may be a variant of a Mycenaean Type B sword dating to the fifteenth century B.C., a type more frequently found on the Greek mainland, but that it could also reflect Mycenaean influence rather than Mycenaean manufacture.

The Assuwa rebellion was one of the most important military events to occur in northwestern Anatolia prior to the Trojan War and one of the few events to which the Mycenaeans may be linked by textual evidence.[2] Conceivably, it was the historical basis for contemporary Hittite tales of Mycenaean warriors or mercenaries in Anatolia, which in turn generated stories of pre–Trojan War Achaean forays on the Anatolian mainland.   EHC

1. Translation and transliteration after Ünal, Ertekin, and Ediz 1991, esp. p. 51; Ünal 1993; Ertekin and Ediz 1993, esp. p. 721.
2. Hittite letter KUB XXVI 91.

THE LEGACY OF IVORY-WORKING TRADITIONS IN THE EARLY FIRST MILLENNIUM B.C.

MARIAN FELDMAN

Ivory, which played such a fundamental role in the international exchanges of the second millennium B.C., almost entirely disappears with the collapse and decline of many of the Bronze Age societies at the end of the era. The final centuries of the Late Bronze Age (the 14th and 13th centuries B.C.) had fostered an internationalism tied to highly centralized palaces that in large part controlled both the human and the material resources needed to procure and produce luxury objects. These objects in turn served a critical function in defining the elite classes. When this palace-centered international system imploded (whether because of external forces or internal instabilities or, more likely, a combination of the two), trade routes were disrupted, the demand for luxury items fell, and ivory working nearly ceased for several hundred years. Yet when ivories do reappear—and in significantly large quantities—from the late tenth through the seventh century B.C., they exhibit a remarkable continuity of tradition.[1] At the same time, this later ivory-working tradition expanded upon and reworked the earlier one in response to a dramatically different social, political, and economic landscape.

Many second-millennium B.C. ivories share motifs that circulated in the intensely international climate of the time. Popular themes include hunting animals from a chariot; heroic combats between humans and lions, sphinxes, and griffins; and lions, bulls, wild goats, and composite creatures attacking one another or posed around elaborate vegetation (cat. nos. 264–269). Disentangling styles and places of manufacture for many of these pieces has proved a daunting task, and indeed their resistance to regional attribution may have been a prime aspect of their value as internationally exchanged items of an elite brotherhood.[2]

The situation is more straightforward in the first millennium B.C., with regionally identifiable ivories appearing from Etruria (and even farther west) to Iran. The exceptionally large number of these ivories has permitted sophisticated analyses according to style and distribution. The two most widespread

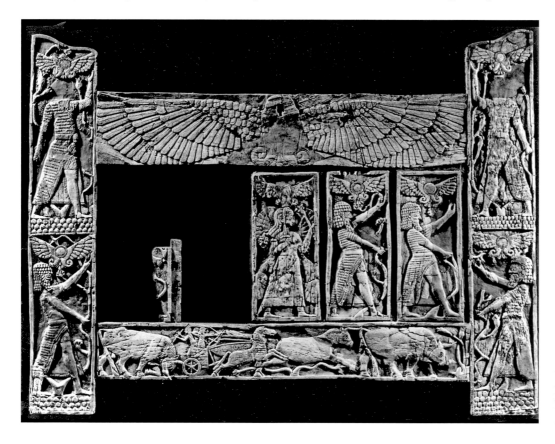

Figure 142. Carved ivory chair back. Nimrud, Fort Shalmaneser, Room SW7. Neo-Assyrian period. Iraq Museum, Baghdad IM 62722

Figure 143. Silver-gilt bowl. Phoenician with Cypro-Archaic period inscription. The Metropolitan Museum of Art, New York, The Cesnola Collection, Purchased by subscription, 1874–76 74.51.4554

and abundant of the stylistic groups, associated with Phoenicia and Syria, show the closest connections with their second-millennium B.C. predecessors, carrying over many of the earlier motifs. In one example, a chariot hunt on an eighth-century B.C. Syrian ivory chair (fig. 142) displays very much the same theme and composition seen on a Late Bronze Age game board from Enkomi (cat. no. 265). Combats between lions, griffins, sphinxes, and hunters, as well as hieratically arranged animals, provide further echoes of popular Late Bronze Age motifs. Moreover, ivory carving did not exist on its own, but was part of a larger luxury craft tradition that included metalworking, which also exhibits strong associations with the Late Bronze Age (fig. 143).

Although Phoenician and Syrian ivories share many iconographic themes, stylistically they can easily be distinguished from one another.[3] An overall sense of balance—created by stable compositions, ornate but refined decoration, and figures with long, slender limbs—characterizes the Phoenician style, along with a heavy use of Egyptianizing elements such as pharaonic attire and religious symbols. Syrian ivories exhibit fewer Egyptianizing features and display a vigorous energy derived from squatter proportions and dynamic poses that fill the space, with figures often pressing against borders as if about to escape (fig. 142). In both traditions, multicolored decoration such as

gold leaf and glass inlays often embellish the ivory, but Phoenician ivories especially boast elaborate cutout cells simulating, when filled, the metalworking technique of champlevé (fig. 144). As single objects or as part of larger furnishings, these ivories must have presented a jewel-like image of grandeur and luxury. Indeed, it is this very opulence, viewed with suspicion, that underlies the biblical declamation, "[Woe to them] that lie upon beds of ivory, and stretch themselves upon their couches" (Amos 6:4). Just such a couch may be depicted in a seventh-century B.C. carved relief of the Assyrian king Ashurbanipal (ca. 668–627 B.C.), who reclines under a grape arbor, his queen nearby in an equally elegant high-backed chair.[4]

While there are strong ties of continuity in the ivory-carving tradition between the Bronze and Iron Ages, which spans the so-called Dark Ages, in the first millennium B.C. these luxury items participated in a dramatically changed world.[5] With the collapse of the Late Bronze Age, the unusually integrated and interdependent international system of palaces, which was largely rooted in prestige, fragmented into an array of decentralized and entrepreneurial endeavors involving mercantilism, colonization, and the territorial expansion of Assyria.[6] Many Late Bronze luxury arts, including ivories, projected a generalized concept of heroic kingship and were part of an exchange system that was cloaked in terms of diplomacy and gifting. In contrast, first-millennium B.C. ivories appear to have circulated in more nakedly commercial and imperialist endeavors.

There are enough differences between Late Bronze and Iron Age ivories to indicate that more is going on than simply the continuation of an earlier tradition. The new political and economic situation of the first millennium B.C. is evident in their greater quantities, which number in the hundreds, and their wider geographic distribution from the western Mediterranean to Iran, which greatly expands the geographic spread of the Late Bronze Age luxury arts that were concentrated in the eastern Mediterranean. Distribution studies of Phoenician and Syrian ivories suggest not only that the two regions operated within different spheres of influence, but that they were highly competitive, guarding exclusive access to routes and markets.[7]

In addition, while Phoenician and Syrian ivories incorporate many motifs from the Late Bronze Age, these are combined with a richer thematic repertoire and a greater diversity of styles. The increased heterogeneity points to a more decentralized system of production than in the second millennium B.C., when it appears that large institutions and especially the palace controlled most ivory working.[8] The Phoenicians, in particular—though we can probably also infer the same for the Syrians—were renowned in antiquity for their mercantile activities, and the eclecticism of their crafts may be partly the result of finely tuned attention to different market demands.[9] This accords with literary evidence that Phoenicians marketed their products to specific foreign clientele, taking differing preferences into account in their selection of artistic forms.[10] In this light, it is not surprising that ivories appear in a variety of locations throughout the Mediterranean, including wealthy Etruscan and Greek tombs.

Enormous numbers of Phoenician and Syrian ivories also have been excavated in the capitals of the great Neo-Assyrian kings of the ninth through the seventh century B.C. Here we can trace a means of acquisition rather different from that of commercial activity. Instead, it is most likely that these and other luxury items were procured by the Assyrian kings as either tribute given by subject states or booty taken in military raids. Kalhu (Nimrud), the capital of Assyria during the ninth century B.C., has revealed massive collections of ivories in the northwest palace of Ashurnasirpal II (883–859 B.C.) and Fort Shalmaneser, a military arsenal built by Ashurnasirpal's successor, Shalmaneser III (858–824 B.C.).[11] Similarly, annals recording the military deeds of the Assyrian rulers include ivory among the lists of tribute and booty. The looted ivories, however, do not seem to have had much impact on Assyrian arts. Indeed, contemporary Assyrian ivories replicate the themes and styles found on the large-scale carved wall reliefs for which Assyria is famous rather than the motifs on the collected foreign ivories. These foreign items appear to have been valued for their qualities as hoarded booty—physical evidence of conquest and imperialism—rather than appreciated for their aesthetic value.[12]

Despite the apparent eclecticism of the first-millennium B.C. works, the artistic continuity of many motifs, themes, and compositional devices, such as heroic combats and antithetically

Figure 144. Carved ivory plaque. Nimrud, Fort Shalmaneser, Room SW37. Neo-Assyrian period. The Metropolitan Museum of Art, New York, Rogers Fund, 1961 61.197.1

arranged animals, nevertheless suggests that ties to the Late Bronze Age remained. The echoes of a Bronze Age past may be attributed to a nostalgia for a "heroic" Golden Age that predated the social, political, and economic transformations of the Dark Ages. This might be compared with the roughly contemporaneous recording in written form of the epic poems of Homer and Hesiod, which recount more glorious, but long gone, days, when proper courtly code governed interactions. Hesiod, in his telling of the five generations of humankind in *Works and Days* (106–201), traces the steady decline of human society from its first Golden Age. He laments the current generation, the men of iron, who lack the heroic qualities of preceding generations. While the sociopolitics of the early Iron Age took increasingly "crass" forms, tied to mercantilism and imperialism, cultural life and the production of luxury arts point to strategies for the active creation and deployment of a courtly and heroic Golden Age. The survival or revival of Late Bronze Age forms in the early centuries of the first millennium B.C. depended in large part on their prior level of prestige and their association with this heroic past. The reliance on, or even active creation of, a nostalgia for a past Golden Age may have served to mask commercial and imperial interests that dominated the Iron Age, as seems to be the case for many of the literary works of the period. The reuse of Late Bronze Age motifs on first-millennium B.C. luxury goods may have been motivated by their references to a courtly royal past of the Late Bronze Age, offsetting the new economic and political realities of the time.

1. Barnett 1982, p. 43; Lagarce 1983.
2. Feldman 2006b.
3. While scholars accept the two broad categories of Phoenician and Syrian ivories, there remains much discussion about subgroups within each, as well as a probable third group, termed South Syrian or Intermediate (Cecchini, Mazzoni, and Scigliuzzo n.d. [forthcoming]; Winter 1981; Herrmann 1992).
4. *Art and Empire* 1995, p. 122.
5. Similarities between ivory and woodworking techniques probably account for the mechanism by which an ivory-carving tradition was transmitted from the end of the Bronze Age into the first centuries of the first millennium B.C. The coexistence of unworked ivory and African blackwood (ebony) discovered on the Late Bronze Age Uluburun ship reinforces the close association between these two crafts (Pulak 1998, p. 203).
6. Liverani 1990; Liverani 2003; S. Sherratt 2003.
7. Winter 1976.
8. Winter 2005, p. 32.
9. Hoffman 2005, p. 356 n. 42.
10. Markoe 2000, p. 143.
11. Ivories have also been found elsewhere at Nimrud (Oates and Oates 2001, pp. 226–35), as well as at the later Assyrian capitals of Khorsabad and Nineveh (Barnett 1982, pp. 44–47).
12. Herrmann n.d. (forthcoming).

PROBLEMS OF CHRONOLOGY: MESOPOTAMIA, ANATOLIA, AND THE SYRO-LEVANTINE REGION

GLENN M. SCHWARTZ

Without an appreciation of where events stand in temporal relation to one another, students of the human past flounder in a sea of confusion. If, for example, we thought that the American Revolution occurred after World War I, our understanding of the past few centuries would be severely hampered. In consequence, chronology provides an important foundation for the investigation of past human behavior. When studying the ancient world, scholars use two principal approaches to assess the passage of time. One is relative chronology, which aims to establish the order of events as they occurred without any concern for the length of time involved. The other, absolute chronology, assigns events in the past to specific calendar years.

The relative chronology of the second millennium B.C. in western Asia is generally straightforward. When it works best, it is based on sequences of changing artifact styles anchored to stratigraphic contexts. Archaeologists in the Levant and Anatolia usually subdivide the millennium into the Middle Bronze Age (early second millennium B.C.), Late Bronze Age (mid- to late second millennium B.C.), and early Iron Age (ca. 1200–1000 B.C.), with each phase characterized by diagnostic pottery and other material culture types.[1] In Mesopotamia, where written records are more profuse than in the Levant or Anatolia, archaeologists employ historically defined periods such as Isin-Larsa, Old Babylonian, and Kassite, whose names refer to ruling dynasties discussed in ancient texts.[2] A problem with this type of periodization is that ceramic, architectural, and artistic styles do not necessarily change at the same time as ruling dynasties or predominant metals do. Even so, archaeologists can usually identify artifact types peculiar to the chronological subdivisions in general use, and the system works reasonably well.

In the case of absolute chronology, we are relatively confident in addressing the last four centuries of the second millennium B.C. This period is well dated because the record of a solar eclipse in 763 B.C. is anchored to a list of Assyrian eponyms, officials whose names were used to designate individual years. The lists of eponyms and kings kept by the Assyrians and Babylonians allow us to date events back from the first millennium B.C. to the fourteenth century B.C.[3] Mesopotamian chronology in the fourteenth century B.C. can also be linked to adjacent regions based on the diplomatic archives discovered at Tell el-Amarna, the capital of the "heretic" pharaoh

Akhenaten, which reveal that Akhenaten was a contemporary of Tushratta, king of Mitanni in Upper Mesopotamia, as well as Suppiluliuma I, king of the Hittites in Anatolia, and the Kassite king Burnaburiash II of Babylon.

By contrast, establishing an absolute chronology for the period before the fourteenth century B.C. has been a frustrating process marked by controversy and disagreement. Most problematic is the paucity of written records and archaeological evidence for the epoch between the downfall of the First Dynasty of Babylon and the appearance of the subsequent Kassite dynasty. The absence of documentation for this so-called Dark Age, whose length is uncertain, prevents us from connecting the well-dated events of the fourteenth century to the chronology of the earlier second millennium B.C. Although Hittite records in Anatolia span this poorly understood era, they add little to the chronological discussion because the Hittite scribes failed to use a system of chronological reckoning such as eponyms or year names. Complicating matters, Hittite kings often adopted the names of their predecessors, and the scribes neglected to distinguish one from the other.[4]

Partly ameliorating the problem are texts from periods of increased international contact which demonstrate that a ruler in one area lived at the same time as a ruler in another area. For example, we know that in the earlier part of the millennium, Zimri-Lim, king of Mari on the Syrian Euphrates, was a contemporary of Hammurabi of the First Dynasty of Babylon, while a different Hammurabi ruled the powerful Yamhad kingdom in northern Syria. In the middle of the millennium, Mursili I, king of the Hittites, conquered both Yamhad and the First Dynasty of Babylon.

The challenge is to relate these synchronisms and their associated regional chronologies with absolute dates. To do this, earlier generations of scholarship relied on observations of the planet Venus recorded in a group of Mesopotamian omen tablets called the Enuma Anu Enlil series, which dated to the reign of Ammi-saduqa of the First Dynasty of Babylon. These observations were related to a celestial cycle that repeats every sixty-four years, resulting in the proposal of three possible absolute chronologies, each associated with a different turn of the cycle ("high," "middle," and "low").[5] The majority of scholars adopted the Middle Chronology, dating Hammurabi of Babylon's reign to 1792–1750 B.C. and the fall of his dynasty to 1595 B.C.; this remains the chronological scheme in common use. Unfortunately, the credibility of the Venus text and its observations has been seriously questioned in recent years.[6]

Largely rejecting the use of the Venus tablets, a team of scholars led by Hermann Gasche has recently made a formidable attack on the Middle Chronology, advocating an "ultra-low" system that would place the fall of the First Dynasty of Babylon in 1499 B.C., roughly a century later than the date established by the Middle Chronology.[7] This proposal, based on a consideration of pottery, stratigraphy, texts, and astronomical data, would eliminate the Dark Age traditionally assigned to the sixteenth century B.C. and place the fall of Babylon just prior to the well-dated Kassite rulers of the fourteenth century B.C. Its proponents argue that the styles of pottery and other material culture from the era before the fall of Babylon are too similar to the styles of the fourteenth century B.C. to have been separated by such a long period of time. According to Gasche and his colleagues, "The pace of the shape-evolution of the vessels we have examined, especially the goblets, would be retarded tremendously in comparison with what happened before and after."[8] While this conclusion may well prove to be correct, it is by no means clear that modern scholars are able to assess the likelihood of different rates of material culture change in antiquity.[9] One might note, for example, the extraordinary conservatism of the texts from Terqa on the Middle Euphrates, in which tablets from the early second millennium B.C. were so similar to those from late in the millennium that scholars had first assumed they were written within a few decades of each other.[10]

If the Ultra-Low Chronology is correct and the Dark Age century eliminated,[11] a century must be added to one of the periods prior to the second millennium B.C. Champions of the Ultra-Low Chronology have not yet indicated which earlier period they would propose to lengthen.

Possible support for the Ultra-Low Chronology has been offered from the results of the excavations at Hazor in the southern Levant, a site mentioned in the Mari texts as an important city and a trading partner of the Mari king. According to its excavators, Hazor did not achieve an urban size and prosperity until the Middle Bronze IIB period, which must therefore correspond to the period of the Mari texts.[12] At Tell el-Dabʻa (Avaris) in northeastern Egypt, Levantine-style Middle Bronze IIB pottery was found in contexts associated with Dynasty 13 and assigned to the early seventeenth century B.C. As a result, excavators date the Middle Bronze IIB city of Hazor and, by extension, the Mari texts to the early seventeenth century B.C.[13] This conclusion is based on the assumption that Egyptian absolute chronology is relatively secure compared with that of western Asia. An early seventeenth-century B.C. date for the Mari archives diverges from the early- to mid-eighteenth-century B.C. date assigned by the Middle Chronology and conforms to the Ultra-Low Chronology. It remains to be seen whether the various strands of this argument, including the archaeological interpretation of Hazor's urban status, the ceramic parallels at Tell el-Dabʻa, and the absolute dating of the strata at Tell el-Dabʻa, are upheld.

Manfred Bietak, the excavator of Tell el-Dabʻa, has proposed that, apart from the dating of Hazor, the Egyptian dating of the Levantine materials from his site has wide repercussions for second-millennium B.C. Levantine chronology. He has proposed a lowering of the traditional dates for the Levantine Middle Bronze Age, placing its beginning at about 1900 B.C. as opposed to 2000 B.C. and the transition from Middle Bronze IIA to Middle Bronze IIB at about 1700 B.C. rather than 1800 B.C.[14] While some archaeologists working in the southern Levant have been amenable to this proposition, others, chief among them William G. Dever, have vehemently opposed it, rejecting Bietak's interpretation of both the Egyptian and Canaanite evidence.[15]

Turning to the natural sciences, two absolute dating methods are particularly relevant, although neither is without its problems. Dendrochronology dates samples of ancient wood by counting annual growth rings, a satisfyingly precise method. However, dendrochronology can inform only as to the year a tree was cut down, while wood components found in excavated buildings may have been used and reused for centuries after the tree was felled. Peter Kuniholm and his colleagues have been instrumental in providing a sequence of tree-ring dates for Anatolia spanning a millennium and a half, from the late third to the early first millennium B.C. Unfortunately, this sequence is "floating," that is, not yet anchored to a deposit with a known calendar-year date. A date range for this floating sequence has been proposed through the use of high-precision carbon-14 dates of wood samples from within the sequence.[16] The uncertainties of these methods are illustrated by the fact that the date range proposed in 1996 was in 2003 revised upward by twenty-two years.

Carbon-14 (radiocarbon) analysis allows for the dating of organic material through estimation of the number of years since the organism died, calculated through the assessment of the amount of decay of carbon-14 absorbed during the organism's lifetime. Contrary to the assumptions of the method's originators, however, the levels of atmospheric carbon-14 were not consistent through time, and thus carbon-14 dates must be calibrated by comparison to tree-ring data of known age (note how carbon-14 and dendrochronology are used as checks on one another). Adding a further note of uncertainty is the steady modification and revision of calibration methods and results over the past few decades.[17] Once a carbon-14 date is calibrated, it will often have a standard deviation that allows a confident assignment only within a century or two. Because the uncertainties in absolute chronology during the second millennium B.C. rarely involve much more than a century, the usefulness of the carbon-14 method has been limited. Radiocarbon dating, however, has grown increasingly precise in recent years, and the technique may provide much-needed assistance in the near future.

The most significant use of natural-science methods in addressing the problems of second-millennium B.C. chronology has involved a combination of dendrochronological and historical evidence. Excavations of the Sarıkaya palace at Acemhöyük in central Anatolia revealed clay seal impressions associated with the northern Mesopotamian king Shamshi-Adad I, presumably removed from deliveries of goods sent from his realm. Dendrochronological analysis of wood beams from the palace yielded a date of 1774 +4/-7 B.C., suggesting that Shamshi-Adad died sometime after that date—unless the sealings had been moved from an earlier building.[18] This result is important because Shamshi-Adad is known to have died midway through the reign of Hammurabi of Babylon. Dating Shamshi-Adad's reign from the late nineteenth to the early eighteenth century B.C. coincides with the traditional Middle Chronology dates.

Related data has recently been provided by analysis of the so-called Mari Eponym Chronicle, which records a solar eclipse observed in the year after Shamshi-Adad's birth. Bearing the Acemhöyük results in mind, Cécile Michel reviewed the years during which total solar eclipses occurred and proposed a date of 1834 B.C. for the birth of Shamshi-Adad.[19] Because Shamshi-Adad is said to have died seventy-three years after the eclipse, his death would be assigned to 1760 B.C., requiring a "modified" Middle Chronology that lowers the dates used for him in this volume by sixteen years. It must be noted, however, that the authenticity of the recorded event could be doubted, given the likely propagandistic intentions of the document from which it originated. Even if the eclipse were historical, it is uncertain where it was observed and whether it was total or partial.[20]

At present, there is no conclusive evidence to favor any of the competing approaches to absolute chronology for the early to mid-second millennium B.C. Scientific methods and historical sources all involve problems and uncertainties. Nevertheless, continuing refinement of natural-science methods, new or reanalyzed texts, bold reappraisals such as that of Gasche and his colleagues, and international chronological projects such as that organized by Bietak[21] bode well for future progress.

1. A. Ben-Tor 1992; Mellink 1992; Levy 1995; Akkermans and Schwartz 2003.
2. Porada et al. 1992.
3. Hagens 2005.
4. Beckman 2000; Wilhelm 2004.
5. Brinkman 1977; P. Åström 1987–89.
6. Cryer 1995; Reiner and Pingree 1975. Attempts to use lunar eclipses recorded in Enuma Anu Enlil are now subject to even greater doubt (Hunger 2000).
7. Gasche et al. 1998a; Gasche et al. 1998b.
8. Gasche et al. 1998a, p. 43.
9. For discussions of the Gasche chronology, see articles in *Just in Time: Akkadica* 199–120 (2000) and Seal 2001; Hunger and Pruzsinszky 2004; and Liverani 2005.
10. Podany 2002, p. 12.
11. Reade 2001, p. 15.
12. A. Ben-Tor 2004; Yadin 1972, pp. 2, 107–8.
13. A. Ben-Tor 2004.
14. Bietak 1997, pp. 124–28; Bietak 1991a. The Middle Bronze Age IIA is also referred to as Middle Bronze I by some archaeologists, and Middle Bronze IIB is termed Middle Bronze II.
15. Dever 1992; Dever 1997, pp. 294–95.
16. Kuniholm et al. 1996; Manning et al. 2001, Manning et al. 2003; Wiener 2003, Manning 2007; Wiener 2007.
17. See, e.g., Stuiver and Van der Plicht 1998 and Stuiver et al. 1998.
18. Manning et al. 2001. For questions concerning the context of the wood samples and sealings, see Pruzsinszky 2006, p. 74.
19. Michel and Rocher 1997–2000; Michel 2002.
20. Warburton 2002. See also C. Eder 2004 and Sassmanshausen 2006 for other recent chronological proposals.
21. Bietak's project is entitled SCIEM 2000: *The Synchronisation of Civilisations in the Eastern Mediterranean in the Second Millennium B.C.*

PROBLEMS OF CHRONOLOGY: EGYPT AND THE AEGEAN

ERIC H. CLINE

Relative dating is essentially settled for the second millennium B.C. in both the Aegean and Egypt. For example, we know the order in which the New Kingdom pharaohs ruled: Amenhotep III ruled earlier than did Tutankhamun, who in turn ruled earlier than did Ramesses II. We also know that the Late Bronze Age followed the Middle Bronze Age in both the Aegean and the ancient Near East. It is the absolute dating that poses the problems in both the Aegean and Egypt during the second millennium B.C. Attempting to determine the years during which a pharaoh ruled, or when an event such as the eruption of the Thera volcano in the Aegean took place, is not easy when dealing with people and events that occurred nearly four thousand years ago.

For example, until fairly recently, it was accepted by most Aegean prehistorians that the eruption of the volcanic island of Thera took place in approximately 1480 +/- B.C. (ca. 1525 B.C. when modified) and that the resulting volcanic ash, tephra, and other debris may have rained down upon the nearby island of Crete, dramatically affecting the crops and perhaps even paving the way for an invasion of Crete by Mycenaeans from the Greek mainland.[1] In the late 1980s and early 1990s, however, Philip

Betancourt and Sturt Manning published a series of initially independent articles suggesting that the eruption had taken place nearly 150 years earlier, in about 1628 B.C.[2] Their evidence, which eventually included radiocarbon dates from short-lived plants on the island of Thera itself as well as data from ice cores taken from as far away as Greenland, provoked a chronological debate that has to date lasted more than two decades and shows no indication of being resolved. As a result, two sets of chronologies for the Aegean area are currently in use: the so-called Traditional Chronology, which begins the Late Helladic and Late Minoan periods at about 1625 B.C. (in the modified version used in this catalogue),[3] and the High Chronology, which begins those periods at about 1700 B.C. (fig. 145).

There are similar problems in Egypt, where one finds High, Middle, Low, and Ultra-Low Chronologies in use by various archaeologists and Egyptologists.[4] While convention usually dictates the use of the Middle Chronology as a compromise, some scholars adhere vigorously to alternative schemes. As long as a scholar makes clear which chronology is being used and provides absolute dates (e.g., 1390–1352 B.C. for the reign of Amenhotep III), others can accordingly adjust their own dating schemes.

Aegean Period	Modified Traditional Chronology	High Chronology
LH I/LM IA	ca. 1625–1525 B.C. End of Hyksos period–beginning of Dynasty 18 Eruption of Thera, ca. 1525 B.C. (?)	ca. 1700–1610 B.C. Late Dynasty 13–Hyksos period Eruption of Thera, ca. 1628 B.C.
LH IIA/LM IB	ca. 1525–1450 B.C Early Dynasty 18–late in reign of Thutmose III	ca. 1610–1500 B.C Begins toward end of Hyksos period–early Dynasty 18
LH IIB/LM II	ca. 1450–1425 B.C Late in reign of Thutmose III–early reign of Amenhotep II	ca. 1500–1475 B.C Early Dynasty 18–early reign of Thutmose III
LH/LM IIIA:1	ca. 1425–1375 B.C Reign of Amenhotep II–early years of Amenhotep III	ca. 1475–1375 B.C Begins during reign of Thutmose III–reign of Amenhotep III
LH/LM IIIA:2 (early)	ca. 1375–1325 B.C Begins during reign of Amenhotep III–reign of Tutankhamun	ca. 1375–1325 B.C Begins during reign of Amenhotep III–reign of Tutankhamun
LH/LM IIIA:2 (late)– LH/LM IIIB	ca. 1325–1200 B.C Reign of Ay–reign of Merneptah	ca. 1325–1200 B.C Reign of Ay–reign of Merneptah
LH/LM IIIC	ca. 1200–1125 B.C Reign of Seti II–middle of Dynasty 20	ca. 1200–1125 B.C Reign of Seti II–middle of Dynasty 20

Figure 145. Modified Traditional versus High Chronology in the second millennium B.C.

Mycenaean pottery, a relatively rare import found at approximately thirty sites in Egypt—from Marsa Matruh on the northwest coast to Sesebi in the far south, including Tell el-Amarna, Rifeh, Gurob, Saqqara, Deir el Medina, and Qantir—has frequently been used to date stratigraphic levels at these sites. This creates a cycle of uncertainty, however, because Egyptian imports are frequently used to date stratigraphic levels in the Bronze Age Aegean, in part because they are also relatively rare imports and because they sometimes are inscribed with a king's or a queen's cartouche. Examples of such imports include two Egyptian Blue monkey figurines with the cartouche of Amenhotep II (1427–1400 B.C.), one found at Mycenae and one at Tiryns; an alabaster vase inscribed with the cartouche of Thutmose III (1479–1425 B.C.) at Katsamba on Crete; various objects of Amenhotep III (1390–1352 B.C.) and queen Tiye, including scarabs or seals at Knossos, Ayios Ilias, and Ayia Triada, and faience plaques at Mycenae; and two faience cartouches of Ramesses II (1279–1213 B.C.), found at Perati.[5]

Despite the inherent problems, general chronological correlations between the two areas can be made, in part because tomb paintings and literary references in Egypt during this time provide further evidence for contacts with the Late Bronze Age Aegean. For example, depictions of Aegean peoples, some specifically labeled as such, have been found in a number of Egyptian tombs primarily spanning the reigns of Thutmose III and Amenhotep III, including those of Senenmut, Rekhmire, Menkheperreseneb, Amenemhab, Kenamun, and Anen.[6] These images frequently include distinctive Aegean objects brought as gifts, or perhaps tribute, to the Egyptian pharaoh.

Of all the Egyptian paintings depicting Aegean peoples, places, or goods, the most recently discovered, and perhaps the most interesting, are those found by Manfred Bietak at Tell el-Dabʿa in the Nile Delta region of Egypt. Now identified as the site of ancient Avaris, capital city of the Hyksos, who ruled Lower Egypt from about 1640 to 1550 B.C., Tell el-Dabʿa was also rebuilt and reoccupied by the Egyptian rulers of Dynasty 18. The fragmentary paintings that adorned the walls of one or more palaces at the site were originally dated by Bietak and his team to the Hyksos period, just prior to the New Kingdom, but are now thought by the excavators to date to the fifteenth century B.C., the time of Thutmose III and a period of known—and relatively intense—contacts between Egypt and the Aegean.[7] The paintings have no identifying labels but depict unmistakably Aegean-looking people, including some leaping over bulls in front of a maze (fig. 39). It is startling to see such a fresco in Egypt, for these scenes are more usually associated with bull-leaping rituals on Minoan Crete.

In addition, references to Bronze Age Aegean peoples are far more common in Egypt than in any Near Eastern country during the second millennium B.C. For example, the term *Kft(j)w*, vocalized as Keftiu, is most likely the Egyptian name for the island of Crete and the Bronze Age Minoans. The term *Iww hryw-ib nw W3d-wr*, translated as "the Isles in the Midst of the Great Green," is usually taken as a reference to the Cycladic islands of the Aegean, perhaps including Crete. The term *Tj-n3-jj* is read as Tanaja (possibly vocalized as a variation of Danaoi) and is most likely a specific reference to the land of the Mycenaeans, situated in the Late Bronze Age Peloponnese on the Greek mainland. These three terms occur primarily during Dynasties 18, 19, and 20, but earlier references to Keftiu and to the Isles do occur. Later examples of all three terms can be found as well, although they probably represent copies rather than new occurences of these names.[8]

Textual references to Egypt and the Egyptians have been found in the Linear B texts of Bronze Age Aegean scribes. These appear in the tablets found at Knossos: *mi-sa-ra-jo* translates as "Egyptian" and *a₃-ku-pi-ti-jo* as "Memphite" or "Egyptian." The former term apparently derives from the Semitic word for Egypt, *Misr*, more commonly found in Akkadian and Ugaritic documents. The latter term may also derive from a Syro-Levantine reference to Egypt, for an Ugaritic name for both Egypt and the city of Memphis was *Hikupta*, which corresponds to the *Hikuptah* of the Amarna Letters and to *Hwt-k3-Pth* in Egyptian. It is found in a Linear B tablet at Knossos as the name of an individual who was in charge of a flock of eighty sheep at the Cretan site of Su-ri-mo. It is perhaps noteworthy that these two terms appear only at Knossos and not in the Linear B tablets found at other sites in the Aegean area.[9] Because debate continues and problems of chronology persist, correlations between the Bronze Age Aegean and Egypt during the second millennium B.C. will vary depending on whether the Traditional or the High Chronology is used.

Debate over the absolute dating of both the Aegean region and Egypt during the second millennium B.C. will undoubtedly continue for the foreseeable future. Changes in absolute dates, however, will probably be relatively minor, and we can rest assured that, at the very least, we have a fairly good grasp of the relative chronology of these two regions.

1. See Hankey and Warren 1974; Hankey 1987; Warren 1987; Warren and Hankey 1989; and Warren 1990.

2. Betancourt 1987; Manning 1988; Betancourt 1990; Manning 1991; see also Manning 1999; Friedrich et al. 2006; and Manning et al. 2006.

3. Koehl 2006, fig. 1, p. xxxiv.

4. See Helck 1987; Hornung 1987; Kitchen 1987; Kitchen 2000; Kitchen 2002; Wiener 2006a; Wiener 2006b; and, most recently, Hornung, Krauss, and Warburton 2006 and Bietak and Czerny 2007, with relevant bibliography.

5. For Bronze Age Aegean imports found in Egypt and Egyptian imports found in the Bronze Age Aegean, see Cline 1994, with updates in Cline 1999 and Cline 2007.

6. See Vercoutter 1956; Wachsmann 1987; and Cline 1994.

7. Bietak 1996; Bietak 2004 (with previous bibliography).

8. See Vercoutter 1956; Wachsmann 1987; and Cline 1994.

9. See discussions in Cline 1994 and Cline 1999.

INDEX TO FIGURES

BIBLIOGRAPHY

COMPILED BY JEAN WAGNER

ABBREVIATIONS USED IN NOTES

ARM = Archives royales de Mari
CMS = Corpus der minoischen und mykenischen Siegel
EA = Amarna (el-Amarna) Letters
LAPO = Littératures anciennes du Proche-Orient
PM I–IV = Arthur Evans, *The Palace of Minos at Knossos*, 1921–35.

WORKS CITED

Abdallah, F.
1996   "Palmyre dans le complexe économico-politique du XVIIIe
          siècle av. J.-C." *Annales archéologiques arabes syriennes* 42,
          pp. 131–35.

Adler, Hans-Peter
1976   *Das Akkadische des Königs Tušratta von Mitanni.* Neukirchen.

Adler, Wolfgang
1994   *Kamid el-Loz 11. Das "Schatzhaus" im Palastbereich: Die Befunde
          des Königsgrabes.* Saarbrücker Beiträge zur Altertumskunde 47.
          Bonn.
1996   "Die spätbronzezeitlichen Pyxiden in Gestalt von Wasser-
          vögeln." In *Kamid el-Lōz 16. "Schatzhaus"-Studien*, edited by
          Rolf Hachmann, pp. 29–117. Saarbrücker Beiträge zur
          Altertumskunde 59. Bonn.

Ägyptisches Museum Berlin
1967   *Ägyptisches Museum Berlin.* Foreword by Werner Kaiser. West
          Berlin: Staatliche Museen Preussischer Kulturbesitz.

Ahlström, Gösta
1993   *The History of Ancient Palestine.* Minneapolis.

Ahrens, Alexander
2005   "Einfluss—Übernahme—Variation: Die ägyptischen und
          ägyptisierenden Steingefässe aus der königlichen Grabanlage
          von Tall Mišrife/Qatna. Eine Untersuchung zu den Bezieh-
          ungen zwischen der nördlichen Levante und Ägypten im 2.
          Jahrtausend v. Chr." Master's thesis, Universität Tübingen.
2006   "A Journey's End—Two Egyptian Stone Vessels with
          Hieroglyphic Inscriptions from the Royal Tomb at Tell
          Mišrife/Qatna." *Ägypten und Levante/Egypt and the Levant* 16,
          pp. 15–36.

Akhenaten and Nefertiti
1973   *Akhenaten and Nefertiti.* Exhibition, Brooklyn Museum.
          Catalogue by Cyril Aldred. Brooklyn.

Akkermans, Peter M. M. G.
2006   "The Fortress of Ili-Pada: Middle Assyrian Architecture at
          Tell Sabi Abyad, Syria." In *Les espaces syro-mésopotamiens:
          Dimensions de l'expérience humaine au Proche-Orient ancien;
          volume d'hommage offert à Jean-Claude Margueron*, edited by
          P. Butterlin et al., pp. 201–11. Subartu, vol. 17. Turnhout.

Akkermans, Peter M. M. G., J. Limpens, and R. H. Spoor
1993   "On the Frontier of Assyria: Excavations at Tell Sabi Abyad,
          1991." *Akkadica* 84–85 (September–December), pp. 1–52.

Akkermans, Peter M. M. G., and Irene Rossmeisl
1990   "Excavations at Tell Sabi Abyad, Northern Syria: A Regional
          Centre on the Assyrian Frontier." *Akkadica* 66 (January–
          February), pp. 13–60.

Akkermans, Peter M. M. G., and Glenn M. Schwartz
2003   *The Archaeology of Syria: From Complex Hunter-Gatherers to
          Early Urban Societies (c. 16,000–300 BC).* Cambridge and
          New York.

Akkermans, Peter M. M. G., and Frans A. M. Wiggermann
1999   "Syrie: La forteresse de Tell Sabi Abyad: Sentinelle de l'empire
          assyrien." *Archéologia*, no. 358 (July–August), pp. 56–65.

Akrivaki, N.
2003   "Τοιχογραφία με παράσταση οδοντόφρακτου κράνους από την
          Ξεστή 4 του Ακρωτηρίου Θήρας." In Vlachopoulos and Birtacha
          2003, pp. 527–41.

Akurgal, Ekrem
1961   *Die Kunst der Hethiter.* Photographs by Max Hirmer. Munich.
1962   *The Art of the Hittites.* Translation of 1961 ed. by Constance
          McNab. Photographs by Max Hirmer. New York.

Albenda, Pauline
2005   "The 'Queen of the Night' Plaque—a Revisit." *Journal of the
          American Oriental Society* 125, pp. 171–90.

Albertarelli, Spartaco
2002   "Senet: A Different 'Gaming Concept.'" In *Step by Step:
          Proceedings of the 4th Colloquium Board Games in Academia*,
          edited by Jean Reschitzki and Rosita Haddah-Zubel,
          pp. 15–23. Fribourg.

Aldred, Cyril
1971   *Jewels of the Pharaohs: Egyptian Jewelry of the Dynastic Period.*
          New York.
1975   "Egypt: The Amarna Period and the End of the Eighteenth
          Dynasty." In *The Cambridge Ancient History*, vol. 2, part 2A,
          History of the Middle East and the Aegean Region, c. 1380–1000 B.C.,
          edited by I. E. S. Edwards et al., pp. 49–97. 3rd ed. Cambridge.
1991   *Akhenaten: King of Egypt.* New York.

Alexander, Robert L.
1985   "The Tyskiewicz Group of Stamp-Cylinders." *Anatolica* 5,
          pp. 141–215.

Al-Khalesi, Yasin M.
1978   *The Court of the Palms: A Functional Interpretation of the Mari
          Palace.* Bibliotheca Mesopotamica, vol. 8. Malibu.

Allen, James P.
2005   *The Art of Medicine in Ancient Egypt.* New York: The
          Metropolitan Museum of Art.
2008   Forthcoming article in *Bulletin of the American Schools of
          Oriental Research.*

Allen, Susan J., and James P. Allen
2006   *Tutankhamun's Tomb: The Thrill of Discovery.* Photographs by
          Harry Burton. New York: The Metropolitan Museum of Art.

Al-Maqdissi, Michel
1996   "Reprise des fouilles à Mishrifeh en 1994." *Akkadica* 99–100,
          pp. 1–14.
2001   "Kurzbericht über die syrischen Ausgrabungen in Misrife-
          Qatna." *Mitteilungen der Deutschen Orient-Gesellschaft zu Berlin*
          133, pp. 141–55.
2002a   "Ergebnisse der sechsten Kampagne der syrischen Aus-
          grabungen in Misrife-Qatna im Jahr 2000." *Mitteilungen der
          Deutschen Orient-Gesellschaft zu Berlin* 134, pp. 193–206.

2002b "Note sur les fouilles syriennes à Mishrifeh/Qatna (1994–2000)." *Florilegium Marianum* 6, pp. 105–17.

2003a "Ergebnisse der siebten und achten syrischen Grabungs-kampagnen 2001 und 2002 im Misrife-Qatna." *Mitteilungen der Deutschen Orient-Gesellschaft zu Berlin* 135, pp. 219–45.

2003b "Recherches archéologiques syriennes à Mishrifeh-Qatna au nord-est de Homs (Émèse)." *Comptes rendus de l'Académie des Inscriptions et Belles Lettres*, pp. 1487–1515.

2005 "Notes d'archéologie levantine, VI: À propos d'une statuette en basalte trouvée à Mishrifeh-Qatna." In "L'archeologia ritro-vata: Omaggio a Paolo Matthiae per il suo sessantacinquesimo anniversario," vol. 2, edited by J. M. Cordoba and L. C. del Cerro, *ISIMU* 8, pp. 49–55 (Arabian part).

2007a "Notes d'archéologie levantine, VI bis: À propos d'une statu-ette en basalte trouvée à Mishrifeh-Qatna." *Al-Rāfidān* 28, pp. 75–82.

2007b "Notes d'archéologie levantine X: Introduction aux travaux archéologiques syriens à Mishrifeh-Qatna au nord-est de Homs (Émèse)." In Morandi Bonacossi 2007, pp. 21–53.

Al-Maqdissi, Michel, et al.
2002 Michel Al-Maqdissi, M. Luciani, Danièle Morandi Bonacossi, M. Novák, and Peter Pfälzner, eds. *Excavating Qatna*. Vol. 1, *Preliminary Report on the 1999 and 2000 Campaigns of the Joint Syrian-Italian-German Archaeological Research Project at Tell Mishrife*. Documents d'archéologie syrienne, vol. 4. Damascus.

2003 Michel Al-Maqdissi, Heike Dohmann-Pfälzner, Peter Pfälzner, and Antoine Suleiman. "Das königliche Hypogäum von Qatna." *Mitteilungen der Deutschen Orient-Gesellschaft zu Berlin*, no. 135, pp. 189–218.

Al-Maqdissi, Michel, and M. Badawi
2002 "Rapport préliminaire sur la sixième campagne de fouilles syriennes à Mishrifeh/Qatna." In Al-Maqdissi et al. 2002, pp. 25–62.

Al-Maqdissi, Michel, and Danièle Morandi Bonacossi
2005 *The Metropolis of the Orontes: Art and Archaeology from the Ancient Kingdom of Qatna. Seven Years of Syrian-Italian Collaboration at Mishrifeh/Qatna*. Damascus.

Alp, Sedat
1950 "Bemerkungen zu den Hieroglyphen des hethtitischen Monuments von Imamkulu: Symboae Hrozny I." *Archiv orientální* 18 (1950), pp. 1–8.

1961–62 "Eine hethitische Bronzestatuette und andere Funde aus Zara bei Amasya." *Anatolia* 6, pp. 217–43.

1968 *Zylinder- und Stempelsiegel aus Karahöyük bei Konya*. Ankara.

1978–80 "Eine Sphinxvase aus Karahöyük bei Konya." *Anatolia* 21, pp. 9–16.

Altenmüller, Hartwig
1965 "Die Apotropaia und die Götter Mittelägyptens." 2 vols. Ph.D. diss., Ludwig-Maximilian-Universität zu München.

1983 "Ein Zaubermesser aus Tübingen." *Die Welt des Orients* 14, pp. 30–45.

1986 "Ein Zaubermesser des Mittleren Reiches." *Studien zur alt-ägyptischen Kultur* 13, pp. 1–27.

1987 "Totenglaube und Magie." In *La magia in Egitto ai tempi dei faraoni: Atti Convegno Internazionale di Studi Milano 29–31 ottobre 1985*, pp. 131–46. Verona.

Altenmüller, Hartwig, and Ahmed M. Moussa
1991 "Die Inschrift Amenemhets II. aus dem Ptah-Tempel von Memphis. Ein Vorbericht." *Studien für altägyptischen Kultur* 18, pp. 1–48.

American Discovery of Ancient Egypt
1995 *The American Discovery of Ancient Egypt*. Exhibition, Los Angeles County Museum of Art; Saint Louis Art Museum; Indianapolis Museum of Art. Catalogue edited by Nancy Thomas. Los Angeles.

Amiet, Pierre
1966 *Elam*. Auvers-sur-Oise.

1976 *Les antiquités du Luristan: Collection David-Weill*. Paris.

1977 *L'art antique du Proche-Orient ancien*. Paris.

1980 *Art of the Ancient Near East*. Translated by John Shepley and Claude Choquet. New York.

1988 *Suse, 6000 ans d'histoire*. Paris.

1992 *Sceaux-cylindres en hématite et pierres diverse*. Vol. 2 of *Corpus des cylindres de Ras Shamra-Ougarit*. Paris.

Amiran, Ruth
1970 *Ancient Pottery of the Holy Land, from Its Beginnings in the Neolithic Period to the End of the Iron Age*. New Brunswick, N.J.

1978 *Early Arad*. [Vol. 1], *The Chalcolithic Settlement and Early Bronze City*. Judean Desert Studies. Jerusalem.

Anati, E.
1959 "The Excavations at the Cemetery of Tell Abu Hawam (1952)." *'Atiqot* (English Series) 2, pp. 89–102.

Andrae, Walter
1925 *Coloured Ceramics from Ashur and Earlier Ancient Assyrian Wall-Paintings*. London.

1935 *Die jüngeren Ischtar-Tempel in Assur*. Wissenschaftliche Veröffentlichung der Deutschen Orient-Gesellschaft, vol. 58. Leipzig.

Andrae, Walter, and Carl Watzinger
1939 *Handbuch der Archäologie I*. Handbuch der Altertumswissen-schaften, ser. 6, part 1. Edited by W. Otto. Munich.

André-Salvini, Béatrice
2008 *Le code de Hammurabi*. 2nd ed. Paris. First published Paris, 2003.

Andrews, Carol
1990 *Ancient Egyptian Jewellery*. London.

1994 *Amulets of Ancient Egypt*. Austin, Tex.

Anthony, David W.
2007 *The Horse, the Wheel, and Language: How Bronze-Age Riders from the Eurasian Steppes Shaped the Modern World*. Princeton.

Aravantinos, V. L.
1984 "The Use of Sealings in the Administration of Mycenaean Palaces." In *Pylos Comes Alive: Industry and Administration in a Mycenaean Palace; Papers of a Symposium*, edited by Cynthia W. Shelmerdine and Thomas G. Palaima, pp. 41–48. New York.

Archanes
1997 Αρχάνες: Μία νέα ματιά στη μινωική Κρήτη. Exhibition, Mouseio Kykladikes Technes, Athens. Catalogue by Yannis Sakellarakis and Efi Sapouna-Sakellaraki [Athens].

Archi, Alfonso, and Paolo Matthiae
1979 "Una coppa d'argento con iscrizione cuneiforme dalla 'Tomba del Signore dei capridi.'" *Studi eblaiti* 1, pp. 191–93.

Areshian, Gregory E.
1988 "Éléments Indoeuropéans dans la mythologie du Plateau Arménien et du Caucase du Sud au IIe av. J.-C." In *Šulmu: Papers on the Ancient Near East*, edited by Petr Vavroušek and Vladimír Souček, pp. 19–37. Prague.

Arik, Remzi Oğuz
1937 *Les fouilles d'Alaca Höyük entreprises par la Société d'histoire turque: Rapport préliminaire sur les travaux en 1935*. Publications de la Société d'Histoire Turque, ser. 5, no. 1. Ankara.

Arnaud, Daniel
1967 "Contribution a l'étude de la métrologie syrienne au II millé-naire." *Revue d'assyriologie* 61, pp. 151–59.

Arnaud, Daniel, Yves Calvet, and Jean-Louis Huot
1979 "Ilšu-ibnišu, orfèvre de l'E.Babbar de Larsa; la Jarre L. 76.77 et son contenu." *Syria* 56, pp. 1–64.

457

Arnold, Dorothea
1977 "Zur Keramik aus dem Taltempelbereich der Pyramide Amenemhets III. in Daschur." *Mitteilungen des Deutschen Archäologischen Instituts Abteilung Kairo* 33, pp. 21–26.
1995 "An Egyptian Bestiary." *Metropolitan Museum of Art Bulletin*, n.s., 52, no. 4 (Spring).
2008 "Image and Identity: Egypt's Eastern Neighbours, East Delta People and the Hyksos." In *The Second Intermediate Period (13th–17th Dynasties): Current Research, Future Prospects*, edited by M. Marée. Leuven. In press.

Art of the First Cities
2003 *Art of the First Cities: The Third Millennium B.C. from the Mediterranean to the Indus*. Exhibition, Metropolitan Museum of Art, New York. Catalogue edited by Joan Aruz, with Ronald Wallenfels. New York.

Art Treasures of Turkey
1966 *Art Treasures of Turkey*. Exhibition circulated by the Smithsonian Institution; National Gallery of Art, Washington, D.C. Catalogue. Washington, D.C.

Artzy, Michal
1993 "Nami: Eight Years Later." *University of Haifa, Center for Maritime Studies News* 20, pp. 11–14.

Aruz, Joan
1993 "Crete and Anatolia in the Middle Bronze Age: Sealings from Phaistos and Karahöyük." In Mellink, Porada, and Özgüç 1993, pp. 35–54.
1995a "Syrian Seals and the Evidence for Cultural Interaction between the Levant and Crete." In *Sceaux minoens et mycéniens*, edited by Walter Müller, pp. 1–21. Corpus der minoischen und mykenischen Siegel, Beiheft 5. Berlin.
1995b "Imagery and Interconnections." *Ägypten und Levante / Egypt and the Levant* 5, pp. 33–48.
1995c "Cylinder Seal." In *Assyrian Origins* 1995, pp. 60–61, no. 41.
1997 "Cypriot and Cypro-Aegean Seals." In Caubet 1997, pp. 271–88.
1998 "The Aegean and the Orient: The Evidence of Stamp and Cylinder Seals." In Cline and Harris-Cline 1998, pp. 301–10.
2003 "Art and Interconnections in the Third Millennium, B.C." In *Art of the First Cities* 2003, pp. 239–50.
2005 "Unravelling the Mysteries of the Well-Travelled Seal." In Laffineur and Greco 2005, pp. 751–58.
2008a *Marks of Distinction: Seals and Cultural Exchange between the Aegean and the Orient (ca. 2600–1360 B.C.)*. Corpus der minoischen und mykenischen Siegel, Beiheft 7. Mainz am Rhein.
2008b "The Aegean or the Near East: Another Look at the Aigina Master of Animals." In Fitton 2008. In press.

Aslanidou, K.
2002 "Der Minoische Spiralfries aus dem Grabungsareal H/IV in Tell el-Dab'a: Malvorgang und Rekonstruktion." *Ägypten und Levante / Egypt and the Levant* 12, pp. 13–27.

Assante, Julia
2002 "Style and Replication in 'Old Babylonian' Terracotta Plaques." In *Ex Mesopotamia et Syria Lux: Festschrift für Manfried Dietrich zu seinem 65. Geburtstag*, edited by Oswald Loretz, Kai A. Metzler, and Hanspeter Schaudig, pp. 1–29. Alter Orient und Altes Testament, vol. 281. Münster.

Assmann, Jan
1983–84 "Krieg und Frieden im alten Ägypten: Ramses II, und die Schlacht bei Kadesh." *Mannheimer Forum* 83–84, pp. 175–231.
1995 *Egyptian Solar Religion in the New Kingdom: Re, Amun, and the Crisis of Polytheism*. Translated by Anthony Alcock. London and New York.
2002 "Echnaton, Tutanchamun und Moses: Ägypten im kulturellen Gedächtnis des Abendlandes." In *Mythos Tutanchamun*, edited by Wolfgang Wettengel, pp. 62–72. Karlsruhe.

Assyrian Origins
1995 *Assyrian Origins: Discoveries at Ashur on the Tigris. Antiquities in the Vorderasiatiches Museum, Berlin*. Exhibition, The Metropolitan Museum of Art, New York, May 2–August 13, 1995. Catalogue edited by Prudence O. Harper et al. New York.

Aston, Barbara, James A. Harrell, and Ian Shaw
2000 "Stone." In Nicholson and Shaw 2000, pp. 5–77.

Astour, Michael G.
2000 "Overland Trade Routes in Ancient Western Asia." In Sasson 2000, pp. 1401–20.

Åström, Lena
1967 *Studies on the Arts and Crafts of the Late Cypriote Bronze Age*. Lund.
1972 *The Late Cypriote Bronze Age: Other Arts and Crafts*. Contributions by Paul Åström, V. E. G. Kenna, and M. R. Popham. vol. 4, part 1D of *The Swedish Cyprus Expedition*. Lund.

Åström, Paul
1987–89 as editor. *High, Middle or Low?: Acts of an International Colloquium on Absolute Chronology Held at the University of Gothenburg 20th–22nd August 1987*. 3 vols. Göteborg.
1989 *Katydhata: A Bronze Age Site in Cyprus*. Studies in Mediterranean Archaeology, vol. 86. Göteborg.
1999 "The Cypriot Pottery from the Iria Shipwreck." In Phelps, Lolos, and Vichos 1999, pp. 131–38.

At That Time the Canaanites Were in the Land
1990 *Yeha-Kena'ani az ba-arets: Ḥaye yom-yom bi-Khena'an bi-teḳufat ha-Bronzah ha-tikhonah 2, 2000–1550 li-fen. ha-s. / At That Time the Canaanites Were in the Land: Daily Life in Canaan in the Middle Bronze Age 2, 2000–1550 B.C.E.* Exhibition, Eretz Israel Museum, Tel Aviv. Catalogue by Irit Ziffer. Tel Aviv.

Au pays de Baal et d'Astarté
1983 *Au pays de Baal et d'Astarté: 10,000 ans d'art en Syrie*. Exhibition, Musée du Petit Palais, Paris. Catalogue. Paris.

Avetisyan, Pavel, and Arsen Bobokhyan
2007 "The Pottery Traditions of the Armenian Middle to Late Bronze Age 'Transition' in the Context of Bronze and Iron Age Periodization." In *Ceramics in Transition: Chalcolithic through Iron Age in the Caucasus and Anatolia*, edited by Karen S. Rubinson and Antonia Sagona. Leuven. In press.

Avila, Robert A. J.
1983 *Bronzene Lanzen- und Pfeilspitzen der griechischen Spätbronzezeit*. Prähistorische Bronzefunde, ser. 5, vol. 1. Munich.

Babylone
2008 *Babylone*. Exhibition, Musée du Louvre, Paris; Pergamon Museum, Berlin; British Museum, London. Catalogue edited by Béatrice André-Salvini. Paris.

Bachhuber, Christoph
2003 "Aspects of Late Helladic Sea Trade." M.A. thesis, Texas A&M University, College Station, Tex.
2006 "Aegean Interest on the Uluburun Ship." *American Journal of Archaeology* 110, pp. 345–63.

Bachvarova, Mary R.
2005 "The Eastern Mediterranean Epic Tradition from *Bilgames and Akka* to the *Song of Release* to Homer's *Iliad*." *Greek, Roman, and Byzantine Studies* 45, no. 2 (Summer) pp. 131–53.

Baer, N. S., et al.
1971 N. S. Baer, N. Indictor, J. H. Frantz, and B. Appelbaum. "The Effect of High Temperature on Ivory." *Studies in Conservation* 16, pp. 1–8.

Baer, N. S., T. Jochsberger, and N. Indictor
1978 "Chemical Investigations on Ancient Near Eastern Archaeological Ivory Artifacts: Fluorine and Nitrogen Composition."

In *Archaeological Chemistry II: Based on a Symposium Sponsored by the Division of the History of Chemistry at the 174th Meeting of the American Chemical Society, Chicago, August 31–September 1, 1977*, edited by Giles F. Carter, pp. 139–49. Advances in Chemistry Series, no. 171. Washington, D.C.

Bahrani, Zainab
2000   "Jewelry and Personal Arts in Ancient Western Asia." In Sasson 2000, pp. 1635–45.
2001   *Women of Babylon: Gender and Representation in Mesopotamia.* London.
2002   "Performativity and the Image: Narrative, Representation, and the Uruk Vase." In *Leaving No Stones Unturned: Essays on the Ancient Near East and Egypt in Honor of Donald P. Hansen*, edited by Erica Ehrenberg, pp. 15–22. Winona Lake, Ind.
2003   *The Graven Image: Representation in Babylonia and Assyria.* Philadelphia.
2007   "The Babylonian Visual Image." In *The Babylonian World*, edited by Gwendolyn Leick, pp. 155–70. New York and London.

Baines, John, and Jaromír Malék
2000   *Cultural Atlas of Ancient Egypt.* New York.

Balkan, Kemal
1957   *Letter of King Anum-hirbi of Mama to King Warshama of Kanish.* Türk Tarih Kurumu Yayınlarından 7, no. 31a. Ankara.

Ballard, Robert D., et al.
2002   Robert D. Ballard, Lawrence E. Stager, Daniel Master, Dana Yoerger, David Mindell, Louis L. Whitcomb, Hanumant Singh, and Dennis Piechota. "Iron Age Shipwrecks in Deep Water off Ashkelon, Israel." *American Journal of Archaeology* 106, pp. 151–68.

Banks, Edgar J.
1912   *Bismaya; or, The Lost City of Adab: A Story of Adventure, of Exploration, and of Excavation among the Ruins of the Oldest of the Buried Cities of Babylonia.* New York and London.

Baqir, Taha
1944   *Iraq Government Excavations at 'Aqar Qūf: First Interim Report, 1942–1943.* Iraq Supplement. London.
1945   *Iraq Government Excavations at 'Aqar Qūf: Second Interim Report, 1943–1944.* Iraq Supplement. London.
1946   "Iraq Government Excavations at 'Aqar Qūf: Third Interim Report, 1944–1945." *Iraq* 8, pp. 73–93.

Barag, Dan
1970   "Mesopotamian Core-formed Glass Vessels." In Oppenheim et al. 1970, pp. 131–97.
1988   Reprint of Barag 1970.

Baramki, Dimitri C.
1967   *The Archaeological Museum of the American University of Beirut.* Beirut.
1973   "A Tomb of the Early and Middle Bronze Age at Byblos." *Bulletin du Musée de Beyrouth* 26, pp. 27–30.

Barber, E. J. W.
1991   *Prehistoric Textiles: The Development of Cloth in the Neolithic and Bronze Ages, with Special Reference to the Aegean.* Princeton.

Barclay, Alison
2001   "The 'Potnia Theron': Adaptation of a Near Eastern Image." In Laffineur and Hägg 2001, pp. 373–86.

Bardet, Guillaume, et al., eds.
1984   *Archives administratives de Mari.* Vol. 1. Archives royales de Mari (Romanized version), vol. 23. Paris.

Barjamovic, Gojko
2008   "The Geography of Trade: Assyrian Colonies in Anatolia, c. 1975–1725 BC and the Study of Early Interregional Networks of Exchange." In *Anatolia and the Jazira during the Old Assyrian Period*, edited by J. G. Dercksen, pp. 87–100. Old Assyrian Archives, Studies, vol. 3. Leiden.

Barnett, Richard D.
1935   "The Nimrud Ivories and the Art of the Phoenicians." *Iraq* 2, pp. 179–210.
1939   "Phoenician and Syrian Ivory Carving." *Palestine Exploration Quarterly* 71, pp. 4–19.
1969   "Anat, Ba'al, and Pasargadae." *Mélanges de l'Université Saint-Joseph* 45, pp. 407–11.
1975   *A Catalogue of the Nimrud Ivories; with Other Examples of Ancient Near Eastern Ivories in the British Museum.* 2nd ed. London.
1982   *Ancient Ivories in the Middle East.* Qedem 14. Jerusalem: Institute of Archaeology, Hebrew University of Jerusalem.

Barrelet, Marie-Thérèse
1955   "Les déesses armées et ailées." *Syria* 32, pp. 222–60.
1958   "Deux déesses syro-phéniciennes sur un bronze du Louvre." *Syria* 35, pp. 27–44.

Basedow, Maureen
2007   "Troy without Homer: The Bronze Age–Iron Age Transition in the Troad." In Morris and Laffineur 2007, pp. 49–58.

Bass, George F.
1963   "Mycenaean and Protogeometric Tombs in the Halicarnassus Peninsula." *American Journal of Archaeology* 67, pp. 353–61.
1967   *Cape Gelidonya: A Bronze Age Shipwreck.* Transactions of the American Philosophical Society 57, part 8. Philadelphia.
1973   "Cape Gelidonya and Bronze Age Maritime Trade." In *Orient and Occident: Essays Presented to Cyrus H. Gordon on the Occasion of His Sixty-fifth Birthday*, edited by Harry A. Hoffner, pp. 29–38. Alter Orient und Altes Testament, vol. 22. Kevelaer.
1986   "A Bronze Age Shipwreck at Ulu Burun (Kaş): 1984 Campaign." *American Journal of Archaeology* 90, pp. 269–96.
1990   "A Bronze-Age Writing-Diptych from the Sea of Lycia." *Kadmos: Zeitschrift für vor- und frühgriechische Epigraphik* 29, no. 2, pp. 168–69.
1991   "Evidence of Trade from Bronze Age Shipwrecks." In Gale 1991a, pp. 69–82.
1997   "Prolegomena to a Study of Maritime Traffic in Raw Materials to the Aegean during the Fourteenth and Thirteenth Centuries, B.C." In Laffineur and Betancourt 1997, pp. 153–70.
2000   "Sea and River Craft in the Ancient Near East." In Sasson 2000, pp. 1421–31.
2004   "Personal Effects." In *Serce Limani: An Eleventh-Century Shipwreck.* Vol. 1, *The Ship and Its Anchorage, Crew, and Passengers*, edited by Geoge F. Bass, pp. 275–87. College Station, Tex.

Bass, George F., et al.
1989   George F. Bass, Cemal Pulak, Dominique Collon, and James Weinstein. "The Bronze Age Shipwreck at Ulu Burun: 1986 Campaign." *American Journal of Archaeology* 93, pp. 1–29.

Bass, George F., D. A. Frey, and Cemal Pulak
1984   "A Late Bronze Age Shipwreck at Kaş, Turkey." *International Journal of Nautical Archaeology* 13, no. 4, pp. 271–79.

Baumann, Hellmut
1982   *Die griechische Pflanzenwelt in Mythos, Kunst und Literatur.* Munich.

Baurain, Claude, and Corinne Bonnet
1992   *Les Phéniciens: Marins des trois continents.* Paris.

Bayliss, Miranda
1973   "The Cult of Dead Kin in Assyria and Babylonia." *Iraq* 35, pp. 115–25.

Beck, Horace C.
1981   *Classification and Nomenclature of Beads and Pendants.* York, Pa. Reprint of paper published in *Archaeologia* 77 (1928).

Becker, Andrea
2007   "The Royal Game of Ur." In Finkel 2007a, pp. 11–15.

Beckman, Gary
1996   *Hittite Diplomatic Texts.* Writings from the Ancient World, vol. 7. Atlanta.
1999   *Hittite Diplomatic Texts.* 2nd ed. Writings from the Ancient World, vol. 7. Atlanta.
2000   "Hittite Chronology." *Akkadica* 119–20 (September–December), pp. 19–32.
2003   "International Law in the Second Millennium, Late Bronze Age." In *A History of Ancient Near Eastern Law*, edited by Raymond Westbrook, pp. 753–74. Handbook of Oriental Studies, section 1, The Near and Middle East, vol. 72. Leiden and Boston.

Bellamy, Ralph
1989   "Bellerophon's Tablet." *Classical Journal* 84, no. 4, pp. 289–307.

Ben-Arieh, S., and G. Edelstein
1977   "Tombs near the Persian Garden: The Tombs and Their Contents." *'Atiqot* (English Series) 12, pp. 1–44.

Benson, J. L.
1972   *Bamboula at Kourion: The Necropolis and the Finds Excavated by J. F. Daniel.* Museum Monograph of the University Museum. Philadelphia.
1973   *The Necropolis of Kaloriziki. Excavated by J. F. Daniel and G. H. McFadden for the University Museum, University of Pennsylvania, Philadelphia.* Studies in Mediterranean Archaeology, vol. 36. Göteborg.

Bentley, Jerry H.
2006   "Beyond Modernocentrism: Toward Fresh Visions of the Global Past." In *Contact and Exchange in the Ancient World*, edited by Victor H. Mair. Honolulu.

Ben-Tor, Amnon
1992   as editor. *The Archaeology of Ancient Israel.* Translated by R. Greenberg. New Haven.
2004   "Hazor and Chronology." *Ägypten und Levante / Egypt and the Levant* 14, pp. 45–68.

Ben-Tor, Daphna
2007   *Scarabs, Chronology, and Interconnections: Egypt and Palestine in the Second Intermediate Period.* Orbis Biblicus et Orientalis, Series Archaeologica, vol. 27. Fribourg and Göttingen.

Ben-Tor, Daphna, Susan J. Allen, and James P. Allen
1999   "Seals and Kings," review of Ryholt 1997. *Bulletin of the American Schools of Oriental Research*, no. 315, pp. 47–74.

Benzi, Mario
1984   "Evidence for a Middle Minoan Settlement on the Acropolis at Ialysos (Mt. Philerimos)." In Hägg and Marinatos 1984, pp. 93–104.
1992   *Rodi e la civiltà micenea.* 2 vols. Incunabula Graeca, vol. 94. Rome.
1999   "Riti di passagio sulla larnax della tomba 22 di Tanagra?" In *Epi ponton plazomenoi: Simposio italiano di studi egei dedicato a Luigi Bernabò Brea e Giovanni Pugliese Carratelli*, edited by Vincenzo La Rosa, Dario Palermo, Lucia Vagnetti, pp. 215–33. Rome.

Beran, Th.
1958   "Die babylonische Glyptik der Kassitenzeit." *Archiv für Orientforschung* 18, pp. 255–78.

Berman, L. M., and Betsy M. Bryan
1992   "Three Carved Gems." In *Egypt's Dazzling Sun* 1992, pp. 442–44.

Betancourt, Philip P.
1985   *The History of Minoan Pottery.* Princeton.
1987   "Dating the Aegean Late Bronze Age with Radiocarbon." *Archaeometry* 29, pp. 45–49.
1990   "High Chronology or Low Chronology: The Archaeological Evidence." In Hardy and Renfrew 1990, vol. 3, *Chronology*, pp. 19–23.
1997   "Relations between the Aegean and the Hyksos at the End of the Middle Bronze Age." In Oren 1997a, pp. 429–32.
1998   "Middle Minoan Objects in the Near East." In Cline and Harris-Cline 1998, pp. 5–10.

Betancourt, Philip P., et al.
1999   Philip P. Betancourt, Vassos Karageorghis, Robert Laffineur, and Wolf-Dietrich Niemeier, eds. *Meletemata: Studies in Aegean Archaeology Presented to Malcolm H. Weiner as He Enters His 65th Year.* Aegaeum 20. Liège and Austin.

Betts, John H.
1997   "Minoan and Mycenaean Seals." In *7000 Years of Seals*, edited by Dominique Collon, pp. 54–73. London: British Museum Press.

Beyer, Dominique
1982   *Meskéné–Emar: Dix ans de travaux, 1972–1982.* Paris.
1997   "Emar et Ougarit: Réflexions sur la glyptique de deux villes de Syrie du Nord vers la fin de l'Âge du Bronze." In Caubet 1997, pp. 169–83.

Bichta, K.
2003   "Luxuria ex Oriente: Ένα Προϊστορικό Ταξίδι από τη Θήρα στην Ανατολή." In Vlachopoulos and Birtacha 2003, pp. 545–47.

Bietak, Manfred
1975   *Tell el-Dab'a II: Der Fundort im Rahmen einer archäologisch-geographischen Untersuchung über das ägyptische Ostdelta.* Untersuchungen der Zweigstelle Kairo des Österreichischen Archäologischen Institutes 2. Vienna.
1981   *Avaris and Piramesse. Archaeological Exploration in the Eastern Nile Delta.* Ninth Mortimer Wheeler Archaeological Lecture. Oxford. Originally published in the *Proceedings of the British Academy, London* 65 (1979), pp. 225–90. 2nd ed., Oxford, 1986.
1991a   "Egypt and Canaan during the Middle Bronze Age." *Bulletin of the American Schools of Oriental Research*, no. 281, pp. 27–72.
1991b   *Tell el-Dab'a V: Ein Friedhofsbezirk der Mittleren Bronzezeitkultur mit Totentempel und Siedlungsschichten.* Part 1. Vienna.
1996   *Avaris, the Capital of the Hyksos: Recent Excavations at Tell el-Dab'a.* London: British Museum Press.
1997   "Avaris, Capital of the Hyksos Kingdom: New Results of Excavations." In Oren 1997a, pp. 87–140.
2000a   as editor. *The Synchronisation of Civilisations in the Eastern Mediterranean in the Second Millennium B.C.: Proceedings of an International Symposium at Schloss Haindorf, 15th–17th of November 1996 and at the Austrian Academy, Vienna, 11th–12th of May 1998.* Contributions to the Chronology of the Eastern Mediterranean, vol. 1; Österreichische Akademie der Wissenschaften, Denkschriften der Gesamtakademie, vol. 19. Vienna.
2000b   "'Rich beyond the Dreams of Avaris': Tell el-Dab'a and the Aegean World—A Guide for the Perplexed." A Response to Eric H. Cline. *Annual of the British School at Athens* 95, pp. 185–205.
2002a   as editor. *The Middle Bronze Age in the Levant: Proceedings of an International Conference on MB IIA Ceramic Material, Vienna, 24th–26th of January 2001.* Contributions to the Chronology of the Eastern Mediterranean, vol. 3. Vienna.
2002b   "Relative and Absolute Chronology of the Middle Bronze Age: Comments on the Present State of Research." In Bietak 2002a, pp. 29–41.
2004   Review of Manning 1999. *Bibliotheca Orientalis* 61, pp. 199–222.
2007   "Bronze Age Paintings in the Levant: Chronological and Cultural Considerations." In Bietak and Czerny 2007, pp. 269–300.

Bietak, Manfred, et al.

1994   Manfred Bietak, J. Dorner, I. Hein, and Peter Jánosi. "Neue Grabungsergebnisse aus Tell el-Dab'a und Ezbet Helmi im Östlichen Nildelta 1989–1991." *Ägypten und Levante / Egypt and the Levant* 4, pp. 9–80.

Bietak, Manfred, and Ernst Czerny, eds.

2003   *The Synchronisation of Civilisations in the Eastern Mediterranean in the Second Millennium B.C. II.: Proceedings of the SCIEM 2000—EuroConference Haindorf, 2nd of May–7th of May 2001.* Contributions to the Chronology of the Eastern Mediterranean, vol. 4; Österreichische Akademie der Wissenschaften, Denkschriften der Gesamtakademie, vol. 29. Vienna.

2004   *Scarabs of the Second Millennium BC from Egypt, Nubia, Crete, and the Levant: Chronological and Historical Implications. Papers of a Symposium, Vienna, 10th–13th of January 2002.* Contributions to the Chronology of the Eastern Mediterranean, vol. 8; Österreichischen Akademie der Wissenschaften Denkschriften der Gesamtakademie, vol. 35. Vienna.

2007   *The Synchronisation of Civilisations in the Eastern Mediterranean in the Second Millennium B.C. III: Proceedings of the SCIEM 2000 – 2nd EuroConference, Vienna, 28th of May–1st of June 2003.* Contributions to the Chronology of the Eastern Mediterranean, vol. 9; Österreichische Akademie der Wissenschaften, Denkschriften der Gesamtakademie, vol. 37. Vienna.

Bietak, Manfred, and Irene Forstner-Müller

2005   "Ausgrabung eines Palastbezirkes der Tuthmosidenzeit bei 'Ezbet Helmi / Tell El-Dab'a, Vorbericht für Herbst 2004 und Frühjahr 2005." *Ägypten und Levante / Egypt and the Levant* 15, pp. 65–100.

2008   "The Topography of New Kingdom Avaris and Pi-Ramesse." In *Ramesside Studies*, edited by S. Snape and M. Collier. Bolton: Rutherford Press. In press.

Bietak, Manfred, and Nannó Marinatos

2000   "Avaris and the Minoan World." In Karetsou 2000, pp. 40–44.

Bietak, Manfred, Nannó Marinatos, and Klaire Palyvou

2000   "The Maze Tableau from Tell el Dab'a." In Sherratt 2000, pp. 77–90.

2007   *Taureador Scenes in Tell el-Dab'a (Avaris) and Knossos.* With a contribution by Ann Brysbaert. Untersuchungen der Zweigstelle Kairo des Österreichischen Archäologischen Institutes 27. Vienna.

Biran, Avraham

1970   "Notes and News: Tel Dan." *Israel Exploration Journal* 20, pp. 118–19.

1971   "Laish-Dan: Secrets of a Canaanite City and an Israelite City." *Qadmoniot* 4, pp. 2–10.

1994   *Biblical Dan.* Jerusalem.

Biran, Avraham, and Rachel Ben-Dov

2002   *Dan II: A Chronicle of the Excavations and the Late Bronze Age "Mycenaean" Tomb.* Annual of the Nelson Glueck School of Biblical Archaeology. Jerusalem.

Birot, Maurice, trans.

1974   *Lettres de Yaqqim-Addu, gouverneur de Sagarâtum.* Archives royales de Mari, vol. 14. Paris.

von Bissing, Friedrich Wilhelm, Freiherr, ed.

1900   *Ein thebanischer Grabfund aus dem Anfang des Neuen Reichs.* Berlin.

Bisson de la Roque, Fernand

1937   *Tôd.* Fouilles de l'Institut Français d'Archéologie Orientale, vol. 17. Cairo.

1950   *Catalogue général des antiquités égyptiennes du musée du Caire: Trésor de Tôd.* Cairo.

Bisson de la Roque, Fernand, Georges Contenau, and Fernand Chapouthier

1953   *Le trésor de Tôd.* Documents de fouilles, vol. 11. Cairo.

Bittel, Kurt

1955   "Vorläufiger Bericht über die Ausgrabungen in Boğazköy im Jahre 1954." *Mitteilungen der Deutschen Orient-Gesellschaft zu Berlin* 88, pp. 1–36.

1957a   "Armförmige Libationsgefässe." In Bittel et al. 1957, pp. 33–42.

1957b   "Vorläufiger Bericht über die Ausgrabungen in Boğazköy im Jahre 1956." *Mitteilungen der Deutschen Orient-Gesellschaft zu Berlin* 89, pp. 6–25.

1976a   *Beitrag zur Kenntnis hethitischer Bildkunst* [lecture delivered on June 21, 1975]. *Sitzungsberichte der Heidelberger Akademie der Wissenschaften, Philosophisch–historische Klasse, Jahrg. 1976, 4. Abhandlung* [Winter]. Heidelberg.

1976b   *Die Hethiter: Die Kunst Anatoliens vom Ende des 3. bis zum Anfang des 1. Jahrtausends v. Chr.* Universum der Kunst, vol. 24. Munich.

1976c   *Les Hittites.* Translated from German by François Poncet. L'univers des formes 24. Paris.

1976d   "Tonschale mit Ritzzeichnung von Boğazköy." *Revue archéologique: Études sur les relations entre Grèce et Anatolie offertes à Pierre Demargne*, n.s., 1, no. 1, pp. 9–14.

Bittel, Kurt, et al.

1957   Kurt Bittel, Rudolf Naumann, Th. Beran, Rolf Hachmann, and G. Kurth. *Boğazköy.* Vol. 3, *Funde aus den Grabungen, 1952–1955.* Berlin.

1975   *Das hethitische Felsheiligtum Yazilikaya.* Vol. 9 of *Boğazköy-Hattuša.* Berlin.

Black, Jeremy, and Anthony Green

1992   *Gods, Demons, and Symbols of Ancient Mesopotamia: An Illustrated Dictionary.* London: British Museum Press.

Blackman, Aylward M.

1914   *The Rock Tombs of Meir.* Vol. 1, *The Tomb-Chapel of Ukh-Hotp's Son senbi (B, no. 2).* London.

Blegen, Carl W., and Elizabeth P. Blegen

1937   *Prosymna: The Helladic Settlement Preceding the Argive Heraeum.* 2 vols. Cambridge.

Blegen, Carl W., John L. Caskey, and Marion Rawson

1953   *Troy.* Vol. 3, *The Sixth Settlement, Part 1.* Princeton.

Bloedow, Edmund F.

1992   "On Lions in Mycenaean and Minoan Culture." In Laffineur and Crowley 1992, pp. 295–304.

1999   "On Hunting Lions in Bronze Age Greece." In Betancourt et al. 1999, vol. 1, pp. 53–61.

2007   "Homer and the *Depas Amphikypellon*." In Morris and Laffineur 2007, pp. 87–95.

Boardman, John

1967   *Excavations in Chios, 1952–1955: Greek Emporio.* British School of Archaeology at Athens Supplementary Series, no. 6. London.

1970   *Greek Gems and Finger Rings: Early Bronze Age to Late Classical.* London.

Bodinaku, N.

1995   "The Late Bronze Age Culture of Albania and the Relations with the Balcanic and Aegean-Adriatic Areas." In *Handel, Tausch und Verkehr im bronze- und früheisenzeitlichen Südosteuropa*, edited by Bernhard Hänsel, pp. 259–68. Südosteuropa-Schriften, vol. 17; Prähistorische Archäologie in Südosteuropa, vol. 11. Munich and Berlin.

Boehmer, Rainer Michael

1965   *Die Entwicklung der Glyptik während der Akkad-Zeit.*
        Untersuchungen zur Assyriologie und vorderasiatischen
        Archäologie, vol. 4. Berlin.

1972   *Die Kleinfunde von Boğazköy aus der Grabungskampagnen
        1931–1939 und 1952–1969.* Wissenschaftliche Veröffent-
        lichung der Deutschen Orient-Gesellschaft, vol. 87. Berlin.

Boehmer, Rainer Michael, and Heinz-Werner Dämmer

1985   *Tell Imlihiye, Tell Zubeidi, Tell Abbas.* Baghdader Forschungen
        7. Mainz am Rhein.

Boehmer, Rainer Michael, and Hans-Gustav Güterbock

1987   *Glyptik aus dem Stadtgebiet von Boğazköy: Grabungskampagnen,
        1931–1939, 1952–1978.* Part 2 of *Die Glyptik von Boğazköy.*
        Berlin.

Boehmer, Rainer Michael, and Georg Kossack

2000   "Der figürlich verzierte Becher von Karašamb." In *Variatio
        Delectat: Iran und der Westen; Gedenkschrift für Peter Calmeyer,*
        edited by Reinhard Dittmann, pp. 9–71. Alter Orient und
        Altes Testament, vol. 272. Münster.

Boessneck, Joachim

1988   *Die Tierwelt des alten Ägypten: Untersucht anhand kulturgeschicht-
        licher und zoologischer Quellen.* Munich.

Bonnet, Charles

1986   *Kerma, territoire et métropole: Quatre leçons au Collège de France.*
        Institut Français d'Archéologie Orientale du Caire, Bibliothèque
        Générale, vol. 9. Cairo.

2004   "The Kerma Culture" and "Kerma." In *Sudan: Ancient Treasures,*
        edited by Derek A. Welsby and Julie R. Anderson, pp. 70–77,
        78–82. London.

Borchardt, Ludwig

1907   *Das Grabdenkmal des Königs Ne-user-re'.* Ausgrabungen der
        Deutschen Orient-Gesellschaft in Abusir, 1902–1904, vol. 1.
        Leipzig.

1910   *Das Grabdenkmal des Königs S'aʒḥu-re'.* 2 vols. Ausgrabungen
        der Deutschen Orient-Gesellschaft in Abusir, 1902– ,
        vols. 6–7. Leipzig.

1911   *Der Porträtkopf der Königin Teje im Besitz von Dr. James Simon
        in Berlin.* Deutsche Orient-Gesellschaft, Ausgrabungen in Tell
        el-Amarna, vol. 1. Leipzig.

Borchhardt, Jürgen

1972   *Homerische Helme: Helmformen der Ägäis in ihren Beziehungen
        zu orientalischen und europäischen Helmen in der Bronze- und
        Frühen Eisenzeit.* Mainz am Rhein.

Börker-Klähn, Jutta

1982   *Altvorderasiatische Bildstelen und vergleichbare Felsreliefs.*
        2 vols. Baghdader Forschungen, vol. 4. Mainz am Rhein.

Boss, M., and Robert Laffineur

1997   "Mycenaean Metal Inlay: A Technique in Context." In
        Laffineur and Betancourt 1997, pp. 191–97.

Bossert, Helmuth T.

1942   *Altanatolien: Kunst und Handwerk in Kleinasien von den Anfängen
        bis zum völligen Aufgehen in der griechischen Kultur.* Berlin.

1951   as editor. *Altsyrien: Kunst und Handwerk in Cypern, Syrien,
        Palästina, Transjordanien und Arabien von den Anfängen bis zum
        völligen Aufgehen in der griechisch-römischen Kultur.* Tübingen.

Boulotis, C.

1988   "Fresco Fragment" and "Plaque with Cult Scene ('Palladion')."
        In *Mycenaean World: Five Centuries* 1988, pp. 181–82, 189.

Bourgeois, B.

1992   "An Approach to Anatolian Techniques of Ivory Carving
        during the Second Millennium B.C." In Fitton 1992, pp. 61–66.

Bourriau, Janine

1994   "Delphinkrug." In *Pharaonen und Fremde* 1994, pp. 233–34,
        no. 288.

1997   "The Dolphin Vase from Lisht." In *Studies in Honor of William
        Kelly Simpson,* edited by Peter der Manuelian, vol. 1, pp. 101–16.
        Boston.

Bourriau, Janine, Laurence Smith, and Margaret Serpico

2001   "The Provenance of Canaanite Amphorae Found at Memphis
        and Amarna in the New Kingdom." In *The Social Context of
        Technological Change: Egypt and the Near East, 1650–1550 BC:
        Proceedings of a Conference Held at St. Edmund Hall, Oxford
        12–14 September 2000,* edited by Andrew J. Shortland,
        pp. 113–46. Oxford.

Bouzek, Jan

1985   *The Aegean, Anatolia, and Europe: Cultural Interrelations in the
        Second Millennium B.C.* Studies in Mediterranean Archaeology,
        vol. 29. Göteborg.

Bovot, Jean-Luc

1994   "Kachel gebundener Asiate." In *Pharaonen und Fremde* 1994,
        p. 277, no. 386.

Boysal, Yusuf

1964   "Milli Eğitim Bakanlığı Müsgebi Kazisi 1963 Yılı Kısa
        Raporu." *Türk Arkeoloji Dergisi* 13, no. 2, pp. 81–85.

1969a   "New Excavations in Caria." *Anadolu* 11, pp. 31–56.

1969b   *Katalog der Vasen im Museum in Bodrum.* Vol. 1, *Mykenisch,
        Protogeometrisch.* Ankara.

Braidwood, Robert J.

1937   *Mounds in the Plain of Antioch: An Archaeological Survey.*
        University of Chicago, Oriental Institute Publications, vol. 48.
        Chicago.

Braudel, Fernand

2001   *Memory and the Mediterranean.* Translated by Siân Reynolds.
        New York.

Braun-Holzinger, Eva Andrea

1984   *Figürliche Bronzen aus Mesopotamien.* Prähistorische Bronze-
        funde, ser. 1, vol. 4. Munich.

Breasted, James H.

1906   *Ancient Records of Egypt: Historical Documents from the Earliest
        Times to the Persian Conquest.* Vol. 2, *The Eighteenth Dynasty.*
        Chicago.

1962   *Ancient Records of Egypt: Historical Documents from the Earliest
        Times to the Persian Conquest, Collected, Edited, and Translated
        with Commentary.* 5 vols. New York.

Brill, Robert H.

1999   *Chemical Analyses of Early Glasses.* 2 vols. Corning, N.Y.:
        Corning Museum of Glass.

Brill, Robert H., and H. Shirahata

1997   "Laboratory Analysis of Some Glasses and Metals from Tell
        Brak." In Oates, Oates, and McDonald 1997, pp. 89–94.

Brinkman, J. A.

1976   *Materials and Studies for Kassite History.* Vol. 1, *A Catalogue of
        Cuneiform Sources Pertaining to Specific Monarchs of the Kassite
        Dynasty.* Chicago.

1976–80 "Kassiten." In *Reallexikon der Assyriologie und Vorderasiatischen
        Archäologie,* edited by E. Ebeling and B. Meissner, vol. 5,
        pp. 464–73. Berlin.

1977   "Appendix: Mesopotamian Chronology of the Historical
        Period." In *Ancient Mesopotamia: Portrait of a Dead Civilization,*
        by A. Leo Oppenheim, pp. 335–48. Rev. ed. completed by Erica
        Reiner. Chicago.

1980–83 "Kudurru: A Philologisch." In *Reallexikon der Assyriologie und
        Vorderasiatischen Archäologie,* vol. 6, pp. 267–74. Berlin.

1981–82 "The Western Asiatic Seals Found at Thebes in Greece: A Preliminary Edition of the Inscriptions." *Archiv für Orientforschung* 28, pp. 73–78.

Briquel-Chatonnet, Françoise
2004 "Les texts rélatifs au cèdre du Liban dans l'Antiquité." In Doumet-Serhal 2004c, pp. 464–71.

Brody, Aaron J.
1998 *"Each Man Cried Out to His God": The Specialized Religion of Canaanite and Phoenician Seafarers.* Harvard Semitic Monographs, no. 58. Atlanta.

Brown, John P.
1969 *The Lebanon and Phoenicia: Ancient Texts Illustrating Their Physical Geography and Native Industries.* Vol. 1, *The Physical Setting and the Forest.* Beirut.

Brunner-Traut, Emma
1977 "Heuschrecke." In *Lexikon der Ägyptologie*, edited by Wolfgang Helck and Wofhart Westendorf, vol. 2, cols. 1179–80. Wiesbaden.

Brunton, Guy, and Reginald Engelbach
1927 *Gurob.* Publications of the Egyptian Research Account and British School of Archaeology in Egypt, vol. 41. London.

Bruyère, Bernard
1937 *Rapport sur les fouilles de Deir el Médineh (1934–1935).* Fouilles de l'Institut Français du Caire, vol. 15. Cairo.

Bryan, Betsy M.
1991 *The Reign of Thutmose IV.* Baltimore.
1996 "Art, Empire, and the End of the Late Bronze Age." In *The Study of the Ancient Near East in the Twenty-first Century, The William Foxwell Albright Centennial Conference*, edited by Jerrold S. Cooper and Glenn M. Schwartz, pp. 33–79. Winona Lake, Ind.
2000 "The 18th Dynasty before the Amarna Period." In *The Oxford History of Ancient Egypt*, edited by Ian Shaw, pp. 218–71. New York.

Bryce, Trevor
1998 *The Kingdom of the Hittites.* Oxford.
2003 *Letters of the Great Kings of the Ancient Near East: The Royal Correspondence of the Late Bronze Age.* London and New York.

Buccellati, Giorgio
1994 "The Kudurrus as Monuments." In *Cinquante-deux réflexions sur le Proche-Orient ancien: Offertes en hommage à Léon De Meyer*, edited by H. Gasche et al., pp. 283–91. Mesopotamian History and Environment, Occasional Publications, vol. 2. Leuven.

Buchanan, Briggs
1957 "On the Seal Impressions on Some Old Babylonian Tablets." *Journal of Cuneiform Studies* 11, pp. 45–52.
1966 *Catalogue of Ancient Near Eastern Seals in the Ashmolean Museum.* Vol. 1, *Cylinder Seals.* Oxford.
1968 "A Cypriote Cylinder at Yale (Newell Collection 358)." *Bulletin de correspondance hellénique* 92, pp. 410–15.

Buchholz, Hans-Günter
1959 "Keftiubarren und Erzhandel im Zweiten Vorchristlichen Jahrtausend." *Praehistorische Zeitschrift* 38, pp. 1–40.
1966 "Talanta, Neues über Metallbarren der ostmediterranean Spätbronzezeit." *Schweizer Münzblätter* 16 (62), pp. 58–72.
1999 "Ein aussergewöhnliches Steinzepter in östlichen Mittelmeer." *Praehistorische Zeitschrift* 74, pp. 68–78.

Buchholz, Hans-Günter, and Vassos Karageorghis
1973 *Prehistoric Greece and Cyprus: An Archaeological Handbook.* Translated by Francisca Garvie. London.

Buchholz, Hans-Günter, and G. Weisgerber
2005 "Prominenz mit Steingerät." In *Das Schiff von Uluburun* 2005, pp. 149–53.

Burkert, Walter
1992 *The Orientalizing Revolution: Near Eastern Influence on Greek Culture in the Early Archaic Age.* Translated by Walter Burkert and Margaret E. Pinder. Cambridge, Mass.

Cabrol, Agnès
2000 *Amenhotep III: Le magnifique.* Monaco.

Cadogan, Gerald
1973 "Patterns in the Distribution of Mycenaean Pottery in the East Mediterranean." In *Acts of the International Archaeological Symposium "Mycenaeans in the Eastern Mediterranean," Nicosia, 27th March–2nd April 1972*, edited by Vassos Karageorghis, pp. 166–74. Nicosia.
1980 *Palaces of Minoan Crete.* London.
1983 "Early Minoan and Middle Minoan Chronology." *American Journal of Archaeology* 87, pp. 507–18.

Callot, Olivier
1994 *La tranchée "Ville Sud": Études d'architecture domestique.* Ras Shamra-Ougarit, vol. 10. Paris.

Caminos, Ricardo A.
1954 *Late-Egyptian Miscellanies.* Brown Egyptological Studies, vol. 1. London.

Campbell, Edward F.
1964 *The Chronology of the Amarna Letters: With Special Reference to the Hypothetical Coregency of Amenophis III and Akhenaten.* Baltimore.

Canby, Jeanny Vorys
1969 "Some Hittite Figurines in the Aegean." *Hesperia* 38, no. 2 (April–June), pp. 141–149.
1975 "The Walters Gallery Cappadocian Tablet and the Sphinx in Anatolia in the Second Millennium B.C." *Journal of Near Eastern Studies* 34, pp. 225–48.
1989 "Hittite Art." *Biblical Archaeologist* 52, nos. 2–3 (June–September), pp. 109–29.
2002 "Falconry (Hawking) in Hittite Lands." *Journal of Near Eastern Studies* 61, pp. 161–201.

Cancik-Kirschbaum, Eva Christiane
1996 *Die mittelassyrischen Briefe aus Tall Šēḫ Hamad.* Berichte der Ausgrabung Tall Šēḫ Hamad/Dūr-Katlimmu (Batsh), vol. 4. Berlin.

Caquot, André, Maurice Sznycer, and Andrée Herdner
1974 *Textes ougaritiques.* Vol. 1, *Mythes et légendes.* Paris.

Carnarvon, George Edward Stanhope Molyneux Herbert, Earl of, and Howard Carter
1912 *Five Years' Explorations at Thebes: A Record of Work Done 1907–1911.* London.

Carter, Howard, and Arthur C. Mace
1923–33 *The Tomb of Tutankhamen: Discovered by the Late Earl of Carnarvon and Howard Carter.* 3 vols. New York.

Cartwright, Caroline
2004 "*Cedrus Libani* under the Microscope: The Anatomy of Modern and Ancient Cedar of Lebanon Wood." In Doumet-Serhal 2004c, pp. 473–79.

Casanova, Michèle
1992 "The Sources of the Lapis-Lazuli Found in Iran." In *South Asian Archaeology* 1989, edited by Catherine Jarrige, pp. 49–56. Madison, Wisc.
1995 "Le lapis-lazuli dans l'Orient antique (les gisements, production et circulation)" and "La fabrication des perles en lapis-lazuli." In *Les pierres précieuses de l'Orient ancien, des Sumériens*

aux Sassanides, edited by Françoise Tallon, pp. 15–20 and 45–46. Paris.

2002 "Le lapis-lazuli, joyau de l'Orient ancien." In *Matériaux, productions, circulations du Néolithique à l'Âge du Bronze*, edited by Jean Guilaine, pp. 169–90. Paris.

2006 "L'émergence du marché au Proche-Orient ancien (4e–2e millénaires av. J.C.)." *La pensée*, no. 347 (July–September), pp. 19–31.

Caskey, Miriam E.
1986 *The Temple at Ayia Irini*. Part 1, *The Statues*. Keos, vol. 2. Princeton.

Catling, H. W.
1964 *Cypriot Bronzework in the Mycenaean World*. Oxford.
1986 "Cypriot Bronzework—East or West?" In *Acts of the International Archaeological Symposium "Cyprus between the Orient and the Occident," Nicosia, 8–14 September 1985*, edited by Vassos Karageorghis, pp. 91–103. Nicosia.

Caubet, Annie
1983 "Les oeufs d'autruche au Proche Orient ancien." *Report of the Department of Antiquities, Cyprus*, 1983, pp. 193–98.
1990 "Ougarit, grandeur d'un petit royaume." *Le Monde de la Bible*, no. 67 (November–December), pp. 31–34.
1991 "Ivoires de Cappadoce." In Charpin and Joannès 1991, pp. 223–25.
1996 "La musique à Ougarit: Nouveaux témoignages matériels." In *Ugarit, Religion and Culture: Proceedings of the International Colloquium on Ugarit, Religion and Culture, Edinburgh, July 1994: Essays Presented in Honour of Professor John C. L. Gibson*, edited by N. Wyatt, W. G. E. Watson, and J. B. Lloyd, pp. 9–31. Münster.
1997 as editor. *De Chypre à la Bactriane: Les sceaux du Proche-Orient ancien; Actes du colloque international organisé au Musée du Louvre par le service culturel, le 18 mars 1995*. Paris.
1998a "Le travail de l'ivoire." In *Liban: L'autre rive* 1998, p. 89.
1998b "Les trésors d'orfèvrerie de Byblos." In *Liban: L'autre rive* 1998, pp. 83–85.
1998c "The International Style: A Point of View from the Levant and Syria." In Cline and Harris-Cline 1998, pp. 105–13.
1999a as editor. *L'acrobate au taureau: Les découvertes de Tell el-Dab'a (Égypte) et l'archéologie de la Méditerranée orientale (1800–1400 av. J.-C.): Actes du colloque organisé au Musée du Louvre . . . 3 décembre 1994*. Paris.
1999b as editor. *Cornaline et pierres précieuses: La Méditerranée de l'antiquité à l'Islam; Actes du colloque organisé au Musée du Louvre par le Service culturel les 24 et 25 novembre 1995*. Paris.
1999c "Ougarit au Louvre." *Le monde de la Bible*, no. 120 (July–August), pp. 32–38.
2000 "Ugarit at the Louvre Museum." *Near Eastern Archaeology* 63, no. 4, pp. 216–19.
2007 as editor. *Faïences et matières vitreuses de l'Orient ancien: Études physico-chimique et catalogue des œuvres du Departement des Antiquités orientales*. Contributions by Anne Bouquillon et al. Paris: Musée du Louvre.
2008 "A Tale of Two Cities: Le coffre en ivoire d'Enkomi et la coupe d'or d'Ougarit." In Fitton and Kiely 2008. In press.

Caubet, Annie, and V. Matoïan
1995 "Ougarit et l'Egée." In *Le pays d'Ougarit autour de 1200 av. J.-C.: Histoire et archéologie: Actes du Colloque International, Paris, 28 juin–1er juillet 1993*, edited by Marguerite Yon, Maurice Sznycer, and Pierre Bordreuil, pp. 99–110. Ras Shamra-Ougarit, vol. 11. Paris.

Caubet, Annie, and Geneviève Pierrat-Bonnefois, eds.
2005 *Faïences de l'antiquité: De l'égypte à l'Iran*. Paris.

Caubet, Annie, and François Poplin
1987 "Les objets de matière dure animale: Étude du matériau." In *Le centre de la ville, 38e–44e campagnes (1978–1984)*, edited by Marguerite Yon et al., pp. 273–306. Ras Shamra-Ougarit, vol. 3. Paris.
1992 "La place des ivoires d'Ougarit dans la production du Proche Orient ancien." In Fitton 1992, pp. 91–100.

Caubet, Annie, and Patrick Pouysségur
1997 *L'Orient ancien: Aux origines de la civilisation*. Paris.

Cauvin, Jacques
1998 "Un aperçu sur la préhistoire du Liban." In *Liban: L'autre rive* 1998, pp. 38–46.

Cecchini, Serena M.
1965 *La ceramica di Nuzi*. Studi semitici 15. Rome.

Cecchini, Serena M., S. Mazzoni, and E. Scigliuzzo, eds.
n.d. *Syrian and Phoenician Ivories of the Early First Millennium BCE: Chronology, Regional Styles, and Iconographic Repertories*. Pisa. Forthcoming.

Chapouthier, Fernand
1938 *Deux épés d'apparat découvertes en 1936 au palais de Mallia*. École Française d'Athènes, Études crétoises, vol. 5. Paris.

Charpin, Dominique
2003 *Hammu-rabi de Babylone*. Paris.
2004a "La circulation des commerçants, des nomades et des messagers dans le Proche-Orient Amorrite (XVIIIe siècle av. J.-C.)." In *La mobilité des personnes en Méditerranée de l'antiquité à l'époque moderne*, edited by Claudia Moatti, pp. 51–69. Rome.
2004b "Histoire politique du Proche-Orient amorrite (2002–1595)." In Charpin, Edzard, and Stol 2004, pp. 25–480.

Charpin, Dominique, et al., eds.
1988 *Archives épistolaires de Mari*. Part 2. Archives royales de Mari, vol. 26, no. 2. Paris.

Charpin, Dominique, and Jean-Marie Durand
1985 "La prise de pouvoir par Zimri-Lim." *Mari: Annales de recherches interdisciplinaires* 4, pp. 293–343.

Charpin, Dominique, Dietz Otto Edzard, and Marten Stol
2004 *Mesopotamien: Die altbabylonische Zeit*. Orbis Biblicus et Orientalis, vol. 160, no. 4. Fribourg and Göttingen.

Charpin, Dominique, and Francis Joannès, eds.
1991 *Marchands, diplomates et empereurs: Études sur la civilisation mésopotamienne offertes à Paul Garelli*. Paris.
1992 *La circulation des biens, des personnes et des idées dans le Proche-Orient ancien: Actes de la XXXVIIIe Rencontre assyriologique internationale, Paris, 8–10 juillet 1991*. Paris.

Charpin, Dominique, and Nele Ziegler
1997 "Mekum, roi d'Apišal." *Mari: Annales de recherches interdisciplinaires* 8, pp. 243–47.
2003 *Florilegium marianum V. Mari et le proche-orient à l'époque amorrite: Essai d'histoire politique*. Mémoires de N.A.B.U., vol. 6. Paris.

Chavane, M.-J.
1987 "Instruments de bronze." In *Le centre de la ville, 38e–44e campagnes (1978–1984)*, edited by Marguerite Yon, pp. 357–74. Ras Shamra-Ougarit, vol. 3. Paris.

Chernykh, Evgenii Nikolaevich
1976 *Drevniaia Metallo-obrabotka na Iugo-zapade SSSR*. Moscow: Academy of Sciences.

Chesson, Meredith S.
2007 "Remembering and Forgetting in Early Bronze Age Mortuary Practices on the Southeastern Dead Sea Plain, Jordan." In *Performing Death: Social Analyses of Funerary Traditions in the Ancient Near East and Mediterranean*, edited by Nicola Laneri, pp. 109–23. University of Chicago Oriental Institute Seminars, no. 3. Chicago.

Chicago Assyrian Dictionary
1956–   *The Assyrian Dictionary of the Oriental Institute of the University*
2005   *of Chicago.* Edited by Ignace J. Gelb, Miguel Civil, Robert D.
         Biggs, et al. 21 vols. Chicago.

Clamer, C.
1980   "A Gold Plaque from Tel Lachish." *Tel Aviv* 7, pp. 152–62.

Clark, Grahame
1986   *Symbols of Excellence: Precious Materials as Expressions of Status.*
         Cambridge.

Cline, Eric H.
1987   "Amenhotep III and the Aegean: A Reassessment of Egypto-
         Aegean Relations in the 14th Century B.C." *Orientalia* 56,
         pp. 1–36.
1991   "Hittite Objects in the Bronze Age Aegean." *Anatolian Studies*
         41, pp. 133–43.
1994   *Sailing the Wine-Dark Sea: International Trade and the Late
         Bronze Age Aegean.* B.A.R. International Series 591. Oxford.
1995   "Egyptian and Near Eastern Imports at Late Bronze Age
         Mycenae." In W. Davies and Schofield 1995, pp. 91–115.
1996   "Assuwa and the Achaeans: The 'Mycenaean' Sword at
         Hattusas and Its Possible Implications." *Annual of the British
         School at Athens,* no. 91, pp. 137–51.
1999   "The Nature of the Economic Relations of Crete with Egypt
         and the Near East during the Bronze Age." In *From Minoan
         Farmers to Roman Traders: Sidelights on the Economy of Ancient
         Crete,* edited by Angelos Chaniotis, pp. 115–43. Stuttgart.
2007   "Rethinking Mycenaean International Trade with Egypt and
         the Near East." In *Rethinking Mycenaean Palaces II,* edited by
         Michael L. Galaty and William A. Parkinson, pp. 190–200.
         2nd ed. Los Angeles: Cotsen Institute of Archaeology.

Cline, Eric H., and Diane Harris-Cline, eds.
1998   *The Aegean and the Orient in the Second Millennium: Proceedings
         of the 50th Anniversary Symposium, Cincinnati, 18–20 April 1997.*
         Aegaeum 18. Liège and Austin.

Cline, Eric H., and David O'Connor, eds.
2006   *Thutmose III: A New Biography.* Ann Arbor.

Cline, Eric H., and Assaf Yassur-Landau
2007   "Poetry in Motion: Canaanite Rulership and Minoan
         Narrative Art at Tel Kabri." In Morris and Laffineur 2007,
         pp. 157–66.

Cochavi-Rainey, Zipora
2003   *The Alashia Texts from the 14th and 13th Centuries BCE: A
         Textual and Linguistic Study.* Alter Orient und Altes
         Testament, vol. 289. Münster.

Cohen, Raymond, and Raymond Westbrook, eds.
2000   *Amarna Diplomacy: The Beginnings of International Relations.*
         Baltimore.

Collins, Billie Jean
2002   as editor. *A History of the Animal World in the Ancient Near East.*
         Handbuch der Orientalistik, ser. 1, Nahe und der Mittlere
         Osten, vol. 64. Leiden.

Collins, Paul
2006   "Trees and Gender in Assyrian Art." *Iraq* 68, pp. 99–108.
2008   *The International Age: From Egypt and Greece to Iran, 1500–
         500 B.C.* London. Forthcoming.

Collon, Dominique
1972   "The Smiting God: A Study of a Bronze in the Pomerance
         Collection in New York." *Levant* 4, pp. 111–34.
1977   "Ivory." *Iraq* 39, no. 2, pp. 219–22.
1980–83 "Krummstab." In *Reallexikon der Assyriologie und Vorder-
         asiatischen Archäologie,* vol. 6, pp. 252–53. Berlin.

1981   "The Aleppo Workshop: A Seal-Cutter's Workshop in Syria in
         the Second Half of the Eighteenth Century, B.C." *Ugarit
         Forschungen* 13, pp. 33–43.
1982   *The Alalakh Cylinder Seals: A New Catalogue of the Actual Seals
         Excavated by Sir Leonard Woolley at Tell Atchana and from
         Neighboring Sites on the Syrian-Turkish Border.* BAR Inter-
         national Series 132. Oxford.
1985a   *Catalogue of the Western Asiatic Seals in the British Museum.*
         [Vol. 2], *Akkadian, Post Akkadian, Ur III Periods.* London.
1985b   "A North Syrian Cylinder Seal Style: Evidence of
         North–South Links with 'Ajjul.'" In *Palestine in the Bronze and
         Iron Ages: Papers in Honour of Olga Tufnell,* edited by Jonathan
         N. Tubb, pp. 57–70. London.
1987   *First Impressions: Cylinder Seals in the Ancient Near East.*
         London: British Museum Publications.
1989   "Cylinder Seals from Ulu Burun." In Bass et al. 1989, pp. 12–16.
1994   "Bull Leaping in Syria." *Ägypten und Levante / Egypt and the
         Levant* 4, pp. 81–85.
1995   *Ancient Near Eastern Art.* London.
2000   "Syrian Glyptic and the Thera Wall Paintings." In S. Sherratt
         2000, pp. 283–93.
2005a   *First Impressions: Cylinder Seals in the Ancient Near East.*
         Rev. ed. London: British Museum Press.
2005b   *The Queen of the Night.* British Museum Objects in Focus.
         London: British Museum Press. Reprinted 2007, with updated
         bibliography.
2007   "The Queen under Attack: A Rejoinder." *Iraq* 69, pp. 43–51.
2008   "The Aigina Treasure: Near Eastern Connections." In Fitton
         2008. In press.

Connan, J., et al.
1999   J. Connan, R. P. Evershed, L. Biek, and G. Eglinton. "Use and
         Trade of Bitumen in Antiquity and Prehistory: Molecular
         Archaeology Reveals Secrets of Past Civilizations." *Royal Society,
         Philosophical Transactions: Biological Sciences* 354, no. 1379
         (January 29), pp. 33–50.

Connan, J., O. Deschesne, and D. Dessort
1991   "L'origine des bitumes archéologiques." In *Arts et industries de
         la pierre,* edited by Marguerite Yon, pp. 101–26. Ras Shamra-
         Ougarit, vol. 6. Paris.

Contenau, Georges
1949   *La civilisation phénicienne.* New ed. Paris: Payot.

Conwell, David
1987   "On Ostrich Eggs and Libyans." *Expedition* 29, no. 3, pp. 25–34.

Cook, Erwin
2004   "Near Eastern Prototypes of the Palace of Alkinoos." *American
         Journal of Archaeology* 108, pp. 43–78.

Cornelius, Izak
1994   *The Iconography of the Canaanite Gods Reshef and Ba'al: Late
         Bronze and Iron Age I Periods (c 1500–1000 BCE).* Orbis Biblicus
         et Orientalis, vol. 140. Fribourg and Göttingen.
2004   *The Many Faces of the Goddess: The Iconography of the Syro-
         Palestinian Goddesses Anat, Astarte, Quedeshet, and Asherah,
         c. 1500–1000 BCE.* Orbis Biblicus et Orientalis, vol. 204.
         Fribourg and Göttingen.

Cour-Marty, M. A.
1985   "Informations et documents: La collection de poids du Musée
         du Caire revisitée." *Revue d'égyptologie* 36, pp. 189–200.
1990   "Les poids égyptiens, de précieux jalons archéologiques." In
         Sociétés urbaines en Égypte et au Soudan, pp. 17–55. Cahiers de
         recherches de l'Institut de Papyrologie et d'Égyptologie de
         Lille, vol. 12. Lille.

Courtois, Jacques-Claude
1979   "Ras Shamra I: Archéologie." *Supplément au Dictionnaire de la
         Bible* 9, nos. 52–53, pp. 1165–95.

1983 "Le trésor de poids de Kalavassos-Ayois Dhimitrios 1982." *Report of the Department of Antiquities, Cyprus*, 1983, pp. 117–30.

1984 *Alasia III: Les objects des niveaux stratifiés d'Enkomi (fouilles C. F.-A. Schaeffer, 1947–70)*. Paris.

Courtois, Jacques-Claude, Jacques Lagarce, and Elisabeth Lagarce
1986 *Enkomi et le bronze récent à Chypre*. Nicosia.

Crete–Egypt
2000 *Crete–Egypt: Three Thousand Years of Cultural Links: Catalogue*. Exhibition, Heraklion Archaeological Museum. Catalogue edited by Alexandra Karetsou and Maria Andreadaki-Vlazaki, with the collaboration of Nikos Papadakis. Heraklion.

Crewe, Lindy
2008 "Feasting with the Dead? Tomb 66 at Enkomi." In Fitton and Kiely 2008. In press.

Crowfoot, John W., and Grace M. H. Crowfoot
1938 *Early Ivories from Samaria*. London.

Cryer, Frederick H.
1995 "Chronology: Issues and Problems." In Sasson 1995, pp. 651–64.

Culican, William
1971 *The First Merchant Venturers: The Ancient Levant in History and Commerce*. [2nd ed.] New York.

Curtin, Philip D.
1984 *Cross-Cultural Trade in World History*. Cambridge.

Curtis, J., and Dominique Collon
1996 "Ladies of Easy Virtue." In *Collectanea Orientalia: Histoire, arts de l'espace et industrie de la terre. Études offertes en hommage à Agnès Spycket*, edited by Hermann Gasche and Barthel Hrouda, pp. 89–95. Civilisations du Proche-Orient, Série I, Archéologie et environnement, vol. 3. Neuchâtel and Paris.

Czerny, Ernst, et al., eds.
2006 *Timelines: Studies in Honour of Manfred Bietak*. 3 vols. Orientalia Lovaniensia analecta, vol. 149. Leuven.

Dajani, R. W.
1970 "A Late Bronze-Iron Age Tomb Excavated at Sahab, 1968." *Annual of the Department of Antiquities of Jordan* 15, pp. 29–34.

Dakoronia, Phanouria, et al.
1996 Phanouria Dakoronia, Sigrid Deger-Jalkotzy, and Agnes Sakellariou, in collaboration with Ingo Pini. *Kleinere griechische Sammlungen*. Suppl. 2, *Die Siegel aus der Nekropole von Elatia-Alonaki*. Berlin.

Dakouri-Hild, Anastasia
2005 "Something Old, Something New: Current Research on the Old Kadmeion of Thebes." *Bulletin of the Institute of Classical Studies of the University of London* 48, pp. 173–86.

D'Albiac, C.
1992 "The Griffin Combat Theme." In Fitton 1992, pp. 105–12.

Daressy, Georges
1906 "Un poignard du temps des rois pasteurs." *Annales du Service des Antiquités de l'Égypte* 7, pp. 115–20.

1928–29 "Les branches du Nil sous la XVIIIe dynastie." *Bulletin de la Société de Géographie d'Égypte* 16, pp. 225–54, 293–329.

Darga, A. Muhibbe
1992 *Hitit Sanatı*. Akbank kültür ve sanat kitapları 56. Istanbul.

Dasen, Véronique
1993 *Dwarfs in Ancient Egypt and Greece*. Oxford.

von Dassow, Eva
2006a "EA 4: From the King of Karduniash to the King of Egypt." In von Dassow and Greenwood 2006, pp. 193–94.

2006b "Rib-Hadda, Mayor of Gubla, to Amenhotep III, King of Egypt." In von Dassow and Greenwood 2006, p. 203.

von Dassow, Eva, and Kyle Greenwood
2006 "Correspondence from El-Amarna in Egypt." In *The Ancient Near East: Historical Sources in Translation*, edited by Mark W. Chavalas, pp. 182–214. Malden, Mass.

Davaras, Costis, and Jeffrey Soles
1995 "A New Oriental Cylinder Seal from Mochlos. Appendix: Catalogue of the Cylinder Seals Found in the Aegean." Αρχαιολογική Εφημερίς (*Archaiologike ephemeris*) 134 (pub. 1997), pp. 29–66.

Davies, Nina de G.
1963 *Scenes from Some Theban Tombs (Nos. 38, 66, 162, with Excerpts from 81)*. Private Tombs at Thebes 4. Oxford.

Davies, Norman de Garis
1906 *The Rock Tombs of El Amarna*. Part 4, *Tombs of Penthu, Mahu, and Others*. London.

1922–23 *The Tomb of Puyemrê at Thebes*. 2 vols. New York: The Metropolitan Museum of Art.

1930 *The Tomb of Ken-Amun at Thebes*. The Metropolitan Museum of Art Egyptian Expedition. 2 vols. New York.

1933 *The Tombs of Menkheperrasonb, Amenmose and Another (Nos. 86, 112, 42, 226)*. Theban Tomb Series, 5th memoir. London.

1973 *The Tomb of Rekh-mi-rē at Thebes*. Reprint of 1943 ed. Publications of the Metropolitan Museum of Art Egyptian Expedition, vol. 11. 2 vols. in 1. New York.

Davies, Norman de Garis, and R. O. Faulkner
1947 "A Syrian Trading Venture to Egypt." *Journal of Egyptian Archaeology* 33, pp. 40–46.

Davies, W. Vivian, and Louise Schofield, eds.
1995 *Egypt, the Aegean, and the Levant: Interconnections in the Second Millennium BC*. London.

Davis, Ellen
1973 "The Vapheio Cups and Aegean Gold and Silver Ware." Ph.D., New York University.

1977 *The Vapheio Cups and Aegean Gold and Silver Ware*. Outstanding Dissertations in the Fine Arts. New York and London.

1986 "Youth and Age in the Thera Frescoes." *American Journal of Archaeology* 90, pp. 399–406.

Davis, Frank
1936 "A Puzzling 'Venus' of 2000 B.C.: A Fine Sumerian Relief in London." *Illustrated London News*, no. 5069 (June 13), p. 1047.

Davis, Jack L.
1981 "Mycenaeans at Thera: Another Look." *American Journal of Archaeology* 85, pp. 69–70.

Davis, Jack L., and John Bennet
1999 "Making Mycenaeans: Warfare, Territorial Expansion, and Representations of the Other in the Pylian Kingdom." In Laffineur 1999, vol. 1, pp. 105–21.

Dawkins, R. M.
1904 "Excavations at Palaikastro. III." *Annual of the British School at Athens* 10, pp. 192–226.

Dawson, Warren R.
1925 "A Bronze Dagger of the Hyksos Period." *Journal of Egyptian Archaeology* 11, no. 3–4 (October), pp. 216–17.

Delange, E.
1993 "Boîte à parfum." In *Aménophis III: Le pharaon-soleil*, pp. 358–59. Exh. cat. Paris: Galeries Nationales du Grand Palais.

Demakopoulou, Katie
1974 "Mycenaean Jewellery Workshop in Thebes." ." Αρχαιολογικά Ανάλεκτα εξ Αθηνών / *Athens Annals of Archaeology* 7, pp. 162–73.

Demakopoulou, Katie, et al.
1995   Katie Demakopoulou, E. Mangou. R. E. Jones, and E. Photos-Jones. "Mycenaean Black Inlaid Metalware in the National Archaeological Museum, Athens: A Technical Examination." *Annual of the British School at Athens* 90, pp. 137–53.

Demakopoulou, Katie, and J. H. Crouwel
1993   "More Cats or Lions from Thera?" Δύο Νεόσχημοι Πυξίδες εξ Έγκωμης." Αρχαιολογική Εφημερίς (*Archaiologike ephemeris*) 132 (pub. 1995), pp. 1–11.

Demakopoulou, Katie, and Dora Konsola
1981   *Archaeological Museum of Thebes: Guide.* Translated by Helen Zigada. Athens.

Demargne, P.
1939   "Le maître des animaux sur une gemme crétoise du MM I." In *Mélanges syriens offerts à M. René Dussaud*, pp. 121–27. Paris.

De Martino, Stefano
2003   *Annali e "Res gestae" antico ittiti.* Studia Mediterranea, vol. 12. Pavia.

Dercksen, Jan Gerrit
1996   *The Old Assyrian Copper Trade in Anatolia.* Istanbul.
2004   as editor. *Assyria and Beyond: Studies Presented to Mogens Trolle Larsen.* Leiden.

Desroches-Noblecourt, Christiane
1963   *Tutankhamen: Life and Death of a Pharaoh.* New York.

Dever, William G.
1991   "Tell el Dab'a and Levantine Middle Bronze Age Chronology: A Rejoinder to Manfred Bietak." In "Egypt and Canaan in the Bronze Age," *Bulletin of the American Schools of Oriental Research*, no. 281, pp. 73–79.
1992   "The Chronology of Syria-Palestine in the Second Millennium B.C.E.: A Review of Current Issues." *Bulletin of the American Schools of Oriental Research*, no. 288, pp. 1–25.
1997   "Settlement Patterns and Chronology of Palestine in the Middle Bronze Age." In Oren 1997a, pp. 285–302.

Dickers, Aurelia
2001   *Die spätmykenischen Siegel aus weichem Stein: Untersuchen zur spätbronzezeitlichen Glyptik auf dem griechischen Festland und in der Ägäis.* Rahden.

Dietz, Søren
1984   *Lindos IV, 1. Excavations and Surveys in Southern Rhodes: The Mycenaean Period.* Publications of the National Museum, Archaeological-Historical Series, vol. 22, part 1. Copenhagen.

Dikaios, Porphyrios
1969   *Enkomi: Excavations, 1948–1958.* Mainz am Rhein.

Dittman, Reinhard
1992   "Assur and Kar-Tukulti-Ninurta." *American Journal of Archaeology* 96, pp. 307–12.

Dobel, Alan, Frank Asaro, and H. V. Michel
1977   "Neutron Activation Analysis and the Location of Wassukanni." *Orientalia* 46, no. 3, pp. 375–82.

Dohmann-Pfälzner, Heike, and Peter Pfälzner
2006   "Ausgrabungen und Forschungen in Tell Mišrife/Qatna 2004 und 2005: Vorbericht der deutschen Komponente des internationalen Kooperationsprojektes." Contributions by M. Abbado, A. Ahrens, R. Evershed, E. Formigli, E. Geith, A. Mukherjee, V. Paoletti, C. Pümpin, E. Rossberger, C. von Rüden, J. Schmid, C. Schmidt, A. Stauffer, and C. Witzel. *Mitteilungen der Deutschen Orient-Gesellschaft zu Berlin* 138, pp. 57–107.
2008   "Ausgrabungen und Forschungen 2006 im Königspalast von Qatna: Vorbericht des syrisch-deutschen Kooperationsprojektes in Tall Mišrife/Qatna." Contributions by Eva Geith, Valeria Paoletti, Jochen Schmid, Conrad Schmidt, and Anne Wissing. *Mitteilungen der Deutschen Orient-Gesellschaft zu Berlin* 139. In press.

Donadoni, Sergio
1989   "Image and Form: the Experience of Sculpture." In *Egyptian Civilization: Monumental Art*, edited by Anna Maria Donadoni-Roveri, pp. 98–185. Milan.

Dossin, Georges
1937   "Transcription of Text in 'Les Fouilles de Mari, troisième campagne (hiver 1935–36),' by André Parrot." *Syria* 18, pp. 54–84.
1938   "Les archives épistolaires du palais de Mari." *Syria* 19 (1938), pp. 105–26.
1950   as translator. *Correspondance de Šamši-Addu et de ses fils.* Vol. 1. Archives royales de Mari, vol. 1. Paris.
1952   as translator. *Correspondance de Iasmah-Addu.* Archives royales de Mari, vol. 5. Paris.
1954   "Le royaume de Qatna au XVIIIe siècle avant notre ère, d'après les 'Archives royales de Mari.'" *Bulletin de l'Académie Royale de Belgique, Classe de lettres*, ser. 5, 40, pp. 417–25. Reprinted in *Recueil Georges Dossin: Mélanges d'assyriologie (1934–1959)*, pp. 300–310. Akkadica Supplementum 1. Louvain, 1983.
1970   "La route de l'étain en Mésopotamie au temps de Zimri-Lim." *Revue d'assyriologie* 64, pp. 97–106.
1978   as translator. *Correspondance féminine.* With the collaboration of André Finet. Archives royales de Mari, vol. 10. Paris.

Dothan, Moshe, and Y. Porath
1993   *Ashdod V: Excavation of Area G: The Fourth–Sixth Seasons of Excavations, 1968–1970.* 'Atiqot (English Series), vol. 23. Jerusalem.

Dothan, Trude, Sharon Zuckerman, and Yuval Goren
2000   "Kamares Ware at Hazor." *Israel Exploration Journal* 50, pp. 1–15.

Doumas, Christos G.
1978–80 as editor. *Thera and the Aegean World: Papers Presented at the Second International Scientific Congress, Santorini, Greece, August 1978.* 2 vols. London.
1985   "Conventions artistiques à Thera et dans la Méditerranée orientale." In *L'iconographie minoenne: Actes de la table ronde d'Athènes (21–22 avril 1983)*, edited by Pascal Darcque and Jean-Claude Poursat, pp. 29–34. Bulletin de correspondance hellénique, Supplément 11. Athens.
1987   "Η Ξεστή 3 και οι κυανοκέφαλοι της Θήρας." In Ειλαπίνη. Τόμος τιμητικός για τον Νικ. Πλάτωνα, pp. 151–59. Heraklion.
1992   *The Wall-Paintings of Thera.* Translated by Alex Doumas. Athens. Greek title.: Οι τοιχογραφίες της Θήρας.
1993   "Ανασκαφές Θήρας." Πρακτικα της εν Αθήναις Αρχαιολογικής Εταιρείας (*Praktika tes en Athenais Archaiologikes Hetaireias*) 1990 (pub. 1993), pp. 224–35.
1995   *Die Wandmalereien von Thera.* Munich.
2000   "Age and Gender in the Theran Wall Paintings." In S. Sherratt 2000, vol. 2, pp. 971–81.
2005   "La répartition topographique des fresques dans les bâtiments d'Akrotiri à Théra." In *Kres technites/L'artisan crétois: Recueil d'articles en l'honneur de Jean-Claude Poursat, publié à l'occasion des 40 ans de la découverte du Quartier Mu*, pp. 73–81. Aegaeum 26. Liège and Austin.

Doumet-Serhal, Claude
2004a   "Sidon (Lebanon): Twenty Middle Bronze Age Burials from the 2001 Season of Excavation." *Levant* 36, pp. 89–154.
2004b   "Sidon: A Jar with Fish or Dolphin Decoration." *Archaeology and History in the Lebanon* 19 (Spring), pp. 106–9.
2004c   as editor. *Decade: A Decade of Archaeology and History in the Lebanon (1995–2004).* London.
2006   "Sidon: Mediterranean Contacts in the Early and Middle Bronze Age, Preliminary Report." *Archaeology and History in the Lebanon* 24 (Winter), pp. 34–47.

Doumet-Serhal, Claude, et al.
[1998]   *Stones and Creed: One Hundred Artifacts from Lebanon's Antiquity*. Translated by Jennifer Curtiss Gage. Beirut.

Dreyfus, Renée
2005   "Game Box with Lions, Gazelles, and a Hound." In *Hatshepsut 2005*, pp. 255–56.

Driessen, J. M., and C. MacDonald
1984   "Some Military Aspects of the Aegean in the Late Fifteenth and Early Fourteenth Centuries B.C." *Annual of the British School at Athens* 79, pp. 49–74.

Drioton, Étienne
1940   "Un ancien jeu copte." *Bulletin de la Société d'Archéologie Copte* 6, pp. 177–206.
1949   *Encyclopédie photographique de l'art: Le Musée du Caire*. Paris.

Dubin, Lois Sherr
1987   *The History of Beads from 30,000 B.C. to the Present*. New York.

Du Mesnil du Buisson, Robert
1926   "Les ruines d'el-Mishrifé au nord-est de Homs (Émèse)." *Syria* 7, pp. 289–325.
1928   "L'ancienne Qatna ou les ruines d'el Mishrifeh au Nord-est de Homs (Émèse). Deuxième campagne de fouilles (1927)," part 2. *Syria* 9, pp. 6–24.
1935   *Le site archéologique de Mishrifé-Qatna*. Paris.

Dunand, Maurice
1937   *Fouilles de Byblos*. Vol. 1, *1926–1932: Atlas*. Paris.
1939   *Fouilles de Byblos*. Vol. 1, *1926–1932: Texte*. Paris.
1945   *Byblia Grammata: Documents et recherches sur le développement de l'écriture Phénicie*. Ministère de l'Éducation Nationale et des Beaux-Arts, République Libanaise, Études et documents d'archéologie, Vol. 2. Beirut.
1950   *Fouilles de Byblos*. Vol. 2, *1933–1938: Atlas*. Paris.
1954   *Fouilles de Byblos*. Vol. 2, *1933–1938: Texte*. Paris.
1958   *Fouilles de Byblos*. Vol. 2, part 2, *1933–1938: Texte*. Paris.

Dunham, Dows
1978   *Zawiyet El-Aryan, the Cemeteries adjacent to the Layer Pyramid*. Boston: Department of Egyptian and Near Eastern Art, Museum of Fine Arts.

Dunham, Sally
1989   "Metal Animal Headed Cups at Mari." In *To the Euphrates and Beyond: Archaeological Studies in Honour of Maurits N. Van Loon*, edited by O. M. C. Haex, H. H. Curvers, and P. M. M. G. Akkermans, pp. 213–20. Rotterdam.

Dupré, Sylvestre
1993   *Bestiaire de Cappadoce: Terres cuites zoomorphes anatoliennes du IIè millénaire avant J.-C. au Musée du Louvre*. Notes et documents des musées de France 25. Paris.

Durand, Jean-Marie
1987   "Documents pour l'histoire du royaume de Haute Mésopotamie, I/C: Les trois routes de l'Euphrate à Qatna à travers le Désert." *Mari: Annales de recherches interdisciplinaires* 5, pp. 159–66.
1988   as editor. *Archives épistolaires de Mari*. Part 1. Archives royales de Mari, vol. 26, no. 1. Paris.
1992   "Unité et diversité au Proche-Orient à l'époque amorrite." In Charpin and Joannès 1992, pp. 97–128.
1997–   as compiler and translator. *Les documents épistolaires du palais
2000   de Mari*. 3 vols. Littératures anciennes du Proche Orient, vols. 16–18. Paris.

Duru, Refik, and Gülsün Umurtak
2005   *Höyücek: 1989–1992 yılları arasında yapılan kazıların sonuçları/Results of the Excavations, 1989–1992*. Türk Tarih Kurumu yayınları, ser. 5, vol. 49. Ankara.

Dussaud, René
1924   "Les inscriptions phéniciennes du tombeau d'Ahiram, roi de Byblos." *Syria* 5, pp. 135–57.
1926   "L'art syrien du deuxième millénaire avant notre ère." *Syria* 7, pp. 336–46.
1930   "Les quatre campagnes de fouilles de M. Pierre Montet à Byblos." *Syria* 11, pp. 164–87.
1931   "La mythologie phénicienne d'après les tablettes de Ras Shamra." *Revue de l'histoire des religions* 104, no. 6, pp. 353–408.
1933   "Ex-voto au dieu Amourrou pour la vie de Hammourabi (Musée du Louvre)." *Monuments et mémoires Piot* 33, pp. 1–10.
1949   *L'art phénicien au IIe millénaire*. Paris.

Eaton-Krauss, Marianne
1990   "The Coffins of Queen Ahhotep, Consort of Sequenen-Re and Mother of Ahmose." *Chronique d'Egypte* 65, pp. 195–205.
2003   "Encore: The Coffins of Ahhotep, Wife of Seqeni-en-Re Tao and Mother of Ahmose." In *Ägypten–Münster: Kulturwissenschaftliche Studien zu Ägypten, dem Vorderen Orient und verwandten Gebieten* [Festschrift E. Graefe], edited by Anke Ilona Blöbaum, Jochem Kahl, and Simon D. Schweitzer, pp. 75–89. Wiesbaden.

Ebeling, Erich
1932   "Apotropaeen." In *Reallexikon der Assyriologie und Vorderasiatischen Archäologie*, vol. 1, pp. 121–22. Berlin.
1971   "Fliege" and "Frosch." In *Reallexikon der Assyriologie und Vorderasiatischen Archäologie*, vol. 3, pp. 87 and 118. Berlin.

Ebla
1995   *Ebla: Alle origini della civiltà urbana; trent'anni di scavi in Siria dell'Università di Roma "La Sapienza."* Exhibition, Palazzo Venezia, Rome. Catalogue by Paolo Matthiae, Frances Pinnock, and Gabriella Scandone Matthiae. Milan.

Ebla to Damascus
1985   *Ebla to Damascus: Art and Archaeology of Ancient Syria*. Exhibition, Walters Art Gallery, Baltimore, and other venues. Catalogue edited by Harvey Weiss. Washington, D.C.: Smithsonian Institution Traveling Exhibition Service.

Echt, R.
1983   "Frühe phönizische Elfenbeine." In *Frühe Phöniker im Libanon 1983*, pp. 79–91.

Ecker, Heather L.
1989   "The Characterization of Weathering Effects and the Conservation of a Mammoth Tusk from Roxton, Bedfordshire." *Bulletin of the British School of Archaeology* 26, pp. 183–223.

Edel, Elmar
1976   *Ägyptische Ärzte und ägyptische Medizin am hethitischen Königshof: Neue Funde von Keilschriftbriefen Ramses' II. aus Bogazköy*. Opladen.
1994   as editor. *Die ägyptisch-hethitische Korrespondenz aus Boghazköi in babylonischer und hethitischer Sprache*. 2 vols. Abhandlungen der Rheinisch-Westfälischen Akademie der Wissenschaften, vol. 77. Opladen.
1997   *Der Vertrag zwischen Ramses II. von Ägypten und Hattušili III. von Hatti*. Wissenschaftliche Veröffentlichung der Deutschen Orient-Gesellschaft, no. 95. Berlin.

Eder, Birgitta, and Reinhard Jung
2005   "On the Character of Social Relations between Greece and Italy in the 12th–11th Century." In Laffineur and Greco 2005, pp. 485–95.

Eder, Christian
1995   *Die ägyptischen Motive in der Glyptik des östlichen Mittelmeerraumes zu Anfang des 2. Jts. v. Chr.* Orientalia Lovaniensia Analecta, vol. 71. Leuven.
2004   "Assyrische Distanzangaben und die absolute Chronologie Vorderasiens." *Altorientalische Forschungen* 31, no. 2, pp. 191–236.

Edwards, Iowerth E. S.
1976 *Tutankhamun's Jewelry*. New York: The Metropolitan Museum of Art.

Edzard, Dietz Otto
1997 *Gudea and His Dynasty*. Royal Inscriptions of Mesopotamia, Early Periods, vol. 3, part 1. Toronto.
2004 "Altbabylonische Literatur und Religion." In Charpin, Edzard, and Stol 2004, pp. 483–640.

Effinger, Maria
1996 *Minoischer Schmuck*. BAR International Series 646. Oxford.

Eggebrecht, Eva
1975 "Dolch." In *Lexikon der Ägyptologie*, edited by Wolfgang Helck and Wolfhart Westendorf, vol. 1, cols. 1113–16. Wiesbaden.
1977 "Greif." In *Lexikon der Ägyptologie*, edited by Wolfgang Helck and Wolfhart Westendorf, vol. 2, cols. 895–96. Wiesbaden.

Egypt's Dazzling Sun
1992 *Egypt's Dazzling Sun: Amenhotep III and His World*. Exhibition, Cleveland Museum of Art; Kimbell Art Museum, Fort Worth; Galeries Nationales du Grand Palais, Paris. Catalogue by Arielle P. Kozloff and Betsy M. Bryan; with Lawrence M. Berman and Elisabeth Delange. Cleveland.

Egypt's Golden Age
1982 *Egypt's Golden Age: The Art of Living in the New Kingdom, 1558–1085 B.C.* Exhibition, Museum of Fine Arts, Boston; Houston Museum of Natural Science; Walters Art Gallery, Baltimore. Catalogue. Boston.

Eichler, Seyyare, and Markus Wäfler, eds.
1990 *Tall al-Hamadiya*. Vol. 2, *Symposion: Recent Excavations in the Upper Khabur Region, Berne, December 9–11, 1986*. Orbis Biblicus et Orientalis, Series Archaeologica, vol. 6. Fribourg and Göttingen.

Eickhoff, Tilman
1985 *Kār Tukulti Ninurta: Eine mittelassyrische Kult- und Residenzstadt*. Abhandlungen der Deutschen Orient-Gesellschaft, no. 21. Berlin.

Elmer-De Witt, Philip
1989 "The Golden Treasures of Nimrud." *Time Magazine* 134, no. 18 (October 30), pp. 80–81.

Elsen-Novák, Gabriele
2002 "Die altsyrische Glyptik aus Qatna: Eine erste Einordnung." *Mitteilungen der Deutschen Orient-Gesellschaft zu Berlin*, no. 134, pp. 257–74.

Emre, Kutlu
1971 *Anadolu kurşun figürinleri ve taş kalıpları / Anatolian Lead Figurines and Their Stone Moulds*. Türk Tarih Kurumu yayınları, ser. 5, vol. 14. Ankara.
2002 "Felsreliefs, Stelen, Orthostaten: Grossplastik als monumentale Form staatlicher und religiöser Repräsentation." In *Die Hethiter und ihr Reich* 2002, pp. 218–33.

Eran, A., and G. Edelstein
1977 "Tombs near the Persian Garden: The Weights." *'Atiqot* (English Series) 12, pp. 52–62.

Erkanal, Armağan
1986 "Panaztepe Kazısının 1985 Yılı Sonuçları." *Kazı Sonuçları Toplantısı* (Ankara) 8, no. 1, pp. 253–61.
1995 "Bir kült kabı üzerine Düşünceler." *Belleten* 59, pp. 593–99.

Erkanal, Hayat
1977 *Die Äxte und Beile des 2. Jahrtausends in Zentralanatolien*. Prähistorische Bronzefunde, ser. 9, vol. 8. Munich.

Erlenmeyer, M., and H. Erlenmeyer
1964 "Über Philister und Kreter, 4." *Orientalia* 33, pp. 199–237.

Ersoy, Yasar
1988 "Finds from the Menemen / Panaztepe in the Manisa Museum." *Annual of the British School at Athens* 83, pp. 56–82.

Ertekin, Ahmet, and Ismet Ediz
1993 "The Unique Sword from Boğazköy / Hattuša." In Mellink, Porada, and Özgüç 1993, pp. 719–25.

Eshmawy, Aiman
2007 "Names of Horses in Ancient Egypt." In *Proceedings of the Ninth International Congress of Egyptologists, Grenoble, 6–12 September 2004*, edited by Jean-Claude Goyon and Christine Cardin, pp. 665–76. Leuven, Paris, and Dudley.

Evans, Arthur J.
1892–93 "A Mykenaean Treasure from Aegina." *Journal of Hellenic Studies* 13, pp. 195–226.
1906 *The Prehistoric Tombs of Knossos*. Vol. 1, *The Cemetery at Zafer Papoura*. Vol. 2, *The Royal Tomb of Isopata*. London. Reprinted from *Archaeologia* 59.
1921 "On a Minoan Bronze Group of a Galloping Bull and Acrobatic Figure from Crete." *Journal of Hellenic Studies* 41, pp. 247–59.
1921–35 *The Palace of Minos: A Comparative Account of the Successive Stages of the Early Cretan Civilization as Illustrated by the Discoveries at Knossos*. 5 vols. in 7 parts. Reprint. London.
1925 "'The Ring of Nestor': A Glimpse into the Minoan After-World and a Sepulchral Treasure of Gold Signet-Rings and Bead-Seals from Thisbê, Boeotia, Part I." *Journal of Hellenic Studies* 45, part 1, pp. 1–75.
1964 *The Palace of Minos: A Comparative Account of the Successive Stages of the Early Cretan Civilization as Illustrated by the Discoveries at Knossos*. 4 vols. in 6 parts. Reprint. London.

Evans, John D.
1959 *Malta*. Ancient People and Places, vol. 11. New York.

Evely, R. D. G.
1993– *Minoan Crafts: Tools and Techniques*. 2 vols. Studies in
2000 Mediterranean Archaeology, vol. 92. Jonsered.

Faist, Bettina
2001 *Der Fernhandel des assyrischen Reiches zwischen dem 14. und 11. Jh. v. Chr.* Münster.

Falsone, Gioacchino
1986 "Anath or Astarte: A Phoenician Bronze Statuette of the Smiting Goddess." In *Religio Phoenicia: Acta colloquii Namurcensis habiti diebus 14 et 15 mensis Decembris anni 1984*, edited by Corinne Bonnet, Edward Lipiński, and Patrick Marchetti, pp. 53–76. Studia Phoenicia 4. Namur.
1988 "La Fenicia come centro di lavorazione del bronzo nell'età del Ferro." *Dialoghi di archaeologia*, ser. 3, 6, no. 1, pp. 79–110.

Farao's van de Zon
2000 *Farao's van de Zon: Achnaton. Nefertiti. Toetanchamon.* Exhibition, Museum of Fine Arts, Boston; Los Angeles County Museum of Art; Art Institute of Chicago; Rijksmuseum van Oudheden te Leiden. Catalogue edited by Rita E. Freed, Yvonne J. Markowitz, and Sue H. D'Auria. Amsterdam.

Fay, Biri
1996 *The Louvre Sphinx and Royal Sculpture from the Reign of Amenemhat II*. Mainz am Rhein.

Fazzini, Richard A., James F. Romano, and Madeleine E. Cody
1999 *Art for Eternity: Masterworks from Ancient Egypt*. Brooklyn: Brooklyn Museum of Art.

Feldman, Marian H.
2002 "Luxurious Forms: Redefining a Mediterranean 'International Style,' 1400–1200 B.C.E." *Art Bulletin* 84 (March), pp. 6–29.
2006a "Assur Tomb 45 and the Birth of the Assyrian Empire." *Bulletin of the American Schools of Oriental Research*, no. 343, pp. 21–43.

2006b   *Diplomacy by Design: Luxury Arts and an "International Style" in the Ancient Near East, 1400–1200 BCE.* Chicago.

2007   "Frescoes, Exotica, and the Reinvention of the Northern Levantine Kingdoms during the Second Millennium B.C.E." In *Representations of Political Power: Case Histories from Times of Change and Dissolving Order in the Ancient Near East*, edited by Marlies Heinz and Marian H. Feldman, pp. 39–65. Winona Lake, Ind.

I Fenici

1988   *I Fenici.* Exhibition, Palazzo Grassi, Venice. Catalogue edited by Sabatino Moscati. Milan.

Finet, A.

1969   "L'Euphrate route commerciale de la Mésopotamie." *Annales archéologiques arabes syriennes* 19, pp. 37–48.

Finkel, Irving L.

2007a   as editor. *Ancient Board Games in Perspective: Papers from the 1990 British Museum Colloquium, with Additional Contributions.* London.

2007b   "On the Rules for the Royal Game of Ur." In Finkel 2007a, pp. 16–32.

Finkelstein, Israel, Shlomo Bunimovitz and Zvi Lederman

1993   *Shiloh: The Archaeology of a Biblical Site.* Institute of Archaeology of Tel Aviv University, Monograph Series 10. Tel Aviv.

Firth, Cecil M., and Battiscombe Gunn

1926   *Teti Pyramid Cemeteries.* 2 vols. Excavations at Saqqara. Cairo.

Fischer, Franz

1963   *Die hethitische Keramik von Boğazköy.* Vol. 4 of *Boğazköy-Hattuša: Ergebnisse der Ausgrabungen des Deutschen Archäologischen Instituts und der Deutschen Orient-Gesellschaft in den Jahren 1931–1939.* Wissenschaftliche Veröffentlichung der Deutschen Orient-Gesellschaft, vol. 75. Berlin.

Fischer, Henry G.

1963   "Varia Aegyptiaca." *Journal of the American Research Center in Egypt* 2, pp. 17–52.

1969   "Egyptian Art." *Metropolitan Museum of Art Bulletin*, n.s., 28, no. 2 (October), pp. 69–70.

Fitton, J. Lesley

1992   as editor. *Ivory in Greece and the Eastern Mediterranean from the Bronze Age to the Hellenistic Period.* British Museum Occasional Paper, no. 85. London.

2002   *Minoans.* London.

2008   as editor. *The Aigina Treasure.* London. In press.

Fitton, J. Lesley, and T. Kiely, eds.

2008   *Cyprus in the British Museum: Cypriot Studies in Honour of Dr. Veronica Tatton-Brown.* London. In press.

Forlanini, M.

2008   "The Historical Geography of Anatolia and the Transition from the Karum-Period to the Early Hittite Empire." In *Anatolia and the Jazira during the Old Assyrian Period*, edited by J. G. Dercksen, pp. 57–86. Old Assyrian Archives, Studies, vol. 3. Leiden.

Forstner-Müller, Irene

2008   *Tell el-Dab'a XVI. Die Gräber des Areals A/II.* Untersuchungen der Zweigstelle Kairo des Österreichischen Archäologischen Institutes 28. Vienna.

Foster, Benjamin R.

1987   "The Late Bronze Age Palace Economy: A View from the East." In Hägg and Marinatos 1987, pp. 11–16.

2005   "Diurnal Prayers of Diviners." In *Before the Muses: An Anthology of Akkadian Literature*, edited by Benjamin R. Foster, pp. 209–11. 3rd ed. Bethesda, Md.

Foster, E. D.

1977   "An Administrative Department at Knossos Concerned with Perfumery and Offerings." *Minos* 16, pp. 19–51.

Foster, Karen P.

1979   *Aegean Faience of the Bronze Age.* New Haven.

Foster, Karen P., and Robert Laffineur, eds.

2003   *Metron: Measuring the Aegean Bronze Age. Proceedings of the 9th International Aegean Conference, New Haven, Yale University, 18–21 April 2002.* Aegaeum 24. Liège and Austin.

Franco, Isabelle

2002   "The Daggers of Kamose." In *Pharaohs* 2002, p. 428, no. 103.

Frankfort, Henri

1936–37 "Notes on the Cretan Griffin." *Annual of the British School at Athens* 37, pp. 106–22.

1937–39 "The Burney Relief." *Archiv für Orientforschung* 12, pp. 128–35.

1939   *Cylinder Seals: A Documentary Essay on the Art and Religion of the Ancient Near East.* London.

1955   *The Art and Architecture of the Ancient Orient.* Pelican History of Art. Harmondsworth.

1970   *The Art and Architecture of the Ancient Orient.* 4th rev. ed. Pelican History of Art. Harmondsworth.

1977   *The Art and Architecture of the Ancient Orient.* 4th rev. printing of 1970 ed. Pelican History of Art. Harmondsworth.

Frayne, Douglas R.

1990   *Old Babylonian Period (2003–1595 BC).* Royal Inscriptions of Mesopotamia; Early Periods, vol. 4. Toronto.

1993   *Sargonic and Gutian Periods (2334–2113 BC).* Royal Inscriptions of Mesopotamia, Early Periods, vol. 2. Toronto.

1997   *Ur III Period (2112–2004 BC).* Royal Inscriptions of Mesopotamia: Early Periods, vol. 3, part 2. Toronto.

French, Elizabeth B.

2002   *Mycenae: Agamemnon's Capital. The Site and Its Setting.* Stroud, Gloucestershire.

2004   "The Contribution of Chemical Analysis to Provenance Studies." In *La céramique mycénienne de L'Égée au Levant: Hommage à Vronwy Hankey*, edited by Jacqueline Balensi, Jean-Yves Monchambert, and Sylvie Müller Celka, pp. 15–25. Travaux de la Maison de l'Orient et de la Méditerranée, no. 41. Lyon.

Friedrich, W. L., et al.

2006   W. L. Friedrich, Bernd Kromer, M. Friedrich, J. Heinemeier, T. Pfeiffer, and S. Talamo. "Santorini Eruption Radiocarbon Dated to 1627–1600 B.C." *Science* 312, no. 5773, p. 548.

Frost, H.

1969a   "The Stone-Anchors of Byblos." *Mélanges de l'Université Saint-Joseph* 45, pp. 425–42.

1969b   "The Stone Anchors of Ugarit." In *Ugaritica VI: La XXXe campagne de fouilles à Ras Shamra (1968)*, edited by Claude F. A. Schaeffer, pp. 235–45. Mission de Ras Shamra, vol. 17. Paris.

1985   "Appendix I: The Kition Anchors." In Karageorghis and Demas 1985, pp. 281–321.

1991   "Anchors Sacred and Profane: Ugarit-Ras Shamra, 1986; the Stone Anchors Revised and Compared." In *Arts et industries de la pierre*, edited by Marguerite Yon, pp. 355–410. Ras Shamra-Ougarit, vol. 6. Paris.

Frühe Phöniker im Libanon

1983   *Frühe Phöniker im Libanon, 20 Jahre deutsche Ausgrabungen in Kāmid el-Lōz.* Exhibition, Rheinisches Landesmuseum Bonn. Catalogue edited by Rolf Hachmann; contributions by Johannes Boese, Rudolf Echt, and Andrei Miron. Mainz am Rhein.

Fugmann, E

1958   *Hama: Fouilles et recherches de la Fondation Carlsberg, 1931–38.*

Vol. 2, *Les premiers habitates et la ville pré-hellénistique de Hamath*, part 1, *L'architecture des périodes pré-hellénistiques*. Copenhagen.

Furumark, Arne
1941   *The Mycenaean Pottery: Analysis and Classification*. Stockholm.

Fuscaldo, P.
2003   "Tell el-Dab'a: Two Execration Pits and a Foundation Deposit." In *Egyptology at the Dawn of the Twenty-first Century: Proceedings of the Eighth International Congress of Egyptologists, Cairo, 2000*, edited by Zahi Hawass, vol. 1, pp. 185–88. Cairo and New York.

Gaballa, G. A.
1976   *Narrative in Egyptian Art*. Mainz am Rhein.

Gabolde, Marc
1998   *D'Akhenaton à Toutânkhamon*. Collection de l'Institut d'Archéologie et d'Histoire de l'Antiquité, vol. 3. Lyon.

Gachet, Jacqueline
1992   "Ugarit Ivories: Typology and Distribution." In Fitton 1992, pp. 67–89.

Gachet-Bizollon, Jacqueline
2007   *Les ivoires d'Ougarit et l'art des ivoiriers du Levant au bronze récent*. Ras Shamra-Ougarit, vol. 16. Paris.

Galán, J.
1994   "Bullfight Scenes in Ancient Egyptian Tombs." *Journal of Egyptian Archaeology* 80, pp. 81–96.

Gale, Noel H.
1991a   as editor. *Bronze Age Trade in the Mediterranean: Papers Presented at the Conference Held at Rewley House, Oxford, in December 1989*. Studies in Mediterranean Archaeology, vol. 90. Jonsered.
1991b   "Copper Oxhide Ingots: Their Origin and Their Place in the Bronze Age Metals Trade in the Mediterranean." In Gale 1991a, pp. 197–239.

Gale, Noel H., and Sophie Stos-Gale
2002   "Archaeometallurgical Research in the Aegean." In *The Beginnings of Metallurgy in the Old World*, edited by Martin Bartelheim, Ernst Pernicka, and Rüdiger Krause, pp. 277–302. Forschungen zur Archäometrie und Altertumswissenschaft, vol. 1. Rahden.
2005   "Zur Herkunft der Kupferbarren aus dem Schiffswrack von Uluburun und der Spätbronzezeitliche Metallhandel in Mittelmeerraum." In *Das Schiff von Uluburun* 2005, pp. 117–31.

Gale, Noel H., Zofia A. Stos-Gale, and G. Maliotis
2000   "Copper Oxhide Ingots and the Mediterranean Metals Trade: A New Perspective." In *Proceedings of the Third International Congress of Cyprus Studies*, pp. 327–44. Nicosia.

Galili, E.
1985   "A Group of Stone Anchors from Newe-Yam." *International Journal of Nautical Archaeology* 14, no. 2, pp. 143–53.

Galili, E., J. Shavrit, and M. Artzy
1994   "Reconsidering Byblian and Egyptian Stone Anchors Using Numeral Methods: New Finds from the Israeli Coast." *International Journal of Nautical Archaeology* 23, no. 2, pp. 93–107.

Galili, E., N. Shmueli, and M. Artzy
1986   "Bronze Age Ship's Cargo of Copper and Tin." *International Journal of Nautical Archaeology* 15, no. 1, pp. 32–34.

Gallet de Santerre, Hubert
1987   "Les statuettes de bronze mycéniennes au type dit du 'dieu Reshef' dans leur contexte égéen." *Bulletin de correspondance hellénique* 111, pp. 7–29.

Gallis, Konstantinos
1973   "Δύο Νεόσχημοι Πυξίδες εξ Εγκωμης." Αρχαιολογική Εφημερίς (*Archaiologike ephemeris*) 112, pp. 120–29.

Gardiner, Alan Henderson
1927   *Egyptian Grammar: Being an Introduction to the Study of Hieroglyphs*. Oxford.
1950   *Egyptian Grammar: Being an Introduction to the Study of Hieroglyphs*. 2nd ed. London.
1960   *The Kadesh Inscriptions of Ramesses II*. Oxford.
1988   *Egyptian Grammar, Being an Introduction to the Study of Hieroglyphs*. Reprint of 3rd rev. ed. of 1957. Oxford.

Garelli, Paul
1964   "Tablettes cappadociennes de collections diverses," parts 1, 2. *Revue d'assyriologie* 58, no. 2, pp. 53–68; no. 3, pp. 111–35.
1965   "Tablettes cappadociennes de collections diverses." *Revue d'assyriologie* 59, no. 1, pp. 19–48; no. 4, pp. 149–76.
1966   "Tablettes cappadociennes de collections diverses." *Revue d'assyriologie* 60, no. 2, pp. 93–152.

Garstang, John
1928   "An Ivory Sphinx from Abydos (British Museum, No. 54678)." *Journal of Egyptian Archaeology* 14, no. 1–2 (May), pp. 46–47.

Gasche, Hermann, et al.
1998a   Hermann Gasche, James A. Armstrong, Stephen W. Cole, and Vahe G. Gurzadyan. *Dating the Fall of Babylon: A Reappraisal of Second-Millennium Chronology*. Ghent and Chicago.
1998b   "A Correction to *Dating the Fall of Babylon: A Reappraisal of Second-Millennium Chronology (=MHEM 4)*, Ghent and Chicago, 1998." *Akkadica* 108, pp. 1–4.

Gaspar, Camille
1901   *Le legs de la baronne de Hirsch à la Nation Belge*. Brussels.

Gates, Marie-Henriette
1984   "The Palace of Zimri-Lim at Mari." *Biblical Archaeologist* 47, no. 2, pp. 70–87.
1992   "Mycenaean Art for a Levantine Market? The Ivory Lid from Minet el-Beidha/Ugarit." In Laffineur and Crowley 1992, pp. 77–84.

Gelb, I. J.
1984   "The Inscription of Jibbit-Lim, King of Ebla." *Studia Orientalia* 55, pp. 213–29.

Genouillac, Henri de
1910   "Ancienne stèle de victoire." *Revue d'assyriologie* 7, no. 3, pp. 151–56.
1926   *Céramique cappadocienne*. Vol. 2, *Acquisitions du Musée du Louvre*. Paris.

George, Andrew
1999   as translator. *The Epic of Gilgamesh: The Babylonian Epic Poem and Other Texts in Akkadian and Sumerian*. London.
2004   "Gilgamesh and the Cedars of Lebanon." In Doumet-Serhal 2004c, pp. 450–55.

Germer, Renate
1985   *Flora des pharaonischen Ägypten*. Deutsches Archäologisches Institut, Abteilung Kairo, Sonderschrift 14. Mainz am Rhein.

Gessel, Geraldine C.
1985   *Town, Palace, and House Cult in Minoan Crete*. Studies in Mediterranean Archaeology, vol. 67. Göteborg.

Ghirshman, Roman
1938–39 *Fouilles de Sialk près de Kashan, 1933, 1934, 1937*. 2 vols. Musée du Louvre, Département des Antiquités Orientales, Série archéologique, vols. 4, 5. Paris.
1953   "Uncovering the 'Tower of Babel' of Choga-Zambil: New Excavations in and around the Great Ziggurat of the Elamite

King Untash-Huban." *Illustrated London News* 223 (August 8), pp. 226–27.

1966   *Tchoga Zanbil (Dur-Untash)*. Vol. 1, *La ziggurat*. Mémoires de la Délégation Archéologique en Iran, vol. 39. Paris.

Gibson, McGuire

1992   "Patterns of Occupation at Nippur." In *Nippur at the Centennial: Papers Read at the 35e Rencontre assyriologique internationale, Philadelphia, 1988*, edited by Maria deJong Ellis, pp. 33–54. Philadelphia.

1993   "Nippur, Sacred City of Enlil, Supreme God of Sumer and Akkad." *Al-Rāfidān* 14, pp. 1–18.

Gifts of the Nile

1998   *Gifts of the Nile: Ancient Egyptian Faience.* Exhibition, Cleveland Museum of Art; Museum of Art, Rhode Island School of Design, Providence; Kimbell Art Museum, Fort Worth. Catalogue edited by Florence Dunn Friedman. London.

Gill, M. A. V.

1964   "The Minoan Genius." *Athenische Mitteilungen* 79, pp. 1–21.

Giumlia-Mair, Alessandra R., and Paul T. Craddock

1993   *Das schwarze Gold der Alchimisten: Corinthium aes.* Mainz am Rhein.

Giveon, Raphael

1971   *Les Bédouins Shosou des documents égyptiens.* Documenta et monumenta orientis antique, vol. 18. Leiden.

Glories of the Past

1990   *Glories of the Past: Ancient Art from the Shelby White and Leon Levy Collection.* Exhibition, The Metropolitan Museum of Art, New York. Catalogue edited by Dietrich von Bothmer. New York.

Gnirs, Andrea Maria

1996   *Militär und Gesellschaft: Ein Beitrag zur Sozialgeschichte des Neuen Reiches.* Studien zur Archäologie und Geschichte Altägyptens, vol. 17. Heidelberg.

2004   "Die 18. Dynastie: Licht und Schatten eines internationalen Zeitalters." In *Tutanchamun. Das Goldene Jenseits: Grabschätze aus dem Tal der Könige*, edited by André Wiese and Andreas Brodbeck, pp. 27–44. Exh. cat., Antikenmuseum Basel and Sammlung Ludwig, Basel. Munich.

2006   "Das Motiv des Bürgerkriegs in Merikare und Neferti: Zur Literatur der 18. Dynastie." In *Jn.t dr.w: Festschrift für Friedrich Junge*, edited by Gerald Moers et al., vol. 1, pp. 207–65. Göttingen.

Gods and Heroes of the Bronze Age

1999   *Gods and Heroes of the Bronze Age: Europe at the Time of Ulysses.* Exhibition, National Museum of Denmark, Copenhagen; Kunst- und Ausstellungshalle der Bundesrepublik Deutschland, Bonn; Galeries Nationales du Grand Palais, Paris; National Archaeological Museum, Athens. Catalogue by Katie Demakopoulou et al.; edited by Jørgen Jensen; translations by Melissa Thorson Hause, Steven Lindberg, and John S. Southard. London.

Goedicke, Hans

1975   *The Report of Wenamun.* Baltimore.

1988   "The Scribal Palette of Athu." *Chronique d'Égypte* 63, no. 125, pp. 42–56.

Goelet, O.

1993   "Nudity in Ancient Egypt." *Source* 12, no. 2, pp. 20–31.

Gogadze, E. M. (E. Gogaże)

1972   *T'rialet'is qorġanuli kulturis periodizaci'a da genezisi.* T'bilisi.

Gold der Thraker

1979   *Gold der Thraker: Archäologische Schätze aus Bulgarien.* Exhibition, Römisch-Germanisches Museum, Cologne;

Münchner Stadtmuseum, Munich; Roemer-Museum, Hildesheim. Catalogue by J. N. Chernykh et al. Mainz am Rhein.

Goldstein, Sidney M.

1979   *Pre-Roman and Early Roman Glass in the Corning Museum of Glass.* Corning, N.Y.

Gonen, Rivka

1992a   "The Late Bronze Age." In A. Ben-Tor 1992, pp. 211–57.

1992b   *Burial Patterns and Cultural Diversity in Late Bronze Age Canaan.* Winona Lake, Ind.

Gorelick, L., and A. J. Gwinnett

1987   "A History of Drills and Drilling." *New York State Dental Journal* 53, no. 1, pp. 35–39.

Goren, Yuval, Israel Finkelstein, and Nadav Na'aman

2004   *Inscribed in Clay, Provenance Study of the Amarna Tablets and Other Ancient Near Eastern Texts.* Tel Aviv University, Sonia and Marco Nadler Institute of Archaeology, Monograph Series, no. 23. Tel Aviv.

Grandet, Pierre

1993   *Ramsès III: Histoire d'un règne.* Paris.

Gray, J.

1964   *The Canaanites.* Ancient Peoples and Places, vol. 38. New York.

Grayson, A. Kirk

1987   *Assyrian Rulers of the Third and Second Millennia B.C. (to 1115 BC).* With the assistance of Grant Frame and Douglas Frayne and a contribution by Maynard Maidman. The Royal Inscriptions of Mesopotamia, Assyrian Periods, vol. 1. Toronto.

1991   *Assyrian Rulers of the Early First Millennium BC I (1114–859 BC).* The Royal Inscriptions of Mesopotamia, Assyrian Periods, vol. 2. Toronto.

Greenberg, Moshe

1955   *The Hab/piru.* American Oriental Series, vol. 39. New Haven.

Greenwell, W.

1902   "On Some Rare Forms of Bronze Weapons and Implements." *Archaeologia* 58, no. 1, pp. 1–16.

Griffiths, Dafydd

2004   "The Fabric of a Ceramic Jar from Sidon Decorated with Fish or Dolphins." *Archaeology and History in the Lebanon* 19 (Spring), pp. 110–17.

Grose, David F.

1989   *Early Ancient Glass: Core-formed, Rod-formed, and Cast Vessels and Objects from the Late Bronze Age to the Early Roman Empire, 1600 B.C. to A.D. 50.* New York.

Grumach-Shirun, I.

1977   "Federn und Federkrone." In *Lexikon der Ägyptologie*, edited by Wolfgang Helck and Wolfhart Westendorf, vol. 2, cols. 142–45. Wiesbaden.

Guichard, Michaël

1999   "Les mentions de la Crète à Mari." In Caubet 1999a.

2005   *La vaisselle de luxe des rois de Mari: Matériaux pour le diction-naire de Babylonien de Paris.* Vol. 2. Archives royales de Mari, vol. 31. Paris.

Günbattı, C.

2004   "Two Treaty Texts Found at Kültepe." In Dercksen 2004, pp. 249–68.

Gundlach, R.

1986   "Thoeris." In *Lexikon der Ägyptologie*, edited by Wolfgang Helck and Wolfhart Westendorf, vol. 6, pp. 494–98. Weisbaden.

Günel, Sevinç

1999   *Panaztepe II: Die Keramik von Panaztepe und ihre Bedeutung für Westkleinasien und die Ägäis im 2. Jahrtausend.* Ankara.

Güterbock, Hans G.

1971   "Ivory in Hittite Texts." *Anatolia/Anadolu* 15, pp. 1–7.

1975   "Die Inschriften." In Bittel et al. 1975, pp. 167–87.

1981–83 "A Note on the Friezes of the Stag Rhyton in the Schimmel Collection." *Anadolu* 22 (1981–83), pp. 1–4.

1983   "Hethitische Götterbilder und Kultobjekte." In *Beiträge zur Altertumskunde Kleinasiens: Festschrift für Kurt Bittel*, edited by Rainer M. Boehmer and Harald Hauptmann, pp. 211–14. Mainz am Rhein.

1984   "Hittites and Akhaeans: A New Look." *Proceedings of the American Philosophical Society* 128, no. 2 (June), pp. 114–22.

Güterbock, Hans G., and Timothy Kendall

1995   "A Hittite Silver Vessel in the Form of a Fist." In *The Ages of Homer: A Tribute to Emily Townsend Vermeule*, edited by Jane B. Carter and Sarah P. Morris, pp. 45–60. Austin.

Guy, P. L. O., and Robert M. Engberg

1938   *Megiddo Tombs.* University of Chicago Oriental Institute Publications, vol. 33. Chicago.

Haas, Georg

1953   "On the Occurrence of Hippopotamus in the Iron Age of the Coastal Area of Israel (Tell Qasîleh)." *Bulletin of the American Schools of Oriental Research*, no. 132, pp. 30–34.

Haas, Volkert

1994   *Geschichte der hethitischen Religion.* Handbuch der Orientalistik, ser. 1, Der Nahe und Mittlere Osten, vol. 15. Leiden.

Haas, Volkert, and Markus Wäfler

1985   *Tall al-Ḥamīdīya.* Vol. 1, *Vorbericht 1984.* Orbis Biblicus et Orientalis, Series Archaeologica, vol. 4. Fribourg and Göttingen.

Habachi, Labib

1972   *The Second Stela of Kamose and His Struggle against the Hyksos Ruler and His Capital.* Abhandlungen des Deutschen Archäologischen Instituts Kairo, Ägyptologische Reihe, vol. 8. Glückstadt.

2001   *Tell el-Dabʿa I, Tell el-Dabʿa and Qantir: The Site and Its Connection with Avaris and Piramesse* II. Untersuchungen der Zweigstelle Kairo des Österreichischen Archäologischen Institutes, vol. 2. Vienna.

Hachmann, Rolf, and Arnulf Kuschke

1966   *Bericht über die Ergebnisse der Ausgrabungen in Kamid el-Loz (Libanon) in den Jahren 1963 und 1964.* Bonn.

Hadjioannou, Kyrianos

1971   "On the Identification of the Horned God of Engomi-Alasia." In *Alasia I*, edited by Claude F. A. Schaeffer, pp. 33–42. Paris: Mission Archéologique d'Alasia.

Hagens, Graham

2005   "The Assyrian King List and Chronology: A Critique." *Orientalia* 74, pp. 23–41.

Hägg, Robin, and Nanno Marinatos, eds.

1984   *The Minoan Thalassocracy: Myth and Reality. Proceedings of the Third International Symposium at the Swedish Institute in Athens, 31 May–5 June 1982.* Skrifter utgivna av Svenska Institutet i Athen, ser. 4, vol. 32. Stockholm.

1987   *The Function of the Minoan Palaces: Proceedings of the Fourth International Symposium at the Swedish Institute in Athens, 10–16 June 1984.* Skrifter utgivna av Svenska Institutet i Athen, ser. 4, vol. 35. Stockholm.

Hairfield, H. H., Jr., and E. M. Hairfield

1990   "Identification of a Late Bronze Age Resin." *Analytical Chemistry* 62, no. 1, pp. 41A–45A.

Hakemi, Ali

1997   *Shahdad: Archaeological Excavations of a Bronze Age Center in Iran.* Translated and edited by S. M. S. Sajjadi. Istituto Italiano per il Medio ed Estremo Oriente Centro Scavi e Ricerche Archeologiche, Reports and Memoirs, vol. 27. Rome.

Hakulin, Lena

2004   *Bronzeworking on Late Minoan Crete: A Diachronic Study.* BAR International Series 1245. Oxford.

Haldane, Cheryl Ward

1990   "Shipwrecked Plant Remains." *Biblical Archaeologist* 53, no. 1, pp. 55–60.

1991   "Recovery and Analysis of Plant Remains from Some Mediterranean Shipwreck Sites." In *New Light on Early Farming: Recent Developments in Paleoethnobotany*, edited by Jane M. Renfrew, pp. 213–23. Edinburgh.

1993   "Direct Evidence for Organic Cargoes in the Late Bronze Age." *World Archaeology* 24, no. 3, pp. 348–60.

Hall, H. R.

1928   "Minoan Fayence in Mesopotamia." *Journal of Hellenic Studies* 48, pp. 64–74.

Hallager, B. P., and E. Hallager

1995   "The Knossian Bull: Political Progaganda in Neo-Palatial Crete?" In *Politeia, Society and State in the Aegean Bronze Age: Proceedings of the 5th International Aegean Conference/5e Rencontre égéenne internationale, University of Heidelberg, Archäologisches Institut, 10–13 April 1994*, edited by Robert Laffineur and Wolf-Dietrich Niemeier, pp. 547–56. Liège.

Haller, Arndt

1954   *Die Gräber und Grufte von Assur.* Wissenschaftliche Veröffentlichung der Deutschen Orient-Gesellschaft, vol. 65. Berlin.

Hamilton, R. W.

1935   "Excavations at Tell Abu Hawām." *Quarterly of the Department of Antiquities in Palestine* 4, pp. 1–69.

Hammade, Hamido

1987   *Cylinder Seals from the Collections of the Aleppo Museum, Syrian Arab Republic.* BAR International Series 335. Oxford.

Hankey, Vronwy

1973   "The Aegean Deposit at Tell el-Amarna." In *Acts of the International Archaeological Symposium 'Mycenaeans in the Eastern Mediterranean,' Nicosia, 27th March–2nd April 1972*, edited by Vassos Karageorghis, pp. 128–36. Nicosia.

1987   "The Chronology of the Aegean Late Bronze Age." In P. Åström 1987–89, vol. 2, pp. 39–59.

Hankey, Vronwy, and D. Aston

1995   "Mycenaean Pottery at Saqqara: Finds from Excavations by the Egypt Exploration Society of London and the Rijksmuseum van Oudheden, Leiden, 1975–1990." In *The Ages of Homer: A Tribute to Emily Townsend Vermeule*, edited by Jane B. Carter and Sarah P. Morris, pp. 67–91. Austin.

Hankey, Vronwy, and P. M. Warren

1974   "The Absolute Chronology of the Aegean Late Bronze Age." *Bulletin of the Institute of Classical Studies of the University of London* 21, pp. 142–52.

Hänsel, Bernhard

1976   *Beiträge zur regionalen und chronologischen Gliederung der älteren Hallstattzeit an der unteren Donau.* 2 vols. Bonn.

Hansen, Donald P.

1969   "Some Remarks on the Chronology and Style of Objects from Byblos." *American Journal of Archaeology* 73, pp. 281–84.

1975   "Frühsumerische und frühdynastische Flachbildkunst." In Orthmann 1975, pp. 179–93.

Hansen, O.
1994   "A Mycenaean Sword from Boğazköy-Hattusa Found in 1991."
        Annual of the British School at Athens, no. 89, pp. 213–15.

Hansen, S.
2005   "Neue Forschungen zur Metallurgie der Bronzezeit in
        Südosteuropa." In *Anatolian Metal*, vol. 3, edited by Ünsal
        Yalçin, pp. 89–104. Der Anschnitt, Beiheft 18. Bochum:
        Deutches Bergbau-Museum Bochum.

Harden, Donald B.
1981   *Catalogue of Greek and Roman Glass in the British Museum.*
        Vol. 1, *Core- and Rod-formed Vessels and Pendants and
        Mycenaean Cast Objects.* London.

Hardy, David A., and A. C. Renfrew, eds.
1990   *Thera and the Aegean World III: Proceedings of the Third Inter-
        national Congress, Santorini, Greece, 3–9 September, 1989.* 3 vols.
        Vol. 1, *Archaeology*, edited by David A. Hardy, with C. G.
        Doumas, J. A. Sakellarakis, and P. M. Warren. Vol. 3,
        Chronology, edited by David A. Hardy and A. C. Renfrew.
        London.

Harper, Prudence Oliver
1969   "Dating a Group of Ivories from Anatolia." *Connoisseur* 172,
        no. 693 (November), pp. 156–62.

Harrak, Amir
1987   *Assyria and Hanigalbat: A Historical Reconstruction of Bilateral
        Relations from the Middle of the Fourteenth to the End of the
        Twelfth Centuries B.C.* Texte und Studien zur Orientalistik,
        vol. 4. Hildesheim.

Hart, Henry C.
1888   *Scripture Natural History II. The Animals Mentioned in the Bible.*
        Oxford.

Hartwig, Melinda K.
2004   *Tomb Painting and Identity in Ancient Thebes, 1419–1372 BCE.*
        Monumenta Aegyptiaca, vol. 10; Série imago, no. 2. Brussels
        and Turnhout.

Harvey, Stephen P.
1998   "The Cults of King Ahmose at Abydos." Ph.D. diss., University
        of Pennsylvania, Philadelphia.

Hasel, Michael G.
1998   *Domination and Resistance: Egyptian Military Activity in the
        Southern Levant, ca. 1300–1185 B.C.* Probleme der Ägyptologie,
        vol. 11. Leiden.

Haskell, H. W.
1984   "Pylos: Stirrup Jars and the International Oil Trade." In *Pylos
        Comes Alive: Industry and Administration in a Mycenaean Palace;
        Papers of a Symposium*, edited by Cynthia W. Shelmerdine and
        Thomas G. Palaima, pp. 97–107. New York.

Hatshepsut
2005   *Hatshepsut: From Queen to Pharaoh.* Exhibition, Fine Arts
        Museums of San Francisco/de Young; The Metropolitan
        Museum of Art, New York; Kimbell Art Museum, Fort Worth.
        Catalogue edited by Catharine H. Roehrig. New York.

Hauptmann, A., and R. Maddin
2005   "Die Kupferbarren von Uluburun. Teil 1: Qualitätsmetall für
        den Weltmarkt?" In *Das Schiff von Uluburun* 2005, pp. 133–40.

Hauptmann, A., R. Maddin, and M. Prange
2002   "On the Structure and Composition of Copper and Tin Ingots
        Excavated from the Shipwreck of Uluburun." *Bulletin of the
        American Schools of Oriental Research*, no. 328, pp. 1–30.

Haussoullier, Bernard
1878   "Catalogue descriptif des objets découverts à Spata." *Bulletin de
        correspondance hellenique* 2, pp. 185–228.

Hayes, William C.
1937   *Glazed Tiles from a Palace of Ramesses II at Ḳanṭîr.* Metropolitan
        Museum of Art, Papers, no. 3. New York.
1953   *The Scepter of Egypt: A Background for the Study of the Egyptian
        Antiquities in The Metropolitan Museum of Art.* Vol. 1, *From the
        Earliest Times to the End of the Middle Kingdom.* New York.
1959   *The Scepter of Egypt: A Background for the Study of the Egyptian
        Antiquities in The Metropolitan Museum of Art.* Vol. 2, *The Hyksos
        Period and the New Kingdom (1675–1080 B.C.).* New York.
1990   *The Scepter of Egypt: A Background for the Study of the Egyptian
        Antiquities in The Metropolitan Museum of Art.* 2 vols. New
        York: The Metropolitan Museum of Art.

Hayward, L. G.
1990   "The Origin of the Raw Elephant Ivory Used in Greece and
        the Aegean during the Late Bronze Age." *Antiquity* 64, no. 242,
        pp. 103–9.

Hazzidakis, Joseph
1921   *Étude de préhistoire crétoise: Tylissos à l'époque Minoenne.*
        Translated by L. Franchet. Paris.

Hein, Irmgard
1994   "Dolch des Kamose." In *Pharaonen und Fremde* 1994, p. 272,
        no. 382.

Heinrich, Ernst
1982   *Die Tempel und Heiligtümer im alten Mesopotamien: Typologie,
        Morphologie und Geschichte.* 2 vols. Denkmäler antiker
        Architektur, vol. 14. Berlin.

Helck, Wolfgang
1971   *Die Beziehungen Ägyptens zu Vorderasien im 3. und 2. Jahrtausend
        v. Chr.* 2nd ed. Wiesbaden.
1979   *Die Beziehungen Ägyptens und Vorderasiens zur Ägäis bis ins 7.
        Jahrhundert v. Chr.* Darmstadt.
1987   "'Was kann die Ägyptologie wirklich zum Problem der abso-
        luten Chronologie in der Bronzezeit beitragen?': Chronologische
        Annäherungswerte in der 18. Dynastie." In P. Åström
        1987–89, vol. 1, pp. 18–26.
1995   *Die Beziehungen Ägyptens und Vorderasiens zur Ägäis bis ins 7.
        Jahrhundert v. Chr.* [2nd ed.] Darmstadt.

Hellenkemper, Hansgerd, and Jörg Wagner
1977   "The God on the Stag: A Late Hittite Rock-Relief on the River
        Karasu." *Anatolian Studies* 27, pp. 167–73.

Helms, Mary W.
1993   *Craft and the Kingly Ideal: Art, Trade, and Power.* Austin.

Heltzer, Michael
1978   *Goods, Prices, and the Organization of Trade in Ugarit (Marketing
        and Transportation in the Eastern Mediterranean in the Second
        Half of the Second Millennium B.C.E.).* Wiesbaden.
1989   "Some Questions of the Ugaritic Metrology and its Parallels
        in Judah, Phoenicia, Mesopotamia and Greece." *Ugarit-
        Forschungen: Internationales Jahrbuch für die Altertumskunde
        Syrien-Palästinas* 21, pp. 195–208.

Henderson, J.
1997   "Scientific Analysis of Glass and Glaze from Tell Brak and Its
        Archaeological Implications." In Oates, Oates, and McDonald
        1997, pp. 94–100.

Hepper, F. Nigel
1977   "On the Transference of Ancient Plant Names." *Palestine
        Exploration Quarterly* 109 (July–December), pp. 129–30.

Hermann, Alfred
1932   "Das Motiv der Ente mit zurückgewendetem Kopfe im ägyp-
        tischen Kunstgewerbe." *Zeitschrift für ägyptische Sprache und
        Altertumskunde* 68, pp. 86–105.

Herold, Anja
1998   "Piramesses—the Northern Capital: Chariots, Horses, and

Foreign Gods." In *Capital Cities: Urban Planning and Spiritual Dimensions; Proceedings of the Symposium Held on May 27–29, 1996, Jerusalem, Israel*, edited by Joan Goodnick Westenholz, pp. 129–46. Jerusalem.

Herrmann, Georgina
1968 "Lapis Lazuli: The Early Phases of Its Trade." *Iraq* 30, pp. 21–57.
1992 "The Nimrud Ivories, 2: A Survey of the Traditions." In *Von Uruk nach Tuttul: Eine Festschrift für Eva Strommenger*, edited by Barthel Hrouda, Stephan Kroll, and Peter Z. Spanos, pp. 65–79. Munich.
n.d. "Ivories from the North West Palace at Nimrud." In Cecchini, Mazzoni, and Scigliuzzo n.d. Forthcoming.

Herrmann, G., and P. R. S. Moorey
1980–83 "Lapis-lazuli, B. Archäologie." In *Reallexikon der Assyriologie und Vorderasiatischen Archäologie*, vol. 6, pp. 489–92. Berlin.

Hesiod
1914 *Hesiod; the Homeric Hymns; and, Homerica.* English translation by Hugh G. Evelyn-White. Loeb Classical Library, Greek Authors, vol. 57. Cambridge, Mass.

Hess, Richard S.
1993 *Amarna Personal Names.* American Schools of Oriental Research, Dissertation Series, vol. 9. Winona Lake, Ind.

Die Hethiter und ihr Reich
2002 *Die Hethiter und ihr Reich: Das Volk der 1000 Götter.* Exhibition, Kunst- und Ausstellungshalle der Bundesrepublik Deutschland in Bonn, January 18–April 28, 2002. Catalogue edited by Tahsin Özgüç. Stuttgart.

Higginbotham, Carolyn R.
2000 *Egyptianization and Elite Emulation in Ramesside Palestine: Governance and Accommodation on the Imperial Periphery.* Leiden.

Higgins, Reynold A.
1957 "The Aegina Treasure Reconsidered." *Annual of the British School at Athens* 52, pp. 42–57.
1979 *The Aegina Treasure: An Archaeological Mystery.* London.
1987 "A Gold Diadem from Aegina." *Journal of Hellenic Studies* 107, p. 182.

Hiller, Stefan
1999 "Scenes of Warfare and Combat in the Arts of Aegean Late Bronze Age: Reflections on Typology and Development." In Laffineur 1999, vol. 2, pp. 319–30.

Hilzheimer, M.
1938 "Ente." In *Reallexikon der Assyriologie und Vorderasiatischen Archäologie*, vol. 2, pp. 399–400. Berlin.

Hirschfeld, Nicolle
1993 "Incised Marks (Post-Firing) on Aegean Wares." In *Proceedings of the International Conference, Wace and Blegen: Pottery as Evidence for Trade in the Aegean Bronze Age, 1939–1989; Held at the American School of Classical Studies at Athens, . . . December 2–3, 1989*, edited by Carol Zerner, Peter Zerner, and John Winder, pp. 311–18. Amsterdam.
1999 "Potmarks of the Late Bronze Age Eastern Mediterranean." Ph.D. diss., University of Texas at Austin.

Hochstetter, A.
1987 *Kastanas: Ausgrabungen in einem Siedlungshügel der Bronze- und Eisenzeit Makedoniens, 1975–1979.* [Vol. 5], *Die Kleinfunde.* Prähistorische Archäologie in Südosteuropa 6. Berlin.

Höckmann, O.
1980 "Lanze und Speer im spätminoischen und mykenischen Griechenland." *Jahrbuch des Römisch-germanischen Zentralmuseums, Mainz* 27, pp. 13–158.

Hoerth, Alfred J.
2007 "The Game of Hounds and Jackals." In Finkel 2007a, pp. 64–68.

Hoffman, Gail L.
2005 "Defining Identities: Greek Artistic Interaction with the Near East." In *Crafts and Images in Contact: Studies on Eastern Mediterranean Art of the First Millennium BCE*, edited by Claudia E. Suter and Christoph Uehlinger, pp. 351–89. Fribourg: Academic Press; Göttingen: Vandenhoeck and Ruprecht.

Hoffmeier, James K., and Kenneth A. Kitchen
2007 "Reshep and Astarte in North Sinai: A Recently Discovered Stela from Tell el-Borg." *Ägypten und Levante / Egypt and the Levant* 17, pp. 127–36.

Hogarth, D. G.
1914 *Carchemish: Report on the Excavations at Djerabis on Behalf of the British Museum.* Part 1. London.
1922 "Engraved Hittite Objects." *Journal of Egyptian Archaeology* 8, pp. 211–18.

Holmes, J. L.
1975 "The Foreign Trade of Cyprus during the Late Bronze Age." In *The Archaeology of Cyprus: Recent Developments*, edited by Noel Robertson, pp. 90–110. Park Ridge, N.J.

Hölscher, Uvo
1951 *The Excavation of Medinet Habu.* Vol. 4, *The Mortuary Temple of Ramses III.* Part 2. Translated by Mrs. Keith C. Steele and Elizabeth B. Hauser. Chicago.

Homer
1990 *The Odyssey.* Translated by Robert Fitzgerald. New York.

Hood, M. S. F.
1959–60 "Archaeology in Greece, 1959." *Archaeological Reports*, no. 6, pp. 3–26.
1978 *The Arts in Prehistoric Greece.* Harmondsworth.

Hood, Sinclair [M. S. F.], George Huxley, and Nancy K. Sandars
1958–59 "A Minoan Cemetery on Upper Gypsades." *Annual of the British School at Athens* 53–54, pp. 194–262.

Horden, Peregrine, and Nicholas Purcell
2000 *The Corrupting Sea: A Study of Mediterranean History.* Oxford.

Hornemann, Bodil
1969 *Types of Ancient Egyptian Statuary.* Vol. 6. Copenhagen.

Hornung, Erik
1987 "'Lang oder kurz?': Das Mittlere und Neue Reich Ägyptens als Prufstein." In P. Åström 1987–89, vol. 1, pp. 27–36.
1999 *Akhenaten and the Religion of Light.* Translated by David Lorton. Ithaca, N.Y.

Hornung, Erik, Rolf Krauss, and David A. Warburton, eds.
2006 *Ancient Egyptian Chronology.* Leiden: E. J. Brill.

Hornung, Erik, and Elisabeth Staehelin, eds.
1976 *Skarabäen und andere Siegelamulette aus Basler Sammlungen.* Ägyptische Denkmäler in der Schweiz, vol. 1. Mainz am Rhein.

Horsnell, Malcom John Albert
1999 *The Year-Names of the First Dynasty of Babylon.* 2 vols. Hamilton, Ont.

Horwitz, L. K., and E. Tchernov
1990 "Cultural and Environmental Implications of Hippopotamus Bone Remains in Archaeological Contexts in the Levant." *Bulletin of the American Schools of Oriental Research*, no. 280, pp. 67–76.

Houlihan, Patrick F.
1986 *The Birds of Ancient Egypt.* Warminster.
1996 *The Animal World of the Pharaohs.* London.

Hrouda, Barthel
1991   *Der Alte Orient: Geschichte und Kultur des alten Vorderasien.* Contributions by Jean Bottéro et al. Munich.

Hrozný, Frédéric
1927   "Rapport préliminaire sur les fouilles tchécoslovaques de Kültépé." *Syria* 8, pp. 1–12.

Huehnergard, John
1989   *The Akkadian of Ugarit.* Atlanta.

Hughes-Brock, Helen
1993   "Amber in the Aegean in the Late Bronze Age: Some Problems and Perspectives." In *Amber in Archaeology: Proceedings of the Second International Conference on Amber in Archaeology, Liblice 1990,* edited by C. W. Beck and J. Bouzek, pp. 219–29. Prague: Institute of Archaeology, Czech Academy of Sciences.
1999   "Mycenaean Beads: Gender and Social Contexts." *Oxford Journal of Archaeology* 18, pp. 277–96.
2000   "Animal, Vegetable, Mineral: Some Evidence from Small Objects." In *Krete–Aigyptos, politismikoi desmoi trion chilietion: Meletes,* pp. 120–27. Athens.

Huit millénaires de civilisation anatolienne
1981   *Huit millénaires de civilisation anatolienne: Objets prêtés par le Musée du Louvre.* Exhibition, Maison de l'Unesco, Paris. Catalogue. Ankara and Paris.

Hunger, Hermann
2000   "Uses of Enūma Anu Enlil for Chronology." *Akkadica* 119–20 (September–December), pp. 155–58.

Hunger, Hermann, and Regine Pruzsinszky, eds.
2004   *Mesopotamian Dark Age Revisited: Proceedings of an International Conference of SCIEM 2000, Vienna 8th–9th November 2002.* Contributions to the Chronology of the Eastern Mediterranean, vol. 6; Österreichische Akademie der Wissenschaften, Denkschriften der Gesamtakademie, vol. 32. Vienna.

Huot, Jean-Louis, Jean-Paul Thalmann, and Dominique Valbelle
1990   *Naissance des cités.* Paris.

Iakovidis, Sp.
1979   "Thera and Mycenaean Greece." *American Journal of Archaeology* 83, pp. 101–2.

Ibraham, Moawiyah
1982   *Excavations of the Arab Expedition at Sār el-Jisr Bahrain.* [Manama]: State of Bahrain, Ministry of Information.

Ilasli, A.
1993   "A Hittite Statue in the Area of Ahurhisar." In Mellink, Porada, and Özgüç 1993, pp. 301–8.

Im Labyrinth des Minos
2000   *Im Labyrinth des Minos: Kreta, die erste europäische Hochkultur.* Exhibition, Badisches Landesmuseum Karlsruhe. Catalogue by Susanne Erbelding, Sabine Albersmeier, and Klaus Eckerle. Munich.

Immerwahr, Sara A.
1990   *Aegean Painting in the Bronze Age.* University Park, Pa.
2005   "Left or Right? A Study of Hands and Feet." In *Aegean Wall Painting: A Tribute to Mark Cameron,* edited by Lyvia Morgan, pp. 173–83. British School at Athens Studies, vol. 13. London.

Ingram, R.
2005   "Faience and Glass Beads from the Late Bronze Age Shipwreck at Uluburun." M.A. thesis, Texas A&M University, College Station, Tex.

Invernizzi, Antonio
1980   "Excavations in the Yelki Area (Hamrin Project, Iraq)." *Mesopotamia* 15, pp. 19–49.

Ismail, Bahija Khalil, and Antoine Cavigneaux
2003   "Dāduša's Siegesstele IM 95200 aus Ešnunna: Die Inschrift." *Baghdader Mitteilungen* 34, pp. 129–56.

Ivoires
2004   *Ivoires: De l'Orient ancien aux temps modernes.* Exhibition, Musée du Louvre, Paris. Catalogue by Annie Caubet and Danielle Gaborit-Chopin, with the collaboration of François Poplin. Paris.

Izre'el, Shlomo
1991   *Amurru Akkadian: A Linguistic Study.* 2 vols. Harvard Semitic Studies, nos. 40–41. Atlanta.
1997   *The Amarna Scholarly Tablets.* Cuneiform Monographs, vol. 9. Groningen.

Jack, J. W.
1935   *The Ras Shamra Tablets: Their Bearing on the Old Testament.* Old Testament Studies, no. 1. Edinburgh.

Jacobsen, M., V. M. Bryant Jr., and J. G. Jones
1998   "Preliminary Pollen Analysis of Terebinth Resin from a Bronze Age Mediterranean Shipwreck." In *New Developments in Palynomorph Sampling, Extraction, and Analysis,* edited by Vaughn M. Bryant and John H. Wrenn, pp. 75–82. American Association of Stratigraphic Palynologists Foundation, Contribution Series, no. 33. Houston.

Jacobsson, Inga
1994   *Aegyptiaca from Late Bronze Age Cyprus.* Studies in Mediterranean Archaeology, vol. 112. Jonsered.

Jacoby, Felix, ed.
1958   *Die Fragmente der griechischen Historiker.* Leiden.

Jaeger, Bertrand
1982   *Essai de classification et datation des scarabées Menkhéperrê.* Orbis Biblicus et Orientalis, Series Archaeologica, vol. 2. Fribourg and Göttingen.

Jaeger, Bertrand, and R. Krauss
1990   "Zwei Skarabäen aus der mykenischen Fundstelle Panaztepe." *Mitteilungen der Deutschen Orient-Gesellschaft zu Berlin* 122, pp. 153–56.

Jakob, Stefan
2003   *Mittelassyrische Verwaltung und Sozialstruktur: Untersuchungen.* Cuneiform Monographs, vol. 29. Leiden and Boston.

James, Frances W., and Patrick E. McGovern
1993   *The Late Bronze Egyptian Garrison at Beth Shan: A Study of Levels VII and VIII.* 2 vols. University Museum Monograph 85. Philadelphia.

James, Thomas G. H.
2000   *Tutanchamun: Der ewige Glanz des jungen Pharaos.* Photography by Araldo De Luca. Cologne.

Jánosi, Peter
1992   "The Queens Ahhotep I and II and Egypt's Foreign Relations." *Journal of the Ancient Chronology Forum* 5, pp. 99–105.
1994   "Dolch des Nehemen." In *Pharaonen und Fremde* 1994, p. 155.
1995   "Die Stratigraphische Position und Verteilung der Minoischen Wandfragmente in den Grabungplätzen H/I und H/IV von Tell el-Dab'a." *Ägypten und Levante/Egypt and the Levant* 5, pp. 63–72.

Jansen-Winkeln, K.
2002   "Ägyptische Geschichte im Zeitalter der Wanderungen von Seevölkern und Libyern." In *Die nahöstlichen Kulturen und Griechenland an der Wende vom 2. zum 1. Jahrtausend v. Chr.: Kontinuität und Wandel von Strukturen und Mechanismen kultureller Interaktion; Kolloquium des Sonderforschungsbereiches 295 "Kulturelle und sprachliche Kontakte" der Johannes Gutenberg-*

Universität Mainz, 11.–12. Dezember 1998, edited by Eva A. Braun-Holzinger and Hartmut Matthäus, pp. 123–42. Möhnesee.

Janssen, Jozef M. A.
1951   "Fonctionnaires sémites au service de l'Égypte." *Chronique d'Égypte* 26 (January), pp. 50–62.

Jéquier, Gustave
1921   *Les frises d'objets des sarcophages du Moyen Empire.* Mémoires publiés par les membres de l'Institut Français d'Archéologie Orientale du Caire, vol. 47. Cairo.

Jidejian, Nina
1968   *Byblos through the Ages.* Beirut.

Joannès, Francis
1991   "L'étain, de l'Élam à Mari." In *Mesopotamie et Élam: Actes de la XXXVIème Rencontre assyriologique internationale, Gand, 10–14 juillet 1989*, pp. 67–76. Ghent.
1997   "Palmyre et les routes du désert au début du deuxième millé-naire av. J.-C." *Mari: Annales de recherches interdisciplinaires* 8, pp. 393–415.

Johnson, Jane
1980   *Maroni de Chypre.* Studies in Mediterranean Archaeology, vol. 59. Göteborg.

Johnson, W. Raymond
1991   "The Dazzling Sun Disk: Iconographic Evidence that Amenhotep III Reigned as the Aten Personified." *KMT* 2, no. 2, pp. 14–23, 60–63, 65–66.

Jones, B. R.
2005   "The Clothes-Line: Import and Export of Aegean Cloth(es) and Iconography." In Laffineur and Greco 2005, pp. 707–15.

Jones, Dilwyn
1995   *Boats.* Austin, Tex.

Jung, Reinhard
2007   "Tell Kazel and the Mycenaean Contacts with Amurru (Syria)." In Bietak and Czerny 2007, pp. 551–70.
2007–8   "Pharaohs, Swords, and Sea Peoples: European Long Swords in Egypt and the Levant." In "Archaeological and Historical Studies Presented to Jean-Paul Thalmann on the Occasion of His Sixtieth Birthday," *Archaeology and History in the Lebanon*, nos. 26–27, pp. 212–15.

Kamrin, Janice
1999   *The Cosmos of Khnumhotep II at Beni Hasan.* London and New York.

Kantor, Helene
1945   "Plant Ornament: Its Origin and Development in the Ancient Near East." Ph.D. diss., University of Chicago, 1945. Reissued in 1999 as an e-text: http://oi.uchicago.edu/research/library/dissertation/kantor.html.
1947   "The Aegean and the Orient in the Second Millennium B.C." *American Journal of Archaeology* 51, pp. 1–103. Reprinted as Kantor 1997.
1948   "A Predynastic Ostrich Egg with Incised Decoration." *Journal of Near Eastern Studies* 7, pp. 46–51.
1956   "Syro-Palestinian Ivories." *Journal of Near Eastern Studies* 15, pp. 153–74.
1958   "The Glyptic." In *Soundings at Tell Fakhariyah*, edited by Calvin W. McEwan et al., pp. 69–85. Oriental Institute Publications, vol. 79. Chicago.
1960   "Ivory Carving in the Mycenaean Period." *Archaeology* 13, pp. 14–25.
1965   "The Relative Chronology of Egypt and Its Foreign Corre-lations before the Late Bronze Age." In *Chronologies in Old World Archaeology*, edited by Robert W. Ehrich, pp. 1–46. Chicago.

1997   *The Aegean and the Orient in the Second Millennium B.C.* Archaeological Institute of America, Monographs, no. 1. Boston. Originally published as Kantor 1947.

Kapitän, G.
1984   "Ancient Anchors—Technology and Classification." *International Journal of Nautical Archaeology* 13, no. 1, pp. 33–36.

Kaplan, Maureen F.
1980   *The Origin and Distribution of Tell el Yahudiyeh Ware.* Studies in Mediterranean Archaeology, vol. 62. Göteborg.

Kaplony, Peter
1981   *Die Rollsiegel des Alten Reichs. A. Text.* Monumenta Aegyptiaca, vol. 3A. Brussels.

Karageorghis, Vassos
1964   "Chronique des fouilles et découvertes archéologiques à Chypre en 1963." *Bulletin de correspondance hellénique* 88, pp. 289–370.
1965   *Nouveaux documents pour l'étude du bronze récent à Chypre.* Translated from English by Robert-P. Charles and Mme. Vassos Karageorghis. Études chypriotes, vol. 3. Paris.
1968   *Mycenaean Art from Cyprus.* Republic of Cyprus, Department of Antiquities, Picture Book, no. 3. Nicosia.
1976a   *Kition: Mycenaean and Phoenician Discoveries in Cyprus.* London.
1976b   *The Civilization of Prehistoric Cyprus.* Athens.
1980   "Chronique des fouilles et decouvertes archéologiques à Chypre en 1979." *Bulletin de correspondance hellénique* 104, pp. 761–803.
1983   *Palaepaphos-Skales: An Iron Age Cemetery in Cyprus.* 2 vols. Ausgrabungen in Alt-Paphos auf Cypern, vol. 3. Konstanz.
1993   "Le commerce chypriote avec l'Occident au Bronze récent: Quelques nouvelles découvertes." *Comptes rendus des séances de l'Académie des Inscriptions* 1993, fasc. 2, pp. 577–88.
1998   *Greek Gods and Heroes in Ancient Cyprus.* Athens.
2002   *Early Cyprus. Crossroads of the Mediterranean.* Los Angeles: J. Paul Getty Museum.

Karageorghis, Vassos, and M. Demas, eds.
1985   *Excavations at Kition V: The Pre-Phoenician Levels.* 4 vols. Nicosia: Department of Antiquities.

"Karahöyük kazısı"
1962   "Karahöyük kazısı." In "Haberler: Türk Tarih Kurumu'nun 1962 Yılı Genel Kurul Toplantısı," *Belleten* 26, pp. 620–22. Athens.

Karantzali, Efi
1998   "A New Mycenaean Pictorial Rhyton from Rhodes." In *Eastern Mediterranean: Cyprus, Dodecanese, Crete, 16th–6th Centuries B.C.; Proceedings of the International Symposium, Rethymnon, 13–16 May 1997*, edited by Vassos Karageorghis and Nikolaos Stampolidis, pp. 87–103. Athens.
2001   *The Mycenaean Cemetery at Pylona on Rhodes.* Contributions by P. J. P. McGeorge et al. BAR International Series 988. Oxford.

Karetsou, Alexandra, ed.
2000   *Krete–Aigyptos: Politismikoi desmoi trion chilietion: [Meletes] / Crete–Egypt: Three Millennia of Cultural Connections: [Essays].* Athens.

Keel, Othmar
1993   "Hyksos Horses or Hippopotamus Deities?" *Levant* 25, pp. 208–12.

Keimer, Ludwig
1932   "Pendeloques en forme d'insectes." *Annales du Service des Antiquités de l'Égypte* 32, pp. 129–50.
1933   "Pendeloques en forme d'insectes." *Annales du Service des Antiquités de l'Égypte* 33, pp. 97–130, 193–200.
1935   "Sur un fragment de statuette en calcaire ayant la forme d'un oiseau (vautour?) à tête de reine." *Annales du Service des Antiquités de l'Égypte* 35, pp. 182–92.

1937 "Pendeloques en forme d'insectes." *Annales du Service des Antiqutés de l'Égypte* 37, pp. 143–72.

Kemp, Barry J., and Robert S. Merrillees
1980 *Minoan Pottery in Second Millennium Egypt.* Mainz am Rhein.

Kempinski, Aharon, and Wolf-Dietrich Niemeier, eds.
1992 *Kabri:'onat ha-ḥafirot 1991: din ye-ḥeshbon rishoni 6.* Tel Aviv.

Kendall, Timothy
1978 *Passing through the Netherworld: The Meaning and Play of Senet, an Ancient Egyptian Funerary Game.* Monograph accompanying commercial senet board and playing pieces issued by the Kirk Game Company. Belmont, Mass.
1982 "Games." In *Egypt's Golden Age* 1982, pp. 263–72.
1989 "An Ancient Egyptian Boardgame among the Kababish? An Ethnoarchaeological Ponderable in Kordofan," section III.C.2.d of "Ethnoarchaeology in Meroitic Studies." In *Studia Meroitica 1984: Proceedings of the Fifth International Conference for Meroitic Studies, Rome 1984,* edited by Sergio Donadoni and Steffen Wenig, pp. 711–15. Meroitica, vol. 10. Berlin.
1997 *Kerma and the Kingdom of Kush, 2500–1500 B.C.: The Archaeological Discovery of an Ancient Nubian Empire.* Washington, D.C.: National Museum of African Art, Smithsonian Institution.
2007 "Mehen." In Finkel 2007a, pp. 33–45.

Kenna, Victor E. G.
1964 "Cretan and Mycenaean Seals in North America." *American Journal of Archaeology* 68, pp. 1–12.
1967a as editor. *Die englischen Museen II.* Corpus der minoischen und mykenischen Siegel, vol. 7. Berlin.
1967b "An Unpublished Cypriote Cylinder," with appendix "Les signes Chypro-Minoens," by O. Masson. *Bulletin de correspondance hellénique* 91, pp. 252–54.
1971 *Corpus of Cypriote Antiquities.* Vol. 3, *Catalogue of the Cypriote Seals of the Bronze Age in the British Museum.* Studies in Mediterranean Archaeology, vol. 20. Göteborg.

Kenoyer, Jonathan Mark
1997 "Trade and Technology of the Indus Valley: New Insights from Harappa, Pakistan." *World Archaeology* 29, pp. 262–80.

Kenyon, Kathleen M., and Thomas A. Holland
1983 *Excavations at Jericho.* Vol. 5, *The Pottery Phases of the Tell and Other Finds.* London: British School of Archaeology in Jerusalem.

Kepinski, Ch.
1977 "Un object 'en forme d'avant-bras.'" In *Problèmes concernant les Hurrites,* vol. 1, *Méthodologie et critiques,* by M. T. Barrelet et al., pp. 71–113. Paris.
1987–90 "Libationsarm. B. Archäologisch." In *Reallexikon der Assyriologie und Vorderasiatischen Archäologie,* vol. 7, pp. 12–14. Berlin.

Keramopoullos, Ant.
1930 ""Αι βιομηχανίαι και το εμπόριον του Κάδμου." *Αρχαιολογική Εφημερίς* (*Archaiologike ephemeris*), pp. 29–58.

Kerrn-Lillesø, Ebba
1986 "Stirnband und Diademe." In *Lexikon der Ägyptologie,* edited by Wolfgang Helck and Wolfhart Westendorf, vol. 6, cols. 45–49. Wiesbaden.

Kessler, D.
1987 "Die Asiatiatenkarawane von Beni Hassan." *Studien zur altägyptischen Kultur* 14, pp. 147–65.

Kilian-Dirlmeier, Imma
1987 "Das Kuppelgrab von Vapheio: Die Beigabenausstattung in der Steinkiste. Untersuchungen zur Sozialstruktur in späthelladischer Zeit." *Jahrbuch des Römisch-Germanischen Zentralmuseums, Mainz* 34, pp. 197–212.

1993 *Die Schwerter in Griechenland (ausserhalb der Peloponnes), Bulgarien und Albanien.* Prähistorische Bronzefunde, ser. 4, vol. 12. Stuttgart.
1997 *Das mittelbronzezeitliche Schachtgrab von Ägina.* Alt-Ägina 4, no. 3. Mainz am Rhein.

Killen, Geoffrey
1980 *Ancient Egyptian Furniture.* Warminster.

Kitchen, Kenneth A.
1979 *Ramesside Inscriptions: Historical and Biographical.* Vol. 2. Oxford.
1987 "The Basics of Egyptian Chronology in Relation to the Bronze Age." In P. Åström 1987–89, vol. 1, pp. 37–55.
1996 *Ramesside Inscriptions: Translated and Annotated; Translations.* Vol. 2, *Ramesses II, Royal Inscriptions.* Oxford and Cambridge, Mass.
1999 *Ramesside Inscriptions: Translated and Annotated; Notes and Comments.* Vol. 2, *Ramesses II, Royal Inscriptions.* Oxford and Cambridge, Mass.
2000 "Regnal and Genealogical Data of Ancient Egypt (Absolute Chronology I): The Historical Chronology of Ancient Egypt: A Current Assessment." In Bietak 2000a, pp. 39–52.
2002 "Ancient Egyptian Chronology for Aegeanists." *Mediterranean Archaeology and Archaeometry* 2, no. 2, pp. 5–12.

Klein, Harald
1992 *Untersuchung zur Typologie bronzezeitlicher Nadeln in Mesopotamien und Syrien.* Schriften zur vorderasiatischen Archäologie, vol. 4. Saarbrücken.

Klengel, Horst
1999 *Geschichte des hethitischen Reiches.* Handbuch der Orientalistik, ser. 1, Nahe und der Mittlere Osten, vol. 34. Leiden.
2000 "Qatna: Ein historischer Überblick." *Mitteilungen der Deutschen Orient-Gesellschaft zu Berlin* 132, pp. 239–52.

Knapp, A. Bernard
1986 *Copper Production and Divine Protection: Archaeology, Ideology and Social Complexity on Bronze Age Cyprus.* Studies in Mediterranean Archaeology, Pocket-book 42. Göteborg.
1991 "Spice, Drugs, Grain, and Grog: Organic Goods in Bronze Age East Mediterranean Trade." In Gale 1991a, pp. 21–68.
1993 "Thalassocracies in Bronze Age Eastern Mediterranean Trade: Making and Breaking a Myth." *World Archaeology* 24, pp. 332–47.
2000 "Island Cultures: Crete, Thera, Cyprus, Rhodes, and Sardinia." In Sasson 2000, pp. 1433–49.

Knudtzon, Jørgen Alexander
[1908]– *Die El-Amarna-Tafeln.* Vorderasiatische Bibliothek, vol. 2.
 15 Leipzig.

Kochavi, M.
1977 *Aphek-Antipatris: Five Seasons of Excavation at Tel Aphek-Antipatris (1972–1976).* Tel-Aviv: Tel-Aviv University, Institute of Archaeology.

Koehl, Robert B.
1995 "The Silver Stag 'Bibru' from Mycenae." In *The Ages of Homer: A Tribute to Emily Townsend Vermeule,* edited by Jane B. Carter and Sarah P. Morris, pp. 61–66. Austin.
1999 "The Creto-Mycenaean Earrings of Queen Nofretari." In Betancourt et al. 1999, vol. 2, pp. 300–305.
2003 *Aegean Bronze Age Rhyta.* Archaeological Institute of America, Monograph 7. Boston.
2005 "Preliminary Observations on the Unpublished Mycenaean Pottery from Woolley's Dig-House at Tell Atchana (Ancient Alalakh)." In Laffineur and Greco 2005, pp. 415–22.
2006 *Aegean Bronze Age Rhyta.* Philadelphia.

Koehl, Robert B., and J. Yellin
2007 "What Aegean 'Simple Style' Pottery Reveals about

Interconnections in the 13th-Century B.C.E. Eastern Mediterranean." In *Krinoi kai Limenes: Studies in Honor of Joseph and Maria Shaw*, edited by Philip P. Betancourt, Michael C. Nelson, and Hector Williams, pp. 199–207. Philadelphia.

Koitabashi, M.
1992   "Significance of Ugaritic *mṣltm* 'Cymbals' in the Anat Text." In *Cult and Ritual in the Ancient Near East*, edited by Takahito Mikasa, pp. 1–5. Bulletin of the Middle Eastern Culture Center in Japan, vol. 6. Wiesbaden.

Koldewey, Robert
1908   "Aus den Berichten Professor Dr. Koldeweys aus Babylon." *Mitteilungen der Deutschen Orient-Gesellschaft zu Berlin* 38 (December), pp. 5–21.
1913   *Das wieder erstehende Babylon: Die bisherigen Ergebnisse der deutschen Ausgrabungen.* Leipzig.

Koliński, Rafał
2001   *Mesopotamian dimatu of the Second Millennium B.C.* BAR International Series 1004. Oxford.

Königliche Museen zu Berlin
1899   *Ausführliches Verzeichnis der aegyptischen Altertümer und Gipsabgüsse.* 2nd ed. Berlin. Electronic edition available at http://www.archive.org/stream/ausfuhrlichesver00koni.

Kontorli-Papadopoulou, Litsa
1999   "Fresco Fighting-Scenes as Evidence for Warlike Activities in the LBA Aegean." In Laffineur 1999, vol. 2, pp. 331–39.

Kopcke, Günter
1987   "The Cretan Palaces and Trade." In Hägg and Marinatos 1987, pp. 255–60.

Korres, G.
1969   "Η μεγαλοπρέπεια των μυκηναϊκών κρανών." *Αρχαιολογικά Ανάλεκτα εξ Αθηνών* / *Athens Annals of Archaeology* 2, no. 3, pp. 446–55.

Košak, Silvin
1982   *Hittite Inventory Texts: (CTH 214–250).* Texte der Hethiter, no. 10. Heidelberg.

Koşay, Hamit Z.
1944   *Ausgrabungen von Alaca Höyük: Ein Vorbericht über die im Auftrage der Türkischen Geschichtskommission im Sommer 1936 durchgeführten Forschungen und Entdeckungen.* Veröffentlichungen der Türkischen Geschichtskommission, ser. 5, no. 2a. Ankara.

Koşay, Hamit Z., and Mahmut Akok
1947   "The Pottery of Alaça Höyük." *American Journal of Archaeology* 51, pp. 155–57.
1966   *Türk Tarih Kurumu tarafindan yapılan Alaca Höyük kazısı; 1940–1948 deki çalışmalara ve keşiflere ait ilk rapor* / *Ausgrabungen von Alaca Höyük. Vorbericht über die Forschungen und Entdeckungen von 1940–1948.* Ankara.

Kostourou, M.
1972   "Mycenaean Offensive Weapons." *Αρχαιολογικά Ανάλεκτα εξ Αθηνών* / *Athens Annals of Archaeology* 5, pp. 331–37.

Kozloff, Arielle P.
1992a   "Ritual Implements and Related Statuettes." In *Egypt's Dazzling Sun* 1992, pp. 331–48.
1992b   "Spoon with Sky Goddess Holding a Lotus" and "Spoon with Sky Goddess Holding a Duck." In *Egypt's Dazzling Sun* 1992, pp. 346–47, nos. 74, 75.
1992c   "Tomb Decoration: Paintings and Relief Sculpture." In *Egypt's Dazzling Sun* 1992, pp. 261–83.
2006   "Bubonic Plague in the Reign of Amenhotep III?" *KMT* 17, no. 3, pp. 36–46, 83–84.

Krete–Aigyptos
2000   *Κρήτη–Αίγυπτος: Πολιτισμικοί δεσμοί τριώνχιετιών.* Exhibition, Heraklion Archaeological Museum. Catalogue edited by Alexandra Karetsou and Maria Andreadaki-Vlazaki. Heraklion.

Krzyszkowska, Olga
1984   "Ivory from Hippopotamus Tusk in the Aegean Bronze Age." *Antiquity* 58, pp. 123–25.
1988   "Ivory in the Aegean Bronze Age: Elephant Tusk or Hippopotamus Ivory?" *Annual of the British School at Athens* 83, pp. 209–34.
1990   *Ivory and Related Materials: An Illustrated Guide.* Institute of Classical Studies, University of London, Bulletin Supplement, no. 59. London.

Kuentz, Charles
1928–34   *La bataille de Qadech. Les texts ("Poème de Pentaour" et "Bulletin de Qadech") et les bas-reliefs.* 3 parts. Mémoires publiés par les membres de l'Institut Français d'Archéologie Orientale du Caire, vol. 55. Cairo.

Kuftin, Boris Alekseevich
1941   *Archeologicheskiye Raskopki v Trialeti.* Vol. 1. Tbilisi: Akademii nauk Gruzinskoi SSR.

Kuhlmann, Klaus P.
1977   *Der Thron im alten Ägypten: Untersuchungen zu Semantik, Ikonographie und Symbolik eines Herrschaftszeichens.* Glückstadt.

Kühne, Hartmut
1984   "Tall Seh Hamad/Dur-katlimmu, 1981–1983." *Archiv für Orientforschung* 31, pp. 166–78.
2000   "Dur-katlimmu and the Middle-Assyrian Empire." In *La Djéziré et l'Euphrate Syriens de la Protohistoire à la fin du IIe millénaire av. J.-C.: Tendances dans l'interprétation historique des données nouvelles*, edited by Olivier Rouault and Markus Wäfler, pp. 271–79. Subartu, vol. 7. Turnhout, Belgium.

Kuhrt, Amélie
1995   *The Ancient Near East, c. 3000–330 BC.* Vol. 1, *From c. 3000 BC to c. 1200 BC.* London and New York.

Kuniholm, Peter Ian
1997   "Wood." In *The Oxford Encyclopedia of Archaeology in the Near East*, edited by Eric M. Meyers, vol. 5, pp. 347–49. New York.

Kuniholm, Peter Ian, et al.
1996   Peter Ian Kuniholm, Bernd Kromer, Sturt Manning, M. Newton, C. Latini, and M. Bruce. "Anatolian Tree Rings and the Absolute Chronology of the Eastern Mediterranean, 2220–718 BC." *Nature* 381 (June), pp. 780–83.

Kupper, Jean-Robert
1966   "Northern Mesopotamia and Syria." In *Cambridge Ancient History*, rev. ed., vol. 2, pp. 3–46. Cambridge.
1992   "Le bois a Mari." *Bulletin on Sumerian Agriculture* 6, pp. 163–70.

Kushnareva, Kariné Khristoforovna
1997   *The Southern Caucasus in Prehistory: Stages of Cultural and Socioeconomic Development from the Eighth to the Second Millennium B.C.* Translated by H. N. Michael. University Museum Monograph, vol. 99. Philadelphia.

Lacau, Pierre
1904   *Sarcophages antérieurs au Nouvel Empire.* Vol. 1. Cairo.

Lacovara, P.
1997   "Egypt and Nubia during the Second Intermediate Period." In Oren 1997a, pp. 69–82.

Laffineur, Robert
1988   "Réflexions sur le trésor de Tôd." *Aegaeum* 2, pp. 17–30.
1998   "From West to East: The Aegean and Egypt in the Early Late Bronze Age." *Aegaeum* 18, pp. 53–67.

1999   as editor. *Polemos: Le contexte guerrier en Égée à l'Âge du Bronze: Actes de la 7e Rencontre égéenne internationale Université de Liège, 14–17 avril 1998.* 2 vols. Aegaeum 19. Liège and Austin.

2007   "Homeric Similes: A Bronze Age Background?" In Morris and Laffineur 2007, pp. 79–85.

Laffineur, Robert, and Philip P. Betancourt, eds.

1997   *Technē: Craftsmen, Craftswomen, and Craftsmanship in the Aegean Bronze Age; Proceedings of the 6th International Aegean Conference, Philadelphia, Temple University, 18–21 April 1996.* 2 vols. Aegaeum 16. Liège and Austin.

Laffineur, Robert, and Janice L. Crowley, eds.

1992   *Eikon: Aegean Bronze Age Iconography, Shaping a Methodology. Proceedings of the 4th International Aegean Conference, University of Tasmania, Hobart, Australia, 6–9 April 1992.* Aegaeum 8. Liège.

Laffineur, Robert, and Emanuele Greco, eds.

2005   *Emporia: Aegeans in the Central and Eastern Mediterranean: Proceedings of the 10th International Aegean Conference, Athens, Italian School of Archaeology, 14–18 April 2004.* Aegaeum 25. Liège and Austin.

Laffineur, Robert, and Robin Hägg, eds.

2001   *Potnia: Deities and Religion in the Aegean Bronze Age; Proceedings of the 8th International Aegean Conference / 8e Rencontre égéenne internationale, Göteborg, Göteborg University, 12–15 April 2000.* Aegaeum 22. Brussels and Austin.

Lafont, Bertrand

1987   "Les filles de roi de Mari." In *La femme dans le Proche-Orient antique: XXXIIIe Rencontre assyriologique internationale, Paris, 7–10 juillet 1986,* edited by Jean-Marie Durand, pp. 113–21. Paris.

2001   "Relations internationales, alliances et diplomatie au temps des royaumes amorrites. Essai de synthèse." *Amurru* 2, pp. 213–328.

Lagarce, E.

1983   "Le rôle d'Ugarit dans l'élaboration du repertoire icono-graphique syro-phénicien du premier millénaire avant J.C." In *Atti del I Congresso internazionale di studi Fenici e Punici, Roma, 5–10 Novembre 1979,* vol. 2, pp. 547–61. Rome: Consiglio Nazionale delle Ricerche.

1990   "Un baton magique égyptien en ivoire a Ras Shamra." In *Resurrecting the Past: A Joint Tribute to Adnan Bounni,* edited by Paolo Matthiae, Maurits van Loon, and Harvey Weiss, pp. 171–88. Istanbul.

Lambert, W. G.

1957–58   "Three Unpublished Fragments of the Tukulti-Ninurta Epic." *Archiv für Orientforschung* 18, pp. 38–51.

1983   "The God Aššur." *Iraq* 45, pp. 82–86.

2002   "The Name of Nuska." *Revue d'assyriologie et d'archéologie orientale* 96, no. 1, pp. 57–60.

Lamon, Robert S., and Geoffrey M. Shipton

1939   *Megiddo.* Vol. 1, *Seasons of 1925–34, Strata I–V.* University of Chicago Oriental Institute Publications, vol. 42. Chicago.

Land des Baal

1982   *Land des Baal: Syrien—Forum der Völker und Kulturen.* Exhibition, Museum für Vor- und Frühgeschichte, Schloss Charlottenburg, Berlin, and other venues. Catalogue edited by Kay Kohlmeyer and Eva Strommenger; contributions by Ali Abou Assaf et al. Mainz am Rhein.

Landström, Björn

1970   *Ships of the Pharaohs: 4000 Years of Egyptian Shipbuilding.* Garden City, N.Y.

Lang, Mabel L.

1969   *The Palace of Nestor at Pylos in Western Messenia,* edited by Carl W. Blegen and Marion Rawson. Vol. 2, *The Frescoes.* Princeton.

Lange, Kurt, and Max Hirmer

1967   *Ägypten: Architektur, Plastik, Malerei in drei Jahrtausenden.* 4th ed. Munich.

1978   *Ägypten: Architektur, Plastik, Malerei in drei Jahrtausenden.* Reprint of 4th ed. Munich.

Lansing, Ambrose

1941   "An XVIII Dynasty Saluki Hound." *Bulletin of The Metropolitan Museum of Art* 36, no. 1, part 1 (January), pp. 10–12.

Laroche, Emmanuel

1960   *Les hieroglyphes hittites.* Paris.

1971   *Catalogue des textes hittites.* Études et commentaires, no. 75. Paris. Electronic edition available at: http://www.mesas.emory.edu/hittitehome/стннр.html.

Larsen, Mogens Trolle

1967   *Old Assyrian Caravan Procedures.* Uitgaven van het Nederlands Historisch-Archaeologisch Instituut te Istanbul 22. Istanbul.

1976   *The Old Assyrian City-State and Its Colonies.* Copenhagen.

1982   "Your Money or Your Life! A Portrait of an Assyrian Business-man." In *Societies and Languages of the Ancient Near East: Studies in Honour of I. M. Diakonoff,* pp. 213–45. Warminster.

1987   "Commercial Networks in the Ancient Near East." In Rowlands, Larsen, and Kristiansen 1987, pp. 47–56.

2001   "Affect and Emotion." In *Veenhof Anniversary Volume: Studies Presented to Klaas R. Veenhof on the Occasion of His Sixty-fifth Birthday,* edited by W. H. van Soldt et al., pp. 275–86. Leiden.

2002   *The Aššur-nādā Archive.* Old Assyrian Archives, vol. 1. Leiden.

Lassen, H.

1994   "Zu den beiden Bronzebeinringen aus dem Gräberfeld an der Beşik-Bucht in der Troas." *Studia Troica* 4, pp. 128–42.

2000   "Introduction to Weight Systems in the Bronze Age East Mediterranean: The Case of Kalavasos-Ayios Dhimitrios." In *Metals Make the World Go Round: The Supply and Circulation of Metals in Bronze Age Europe. Proceedings of a Conference Held at the University of Birmingham in June 1997,* edited by C. F. E. Pare, pp. 233–46. Oxford.

Latacz, Joachim

2004   *Troy and Homer: Towards a Solution of an Old Mystery.* Translated by Kevin Windle and Rosh Ireland. Oxford.

Leahy, Anthony, ed.

1990   *Libya and Egypt, c1300–750 BC.* London: Centre of Near and Middle Eastern Studies.

Leclant, Jean

1960   "Astarté à cheval d'après les representations égyptiennes." *Syria* 37, pp. 1–60.

1978   as editor. *Le temps des pyramides: De la préhistoire aux Hyksos (1560 av. J.-C.).* Part 1 of *Le monde égyptien: Les pharaons.* Contributions by Cyril Aldred et al. Paris.

Ledrain, E. (Eugène)

1888   *Notice sommaire des monuments phéniciens du Musée du Louvre.* Paris.

Lehmann, G. A.

1985   *Die mykenisch-frühgriechische Welt und der östliche Mittelmeerraum in der Zeit der "Seevölker"-Invasionen um 1200 v. Chr.* Rheinisch-Westfälische Akademie der Wissenschaften, Vorträge, no. G276. Opladen.

1996   "Umbrüche und Zäsuren im östlichen Mittelmeerraum und Vorderasien zur Zeit der 'Seevölker'-Invasionen um und nach 1200 v. Chr.: Neue Quellenzeugnisse und Befunde." *Historische Zeitschrift* 262, pp. 1–38.

Leonard, Albert, Jr.

1994   *An Index to the Late Bronze Age Aegean Pottery from Syria-*

Palestine. Studies in Mediterranean Archaeology, vol. 114. Jonsered.

1996 "'Canaanite Jars' and the Late Bronze Age Aegeo-Levantine Wine Trade." In McGovern, Fleming, and Katz 1996, pp. 233–54.

Leonard, Albert, Jr., et al.
1993 Albert Leonard Jr., M. Hughes, A. Middleton, and Louise Schofield. "The Making of Aegean Stirrup Jars: Techniques, Tradition, and Trade." *Annual of the British School at Athens* 88, pp. 105–23.

Leospo, Enrichetta, and Mario Tosi
2005 *Il potere del re, il predominio del dio: Amenhotep III e Akhenaten.* Turin.

Lerouxel, François
2002 "Les échanges de présents entre souverains amorrites au XVIIIe siècle av. n. è. d'après les Archives royales de Mari." In *Recueil d'études à la mémoire d'André Parrot*, edited by Dominique Charpin and Jean-Marie Durand, pp. 413–64. Florilegium marianum, vol. 6. Paris.

Levi, Doro
1925–26 "Le cretule di Zakro." *Annuario della Scuola Archeologica di Atene e delle Missioni italiane in Oriente* 8–9, pp. 157–201.

Lévi-Strauss, Claude
1953 "Social Structure." In *Anthropology Today: An Encyclopedic Inventory*, edited by A. L. Kroeber, pp. 524–53. International Symposium on Anthropology, 1952, New York. Chicago.

Levy, Thomas E., ed.
1995 *The Archaeology of Society in the Holy Land.* New York.

Lewartowski, Kazimierz
2000 *Late Helladic Simple Graves: A Case Study of Mycenaean Burial Customs.* BAR International Series 878. Oxford.

Liban: L'autre rive
1998 *Liban: L'autre rive.* Exhibition, Institut du Monde Arabe, Paris. Catalogue edited by Valérie Matoïan. Paris.

Lichardus, J., et al.
2002 J. Lichardus, R. Echt, I. K. Iliev, C. J. Christov, J. S. Becker and W.-R. Thiele. "Die Spätbronzezeit an der unteren Tundža und die ostägäischen Verbindungen in Südostbulgarien." *Eurasia Antiqua: Zeitschrift für Archäologie Eurasiens* 8, pp. 135–83.

Lichtheim, Miriam
1973 *Ancient Egyptian Literature.* Vol. 1, *The Old and Middle Kingdoms.* Berkeley.
1976 *Ancient Egyptian Literature.* Vol. 2, *The New Kingdom.* Berkeley.

Lilyquist, Christine
1988 "The Gold Bowl Naming General Djehuty: A Study of Objects and Early Egyptology." *Metropolitan Museum Journal* 23, pp. 5–68.
1993 "Granulation and Glass: Chronological and Stylistic Investigations at Selected Sites, ca. 2500–1400 B.C.E." *Bulletin of the American Schools of Oriental Research*, nos. 290–91, pp. 29–94.
1994 "The Dilbat Hoard." *Metropolitan Museum Journal* 29, pp. 5–36.
1998 "The Use of Ivories as Interpreters of Political History." *Bulletin of the American Schools of Oriental Research*, no. 310, pp. 25–33.
1999a "On the Amenhotep III Inscribed Faience Fragments from Mycenae." *Journal of the American Oriental Society* 119, pp. 303–8.
1999b "The Objects Mentioned in the Texts." In *Royal Gifts in the Late Bronze Age, Fourteenth to Thirteenth Centuries, B.C.E.: Selected Texts Recording Gifts to Royal Personages*, translated by Zipora Cochavi-Rainey, pp. 211–18. Be'er-Sheva, vol. 13. [Beersheba.]

2003 *The Tomb of Three Foreign Wives of Tuthmosis III.* New York: The Metropolitan Museum of Art.

Lilyquist, Christine, and Robert H. Brill
1993 *Studies in Early Egyptian Glass.* New York: The Metropolitan Museum of Art.

Limet, Henri
1986 *Textes administratifs relatifs aux métaux.* Archives royales de Mari, vol. 25. Paris.

Lipinska, Jadwiga
2001 "Thutmose III." In The *Oxford Encyclopedia of Ancient Egypt*, edited by Donald B. Redford, vol. 3, pp. 401–3. Oxford.

Lipke, Paul
1984 *The Royal Ships of Cheops: A Retrospective Account of the Discovery, Restoration, and Reconstruction. Based on Interviews with Hag Ahmed Youssef Moustafa.* BAR International Series 225. Oxford.

Littauer, M. A., and J. H. Crouwel
1979 *Wheeled Vehicles and Ridden Animals in the Ancient Near East.* Handbuch der Orientalistik, ser. 7, Kunst und Archäologie, vol. 1. Leiden.

Liverani, Mario
1979 "Irrational Elements in the Amarna Trade." In *Three Amarna Essays*, pp. 21–33. Translated by Matthew L. Jaffe. Malibu.
1983 "Political Lexicon and Political Ideologies in the Amarna Letters." *Berytus* 31, pp. 41–56.
1987 "The Collapse of the Near Eastern Regional System at the End of the Bronze Age: The Case of Syria." In Rowlands, Larsen, and Kristiansen 1987, pp. 66–73.
1990 *Prestige and Interest: International Relations in the Near East, ca. 1600–1100 B.C.* Padua.
2001 *International Relations in the Ancient Near East, 1600–1100 B.C.* London and New York.
2003 "The Influence of Political Institutions on Trade in the Ancient Near East (Late Bronze to Early Iron Age)." In *Mercanti e politica nel mondo antico*, edited by Carlo Zaccagnini, pp. 119–37. Saggi di storia antica 21. Rome: L'Erma di Bretschneider.
2005 Review of H. Gasche et al. 1998a. *Journal of Near Eastern Studies* 64, pp. 214–15.

Lloyd, Seton, and Fuad Safar
1943 "Tell Uqair Excavations by the Iraq Government's Directorate of Antiquities in 1940 and 1941." *Journal of Near Eastern Studies* 2, pp. 131–58.

Lolos, Y.
1989 "The Gold Chalice from the Late Bronze Age Wreck at Akroterion (Ulu Burun) in Lycia." *Enalia* 1, pp. 8–9.

Longpérier, Adrien de
[1882] *Musée Napoléon III: Choix de monuments antiques pour servir à l'histoire de l'art en Orient et Occident.* Paris.

Loret, V.
1949 "La résine de térébinthe (sonter) chez les anciens Égyptiens." In *Recherches d'archéologie, de philologie et d'histoire* 19, pp. 1–61. Cairo: L'Institut Français d'Archéologie Orientale.

Lo Schiavo, Fulvia
1995 "Ancore di pietra dalla Sardegna: Una riflessione metodologica e problematica." In *I fenici: Ieri oggi domani. Richerche, scoperte, progetti. Atti del Convegno (Roma, 3–5 marzo 1994)*, pp. 409–21. Rome.

Loud, Gordon
1939 *The Megiddo Ivories.* University of Chicago Oriental Institute Publications, vol. 52. Chicago.
1948 *Megiddo II: Seasons of 1935–39.* 2 vols. University of Chicago Oriental Institute Publications, vol. 62. Chicago.

Lucas, Alfred, and John R. Harris
1962   *Ancient Egyptian Materials and Industries.* London.

Luciani, M.
2006   "Ivory at Qatna." In Czerny et al. 2006, vol. 3, pp. 17–38.

Luckenbill, Daniel David
1926–27 *Ancient Records of Assyria and Babylonia.* 2 vols. Chicago.

Luiselli, Maria Michela
2007   "Religion und Literatur: Überlegungen zur Funktion der 'persönlichen Frömmigkeit' in der Literatur des Mittleren und Neuen Reiches." *Studien zur altägyptischen Kultur* 36, pp. 157–82.

Luppert-Barnard, Shelley
2001   Review of Cancik-Kirschbaum 1996. *Journal of Near Eastern Studies* 60, pp. 56–59.

Macalister, R. A. Stewart
1912   *The Excavation of Gezer, 1902–1905 and 1907–1909.* Vol. 2. London.

MacDonald, Eann
1932   *Beth-Pelet.* Vol. 2, *Prehistoric Fara.* Publications of the British School of Archaeology in Egypt and Egyptian Research Account, vol. 52. London.

Mace, Arthur C.
1921   "The Egyptian Expedition 1920–1921: I. Excavations at Lisht." In "Egyptian Expedition for MCMXX–MCMXXI," *Bulletin of The Metropolitan Museum of Art* 16, no. 11, part 2 (November), pp. 5–19.

Mace, Arthur C., and Herbert E. Winlock
1916   *The Tomb of Senebtisi at Lisht.* Publications of The Metropolitan Museum of Art Egyptian Expedition 1. New York.

MacGillivray, Joseph A.
1998   *Knossos: Pottery Groups of the Old Palace Period.* British School at Athens Studies, vol. 5. London.
2003   "A Middle Minoan Cup from Sidon." *Archaeology and History in the Lebanon* 18, pp. 20–24.
2004   "A Middle Minoan Cup from Sidon." In Doumet-Serhal 2004c, pp. 125–31.

MacGillivray, Joseph A., et al.
1991   MacGillivray, Joseph A., L. H. Sackett, Jan M. Driessen, A. Farnoux, and D. Smyth. "Excavations at Palaikastro, 1990." *Annual of the British School at Athens* 86, pp. 121–47.

MacGillivray, Joseph A., L. H. Sackett, and Jan M. Driessen
1998   "Excavations at Palaikastro, 1994 and 1996." *Annual of the British School at Athens* 93, pp. 221–68.

Machinist, Peter B.
1978   "The Epic of Tukulti-Ninurta I: A Study in Middle Assyrian Literature." Ph.D. diss., Yale University, New Haven.

Mackay, E. J. H.
1925   *Report on the Excavation of the "A" Cemetery at Kish, Mesopotamia.* Part 1. Field Museum of Natural History, Anthropology, Memoirs, vol. 1, no. 1. Chicago.
1929   *A Sumerian Palace and the "A" Cemetery at Kish, Mesopotamia,* Part 2. Field Museum of Natural History, Anthropology, Memoirs, vol. 1, no. 2. Chicago.

Macnamara, E., and N. Meeks
1987   "The Metallurgical Examination of Four Late Cypriot III Stands Now in the British Museum." *Report of the Department of Antiquities, Cyprus,* 1987, pp. 57–60.

Malamat, Abraham
1970   "Northern Canaan and the Mari Texts." In *Near Eastern Archaeology in the Twentieth Century: Essays in Honor of Nelson Glueck,* edited by James A. Sanders, pp. 164–77. Garden City, N.Y.
1971   "Syro-Palestinian Destinations in a Mari Tin Inventory." *Israel Exploration Journal* 21, pp. 31–38.

Mallowan, M. E. L.
1954   "The Excavations at Nimrud (Kalhu) 1953." *Iraq* 16, pp. 59–163.

Manlius, N.
2001   "The Ostrich in Egypt: Past and Present." *Journal of Biogeography* 28, no. 8, pp. 945–53.

Manniche, Lise
1989   *An Ancient Egyptian Herbal.* London: British Museum Publications.
1991   *Music and Musicians in Ancient Egypt.* London: British Museum Press.

Manning, Sturt W.
1988   "The Bronze Age Eruption of Thera: Absolute Dating, Aegean Chronology and Mediterranean Cultural Interrelations." *Journal of Mediterranean Archaeology* 1, no. 1 (June), pp. 17–82.
1991   "Response to J. D. Muhly on Problems of Chronology in the Aegean Late Bronze Age." *Journal of Mediterranean Archaeology* 4, pp. 249–62.
1999   *A Test of Time: The Volcano of Thera and the Chronology and History of the Aegean and East Mediterranean in the mid-Second Millennium BC.* Oxford: Oxbow Books.
2007   "Clarifying the 'High' v. 'Low' Aegean/Cypriot Chronology for the mid-Second Millennium BC: Assessing the Evidence, Interpretive Frameworks, and Current State of the Debate." In Bietak and Czerny 2007, pp. 101–37.

Manning, Sturt W., et al.
2001   Sturt W. Manning, Bernd Kromer, Peter Ian Kuniholm, and Maryanne W. Newton. "Anatolian Tree Rings and a New Chronology for the East Mediterranean Bronze-Iron Ages." *Science* 294, no. 5551 (December 21, 2001), pp. 2532–35.
2003   Sturt W. Manning, Bernd Kromer, Peter Ian Kuniholm, and Maryanne W. Newton. "Confirmation of Near-Absolute Dating of East Mediterranean Bronze-Iron Dendrochronology." *Antiquity* 77, project gallery 295 (electronic edition only: www.antiquity.ac.uk).
2006   Sturt W. Manning, C. B. Ramsey, W. Kutschera, T. Higham, Bernd Kromer, P. Steier, and E. M. Wild. "Chronology for the Aegean Late Bronze Age, 1700–1400 B.C." *Science* 312, no. 5773, pp. 565–69.

Manning, Sturt W., and Linda Hulin
2005   "Maritime Commerce and Geographies of Mobility in the Late Bronze Age of the Eastern Mediterranean: Problematizations." In *The Archaeology of Mediterranean Prehistory,* edited by Emma Blake and A. Bernard Knapp, pp. 270–302. Blackwell Studies in Global Archaeology, vol. 6. Malden, Mass.

Maran, Josephy
1987   "Die Silbergefässe von el-Tôd und die Schachtgräberzeit auf dem griechischen Festland." *Praehistorische Zeitschrift* 62, no. 2, pp. 221–27.
2004   "The Spreading of Objects and Ideas in the Late Bronze Age Eastern Mediterranean: Two Case Examples from the Argolid of the 13th and 12th Centuries B.C." *Bulletin of the American School of Oriental Research* 336 (November), pp. 11–30.
2006   "Coming to Terms with the Past: Ideology and Power in Late Helladic IIIC." In *Ancient Greece: From the Mycenaean Palaces to the Age of Homer,* edited by Sigrid Deger-Jalkotzy and Irene S. Lemos, pp. 123–50. Edinburgh Leventis Studies, vol. 3. Edinburgh.

Marcus, Michelle I.
1991   "The Mosaic Glass Vessels from Hasanlu, Iran: A Study in Large-Scale Stylistic Trait Distribution." *Art Bulletin* 73 (December), pp. 536–60.

Margueron, Jean-Claude

1989   "Problèmes de transports au début de l'âge du bronze." In *Reflets des deux fleuves: Volume de mélanges offerts à André Finet*, edited by Marc Lebeau and Philippe Talon, pp. 119–26. Leuven.

2000   "Mari: A Portrait in Art of a Mesopotamian City-State." In Sasson 2000, pp. 885–99.

Marinatos, Nannó

1990a   "Celebrations of Death and the Symbolism of the Lion Hunt." In *Celebrations of Death and Divinity in the Bronze Age Argolid: Proceedings of the Sixth International Symposium at the Swedish Institute at Athens 11–13 June 1988*, edited by Robin Hägg and Gullög C. Nordquist, pp. 143–48. Skrifter utgivna av Svenska Institutet i Athen, ser. 4, vol. 40. Stockholm.

1990b   "Reshef or 'Smiting God' Figure." In *Troy, Mycenae, Tiryns, Orchomenos: Heinrich Schliemann, the 100th Anniversary of His Death*, edited by Katie Demakopoulou, p. 370, no. 356. Exh. cat. Athens: National Archaeological Museum.

1993   *Minoan Religion: Ritual, Image, and Symbol.* Columbia, S.C.

1994   "The 'Export' Significance of Minoan Bull Hunting and Bull Leaping Scenes." *Ägypten und Levante / Egypt and the Levant* 4, pp. 89–93.

1995   "Divine Kingship/Queenship in Minoan Crete." In *The Role of the Ruler in the Prehistoric Aegean: Proceedings of a Panel Discussion Presented at the Annual Meeting of the Archaeological Institute of America, New Orleans, Louisiana, 28 December 1992*, edited by Paul Rehak, pp. 37–48. Aegeum 11. Liège.

Marinatos, Spyridon

1972   *Excavations at Thera V: (1971 Season).* Bibliotheke tes en Athenais Archaiologikes Hetaireias, vol. 64. Athens.

1976   *Excavations at Thera VII: (1973 Season).* Translated by Mrs. H. Tsigadas. Archaioi topoi kai mouseia tēs Hellados, vol. 4. Athens.

Marinatos, Spyridon, and Max Hirmer

1973   *Kreta, Thera und das mykenische Hellas.* 2nd ed. Munich.

Marketou, Toula

1988   "New Evidence on the Topography and Site History of Prehistoric Ialysos." In *Archaeology in the Dodecanese*, edited by Søren Dietz and Ioannes Papachristodoulou, pp. 27–33. Copenhagen: National Museum of Denmark.

1990   "Santorini Tephra from Rhodes and Kos: Some Chronological Remarks Based on the Stratigraphy." In Hardy and Renfrew 1990, vol. 3, *Chronology*, pp. 100–119.

1998   "Excavations at Trianda (Ialysos) on Rhodes: New Evidence for the Late Bronze Age I Period." *Rendiconti della Accademia nazionale dei Lincei, Classe di scienze morali, storiche e filologiche*, ser. 9, 9, pp. 39–82.

n.d.   "Ialysos and Its Neighbouring Areas in the MBA and LB I Periods: A Chance for Peace." In *The Minoans in the Central, Eastern, and Northern Aegean: New Evidence. Acts of a Minoan Seminar 22–23 January 2005 in Collaboration with the Danish Institute at Athens and the German Archaeological Institute at Athens*, edited by Eric Hallager, Colin F. Macdonald, and Wolf-Dietriech Niemeier. Monographs of the Danish Institute at Athens, vol. 8. Athens. Forthcoming.

Markoe, Glenn

1990   "The Emergence of Phoenician Art." *Bulletin of the American Schools of Oriental Research*, no. 279, pp. 13–26.

2000   *Phoenicians.* Berkeley: University of California Press.

Marshall, Frederick H.

1969   *Catalogue of the Jewellery, Greek, Etruscan, and Roman, in the Department of Antiquities, British Museum.* [Reprint of 1911 ed.] London.

Martelli, Marina

1988   "La stipe votiva dell'Athenaion di Ialysos: Un primo bilancio."

In *Archaeology in the Dodecanese*, edited by Søren Dietz and Ioannes Papachristodoulou, pp. 104–20. Copenhagen.

2000   "La stipe di Ialysos: Avori orientali e Greci." In *Un ponte fra l'Italia e la Grecia: Atti del Simposio in onore di Antonino di Vita, Ragusa, 13–15 febbraio.* Padua.

Marthari, M.

1987   "The Local Pottery Wares with Painted Decoration from the Volcanic Destruction Level at Akrotiri, Thera: A Preliminary Report." *Archäologischer Anzeiger*, 1987, pp. 359–79.

Martin, Lutz

2007   "Die Statuette VA4853 — Eine Darstellung des Wettergottes?" In *Belkıs Dinçol ve Ali Dinçol'a Armağan, Vita: Festschrift in Honor of Belkıs Dinçol and Ali Dinçol*, edited by Metin Alparslan, Meltem Doğan-Alparslan, and Hasan Peker, pp. 475–78. Istanbul.

Mastrokostas, Euthumios

1966   "Ἀνασκαφὴ Ἁγίου Ἠλία Μεσολογγίου-Ἰθωρίας." Πρακτικά της εν Αθήναις Αρχαιολογικής Εταιρείας (*Praktika tes en Athenais Archaiologikes Hetaireias*) 1963 (pub. 1966), pp. 203–17.

Matthäus, Hartmut

1980   *Die Bronzegefässe der kretisch-mykenischen Kultur.* Prähistorische Bronzefunde, ser. 2, vol. 1. Munich.

1985   *Metallgefässe und Gefässuntersätze der Bronzezeit, der geometrischen und archaischen Periode auf Cypern.* Prähistorische Bronzefunde, ser. 2, vol. 8. Munich.

1995   "Representations of Keftiu in Egyptian Tombs and the Absolute Chronology of the Aegean Late Bronze Age." *Bulletin of the Institute of Classical Studies* 40, pp. 177–94.

Matthews, Donald M.

1990   *Principles of Composition in Near Eastern Glyptic of the Later Second Millennium B.C.* Orbis Biblicus et Orientalis, Series Archaeologica, vol. 8. Fribourg and Göttingen.

1992   *The Kassite Glyptic of Nippur.* Orbis Biblicus et Orientalis, vol. 116. Fribourg and Göttingen.

Matthiae, Paolo

1981   "Osservazioni sui gioielli delle tombe principesche di Mardikh IIIB." *Studi eblaiti* 4, pp. 205–25.

1989a   "Masterpieces of Early and Old Syrian Art: Discoveries of the 1988 Ebla Excavations in a Historical Perspective." *Proceedings of the British Academy* 75, pp. 25–56.

1989b   *Ebla: Un impero ritrovato. Dai primi scavi alle ultime scoperte.* Turin.

2007   "About the God Rashap's Old Syrian Iconography." In *Refik Duru'ya armağan / Studies in Honour of Refik Duru*, edited by Gülsün Umurtak, Şevket Dönmez, Aslıhan Yurtsever, pp. 187–98. Istanbul: Ege Yayınları.

Mauss, Marcel

1923–24 "Essai sur le don." *Année sociologique* 1, pp. 30–186. Translated in 1967.

1967   *The Gift: Forms and Functions of Exchange in Archaic Societies.* Translated by Ian Cunnison. New York.

Maxwell-Hyslop, K. R. (Rachel)

1946   "Daggers and Swords in Western Asia: A Study from Prehistoric Times to 600 B.C." *Iraq* 8, pp. 1–65.

1971   *Western Asiatic Jewellery, c. 3000–612 B.C.* London.

1995   "A Note on the Anatolian Connections of the Tôd Treasure." *Anatolian Studies* 45, pp. 243–50.

Mazar, A.

1975   "Excavations at Tell Qasîle, 1973–1974 (Preliminary Report)." *Israel Exploration Journal* 25, nos. 2–3, pp. 77–88.

Mazzoni, Stefania

2002   "The Ancient Bronze Age Pottery Tradition in Northwestern Central Syria" and "Late Bronze Age Pottery Production in Northwestern Central Syria." In *Céramique de l'âge du bronze en Syrie*, vol. 1, *La Syrie du sud et la Vallée de l'Oronte*, edited by Michel al-Maqdissi, Valérie Matoïan, and Christopher Nicolle, pp. 69–96, and 129–42. Beirut.

McFadden, George H.
1954 "A Late Cypriote III Tomb from Kourion: Kaloriziki No. 40." *American Journal of Archaeology* 58, pp. 131–42.

McGovern, Patrick E.
1985 *Late Bronze Palestinian Pendants: Innovation in a Cosmopolitan Age.* Sheffield.
1997 "Wine of Egypt's Golden Age: An Archaeochemical Perspective." *Journal of Egyptian Archaeology* 83, pp. 69–108.

McGovern, Patrick E., et al.
1994 Patrick E. McGovern, Janine Bourriau, Garman Harbottle, and Susan J. Allen. "The Archaeological Origin and Significance of the Dolphin Vase as Determined by Neutron Activation Analysis." *Bulletin of the American Schools of Oriental Research*, no. 296, pp. 31–43.

McGovern, Patrick E., Stuart J. Fleming, and Solomon H. Katz, eds.
1996 *The Origins and Ancient History of Wine.* Food and Nutrition in History and Anthropology 11. Amsterdam.

McGovern, Patrick E., Stuart J. Fleming, and C. P. Swann
1993 "The Late Bronze Egyptian Garrison at Beth Shan: Glass and Faience Production and Importation in the Late New Kingdom." *Bulletin of the American Schools of Oriental Research*, nos. 290–91, pp. 1–27.

Medvedskaya, I. N.
1982 *Iran: Iron Age I.* Translated by S. Pavlovich. BAR International Series 126. Oxford.

Mee, Christopher
1978 "Aegean Trade and Settlement in Anatolia in the Second Millennium B.C." *Anatolian Studies* 28, pp. 121–56.
1982 *Rhodes in the Bronze Age: An Archaeological Survey.* Warminster.

Meekers, Marijke
1987 "The Sacred Tree on Cypriote Cylinder Seals (Plate XX)." *Report of the Department of Antiquities, Cyprus*, 1987, pp. 67–76.

Meeks, Dimitri
2001 "Fantastic Animals." In The *Oxford Encyclopedia of Ancient Egypt*, edited by Donald B. Redford, vol. 1, pp. 504–7. Oxford.

Meiggs, Russell
1982 *Trees and Timber in the Ancient Mediterranean World.* Oxford.

Mekhitarian, Arpag
1978 *La peinture égyptienne.* Geneva.

Melena, J. L.
1976 "La producción de plantas aromáticas en Cnoso." *Estudios clásicos* 20, pp. 177–90.

Mellaart, James
1962 "The Late Bronze Age Monuments of Eflatun Pinar and Fasillar near Beyşehir." *Anatolian Studies* 12, pp. 111–17.
1966 *The Chalcolithic and Early Bronze Ages in the Near East and Anatolia.* Beirut.

Mellink, Machteld J.
1969 "The Pratt Ivories in The Metropolitan Museum of Art—Kerma—Chronology and the Transition from Early Bronze to Middle Bronze." *American Journal of Archaeology* 73, pp. 285–87.
1983 "The Hittites and the Aegean World: Part 2, Archaeological Comments on Ahhiyawa-Achaians in Western Anatolia." *American Journal of Archaeology* 87, pp. 138–41.
1987 "Anatolian Libation Pourers and the Minoan Genius." In *Monsters and Demons in the Ancient and Medieval Worlds: Papers Presented in Honor of Edith Porada*, edited by Ann E. Farkas, Prudence O. Harper, and Evelyn B. Harrison, pp. 68–71. Mainz am Rhein.
1992 "Anatolian Chronology." In *Chronologies in Old World Archaeology*, edited by Robert W. Ehrich, vol. 1, pp. 207–20, vol. 2, pp. 171–84. 3rd ed. Chicago.
1993 "Aspects of Minor and Major Arts in Kanish and Acemhöyük." In Mellink, Porada, and Özgüç 1993, pp. 727–30.

Mellink, Machteld J., Edith Porada, and Tahsin Özgüç, eds.
1993 *Nimet Özgüç Armağan. Aspects of Art and Iconography: Anatolia and Its Neighbors: Studies in Honor of Nimet Özgüç.* Ankara.

Merrillees, Robert S.
1982 "Metal Vases of Cypriot Type from the 16th to 13th Centuries B.C." In *Early Metallurgy in Cyprus, 4000–500 B.C.: Acta of the International Archaeological Symposium, Larnaca, Cyprus, 1–6 June 1981*, edited by James D. Muhly et al., pp. 233–50. Nicosia.
2003 "The First Appearances of Kamares Ware in the Levant." *Ägypten und Levante/Egypt and the Levant* 13, pp. 127–42.

Meskell, Lynn
2004 *Private Life in New Kingdom Egypt.* Princeton.

Metzger, Martin
1993 *Kāmid el-Lōz 8. Die spätbronzezeitlichen Tempelanlagen. Die Kleinfunde.* 2 vols. Saarbrücker Beiträge zur Altertumskunde 40. Bonn.

Meyer, Jan-Waalke
1986 "Die Spielbretter KL 78:534 und KL 78:536bis." In *Kāmid el-Lōz in den Jahren 1977 bis 1981*, edited by Rolf Hachmann, pp. 123–43. Saarbrücker Beiträge zur Altertumkunde 36. Bonn.

Michel, Cécile
1996 "Le commerce dans les textes de Mari." In *Amurru I: Mari, Ébla, et les Hourrites; dix ans de travaux. Actes du colloque international (Paris, mai 1993)*, edited by Jean-Marie Durand, pp. 385–426. Paris.
1997 "Les malheurs de Kunnanîya, femme de marchand." *Archivum Anatolicum* 3, pp. 239–53.
1999 "Les joyaux des rois de Mari." In Caubet 1999b, pp. 401–32.
2001 *Correspondance des marchands de Kaniš au début de IIe millénaire avant J.-C.* Littératures anciennes du Proche-Orient 19. Paris.
2002 "Nouvelles données pour la chronologie du IIe millénaire." *Nouvelles assyriologiques brèves et utilitaires*, no. 1 (March), pp. 17–18, no. 20.

Michel, Cécile, and Patrick Rocher
1997– "La chronologie du IIe millénaire revue à l'ombre d'une éclipse
2000 de soleil." *Jaarbericht "Ex Oriente Lux"* 35–36, pp. 111–26.

Mikesell, Marvin W.
1969 "The Deforestation of Mount Lebanon." *Geographical Review* 59, no. 1 (January), pp. 1–28.

Militello, Pietro
1999 "Influenza orientale sui palazzo minoici? Il caso della decorazione parietale." In *Simposio italiano di studi egei dedicato a Luigi Bernabò Brea e Giovanni Pugliese Carratelli*, edited by Vincenzo LaRosa, Dario Palermo, and Lucia Vagnetti, pp. 91–108. Rome.

Mills, J. S., and R. White
1989 "The Identity of the Resins from the Late Bronze Age Shipwreck at Ulu Burun (Kaş)." *Archaeometry* 31, pp. 37–44.

Minoans and Mycenaeans
1999 *Minoans and Mycenaeans: Flavours of Their Time.* Exhibition, National Archaeological Museum, Athens. Catalogue edited by Yannis Tzedakis and Holley Martlew. Athens.

Miron, Renate
1990 *Kāmid el-Lōz 10: Das "Schatzhaus" im Palastbereich. Die Funde.* Saarbrücker Beiträge zur Altertumskunde, vol. 46. Bonn.

Mlinar, Christa
2004 "The Scarab Workshops of Tell el-Dab'a." In Bietak and Czerny 2004, pp. 107–40.

Mommsen, Hans
2006 "Neutron Activation Analysis: Where Was the Dolphin Jar Made?" *Archaeology and History in the Lebanon* 24, pp. 48–51.

Montet, Pierre
1923 "Nouvelles archéologiques: Les fouilles de Byblos en 1923." *Syria* 4, pp. 334–44.
1928–29 *Byblos et l'Égypte: Quatre campagnes de fouilles à Gebeil, 1921–1922–1923–1924.* Bibliothèque archéologique et historique, vol. 11. Paris.
1998 *Byblos et l'Égypte.* Reprint of Montet 1928–29. Bibliothèque archéologique et historique, vol. 11, Texte. Beirut.

Montserrat, Dominic
2000 *Akhenaten: History, Fantasy, and Ancient Egypt.* London.

Moorey, P. R. S.
1970 "Cemetery A at Kish: Grave Groups and Chronology." *Iraq* 32, no. 2, pp. 86–128.
1978 *Kish Excavations, 1923–1933.* Oxford.
1994 *Ancient Mesopotamian Materials and Industries: The Archaeological Evidence.* Oxford.
1999 "Blue Stones in the Ancient Near East: Turquoise and Lapis Lazuli." In Caubet 1999b, pp. 175–88.

Moorey, P. R. S., and S. Fleming
1984 "Problems in the Study of Anthropomorphic Metal Statuary from Syria-Palestine before 330 B.C." *Levant* 14, pp. 67–90.

Moortgat, Anton
1967 *Die Kunst des Alten Mesopotamien: Die klassische Kunst Vorderasiens.* Cologne.

Moortgat, Anton, and Ursula Moortgat-Correns
1976 *Tell Chuēra in Nordost-Syrien: Vorläufiger Bericht über die siebente Grabungskampagne 1974.* Berlin.

Moran, William L., ed. and trans.
1992 *The Amarna Letters.* Baltimore.

Morandi Bonacossi, Danièle, ed.
2007 *Urban and Natural Landscapes of an Ancient Syrian Capital: Settlement and Environment at Tell Mishrifeh/Qatna and in Central-Western Syria. Proceedings of the International Conference Held in Udine, 9–11 December 2004.* Studi Archeologici su Qatna 1. Udine.

Morenz, Ludwig D.
1996 *Beiträge zur Schriftlichkeitskultur im Mittleren Reich und in der 2. Zwischenzeit.* Ägypten und Altes Testament, vol. 29. Wiesbaden.
2000 "Stierspringen und die Sitte des Stierspiels im altmediterranen Raum." *Ägypten und Levante / Egypt and the Levant* 10, pp. 195–204.

de Morgan, Jacques
1900 *Recherches archéologiques; 1ère série: Fouilles à Suse en 1897–1898 et 1898–1899.* Vol. 1 of *Mémoires de la Délégation en Perse.* Paris.

Morgan, Lyvia
1988 *The Miniature Wall Paintings of Thera: A Study in Aegean Culture and Iconography.* Cambridge.
1998 "Power of the Beast: Human-Animal Symbolism in Egyptian and Aegean Art." *Ägypten und Levante / Egypt and the Levant* 7, pp. 17–31.
2004 "Feline Hunters in the Tell el-Dab'a Paintings: Iconography and Dating." *Ägypten und Levante / Egypt and the Levant* 14, pp. 285–98.
2007 Contributions by Mark Cameron. "The Painted Plasters and Their Relation to the Wall Painting of the Pillar Crypt." In *Excavations at Phylakopi in Melos, 1974–77,* by Colin Renfrew, co-edited by Neil Brodie, Christine Morris, and Chris Scarre, pp. 371–99. British School at Athens, Supplementary vol. 42. London.

Morris, Ellen Fowles
2005 *The Architecture of Imperialism: Military Bases and the Evolution of Foreign Policy in Egypt's New Kingdom.* Probleme der Ägyptologie 22. Leiden.

Morris, Sarah P.
1989 "A Tale of Two Cities: The Miniature Frescoes from Thera and the Origins of Greek Poetry." *American Journal of Archaeology* 93, pp. 511–35.
1992 *Daidalos and the Origins of Greek Art.* Princeton.
1997 "Homer and the Near East." In *A New Companion to Homer,* edited by Barry Powell and Ian Morris, pp. 599–623. Leiden.

Morris, Sarah P., and Robert Laffineur, eds.
2007 *Epos: Reconsidering Greek Epic and Aegean Bronze Age Archaeology: Proceedings of the 11th International Aegean Conference. Los Angeles, UCLA— The J. Paul Getty Villa, 20–23 April 2006.* Aegaeum 28. Liège and Austin.

Mountjoy, P. A.
1998 "The East Aegean—West Anatolian Interface in the Late Bronze Age: Mycenaeans and the Kingdom of Ahhiyawa." *Anatolian Studies* 48, pp. 33–67.

Mountjoy, Penelope A., and Hans Mommsen
2001 "Mycenaean Pottery from Qantir-Piramesse, Egypt." *Annual of the British School at Athens* 96, pp. 123–55.

Muhly, James D.
1985 "Sources of Tin and the Beginnings of Bronze Metallurgy." *American Journal of Archaeology* 89, pp. 275–91.
2000 "Mining and Metalwork in Ancient Western Asia." In Sasson 2000, pp. 1501–21.

Muhly, James D., R. Maddin, and T. Stech
1988 "Cyprus, Crete, and Sardinia: Copper Ox-Hide Ingots and the Bronze Age Metals Trade." *Report of the Department of Antiquities, Cyprus,* 1988, pp. 281–98.

Müller, Hans-Wolfgang
1987 *Der Waffenfund von Balâṭa-Sichem; und, Die Sichelschwerter.* Bayerische Akademie der Wissenschaften, Philosophisch-Historische Klasse, Abhandlungen, n.s., no. 97. Munich.

Müller, Hans-Wolfgang, and Eberhard Thiem
1999 *Gold of the Pharaohs.* Translated by Pierre Imhoff and Dafydd Roberts. Ithaca, N.Y.

Müller, Walter
2003 "Precision Measurements of Minoan and Mycenaean Gold Rings with Ultrasound, Metron, Measuring the Aegean Bronge Age." *Aegaeum* 24, pp. 475–81.
2005 "Gold Rings on Minoan Fingers." In *Kres technites / L'artisan crétois: Recueil d'articles en l'honneur de Jean-Claude Poursat, publié à l'occasion des 40 ans de la découverte du Quartier Mu,* pp. 171–76. Aegaeum 26. Liège and Austin.

Müller-Karpe, H.
1977 "Zur altbronzezeitlichen Geschichte Europas." *Jahresbericht des Instituts für Vorgeschichte der Universität Frankfurt am Main,* 1977, pp. 39–64.

Murnane, William J.
1990   *The Road to Kadesh: A Historical Interpretation of the Battle Reliefs of King Sety I at Karnak*. Studies in Ancient Oriental Civilization, no. 42. 2nd rev. ed. Chicago.

Murray, A. S., A. H. Smith, and H. B. Walters
1900   *Excavations in Cyprus (Bequest of Miss E. T. Turner to the British Museum)*. London.
1970   *Excavations in Cyprus (Bequest of Miss E. T. Turner to the British Museum)*. Reprint of 1900 ed. London.

Murray, Margaret A.
1934   *Corpus of the Bronze Age Pottery of Malta*. London.

Muscarella, Oscar White
1988   *Bronze and Iron: Ancient Near Eastern Artifacts in The Metropolitan Museum of Art*. New York.
1992   "Vessel in the Form of a Stag." In "Ancient Art: Gifts from the Norbert Schimmel Collection." *Metropolitan Museum of Art Bulletin*, n.s., 49, no. 4 (Spring), pp. 6–7.

Musche, Brigitte
1988   *Vorderasiatischer Schmuck zur Zeit der Arsakiden und der Sasaniden*. Handbuch der Orientalistik, ser. 7, Kunst und Archäologie, vol. 1, Der Alte Vordere Orient 2. Abschnitt, die Denkmäler, B, Vorderasien, part 5. Leiden.

Mycenaean World: Five Centuries
1988   *The Mycenaean World: Five Centuries of Early Greek Culture, 1600–1100 B.C.* Exhibition, National Archaeological Museum, Athens. Catalogue edited by Kaite Demakopoulou; translated by Miriam E. Caskey and David A. Hardy. Athens.

Mylonas, George E.
1966   *Mycenae and the Mycenaean Age*. Princeton.

Na'aman, Nadav
1992   "Amarna letters." In *The Anchor Bible Dictionary*, edited by David N. Freedman, vol. 1, pp. 174–81. New York.

Nagel, Wolfram
1972   "Mittelassyrischer Schmuck aus der Gruft 45 in Assur." *Acta Praehistorica et Archaeologica* 3, pp. 43–55.

Naissance de l'écriture
1982   *Naissance de l'écriture. Cunéiformes et hiéroglyphes*. Exhibition, Galeries Nationales du Grand Palais, Paris. Catalogue edited by Béatrice André-Leicknam and Christiane Ziegler. Paris.

Naster, Paul
1975–76 "Le poignard de Kamosis au Cabinet des Médailles à Bruxelles." In *Miscellanea in Honorem Josephi Vergote*, edited by Paul Naster, Herman de Meulenaere, and Jan Quaegebeur, pp. 419–26. Orientalia Lovaniensia Periodica 6–7. Leuven.

Naville, Édouard
1886   *Das ägyptische Todtenbuch der XVIII. bis XX. Dynastie*. Berlin.
1896   *The Temple of Deir el Bahari: Its Plan, Its Founders, and Its First Explorers*. Part 2, *The Ebony Shrine, Northern Half of the Middle Platform: Plates XXV–LV*. Memoir of the Egypt Exploration Fund, vol. 14. London.

Negbi, Ora
1970   *The Hoards of Goldwork from Tell el'Ajjul*. Studies in Mediterranean Archaeology, vol. 25. Göteborg.
1976   *Canaanite Gods in Metal: An Archaeological Study of Ancient Syro-Palestinian Figurines*. Publications of the Institute of Archaeology, no. 5. Tel Aviv.
1978   "The 'Miniature Fresco' from Thera and the Emergence of Mycenaean Art." In Doumas 1978–80, vol. 1, pp. 645–56.
1989   "Bronze Age Pottery (Strata XVII–XV)." In *Excavations at Tel Michal, Israel*, edited by Ze'ev Herzog, George Rapp Jr., and Ora Negbi, pp. 43–63. Publications of the Sonia and Marco Nadler Institute of Archaeology, no. 8. Minneapolis.

Neu, Erich
1974   *Der Anitta-Text*. Wiesbaden.

Neve, Peter
1965   "Die Grabungen auf Büyükkale im Jahre 1963." *Mitteilungen der Deutschen Orient-Gesellschaft zu Berlin* 95, pp. 35–68.
1982   *Büyükkale: Die Bauwerke; Grabungen 1954–1966*. Berlin.
1983   "Die Ausgrabungen in Bogazköy-Hattusha 1982." *Archäologische Anzeiger*, 1983, pp. 427–54.
1992   "Hattusha: Stadt der Götter und Tempel. Neue Ausgrabungen in der Hauptstadt der Hethiter." *Antike Welt* 23, Sondernummer, pp. 2–88.

Newberry, Percy E.
1893   *Beni Hasan*. Part 1. London.
1894   *Beni Hasan*. Part 2. London.

Nibbi, Alessandra
1981   *Ancient Egypt and Some Eastern Neighbours*. Park Ridge, N.J.

Nicholson, Paul T.
1993   *Egyptian Faience and Glass*. Shire Egyptology, vol. 18. Princes Risborough.
1995a   "Industrial Archaeology at Amarna." *Egyptian Archaeology* 7, pp. 14–16.
1995b   "Glassmaking and Glassworking at Amarna: Some New Work." *Journal of Glass Studies* 37, pp. 11–19.
1995c   "Recent Excavations at an Ancient Egyptian Glassworks: Tell el-Amarna 1993." *Glass Technology* 36, pp. 125–28.
2000   "Egyptian Faience." In Nicholson and Shaw 2000, pp. 177–94.
2007   *Brilliant Things for Akhenaten: The Production of Glass, Vitreous Materials, and Pottery at Amarna Site O45.1*. Egypt Exploration Society, Excavation Memoir 80. London.

Nicholson, Paul T., C. M. Jackson, and K. M. Trott
1997   "The Ulu Burun Glass Ingots, Cylindrical Vessels and Egyptian Glass." *Journal of Egyptian Archaeology* 83, pp. 143–53.

Nicholson, Paul T., and Ian Shaw, eds.
2000   *Ancient Egyptian Materials and Technology*. Cambridge.

Niemeier, Wolf-Dietrich
1980   "Die Katastrophe von Thera und die spätminoische Chronologie." *Jahrbuch des Deutschen Archäologischen Instituts* 95, pp. 1–76.
1986   "Zur Deutung des Thronraumes im Palast von Knossos." *Mitteilungen des Deutschen Archäologischen Instituts, Athenische Abteilung* 101, pp. 63–95.
1990   "Mycenaean Elements in the Miniature Fresco from Thera?" In Hardy and Renfrew 1990, vol. 1, *Archaeology*, pp. 267–84.
1991   "Minoan Artisans Travelling Overseas: The Alalakh Frescoes and the Painted Plaster Floor at Tel Kabri (Western Galilee)." In *Thalassa, l'Égée préhistorique et la mer: Actes de la troisième Rencontre égéenne internationale de l'Université de Liège, Station de recherches sous-marines et océanographiques (StaReSo), Calvi, Corse, 23–25 avril 1990*, edited by Robert Laffineur and Lucien Basch, pp. 189–200. Aegaeum 7. Liège.
1995   "Tel Kabri: Aegean Fresco Paintings in a Canaanite Palace." In *Recent Excavations in Israel: A View to the West*, edited by S. Gitin, pp. 1–15. Archaeological Institute of America, Colloquia and Conference Papers, vol. 1. Dubuque, Iowa.
1998a   "The Minoans in the South-Eastern Aegean and in Cyprus." In *Eastern Mediterranean: Cyprus, Dodecanese, Crete, 16th–6th Centuries B.C.; Proceedings of the International Symposium, Rethymnon, 13–16 May 1997*, edited by Vassos Karageorghis and Nikolaos Stampolidis, pp. 29–47. Athens.
1998b   "The Mycenaeans in Western Anatolia and the Problem of the Origins of the Sea Peoples." In *Mediterranean Peoples in Transition: Thirteenth to Early Tenth Centuries BCE*, edited by S. Gitin, A. Mazar, and E. Stern, pp. 17–65. Jerusalem.

1999 "Mycenaeans and Hittites in War in Western Asia Minor." In Laffineur 1999, vol. 1, pp. 141–55.

2002 "Hattusa und Ahhijawa im Konflikt um Millawanda/Milet." In *Die Hethiter und ihr Reich* 2002, pp. 294–99.

2003 "The Helladic Territory and the Hittite Empire: Mycenaeans and Hittites in West Asia Minor." In *Sea Routes* 2003, pp. 103–7.

2005a "The Minoans and Mycenaeans in Western Asia Minor: Settlement, Emporia or Acculturation? In Laffineur and Greco 2005, pp. 415–22.

2005b "Minoans, Mycenaeans, Hittites, and Ionians in Western Asia Minor: New Excavations in Bronze Age Miletus-Millawanda." In *The Greeks in the East*, edited by Alexandra Villing, pp. 1–36. British Museum Research Publication, no. 157. Oxford.

Niemeier, Wolf-Dietrich, and B. Niemeier
1998 "Minoan Frescoes in the Eastern Mediterranean." In Cline and Harris-Cline 1998, pp. 69–97.

1999 "The Minoans of Miletos." In Betancourt et al. 1999, vol. 2, pp. 543–54.

Niklasson, Karin
1983 "Tomb 23. A Shaft-Grave of the Late Cypriot III Period." In *Hala Sultan Tekke. 8: Excavations, 1971–79*, edited by Paul Åström et al., pp. 169–213. Studies in Mediterranean Archaeology, vol. 45.8. Göteborg.

Nougayrol, Jean
1939 *Cylindres-sceaux et empreintes de cylindres trouvés en Palestine.* Paris.

1955 *Textes accadiens et hourrites des archives est, ouest et centrales.* Vol. 3, part 1 of *Palais royal d'Ougarit III*, edited by Claude F. A. Schaeffer. Paris.

1970 *Le palais royal d'Ugarit VI: Textes en cunéiformes babyloniens des archives du Grand Palais et du Palais Sud d'Ugarit.* Mission de Ras Shamra, vol. 12. Paris.

Novák, Mirko
2006 "Fundamentierungstechniken im Palast von Qatna." In Czerny et al. 2006, vol. 3, pp. 63–71.

Novák, Mirko, and Peter Pfälzner
2001 "Ausgrabungen in Tall Mišrife-Qatna 2000: Vorbericht der deutschen Komponente des internationalen Kooperationsprojektes." *Mitteilungen der Deutschen Orient-Gesellschaft zu Berlin*, no. 133, pp. 157–98.

2002 "Ausgrabungen in Tall Mišrife-Qatna 2001: Vorbericht der deutschen Komponente des internationalen Kooperationsprojektes." *Mitteilungen der Deutschen Orient-Gesellschaft zu Berlin*, no. 134, pp. 207–46.

2003 "Ausgrabungen im bronzezeitlichen Palast von Tall Mišrife–Qatna 2002: Vorbericht der deutschen Komponente des internationalen Kooperationsprojektes." *Mitteilungen der Deutschen Orient-Gesellschaft zu Berlin*, no. 135, pp. 131–65.

Nylander, Carl
1970 *Ionians in Pasargadae: Studies in Old Persian Architecture.* Uppsala.

1979 "Achaemenid Imperial Art." In *Power and Propaganda: A Symposium on Ancient Empires*, edited by Mogens Trolle Larsen, pp. 345–59. Mesopotamia, vol. 7. Copenhagen.

Oates, David, Joan Oates, and Helen McDonald
1997 *Excavations at Tell Brak.* Vol. 1: *The Mitanni and Old Babylonian Periods.* McDonald Institute Monographs, vol. 1363. Cambridge.

Oates, Joan
2005 *Babylon.* Rev. ed. London.

Oates, Joan, and David Oates
2001 *Nimrud: An Assyrian Imperial City Revealed.* London: British School of Archaeology in Iraq.

Obsomer, Claude
1995 *Sésostris Ier: Étude chronologique et historique du règne.* Brussels.

O'Connor, David
1997 "The Hyksos Period in Egypt." In Oren 1997a, pp. 45–68.

O'Connor, David, and Eric H. Cline, eds.
1998 *Amenhotep III: Perspectives on His Reign.* Ann Arbor.

O'Connor, David, and Stephen Quirke, eds.
2003 *Mysterious Lands.* London.

Oganesian, V. E.
1988 "Serebrianyi kubok iz Karashamba." *Istoriko-filologicheskii zhurnal*, no. 4, pp. 145–61.

1992a "A Silver Goblet from Karashamb." *Soviet Anthropology and Archeology* 30, no. 4, pp. 84–102.

1992b "Raskopki Karashambskogo mogil'nika v 1987 g." *Arkheologicheskiye raboty no novostroikakh armenii*, vol. 1, pp. 26–36.

Ogden, Jack
1982 *Jewellery of the Ancient World.* New York.

1993 "Aesthetic and Technical Considerations Regarding the Colour and Texture of Ancient Goldwork." In *Metal Plating and Patination: Cultural, Technical, and Historical Developments*, edited by Susan La Niece and Paul Craddock, pp. 39–49. London.

2000 "Metals." In Nicholson and Shaw 2000, pp. 148–76.

Oguchi, K.
1992 "Shells and Shell Objects from Area A of 'Usiyeh." *al-Rāfidān: Journal of Western Asiatic Studies* 13, pp. 61–85.

Oller, Gary H.
2000 "Messengers and Ambassadors in Ancient Western Asia." In Sasson 2000, pp. 1465–73.

Oppenheim, A. Leo
1970 "The Cuneiform Tablets with Instructions for Glassmakers." In Oppenheim et al. 1970, pp. 22–101.

1973 "Towards a History of Glass in the Ancient Near East." *Journal of the American Oriental Society* 93, pp. 259–66.

Oppenheim, A. Leo, et al.
1970 A. Leo Oppenheim, Robert H. Brill, Dan Barag, and Axel von Saldern, eds. *Glass and Glassmaking in Ancient Mesopotamia: An Edition of the Cuneiform Texts Which Contain Instructions for Glassmakers with a Catalogue of Surviving Objects.* Corning Museum of Glass Monographs, vol. 3. Corning, N.Y.

Oren, Eliezer D.
1973 *The Northern Cemetery of Beth Shan.* Museum Monograph of the University Museum of the University of Pennsylvania. Leiden.

1997a as editor. *The Hyksos: New Historical and Archaeological Perspectives.* University Museum Monograph, vol. 96; University Museum Symposium Series, vol. 8. Philadelphia.

1997b "The 'Kingdom of Sharuhen' and the Hyksos Kingdom." In Oren 1997a, pp. 253–84.

2000 *The Sea Peoples and Their World: A Reassessment.* University Museum Monograph, vol. 108. Philadelphia.

Orthmann, Winfried, ed.
1975 *Der alte Orient.* Propyläen-Kunstgeschichte, vol. 14. Berlin.

1995 *Ausgrabungen in Tell Chuēra in Nordost-Syrien.* Vol. 1, *Vorbericht über die Grabungskampagnen 1986 bis 1992.* Vorderasiatische Forschungen der Max Freiherr von Oppenheim Stiftung, vol. 2. Saarbrücken.

Osing, Jürgen
1982 "Namensopfer." In *Lexikon der Ägyptologie*, edited by Wolfgang Helck and Wolfhart Westendorf, vol. 4, col. 337. Wiesbaden.

von der Osten, Hans Henning
1934 *Ancient Oriental Seals in the Collection of Mr. Edward T. Newell.* Chicago.

Otto, Adelheid
2000   *Die Entstehung und Entwicklung der Klassisch-Syrischen Glyptik.* Untersuchungen zur Assyriologie und vorderasiatischen Archäologie, vol. 8. Berlin and New York.

Özgüç, Nimet
1949   "Dövlek köyünden (Şarkişla ilcesi) getirilen Eti heykelciği." *Türk Tarih, Arkeologya ve Etnografya Dergisi* 5, pp. 45–52. English summary.
1956   "Ein hethitischer Stierkopf aus Tokat." *Anatolia / Anadolu* 1, pp. 53–58.
1965   *Kültepe mühür baskılarında Anadolu grubu / The Anatolian Group of Cylinder Seal Impressions from Kültepe.* Türk Tarih Kurumu Yayınları, ser. 5, no. 22. Ankara.
1966   "Excavations at Acemhöyük." *Anatolia* 10, pp. 1–52.
1968   *Kanis Karumu Ib kati mühürleri ve mühür baskilari / Seals and Seal Impressions of Level Ib from Karum Kanish.* Türk Tarih Kurumu Yayınlarından, ser. 5, vol. 25. Ankara.
1969   "Assyrian Trade Colonies in Anatolia." *Archaeology* 22, pp. 250–55.
1971   "A Stamp Seal from Niğde Region and Four Seal Impressions Found in Acemhöyük." *Anatolia* 15 (1971), pp. 17–26.
1976   "Acemhöyük'te bulunmuş olan bir fildişi kutu ve bir kurşun figürin kalıbı /An Ivory Box and a Stone Mould from Acem-höyük." *Belleten* 40, pp. 547–60.
1980   "Seal Impressions from the Palaces at Acemhöyük." In Porada 1980, pp. 61–80.
1983   "Sealings from Acemhöyük in The Metropolitan Museum of Art, New York." In *Beiträge zur Altertumskunde Kleinasiens: Festschrift für Kurt Bittel*, edited by R. M. Boehmer and H. Hauptmann, pp. 413–26. Mainz am Rhein.
1991   "The Composite Creatures in Anatolian Art during the Period of the Assyrian Trading Colonies." In *Near Eastern Studies: Dedicated to H.I.H. Prince Takahito Mikasa on the Occasion of His Seventy-fifth Birthday*, edited by Masao Mori et al., pp. 293–317. Wiesbaden.

Özgüç, Tahsin
1953   "Kültepe' de 1950 Yılında Türk Tarih Kurumu Adına Yapılan Kazılar Hakkında Ön-Rapor / Vorliufiger Bericht über die Grabungen von 1950 in Kültepe Ausgeführt im Auftrage des Türk Tarih Kurumu." *Belleten* 17, no. 65, pp. 101–8 (Turkish), 109–18 (German).
1978   *Maşat Höyük kazıları ve çevresindeki araştırmalar / Excavations at Maşat Höyük and Investigations in Its Vicinity.* Tarih Kurumu Yayınlarından, ser. 5, vol. 38. Ankara.
1986a   "The Hittite Cemetery at Ferzant: New Observations on the Finds." *Belleten* 50, no. 197 (August), pp. 393–402.
1986b   *Kültepe-Kaniş II: Eski Yakindoğu'nun ticaret merkezinde yeni araştırmalar / New Researches at the Trading Center of the Ancient Near East.* Türk Tarih Kurumu Yayınlarından, ser. 5, vol. 41. Ankara.
1986c   "Glazed Faience Objects from Kanish." In *Insight through Images: Studies in Honor of Edith Porada*, edited by Marilyn Kelly-Buccellati in collaboration with Paolo Matthiae and Maurits van Loon, pp. 201–8. Bibliotheca Mesopotamica, vol. 21. Malibu.
1986d   "New Observations on the Relationship of Kültepe with Southeast Anatolia and North Syria during the Third Millennium B.C." In *Ancient Anatolia: Aspects of Change and Cultural Development. Essays in Honor of Machteld J. Mellink*, edited by Jeanny Vorys Canby, pp. 31–47. Madison.
1988   *İnandıktepe: Eski Hitit Çağında önemli bir kült merkezi / An Important Cult Center in the Old Hittite Period.* Türk Tarih Kurumu Yayınlarından, ser. 5, vol. 43. Ankara.
1999   *Kültepe-Kaniş / Neša: The Palaces and Temples of Kültepe-Kaniş / Neša.* Türk Tarih Kurumu Yayınlarından, ser. 5, vol. 46. Ankara.
2002a   "Die Keramik der althethitischen Zeit. Kultgefässe." In *Die Hethiter und ihr Reich* 2002, pp. 248–55.

2002b   "Opfer und Libation." In *Die Hethiter und ihr Reich* 2002, pp. 122–27.
2003   *Kültepe-Kaniş / Neša: The Earliest International Trade Center and the Oldest Capital City of the Hittites.* [Istanbul]: Middle Eastern Culture Center in Japan.

Özgüç, Tahsin, and Nimet Özgüç
1953   "Türk Tarih Kurumu tarıfından yapılan Kültepe Kazısı Raporu 1949 / Ausgrabungen in Kültepe." *Ankara* 6, pp. 251–68 (Turkish), 269–88 (German).
1959   *Kültepe-Kaniš: New Researches at the Center of the Assyrian Trade Colonies.* Türk Tarih Kurumu Yayınlarından, ser. 5, vol. 19. Ankara.

Özgünel, Coşkun
1996   *Mykenische Keramik in Anatolien.* Asia Minor Studien, vol. 23. Bonn.

Panagiotaki, M.
1998   "The Vat Room Deposit at Knossos: The Unpublished Notes of Sir Arthur Evans." *Annual of the British School at Athens* 93, pp. 167–84.
2000a   "Crete and Egypt: Contacts and Relationships Seen through Vitreous Materials." In *Crete–Egypt* 2000, pp. 154–61.
2000b   "Φαγεντιανή, κοσμήματα και πολύτιμα αντικείμενα." In *Krete–Aigyptos* 2000, pp. 93–96, 103, no. 103.

Panagiotaki, M., et al.
2003   M. Panagiotaki, L. Papazoglou-Manioudaki, G. Chatzi-Spiliopoulou, E. Andreopoulou-Mangou, Y. Maniatis, M. S. Tite, and A. Shortland. "A Glass Workshop at the Mycenaean Citadel of Tiryns in Greece." *Annales du 16ème Congrès de l'Association Internationale pour l'Histoire du Verre*, pp. 14–18.

Panagiotopoulos, D.
2001   "Keftiu in Context: Theban Tomb Paintings as a Historical Source." *Oxford Journal of Archaeology* 20, pp. 263–83.
2006   "Foreigners in Egypt in the Time of Hatshepsut and Thutmose III." In Cline and O'Connor 2006, pp. 370–412.

Pantazis, Th., et al.
2003   Th. Pantazis, A. G. Karydas, Christos Doumas, A. Vlacho-poulos, P. Nomikos, and M. Dinsmore. "X-Ray Fluorescence Analysis of a Gold Ibex and Other Artifacts from Akrotiri." In K. Foster and Laffineur 2003, pp. 155–60.

Papadopoulos, Thanasis J.
1998   *The Late Bronze Age Daggers of the Aegean, I: The Greek Mainland.* Prähistorische Bronzefunde, ser. 6, vol. 11. Stuttgart.

Papasavvas, Giorgos
2001   Χάλκινοι Υποστάτες από την Κύπρο και την Κρήτη. Leukosia.

Papazoglou-Manioudaki, Lena
1994   "A Mycenaean Warrior's Tomb at Krini, near Patras." *Annual of the British School at Athens* 89, pp. 171–200.
2003   "Rhyta, Figures, and Figurines in the Shape of the Bull in Prehistoric Greece." In *The Bull in the Mediterranean World: Myth and Cults*, edited by S. Athanassopoulou and Yannis Tzedakis, pp. 122–24. Exh. cat. Athens: Benaki Museum.

Pardee, Dennis
2002   *Ritual and Cult at Ugarit.* Atlanta.

Parfums et cosmétiques
2002   *Parfums et cosmétiques dans l'Égypte ancienne.* Exhibition, Musée d'Archéologie Méditerranéenne, Marseille. Catalogue by Alain Charron, Gisèle Piérini, and Philippe Walter. Marseille.

Parise, Nicola F.
1968   "I pani di rame del II millennio a.C.: Considerazioni prelimi-nari." In *Atti e memorie del I Congresso internazionale di miceno-logia*, pp. 117–33. Rome.

1984   "Unità ponderali e rapporti di cambio nella Siria del Nord." In *Circulation of Goods in Non-Palatial Context in the Ancient Near East: Proceedings of the International Conference Organized by the Instituto per gli Studi Micenei ed Egeo-Anatolici*, edited by Alfonso Archi, pp. 125–38. Incunabula Graeca, vol. 82. Rome.

Parkinson, R. B.
2002   *Poetry and Culture in Middle Kingdom Egypt: A Dark Side to Perfection*. London.

Parrot, André
1937   "Les fouilles de Mari, troisième campagne (hiver 1935–1936)." *Syria* 18, pp. 54–84.
1938   "Les fouilles de Mari, quatrième campagne (hiver 1936–37)." *Syria* 19, pp. 1–29.
1950   "'Cérémonie de la Main' et Réinvestiture." In *Studia Mariana*, edited by André Parrot, pp. 37–40. Leiden.
1956   *Mission Archéologique de Mari*. Vol. 1, *Le temple d'Ishtar*. Paris.
1958   *Mission Archéologique de Mari*. Vol. 2, *Le palais*. Parts 1 (*Architecture*), 2 (*Peintures murales*). Paris.
1959   *Mission Archéologique de Mari*. Vol. 2, *Le palais*. Part 3, *Documents et monuments*. Paris.
1967   *Mission Archéologique de Mari*. Vol. 3, *Les temples d'Ishtarat et de Ninni-zaza*. With the collaboration of Georges Dossin and Lucienne Laroche. Paris.

Parrot, André, Maurice H. Chéhab, and Sabatino Moscati
1975   *Les Phéniciens: L'expansion phénicienne, Carthage*. L'univers des formes, vol. 23. Paris.
1977   *Die Phönizier: Die Entwicklung der phönizischen Kunst von den anfängen bis zum Ende des dritten punischen Krieges*. Translated by Franz Graf von Otting and Wolf-Dieter Bach. Munich.
2007   *Les Phéniciens: L'expansion phénicienne, Carthage*. L'univers des formes. Paris.

Paschalidis, C. P.
2002–3   "Στα Ίχνη των Πήλινων Υποδημάτων. Πήλινα Ιδιότυπα Ρυτά από τη Μυκηναϊκή Αττική στο Εθνικό Αρχαιολογικό Μουσείο." *το Μουσείον* [To Mouseion] 3, pp. 93–110.

Patai, Raphael
1998   *The Children of Noah: Jewish Seafaring in Ancient Times*. Princeton.

Patch, Diana Craig
2005   "Jewelry in the Early Eighteenth Dynasty." In *Hatshepsut* 2005, pp. 191–215.

Patch, Diana Craig, and Cheryl Ward Haldane
1990   *The Pharaoh's Boat at the Carnegie*. Pittsburgh: Carnegie Museum of Natural History.

Payton, R.
1991   "The Uluburun Writing-Board Set." *Anatolian Studies* 41, pp. 99–106.

Peck, William H.
1978   *Egyptian Drawings*. New York.

Pecorella, Paolo E., ed.
1998   *Tell Barri/Kahat 2: Relazione sulle campagne 1980–1993 a Tell Barri/Kahat, nel bacino del Habur (Siria)*. Documenta asiana, vol. 5. Rome.

Peltenburg, E. J.
1972   "On the Classification of Faience Vases from Late Bronze Age Cyprus." In *Πρακτικά του πρώτου Διεθνούς Κυπριολογικού Συνεδρίου* [Acts of the First International Congress of Cypriot Studies], vol. 1, pp. 129–36. Nicosia.
1985   "Appendix II: Glazed Vessels from Bronze and Iron Age Kition." In Karageorghis and Demas 1985, pp. 255–79.
1991   "Greeting Gifts and Luxury Faience: A Context for Orientalising Trends in Late Mycenaean Greece." In Gale 1991a, pp. 162–79.

Pendlebury, J. D. S.
1931   "Preliminary Report of Excavations at Tell El-'Amarnah 1930–1." *Journal of Egyptian Archaeology* 17, pp. 233–44.
1951   *The City of Akhenaten, Part 3: The Central City and the Official Quarters: The Excavations at Tell el-Amarna During the Seasons 1926–1927 and 1931–1936*. 2 vols. Memoir of the Egypt Exploration Society 44. London.

Perrot, Georges, and Charles Chipiez
1885   *History of Art in Phoenicia and Its Dependencies*. Translated by Walter Armstrong. London. Originally published as: *Histoire de l'art dans l'antiquité*. Vol. 3, *Phénicie, Cypre*. Paris.

Perrot, J. F. A.
1955   "The Excavations at Tell Abu Matar, near Beersheba." *Israel Exploration Journal* 5, pp. 167–89.

Persson, Axel W.
1931   *The Royal Tombs at Dendra near Midea*. Acta Regiae Societatis Humaniorum Litterarum Lundensis, vol. 15. Lund.

Persson, Axel W., Nils Hammarstrand, and John R. C. Hamilton
1942   *New Tombs at Dendra near Midea*. Acta Regiae Societatis Humaniorum Litterarum Lundensis, vol. 34. Lund.

Petrie, W. M. Flinders
1891   *Illahun, Kahun, and Gurob, 1889–90*. London.
1894   *Tell el Amarna*. Warminster. Reprinted 1974.
1901   *The Royal Tombs of the Earliest Dynasties, 1901*. Part 2. Memoir of the Egypt Exploration Fund 21. London.
1909   *Qurneh*. British School of Archaeology in Egypt and Egyptian Research Account, Fifteenth Year, 1909 [Publication 16]. London.
1925   *Buttons and Design Scarabs, Illustrated by the Egyptian Collection in University College, London*. Publications of the Egyptian Research Account and British School of Archaeology in Egypt, vol. 38. London.
1926   *Ancient Weights and Measures*. British School of Archaeology in Egypt, Publications of the Egyptian Research Account 39. London.
1927   *Objects of Daily Use: The Petrie Egyptian Collection and Excavations*. British School of Archaeology in Egypt, vol. 42. London.
1932a   *Ancient Gaza I: Tell el Ajjūl*. Vol. 2. Publications of the Egyptian Research Account and British School of Archaeology in Egypt, vol. 54. London.
1932b   "The Palaces of Ancient Gaza. Tell el Ajjūl." *Ancient Egypt* 17, nos. 1–2, pp. 1–9, 41–46.
1934   *Ancient Gaza: Tell el-Ajjūl*. Vol. 4. Publications of the Egyptian Research Account and British School of Archaeology in Egypt 56. London.
1974   *Objects of Daily Use*. British School of Archaeology in Egypt, Catalogue of Egyptian Antiquities 6. Warminster. Reprint of 1927 ed.

Petrie, W. M. Flinders, Ernest J. Mackay, and Margaret A. Murray
1952   *Ancient Gaza*. Vol. 5, *City of Shepherd Kings and Ancient Gaza*. London.

Petruso, Karl M.
1984   "Prolegomena to Late Cypriot Weight Metrology." *American Journal of Archaeology* 88, pp. 293–304.

Petschel, Susanne
2004   "Ehrendolch des Djehuty." In *Pharao siegt immer* 2004, p. 87, no. 76.

Pettinato, Giovanni
1981   *The Archives of Ebla: An Empire Inscribed in Clay*. Garden City, N.Y.

Pfälzner, Peter
1995   *Mittanische und mittelassyrische Keramik: Eine chronologische, funktionale und produktionsökonomische Analyse*. 2 vols. Berichte

der Ausgrabund Tall Šēḫ Ḥamad/Dūr-katlimmu, vol. 3. Berlin.

2005   "Syrien: Qatna. Ahnenkult im 2. Jahrtausend v. Chr." *Welt und Umwelt der Bibel*, no. 2, pp. 56–59.

2006   "Syria's Royal Tombs Uncovered." *Current World Archaeology* 15, pp. 2–13.

2007a   "Archaeological Investigations in the Royal Palace of Qatna." In Morandi Bonacossi 2007, pp. 21–53.

2007b   "Das System des 'kommerzialisierten Geschenkaustausches' im 2. Jahrtausend v. Chr. in Syrien." In *Geschenke und Steuern, Zölle und Tribute: Antike Abgabenformen in Anspruch und Wirklichkeit*, edited by H. Klinkott and S. Kubisch, pp. 117–31. Leiden.

2007c   "Where the Living Feasted with the Dead: The Royal Tombs of Qatna, Syria." In *Discovery!: Unearthing the New Treasures of Archaeology*, edited by Brian M. Fagan, pp. 62–65. London.

2007d   "The Late Bronze Age Ceramic Traditions of the Syrian Jazirah." In *Céramique de l'âge du bronze en Syrie*, vol. 2, edited by Michel al-Maqdissi, Valérie Matoïan, and Christopher Nicolle. Beirut.

Pfälzner, Peter, and Constance von Rüden

2008   "Between the Aegean and Syria: The Wall Paintings from the Royal Palace of Qatna." In *Fundstellen: Gesammelte Schriften zur Archäologie und Geschichte Altvorderasiens ad Honorem Hartmut Kühne*, edited by D. Bonatz, R. M. Czichon, and F. J. Kreppner, pp. 95–118. Wiesbaden.

Pharao: Kunst und Herrschaft

1997   *Pharao: Kunst und Herrschaft im alten Ägypten*. Exhibition, Kunsthaus Kaufbeuren. Catalogue by Alfred Grimm, Sylvia Schoske, and Dietrich Wildung. Munich.

Pharaohs

2002   *The Pharaohs*. Exhibition, Palazzo Grassi, Venice. Catalogue edited by Christiane Ziegler. Milan.

Pharaohs and Mortals

1988   *Pharaohs and Mortals: Egyptian Art in the Middle Kingdom*. Exhibition, Fitzwilliam Museum, Cambridge, and Liverpool. Catalogue by Janine Bourriau, with a contribution by Stephen Quirke. Cambridge.

Pharaohs of the Sun

1999   *Pharaohs of the Sun: Akhenaten. Nefertiti. Tutankhamun.* Exhibition, Museum of Fine Arts, Boston; Los Angeles County Museum of Art; Art Institute of Chicago; Rijks-museum van Oudheden te Leiden. Catalogue edited by Rita E. Freed, Yvonne J. Markowitz, and Sue H. D'Auria. Boston.

Pharaonen und Fremde

1994   *Pharaonen und Fremde: Dynastien im Dunkel*. Exhibition, Historisches Museum der Stadt Wien. Catalogue by Irmgard Hein et al. Vienna.

Le pharaon-soleil

1993   *Le pharaon-soleil: Aménophis III*. Exhibition, Cleveland Museum of Art; Kimbell Art Museum, Fort Worth; Galeries Nationales du Grand Palais, Paris. Catalogue by Arielle P. Kozloff and Betsy M. Bryan; with Lawrence M. Berman and Elisabeth Delange. Paris.

Pharao siegt immer

2004   *Pharao siegt immer: Krieg und Frieden im alten Ägypten*. Exhibition, Gustav-Lübcke-Museum, Hamm. Catalogue edited by Susanne Petschel and Martin von Falck; contribu-tions by Christian Bayer et al. Bönen.

Phelps, William, Yannos Lolos, and Yannis Vichos, eds.

1999   *The Point Iria Wreck: Interconnections in the Mediterranean, ca. 1200 BC; Proceedings of the International Conference, Island of Spetses, 19 September 1998*. Athens.

Philip, Graham

2006   *Tell el-Dab'a XV: Metalwork and Metalworking Evidence of the Late Middle Kingdom and the Second Intermediate Period*. Untersuchungen der Zweigstelle Kairo des Österreichischen Archäologischen Institutes, vol. 26. Vienna.

Phillips, Jacqueline S.

1991   "The Impact and Implications of the Egyptian and 'Egyptianizing' Material Found in Bronze Age Crete ca. 3000–ca. 1100 B.C." 3 vols. Ph.D. diss., University of Toronto.

2008   *Aegyptiaca on the Island of Crete in Their Chronological Context: A Critical Review*. Contributions to the Chronology of the Eastern Mediterranean, vol. 18; Österreichische Akademie der Wissenschaften, Denkschriften der Gesamtakademie, vol. 49. Vienna.

Phillips, Jacqueline S., and Eric Cline

2005   "Amenhotep III and Mycenae: Further Evidence." In *Autochthon*: Österreichische Akademie der Wissenschaften, *Papers Presented to O.T.P.K. Dickinson on the Occasion of His Retirement* [Institute of Classical Studies, University of London, 9 November 2005], edited by Anastasia Dakouri-Hild and Sue Sherratt, pp. 317–28. Oxford.

Photos, E., R. E. Jones, and Thanasis Papadopoulos

1994   "The Black Inlay Decoration on a Mycenaean Bronze Dagger." *Archaeometry* 36, no. 2, pp. 267–75.

Piankoff, Alexandre, trans.

1957   *Mythological Papyri*. Edited by Natacha Rambova. 2 vols. New York.

Piccione, Peter A.

2007   "The Egyptian Game of Senet and the Migration of the Soul." In Finkel 2007a, pp. 54–63.

Pierrat, Geneviève

1994   "À propos de la date et de l'origine du trésor de Tôd." *Bulletin de la Société Française d'Égyptologie* 130 (June), pp. 18–28.

Pierrat-Bonnefois, Geneviève

1999   "Les objets en lapis-lazuli dans le trésor de Tôd." In Caubet 1999b, pp. 285–302. Paris.

Pierre[-Müller], Beatrice

1987   "Décor peint à Mari et au Proche-Orient." *Mari: Annales de recherches interdisciplinaires* 5, pp. 551–76.

Pini, Ingo

1970   as editor. *Die Siegelabdrücke von Phästos*. Vol. 5 of *Iraklion, Archäologisches Museum*. Corpus der minoischen und mykenis-chen Siegel, vol. 2. Berlin.

1977–78 "Ein orientalischer Rollsiegelabdruck auf der Tonplombe, Iraklion Museum, Inv. Nr. 508 aus Aj. Triada." *Marburger Winckelmann-Programm*, 1977–78, pp. 3–9.

1979   "Cypro-Aegean Cylinder Seals: On the Definition and Origin of the Class." In *Acts of the International Archaeological Sym-posium: The Relations between Cyprus and Crete ca. 2000–500 B.C.*, pp. 121–27. Nicosia.

1980   "Kypro-ägaische Rollsiegel: Ein Beitrag zur Definition und Ursprung der Gruppe." *Jahrbuch des Deutschen Archäologischen Instituts* 95, pp. 77–108.

1992   *Kleinere griechische Sammlungen*. Corpus der minoischen und mykenischen Siegel, vol. 5, suppl. 1A, *Ägina–Korinth*. Berlin.

1993   *Kleinere griechische Sammlungen*. Corpus der minoischen und mykenischen Siegel, vol. 5, suppl. 1B, *Lamia–Zakynthos und Weitere Lander des Ostmittelmeerraums*. Berlin.

1997   as editor. *Die Tonplomben aus dem Nestorpalast von Pylos*. Mainz am Rhein.

490

2004   *Kleinere griechische Sammlungen*. Corpus der minoischen und mykenischen Siegel, vol. 5, suppl. 3. Part 1, *Neufunde aus Greichenland und der westlichen Türkei*. Part 2, *Nafplion—Volos*. Berlin.

Pini, Ingo, et al.
1975   Ingo Pini, J. L. Caskey, M. Caskey, O. Pelon, M. H. Wiencke, and J. G. Younger. *Kleinere griechische Sammlungen*. 2 vols. Corpus der minoischen und mykenischen Siegel, vol. 5. Berlin.

Pittman, Holly
2000   "Cylinder Seals and Scarabs in the Ancient Near East." In Sasson 2000, pp. 1589–1603.
2003a   "Kneeling Bull Holding a Vessel." In *Art of the First Cities* 2003, p. 43, no. 13.
2003b   "Standing Lioness Demon." In *Art of the First Cities* 2003, pp. 44–45, no. 14.

Platon, Nikolaos
1966   "Ανασκαφαί Ζάκρου." *Πρακτικά της εν Αθήναις Αρχαιολογικής Εταιρείας (Praktika tes en Athenais Archaiologikes Hetaireias)*, 1963 (pub. 1966), pp. 160–88.
1969   *Iraklion Archäologisches Museum*. Vol. 1, *Die Siegel der Vorpalast-zeit*. Corpus der minoischen und mykenischen Siegel, vol. 2, Berlin.
1971   *Zakros: The Discovery of a Lost Palace of Ancient Crete*. New York.

Platon, Nikolaos, Walter Müller, and Ingo Pini, eds.
1999   *Iraklion Archäologisches Museum, 6: Die Siegelabdrücke von Aj. Triada und anderen zentral- und ostkretischen Fundorten, unter Einbeziehung von Funden aus anderen Museen*. Corpus der minoischen und mykenischen Siegel, vol. 2. Berlin.

Platt, Elizabeth Ellen
1976   "Triangular Jewelry Plaques." *Bulletin of the American Schools of Oriental Research*, no. 221, pp. 103–11.
1979   "Jewelry of Bible Times and the Catalogue of Isa 3:18-23, Part 1." *Andrews University Seminary Studies* 17, no. 1, pp. 71–84.

Podany, Amanda H.
2002   *The Land of Hana: Kings, Chronology, and Scribal Tradition*. Bethesda, Md.

Politis, Thea
2001   "Gold and Granulation: Exploring the Social Implications of a Prestige Technology in the Bronze Age Mediterranean." In *The Social Context of Technological Change: Egypt and the Near East, 1650–1550 B.C.: Proceedings of a Conference Held at St. Edmund Hall, Oxford, 12–14 September 2000*, edited by Andrew J. Shortland, pp. 161–94. Oxford.

Pollard, A. M.
1987   "Report on the Analysis of Failaka Glass, Glazed Pottery, and Faience." In *Failaka/Dilmun: The Second Millennium Settlements*, vol. 2. *The Bronze Age Pottery*, edited by F. Højlund, pp. 185–89. Jutland Archaeological Society Publications, vol. 17.2. Århus.

Polz, Daniel
2007   *Der Beginn des Neuen Reiches: Zur Vorgeschichte einer Zeitenwende*. Sonderschrift, Deutsches Archäologisches Institut, Abteilung Kairo, vol. 31. Berlin.

Popham, M., E. Catling, and H. Catling
1974   "Sellopoulo Tombs 3 and 4, Two Late Minoan Graves near Knossos." *Annual of the British School at Athens* 69, pp. 195–257.

Popham, Mervyn, E. Touloupa, and L. H. Sackett
1982   "The Hero of Lefkandi." *Antiquity* 56 (1982), pp. 169–74.

Porada, Edith
1947   *Seal Impressions of Nuzi*. Annual of the American Schools of Oriental Research, vol. 24. New Haven.
1948   *Corpus of Ancient Near Eastern Seals in North American Collections*. Vol. 1, *The Collection of the Pierpont Morgan Library*. Catalogued and edited by Edith Porada for the Committee of Ancient Near Eastern Seals, a project of the Iranian Institute, the Oriental Institute of the University of Chicago, and the Yale Babylonian Collection; contributions by Briggs Buchanan. Bollingen Series, vol. 14. New York.
1952   "On the Problem of Kassite Art." In *Archaeologica Orientalia in Memoriam Ernst Herzfeld*, edited by George C. Miles, pp. 179–87. Locust Valley, N.Y.
1973a   "Notes on the Sarcophagus of Ahiram." *Journal of the Ancient Near Eastern Society of Columbia University* 5, pp. 355–72.
1973b   "On the Complexity of Style and Iconography in Some Groups of Cylinder Seals from Cyprus." In *Acts of the International Archaeological Symposium 'The Mycenaeans in the Eastern Mediterranean', Nicosia, 27th March–2nd April 1972*, pp. 260–73. Nicosia: Department of Antiquities.
1974   "Mesopotamien und Iran." In *Frühe Stufen der Kunst*, edited by Machteld J. Mellink and Jan Filip, pp. 141–65. Propyläen Kunstgeschichte, vol. 13. Berlin.
1975   "Standards and Stools on Sealings of Nuzi and Other Examples of Mitannian Glyptic Art." In *Le temple et le culte: Compte rendu de la 20e Rencontre Assyriologique Internationale organisée à Leiden du 3 au 7 juillet 1972 sous les auspices du Nederlands Instituut voor het Nabije Oosten*, pp. 164–72. Leiden.
1980   as editor. *Ancient Art in Seals*. Princeton.
1981–82 "The Cylinder Seals Found at Thebes in Boeotia." *Archiv für Orientforschung* 28, pp. 1–70.
1982   "Remarks on the Tôd Treasure in Egypt." In *Societies and Languages of the Ancient Near East: Studies in Honour of I. M. Diakonoff*, pp. 285–303. Warminster.
1985   "Mesopotamien und Iran." In *Frühe Stufen der Kunst*, edited by Machteld J. Mellink and Jan Filip, pp. 141–65. Propyläen Kunstgeschichte. Reprint. Berlin.

Porada, Edith, et al.
1992   Edith Porada, Donald P. Hansen, Sally Dunham, and Sidney H. Babcock. "The Chronology of Mesopotamia, ca. 7000–1600 B.C." In *Chronologies in Old World Archaeology*, edited by Robert W. Ehrich, vol. 1, pp. 77–121, vol. 2, pp. 90–124. 3rd ed. Chicago.

Porter, Bertha, and Rosalind L. B. Moss
1934   *Topographical Bibliography of Ancient Egyptian Hieroglyphic Texts, Reliefs, and Paintings*. Vol. 4, *Lower and Middle Egypt*. Oxford. Reissued 1968.
1972   *Topographical Bibliography of Ancient Egyptian Hieroglyphic Texts, Reliefs, and Paintings*. Vol. 2, *Theban Temples*. 2nd ed. Oxford.

Porter, Bertha, and Rosalind L. B. Moss, revised by Jaromír Málek
1978   *Topographical Bibliography of Ancient Egyptian Hieroglyphic Texts, Reliefs, and Paintings*. 2nd ed. Vol. 3, *Memphis*, part 2, *Saqqâra to Dahshûr*. Oxford.

Posener, Georges
1971   "Syria and Palestine, ca. 2160–1780 B.C." In *The Cambridge Ancient History*, vol. 1, part 2, edited by I. E. S. Edwards, C. J. Gadd, and N. G. L. Hammond, pp. 532–58. Cambridge.

Postgate, Carolyn, David Oates, and Joan Oates
1997   *The Excavations at Tell Al Rimah: The Pottery*. Iraq Archaeo-logical Reports, vol. 4. Warminster.

Postgate, J. N.
1990   "Trees and Timber in the Assyrian Texts." *Bulletin on Sumerian Agriculture* 5, pp. 177–92.

Pottier, Edmond
1922   "Observations sur quelques objets trouvés dans le sarcophagi de Byblos." *Syria* 3, pp. 298–306.

Potts, Daniel T.
1990   *The Arabian Gulf in Antiquity.* Vol. 1, *From Prehistory to the Fall of the Achaemenid Empire.* Oxford and New York.
2000   "Distant Shores: Ancient Near Eastern Trade with South Asia and Northeast Africa." In Sasson 2000, pp. 1451–63.

Poursat, Jean-Claude
1973   "Le Sphinx minoen: Un nouveau document." In *Antichità Cretesi: Studi in onore di Doro Levi*, vol. 1, pp. 111–14. Catania.
1977a   *Catalogue des ivoires myceniens du Musée National d'Athènes.* Athens: Ethnikon Archaiologikon Mouseion.
1977b   *Les ivoires mycéniens: Essai sur la formation d'un art mycénien.* 2 vols. Bibliothèque des Écoles Françaises d'Athènes et de Rome, no. 230. Athens.
1980   "Fouilles exécutées à Mallia." In *Mallia: Le quartier Mu*, vol. 2, pp. 116–32. Études crétoises, vol. 26. Paris.
1999   "Ivoires chypro-égéens: De Chypre à Minet el-Beida et Mycènes." In Betancourt et al. 1999, vol. 3, pp. 683–88.

Powell, Marvin A.
1987–90 "Masse und Gewichte." In *Reallexikon der Assyriologie und Vorderasiatischen Archäologie*, edited by Erich Ebeling and Bruno Meissner, vol. 7, pp. 457–517. Berlin.

Preziosi, Donald, and Louise A. Hitchcock
1999   *Aegean Art and Architecture.* Oxford.

Priese, Karl-Heinz, ed.
1991   *Ägyptisches Museum: Museumsinsel Berlin.* Contributions by Caris-Beatrice Arnst et al. Mainz am Rhein and Berlin.

Primas, M., and E. Pernicka
1998   "Der Depotfund von Oberwilflingen: Neue Ergebnisse zur Zirkulation von Metallbarren." *Germania* 76, pp. 25–65.

Pritchard, James B.
1963   *The Bronze Age Cemetery at Gibeon.* University Museum, University of Pennsylvania, Museum Monographs. Philadelphia.
1969   as editor. *Ancient Near Eastern Texts Relating to the Old Testament.* Translated and annotated by W. F. Albright et al. 3rd ed. Princeton.
1975   *Sarepta. A Preliminary Report on the Iron Age: Excavations of the University Museum of the University of Pennsylvania, 1970–72.* University Museum, University of Pennsylvania, Museum Monographs. Philadelphia.

Protonotariou-Deilaki, E.
1968   "Θολωτός τάφος Καζάρμας." Αρχαιολογικά Ανάλεκτα εξ Αθηνών / *Athens Annals of Archaeology* 1, pp. 236–38.
1969   "Θολωτός τάφος Καζάρμας." Αρχαιολογικά Ανάλεκτα εξ Αθηνών / *Athens Annals of Archaeology* 2, pp. 3–6.

Pruss, Alexander, and Abd Al-Masīh Bagdo
2002   "Tell Fecheriye. Bericht über die erste Kampagne der deutsch-syrischen Ausgrabungen 2001." *Mitteilungen der Deutschen Orient-Gesellschaft* 134, pp. 311–29.

Pruzsinszky, Regine
2006   "Šamšī-Adad I. 'neue' Regierungsdaten und assyrische Distanzangaben." In Czerny et al. 2006, vol. 3, pp. 73–80.

Pulak, Cemal
1988   "The Bronze Age Shipwreck at Ulu Burun, Turkey: 1985 Campaign." *American Journal of Archaeology* 92, pp. 1–37.
1995   "Das Schiffswrack von Uluburun." In *In Poseidons Reich: Archäologie unter Wasser*, pp. 43–58. Zaberns Bildbände zur Archäologie 23. Mainz am Rhein.
1997   "The Uluburun Shipwreck." In *Res Maritimae: Cyprus and the Eastern Mediterranean from Prehistory to Late Antiquity; Proceedings of the Second International Symposium "Cities on the Sea," Nicosia, Cyprus, October 18–22, 1994*, edited by Stuart Swiny, Robert L. Hohlfelder, and Helena Wylde Swiny,

pp. 233–62. Cyprus American Archaeological Research Institute Monograph Series 1. Atlanta.
1998   "The Uluburun Shipwreck: An Overview." *International Journal of Nautical Archaeology* 27, no. 3, pp. 188–224.
1999   "The Late Bronze Age Shipwreck at Uluburun: Aspects of Hull Construction." In Phelps, Lolos, and Vichos 1999, pp. 209–38.
2000a   "The Balance Weights from the Late Bronze Age Shipwreck at Uluburun." In *Metals Make the World Go Round: The Supply and Circulation of Metals in Bronze Age Europe. Proceedings of a Conference Held at the University of Birmingham in June 1997*, edited by C. F. E. Pare, pp. 247–66. Oxford: Oxbow.
2000b   "The Cargo of Copper and Tin Ingots from the Late Bronze Age Shipwreck at Uluburun." In *Anatolian Metal*, vol. 1, edited by Ü. Yalçın, pp. 137–57. Der Anschnitt 13. Bochum: Deutsches Bergbau-Museum Bochum.
2001   "The Cargo of the Uluburun Ship and Evidence for Trade with the Aegean and Beyond." *In Italy and Cyprus in Antiquity, 1500–450 B.C.: Proceedings of an International Symposium Held at the Italian Academy for Advanced Studies in America at Columbia University, November 16–18, 2000*, edited by Larissa Bonfante and Vassos Karageorghis, pp. 13–60. Nicosia.
2002   "The Uluburun Hull Remains." In *Tropis VII: 7th International Symposium on Ship Construction in Antiquity: Pylos 1999 Proceedings*, edited by H. E. Tzalas, pp. 615–34. 2 vols. Athens.
2004   "Museen in der westlichen Türkei: Bodrum Archäologisches Museum." In Pini 2004, part 2, pp. 651–52.
2005a   "Who Were the Mycenaeans aboard the Uluburun Ship?" In Laffineur and Greco 2005, pp. 295–312.
2005b   "Discovering a Royal Ship from the Age of King Tut: Uluburun, Turkey." In *Beneath the Seven Seas: Adventures with the Institute of Nautical Archaeology*, edited by G. F. Bass, pp. 34–47. London.
2005c   "Das Schiffswrack von Uluburun." In *Das Schiff von Uluburun* 2005, pp. 55–102, with accompanying catalogue, pp. 559–633.

Pulak, Cemal, and D. Frey
1985   "The Search for a Bronze Age Shipwreck." *Archaeology* 38, no. 4, pp. 18–24.

Pulak, Cemal, and E. Rogers
1994   "The 1993–1994 Turkish Shipwreck Surveys." *Institute of Nautical Archaeology Quarterly* 21, no. 4, pp. 17–21.

Pusch, Edgar B.
1977   "Ein unbeachetete Brettspielart." *Studien zur altägyptischen Kultur* 5, pp. 199–212.
1979   *Das Senet-Brettspiel im alten Ägypten.* 2 vols. Münchener ägyptischer Studien 38. Munich and Berlin.
2007   "The Egyptian 'Game of Twenty Squares': Is It Related to 'Marbles' and the Game of the Snake?" In Finkel 2007a, pp. 69–86.

Pusch, Edgar B., H. Becker, and J. Fassbinder
1999   "Wohnen und Leben; oder, Weitere Schritte zu einem Stadt-plan der Ramsesstadt." *Ägypten und Levante / Egypt and the Levant* 9, pp. 155–70.

Pusch, Edgar B., and Anja Herold
1999   "Qantir / Pi-Ramesses." In *Encyclopedia of the Archaeology of Ancient Egypt*, edited by Kathryn A. Bard, pp. 647–49. London and New York.

Putnam, James
1990   *Egyptology: An Introduction to the History, Art, and Culture of Ancient Egypt.* New York.

Puturidze, Marina
2003   "Social and Economic Shifts in the South Caucasian Middle Bronze Age." In A. Smith and Rubinson 2003, pp. 111–27.
2005   "About the Problem of South Caucasian-Near Eastern Cultural Relations According to the Items of Artistic Craft during the First Half of the 2nd Millennium B.C." *Metalla* 12, no. 1–2, pp. 8–22.

Quibell, James Edward
1912   *Excavations at Saqqara (1908–9, 1909–10): The Monastery of Apa Jeremias.* Excavations at Saqqara, vol. 4. Cairo.

Quirke, Stephen
1991   "Royal Power in the 13th Dynasty." In *Middle Kingdom Studies*, edited by Stephen Quirke, pp. 123–39. New Malden, Surrey.

Rainey, Anson F.
1996   *Canaanite in the Amarna Tablets: A Linguistic Analysis of the Mixed Dialect Used by Scribes from Canaan.* 4 vols. Handbuch der Orientalistik; erste Abteilung, Der Nahe und Mittlere Osten 25. Leiden.

Randall-MacIver, David, and Arthur C. Mace
1902   *El Amrah and Abydos: 1899–1901.* London: Egypt Exploration Fund.

Raven, Maartin J.
2004   "Dolch." In *Pharao siegt immer* 2004, p. 133, no. 134.

Reade, Julian
2001   "Assyrian King Lists: The Royal Tombs of Ur, and Indus Origins." *Journal of Near Eastern Studies* 60, pp. 1–29.
2004   "The Assyrians as Collectors: From Accumulation to Synthesis." In *From the Upper Sea to the Lower Sea: Studies on the History of Assyria and Babylonia in Honour of A. K. Grayson*, edited by Grant Frame, pp. 255–68. Istanbul.

von Reden, Sibylla
1992   *Ugarit und seine Welt: Die Entdeckung einer der ältesten Handelsmetropolen am Mittelmeer.* Bergisch Gladbach.

Redford, Donald B.
1967   *History and Chronology of the Eighteenth Dynasty of Egypt: Seven Studies.* Toronto.
1992   *Egypt, Canaan, and Israel in Ancient Times.* Princeton.
1997   "Textual Sources for the Hyksos Period." In Oren 1997a, pp. 1–44.
2003   *The Wars in Syria and Palestine of Thutmose III.* Culture and History of the Ancient Near East, vol. 16. Leiden.

Reese, D. S.
1980   "Industrial Exploitation of Murex Shells: Purple Dye and Lime Production at Sidi Khrebish, Benghazi (Berenice)." *Libyan Studies* 11, pp. 79–93.
1984   "Topshell Rings in the Aegean Bronze Age." *Annual of the British School at Athens* 79, pp. 237–38.
1985a   "Appendix VIII(B): The Kition Ostrich Eggshells." In Karageorghis and Demas 1985, part 2, pp. 371–82.
1985b   "Appendix VIII(D), Hippopotamus and Elephant Teeth from Kition." In Karageorghis and Demas 1985, part 2, pp. 391–409.
1987   "Palaikastro Shells and Bronze Age Purple-Dye Production in the Mediterranean Basin." *Annual of the British School at Athens* 82, pp. 201–6.
1998   "Appendix III: A Hippopotamus Tooth from Hala Sultan Tekke, Cyprus." In *Hala Sultan Tekke 10: The Wells*, edited by Paul Åström, pp. 140–45. Jonsered.

Reese, D. S., and O. Krzyszkowska
1996   "Elephant Ivory at Minoan Kommos." In *Kommos*, vol. 1, *The Kommos Region and Houses of the Minoan Town*, part 2, *The Minoan Hilltop and Hillside Houses*, edited by Joseph W. Shaw and Maria C. Shaw, pp. 324–28. Princeton.

Reeves, Nicholas
1995   *The Complete Tutankhamun: The King, the Tomb, the Royal Treasure.* New York. First published London, 1990.
2000   *Ancient Egypt: The Great Discoveries; a Year-by Year Chronicle.* London.
2001   *Akhenaten: Egypt's False Prophet.* London.

Reeves, Nicholas, and John H. Taylor
1992   *Howard Carter before Tutankhamun.* London: British Museum.
1993   *Howard Carter before Tutankhamun.* New York.

Regling, K.
1926   "Geld." In *Reallexikon der Vorgeschichte*, edited by Max Ebert, vol. 4, pp. 204–38. Berlin.

Rehak, Paul
1992   "The Fresco from Room 31 in the Cult Center at Mycenae." In Laffineur and Crowley 1992, pp. 39–62.
1994   "The 'Aegean Priest' on CMS I 223." *Kadmos* 33, pp. 81–102.
1996   "Aegean Breechcloths, Kilts, and the Keftiu Paintings." *American Journal of Archaeology* 100, pp. 35–51.
1997   "Aegean Art before and after the LM IB Cretan Destructions." In Laffineur and Betancourt 1997, vol. 1, pp. 51–67.

Rehak, Paul, and John G. Younger
1998   "International Styles in Ivory Carving in the Bronze Age." In Cline and Harris-Cline 1998, pp. 229–57.

Rehm, Ellen
1997   *Kykladen und Alter Orient. Bestandskatalog des Badischen Landesmuseums Karlsruhe.* Karlsruhe.

Rehren, T.
2005   "Der Handel mit Glas in der Spätbronzezeit." In *Das Schiff von Uluburun* 2005, pp. 533–56.

Rehren, T., and E. B. Pusch
1997   "New Kingdom Glass-Melting Crucibles from Qantir-Piramesses." *Journal of Egyptian Archaeology* 83, pp. 127–41.

Rehren, T., E. Pusch, and A. Herold
1998   "Glass Coloring Works Within a Copper-Centered Industrial Complex in Late Bronze Age Egypt." In *The Prehistory and History of Glassmaking Technology*, edited by P. McCray and D. Kingery, pp. 227–50. Ceramics and Civilization, vol. 8. Westerville, Ohio.

Reiner, Erica, and David Pingree
1975   *Babylonian Planetary Omens.* Part 1, *Enūma Anu Enlil Tablet 63: The Venus Tablets of Ammisaduqa.* Bibliotheca Mesopotamica, vol. 2, fasc. 1. Malibu.

Renfrew, Colin, and J. Cherry
1985   "The Finds." In *The Archaeology of Cult: The Sanctuary at Phylakopi*, edited by Colin Renfrew, pp. 299–360. London: British School of Archaeology at Athens.

Reusch, Helga
1958   "Zum Wandschmuck des Thronsaales von Knossos." In *Minoica: Festschrift zum 80. Geburtstag von Johannes Sundwall*, edited by Ernst Grumach, pp. 334–58. Berlin.

Reuther, Oskar
1926   *Die Innenstadt von Babylon (Merkes).* Wissenschaftliche Veröffentlichung der Deutschen Orient-Gesellschaft, vol. 47. Leipzig.

Richter, Thomas
2003   "Das 'Archiv des Idanda.'" In "Bericht über Inschriftenfunde der Grabungskampagne 2002 in Mišrife/Qatna," *Mitteilungen der Deutschen Orient-Gesellschaft zu Berlin*, no. 135, pp. 167–88.
2005   "Qatna in the Late Bronze Age. Preliminary Remarks." In *General Studies and Excavations at Nuzi 11/1*, edited by David I. Owen and Gernot Wilhelm, pp. 109–26. Studies on the Civilization and Culture of Nuzi and the Hurrians, vol. 15. Bethesda, Md.

Ricketts, M.
1960   "Appendix B: Furniture from the Middle Bronze Age." In *Excavations at Jericho I: The Tombs Excavated in 1952–54*, edited by Kathleen M. Kenyon, pp. 527–34. London: British School of Archaeology in Jerusalem.

Riemschneider, Margarete
1954   *Die Welt der Hethiter.* Stuttgart.

Rigault, Patricia
1999   "Dress in Beaded Netting." In *Egyptian Art in the Age of the Pyramids*, pp. 306–7, no. 94. Exh. cat. New York: The Metropolitan Museum of Art.

Riis, P. J.
1948   *Hama: Fouilles et recherches de la Fondation Carlsberg 1931–1938*, vol. 2, part 3, *Les cimetières à crémation*. Nationalmuseets Skrifter, Større Beretninger 1. Copenhagen.

Rival, Michel
1991   *La charpenterie navale romaine: Matériaux, méthodes, moyens*. Travaux du Centre Camille Jullian 4. Paris.

Roaf, M., and John Boardman
1980   "AQ Greek Painting at Persepolis." *Journal of Hellenic Studies* 100, pp. 204–6.

Robins, Gay
1986   *Egyptian Painting and Relief*. Shire Egyptology, no. 3. Princes Risborough.

Roeder, Günther
1956   *Ägyptische Bronzefiguren*. Mitteilungen aus der Ägyptischen Sammlung 6. Berlin: Staatliche Museen zu Berlin.

Röllig, W.
1983   "Ein Itinerar aus Dur-katlimmu." *Damaszener Mitteilungen* 1, pp. 279–84.

Das Rollsiegel in Syrien
1980   *Das Rollsiegel in Syrien: Zur Steinschneidekunst in Syrien zwischen 3300 und 330 vor Christus*. Exhibition, Eberhard-Karls-Universität Tübingen and Kunsthalle Tübingen. Catalogue by Hartmut Kühne; contributions by Claude F. A. Schaeffer-Forrer, Gerti Preuss, and Andrea Moritz. Ausstellungskataloge der Universität Tübingen, no. 11. Tübingen.

Romano, James F.
1980   "The Origin of the Bes-Image." *Bulletin of the Egyptological Seminar* 2, pp. 39–56.
1989   "The Bes-Image in Pharaonic Egypt." Ph.D. diss., New York University.
1998   "Notes on the Historiography and the History of the Bes-Image in Ancient Egypt." *Bulletin of the Australian Centre for Egyptology* 9, pp. 89–105.

Romer, John
1994   *Valley of the Kings, Exploring the Tombs of the Pharaohs*. New York.

Rommelaere, Catherine
1991   *Les chevaux du Nouvel Empire égyptien: Origines, races, harnachement*. Brussels.

Rose, P.
2007   *The Eighteenth Dynasty Pottery Corpus from Amarna*. Egypt Exploration Society, Excavation Memoir 83. London.

Roßberger, Elisa
2006   "Der Perlenschmuck aus der Königsgruft von Qatna." M.A. thesis, Universität Tübingen.

Rössler-Köhler, Ursula
1980   "Löwe, L.-Köpfe, L.-Statuen." In *Lexikon der Ägyptologie*, edited by Wolfgang Helck and Wolfhart Westendorf, vol. 3, cols. 1080–90. Wiesbaden.

Rost, Liane
1961–63 "Zu den hethitischen Bildbeschreibungen." *Mitteilungen des Instituts für Orientforschung* 8, no. 2 (1961–63), pp. 161–217; 9, nos. 2–3 (1963), pp. 175–239.

Roth, Ann Macy
1999   "The Ahhotep Coffins: The Archaeology of an Egyptological Reconstruction." In *Gold of Praise: Studies on Ancient Egypt in Honor of Edward F. Wente*, edited by Emily Teeter and John A. Larson, pp. 361–77. Studies in Ancient Oriental Civilization, no. 58. Chicago.
2005   "Grips from a Dagger Handle of Thutmose I." In *Hatshepsut* 2005, p. 15, no. 1.

Rowe, Alan
1936   *A Catalogue of Egyptian Scarabs, Scaraboids, Seals and Amulets in the Palestine Archaeological Museum*. Cairo.
1940   *The Four Canaanite Temples of Beth-Shan*. Vol. 1, *The Temples and Cult Objects*. Publications of the Palestine Section of the University Museum, University of Pennsylvania, vol. 2. Philadelphia.

Rowe, Louis Earle
1908   "Egyptian Portraiture of the XX Dynasty." *Museum of Fine Arts Bulletin* 6, no. 36 (December), pp. 47–50.

Rowlands, Michael, Mogens Trolle Larsen, and Kristian Kristiansen, eds.
1987   *Centre and Periphery in the Ancient World*. Cambridge and New York.

Royal City of Susa
1992   *The Royal City of Susa: Ancient Near Eastern Treasures in the Louvre*. Exhibition, The Metropolitan Museum of Art, New York. Catalogue edited by Prudence O. Harper, Joan Aruz, and Françoise Tallon. New York.

Royal Women of Amarna
1996   *The Royal Women of Amarna: Images of Beauty from Ancient Egypt*. Exhibition, The Metropolitan Museum of Art, New York. Catalogue by Dorothea Arnold; contributions by James P. Allen and Lyn Green. New York.

Le royaume d'Ougarit
2004   *Le royaume d'Ougarit: Aux origines de l'alphabet*. Exhibition, Musée des Beaux-Arts, Lyon. Catalogue edited by Geneviève Galliano and Yves Calvet. Paris and Lyon.

Rubinson, Karen
1977   "The Chronology of the Middle Bronze Age Kurgans at Trialeti." In *Mountains and Lowlands: Essays in the Archaeology of Greater Mesopotamia*, edited by Louis D. Levine and T. Cuyler Young Jr., pp. 235–49. Bibiotheca Mesopotamica, vol. 7. Malibu.
2003   "Silver Vessels and Cylinder Sealings: Precious Reflections of Economic Exchange in the Early Second Millennium BC." In A. Smith and Rubinson 2003, pp. 128–43.
2006   "Over the Mountains and through the Grass: Visual Information as 'Text' for the 'Textless.'" In *Beyond the Steppe and the Sown*, edited by D. L. Peterson, L. M. Popova, and A. T. Smith, pp. 247–63. Colloquia Pontica 13. University of Chicago Conference on Eurasian Archaeology, 1st, 2002. Leiden

von Rüden, Constance
2006   "Die Wandmalereien von Tall Mishrife/Qatna im Kontext interregionaler Kommunikation." Doctoral diss., Albert-Ludwigs-Universität, Fribourg. Currently being prepared for publication.

Rudolph, Wolf
1973   "Die Nekropole am Prophitis Elias bei Tiryns." In *Tiryns: Forschungen und Berichte* 6, pp. 23–126.

Russell, P.
2002   "Aegean Pottery and Selected Cypriot Pottery." In White 2002, vol. 2, pp. 1–16.

Russmann, Edna R.
2005   "Sphinx of a Queen of Thutmose III." In *Hatshepsut* 2005, pp. 32–33, no. 11.

Rutten, M.
1938   "Les animaux à attitudes humaines dans l'art de l'ancienne Mésopotamie." *Revue des études sémitiques*, no. 3, pp. 97–119.

Rutter, J. B.
2005   "Assessing the Shipboard Profile of a Regional Ceramic
        Assemblage: The Aegean Pottery from the Uluburun
        Shipwreck." Paper presented at the annual meeting of the
        Archaeological Institute of America, Boston, January 7, 2005.

Ryholt, K. S. B.
1997   *The Political Situation in Egypt during the Second Intermediate
        Period, c. 1800–1550 B.C.* Copenhagen.

Sadek, Ashraf I.
1980–85 *The Amethyst Mining Inscriptions of Wadi el-Hudi.* 2 vols.
        Warminster.

Sader, Hélène
1998   "Les textes en écriture dite pseudo-hiéroglyphique de Byblos."
        In *Liban: L'autre rive* 1998, p. 61.

el-Safadi, Hishām
1974   *Die Entstehung der syrischen Glyptik und ihre Entwicklung in der
        Zeit von Zimrilim bis Ammitaqumma.* Kevelaer.

Saidah, H.
1993–94 "Beirut in the Bronze Age: The Kharji Tombs." *Berytus* 41,
        pp. 137–207.

Saidel, Benjamin Adam
2002   "The Excavations at Rekhes Nafha 396 in the Negev High-
        lands, Israel." *Bulletin of the American Schools of Oriental
        Research,* no. 325, pp. 37–63.

Sakellarakis, J. A.
1971   "Ελεφάντινον πλοίον εκ Μυκηνών." *Αρχαιολογική Εφημερίς*
        (*Archaiologike ephemeris*) 110, pp. 188–233.
1979   *Το ελεφαντόδοντο και η κατεργασία του στα μυκηναϊκά χρόνια.*
        Athens.
1982   *Athen, Nationalmuseum.* Corpus der minoischen und myken-
        ischen Siegel, vol. 1, supplement. Berlin.
1990   "The Fashioning of Ostrich-Egg Rhyta in the Creto-
        Mycenaean Aegean." In Hardy and Renfrew 1990, vol. 1,
        Archaeology, pp. 285–308.

Sakellariou, Agnès
1964   as editor. *Die minoischen und mykenischen Siegel des National
        Museums in Athen.* Corpus der minoischen und mykenischen
        Siegel, vol. 1. Berlin.
1966   *Μυκηναϊκή Σφραγιδογλυφία.* Athens.

Saleh, Mohamed, and Hourig Sourouzian
1987   *The Egyptian Museum, Cairo: Official Catalogue.* Mainz am Rhein.

Salje, Beate
1990   *Der "Common Style" der Mitanni-Glyptik und die Glyptik der
        Levante und Zyperns in der Späten Bronzezeit.* Baghdader
        Forschungen, vol. 11. Mainz am Rhein.
1997   "Sceaux-cylindres proche-orientaux du Bronze récent trouvés
        dans l'aire égéenne." In Caubet 1997, pp. 249–67.

Salles, Jean-François
1998   "Byblos: Métropole maritime." In *Liban: L'autre rive* 1998,
        pp. 66–70.

Sandars, Nancy K.
1961   "The First Aegean Swords and Their Ancestry." *American
        Journal of Archaeology* 65, pp. 17–29.
1963   "Later Aegean Bronze Swords." *American Journal of
        Archaeology* 67, pp. 117–53.
1983   "North and South at the End of the Mycenaean Age: Aspects
        of an Old Problem." *Oxford Journal of Archaeology* 2, no. 1,
        pp. 43–68.

Saretta, Phyllis
1997   "Egyptian Perceptions of West Semites in Art and Literature
        during the Middle Kingdom: An Archaeological, Art Histor-
        ical, and Textual Survey." Ph.D. diss., New York University.

Sassmannshausen, Leonhard
2006   "Zur mesopotamischen Chronologie des 2. Jahrtausends."
        Baghdader Mitteilungen 37, pp. 157–78.

Sasson, Jack M.
1968   "Instances of Mobility among Mari Artisans." *Bulletin of the
        American Schools of Oriental Research,* no. 190, pp. 46–54.
1995   as general editor. *Civilizations of the Ancient Near East.* 4 vols.
        New York.
2000   as general editor. *Civilizations of the Ancient Near East.* 2 vols.
        Peabody, Mass.
2006   "The Servant's Tale: How Rebekah Found a Spouse." *Journal
        of Near Eastern Studies* 65, pp. 241–65.

Säve-Söderburgh, Torgny
1953   *On Egyptian Representations of Hippopotamus Hunting as a
        Religious Motive.* Lund.

Scandone Matthiae, Gabriella
1979   "Un oggetto faraonico della XIII dinastia dall 'Tomba del
        Signore dei capridi.'" *Studi eblaiti* 1, pp. 119–28.
1988   "Les relations entre Ébla et l'Égypte au IIIème et au IIème
        millénaire av. J.-Chr." In *Wirtschaft und Gesellschaft von Ebla,*
        edited by H. Waetzoldt and H. Hauptmann, pp. 67–73.
        Heidelberg.
1991a   "Una testa paléosiriana in avorio con corona atef." *La parola
        del passato: Rivista di studi antichi* 46, pp. 372–93.
1991b   "Gli intarsi egittizzanti del palazzo settentrionale di Ebla."
        Scienza all'antichita 5, pp. 423–59.
2002   *Gli avori egittizzanti dal Palazzo Settentrionale.* Materiali e
        studi archeologici di Ebla, vol. 3. Rome.

Schachermeyr, Fritz
1967   *Ägäis und Orient: Die überseeischen Kulturbeziehungen von
        Kreta und Mykenai mit Ägypten, der Levante und Kleinasien
        unter besonderer Berücksichtigung des 2. Jahrtausends v.
        Chr.* Graz.

Schaeffer, Claude F. A.
1929   "Les fouilles de Minet el-Beida et de Ras Shamra." *Syria* 10,
        pp. 285–97.
1931   "Les fouilles de Minet-el-Beida et de Ras Shamra: Deuxième
        campagne (printemps 1930). Rapport sommaire." *Syria* 12,
        pp. 1–14.
1932   "Les fouilles de Minet el-Beida et de Ras-Shamra: Troisième
        campagne (printemps 1931). Rapport sommaire." *Syria* 13,
        pp. 1–27.
1933   "Les fouilles de Minet-el-Beida et de Ras-Shamra: Quatrième
        campagne (printemps 1932). Rapport sommaire." *Syria* 14,
        pp. 93–127.
1934   "Les fouilles de Ras Shamra: Cinquième campagne (printemps
        1933)." *Syria* 15, pp. 105–31.
1936a   "Les fouilles de Ras Shamra-Ugarit: Septième campagne
        (printemps 1935). Rapport sommaire." *Syria* 17, pp. 105–48.
1936b   *Missions en Chypre: 1932–1935.* Paris.
1937   "Les fouilles des Ras Shamra-Ugarit: Huitième campagne
        (printemps 1936). Rapport sommaire." *Syria* 18, pp. 125–54.
1939a   *The Cuneiform Texts of Ras Shamra-Ugarit.* Schweich Lectures
        of the British Academy for 1936. London.
1939b   *Ugaritica: Études relatives aux découvertes de Ras Shamra.
        Première série.* Mission de Ras Shamra, vol. 3. Paris.
1943   "La date des kourganes de Trialeti." *Antiquity* 17, no. 68,
        pp. 183–87.
1949   *Ugaritica II: Nouvelles études relatives aux découvertes de Ras
        Shamra.* Mission de Ras Shamra, vol. 5; Bibliothèque
        archéologique et historique, vol. 47. Paris.
1951   "Un industrie d'Ugarit: La pourpre." *Annales archéologiques
        arabes syriennes* 1, pp. 188–92.
1954   "Les fouilles de Minet-el-Beida et de Ras Shamra: Quinzième,
        seizième et dix-septième campagnes (1951, 1952 et 1953).
        Rapport sommaire." *Syria* 31, pp. 54–59.

| 1956 | *Ugaritica III: Sceaux et cylindres hittites, épée gravée du cartouche de Mineptah, tablettes cypro-minoennes et autres découvertes nouvelles de Ras Shamra.* Mission de Ras Shamra, vol. 8. Paris. |

1961–62 "Résumé des résultats de la XXIIIe campagne de fouilles à Ras Shamra-Ugarit (automne 1960)." *Annales archéologiques arabes syriennes* 11–12, pp. 187–96.

1962 *Ugaritica IV: Découvertes des XVIIIe et XIXe campagnes, 1954–1955; fondements préhistoriques d'Ugarit et nouveaux sondages; études anthropologiques; poteries grecques et monnaies islamiques de Ras Shamra et environs.* Mission de Ras Shamra, vol. 15. Paris.

1963 "Ausgrabungen und Forschungsreisen. Neue Entdeckungen in Ugarit (23. und 24. Kampagne, 1960–1961)." *Archiv für Orientforschung* 20, pp. 206–15.

1966a "Neue Entdeckungen und Funde in Ugarit (1962–1964)." *Archiv für Orientforschung* 21, pp. 131–37.

1966b "Nouveaux témoignages du culte de El et de Baal a Ras Shamra-Ugarit et ailleurs en Syrie-Palestine." *Syria* 43, pp. 1–19.

1978 *Ugaritica VII.* Mission de Ras Shamra, vol. 18. Paris.

Schaeffer-Forrer, Claude F. A.

1983 *Corpus des cylindres-sceaux de Ras Shamra-Ugarit et d'Enkomi-Alasia.* Vol. 1. Paris.

Schafer, E. H.

1955 "Orpiment and Realgar in Chinese Technology and Tradition." *Journal of the American Oriental Society* 75, pp. 73–89.

Schäfer, Heinrich

1974 *Principles of Egyptian Art.* Edited by Emma Brunner-Traut; translated and edited by John Baines. Oxford.

Scharff, Alexander

1923 *Die Götter Ägyptens.* Berlin.

Scheil, Vincent

1900 "Kudurru de Nazimaruttaš." In "Textes élamites et sémitiques," *Mémoires de la Délégation en Perse* 2, pp. 86–92.

Schiaparelli, Ernesto

1927 *Relazione sui lavori della missione archaeologica italiana in Egitto (anni 1903–1920).* Vol. 2, *La tomba intatta dell'architetto Cha, nella necropoli di Tebe.* Turin.

Schiering, Wolfgang

1998 *Minoische Töpferkunst: Die bemalten Tongefässe der Insel des Minos.* Kulturgeschichte der antiken Welt, vol. 73. Mainz am Rhein.

Schiestl, R.

2000 "Eine archäologische Notiz: Eine neue Parallele zum An-hänger aus Tell el-Dab'a aus dem Petrie Museum, University College London." *Ägypten und Levante / Egypt and the Levant* 10, pp. 127–28.

2006 "The Statue of an Asiatic Man from Tell el-Dab'a, Egypt." *Ägypten und Levante / Egypt and the Levant* 16, pp. 173–85.

2008 "Three Pendants: Tell el-Dab'a, Aigina and a New Silver Pendant from the Petrie Museum." In Fitton 2008. In press.

Das Schiff von Uluburun

2005 *Das Schiff von Uluburun: Welthandel vor 3000 Jahren.* Exhibition, Deutsches Bergbau-Museum Bochum. Catalogue edited by Ünsal Yalçin, Cemal Pulak, and Rainer Slotta. Veröffentlichungen aus dem Deutschen Bergbau-Museum Bochum, no. 138. Bochum.

Schliemann, Heinrich

1878 *Mycenae: A Narrative of Researches and Discoveries at Mycenae and Tiryns.* London.

1886 *Tiryns: Der prähistorische Palast der Könige von Tiryns.* Leipzig. Eng. ed.: *Tiryns: The Prehistoric Palace of the Kings of Tiryns; the Results of the Latest Excavations.* New York.

Schneider, Thomas

1998 *Ausländer in Ägypten während des Mittleren Reiches und der Hyksoszeit.* Vol. 1, *Die ausländischen Könige.* Ägypten und altes Testament, vol. 42, no. 1. Wiesbaden.

2002 "Sinuhes Notiz über die Könige: Syrisch-anatolische Herrscher-titel in ägyptischer Überlieferung." *Ägypten und Levante / Egypt and the Levant* 12, pp. 257–72.

2003 *Ausländer in Ägypten während des Mittleren Reiches und der Hyksoszeit.* Vol. 2, *Die ausländische Bevölkerung.* Ägypten und altes Testament, vol. 42, no. 2. Wiesbaden.

Schofield, Louise, and R. B. Parkinson

1994 "Of Helmets and Heretics: A Possible Egyptian Representation of Mycenaean Warriors on a Papyrus from el-Amarna." *Annual of the British School at Athens* 89, pp. 157–70.

Schönheit, Abglanz der Göttlichkeit

1990 *Schönheit, Abglanz der Göttlichkeit: Kosmetik im Alten Ägypten.* Exhibition, Deutsches Medizinhistorisches Museum, Ingol-stadt; Staatliche Sammlung Ägyptischer Kunst, Munich; Ägyptischer Museum der Staatliche Museen Preussischer Kulturbesitz, Berlin. Catalogue by Sylvia Schoske, with contri-butions by Alfred Grimm and Barbars Kreissl. Munich.

Schönheit im Alten Ägypten

2006 *Schönheit im Alten Ägypten: Sehnsucht nach Vollkommenheit.* Exhibition, Roemer- und Pelizaeus-Museum Hildesheim; Badisches Landesmuseum, Karlsruhe. Catalogue edited by Katja Lembke and Bettina Schmitz. Hildesheim.

Schott, Siegfried

1958 "Eine Kopfstütze des Neuen Reiches." *Zeitschrift für Ägyptische Sprache* 83, pp. 141–44.

Schweitzer, Ursula

1948 *Löwe und Sphinx im Alten Ägypten.* Ägyptologische For-schungen, vol. 15. Glückstadt.

Scullard, H. H.

1974 *The Elephant in the Greek and Roman World.* Ithaca, N.Y.

Seal, Th.

2001 Review of Gasche et al. 1998a. *Bibliotheca Orientalis* 58, no. 1–2 (January–April), pp. 163–72.

Sea Routes

2003 *Sea Routes—From Sidon to Huelva: Interconnections in the Mediterranean, 16th–6th c. BC. Cultural Olympiad.* Exhibition, Museum of Cycladic Art, Athens. Catalogue edited by Nicholaos Chr. Stampolidis. Athens.

Seeden, Helga

1980 *The Standing Armed Figurines in the Levant.* Prähistorische Bronzefunde, ser. 1, vol. 1. Munich.

1982 "Peace Figurines in the Levant." In *Archéologie au Levant: Recueil à la mémoire de Roger Saïdah,* pp. 107–21. Collection de la Maison de l'Orient Méditerranéen 12, série archéologique 9. Lyon.

1998 "Dieux de bronze, d'or et d'argent." In *Liban: L'autre rive* 1998, p. 95.

Seger, Joe D.

1988 *Gezer V: The Field I Caves.* Annual of the Nelson Glueck School of Biblical Archaeology, vol. 5. Jerusalem.

Seidl, Ursula

1989 *Die babylonischen Kudurru-Reliefs: Symbole mesopotamischer Gottheiten.* Orbis Biblicus et Orientalis, vol. 87. Fribourg and Göttingen.

Serpico, M., and R. White

2000 "The Botanical Identity and Transport of Incense during the Egyptian New Kingdom." *Antiquity* 74, no. 286, pp. 884–97.

Seyrig, H.
1954   "Notes sur le trésor de Tôd." *Syria* 31, pp. 218–24.
1955   "Antiquités syriennes, 2: Tauromachie égéene." *Syria* 32,
        pp. 34–37.

Shalev, Sariel
2004   *Swords and Daggers in Late Bronze Age Canaan.* Prähistorische
        Bronzefunde, ser. 4, vol. 13. Stuttgart.

Shaw, Ian, and Robert Jameson
1993   "Amethyst Mining in the Eastern Desert: A Preliminary
        Survey at Wadi el-Hudi." *Journal of Egyptian Archaeology,*
        no. 79, pp. 81–97.

Shaw, Joseph W.
1978   "Evidence for the Minoan Tripartite Shrine." *American Journal
        of Archaeology* 82, pp. 429–48.
1995   "Two Three-Holed Anchors from Kommos, Crete: Their
        Context, Type, and Origin." *International Journal of Nautical
        Archaeology* 24, pp. 279–91.

Shaw, Maria C.
1972   "The Miniature Frescoes of Tylissos Reconsidered."
        Archäologischer Anzeiger, no. 2, pp. 171–88.

Shear, I. M.
1998   "Bellerophon Tablets from the Mycenaean World? A Tale of
        Seven Bronze Hinges." *Journal of Hellenistic Studies* 118,
        pp. 187–89.

Shelmerdine, Cynthia W.
1985   *The Perfume Industry of Mycenaean Pylos.* Studies in
        Mediterranean Archaeology, Pocket-book 34. Göteborg.
1998   "The Perfumed-Oil Industry." In *Sandy Pylos: An Archaeo-
        logical History from Nestor to Navarino,* edited by Jack L. Davis,
        pp. 101–9. Austin.

Sherratt, Andrew, and Susan Sherratt
1991   "From Luxuries to Commodities: The Nature of Mediter-
        ranean Bronze Age Trading Systems." In Gale 1991a,
        pp. 351–86.

Sherratt, Susan
1994   "Comment on Ora Negbi, The 'Libyan Landscape' from Thera:
        A Review of Aegean Enterprises Overseas in the Late Minoan
        IA Period." *Journal of Mediterranean Archaeology* 7, pp. 237–40.
2000   as editor. *The Wall Paintings of Thera: Proceedings of the First
        International Symposium, Petros M. Nomikos Conference Centre,
        Thera, Hellas, 30 August–4 September 1997.* 3 vols. Athens.
2003   "The Mediterranean Economy: 'Globalization' at the End of
        the Second Millennium B.C.E." In *Symbiosis, Symbolism, and the
        Power of the Past: Canaan, Ancient Israel, and Their Neighbors
        from the Late Bronze Age through Roman Paleastina; Proceedings
        of the Centennial Symposium, W. F. Albright Institute of Archaeo-
        logical Research and American Schools of Oriental Research,
        Jerusalem, May 29–31, 2000,* edited by William G. Dever and
        Seymour Gitin, pp. 37–62. Winona Lake, Ind.

Shortland, Andrew J.
2000   *Vitreous Materials at Amarna: The Production of Glass and
        Faience in 18th Dynasty Egypt.* BAR International Series 827.
        Oxford.

Shortland, Andrew J., and M. S. Tite
2000   "Raw Materials of Glass from Amarna and Implications for
        the Origins of Egyptian Glass." *Archaeometry* 42, no. 1,
        pp. 141–51.

Silverman, David P., Josef W. Wegner, and Jennifer Houser Wegner
2006   *Akhenaten and Tutankhamun: Revolution and Restoration.*
        Philadelphia: University of Pennsylvania Museum of
        Archaeology and Anthropology.

Simpson, Elizabeth
2000   "Furniture in Ancient Western Asia." In Sasson 2000,
        pp. 1647–71.

Simpson, St John
2007   "Homo Ludens: The Earliest Board Games in the Near East."
        In Finkel 2007a, pp. 5–10.

Sipahi, Tunç
2000   "Eine althethitische Reliefvase vom Hüseyindede Tepesi."
        Istanbuler Mitteilungen 50, pp. 63–85.
2001   "New Evidence from Anatolia Regarding Bull-Leaping Scenes
        in the Art of the Aegean and the Near East." *Anatolica* 27,
        pp. 107–26.
2005   "Hüseyindede'den Hitit Tasvir Sanatı için Yeni Bir Sahne."
        In *V. Uluslararası Hititoloji Kongresi bildirileri Çorum 02–08
        Eylül 2002 / Acts of the Vth International Congress of
        Hititology, Çorum, September 02–08, 2002,* pp. 661–78.
        Ankara.

Skinner, Frederick G.
1954   "Measures and Weights." In *A History of Technology,* vol. 1,
        edited by Charles J. Singer, E. J. Holmyard, and A. R. Hall,
        pp. 774–84. Oxford.
1967   *Weights and Measures: Their Ancient Origins and Their Develop-
        ment in Great Britain up to A.D. 1855.* London.

Slanski, Kathryn E.
2000   "Classification, Historiography and Monumental Authority:
        The Babylonian Entitlement *narûs (kudurrus)*." *Journal of
        Cuneiform Studies* 52, pp. 95–114.
2003   *The Babylonian Entitlement narûs (kudurrus): A Study in Their
        Form and Function.* American Schools of Oriental Research
        Books, ser. 9. Boston.

Smith, Adam T.
2001   "The Limitations of Doxa: Agency and Subjectivity from an
        Archaeological Point of View." *Journal of Social Archaeology* 1,
        no. 2, pp. 155–71.

Smith, Adam T., and Karen Sydney Rubinson, eds.
2003   *Archaeology in the Borderlands Investigations in Caucasia and
        Beyond.* Los Angeles: Cotsen Institute of Archaeology,
        University of California.

Smith, William Stevenson
1965   *Interconnections in the Ancient Near-East: A Study of the
        Relationships between the Arts of Egypt, the Aegean, and Western
        Asia.* New Haven.
1981   *Art and Architecture of Ancient Egypt.* 2nd ed. Pelican History
        of Art. New York.

Soles, Jeffrey
2004   "The 2004 Greek-American Excavations at Mochlos." *Kentro:
        The Newsletter of the INSTAP Study Center for East Crete* 7,
        pp. 2–5.
2008   "100 Years at Mochlos, Gateway to Crete." Paper presented on
        January 4 at the Archaeological Institute of America, 109th
        Annual Meeting, Chicago.

Soles, J., and C. Davaras
1992   "Excavations at Mochlos, 1989." *Hesperia* 61, pp. 413–45.

Sollberger, Edmond
1969   "Old-Babylonian Worshipper Figurines." *Iraq* 31, pp. 90–93.

Sollberger, Edmond, and Jean-Robert Kupper
1971   *Inscriptions royales sumeriennes et akkadiennes.* Littératures
        anciennes du Proche-Orient, vol. 3. Paris.

Sommerfeld, Walter
1995   "The Kassites of Ancient Mesopotamia: Origins, Politics and
        Culture." In Sasson 1995, vol. 2, pp. 917–30.

Sotiropoulou, S., K. Andrikopoulos, and E. Chryssikopoulou
2003   "The Use of Tyrian Purple in the Wall Paintings of Thera." In *Fourth Symposium on Archaeometry: Athens, Greece, May 28–31, 2003*. Electronic edition by Hellenic Society for Archaeometry: www.archaeometry.gr/oldv/symposium2003/pages_en/abstracts/papers/pigments/pigment11.htm.

Spaey, Johanna
1993   "Emblems in Rituals in the Old Babylonian Period." In *Ritual and Sacrifice in the Ancient Near East: Proceedings of the International Conference Organized by the Katholieke Universiteit Leuven from the 17th to the 20th of April 1991*, edited by J. Quaegebeur, pp. 411–20. Orientalia Lovaniensia analecta, vol. 55. Leuven.

Spalinger, Anthony J.
1985   "Remarks on the Kadesh Inscriptions of Ramesses II: The 'Bulletin.'" In *Perspectives on the Battle of Kadesh*, edited by Hans Goedicke, pp. 43–75. Baltimore.
2002   *The Transformation of an Ancient Egyptian Narrative: P. Sallier III and the Battle of Kadesh*. Göttinger Orientforschungen, ser. 4, Ägypten, vol. 40. Wiesbaden.
2005   *War in Ancient Egypt: The New Kingdom*. Malden, Mass., and Oxford.
2006   "Datings of the Kadesh Reliefs." In *Five Views on Egypt*, by Anthony J. Spalinger, pp. 137–56. Göttingen: Seminar für Ägyptologie und Koptologie.

Spar, Ira, ed.
1988   *Cuneiform Texts in the Metropolitan Museum of Art*. Vol. 1, *Tablets, Cones, and Bricks of the Third and Second Millennia, B.C.* New York.

Spartz, Edith
1962   *Das Wappenbild des Herrn und der Herrin der Tiere in der minoisch-mykenischen und frühgriechischen Kunst*. Munich.

Speiser, E. A.
1950   "On Some Articles of Armor and Their Names." *Journal of the American Oriental Society* 70, pp. 47–49.

Spycket, Agnès
1981   *La statuaire du Proche-Orient ancien*. Handbuch der Orientalistik, Abteilung 7, Kunst und Archäologie, vol. 1, Der Alte Vordere Orient, part 2, Die Denkmäler. B, Vorderasien; Lfg. 2. Leiden and Cologne.

Stadelmann, Rainer
1967   *Syrisch-palästinensische Gottheiten in Ägypten*. Probleme der Ägyptologie, vol. 5. Leiden.

Stager, L.
2002   "The MBIIA Ceramic Sequence at Tel Ashkelon and its Implications for the 'Port Power' Model of Trade." In Bietak 2002a, pp. 353–62.
2003   "Phoenician Shipwrecks in the Deep Sea." In *Ploes: Sea Routes: Interconnections in the Mediterranean, 16th–6th c. BC: Proceedings of the International Symposium Held at Rethymnon, Crete, September 29th–October 2nd, 2002*, edited by N. C. Stampolides and Vassos Karageorghis, pp. 233–47. Athens.

Stanley, Phillip V.
1982   "KN Uc 160 and Mycenaean Wines." *American Journal of Archaeology* 86, pp. 577–78.

Starr, Richard F. S.
1937–39 *Nuzi: Report on the Excavation at Yorgan Tepa near Kirkuk, Iraq, Conducted by Harvard University in Conjunction with the American Schools of Oriental Research and the University Museum of Philadelphia, 1927–1931*. 2 vols. Cambridge, Mass.

Staubli, Thomas
1991   *Das Image der Nomaden im alten Israel und in der Ikonographie seiner sesshaften Nachbarn*. Orbis Biblicus et Orientalis, vol. 107. Fribourg and Göttingen.

Steffy, J. Richard
1994   *Wooden Ship Building and the Interpretation of Shipwrecks*. College Station, Tex.

Stein, Diana L.
1984   *Khabur Ware and Nuzi Ware: Their Origin, Relationship, and Significance*. Assur, vol. 4, no. 1. Malibu.
1989   "Art and Architecture of the Hurrians." In *The Hurrians*, by Gernot Wilhelm, pp. 80–90. Warminster.
1997   "Nuzi." In *The Oxford Encyclopedia of Archaeology in the Near East*, edited by Eric M. Meyers, vol. 4, pp. 171–75. New York.

Steindorff, George
1946   "The Magical Knives of Ancient Egypt." *Journal of the Walters Art Gallery* 9, pp. 41–51.

Stern, B., et al.
2000   B. Stern, C. Heron, M. Serpico, and J. Bourriau. "A Comparison of Methods for Establishing Fatty Acid Concentration Gradients Across Potsherds: A Case Study Using Late Bronze Age Canaanite Amphorae." *Archaeometry* 42, pp. 399–414.

Stol, Marten
1979   *On Trees, Mountains, and Millstones in the Ancient Near East*. Ex Oriente Lux, Mededelingen en verhandelingen van het Vooraziatisch-Egyptisch Genootschap, vol. 21. Leiden.
2004   "Wirtschaft und Gesellschaft in Altbabylonischer Zeit." In Charpin, Edzard, and Stol 2004, pp. 641–976.

Stos-Gale, Z. A., et al.
1997   Z. A. Stos-Gale, G. Maliotis, N. H. Gale, and N. Annetts. "Lead Isotope Characteristics of the Cyprus Copper Ore Deposits Applied to Provenance Studies of Copper Oxhide Ingots." *Archaeometry* 39, pp. 83–123.
1998   Z. A. Stos-Gale, N. H. Gale, G. Bass, C. Pulak, E. Galili, and J. Sharvit. "The Copper and Tin Ingots of the Late Bronze Age Mediterranean: New Scientific Evidence." In *The Fourth International Conference on the Beginning of the Use on Metals and Alloys, May 25–27, 1998, Kunibiki Messe, Matsue, Shimane, Japan*, pp. 115–26. Shimane.

Strudwick, Nigel
2006   *The British Museum. Masterpieces of Ancient Egypt*. London.

Stubbings, Frank H.
1951   *Mycenaean Pottery from the Levant*. Cambridge.

Stuiver, Minze, et al.
1998   Minze Stuiver, Paula J. Reimer, Édouard Bard, J. Warren Beck, G. S. Burr, Konrad A. Hughen, Bernd Kromer, Gerry McCormac, Johannes van der Plicht, and Marco Spurk. "INTCAL98 Radiocarbon Age Calibration, 24,000-0 cal BP." *Radiocarbon* 40, pp. 1041–84.

Stuiver, Minze, and Hans van der Plicht
1998   "Editorial Comment." *Radiocarbon* 40, no. 3, pp. xii–xiv.

Symeonoglou, Sarantis
1973   *Kadmeia, I. Mycenaean Finds from Thebes, Greece: Excavations at 14 Oedipus St.* Studies in Mediterranean Archaeology, vol. 35. Göteborg.

Symington, D.
1991   "Late Bronze Age Writing-Boards and Their Uses: Textual Evidence from Anatolia and Syria." *Anatolian Studies* 41, pp. 111–23.

Tadmor, Hayim
1979   "The Decline of Empires in Western Asia c. 1200 B.C.E." In *Symposia Celebrating the 75th Anniversary of the Founding of the American Schools of Oriental Research (1900–1975)*, edited by Frank Moore Cross, pp. 1–14. Cambridge, Mass.

Tadmor, M.
1970   "A Sickle Sword and a Straight Sword: New Acquisitions in the Israel Museum." *Qadmoniot 3*, no. 2, pp. 63–64.

Tait, W. J.
1982   *Game-Boxes and Accessories from the Tomb of Tut'ankamūn*. Tut'ankamūn's Tomb Series 7. Oxford.

Taylor, John H.
1991   *Egypt and Nubia*. Cambridge, Mass.

Tefnin, Roland
1990   "Une figurine en plomb du 'Maitre des Antilopes' découverte à Oumm El-Marra." In *Resurrecting the Past: A Joint Tribute to Adnan Bounni*, edited by Paolo Matthiae, Maurits van Loon, Harvey Weiss, pp. 307–16. Istanbul.

Teissier, Beatrice
1987   "Glyptic Evidence for a Connection between Iran, Syro-Palestine, and Egypt in the Fourth and Third Millennia." *Iran 25*, pp. 27–53.
1994   *Sealing and Seals on Texts from Kültepe Kārum Level 2*. Uitgaven van het Nederlands Historisch-Archaeologisch Instituut te İstanbul 70. Leiden.
1996   *Egyptian Iconography on Syro-Palestinian Cylinder Seals of the Middle Bronze Age*. Orbis Biblicus et Orientalis, Series Archaeologica, vol. 11. Fribourg and Göttingen.

Televantou, Christinas A.
1994   *Ακρωτήρι Θήρας. Οι τοιχογραφίες της Δυτικής Οικίας*. 2 vols. Athens. Summary in English.
2000   "Aegean Bronze Age Wall Painting: The Theran Workshop." In S. Sherratt 2000, pp. 831–43.
2007   "Επίχριστες τράπεζες προσφορών." In *Ακρωτήρι Θήρας. Δυτική οικία. Τράπεζες-λίθινα-μετάλλινα-ποικίλα*, edited by Christos G. Doumas, pp. 49–70. Η εν Αθήναις Αρχαιολογική Εταιρεία, no. 246. Athens.

Temizer, Raci
1979   *Ankara Anadolu Medeniyetleri Müzesi / Museum of Anatolian Civilizations*. Ankara.

Terrace, Edward L. B., and Henry G. Fischer
1970   *Treasures of the Cairo Museum: From Predynastic to Roman Times*. London.

Thalmann, Jean-Paul
1991   "Tell'Arqa, 1981–1991, bilan et perspectives." *Berytus 39*, pp. 21–38.
1998   "Le Liban à l'Âge du Bronze, du village à la cite-Étàt." In *Liban: L'autre rive* 1998, pp. 50–70.
1999   "Les découvertes de Tell el-Dab'a et l'archéologie de la Méditerranée orientale." In Caubet 1999a, pp. 101–21.

Thomas, Nancy
2005   "Niello or Not? Laboratory Analyses of the Black-Inlaid Weapons of the Aegean, Egypt, and the Levant." In Laffineur and Greco 2005, pp. 717–30.

Tomabechi, Yoko
1983   "Wall Paintings from Dur Kurigalzu." *Journal of Near Eastern Studies 42*, pp. 123–31.

Tončeva, G.
1982   "Thracia Pontica à l'age de Bronze récent." In *Thracia Pontica I: Premier symposium international, Sozopol, 9–12 octobre 1979*, edited by A. Fol, pp. 176–82. Sofia.

Tosi, M.
1974   "The Lapis Lazuli Trade across the Iranian Plateau in the 3rd Millennium B.C." In *Gururājamañjarikā: Studi in onore di Giuseppe Tucci*, pp. 3–22. Naples.

Tournavitou, Iphigenia
1995   "The Mycenaean Ivories from the Artemision at Delos." *Bulletin de correspondance hellénique* 119, no. 2, pp. 479–527.

1997   "Jewellers' Moulds and Jewellers' Workshops in Mycenaean Greece: An Archaeological Utopia." In *Trade and Production in Premonetary Greece: Production and the Craftsman; Proceedings of the 4th and 5th International Workshops, Athens 1994 and 1995*, edited by Carole Gillis, Christina Risberg, and Birgitta Sjöberg, pp. 209–56. Studies in Mediterranean Archaeology, Pocket-book 143. Jonsered.
1999   *The "Ivory Houses" at Mycenae*. Annual of the British School at Athens, supplement 24. London.

Tsukimoto, Akio
1985   *Untersuchungen zur Totenpflege (kispum) im alten Mesopotamien*. Alter Orient und Altes Testament, vol. 216. Kevelaer.

Tuchelt, Klaus
1962   *Tiergefässe in Kopf- und Protomengestalt: Untersuchungen zur Formengeschichte tierförmiger Giessgefässe*. Istanbuler Forschungen, vol. 22. Berlin.

Tufnell, Olga
1958   *Lachish (Tell ed Duweir)*. Vol. 4, *The Bronze Age*. 2 vols. London.
1983   "Some Gold Bird Ornaments, Falcon or Wryneck?" *Anatolian Studies 33*, pp. 57–66.
1984   *Studies on Scarab Seals*. Vol. 2, *Scarab Seals and Their Contribution to History in the Early Second Millennium B.C.* 2 parts. Warminster.

Tufnell, Olga, C. H. Inge, and L. Harding
1940   *Lachish II (Tell ed Duweir): The Fosse Temple*. London.

Tyszkiewicz sale
1898   *Collection d'antiquités du Comte Michel Tyszkiewicz*. Sale, Hôtel Drouot, June 8. Catalogue by Wilhelm Froehner. Paris.

Ünal, Ahmet
1993   "Boğazköy Kılıcının Üzerindeki Akadca Adak Yazısı Hakkında Yeni Gözlemler." In Mellink, Porada, and Özgüç 1993, pp. 727–30.

Ünal, Ahmet, Ahmet Ertekin, and Ismet Ediz
1991   "The Hittite Sword from Bogazköy-Hattusa, Found 1991, and Its Akkadian Inscription." *Müze* 4 (pub. 1992), pp. 46–52.

Unger, Eckhard
1931   "Topographie der Stadt Dilbat." *Archiv Orientální 3*, pp. 21–48.

Unterwegs zum goldenen Vlies
1995   *Unterwegs zum goldenen Vlies: Archäologische Funde aus Georgien*. Exhibition, Museum für Vor- und Frühgeschichte, Saarbrücken. Catalogue edited by Andrei Miron and Winfried Orthmann. Saarbrücken.

Vagnetti, Lucia
1999   "Mycenaeans and Cypriots in the Central Mediterranean before 1200 B.C." In Phelps, Lolos, and Vichos 1999, pp. 187–208.

Vagnetti, Lucia, and Fulvia Lo Schiavo
1989   "Late Bronze Age Long Distance Trade in the Mediterranean: The Role of the Cypriots." In *Early Society in Cyprus*, edited by Edgar J. Peltenburg, pp. 217–43. Edinburgh.

Valbelle, Dominique
1981   *Satis et Anoukis*. Deutsches Archäologisches Institut, Abteilung Kairo. Mainz am Rhein.

Vallogia, Michel
1986   *Le mastaba de Medou-Nefer*. 2 vols. Cairo.

Van Buren, E. Douglas
1945   *Symbols of the Gods in Mesopotamian Art*. Analecta Orientalis 23. Rome.

Van de Mieroop, Marc

1992   "Wood in the Old Babylonian Texts from Southern Babylonia." *Bulletin on Sumerian Agriculture* 6, pp. 155–61.

2002   "In Search of Prestige: Foreign Contacts and the Rise of an Elite in Early Dynastic Babylonia." In *Leaving No Stones Unturned: Essays on the Ancient Near East and Egypt in Honor of Donald P. Hansen*, edited by Erica Ehrenberg, pp. 125–37. Winona Lake, Ind.

2003   *A History of the Ancient Near East, ca. 3000–323 B.C.* Oxford.

2004   *A History of the Ancient Near East, ca. 3000–323 B.C.* Blackwell History of the Ancient World, vol. 1. Malden, Mass.

2007   *The Eastern Mediterranean in the Age of Ramesses II.* Malden, Mass.

Vandersleyen, Claude

1975   *Das Alte Ägypten.* Propyläen Kunstgeschichte, vol. 15. Berlin.

Vandier, J.

1937   "À propos d'un dépôt de provenance asiatique trouvé a Tôd." *Syria* 18, pp. 174–82.

Vandier d'Abbadie, Jeanne

1972   *Catalogue des objets de toilette égyptiens.* Paris.

Vanschoonwinkel, J.

1990   "Animal Representations in Theran and Other Aegean Arts." In Hardy and Renfrew 1990, vol. 1, *Archaeology*, pp. 327–47.

Varvarrigos, Anast. P.

1981   *Το οδοντόφρακτον μυκηναϊκόν κράνος (ως προς την τεχνικής της κατασκευής του).* Athens. Doctoral thesis, Philosophike Schole Panepistemiou, Athens, 1980.

Veenhof, Klaas R.

1972   *Aspects of Old Assyrian Trade and Its Terminology.* Leiden.

1991   "Assyrian Commercial Activities in Old Babylonian Sippar." In Charpin and Joannès 1991, pp. 287–304.

1993   "On the Identification and Implications of Some Bullae from Acemhöyük and Kültepe." In Mellink, Porada, and Özgüç 1993, pp. 645–57.

2000   "Kanesh: An Assyrian Colony in Anatolia." In Sasson 2000, pp. 859–71.

n.d.   "The Old Assyrian Period." forthcoming in the series Orbis Biblicus et Orientalis.

Venedikov, Ivan

1988   *The Vulchitrun Treasure.* Translated by Nedyalka Chakalova. Sofia.

Venit, Marjorie

1986   "Toward a Definition of Middle Assyrian Style." *Akkadica* 50, pp. 1–21.

Ventris, Michael, and John Chadwick

1973   *Documents in Mycenaean Greek.* 2nd ed. Cambridge.

Vercoutter, Jean

1956   *L'Égypte et le monde égéen préhellènique: Étude critique des sources égyptiennes (du début de la XVIIIe à la fin de la XIXe dynastie).* Institut Français d'Archéologie Orientale, Bibliothèque d'étude, vol. 22. Cairo.

Verhoeven, Ursula

1986   "Tefnut." In *Lexikon der Ägyptologie*, edited by Wolfgang Helck and Wolfhart Westendorf, vol. 6, cols. 296–304. Wiesbaden.

Vermaak, P. S.

2007   "Relations between Babylonia and the Levant during the Kassite Period." In *The Babylonian World*, edited by Gwendolyn Leick. New York and London.

Vermeule, Emily

1964   *Greece in the Bronze Age.* Chicago.

1970   Review of Lang 1969. *Art Bulletin* 52, pp. 428–30.

Vermeule, Emily, and Vassos Karageorghis

1982   *Mycenaean Pictorial Vase Painting.* Cambridge, Mass.

Vermeule, Emily, and Florence Z. Wolsky

1990   *Toumba Tou Skourou: A Bronze Age Potters' Quarter on Morphou Bay in Cyprus.* Boston.

Verner, Miroslav

1970   "Statue of Taweret (Cairo Museum No. 39145) Dedicated by Pabesi and Several Remarks on the Role of the Hippopotamus Goddess." *Zeitschrift für ägyptische Sprache* 96, pp. 52–63.

Vernier, Émile

1927   *Bijoux et orfèvreries.* 2 vols. Catalogue général des antiquités égyptiennes du Musée du Caire, nos. 52001–53855. Cairo.

Villard, Pierre

1986   "Un roi de Mari à Ugarit." *Ugarit Forschungen* 18, pp. 387–412.

2000   "Shamshi-Adad and Sons: The Rise and Fall of an Upper Mesopotamian Empire." In Sasson 2000, pp. 873–83.

Virolleaud, C.

1922   "Découverte à Byblos d'un hypogée de la douzième dynastie égyptienne." *Syria* 3, pp. 273–90.

Vlachopoulos, A., and K. Birtacha, eds.

2003   *Αργοναύτης: Τιμητικός τόμος για τον καθηγητή Χρήστο Ντούμα από τους μαθητές του στο Πανεπιστήμιο Αθηνών (1980–2000).* Athens.

Vogel, J. C., B. Eglington, and J. M. Auret

1990   "Isotope Fingerprints in Elephant Bone and Ivory." *Nature* 346 (August 23), pp. 747–49.

Vollenweider, Marie-Louise

1967   *Catalogue raisonné des sceaux cylindres et intailles.* Vols. 1–3. Geneva.

Von Troja bis Amarna

1978   *Von Troja bis Amarna: The Norbert Schimmel Collection, New York.* Exhibition, Ägyptischen Museum, Berlin; Museum für Kunst und Gewerbe, Hamburg; Prähistorischen Staats- sammlung, Munich. Catalogue edited by Jürgen Settgast; contributions by Ulrich Gehrig, Eva Strommenger, and Klaus Vierneisel. Mainz am Rhein.

Vulpe, Alexandru

1970   *Die Äxte und Beile in Rumänien.* Vol. 1. Prähistorische Bronzefunde, ser. 9, vol. 2. Munich.

Wace, Alan J. B.

1932   *Chamber Tombs at Mycenae.* Archaeologica, vol. 82. Oxford.

1949   *Mycenae: An Archaeological History and Guide.* Princeton.

Wachsmann, Shelley

1987   *Aegeans in the Theban Tombs.* Orientalia Lovaniensia Analecta 20. Leuven.

1998   *Seagoing Ships and Seamanship in the Bronze Age Levant.* College Station, Tex.

Wainwright, G. A.

1925   "A Dagger of the Early New Kingdom." *Annales du Service des Antiquités de l'Égypte* 25, pp. 135–48.

1956   "The Cappadocian Symbol." *Anatolian Studies* 6, pp. 137–43.

Walberg, Gisela E.

1976   *Kamares: A Study of the Character of Palatial Middle Minoan Pottery.* Acta Universitatis Upsaliensis; Boreas, vol. 8. Uppsala.

1991a   "A Gold Pendant from Tell el-Daba." *Ägypten und Levante/Egypt and the Levant* 2, pp. 111–12.

1991b   "The Finds at Tell el-Dab'a and Middle Minoan Chronology." *Ägypten und Levante/Egypt and the Levant* 2, pp. 115–18.

1998   "The Date and Origin of the Kamares Cup from Tell el-Dab'a." *Ägypten und Levante/Egypt and the Levant* 8, pp. 107–8.

Waldbaum, Jane C.
1980   "The First Archaeological Appearance of Iron and the
         Transition to the Iron Age." In *The Coming of the Age of Iron*,
         edited by Theodore A. Wertime and James D. Muhly,
         pp. 69–98. New Haven.

Wallerstein, Immanuel
1974–89 *The Modern World-System, I–III*. New York and San Diego.

Warburton, David A.
2002   "Eclipses, Venus-Cycles, and Chronology." *Akkadica* 123, no. 1,
         pp. 108–14.
2003a   "Les valeurs commerciales et idéologiques au Proche-Orient
         ancien." *La pensée*, no. 336, pp. 101–12.
2003b   *Macroeconomics from the Beginning: The General Theory, Ancient
         Markets, and the Rate of Interest*. Civilisations du Proche-Orient,
         ser. 4, Histoire, essays, no. 2. Neuchâtel.

Ward, Cheryl
2003   "Pomegranates in Eastern Mediterranean Contexts during the
         Late Bronze Age." *World Archaeology* 34 (February), pp. 529–41.

Wardle, D.
1988   "Does Reconstruction Help?" In *Problems in Greek Prehistory:
         Papers Presented at the Centenary Conference of the British School
         of Archaeology at Athens, Manchester, April 1986*, edited by
         Elizabeth B. French and K. A. Wardle. Bristol.

Wardle, K. A.
1973   "A Group of Late Helladic IIIB2 Pottery from within the
         Citadel at Mycenae: 'The Causeway Deposit.'" *Annual of the
         British School at Athens* 68, pp. 297–348.

Warnock, P., and M. Pendleton
1991   "The Wood of the Uluburun Diptych." *Anatolian Studies* 41,
         pp. 107–10.

Warren, Peter M.
1969   *Minoan Stone Vases*. Cambridge.
1976   "Did Papyrus Grow in the Aegean?" Αρχαιολογικά Ανάλεκτα εξ
         Αθηνών / *Athens Annals of Archaeology* 9, pp. 89–95.
1987   "Absolute Dating of the Aegean Late Bronze Age." *Archae-
         ometry* 29, pp. 205–11.
1990   "Summary of Evidence for the Absolute Chronology of the
         Early Part of the Aegean Late Bronze Age Derived from
         Historical Egyptian Sources." In Hardy and Renfrew 1990,
         vol. 3, *Chronology*, pp. 24–26.
1995   "Minoan Crete and Pharaonic Egypt." In W. Davies and
         Schofield 1995, pp. 1–18.
2000   "From Naturalism to Essentialism in Theran Minoan Art." In
         S. Sherratt 2000, pp. 364–80.

Warren, Peter M., and Vronwy Hankey
1989   *Aegean Bronze Age Chronology*. Bristol.

Wartke, Ralf-Bernhardt
1992   "Die Backsteingruft 45 in Assur: Entdeckung, Fundzusammen-
         setzung und Präsentation im Berliner Vorderasiatisches
         Museum." *Mitteilungen der Deutschen Orient-Gesellschaft zu
         Berlin* 124, pp. 97–130.
1995   "Old Assyrian Merchant's Grave (Grave 20)" and "Wealth of
         Ashur: The Middle Assyrian Period." In *Assyrian Origins* 1995,
         pp. 44–47 and 81–83.

Watkins, Calvert
1986   "The Language of the Trojans." In *Troy and the Trojan War: A
         Symposium Held at Bryn Mawr College, October 1984*, edited by
         Machteld J. Mellink, pp. 45–62. Bryn Mawr, Pa.

Watrous, Livingston Vance
1992   *Kommos*. Vol. 3, *The Late Bronze Age Pottery*. Princeton.

Webb, Jennifer M.
1999   *Ritual Architecture, Iconography, and Practice in the Late Cypriot*

Bronze Age. Studies in Mediterranean Archaeology and
Literature, Pocket-book 75. Jonsered.

Weeks, Kent R.
2005   *The Treasures of Luxor and the Valley of the Kings*. Vercelli.

Weeks, L.
1999   "Lead Isotope Analyses from Tell Abraq, United Arab Emirates:
         New Data Regarding the 'Tin Problem' in Western Asia."
         Antiquity 73, pp. 49–64.

Weigall, A. E. P.
1901   "Some Egyptian Weights in Professor Petrie's Collection."
         Proceedings of the Society of Biblical Archaeology 23, pp. 378–94.

Weingarten, Judith
1991   *The Transformation of Egyptian Taweret into the Minoan Genius:
         A Study in Cultural Transmission in the Middle Bronze Age*.
         Studies in Mediterranean Archaeology, vol. 88. Partille.
1996   "The Impact of Some Aegean Gem Engravers on Cypriot
         Glyptic Art: Thoughts on a 'Chicken or Egg' Problem." In
         *Minotaur and Centaur: Studies in the Archaeology of Crete and
         Euboea Presented to Mervyn Popham*, edited by Doniert Evely,
         Irene S. Lemos, and Susan Sherratt, pp. 79–86. BAR
         International Series 638. Oxford.

Weinstein, James
1989   "The Bronze Age Shipwreck at Ulu Burun: 1986 Campaign,
         Part 3: The Gold Scarab of Nefertiti from Ulu Burun: Its
         Implications for Egyptian History and Egyptian-Aegean
         Relations." In Bass et al. 1989, pp. 17–29.

Weippert, Helga
1988   *Palästina in vorhellenistischer Zeit*. Contribution by Leo Milden-
         berg. Munich.

Welter-Schultes, F. W.
2008   "Bronze Age Shipwreck Snails from Turkey: First Direct
         Evidence for Oversea Carriage of Land Snails in Antiquity."
         Journal of Molluscan Studies 74, pp. 79–87.

Werblowsky, R. J. Zwi, and Geoffrey Wigoder
1966   *The Encyclopedia of the Jewish Religion*. Jerusalem.

West, Martin L.
1997   *The East Face of Helicon: West Asiatic Elements in Greek Poetry
         and Myth*. Oxford.

Weszeki, M.
2003–5   "Pferd. A. 1." In *Reallexikon der Assyriologie und Vorder-
         asiatischen Archäologie*, vol. 10, pp. 469–71. Berlin.

White, Donald
1986   "1985 Excavations on Bates's Island, Marsa Matruh."
         Journal of the American Research Center in Egypt 23,
         pp. 51–84.
2002   *Marsa Matruh: The University of Pennsylvania Museum of
         Archaeology and Anthropology's Excavations on Bates's Island,
         Marsa Matruh, Egypt, 1985–1989*. Vols. 1, 2. Philadelphia.

Whiting, Robert M.
2000   "Amorite Tribes and Nations of Second-Millennium Western
         Asia." In Sasson 2000, pp. 1231–42.

Wiener, Malcolm H.
1987   "Trade and Rule in Palatial Crete." In Hägg and Marinatos 1987,
         pp. 261–66.
1991   "The Nature and Control of Minoan Foreign Trade." In Gale
         1991a, pp. 325–50.
2003   "Time Out: The Current Impasse in Bronze Age Archaeological
         Dating." In K. Foster and Laffineur 2003, pp. 363–99.
2006a   "Egypt and Time." *Ägypten und Levante / Egypt and the Levant*
         16, pp. 325–39.
2006b   "Chronology Going Forward (with a Query about 1525/4 B.C.)."
         In Czerny et al. 2006, vol. 3, pp. 317–28.

2007 "Times Change: The Current State of the Debate in Old World Chronology." In Bietak and Czerny 2007, pp. 25–47.

Wiggermann, F. A. M.
2000 "Agriculture in the Northern Balikh Valley: The Case of Middle Assyrian Tell Sabi Abyad." In *Rainfall and Agriculture in Northern Mesopotamia: Proceedings of the Third MOS Symposium (Leiden 1999)*, edited by Remko M. Jas, pp. 171–231. Istanbul.

van Wijngaarden, Gert Jan
2002 *Use and Appreciation of Mycenaean Pottery in the Levant, Cyprus, and Italy (1600–1200 B.C.)*. Amsterdam.

Wild, Anne
2008 "Ursprung und Entwicklung des Greifenmotivs im östlichen Mittelmeerraum und in Vorderasien." M.A. thesis, Universität Tübingen.

Wildberger, Hans
2002 *Isaiah 1–12: A Commentary*. Translated by Thomas H. Trapp. Reprint of 1991 ed. Minneapolis.

Wilde, Heike
2003 *Technologische Innovationen im zweiten Jahrtausend vor Christus: Zur Verwendung und Verbreitung neuer Werkstoffe im ostmediterranen Raum*. Göttinger Orientforschungen, ser. 4, no. 44. Wiesbaden.

Wildung, Dietrich
1980 *Fünf Jahre: Neuerwerbungen der Staatlichen Sammlung Ägyptischer Kunst München, 1976–1980*. Mainz am Rhein.
1982 "Niello." In *Lexikon der Ägyptologie*, edited by Wolfgang Helck and Wolfhart Westendorf, vol. 4, col. 479. Weisbaden.

Wilhelm, Gernot
1983 "Die Keilschrifttafeln aus Kāmid el-Lōz." In *Frühe Phöniker im Libanon 1983*, pp. 401–42.
2004 "Generation Count in Hittite Chronology." In Hunger and Pruzsinszky 2004, pp. 71–79.

Wilkinson, Alix
1971 *Ancient Egyptian Jewellery*. London.

Wilkinson, Charles K., and Marsha Hill
1983 *Egyptian Wall Paintings: The Metropolitan Museum of Art's Collection of Facsimiles*. Text by Charles K. Wilkinson; catalogue compiled by Marsha Hill. New York.

Wilkinson, Richard H.
1992 *Reading Egyptian Art: A Hieroglyphic Guide to Ancient Egyptian Painting and Sculpture*. London.
1994 *Symbol and Magic in Egyptian Art*. New York.

Wilson, J.
1969 "Egyptian Myths, Tales, and Mortuary Texts." In Pritchard 1969, pp. 3–36.

Wilson, Veronica
1975 "The Iconography of Bes with Particular Reference to the Cypriote Evidence." *Levant* 7, pp. 77–103.

Winlock, Herbert E.
1914 "Excavations at Thebes in 1912–13 by the Museum's Egyptian Expedition." *Bulletin of The Metropolitan Museum of Art* 9, no. 1 (January), pp. 11–23.
1924 "The Tombs of the Kings of the Seventeenth Dynasty at Thebes." *Journal of Egyptian Archaeology* 10, pp. 217–77.
1932 *The Tomb of Queen Meryet-Amūn at Thebes*. New York.
1937 "An Egyptian Headdress." *Bulletin of The Metropolitan Museum of Art* 32, no. 7 (July), pp. 173–75.
1955 *Models of Daily Life in Ancient Egypt from the Tomb of Meket-Rē' at Thebes*. Publications of The Metropolitan Museum of Art Egyptian Expedition, vol. 18. Cambridge.

Winter, Irene J.
1976 "Phoenician and North Syrian Ivory Carving in Historical Context: Questions of Style and Distribution." *Iraq* 38, pp. 1–22.
1981 "Is There a South Syrian Style of Ivory Carving in the Early First Millennium B.C.?" *Iraq* 43, pp. 101–30.
2000 "Thera Paintings and the Ancient Near East: The Private and Public Domains of Wall Decoration." In S. Sherratt 2000, pp. 745–62.
2005 "Establishing Group Boundaries: Toward Methodological Refinement in the Determination of Sets as a Prior Condition to the Analysis of Cultural Contact and/or Innovation in First Millennium BCE Ivory Carving." In *Crafts and Images in Contact: Studies on Eastern Mediterranean Art of the First Millennium BCE*, edited by Claudia E. Suter and Christoph Uehlinger, pp. 23–42. Fribourg: Academic Press; Göttingen: Vandenhoeck and Ruprecht.

Winter, Urs
1983 *Frau und Göttin: Exegetische und ikonographische Studien zum Weiblichen Gottesbild im alten Israel und in dessen Umwelt*. Orbis Biblicus et Orientalis, vol. 53. Fribourg and Göttingen.

Wiseman, D. J.
1955 "Assyrian Writing-Boards." *Iraq* 17, pp. 3–13.

Wolf, Walther
1926 *Die Bewaffnung des altägyptischen Heeres*. Leipzig.

Wolters, Jochem
1983 *Die Granulation: Geschichte und Technik einer alten Goldschmiedekunst*. Munich.

Woolley, Leonard
1934 *The Royal Cemetery: A Report on the Predynastic and Sargonid Graves Excavated between 1926 and 1931*. Publications of the Joint Expedition of the British Museum and of the Museum of the University of Pennsylvania to Mesopotamia: Ur Excavations, vol. 2. [Oxford].
1939 "Excavations at Atchana-Alalakh, 1938." *Antiquaries Journal* 19, no. 1, pp. 1–37.
1953 *A Forgotten Kingdom, Being a Record of the Results Obtained from the Excavation of Two Mounds, Atchana and Al Mina, in the Turkish Hatay*. Melbourne and Baltimore.
1955 *Alalakh: An Account of the Excavations at Tell Atchana in the Hatay, 1937–1949*. Society of Antiquaries, Research Committee, Reports, no. 18. Oxford.

Woolley, Leonard, and Max E. L. Mallowan
1976 *The Old Babylonian Period*. Edited by T. C. Mitchell. Publications of the Joint Expedition of the British Museum and of the Museum of the University of Pennsylvania to Mesopotamia: Ur Excavations, vol. 7. London.

Wright, J. C.
1996 "Empty Cups and Empty Jugs: The Social Role of Wine in Minoan and Mycenaean Societies." In McGovern, Fleming, and Katz 1996, pp. 287–309.

Wulstan, D.
1973 "The Sounding of the Shofar." *Galpin Society Journal* 26, pp. 29–46.

Wyart, Jean, Piere Bariand, and Jean Filippi
1981 "Lapis Lazuli from Sar-e-Sang, Badakhshan, Afghanistan." *Gems and Gemmology* 17, no. 4, pp. 184–90.

Xénaki-Sakellariou, Agnès
1953 "La representation de Casque en Dents de Sanglier." *Bulletin de correspondance hellenique* 77, pp. 46–58.
1985 Οι θαλαμωτοί τάφοι των Μυκηνών. Ανασκαφής Χρ. Τσούντα 1887–1898 / *Les tombes à chambre de Mycènes: Fouilles de Chr. Tsountas, 1887–1898*. Paris.

1989   "Techniques et évolution de la bague-cachet dans l'art créto-mycénien." In *Fragen und Probleme der bronzezeitlischen ägäischen Glyptik: Beiträge zum 3. Internationalen Marburger Siegel-Symposium, 5.–7. September 1985*, edited by Walter Müller, pp. 323–38. Corpus der minoischen und mykenischen Siegel, Beiheft 3. Berlin.

1995   "Les bagues-cachets crétomycéniennes: Art et fonction." In *Sceaux minoens et mycéniens*, pp. 313–29. Corpus der minoischen und mykenischen Siegel, Beiheft 5. Berlin.

Xénaki-Sakellariou, Agnès, and Christos Chatziliou
1989   *"Peinture en metal" à l'époque mycenienne: Incrustation damasquinage niellure*. Athens.

Yadin, Yigael
1963   *The Art of Warfare in Biblical Lands in the Light of Archaeological Studies*. 2 vols. New York.
1972   *Hazor*. London.

Yadin, Yigael, et al.
1960   Yigael Yadin, Y. Aharoni, R. Amiran, T. Dothan, I. Dunayevsky, and J. Perrot. *Hazor*. Vol. 2, *An Account of the Second Season of Excavation, 1956*. Jerusalem.

Yakar, Jak
1976   "Hittite Involvement in Western Anatolia." *Anatolian Studies* 26, pp. 117–28.

Yalouris, N.
1968   "An Unreported Use for Some Mycenaean Glass Paste Beads." *Journal of Glass Studies* 10, pp. 9–16.

Yener, K. A.
2005   *The Amuq Valley Regional Projects*. Vol. 1, *Surveys in the Plain of Antioch and Orontes Delta, Turkey, 1995–2002*. Oriental Institute Publications, vol. 131. Chicago.
2007   "A Zoomorphic Vessel from Alalakh: Diplomatic Emblems in Three Dimensional Form." In *Refik Duru'ya armağan / Studies in Honour of Refik Duru*, edited by Gülsün Umurtak, Şevket Dönmez, and Aslıhan Yurtsever, pp. 217–29. Istanbul.

Yıldırım, Tayfun
2000   "Yörüklü / Hüseyindede: Eine neue hethitische Siedlung im Südwesten von Çorum." *Istanbuler Mitteilungen* 50, pp. 43–62.
2005   "Hüseyindede Tepesi'nde Bulunan Yeni Bir Kült Vazosu." In *V. Uluslararası Hititoloji Kongresi bildirileri Çorum 02–08 Eylül 2002 / Acts of the Vth International Congress of Hititology, Çorum, September 02–08, 2002*, pp. 761–78. Ankara.

Yoffee, Norman
2000   "The Economy of Ancient Western Asia." In Sasson 2000, pp. 1387–99.

Yon, Marguerite
1980   "Rhytons chypriotes à Ougarit." *Report of the Department of Antiquities, Cyprus*, 1980, pp. 79–83.
1986   "Instruments de culte en Mediterranee orientale." In *Acts of the International Archaeological Symposium "Cyprus between the Orient and the Occident," Nicosia, 8–14 September 1985*, edited by Vassos Karageorghis, pp. 275–78. Nicosia.
1990   "El, le père des dieux." *Mémoires et monuments Piot* 71, pp. 1–9.
1991   "Notes sur la sculpture de pierre." In *Arts et industries de la pierre*, edited by Marguerite Yon, pp. 345–53. Ras Shamra-Ougarit, vol. 6. Paris.
2006   *The City of Ugarit at Tell Ras Shamra*. Winona Lake, Ind. Originally published in French, Paris, 1997.

Yon, Marguerite, and Jacqueline Gachet
1989   "Une statuette du dieu El à Ougarit." *Syria* 66, p. 349.

Yon, Marguerite, Vassos Karageorghis, and Nicolle Hirschfeld
2000   *Céramiques mycéniennes d'Ougarit*. With the collaboration of Annie Caubet. Ras Shamra-Ougarit, vol. 13. Paris.

Yoselevich, Noga
2006   "The Utilization of Chalices as Incense Burners on Boats and in Coastal Sites." *R.I.M.S. News* (University of Haifa, Leon Recanati Institute for Maritime Studies), no. 32, pp. 27–28.

Yoshimura, Sakuji, Nozomu Kawai, and Hiroyuki Kashiwagi
2005   "A Sacred Hillside at Northwest Saqqara: A Preliminary Report on the Excavations, 2001–2003." *Mitteilungen des Deutschen Archäologischen Instituts, Abteilung Kairo* 61, pp. 361–402.

Younger, John G.
1976   "Bronze Age Representations of Aegean Bull-Leaping." *American Journal of Archaeology* 80, pp. 125–37.
1979   "Semi-Precious Stones to the Aegean." *Archaeological News* 8, nos. 2–3, pp. 40–44.
1985   "The Sealstones." In *The Archaeology of the Cult: The Sanctuary at Phylakopi*, edited by Colin Renfrew, pp. 281–97. London: British School of Archaeology at Athens.
1986   "Aegean Seals of the Late Bronze Age: Stylistic Groups: Minoan Groups of the Early Fifteenth Century B.C." *Kadmos* 25, pp. 119–40.
1987   "Aegean Seals of the Late Bronze Age: Stylistic Groups VI. Fourteenth-Century Mainland and Fourteenth-Century Cretan Workshops." *Kadmos* 26, pp. 44–73.
1988   *The Iconography of Late Minoan and Mycenaean Sealstones and Finger Rings*. Bristol.
1989   "Aegean Seals of the Late Bronze Age: Stylistic Group VII, Concordance." *Kadmos* 28, pp. 101–36.
1992   "Representations of Minoan-Mycenaean Jewelry." In Laffineur and Crowley 1992, pp. 257–93.
1995   "Bronze Age Representations of Aegean Bull-Games, III." In *Politeia, Society and State in the Aegean Bronze Age: Proceedings of the 5th International Aegean Conference / 5e Rencontre égéenne internationale, University of Heidelberg, Archäologisches Institut, 10–13 April 1994*, edited by Robert Laffineur and Wolf-Dietrich Niemeier, pp. 507–45. Liège.

Yoyotte, Jean
1981   "Le général Djéhouty et la perception des tributs syriens: Causerie au sujet d'un objet égaré." *Bulletin de la Société Française d'Égyptologie* 92 (October), pp. 33–51.

Yule, P.
1985   Appendix. In Paul Åström, "Middle Minoan Chronology Again," in Πεπραγμένα του Ε′ Διεθνούς Κρητολογικού Συνεδρίου (Hagios Nikolaos, 25 Septembriou–1 Oktovriou 1981), edited by Theochares Detorakes, [part] A, pp. 42–44. Heraklion.

Zaccagnini, Carlo
1983   "Patterns of Mobility among Ancient Near Eastern Craftsmen." *Journal of Near Eastern Studies* 42, pp. 245–64.
1986   "Aspects of Copper Trade in the Eastern Mediterranean during the Late Bronze Age." In *Traffici Micenei nel Mediterraneo*, edited by M. Marazzi, S. Tusa, and L. Vagnetti, pp. 413–24. Taranto: Istituto per la Storia e l'Archeologia della Magna Grecia.
1987   "Aspects of Ceremonial Exchange in the Near East during the Late Second Millennium B.C." In Rowlands, Larsen, and Kristiansen 1987, pp. 57–65.

Zawadzki, Stefan
2006   *Garments of the Gods: Studies on the Textile Industry and the Pantheon of Sippar According to the Texts from the Ebabbar Archive*. Orbis Biblicus et Orientalis, vol. 218. Fribourg and Göttingen.

Zettler, Richard
1993   *Nippur, III. Kassite Buildings in Area WC-1*. Contributions by James A. Armstrong et al. Oriental Institute Publications, vol. 3. Chicago.

Zevit, Ziony
2001   *The Religions of Ancient Israel: A Synthesis of Parallactic Approaches.* London.

Zevulun, U.
1987   "A Canaanite Ram-Headed Cup." *Israel Exploration Journal* 37, pp. 88–104.

Zeyrek, Turgut H., and Zeynep Kızıltan
2005   "Some Selected Mesopotamian Weights from Istanbul Archaeological Museums/İstanbul Arkeoloji Müzelerinden Seçilmiş Mezopotamya Ağırlıkları." *Jahrbuch für Kleinasiatische Forschung. Anadolu Araştırmaları* 18, no. 1, pp. 15–63.

Ziegler, Christiane
2001   "Une nouvelle statue royal du Moyen Empire au Musée du Louvre: La reine Khénémet-Nefer-Hedjet-Ouret." In *Monuments et mémoires de la Fondation Eugène Piot* (Académie des Inscriptions et Belles-Lettres), vol. 24. Paris.

INDEX

PHOTOGRAPH CREDITS